MITCHELL BEAZLEY WINE LIBRARY

THE COMPLETE
BORDEAUX

MITCHELL BEAZLEY WINE LIBRARY

THE COMPLETE
BORDEAUX

The Wines | The Châteaux | The People

STEPHEN BROOK

The Complete Bordeaux
The Wines – The Châteaux – The People
by Stephen Brook

First published in Great Britain in 2007 by Mitchell Beazley,
a division of Octopus Publishing Group Limited,
2–4 Heron Quays, London E14 4JP.
An Hachette UK company
www.hachettelivre.co.uk

Distributed in the U.S. and Canada by Octopus Books USA:
c/o Hachette Book Group USA, 237 Park Avenue, New York NY 10017

Reprinted 2009

ISBN 978 1 84000 980 4

A CIP catalogue record for this book is available from the British Library.
Set in Bembo

Printed and bound in China

The author and publishers will be grateful for any information which will assist them
in keeping future editions up-to-date. Although all reasonable care has been taken in
the preparation of this book, neither the publishers nor the author can accept any
liability for any consequences arising from the use thereof, or the information
contained therein.

Commissioning Editor: Hilary Azziz, Rebecca Spry
General Editor: Margaret Rand
Executive Art Editor: Yasia Williams-Leedham
Layout Design: Trevor Bounford
Maps: Encompass Graphics
Editor: Philippa Bell
Proofreader: Patricia Carroll
Indexer: C S Heath
Production: Lucy Carter

HALF TITLE: This sign identifies the D2 road that runs from the northern
Médoc to the outskirts of the city.

TITLE: Modern Bordeaux cellars combine functionality with artistic flair.
This new winery at André Lurton's Château Rochemorin in Pessac-Léognan
was completed in 2004.

BELOW: Old vines, they say, make the best wines. These venerable plants
in St-Emilion are preparing to carry a new crop of concentrated fruit.

A book of this scope could never have been written without the active cooperation and assistance of numerous individuals and organizations. Organizing my many visits to the region was undertaken by the following, and I am most grateful to them for their patience at assembling some very complex programmes: Florence Raffard and Pauline Léonard of the CIVB organized many of the visits; Françoise Peretti and her team in London representing the CIVB were helpful intermediaries, as subsequently were Rosamund Hitchcock and Natasha Claxton of R&R Public Relations. Elodie Juan, then at the Alliance des Crus Bourgeois, and Sylvain Boivert of the Conseil des Crus Classés organized the lion's share of my visits in the Médoc. Local syndicats assisted me with their knowledge as well as their skills in putting together complex itineraries. I am also indebted to Sybil Marquet (Maison du Vin at St-Estèphe), Caroline Barbier (Pessac-Léognan), and Marie Laurence Prince Dutrouloux (Conseil des Vins de Graves).

In St-Emilion Nadine Couraud and her team did a fantastic job ensuring I crammed as many visits as possible into the time available. In Pomerol Bruno de Lambert and Jean-Marie Garde organized my visits, and Jean-Noël Boidron made appointments for me in St-Georges-St-Emilion at very short notice. I also indebted to Michel Ponty (Maison du Vin de Fronsac), Didier Gontier (Côtes de Bourg), Jean Lissague (Côtes de Blaye), the Côtes de Francs Syndicat, Christophe Château, and Florent Dubard.

Marie-Stéphane Malbec and Sandrine Tulasne of Lettres et Châteaux in Bordeaux organized my visits to Sauternes, and Emma Baudry put together a fine refresher course in the sweet wines of the Right Bank. Catherine di Costanzo smoothed my path as I visited a number of the properties that she so efficiently represents. Frédéric Lospied of J.P. Moueix patiently answered innumerable queries. Jeffrey Davies organized a tasting for me so that I could be exposed to little-known properties that were producing wines of great interest.

I am enormously grateful to the following, who invited me to stay at their properties while researching the book. The privacy and comfort they offered me were much appreciated. Christian Seely, Marie-Louise Schÿler, and Patricia Doré, who gave me the run of Pichon-Longueville on more than one occasion; Mme. May-Eliane de Lencquesaing at Pichon-Lalande; John Kolasa at Rauzan-Ségla and Canon; André Lurton at La Louvière; Michel Garat at St-Robert; Daniel and Florence Cathiard at Smith-Haut-Lafitte; Caroline Frey at La Lagune; Mme. Marie-Françoise Nony at Grand-Mayne; Dominique and Florence Decoster at Fleur Cardinale; James Grégoire at La Rivière; Gavin and Angela Quinney at Bauduc; and Josette Germain and Philippe Peiffer at Peyredoulle. At Canon Florence Defrance and Béatrice Amadieu let me have the run of their office, which was an enormous help.

I am also grateful to the dozens of proprietors who invited me to join them for lunch or dinner, thus providing the perfect context in which to enjoy both their wines and their company. It would be impossible to list them all, but I would like specifically to mention Christophe Anney, Jean-Claude Aubert, Bernard Audoy, Jean-Noël Belloc, Olivier and Anne Bernard, Alfred-Alexandre and Michèle Bonnie, Philippe Castéja, Sophie and Laurent Cogombles, Didier Cuvelier, Pascal Delbeck, Henri Dubosq, Philippe Lacoste, Jonathan and Lyn Maltus, Didier Marcelis, Jean-Christophe Mau, Patrick Monjanel, Christian Moueix, Stephan von Neipperg, Patrick Pagès, Gérard Perse, Michel Querre, Pierre and Josette Taïx, Nicolas Thienpont, Yves and Stéphanie Vatelot, Alain Vauthier, and Xavier and Dominique Vayron.

I must thank Patrick Bernard, who has twice invited me to the comprehensive tastings organized over two days in his Millésima cellars in Bordeaux. Janet Burns and Colin Deane of Accent PR facilitated this process. Jean-Marie Chadronnier of CVGB has always been a candid and invaluable source of information as well as opinion, and at the same company Marie-Hélène Inquimbert gave up a day to show me their properties. Bernard Magrez went out of his way to show me his wines and give me a complete understanding of his ever-expanding portfolio. Olivier Bernard and Thomas Stonestreet gave up a good deal of time at Domaine de Chevalier to help me attain a better technical understanding of viticulture and winemaking, and Paul Pontallier at Château Margaux has done the same on many occasions. Philippe Dhalluin devoted a great deal of time to my visits to Mouton-Rothschild on more than one occasion. I also want to thank Jean-Michel Cazes for his extraordinary accessibility and frankness, and I would not want to neglect mentioning his sister Sylvie Cazes-Régimbeau, who facilitated so many visits over the years.

Fine old vintages of Bordeaux do not just fall into one's lap. We are privileged to taste them because friends and hosts take the trouble and exhibit the generosity to open venerable and treasured wines for their guests. In this regard I particularly want to thank Jean-Michel Cazes (Lynch-Bages and Ormes de Pez), Christian Seely (Pichon-Longueville), Daniel and Florence Cathiard (Smith-Haut-Lafitte), Henri Dubosq (Haut-Marbuzet), Olivier Bernard (Domaine de Chevalier), Jean Bouquier (Domaine de Grandmaison), Bernard de Laage (Palmer), André Lurton (La Louvière, Couhins-Lurton, etc.), Anthony Hanson MW, Dr Andrew Au, Professor Bipin Desai, Hardy Rodenstock, Jacques and Roz Seysses, and James Suckling. Christelle Guibert, the tastings organizer at *Decanter*, grandly did her best to organize blind tastings of Bordeaux during one of my increasingly rare spells in London, and Philippe Capdouze of Ficofi has invited me to some of his magnificent tasting events in London.

Finally, I would like to thank those who, over the past two decades, have helped me understand Bordeaux and its wines: Richard Bampfield MW, Michael Broadbent MW, Emile Castéja, Philippe Castéja, Charles Chevallier, Stéphane Derenoncourt, Pierre Dubourdieu, Professor Denis Dubourdieu, Nicholas Faith, Jo Gryn, James Lawther MW, Kees Van Leeuwen, Daniel Llose, Comte Alexandre de Lur-Saluces, Jonathan Maltus, Fiona Morrison MW, Douglas Morton, Xavier Planty, Steven Spurrier, Nicole Tari and Nicolas Heeter-Tari, Alfred Tesseron, Michel Tesseron, and Jean-Luc Thunevin.

I feel honoured that Hilary Lumsden of Mitchell Beazley gave me the opportunity to write this book. I follow in very distinguished footsteps, and over the years I have learned a great deal from the wise reflections, in print and in person, of David Peppercorn MW. My editor, Margaret Rand, has uncomplainingly worked through countless drafts and deftly spotted some errors, but of course any that remain are entirely my own responsibility.

I am aware that a number of properties I would have liked to include in this book are absent. In some cases this is because their owners neglected to turn up for my appointment. This is regrettable on two counts: it deprives readers of information I was intending to include, and it resulted in my hanging about in the cold (often) and the dark (sometimes) hoping someone would show up.

My wife Maria has tolerated my long absences with good humour, despite having to deal with all the things that go wrong the moment one leaves the country. Our cats Dweezil and Delilah provided some comic relief during those long days in front of the computer.

Contents

Château d'Yquem turns on the floodlights to welcome hundreds of guests to dinner during the Vinexpo Wine Fair.

LEFT: In the gently undulating Entre Deux Mers region, the vineyards, refreshed by mists at dawn, await a new day of sunshine and ripening.

FOLLOWING PAGE: Ancient limestone quarries are burrowed beneath the vineyards of St Emilion. Here at Château Belair they are used as a cellar for barrel-ageing.

ATLANTIC OCEAN

Gironde

St-Christoly-
Médoc

Lesparre-
Médoc

St-Seurin-de-
Cadourne

St-Estèphe

St-Palais

St-Ciers-
sur-Gironde

Braud-et-St-Louis

Reign

Etauliers

Pauillac

St-Julien-
Beychevelle

St-Laurent-Médoc

Beychevelle

Eyrans

Saugon

Blaye

St-Christoly-
de-Blaye

St-Sav

Lac d'Hourtin
Carcans

Lamarque

Villeneuve

Listrac-Médoc

Moulis-en-Médoc

Margaux

Macau

Bourg

Dordogne

Ambès

St-And
de-Cubz

Castelnau-
de-Médoc

Etang de
Lacanau

Lacanau

Ambarès-
Lagrave

Louens

Blanquefort

St-Médard-en-Jalles

Eysines

Basse

Bruges

Lormont

le Bouscat

Cenon

Mérignac

Floirac

Bouliac

BORDEAUX

Talence

Bègles

Pessac

Garonne

Cén

Gradignan

Cestas

Léognan

la Prade

Cambé

la Brède

Saucats

Cabanac-et-
Villagrains

	Haut-Médoc		Premières Côtes de Bordeaux
	St-Émilion		Graves de Vayres
	Médoc		Ste-Foy-Bordeaux
	Pomerol		Côtes de Bordeaux-St-Macaire
	St-Émilion Satellites		Pessac-Léognan
	Fronsac and Canon-Fronsac		Graves
	Bordeaux Haut-Benauge and Entre-Deux-Mers Haut-Benauge		Cérons
	Côtes de Castillon		Sauternes and Barsac
	Lalande-de-Pomerol		Loupiac
	Côtes de Francs		Ste-Croix-du-Mont
	Blaye, Côtes de Blaye, and Premières Côtes de Blaye		Entre-Deux-Mers
	Bourg, Côtes de Bourg, and Bourgeais		Bordeaux Appellation

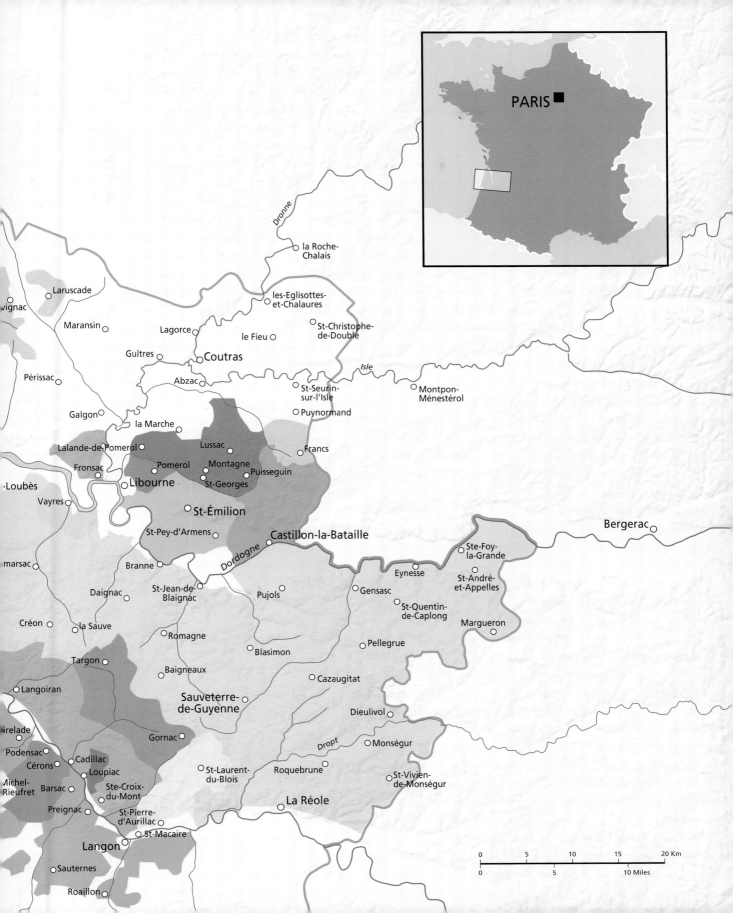

PARIS

Dronne

la Roche-
Chalais

Laruscade

vignac

Maransin

Lagorce

le Fieu

les-Eglisottes-
et-Chalaures

St-Christophe-
de-Double

Guîtres

Coutras

Périssac

Abzac

Isle

St-Seurin-
sur-l'Isle

Montpon-
Ménestérol

Galgon

Puynormand

la Marche

Lalande-de-Pomerol

Lussac

Francs

Fronsac

Pomerol

Montagne

Puisseguin

-Loubès

Libourne

St-Georges

Vayres

St-Émilion

St-Pey-d'Armens

Castillon-la-Bataille

Bergerac

Ste-Foy-
la-Grande

Dordogne

Eynesse

St-André-
et-Appelles

marsac

Branne

St-Jean-de-
Blaignac

Pujols

Gensasc

St-Quentin-
de-Caplong

Daignac

Margueron

Créon

la Sauve

Romagne

Blasimon

Pellegrue

Targon

Baigneaux

Cazaugitat

Langoiran

Sauveterre-
de-Guyenne

Dieulivol

Gornac

Dropt

Monségur

irelade

Podensac

Cadillac

St-Laurent-
du-Blois

Roquebrune

St-Vivien-
de-Monségur

Cérons

Loupiac

Michel-
Rieufret

Barsac

Ste-Croix-
du-Mont

La Réole

Preignac

St-Pierre-
d'Aurillac

Langon

St-Macaire

Sauternes

Roaillon

0   5   10   15   20 Km

0   5   10 Miles

1855 Classification

Premiers Crus (First Growths)

Lafite-Rothschild (Pauillac)

Margaux (Margaux)

Latour (Pauillac)

Haut-Brion (Pessac-Léognan)

Mouton-Rothschild (Pauillac)

Deuxièmes Crus (Second growths)

Rauzan-Ségla (Margaux)

Rauzan-Gassies (Margaux)

Léoville-Las-Cases (St-Julien)

Léoville-Poyferré

Leoville-Barton (St-Julien)

Durfort-Vivens (Margaux)

Gruaud-Larose (St-Julien)

Lascombes (Margaux)

Brane-Cantenac (Margaux)

Pichon-Longueville Baron (Pauillac)

Pichon-Longueville Comtesse de Lalande (Pauillac)

Ducru-Beaucaillou (St-Julien)

Cos-d'Estournel (St-Estèphe)

Montrose (St-Estèphe)

Troisièmes Crus (Third Growths)

Kirwan (Margaux)

D'Issan (Margaux)

Lagrange (St-Julien)

Langoa-Barton (St-Julien)

Giscours (Margaux)

Malescot-St-Exupéry (Margaux)

Boyd-Cantenac (Margaux)

Cantenac-Brown (Margaux)

Palmer (Margaux)

La Lagune (Ludon)

Desmirail (Margaux)

Calon-Segur (St-Estèphe)

Ferrière (Margaux)

Marquis d'Alesme-Becker (Margaux)

Quatrièmes Crus (Fourth Growths)

St-Pierre (St-Julien)

Talbot (St-Julien)

Branaire-Ducru (St-Julien)

Duhart-Milon (Pauillac)

Pouget (Margaux)

La Tour-Carnet (St-Laurent)

Lafon-Rochet (St-Estèphe)

Beychevelle (St-Julien)

Prieuré-Lichine (Margaux)

Marquis-de-Terme (Margaux)

Cinquièmes Crus (Fifth Growths)

Pontet-Canet (Pauillac)

Batailley (Pauillac)

Haut-Batailley (Pauillac)

Grand-Puy-Lacoste (Pauillac)

Grand-Puy-Ducasse (Pauillac)

Lynch-Bages (Pauillac)

Lynch-Moussas (Pauillac)

Dauzac (Margaux)

D'Armailhac (Pauillac)

Du Tertre (Margaux)

Haut-Bages-Libéral (Pauillac)

Pédesclaux (Pauillac)

Belgrave (St-Laurent)

Camensac (St-Laurent)

Cos-Labory (St-Estèphe)

Clerc-Milon (Pauillac)

Croizet-Bages (Pauillac)

Cantemerle (Macau)

Bordeaux is more than a wine. It is an interconnected universe of interests, all focusing on the fate of millions of vines as they negotiate their way through an uncertain climate, beset by pests and maladies. Then comes their harvesting and transformation into glorious wine. Only at that point does an army of brokers, merchants, journalists, PR men and women, consultants, and speculators come into the picture. On the sidelines stand squads of researchers and academics, restaurateurs and catering managers, label designers, coopers, closure technicians. All social classes are involved: a prince here and there, barons and counts galore, super-rich industrialist proprietors, slick merchants, struggling peasant farmers, and doughty *vignerons*, braving the December winds to prune the slumbering vines. Wine, and wine alone, the pleasure it gives, the wealth it generates, is the focus of this relentless labour and attention.

The visitor sees little of this, other than the vines, vast waves of them in the Médoc, patchworks buried in woodland in the Graves, rippling along the plateau or river plain in St-Emilion. Some may visit a château and tour its industrial winery, its sombre *chais*. But that will give them only a snapshot of the wine year. They may see the well-stocked wine shops in Margaux, St-Emilion, or Bordeaux itself, but few will glimpse the ancient cellars behind the Quai de Chartrons or the warehouse facilities of the big négociant houses. They will glimpse the great châteaux behind their ornate iron gates; few will be ushered in to be served lunch by elderly retainers, or more likely these days, sophisticated *traiteurs*.

There is a gulf that separates the visitor from the insider. I know of no other wine region remotely like it. Napa's tasting rooms, Barossa's cellar doors, the medieval cellars of Beaune, they all make an effort to communicate, to welcome the outsider. Bordeaux, essentially, couldn't care less about the outsider. The consumer's primary function in Bordelais eyes is to consume, not to inquire too deeply into the sacred mysteries of vine and wine. It's not as bad as it used to be – today there are wine schools, and a handful of great châteaux that are happy to whisk thousands of visitors around each year – but it's still a dismal destination for the tourist on a pilgrimage to what he or she still perceives as the world's greatest wine Mecca.

To the professional, whether merchant or journalist, consultant or expert, Bordeaux presents a very different face. To us it is infinitely welcoming, offering tastings, lavish meals, long cosy chats. An inner circle is routinely invited to feasts where a thousand guests – drawn from London or Houston, Seoul or Hamburg – dine on exquisitely prepared food, washed down with great vintages, and illuminated by prolonged firework displays. So effortless is the hype that we, on the receiving end, sometimes forget that it is indeed hype, just another cog in the vast promotional machine of Bordeaux. To bypass it, which one can indeed do, is, however, to lose out on a crucial source of information. All the great and good of Bordeaux gather on its state occasions, and those invited to meet them have an opportunity to chat to, or even quiz, the most powerful merchants, the grandest proprietors, the cleverest academics, the canniest importers.

Like most other writers on Bordeaux, I have preferred to be on the inside than the outside. But Bordeaux also sucks you in. We, the privileged, stay in its châteaux, embrace its grand old (and young) ladies, scoff its meals, show a genuine awed gratitude when we are unexpectedly served a rare old vintage. We are even friends with many proprietors and winemakers and administrators. After all, we see them regularly in the most convivial of surroundings; they are pleased to see us and we are delighted to see them, with a handful of exceptions. We become part of the system.

Despite all these blandishments, to which I easily succumb, I have tried to retain my impartiality, but it is not always easy. I try to keep in mind that there is another side to Bordeaux: that first and foremost it's all about wine as a business. Journalists are targeted because one of our roles is perceived to be maintaining the prestige of Bordeaux, its self-proclaimed superiority, its iconic status.

The Bordeaux wine business is rather strange; it is one in which the notion of traceability and personal contact is thought of very little account. The Burgundy buyer will make his or her decisions down in a dark, damp cellar with a row of glasses balanced precariously on an upturned barrel. The California wine buyer will make his or her decisions on a sun-dappled terrace. The Bordeaux buyer will decide on his or her purchases in an office.

The wine is dispatched into a series of oubliettes. First, from château to négociant cellar, thence to the Carrefour warehouse or the Rome cellars of an importer, thence to a retailer or a wine club, and eventually into the hands of the consumer. It's as if the millions of bottles produced each year are scattered around the world by benign gnomes. Such is the bizarre nature of the Bordelais distribution system that most producers have no idea where their wines end up. I've seen bottles of Lafite in a dark, humid grocery shop in a dingy border town on the Thai/Burmese border, their corks probably rotten, their contents steamed and oxidized. How did they get there? Almost impossible to find out, for proprietor and nosy wine writer alike.

Bordeaux châteaux can't woo their clients, because they don't know who they are. Consumers are at the end of a chain with so many links that no one can follow them to the end. Hence the importance of wooing everyone who might have some influence over clients, actual and potential. Promotion is a team effort, whether in the form of a vacuous generic advertising campaign or a Union des Grands Crus roadshow.

Some properties, however, and usually those with the highest reputations and largest profits, are increasingly loath to welcome visitors. And when they deign to give you an appointment, visits are organized strictly on their terms. For the wine writer this can be irksome. It is hard to learn about a property and its wines if visits are severely limited in their scope, and if one is placed in the well-manicured but indifferent hands of a smartly dressed PR, who gives answers only to a set number of questions and ignores the rest.

Many years ago, as a writer with rather slender credentials, I asked to visit a top Médoc château. I was received by the owner, and we tasted at least six different vintages. It was a fascinating meeting, as it enabled me not just to taste his wines but to understand what the proprietor was seeking to achieve. Furthermore, I could listen to his own assessment of the extent to which he felt he had succeeded. In 2004 it took five telephone calls over a number of days to obtain an appointment at the same property at a quiet time of the year. I was received courteously enough by the estate director and walked through the winery; he answered my questions, but in a fairly perfunctory way. The tasting consisted of two cask samples, the *grand vin* and the second wine. Then a handshake and a walk to the exit. This experience was repeated at various times in the course of my researches. Nonetheless, parsimonious wine estates run like soulless corporations are very much in the minority. Most estates, large or small, prestigious or little known, are eager to show their wine and discuss it, and without their cooperation this book would scarcely have been possible.

Every effort has been made to ensure that the factual information provided in entries on individual châteaux is accurate. Whenever possible, statistical information about percentages of grape varieties, production figures, and so forth has been obtained directly from the estates. However, my experience is that such statistics can be wildly unreliable. Even a press kit or other printed information disseminated by estates themselves can be full of contradictions. Nor can I be entirely certain that the response given to direct inquiries is truthful. The practice of filtration is a notorious example. Because it has come to be thought undesirable to filter a wine, many châteaux gloss over this aspect of wine production. So when the answer "no" is given to an inquiry about whether the wine is filtered, that may not be strictly true. What "no" sometimes means is: "We used to do a sterile filtration in the past, but we recognize that this can strip the wine of some of its flavour and aroma, so we no longer do so. But we do a light filtration just before bottling to remove any gross impurities that still may be present in the wine." Fair enough, but that is not quite the same thing as "unfiltered". So the reader is implored to take such information with a large pinch of salt.

One statistically uncertain area is that of *encépagement*, the distribution of grape varieties within the vineyard. Few will be greatly bothered whether the proportion of Merlot in the vineyard is forty or forty-five per cent, but in a book such as this one looks for veracity, and it isn't always going to be there, despite the author's best efforts. (These include emails to châteaux to check certain details, emails that as often as not are unanswered.) Exact percentages are difficult to calculate, especially if, as is often the case in Bordeaux, a property's vineyards are scattered over various communes and dozens of parcels, and subject to regular replanting.

Percentages of grape varieties cited at each property refer to their presence in the vineyard. Some varieties are more productive than others, and thus will be more present in the final wine. The age of the vines is another important factor, since young vines tend to give generous crops whereas very old vines are more niggardly in their production. Moreover, some vintages favour one variety, whereas another may have succumbed to *coulure* or may simply have failed to ripen. This frequently happens with Petit Verdot, a late-ripening variety that does not always measure up. To enter into great detail about the precise composition of each wine smacks of the anorak, but the reader should be aware that forty per cent Merlot, for example, in a vineyard may well translate in certain vintages into sixty per cent Merlot in the wine. Production figures relate to total production from that estate, not to the *grand vin* alone. Of course such figures are approximate, as the quantity of wine produced will vary from year to year.

There are some areas where I have been deliberately sparse on details on the grounds that they would soon induce tedium in the reader. These include:

(1) Cooling methods. Nowadays almost all tanks are efficiently temperature-controlled, although in different ways.

(2) Presses. It can safely be assumed that the majority of presses are now pneumatic presses, and that except in Bordeaux's backwaters the horizontal press has been consigned to the equivalent of the knacker's yard. Some estates have either retained or reverted to vertical presses, which I do sometimes single out, as it shows that the property is willing to adopt the most labour-intensive method in its quest for quality.

(3) Coopers and toasts. Every winemaker has his or her favourites, but most estates are continuously conducting trials to see which oak and cooper works best for their wine. While the wine buff may be enthralled by the nuances between Radoux medium-toast and the same wine in Vicard medium-toast-plus, I believe these nuances are of little interest to the reader. Moreover, the visiting journalist has no way of assessing the choices made with regard to oak other than by tasting the final product.

(4) Second wines. Second wines are second-best. Their function is to improve the quality of the main wine by mopping up wines deemed second-rate either because they are made from young vines or just don't contribute to the blend. Some second wines are excellent, and the best are indeed mentioned. But the majority are of marginal interest to the Bordeaux lover, since they are designed to be drunk young and are unlikely to be cellared.

I have thought long and hard about the role that tasting notes should play in this book. My primary aim has been to explain the wine culture of Bordeaux, and that of course includes a detailed look at each of its major wine estates, and the wines it produces. I have decided against providing formal tasting notes, both because it would expand the book to elephantine proportions, and because other writers – notably Robert Parker, Clive Coates MW, Michael Broadbent MW, Michel Bettane – have already done so, and my experience, especially of old vintages, can scarcely match theirs. On the other hand, I have, in the case of important properties, given a more detailed account of the vintages I have tasted, so that the reader can gain some notion of what the wines are like to drink.

Yet the more I taste, the more I am aware that an assessment based on a single tasting can be misleading. Faulty bottles are not uncommon, especially among older vintages. It is not always easy to know whether, for example, some slight oxidation is a characteristic of a particular wine at a particular age, or a consequence of poor storage or inept bottling. The 1961 Château Lafite is apparently notorious for its inconsistency. I have tasted 1983 Château Margaux six times, with half the bottles distinctly inferior to the best three. Which is the real 1983? The answer is that I give the wine the benefit of the doubt. When comparing notes with other writers on museum-piece vintages, I am often struck by the widely different assessments we make. I may find the wine tired and drying out, Robert Parker (or whoever) may find it splendid and vibrant. Or vice versa. This confirms the old adage that there is no such thing as a great vintage, only great bottles.

It is a sad feature of our age that one cannot always be certain that a rare wine one is privileged to taste or drink is authentic. I reported on certain venerable clarets that I drank assuming them to be the genuine article, but in 2007 information was published that implied that some of these wines may well have been fakes. I am in no position to confirm or deny this, but serious questions have been raised about, for instance, the Pétrus vintages from the 1920s and the 1870 Lafite that I tasted in 2002. So my comments on these wines should be read with a high degree of scepticism.

At a magnificent dinner at Yquem in June 2005, the hundreds of guests were served marvellous First Growths from 1975 to 1983, mostly from magnum (and almost certain to be authentic since they came from the châteaux' own cellars). Inevitably, the writers and other guests present couldn't help comparing notes. It was remarkable how opinions differed. There were no corked wines on the tables, but the bottle variation was significant and perhaps inevitable. So I think it is important for readers of wine books to be aware of the subjectivity of many tasting notes and assessments, unless the same wine has been tasted repeatedly on different occasions.

With very few exceptions I have excluded my tasting notes from *primeur* tastings, as they are too early to allow anything like a definitive judgment on the wines.

There is no point debating whether Bordeaux is indeed the greatest wine region in the world. But there can be no doubt that it has beguiled the palates of generations of wine drinkers. Certainly in Britain it has been a hereditary taste, with country gentlemen laying down cases of their favourite wines for future generations, and their children following suit. Great Bordeaux has longevity. A wine from a fine vintage can be tasted young, and then retasted and drunk for decades. It evolves, slowly, mysteriously, subtly. A great bottle of wine is not a work of art; it is a work of nature, sleepily alive, constantly changing.

It is not easy to pin down what it is about Bordeaux that has such a firm grip on generations of wine-lovers around the world. It cannot be the varietal flavours alone, as the flavours of ripe Cabernet and Merlot are easily replicated, even amplified, in vineyards worldwide. Sometimes, in books about the wines of Bordeaux, I encounter the word "digestible". It doesn't make much sense, yet I think I know exactly what is meant by the term. It includes modest degrees of alcohol – classic Bordeaux ranges from twelve degrees of alcohol to 13.5 degrees – that allow the consumption of a fair volume without serious damage to one's sobriety. It includes balance and freshness, qualities that make one eager to reach for the bottle and enjoy a second glass.

But Bordeaux has more than elegance and balance, crucial as those are as defining characteristics of its wines. I also find in good Bordeaux what I can only call force. Bordeaux exudes a strength of personality that can be described as virile. It's a mixture of robustness and vigour. It has a punch that is lacking, say, in Burgundy, although a great Burgundy can offer other, more sensual experiences that can't be encountered in Bordeaux. Hugh Johnson, in his characteristic blend of precision and poetry, has captured the spirit of Bordeaux as well as anyone else when he wrote recently: "Its power as it washes the tongue, a strangely ascetic draft, comes from ripeness held in a precisely calculated grip of astringency, warm and cold at once."

1. The Rise of Bordeaux

 The history of the vineyards of Bordeaux is a commercial history. This has never been a region dominated by peasant farmers. Already by the seventeenth century a Bordeaux vineyard was an investment, and the owner tended to be divorced both from the agricultural and winemaking operations of his property, and from the commercialization of the finished product. So any account of the development of Bordeaux as a wine region is inextricably linked to its political and commercial history.

From earliest times, Bordeaux and its wines were internationalized. The Romans, as so often, were the first to plant vines, probably in the first century BC. They seem to have planted their vines in St-Emilion, on the heights of Loupiac, on the plateau of Blaye. The arrival of Goths and Vandals put the brakes on this nascent wine industry, which did not revive until the second millennium. Those who grew the vines from medieval times were peasants on the one hand, aristocratic landlords and ecclesiastical institutions on the other. They were French, but those who sold the wines throughout Europe, and later throughout the world, were usually foreigners, although some would put down deep roots.

From 1152, when the future Henry II married Eleanor of Aquitaine, until the mid-fourteenth century the major ports of Bordeaux and Libourne were in English hands. Privileges were granted to the outskirts of the city, where most of the vineyards were planted, placing their produce ahead of the queue of other wines passing through the port of Bordeaux. That gave them a tremendous head start on international markets. Moreover, as vineyard development rapidly expanded away from Bordeaux, into the southern Médoc and the Graves, the privileges followed the vines.

In the fourteenth century the vineyards continued to expand to meet the demand from England and other markets. The gravelly hillocks of Léognan, Martillac, Gradignan, and other villages close to the city, as well as areas around Blaye and Libourne, were soon planted with vines. According to wine historian René Pijassou, the wines made here had little resemblance to modern Bordeaux. They would have been light in body and colour and intended for rapid consumption.

After the battle of Castillon of 1453, when Aquitaine reverted to the French, the *vignerons* of the region suffered from the loss of their principal markets, but gradually they recovered. Although the territory had reverted to French rule, that did not lead to the end of foreign participation, as the new rulers had no interest in stifling a profitable trade. English commercial influence may have diminished, but other north Europeans muscled in, notably the Dutch, Irish, and Germans, many of whose descendants are still influential in present-day Bordeaux.

Its best-known region in medieval times was the Graves, where both red and (mostly sweet) white wines were produced. In the 1530s Jean de Pontac began planting at Haut-Brion, a property that would later assume importance as the precursor of the "château" system, whereby status would attach to individual estates rather than to regions as such. A century after Jean de Pontac completed planting his vineyards, Haut-Brion would become the first wine to be sought after by name in London, thanks to Arnaud de Pontac, who inaugurated Bordeaux's first modern marketing campaign in the English capital.

There were also important vineyards on the east side of the Gironde, around Bourg and Blaye, though they were less prestigious than those of the Graves. The Médoc was a late developer: low-lying and swampy, its marshes needed to be drained. The infrastructure was poor, and this was clearly a barrier to economic development. There was some viticulture in the Médoc even in medieval times, but it became an important region only in the seventeenth century, after the marshes had been drained by Dutch engineers. Drainage liberated the gravel terraces and altered their water table, making them suitable for human habitation and creating, perhaps as an afterthought, what was to become the ideal habitat for vines.

MEDOC LAND-GRAB

The heyday of the Médoc's viticultural expansion and cultivation was the first half of the eighteenth century. The *noblesse de la robe*, a new, commercially and professionally based elite that was replacing the ancient nobility of the *noblesse d'épée*, rushed to invest its wealth in land. The planting of new vineyards proceeded at such a pace that the authorities feared that the growing of cereals in the Médoc would so diminish that the local population could go hungry. In 1725 the Conseil d'Etat imposed a ban on new plantings without royal approval, but the sporadically imposed system of fines did little to deter further vineyard development.

It did not take long for the excellence of Médoc reds to become recognized and the wines were soon fetching higher prices than those from all other regions of Bordeaux. The once-renowned Graves was eclipsed, and has remained so, with the mighty exception of Haut-Brion.

It was already apparent that the specificity of Bordeaux's gravel soils played a crucial part in establishing which vineyards were likely to produce the top wines. There were two major factors. The first was the gravel soils from which the Graves took its name. Such soils tended to be on shallow ridges known as *croupes* and they had two overriding advantages as a soil type. The drainage was excellent, so that even in the uncertain maritime climate of Bordeaux, a spell of wet weather did not lead to disaster. In addition, the very stoniness of the gravel retained heat until well into the evening, and this heat was directed upwards onto the grapes, helping them to achieve ripeness, this too being no certainty in the Bordeaux climate.

The second factor, which would lead to the supremacy of the Médoc in the long term, was proximity to the Gironde estuary, which exercised a moderating influence on the climate, ironing out extremes. It was rare for vineyards close to the river to freeze, whereas those lying just a few kilometres inland were far more likely to be ravaged by dangerous spring frosts. More westerly vineyards were colder in general, so that full maturation was hard to achieve; tannins were more green, more robust. This was common knowledge, reflected in land prices and in the renown of specific estates in the eyes of brokers and the wine trade in general. It is instructive to look at seventeenth-century maps of the Médoc. Not only did cartographers have only the vaguest idea of the peninsula's true shape, but the interior was mostly left blank, suggesting that even at this date it was scarcely explored.

THE RISE OF THE BROKERS

As the Médoc was gradually developed from the early seventeenth century onwards, the *courtier* came into his own. The vineyards of the northern Médoc were terra incognita to the Bordeaux-based merchants, who became increasingly dependent on the knowledge and expertise of the brokers. The Dutch firm of Beyerman, founded in 1620, was by a long way Bordeaux's most ancient *courtier* house. Many others were to follow a century later: Schröder & Schÿler (now transformed into négociants) in 1739, the Lawtons (whose descendants are still active in the profession), and the Miailhes, who are still very much around, but principally as proprietors of important vineyards. The Dutch and the British were to prove complementary masters of Bordeaux commerce: the former favoured wines that were as cheap as could be compatible with drinkability, whereas the British market went for quality even if the price was considerably higher. This British preference was not just a reflection of intrinsic good taste, compared to the Dutch predilection for soapy cheese, stewed eels, caravanning, and cheap, sweet wine. The British government had imposed high duties on wines imported from France. Thus the thin, light fare that had supplied British palates from medieval times was no longer good value, whereas there was a market, even at relatively high prices, for red wine of high quality, which the Pontacs and Ségurs were only too ready to supply.

The hierarchy of vineyards embodied in the 1855 classification was essentially in place by the end of the eighteenth century. An advertisement in the *London Gazette* as early as 1707 announced the sale of parcels of new wine from Châteaux Lafite, Margaux, and Latour.[1] From the eighteenth century until the 1855 classification, there was little or no dispute about the First and Second Growths; lower down the scale it was a different matter.

1 Ray, *Lafite*, Peter Davies, London, 1968, 19

If during the eighteenth century the typical owner of a well-regarded property in the Médoc or Graves had been a nobleman, lawyer, or politician, in the century that followed the purchaser was more likely to be a banker, businessman, or Bordeaux négociant. The Revolution spelled doom to many an aristocratic proprietor. Those who managed to retain their heads found that their estates were confiscated as *biens publics* ("national property"), which were subsequently offered for sale. Nor did the Napoleonic era bring long-term stability. Trade with Britain came to a halt during the Napoleonic wars, and although conditions returned to normal after Napoleon's final banishment, another spate of property sales took place after 1814 because of the continuing economic crisis.

Those who deplore the influx of new money into Bordeaux (from Belgian industrialists, hypermarket proprietors, or New York perfumers, to give but a few examples) should recall that the acquisition of a Bordeaux estate as both a business venture and a fashion accessory is nothing new. The eighteenth-century *parlementaires* set the trend. The Marquis de las Marismas who bought Château Margaux in 1836 was, despite the aristocratic handle, a banker from Paris. And so were the Rothschilds, the Péreires of Palmer, and the Foulds of Beychevelle. And if the expected profits should not materialize, it was always possible to regard the property as a rural retreat.

THE 1855 CLASSIFICATION

The American wine historian Dewey Markham has exhaustively chronicled how the celebrated 1855 classification came into being. As he points out, this was just the latest in a series of classifications, compiled with varying degrees of authority by brokers and merchants since the mid-eighteenth century. Ranking was closely allied to the prices obtained for the wine of each property. The 1855 classification was compiled by the brokers of Bordeaux at the request of the Bordeaux Chamber of Commerce as an aid to the presentation of the region's best wines at the Paris Exposition of 1855. Before 1855 classifications were commercial props for the wine trade; the 1855 version, in contrast, took on a life of its own, and soon became established as a definitive rather than an evolving hierarchy. Although in theory it was possible to amend the rankings, there were too many vested interests at stake for this to be easily accomplished. Château Cantemerle was added to the list of Fifth Growths, having originally been overlooked because its sales were virtually monopolized by Dutch importers, so its qualities were hardly known at all by the Bordeaux brokers. A court later ruled that:

> There is nothing official about the classification of the Médoc's wines, nor is it definitive and irrevocable.... The classification always leaves open the hope for all proprietors of a new and higher standing for their wines.[2]

In theory, maybe; in practice the classification was almost set in tablets of stone. It took Baron Philippe de Rothschild decades to secure the promotion of Mouton to the ranks of the Firsts in 1973, even though for close to two centuries it had secured prices that equalled those for Lafite and Latour.

Although not intended as such, the 1855 classification became a wonderful PR tool for Bordeaux as a whole. Burgundy would develop its *cru* system, but that would be based, in an apotheosis of the *appellation contrôlée* system, on terroir alone. In Bordeaux this was never the case. The classification rewarded, or penalized, properties that were themselves continuously in flux. Estates bought, sold, and exchanged parcels of vines with great regularity, seeking to improve, expand, or rationalize their holdings. Châteaux became brands, not geographical entities. Yet their status was unaffected in the eyes of the classification, and, consequently, in the eyes of the buying public, who came increasingly to regard the classification as holy writ. The lack of a classification at this time in the Graves allowed châteaux a good deal of licence. In 1928 Château Haut-Bailly was proudly labelled "1er Grand Cru", but by 1944 the self-promotion had been moderated to "Grand Cru Exceptionnel".

---

2 Quoted in Markham, *1855: A History of the Bordeaux Classification*, Wiley, New York, 1998, 167

Because the classification can, in theory, be revised at any time, pressure has been exerted over the decades, by the likes of the late Henri Martin and André Cazes, to institute a revision. Such pressure comes from below, from aspiring proprietors, not from those at the top of the tree. Anthony Barton, owner of two classified growths in St-Julien, shrinks with horror at the mere suggestion:

> *There's plenty of conflict and envy between owners as it is. Just imagine the repercussions if some of their properties were demoted in a new classification. There'd be blood on the streets.*

So one can safely predict that no significant revision of the 1855 classification will ever take place.

The four-tier St-Emilion classification, being of much more recent devising, is required to be revised every ten years. This obligation is taken very seriously, and properties have been demoted as well as promoted. The Graves hierarchy is slightly more rigid and, as is well known, Pomerol has got by very nicely without any classification at all.

The 1855 classification became transformed from an insider's guide to an outsider's vade mecum. All cited properties had status, even if that status varied from stellar to modest. Subsequently even the lesser estates, the *crus bourgeois*, would establish their own classification, although it was really too amorphous to be of much practical use to the consumer.

BORDEAUX'S INTERNAL MARKET

The classification would have been unthinkable without the long-standing structure of Bordeaux's unique commercial system, known as the *Place de Bordeaux*. Many other wine regions had a two-tier system of growers and merchants, but nowhere was this as marked as in Bordeaux. It was not only that the two professions were utterly distinct and therefore drew on entirely different skills. Snobbery played its part too: the noblemen and parliamentarians who owned the most important vineyards of Bordeaux did not want to sully their hands with commerce, and were happy to leave sales and distribution to specialist merchants.

The *Place* soon developed into a three-tier system with brokers (*courtiers*) operating as middlemen. As the vineyards of Bordeaux spread and ownership proliferated, it became the role of the broker to inform the merchant of recent developments – which property was in the ascendancy, which in decline, which proprietor was in financial trouble, which vineyard had been recently replanted, and so forth – and to negotiate sales of wine from property to merchant.

Inevitably a tug of war developed between the proprietor and the merchant, with the former seeking the highest possible price, the latter the lowest. Occasionally a temporary equilibrium, based on a gratifying margin of profit for both sectors, was achieved. Somehow it was a system that for all its imperfections, even cruelties, stood the test of time. There were economic cycles in Bordeaux as everywhere else, but owners and merchants usually prospered in the long haul. Yet because an element of instability was built into the system, there were periods of economic depression when properties had to be sold as a last resort. In the century and a half since 1855, only three classified properties still remain in the ownership of the original family (Léoville-Barton, Langoa-Barton, and Mouton-Rothschild).

That constant turnover in properties was just as common in the century and a half before the classification, too. By the late nineteenth century the new proprietors often turned out to be the Bordeaux merchants: families such as Eschenauer, Cruse, Borie, and Castéja gained status after they became the owners of some of the region's most important properties. Mutually interdependent, the château owners and the négociants prospered over the years, even if at the expense of the other. The merchant Hermann Cruse took a daring gamble when he bought vast quantities of the 1847 vintage. Fear of imminent revolution across Europe was deterring other négociants, but Cruse went ahead regardless. The revolutions duly took place, but without too great an upheaval, and a relieved populace rushed to buy the 1847s, and had to beat a path to M. Cruse's door if they wanted some. His fortune was made.

Speculation has always been part and parcel of the Bordeaux system. Numerous formulae were devised – subscriptions, futures, exclusivities, and so forth – to facilitate the sales of wines. In 1917 three of the First Growths signed five-year agreements with négociants to sell their crop at a fixed price, which would at least guarantee the proprietors a certain and constant income, regardless of climatic conditions. Once the world war ended, prices rose, and although the proprietors tried to negotiate better terms with the merchants, the négociants wouldn't budge. They were making money, largely at the expense of the owners, but that was the nature of the gamble.

In periods of economic depression, such as the 1930s, everyone suffered. If there were no transactions, there was no commission for the brokers, many of whom ran separate businesses (real estate for the Miailhes) in order to make ends meet. (Visiting Jean-Michel Cazes in the late 1990s, I was astonished to find myself interviewing him not in the comfortable surroundings of Château Lynch-Bages, but in the AXA insurance offices in central Pauillac. Cazes owned three properties, the best hotel in the Médoc, a successful négociant business, and was the manager of the powerful AXA Millésimes group of properties, yet until the day he retired he kept his hand in as an insurance broker. This was a legacy from the insecure days of the 1930s and 1950s, when it had been all but impossible to earn a living from wine production.)

The strength of the négociants lay in their diversity. This is as true today as it was in the nineteenth century. Some specialize in the domestic market, others in exporting to South America or South Korea, others in sales to supermarkets, others deal with top restaurants and private customers. The proprietors, working through the brokers, divide up their allocations between dozens, even hundreds, of négociants, using higher allocations as rewards for good service (and withdrawing their custom from négociants whose performance has been disappointing), just as the merchants themselves use the same system of rewards and punishments to cajole their own customer base.

In the flurry of activity that is the *Place de Bordeaux*, it is easy to forget that there is such a person as the final customer. Nobody has ever given much thought to that ephemeral creature. Whereas all other wine regions foster a rapport between supplier and customer, that is not the Bordeaux way. The absence of direct sales to the consumer, except in some of the more marginal regions, means that the château owner has no idea who, at the end of the line, has bought the wine. Once the crop has been sold to the *Place* in the spring following the vintage, the work is done. There is no point nurturing relationships with loyal consumers whose identities are largely unknown. Hence the notorious aloofness of the Bordeaux proprietors. Hospitable and attentive to the trade and their hangers-on (such as journalists), their doors remain closed to the general public.

All of this applies mostly to the proprietors of the leading châteaux, and the négociants who buy from them. But there is another side to Bordeaux, and always has been: that of the outlying vineyards producing substantial crops of inexpensive wines for everyday consumption. In the Entre-Deux-Mers, the southern Graves, the Côtes de Bourg, the Premières Côtes, and the areas entitled solely to the lowly Bordeaux appellation, there is no market for high-priced wines, no classification to hang your hat on. The vast majority of the wine that flows through the port of Bordeaux is frankly mediocre.

Indeed, in the past much of it, whatever it said on the label, was not even from Bordeaux. It was common practice throughout the nineteenth century – and, some claim, to this day – to "improve" the wines when nature was less than obliging. The blending wine of choice was Hermitage from the Rhône, and the 1795 Lafite, no less, was beefed up with a proportion of deep-coloured Hermitage. Only the top growths could afford to plump up their wine this way. Lesser Bordeaux had to make do with dark Spanish wines from Alicante or Benicarlo. Sometimes "stum wine" (unfermented grape juice) was added as a surreptitious chaptalization, as the unfermented juice would ferment, giving more body and alcohol to the doctored wine. The practice was not a secret, and there are apparently references in the account books of established importers to "Lafite Hermitaged".[3] Presumably the shippers, and their clients, would rather have a beefed-up Lafite from a modest vintage than a pure but weedy wine from the same year.

3 Ray, *Lafite*, 22

COMMITTING ADULTERATION

There was considerable suspicion across the land when it became known that the financiers of the handy railway line from Sète on the Mediterranean coast (a natural destination for casks of wine from North Africa) to Bordeaux were none other than the Péreire brothers, Parisian bankers and owners of Château Palmer. Some of this blending activity was perfectly legal; in other cases it was simply fraudulent. Much depended on how the wine was sold and thus what it claimed to be. Because many of these frauds involved classed growths, the proprietors grouped together in 1901 to found the Syndicat des Grands Crus Classés du Médoc; one of its functions was to deter such deceptions from taking place and to punish the perpetrators.

Adulteration and fraud worsened after phylloxera reached Bordeaux in 1869. The louse, which attacks the vine's roots, took its time inflicting damage on the vineyards, but by the 1880s almost the entire region had been affected. Many châteaux were in no hurry to replant on American rootstocks, the only solution to the problem, if only because the replanting of an entire vineyard was very costly. But the ravages of the louse did lead to a shortage of wine. If négociants had orders that needed to be filled, then the wine had to come from somewhere and it wasn't Bordeaux.

There is much discussion among connoisseurs about whether the quality of top Bordeaux has declined since replanting on American rootstocks. Edmund Penning-Rowsell was unconvinced: "I see no reason to believe the wines less good than the 1880s. I believe that the great pair of 1899 and 1900 proved the pessimism unfounded."[4]

In most cases it was the négociants rather than the proprietors who took care of the *élevage* of the wine, that is, its nurturing in barrel until it was deemed ready for bottling. Barrels of new wine, often already divided into different lots according to quality, were shipped down the Gironde to the warehouses in Bordeaux. These lined the quayside, especially along the stretch known as the Quai des Chartrons. Behind the stately façades of the traditional négociant houses established here are immense cellars stretching back from the quayside for hundreds of metres. Even today it is an awe-inspiring promenade to stroll through the immense cellars of the traditional négociant house of Mähler-Besse, staring at the stacks of wooden cases containing priceless vintages of top growths from the 1940s to the present day. These cellars now house stocks of bottled wine; in the past they were filled with rows of barrels. Bottling rarely took place until the wines had been aged three or four years in barrel.

Today most serious Bordeaux is barrel-aged and then bottled at the château. That is a change that took place some thirty or forty years ago. It is still possible to find classed-growth Bordeaux that was bottled in England or Scotland or Belgium. Importers would buy barrels from the négociants, then have them shipped to the home base for further ageing and subsequent bottling. The presence of thousands of barrels of wine in each négociant's or importer's warehouse offered them a wonderful opportunity to doctor the wine should they choose to do so. The addition of a bucket of inky Alicante might indeed do wonders for a lacklustre claret from a washed-out vintage, but for the cheapest wines even Alicante was probably considered an expensive option. Wretched hybrid vines were widely cultivated, and these often formed the basis for *vins de teinturiers*, which were the dark wines used to beef up mediocre Bordeaux. And there was worse: liquids concocted from plants, lichens, and flowers were often used as additives.

Viticultural and other improvements, not to mention climatic change, have ensured that most vintages can yield a drinkable wine at the very least, but in the past this was not so. *Oïdium* was the fungal disease that wrecked most wine production in the Médoc throughout the 1850s. The average yield in the mid-1850s at Gruaud-Larose was a pitiful five hectolitres per hectare.[5] Even though an effective treatment against *oïdium* had been discovered by 1855, sulphuring the vines was slow to be adopted at many estates for fear (unfounded) that the wines would smell or taste of sulphur. Once *oïdium* had been mastered, prosperity returned to the wine estates in the 1860s, but before very long phylloxera began to make its unwelcome appearance in the late 1870s.

4 Penning-Rowsell, *The Wines of Bordeaux*, Penguin, London, 1989, 15

5 Pijassou and Ters, *Gruaud-Larose*, Stock, Paris, 1997, 70

To make matters worse, there were simultaneous outbreaks of mildew from 1882 onwards. Downy mildew, which mostly affects the leaves, was the next malady to affect Bordeaux, in the 1880s. Fortunately a cure, doses of copper sulphate, was discovered in 1888.

PROSPERITY AND DISEASE

Nonetheless the mid- to late nineteenth century was a time of considerable prosperity for the Médoc in particular. France became a rich country under Napoleon III, and much of the population enjoyed far higher living standards than earlier in the century. From the 1840s onwards it became feasible and even profitable for businessmen, such as Parisian banking families, to invest in vineyards and châteaux. It was not the Médocains who made the Médoc prosperous. In the 1860s Bordeaux was producing wines of such quality that some of them are still drinking well today.

One of the mysteries of great claret is why the outstanding vintages from such decades as the 1860s, 1870s, and 1890s are often still in fine condition when tasted today. Some attribute this longevity and vigour to the presence of pre-phylloxera vines. When I put the question to Bruno Prats, former owner of Château Cos d'Estournel, he believed the answer was more complex, a combination of low yields, old vines, and good-quality oak barrels at the top châteaux. Whatever the explanation, the last part of the nineteenth century, despite the ravages of disease, was a golden age for Bordeaux.

LET THE BAD TIMES ROLL

Unfortunately the first decade of the twentieth century was fairly disastrous, with bad vintages greatly outnumbering the good. Prices dropped by about one-third. Although nature was not in a generous mood, the growers made matters worse by overcropping. Edmund Penning-Rowsell observed:

> There was no real delimitation of the Gironde vignoble and no control of production; much of the wine was inferior and badly made; this was made worse by the poor vintages. After three disastrous crops in 1901–3, there was not one outstanding year up to 1910, the best being 1906. This over-production had been made worse by chaptalization.... It was not uncommon for producers to sell more wine than they had made by watering it, a highly illegal operation.[6]

During this appalling decade, numerous properties were put up for sale, and, to make matters worse, they changed hands at prices far lower than the prices prevailing some decades earlier. Even so, many properties failed to find purchasers easily. René Pijassou and Didier Ters cite the example of Malescot-St-Exupéry.[7] Acquired in 1869 for just over one million francs, it was put up for sale in 1900 at 400,000 francs. There was no interest, and a year later a deal was finally concluded for a paltry 155,000 francs.

With poor economic conditions and proprietors strapped for cash, subscription sales came into their own. More and more châteaux entered into fixed-term contracts with négociants for up to ten years. Such arrangements usually benefited the merchants more than the owners, especially since slumps were invariably followed by periods of growing prosperity and rising prices. The proprietors were guaranteed a steady, if reduced, income, and would not be burdened with high levels of stock, since every vintage was shipped to the négociants with whom the contract, or *abonnement*, had been signed. Provided the owners had got their sums right, they could at least be certain of surviving a rough patch, whereas other properties, entirely at the mercy of the whims of the market, would have a much more rocky ride, one that often concluded with the sale of the estate. Of the

6 Penning-Rowsell, *The Wines of Bordeaux*, 121–3

7 Pijassou and Ters, *Gruaud-Larose*, 81

hundred or so properties that changed hands in the late nineteenth and early twentieth centuries, more than half came onto the market because of bankruptcy.[8]

The *abonnement* system could also be good news for the consumer, since it stabilized the market. The major drawback of the system, as Edmund Penning-Rowsell pointed out, was that "the growers had little incentive to improve their vineyards and their wines".[9]

DEPRESSION AND OCCUPATION

Despite the more buoyant conditions in the 1920s, there was worse to come in the 1930s. The worldwide economic depression flattened demand. Prohibition had killed off the American market, Revolution had done for the Russian market. If some individuals still had money to burn, they were unlikely to fritter it on a vineyard. The broker Hugues Lawton recalled: "Everything was up for sale, but there were no purchasers. Vines were being pulled up everywhere in the Médoc."[10] In 1929 there were 17,100 hectares under vine in the Médoc; nine years later there were just 13,300. In 1918 Château Citran had seventy-three hectares in production; by 1938 just four remained. The situation was made worse by the sparseness of good vintages in the 1930s, other than 1934 and 1937.[11] A government decree of 1935 even awarded subsidies for each hectare pulled out. Many growers, on the brink of financial ruin, created cooperatives in order to cut costs. Some of the more established proprietors were able to weather the storm thanks to their ownership of forests in the Landes between the vineyards and the Atlantic shore, but by the 1930s the price of wood had plummeted, so even this standby was in decline. Outbreaks of black rot, against which there were few effective treatments, didn't help.

World War II was not an unmitigated disaster for Bordeaux, at least in commercial terms. There had been a vigorous trade between Bordeaux and Germany for centuries, and some négociants of German origin were encouraged to maintain those business links. The Bordeaux merchants with long-standing links to the historic German wine trade in Bremen and other cities were in an uncomfortable position. Before the war Herr X from Hamburg might have been a close business associate, even a family friend; now he was on the doorstep in an officer's uniform, and it was hard to slam the door in his face. Since the port of Bordeaux itself was blockaded, the sole significant export destination was Germany, and it was asking a good deal of families with ancient links to Germany to abandon their business.

Indeed, the Germans would buy wines of top quality only from merchants with whom they had traded in the pre-war years. A so-called Weinführer, Heinz Böhmers from Bremen, was appointed by the German authorities to keep a close eye on the wine trade and to offer assurances that venerable cellars would not be raided by predatory soldiers. For those négociants who continued to trade there was a fine line between business and collaboration. After the war merchants who were deemed to have been too close to the German authorities found their businesses subject to confiscation, and their persons subject to arrest. However, only two of them, Louis Eschenauer and Roger Descas, ended up serving prison sentences, and none was executed, even though that was a possible penalty for collaborators.

For those certain to be branded as enemies of the Reich, Bordeaux was no place to be in the early 1940s. For the Sichels, négociants and co-owners of Château Palmer, their links to England and their Jewish heritage ensured that they would have been rounded up had they stayed, so they sold their stock and left. Nor did the Rothschilds hang around for any longer than was necessary. Proprietors tended to keep their heads down and their cellars firmly locked, especially since the Weinführer was quite insistent in his demands for fresh stock to furnish the tables of the upper echelons of the Nazi regime. Böhmers managed to extract 5,000 cases

---

8 Penning-Rowsell, *The Wines of Bordeaux*, 114

9 Ibid., 117–19

10 Lawton and Miailhe, *Conversations et souvenirs autour du vin de Bordeaux*, Editions Confluences, Bordeaux, 1999, 31

11 Penning-Rowsell, *The Wines of Bordeaux*, 129

(including many rare vintages) from Lafite. The depredations could have been worse, had not the *maître de chai* at Lafite cunningly insisted that many of the rarest wines in the cellars were the personal property of the Führer and therefore not to be touched.

Once the war had ended the wine trade was slow to recover, and it was only at the very end of the 1940s that conditions improved, despite a number of superb vintages. Château-owners continued to struggle, doing their best to maintain their properties despite low prices for their wines. Many of them resorted to sales *sur souche*, which meant that a price, usually based on that for the previous vintage, was agreed with the négociants a few months before the grapes were even picked. Again, this method of sales was a gamble, but it ensured some cash flow. Much of the celebrated 1955 and 1961 vintages were sold in this way.

Peter Sichel recalls:

> The first vintages I sold were the 1952 and 1953. Nearly all our sales in those days were in cask – our clients each did their own bottling. Prices were the equivalent of around 550 francs per hogshead of 225 litres – about 1.83 francs per bottle! But it was difficult to sell, and when I returned from a week travelling with an order for a hogshead or two I was congratulated! One of our regular customers was British Railways, who served half bottles of Château Palmer as their vin de maison in the restaurant cars! [12]

THE FIFTIES: STILL STRUGGLING

For the first half of the 1950s, even some of the most prestigious estates, such as Mouton, were unprofitable. In 1948 Philippe de Rothschild had struck a deal with one sole négociant to buy the entire crop, a situation unimaginable today. Some growers could not afford the remedial treatments necessary to counter outbreaks of disease and climatic disasters. Once again it seemed that half the properties of the Médoc were up for sale as proprietors despaired of seeing their way back to profitability. The devastating frost of 1956 compounded the problems; many vineyards needed to be replanted, but that for some was an unaffordable expense. In any event, vineyards remained out of production for some years until the new vines were a few years old.

It was galling for proprietors to realize that in outstanding years, such as 1961, they had sold their wines for what proved with hindsight to be very low prices. They knew they were gambling, but it was dispiriting to find oneself time and again on the losing side. But gradually conditions improved once again. In the late 1960s proprietors regained much of the initiative by deciding to bottle most of their wines at the châteaux, rather than selling them in barrel to the *Place*. Of course some of the top properties, notably Mouton, had already been doing that for decades, but it was not common practice. The role of the négociants began to change accordingly. No longer entrusted with the *élevage*, they could devote more of their energies to the profitable distribution of the wines still in the care of the châteaux. The négociants were not slow to adapt to these changing circumstances, but by the 1980s there was an entire breed of négociants who held no stock but conducted all their business from a small office with a fax machine. Their role was, indeed, closer to that of the traditional broker.

The négoce was also delivered a severe blow by the scandal that shook the industry in 1973. It erupted when Lionel Cruse refused to allow inspectors into his cellars, on the grounds that there was a gentleman's agreement that notice should be given before inspections. It appears that the inspectors were not gunning for the house of Cruse, but were gathering evidence against an unscrupulous merchant called Pierre Bert, who had bought cheap table wines and then altered the documents to make it appear that these wines were good Bordeaux. Having done this, he could then sell these bogus bulk wines to the négociants at a very good profit, and supply false documents attesting to their authenticity. Cruse was by no means the only merchant to be involved with Bert, but it did appear that they were not unaware of what Bert was up to. The long-term consequence was that Bert went to prison for a year, and one of the Cruse family committed suicide.

To make matters worse, the scandal coincided with one of Bordeaux's periodic commercial crises. The dreadful 1972 vintage had been wildly overpriced, as were the two succeeding vintages. When the market crashed, as it inevitably did when oil prices went through the roof in 1973, the négociants were left holding the parcel. They were stuck with overpriced wine that no one wanted.

Jean-Michel Cazes recalls the desperation of some négociants at this time:

> *I had been working in Paris and arrived here just in time for the Bordeaux crisis and the oil crisis. It was also a time of major technical changes. People were just beginning to understand malolactic fermentation, and many négociants said they wouldn't accept wines such as 1972s that hadn't gone through malo. It was a way for them to wriggle out of their agreements, as their businesses were in peril.*

Prices dropped by seventy per cent, but it was too late. It was the end for some individual merchants, and the beginning of the end for the system by which négociants carried vast stocks. At this time, many négociants still had "exclusivity" arrangements with certain properties. This monopoly arrangement could be an advantage, but not in the 1970s, when such négociants found themselves locked into agreements to buy substantial quantities of wine for which there was no longer any market. This crisis was to provide an additional spur to develop the futures system for consumers as well as the trade, since the new wines were passed on rapidly to the customers and the go-between merchants no longer needed to hold stock.

NEW OWNERS, NEW FLAVOURS, NEW CRITICS

Patterns of ownership were changing too, especially in the Médoc. Inheritance taxes doubled in 1981, and many families found it impossible to hang onto their estates, especially when they had to be divided into equal shares among the children. More and more properties fell into the hands of insurance companies and other corporate giants, such as British brewers and Japanese drinks companies. Wealthy négociants such as the Merlauts were also in a position to buy estates. In some cases these new owners managed their properties well; in other cases they seemed interested solely in improving their profitability, which led to a lowering of quality. The large properties of the Médoc were affordable only to corporate purchasers or individuals of enormous wealth, such as François Pinault at Latour and the Wertheimers at Rauzan-Ségla. Many rich individuals looked elsewhere, such as Alfred-Alexandre Bonnie at Malartic-Lagravière and the Cathiards at Smith-Haut-Lafitte in Pessac-Léognan, and the dozens of businessmen who were attracted by the smaller, more manageable properties of St-Emilion.

If the structure of the *Place* was changing, that was in response to a changing international market. The turning point was the sumptuous 1982 vintage, which reached a very wide customer base, in large part thanks to the enthusiastic endorsement of the vintage by an astute wine critic named Robert Parker. Where many British wine writers mused about the nuances of each growth in their cultivation of connoisseurship, Parker, and later the *Wine Spectator* and other American journals, took a more dogmatic stand, by scoring each wine as though it were sitting an examination. Although Parker always insisted that his written comments were more important than his score, a new generation of wine drinkers (and wine investors) was more influenced by the number than by the varying cocktail of fruits discerned in each wine.

The kind of publicity that Parker (and others) were giving to Bordeaux and its wines from 1982 onwards also played a part in improving quality. Michel Tesseron of Château Lafon-Rochet recalls:

Before 1982 nobody ever talked about fruit in a wine. But ever since 1982 we all tried to pick only when the grapes were properly ripe. Before then, you picked the first vines when they were still unripe and the last vines when they were overripe.

This was also the time when selection became much more important, and many leading estates created second wines.

For merchants and importers, the Parker score in particular became an invaluable sales tool. Indeed it was logical to do so, given the reliance on those scores by the final customers. The aspiring claret drinkers of Hong Kong or Kyoto no longer needed to scratch their heads while wondering whether Lafite was a better buy than Latour, or whether Trotanoy was outgunned in this particular vintage by Lafleur. A very high Parker score was taken as proof that not only was the rewarded wine likely to be outstanding, but it was also likely to be a sound long-term investment.

The growing influence of the wine press went hand in hand with the development of the *en primeur* or futures system, by which wine was sold to consumers long before it was bottled. Historically, futures purchases had been an internal mechanism. By the 1980s everybody could play. Wine writers as well as importers were encouraged to visit Bordeaux six months after the vintage to taste the new wines. Although traditional merchants make their own recommendations to their customers based on their own expert tastings, newcomers promote the futures campaign on the back of wine critics' assessments, often appending the crucial scores to their mail-order offers. And it works. The merchant has a vested interest in selling on the wines bought *en primeur*; the wine critic is supposed to be independent and dispassionate.

I have expounded in an earlier book (*Bordeaux: People, Power, Politics*) on the deficiencies of the *en primeur* system, which is adored by the proprietors because it provides much welcome cash flow. But it requires journalists and importers alike to judge a wine that has only just begun its *élevage*. There can be many a slip between barrel and lip. Numerous factors will alter the aroma, flavour, and structure of the wine in the period to follow before bottling. There will be the effects of oak-ageing, possibly of micro-oxygenation, of the addition of press wine or other adjustments to the blend, of fining and filtration. Nor is there any control over the samples submitted, and whereas most owners and their *maîtres de chai* make an honest attempt to cobble together a representative sample of the final blend, the temptation to tweak that sample must be hard to resist. Attempts by some conscientious proprietors to introduce some measures of control and verification have met with stubborn resistance, as have attempts to postpone the *primeur* tastings until later in the year, when a more definitive judgment would be easier to make. The whole dubious system is further fuelled by the ingrained competitiveness between journalists, each keen to be the first on-line with the "story" and with detailed comments on infant wines. Particularly absurd is the sight of wine writers studiously tasting and writing up a range of wines that are never offered *en primeur*.

The vagaries of wine criticism have contributed to the speculative nature of the Bordeaux market. This is regrettable. Pricing itself has become closely linked to the palates of a small handful of tasters. This has reinforced what has always been the great weakness of the *Place de Bordeaux*, its lack of stability. Pricing has never been linked to quality but to market conditions. The prices demanded for the 1972 were simply absurd, given the abysmal quality of the wines. Despite the ensuing crisis, the *Place* went through the whole thing again in the 1980s, when the thin 1984s were priced at more than the fine 1983s. Many trade customers just gritted their teeth and went along with it, fearing that a refusal to buy might lose them their future allocations of vintages such as, it transpired, the excellent 1985.

Bordeaux has no collective memory, or, if it does, it chooses to suppress it. A similar situation arose yet again in 1997, a light rather than poor vintage, yet considerably more expensive than the excellent 1996s. A handful of proprietors, a brave few, refused to increase their prices because they knew the wines didn't deserve it, but the majority – citing strong if mysterious demand from overseas clients – jacked up their prices. Five years on, those who bought the wines *en primeur* could, in many cases, have bought them for half the price from the shelves of merchants swiftly unloading their stocks of these unwanted wines.

In most wine regions, the producer sets the price and then attempts to sell the wine in any way he or she sees fit. Buyers will not tolerate extreme swings of price, so there is a modicum of stability. In Bordeaux the concept of stability is alien to growers and négociants alike. The *primeur* campaigns are used to whip up the maximum excitement, and only after the trade and the press have departed do the growers begin to release their prices.

No one should be under any illusion that those release prices are based on the quality of the wine. To be sure, if the quality is high, then the temptation to increase prices is all but irresistible. But it's easy for growers to find an excuse to raise prices. If the crop is short, then a price rise is deemed necessary. If a particular market, such as the Far East, seems to be awash in cash and eager to buy, then up go the prices.

Whenever a really fine vintage comes along – and there have been many over the past twenty years – the trade and, often, the press urge the growers to exercise restraint. The latter rarely listen, and most proprietors do not take kindly to being lectured on greed by the *Place*. If a producer senses that demand is going to be high, as it was in 2000, then it is natural for him or her to wish to benefit financially, rather than allow the négociants and other middlemen to cash in. Anthony Barton, the least greedy of proprietors, increased his prices only very moderately in 2000, despite the undoubted excellence of the vintage. Within a few weeks of announcing his *prix de sortie*, his opening price to the trade, the wine was changing hands for about three times that price. The trade and consumers were soon aware that the wine was of fabulous quality, so up went the prices. In this case the middlemen made higher profits than the proprietor.

It is hard to underestimate the competitiveness of Bordeaux estates. Many customers, or potential customers, assume that if a wine is relatively inexpensive, then it can't be of the highest quality. If a handful of properties in a village are obtaining very high prices, then it is natural for the other producers to think they can, and should, do the same. Nicolas de Bailliencourt, owner of Château Gazin in Pomerol, is a modest and unassuming man who produces excellent wine. In 2000 he was unsure what to do:

> In 2000 we were tempted to keep our prices at the same level as the 1999s, but others were advising us to "follow the market". If everybody increases their prices and you don't, then you are made to look stupid. My prix de sortie tends to be reasonable. Then I see the wine selling for enormous prices in New York retailers. But it's not Gazin that is making this enormous profit. And when the market calms down, châteaux such as ours that have tried to stay reasonable still need to come down along with the greedier châteaux. So it is very tempting to keep putting up the prices when the going is good.

2003: A CASE STUDY

The 2003 campaign was a fine illustration of the turbulence of the Bordeaux market. Growing conditions had been unique, with week after week in August at temperatures of over 40°C (104°F), provoking scorched berries, unripe tannins, and many other problems leading to high alcohols and unbalanced wines. Although it should have been obvious that this was a very mixed vintage, the overall judgments tended to stoke up interest in the wines. "Many châteaux have produced their finest ever wines," wrote Steven Spurrier in *Decanter* in June 2004, and in the same month Robert Parker heated up the American and Asian markets by writing in the *Wine Advocate*: "If you don't jump in and buy them quickly, you will pay an even dearer price when they show up in bottle."

Other critics were more prudent. The indispensable *Vintage and Market Report* published by the négociant house of Sichel declared: "The 2003 vintage is certainly exceptional but it would be misleading to label it a great vintage." The British wine trade was also cautious. "It is important", intoned Tanners in its opening offer, "to select carefully as some wines have unbalanced tannins and some are too jammy and alcoholic."

The top châteaux were slow to declare their hand. When the First Growths announced, they essentially doubled their 2002 opening price. The "super-seconds" followed in their wake. In addition, these prices applied only to the all but unobtainable first *tranche* ("portion"); subsequent *tranches* were considerably more expensive. It is true that the prices for the 2002, with which comparisons were inevitably made, were on the low side, because of slack demand. Nonetheless, some fifty properties came out with *prix de sortie* higher than those for the very expensive 2000 vintage. The fine Montrose was released at 38 Euros (compared to 22 Euros for its 2002, 33 Euros for 2000, and, hilariously, 35 Euros for 1997), but very strong demand caused its price to treble within a few days on the *Place de Bordeaux*. By late June all commercial activity by such châteaux had ceased, so everyone could pack their bags and go to Biarritz until it was time for the next harvest.[13] (In the meantime, growers in the more marginal areas of Bordeaux were queuing up to file for bankruptcy.)

How do these crucial opening prices come to be set? That is not an easy question to answer. The First Growths set the tone and pattern for the campaign to follow, and there is no doubt that their directors do discuss pricing strategy among themselves, although they deny overt collusion. But it is no coincidence that each vintage the Firsts' *prix de sortie*, while not uniform, are set within a fairly narrow band. Some châteaux are owned by individuals, so the proprietors can do as they please. Others are owned by corporations, whose boards may well overrule the advice of the château directors. Latour is owned by François Pinault and managed by Frédéric Engerer, who explained to me how things were done at that property: "I suggest, Pinault listens, Pinault decides."

There is no doubt that rivalry among proprietors is an important factor. Pricing has as much to do with market positioning as with fair value in any vintage. As Nicolas de Bailliencourt of Gazin made clear, no proprietor wishes his or her wines to be perceived as too cheap, as low prices may be associated by the consumer with modest quality. But the rivalry is often taken to absurd lengths, with proprietors absolutely determined to trump their immediate neighbours. So unfortunate consumers are asked to reach into their pockets to assuage the pride of their favourite wines' owners.

Some owners point to the enormous investments made at the estates in recent years, and this is frequently the case. But that does not mean that the château is entitled to claw back all that supposedly long-term investment in just a few vintages by putting up its prices to extortionate levels. Gérard Perse, owner of Pavie and Pavie-Decesse, used this argument to me to justify his steadily increasing prices. Fortunately the common sense of the consumer eventually steps in with a shake of the head when it is time to decide whether or not to buy.

Anthony Barton told me in 2004:

> *The pricing of the top growths has got completely out of hand. I asked one of my neighbours, who is fairly open about these things, what he planned to do in a recent vintage. Oh, he said, I'll probably increase my prices by ten or fifteen per cent. Needless to say, he came out about forty per cent higher. When I taunted him gently about this a few weeks later, he shrugged his shoulders and murmured: "Quand le train passe, je monte dessus." ("When the train passes by, I climb aboard.")*
>
> *I'm known for keeping my prices fairly stable, and let me tell you, I'm still making good money. We have a new pool, and I've lashed out on a Jaguar — even though my wife won't let me drive it because she doesn't like me taking my dog with me. The problem with ridiculous price increases is that it turns Bordeaux into a speculative market. Of course it has always been that way, but it's becoming more exaggerated. And that makes it impossible for smaller properties to get by. They can't possibly match the prices of the top growths, so there is a vast pool of well-made wine, especially from* crus bourgeois, *for which there is little*

---

13 I am indebted to Neil Beckett's detailed reports in *Harpers* in June and July 2004 for much of this information.

market. And while the top properties keep ratcheting up their prices, they ignore the fact that there is a good deal of unsold stock in Bordeaux.

The producers argue that the system maintains a certain stability because the négociants have one powerful weapon in their hands: they can refuse to buy the wine if they deem the price is too high. But it's not that simple. The top wines of Bordeaux are allocated between a number of négociants. If a négociant regularly orders, and receives, 300 cases from a top property, he or she can be reasonably sure, in a good vintage, of selling it all at a good profit. That, after all, is how négociants make their living. Should, one year, the wine seem poor value and/or hard to sell because of market conditions, there is indeed the option to refuse to buy.

This sound commercial decision can have dire consequences. Regular customers will be obliged to look elsewhere for the wine, and may not return in subsequent vintages. Even worse, when the time comes to place an order for the next vintage, the château may respond: "I'm awfully sorry, but since you chose not to support us during the preceding vintage, we shall look for another merchant to take your usual allocation." Or that allocation may be cut. It may be a kind of blackmail, but it's effective, and it's not only the wine industry that rewards loyalty.

Thus the négociants often feel obliged to buy wines for which the market may be thin, simply to retain their relations, and allocations, with the châteaux with which they work most closely. The same system of rewards and sanctions operates all the way down the line. Importers also feel obliged to buy wines they don't particularly want, or suspect they can't sell, in order to stay on good terms with négociants they have long worked with.

This arm-twisting is the cause of the routine over-stocking that plagues the Bordeaux wine trade. Prices soared, predictably, in 2000 both because the wines were uniformly excellent and because there was some bizarre magic that attached to zeros in the vintage year. Along come the 2001s and 2002s, both very good vintages on the Left Bank, if not quite as stellar as 2000. The *Place* and the importers urge the châteaux, who made huge profits in 2000, to reduce their prices. They respond, though in many cases those reductions are dwarfed by the increases of the previous year, and thus the prices remain high. Everyone dutifully buys, but the public, having overspent on the 2000s, is not eager to buy the succeeding vintages. Stocks build up in négociants' and importers' warehouses. Understandably they are in no mood to buy any wine for which they do not discern an immediate sales possibility. Many fine *crus bourgeois*, especially in the northern Médoc, where the richer, more water-retentive soils proved advantageous in 2003, made excellent wines in that year, but found there was no demand for them.

Thus the speculative nature of the Bordeaux market has benefited the few at the expense of the many. If, as in 2003, the *Place* has no interest in buying and selling your wine, then you, as a producer, are well and truly stuck. There are few other outlets. Direct sales are not a Bordeaux tradition, especially in the Médoc. Because of the dominance of the *Place*, indeed so effective from time to time, few châteaux find it worthwhile to develop an independent sales or promotional network. Demand was slack for the mostly excellent 2004s, but the justifiable hype around the 2005s set new pricing records – but only for the most sought-after wines. In spring 2006 a Texan importer told me he had many clients lined up for a case or more of each First Growth. Price wasn't an issue for these buyers, who could no doubt be replicated in Hong Kong or Geneva.

However, for large numbers of growers the situation by 2005 was that Bordeaux as a whole was no longer capable of selling the substantial quantities of wine it routinely produced. Most of that wine came from areas that had been recently developed and should never have been planted with vines in the first place. For such growers, especially with a dominance of white grapes, the future looks bleak, and many bankruptcies are likely. If, in the long term, this means the quantity of Bordeaux wine on the market is more closely attuned to international demand and that its overall quality is better, then the disappearance of many mediocre properties will be no bad thing.

But the fall in demand for Bordeaux on both domestic and international markets is affecting prestigious as well as mediocre properties. The director of one classed growth told me in 2003 that he had sold only forty per cent of his very good 2001s. The owner of a Second-Growth Sauternes estate told me he hadn't sold a single case of his 2004 *en primeur*. Will he fare any better with the mostly overpriced 2006s?

Bordeaux has always been a speculative marketplace, but it was not always a system of extremes. The gap between even a sound classified growth and a First Growth has continued to expand (not to mention the ever-widening gap between a well-made *cru bourgeois* and a First Growth), a gap that widened even further with the superb 2005 vintage. One consequence of this is that the "traditional" Bordeaux lover, always prepared to pay a high but not foolish price for the wine, is being increasingly priced out of the market. The proprietors may not care, because the place of this "traditional" market has been taken by the new rich, who eagerly follow orders from the gurus of the wine press and for whom price is a minor consideration. Whether these new buyers will remain steadfast is another matter. If the "traditional" claret lover was sometimes absurdly loyal, placing his order year in, year out for his favourite Montrose or La Mission, the new well-heeled wine drinker is likely to switch allegiance from year to year, depending on fad and fashion — and scores.

Many of us stubbornly persist in seeing fine wine not just as another luxury brand, but as a drink that forms part of a culture of good living. There may be many customers who are happy to drink labels rather than wines, but the bedrock of any region's support has to be those who drink wines rather than labels.

The way in which the sought-after wines are marketed also does no favours to the trade or the consumer. It is no secret that owners with a number of properties attach the lesser growths to the coat-tails of their finest wine. So if a négociant (or importer, or retailer) wants fifty cases of Château Fabulous, he or she will be politely informed that the order can be secured by also taking 100 cases of Château Middling and 200 of Château Humdrum. The unfortunate retailer, having flogged Château Fabulous, is then stuck with the task of persuading customers of the remarkable if unusual merits of those greatly underrated wines, Château Middling and Château Humdrum.

SAUTERNES AND OTHERS

This book also considers the sweet wines of Bordeaux, which have been unaffected by the speculative fever that characterizes the market for the region's great red wines. Sauternes and Barsac are prestigious wines, miracles of perfectly wedded agriculture and a benign freakishness of nature. They are wines that have gone through cycles of success and slump. By the 1970s a lack of investment was having dire consequences. A handful of properties such as Yquem, Climens, Coutet, Nairac, and Raymond-Lafon were dedicated to maintaining the costly and labour-intensive practices of the past, all aimed at producing a good crop of perfectly botrytized grapes that would then be vinified and aged with care. But many properties, including First Growths, had thrown out their oak barrels, chaptalized routinely, over-sulphured, and did everything possible to rob their wines of personality and drinkability. The 1983 vintage, widely acclaimed, brought in profits that were often invested in restoring traditional practices, and standards improved across the region. Most classified growths were making very good wines by the time the glorious trio of vintages from 1988 to 1990 came around.

More recently, vintages such as 2001 and 2005 have sold well, and for good prices. Yet the commercial progress of Sauternes remains sporadic. In large part this is the fault of the Sauternais, who seem incapable of teaming up to promote their wines, despite the fact that wine critics have swooned over the terrific quality of the wines themselves. But sweet wine producers worldwide have to fight against those who decry sweet wines in general as injurious to health because of high sugar content, as incompatible with the vast majority of foods, as relics of the past when sweetness was equated with nutrition. This is a battle the Sauternais are poorly equipped to fight. And once again, the entrenched *Place de Bordeaux* dissuades producers and merchants alike from making much of an effort to promote the wines. The producers cannot negotiate direct sales on the back of promotional efforts, and for merchants the volumes involved are too insignificant. So Sauternes remains a cult wine, adored by a few, ignored by most. Given the enormous costs of production, one can't help wondering from time to time whether such a hand-crafted style of wine can survive.

The growers of the lesser sweet wine regions are facing the same problems but with even fewer resources for combating them. In outstanding vintages there is no doubt that regions such as Loupiac and Cérons are capable of making great sweet wines. But often the results in the bottle are disappointing. With very few exceptions, prices for these wines are significantly lower than for Sauternes and Barsac. Lower returns mean that growers are less able or willing to make the investments and efforts in vineyards and wineries that will result in great wines. On the other hand, relatively low prices clearly appeal to certain markets and consumers, so all is not lost. Since the *Place de Bordeaux* has no interest in these wines, many properties have successfully built up networks of private customers and retailers.

If the confusion and mendacity that infest the *Place* are enduring blots on its reputation and a grave disservice to the often deluded consumer, there is nonetheless much that is positive in modern-day Bordeaux. I doubt that the overall quality of wine, even at relatively modest levels, has ever been higher. Enormous advances have been made in viticulture and oenology, often thanks to the close involvement of the University of Bordeaux's renowned faculty of oenology in the wine industry on its doorstep. There is no longer any excuse for producing bad wine in Bordeaux. There will always be vintage variation, but the truly ghastly vintages of years such as 1968 and 1972 are unlikely ever to be repeated. Global warming has played its part, but so have the factors mentioned above.

The introduction of second wines has done wonders for the quality of the *grand vin*. In the past the entire crop was picked, vinified, and bottled together, with little or no selection. That is unthinkable today. Wines are no longer tainted by hail or rot, since affected bunches are eliminated at sorting tables. There may be some faint justification in the complaint that the ubiquitous presence of consultant oenologists such as Michel Rolland, Denis Dubourdieu, and Jacques Boissenot is "standardizing" the wines of Bordeaux, but one must also recognize that their expertise and vigilance have helped to raise quality. With parcel selection becoming ever more detailed, as growers seek to identify the typicity of their best vineyards, so the blending process becomes more complex and more crucial. Here too the experience of the consultant is an essential supplement to the taste of the owner and the palate of the cellarmaster.

Proprietors may be cynical in their manipulation of the market, but almost without exception the important estates are offering wines of sound quality at the very least. Twenty years ago, there were a good number of classified growths that produced mediocre wines. Today they can be counted on the fingers of two hands. The growers know there is no future in mediocrity, that regions such as Napa, Stellenbosch, Margaret River, and Tuscany are capable of producing superb wines based on the Bordeaux varieties. Some Bordelais may look down their noses at what they regard as the meretriciousness of the "New World" but their ranks are dwindling. May-Eliane de Lencquesaing, Jean-Guillaume Prats, Christian Seely, Pierre Lurton, Christian Moueix, and many other leading figures are fully aware that the international competition is intense and that Bordeaux cannot afford to take short cuts. Such producers strive for ever-higher quality and consistency, and for the most part they deliver the goods. It is in their long-term interests to do so, but we the consumers also benefit enormously. We are right to grumble that many Bordeaux wines are grossly overpriced, but we are under no obligation to buy them, and if we are fortunate enough to be able to afford them, then it is unlikely we will be disappointed by their quality. A great Médoc from 1990, a great Pomerol from 1998, a great Sauternes from 2001, a great white Pessac-Léognan from 2000 – these are wines that satisfy the senses and stimulate the intellect. What more can we ask of a fine wine?

2. The Land

Robert Louis Stevenson once described the wine of Napa as "bottled poetry". In which case, Bordeaux is bottled history. But it is of course more than that. Like any other great wine, Bordeaux is defined by its soils and its climate. These are the factors that determine its typicity, aided by support systems such as grape varieties and human intervention. Like most of the world's great wine regions, Bordeaux is essentially marginal. The climate is usually benign enough to ensure that the grapes ripen properly, but sufficiently hazardous to ensure that from time to time vintages can be hellish compounds of frost, hail, chill, and downpours, all adding up to a riot of rot and unripeness. When grapes do ripen, they ripen in different ways, leading to considerable vintage variations, which are indeed part of the fascination of Bordeaux. The vintages of 1989 and 1990, for example, are both excellent, but excellent in different ways.

Average rainfall measured at Bordeaux's airport is 851 millimetres (33.5 inches), but there are significant variations from year to year. Almost until the last moment the grower cannot be certain of a good harvest. The history books are crammed with years that were all set to be "vintages of the century" but were wrecked by late rains.

Yet even climate is not constant in its inconstancy. Global warming has undoubtedly affected the wines of Bordeaux. Records kept at Mouton-Rothschild confirm that the average temperature throughout the year has risen by one degree Centigrade over the past decade. Analyses by Pascal Ribéreau-Gayon at the University of Bordeaux have established that from 1990 to 1995 the average start of flowering was June 14. In 1997 it was May 23, and in 1999 May 31. From 1990 to 1995 *véraison* began, on average, on August 18; in 1999, it was on August 4.

Early flowering usually leads to an early harvest, which in turn decreases the risk of encountering inclement weather in the mid- to late autumn. Harvesting in mid- to late September is less risky than harvesting two weeks later in October. Decades such as the 1930s and 1950s produced numerous vintages that were frankly abysmal. Who can recall with pleasure the taste of a 1935 or 1954? Or for that matter 1963 or 1968? Yet since 1984 there have been no truly poor vintages. The 1987s and 1997s are on the light side, but they are far from undrinkable. The 1992s and 1993s are not easy to love, but some good, if short-lived, wines were made in those sodden years. Technological improvements in the vineyard and the winery have lessened the wretchedness of wretched years, but, even taking that into account, the climate for grape-farming in Bordeaux has been more benign in the past fifteen years than in living memory.

This is bound to have an effect on the taste of the wines. Kees Van Leeuwen at Château Cheval Blanc does believe that global warming is a reality. So far,

> *global warming has been largely positive for late-maturing grapes in Bordeaux like Cabernet Sauvignon or Petit Verdot, as there's a better chance of ripening fully. But for early-ripening varieties such as Merlot and Sauvignon Blanc, you risk losing aromatic freshness.*[1]

Hail is a more random hazard. Although usually highly localized, it can cause considerable devastation. In 1999 a hailstorm in St-Emilion cut a swathe 500 metres (1,640 feet) wide, cutting through 500 hectares of vineyards, including Angélus, Beau-Séjour-Bécot, and Canon. Hail, which usually clatters down in the early summer, has the power to destroy part of the crop, and to damage the skins of ripening berries, opening the gate to rot. It can also scar the wood, which can affect the next year's crop.

There is not much a grower can do to protect vines against hail, though at Château Le Pape in Pessac-Léognan I have inspected a remarkable piece of machinery in the middle of the vineyards. When the risk is high, an alarm sounds in the château. Patrick Monjanel then triggers the device, which uses various gases to shoot heat seven kilometres (4.3 miles) high into the sky. This provides protection over a five-kilometre (3.1-mile) radius. He claims that this too-good-to-be-true device is effective. Daniel Cathiard of Smith-Haut-Lafitte came round to take a look at this device, as he was thinking of having this system installed at Smith. But he was advised that his vineyards were covered by Le Pape's.

Frost is an annual hazard, and the most damaging frosts take place during the spring, when the leaves begin shyly to unfurl. Some vineyards particularly prone to frost, such as Domaine de Chevalier, are equipped with windmills that circulate the air and deter frost.

TERROIR

Climate has a powerful role to play in determining the ripeness and the balance of a wine, but it has only a limited influence on the flavour of a wine. Here the notion of terroir comes into its own. Climate, to be sure, is part and parcel of the catch-all concept of terroir, but soil is paramount. When we think of the terroir of Chablis we think of the shimmering limestone slopes; when we contemplate the terroir of the Mosel, we recall the near-vertical scree of slate looming over the river. We should also think of the climate, but it is still the soil that seems to determine flavour.

There are two major soil types in the Bordeaux region: gravel and clay-limestone. The former is crucial to the typicity of the Médoc and Graves. The latter, known in French as *argilo-calcaire*, is more commonly encountered in the Côtes and the Entre-Deux-Mers and the more westerly areas of the Médoc and Graves.

Clay-limestone is unremarkable. It is a soil type found all over Europe, and it can be the source of excellent wines. It is dominant on the Right Bank, especially in St-Emilion and its satellites, and in the various Côtes. However, there is considerable variation in the depth of clay and the porous quality of the limestone. If the clay is too thick and rich, there is a danger of waterlogging, but in dry years its water-retentive properties are an advantage. Limestone is more discreetly water-retentive and on the great terroirs of the St-Emilion plateau it keeps hydric stress at bay without soaking the roots in water, which could result in bloated bunches and excessive yields. The Libournais soils are discussed in greater detail in the introduction to St-Emilion.

Gravel, however, is more unusual. It is the scattered seed of the Pleistocene Ice Age, in the early Quaternary period of earth's geological epic. As James Wilson explains in his useful book, *Terroir*, the Ice Age was not a single event, but a series of alternating periods of freeze and thaw. These floods released huge volumes of rock and pebbles. Those that helped create the soils of Bordeaux came primarily from two sources: the Pyrenees and the Massif Central. Grinding and coursing their way down from those mountain ranges, the rock splattered into pebbles and stones and gravel, and when the force of its propulsion weakened, it settled down comfortably on riverside terraces in Bordeaux. The gravel and rock were not pure mineral matter, of course; they were mixed with sand, mud, clay, and any other material scooped up in their downward trajectory. The special contribution of the Massif Central was quartz and agates, while the Pyrenees deposited black and red Lydian (*lydenne*) stones. Quartz is easily the most important element in the gravel terraces. This complexity of composition accounts for the lack of uniformity within the Bordeaux vineyards. Thus the gravel of Pauillac, in its depth, composition, and consistency, differs from that of Margaux or Léognan.

There were four major stages of gravel migration and deposit in the Bordeaux region: the Günz, Mindel, Riss, and Würm. We can more or less forget about the last two, which were inundated toward the end of the last Ice Age, when the Gironde rose by some sixty metres (197 feet). By far the most significant stage is the Günzian. Almost all the most renowned gravel *croupes* (or ridges) in the Médoc, Graves, and Pomerol are of Günzian gravel. It was not at first apparent to the hesitant settlers of the marshy Médoc that its soils would prove ideal for viticulture. It was only when Dutch engineers drained the areas along the estuary in the eighteenth century that the water table of the nearby gravel terraces was lowered, facilitating cultivation and improving the natural drainage, which is so essential to good grape-farming.

The gravel terraces rest on bands of rock of varying types. Limestone is common, and so is a sandstone-dominated hardpan known as *alios*. The depth of the gravel is another variable factor. In parts of Pauillac it can be nine metres (twenty-nine feet) or more in depth; elsewhere, where the bedrock is closer to the surface, it is considerably shallower. Deep gravel assures good drainage, but beyond that it is the composition of the bed that will contribute to the flavour and structure of the wine emanating from it. The bands of clay and marl on which the gravel rests are a source of moisture, so that in the best vineyards the vines will never suffer hydric stress, even in the hottest years. Nor is a gravel terrace inert; it contains mineral elements and micro-organisms, which can stimulate the vines. In addition, gravel retains heat, and can reflect warmth accumulated during daylight back onto the leaves and vines. This will accelerate the ripening of the vines.

Possession of a gravelly soil is in itself no guarantor of exceptional quality. There can be significant variations within what appears to be a uniform site. Philippe Courrian of Château Tour-Haut-Caussan stresses the sheer diversity of the Médocain soils. "Neighbourly proximity", he has written, "doesn't exist in the Médoc vineyards, and to claim that your vines are great because they adjoin those of Latour or Mouton is a falsification. Just one centimetre away from the finest soil in the world there could be a terroir completely unsuited to the vine."[2]

In the Médoc, and to a slightly lesser extent in the Graves, proximity to the river is regarded as beneficial. It is certainly a boon in years when temperatures plummet during the spring, bringing a risk of frost. The vines of Latour, famously, are hardly ever affected by frost, and even in devastating years such as 1991 manage to deliver a moderate crop of good wine. The other benefit is that these vineyards are on terraces that slope down to the alluvial *palus* soils by the river, and those slopes provide excellent drainage.

Soils that lie inland from the river-bordering communes certainly differ from the often deep gravel terraces by the estuary. Soils with a higher clay content, as is common in the western parts of the appellations and in large swathes of St-Estèphe, for example, are colder than the terraces. They are more prone to frost, and the vines may well ripen later than those on gravel. This makes them more suitable for Merlot than for late-ripening Cabernet.

Kees Van Leeuwen of Cheval Blanc has undertaken very detailed soil studies for various estates. Philippe Blanc at Beychevelle has found it helps him work out how to use his soils to the best advantage. However, Vincent Faure of Sociando-Mallet, who was born at Château Latour, finds the studies fascinating but argues that they serve no useful purpose, since experience counts for as much as scientific data when it comes to best exploiting one's terroir.

Proving the idea of terroir

I am a firm believer in the notion of terroir, but I also believe it is essentially mysterious. The experience of centuries informed growers where the vines thrived best. The superiority of the vineyards of, say, Latour over those of Lynch-Moussas is demonstrated by experience, and can be supported by comparing the soil structure and microclimates of each. But it is far more difficult to establish any direct correlation between those micro-conditions and the quality and character of the wine that results from them. Recently I stood in the vineyards of Le Musigny, one of Burgundy's finest vineyards, and asked the growers how they accounted for the greatness of the wines. Nobody could give a clear answer. That the wines were greater than those from neighbouring *crus*, no one doubted; but there was no single factor that accounted for it. I believe the same holds true in Bordeaux. Vineyard and estate managers have become passionate about conducting soil analyses (such as at Lascombes and Olivier), simply in order to understand better the raw material they are dealing with. They end up with as many as eighty different parcels, and may even vinify most of them separately,

2 Courrian and Creignou, *Vigneron du Médoc*, Payot, Paris, 1996, 38–40

knowing that each will give a subtly different wine. But knowing and manipulating those nuances is not the same as understanding precisely why they exist.

The notion of terroir, at least in Bordeaux, is muddied by the fact that it is the estate rather than the soil itself that is classified. The owner of a small property once took me into his vineyards in northern Pauillac, and pointed to some rows of vines. "They used to belong to me, and I'm *cru bourgeois*. Then a few years ago I sold them to Mouton, so now they're *premier cru*." I put this point to Mouton subsequently, and the response was that legally those vines were now part of the *premier cru* estate, but that did not mean they would necessarily enter the blend for the *grand vin*. Nonetheless, this anecdote illustrates that since a Bordeaux château is a brand, the notion of terroir is diluted. Sales and exchanges of blocks of vines are nothing new. The wine historian Dewey Markham points out that between 1841 and 1850 there were fifteen such transactions between Latour and other properties in Pauillac.[3]

There are some classified growths that own roughly the same vineyards as they controlled in 1855, but not that many. Nor is there anything illegitimate about tinkering with one's vineyard area, though the law does not permit exchanges of parcels between different communes. It is well known that after Alexis Lichine bought Château Lascombes in Margaux, he went on a buying spree to expand the run-down property. Clearly many of those parcels were not of the quality one would associate with a Second Growth. The current team at Lascombes admit that about one-third of the property is not up to standard, and those wines are never used for the *grand vin*. But such scruples are voluntary. In tougher times, especially before selection became widespread, I do not doubt that there were years when proprietors felt tempted or compelled to use every single drop from their vineyards.

Stunning conjuring tricks have been undertaken over the years. When Baron Philippe de Rothschild bought the growth now known as Armailhac, he had every right to incorporate its vineyards into those of Mouton, though he did not do so. The same would have been true when Lafite acquired Duhart-Milon. Five hectares of Château Gazin were absorbed by Pomerol's Château Pétrus in 1969. A parcel of Château Haut-Bages-Libéral that lay close to Pontet-Canet was incorporated into the latter estate by the Cruse family, who happened to own both of them at the time. The reader who wishes to be thoroughly confused can look at the chapter on Margaux and ponder the history of Durfort-Vivens, Desmirail, and Brane-Cantenac, and the frequent transfers of vines and names that occurred in the past.

There is no conspiracy afoot here. The Bordelais system differs from the Burgundian model, where the vine and its location are paramount. In Burgundy the vineyard was assessed; in Bordeaux it has always, since the mid-eighteenth century, been the brand that has been rated. Nor should too much be made of this very fluid notion of terroir. Certainly it is open to abuse, but these days few châteaux would be doing themselves any favours by wilfully using inferior wine in their *grand vin*. Most (though certainly not all) estates are trying to do the best they can. With posses of experienced wine critics and knowledgeable merchants on the prowl, there is no point in aiming for mediocrity.

Finally, it is impossible to gauge the influence of the winemaker. With so many choices available to any winemaker, the style, flavour, and structure of any wine are easily manipulated, and this is not meant as a criticism. It is perfectly legitimate to ferment at 28°C (82°F) or at 32°C (90°F), to age in older barrels or eighty per cent new oak, to fine with egg white or not at all, to blend early or to blend late. Yet these are all decisions that will have some bearing on the final product. At a blind tasting of St-Emilion top growths at *Decanter* magazine a few years ago, I was impressed when one of England's top wine merchants correctly identified about half the wines. It later occurred to me to wonder whether he was astutely recognizing the terroir of Ausone or Figeac, or simply identifying the winemaking signature of each property. Terroir, in short, does not exist in isolation.

3 Markham, *1855: A History of the Bordeaux Classification*, Wiley, New York, 1998, 188

GRAPE VARIETIES

Clearly there is a close relation between the flavour of any wine and the grape variety/varieties from which it is made. It would be wrong to suppose that any variety has the same flavour profile wherever it is grown. Bordeaux winemakers insist that Merlot grown in the Médoc is very different from the same variety grown in Pomerol or St-Emilion. Sauvignon Blanc grown in the Graves tastes different from the variety cultivated in Sancerre; the same is true of Cabernet Franc in St-Emilion and the same variety in Chinon.

There are eight varieties planted in Bordeaux, as well as tiny areas of varieties such as Carmenère. The reds are Cabernet Sauvignon, Cabernet Franc, Merlot, Petit Verdot, and Malbec; the whites are Sauvignon Blanc, Sémillon, and Muscadelle. Although Cabernet Sauvignon is associated with the Left Bank and Merlot with the Right, it has to be recalled that there is an increasing amount of Merlot being planted in the Médoc and Graves, and that top estates such as Pichon-Lalande, Palmer, and Haut-Brion have long had a large proportion of Merlot in the blend. Similarly, there are St-Emilion properties such as Ausone, Figeac, Cheval Blanc, and Jean Fauré with a great deal of Cabernet Franc and/or Cabernet Sauvignon.

The number of varieties planted has been greatly reduced since phylloxera required the replanting of Bordeaux's vineyards. In 1794 there were records of thirty-four red varieties and twenty-nine white in the Libournais, though there were fewer in the Médoc.[4] There were undoubtedly more if sub-varieties were included. When vineyards were replanted, it was inevitable that the varieties selected were those that were most resistant to disease and most productive, though one hopes that quality too was a factor. Philippe Dhalluin of Château Mouton-Rothschild suspects the taste of Bordeaux has improved since that replanting. He has encountered a near-defunct Bordeaux variety called Pardotte, but finds the wine incredibly acidic. It was therefore a positive development to have this variety suppressed after phylloxera.

In the 1850s the writer Armand d'Armailhacq published an important book on the Médoc, and here he cites the principal varieties as Gros Cabernet (probably Cabernet Franc), Cabernet Sauvignon, Cabarnelle (this seems to be the same as Carmenère), Merlau, Malbec, and Verdot. In other nineteenth-century texts I have found references to Carmenet and Cabernet Blanc (at Château Montrose). In 1874 the classic reference book by Féret states that at Pauillac seventy-five per cent of vineyards were planted with Cabernet Sauvignon, the remainder with Merlot and Malbec; in Pessac, however, the proportion of Cabernet was around fifty per cent, the remainder Merlot and Malbec.

It should also be remembered that many hybrid varieties were planted in Bordeaux until fairly recently. Jean Miailhe recalls seeing hybrid vines in the vineyards of Giscours and other properties in the 1940s.[5] Indeed, by the late 1950s one-third of all French vineyards were planted with hybrids. Such vines were very productive but the wine itself was, in the succinct word of Philippe Courrian, *infâme*. The invention of chromatography made the use of such vines detectable in the early 1960s and hastened the long-overdue uprooting of hybrids.

As in most wine regions of the world, there are numerous rootstocks and clones developed for each variety. These are selected on the basis of resistance to disease, productivity, size of berries, and so forth. It is widely admitted that rootstocks such as SO4 are usually too prolific, and the same is true, for example, of many modern clones of Cabernet Franc. With no incentive for high crops, vineyard managers tend to be cautious in their choice of both rootstocks and clones, avoiding those developed primarily for the generosity of their crop. Much research has been done, notably at Haut-Brion since 1977, when, in collaboration with the French agricultural research institute INRA, 370 red clones have been assessed.

Most Bordeaux wines blend two or more varieties. There are exceptions, such as Pomerols or St-Emilions that are pure Merlot, Sauternes or Barsacs that are pure Sémillon, or Graves that are pure Sauvignon Blanc. The long-established custom of blending is surely derived from a kind of insurance

4 Peppercorn, *Bordeaux*, Faber, London, 1991, 9

5 Lawton and Miailhe, *Conversations et souvenirs autour du vin de Bordeaux*, Editions Confluences, Bordeaux, 1999, 26

policy practised by grape-growers in all marginal regions. The old vineyards of Portugal or Austria were field blends, with varieties all mixed up and interplanted. If one or more failed to ripen or was attacked by pests, there was a fighting chance some of the others would make it through to harvest. There have been plenty of vintages in Bordeaux, especially in the Médoc, where one or another variety has been virtually eliminated, thanks to *coulure* or rot. So it is not surprising that the growers have saved themselves from wipe-out by planting two or more varieties.

Cabernet Sauvignon

By the mid-nineteenth century this was becoming established as the most important variety in the Médoc, and with good reason. It is less susceptible to spring frost than Merlot, and it resists rot quite successfully, which is just as well, given that the variety is late-ripening and often needs to survive autumn downpours. However, it is more prone to suffer from powdery mildew than Merlot. The berries are fairly small, so there is a high ratio of skin to juice. Colour is deep and the natural concentration of phenolics high. The consequence is a dark wine with a good deal of tannin that provides the backbone for most long-lived Bordeaux.

Its flavour is distinctive. Blackcurrants are the dominant fruit aroma, but other dark fruits are often discernible, such as blackberries and black cherries. In the New World, Cabernet can be a fruit bomb, but in Bordeaux it is prized more for its elegance. Unripe Cabernet Sauvignon can be unpleasant, with marked vegetal aromas. In small doses these can be attractively grassy; in excess, aromas of green peppers and asparagus take over, and these are undesirable in a red wine.

Merlot

Wine writer Benoît de Coster maintains that Merlot is "*sans nul doute*" the finest Bordeaux variety because it almost always achieves complete maturity and remains healthy. De Coster is a Belgian, predisposed to the Right Bank, so that may colour his view, which is not widely shared. On the other hand, it makes perfect sense to say that if Cabernet Sauvignon is king in the Médoc, then Merlot can claim sovereignty in St-Emilion and Pomerol. It ripens about two weeks earlier than Cabernet, which is an undoubted advantage, but it is also more susceptible to spring frosts because it buds earlier. Cabernet can deliver excellent wine even at fairly high yields, but that is not the case with Merlot, which yearns to overproduce and will do so unless severely pruned and, if necessary, green-harvested. It also shows some fragility during flowering, when it often succumbs to *coulure*. It can also suffer from downy mildew.

Its sensory appeal is easy to understand. It gives rich fruit and doesn't lack tannin and structure, but it rarely has the harsh edge that Cabernet can demonstrate. It is supple and lush, easy-going from lesser sites, powerfully structured from outstanding terroir. Sugar, and therefore alcohol, levels tend to be considerably higher than for the Cabernets.

The variety is definitely gaining ground on the Left Bank, as Cabernet makes a steady retreat. Already by 1988, half the Bordeaux vineyards were planted with it. In some areas, such as St-Estèphe and Listrac, Cabernet Sauvignon struggles to ripen, and is often being replaced by Merlot. The same is true in some inland areas of the Graves. In such cases it makes sense to replace Cabernet with Merlot, especially on colder soils with some clay and limestone content. It is tempting to think that the main reason for planting more Merlot is commercial. However, Dominique Befve of Château Lascombes insists this is not so, as Merlot's yields are often lower than those from Cabernet. It is also more likely to suffer from rot.

Cabernet Franc

This variety rarely dominates any blend in Bordeaux; Cheval Blanc and Le Dôme in St-Emilion are among the few exceptions. But it plays a strong supporting role in St-Emilion, where it has flourished since the late eighteenth century, and is present in many vineyards in other parts of the region, including the Médoc. It buds and ripens about a week earlier than Cabernet Sauvignon. Unripe Cabernet Franc can be nastily green and vegetal, so it is important to keep yields to no more than fifty hectolitres per hectare to ensure it ripens properly. It is unpopular in certain quarters because clonal selections of the variety tend to be too productive. Massal selections, on the other hand, can be excellent. Despite its relatively light colour and medium body, it can, as Château Cheval Blanc gloriously illustrates, age extremely well if grown on the right soils.

Its unpopularity in much of the Médoc is due to many factors, notably its susceptibility to disease and rot. Marcel Ducasse at Château Lagrange finds the variety green and watery, except when the vines are very old. Philippe Dhalluin agrees, saying Cabernet Franc gives good wine at Mouton only because of the age of the vines. He does not dislike Cabernet Franc, but finds that Cabernet Sauvignon in the Médoc is invariably better. Didier Furt at Château Carmes Haut-Brion, in contrast, is an enthusiast, finding that the variety contributes acidity, vigour, and power to the wine. It can have high tannins, and needs to be handled gently during fermentation so as not to extract bitter elements.

Cabernet Franc has more freshness and perfume than Merlot, and thus provides a useful balance to that dominant variety on the Right Bank. Growers in St-Emilion insist that the vine needs heat, doesn't like stress, and needs soils with good drainage, which rules out most sandy soils. Hubert de Boüard of Château Angélus believes some clay or limestone in the subsoil is essential. Unlike Merlot, he points out, Cabernet Franc needs to be at least fifteen years old to produce top-quality fruit. Olivier Decelle at Château Jean Faure believes that although you need to wait to ensure the grapes are fully ripe, once that moment is reached, it's important to pick fast, as after a few days its quality will tumble.

Carmenère

Better known in Chile than in Bordeaux, this ancient variety, which all but disappeared after phylloxera, is making a very modest comeback in St-Emilion and the Médoc. A few properties such as Belle-Vue in the Haut-Médoc are planting it, and there has always been a small block of it at Mouton and Haut-Bailly. It is prized for its richness and concentration when fully ripe, but is susceptible to *coulure* and to *oïdium*.

Malbec

Known for centuries as Pressac in St-Emilion, this variety has a reputation in decline. It arrived in St-Emilion from Cahors, as the purchaser of Château de Pressac in the 1730s was from that region of the southwest. The variety became known as Noir de Pressac. When it was subsequently transported by a M. Malbec to the Médoc, its name changed again.

It was the variety that probably dominated the vineyards of Lafite in the late eighteenth century.[6] Pierre Lurton, director of Cheval Blanc and Yquem, points out that in the early nineteenth century about sixty per cent of Bordeaux's vineyards were planted with the variety. Today the consensus is that it has little to contribute to a great wine from Bordeaux. Not only is it susceptible to mildew and *coulure*, but it has large berries and easily overcrops, resulting in soft wine with little character. Indeed, Gérard Bécot of Beau-Séjour-Bécot points out that its large berries were the reason it was cultivated, as planting Malbec was an easy way to boost yields. On the other hand it does ripen early, which can be an advantage in Bordeaux. However, one Blaye grower observed that because it is susceptible to rot, it is often picked too early, resulting in vegetal flavours. It has largely disappeared from the most prestigious vineyards, though it retains some popularity in the Côtes de Bourg and Blaye. Gruaud-Larose conserves a one-hectare block, and maintains that in the late eighteenth century it was the most popular variety in the Médoc. It represents ten per cent of the vineyard at Château de Gaillat in the southern Graves, where owner Hélène Bertrand-Coste says she likes its spiciness despite its capriciousness and high yields. If Malbec seems to perform far better in Argentina than in France, that is almost

6 Johnson, *The Story of Wine*, Mitchell Beazley, London, 1989, 261

certainly because the cuttings sent to Argentina were from pre-phylloxera vines. Clonal selections available in France tend to be groomed for productivity rather than quality.

Petit Verdot

This was the grape of choice for those planting vines on the alluvial soils of the *palus* along the shores of the Gironde from the seventeenth century onwards. This muscular variety is now enjoying a renaissance. It is almost chic. It crops up as a single-varietal wine in the oddest places, such as the Hunter Valley in Australia. There are even such wines in Bordeaux, though the quantities are minuscule. Petit Verdot in the Médoc is usually regarded as a pungent spice to be added to the blend with care. It needs to be very ripe to succeed, and it ripens very late. It is usually picked after Cabernet Sauvignon, though in areas such as Listrac, where Cabernet struggles to ripen, Petit Verdot can ripen first. However, according to Patrice Pagès of Fourcas-Dupré, if you wait too long before picking Petit Verdot, the grapes can turn to mush as they veer toward overmaturity.

A number of properties in Margaux have a few hectares of Petit Verdot, but in dubious vintages it is excluded from the *grand vin*. However, in good years châteaux such as Lagrange and Léoville-Poyferré can include a good ten per cent in the blend. When not fully ripe, its tannins can be overbearing. It is admired for its colour, its finesse, its backbone, its fullness of flavour, its hints of liquorice and spice, and its suitability for blending with Cabernet Sauvignon. In general, Cabernet from Margaux is more fragile than the same vine planted farther north, so a dash of Petit Verdot can add colour and weight. Its drawbacks are a susceptibility to *coulure* and rot; it also has fragile stems that can snap in a strong wind. Clonal selections can be too vigorous; Caroline Frey at La Lagune got rid of the clonal Petit Verdot (clone 400 is the major culprit) and replaced it with massal selections. Thomas Duroux at Palmer says it needs to be very carefully managed, with yields kept down to no more than thirty-five hl/ha; if this is done, then it can ripen every year, and not only in top vintages. Ripe Petit Verdot, says Duroux, contributes structure, aroma, and tannins to the blend.

Not everyone shares the new enthusiasm for Petit Verdot. I believe it was the late Peter Sichel who remarked that in good vintages you don't need it; and in poor ones, it doesn't ripen at all. At Brane-Cantenac in Margaux, it has been phased out over recent years, perhaps because of the high proportion of Cabernet Sauvignon in the vineyards.

Petit Verdot is not associated with the Right Bank. However, when INAO was reviewing the rules and regulations for AC Pomerol, Christian Moueix did suggest that Petit Verdot should be an authorized variety. INAO did not agree.

Colombard

This white variety has no great reputation, yet a good deal survives in Blaye, where it produces aromatic wines that are charming when young but do not age well.

Sémillon

This is the most widely planted white variety. It is vigorous, and its golden berries are larger than those of Sauvignon Blanc. So if good wine is to be made, the yield must be kept low. Sémillon is thin-skinned and thus susceptible to botrytis, which makes it a variety of choice for sweet wines rather than dry ones. Nonetheless it has a strong following in the Graves, where the grape gives rich, unctuous, full-bodied wines, with some tropical fruit and honeyed aromas. The texture is waxy, in contrast to the more pungent, perkier Sauvignon Blanc. It also has the ability to age well. The vine itself is very long-lived – centenarian parcels are not unusual in the Premières Côtes – which appeals to growers anxious to avoid the costs involved in regular replanting. It is often blended with Sauvignon Blanc, which balances the plumpness of Sémillon with its leaner, racier, more acidic structure. But the introduction of cool-fermentation techniques in the late 1980s revealed a hitherto unsuspected finesse and vigour in Sémillon, which, when poorly vinified, could be rounded, flat, and dull.

Sauvignon Blanc

The variety ripens early and retains good acidity, giving a zesty, tangy, refreshing character. It is versatile enough to give simple, racy, unoaked wines for immediate consumption, as in the Entre-Deux-Mers and parts of the southern Graves, and more solid, structured, and complex wines when barrel-fermented. The variety has had a rough ride from commentators as diverse as Jancis Robinson and Brian Croser, and is often criticized for its simplicity and its inability to age. But this is to do it an injustice, as anyone who has drunk a mature Couhins-Lurton or Smith-Haut-Lafitte can confirm. In Pessac-Léognan the white wine must contain at least thirty per cent Sauvignon.

Muscadelle

Although not directly related to the Muscat family, this variety does have a perfumed aroma that many growers relish. Muscadelle is hardly ever vinified as a varietal (though I have encountered one from Bergerac), and rarely represents more than fifteen per cent of any vineyard. Although it ripens early, it has all kinds of drawbacks: it is productive, it can succumb to *coulure*, as well as to powdery mildew, grey rot, and botrytis. For this reason many growers find it too tiresome to work with, but it retains its stubborn admirers, as a component in both dry and sweet wines.

Sauvignon Gris

This offshoot of Sauvignon Blanc was developed at the wine college at Château La Tour-Blanche in Sauternes. Its principal characteristics are good sugar levels, earlier ripening than Sauvignon Blanc, and floral rather than grassy aromas. It has attracted quite a following in the Graves, and is discussed further in those sections.

DISEASES

The humid Bordeaux climate requires a constant struggle against maladies that affect the vine's development. The high density of plantation can also encourage the spread of disease. Since the nineteenth century treatments have been developed to combat these maladies, and many are highly effective. But there are understandable concerns these days about the toxicity of some of these remedies. The conscientious grower needs to achieve the right balance between unavoidable and excessive treatments.

Oïdium

This disease, also known as powdery mildew, has been a constant vexation to Bordeaux growers ever since its arrival in 1851. It is a fungal growth that attacks young leaves and grapes by forming white spots that spread across the surface of the affected part. It is wind-borne and spreads most rapidly in warm weather. If left untreated the leaves will drop off and the grapes split and dry. The cure is sulphur treatments. The custom of planting roses at the end of each row derives from the belief that roses act as an early warning system for *oïdium*.

Mildew

(Also called downy mildew.) The malady primarily affects the leaves, which become discoloured and can eventually drop off. The effect is to reduce significantly the process of photosynthesis, which in turn slows maturation. Like *oïdium*, it cannot be left untreated. In the 1880s a treatment was found in the form of copper sulphate blended with lime (*bouillie bordelaise* or Bordeaux mixture). Despite the ready availability of a treatment, the problem cannot be eliminated entirely, and mildew has ruined certain vintages such as 1910 and 1915. It is still very much present in the vineyards, and posed severe problems in 1999 and 2000; early treatment was essential. Sprays more effective than *bouillie bordelaise* have now been developed. A related ailment, called *mildiou mosaïque*, turns the leaves purple before harvest and slows down further maturation. However, it leaves the grapes unaffected.

Coulure and *millerandage*

These are not diseases but problems that occur during the flowering, which usually takes place in June. If the weather is too cold, problems will arise. *Coulure* is the dropping off of the infant flowers or berries, which fail to set normally. This has no effect on the quality of the wine, but reduces the yield. For some growers a bit of *coulure* is a welcome alternative to sending teams into the vineyards to green-harvest. *Millerandage* is the failure of some berries within a bunch to develop normally. The outcome is usually a mix of normal and seriously underripe berries within the same bunch, which results in uneven ripening. If the undeveloped berries are not removed, they will contribute a harsh, acidic edge to the wine.

Eutypiose

This is a disease of the wood, and it particularly affects Cabernet Sauvignon. A minute fungus invades the wood, usually through scars left by the pruning process, and it gradually rots the vine from the inside. It can take three to ten years before the vine dies. There is no definitive cure, though there are treatments that will sometimes slow down the progress of the disease. Jean-Louis Camp of Château Croizet-Bages estimates that the Médoc vineyards lose about two per cent of their Cabernet vines each year to eutypiose, though others believe the mortality rate is only one per cent. Olivier Sèze of Château Charmail told me that its old vines can resist the disease quite successfully, whereas productive clones have less dense wood and are more likely to succumb.

Esca

Like eutypiose, this is a disease of the wood, and it functions by destroying the sap. It seems to be on the increase and affects Merlot and Cabernet Sauvignon. Pascal Delbeck of Bélair in St-Emilion treats it by cutting a broad vertical slash into the stem to allow air and sunlight to penetrate. He says this is based on ancestral practice, but does seem to work.

Vers de la grappe

The larva of a small butterfly called *Polychrosis botrana* does enormous damage by burrowing into the grapes and provoking grey rot. Rather than use pesticides, most conscientious estates use a technique called *confusion sexuelle*. Sachets are attached to the wires along the rows, and they emit artificial pheromones. This arouses and confuses the butterflies and curbs their ability to reproduce. It seems to be reasonably effective.

Botrytis

A detailed account of botrytis is given in Chapter Twenty-Eight, where its crucial role in the production of Sauternes is explained. However, botrytis can also affect red grapes, and in such cases the rot is anything but noble. There are natural methods to protect the bunches, such as deleafing which improves ventilation. Most vineyard managers employ anti-botrytis sprays, which can protect the vines for about one week, at the same time prolonging the growing season, which is an advantage when the grapes need more time to achieve full ripeness. If botrytis can be a positive form of rot in the right circumstances, that cannot be said for the wholly malevolent black rot.

PRUNING

There are two basic methods of training the vine: cane-pruning and spur-pruning. The latter forms a bush vine, and this is rarely encountered in Bordeaux. Cane-pruning creates one or two canes that are trained along wires. Where there is one cane, the system is known as *guyot simple*; when two, *guyot double*. In the Médoc and the Graves the *guyot double* is more common; on the Right Bank, the *guyot simple* prevails. The drawback of *guyot simple* is that you have only one choice of cane, whereas with *guyot double* you have two to choose from. There is a variation on spur-pruning called cordon-training, when two spurs are trained along wires. Cordon-training is rare, but it is preferred by some estates, such as Domaine de Grandmaison in Pessac-Léognan, which believe it gives better aeration and lower productivity. Other growers are more sceptical and believe the main reason some producers opt for it is that certain operations, such as pre-pruning, can be carried out mechanically, thus reducing costs.

The form of pruning is decided by the grower. The act of pruning is to select the best wood on which the next year's buds will grow, and to eliminate all old wood. How the pruning is done will affect the quality of the fruit and the quantity of bunches per vine. Pruning begins from late November and continues through the winter. Some like to prune late in the belief that this will protect the vines from spring frosts.

At Mouton, the pruning is usually completed by late February. The aim of the exercise is to try to manipulate the vine into delivering the most homogeneous conditions of ripeness at harvest. Thus the pruning at top estates is not done by formula, but is adapted to the nature and precocity of the soils. "What is important", says Philippe Dhalluin, "is that when the growing season begins, the various parcels at Mouton and our other estates are predicted to attain maturity at the same time. But it's not a scientific procedure and it doesn't always work out."

It is often said that pruning short is essential in order to reduce yields. Excessively short pruning, says St-Emilion winemaker Jonathan Maltus, can result in the vines producing very large berries that will not give good-quality wine. Thomas Stonestreet of Domaine de Chevalier agrees that if the pruner leaves only a single bud, then the vine will focus all its energies on it, resulting in a very large bunch. The pruners at Chevalier are encouraged to assess the vigour of each vine and deal with it accordingly. This is why, at most top estates, the same workers deal with the same parcels of vines each year, to maximize their familiarity with each individual vine and its needs.

After the initial winter pruning, the vineyard team returns to the vineyards to attach the canes to the wires. With close planting, care must be taken to separate the potential bunches so as to avoid crowding and poor ventilation. Errors made in pruning young vines can be difficult to correct and can have lasting consequences.

TRELLISING

Related to the pruning of the vine is its trellising, the way its foliage and bunches are dispersed along the wires. Over the last decade it has become fashionable to raise the height of the trellis. The traditional low trellising was created with the comfort of the *vigneron* in mind: the vines were hedged in such a way that they could be worked on with relative ease.

The argument in favour of a heightened trellis is that it increases the leaf surface of each vine, which in turn creates more sugar in the grapes. It also facilitates summertime operations such as leaf-pulling. Having more foliage above the bunches means that you can remove leaves without this having too marked an effect on the ability of the remaining leaves to photosynthesize. At Château de Pez the director is convinced that higher trellising will speed up maturation and allow an earlier harvest. The new height is not uniformly imposed, as it depends on the spacing and density within any vineyard. Raising the trellis must not be overdone, otherwise one ends up with a wall of foliage that can shade neighbouring rows of vines and increase the risk of herbaceousness or unripeness.

Since the 1980s there have been some experimental plantings of lyre-trained vines, under the supervision of INRA, the French agricultural institute. This form of trellising divides the top of the canopy, allowing excellent sun exposure which encourages high yields without, it seems, any diminution of quality. The system has been used at Château La Rame in Ste-Croix-du-Mont, and at Château Bertinierie in Blaye. Here the owners, the Bantegnies family, found that the grapes ripened a week earlier, which was clearly advantageous, but that lyre-training is very costly to farm.

VITICULTURE

If the 1980s were the decade of innovative vinification, then the 1990s and 2000s were and are the decades of viticultural improvements. It's a truism that great wine is made in the vineyard, but one that many Bordeaux producers have started taking seriously only in recent years. In the 1960s and 1970s there was much abuse of vineyards by the over-use of chemical fertilizers and pesticides, which may have given the vineyard manager a quiet life, but didn't improve wine quality. It is still a depressing sight to tour the Bordeaux vineyards and see how many are still routinely poisoned with chemical herbicides.

All this is beginning to change. Fertilizers are still applied to the vineyards, but as compost rather than chemicals. Jean-Michel Comme at Pontet-Canet is opposed to fertilizers, especially those with a high potassium content, because their use encourages the vine's roots to remain near the surface rather than plunging deep in search of nutrients in the soil below. He also observes that excessive fertilizer use can lead to high pH, which is detrimental to the balance of the wine. The veteran winemaker Georges Pauli believes that adding compost not only enlivens the soil but increases its water-retentive capacity.

Herbicides are still visibly in use in Bordeaux, but many top estates are now ploughing their vineyards, a procedure that allows the soil to breathe and encourages the growth of micro-organisms. The plough also cuts any roots that lie close to the surface, thus forcing them to look below for water and nutrients. Olivier Sèze at Château Charmail believes that the reason why ploughing is far less common here than in Burgundy is that the estates are much larger, which makes the process even more time-consuming. Nonetheless, he believes that any property that aspires to be irreproachable in terms of quality should not hesitate to adopt ploughing.

Essentially what has been happening is not innovation so much as a return to the good practices of the past. Hubert de Boüard of Château Angélus claims to have been one of the first to practise a more scrupulous viticulture in St-Emilion:

> In the 1980s I began cutting back on fertilizers, improving drainage, lowering yields, green-harvesting, and leaf-pulling. This was all considered revolutionary at the time, but a few years later everyone was doing the same thing, at least among the top estates. But there is nothing new about these practices. They were all known in the nineteenth century, and even in the fifteenth century growers were asking their workers to remove leaves. It was the only way to avoid rot.

> The point of all these techniques is to reveal the terroir in the wines. The 1960s were also a period of tremendous research at the faculty of oenology here in Bordeaux. The problem was that hardly any of their findings were actually implemented in the vineyards and wineries at the time. My generation has been able to analyse all this information and apply it. By the 1980s we were returning to the essentials of the vineyard, which is the source of any great wine.

Some deleafing is now done by machine or by a technique known as *effeuillage thermique*, by which the leaves on one side of the row are scorched by a machine and eventually drop off. Any burn on the grape skins is replaced by new growth, as with a human skin burn. But some producers steer clear of the technique. Philibert Perrin of Château Carbonnieux worries that white vines in particular are fragile and even with slight damage to the berries there is an increased risk of rot. Olivier Sèze of Château Charmail, who began deleafing in the 1980s, counters that with manual deleafing there is an even higher risk of damage, as the workers can tug at the leaves and bruise the bunches.

Deleafing, whether manual or mechanical, is not a risk-free procedure. Although it undoubtedly ventilates the vines and reduces the risk of rot, it also exposes the bunches to direct sunlight. Timing, especially when both sides of the row are deleafed, can be crucial, as some growers discovered to their cost in 2003, when the equatorial heat in August burned and shrivelled bunches that were directly exposed to sunlight.

The practice is not universal. At Château Margaux, which is hardly a slacker when it comes to quality, Paul Pontallier opposes the practice. He is wary of the tendency to distrust nature and continually interfere in growth patterns:

> *It's important to remember that leaves are factories of sugar, so removing too many of them could interfere with the ripening process. It's not essential for the bunches to have direct exposure to sunlight, and this can damage or raisin the grapes, as happened in 2003. But this is not a dogma. In parcels where we find the vigour excessive, we will remove leaves. But I have never seen a vine that habitually produces our second wine, Pavillon Rouge, give us wine for the grand vin after leaf-pulling. At best it can give us a better Pavillon Rouge.*

The planting of green cover between the rows is another technique used to restrain vigour, since the grass provides competition to the vine roots. This is widely practised, and the green cover is later ploughed into the soil, thus adding organic matter.

Other practices are rarely discussed, such as the application of a product called Sierra that was originally developed to speed up the colouring of tomatoes. If vines are treated with it during *véraison*, it aborts and shrinks any green berries, allowing them to be eliminated. This in turn speeds up the maturation process, since the vine doesn't need to expend energy on grapes that will never ripen fully. Sierra can be effective but it is also expensive.

It has its opponents too. Charles Chevallier of Lafite observes that if you apply it too early, you can damage some ripening fruit; apply it too late, and it has no effect. He prefers to green-harvest in order to eliminate berries that will never ripen. "That way you can at least see what you're doing." Alexandre Thienpont at Vieux-Château-Certan finds that parcels treated with Sierra end up with lower acidity, which he doesn't want. For Thomas Stonestreet of Domaine de Chevalier, it's a way of correcting errors that should have been avoided earlier. Moreover, if you remove some small berries, there is a possibility that the remaining berries will grow larger, thus altering the ratio of juice to skins. "What's more, it's a hormonal treatment, and I think it's stupid to use such applications in our vineyards."

Rather surprisingly there is very little organic or biodynamic viticulture in Bordeaux, although there are outcrops of the latter in St-Emilion. Bruno Prats, formerly of Cos d'Estournel, told me that he believes fully organic viticulture is rare because the climate in Bordeaux is far more humid than in Burgundy or Alsace. This would certainly be a widely accepted rationale for hesitancy to move in that direction. However, many estates practise *lutte raisonnée*, which is a somewhat loosely defined approach that turns to chemical treatments only as a last resort. Some estates have opted for the Cousinié method, which was created by a viticulturalist from southwest France. He opposed subjecting the vines to too much stress, as he felt it would increase their susceptibility to disease. The method conducts analyses of the soil, the vine stems, and the leaves, and then corrects any deficits. Prescribed treatments are organic, although that does not make the vineyard or wine organic as a consequence. Châteaux Lamarque and Tayac are among the properties that have adopted this method.

Green-harvesting

The *vendange verte* has become an almost religious ritual during the summer months. Its practice is an acknowledgment that many vines in Bordeaux are intrinsically too vigorous, either because of the clonal or rootstock material, or because of the soil or choice of grape variety. The theory is simple enough: remove bunches, and the vine will devote its energies to the handful that remain, giving low yields and good concentration. The problem, as so often, lies in the timing. Green-harvest at the wrong time, and the vine will simply compensate by pumping up the remaining bunches, when the goal of the *vigneron* is to create small berries with a low ratio of juice to skin.

Jean Gautreau at Château Sociando-Mallet is notoriously opposed to green-harvesting, but most growers see it as a palliative. While opposed to routine green-harvesting, they are fully prepared to resort to it if no other method remains of restraining yields and speeding up maturation. This applies especially to vigorous young vines. Gonzague Lurton of Château Durfort-Vivens argues that:

> With systematic green-harvesting the vine will adjust and simply increase its crop the following year. I prefer to prune short and remove buds. But that's more costly and also more risky, as you open yourself to the possibility that hail or disease could lead to the loss of much of the crop. So instead, growers retain as much fruit as possible and then remove it at the last moment.

Charles Chevallier suspects that the more you green-harvest, the more you need to keep doing it in the future. So at Lafite, while they do practise it, it is not systematic.

Gautreau is scornful:

> On a large property here you could have 700,000 vines. It would take a team of workers five months to deal with them! I don't dispute that large estates that claim to green-harvest may do so, but they must use students or other labour that doesn't know what it is doing. I prefer to follow nature. Bordeaux's greatest vintages were all high-yielding years, and great vintages of the past such as 1929 and 1947 were made without green-harvesting.
>
> If you have twenty bunches, and remove half, the remaining ten will compensate by producing larger berries — and possibly more juice from the ten bunches than would have been obtained if all twenty had been left. I'll leave and pick all twenty, but then I'll taste and bleed the tanks.

Olivier Bernard agrees with Gautreau that if you have healthy, well-tended vines, especially old vines, you shouldn't need to green-harvest.

> At Domaine de Chevalier we rarely need to drop more than five per cent from our old vines. But with the young vines we sometimes remove fifty per cent. It's hard to avoid. It also depends on the year and the climate. Timing is crucial. If you green-harvest early, in July, the vine will compensate. It's better to do it at the end of véraison, when you can eliminate green and uneven bunches that are clearly visible. That will also give you more even maturation.

It's worth pointing out that Gautreau has long-established vineyards. Those with a lot of young vines or vines planted on productive rootstocks such as SO4 may not be able to adopt the same approach.

Vine age

It is one of the most strongly held beliefs of French viticulture that old vines are intrinsically superior to young vines in the quality of their wine. At many top estates in Bordeaux, vines younger than fifteen or even twenty years are systematically excluded from the *grand vin*. Such a decision clearly has to be based on empirical evidence rather than dogma. On the other hand, New World viticulturalists believe that, in their vineyards at any rate, young vines can produce excellent wine. It is a view I can confirm, as I have drunk superb Pinot Noir and Syrah from southern Californian vineyards a mere three or four years old.

The response of Etienne de Montille from Burgundy, a region even more devoted to the cult of the old vine than Bordeaux, is that New World growers have no choice in the matter. There are regions where there are scarcely any old vines, so winemakers have to learn how to make the best wine from the material at their disposal. "In France we have a choice. Old vines are plentiful, so there is no reason for us to make those same efforts with the young vines. We can afford to wait."

Thomas Stonestreet believes the French approach is sensible:

> Young vines give large berries, which is not what we are looking for. It's incontestable that old vines give smaller berries and more concentrated fruit. However, four-year vines can be very good, but overall their juice tends to be more dilute. You can try to compensate with short pruning, but you still won't achieve the same balance and concentration as with old vines. The climate also affects the development of vines – in hot climates such as California the vines will develop faster than here in Bordeaux.

One rule of thumb for restraining the youthful vigour of young vines is to prune to two bunches less than the age of the vines: thus, retain three bunches for a five-year vine, five bunches for a seven-year vine.

When visiting an estate, I always ask about the average age of the vines. The response is often fairly precise. So it was a surprise to hear Jean-Michel Cazes respond: "Who knows?" He expanded:

> There are many parcels where we know the date of planting, but vines frequently need to be replaced, and it's impossible to keep precise records. One day, when I have more time, I may try to make a more exact estimate of the vine age at Lynch-Bages, but for the moment the best I can do is offer you a reasonably accurate guess.

I have no doubt the same would be true at most large properties.

Dr. Richard Smart, the well-known viticulturalist from Australia, has long rejected the notion that old vines necessarily give better quality than young ones. I asked him what he would do if he were given control of a major Médoc vineyard.

> The top sites are clearly doing well. But I believe their success is based not on low yield but on low vigour. But my job is essentially remedial, and I think I could improve sites that were not performing at their full potential. I'm not convinced that high-density planting is always the right choice, and it certainly adds to the cost of vineyard management.

YIELDS

One aim of pruning is to ensure the vine is balanced and will produce a uniformly ripe crop in a reasonable but not excessive quantity. But the notion of a correct or reasonable yield is controversial. It is argued, on the one hand, that high yields lead to dilution, since the energies of the vines have been too dispersed in serving too many bunches. Thus reducing the yields, by whatever means, will increase concentration and intensity of flavour. On the other hand, many château directors point out that many of the greatest vintages of recent years (such as 1990) were high-yielding, without any evident reduction in quality or structure. Thus, they argue, there is no direct correlation between yield and quality, although everyone agrees that ludicrously high yields will never produce good wines.

There is no doubt that improved viticultural practices, more productive clones and rootstocks, and a generous hand with the fertilizers have led to higher yields than a few decades ago. Effective treatments against maladies have certainly had an impact on yields. In the late eighteenth century the average yield at Latour was sixteen hl/ha, and from 1920 to 1973 it was still, on average, a modest thirty-three hl/ha.[7] In years such as 1959, the yield at Palmer was thirty-seven hl/ha; in 1961 it was a mere twelve, in 1955 a relatively high forty-five. Most vintages had yields in the twenties.[8] Such low yields, common in the Médoc in the first half of the twentieth century, were almost certainly the consequence of maladies and missing vines. No one believes such exaggeratedly low yields were deliberately sought as a means of attaining high quality.

Philippe Courrian admits that in 1974, with the help of fertilizers, he obtained average yields at Tour-Haut-Caussan of 106 hl/ha. In 1982 his yields were seventy-five hl/ha without any detrimental effect on quality. In 1990 the average for the Médoc was about eighty-six hl/ha; since the maximum permitted yield was around sixty, the excess had to be sent for distillation. (Officially established yields are always boosted by a legal trump card called the PLC, or *plafond limite de classement*, which can increase the maximum quantity by a further twenty per cent.) But the wine that ended up in the bottle was presumably of similar quality (or lack of it) as that dispatched to the distillery. Courrian remarks that the wine in 1990 happened to be very good, and the upshot of the over-production was that it persuaded many growers that there was no point in aiming for excessive yields.

Each year the négociant Maison Sichel issues an invaluable report on the vintage, and this often includes some reflections on other pertinent issues. In 1999 the report sagely observed:

> In the case of a plot that has been allowed to over-produce, it is not only the quantity over
> the PLC which will be diluted but the total crop. To ensure maximum allowable yield
> regulation that actually results in better quality would require that the whole crop be sent
> to the distillery, or at least be denied the right to Bordeaux origin: a measure which would
> have such dramatic consequences that it is not even worth contemplating.

It was not just growers who wanted to sell the maximum amount of grapes to the local cooperative who opted for over-production. Generous yields were common at prestigious properties too. Jean-Guillaume Prats at Cos d'Estournel admits that his father Bruno had no problems with high yields in the 1980s.

> In 2000 we had yields of forty-five to forty-six hl/ha in the vineyard, whereas a few years ago
> the yields were closer to sixty. That's because until fairly recently there was no economic incentive
> to have low yields. As my father used to say, the practice was not rewarded by the market.

Despite the lip service paid to low yields, there is no denying that many estates crop the legal maximum. The owner of a lesser estate in Pauillac told me that he never green-harvested because he couldn't afford to dispense with so much potential wine. At the other end of the scale, a respected estate director told me just before the 2000 vintage that he expected many estates to make as much wine as possible, simply to exploit the predicted demand for the vintage.

Statistics on yields need to be treated with some caution, especially when the source is a property that prides itself on a very low crop. The yield figure is supposed to refer to the amount of juice produced per hectare. (Some argue that a more useful figure is that of grape weight per vine, but that is a topic for another place.) However, it seems likely that some estates do not include juice removed by bleeding the tanks or lots subjected to mechanical concentration. It is also legal to boost the yields of parcels of younger vines to compensate for the naturally low-yielding old vines on the same property. As long as the average does not exceed the PLC, there is no prohibition of this kind of manipulation. Claims of very low yields were made for the *garagiste* wine Marojallia from Margaux. A cursory glance at the *déclaration de récolte*, the legally required annual crop report

7 Penning-Rowsell, *The Wines of Bordeaux*, Penguin, London, 1989, 89

8 Pijassou, *Château Palmer*, Stock, Paris, 1997, 90

deposited at the town hall of every commune, soon revealed that the yields for Marojallia were a generous fifty-eight hl/ha. The directors had simply cited the yield for that proportion of the wine that ended up as *grand vin*. This was clearly dubious practice. More admirable is the transparency practised by Château Prieuré-Lichine, which cites both figures, that for its vineyards as a whole, and that for its *grand vin*.

So if it is possible to make great wine at a maximum yield of sixty hl/ha, what is the point of reducing yields further, a costly process both in terms of labour costs and lost volume? The answer is that not every vintage is a 1982 or 1990, when everything ripens with ease. Olivier Bernard argues that there is no such thing as a calculable "correct yield":

> *The question is what is the right yield for a vine? It depends on various factors: the age of the vine, the density of planting. The definition of a great terroir in Bordeaux is that it's a warm one. It's not easy to get maturity here; hence all the operations during the summer to increase the chances of maturation. But in hot years high yields are acceptable because everything can ripen, except perhaps for young vines with shallow root systems. But in cooler years you can only get mature bunches if the yields are low. So during the summer you need to guess what the year ahead will be like. Certainly by véraison you have a shrewd idea of the harvesting date. Maturation also depends on access to moisture. Low-lying parcels in the vineyard have to be handled differently from parcels planted on warm gravel soils. Experience and observation are essential to help you to regulate your vines.*

The practice of brutal crop reduction, usually by bunch-thinning during the summer, has its origins on the Right Bank. There some *garagistes* would plant vines on a mediocre terroir; to compensate for this mediocrity, the concentration of the wine (and its depth of colour and alcoholic degree) would be pumped up by halving normal yields and by mechanical concentration or other procedures in the winery. It certainly worked, to judge by the high scores obtained from certain critics for these wines. Gérard Perse of Pavie, no friend of high yields, observed to me:

> *If you are growing vines on a mediocre soil then you need to have low yields to make decent wine. But a great terroir allows you to get exceptional quality at thirty-five hl/ha; to obtain the same quality on poor soil you need to crop at twenty. It's better to crop at forty on a great terroir than twenty on a mediocre one.*

That some yields are absurdly low is clear, yet the Médoc estates have taken a leaf or two from the *garagistes'* book. Jean-Guillaume Prats remarks:

> *The emphasis on lower yields is a direct consequence of the* garagistes, *who have shaken things up. The Médoc is learning that lesson from them. It's true that many* garagistes *practise very low yields because their terroir is poor. Indeed I do the same. Our most mediocre parcels at Cos are cropped at twenty-five hl/ha, but such strictness is pointless on a great terroir. In fact, cropping at less than forty hl/ha doesn't make sense if you have great soils.*

Frédéric Engerer, the director of Château Latour, is especially sceptical when it comes to very low yields:

> *If there were an exact correlation between yields and quality, everyone would know about it. At Latour we aim for about eight bunches per vine, but of course it depends on the vine's age and vigour. Yields also have to do with the size of the bunches, which vary*

according to the amount of rainfall. I am not going to play the game of what I call "low yield madness". We have old vines that never bear more than four bunches, but we also have young vines where it is impossible to have yields below forty hl/ha. Our average yield in 2000 was fifty hl/ha. But we don't have targets. We respect each vine and parcel and its needs to stay healthy. In 1999 we had forty hl/ha, but again that was not a target. We have a great terroir here. It's like a Ferrari and we need to drive it properly. We don't want to mess around with the terroir.

Charles Chevallier of Lafite also says there are no firm rules:

There are parcels at Lafite that always yield sixty hl/ha and the wine always ends up in the grand vin. There are other parcels that give considerably less but never make it into the grand vin. So it's hard to generalize.

Thierry Gardinier of Château Phélan-Ségur argues that with the high-density planting in the Médoc it is difficult to obtain very low yields, especially if the vines are all healthy and there are no missing vines. Jean-Michel Cazes of Lynch-Bages agrees:

When people talk about yields they forget about density. Here in the Médoc we have 10,000 vines per hectare. The crop expressed in hectolitres tells you nothing. Here in Pauillac and St-Julien and St-Estèphe I am sure that fifty to sixty is about right. Latour always had some of the highest yields in the region, but that was because none of their vines were missing.

Anthony Barton in St-Julien makes a similar observation, noting that Ducru-Beaucaillou and Léoville-Las-Cases always seemed to have higher yields than their neighbours, "but that's because their vineyards were better cared for".

Vines are planted to a lower density in the Right Bank zones, so yields tend to be lower than in the Médoc and Graves. Moreover Merlot is a productive variety, with larger berries than Cabernet Sauvignon, so most growers do make a serious attempt to keep yields at a sensible level.

By now it should be clear that there is no simple answer to the question of yields. Very low yields need not necessarily result in an exceptional wine, and yields near the legal maximum need not be a cynical wish to make the maximum volume at the expense of quality. Yield has to vary according to the balance of individual vines. But that raises the question of what a balanced vine is. Paul Pontallier replies:

A balanced vine is one that shows the correct relationship between vigour and yield. But that balance varies according to a variety of factors, such as terroir, density, and many other factors.

Olivier Bernard adds:

By its nature, "balance" is unstable. It has to do with the leaf surface, with the vegetative vigour of the vines, with the productivity of the soil − its moisture content, its physical properties − and with density. The wood of the vine needs to be balanced too − sometimes you need to leave more buds than usual in order to reduce the vigour of the wood itself. And you need to rein back vigorous vines, otherwise the sap has to travel too far to the extremities of the vine.

Fortunately most good estates practise what they preach. You won't find many dilute wines among the classified growths anywhere in Bordeaux. If there is any excess, it lies in the direction of exaggeratedly low yields with the aim of producing super-concentrated wines that impress palates that mistake power and heft for quality.

THE HARVEST

The final operation of the growing season is harvesting. Because of the often perilous autumnal climate of Bordeaux, it is the aim of every vineyard manager to achieve even and precocious maturation. Very late years have rarely been of exceptional quality, and producers rejoice when the harvest can take place relatively early and in sound conditions. Techniques such as raising the trellis, leaf removal, and green-harvesting all contribute to speeding up the rate of maturation, allowing vineyard managers to delay the harvest as long as the fine weather holds up. In the past, especially during difficult economic periods, growers tended to pick earlier than they should have done, which often accounts for the harsh tannins still discernible in many venerable vintages.

Some vineyards are picked by hand, others by machine. Strong views are expressed by the proponents of both methods. I believe the first harvesting machines were introduced at Château Larose-Trintaudon in 1970. Jean Miailhe describes the results of machine-picking in the 1970s as "*un travail affreux*".[9] But the technology has improved radically, and modern machines inflict far less damage on the vines than the bruisers of old. Today the extensive Médoc estates run by Jean Miailhe's son Eric are almost entirely picked by machine.

There are clear advantages to machine-harvesting. One is greater flexibility. It makes it possible to pick at night, which is preferable during very hot weather, since the grapes will reach the winery at a cooler temperature, which can reduce problems during fermentation. It also speeds up the harvesting process, allowing growers to wait longer, since they can react more swiftly to any onset of bad weather. There is also an economic advantage to using machines, by eliminating the need to hire, feed, and often house teams of pickers.

Proponents of manual harvesting insist that, despite technological advances, machines are still less gentle than a pair of human hands, and less adept at excluding extraneous matter such as leaves and bugs. White wines are particularly prone to oxidation, so some estates use machines to pick red vines but still hand-pick their whites. But it is true that teams of pickers, unless one is fortunate enough to work each year with the same crew, are less flexible in their working hours, often require time off at weekends whatever the weather, and need close supervision, especially if one is relying on students or untrained workers. There are geographical constraints as well. Estates in the Graves, Margaux, or the Libournais are close to cities with a good supply of potential harvesters. If your property lies in the northern Médoc, some two hours' drive from Bordeaux, it may be difficult to find teams of qualified pickers prepared to turn up when you need them. Patrice Ricard of Château Patache d'Aux recalls that years ago the pickers would telephone from Spain to ask when the harvest was going to begin. He gave them a date, they arrived as agreed, and they started to harvest whether or not the grapes were fully ready.

A more recent development has been the formation of companies that lease out pickers. Estates contract with them to pick a certain number of hectares per day, and can specify the days when the grapes are likely to be fully mature. This allows the estate to have its fruit hand-picked without the inconvenience of having to house the workers.

There are still a number of classified growths that pick by machine. There seems little excuse for this, even if machines are more delicate than in the past. There is surely no substitute for the careful grape selection inherent in trained manual harvesting, and in the close surveillance of hand-pickers by experienced workers from the château's permanent team. On the other hand, machine-harvesting in more remote and less prestigious regions such as the northern Médoc, southern Graves, and Entre-Deux-Mers is here to stay. Very high prices cannot be charged for these wines, and proprietors need to keep a close control over their costs.

9 Lawton and Miailhe, *Conversations*, 50

The containers in which the bunches are harvested have also changed. In the past (and at many estates this is still the case) the grapes were dumped into fairly large bins which were then conveyed to the winery by tractor. The risk was and is that the weight of the bunches could squeeze out juice into the bottom of the bin, and this juice could oxidize unless the grapes were processed rapidly. Today the quality-oriented properties pick in small plastic crates called *cagettes*. These have a capacity of about eight kilos (17.6 pounds) of grapes, so the bunches remain intact and unbruised. Perforated bases allow any escaping juice to run off, and the *cagettes* are grooved so that they can be stacked without crushing the grapes.

The harvest itself has become much more selective. A handful of properties, such as Domaine de Chevalier for its white vines, have always practised *tries successives*, whereby the harvesters are sent repeatedly into the vineyards in order to select only those bunches that are fully ripe. This is routine practice in Sauternes, where only botrytis-affected bunches are sought. But in the past proprietors were keen to pick fast and early. Jacques Merlaut, the patriarch of the Taillan group of négociants, recalls:

> *Thirty years ago almost all the vineyards of any château would have been picked all at once.*
> *Now everyone picks parcel by parcel according to maturity. That's a huge advance. It means*
> *that nowadays one can always make decent wine, if not great wine. Unfortunately this*
> *doesn't apply to generic Bordeaux.*

Another veteran, Thierry Manoncourt of Château Figeac, remembers: "In the past the whole vineyard would have been picked in eight days. Today it takes us twenty to thirty days."

Paul Pontallier sounds a cautionary note regarding the assumption that rain at harvest is necessarily disastrous. "The crucial factor is the condition of the grapes before the rain falls. Rain doesn't modify maturity, and the worst it can do is cause dilution. In the same way, if you wash a table grape, the berry doesn't taste any less sweet." Dilution can be corrected by various means: slatted sorting tables, drying tunnels, reverse osmosis, and bleeding tanks are all techniques that can be employed to remove excess water. But of course a harvest in dry conditions is preferable to conditions that require remedial action.

How is maturity to be defined? In the past, and to a large extent this is still true, the two criteria were sugar and acidity. The notion of phenolic ripeness – essentially ripe pips and tannins as well as sweet fruit – is relatively new. Phenolic ripeness requires leaving the bunches longer on the vine, weather permitting. The danger, even in ideal conditions, is that as the phenolic ripeness develops, the acidity declines and the pH rises. The sugar levels may also rise to levels that not everyone will find acceptable. In the end it is a matter of taste. Bernard Magrez poured me a wine he had produced as a *micro-cuvée* at one of his estates. The high alcohol and overripe fruit were detectable, and I confessed I didn't much like the wine (it had 15.5 degrees of alcohol). Neither, it turned out, did he. But overripe wines have their following, especially among American tasters, so it is not surprising that some Bordeaux producers are deliberately producing these late-harvested but highly atypical styles. (Christian Dauriac, with properties in St-Emilion and Pomerol and a disciple and friend of Michel Rolland's told me: "If you don't have five per cent rot in your vineyards, then your grapes aren't ripe.")

I asked certain managers what their criteria were for "ripeness". Thomas Stonestreet at Chevalier replied:

> *There is certainly a minimum level of sugar required for real maturity, but we consider white*
> *grapes mature when we have the right balance of sugar and acidity, not just high sugars. For*
> *reds the balance tends to be between sugars and tannins as well as acidity. I'm convinced that*
> *overmature vines won't produce wines that will age well. The only reason why certain estates*
> *aim for systematic overmaturity is that they think the resulting wine, with its deep colour*
> *and high alcohol, will appeal to the critics.*

Philippe Dhalluin notes that tannin levels seem to be higher than in the past, though he has no explanation for the phenomenon:

> So winemakers compensate for that with higher ripeness in the grapes, which gives a more suave attack, and high sugars help to balance the high tannins — at least initially.

But this does not make him an apologist for overmaturity.

I asked Paul Pontallier whether there was a direct correlation between sugar levels and "quality", bearing in mind that many of the classic vintages of a century ago had low alcoholic levels and probably would not have qualified as "ripe" by today's criteria. He replied:

> If the grape sugars at harvest are very low, then the most likely explanation is either a lack of maturity or dilution. There were low sugars in the past because chaptalization was rare, and expensive. On a great gravel terroir, twelve degrees of alcohol for Cabernet Sauvignon is unusually high — eleven degrees would be more usual. A little chaptalization brings back the balance into the wine. Chaptalization became widespread in the 1950s in the Médoc, but before then people were accustomed to a lighter style of Bordeaux wine. However, we know that the greatest years such as 1900, 1928, and 1929 had higher sugars and much more richness. We have higher sugars on a more routine basis today because everyone is picking later than in the past. That means the wines have lower acidity. High acidity reinforces the astringency of tannins, so that means nowadays we have rounder, more supple tannins.

Another explanation for the earlier harvesting in times past is that the producers were wary of stuck fermentations, which were more likely to occur with very rich musts. Hence there were a great number of wines in the nineteenth and early twentieth centuries with as little as eight or nine degrees of alcohol. In 1840 the First Growths ranged from 8.7 degrees to 9.3 degrees. Some of them nonetheless had the structure to last, but the acidity levels would have been very high and they would have required prolonged barrel-ageing to make them palatable. As recently as 1952 the average strength of claret was only 11.2 degrees. It is doubtful that modern wine drinkers would have taken much pleasure from a very young nineteenth-century claret. Nor would anyone seriously advocate a return to the practices that resulted in such wines, even if over the long term some of them proved to be excellent.

3. Wine and Style

The Bandol producer and autodidact Come Henri de St-Victor once told me that he learnt the rudiments of winemaking in about twenty minutes. At colleges in Dijon, Montpellier, and Bordeaux, students can spend three years acquiring their degrees in oenology. Hugh Johnson and James Halliday have written a lengthy book with the telling title *The Art and Science of Wine*. Winemaking is too intuitive to be a mere science, too rooted in practical considerations and consequences to be considered a form of art.

These days, it has become fashionable to favour "non-interventionist" winemaking, which suggests that all the winemaker has to do is sit back and allow nature to take its course as the wine ferments and ages, intervening only when something goes wrong. This is the concept of winemaker as physician. François Mitjaville of Château Tertre-Rôteboeuf briskly disposes of this approach: "The only part of a wine that is purely natural is the fruit. Once we have that fruit, the rest is the result of intervention. We are not animals. We have minds and we make choices."

Nonetheless, the winemaking process for red Bordeaux is relatively simple. The red grapes are harvested, brought to the winery ("*cuvier*"), often sorted, usually destemmed, usually crushed, and sometimes given a pre-fermentation maceration at a cold temperature before fermentation begins with the aid of either indigenous or cultivated yeasts. During fermentation, extraction is aided by regularly pumping over the must, or by punching down the cap, or sometimes by *délestage*, a technique that involves emptying the tank and then refilling it – or by all three. The young wine may receive an extended maceration, before being drawn off the *marc*, the residue of skins and pips. The *marc* is then pressed and the press wine set aside for subsequent blending. The wine that has been drawn off then undergoes its malolactic fermentation. Thereafter the wine is aged in small barrels or tanks until the winemaker considers it is ready for bottling, which is usually preceded by fining and/or filtration. The blending of the *grand vin* may take place at any time during the ageing process, although most winemakers like to complete it during the winter immediately after the harvest.

White wine fermentation is also a relatively straightforward process. After harvesting the grapes may be pressed directly and then fermented, or the grapes may be given a period of maceration (also known as skin contact) that can last from four to twenty-four hours. Skin contact extracts aromas and can give the wine greater complexity, but is beneficial only if the grapes are very healthy. If there is damage or bruising, then oxidation and bacterial problems can result. Skin contact is usually reserved for the naturally aromatic Sauvignon Blanc in preference to the more rounded, fleshy Sémillon.

Simpler white wines are fermented in tanks, given a short period of ageing, perhaps four to six months, also in tanks, but often on the fine lees, and are then filtered and bottled. Wines with some pretensions to quality and ageability are often fermented in barriques, with a varying proportion of new oak. The wines are usually aged on the fine lees, with regular stirring ("*bâtonnage*"). They may or may not go through malolactic fermentation. Some winemakers favour a blend of oaked and unoaked wine. (The vinification of sweet white wines will be discussed in Chapter Twenty-Eight.)

In the past vinification was a much more haphazard process, because little was known about the science of fermentation. Nor was it easy to determine the level of maturity of the grapes harvested. A painting shown to me at Château Batailley by Emile Castéja illustrated how wine would have been made in the late nineteenth century. The bunches were destemmed by hand, by rubbing the grapes through a box with slats; the grapes were then put into large wooden troughs, in which they were broken up. The must was placed in containers and lifted into the wooden fermentation vats. It could take two or three days to fill a vat. Once fermentation began, the cap was broken up with a stick to which a kind of ball was attached. Since there was no temperature control, the grapes were often picked in the evenings to ensure that the grapes added to the vat were relatively cool.

Fermentation was faster than it is today. (Alfred Danflau records that in the 1860s Château Belair had a *cuvaison* of no more than forty-eight hours.) The vat was covered and, from a hole near the top, a pipe curved down into a bucket of water, thus insulating the wine from the air while allowing gases to escape. Four to six weeks later the vats were emptied, and the wine poured into barrels, where it stayed for two to three years, with quite frequent rackings. Quite a lot of press wine would have been added.

The fermentation process would have been bedevilled by excessively high temperatures, especially in hot years. If the temperature rose too high, the yeasts would die and the fermentation would grind to a halt. The risk of spoilage was very high. Primitive methods such as lowering ice wrapped in canvas into the vats were resorted to in order to keep the temperature from rising too high. This method was still in use in 1961, but by the 1970s efficient temperature control, which nowadays is usually computerized, had eliminated this particular problem. Bacterial problems were common, since it was difficult to maintain the wooden vats in perfect sanitary condition. A vintage could easily be spoilt, either because of bacterial contamination or because of volatile acidity engendered by fermentation at excessive temperatures. Chaptalization, the addition of sugar to the fermenting must, was legalized in Bordeaux only as recently as 1951, though there seems little doubt that it was practised surreptitiously long before that.[1] It is only during the recent spate of very warm vintages that many châteaux have made an effort to dispense with chaptalization. Until quite recently, it was a routine operation on the Left Bank, with the intention of boosting the alcoholic degree of the wine by about one degree, especially in the case of Cabernet Sauvignon, which often struggled to attain a potential alcohol level higher than eleven degrees.

During the spring following the vintage, the barrels would be shipped by barge from the château to the négociants' cellars in Bordeaux, where the *élevage* would have been completed. Often the finished wine was sold in cask to purchasers, who would bottle it in their own cellars.

Given the myriad ways in which the winemaking process could go wrong, it seems astonishing that truly great wines could be made at all. Until a few decades ago, no one subjected the crop to a rigorous selection process, no one knew how malolactic fermentation functioned, no one had efficient ways of controlling temperature, no one could be sure that every vat and barrel was uncontaminated, no one had heard of a polyphenol or anthocyanin. Nonetheless, there were certain years when all the factors conducive to quality coincided. The great years were those when all the grapes ripened more or less simultaneously, and when the resulting wines survived the lottery of vinification.

SORTING AND DESTEMMING

Although it was not that long ago that all or some stems were retained during vinification, it has been common practice for some decades to detach the berries from their stalks. Although there are some advantages to retaining stems, they are outweighed by the likelihood of extracting bitter tannins. By the 1920s routine destemming had been introduced at many properties, though stems were retained, on a pragmatic basis, in very hot vintages such as 1959, when the organic matter of the stalks would increase the otherwise low acidity of the wine. Small estates such as Le Pin in Pomerol still incorporate a proportion of the stems if acidity is deemed too low.

Many years ago a perfectly efficient machine for destemming grapes was invented, and over the years it has been refined to ensure that the mechanical handling of the grapes is as gentle as possible. Nonetheless, enormous efforts have been made in the search for ever-better ways to perform an essentially straightforward operation. It is, I think, illustrative of modern Bordeaux that so much energy and expense are devoted to a process that is essentially routine.

At Château La Garde and Château La Conseillante (and more recently at Gigault in Blaye), I inspected a new destemming machine called an *égreneur*, which is a conveyor belt that moves the bunches upwards. Four steel hoods cover this belt. The first two contain rubber truncheons that gently pummel the bunches, so that

1 Penning-Rowsell, *The Wines of Bordeaux*, Penguin, London, 1989, 24

only the ripest grapes are dislodged from the stems. The remaining attached berries pass beneath the next two hoods, where the pummelling is more violent. About eighty per cent of the bunches are destemmed beneath the first two hoods, and these are clearly the ripest grapes. The remaining twenty per cent (though the proportions can be mechanically altered) are sorted again, and usually end up in the second wine. Thus destemming and selection can be combined in the same operation.

In St-Emilion I have seen another machine called La Tribaie, which was invented by grower Philippe Bardet. He set about creating a machine specifically designed to sort machine-harvested grapes by borrowing and adapting technology originally created for sorting vegetables. A hopper conveys the grapes onto a vibrating belt, which eliminates any *millerandé* berries that are small, green, and unripe. The belt then drops the berries into a rotating drum. Damaged berries stick to the drum, while healthy berries bounce off it into a trough filled with must. Depending on their specific gravity, ripe grapes will sink to the bottom of the must, while unripe berries will float. The latter can be skimmed off and eliminated. The healthy berries can be dispatched to another conveyor belt if the producer wishes to sort the grapes a second time. It is up to the producer to discard the berries that don't make the grade, or to retain them for a second wine or for bulk wine. Bardet estimates that the team of six required to harvest the grapes and run the machine perform the same work as 150 people working entirely by hand. However, the vines need to be carefully prepared before the machine-harvesting in order to minimize the proportion of damaged bunches.

Bardet believes the Tribaie can have a positive effect on quality:

> *In my experience, destemming can damage berries more than machine-harvesting. In 2001 I compared picking into* cagettes *with machine-picking, and I found I had more whole berries after using the machine. The other major advantage is in the quality of the press wine. Because there are no unripe grapes going into the press, the press wine is good enough to be used in its entirety in the blend.*

The system has been purchased by André Lurton for his new winery at Château Rochemorin. There I tasted wines made from "sunken" and from "floating" berries. In terms of their sugar content, there was a whole degree of potential alcohol between them. The floating berries made a wine that was decidedly thinner and slightly vegetal; it was made clear that this quality of wine would never enter the *grand vin*. Lurton is also impressed by the speed of the machine, since in one hour it can process as much fruit as ten people sorting the grapes by hand.

Such sophisticated mechanical aids are clearly of interest to owners of large properties, but probably not cost-effective for smaller estates. Here the grapes are going to be sorted by hand. There is often a preliminary sorting in the vineyards, where the foreman of any picking team will fix a beady eye on the bunches and chuck out any that don't seem up to standard; or there may be a conveyor belt ("*table de tri*") set up between the rows, with six or eight sorters. There will often be a further sorting table at the winery, usually perforated and vibrating so as to keep small unripe berries, bugs, dirt, and other extraneous matter from entering the destemmer. In some wineries there is yet another sorting process after destemming.

Although sorting tables of varying degrees of severity are now routine installations at most quality-conscious properties, there are some who view them with a certain scepticism. Observing the 2005 harvest at Château Margaux, I was astonished to see that the grapes were not transported in *cagettes* but instead were moved in much larger containers; just as shockingly, there was no sorting at the reception area. The grapes were simply dumped into the reception bins on their way to the destemmer. When I confronted director Paul Pontallier with this unorthodox procedure, he explained that his staff carefully trained the harvesters, and if a supervisor noticed someone who was not picking as selectively as required, he or she would be singled out for re-education.

It may seem logical to treat grapes gently, but within seconds of arrival here they are going to be destemmed and crushed, so what actually is the point of all the careful handling? It wouldn't cost us much to install a vibrating table de tri *but all it does is vibrate – it doesn't select. For me it is more important to ensure that our vines are impeccable immediately before harvest, and that there is no trace of rotten fruit. We did once conduct an experiment over four vintages, comparing parcels that had been picked in* cagettes *with those that had not been, and we found no significant difference in wine quality.*

Pontallier is not entirely alone in his views. I also noticed, during that same vintage, that there was no sorting table at Château L'Eglise Clinet. Denis Durantou was unapologetic:

That's because the vines are prepared carefully just before the harvest. And in any case, how important are the few leaves and other odds and ends that you can eliminate by sorting?

Even though efficient mechanical destemmers have been in existence for many decades, some perfectionist properties reject such aids and destem the grapes manually. The idea originated at tiny Right Bank properties where the owner couldn't afford a machine. But now the practice has been adopted by some quite sizeable estates. Many of the wines produced by Bernard Magrez are made from grapes destemmed by hand. I once asked Magrez whether he was sure that manual destemming made any difference to the final quality of the wine. He replied that he couldn't be absolutely certain since his team hadn't been doing it for long enough, but he was keen on the idea nonetheless. Château Clinet in Pomerol recently began experimenting with manual destemming, and although the results were not conclusive, they did seem to think the procedure resulted in softer wines, though whether that is in itself desirable they did not say. Paul Pontallier at Château Margaux says he is not convinced that manual destemming necessarily gives better-quality wine. "But conscientious destemming by hand is certainly superior to bad mechanical destemming."

The practice does attract attention from wine writers, always in search of the latest novelty, and it certainly sounds perfectionist. I have no way of assessing whether the labour and thus expense involved are worth it, but what is certain is that it adds considerably to the cost of production, and in the end it is the consumer who is paying for what may well be a media-inspired indulgence.

CRUSHING

After the grapes have been destemmed, they are usually crushed. This operation needs to be handled with care, since crushing that is too brutal can bruise the pips and allow harsh tannins to seep into the must. A few winemakers now dispense with crushing. At Château Smith-Haut-Lafitte, Fabien Tietgen argues that by not crushing he allows the weight of the berries in the vats to force out some juice, which gradually ferments, as does the juice remaining inside the berries. This creates a very slow fermentation process resulting, he believes, in finer-grained tannins. It's a plausible argument, since if the berries are uncrushed the yeasts will have to work more slowly, thus retarding fermentation. But a similar result can be achieved by chilling the must, as is done at many wineries.

Oenologist Dany Rolland also favours dispensing with crushing:

Crushing is brutal and can oxidize the grapes. By not crushing, the release of the juice is more progressive and gentle, which gives better extraction and better press wine. We have done experiments to establish this.

At an increasing number of wineries pumping the grapes is being eliminated. Thus after destemming and crushing, the grapes are raised by a conveyor belt to a spot over the destined fermentation tank, and gently tipped into the vat. (The most dazzling and architecturally satisfying model for this kind of gravity-operated *cuvier* is at Château La Lagune.) In some cases, the destemming and/or crushing take place on a platform just above the tanks, facilitating the tipping of the fruit into the vats without pumping. At Pontet-Canet, Jean-Michel Comme crushes the grapes lightly, then lets them fall into the vats by gravity. He is convinced this has an important effect on wine quality. He has found that the unbruised berries take on colour and ferment more slowly, giving a more gentle extraction and more supple tannins.

Paul Pontallier is not entirely persuaded that using gravity in this way makes much of a difference in the long term:

> *It's a sincere practice, but I'm not sure it's scientifically based. We need to be able to make precise comparisons. If some of the grapes that end up in the tank are bruised or slightly damaged, so what? Why treat grapes like caviar, if you then crush them? What often baffles me is that the estates that are the most finicky in terms of grape handling and sorting are often the ones that choose to produce the most extracted wines.*

COLD SOAK

This Burgundian technique, also known as pre-fermentation maceration, delays the onset of fermentation by chilling the must to a low temperature at which yeasts cannot work. While the grapes and must are chilled down, a certain extraction begins nonetheless. The process extracts colour and stabilizes it, and it also extracts fruit. However, it is essential to protect the unfermented juice from oxidation. This is done by injecting sulphur dioxide; if this is done to excess, which may be necessary if the cold soak is prolonged for more than four days, the SO_2 can itself extract bitter tannins. Another method is to protect the must with dry ice.

There seems to be no strong argument against a cold soak. On the other hand, there seems to be no firm evidence that it has any long-term beneficial effect either. Denis Dubourdieu has argued that there is no reason to believe that by the time the wine is ready for bottling, it makes the slightest difference whether it has been through a cold soak or not. Paul Pontallier also finds no pragmatic reason to adopt the procedure, and the veteran winemaker Daniel Llose is also not convinced it makes a difference.

FERMENTATION VATS

Before the twentieth century fermentation always took place in wooden vats. Their sole drawback was the need to maintain them in exemplary condition. Leaking staves needed to be mended or replaced, and the interiors had to be cleaned and disinfected (often with brandy) to avoid bacterial contamination. From the 1920s onwards many wooden vats were replaced with cement tanks, lined with epoxy resin to help keep them pristine. They were ugly and they were immoveable, but they served their purpose. From the early 1960s stainless-steel vats were introduced. These had obvious advantages: they were easy to keep clean and there were various methods by which the temperature of the liquid within could be controlled.

Stainless-steel vats seemed to be the *dernier cri*, but, as always happens, some retro-chic entered the picture. In the late 1980s wineries began discarding their steel tanks and replacing them with wooden vats, often expensively made with top-quality French oak. It was argued that the staves permitted a gradual and beneficial exchange of oxygen. A decade later wineries still equipped with cement tanks came to the realization that they weren't so bad after all, since they maintained a stable temperature more efficiently than stainless steel, which tended to heat up fast and cool down equally fast. Furthermore, steel could give the wine some reductive aromas. Some estates gave their old cement tanks a scrub and put them back into service. Claire Villars, at Ferrière and Haut-Bages-Libéral, ordered new ones.

The consensus among winemakers, except for those who are furiously partisan, is that the nature of the vat is not of great importance. There are advantages and drawbacks to each type. Some wineries will ferment most of their wine in steel, but reserve the very finest batches for fermentation in wood. Wooden vats are expensive to purchase, costly to maintain, and have a limited lifespan. After about five years a wooden vat can be shaved and renewed, but after eight or ten years it will be necessary to replace it. Hubert de Boüard at Château Angélus believes the nature of the container is far less important than the quality of the grapes you put into them.

The ability to control the temperature, and indeed manipulate it throughout the fermentation process, is crucial too. Some winemakers prefer to ferment at relatively high temperatures (over 30°C/86°F) for at least part of the process in order to maximize extraction and richness. Others will take a different approach, opting for a cooler temperature overall, so as to retain more freshness and aroma. It comes down to a question of personal stylistic preference. With every new day, the winemaker must make a myriad of small decisions, some trivial in themselves, but cumulatively they will define the balance, style, flavour, and structure of the wine.

Few good winemakers work by rote. Gonzague Lurton of Château Durfort-Vivens states: "Vinification is about adapting to circumstances, not about applying a set of rules." Olivier Bernard concurs:

> I am wary of anything that seems excessive, such as doing a cold maceration for a week, then heating the must to 24°C (75°F) to get fermentation going. Or raising the temperature after fermentation to 37 or 42°C (99 or 108°F). We should keep our winemaking as natural as possible. In the 1960s and 1970s a lot of traditional cellar-work was forgotten and replaced by mechanical solutions. But it's important that we recover those methods.

To complicate their lives further, some winemakers have been experimenting with fermentation in barriques. This is not an entirely new method, but seems to have reached Bordeaux in the late 1990s. Smith-Haut-Lafitte and Château du Seuil in the Graves, Labégorce-Margaux, and Quinault in St-Emilion are among those trying it out. For obvious practical reasons, it can be done only with fairly small volumes. One advantage of the technique is that temperatures tend to be self-regulating and rarely exceed 25°C (77°F). Fabien Tietgen at Smith finds that this slow barrique-fermentation gives more sweetness and body than conventional fermentation. The drawback is that the wine absorbs a lot of oak, since each barrel can be only partially filled to allow for the cap and to allow gases to escape. Thus the barrel, which is often larger than the standard barrique bordelaise, can be only half-filled. (Paul Pontallier concedes that barrel-fermentation of red wines, if done with care, can produce very good wines, but is not convinced that they are sufficiently different or superior to justify the expense and labour.)

A significant change, visible in most cuviers, is the replacement of very large fermentation tanks by batteries of much smaller tanks. This is to allow the separate vinification of the various parcels of which the property is composed. As more and more estates analyse their soils and parcels, they seek to maximize the number of blending components. It also allows individual parcels to be picked at optimal maturity, rather than because the grapes are needed to top up a large tank. Everyone agrees this is a positive development, though Henri Dubosq of Château Haut-Marbuzet does wonder whether sometimes it is taken to extremes: "If you take a sausage and cut it into many small pieces, you can no longer taste the sausage."

CONCENTRATORS

A new technology was devised in the late 1980s for removing excess water from grapes. The idea behind it was that many potentially fine vintages are ruined, or partly ruined, by untimely rainfall. New machines, called concentrators, allowed a proportion of such musts to be removed, thus improving the concentration of the fruit. The traditional way to deal with diluted must was to bleed the tanks during fermentation; this eliminated ten to fifteen per cent of the juice, which could be fermented separately to make a rosé. The drawback is that more than water is removed by this process: sugar, anthocyanins, and acids are also bled off. However, blind tastings at Bordeaux University don't show much difference in a wine concentrated by machine and one produced by bleeding the tanks.

There are two types of *concentrateur*: reverse osmosis and vacuum concentration ("*évaporation sous-vide*"). Reverse osmosis was first used at Léoville-Las-Cases in 1987. The technique is based on the difference in pressure of cells on either side of a membrane. When the must is introduced into the machine, the liquid redresses the balance by forcing water from one side of the membrane to the other. The vacuum system works by pumping the must into a tank free of oxygen. Deprived of oxygen, the must will boil at 23°C (73°F), allowing evaporation without heating the liquid excessively.

The vacuum system is cheaper but slower to run than reverse osmosis. The drawback to both systems is that every element in the must is concentrated. Any trace of rot or oxidation will be concentrated too. Therefore a concentrator must be employed with great caution in a difficult vintage. But in trouble-free, healthy vintages there is unlikely to be any need for it. Most large properties, including some First Growths, openly admit that they are equipped with one system or another, but they also say that with the mostly fine vintages of the past decade, there has been very little need to use it.

There are certain regulations to prevent excessive dependence on concentrators. The maximum proportion of must that can be removed is twenty per cent; and if concentration is used, then no chaptalization is permitted. Concentration cannot be applied once fermentation has begun. Nor is it permitted to overcrop and then use a concentrator to bring the must down to the maximum permitted yield. Most estate directors are satisfied that there is no intrinsic harm in either system, so long as it is not abused. Many châteaux have conducted experiments and micro-vinifications to assess the long-term consequences of concentration. It is also a technique that is never applied to an entire crop, but just to one or two lots that are rain-diluted. Many properties also claim that concentrated must is used only for the second wine. Hubert de Boüard, who experimented with reverse osmosis in the mid-1990s, isn't so sure:

> It clearly has no detrimental effect on the ageing capacity of a wine, but it's only useful for
> great wines. With mediocre wines you just concentrate whatever makes them mediocre.

Some, such as Christian Moueix in Libourne (Château Pétrus, among others), remain opposed to concentrators. Many traditional winemakers argue that reliance on concentrators can encourage estates to overcrop in the expectation that they can adjust the must later. Anthony Barton of Léoville- and Langoa-Barton would rather chaptalize; Alexandre Thienpont of Vieux-Château-Certan would rather bleed the tanks. Olivier Bernard at Chevalier worries that concentration can harden a wine, but finds it acceptable to boost the alcohol of Cabernet Sauvignon by half a degree or so.

Philippe Dhalluin at Mouton is not strongly opposed, but has reservations:

> The appeal of the concentrator is that you're not using any extraneous elements, such as
> sugar. But these are violent processes. With sous-vide [the vacuum system] you are actually
> boiling the must, even if at a relatively low temperature. And osmosis means that you are
> using very high pressure to force the wine through a membrane.

There is no doubt that concentration is open to abuse. There is nothing to stop a grower reducing yields to obtain a highly concentrated wine, and then removing up to twenty per cent of the liquid by concentration to end up with an ultra-concentrated and alcoholic wine. If used in a reckless way, as sometimes it has been on the Right Bank, concentration can alter the natural balance of a wine and its traditional character. On the other hand, to criticize concentration as a technological manipulation is absurd, since many traditional interventions in the winemaking process are no less manipulative. At Château Pomeaux in Pomerol, up to forty per cent of the wine is bled during fermentation, which also has a dramatic effect on its structure.

(For manipulation red in tooth and claw, how about "*Flash Détente*". This system, which I do not claim fully to understand, involves heating the grapes after destemming to around 60°C/140°F, which not surprisingly causes the cell structure within the skin to explode and in the process extracts elements in the grape not usually accessible. Then the fruit is chilled down to around 20°C/68°F, so that normal fermentation can begin. The idea is to give greater concentration and aroma and minimize the risk of volatile acidity; but its main function is to soften green tannins. It's a very expensive system and is used only at very large estates, such as Château Lesparre in Graves de Vayres.)

Professor Denis Dubourdieu has no fundamental objections to concentration:

> *Osmosis is like using a pail when your boat has taken in some water. Its misuse is when there is dilution in the grapes because of excess yields, in which case the technique won't work, as you don't change the character of the wine. If a wine is dilute because of high yields, chances are it's also not ripe. But if the grapes are fully ripe and healthy but picked in wet weather, then osmosis can be useful.*

YEASTS

There is no uniform practice when it comes to yeast selection. Many wineries are happy to rely on the native yeast population in the vineyard and *cuvier*. Other wineries, especially those producing a less expensive and more commercial style of wine, opt for selected (also known as cultivated or cultured) yeasts, so as to avoid the risk of stuck fermentations. Winemakers have their own justifications for their personal preferences. The *maître de chai* at Ducru-Beaucaillou prefers natural yeasts, since they work more slowly than selected yeasts, and he believes the extraction is better with a slower fermentation. Marie-Laure Lurton of Villegorge prefers selected yeasts, so as to deter high volatile acidity and prevent the simultaneous onset of malolactic fermentation. She also points out that should any bacterial infection afflict the wine during fermentation with natural yeasts, you need to use very high doses of SO_2 to combat it.

Many wineries compromise. When the first grapes arrive at the winery, some of the must is inoculated with selected yeasts to provide a *pied de cuve*, essentially a starter batch. Once the first vat begins to ferment, the natural yeasts present in the winery get their skates on and start working on the other vats.

All things considered, the individual aromas and subtleties imparted by yeast strains native to the environment of the estate are more welcome than the more standardized aromas from cultivated yeasts, especially in white wines. But it cannot be denied that some very good and characterful Bordeaux is made with selected yeasts.

The real problem is likely to arise in a decade or so, if the use of genetically modified yeasts is authorized. Many estates throughout France have warned of the catastrophic consequences of GM strains that could suppress and destroy the native yeast populations. But this is still many years off.

PIGEAGE

The traditional Bordelais method of extraction is to pump the juice over the cap with regular frequency. Its drawback is that, although it keeps the cap moist and disperses the must, it is not that effective at breaking up the thick mass of the cap. In recent years some winemakers have opted instead, or additionally, for the Burgundian method of *pigeage*. In its traditional form this involves naked men jumping into fermentation tanks and stomping on the cap to break it up. The process is quite dangerous, and workers have passed out and drowned. So today *pigeage* is often done manually by forcing plungers into the cap, or mechanically.

Although *pigeage* is always associated with Burgundy, there are those who claim that there are Bordelais precedents too. Jean-Luc Thunevin of St-Emilion believes it was practised at Domaine de Chevalier half a century ago, and elsewhere. The technique fell from favour, he claims, after it was used with insufficiently ripe grapes, in which case vegetal flavours intruded into the wine.

There are clear benefits from *pigeage*. It does indeed break up the cap, it distributes the must more evenly than pumpovers, it extracts good colour, and can give more *gras* or fat to the wine. But it has its critics too. Philippe Dhalluin observes:

> Pigeage *evolved as an ideal means of extraction for Pinot Noir. But if you use the technique with Cabernet, you can extract more than is ideal. It's better to use a gentle pumpover and a longer* cuvaison. *But my mind isn't closed, and we may do some experiments at Mouton.*

Gonzague Lurton is against its use with Cabernet Sauvignon and Merlot:

> *These are varieties that need oxygen, unlike Pinot Noir. No one knows how to regulate* pigeage − *how often and when to do it − so it's risky as a means of extraction. I have a feeling it is being introduced in some properties because it attracts media attention, and wine writers are always in need of a new story.*

There is a compromise method known as the Socma system, which has been acquired by Brane-Cantenac, Pédesclaux, and other properties. With this system a pump is immersed in the cap; every few minutes (the timing can be regulated) the juice is forced up a central column and floods the cap, thereby causing it to break up after repeated assaults.

PRESSING

There are three kinds of press in common use. The least esteemed is the horizontal press, which presses the skins between two plates. This is the harshest form of press and thus the most likely to extract bitter tannins. It is now seen only at estates that either cannot afford or cannot be bothered to work with a more delicate machine. The horizontal press was succeeded by the pneumatic press, in which an inflatable rubber bladder presses the grapes against the sides of the machine. This is both gentle and flexible, as the intensity and duration of the pressing cycle can be programmed. It is easily the best option for white wine.

The most traditional press is the vertical or hydraulic press, which has been around since the nineteenth century. This too is very gentle, but it is also slow and labour-intensive. It is favoured at many top Sauternes estates. It is also making a comeback in the form of a more mechanized, programmable version, as gentle as the old type of press but easier to handle.

The amount of press wine added to the blend is usually determined by tasting both elements. The riper the year, the better the quality of the press wine is likely to be; in leaner years, it must be added with caution, since it can easily impart astringency to the final blend.

MICRO-OXYGENATION

Many years ago I was visiting Madiran in southwest France and encountered a young man called Patrick Ducournau. He was happy to pour me his wines but he also showed me a system he had developed for inoculating controlled doses of oxygen into a fermenting wine. Its primary function was to soften the green tannins often present in the ultra-tannic Tannat variety that dominates Madiran. Within a few years Ducournau was selling thousands of micro-oxygenation kits to wineries across the world.

It caught on in Bordeaux as it did elsewhere, and became legally sanctioned in 1998. Although the Bordeaux varieties are intrinsically less tannic than Tannat, green tannins and excessive herbaceousness can often be encountered in difficult vintages. So micro-oxygenation has been adopted by many oenologists, especially in sub-regions such as Bourg and Blaye where rusticity can characterize the wines. If micro-oxygenation is performed during *fermentation sous marc*, the wine rapidly absorbs the dose of oxygen and it helps to stabilize tannins and anthocyanins. Opponents of the technique point out that pumpovers perform a similar function by aerating the wine. In the prestigious areas, where higher prices for the wine support a scrupulous viticulture and careful selection, it seems to have less of a role to play. One does not, after all, expect Lafite or Haut-Brion to harvest grapes with green tannins in the first place.

There is a second application of micro-oxygenation, often known as *cliquage*. This too involves the controlled inoculation of oxygen, but it is done during the *élevage*. This has proved much more controversial, as it is a technique often applied not to run-of-the-mill wines but to some of Bordeaux's most prized growths. The idea behind *cliquage* is that it makes racking redundant. The Bordeaux tradition is to rack (essentially, aerate) wine in barrel every three months. Its purpose is to combat reduction and expose the wine to oxygen; it also allows the winery team to draw the liquid off the lees at each racking, thus slowly clarifying the wine. Enthusiasts for *cliquage* point out that with this system the doses of oxygen can be scientifically regulated, whereas racking is a more brutal, and less controllable, means of achieving the same end. Moreover, since no racking is required, it is possible to age the red wine on the fine lees, should you wish to do so.

Opponents of *cliquage* fear that its long-term impact is as yet unknown. Some believe it can increase the chances of brettanomyces infection in the wine. Hubert de Boüard of Angélus is very wary of the system, suspecting that it prompts the wine to evolve too rapidly. Stéphane Derenoncourt, an enthusiast for the method, which he applies widely to the wines he makes in St-Emilion, argues the precise opposite, that the wine will age better if subjected to micro-oxygenation. The veteran Moueix winemaker, Jean-Claude Berrouet, argues that Merlot is aromatically fragile, so applying micro-oxygenation to vats or barrels of Merlot is to invite a loss of freshness.

Another winemaker observes:

> I've experimented with micro-oxygenation but there have been lots of variations in the results. It's like driving and braking at the same time. The lees encourage reduction, the oxygen speeds up the evolution. It's a bit like giving a Ferrari to people who can't drive. The useful idea behind it is that the élevage *begins before the malolactic fermentation, while the wine is still on its lees, which used to be a period that was neglected by winemakers.*

Denis Dubourdieu is sceptical too:

> Racking is a brutal form of aeration, and it's irregular. So it can be replaced by introducing the equivalent amount of oxygen artificially and leaving the wine on its lees without racking. A lot depends on whether you are using new or older oak. But racking is not only done to oxygenate the wine. It's also important to disinfect the barrel to avoid brettanomyces and other bacterial problems. Barrique-ageing imposes racking. Good élevage *involves knowing how much oxygen is being introduced, whether at racking or bottling. My view is that micro-oxygenation while the wine is* sous marc *is of little use with great wines, because they are going to receive prolonged barrel-ageing anyway. The only reason to do it* sous marc *is to make the wine more accessible by the* primeur *tastings in March. There is no oenological case for it.*

It is very difficult to assess the merits and drawbacks of micro-oxygenation, especially since its use requires the winemakers to make numerous choices about doses and timing. The 200-page documentation given me by Ducournau looks like a chemistry textbook, and it is way beyond my competence to judge the scientific basis for the method. But it's an important issue, since the technique is widely used. For an outside view I turned to Dr. Terry Lee, for many years head of research and development at Gallo in California. He too had serious doubts:

> *No one knows how micro-oxygenated wines will evolve because there hasn't been enough research. You need to know how much oxygen has been injected, and you also need a qualified team to make a sensory evaluation of various wines. None of this has been done. And if it seems to be the case that micro-oxygenation makes wines softer and more approachable you have to keep in mind that the Bordelais use other techniques, such as picking riper fruit and giving extended maceration, to achieve the same ends.*

BARREL-AGEING

Most Bordeaux wines with pretensions to quality undergo their *élevage* in barriques rather than tanks. The gentle infusion of wine with oxygen through the slight porosity of the staves gives the wine a greater roundness and harmony. It reduces astringency and gives the wine more fatness and texture. In the nineteenth century wines were so tannic that it often required at least three years of ageing in barrel before they were ready for bottling. Today a period of eighteen or twenty months is usually the maximum, though many châteaux age the wine for only twelve months, for the purely practical reason that the barrels need to be emptied to receive the next crop.

As has already been mentioned, the wine needs to be racked regularly, or oxygenated by *cliquage*. However, this received wisdom is being challenged, and quite a few serious red wines are being aged on the fine lees with minimal racking. The technique is common enough for the ageing of white wines, which are often kept on the fine lees and regularly stirred to keep those lees in suspension. The object of the exercise is to give the wine more richness and succulence. Some oenologists decided the same method could be used with red wines, and for much the same reasons. Another advantage is that you can reduce the doses of sulphur dioxide normally required during racking. Others reject the method as pointless, pointing out that one reason for keeping wine on the fine lees is to protect it from oxidation, but Bordeaux varieties are quite capable of resisting oxidation during a normal *élevage*. Cynical observers believe the real reason behind this modish innovation is to make the wines more flattering during the crucial *primeur* tastings. What both proponents and opponents agree on is that the quality of the fine lees is crucial: if the grapes lack maturity or are in some way unhealthy, then those defects will be exaggerated in the final wine if it is aged on the lees. Extreme vigilance is required, as extended lees-ageing does increase the risk of volatile acidity and bacterial infection.

In order to stir the lees into the wine, some châteaux have invested in a system of special racks called Oxoline. This allows the barrels to be gently rolled without removing them from the racks; nor is it necessary to open the bung and stir the lees by hand, as is done with white wines. Some winemakers believe the system is flawed, since the lees tend to stick to the interior of the barrel, and mere rolling won't stir them up sufficiently.

Some properties are conducting discreet experiments to modify and improve the *élevage*. At Château La Garde in Pessac-Léognan, lees are separated from the white wine after malolactic fermentation, then stirred for one month in a tank in order to semi-liquefy them. This liberates proteins and other compounds. Then the lees are redistributed to barrels that would benefit from some fattening up. The lees are then stirred by rolling. It is hard for an outsider to assess such experiments, but it confirms that Bordeaux winemakers are rarely inclined to rest on their laurels.

Château Margaux, that bastion of traditional winemaking in tandem with scientific rigour, is a strong believer in racking. Paul Pontallier explains:

> *I am not at all sure that ageing a red wine on its fine lees is necessarily a positive process. I believe it is fundamental to good* élevage *to get oxygen into the wine and to remove lees at the same time. What we do at Margaux is to retain after racking the small volume of wine*

that contains the lees. With hundreds of barrels in the chai, *that can add up to a lot of wine. We filter it, then add it to our second wine. If lees-ageing were so beneficial in terms of quality, then surely the* vin de lie *would end up as equal in quality to our grand vin. But it never is, and that's why we blend it with Pavillon. I suspect that the real reason for the popularity of ageing Bordeaux* sur lie *is to improve texture and mouthfeel, not the quality of the wine itself. But we are adamant in wanting to create wines that will give pleasure to drinkers rather than satisfy the criteria of tasters and critics.*

The volume of the *barrique bordelaise* was officially defined in the 1860s at 225 litres. Most barrels found in the *chais* of Bordeaux are of French oak, though some properties use a proportion of American or East European oak, which is considerably cheaper, for second wines. There are countless variations on the theme of barrel: source of wood, length of drying, degree of toasting, age of barrel, and the stylistic signature of the cooper all offer the winemaker different nuances to work with. Experimentation is constant, as winemakers seek to fine-tune the *élevage*, and they often invite the coopers to participate in tastings to assess the suitability of their barrels.

Red wine always goes through malolactic fermentation, which lowers the level of sometimes harsh malic acid by converting it into more supple lactic acid. This process can either take place in tanks following the alcoholic fermentation, or the newly fermented wine can be decanted into barriques for the malolactic to take place in oak. Some winemakers will inoculate to provoke the malolactic; others will let nature take its course, and should it be reluctant to do so, nature can be given a gentle prodding by heating the *chai*.

Malolactic fermentation *en barrique* is nothing new. The Burgundians have always practised it. But it is relatively recent in Bordeaux, where estates are much larger, making the process far more labour-intensive. Those who favour the technique argue that it speeds up the integration of oak into the wine. There is also widespread agreement that the method enhances the initial fruitiness of a wine. The veteran winemaker Georges Pauli believes it also stabilizes the colour and harmonizes the tannins. However, there is also a strong commercial reason for the practice. With thousands of tasters descending on Bordeaux for the *primeur* tastings, it is understandable that winemakers will do everything possible to ensure the wine is as palatable as possible. There is no doubt that the sooner the new wine goes into barrel, the rounder and more flattering it will appear by the spring. With crucial commercial decisions, not to mention wine writers' scores, being determined at the spring tastings, it is quite understandable that châteaux want their wines to be as sexy as possible. Dany Rolland is completely open about it: "Probably after ten years in bottle there is no discernible difference. But wines are judged early by the trade and the press, so it's very important that it tastes good by March."

Jean-Louis Camp of Château Rauzan-Gassies admits that he uses partial *malo en barrique* essentially for cosmetic purposes, to make the wine look good young. But he is certain that six months later it is impossible to distinguish between those lots that have gone through malolactic in barrel and those that have completed it in tanks. On this there is widespread agreement from other winemakers such as Philippe Dhalluin of Mouton and from researchers such as Dr. Gilles de Revel of Bordeaux University.

But there are those who claim that the benefits can be medium- if not long-term. The Gironde chamber of agriculture and Château Brane-Cantenac jointly compared the two techniques. The result, according to Brane-Cantenac, favoured malolactic in barrel. The advantages were:

improvement and stabilization of colour; softening of the wines; increased roundness and fatness; lessening of hard, oak character and an increased range of aromas…. Their bouquet is more complex and fine, the oak flavours are better integrated and the tannins are rounder and more silky. These differences, which are more obvious at the beginning of the ageing process, disappear however in time, but nevertheless remain in evidence after the wine has been bottled for three years or more.

The composition of the final blend can take place at various times. Most estates will begin making up their blends in January or February following the vintage. Although one motive is the wish, or need, to have a blend made up by the time the merchants and wine press arrive in March to taste the new wine, an equally important one is the belief that the sooner the wine is blended, the more harmonious it will be after its *élevage*. There are those, notably Michel Rolland, who take the opposite view, preferring to blend at the last moment, after surveying all the various components during their sojourn in barrel. Another argument for blending late is that keeping the components separate for as long as possible allows winemakers and consultants, especially recently hired ones, to attain a better understanding of the various parcels and grape varieties that make up the estate.

After the *élevage* is completed, the wine is usually fined with fresh eggwhite (gelatine at less quality-conscious properties) and filtered before being bottled. Fining helps to take the rough edges off the tannins in the wine, and filtration is designed to remove impurities. Both operations can be regulated to some extent: the ratio of eggwhite per barrel can be decreased to give a more gentle fining, and there are various systems of filtration, from rather brutal sterile filtration to laxer systems that are less likely to strip the wine of flavour and aroma. Some properties fine but don't filter; others filter but don't fine. It depends on the state of the wine – its clarity, its stability – and on the philosophy of the winemaker. Many wines are bottled without fining or filtration, which is certainly the best solution so long as the wine is clear and stable. Fortunately I have yet to see in Bordeaux the cloudy wines that some Italian and Californian winemakers (and their ill-informed supporters in the wine press) consider grittily authentic rather than microbiological time-bombs.

TCA

This nasty compound, 2,4,6-trichloranisole, is related to cork taint, a problem scarcely unique to Bordeaux's wine. However, the taint has other ways of entering the wine. In the late 1980s and 1990s it became apparent that a few wines, including Ducru-Beaucaillou and Canon, had distinctly unpleasant aromas and flavours. Although similar in character to cork taint, this problem was far more widespread than that haphazardly occurring complaint. The source of the problem turned out to be treatments used on wooden rafters in *chais*. The products that caused the taint were banned by the mid-1990s, so the problem is, or should be, consigned to history. It was ironic that properties that invested in expensive, air-conditioned *chais* were most likely to be affected. The actual contamination occurred when the wine was being racked and exposed to oxygen, which carried the taint.

SELECTION AND SECOND WINES

As has already been mentioned, one of the most important developments in recent decades has been the widespread creation of second wines. Although a few top properties have long released such wines, the idea really took off after 1982. Curiously, Mouton was among the last important estates to produce a second wine. When I asked the director about this many years ago, he explained that the absence of a second wine forced his team to put all their efforts into ensuring the *grand vin* was as good as possible. I am not sure he believed his own argument, as a few years later Mouton did indeed begin releasing Le Petit Mouton.

The logic is simple enough. In order to maintain the quality of the *grand vin*, estates will automatically exclude from it wine made from very young vines or from vines grown on parcels known to be inferior. At various stages during the vinification and *élevage*, the winemakers have the option to declassify lots that they are unhappy with. They are consigned to the second wine or, if they are really unsatisfactory, may be sold off to wholesalers.

Estates have different views about how much *grand vin* to produce. At Lynch-Bages, relatively little wine is declassified into the second wine; at Léoville-Las-Cases it is always more than fifty per cent, and sometimes as much as two-thirds. There is no right answer. It's a safe guess that at Lynch-Bages, Jean-Michel Cazes aims to produce a substantial quantity of excellent wine at a fair price. He has no wish to make a cult of Lynch-Bages.

I would also guess that the Delons at Léoville deliberately curbed the production of *grand vin* in order to maximize its quality and concentration – and price. It has long been the Léoville ambition to produce a wine at the same quality level as the First Growths, and to obtain similar prices to those obtained by the Firsts. So the proportion of *grand vin* is manipulated to suit the agendas of proprietors. There is nothing wrong with that, but there is no clear line in the sand between the quality required for the *grand* and second wines. It's a subjective decision. Commercial factors may also persuade estate directors to vary the proportions according to demand, and how much *grand vin* they can realistically expect to sell in any given vintage. The principle to remember is that a second wine is always the second-best wine. When the first wine is a First Growth, then the chances are that the second wine will still be worthwhile; when the first wine is modest, then you can be sure its second wine will be exceedingly so.

THE OENOLOGISTS

It is hard to overestimate the role that professional oenologists have played in the evolution of Bordeaux and its wines. The industry is fortunate to have the renowned faculty of oenology of the University of Bordeaux on its doorstep. Other wine regions have comparable institutes. But, to take one distinguished example, the University of California at Davis teaches viticulture and oenology, but has always had a reputation for teaching its students how to play safe and avoid winemaking errors. Such a winemaking technique was tailored more to the requirements of the big producers than the quality-conscious demands of smaller wineries. Bordeaux has focused on research as well as teaching, with a view to furthering the understanding and application of the winemaking process. Its luminaries, beginning with Emile Peynaud, have enabled winemakers to avoid the pitfalls of the past by having a clearer understanding of the art and chemistry of vinification and *élevage*.

Emile Peynaud, who was born in 1912, retired in 1990, and died in 2004, was the founding father of modern oenology, and a much sought-after consultant to many leading estates. The fact that his most important recommendations were that grapes should be picked ripe, that poor-quality or musty barrels should be thrown out, and that temperatures should be controlled during fermentation tells us something about the state of winemaking before his days as a consultant.

The consultants have become important because most proprietors of Bordeaux estates are not winemakers. They may have taken some courses in oenology, but their primary role is to maintain the estate's profitability. Thus the winemaking is entrusted to the *maître de chai*. These cellarmasters are the unsung heroes of Bordeaux, monitoring all aspects of the winemaking and ensuring that operations such as pumpovers and rackings are performed promptly and correctly. Many *maîtres de chai* may stomp around in blue overalls and speak in a barely intelligible Médocain accent, but their skill and experience are crucial to the running of the winery.

It is not, however, the primary job of the *maître de chai* to decide when to pick or how the final blend should be made up; nor can he make commercial decisions such as how much wine should be declassified. Hence the proprietors' growing dependence on consultant oenologists. Many consultants emerged from laboratories, where their skills gave them an analytical understanding of winemaking and an expertise at correcting faults that can arise. Others have emerged from the faculty of oenology at Bordeaux University. Emile Peynaud was the first of this distinguished band, and was later joined by Yves Glories, Pascal Ribéreau-Gayon, and Denis Dubourdieu. Some of these distinguished oenologists have employed their brightest students to assist them, and some of them in turn have set up independent consultancies.

The role of the consultant oenologist will vary. Some do little more than perform analyses on young wines and suggest solutions to any emerging problems. Others focus on vineyard development, analysing soil structures and proposing remedies to diseases or other problems in the vineyard, or altering trellising systems or densities. Companies have been set up that can call on the varying specializations of their employees, since no single person can be omni-competent. Other consultants are valued for their skills at *assemblage*, that crucial moment when the dozens of different lots must be unified into a final blend.

Consultants are sometimes accused of imposing a style on their clients. I believe this to be an over-simplification. If there is a family resemblance between some of the wines produced by estates that employ Michel Rolland, for example, it is because he insists on certain basic principles, such as the harvesting of fully ripe fruit, and proposes others, such as blending late, shortly before bottling, rather than during the winter after the vintage, which is still common practice. At the end of the day it is the owner who gives the orders. Some use their consultants to give a view from outside the domaine but do not necessarily follow their recommendations. Others rely slavishly on their advice.

Overall they have been a force for good. If they cannot by themselves create great wines, especially from a less-than-great terroir, they can at least prevent the production of poor or faulty wines. The best oenologists command a high price for their skills, and, in some cases, their influence with the wine press. It is no secret that Robert Parker has relied heavily on Michel Rolland for advice. Parker admires the rich, ripe style that is the Rolland hallmark. This makes it tempting for proprietors to hire a man of influence, in the hope that it will bring their wine to the attention of those, like Parker, who can make the reputation of a little-known or previously underperforming property.

Good advice doesn't come cheap, and there are plenty of second-raters in the business. My heart sinks when a proprietor, keen to show me his estate and wines, nonetheless delegates the task to his *oenologue*, who, in many cases, is unlikely to be Professor Dubourdieu and more likely to be a pompous, self-satisfied martinet, whose principal concern is to play safe. Great winemaking involves risk-taking, but some oenologists will use every trick in the book to clean up the wine to the greatest possible extent. There may be no bacteria within a mile of the winery, but there is no flavour either.

The following are the best known of the Bordeaux consultants and their clients, although I do not claim these lists are definitive. With the best-known consultants such as Michel Rolland or Gilles Pauquet, proprietors like to claim an affiliation when in some cases they merely use the services of their laboratories rather than those of the great men in person. If more than one oenologist seems to be working for the same estate, that is often because more than one opinion is sought.

Jacques Boissenot

He worked closely with Emile Peynaud for almost twenty years, and works with many of the most prestigious and traditional estates of the Médoc. His stylistic benchmarks would be harmony and balance rather than power; he likes a good dose of press wine to give structure and length to a wine, and is wary of excessive new oak. He has the reputation of being a precise taster but is none too keen on experimentation. Today he is increasingly assisted by his son Eric, who shares his general approach. The properties for which they consult include:

Margaux: Margaux, Brane-Cantenac, Desmirail, Giscours, Tertre, Issan, Palmer, Rauzan-Ségla, Labégorce-Zédé, Ferrière, Dauzac, Terrey-Gros-Caillou, Tour de Mons.

St-Julien: Branaire-Ducru, Ducru-Beaucaillou, Léoville-Las-Cases, Beychevelle, Lagrange, St-Pierre, Talbot.

Pauillac: Lafite, Latour, Pichon-Lalande, Grand-Puy-Lacoste, Haut-Batailley, Lynch-Moussas, Pédesclaux, Pibran, Pontet-Canet.

St-Estèphe: Cos d'Estournel, Phélan-Ségur.

Others: Tour-de-By, La Cardonne, Ramafort, Anthonic, Chasse-Spleen, Beaumont, Coufran, Fourcas-Hosten, Lamarque, Lanessan, Patache d'Aux, Peyrabon, Sénéjac, Soudars, Verdignan, Villegorge.

Pascal Chatonnet

An expert in TCA contamination, and the owner of some good Right Bank properties. He consults for some sixty estates in nine countries. In Bordeaux he focuses on St-Emilion and its satellites, where his clients include Branda (Puisseguin).

Olivier Dauga

As a former vineyard manager, it is not surprising that Dauga's priority is viticulture. His clients include Bellevue-Gazin, Cantinot, Caronne-Ste-Gemme, Lousteauneuf, Sérilhan.

Stéphane Derenoncourt

The modest Derenoncourt is a self-taught winemaker who came to Bordeaux from northern France in 1982, and began working in the vineyards of Fronsac. Later he was taken on as winemaker by Stephan von Neipperg at Canon-La-Gaffelière, La Mondotte, and his other properties. The estates he works for are primarily on the Right Bank and include Aiguilhe, Beaulieu (Bordeaux), Beauséjour (Montagne-St-Emilion), Bellevue, Cadet-Bon, Canon-La-Gaffelière, Clos Fourtet, Clos de l'Oratoire, Faurie-de-Souchard, La Gaffelière, Gigault, Grands Marechaux, Grée-Laroque, Guadet, Haut-Gay, Hostens-Picant, L'Isle Fort, Larcis-Ducasse, Lucia, La Mondotte, Pavie-Macquin, Le Pin Beausoleil, La Prade, Le Prieuré, Puygueraud, Richelieu, Rol Valentin, La Rousselle, Sanctus, Sansonnet, Tertre Daugay, La Tour Figeac, Vieux Manoir, Vrai Canon Bouché, and Vray Croix de Gay. In Pessac-Léognan he consults for Clos Marsalette, Brown, Domaine de Chevalier (red only), Smith-Haut-Lafitte, and Le Thil Comte Clary. He makes a close study of the soil at the properties where he works, believing this is crucial to wine quality, and often teams up with soil scientist Claude Bourguignon. Like Michel Rolland, he prefers to blend late. As a Right Bank specialist and a leading enthusiast for micro-oxygenation and whole-berry fermentation, some eyebrows were raised when he was taken on by Prieuré-Lichine in Margaux, Branas Grand Poujeaux, and Preuillac in the Médoc. In 2007 he added Sérilhan in St-Estèphe to his portfolio. He owns his own small estate in the Côtes de Castillon. He is now assisted by Julien Lavenu.

Denis Dubourdieu

Somehow this clever and sharp-minded man finds the time to teach and head research projects at the University of Bordeaux, to run his own estates in the Graves, Premières Côtes, and Barsac, and to consult for a growing band of top properties, primarily but not exclusively in Pessac-Léognan. There he advises Barret, Carbonnieux, Domaine de Chevalier, Couhins-Lurton, Feran, La Louvière, Latour-Martillac, Haut-Bailly, Olivier, Rochemorin, and Le Sartre. In the 1980s Dubourdieu was the leading expert on white wine vinification, introducing Bordeaux to skin contact, barrel-fermentation, and *bâtonnage*. He pays close attention to vineyards too, and ensuring that vines (and wines) are in balance. He has recently expanded his consultancy work to include the red wines from Siran, Batailley, Arsac, Beau Site, du Glana, La Lagune, Lynch-Moussas, de Pez, Lamothe-Bergeron, and Grand-Puy-Ducasse. His scientific training leads him to cast a sceptical eye on any winemaking innovation he suspects owes more to fashion than substance.

On the Right Bank he consults for Bergat, Bourgneuf-Vayron, Canon de Brem, Cheval Blanc, Couvent des Jacobins, La Dauphine, Domaine de l'Eglise, L'Enclos, La Grangère, Plaisance (Premières Côtes), de Pressac, Quinault, Taillefer, Tauzinat L'Hermitage, and Trottevieille. In Sauternes he advises de Malle, Rayne-Vigneau, and Yquem.

Jean-Philippe Fort

Although still attached to the Rolland laboratory in Libourne, Fort, an enthusiast for micro-oxygenation, has been developing his own clientele, a list that is growing fast. It includes: Balestard-La-Tonnelle, Beau-Séjour-Bécot, Cap de Mourlin, Chauvin, Franc Maillet, La Gomerie, Grand Corbin-Despagne, Les Hauts Conseillants, Joanin-Bécot, Laniote, Larmande, Laurets, de Lussac, Perron, Petit-Faurie-de-Soutard, Producteurs Réunis de Puisseguin, Roudier, St-Georges, St-Jean-de-Lavaud, Tour Maillet, Vieux-Ch-Champs-de-Mars, Vieux-Guillou, and Vieux Maillet.

Gilles Pauquet

This self-effacing consultant is a Right Bank specialist, who set up his Libourne laboratory in 1977. In St-Emilion he works with L'Arrosée, Bellefont-Belcier, Bergat, Cadet-Piola, Canon, Cheval Blanc, Le Dôme, Figeac, Fleur de Jauge, Fleur Pourret, Fonbel, La Grace Dieu, Laforge, Laroque, Moulin-St-Georges, de Pressac, Rozier, St-Georges-Côte-Pavie, Teyssier, La Tour du Pin Figeac (Giraud-Bélivier), Trianon, Trottevieille, and Vieux Fortin. And in Pomerol: Bourgneuf-Vayron, La Cabanne, Le Caillou, La Conseillante, Croix du Casse, L'Enclos, Gazin, Gombaude-Guillot, Mazeyres, La Patache, and Plincette. And in the satellite appellations: Laborde. (*See also* Stéphane Toutoundji.)

Michel Rolland

Rolland, who owns Château Le Bon Pasteur in Pomerol and some lesser properties, has, with his wife Dany, run an oenological laboratory in Libourne since the 1970s and began consulting in 1982. A flamboyant character who does not take kindly to criticism, Rolland has a reputation for arrogance that is only partly deserved. Estimates vary, but it is said that he consults, in some degree or another, for between 110 and 200 properties around the world. (I have met him more frequently in Napa Valley and Argentina than in Bordeaux.) He commands very high fees and his clients believe he is worth every penny, and not just because of his undoubted influence with Robert Parker. Their stylistic preferences overlap: Rolland, like Parker, likes big, dark, rich wines with supple tannins and little pronounced acidity. He believes in picking the grapes when fully ripe – hardly revolutionary these days. He often recommends techniques such as parcel selection, extended maceration, occasional micro-oxygenation, a high proportion of new oak, malolactic fermentation in barrique, and late blending. These are principles, not formulae, and he does adapt winemaking techniques to the specificity of each estate. It is simply untrue to state, as some have done, that he makes all his wines in the same way. Everyone accepts that he is a superb blender, often composing the *assemblage* without needing to take notes, thanks to an excellent memory.

The accusation that all Rolland wines taste the same is absurd, but he does leave an often discernible signature on them. A pertinent example is the underperforming Margaux estate of Château Kirwan, where he rapidly improved quality. Whether the wine is a "typical" Margaux is open to question. He has done much the same at Château Clarke in Listrac, and a discussion of his reforms is given in the appropriate entry.

Consultancies come and go but the following is a list, current at the time of writing, of the principal Bordeaux properties where his car is sometimes parked:

St-Emilion: Angélus, Armens, Ausone, Bellefont-Belcier, de Candale, Clos des Jacobins, Clos St-Martin, Corbin, Côte de Baleau, La Couspaude, Croix de Labrie, Dassault, Destieux, La Dominique, Faugères, Fombrauge, Fonplégade, Franc-Mayne, Grand-Mayne, Grand-Pontet, Grandes Murailles, Haut Brisson, Jean Faure, Larmande, Monbousquet, Pavie, Pavie-Decesse, Ripeau, Rochebelle, Rocher Bellevue-Figeac, St Hubert, Troplong-Mondot, Valandraud.

Pomerol: Beauregard, Bonalgue, Certan-de-May, La Clémence, Clinet, Clos du Clocher, La Commanderie de Mazeyres, Croix Toulifaut, L'Evangile, Le Gay, Petit-Village, Pomeaux, Prieurs de la Commanderie, Rouget, La Violette.

Satellites: Fleur de Boüard, Garraud, Grand Ormeau, Jean de Gué, Messile Aubert.

Other Right Bank properties: Bellevue (Canon-Fronsac), Le Doyenné, Girolate, La Gravière, Haut-Ballet, Lagarosse, Lagrave Aubert, Marsau, Pey La Tour, Reignac, Les Laurets de Viaud.

Médoc: Lascombes, Clarke, Léoville-Poyferré, Pontet-Canet, La Tour-Carnet, Clément-Pichon, Le Crock, Loudenne, Brillette, Phélan-Ségur.

Pessac-Léognan: Smith-Haut-Lafitte, Larrivet-Haut-Brion, Malartic-Lagravière, Latour-Martillac, La Garde, de France, Pape-Clément (and other properties owned by Bernard Magrez).

Rolland has a team of seven oenologists, some of whom – Jean-Philippe Fort – operate independently in following certain properties. So the degree of personal attention given by Rolland himself to the above list will vary.

Stéphane Toutoundji

An associate of Gilles Pauquet, Toutoundji advises the following properties in St-Emilion: Fonroque, Moulin du Cadet, Clos de la Cure, de Ferrand, La Grâce Dieu Les Menuts, Milon, La Serre, Laborde, and Croque-Michotte. And in Pomerol: Guillot, Plince, La Pointe, and Valois.

Christian Veyry

A serious young man now entering middle age, Veyry has become an important consultant on the Right Bank, especially in Fronsac. In Pomerol he advises Bel-Air, Bellegrave, Bonalgue, Clos du Clocher, Croix de Gay, and Montviel. In the satellites: Courlat and Faizeau. In Canon-Fronsac: Beauséjour, de Carles, Chadenne, Dalem, Haut Larriveau, Moulin Haut-Laroque, Moulin Pey Labrie, Puy Guilhem, Renard Mondésir, and Vieille Cure. In Blaye and Bourg: Bel Air La Royère and Martinat.

Other important winemaking figures in Bordeaux are Jean-Claude Berrouet, who supervises all the wines produced by J.P. Moueix, Pétrus included, but also consults for Rochebelle; Georges Pauli, former winemaker for the Cordier group, now overseeing Gruaud-Larose, Tourteau-Chollet, de Portets, and Grand Lartigue; Daniel Llose, former technical director of AXA Millésimes, who is now looking after the properties of the Cazes family; Denis Durantou keeps an eye on Moulinet; Jean-Luc Colombo from the Rhône has been hired by the Milhade family to consult for the properties they own or manage, which includes St-Georges-Côte-Pavie and Lyonnat; Alain Raynaud advises Haute-Barde and for the Rollan-de-By group of estates in the Médoc and Château de Carles in Fronsac; Patrick Valette consults for Berliquet and Plaisance in St-Emilion; and Hubert de Boüard consults for Clos des Jacobins and La Commanderie for Pichon-Longueville, Chantegrive in the Graves, and Château Clos Chaumont in the Premières Côtes. Jean-Luc Thunevin, as well as being a proprietor and négociant, acts as a consultant for Château de Carles (together with Alain Raynaud) and Fleur Cardinale.

THE TASTE OF BORDEAUX

Because of the great advances in viticulture and vinification in Bordeaux, certainly since 1982, it has become possible for winemakers to manipulate their wines much more than in the past. The number of choices to be made during the process of bringing a wine to bottle has risen. I have already mentioned the St-Emilion wine I recently tasted with 15.5 degrees of alcohol. That would have been both inconceivable and technically impossible twenty years ago. Today anything is possible. That is both liberating and disturbing.

John Kolasa, who runs both Rauzan-Ségla and Canon, is very wary of new techniques such as concentration, micro-oxygenation and lees-stirring. I doubt that he is opposed to innovation as such; what worries him is a possible, perhaps actual, loss of typicity. He strongly believes that "Bordeaux must remain Bordeaux." It's not that all Bordeaux wines should taste the same, but there is a family resemblance between them. Even a modest Médoc or Graves has a regional signature, that balance of fruit, acidity, and tannin, perhaps a slight austerity, and an easy drinkability. A top Bordeaux may lack that individuality when young: the sheen of full ripeness, supple tannins, and new oak may make the wine hard to distinguish from a great New World or Italian Cabernet. But with bottle-age that Bordeaux typicity will re-emerge: those cedary aromas, those whiffs of cigar-box and damp earth, and a savoury tone on the palate – they are unlikely to have come from Coonawarra or Sonoma.

Bruno Prats, late of Cos d'Estournel, once made a wise observation:

> The great advantage Bordeaux enjoys is the existence of benchmarks. If we are lucky enough, we can still taste a wine such as 1900 Margaux that establishes what a great claret should taste like. When Piero Antinori was talking to me in the 1970s about improving quality in Tuscany, one of his problems was that there were no comparable benchmarks in Italy.

Yet Bordeaux is changing, but not necessarily for the worse. Prats' son Jean-Guillaume confirms:

> There is no doubt that styles have changed. At Cos d'Estournel our wines used to be
> austere, intense, and oaky when young, even in vintages such as 1990 and 1995. But today
> we find that the wines need to be charming as soon as they are in bottle. We can achieve this
> by not going for overripeness and losing the fresh acidity in our wines. Of course the grapes
> must have phenolic ripeness, and I believe in malo en barrique. But I don't want overripe
> fruit and long macerations and pigeage and over-extraction, all of which in my view could
> harm the capacity of the wine to age.

The American wine importer Kermit Lynch fears things have already gone too far. He laments:

> Nineteen-eighty-two was an atypical vintage, but ever since producers have been trying to
> make wines that taste like it. By now I can no longer distinguish one vintage from another,
> one château from another. It has to do with technology too. With concentrators you increase
> the resemblance of one vintage to every other. I like to accept, as one did in the past, that
> there are some lighter vintages. So what? You can take a bigger swallow! I want variety in
> Bordeaux, and not just a succession of tannic monsters.

Lynch is surely over-pessimistic. If "light" means thin and dilute, I am happy to see the back of those wines. But if "light" means elegant, graceful, harmonious, and digestible, I have no trouble finding those wines among many *crus bourgeois*, Pomerols, and Graves, as well as classified growths. On the other hand, I wouldn't dispute that there are too many ungainly, top-heavy wines that are scarcely recognizable as Bordeaux. When I blind-tasted the 2004 Château Pavie among its peers in St-Emilion, I had no difficulty guessing its identity simply because it was the most extracted and least drinkable of the wines before me. If Parker and would-be Parkers think these are great wines, and if their readers still seek them out as overpriced "collectibles", well, that doesn't mean "the end of Bordeaux as we know it". Bordeaux and its marketplace accept diversity. For every devotee of Pavie, there is a worshipper at the shrine of Margaux or La Conseillante. I am prepared to accept a little deviation from the classic perception of Bordeaux, and even a slight move toward homogenization, in order to enjoy all the improvements cited in this and the previous chapter that have made the overall standard of the wines so much higher than it was twenty or more years ago.

Christian Moueix accepts that Bordeaux has become richer and more alcoholic over recent decades:

> There are two aspects to this. Techniques such as green-harvesting and leaf removal both
> speed maturation and result in higher grape sugars. The other aspect is going for exaggerated
> hang-time, which is the intentional factor.

By way of conclusion, I like the observation of CVBG boss Jean-Marie Chadronnier:

> Styles have certainly changed. In the past a lot of grapes were not destemmed and there were
> many wines that were very tannic in their youth. But the important thing to remember is
> that we have the same raw materials as a century ago. The terroir doesn't change, and the
> grape varieties haven't changed. Today we are just better at ripening fruit. The great vintages
> of the 1940s were not that different in style from the great vintages of more recent times,
> simply because they were very ripe years. But what has changed is that since 1982 there
> have been huge advances in knowledge, an understanding that we need full ripeness, sensible
> yields, efficient temperature control, and hygiene in the winery.

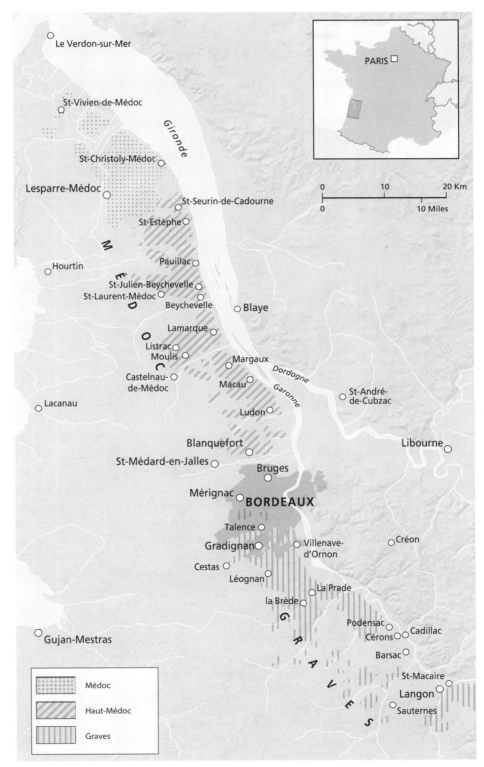

The Left Bank

4. The Médoc

 The Médoc is a geographical name for the entire peninsula that stretches northwards from the city of Bordeaux to the remote port of Le Verdon. A coastal strip running up the eastern side of the peninsula is where the vast majority of the Médoc's vineyards are situated. The most prestigious communes are Margaux, St-Julien, Pauillac, and St-Estèphe, with the two less esteemed communes of Moulis and Listrac, west of Margaux, trying out as understudies. The remainder of the peninsula's vineyards fall under two ACs: Médoc and Haut-Médoc. These two appellations are home to the great majority of the region's *crus bourgeois* as well as to five classed growths: La Lagune, Cantemerle, Belgrave, Camensac, and La Tour-Carnet. Until the 1940s what is today known simply as AC Médoc was called Bas-Médoc, as the more northerly counterpart of the Haut-Médoc. Its growers, arguing that Bas-Médoc implied a more lowly standing than Haut-Médoc, successfully petitioned to have the name changed.

Broadly speaking, the AC Médoc lies west and north of St-Estèphe, whereas the Haut-Médoc vineyards flank the more prestigious communes to the west and south, with the exception of St-Seurin-de-Cadourne, which lies between St-Estèphe and the AC Médoc vineyards. Both are very large regions: AC Médoc is composed of 5,580 hectares, and is responsible for thirty-four per cent of the entire production of the Médoc, or an average of thirty-eight million bottles. The Haut-Médoc is slightly smaller, at 4,615 hectares, representing 28.5 per cent of the Médoc's production, or an average of thirty-three million bottles. The minimum density for AC Médoc vineyards is 5,000 vines per hectare; that for the Haut-Médoc is 6,500 vines per hectare. Many vineyards in the latter appellation are still planted at 5,000 vines per hectare, but have until 2020 to replant at a higher density. Only red wines can be AC Médoc; white wines, which exist, though in small quantities, are only entitled to be labelled AC Bordeaux.

The estates of the Haut-Médoc, it is fair to say, are often considered superior to those of AC Médoc, but this is a very broad generalization. There are certainly many fine properties in AC Médoc, especially those that lie close to the estuary. Their proprietors would probably argue that it was their isolation from the city of Bordeaux in the eighteenth and nineteenth centuries, rather than the intrinsic inferiority of their soils and microclimates, that led to their being omitted entirely from the 1855 classification. Quality in the northern Médoc demands unremitting efforts on the part of the owners and management. This is an area where low yields, grape selection, and other human interventions play a major role.

The French wine writer Denis Hervier finds the landscape of the northern Médoc utterly enchanting. I doubt that this impression is widely shared. Having once toured these vineyards on a wet and blustery November day, I soon found the bleak, almost treeless landscape oppressive, with the leaf-stripped vines at their most skeletal and scarcely a sign of human habitation anywhere around me. Only close to the little ports that dot the estuary shoreline is there some vestigial charm. Standing in the almost hilly, gravelly vineyards of Tour-de-By, with its stirring view across the estuary, it is not hard to imagine the staunch pride of the founders and early owners, who had developed the finest terroirs close to the water, the same water that would transport their wines to Bordeaux.

The northern Médoc, with a few exceptions, is no longer dominated by Cabernet Sauvignon. This shift from Cabernet – said to be around eighty-five per cent in the early twentieth century – to more widespread plantings of Merlot has probably benefited quality. Cabernet Sauvignon does not always ripen easily on the chilly clay and sand soils of AC Médoc, and Merlot, which ripens earlier, is a sounder choice. Needless to say, where the soil is gravelly or particularly well drained, then Cabernet has been retained. The Médoc also suffers from an excess of productive rootstocks such as SO4; the richer classified estates could afford to replant vineyards still on SO4, but that is not an easy option farther north where the wines fetch a much more modest price. The quality of the wines produced in the Médoc is extremely variable, both because of the great variations in soil and exposition, and because not all *vignerons* are equally skilled as winemakers. Jean-Louis Camp, a veteran winemaker, believes that there is little significant difference in climate between, say, Pauillac and the northern Médoc until you reach north of Château Loudenne at St Christoly. Jean-Michel Lapalu, who owns a clutch of properties in the northern Médoc, says there is a climatic difference between the north and south of the Médoc, with his vineyards up at Bégadan ripening about eight days later than vines in Margaux.

That the Haut-Médoc enjoys a higher reputation than the former Bas-Médoc is hardly surprising. Many of its vineyards lie a stone's throw away from those of classed estates. The gravel *croupes* that are the glory of Margaux and the other prestigious communes are also found throughout the Haut-Médoc, but since the latter vineyards lie farther inland, ripening is more of a problem. In fine vintages the Haut-Médoc (and for that matter the Médoc) is capable of producing superb wines, but they do not enjoy the consistency of the better-located classed growths.

THE CRUS BOURGEOIS

The estates of these two appellations dominate the *crus bourgeois*, even though a fair number lie within the boundaries of the prestigious communes, especially Margaux and St-Estèphe. The term *cru bourgeois* is an ancient one, and the 1850 edition of the standard reference work on the wines of Bordeaux, *Cocks & Féret*, divides the category into *bourgeois supérieurs*, *bons bourgeois*, and plain *bourgeois*. Later in the century some of these properties were singled out as *exceptionnels*. Denis Hervier quotes a wine book of 1868, which listed the top *crus bourgeois* as Citran, Monbrison, Siran, Seguineau, Labégorce, Lynch-Pontac, Belair, Paveil, Poujeaux, Chasse-Spleen, Angludet, Fourcas-Dupré, Fonréaud, Mauvezin, Duplessis, Lanessan, Ducluseau, and Labaut. This list includes many of the properties that are still recognized as the top *crus bourgeois* today. There were other categories employed in the nineteenth century to indicate the quality and status of certain properties, such as *cru artisan* and *cru paysan*, both with similar connotations of class and hierarchy.

Despite this Bordelais passion for placing all wine estates within an appropriate category, it was not until 1932 that any attempt was made to classify the *crus bourgeois*. It proved generous, classifying 444 estates, of which ninety-nine were *crus bourgeois supérieurs* and six (later expanded to eighteen) *supérieurs exceptionnels*. Curiously the 1932 classification never had official recognition. Jointly devised by the Bordeaux chamber of commerce and the Gironde chamber of agriculture, it was widely accepted and respected, but could never be subject to close regulation.

Moreover, other regions, such as Bourg and Blaye, borrowed the term "*cru bourgeois*" for some of their leading wines, which caused some confusion, since the 1932 classification was restricted to the Médoc. Its growers sued the Bourg Syndicat, claiming it had no right to use the term, but the case was lost. In 1962 a Syndicat promoting and defending the interests of the *crus bourgeois* was formed. Jean Miailhe, who owned a number of *cru bourgeois* properties, recalls visiting some estates that expressed an interest in joining the proposed Syndicat, and was appalled by the condition of many of the vineyards and cellars, which he called "*catastrophique*"; tasting samples from barrel were offered in old mustard jars.[1]

Miailhe was among those pressing for the 1932 classification to be given official status. Jacques Chirac, minister of agriculture at the time, was sympathetic, but the classified growths, whose consent was required for such a move, were less keen. Nothing happened. As time went by, the 1932 classification was increasingly abused. Some négociants simply invented *cru bourgeois* labels, but the Syndicat had no authority to take action against them. Other properties used them as labels for their second wines, despite not being entitled to do so. And inevitably certain properties had either declined in quality or disappeared altogether.

The Syndicat kept its members' wines in the public eye by organizing the annual Coupe des Crus Bourgeois, a contest first held in 1985. The judges were primarily journalists from various parts of the world, and wines were judged blind three at a time, the weakest being eliminated from contention. For the final rounds a jury of experts was convened (usually friends of the best-known journalists present), and eventually a winner

---

1 Lawton and Miailhe, *Conversations et souvenirs autour du vin de Bordeaux*, Editions Confluences, Bordeaux, 1999, 64

emerged. The Coupe had the merit of not taking itself too seriously. Yet the list of winners showed that the informal judging process did nonetheless select the top estates on a fairly regular basis, with the occasional surprise, such as Château d'Escurac, which well merited its prize with the 1996 vintage. Once the Syndicat announced its intention to reorganize the classification, the Coupe had to end, so the last of these enjoyable competitions was held in 1999.

By the 1990s the Syndicat was clearly in something of a shambles. Not only were there numerous impostors posing as *crus bourgeois*, but many top properties disdained to use the words on their labels, believing, no doubt with every justification, that the prestige of their marque counted for far more than the modest words "*cru bourgeois*". By 2000 it was widely accepted that the classification would have to be revised. Yet it would not prove easy to establish criteria for a new classification. Eventually it was agreed that all properties that wished to be confirmed as *crus bourgeois* would have to submit a series of vintages (1994–99 inclusive) that would be assessed, blind, by a jury composed of eighteen brokers, négociants, oenologists, and other experts. More controversially, four proprietors were also members of the jury. Journalists, sommeliers, and specialist foreign importers were excluded largely for practical reasons: mostly based outside the Bordeaux region, they would have found it difficult to attend the numerous meetings and tasting sessions. This practical decision did, however, lay the jury open to the charge that it was too parochial.

Rules were drawn up governing criteria for inclusion. Thus, properties with wines that were vinified elsewhere did not qualify as *crus bourgeois*, which needed to be vinified on site. Cooperatives were also excluded, as *crus bourgeois* had to be vinified by the proprietor. In January 2001 the ministry of agriculture decreed that the new classification would have three categories: *crus bourgeois*, *crus bourgeois supérieurs*, and *crus bourgeois exceptionnels*. The classification would be subject to revision every ten years.

The jury set to work. Part of its task was to assess the wines; another part was to visit the properties and ensure their vineyards and cellars were up to scratch. In June 2003 the results were announced. The jury had been severe: about 150 properties lost their right to call themselves "*cru bourgeois*". Just 247 châteaux were approved: 145 were accepted as regular *crus bourgeois*, eighty-six as *supérieurs*, and nine as *exceptionnels*. In terms of area, the 247 estates accounted for 7,200 hectares of vineyards. The nine *exceptionnels* were Haut-Marbuzet, Ormes-de-Pez, de Pez, Phélan-Ségur, Siran, Labégorce-Zédé, Poujeaux, Chasse-Spleen, and Potensac. This top category was to prove uncontroversial, though there were clearly some omissions such as Sociando-Mallet, but this was because this estate (a few others took the same view) had no wish to be considered in the first place. The new classification was greeted positively at first, as it was clear that the panel had had the courage to evict a large number of underperforming estates. New rules were imposed on members, of which the most important were a new logo for all labels and the requirement to print the term "*cru bourgeois*" on the label, which was being neglected by some properties.

There was discontent, however, among some of the *refusés*. A leading critic of the new classification was Jean-Christophe Mau of the négociant house Yvon Mau, which had acquired a Médoc *cru bourgeois* called Preuillac in 1998. Because it was a recent acquisition it was unable to assemble the series of six consecutive vintages required for evaluation. Of itself that should not have eliminated Preuillac from consideration, if a visiting panel of experts had delivered a favourable report on the property and the considerable investments Mau had made. However, according to Mau, the property had not been visited and thus should not have been excluded so peremptorily. Other properties launched similar appeals. Owners such as Mau were simply furious, arguing that they had been denied an opportunity to demonstrate that the wines were indeed worthy of *cru bourgeois* status.

Finally, the Syndicat, now renamed the Alliance des Crus Bourgeois, agreed in November 2004 to re-examine the dossiers and wines of some seventy-seven rejected properties. In early 2006 a Bordeaux judge ruled that, because of potential conflict of interest, the jury was not competent to implement a declassification. A year later a more senior court of appeals judge compounded the embarrassment by asserting that the jury had not been competent to evaluate classified properties either. That threw the entire 2003 three-tier classification into doubt. The judges also agreed that there had been a potential conflict of interest, since four proprietors of *crus bourgeois* had been members of the seventeen-strong jury. After further hearings and tribunals there seemed, by March 2007, no further possibility of appeal, and to all intents and purposes the 2003 classification was dead in the water. Some proprietors understandably bemoaned the fact that the exercise had been a colossal waste of time and money. Some of those who had brought the legal action in the first place seemed convinced that a new process would do the job of classification properly, but it seems inconceivable that the Médoc wine industry would want to go through the whole process a second time.

The upshot is that all the properties designated as *cru bourgeois supérieur* or *cru bourgeois exceptionnel* in 2003 now reverted to the basic *cru bourgeois* status granted in 1932. Since the 1932 classification had become so discredited that everyone had agreed on the need for radical revision in 2003, the current status of *cru bourgeois* has become a meaningless accolade. In the 2006 edition of this book, the precise status of each *cru bourgeois* property, as decided in 2003, was stated in each entry. Rather than revert to the status granted in 1932, I have decided to ignore the label altogether.

In the meantime, a separate jury has re-examined the *cru artisan* category, and in January 2006 forty-four properties were authorized to use this admittedly modest rank on their labels. The list will be reviewed in 2016.

THE VILLAGES OF THE MEDOC

It is difficult, in both appellations, to single out individual villages as unquestionably superior in their terroir to others. Unpromising AC Médoc locations such as Couquèques can deliver the goods, as Château Les Ormes-Sorbet has demonstrated for years. It is even more difficult with the Haut-Médoc, since it covers such a large and diverse area. There is little in common, other than the welcome presence of some gravel *croupes*, between St Laurent, huddled shoulder to shoulder with St-Julien and Pauillac, and the southerly communes of Ludon and Macau. One exception is St-Seurin-de-Cadourne, the northerly extension of St-Estèphe. There are *croupes* aplenty, and yet the soil is very varied, with different kinds of clay, gravel beds of varying depths, and an undulating terrain unusual for the Médoc. The list of fine properties here does, however, demonstrate that St-Seurin is an unusually dependable source of excellent wine at fair prices: Sociando-Mallet, Charmail, Coufran, Soudars, Verdignan, Sénilhac, and Liversan, among others. Olivier Sèze, who makes the wine at Charmail and Château St-Paul, finds that Merlot here has a distinctive character. "I once organized a blind tasting of the three main grape varieties grown here, and invited journalists and others to come and taste them. Everyone got the varieties mixed up. That's because Merlot here has a power and structure that are atypical for the variety."

Broadly speaking, the Haut-Médoc vineyards to the west of the celebrated villages have both a cooler climate and a higher clay content in the soil. The vineyards south of Margaux, which include classed growths such as Cantemerle and Lagune, have gravelly soils of varying density, but also a higher sand content. Even farther south, around Blanquefort and Parempuyre, the soil is heavier with markedly less gravel, and the wines, though fleshy, can lack structure. The reason why the eight-kilometre band of land between Margaux and St-Julien (mostly covered by Lamarque and Cussac) was excluded from those ACs is because the geology is very different, and very little Günzian gravel was deposited there, and where it did exist, it has been subject to erosion. The commune of Avensan can deliver wines that resemble those from Moulis, while St Laurent can claim special status as home to three classed growths.

The following are the principal Haut-Médoc communes with the approximate area of vineyards: St-Seurin-de-Cadourne (611 hectares), Vertheuil (300), Cissac (370), St Sauveur (350), St Laurent (500), Cussac-Fort-Médoc (600), Lamarque (171), Arcins (247), Avensan (200), Macau (237), Ludon (160), Parempuyre (62), Blanquefort (145), Pian-Médoc (80), and Taillan (37).

And these are the principal Médoc communes: Jau-Dignac-et-Loirac (306 hectares), Valeyrac (450), Bégadan (900), St Christoly (360), Couquèques (230), Civrac (400), Prignac (250), Blaignan (445), St Yzans (438), Lesparre (107), Ordonnac (350), and St Germain d'Esteuil (416).

With hundreds of estates within the two appellations, a personal selection has been unavoidable. The main focus is on the five classed growths and a generous selection of *crus bourgeois*, but official status has not itself been the defining criterion. Where tasting experiences have been almost entirely negative, I have omitted the property altogether. There seems little point drawing the reader's attention to the steadfastly mediocre. Where the official status of a property is given, it refers to the 2003 classification.

MEDOC

Château Bégadan

Bégadan. Tel: 0556 415577. Owner: Jean-Pierre Sallette. Cru artisan. 16 ha. 50% Cabernet Sauvignon, 50% Merlot. Production: 100,000 bottles

Jean-Pierre Sallette bought this estate in 1974. The vines are picked by machine, and the wine is aged partly in tanks, partly in barriques. The only vintage I have encountered is the 2001, which showed reasonable fruit concentration, but was marred by coarse tannins.

Château Blaignan

Blaignan. Tel: 0556 112900. Owner: Crédit Agricole Grands Crus. 87 ha. 50% Cabernet Sauvignon, 41% Merlot, 9% Cabernet Franc. Production: 500,000 bottles. Second wine: Ch Prieuré Blaignan

This ancient property traces its history back to 1700, when it was acquired by the Comte de Toulouse. In 1726 it was bought by Jean Taffard, and for the next two centuries the estate was known by his name. Until 2004 it formed part of the Mestrezat group, which also owned Châteaux Rayne-Vigneau, Grand-Puy-Ducasse, and other properties. Blaignan was sold as part of the package to Crédit Agricole. The grapes are machine-harvested and the wine, unusually, sees no oak. The 1996, drunk in 2003, had a silky texture, and was well balanced and still fresh. It had aged remarkably well considering that Blaignan has a reputation for being a Médoc to be drunk young. The 2003 is aromatic, but uncomfortably blends sharp acidity and a hollow structure. Although amiable and fresh, the 2004 lacks personality.

Château Bournac

Civrac. Tel: 0556 735924. Owner: Bruno Secret. 14 ha. 65% Cabernet Sauvignon, 35% Merlot. Production: 60,000 bottles

The Secret family came to the Médoc in 1968, and Bruno Secret took over this property in 1990. The wines have steadily progressed ever since. They are aged for twelve months in fifty per cent new oak. The 2000 steered well clear of overripeness, tasting of slightly sour cherries, and showing ample spice and concentration.

Château Le Breuil-Renaissance

Blaignan. Tel: 0556 415067. Website: www.lebreuil-renaissance.com. Owner: Philippe Bérard. 27 ha. 60% Merlot, 40% Cabernet Sauvignon. Production: 160,000 bottles. Second wine: Ch Haut-Bana

The regular bottling of this wine in 2001 and 2004 was attractive and accessible, though without much weight. M. Bérard also makes a prestige bottling, aged in new oak, from a three-hectare parcel with a higher proportion of Cabernet Sauvignon. The 2001 was dense and oaky, with an attractive spiciness emerging from the plump, concentrated fruit. A touch extracted, perhaps, but more successful than the regular wine. The powerful 2003 has unusual vigour and drive for the vintage.

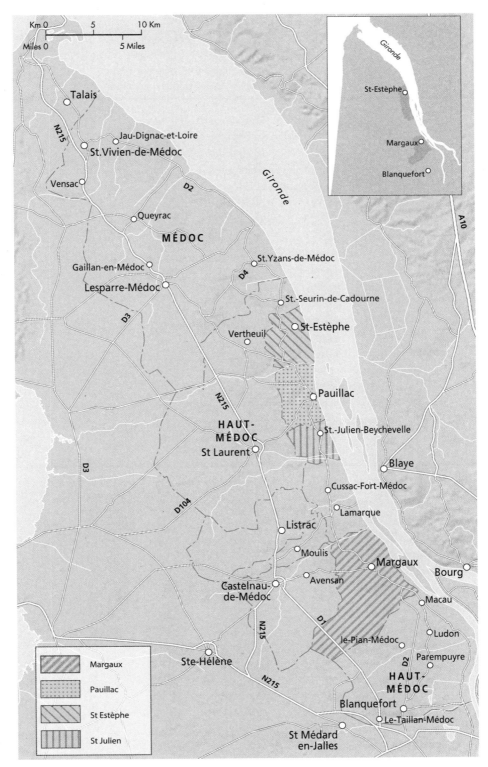

The Médoc and the Haut–Médoc

Château de By

Bégadan. Tel: 0556 732656. Owner: Domaines Codem (Fiat). 15 ha. 40% Merlot, 30% Cabernet Sauvignon,
20% Petit Verdot, 10% Cabernet Franc. Production: 50,000 bottles

Under the same ownership as Château Greysac (*q.v.*), this well-run property makes modest but fruity and enjoyable wines. Both the 2002 and 2003 were successful in their unambitious way.

Château La Cardonne

Blaignan. Tel: 0556 733151. Website: www.domaines-cgr.com. Owner: Guy Charloux (Domaines CGR). 87 ha.
50% Merlot, 45% Cabernet Sauvignon, 5% Cabernet Franc. Production: 430,000 bottles. Second wine: Ch Cardus

La Cardonne is the headquarters of an important group of properties, all run by the same team. The other two estates are Ramafort and Grivière (*qq.v.*), both close by. La Cardonne is quite an ancient property, dating back to the seventeenth century. In 1973 the Rothschilds of Lafite bought and restructured the estate, which was acquired by Guy Charloux in 1990 and run during the 1990s by Eric Fabre, the former technical director at Lafite. In 2000 he was replaced by Magali Guyon. Jacques Boissenot acts as consultant oenologist for all three properties.

All three are run on unashamedly commercial lines. The extensive vineyards, mostly located on a relatively high plateau of sandy gravel with a limestone base, are machine-harvested. La Cardonne was a pioneer of *sous-vide* concentration in the early 1990s. The wine used to be unoaked, but today is aged in one-third new oak for twelve months. None of the CGR wines are sold via the *Place de Bordeaux*. Instead, the company has its own distribution structure, and ages the bottles for about two years in its underground cellars, so that they are drinkable on release.

It would be unreasonable to expect great complexity from these wines. Instead they offer sound fruit, supple texture, a discernible touch of oak, and a modicum of elegance. They are not overly fleshy or even fruit-driven, and thus retain their typicity as wines of the Médoc. The 1991, 1994, and 1995 were all good wines, and the 1996 was very good indeed, with ample ripe tannins and fine acidity. The 2000 is supple and balanced but a disappointment for the vintage, and I prefer the suave, spicy, more concentrated 2001. The 2003 is a success for the vintage, with sweet oaky aromas, plenty of black cherry fruit, and reasonable length. The 2004 has lift and freshness but lacks concentration.

Château La Clare

Bégadan. Tel: 0556 415859. Website: www.rollandeby.com. Owner: Jean Guyon. 20 ha. 45% Merlot,
35% Cabernet Sauvignon, 15% Cabernet Franc, 5% Petit Verdot. Production: 100,000 bottles

This property, which was reconstituted in the 1970s by then-proprietor Paul de Rozières, has been since 2001 under the same ownership as the better-known Château Rollan-de-By (*q.v.*), and is fashioned to be less dense and more approachable than the latter. The vineyards are picked both by hand and by machine. The wine is aged for twelve months in sixty per cent new oak. Quality is high. The 1996 had real flair and personality, svelte in texture yet with invigorating acidity. However, the 2000 is austere and dull. The 2001 has a tangy, red-fruits nose, ample upfront fruit, a supple texture, and moderate length of flavour.

Château d'Escurac

Civrac. Tel: 0556 415081. Owner: Jean-Marc Landureau. 18 ha. 60% Cabernet Sauvignon, 40% Merlot.
Production: 100,000 bottles. Second wine: La Chapelle d'Escurac

Château d'Escurac leaped into view when this formerly obscure property won the 1999 Coupe des Crus Bourgeois with its 1996 vintage. Before 1990 M. Landureau had sold his grapes to the cooperative, so his rise to stardom was rapid, and it was confirmed by promotion to *cru bourgeois supérieur* in 2003. The vineyards are on a lofty *croupe* with deep gravel soil. The wine sees around forty per cent new oak, but the wood is rarely obtrusive. The delicious, sumptuous 1996 is still going strong, with oaky, pruney aromas, and hardly any evolution on the palate. The 2000, with its classic Médoc style blending firm tannins, the merest hint of herbaceousness, and fine acidity, was a worthy successor. As is the bright, vigorous, oaky 2001. The 2003 is plump and full-bodied; although it offers a good mouthful of fruit, it lacks persistence. Lean but concentrated, the 2004 has freshness, grip, and finesse but is overshadowed by the powerful, full-bodied, and altogether splendid 2005.

Château Fontis

Ordonnac. Tel: 0556 733030. Owner: Vincent Boivert. 10 ha. 50% Cabernet Sauvignon, 50% Merlot.
Production: 35,000 bottles

Vincent Boivert is the son of the late Jean Boivert of Château Les Ormes-Sorbet, and in 1995 he acquired this property to develop on his own. He changed its name from Château Hontemieux. Its vineyards are situated on one of the highest *croupes* of the Médoc, and there is also a good deal of clay in the soil. The grapes are picked by hand, and the vinification is similar to that practised at Les Ormes-Sorbet. Boivert ages the wine partly in tanks, but mostly in Taransaud barrels, of which at least one-third are new, for around eighteen months before eggwhite-fining, a light filtration, and bottling.

The 1996 was particularly successful here, marked by ripe Cabernet fruit and a graceful structure. More recent vintages, such as the 1998, 1999, 2000, and even 2003, have been well made, but seem rather light. This is to some extent a stylistic choice, as Boivert does not want extracted wines and favours elegance over power. However, in 2005 Boivert made a splendid wine, full of fruit and with firm, ripe tannins.

Château La Gorce

Blaignan. Tel: 0556 090122. Website: www.chateaulagorce.com. Owner: Denis Fabre. 44 ha. 50% Merlot,
45% Cabernet Sauvignon, 5% Cabernet Franc and Petit Verdot. Production: 300,000 bottles.
Second wine: Ch Canteloup

Twenty years ago this large property, which was bought by the Fabre family in 1980, was planted with a clear majority of Cabernet Sauvignon, which represented sixty per cent of the vineyards.

Aged in fifty per cent new oak, this is a solid, weighty wine, and I have positive notes from older vintages such as 1982, 1985, and 1986. It was never that complex or substantial, but it usually had charm and delicacy. I didn't care for the 1996, but La Gorce seems back on form with the 2001 and 2002, which are wines of considerable heft. Perhaps they are a touch solid and four-square, but they offer a satisfying mouthful of rounded yet moderately tannic wine. The 2003 is excellent, with lush, oaky aromas, considerable richness, weight, and spice, and a welcome long finish. The 2004 has a similar plumpness, but more complexity and vigour than the 2003.

Goulée

*Tel: 0556 731550. Website: www.cosestournel.com. **Owners:** Michel Reybier and Jean-Guillaume Prats.*
*28 ha. 80% Cabernet Sauvignon, 20% Merlot. **Production:** 120,000 bottles*

This is a fairly radical venture emerging from Cos d'Estournel as the brainchild of Jean-Guillaume Prats. He wishes to make a modern-style wine that can be drunk young. As a model he cites the excellent Alion that comes from the Vega Sicilia stable in Ribera del Duero. At first he thought of buying in wine or grapes, but found he couldn't get the quality he wanted. So he then had the idea of blending fruit from different terroirs to blend for consistency. So far he has acquired three parcels in the Médoc – their precise location not stated – and will eventually build a winery in Marbuzet. The winemaker is South African and the first vintage 2003. The 2003 lacked Médocain angularity, and was rather jammy – but it doesn't lack length. In 2004, an abundant vintage, the yield was only thirty-five hectolitres per hectare. Goulée is vinified in conical vats after a cold soak, there is no pumping, the cap is punched down, and the wine is aged in fifty per cent new oak. I have only tasted the 2004 from cask, and it was certainly supple and approachable for a young wine. Production will eventually rise to 15,000 cases.

Château Les Grands Chênes

*St Christoly. Tel: 0556 415312. Website: www.bernard-magrez.com. **Owner:** Bernard Magrez. 12 ha.*
*50% Merlot, 45% Cabernet Sauvignon, 5% Cabernet Franc. **Production:** 60,000 bottles.*
Second wine: Temperance de Grands Chênes

This property was developed from 1981 onwards by Jacqueline Gauzy-Darricade, then bought by Bernard Magrez in 1998. The vines, located on *croupes* within view of the Gironde, were already of a respectable age, and today they are on average about thirty years old. There are two soil types: gravel and clay-limestone. Pre-Magrez vintages such as 1995 and 1996 had been dilute and even a touch astringent, but the new owner went to work immediately to boost quality. Green-harvesting was introduced, as was hand-sorting at the winery. After a four-day cold soak, the must undergoes *pigeage*, and the wine is aged in fifty per cent new barriques for fifteen months.

There used to be a prestige bottling, but this was discontinued by 2002, when the second wine was introduced. Today Grands Chênes is a thoroughly modern wine: plummy, opulent, supple, with a sweet coating of oak. Vintages such as 1998 and 2000 are rather dour and charmless, but the 2001 by 2007 was showing better balance and accessibility, though not much complexity. The 2002 now seems extracted, and the 2003 has the drab, baked character of the vintage and little length. The 2004 shows Grands Chênes at its best: supple, spicy, lively, and balanced. For the vintage, the 2005 is a touch disappointing but doesn't lack body and rich black-cherry fruit. The wine is reasonably priced for the quality and probably offers the best value from M. Magrez's rapidly expanding portfolio.

Château Greysac

Bégadan. Tel: 0556 732656. Website: www.greysac.com.
Owner: Domaines Codem (Fiat). 60 ha. 58 ha red: 50% Merlot, 48% Cabernet Sauvignon, 2% Cabernet Franc.
*2 ha white: 100% Sauvignon Blanc. **Production:** 450,000 bottles. Second wine: Domaine de By*

This well-known property was bought in 1975 by the Agnelli family, owners of Fiat. They renovated the run-down estate and its eighteenth-century château. Since the late 1980s Greysac has been managed by Philippe Dambrine, who also runs Château Cantemerle. The fruit is picked by machine, and the wine is aged for twelve months in twenty per cent new oak. There is also a white wine produced from Sauvignon Blanc, barrel-fermented and aged for six months in fifty per cent new oak. The only vintage I have tasted, the 2001, was fragrant and rich.

There have been some fine wines from Greysac. The 1990 was still going strong in 1999, with bright acidity and vigour, supple yet long, and clearly in its prime. The 1996 was excellent, ripe and oaky on the nose, with ample spice and zest and length. The 1998 was less dour than some wines from this tricky year; it was certainly dense, but enlivened by a racy, peppery tone that didn't impair its concentration and length. The 1999 is less complex, but it's fresh, elegant, and delicious now. The 2000 was not especially concentrated, but it was balanced and fresh, and a copybook example of a good, sturdy Médoc *cru bourgeois*. The 2001 is rather slack and dull, and lacks some concentration. However, the 2002 is zesty and stylish, well balanced though not particularly complex. The 2003 was ungainly at first, but the tannins have softened to reveal a wine of some power and spice.

Château de Monthyl is a twenty-one-hectare *cru bourgeois* under the same ownership, as is Château de By, which produced a simple but attractive wine in 2002 and a chunkier though fruity wine in 2003.

Château Grivière

*Blaignan. Tel: 0556 733151. Website: www.domaines-cgr.com. **Owner**: Guy Charloux (Domaines CGR).*
*18 ha. 55% Merlot, 40% Cabernet Sauvignon, 5% Cabernet Franc. **Production**: 85,000 bottles*

This comes from the same stable as Château La Cardonne (*q.v.*) and is made and commercialized in the same way. The whole vineyard was replanted twenty-five years ago. I have enjoyed the 1996, which has aromatic panache, and lush, juicy, upfront fruit on the palate. By now it should be fully ready to drink. The 2000 was excellent: rich and rounded, with considerable weight, grip, and length. The 2001 shows comparable vigour, with red-fruits aromas and a long, peppery finish. The 2003 is dense, juicy, and packed with fruit, but it's also tannic and has a rather flat finish. The 2004 seems easy-going but has a tough finish.

Château Haut-Canteloup

*St Christoly. Tel: 0556 415898. **Owner**: François Clauzel. 38 ha. 60% Merlot, 30% Cabernet Sauvignon,*
*10% Cabernet Franc. **Production**: 250,000 bottles. **Second wine**: Ch Les Mourlanes*

Most of the vineyards of this property are at St Christoly on gravel soils, but there are also twelve hectares on clay-limestone in Couquèques. They are all harvested mechanically. The wine is aged half in tanks, and half in new barriques. The 2001 is a ripe, coffee-scented wine, sleek and charming and fresh, all adding up to a highly drinkable young Médoc. The 2002 is far simpler and lacks individuality, while the 2003 has density and concentration but little finesse. The elegant, cedary 2004 has ample fruit but perhaps lacks excitement. There is also a 50,000-bottle *cuvée* aged in new oak called Collection, which I have not tasted.

Haut-Condissas

*Bégadan. Tel: 0556 415859. Website: www.rollandeby.com. **Owner**: Jean Guyon. 5 ha. 60% Merlot, 20% Petit Verdot,*
*20% Cabernet Sauvignon and Cabernet Franc. **Production**: 14,000 bottles*

Haut-Condissas is a *micro-cuvée* produced from an exceptionally stony parcel at Château Rollan-de-By (*q.v.*) that lies close to the river on a gravelly clay *croupe*. As at Rollan-de-By, the consultant winemakers are Alain Raynaud and Riccardo Cotarella. The grape blend is unusual, and the average age quite high at thirty-five years. Yields are kept to around forty hl/ha. The grapes are picked (by hand, of course) when ultra-ripe, indeed when close to raisining. After a very severe sorting at the winery, the wine is cold-soaked, then fermented in conical wooden vats. Haut-Condissas is aged entirely in new oak, and the lees are stirred for the first three months of the *élevage*. The first vintages in the mid-1990s were met with acclaim, perhaps to honour one of the first *garagiste* wines of the Médoc. Indeed, the prestigious Grand Jury Européen placed this wine ahead of any classified growth of the Médoc. Make of that what you will.

Not surprisingly, Haut-Condissas, on the evidence of the 2001, 2002, and 2004 vintages, is richly oaky, with dense, plummy aromas; in style it is tight and rather chunky and extracted, a wine designed to impress.

Château Haut-Maurac

*St Yzans. Tel: 0556 090537. **Owner:** Olivier Decelle. 28 ha. 60% Cabernet Sauvignon, 40% Merlot.*
***Production:** 280,000 bottles. **Second wine:** Ch Haut-Maurac-Bellecour*

This is likely to be a property worth watching, as it was bought by Olivier Decelle in 2000. It was Decelle who acquired the large estate of Mas Amiel in Maury in the Roussillon, and did wonders for its international reputation. The terroir at Haut-Maurac is said to be very fine, with a gravel *croupe* close to the Gironde, but the vineyards were in poor shape, and it will be a few years before they are back on form. In 2001, Decelle reduced the yields sharply to thirty-five hl/ha. Eric Boissenot has been hired as the consultant oenologist. The grapes are picked by hand and the wine is aged in one-third new oak. The 2002 is a tremendous success, with sweet, oaky aromas, supple tannins, considerable weight of fruit, and well-integrated oak. The 2003 is more stern and austere, with chewy tannins and a lack of elegance. But the 2004 is spicy and concentrated.

Château Haut-Myles

*Civrac. Tel: 0556 415081. **Owner:** Jean-Marc Landureau. 12 ha. 50% Merlot, 50% Cabernet Sauvignon.*
***Production:** 80,000 bottles*

This property is under the same ownership and management as Château d'Escurac (*q.v.*), but there are significant differences between the two wines.

Haut-Myles is predominantly Merlot, and the wine is aged for six months in American as well as French oak. The 2001 was very well made, with a spicy, oaky nose, while the palate was firm and structured yet without any trace of toughness. (I hope a dire bottle, tasted blind in 2005, was an aberration.)

Château L'Inclassable

*Prignac. Tel: 0556 090217. **Owner:** Rémy Fauchey. 15 ha. 55% Cabernet Sauvignon, 30% Merlot,*
*9% Cabernet Franc, 6% Petit Verdot. **Production:** 90,000 bottles*

Until 2002 this property was known as Château Lafon, but its name had to be changed to avoid confusion with a property of the same name in Listrac. Rémy Fauchey chose the grandiose Château L'Inclassable. The estate, owned by the family since 1900, is tended with care, employing green cover and only natural fertilizers. The wine blends the fruit from two terroirs, one gravelly, the other clay-limestone. After fermentation in cement tanks, the wine is aged in fifty per cent new barriques for around twelve months. Ever since 1995, the first vintage I tasted from Lafon, the wine has been made in a tannic, extracted style that can be rather overwhelming. Yet the fruit quality, compounded of blackcurrants and black cherries, can be impressive, as in 2001 and 2002, so it seems all the more regrettable that this core of fruit is usually obscured by a wall of chunky tannins. The 2003 is both stewed and brutal in its tannins, but the 2004, while robust and structured, is richly fruity and has persistence of flavour.

The property also produces a wine, not strictly a second wine, called Château Fontaine d'Aubier, which is aged in second-fill barriques.

Château Labadie

*Bégadan. Tel: 0556 415558. **Owner:** Yves Bibey. 46 ha. 58% Merlot, 40% Cabernet Sauvignon, 1% Cabernet Franc,*
*1% Petit Verdot. **Production:** 100,000 bottles. **Second wine:** Ch Pontet-Barrail*

Until 1988 Labadie delivered its crop to the local cooperative. The vineyards are machine-harvested, and after a five-day cold soak at 10°C (50°F), the must is fermented at high temperatures. The wine is then aged mostly in tanks and twenty-five per cent in barriques with regular *bâtonnage*. The 2001 is enjoyable and unpretentious, with its cedary aromas and bright, lively flavours. The 2003 is its opposite, with some greenness and astringency.

Château Lacombe–Noaillac

Jau-Dignac-et-Loirac. Tel: 0556 415018. Website: www.domaines-lapalu.com.
Owner: Jean-Michel Lapalu. 30 ha. 47% Cabernet Sauvignon, 45% Merlot, 5% Cabernet Franc, 3% Petit Verdot.
Production: 230,000 bottles. Second wine: Les Rives de Gravelongue

This estate was purchased by the present owner in 1979, and over the next few years he completely replanted the vineyards, which lie on sandy, gravelly soils, with good drainage. Since 1996 the estate has been incorporated into Domaines Lapalu (*see* Patache d'Aux). The wine is aged in a blend of stainless-steel tanks and barriques, of which fifteen per cent are new. This is a medium-bodied, easy-drinking wine, with freshness rather than complexity. It should be drunk young. The 2002 is a touch green and there is more overt fruit and lushness in the 2003, even though the texture is flat.

A ten-hectare parcel nearby, with the same varietal blend, produces 80,000 bottles of another wine called Château Les Traverses.

Château Lafon

See *Château L'Inclassable*

Château Laujac

Bégadan. Tel: 0556 415012. Owner: Bernard Cruse. 30 ha. 60% Cabernet Sauvignon, 30% Merlot,
5% Cabernet Franc, 5% Petit Verdot. Production: 170,000 bottles. Second wine: Ch La Tour-Cordouan

This comfortable country house and its park have formed a rural retreat for members of the Cruse family since 1852. Wine production seems almost an afterthought. The best that can be said for vintages such as 1979, 1981, 1983, and 1985 is that the wines showed some pleasant fruit and little else. They lacked concentration, bite, and length. The 1986 was marginally better and more interesting. The same, fortunately, is true of more recent vintages such as 2001 and 2002, which are gentle, supple, easy-going, somewhat dilute, but enjoyable. The wine is aged both in tanks and a small proportion of new barriques.

Château Loudenne

St Yzans. Tel: 0556 731780. Website: www.lafragette.com. Owner: Jean-Paul Lafragette. 62 ha. 50 ha red:
55% Merlot, 42% Cabernet Sauvignon, 2% Petit Verdot, 1% Cabernet Franc. 12 ha white: 60% Sauvignon Blanc,
40% Sémillon. Production: 300,000 bottles. Second wine: Les Tours de Loudenne

Loudenne was a popular wine in Britain for decades, since it was owned by the British wine merchants IDV. With resident directors such as the late Martin Bamford and, more recently, Charles Eve, the pink chartreuse was a haven for the British wine trade during its buying trips to Bordeaux. Here visitors were assured of good wine, good food, and impish conversation. This era came to a definitive end in 2000, when Loudenne was sold to Cognac tycoon Jean-Paul Lafragette. He also bought Château de l'Hospital in the Graves and Château de Rouillac in Pessac-Léognan (*qq.v.*), and installed his daughter Florence as director of all three. At Loudenne, Lafragette employs both Michel Rolland and Athanase Fakorellis as consultant oenologists.

Loudenne is a beautifully situated property, with its vineyards planted on south-facing *croupes* that are perfectly ventilated and exceptionally close to the estuary. Under IDV ownership, Loudenne was a pleasant but unmemorable wine; the grapes were picked fairly early, and yields were clearly quite high. The Lafragettes introduced immediate changes: heightening the trellis to increase the surface of foliage, ploughing the soil, picking later and entirely by hand. The red is fermented with pumping over and *pigeage* before being aged for twelve months in thirty per cent new barriques.

Loudenne was always well known for its white wine, even though I never found it particularly good. (Indeed in some vintages it was vegetal and decidedly dull.) It is one of the largest white wine vineyards in the Médoc, with some twelve hectares planted with Sauvignon Blanc and Sémillon. Fermentation begins in tanks but is now completed in barrels, in which the wine is aged on the fine lees with *bâtonnage* for six months. Here too the proportion of new oak is around thirty per cent. The result is a lush, fruity wine for drinking fairly young. The range is completed with a rosé and a prestige bottling.

Seahorses used to frolic in the Gironde, so the Lafragettes borrowed the French term for this creature as the name of their prestige bottling, Hippocampus. The grapes come from the highest sectors of the gravel *croupes*, those with a view of the estuary. The vinification is said to be essentially the same as for the red Loudenne, though I find the nose dominated by new oak aromas and the palate a touch too lush and extracted. Only 5,000 bottles are produced.

As for the regular bottling, the 1999 is very odd, with dill aromas and a distinct herbaceous character. The 2000 is riper on the nose, but lacks flesh and charm – mediocre for the vintage. Then there is an immediate leap in quality with the elegant, perfumed liquorice-scented 2001, with its ripe tannin, fresh acidity, and remarkable finesse. The 2002 and 2004 are very much in the same mould, perhaps a touch riper and more rounded. The 2003 is a success for the vintage, and Florence Lafragette attributes this to the influence of sea air from the estuary, which enveloped the vines in a humidity that other vineyards may have lacked.

The Lafragettes have taken a positive approach to tourism in this rather remote spot, offering hotel facilities and a wine museum.

Château Lousteauneuf

*Valeyrac. Tel: 0556 415211. Website: www.chateau-lousteauneuf.com. **Owner:** Bruno Segond. 22 ha.*
*54% Cabernet Sauvignon, 40% Merlot, 4% Cabernet Franc, 2% Petit Verdot. **Production:** 125,000 bottles.*
Second wine: Le Petit Lousteau

In 1962 Serge Segond left Algeria for France, and bought this property, which at that time had only four hectares still in production. He planted more vines and in 1993 constructed a cellar so that the wine could be bottled on the property. In 1988 his son Bruno took over. The soil is varied, with silt and sand as well as gravel and clay-limestone. Most of the fruit is machine-picked.

Bruno Segond has firmly set his tent in the modernist camp. The must is given a cold soak, then fermented with pumping over and *délestage* to ensure thorough extraction for up to thirty days. The wine is aged in forty per cent new barriques for twelve to eighteen months, depending on the vintage. It is then bottled without fining or filtration. There is also a special bottling, the Cuvée Emma, aged for twenty-four months in new oak. For the second wine, about half the oak employed is American.

The 2001 has pungent, black-fruits aromas and rich, supple, damsony fruit – a bit flashy, perhaps, but the fruit quality is excellent and the wine is long and well balanced. The 2003 has muted blackberry aromas, and a rather massive structure, with power and presence and a chocolatey finish. The 2004 is a bit rustic and earthy, but the 2005 translates its power into impressive weight and length.

Magrez Tivoli

*Valeyrac. Website: www.bernard-magrez.com. **Owner:** Bernard Magrez. 2.5 ha. 50% Cabernet Sauvignon,*
*50% Merlot. **Production:** 3,600 bottles*

One of many *micro-cuvées* from Bernard Magrez and his team. It's made from a gravelly parcel of old vines with an average age of forty years. Yields are minuscule, at around twenty hl/ha. The bunches are sorted before and after destemming, then fermented in small wooden vats. The wine is aged for eighteen months in mostly new barriques. The first vintage, the 2002, is much as one might have predicted: opaque in colour, with a dense, blackcurranty nose, while on the palate there is a rich coating of oak, immense concentration, and a certain lack of elegance. Impressive, to be sure, but hard to distinguish from so many other wines fashioned in the same way.

Château Les Ormes-Sorbet

*Couquèques. Tel: 0556 733030. Website: www.ormes-sorbet.com. **Owner:** Hélène Boivert. 22 ha.*
65% Cabernet Sauvignon, 30% Merlot, 2% Petit Verdot, 2% Cabernet Franc, 1% Carmenère.
***Production:** 150,000 bottles. **Second wine:** Ch de Conques*

Jean Boivert was a much liked and well-respected figure in the Médoc, and a familiar face at the annual Marathon. Sadly, he died in 2004, and the fine estate he developed is now run by his widow Hélène and their sons Vincent and François. The vineyards are quite dispersed, but the wines have an average age of thirty years. The soils are mostly clay-limestone, with a limestone subsoil. The vines are picked by hand. Vinification is entirely traditional, other than use of malolactic fermentation in barriques. Ever since 1982 the wine has been aged solely in fifty per cent new Taransaud barrels for eighteen to twenty months, before eggwhite-fining and bottling.

Les Ormes-Sorbet has been a consistently excellent wine for many years. Time and again it demonstrates that Cabernet Sauvignon can perform splendidly even in this northerly sector of the Médoc. I usually discern black cherries rather than blackcurrant aromas, and a distinct oaky presence that is nonetheless well integrated into the wine. Very occasionally, as in 1998, the tannins are slightly dry, but this is very much the exception. In recent vintages the wines have displayed a greater elegance than in the 1990s, without sacrificing richness and grip. I have particularly enjoyed the 1990, 1995, 1996, 2000, 2001, and 2002. The 2003 is a touch heavy and flabby, but has some light acidity and reasonable fruit – to drink young. The 2004 is no heavyweight, but it's lively and balanced, with rich, smoky aromas. Despite initial austerity, the concentrated 2005 has considerable freshness too.

Château Patache d'Aux

*Bégadan. Tel: 0556 415018. Website: www.domaines-lapalu.com. **Owner:** Jean-Michel Lapalu. 43 ha.*
*60% Cabernet Sauvignon, 30% Merlot, 7% Cabernet Franc, 3% Petit Verdot. **Production:** 300,000 bottles.*
***Second wine:** Le Relais de Patache d'Aux*

This is the principal property of the small Médocain empire founded by Claude Lapalu, and now owned by his son Jean-Michel. Claude Lapalu came to Bordeaux from Algeria, and this was the first property he bought, followed in 1972 by Château Lebosq. In 1980 Jean-Michel bought Château Lacombe-Noaillac (which is now his home) and took over the business in 1992. In 1995 they acquired Château Liversan (*q.v.*) and created Domaines Lapalu as a holding company. In 1997 Domaines Lapalu took over the management of Château Larrivaux in Cissac. Two years later, Jean-Michel teamed up with his general manager, Patrice Ricard, to buy Château Lieujean (*q.v.*). By 2000 they controlled 237 hectares, with a total sale of 1.5 million bottles, making them probably the largest single producer of Médoc and Haut-Médoc wines. Olivier Sempé acts as technical director for all the properties, and Eric Boissenot is the consultant oenologist. Each property has its own cellars and *maître de chai*. However, once the wine has been bottled, distribution is centralized.

The estate takes its name from the Chevaliers d'Aux, who were the owners since 1632. Seized by the state during the Revolution, it became a posthouse for carriages travelling through the Médoc, as illustrated on the label. Claude Lapalu bought it in 1964, jointly with Guy Pagès, the brother of the owner of Château Tour-de-By. The soil consists of clay and chalk over a pebbly chalk subsoil, and the average age of the vines is now thirty-five years. The grapes are picked by machine, which Patrice Ricard believes gives them much greater flexibility. After sorting, the must is fermented in various kinds of vats, and the wine is aged for twelve months in twenty-five per cent new oak.

The wines are often stored for up to three years after bottling, so that the owners can offer clients bottles that are ready to drink. As for style, the Lapalu team is looking for drinkability rather than super-concentration. This is exactly what they achieve, and if the wines don't rise to great heights, that's because Lapalu and Ricard have no wish to occupy them. They would rather offer consistent quality, immediate drinkability, and good value. Nonetheless, Patache d'Aux can be very good, with a surprising amount of oakiness on the nose and an attractive fleshiness on the palate. All vintages since 1999 have been in this style, with the exception of the super-ripe, tannic, and rather fatiguing 2003. The 2004 has rich blackberry aromas, and plenty of fruit, vigour, and unusual tannic grip for this property.

There is also a bottling called, rather confusingly, La Patache, which is a blend from different Lapalu properties; it is aged both in vats and in American oak barrels. The only example I have tasted is the 2001, which was almost pure Cabernet Sauvignon, and had a great deal of power and concentration.

Château Potensac

*Ordonnac. **Tel:** 0556 732526. **Website:** www.chateau-potensac.com. **Owners:** Jean-Hubert Delon and Geneviève d'Alton. 67 ha. 46% Cabernet Sauvignon, 36% Merlot, 16% Cabernet Franc, 2% Carmenère. **Production:** 320,000 bottles. **Second wine:** La Chapelle de Potensac*

This large estate has been owned by the Delons and their forebears for over two centuries, and expanded over the years by purchases of neighbouring vineyards. The soils are gravelly clay, giving well-structured wines that age well. The grape blend is unusual, but the *maître de chai* confirms that often the best lots in any vintage are the Cabernet Franc and Petit Verdot. The average age of the vines is thirty years, and the vineyards are picked manually, quite late in the season, by the same team that harvests Léoville-Las-Cases. The vinification is traditional, and the wine is aged for around fifteen months in no more than (and often, as in 2001, much less than) thirty per cent new oak, though before 1997 no new oak at all was used here. Quality is maintained by the routine declassification of around forty per cent of production.

This is a wine of remarkable robustness, vigour, and longevity, short on finesse but packed with fruit. In weaker vintages Potensac can be rather austere. The 1966 was terrific, still ripe and satisfying in 1989. The 1975 also retained its spice and fruit and tannic structure into a prolonged old age. The 1976 was fairly successful for the vintage. The 1978, with its delicious Cabernet fruit, evolved fairly fast, though it was still drinking well in 1996. The 1979, 1980, and 1981 were all unexciting, but Potensac was back on brilliant form in 1982, a big, powerful, brooding wine that has remained imposing for two decades. The 1983 showed far more austerity, but was a classic Médoc that is now past its best. Yet by 2006 the 1985 was still elegantly scented and gorgeously opulent, with well-integrated tannins and quite good length. The 1987, always light, should have been drunk up. The 1989 was similar in style and persistence to the 1982, but the 1990, the only time I have drunk it, was quite chunky. The 1996 is full-bodied and voluptuous, massively fruity and persistent. This classic Médoc still needs a little time to shed its robust tannins. The 1997 is remarkably powerful and spicy for the vintage, though it lacks complexity. The 1998 was tough and ungainly in its youth, and there was more pleasure to be had from the ripe, stylish, yet powerful 1999. The 2000, 2001, 2002, and 2003 are all excellent: big, ripe wines with swagger and broad shoulders; not exactly elegant, but lush and concentrated and powerful.

Potensac is the sole *cru bourgeois exceptionnel* in the AC Médoc and fully deserves its leading role.

Château Preuillac

Lesparre. Tel: 0556 090029. Website: www.chateau-preuillac.com. **Owner:** *Yvon Mau and the Dirkzwager company.*

30 ha. 54% Cabernet Sauvignon, 44% Merlot, 2% Cabernet Franc. **Production:** *170,000 bottles.*

Second wine: Ch Le Preuil

This estate, which lies close to Potensac and La Cardonne in a single block, was established in 1869 by Edmond Adde. In the 1930s it became severely neglected and was revived only in 1969 by Raymond Bouët, who built the winery and *chai*. He also built the château itself, which is a convincing replica of an early-nineteenth-century mansion. Bouët died in 1984, and his heirs subsequently sold the property to the négociant house of Yvon Mau and its Dutch partners in 1998. Jean-Christophe Mau set about restoring the property with great zeal, investing heavily in new drainage and a new *chai*, and replanting over one-third of the property. In 2003 he hired Stéphane Derenoncourt as a consultant oenologist. In that same year, Preuillac lost its *cru bourgeois* status. Jean-Christophe Mau did not take this lying down, protesting that the property had not been properly inspected and no account had been taken of the investments Mau had made.

Mau admits that the terroir – clay-limestone and sandy gravel – is not exceptional, so his team needs to make substantial efforts in the vineyard, by pruning and green-harvesting, to control yields (forty-five to fifty hl/ha) and deliver grapes of high quality. The harvesting is manual, and the grapes are sorted in the vineyard. The *grand vin* has almost sixty per cent Merlot, while the second wine is Cabernet-dominated. The must is fermented with indigenous yeasts in large oak vats with the aid of micro-oxygenation. Since 2004 about one-third of the wine goes through malolactic in barrel. The wine is aged for twelve months in thirty-five to fifty per cent new oak, then fined with eggwhite.

It has taken a while for the investments to bear fruit. The 1998 is a gently flavoury lightweight claret, but the 1999 was rather herbaceous and astringent. However in 2000 and 2001, Preuillac produced well-balanced, oaky wines, with freshness and sound, blackcurrant fruit, but there is some greenness on the 2001. The firm but fresh 2004 is the first vintage here to show real elegance.

Although the château is not inhabited, it is used as the headquarters for a wine school primarily aimed at an international clientele of aspiring professionals.

Château Ramafort

Blaignan. Tel: 0556 733151. Website: www.domaines-cgr.com. **Owner:** *Guy Charloux (Domaines CGR).*

20 ha. 50% Merlot, 50% Cabernet Sauvignon. **Production:** *125,000 bottles.* **Second wine:** *Ch Le Vivier*

Like Château Grivière (*q.v.*), Ramafort has its headquarters at its sister estate of La Cardonne (*q.v.*), and is made in much the same way. The 1995 managed to win the Coupe des Crus Bourgeois in 1998, but this was a bit of a fluke. It was certainly a good wine, if a touch too oaky in its youth, and the 1996 was a worthy successor. But the overall quality doesn't seem to place Ramafort in the top ranks of Médoc wines. On the other hand, it is often underrated, and vintages such as 2000 and 2001 delivered rich, rounded, supple wines with little complexity but very attractive fruit. The 2000 certainly didn't lack robustness and structure, and shows every sign of having a long life ahead of it. The 2003 avoids the heaviness of many wines from this vintage, but is sound and supple rather than exciting. Cherries mark the aromas of the 2004, which is svelte but has an earthy finish.

Château Rollan-de-By

*Bégadan. Tel: 0556 415859. Website: www.rollandeby.com. **Owner:** Jean Guyon. 44 ha. 70% Merlot,*
*20% Cabernet Sauvignon and Cabernet Franc, 10% Petit Verdot. **Production:** 200,000 bottles.*
Second wine: La Fleur-de-By

This is one of the most renowned wines of the Médoc and is almost entirely the creation of Parisian designer Jean Guyon, who expanded the property from two hectares in 1989, when he bought it, to its present forty. The high and somewhat atypical proportion of Merlot ensures the wine always has a certain opulence, with Petit Verdot giving a deep colour. With considerable daring in the conservative Médoc, Guyon also hired an Italian consultant oenologist, Riccardo Cotarella, subsequently joined by Alain Raynaud. The grapes are picked in *cagettes* at optimal ripeness, or just beyond, and fermented in steel tanks in the customary way. The wine is aged in sixty per cent new barriques for twelve months or more, with some *bâtonnage* at the beginning of the process.

I first took notice of this wine in the unpromising 1991 vintage, when Rollan-de-By turned out to be rich, full-bodied, and densely structured, and with an especially lovely minty nose. The 1995 was a bit tough, and the 1996 exhibited dense, succulent fruit and hints of overripeness on the nose. The 2000 has weight and ripeness and the 2001 is exceptionally voluptuous for a Médoc, but it's hard to object to so much lush, toasty oak, especially since the wine doesn't lack acidity. The 2002, tasted very young, showed promise but the 2004 is oddly hard and rigid. If Rollan-de-By were not opulent enough, Guyon also produces a prestige bottling called Haut-Condissas (*q.v.*).

Château Rousseau de Sipian

*Valeyrac. Tel: 0556 415492. Website: www.chateaurousseau.com. **Owner:** Racey family. 14 ha.*
*60% Cabernet Sauvignon, 40% Merlot. **Production:** 70,000 bottles. **Second wine:** Les Tourelles de Sipian*

This was an important estate in the nineteenth century, but the vines were grubbed up after World War II. In 1989 the Laveau-Bock family began restoring the vineyard, a process continued by Roy Racey and his son Christopher, who bought the property in 2000. They have been making significant efforts in the vineyards to improve quality, by ploughing the soil, reducing yields, and harvesting manually. The wine is aged for sixteen months in at least fifty per cent new oak. The 2001 has a dense, chocolatey nose, and a curious structure that shows some vigour but also astringency.

Château Le Temple

*Valeyrac. Tel: 0556 415362. **Owner:** Denis Bergey. 18 ha. 60% Cabernet Sauvignon, 35% Merlot,*
*5% Petit Verdot. **Production:** 90,000 bottles. **Second wine:** Ch Balirac*

Le Temple was the source of a ripe, fleshy wine in 2000, with smoky raspberry aromas and reasonable concentration on the palate. The 2001 showed initially assertive tannins that became more supple with bottle-age, though it remains a fairly chunky wine. The 2002 is similar in style, a solid wine that still has plenty of fruit. The 2003 is jammy and rather coarse. Although not jammy, the 2004 is also rather rugged and coarse, and has a dry finish. I have conflicting notes on the Cuvée Prestige from 1995.

Château Tour Blanche

*St Christoly. Tel: 0557 266804. Website: www.bernard-magrez.com. **Owner:** Bernard Magrez. 39 ha.*
*58% Merlot, 26% Cabernet Sauvignon, 12% Cabernet Franc, 4% Petit Verdot. **Production:** 200,000 bottles.*

Formerly the property of Dominique Hessel of Listrac, Tour Blanche was acquired by Bernard Magrez in 2004. His team completed the production of the 2003, a supple wine with some light spiciness and moderate length.

Château La Tour-de-By

*Bégadan. Tel: 0556 415003. Website: www.la-tour-de-by.com. **Owner:** Marc Pagès. 74 ha.*
*55% Cabernet Sauvignon, 35% Merlot, 5% Petit Verdot, 5% Cabernet Franc. **Production:** 450,000 bottles.*
Second wine: Ch La Roque-de-By

This fine property can trace its history back to 1599, when it was owned by Pierre Tizon. It remained in his family until 1725, when it was sold to Comte Louis de Gramont. Various other proprietors followed, until in 1860 the property was acquired by M. Rubichon, who built the grandiose château in 1876. Later, it came into the hands of Parisian grocer Julien Damoy, who also gave his name to an estate in Gevrey-Chambertin. Finally it was bought in 1965 in a fairly run-down condition by Marc Pagès, who had recently returned from Tunisia, and two partners. In 1999 Pagès and his family became the sole owners.

The Tour of the name refers to a former lighthouse built in 1825 that still stands in the vineyards, a reminder that until quite late in the nineteenth century the property was accessible only by boat. The vineyards are superb, with most of them located on a gravel *croupe* that is the highest point between Pauillac and Le Verdon. There is also a twenty-nine-hectare parcel at St Christoly, where the terroir is considerably less exceptional. The average age of the main parcel is thirty-five years, and one parcel is still struggling along after 110 years in the ground. Since the early 1990s the vineyards have been machine-harvested, it being difficult to find harvesters prepared to work this far north of Bordeaux. The wine is vinified in wooden vats and stainless-steel tanks, and aged for twelve months in fifteen per cent new oak. Each year, consultant Jacques Boissenot and the winemaking team select the best barrel of each variety, and age it in new oak to produce 3,000 bottles of a Cuvée Prestige. Pagès says he does this mostly for the fun of it.

Tour-de-By is a typical Médoc, robust rather than elegant, with ample tannin and vigour. The 1986 and 1990 were both very good examples in this style. The 1995 was excellent in its youth but by 2004 was beginning to lose some fruit. The 1996 also failed to age gracefully, eventually developing rubbery tones on the nose, and some rather dry tannins. The 1997 is solid and charmless, and the 1998, despite a sweet blackberry and blackcurrant nose, is a rather brutal wine that is only now evolving into a classic Médoc style with a touch of austerity. There is a considerable increase in refinement from 1999 onwards, and that vintage has a svelte texture and considerable charm. The 2000 is more in the mould of the virile 1990, but the smoky 2001, while rich and full, is also quite earthy. The 2002 is plummy and rich, with a hint of herbaceousness that adds character to the wine. The 2003 offers a big mouthful of rich black-cherry fruit, but it tails off on the finish and is unlikely to make old bones. Redcurrant aromas mark the 2004, which is a robust, solid wine, and the somewhat more powerful and chunky 2005 is in the same style.

On the whole Tour-de-By is a very reliable property, usually delivering a forceful, concentrated wine with panache at a fair price.

Château Tour Haut-Caussan

Blaignan. Tel: 0556 090077. Owner: Philippe Courrian. 17 ha. 50% Cabernet Sauvignon, 50% Merlot.
Production: 125,000 bottles. Second wine: Ch La Landotte

This property has been in Courrian's family since 1877. Insiders know that few Médoc wines offer such outstanding value and consistent quality as Tour Haut-Caussan. It was Michel Tesseron of Château Lafon-Rochet who first introduced me to this excellent wine, which he served during lunch at his château, a remarkable tribute given the snobbery more often encountered within the hierarchy of Bordeaux. Courrian has also written a candid book on the challenges and rewards of being a wine producer in the northern Médoc, and his observations on the changes, mostly positive, that have taken place over past decades.[2]

His vineyards lie in two sections, the first on clay-limestone around the restored tower from which the property takes its name; the second on the plateau de Potensac, which is more gravelly and better suited to Cabernet Sauvignon. Some of the vines are fifty years old, and the average age is around twenty-five years. No chemical fertilizers or herbicides are used.

However, Philippe Courrian owns a second property down in Corbières, where he now spends most of his time. So Tour Haut-Caussan is now run by his son Fabien and his daughter Véronique. The grapes are picked by hand and there is nothing unusual about the vinification, other than the adoption, since 2003, of malolactic fermentation in barriques. The wine is aged up to fifteen months in thirty-five per cent new oak, then eggwhite-fined.

I have tasted numerous vintages since 1987 and there is not a single wine that I would describe as disappointing. The wine is beautifully judged, delicately perfumed with an occasional smokiness; while on the palate there is always good acidity to balance the vibrant fruit and discreet tannins. Moreover, the wine never fails to show good length of flavour. The 2004, suave and spicy, seems exceptional, but the beautifully stylish and concentrated 2005 is even better.

Courrian has exhibited behaviour most Bordeaux proprietors would regard as perverse by refusing to increase his prices since 1996, making Tour Haut-Caussan a real bargain. This sage policy has enabled the Courrians to hold on to a loyal clientele through thick and thin, while many of their greedier colleagues are now struggling to survive. Long may they continue to thrive.

Château Tour-Seran

St Christoly. Tel: 0556 415859. Website: www.rollandeby.com. Owner: Jean Guyon. 10 ha. 65% Merlot,
15% Cabernet Sauvignon, 10% Cabernet Franc, 10% Petit Verdot. Production: 90,000 bottles

This property, once owned by the Marquis de Ségur, is under the same ownership and management as Rollande-By (*q.v.*). Guyon bought the property in 2000 and his first vintage was 2001. The wine is aged for twelve months in one-third new oak. I didn't care for the debut vintage, which I found opulent but also rather souped-up, plump and fruity yet lacking freshness, vigour, and a clear Médoc signature.

Château Vernous

Lesparre. Tel: 0556 411357. Owner: Bernard Frachet. 23 ha. 60% Cabernet Sauvignon, 36% Merlot,
4% Cabernet Franc. Production: 150,000 bottles. Second wine: Les Hauts-de-Vernous

Frachet practises extended maceration and ages his wine for up to eighteen months in forty per cent new oak. The result is a rich, rounded wine, with a good deal of tannin and an assertively chewy finish. There's little elegance or complexity here, but it's a robust and satisfying mouthful. The robust, juicy 2004 seems distinctly better than preceding vintages.

2 Courrian and Creignou, Vigneron du Médoc, Payot, Paris, 1996

Vieux-Château-Landon

*Bégadan. Tel: 0556 415042. Website: www.vieux-chateau-landon.com. **Owner:** Cyril Gillet. 38 ha.*

*70% Cabernet Sauvignon, 25% Merlot, 5% Malbec. **Production:** 280,000 bottles. **Second wine:** Ch Landon*

This wine is aged in a blend of tanks and barriques, of which about one-third are new. These are typical Médoc wines, robust and tannic in their youth but evolving quite rapidly into cedary, stylish bottles that make for very good medium-term drinking. The 1995, 2001, and the sumptuous yet vigorous 2004 are particularly successful, but the 2003 is one-dimensional. The firm and spicy 2005 is outstanding.

Château Vieux-Robin

*Bégadan. Tel: 0556 415064. Website: www.chateau-vieux-robin.com. **Owners:** Didier and Maryse Roba.*

18 ha red: 55% Cabernet Sauvignon, 40% Merlot, 5% Petit Verdot and Cabernet Franc. 0.5 ha white:

*100% Sauvignon Blanc. **Production:** 120,000 bottles. **Second wine:** Air de Vieux-Robin*

This property has belonged to Maryse Roba's family since the eighteenth century, and her husband Didier began running the estate in 1988. Today they are assisted by their son Olivier. The dynamic and tireless Maryse Roba realized from the outset that a little-known property in Bégadan needed stratagems to ensure wine recognition. By opening the property to visitors and putting on small art shows, and by commissioning striking labels for the wines, Maryse has helped to put Vieux-Robin on the map. But this is no triumph of marketing over content. The wine is very good indeed.

Three-quarters of the vineyards lie in a single parcel near the house and winery; the remainder are some three kilometres (1.9 miles) away. The soils are diverse, with gravel and coarse sand, as well as clay-limestone that is water-retentive. The grapes are harvested both manually and by machine, and there is careful sorting both in the vineyard and at the winery. The vinification is straightforward, and the regular bottling is aged in older barrels for around eighteen months.

Of far greater interest is the bottling called Bois de Lunier, which is produced from older vines and is aged in forty per cent new barriques. This was first produced in 1988 and is the wine that Vieux-Robin is best known for. There is also a wine called Collection, which is identical to Bois de Lunier, except that it is aged for two years in new oak.

A new addition to the range since 1999 is Blanc de Lunier, a Sauvignon Blanc barrel-fermented in fifty per cent new oak, and aged *sur lie* for twelve months. Production at present is very limited, with only 1,200 bottles released.

The principal wine here is clearly Bois de Lunier, and I have rarely encountered the regular bottling. But the 1982, produced long before the creation of Bois de Lunier, was delicious in 1998, with a chocolatey, cedary nose, lush, plump fruit, and a lively finish. Bois de Lunier has been consistently good, with the oak well integrated and the fruit always to the fore; moreover, the wine always has freshness and length. I have particularly enjoyed the 1990, 1996, 1998, and the slightly four-square 2000. Even better is the gorgeous 2002, with its aromas of violets and crystallized fruit, its sleek texture, its zest and elegance. The 2003 is lush but fades fast on the finish. However, the 2004 and 2005 have admirable fruit, vigour, and length. Collection is over the top: too oaky, too meaty, and, when young, far too tannic. The 2002 white wine was very attractive, with apricot aromas and a rich spiciness balanced by zesty acidity.

5. The Haut-Médoc

Château d'Agassac

*Ludon. Tel: 0557 881547. Website: www.agassac.com. **Owner:** Groupama Assurances. 38 ha. 50% Merlot, 47% Cabernet Sauvignon, 3% Cabernet Franc. **Production:** 210,000 bottles. **Second wine:** Ch Pomiès-Agassac*

The château itself is a moated keep rising, improbably, among the suburban developments south of Ludon. The present structure dates from the sixteenth and nineteenth centuries, replacing an older castle that stood on this spot. In the seventeenth century it belonged to the de Pommiès family, and the wine was known until well into the twentieth century as Château Pommiers and Château de Ludon. It was much appreciated on the Dutch market. In the course of the twentieth century, the property fell into a decline, and when in 1996 it was bought from the then-owners, the Gasqueton family of Calon-Ségur, by the French insurance company Groupama, enormous investments were required. Groupama first set about renovating the vineyards, and it turned its attention last to the ruinous château.

The vineyards are located on two gravel *croupes*, both around three metres (ten feet) in depth, though they differ in the composition of their stony topsoil and in their clay content. The average age of the vines is around twenty years. The estate practises *lutte raisonnée*.

Agassac has been run for many years by Jean-Luc Zell, who is clearly engaged by the challenge of restoring Agassac and its reputation. His aim is to capture the fruit from his vineyards, rather than to produce profoundly structured wines. He picks late, especially where Cabernet Sauvignon is concerned, and ferments the wines in squat stainless-steel tanks. Seventy-five per cent of the wine is aged in barriques, of which twenty-five per cent are new; the remaining twenty-five per cent is aged in tanks, with micro-oxygenation.

Vintages from the 1980s were fairly tough, so there was plenty of room for improvement. Zell's first vintages were unimpressive, but that was before the investments in vineyard and winery had taken effect. He himself has been satisfied with the quality only since 2001, and both the 1998 and 1999 are light and need to be drunk up; the 2000 is richer but relatively lean for the year and by 2006 was just about ready. The 2001 is very well balanced, but I marginally prefer the 2002, which is fresh and lively, with good length. The 2003 has welcome freshness, but little complexity or length. Agassac is back on form with the supple but spicy 2004, which Zell offered in both cork-stoppered and screwcapped versions. The 2005 is a forward wine, with fresh red-fruits aromas, ample fruit but a light structure, though none the worse for that.

Château Aney

*Cussac. Tel: 0556 589489. **Owner:** M. Raimond. 24 ha. 65% Cabernet Sauvignon, 25% Merlot, 7% Cabernet Franc, 3% Petit Verdot. **Production:** 130,000 bottles. **Second wine:** Ch Aney-d'Arnaussan*

This property was first established in 1850, and has been owned by the Raimond family since 1972. They have reorganized the vineyards and renovated the *chais*. The average age of the vineyards is eighteen years, and they are machine-picked. Vinification is classic, and the wines are aged twelve months in one-third new barriques. Of the trio of vintages from 1999 to 2001, the 2000 is easily the best, certainly superior to the mediocre 2001. Although slightly overripe, the 2003 is generously fruity and has upfront charm. Aney is a wine of few pretensions: fruity, discreetly oaked, and well balanced; what it lacks is flair and style. But it is modestly priced.

Château d'Arche

Ludon. Tel: 0556 560430. Website: www.mahler-besse.com. Leased by the négociant Mähler-Besse. 9 ha.
45% Cabernet Sauvignon, 40% Merlot, 15% Cabernet Franc, Carmenère, and Petit Verdot.
Production: 70,000 bottles. Second wine: Ch Egmont

This good little property has been owned since the early 1990s by the experienced négociant house of Mähler-Besse. The soil is quite gravelly, and the average age of the vines is thirty years. No chemical herbicides are used, and the soil is ploughed. The grapes are picked manually and the wine is aged in thirty-five per cent new oak. The result is a sound and dependable Médoc. Since 1995 the wine has been strikingly consistent. There is ample sweet, brambly fruit on the nose, and Arche never lacks structure and a degree of tannic density. It ages well, and the slightly herbaceous 1999 was still fresh and concentrated in 2004. The 2000 has evolved beautifully into a voluptuous wine with some weight and ripe tannins that will continue to sustain it. It is closely matched by the 2001, which is ripe, succulent, and long, and far superior to the drab, stewed 2003, as is the energetic, powerful 2004.

Château Arnauld

Arcins. Tel: 0557 888910. Owners: Nathalie Roggy and François Theil. 38 ha. 50% Cabernet Sauvignon,
45% Merlot, 5% Petit Verdot. Production: 250,000 bottles. Second wine: Comte d'Arnauld

This property was bought in 1956 by *pied noir* Maurice Roggy, whose daughters married two of the Theil brothers of Château Poujeaux. Today François Theil manages the estate. Recent vintages have been impressive. Both the 2001 and 2002 show plenty of oak on the nose, and the palate has undeniable weight and no shortage of ripe black fruits. Arnauld seems to have gained in richness and complexity since even good previous vintages such as 1996. The 2002 is particularly fine, with firm tannins and considerable force. It should age well. The 2004 has a worrying herbaceousness, and the 2005 is a disappointment too.

Château d'Aurilhac

St-Seurin-de-Cadourne. Tel: 0556 593532. Owners: M. and Mme. Erik Nieuwaal. 20 ha.
50% Cabernet Sauvignon, 44% Merlot, 3% each Petit Verdot and Cabernet Franc. Production: 145,000 bottles.
Second wine: Ch La Fagotte

Dutchman Erik Nieuwaal married a French bride with a vineyard, and since 1983 he has been making the wine. The entire estate had to be replanted; fortunately it was essentially in a single parcel, which made the task easier. Inevitably the vineyard, on clay-limestone soil, is still relatively young. The vines are picked by machine and the grapes are sorted at the winery. The *cuvaison* is usually at least three weeks, and Nieuwaal employs both pumpovers and *délestage* to extract fruit and tannin. A pneumatic press was acquired in 2002 to improve quality further. The wine is aged in thirty per cent new oak, of which about ten per cent is American. Filtration is the exception rather than the rule.

The lanky Nieuwaal works hard with his wines, and they can be rather too extracted. On the other hand, they are very consistent. I suspect a hint of coarseness in some vintages (such as 1996, 1997, and 2003) may have more to do with the high clay content in the soil than with the vinification. The 1999 is a success for the year. The savoury 2000 is forthright and extracted, and the 2001 shows more finesse. The 2002 is marked by black-cherry flavours, and its tannic structure was refreshed by fine acidity. The 2003 is a pleasant surprise: grippy, but a powerful mouthful of dense fruit. Both the 2004 and 2005 are big, powerful, swaggering wines, both on the verge of overripeness but steering clear.

Château Beaumont

Cussac. Tel: 0556 589229. Website: www.chateau-beaumont.com. Owner: Grands Millésimes de France. 105 ha.
60% Cabernet Sauvignon, 33% Merlot, 4% Cabernet Franc, 3% Petit Verdot. Production: 600,000 bottles.
Second wines: Ch d'Arvigny, Les Tours de Beaumont

This immense property lies in a single block on the plateau of Cussac, at a height of some thirty metres (ninety-eight feet). The Günzian gravel soil is mixed with sand. The vineyards were originally planted in 1824 under the ownership of a M. Bonnin. In 1830 Beaumont was bought by the Marquis d'Aligre, who trebled the area under vine. It was sold again in 1849, and the new owners, the Bonnin brothers (unrelated, it seems, to the previous M. Bonnin), built the rather pompous, low-slung château of 1854. In 1860, they sold the property to the Comte de Gennes, and thereafter it passed through numerous hands, including such unusual owners as a nobleman from Brittany and, from 1966, a Colonel Bolivar from Venezuela. In the early 1980s it was the property of a well-known viticulturalist, Bernard Soulas, who restructured the vineyards and restored the château, before selling the lot to Grands Millésimes de France in 1986. This subsidiary of a giant insurance company is in partnership with the Japanese firm of Suntory; it also owns Château Beychevelle (*q.v.*), and the Hetszóló domaine in Tokaj. Etienne Priou is technical director, and Jacques Boissenot consultant oenologist.

Given the size of the property, it is not surprising that the harvest is mechanical. The wine is aged for up to sixteen months in one-third new barriques. In the 1980s this was an uneven wine, sometimes marked, as in 1985, by vegetal flavours and aromas. The 1990s seem to have brought improvements: the 1990 itself had charm and suppleness, and 1994 was good for the vintage. The 1995 was plump and vibrant when young, with ripe tannins; it seemed more complex than the 1996, which was nonetheless juicy and enjoyable. The 1999 was far more successful here than the astringent 1998, and the 2000, while fairly dilute, was still drinking well in 2007. The 2001 and 2002 are distinctly better. The 2003 is easy-going but finishes short, and should be drunk young. The 2004 is solid but the 2005 seems weak for the vintage. Beaumont is a fairly simple wine, made in large volumes and definitely intended for early or medium-term drinking. It is very reasonably priced and offers good value, but there is no point making claims for the wine that it cannot sustain.

Château Bel Air

Cussac. Tel: 0556 590818. Owner: Françoise Triaud. 37 ha. 65% Cabernet Sauvignon, 35% Merlot.
Production: 160,000 bottles

This property was assembled in the 1980s from diverse parcels acquired by Françoise Triaud, just as her father Henri Martin had done in St-Julien with Château St-Pierre and Château Gloria. The soils are composed of gravel mixed with sand, and about half the vineyard is over thirty years old. The wine is aged for twelve months in both barriques and tanks; any unsatisfactory lots are sold off to wholesalers. It is an unpretentious wine, reasonably fruity, but it lacks stuffing. On the other hand it is inexpensive.

Château Belgrave

St Laurent. Tel: 0556 355300. Website: www.cvbg.com. Owner: a private consortium, but managed since 1979
on long-term leases by CVBG (Dourthe Kressmann). Cinquième cru. 60 ha. 45% Cabernet Sauvignon,
42% Merlot, 8% Cabernet Franc, 5% Petit Verdot. Production: 340,000 bottles.
Second wine: Diane de Belgrave

Belgrave is part of the trio of classified properties that stand shoulder to shoulder just west of Château Lagrange. The Médocains might have you believe that the name of the estate is a tribute to the three fine *croupes* on which the vineyards are planted. Not so: a former owner had a soft spot for the fashionable Belgravia district in London, and borrowed the name for his estate.

Although CVBG has run Belgrave since 1979, it is only in recent years that it has made a substantial effort to improve quality. Jean-Marie Chadronnier, the head of CVBG, believes that the first vintage to show the effects of the company's investments was 1994. The initial task was to restore the vineyards and the drainage. The vineyards were also expanded from the twenty hectares under vine in 1979. More recently CVBG has rebuilt the cellars and in 2004 completed a new *cuvier* in the form of a rather drab box alongside the château itself, which was restored in the 1990s.

The vineyards are in a single parcel around the château. There is a high proportion of Cabernet Franc, but winemaker Frédéric Bonaffous doesn't believe that the variety performs well here, so it will be phased out and replaced with Cabernet Sauvignon or Merlot. The average age of the vines is now a respectable twenty-five years.

After harvesting the grapes are sorted both before and after destemming, and there is no pumping. Then they are given a cold soak at 5°C (41°F) for up to seven days. The winery is now equipped with seven wooden vats reserved for its best parcels. These wooden vats are not pumped over, but punched down instead. Since 2000 Bonaffous has tried to age the wine without racking or micro-oxygenation. He works closely with a range of coopers to ensure the barrels match the style of the wine, which is refined rather than powerful. The wine is aged in about forty per cent new oak for twelve months. It is filtered, but fined only when necessary.

Belgrave's relative obscurity is probably attributable to the fact that it is distributed directly by CVBG rather than through the *Place de Bordeaux*. The older vintages I have tasted – 1982, 1986, 1990 – have been attractive wines, well balanced but lacking in complexity. The vintages of the mid-1990s were lacklustre, but I note a distinct improvement from 1998 and 1999, which show much more flesh and succulence, with a sleeker, more supple texture and quite good length of flavour. The 2000 is plump and reasonably concentrated but lacks some vigour overall. The 2001 is quite concentrated yet rather dull, and outclassed by the structured yet charming 2002, with its lush fruit and sweet tannins. The 2003 is rather baked and drab, lacking lift. The 2004 has charm and vibrancy, with ripe blackcurrant aromas; it may lack depth but it's very appealing and well balanced. Belgrave is an underrated wine, worth watching as the next few years should bring further improvements in quality and a greater expression of personality.

Château Belle-Vue

*Macau. Tel: 0557 881979. Website: www.chateau-belle-vue.com. **Owner**: Vincent Mulliez.*
*10 ha. 42% Cabernet Sauvignon, 38% Merlot, 20% Petit Verdot. **Production**: 50,000 bottles*

This little-known estate was detached from Château Gironville in 1996 and now consists of parcels close to Giscours. The high proportion of Petit Verdot makes it unusual, and there is also a small parcel of Carmenère that came into production in 2003. The average age of the vines, some twenty-five years, is boosted by the survival of some vines from 1907. The grapes are picked manually, and fermented in steel tanks with punching down rather than pumping over. The *cuvaison* can be as long as eight weeks, and malolactic fermentation takes place in new oak. Bizarrely (for Bordeaux) the wine is aged on the lees with *bâtonnage* for around fifteen months in fifty per cent new French and Hungarian oak. The wine is then fined with eggwhite but bottled without filtration.

The excellent 2001 shows plenty of oak on the nose, while on the palate the tannins are bold but ripe, and a certain fleshiness is balanced by spice, length, and finesse. The 2002 I find excessively plummy, soft, and sweetish, a lush, crowd-pleasing style that somehow doesn't shout Médoc. The 2003 suffers from overripeness, and soon induces palate fatigue, but the 2004 is a winning combination of plump fruit, robust tannins, and a fresh, lifted finish. Despite some complex aromas and a velvety texture, the 2005 has a solid finish and lacks flair.

Château Bel-Orme-Tronquoy-de-Lalande

*St-Seurin-de-Cadourne. Tel: 0556 593829. **Owner**: Jean-Michel Quié. 28 ha. 60% Merlot,*
*32% Cabernet Sauvignon, 8% Cabernet Franc. **Production**: 180,000 bottles. **Second wine**: Ch Tour-Carmail*

The pretty little château, little more than a charming villa, lies near the centre of the village. It is occasionally inhabited by the visiting Quié family, who also own Châteaux Rauzan-Gassies and Croizet-Bages (*qq.v.*). The Quiés bought this estate in 1936. All of them are managed by Jean-Louis Camp. He points out that the soil here – which is gravel over a base of clay-limestone – is better suited to Merlot than Cabernet. The vineyards are in three main parcels: Carmail (close to the estuary), Bel Orme (close to the château), and Quimper near the village cemetery. Bel Orme was mostly replanted in 2001, as the vines were suffering from old age, being sixty-three years old at the time. There is a deep gravel bed at Quimper, making it ideal for Cabernet Sauvignon.

Most of the grapes are picked by machine. Vinification is classic, with the use of selected yeasts. The wine is aged for twelve months in barriques, with fifteen per cent new oak. From the 1960s to the late 1980s this wine was a brute. Jean-Louis Camp agrees, and attributes this toughness to an excessive use of press wine. Even in 1997, the 1970 was rather stewed and dry; hopes expressed in my tasting note of the same wine in 1989 that it would shed its austere, chunky tannins were not realized. In the 1990s I have reasonably appreciative notes on the 1995 and 1998, but other good vintages such as 1990, 1999, and 2000 were drab. However, with 2001, 2002, and 2003 M. Camp's diligent efforts seem to be paying off. The wine remained hefty and broad-shouldered, but these vintages show greater concentration, riper fruit, and better length. Curiously, both the 2004 and 2005 showed a lack of concentration and seemed flat-footed.

Château Bernadotte

St Sauveur. Tel: 0556 595704. Website: www.chateau-bernadotte.com. **Owner:** *Champagne Louis Roederer. 39 ha.*
50% Cabernet Sauvignon, 44% Merlot, 4% Cabernet Franc, 2% Petit Verdot. **Production:** *250,000 bottles.*
Second wine: Ch Fournas-Bernadotte

The estate, which adjoins Château Liversan, takes its name from Germaine Bernadotte, who married Jouandou du Pouey in 1615; their son inherited the property and retained his mother's name. One of the family's descendants ended up on the Swedish throne. The château itself dates from 1860. It was bought in 1973 by a Swedish pilot called Curt Eklund. The wines appeared under two labels, as nine hectares lay within the Pauillac appellation. The Pauillac wine was labelled as Bernadotte; the Haut-Médoc wine, which was by far the greater in terms of volume, was called Fournas-Bernadotte. The Eklunds used to vinify the wines at the local cooperative, until they built their own winery and *chai* in 1987. The Pauillac wine was quite good, at least in vintages such as 1989 and 1995; the style was supple and upfront. The 1996, however, was a disappointment: rather light and lacking in complexity.

By this time the Eklunds were becoming disenchanted. They were often absent in Sweden, so the estate was not as well managed as it should have been. So in late 1996 they approached May-Eliane de Lencquesaing of Pichon-Lalande, to ask whether she might be interested in buying the property. Their hunch was correct. She thought it would be useful to have a *cru bourgeois* from a good terroir that could be marketed alongside her much more expensive classified growth. Perhaps even more tempting was the prospect of nine more hectares of AC Pauillac that could theoretically be incorporated into Pichon, though in practice it is now part of the blend of Pichon's second wine.

The Pichon team lightly restructured the vineyards, planting more Merlot in place of Cabernet Sauvignon, since the soils were colder and the Cabernet often struggled to ripen. It took a while for the difference to be felt, and Mme. de Lencquesaing believes it was only in 2000 that an improvement in quality became discernible. In 2006, when Champagne Roederer acquired Pichon-Lalande, it also took over Bernadotte.

The vines are picked manually, and the vinification is similar to that at Pichon-Lalande, except that there is less extraction so as to ensure the wines are approachable relatively young. Bernadotte is aged for twelve months in thirty-five per cent new oak. The efforts are certainly paying off, and the 2000 is indeed a wine with a richness and vigour rarely encountered during the Eklund years. It is far better than the 1999, which lacks grip and has matured rapidly, although it is quite well balanced and unmistakably Médoc in character. The 2002 is elegant and fresh, far from weighty but well balanced. The 2004 was severe in its youth, but its concentration of fruit is impressive. The 2005, tasted just before bottling, seemed slack and slightly bitter – perhaps a poor sample.

Château de Braude

Arsac. Tel: 0556 588451. Website: www.chateau-mongravey.fr. Owner: Régis Bernaleau. 9 ha.
55% Cabernet Sauvignon, 45% Merlot. Production: 50,000 bottles

The Bernaleau family owns Château Mongravey (*q.v.*) in Margaux, and this small property in Arsac. Despite moderate yields and a generous use of new barriques, the wine was unimpressive until the pure and concentrated, blackcurrant-scented 2004. On the other hand, a special *cuvée* called Château Braude Fellonneau, aged for twenty-four months in new oak, does have more weight and finesse. The 2004 is excellent.

Château du Breuil

Cissac. Tel: 0556 595813. Website: www.chateau-cissac.com. Owner: Louis Vialard. 25 ha. 34% Merlot,
28% Cabernet Sauvignon, 23% Cabernet Franc, 11% Petit Verdot, 4% Malbec. Production: 100,000 bottles.
Second wine: Ch Moulin du Breuil

Since 1987, this property has been under the same ownership and management as the better-known Château Cissac (*q.v.*), which it adjoins. Its principal feature is a ruinous fourteenth-century moated castle that once belonged to the English Crown. The gravelly topsoil is somewhat deceptive, since one metre (three feet) beneath the surface lies clay-limestone. This means the vines are quite vigorous, though an effort is made to keep yields down to around fifty hectolitres per hectare. About half the vineyards are picked by machine, and the wines are aged in older barrels, of which up to fifteen per cent are of American oak. The 1995 was a very successful wine, with discreet tannins and reasonable concentration, but more recent vintages such as 2000 and 2001 have been dispiritingly light, lacking in fruit and length. Even though it is sold at a very reasonable price, the wine remains disappointing.

Château Cambon La Pelouse

Macau. Tel: 0557 884032. Website: www.cambon-la-pelouse.com. Owners: Jean-Pierre and Annick Marie.
65 ha. 50% Merlot, 36% Cabernet Sauvignon, 12% Cabernet Franc, 2% Petit Verdot. Production: 325,000 bottles.
Second wine: Ch Trois Moulins

Cambon La Pelouse can trace its history back to the seventeenth century, when the wine was apparently much appreciated in England. In the nineteenth century it belonged to the Baron de Villeneuve, who also owned neighbouring Château Cantemerle. In 1996 the property was bought by Jean-Pierre Marie, who had prospered in the supermarket business in Paris, but at the age of fifty-one decided to invest his money more enjoyably. The vineyards had been abandoned after the frost of 1956, then replanted in 1975, so they are still relatively young.

As well as a block planted close to the modern winery, the main vineyards are located close to Giscours and Cantemerle, where the soil is mostly fine gravel mixed with sand. The parcel near Giscours has more gravel. The density is on the low side, at between 5,000 and 7,000 vines per hectare. But great efforts have been made to improve the viticulture: the vineyards are ploughed, the trellising has been raised to increase the foliage surface by twenty-five per cent, chemical herbicides are not employed, and green cover is planted in parts of the vineyard. Vineyard manager François Baudoux has increased the proportion of Merlot, which he feels is better adapted to the sandier sectors.

Despite this attention to detail, the vineyards are mostly picked by machine. The winemaking is focused on producing a ripe, modern style of claret. From 2005 the grapes are sorted before and after destemming; any juice that runs off the newly picked grapes is simply discarded. Part of the must is cold-soaked for six days. The *cuvaison* lasts for three to four weeks, with pumping over and *délestage*. The wine is aged for up to fourteen months in forty per cent new oak, including some American and Hungarian oak. Racking is kept to the minimum.

Château Trois Moulins is a separate property, acquired by M. Marie at the same time, but it is regarded as a kind of second wine. However, it differs in one major respect from Cambon, since it can contain up to forty per cent Cabernet Franc. The vinification is the same as for Cambon, but only half the wine is aged in barrels.

In the 1980s the wines were unoaked. The new owner soon put a stop to that. Cambon certainly attracted attention in 2000. It was solid and concentrated, and decidedly rich even if not noticeably elegant. The 2001 is very marked by toasty oak; the palate is lush and fruity, rich without being too extracted, plump and plummy. The 2002 and 2004 are in the same mould, with firm tannins balanced by very sweet fruit. They are more stylish than the toasty, liquorice-scented, and rather jammy 2003, which lacks lift and flair. The 2005 has more power but is a touch leaden. Cambon La Pelouse is a crowd-pleaser, not a wine that shows much subtlety, but it is packed with rich, succulent fruit. There is an occasional hint of overripeness, and it is probably not a wine for long cellaring, but it does give terrific pleasure in the short to medium term.

Château Camensac

*St Laurent. Tel: 0556 594169. Website: www.chateaucamensac.com. **Owners:** Jean Merlaut and Céline Villars-Foubet. Cinquième cru. 70 ha. 60% Cabernet Sauvignon, 35% Merlot, 5% Cabernet Franc. **Production:** 300,000 bottles.*
Second wine: La Closerie de Camensac

Known until 1988 as Château de Camensac (and more than a century earlier as Château Popp), this large property is sandwiched between two other classified growths, Belgrave and La Tour-Carnet, just west of St-Julien. From 1965 to 2005 the proprietors were the Forner family, who also own the major Rioja bodega of Marqués de Cáceres. When they bought the property, it was in poor shape. The vineyards consisted of no more than fifteen hectares, of which two were planted with hybrid grapes. Emile Peynaud was hired to turn things around, which he did, and today the consultant is Michel Rolland. Most of the vineyard has had to be replanted, so the density is high, at 10,000 vines per hectare. Today the average age of the vines is around thirty years. By 2005, Forner was ready to retire, and Camensac was bought by Jean Merlaut and his niece Céline Villars-Loubet. In addition to running Chasse-Spleen (*q.v.*) in Moulis, she and her husband have taken over the management of Camensac.

The vines are planted on well-drained, reasonably homogeneous gravel slopes overlooking those of La Tour-Carnet. The largest parcel lies behind the unadorned chartreuse and approaches the vineyards of Lagrange. The vines are picked both manually and by machine. The wine is fermented in cement and steel tanks with automatic pumpovers. The wine is aged in up to sixty per cent new oak, but the proportion does vary considerably depending on the vintage.

M. Forner was a charming old gentleman, so it was distressing to conclude that the wine could surely have been much better than it was. I have tasted numerous vintages from 1975 onwards, and almost without exception they are disappointing on numerous counts, being either green or dilute or short. There are a few exceptions. The 1996 is a savoury wine, with a certain attractive gaminess, although purists may raise an eyebrow and suspect a trace of brettanomyces. The 1998 is somewhat rustic and dull but doesn't lack freshness; drink it soon. The 2000 has a degree of power and tannin rarely found in Camensac; if lacking in elegance, it has some richness and length. The 2001 is acceptable without being remotely exciting, but is superior to the harsh and dull 2002 and the green, rasping 2003.

The quality at the neighbouring properties of Belgrave and La Tour-Carnet has improved considerably over the past decade, and Camensac has been lagging behind. No doubt the Merlauts will work energetically to turn things around.

Château Cantemerle

Macau. Tel: 0557 970282. Website: www.cantemerle.com. Owner: SMABTP insurance company. Cinquième cru.
90 ha. 50% Cabernet Sauvignon, 40% Merlot, 5% Cabernet Franc, 5% Petit Verdot.
Production: 350,000 bottles. Second wine: Les Allées de Cantemerle

As you drive up the D2 road from Blanquefort toward Pauillac, Cantemerle is one of the first great wine estates you come to. Its park, although wrecked by the damaging winter storms of 1999, is still impressive, and in winter you can see the sprawling château behind the trees. From the 1570s until 1892 this was the property of the Villeneuve family. The original château wasn't where it is today; instead its ruins lie on the right side of the D2 behind the modern Cazes winery. In the early nineteenth century Cantemerle sold its entire crop directly to Dutch merchants. This meant the growth was scarcely known within the Bordeaux region. However, with excellent timing, the then-owners offered the wine to the *Place de Bordeaux* for the first time in 1854. The brokers were impressed by the wine, and, in the nick of time, Cantemerle was classified.

In 1892 the well-known Dubos family from Bordeaux bought the estate, and it was well cared for by Pierre Dubos from the 1930s to the 1960s. Cantemerle passed to his nephews, who failed to invest in the property, which slid into a gradual decline. In 1981 it was bought by a large French insurance company. At that time only twenty hectares were planted, a sharp reduction from the 115 hectares in production in 1855. It wasn't hard to find out where the historic Cantemerle vineyards had been located, and the new owners began replanting them throughout the 1980s.

In 1993 Philippe Dambrine, a rather dashing figure with swept-back black hair, was appointed as director of the property, and he has continued to replant, as well as to invest in the winery. Today the vineyards are in three main sectors. Thirty hectares are planted on the plateau north of the château: the soils here are very fine gravel and sand. Another twenty hectares, also on gravelly soils, lie between Cantemerle and La Lagune. This too was part of the historic Cantemerle property, but for many years had been leased to Château de Malleret. In 2003 an additional thirty hectares were planted just north of the Cazes winery as well as farther east. This block includes some fifty-year-old Cabernet Sauvignon vines. Not that long ago Cabernet Franc represented twenty-three per cent of the plantings, but Dambrine was unhappy with the productive clones, and has sharply reduced their quantity by grafting over. In the long term Dambrine would like to see about sixty per cent Cabernet Sauvignon and forty per cent Merlot. The soil is ploughed and the average age of the vines is thirty years, with a density of 9,600 vines per hectare.

The grapes are hand-picked, with sorting both in the vineyard and after destemming. Cantemerle is equipped with a *sous-vide* concentrator and Dambrine says he is happy with it. The must is fermented in steel tanks and in restored wooden vats, with pumpovers and *délestage*, and *pigeage* may be attempted in years to come. Dambrine likes to get the wine into barrel fast to retain its depth of colour. The blending is done progressively, while the wine is ageing in thirty to forty per cent new barriques for twelve months, with regular racking and a light gelatine fining.

There were fine vintages here in the past, but they were not consistent. The 1953 was beautifully balanced, with a lingering finish. More recently the 1978 was sumptuous, spicy, and invigorating, but by the early 1990s seemed to have given all that it was going to deliver. The 1979 was graceful wine, forward and pretty and a pleasure to drink, though hardly great. The 1983 was still drinking well in 2000; it had developed a slight gaminess on the nose, but was rich and supple on the palate. I have had varying bottles of the 1985, which should probably have been drunk up by now. The 1986 initially had the toughness of the vintage, but by the end of the 1990s it had developed some charm and was fully mature.

The 1989 has developed well, with a powerful cedary character emerging on the nose; the palate is soft and lush but slightly earthy. The 1990 was good as far as it went, but, given the splendour of the vintage, the wine lacked complexity and richness on the mid-palate. The 1995 is dense and savoury, with remarkable concentration and weight if not much elegance. The 1996 is very different, a wine with charm, delicacy, and poise, though it seems to be evolving quite fast. The 1998 has a sweet, leafy nose, a lush texture with no rough edges, and is ready to drink. The 1999 is fully ready to drink, with attractive floral aromas, a supple texture, and pleasing length. The 2000 exhibits richer and riper fruit aromas, quite powerful tannins, and good fruit and balance. The 2001, 2002, and 2003 are good wines, quite forward given their youthfulness, supple and slightly hollow. On all the wines since 2000 I detect a stewed-fruit character on the nose that I am at a loss to explain, though it suggests that some of the grapes are picked overripe. It's not disagreeable, but it stamps the wines in a way I find disquieting. At a blind tasting of almost all the 2002 classed growths, I gave my lowest score (as did the other tasters) to Cantemerle, and my note detected a lightness and greenness in the wine that I had not detected on other occasions. Perhaps a duff bottle? At a similar tasting of 2001s, that vintage was supple but just about ready to drink, though the 2000 had more backbone, though it too showed some disquieting greenness. Despite some initial richness the 2003 is a light wine with moderate acidity that should be drunk young. However, it is holding up better than some Médocs from this vintage. The 2004 has more spice and vigour, and seems fresher than preceding vintages. Indeed, it seems to be the finest and most concentrated Cantemerle in many years.

Since the arrival of Philippe Dambrine Cantemerle has certainly made progress and is far more consistent than in the past. And yet, despite his dynamism and professionalism, the wine is still not as good as one feels it could be. Given its location, it is unreasonable to expect great power and richness from Cantemerle, but it does not seem markedly better than many good *crus bourgeois*. Perhaps it will just take more time for the changes in vineyard and winery to make their mark on the bottled wine.

Château Cap-de-Haut
See *Château de Lamarque*

Château Caronne-Ste-Gemme
St Laurent. Tel: 0556 875681. Website: www.chateau-caronne-ste-gemme.com. **Owner:** *François Nony. 45 ha. 65% Cabernet Sauvignon, 33% Merlot, 2% Petit Verdot.* **Production:** *240,000 bottles.* **Second wine:** *Parc Rouge de Caronne*

This property has been in the Nony family for over a century. The vineyards are not far from those of Château Lagrange and Gruaud-Larose, but are more at risk from frost. They are picked both by machine and by hand. With its substantial proportion of Cabernet Sauvignon, this remains a wine of classic style, capable of ageing well in bottle. It is aged in twenty-five per cent new barriques. I have limited experience of Caronne-Ste-Gemme, but have rarely found the wine exciting. Even the 1982 lacks concentration and persistence. The 1996 is attractively perfumed, but somewhat lean and lacking in finesse. The 1998 has lost its fruit, and the 1999 lacks the charm of the vintage, showing modest fruit, earthy tannins, and a drab finish. The supple, fruity 2001 suggests that quality is on the rise. However, the 2003 is earthy and extracted.

Château Charmail
St-Seurin-de-Cadourne. Tel: 0556 597063. **Owner:** *Olivier Sèze. 22 ha. 48% Merlot, 30% Cabernet Sauvignon, 20% Cabernet Franc, 2% Petit Verdot.* **Production:** *125,000 bottles.* **Second wine:** *Tour de Charmail*

The re-creation of Charmail from a run-down estate to one of the stars of the Haut-Médoc has been a labour of love undertaken by Olivier Sèze. He grew up on a wine estate, but in distant Fronsac. After completing his studies, Sèze came across Charmail, a renowned property in the eighteenth century, but in a terrible state in 1980.

I took over the property, but had no money. So I made as much wine as I could from the plots of young vines, just to earn enough money so that I could keep investing in the vineyards and in good equipment. By the end of the 1980s I thought I was ready to make wine that was as good as any from St-Seurin. The first wine I was really proud of was the 1992. Yes, it wasn't a good vintage, but by working correctly and imaginatively in the vineyard in difficult years, I find I can achieve excellent results.

He claims to have been a pioneer both of green-harvesting and deleafing.

Although the Charmail vineyards occupy a single parcel close to Sociando-Mallet, the soils are very varied and essentially clay-limestone. They came up trumps in dry years such as 2003, but the drawback of clay soils is that they can deliver coarse tannins if they are not properly managed. The principal variety is Merlot, and Sèze has also planted a good deal of Cabernet Franc, which, he believes, explains the specific personality of his wine, which exhibits deep colour, spice and liquorice flavours, and high extract. All these qualities are of course conditional on reasonably low yields. In September he goes through the vineyards carefully removing any unripe or uneven bunches; this is in order to prepare them for machine-harvesting. The grapes are then sorted at the winery.

Sèze is one of a handful of winemakers in the Médoc who uses dry ice to bring down rapidly the temperature of the must to around 5°C (41°F) for a lengthy cold soak. The idea is to extract the tannins not from the pips, which don't always ripen properly, but from the skins. After the alcoholic fermentation, using native yeasts, is over, he takes his foot off the pedal so as to avoid extracting any bitter tannins. The wine is aged for twelve months in thirty-five per cent new oak, and blended quite late. There is neither fining nor filtration.

Although Sèze does produce a second wine, his long-term goal is to ensure that the entire crop is good enough to serve as *grand vin*. Ideally, he would like to eliminate the second wine altogether. But he admits he is not there yet. He finds his wines show signs of reduction after bottling, so they need aeration when drunk young.

I have tasted almost every Charmail since 1994 and there is not a poor wine among them. The 1994 wasn't great, but it was spicy and stylish and a fine success for the vintage. The more structured 1995 has ripeness, stuffing, and persistence. The 1996 is superb, rich, full-bodied, but bright and concentrated, with very well-judged oak. The 1997 is sweet and harmonious, and remarkably good for a lacklustre vintage; it is drinking well now. The chocolatey 1998 is concentrated and harmonious and displays no hard tannins. The 2000, predictably, is lush and opulent, with a fine texture and exemplary length. The 2001 is by no means inferior to 2000: it's a classic wine, full-bodied and structured. I took it to have far more Cabernet in the blend than is actually the case. As Sèze observes, even the Merlot here gives dense and structured wines. The 2002 is still closed, but has terrific potential, with real weight and powerful tannins. But it will need more time. I found the 2003 heavy and dull when tasted young, but it may well alter after bottling.

Charmail is reasonably priced for the quality. It is very much an expression not only of the excellent St-Seurin vineyards but of Sèze's own ideas and personality. He gives the impression of having thought long and hard about every aspect of his winemaking, and to have developed empiricism to a high art.

Cave Coopérative Chatellenie de Vertheuil
See *Cave Coopérative Marquis de St-Estèphe (St-Estèphe)*

The Vertheuil cooperative merged some years ago with the more important cooperative in St-Estèphe, but it has retained its own identity with two principal bottlings: Chatellenie is unoaked, while Chesnée des Moines is aged in barrels. Both are simple, straightforward wines that fail to make much of an impression, but the oaked *cuvée* is marginally more interesting.

Château Cissac

*Cissac. Tel: 0556 595813. Website: www.chateau-cissac.com. **Owner**: Louis Vialard. 50 ha.*
*70% Cabernet Sauvignon, 25% Merlot, 5% Petit Verdot. **Production**: 220,000 bottles.*
Second wine: Les Reflets du Ch Cissac

It was in 1945 that Louis Vialard took over this property, in the family since 1885. It was in poor shape in those days, not surprisingly, but he enterprisingly set off for England to sell Cissac's wines. He found buyers, raised badly needed cash, and established a wine-importing company in London. Louis Vialard is still keeping an eye on Cissac, but his granddaughter Marie is more closely involved, as is Laurent St Pasteur, a dynamic manager appointed in 2001.

The vineyards are on gravelly, sandy soil, yields are said to average a moderate forty-five hl/ha, and only the young vines are picked by machine. There used to be a moderate percentage of Cabernet Franc here, but the variety has since been eliminated. The wine is fermented in old wooden vats as well as squat stainless-steel vats. Temperature control was introduced only in 1999. Under St Pasteur, extraction has been stepped up, with bleeding of the tanks, pumping over, and *délestage*, his aim being to produce wines that are structured yet accessible young. Cultivated rather than natural yeasts are used. The wine is aged up to eighteen months in thirty per cent new oak, with a good deal of American oak used for the second wine. In 2003 St Pasteur introduced lees-stirring so as to give the wine more fat and roundness.

Cissac is much admired, but its charms usually escape me. It is, perhaps, as its admirers claim, a "classic" claret, if by that one means that the aromas are sometimes vegetal and the tannins often green and hard. I have tasted almost every vintage from 1970 to 2003, and my notes record a struggle to find much to appreciate. Curiously, Cissac seems to have succeeded in some modest vintages more than in great ones, and I have relatively approving notes of the 1976, 1977, and 1983, though the fine years of 1982 and 1990 resulted in good if not outstanding wines. Since the arrival of St Pasteur the wines have gained some weight and density, but they remain rather brutal in their tannic structure, especially the 2001. Perhaps it will take a few more years for his reforms to bear fruit.

Château Citran

*Avensan. Tel: 0556 582101. Website: www.citran.com. **Owner**: Antoine Merlaut. 90 ha.*
*58% Cabernet Sauvignon, 42% Merlot. **Production**: 550,000 bottles. **Second wine**: Les Moulins de Citran*

The imposing château, now the home of Antoine Merlaut and his family, was built in 1861. Like many other Médoc properties it fell into severe decline after World War I, and by 1938 there were only four hectares under vine. In 1945 this substantial property was acquired by the Miailhe family. In the 1980s, under the stewardship of Jean Miailhe's sister, it was performing poorly, and machine-harvesting didn't help. In 1987 a Japanese property company called Touko-Haus bought the no-longer-profitable estate, and spent a fortune in renovating the vineyards and winery. Despite this investment, it gave up on Citran in 1996, selling the estate to the Taillan group, négociants and owners of Gruaud-Larose, Chasse-Spleen (*qq.v.*), and other important properties.

The vineyards are in two main sections: on sandy soils near Avensan and on gravelly soils nearer the château. Vines in the former are now being grubbed up in favour of new plantings in the latter. Even in the late 1990s this was not a wine that ever excited me, although the 1996 did evolve well. The wine was supple, but lacked excitement and flair. Even the 2000 shows signs of greenness and a lack of generosity. Today there is more selection, and the wine is aged in forty per cent new barriques. The 2001 marks a major improvement in quality, replicated in 2002, with ripe tannins and good underlying acidity and length. The 2003, however, is austere and rather rustic, and there is some puzzling astringency on the simple if savoury 2004. The 2005, however, is richer and more virile, and shows great promise. At long last, Citran could be a property to watch.

Château Clément-Pichon

Parempuyre. Tel: 0556 352379. Website: www.vignobles.fayat.com. Owner: Clément Fayat. 25 ha.
50% Merlot, 40% Cabernet Sauvignon, 10% Cabernet Franc. Production: 125,000 bottles.
Second wine: La Motte de Clément-Pichon

Building magnate Clément Fayat is better known as the owner of Château La Dominique (*q.v.*) in St-Emilion, but since 1976 he has also owned this hideous pile, which is even uglier than Château Lanessan, which is by the same architect (Michel-Louis Garros). It was built in 1881 in the unprepossessing Bordeaux suburb of Parempuyre after a fire destroyed the previous one. A few years after he took over the property, which used to be known as Château Parempuyre, M. Fayat was on the receiving end of a writ from Mme. de Lencquesaing of Pichon-Lalande, objecting to the use of the name "Pichon" here. Fortunately this battle of the titans was settled amicably.

As Fayat replanted the entire property, the first vintage here was 1981. The vines are picked manually, and the must is fermented in steel tanks, with the use of micro-oxygenation. Part of the crop goes through its malolactic fermentation in oak, and the wine as a whole is aged in fifty per cent new oak for up to sixteen months. My experience of the wine is limited, but I have consistently good notes on the 1996, which is stylish, concentrated, and spicy. In contrast, both the 2000 and 2002 seem rather too soft and lacking in structure for the vintages. The 2003 is supple but hollow and it fades fast. The lush but vigorous, blackcurrant-scented 2005 is by far the best Clément-Pichon in years.

Clos du Jaugeyron

Arsac. Tel: 0556 588943. Owner: Michel Théron. 2.3 ha. 62% Cabernet Sauvignon, 36% Merlot,
2% Petit Verdot. Production: 9,000 bottles

This tiny property, with vineyards in Macau and Cantenac, has been owned since 1993 by Michel Théron. The vines are old here, thirty-five years on average, and yields are controlled by planting a cover crop between the rows. The grapes are destemmed in part by hand, then fermented in small cement vats. Malolactic fermentation takes place in barriques, in which the wine is also aged for twelve months. One-third of the barrels are new. Théron uses the system of rolling the barrels in order to keep the lees in suspension. The 2001 had charming red-fruits aromas, and was plump, almost sumptuous, on the palate, but not lacking in forceful tannins to give it structure and length. The 2003 is ultra-ripe, fleshy, spicy, and oaky, but a good wine from a very difficult vintage. After a supple, juicy attack, the enjoyable 2004 finishes on a lively, almost perky, note. The 2005 is a model of fine balance, with sumptuous fruit and firm acidity giving impeccable length. There is also a tiny production of AC Margaux, from an 0.25-hectare parcel at Cantenac.

Château Comtesse du Parc

Vertheuil. Tel: 0556 593289. Website: www.chateautourdestermes.com. Owners: Jean and Christophe Anney. 6 ha.
50% Cabernet Sauvignon, 50% Merlot. Production: 40,000 bottles

The Anneys are better known as the owners of Château Tour des Termes (*q.v.*) in St-Estèphe. This small property, with vines planted on very stony soils, produces supple wines to be enjoyed young. Although the wines are aged in barriques for twelve months, no new oak is used. It is an attractive wine, sleek and lightly spicy, with little depth or length. But then it is without delusions of grandeur.

Château Coufran

*St-Seurin-de-Cadourne. Tel: 0556 593102. Website: www.chateau-coufran.com. **Owner:** Miailhe family.*
*76 ha. 85% Merlot, 15% Cabernet Sauvignon. **Production:** 500,000 bottles.*
Second wine: Ch La Rose-Maréchale

This well-known property was bought by Louis and Edouard Miailhe in 1924, and has passed through the generations to the jovial Eric Miailhe and his brother. Two other properties form the Vignobles Miailhe: Soudars and Verdignan (*q.v.*). Eric's father Jean put these wines on the map, and was also in charge of the Syndicat of the Crus Bourgeois for many years. Jean Miailhe is now enjoying his retirement, but is a welcome figure around the lunch table at Coufran when wine-focused visitors are invited.

The very high proportion of Merlot at Coufran is an oddity. Eric Miailhe explains that, during the 1930s, his grandfather decided in a moment of exasperation that the late-ripening Cabernet Sauvignon was more trouble than it was worth, so he grubbed it up and replaced it with Merlot. In the 1980s some Cabernet was replanted, but Eric believes that the high proportion of Merlot both gives Coufran its own typicity and is largely responsible for its great popularity.

The vines are among the most northerly in the Haut-Médoc. The soil here is sandy gravel, and the vineyards are machine-harvested, though Miailhe stresses that the vines are carefully prepared beforehand to eliminate unripe or damaged bunches. After sorting, fermentation takes place with cultivated yeasts in stainless-steel tanks with pumping over and *délestage*. One-third of the wine is aged in tanks to conserve the fruit; the remainder is aged for twelve months in French and a little Hungarian oak.

It is the policy of Vignobles Miailhe to store the wines after bottling for about two years before releasing a vintage. The idea is to ensure that the wines can be drunk with enjoyment on release, although they can be cellared further. The Bordelais are often reproached for producing their wines without much reference to the eventual market for those wines. This is not the case here, and the Miailhe family is thoroughly commercially minded. Eric Miailhe admits the grape selection here is less strict than at, say, Verdignan, but he seeks to release Coufran at an attractive price that will appeal to and satisfy a specific clientele. He is also not keen on second wines, pointing out that the Miailhe wines are inexpensive in general, so there is no margin in producing an even cheaper second wine.

Coufran delivers the goods. It is not a great wine, and doesn't aim to be. On the other hand, it is very good value and satisfying in all but the weakest vintages. The 1996, for example, retained its fresh, blackcurranty fruit for many years. The 1998 lacks some weight, but is supple, spicy, and balanced, with no obtrusive tannins. The 1999 is in a similar mould, but the 2000, although reasonably concentrated, is unexciting for the vintage and has a dry finish. The 2001 is delicious, with liquorice tones on the nose, and ample tannins behind the plump fruitiness. The 2002 is very good too, quite perfumed on the nose, while on the palate it is fresh, lively, and delicate. The 2003 is easy-going and lacks some vigour, but it will give some pleasure over the next few years.

Château Dasvin–Bel–Air

*Blanquefort. Tel: 0557 880764. **Owner:** Tessandier family. 20 ha. 45% Merlot, 45% Cabernet Sauvignon,*
*10% Cabernet Franc. **Production:** 150,000 bottles*

This property is under the same ownership and management as Château Maucamps (*q.v.*) in Macau. The vines, which are young, are picked by hand and by machine. The wine is vinified with selected yeasts, and the occasional application of micro-oxygenation. It is aged for sixteen months in twenty per cent new oak, with some American oak. The 2000 is fresh with raspberry and blackcurrant aromas, a rather simple wine with little flesh or length, but pleasant enough given its modest price. The 2002 is similar.

Château Duthil

Le Pian-Médoc. Tel: 0557 970909. Website: www.chateau-giscours.fr. Owner: Eric Albada Jelgersma. 6 ha.
55% Cabernet Sauvignon, 45% Merlot. Production: 40,000 bottles

Under the same ownership as the Margaux properties of Giscours and du Tertre (*qq.v.*), this is aged in barrels disposed of by Château Giscours. The 2001 was plumply fruity, persistent, and quite tannic. The plummy 2003 has initially lush fruit, but is marred by rather coarse tannins, but the 2004 is both concentrated and balanced.

Château La Fon du Berger

St Sauveur. Tel: 0556 595143. Website: www.lafonduberger.com. Owner: Gérard Bougès. 20 ha.
60% Cabernet Sauvignon, 30% Merlot, 5% Cabernet Franc, 5% Petit Verdot. Production: 100,000 bottles.
Second wine: Plantey de Lieujean

At one of the roundabouts on the outskirts of Pauillac is a signpost pointing to this property, which is surprising, since La Fon du Berger is not exactly well known. Indeed, until 2003, when it was promoted, it was a mere *cru artisan*. But Gérard Bougès has been justly rewarded for the efforts he has made since 1988, when he left the cooperative to start bottling his own wines. The vineyards are on sandy gravel soil between Châteaux Liversan and Bernadotte. The wine is aged in twenty per cent new barriques for twelve months. One telling detail, however, is that he traded in his modern pneumatic press for two vertical presses, which, he believes, give a superior press wine. The wines have improved since the mid-1990s when they could be astringent, though they retain a trace of rusticity. But they are honest wines with Médocain austerity and abundant vintage character.

Bougès also owns 1.5 hectares within the nearby Pauillac appellation, and this was first bottled in 1998. It is aged in around forty per cent new oak, as the wine is more structured than the Haut-Médoc. The 2001 certainly shows more weight and persistence than the Haut-Médoc.

Château Fontesteau

St Sauveur. Tel: 0556 595276. Website: www.fontesteau.com. Owners: Dominique Fouin, Jean-Christophe Barron,
Joachim Immelenkemper. 30 ha. 60% Cabernet Sauvignon, 25% Merlot, 15% Cabernet Franc.
Production: 185,000 bottles. Second wine: Messire de Fontesteau

This splendid property has a rather complicated history. It had been owned since 1943 by a René l'Eglise, who sold up in 1983 as he had no heirs. The new owner was Dominique Fouin, who bought the existing vineyard of seven hectares and a run-down winery. He set about restoring the property, and took in two partners: Jean-Christophe Barron in 1992, and in 1995 Joachim Immelenkemper from Germany, who helped to finance the purchase of the château itself, which had remained in the l'Eglise family and passed down to an Englishman. The English owner was somewhat dismayed to find himself the proprietor of a large château with no indoor plumbing, and was happy to negotiate its sale. The new owners renovated the château, restored the fine park, and created a new lake within it. A new *chai* was built in 1998.

As for the vineyards, they are sandy-gravelly soils over a limestone base. Barron makes the wine, with the aid of consultant Jacques Boissenot. The younger vines are picked by machine. The wine is fermented in stainless-steel tanks, sometimes, but not systematically, with the aid of micro-oxygenation. The wine is aged for twelve months in twenty per cent new barriques.

The wine is somewhat irregular in quality and style. Some vintages, such as 1996, have lacked concentration and structure; others, such as 2001, have been rather soupy and lacklustre. However, the wine is excellent and unusually lush in 1998. The 2000 is plump and supple, yet has ample tannin that should ensure a good future; and the 2002 is a great success, with sweet, intense cassis aromas, and fine acidity and elegance on the palate. However, I have twice encountered oxidized bottles of the 2003, and the 2004 is disappointingly dilute and astringent. Fontesteau is not distributed via the *Place de Bordeaux*, but through a network of importers and to private customers. This may explain why it is less well known than it usually deserves.

Château de Gironville

Macau. Tel: 0557 881979. Website: www.scgironville.com. Owner: Vincent Mulliez. 10.4 ha. 47% Merlot,
43% Cabernet Sauvignon, 10% Petit Verdot. Production: 60,000 bottles

In the nineteenth century this was a substantial property of thirty-five hectares. The vines were grubbed up in 1929, and not replanted until 1987 by Rémy Fouin, from whom the present owner bought the property in 2004. The gravelly soil is especially deep. The wine is aged twelve to fourteen months in thirty per cent new oak, both French and Hungarian, and bottled without filtration. The 2001 is a delicate, charming wine, now ready to drink. The 2002 and 2003 are surprisingly soft and plush, and seem to lack the grip that should typify a good Médoc. In contrast, the 2004 has generous tannins without excessive extraction, and a long, spicy finish. The 2005 has more density and is tightly structured, and will need time for its fruit to unfurl.

Château Hanteillan

Cissac. Tel: 0556 593531. Website: www.chateau-hanteillan.com. Owner: Catherine Blasco. 82 ha.
46% Cabernet Sauvignon, 45% Merlot, 5% Cabernet Franc, 4% Petit Verdot. Production: 500,000 bottles.
Second wine: Ch Laborde

This large property borders St-Estèphe and the vineyards of Lafon-Rochet. It was owned by the nobility in the seventeenth and eighteenth centuries, but after they failed to survive the Revolution, the property came into the hands of Antoinette Rose de Lapeyrière, who constructed the existing château. In 1852 the estate was sold to a M. Lefort, who made considerable investments. In 1903 Hanteillan was acquired by a family from the Corrèze, who retained ownership until 1973, when it was bought by construction magnate Maurice Mathieu, whose daughter Catherine Blasco has run the property for over two decades.

The soils are varied, with parcels of clay-limestone, marl, and gravel. The average age of the vines is twenty-five years, and the viticulture is essentially organic. The grapes are machine-harvested. Winemaker Béatrice Friquet oversees the vinification and the *élevage* in barrels and vats. I have not tasted the wine for some years, but in the 1990s it was lively and attractive but with little depth or complexity. It seems structured for fairly early drinking.

Château Haut-Bréga

St-Seurin-de-Cadourne. Tel: 0556 596250. Owner: Joseph Ambach. Cru artisan. 8 ha.
60% Cabernet Sauvignon, 40% Merlot. Production: 40,000 bottles

Until 1979 the production from this small property was dispatched to the local cooperative. The vines are planted on clay and gravel soils, and are picked by hand. The wine is aged in forty per cent new barriques for around twelve months. Despite its modest status, I have been impressed by recent vintages, which show ripe, intense aromas, and no lack of concentration, grip, and length. The price is extremely reasonable for the quality.

Château Haut-Madrac

St Sauveur. Tel: 0556 000070. Owner: Philippe Castéja. 20 ha. 75% Cabernet Sauvignon, 25% Merlot.
Production: 120,000 bottles

The négociant Philippe Castéja, who owns Châteaux Batailley and Lynch-Moussas (*qq.v.*) in Pauillac, also owns this property, with vineyards close to Lynch-Moussas, where the wine is actually vinified. It is not often seen, since the production was mostly sold to airlines. Unfortunately, two of those airlines were Sabena and Swissair, which have been obliged to forsake the skyways, so perhaps we will see more of Haut-Madrac in other circuits of distribution. It's a perfectly sound wine, plump and with upfront fruit. It is reasonably concentrated, but simply lacks flair. The wine is usually ready to drink at about five years. The cedary, fresh 1999, the medium-bodied 2002, and the heftier 2003 are all of good quality.

Château Hourtin-Ducasse

*St Sauveur. Tel: 0556 595692. Website: www.hourtin-ducasse.com. **Owner:** Michel Marengo. 24 ha.*
*70% Cabernet Sauvignon, 25% Merlot, 5% Cabernet Franc. **Production:** 170,000 bottles. **Second wine:** Ch Peyrahaut*

This estate seems to date from the eighteenth century, and it was bought by the present owner in 1976. The vines lie close to Pauillac, yet the wine is attractive and easy-going, though often robbed of finesse by rather dry tannins. However, no new oak is used to age the wines, which are supple, approachable young, and inexpensive.

Château Lachesnaye

*Cussac. Tel: 0556 589480. Website: www.lachesnaye.com. **Owner:** Bouteiller family. 20 ha.*
*50% Cabernet Sauvignon, 50% Merlot. **Production:** 120,000 bottles*

Lachesnaye, originally planted in the mid-eighteenth century, was bought by the Bouteillers, who also own the neighbouring Château Lanessan (*q.v.*), in 1961. As you drive from the D2 toward Lanessan, Lachesnaye is the hideous baronial château you pass on the left. The mansion was built in 1880 by its then-owner Frédéric Exshaw. Before 1961 the property was known as Château Ste-Gemme, but after Jean Bouteiller bought the estate he replanted most of it and changed the name. The grapes are picked by machine and only partly aged in oak. It is a soundly made wine that is reasonably robust and concentrated, and can age very well.

Château La Lagune

*Ludon. Tel: 0557 888277. Website: www.chateau-lalagune.com. **Owner:** Jean-Jacques Frey. Troisième cru.*
*75 ha. 60% Cabernet Sauvignon, 30% Merlot, 10% Petit Verdot. **Production:** 450,000 bottles.*
Second wine: Moulin de La Lagune

The substantial property lies on the right side of the D2 as one passes by Ludon on the way north; it is the first of the great Médoc properties. It's easy to overlook the château itself, a chartreuse dating from 1730, as the buildings are partly screened by woods. As chartreuses go, this is on a grand scale, and has been lavishly restored by the present owners, the Frey family. La Lagune was already an important estate in the late sixteenth century, but it was not until the eighteenth century that it developed as a wine estate. It often changed hands, until in 1886 the Sèze family, who were Bordeaux négociants, acquired the property and retained it through several generations. They restored the vineyards after the depredations of phylloxera, but the vines were once again devastated by the frost of 1956, and had to be replanted. In 1958 Georges Brunet began the process of renovating the property, but soon left for Provence to establish Château Vignelaure. The property was becoming run-down, and in 1961 it was bought by René Chayoux, the owner of Champagne Ayala. Chayoux had no direct heirs, so after his death La Lagune (and Ayala) passed to his collaborator Jean-Michel Ducellier, and then in 1998 to Ducellier's son Alain. In 1999 Ayala and Lagune were bought by Jean-Jacques Frey, whose other businesses include property and fashion; he also owns forty-five per cent of Billecart-Salmon. In 2004 Ayala was sold to Bollinger, but La Lagune remains in the Freys' hands. Jean-Jacques Frey's three daughters are each involved in different sectors of his business. La Lagune is supervised by Caroline Frey, a trained oenologist in her late twenties who has worked with Denis Dubourdieu, the consultant oenologist here. The cellarmaster, here for over thirty years, is Patrick Moulin. The first vintage vinified by Caroline was 2004, though she credits Moulin as her mentor. Her striking good looks and relaxed personality have proved no disadvantage in raising the profile of La Lagune.

The sixty hectares of vineyards are in one large parcel on sandy-gravelly soil, with clay-limestone sub-soil in certain sectors. The trellising has been raised in the 2000s and the many missing vines replanted, but the major investment has taken place in the *cuvier*. This stunning building, designed by Patrick Baggio and completed in 2003, is horseshoe-shaped and equipped with squat stainless-steel tanks. The grapes, picked in small *cagettes*, are hauled by lift onto a platform above the tanks. Here they are sorted three times, then crushed lightly and dispatched down a metal tube into one of the tanks. Because the platform is higher than the entry hatches into the tanks, no pumping is required, and the crushed fruit is essentially pushed gently down the tube. The funnel of the tube can be swung round to whichever tank has been chosen as recipient. The process is so gentle that sometimes there are too many whole berries and too little juice in the tanks to get the fermentation going. After a cold soak, selected yeasts are added. Patrick Moulin points out that, as the winery is so new, there is not much of an indigenous yeast population as yet. Vinification takes place with pumping over and *délestage*, and the wine remains in tanks (other than press wine) for the malolactic fermentation. The wine is aged in fifty per cent new oak (it used to be considerably higher in the 1980s) for up to eighteen months, with regular racking. The second wine is a relatively new creation, dating from 1998, and it is aged in one-third new oak.

The soil here in the southern Médoc ensures that La Lagune is never an especially powerful or dense wine. Moulin says the structure of the terroir is closer to Pessac than to Pauillac, and the wine itself often resembles that from Margaux.

There were some good wines made here in the 1970s, and I have positive notes on the 1971, 1973, and 1975, although the latter was distinctly chunky. The 1982 was terrific from the outset, richly fruity on the nose and, despite its tannins and richness, always accessible and enjoyable. It has lacked elegance, but with so much voluptuous fruit it is churlish to complain. The 1983 was a touch more austere, and lacked concentration; the structure of the wine has scarcely altered since I first tasted it in 1989 and last tasted it in 2002. Yet it has held up well. The 1984 is not bad at all for the vintage, but the 1985 has all the charm and silkiness of that lovely vintage. The 1986 is very much in the same mould, and not as obtrusively tannic as so many wines of that year; today it is graceful and long, and probably at its peak. The 1988 is rather lean and has evolved rapidly, and is outgunned by the splendid 1989, still succulent, tannic, and concentrated in 2002. The 1993 is good for the vintage and more appealing than the blunt, tannic 1994. The 1998 has the defects of the vintage, showing too much grip for the actual fruit and lacking interest and length. The 1999, however, is delicious, a cedary, silky wine, with airiness, charm, and some intensity; it may lack structure and depth, but the fruit quality is very seductive. The 2000 is a touch disappointing. Its smoky oakiness doesn't lack elegance, and the palate shows supple fruit and lively acidity, yet the wine lacks excitement and weight. The 2001 is forward, well balanced, and vigorous, with ample fruit; by 2007 it was beginning to drink well. The 2002 shows beautiful pure Cabernet, cassis aromas, stylish and assertive on the palate, with the merest hint of herbaceousness. The 2003 is concentrated and imposing without being too extracted, but the aromas seem a touch candied, and there is another note of crystallized fruits on the finish. It's a good if far from thrilling wine in a tricky vintage. There are attractive blackcurrant aromas on the 2004, which is a fresh, elegant wine, with ripe tannins and excellent balance.

La Lagune, usually reliable, rarely exciting, seems on the edge of a breakthrough in quality and elegance. The counsels of Denis Dubourdieu, and the completion of as well-equipped a winery as any in Bordeaux, suggest that there are great things to come.

Château de Lamarque

Lamarque. Tel: 0556 589003. Website: www.chateaudelamarque.com. Owner: Pierre-Gilles Gromand-Brunet d'Evry.
35 ha. 45% Cabernet Sauvignon, 35% Merlot, 15% Cabernet Franc, 5% Petit Verdot.
Production: 250,000 bottles. Second wine: D de Lamarque

Tourists come to Lamarque to admire the medieval château, with its imposing machiolations and crenellations mostly from the fourteenth century, though the castle is of eleventh-century origin. The charming Romanesque chapel remains intact, and the thirteenth-century undercroft is now the family's private cellar. The castle dates from the time when this was the northern frontier of the Guyenne, and its function was to protect the region from Viking and subsequent incursions. During the Hundred Years War ownership alternated between the French and the English, and tucked into the corner of the drawing room ceiling are the coats of arms of Henry V of England and the Duke of Gloucester. In 1453 Lamarque returned permanently to the French fold. In 1851 it was acquired by the Comte de Fumel (whose family were former owners of Margaux), and the present owner's grandmother, the last of the Fumels, married her cousin, the Marquis d'Evry, from whom the present owner is descended. The present M. d'Evry is a genial and enthusiastic guardian of his heritage, and is actively aided in running the property by his wife Marie-Hélène, who is in charge of the technical aspects of the vineyards and winery.

The vineyards lie away from the castle, which was built on a rare rocky outcrop, in three main parcels, each on a gravelly *croupe*. Twenty hectares lie close to Moulis, bordering the vineyards of Poujeaux, Chasse-Spleen, and Maucaillou. Another parcel lies behind the village church, the third opposite Château Malescasse just to the south. The wines are fermented with a submerged cap, and the tanks are often bled by up to fifteen per cent to improve concentration. The large wooden vats visible in the cellars are false fronts for the cement tanks concealed behind them. M. d'Evry doesn't want too much extraction, and will blend in more press wine to compensate for any apparent lack of structure. The wine is aged in up to fifteen per cent new oak and bottled without filtration.

The oldest vintage I have tasted was the 1986, from magnum in 1998; despite a certain lack of concentration and weight, the wine was sweet and fleshy on the nose, and still fresh and attractive on the palate – ready for drinking. The 1988, in contrast, was rustic and rather raw. The 1998 has considerable aromatic charm; it is sleek, attractive, and with none of the rusticity of some 1998s. The 1999 is lighter and more forward. In their youth the 2000 and 2002 were quite full-bodied and powerful, but with ripe tannins and good persistence of flavour. The 2000 was still rich and firm five years later; it's wine of real weight that will age well. There is good fruit on the 2003, but the tannins are chewy and the wine finishes short and should be drunk young. The 2004 may seem understated, but it's poised and fresh and reasonably long. In contrast, the 2005 is sheer power and weight of fruit, a wine that will evolve over many years. Lamarque is a thoroughly sound and reliable wine, even though it clearly lacks elegance.

The same family owns the eleven-hectare Château Cap-de-Haut at Lamarque, and the wine is made essentially in the same way as its big brother, though with shorter barrel-ageing and less new oak. There is also a rosé rather oddly known as Noblesse Oblige.

Château Lamothe-Bergeron

Cussac. Tel: 0556 599822. Owner: Crédit Agricole Grands Crus. 67 ha. 49% Merlot, 44% Cabernet Sauvignon,
7% Cabernet Franc. Production: 180,000 bottles. Second wine: Ch Romefort

Since 1978 this estate has been owned by the Cordier-Mestrezat négociant house. Then in 2004 the company's properties were sold to the Crédit Agricole bank. The vineyards are well located, being close to the St-Julien border. The grapes are picked by hand as well as by machine, and the wine is nurtured for twelve months in twenty-five per cent new oak.

Older vintages of the wine that I have drunk have been pleasant enough but without much distinction or personality. My experience of recent vintages is limited, but the 1998, while mildly herbaceous, remains fresh and attractive, with a clean, lively finish. The 1999 is in a similar mould, though less herbaceous, and has an attractive savoury tone. The 2001 was excellent, fruit-forward but with supple tannins and ample vigour and concentration. There is an easy-going charm to the 2003, which should be drunk young.

Château Lamothe-Cissac

Cissac. Tel: 0556 595816. Owner: Vincent Fabre. 33 ha. 73% Cabernet Sauvignon, 20% Merlot,
2% Cabernet Franc, 5% Petit Verdot. Production: 240,000 bottles. Second wine: Ch Fonsèche

Gabriel Fabre lived in North Africa until the 1960s, when, like so many other *pieds noirs*, he moved to France and acquired vineyards. Lamothe-Cissac had been gambled away at Biarritz casino, and subsequently abandoned until Fabre bought it in 1964. Since his death in 1991, the property has been run by his son Vincent, who gained international experience in the 1980s by working in Australia and California. The vineyards are located not only in Cissac but on the plateau of Vertheuil. There are two major soil types: clay-limestone and sandy gravel. On average the wines are about forty years old, and, unusually, very much dominated by Cabernet Sauvignon. Since the early 1980s the majority of the vineyards have been machine-harvested.

Fabre favours a lengthy *cuvaison*. Modern technology is unashamedly employed, with reverse-osmosis concentration in some vintages, and micro-oxygenation both during fermentation and barrel-ageing. The wines are aged for up to fifteen months in no more than twenty-five per cent new oak, with some use of 400-litre barrels to moderate the oak influence. In top years Lamothe-Cissac produces a separate Vieilles Vignes bottling, no more than 40,000 bottles, from vines that are sixty years old; this *cuvée* is aged entirely in new oak.

Despite the fact that this is clearly a well-managed estate, I find the wines unremarkable; they are sound and competently made, but lack magic and verve. Nor is the Vieilles Vignes bottling dramatically superior to the regular bottling. Yet the wines can age: a 1989 Vieilles Vignes was still plump and concentrated in 2004, though it suffered from a dry finish. The 1996 and 2000 vintages were fairly successful, but the 2001 and 2002 are distinctly lean, with green edges and a lack of flesh. Forget the flabby 2003, but keep an eye out for the juicy and appealing 2004.

Château Landat

Cissac and Vertheuil. Tel: 0556 595816. Owner: Vincent Fabre. 22 ha. 75% Cabernet Sauvignon,
20% Merlot, 5% Petit Verdot. Production: 120,000 bottles. Second wine: Ch Laride

Like Lamothe-Cissac (*q.v.*), this is owned by the Fabre family, who bought it in 1976. The vineyards are divided between northern Cissac and the plateau of Vertheuil, the soil being a mix of clay-limestone and deep gravel. The wine is aged in twenty per cent new barriques. As at Lamothe-Cissac, there is, vintage conditions permitting, a Vieilles Vignes *cuvée* of up to 20,000 bottles. Both the 2000 and 2001 were lean and almost tart.

Château Lanessan

Cussac. Tel: 0556 589480. Website: www.lanessan.com. Owner: Hubert Bouteiller. 40 ha.
75% Cabernet Sauvignon, 20% Merlot, 5% Cabernet Franc and Petit Verdot. Production: 250,000 bottles.
Second wine: Les Calèches de Lanessan

The Bouteiller family were wine suppliers to the royal house in the eighteenth century – hence their name. They can trace their ownership of this estate back to 1793. A road leads past Château Lachesnaye (*q.v.*), which is also owned by the Bouteillers, to the Victorian pile of Lanessan and its extensive outbuildings, some of which house a museum dedicated to horses and their accoutrements. The estate was owned by the same family from the fourteenth century until its purchase by the Delbos family in 1793. The Delbos family were Bordeaux merchants, who developed the estate both in terms of quality and quantity. According to many wine historians, Lanessan missed out on classification in 1855 because the then-owner, Louis Delbos, couldn't be bothered to submit samples to the brokers organizing the classification.

It was Louis's son André who in 1868 demolished the existing château and replaced it with the pile that stands here today. André Delbos had four daughters but no son. In 1907 one of the daughters, Marie-Louise, married Etienne Bouteiller, the forebear of Hubert. It was André's passion for horses and carriages that led to the establishment of the museum here. This is a hospitable property, with current and older vintages available for tasting and purchase most days of the week.

The vineyards are in one large parcel, not far from those of Gruaud-Larose. The vines are quite old, around forty years on average, and planted to a high density on good gravel soils. The grapes are picked by machine, and fermented in concrete tanks. After blending in February, the wine is aged in thirty per cent new barriques. Old vintages of Lanessan have a very good reputation, for quality and longevity. I have tasted some excellent wines from the 1970s, although I have disappointing notes on some vintages of the 1980s. The 2000, 2001, and 2003 were all very good, but the 2004 and 2005 have been disappointingly flat and dull. Tasted just before bottling, two samples of the latter were volatile and tired – perhaps elderly samples. At its best, Lanessan has aromas of black fruits – often plums and blackberries – and the wine always has a firm tannic structure, and clearly ages well. Prices are far from rapacious.

Château Larose-Perganson

See *Ch Larose-Trintaudon*

Château Larose-Trintaudon

St Laurent. Tel: 0556 594172. Website: www.larose-trintaudon.com. Owner: Assurance Générale de France.
175 ha. 65% Cabernet Sauvignon, 35% Merlot. Production: 1,000,000 bottles.
Second wine: Larose-St Laurent

This is easily the largest wine property in the Médoc. It is well located, right on the border with Pauillac, and indeed a few hectares fall within the Pauillac appellation and are bottled separately as Château La Tourette (*q.v.*). The estate's history can be traced back to the early eighteenth century. In 1858 Comte Ernest de Lahens became the owner, and it was he who built the imposing château. Thereafter the estate had various owners, including a White Russian Count Tchernoff and a Spanish duke who never actually set foot here. In 1966 the estate was acquired by the Forner family of Marqués de Cáceres in Rioja. They had been encouraged to buy the almost derelict property by Emile Peynaud, who detected its potential. The Forners put in new drainage and replanted the vineyards. Family dissension persuaded the Forners to sell up in 1986, though they retained Château Camensac.

The new owner was an insurance company. By the time the Forners sold Larose-Trintaudon, its wines were good despite the high volumes produced, and the AGF built on that reputation. For many years the winemaker here has been Franck Bijon. His task is made easier by the fact that 140 hectares are planted in a single parcel around the château. The soils are mostly deep gravel with a subsoil of clay and sand. The density is 6,000 vines per hectare to facilitate machine-harvesting, which was introduced here by the Forners. The wine is aged for twelve months in twenty-five per cent new barriques.

This is an unashamedly commercial property, making large quantities of typical Médoc at a modest price, so it would be wrong to expect sublime quality. That said, the wine is surprisingly good, and has been for some time. The 1983 and 1990 were attractive and vigorous, and vintages since 2000 have been more than acceptable. The wines are not dilute, but are rounded and supple and have more length and stylishness than many others from neighbouring properties.

In 1996 the owners decided to make a separate bottling from a thirty-three-hectare parcel that they believe is of exceptional quality. For this wine they have revived the name of an estate that existed here in the past but was amalgamated with Trintaudon in the early nineteenth century: Larose-Perganson. About one-third of the grapes are picked by hand, then sorted, and given an extended fermentation before being aged in forty per cent new oak. The wine is good but not significantly better than Larose-Trintaudon, so it is arguable whether it justifies the higher price asked for it. The 2001 and 2004 seem the most successful of recent vintages, but 2002 and 2003 lacked excitement. Perhaps it will be a few years yet before Bijon and his team have defined a separate style for this wine. In the meantime neither Larose-Trintaudon nor Larose-Perganson should be dismissed as merely commercial.

Château Lestage-Simon

St-Seurin-de-Cadourne. Tel: 0556 593183. Owner: Vignobles Leprince. 40 ha. 60% Merlot,
35% Cabernet Sauvignon, 5% Cabernet Franc. Production: 220,000 bottles. Second wine: Ch Troupian

This property, spread out among seventeen parcels, was inherited by Charles Simon in 1976. After his death in 2001, the estate was sold to Vignobles Leprince, a company that leased the property to two négociant houses, J. Lebegue and Antoine Moueix. In 2002 they installed as director Merete Larsen, whose husband, Jean-Marc Landureau, owns Château d'Escurac (q.v.).

Some parcels here are fifty years old, although the average age is twenty-eight years. The soils are very diverse, and include gravel, clay, sand, and clay-limestone. It's the clay that accounts for the high proportion of Merlot here. Larsen was swift to introduce viticultural reform, planting green cover between the rows and heightening the trellising. Most of the vines are machine-harvested, but there is sorting at the winery and again after destemming. The winery is equipped with a reverse-osmosis machine, but Larsen does not practise micro-oxygenation. She likes a cold soak of about six days to get more overt fruit into the wine, which is aged for at least twelve months in one-third new oak, including a few barrels of East European origin. Blending takes place late.

Vintages I have sampled from the 1990s were lacklustre, with the exception of the stylish, cassis-suffused 1996. The first of Larsen's wines, the 2002, shows a modest improvement, and the 2003 is fresher and better balanced than most, but clearly it is too early to judge the effects of the new management.

Château Lieujean

St Sauveur. Tel: 0556 415018. Website: www.domaines-lapalu.com. Owners: Jean-Michel Lapalu and Patrice Ricard.
38 ha. 69% Cabernet Sauvignon, 31% Merlot. Production: 280,000 bottles. Second wine: Ch Lagrave

Lieujean is a recent acquisition of the Lapalu group, bought jointly in 1999 by Jean-Michel Lapalu and his general manager. It's located next door to Château Liversan. The soil is thin gravel over a subsoil of chalk and stones.

Like many other Lapalu wines, this is aged both in barrels and stainless-steel tanks. Judging from the three vintages since 2000, Lieujean is a fairly simple wine, though attractively cherry-scented. In terms of concentration and length, the 2002 seems a step up on the preceding years, and the lush, enjoyable 2004 is even better.

Château Liversan

St Sauveur. Tel: 0556 415018. Website: www.domaines-lapalu.com. **Owner:** *Domaines Lapalu. 39 ha.*
50% Merlot, 49% Cabernet Sauvignon, 1% Cabernet Franc. **Production:** *300,000 bottles.*
Second wine: Les Charmes de Liversan, also sold as Ch Fonpiqueyre

Liversan was bought by Prince Guy de Polignac in 1984, but after his son was killed in a flying accident over the vineyards in 1991, he lost heart and sold the property to the ubiquitous Lapalus in 1995. The average age of the vines here is about twenty-five years, and the wine is aged for twelve months in twenty-five per cent new oak.

The Lapalus strive to make moderately priced wine to a good standard, and Liversan is no exception. During the Polignac years the wines were often dry and lacking in finesse. I have tasted many older vintages of Liversan from 1967 onwards, all of them undistinguished, although in some cases they may simply have been well past their best. The first of these vintages that was a pleasure to drink was the 1986, though it evolved fast. The 1995 and 1996 are solid and four-square, with bitter tones on the finish. The 1999 was attractive but is now tiring. The 2000 is medium-bodied and has some charm as well as ripe tannin. I slightly prefer the 2001, which is fresh, juicy, and easy-going.

Château Magnol

Blanquefort. Tel: 0556 954800. Website: www.barton-guestier.com. **Owner:** *Barton & Guestier. 17 ha.*
50% Merlot, 50% Cabernet Sauvignon. **Production:** *85,000 bottles*

In 1973 the négociant house of Barton & Guestier bought this estate in the southern Médoc. The soil is rather sandy so this is not a wine of great weight. The grapes are partly machine-harvested and vinification is traditional, with ageing in about one-third new oak for twelve months. The 1995 was a conspicuous success, more so than the rather astringent 1996, and the 2001 is a tannic wine of considerable structure yet with ample fruit behind it – more so than the easy-going, forward 2000.

Château Malescasse

Lamarque. Tel: 0556 731520. Website: www.malescasse.com. **Owner:** *Alcatel. 37 ha. 55% Cabernet Sauvignon,*
35% Merlot, 10% Cabernet Franc. **Production:** *240,000 bottles.* **Second wine:** *La Closerie de Malescasse*

The handsome early-nineteenth-century château lies just outside Lamarque. There have been numerous owners during the twentieth century. When in 1970 it was acquired by an American company, only four hectares remained under vine; in 1979, it was sold to Guy Tesseron, the owner of Pontet-Canet and Lafon-Rochet. He sold it to the Alcatel company in 1992. Alcatel was also the owner of Gruaud-Larose, until its decision to sell it in 1997.

Georges Pauli, who still supervises winemaking at Gruaud-Larose and used to do the same for all the properties owned by the Cordier family in the past, remains a consultant here, though Bertrand Chemin is the manager of the property. The vineyards lie on a gravelly *croupe*, the highest in Lamarque. The wine is fermented in steel tanks and is aged for fourteen months in twenty per cent new oak.

Although modestly priced, Malescasse is a wine it is hard to get excited about. Vintages in the early 1990s were coarse and rough-hewn without having much weight of fruit. The 1996 was reasonably concentrated, but today shows to excess the high acidity of the vintage. The 2000 is rather rustic, but the fresher 2001, with its touch of liquorice and suppleness on the palate, is attractive, and matched by the blackberry-scented 2002 and the elegant and graceful 2004. Although they still lack depth and complexity, the Malescasse wines seem fresher and more stylish than they used to be.

Château de Malleret

*Le Pian-Médoc. Tel: 0556 350536. **Owner:** not disclosed. 50 ha. 55% Merlot, 45% Cabernet Sauvignon.*
***Production:** 250,000 bottles*

This large property, with its grandiose château, was owned by the De Vivier family until it was acquired in 2000 by A. de Luze et Fils, part of the Grands Vins de Gironde group. In 2006 it was sold to a mysterious Frenchman, resident in Switzerland, whose identity is not disclosed as other members of his family are not aware of his ownership. He hired as winemaker Bruno Vonderheyden from Château Monbrison in Margaux.

Over the past decade the wine has been sound, rather lean, and utterly lacking in verve and excitement. Perhaps the new owner will realize the potential of the property.

Château Maucamps

*Macau. Tel: 0557 880764. **Owner:** Tessandier family. 14 ha. 65% Cabernet Sauvignon, 30% Merlot,*
*5% Petit Verdot. **Production:** 80,000 bottles*

This fine property, bought by the Tessandier family in 1954, is partly located on an extension of the same gravel *croupe* on which La Lagune is situated, though there are three parcels in all. The vineyards are quite close to the river. The grapes are hand-picked, and fermented in stainless-steel tanks at up to 32°C (90°F), with a lengthy *cuvaison*. Should there be any vegetal tones, micro-oxygenation will be applied. The wine is aged for twelve to fifteen months in forty per cent new barriques, and bottled without filtration. The 1996 was ripe, tannic, and spicy in its youth, and the 2001 is rich and supple, quite forward but with good structure and tannins that should ensure a fairly long life. The 2003 is light and forward and won't make old bones. The 2005 is neutral in its fruit expression and has a rather solid finish.

The Tessandiers and the Maucamps team also produce a wine called Château Dasvin-Bel-Air (*q.v.*). From their *palus* vineyards, two Bordeaux Supérieur wines are produced: Château Lescalle and Château Barreyre.

Château Maurac

*St-Seurin-de-Cadourne. Tel: 0557 880764. **Owner:** Claude Gaudin. 18 ha. 65% Merlot,*
*35% Cabernet Sauvignon. **Production:** 110,000 bottles*

The top wine here is called Les Vignes de Cabaleyran and takes its name from a gravelly nine-hectare parcel. The regular bottling is from vines picked by machine as well as manually, and aged in tanks as well as barrels; in 2001 it showed earthy aromas, and more density than elegance. The 2001 Cabaleyran by 2007 had developed an appealing minerality, freshness, and balance. The 2003 has ripe blackcurrant aromas, plump texture, and a tannic structure. The 2005 is robust and packed with fruit.

Château Le Meynieu

*Vertheuil. Tel: 0556 733210. **Owners:** Jacques and Hervé Pédro. 20 ha. 62% Cabernet Sauvignon, 30% Merlot,*
*8% Cabernet Franc. **Production:** 90,000 bottles. **Second wine:** Ch La Gravière*

This is under the same ownership and direction as Château Lavillotte (*q.v.*) in St-Estèphe, which is close by. When the Pédros bought the estate in 1962, only one hectare of vines remained. The soil is clay-limestone, so it is surprising to find so much Cabernet here. The grapes are partly machine-harvested, and the wine is aged for fifteen months in forty per cent new barriques. The oak does show on the nose of the cherry-scented 2002, which has vanilla scents, but the palate is silky and accessible, and graced with a welcome streak of acidity. Meynieu is an inexpensive wine, making it good value, and the second wine is sold almost entirely through supermarkets.

Château Meyre

*Avensan. Tel: 0556 581077. Website: www.chateaumeyre.com. **Owner:** Corinne Bonne. 18 ha.*

*40% Cabernet Sauvignon, 35% Merlot, 15% Cabernet Franc, 10% Petit Verdot. **Production:** 110,000 bottles*

One of the few properties located within the commune of Avensan, Meyre was bought in 1998 by the present owner and winemaker. As well as the regular bottling, which is aged for twelve months in one-third new oak, there is a special *cuvée* called Optima. The 2000 Optima is very ripe and lush, and seems to have a lot of Merlot in the blend, but it's undeniably attractive. The regular bottling in 2001 was excellent, with a lot of zest and presence, and a long, ripe, tannic finish. The 2002, tasted soon after bottling, seemed very extracted, but a year later it had become more supple and imposing, despite a rather dry finish. The 2004 is straightforward but lacks weight. Corinne Bonne also owns a very small 1.6-hectare property in AC Margaux called L'Enclos Gallen, which, atypically, is planted with eighty per cent Merlot.

Château Mille Roses

*Macau. Tel: 0556 588004. **Owner:** David Faure. 9.5 ha. 52% Merlot, 42% Cabernet Sauvignon,*

*6% Petit Verdot. **Production:** 32,000 bottles*

This property was established fairly recently. The vineyards are fairly mature and picked by hand. Fermentation takes place in steel tanks, with ageing in up to fifty per cent new oak, some of which is Hungarian. The 2001 is a fairly rich, chunky wine, with firm tannins but little finesse. Yet I prefer it to the juicy but less structured 2003. The 2004 is lean and sleek, with ample acidity, but the juicy, lively 2005 has more complexity.

Château Le Monteil d'Arsac

See *Ch d'Arsac (Margaux)*

Château du Moulin Rouge

*Cussac. Tel: 0556 589113. **Owners:** Pelon and Ribeiro families. 17 ha Médoc (and 3ha in AC Bordeaux).*

*50% Merlot, 40% Cabernet Sauvignon, 10% Cabernet Franc. **Production:** 100,000 bottles.*

Second wine: L'Ecuyer du Moulin Rouge

A traditional Médoc, if not that sophisticated, Moulin Rouge has been owned by the same family for over two centuries. The vineyards are well located, on gravelly soils not far from Beychevelle, and they are picked by hand. The wine is aged in one-third new oak for twelve months. Moulin Rouge is quite robust yet lacks some concentration and elegance; even in good recent years such as 2001 and 2002 it has shown some rawness and astringency. The 2003 is rather coarse and dry, but the 2004 and the excellent 2005 both show more richness and balance despite some assertive tannins. The price is reasonable, but there are other, more stylish wines in its price bracket.

Château Moulin de Soubeyran

*Le Pian-Médoc. Tel: 0556 588004. **Owner:** David Faure. 7 ha. 65% Cabernet Sauvignon, 25% Merlot,*

*10% Cabernet Franc. **Production:** 35,000 bottles*

A few years ago this property was purchased by David Faure, who also owns Château Mille Roses. The estate is managed by Laurent Vonderheyden of Château Monbrison. The vines, abandoned after the 1956 frost, were replanted from 1987 onwards, so they are relatively young. The only vintage I have tasted was the 2000, a firm wine with bright acidity and reasonable length of flavour.

Château Paloumey

*Ludon. Tel: 0557 880066. Website: www.chateaupaloumey.com. **Owner:** Martine Cazeneuve. 32 ha.*
*55% Cabernet Sauvignon, 40% Merlot, 5% Cabernet Franc. **Production:** 125,000 bottles.*
Second wine: Les Ailes de Paloumey

The Cazeneuve family owned Château Maine-Gazin in Blaye (now the property of Vignobles Germain) in the 1980s. They were keen to move up the quality ladder, but found it too costly to invest in Blaye, given that the wine, however good, could never fetch a high price that would justify the investment. So they sold up and, after a lengthy search, found Château Paloumey in the southern Médoc. There was a substantial three-storey château on the land, but the vineyards had been abandoned in 1954. But such experienced Médoc winemakers as Daniel Llose (of AXA Millésimes) and Georges Pauli (of the Cordier estates) were sure the terroir was of high quality. The Cazeneuves bought Paloumey in 1990 and began planting, on gravelly soils near Cantemerle and La Lagune.

Although the vines are inevitably rather young, the wine is impressive. Pascal Lamarque makes the wines, and Daniel Llose continues to advise. Martine Cazeneuve favours *lutte raisonnée* in the vineyards, and the grapes are hand-picked in *cagettes*, then sorted before and after destemming. Fermentation takes place with pumpovers and *délestage*. After ageing up to fifteen months in one-third new barriques, the wine is blended relatively late.

The 1996 was bland, but the 1999 has held up well, thanks to lively acidity and some spice and complexity. Overall, quality has taken a leap since 2001, an excellent wine with subtle tobacco aromas and a robust, spicy palate with good acidity and length. In the trickier 2003 vintage, Lamarque kept his nerve and did not over-extract, delivering a well-balanced and supple wine for fairly early consumption. Also well balanced is the supple and concentrated 2004. The 2005 is supple, fleshy, and stylish, but doesn't seem to have the majesty of the vintage.

Quality is aided by declassifying about one-third of the crop into the second wine, and there is also a rosé called Plume de Paloumey. In a region that doesn't lack forceful female personalities, Martine Cazeneuve stands out as among the most determined and tenacious. Paloumey is clearly a property to watch, as are the other properties she leases, Château La Bessane in Margaux and Château La Garricq in Moulis (*qq.v.*). Her ambitious zeal and rapid progress at Paloumey has been widely recognized.

Château Peyrabon

*St Sauveur. Tel: 0556 595710. Website: www.chateaupeyrabon.com. **Owner:** Patrick Bernard. 50 ha. 65% Cabernet*
*Sauvignon, 29% Merlot, 4% Cabernet Franc, 2% Petit Verdot. **Production:** 180,000 bottles. **Second wine:** Ch Pierbone*

This excellent property lies on the border with Pauillac, and indeed five hectares are within AC Pauillac, and released as such under the name La Fleur-Peyrabon (*q.v.*). The estate was already well known in the eighteenth century, when the château was built. In the mid-nineteenth century, owner Arnaud Roux was obtaining
classified-growth prices for his wines and tried to obtain belated recognition of Peyrabon as a classified growth. But without luck, and in 1869 the courts ruled definitively against Roux. There were various owners in the twentieth century, until in 1958 it was bought by René Babeau. In 1976 Babeau's son Jacques inherited Peyrabon. He expanded the property by buying land from Château Liversan but the costs of replanting were too much for him. He also realized no one in his family would be interested in succeeding him. As debts began to mount, Babeau, a genial and courteous man, decided to sell up, and in 1998 the Bordeaux mail-order merchant Patrick Bernard bought the estate.

It was Bernard's ambition to restore Peyrabon to its days of glory a century or more ago. He invested heavily in the vineyards, replanting eleven hectares and installing new drainage and ditches. He also restored the winery and built a new *chai*. He undertook detailed soil analyses, and improved viticultural practices by stopping the use of herbicides and introducing ploughing. Treatments were radically reduced. He even cut down some trees to improve the ventilation of the vineyards. "All small details", he told me, "and perhaps less exciting than using 200 per cent new oak – but important all the same."

The soils at Peyrabon are sandy gravel and clay-limestone. About half the vineyards are picked by machine, but the selection is far stricter than in Babeau's day, when the wines were simple and lacking in substance and length. The wine is aged in one-third new barriques for approximately fourteen months.

Bernard says that the style of wine he is looking for is one that unites power, balance, and fine tannins. He is well on his way. The finest parcel at Peyrabon is reserved for the Pauillac, but the Haut-Médoc has improved substantially since 2000, and subsequent vintages have maintained the high standard. They are wines of considerable body, quite marked by oak when young, and remarkably approachable soon after bottling. Yet they seem to have sufficient structure and length to promise a good future for five years or more. The 2000 and 2002 are the best vintages thus far, the 2003 being agreeable but lacking in concentration and structure. The 2005 seemed rather drab and lacking in lift when tasted just before bottling.

Château Peyre-Lebade

Lamarque. Tel: 0556 583800. Website: www.lcf-rothschild.com. **Owner:** *Benjamin de Rothschild. 56 ha. 65% Merlot, 25% Cabernet Sauvignon, 10% Cabernet Franc.* **Production:** *250,000 bottles*

In 1979, six years after Baron Edmond de Rothschild bought Château Clarke in Listrac, he bought another abandoned property. Peyre-Lebade had been acquired in 1835 by Bertrand Redon, the father of the great painter Odilon Redon. Rothschild had to start from scratch, draining and replanting the whole property. The first vintage was 1988. The soils are mostly limestone and clay-limestone; hence the high proportion of Merlot here. It's a large property, so is picked by machine as well as manually. The wine is aged for up to fourteen months in ten per cent new barriques, and blended late. The 2001 had a mentholly nose, and was rich, ripe, and concentrated, with chewy tannins but not without elegance. However, the 2002 was simple, light, and fairly short.

Château Puy-Castéra

Cissac. Tel: 0556 595880. Website: www.puycastera.com. **Owner:** *Alix Marès. 28 ha. 55% Cabernet Sauvignon, 33% Merlot, 10% Cabernet Franc, 2% Petit Verdot and Malbec.* **Production:** *150,000 bottles.* **Second wine:** *Ch Holden*

This estate, which consists of a single parcel of vineyards, lies quite close to St-Estèphe. The property was bought by the Marès family in the 1960s, when they returned from North Africa. They replanted the vineyards from 1974 onwards, with advice from Emile Peynaud. Today the property is run by the founder's granddaughter, who has introduced significant changes in the vineyard, such as heightened trellising, and she installed a sorting table in the winery in 2002. The soil is mostly clay-limestone with a little gravel, yet the majority of the vines are Cabernet Sauvignon. The grapes are picked by machine, but the vinification is entirely traditional, and the wine is aged for twelve months in twenty-five per cent new barriques. Fining and filtration are usual but not systematic.

Past vintages I have tasted have been patchy, with both good and disappointing bottles from 1996, and a slightly green 1998. But the 1995 was a big, solid, smoky wine, with ample length, and the 2000 was in the same mould, but with more weight and complexity. The 2002 is certainly the best Puy-Castéra I have encountered, with its black-cherry aromas and an undeniable opulence and overt fruitiness on the palate. The 2004 is similar, but shows less concentration and complexity.

Château Ramage-la-Batisse

St Sauveur. Tel: 0556 595724. Owner: MACIF company. 66 ha. 51% Cabernet Sauvignon, 41% Merlot, 6% Cabernet Franc, 2% Petit Verdot. Production: 400,000 bottles. Second wine: Clos de Ramage

This large and well-known estate consists of parcels of vines gradually acquired by Francis Monnoyeur from 1961 onwards, and its wine enjoys very wide distribution. It produces a very dependable wine, aged both in new oak and in tanks. Among older vintages, the 1985, with its cigar-box nose and supple, grassy fruit, stood out, though it would probably be well past its best now. The 1995 is robust, plump, and spicy, a thoroughly stylish and enjoyable wine. It is marginally better than the juicy but rather more simple 1996. The 2000 remains opulent in aroma and flavour, with masses of plump fruit and a long, chewy finish. The 2001 also has the fleshiness and juiciness that seem to be the hallmarks of the wine, but my notes over the years suggest that Ramage-la-Batisse is best enjoyed young, when its fruit and vigour are to the fore. Despite some coarse, dense tannins, the 2003 has abundant fruit and some peppery vigour. The 2004 is supple but rather coarse.

Château du Retout

Cussac. Tel: 0556 589108. Website: www.chateau-du-retout.com. Owner: Gérard Kopp. 33 ha. 56% Cabernet Sauvignon, 35% Merlot, 7% Petit Verdot, 2% Cabernet Franc. Production: 100,000 bottles. Second wines: Ch Camino Salva, Ch Tour Salvet

The property unites two former estates, Château Retout-Pigneguy-Mercadier and Château Salva-de-Camino, and was bought by the Kopp family in the 1950s. The soil is mostly gravel, but there are parcels with a good deal of clay as well. Most of the property is machine-picked. After a traditional vinification, about two-thirds of the wine is aged in twenty-five per cent new barriques.

Retout has a rich nose of plums and black cherries, with coffee tones in some vintages. Judging from the 2000, 2001, and 2002, Retout is made in a burly style, with rather protuberant tannins, but the wine does have swagger and extract, though at the expense of elegance. The 2003 is very solid, and lacks lift and freshness.

Château Reysson

Vertheuil. Tel: 0556 355300. Owner: Mercian Corporation. 70 ha. 50% Merlot, 50% Cabernet Sauvignon. Production: 500,000 bottles

This property has been owned since 1988 by a Japanese corporation but managed since 2001 by the Bordeaux négociant house CVBG. Professor Denis Dubourdieu acts as an adviser. The soil here is primarily clay-limestone with some gravel. The vineyards are planted to a rather low density, but more recent plantings have been at 6,700 vines per hectare. In addition to the regular bottling, there is a Réserve, which receives considerably more barrel-ageing; some 80,000 bottles are produced. The 2002 Réserve shows lively, oaky aromas of considerable purity, and good concentration and freshness on the palate; a good wine just about ready to drink. The regular 2003 is jammy and soupy, but the Réserve is better, but still hard to recommend, despite the reasonable price. However, the 2004 Réserve has ample fruit, though not much personality.

Château St-Ahon

Blanquefort. Tel: 0556 350645. Website: www.saintahon.com. Owner: Comte Bernard de Colbert. 31 ha.
60% Cabernet Sauvignon, 30% Merlot, 8% Cabernet Franc, 2% Petit Verdot. Production: 130,000 bottles.
Second wine: Colbert Cannet du Ch St-Ahon

Some years ago the vineyards of this ancient property were reconstituted. It was bought in 1985 by the present owner, and since 2000 it has been managed by his daughter Françoise and son-in-law Nicolas Chodron de Courcel. The vines are picked by machine and, after a classic vinification, the wine is aged in twenty-five per cent new oak, with a portion remaining in tanks. The 2001 is plump, concentrated, and richly fruity, while the 2003 is a good effort for the vintage, with no more than a hint of cooked fruit. Surprisingly, the 2004 is rather rustic and flat-textured.

Château St-Paul

St Seurin. Tel: 0556 593472. Owner: a consortium of investors. 20 ha. 50% Cabernet Sauvignon, 45% Merlot,
5% Cabernet Franc. Production: 120,000 bottles. Second wine: Antognan de St-Paul

Various families teamed up to invest in this estate, and they wisely asked Olivier Sèze of the neighbouring Château Charmail to manage the property. The vineyards are a single parcel, but, as is often the case at St Seurin, the soils, primarily of gravel and clay, are very varied. The vines are quite old, around forty years on average, and yields are very low at around forty hl/ha. Indeed Sèze wishes the vines were rather more productive, as he feels the wines would be better balanced were they slightly less concentrated. Moreover, a young St-Paul can be exceedingly tannic, even rustic, and demands some bottle-age before it becomes enjoyable. Sèze is very cautious about extraction, and the wine is aged for twelve months in no more than twenty-five per cent new barriques.

My first taste of St-Paul was in 1997, when the 1982 accompanied lunch at a local restaurant. It was remarkably good: smoky, even leathery on the nose, yet lush. On the palate it had clearly softened up, with some mushroomy, leathery characters as well as plump spicy fruit. (However, a 1994, tasted on the same occasion, was dire.) The 1990 and 1995 are coarse and rustic, but the 1996 is far better, with a firm core of fruit behind a robust and initially impenetrable outer casing. Sèze took over in 1999, and it shows. I find the 2003 rather leaden, but both 2001 and 2002 are excellent; these are wines of power and density rather than finesse, and, given their origins, they are unlikely ever to be otherwise. Yet on their own terms they are impressive and rewarding.

Château de Ste-Gemme

Cussac. Tel: 0556 589480. Website: www.sainte-gemme.com. Owner: Hubert Bouteiller. 10 ha. 50% Merlot,
50% Cabernet Sauvignon. Production: 80,000 bottles

The Bouteillers of Château Lanessan (*q.v.*) bought this neighbouring property in 1962. In the past its wine had been blended with that of Château Lachesnaye, as the two estates shared the same owner. The Bouteillers restored its independence. Although originally classified as a *cru bourgeois*, Ste-Gemme apparently lost its status in 2003 not so much on qualitative grounds but because it was not vinified in a separate *chai*. The vineyards are planted on soils of gravel over clay-limestone, and are bordered by panels belonging to Beychevelle and Ducru-Beaucaillou. The location seems promising but the vines are machine-picked. The vinification is about the same as for Lanessan. Although an inexpensive wine intended for early drinking, I found the 1995 still piquant and fresh in 2004, somewhat neutral in its fruit quality but certainly not tiring.

Château Sénéjac

*Le Pian-Médoc. Tel: 0556 702011. **Owner:** Thierry Rustmann. 40 ha. 60% Cabernet Sauvignon, 25% Merlot, 14% Cabernet Franc, 1% Petit Verdot. **Production:** 200,000 bottles. **Second wine:** Artigue de Sénéjac*

Under the stewardship of Comte Charles de Guigné, whose family had owned the estate since 1860, Sénéjac was better known for its white wines than its reds. From 1983 Jenny Dobson was the winemaker, and she brought with her from New Zealand her expertise in this area. Her white wines were consistently good, but far from remarkable. She left in 1993 and in 1999 the count sold the property to Thierry Rustmann, who was then married to one of the Cordier daughters, who co-owned Château Talbot. Most of the white vines had been leased from another property, and when that lease expired, Sénéjac was left with a trifling 0.6 hectares of white vines. Rustmann considered this wasn't a viable quantity, so he grafted them over.

Sénéjac consists of thirty-one hectares in a single parcel. Although the property lies relatively far inland, it contains a high proportion of Cabernet Sauvignon. The grapes are harvested in *cagettes*, and in some years reverse osmosis is used to increase concentration. The wine is aged for twelve to fifteen months in one-third new barriques.

Rustmann introduced a wine called Karolus, the costly product of a single three-hectare plot, with older vines cropped at lower yields than the rest of the estate. The vinification is identical to that of the main wine, but the wine sees up to fifty per cent new oak. Sénéjac was mediocre through most of the 1990s, although the 1998 is fleshy and still drinking well. It took Rustmann a few vintages to get going in terms of ameliorating the quality, but the 2001 was stylish and long. The real breakthrough came in 2002, when he produced a terrific wine, with opulent black-cherry fruit, and remarkable succulence and vigour. And in 2003 Sénéjac was richly fruity and opulent, without the baked character of the vintage. Shortly before bottling, the austere 2005 was hard to judge, but had a long, spicy finish.

The 2001 Karolus has a similar flavour profile, but more overt oakiness and considerable persistence – but it is not superior to the regular 2002. The 2003 Karolus is equally oaky, but supple and forward, though it has surprisingly good acidity. The 2004 was lush and oaky but rather over-extracted, and the regular Sénéjac seemed better balanced. After 2004 Rustmann discontinued production of Karolus, since he believed there was now insufficient difference in quality between it and the regular Sénéjac.

Château Sénilhac

*St Seurin. Tel: 0556 593141. **Owner:** Jean-Luc Grassin. 23 ha. 55% Cabernet Sauvignon, 40% Merlot, 5% Cabernet Franc. **Production:** 130,000 bottles. **Second wine:** Ch Dilhac*

In the late nineteenth century Sénilhac was the largest wine estate in St Seurin, but by 1938 a mere three hectares remained under vine. The Grassins bought the property in 1972 and reconstituted the vineyards, which are in a single parcel planted on clay-limestone soils. They are machine-harvested. I find this quite an extracted wine, with green, tart elements even in ripe years such as 2000. The 2001 is in the same mould: dense and oaky, but tannic and somewhat astringent. In 2002 the same over-extraction is evident, but the fruit is more succulent.

Château Sociando-Mallet

*St Seurin. Tel: 0556 733880. **Owner:** Jean Gautreau. 74 ha. 55% Cabernet Sauvignon, 40% Merlot,*
*5% Cabernet Franc. **Production:** 450,000 bottles. **Second wine:** La Demoiselle de Sociando-Mallet*

The rise to stardom of this outstanding property is one of the more unusual success stories of the Médoc. Jean Gautreau had been working with négociant houses in Bordeaux in the 1940s and then set up his own business. In 1969 he bought Sociando essentially as a holiday home. Although Sociando had enjoyed considerable recognition in the nineteenth century, Gautreau had no intention of planting vines here, but good friends in the industry such as Jean-Paul Gardère of Latour and Jean-Michel Cazes of Lynch-Bages convinced him that the frost-free soils on this *croupe* overlooking the estuary were likely to be of superlative quality. Sociando is in effect a northern extension of the riverside *croupes* of St-Estèphe.

Gautreau kept planting, and today this is one of the largest estates of the Haut-Médoc. Although the soil is rich in well-draining gravel, it also enjoys a subsoil of clay-limestone that serves it well in dry years such as 2002 and 2003. The soil has always been ploughed and composted, but Gautreau is an iconoclast when it comes to other revered practices such as leaf-pulling and green-harvesting, both of which he resolutely opposes. It is Gautreau's loudly expressed view that a top terroir planted at high density should be able to produce a crop of around fifty hl/ha without any drop in quality. Indeed in 2002, when most properties were cropping around thirty to thirty-five hl/ha, and in 2003 when the figure was similar, Sociando was rejoicing in yields of fifty-five and forty-nine respectively, although Gautreau provocatively described the 2003 crop as "*faible*".

Diehard critics who equate lower yields with higher quality are likely to be confounded by Sociando's perverse excellence, for few would dispute its very high quality. As for the winemaking, it is conventional. Should the wine lack concentration, technical director Vincent Faure will bleed the tanks, although the estate is equipped with a reverse-osmosis machine. The *cuvaison* can be as long as thirty days, with temperatures rising to a maximum of 33°C (91°F). A proportion of press wine is always blended in, and the wine is aged in new oak for twelve months and bottled without fining or filtration.

My experience of Sociando is less extensive than I should like, but in most of the vintages I have tasted the wine blends ripe, assertive tannins with richness of fruit, all lushly cosseted in the seductive sheen of new oak. The 1993 and 1999 struck me as exceptional for those vintages, but the 2001 lacks some grip – at least for Sociando. The 2002 is superb, with all the sweet cassis fruit of a ripe Cabernet year. The 2003, in its youth, was a touch jammy and exceedingly tannic. The 2004 has fleshy, oaky aromas and a tannic solidity beneath its sleek texture. Despite formidable tannins, the 2005 is magnificent, a complex wine balancing that robust structure with freshness and complexity.

Sociando is evidently of classified growth quality, and it fetches appropriately high prices. The second wine can be very good too – I recall a deliciously rich and imposing 1995 – but it contains far more Merlot than the *grand vin*, and is aged in a modest twenty-five per cent new oak. There is also a Cuvée Jean Gautreau, a selection of the best barrels from each lot, given additional barrel-ageing; although 4,000 bottles are produced, it is not released commercially. The 1996 was still very assertive and backward in 2007.

Château Soudars

St Seurin. Tel: 0556 593609. Website: www.chateausoudars.com. Owner: Eric Miailhe. 23 ha. 50% Merlot,
49% Cabernet Sauvignon, 1% Cabernet Franc. Production: 140,000 bottles. Second wine: Ch Marquis de Cadourne

Soudars is another of the properties belonging to Eric Miailhe, and the viticulture and vinification are essentially identical to that at Château Coufran (*q.v.*). He bought the property in 1973 and re-created the historic vineyard of Soudars. The soil is stony clay-limestone, but has excellent drainage. The vines are picked by machine, and the wine is aged in twenty-five per cent new oak for up to fourteen months, although one-tenth of the crop stays in tanks to preserve overt fruitiness. Miailhe regards Soudars as the most modern in style of his three principal wines. The wine is soft and forward, with a plump, gentle fruitiness usually enlivened by fresh acidity that gives it some freshness too. Soudars may not rise to very great heights, but it's very dependable. The 2005 is the exception, being a concentrated, somewhat chunky wine of unusual power.

Château La Tempérance

St Seurin. Tel: 0557 267080. Website: www.bernard-magrez.com. Owner: Bernard Magrez. 11 ha. 70% Merlot,
20% Cabernet Sauvignon, 10% Petit Verdot. Production: 50,000 bottles

Another investment by the ubiquitous Bernard Magrez, but since 2003 was the first vintage I have not tasted the finished wine.

Château La Tour-Carnet

St Laurent. Tel: 0556 733090. Website: www.latour-carnet.com. Owner: Bernard Magrez. Quatrième cru.
65 ha. 50% Merlot, 40% Cabernet Sauvignon, 7% Cabernet Franc, 3% Petit Verdot. 35% Sauvignon Blanc,
35% Sémillon, 30% Sauvignon Gris. Production: 270,000 bottles. Second wine: Ch Douves de Carnet

Of the three classified growths side by side in St Laurent, La Tour-Carnet is easily the most impressive as a site. As you drive in from the road, you are soon confronted by an imposing fortified gatehouse which suggests the main structure is a castle. That certainly was the case in the thirteenth century, when it belonged to the counts of Foix, but the medieval castle was destroyed after the English departure from Aquitaine. It appears that this was already a wine estate in the fifteenth century, and that its wines fetched high prices. The gatehouse was preserved, and behind it rises a residential block of eighteenth-century appearance. The interior has been entirely renovated and redecorated by Bernard Magrez, who acquired the estate in 2000. He has opted for a rather startling neo-medieval style, with maxims from Montaigne, whose brother-in-law Thibault de Camin once owned the property, painted onto the ceiling beams. Whether the black and white swans that glide around the moat are also picturesque additions by M. Magrez, I have neglected to ask.

Throughout most of the eighteenth century and the first half of the nineteenth, La Tour-Carnet was the property of a Swedish merchant, Jerome de Luetkens. By the mid-twentieth century the estate was owned by a Bordeaux shipowner, Louis Lipschitz, and subsequently by his daughter, Mme. Pellerin. Unfortunately quality during Mme. Pellerin's tenure was disappointing. Yields were at the maximum, the vineyards were machine-picked, there was no selection, and no new oak was used to age the wine.

Although the vines are in a single substantial parcel, the terroir is very varied. Gravel dominates the *croupes*, to be sure, but there are lacings of clay among the gravel and in most places a subsoil of clay-limestone. Bernard Magrez, as is his wont, came in like a hurricane in order to turn around this underperforming property. The proportion of Merlot was increased from forty-two to fifty per cent, which seems sensible enough given the nature of the soils. Trellising was raised, and green-harvesting keeps yields down to around forty-five hl/ha. The grapes are picked as late as possible, and by hand. Fifty workers are on hand to sort the grapes before and after destemming, and in 2004 they experimented with some hand-destemming. About half the crop is vinified in wooden vats. The winemaking shows the influence of Michel Rolland, although the full-time winemaker here is the young Emmanuel Bonneau. There is a prolonged cold soak at 10–12°C (50–4°F) for up to a week, with *pigeage. Cuvaison* can be as long as forty-five days if extended maceration is deemed advisable, although in such cases Bonneau soft-pedals the *pigeage* and pumpovers.

The long, narrow *chai* has been air-conditioned and humidified. Malolactic fermentation takes place in barriques, and the wine is aged in sixty-five per cent new oak for around eighteen months. During the beginning of its *élevage*, it stays on the fine lees with regular stirring. Should it begin to show reductive aromas, Bonneau will micro-oxygenate the barrels.

From 2003 the team also produced some white wine from just under one hectare of mixed white varieties. These vines were planted close to the château in 2000. The must receives some skin contact, is pressed in a vertical press, and fermented in new oak. There is no malolactic fermentation, but there is regular *bâtonnage* for up to four months.

The improvement in La Tour-Carnet since 2000 has been dramatic, but then the Magrez team started from a fairly low point. With the exception of the 1999, which I quite liked, my notes on vintages of the 1990s are dotted with words such as "green", "simple", and "hollow". You get the idea. As early as 2000, La Tour-Carnet emerged from its wilderness years as a far fleshier wine, plump, sleek, and fruit-forward. Both the 2001 and 2002 are delicious wines, opulent and unashamedly modern in style. The 2003 has cooked aromas but the palate is fresher, and the wine will offer good drinking for a few years to come. The excellent 2004 is a return to the style of the 2001 and 2002. La Tour-Carnet is clearly back on track and showing for the first time in many years the true potential of its vineyards.

The 2003 white, its debut, was very oaky, plump, and full-bodied, yet somehow escaped any suggestion of heaviness. The 2005 and 2006 whites both had more vigour and power but again were very marked by oak. The 2003 has settled down into a medium-bodied wine that's a touch candied but has sufficient zest to sustain it over the medium term. The 2004 shows some youthful austerity but it's concentrated, balanced, and long.

Château Tour du Haut-Moulin

Cussac. Tel: 0556 589110. Owner: Lionel Poitou. 32 ha. 50% Cabernet Sauvignon, 45% Merlot, 5% Petit Verdot. Production: 190,000 bottles. Second wine: Florilège de Tour du Haut-Moulin

Travel toward the estuary from the village of Cussac and you soon come to the winery of this sterling property, though most of the vineyards lie farther inland near Beaumont. It has been in the ownership of the Poitou family since 1870. Half the vineyards are picked by machine, but there is very careful sorting at the winery. After crushing, the must is subjected to a brief cold soak, then fermented with native yeasts in cement tanks. Temperature control was installed in 1998. Poitou likes a very lengthy *cuvaison* that includes an extended maceration. The wine is aged in forty per cent new barriques for fourteen months.

The only veteran vintage I have encountered was the 1979 in 1987, and this proved to be a light, stylish wine with good balance and grip. The 1995 was unremarkable, but the 1996 has surprising complexity. It has complex savoury aromas of plums and liquorice, while the palate is rich, juicy, and concentrated – not much finesse but loads of fruit and a firm, chewy finish. The 1998 is rich, weighty, and solid, but near its peak. The 2000 resembles the 1996 (although I have recently had a lifeless bottle), whereas the 2001, while similarly structured, has a more overt black-fruits character. The 2003 is a success for the vintage, with a similar character to the 2001 and no clumsiness or over-extraction. The 2004 is straightforward but had harsh tannins in its youth. The 2005 is also very chewy, but it has imposing weight and fine damsony fruit. Tour du Haut-Moulin isn't elegant, but it delivers its flavours with panache.

This part of the Médoc is full of small properties that claim to be open (but rarely are) and that claim to offer tastings (but never seem to have a bottle or corkscrew handy). La Tour du Haut-Moulin is a great exception, offering a genuine welcome to visitors and an array of organized wine-related activities to those who seek them.

Château Tour St Joseph

Cissac. Tel: 0557 778888. Website: www.chevalquancard.com. Owners: Marcel and Christian Quancard.
10 ha. 70% Cabernet Sauvignon, 25% Merlot, 5% Cabernet Franc. Production: 50,000 bottles
Second wine: Ch La Croix Margautot

This small property is owned by the négociant house of Cheval Quancard. It produced an oaky, voluptuous, delicious wine in 1996, and a highly commendable and eminently drinkable, if less full-bodied, effort in 2001. The 2003 is a sumptuous wine with ample flesh and weight and surprising length.

Château Verdignan

St Seurin. Tel: 0556 593102. Owner: Miailhe family. 60 ha. 50% Cabernet Sauvignon, 45% Merlot,
5% Cabernet Franc. Production: 400,000 bottles. Second wine: Ch Plantey-de-la-Croix

The pretty, turreted château and vineyards of Verdignan were bought by Jean Miailhe in 1972, and this is now the third estate in the Miailhe portfolio (*see also* Coufran and Soudars); it is owned by Eric Miailhe and his brother. The vines are planted on rich gravel soils with some clay-limestone in the mix. The vinification is the same as for Coufran, and the wine is aged for twelve months in thirty-five per cent new oak, although, as at Soudars, ten per cent of the wine stays in tanks to keep it fresh. Eric Miailhe sees Verdignan as the most classic in style of his three properties, and says its wines bear some resemblance to those of St-Estèphe.

Verdignan is a frankly commercial wine intended to give considerable pleasure at an affordable price. Medium-bodied, with reasonable fruit and concentration, and in some vintages a measure of charm and persistence too, Verdignan rarely thrills, rarely disappoints. Among older vintages, I have enjoyed the 1978, 1995, and 1996. The 2000, 2001, and 2002 are all well made and satisfying; of this trio, the 2001 has more weight and tannin and will probably age best. The 2003 is soupy, earthy, and fairly short.

Château de Villegeorge

Avensan. Tel: 0556 582201. Website: www.vignobles-marielaurelurton.com. Owner: Marie-Laure Lurton-Roux. 20 ha.
53% Cabernet Sauvignon, 47% Merlot. Production: 60,000 bottles. Second wine: Ch Peyremorin

The petite but energetic Marie-Laure Lurton is a trained oenologist, who worked with her father Lucien at his numerous properties from 1984 onwards. In 1992 she, like her siblings, was simply given vineyards to run and develop. In her case she ended up with three properties: Villegorge, which her father had bought in 1973 (vineyards only), Château Duplessis in Moulis, and Château La Tour de Bessan at Margaux (*qq.v.*). Emilie Roullé is the technical director of all three, but Marie-Laure keeps a very tight grasp on them too. Villegeorge was well known in the nineteenth century and fetched high prices; in 1936 it was recognized as *cru bourgeois exceptionnel*.

The soils are deep gravel, and the vineyards are planted in two main sectors, one at Avensan, the other close to Soussans. The microclimate, especially at Avensan, is relatively cold and prone to frost, which explains the high proportion of Merlot. Marie-Laure practises *lutte raisonnée* and has installed a water purification plant, which is unusual at a small property in the Médoc. The grapes are picked manually and each parcel is fermented separately. The vinification is traditional. Although she doesn't like a lot of extraction, she also insists she isn't aiming for an easy-drinking style. Villegeorge is aged in up to thirty per cent new barriques for twelve months.

Despite Marie-Laure's dedication and experience, I find the wines here hard to enjoy. From the pre-Lurton era, the 1961, unlike the vast majority of wines from that glorious vintage, was asparagussy and acidic by 1993. More recently, the 1988 is pretty and leafy but probably already just past its best; the 1996 has some finesse but seems a touch light for the vintage and is certainly ready to drink. The 1997 is rather mean, the 1998 light and fluid, but the 1999 is fresh, medium-bodied, and equally ready to drink. Surprisingly, the 2000, tasted twice, has been green and dour and dull, and is easily bettered by the more supple and concentrated 2001. The 2003 is soupy, rather hollow, and lacks persistence. Even the 2005 is rather dull; despite a suave texture, it lacks lift. What all the wines lack is complexity, which is regrettable considering the relatively high prices asked for them.

6. Moulis and Listrac

 These two appellations, of roughly equal size, are really part of the Haut-Médoc but have been promoted to a higher status. They lie to the west of Lamarque. Taking one of the side roads that head west, it is hard to tell when, or indeed whether, you have entered either of them. Moulis is the more southerly; Listrac, centred round the village of that name, the more sprawling. Since they are neighbouring and quite similar in character, it makes sense to consider them together.

It is easy to get lost here, especially once you leave the area's only highway, the N215 that heads north toward St Laurent and passes through the village of Listrac. The country roads are winding, and the woodlands impede the view. There are no classified growths here, but instead there are a number of highly regarded *crus bourgeois*, especially in Moulis. The best soils in both appellations are gravel *croupes*, but the more westerly location away from the Gironde means that both regions are cooler and the grapes ripen later than in St-Julien and Margaux. Therefore both regions, but especially Listrac, can be disappointing in more difficult years. The tendency to increase the proportion of Merlot in the vineyards, apparent throughout the Médoc and Graves, is evident here too, but perhaps with more justification. Overall, the wines have weight and richness at the expense of finesse and perfume.

MOULIS

The smallest Médoc appellation, granted its AC in 1938, Moulis runs in a fairly narrow band for some twelve kilometres (7.5 miles) from southwest to northeast, squeezed between Avensan to the south and Listrac to the north. For the most part, the vineyards lie closer to the estuary than those of Listrac. Consequently the vines ripen a few days earlier than those in Listrac and are slightly less prone to frost.

The finest terroir in Moulis is the Grand-Poujeaux plateau, where the gravel lies deep over a clay-limestone subsoil and where the drainage is excellent. It does not really differ much from the Günzian gravelly soils of St-Julien or Margaux; it is the microclimate that puts Moulis in the shade when compared to those two appellations. Grand-Poujeaux is where the top estates tend to have their vineyards, some in a single block, others more dispersed. The plateau is by no means uniform, as there are varied expositions and thicknesses of gravel; clay, sand, and large stones called *galets* also feature in certain spots, all contributing to the nuances of the wines. In other parts of the appellation the soil is primarily clay-limestone.

There are 635 hectares under vine, forty-three producers turning out about four million bottles between them, and no cooperative. Fourteen *crus bourgeois* own over sixty per cent of the vineyards. Moulis claims to have been an important wine region in late medieval times, although this is hard to verify. Certainly, the presence of a Romanesque church, as at Listrac, proves that the region has been settled for many centuries. In the late nineteenth century there were still 1,500 hectares under vine, about the double of today's surface.

In the early twenty-first century, the INAO was being petitioned to include Arcins and Lamarque within Moulis, thus promoting them from Haut-Médoc, on the grounds that they are essentially eastward extensions of Moulis and framed to the north and south by the same *jalles*, or streams. The incentive for the Moulis growers to embrace their less prestigious neighbours is that many of them own parcels in Lamarque, which are not at present entitled to the AC Moulis. Although the proposals are relatively uncontroversial, the wheels grind slowly, and it is unlikely that any fusion will take place in the immediate future.

There have also been proposals to unite Moulis and Listrac in a single AC, but to this idea there is significant opposition, especially from the Listrac cooperative. Those who favour the proposal tend to be châteaux such as Clarke and Moulin-à-Vent that have vineyards in both ACs.

The wines are robust, though less so than those of Listrac. Those from the best terroirs have considerable richness and structure, and age very well.

Château Anthonic

Tel: 0556 583460. Owner: Cordonnier family. 29 ha. 57% Merlot, 42% Cabernet Sauvignon, 1% Petit Verdot.
Production: 150,000 bottles. Second wines: Ch Le Malinay, Les Aigles d'Anthonic

By origin the Cordonniers were wine merchants in northeast France and Belgium. François Cordonnier bought this property near the village in 1977, and for some years it has been run by his energetic if earnest nephew Jean-Baptiste. Anthonic has existed under various names since it was first planted around 1840. The estate consists of two main parcels. One is an eighteen-hectare block on clay-limestone soil; the remainder is near the Grand-Poujeaux plateau, on a mix of clay-limestone and gravel. Given the composition of the soil, it is not surprising that Anthonic contains a good deal of Merlot – in vintages such as 2002 and 2003, as much as sixty-six per cent. The older parts of the vineyards are planted at a density of 6,700 vines per hectare, but recent plantings are at 10,000.

Only the older vines are picked by hand. Anthonic is equipped with a *sous-vide* concentrator, but the last time it was used was in 2001. The vinification is traditional, sometimes but not systematically with selected yeasts. The wine is aged for eighteen months in one-third new barriques.

Given the enthusiasm and commitment of Jean-Baptiste Cordonnier, I find the wines surprisingly light and forward, and lacking in persistence: 2000 and 2001 are far from arresting despite some pallid charm, but the fresh and bright 2004 is excellent, showing fine concentration and a welcome briskness and length.

Château Biston-Brillette

Tel: 0556 582286. Website: www.chateaubistonbrillette.com. Owner: Michel Barbarin. 25 ha.
50% Cabernet Sauvignon, 50% Merlot. Production: 165,000 bottles. Second wine: Ch Biston

The property takes its name from the M. Biston who established it on the plateau of Brillette. By 1860 there were thirty hectares under vine. There were various owners later in the century, and in 1930 the vineyard was separated from the château and sold separately to a M. Lagarde. By this time there were only five hectares of vines, and by the time Michel Barbarin's father bought the property, there was just a single hectare left, with the rest of the estate devoted to polyculture. Today Biston-Brillette is managed by Michel's sons Serge and Jean-Paul.

Given the virtual disappearance of the vineyards by the time the Barbarins bought the property, the wine estate has been built up more or less from scratch. Forty per cent of the vines are near the winery on clay-limestone soils, forty per cent are on gravel soils, and the remaining twenty per cent on clay, which is ideal for Merlot. Almost all the vines are picked by machine. The wines were vinified, usually with natural yeasts, in cement tanks until 2002, when these were replaced by steel tanks. The wine is aged for twelve months in one-third new oak, and about one-fifth of the barrels are of American and Hungarian origin.

I was distinctly unimpressed by the wines in the 1990s, other than the reasonably fresh 1996. But since 2000 they have had more body and structure. Cherries dominate the aromas, there is ample freshness to balance the firm tannins, and the occasional earthy, savoury tone, as on the 2001 and 2004, is by no means disagreeable. The wines are inexpensive and now offer good value.

Château Branas Grand Poujeaux

Tel: 0556 589330. Website: www.branasgrandpoujeaux.com. Owner: Justin Onclin. 12 ha. 50% Merlot,
45% Cabernet Sauvignon, 5% Petit Verdot. Production: 40,000 bottles. Second wine: Les Eclats de Branas

Justin Onclin runs the Ballande group's wine interests, primarily Château Prieuré-Lichine. This is his personal property, which he bought in 2002 knowing that the vineyards had been well looked after by the previous owner, Jacques de Pourquéry, and that they had great potential. The soil is Günzian gravel, and the average age of the vines just over twenty-five years. The soil is ploughed and the vines green-harvested twice in order to keep yields at a maximum of forty-five hectolitres per hectare. The winemaking team is the same as at Prieuré, and Michel Rolland acted as consultant until 2006, when he was replaced by Stéphane Derenoncourt.

The approach is frankly *garagiste*. The grapes are picked in *cagettes*, sorted repeatedly at the winery, given a prolonged cold soak, and tipped into the vats by gravity and without crushing. Fermentation takes place with *pigeage*, bleeding of one-third of the must, and micro-oxygenation. After a *cuvaison* of up to thirty-five days, the *marc* is pressed in a vertical press. The wine is aged for eighteen months in new barriques with lees-stirring.

I have not tasted Branas from the Pourquéry years, but it had a good reputation. The first Onclin vintage, the 2002, was affected by hail and the crop was very low. The colour is opaque, the nose sweet, fleshy, and oaky, but not without subtlety. It's a wine that is highly concentrated, with powerful tannins and modest acidity, yet not too extracted. The 2003 was similar, though with more raisiny aromas and even more weight on the palate; but it wasn't flabby and has some persistence. The 2004 has oaky, smoky aromas, and its opulence and concentration are balanced by fair acidity, yet the wine remains rather stolid.

Château Brillette

*Tel: 0556 582209. Website: www.chateau-brillette.fr. **Owner**: Jean-Louis Flageul. 40 ha. 48% Merlot, 40% Cabernet Sauvignon, 9% Cabernet Franc, 3% Petit Verdot. **Production**: 180,000 bottles.*

Second wine: Ch Berthault-Brillette

A well-known property in the late nineteenth century, when it belonged to the Comte du Perier de Larsan, Brillette was bought in 1976 by a business tycoon named Raymond Berthault. He hired Emile Peynaud and Bertrand Bouteiller (then at Pichon-Longueville) as consultants. After Berthault died in 1981, the property passed to his widow, and, from 1994, to her son Jean-Louis Flageul. Recently there has been considerable investment in a new *cuvier* and *chai*, and Michel Rolland has been hired as a consultant. Most of the vineyards are planted on gravel soils, the remainder on clay and sand. The average age of the vines is forty years. The vinification is classic and the wine is aged for twelve months in forty per cent new barriques. I have tasted this wine from time to time over two decades, and, with the exception of the excellent 2001, have always found a certain rusticity and dullness.

Château Caroline

*Tel: 0556 580243. Website: www.chateau-fonreaud.com. **Owner**: Chanfreau family. 9 ha. 62% Merlot, 38% Cabernet Sauvignon. **Production**: 50,000 bottles*

The Chanfreaus are better known as the owners of Château Fonréaud (*q.v.*) in Listrac, but they also own this small property in Moulis. The wines are aged for twelve months in one-third new oak. I have not tasted the wine in many years, but the 1995 was opulent, with firm tannins on the finish, while the 1996 was dilute and rather acidic.

Château Chasse-Spleen

*Tel: 0556 580237. Website: www.chasse-spleen.com. **Owner**: Merlaut family. 113 ha. 58% Cabernet Sauvignon, 35% Merlot, 7% Petit Verdot and Cabernet Franc. **Production**: 450,000 bottles.*

Second wine: L'Oratoire de Chasse-Spleen

This long-established estate came into existence after a larger estate was divided in 1822. There were a number of owners in the twentieth century, notably the Lahary family who bought it in 1922; then it was bought by the négociant Jacques Merlaut in 1976. He put his daughter Bernadette in charge of the property, and she ran it until her untimely death in 1992. Under her management the estate, which was fifty hectares when her father bought it, was expanded to ninety hectares. Today Chasse-Spleen is run by Bernadette Villars' daughter Céline and her husband Jean-Pierre Foubet. There was a further expansion of the estate in 2003 when the Merlaut family acquired the twenty-three-hectare Château Gressier-Grand-Poujeaux, which before 1822 was part of the same property. So the acquisition is a belated reunion. Gressier also has exceptionally deep gravel soils which, say the Foubets, are possibly even better than those of either Chasse-Spleen or Poujeaux. The soils of the Chasse-Spleen vineyards are mostly gravel on the Grand-Poujeaux plateau, but there are sectors of clay-limestone where Merlot is planted.

The estate maintains a relatively high proportion of Cabernet Sauvignon, which gives the wine a firm backbone. It is aged for up to eighteen months in forty per cent new barriques. The wine has been splendid for decades, producing a substantial volume of rich, gutsy, well-structured, traditional claret of great consistency and no hint of rusticity. It is clearly of classified growth status, and arguably the finest wine from either Moulis or Listrac.

I was able to taste some older vintages about twenty years ago. The 1958 was tired and fading. The 1961 was still deep in colour, with a rich, slightly farmyardy nose, and a sweet, generous, complex palate. The 1967 was stylish but fairly light, the 1976 open and generous, and fully ready to drink. The 1980 was balanced but unexciting, the 1981 rather tannic and hard. The 1970, tasted in 2001, was a classic wine: still full-bodied, rich, and spicy, with good vigour and length. The 1978 has always been rather austere and charmless, and I prefer the more elegant and balanced 1979. There's no lack of ripeness and plump fruit on the 1982, but it has always lacked some grip and complexity. It's a good wine but not exceptional for the vintage. Bernadette Villars confided that she preferred the 1983 and I agree. It is still drinking well, with an elegant, cedary nose, sweet fruit with a light tannic backbone, and still sustained and balanced by moderate acidity.

The 1984 was well made, but light and forward. The 1985 was rounded and silky yet had some tannic backbone and reasonable length. There's a lot of oak still showing on the 1986, a medium-bodied, stylish, and vigorous wine with good length. The 1989 has strong Cabernet aromas, and the wine is rich and dense, with good depth and length. The 1990 is similar, perhaps a touch oakier, but it's classic Bordeaux; in 2006 it was still intense, silky, fresh, and long. The 1993 is rather dilute and dull. The 1996 is very fine indeed, with mushroomy, cedary aromas, a supple texture, integrated tannins, and impeccable harmony and balance. This should age very well. The 1998 is quite concentrated and robust, at present rather tough but may well blossom with more bottle-age. The emphasis in the 1999 is on freshness and spiciness; it's not a massive wine, but one with style and complexity. The 2000 is complex, with aromas of blackcurrant pastilles and oak, and a robust, tight palate that is also lively and bright. The 2001 is similar, perhaps leaner than the 2000, but more elegant. The 2002 is a triumph, with exuberant blackcurrant and plum aromas; it's a rich, rounded, full-bodied wine of great generosity, yet not lacking in finesse and length. The 2003 is medium-bodied, pleasant enough, but not that complex. I prefer the plump, full-bodied 2004, with its excellent balance and spicy finish. The 2005 has wonderful smoky, leathery aromas, a seamless texture, and tremendous vigour and complexity.

As for Gressier-Grand-Poujeaux, it is a wine I have tasted often but rarely with pleasure. The 1967, 1970, and 1971 were rather hard and neutral, the 1979 coarse and woody, and the 1981 astringent and dry, but the 1994 was far better, with more fruit and body. The new team made a rather shallow wine in 2003, lacking fruit and finesse.

Château Duplessis

*Tel: 0556 582201. Website: www.vignobles-marielaurelurton.com. **Owner:** Marie-Laure Lurton-Roux. 20 ha.*
*62% Merlot, 24% Cabernet Sauvignon, 12% Cabernet Franc, 2% Petit Verdot. **Production:** 80,000 bottles.*
Second wine: La Licorne de Duplessis

This is one of a number of properties owned and run by Marie-Laure Lurton-Roux (*see* Château de Villegorge in Haut-Médoc). It seems that vines were first planted in the mid-nineteenth century by a M. Fabre. Later in the century, after his death, half the property went to his son, who named his share Duplessis-Fabre; the other portion went to his son-in-law Alcide Hauchecorne. Duplessis had various owners thereafter, and in 1983 Lucien Lurton became the major shareholder. He handed over the property to his daughter in 1992.

The soil is clay, sand, and marl, in varying combinations, over fissured limestone. The harvest is manual. Since 2001 the *marc* has been pressed in a gentle vertical press. The wine is aged for up to fourteen months in around twenty-five per cent new oak, with some American barrels in the mix.

The 1995 is ageing well, with a ripe, oaky nose; the wine is medium-bodied, supple, and spicy, with no rusticity. The 1996, 1997, and 2004 are rather nondescript. The 2001 is excellent, with its ripe, oaky nose, a lush palate, and firm, ripe tannins. It's a robust style but it doesn't lack fruit. The 2003 has ripe cherry aromas, a supple texture, and though slightly cooked, remains a pleasant if fairly simple wine.

Château Duplessis-Fabre, run in the 1980s by Patrice Pagès of Château Fourcas-Dupré in Listrac, is now part of the group of estates owned by Philippe Dourthe of Château Maucaillou (*q.v.*), where the wine is vinified. I have not tasted it since the 1980s, when it was a forward, fruity wine.

Château Dutruch Grand-Poujeaux

Tel: 0556 580255. Owner: Cordonnier family. 26 ha. 53% Merlot, 45% Cabernet Sauvignon, 2% Petit Verdot. Production: 170,000 bottles. Second wine: Ch La Bernède Grand-Poujeaux

This is under the same ownership and management as Château Anthonic (*q.v.*). It was bought by François Cordonnier in 1967. At that time there were only eleven hectares under vine, and since then the property has been expanded. A new *chai* was built in 1999.

Almost all the vineyards are planted on the Grand-Poujeaux plateau, with only ten per cent on clay-limestone. So it is surprising that there is so much Merlot planted. Jean-Baptiste Cordonnier explains that this has always been the case at Dutruch, despite the soil structure, and many of the Merlot vines are very old. About half the crop is picked by machine, and the wine is fermented traditionally, then aged up to eighteen months in one-third new barriques. The selection is quite severe, with about one-third declassified.

The 1994 was a success here, a stylish, medium-bodied wine with some delicacy, but the 1995 is rather coarse and extracted. The 1996 is reasonably fruity but far from exceptional. The 2001 is richer than Anthonic with some underlying austerity but seems to have good potential. The 2002 shows ripe cherry aromas, a rounded palate, and reasonable acidity and length. The 2004 has bacony, savoury aromas, and lacks generosity of fruit; austere when young, it may yet improve. Overall, the Dutruch wine is reliable and good, but I can't help thinking it could be better.

Château La Garricq

Tel: 0557 880066. Website: www.chateaupaloumey.com. Owner: Martine Cazeneuve. 3 ha. 50% Cabernet Sauvignon, 30% Merlot, 20% Cabernet Franc. Production: 16,000 bottles

This small property belongs to Martine Cazeneuve, the energetic proprietor of the more important Château Paloumey (*q.v.*) in the Haut-Médoc. These vines are planted on gravel and clay soils. After a traditional vinification, the wine is aged for twelve to fifteen months in one-third new barriques. This is quite a savoury wine, with black-cherry aromas and fruit. It's robust and reasonably concentrated, but as yet lacks a little flair.

Château Granins Grand-Poujeaux

Tel: 0556 580582. Owner: André Batailley. 12 ha. 45% Merlot, 45% Cabernet Sauvignon, 10% Petit Verdot. Production: 65,000 bottles. Second wine: Ch Tour-Granins-Grand-Poujeaux

The property, established by Edouard Batailley under the name Château Peyrodon, was divided in 1983, and this portion was bought by his son André and renamed. In 1993 he leased the portion of the property belonging to his sister, and thus in effect reunited the estate. As the name suggests, most of the vines (two-thirds, to be precise) are located on the Grand-Poujeaux plateau, and the remainder are on clay-limestone. The average age of the vines is about forty years. The wine is aged for twelve to fifteen months in one-third new barriques.

The 2001 is medium-bodied, reasonably concentrated, and has ample fruit and, notwithstanding, a slight rusticity and chewiness. The 2002 has a stylish, oaky nose, and is supple, juicy, fresh, and forward.

Château Malmaison

*Tel: 0556 583800. Website: www.lcf-rothschild.com. **Owner:** Baron Benjamin de Rothschild. 24 ha. 80% Merlot, 20% Cabernet Sauvignon. **Production:** 140,000 bottles. **Second wine:** Les Granges des Domaines Edmond de Rothschild*

This property, just across the line (and the Listrac/Moulis boundary) from Château Clarke, was bought by Edmond de Rothschild in 1973 and entirely replanted. The vineyards are planted on clay-limestone and sandy clay, which accounts for the very high proportion of Merlot. The grapes are picked by hand and machine, and, after a cold soak, fermented in stainless-steel tanks with some micro-oxygenation. The wine is aged for fourteen to eighteen months in up to fifty per cent new barriques. The only vintage I have tasted, the 1996, was light and uninspired, but perhaps that was unrepresentative of the wine being made today.

Château Maucaillou

*Tel: 0556 580123. Website: www.chateau-maucaillou.com. **Owner:** Philippe Dourthe. 68 ha. 55% Cabernet Sauvignon, 36% Merlot, 7% Petit Verdot, 2% Cabernet Franc. **Production:** 650,000 bottles.*

Second wine: Le No 2 de Maucaillou

This important property was developed in the late nineteenth century by the Petit-Laroche family, who built the grandiose château in 1875. The name is a contraction of *mauvais cailloux*, which literally means "poor pebbles", the implication being that the soil was too poor to be cultivated. In 1929 the estate was bought by the Dourthe family of négociants, but by then there were no more than twenty hectares under vine. Today the vineyards are both expanded and dispersed, but there is a sizeable grouping on the Grand-Poujeaux plateau. The average age of the vines is twenty-five years.

Philippe Dourthe has also created that rarity in the Médoc, a tourist complex that includes quite a large museum devoted to wine arts and crafts. Inside the museum is a cycle of paintings about Bordeaux, each of which features a vignette portrait of himself.

The grapes are picked by hand and by machine, and fermented in stainless-steel tanks. The *marc* used to be pressed in pneumatic presses, but, curiously, Maucaillou has reverted to vertical presses since 1999, which is surprising given the size of the property. The wine is aged for at least eighteen months in seventy per cent new oak, a very high proportion for Moulis.

The 1979 and 1981 were unexpectedly delicious wines when tasted many years ago. The 1983, 1989, and 1997 were all rather simple and even dilute. The 1996 by 2007 was very evolved, with leafy, caramel aromas, and little flesh on the palate. The 1999 is riper, with an appealing gaminess on the nose; it has evolved quite fast and acquired some mentholly, meaty flavours that may be atypical. The 2000 has some spice and zest but is lean for the vintage. The 2001 has lovely aromas of plums and new oak, but the wine is very different: overwrought, with mouth-puckering tannins and some heaviness. The 2003 is in a similar style, powerful but lacking in finesse. No such reservations about the succulent 2004, which is accessible, lively, and balanced.

Château Moulin-à-Vent

*Tel: 0556 581579. Website: www.moulin-a-vent.com. **Owner:** Dominique Hessel. 25 ha. 60% Merlot, 38% Cabernet Sauvignon, 2% Cabernet Franc. **Production:** 150,000 bottles. **Second wine:** Ch Moulin de St-Vincent*

This estate has been owned by oenologist Dominique Hessel since 1977. Just over half the vines are planted on Günzian gravel soils, the remainder on clay-limestone. The grapes are picked by machine and, after fermentation, the wine is aged both in tanks and in barriques, of which twenty-five per cent are new. I usually find this wine disappointing, even in fine years such as 1990 and 1995. The 1996 is better, a wine with elegance and vigour. The 1999 is firm and balanced, not complex but sound and enjoyable. The 2002 has an odd nose of boiled sweets; on the palate it is medium-bodied, easy-going, and rather simple. The 2003 is dull and short, and 2004 similar. However, the rich, juicy 2005 demonstrates the potential of this property; the tannins are firm but by no means harsh.

Château La Mouline
Tel: 0556 171317. Website: www.chateaulamouline.com. Owner: Jean-Louis Coubris. 17 ha.
57% Cabernet Sauvignon, 39% Merlot, 3% Cabernet Franc, 1% Petit Verdot. **Production:** *130,000 bottles.*
Second wine: Domaine de Lagorce du Ch La Mouline

This property has been in the hands of the same family for over a century, and is today managed by Cédric Coubris. Over the past two decades the vineyards have been considerably expanded and a stainless-steel *cuvier* installed. Despite the high proportion of Cabernet Sauvignon, most of the vines are planted on clay-limestone. The grapes are picked by machine and manually. The wine is aged for eighteen months in fifty per cent new barriques, the remainder being one year old.

I find the wines unsatisfactory. Many vintages have cooked aromas and flavours, and a chunky texture that doesn't harmonize with the often aggressive acidity.

The Coubris family also produce a Listrac called Château Palais de l'Orque.

Château Poujeaux
Tel: 0556 580296. Website: www.chateaupoujeaux.com. Owner: Theil family. 52 ha.
50% Cabernet Sauvignon, 40% Merlot, 5% Cabernet Franc, 5% Petit Verdot. **Production:** *350,000 bottles.*
Second wine: La Salle de Poujeaux

It would, I am sure, be widely agreed that together with Chasse-Spleen, Poujeaux is Moulis's finest property. Known since the sixteenth century as La Salle de Poujeaux, it belonged to André Castaing in 1806, and was divided into three sections in 1880. One of these sections was bought by François Theil in 1921. Over the following thirty years his son Jean managed to unite the property once again. In 1981 he handed over the estate to his three sons, Philippe, Jean-Pierre, and François. They in turn are now handing over to their nephew Christophe Labanne.

Most of the vineyards are located around the château in a single parcel on the Grand-Poujeaux plateau. The average age of the vines is thirty-five years. The soil is ploughed and the vineyards green-harvested if necessary. The harvest is manual and sorting is done in the vineyard. Fermentation takes place in tanks of various kinds, all temperature-controlled. The *cuvaison* is often prolonged, malolactic fermentation takes place in tanks, and the wine goes into oak in December. Then it is aged for twelve to eighteen months in fifty per cent new oak. It is eggwhite-fined but not filtered.

I find this an extremely reliable wine. It is rich, it is supple in texture, it has weight but no excessive extraction; it has some density but never lacks fruit. It is sensibly priced, and the Theils' reluctance to jack up their prices in outstanding vintages makes their wine an excellent purchase in top years.

Thirty years on, the 1970 was holding up well, a medium-bodied but robust wine in perfect health, with quite good length. Ready now but by no means flagging. Drunk from double magnum in 2006, the 1982 had developed a light leafiness on the nose and had clearly lost a little fruit, yet it was still stylish and long. There was an atypical jamminess on the 1989, and I much preferred the 1990. This has evolved beautifully, and now has a lovely sweet, gamey nose, with leathery tones; it's super-ripe without portiness, it has vigour as well as concentration, and is delicious to drink. Many 1995s are impressive but rugged, but not Poujeaux, which has elegant, oaky aromas, ripeness and power, a sleek texture, impressive weight, and very good length. Equally fine is the 1996, with its sweet if meaty nose of vanilla, cherries, and cedar; after a surly adolescence, the fruit has emerged as juicy and upfront, with ripe tannins and a zesty finish. The 1997 is a bit vegetal, but the 1998 is splendid: a sweet, spicy, elegant nose marked by blackcurranty fruit; while the tannins are robust but ripe, there is ample fruit, no rawness, and a bracing touch of coffee on the finish. I prefer it to the more one-dimensional 1999, which nonetheless is an attractive medium-bodied wine with concentration and good length.

The 2000 is simply packed with fruit and charm, ripe blackcurrants with a hint of chocolate. The wine is rich, fleshy, boldly flavoured, reasonably forward but well balanced and long. The 2001 is similar, but in a lower key, and perhaps with a touch more finesse than the very fruity 2000. The 2002 is now rather closed, but there is some dense oakiness on the nose, while the palate is very tight and concentrated, with delicious fruit and a finely poised structure. The 2003 is light, rather soupy, and hard-edged. The 2004 is aromatically complex, but seems quite forward, though it doesn't lack tannic backbone. Balance is the hallmark of the delicious and elegant 2005, with its suave texture and judicious extraction.

Château Ruat-Petit-Poujeaux

*Tel: 0556 582515. **Owner**: Pierre Goffre-Viaud. 16 ha. 50% Merlot, 35% Cabernet Sauvignon, 15% Cabernet Franc. **Production**: 100,000 bottles*

This has been owned by the Viaud family since 1871. Most of the vineyards are on limestone soil with some sand and gravel, which justifies the dominance of Merlot. The grapes are picked by hand, and the wine is aged in tanks as well as oak for up to fifteen months. I have tasted some top vintages from this château (1989, 1990, 1995, 1996, 2002) and not cared for any of them. At best these are pleasant wines, but they lack concentration and grip and length.

LISTRAC

There have been vineyards at Listrac for centuries, and the names of both Listrac and Fourcas appear on the eighteenth-century Belleyme map. In 1913 there were 1,380 hectares under vine, but many vineyards disappeared during the economic crisis of the 1930s, from which the region has never fully recovered.

The most important properties in this appellation line either side of the D5 both north and south of the village of Listrac itself. However, the vineyards stretch quite a distance to the east, and a rather shorter distance to the west, where ever-sandier soils make them unsuitable for viticulture. Listrac takes pride in rising to the highest point in the Médoc, a majestic forty-three metres (141 feet). One benefit of these mini-peaks is that the slopes tend to have excellent drainage. Roughly half the vineyards are on Garonnais and Pyrenees gravel, not far from Grand-Poujeaux; the remainder are on clay-limestone. Fourcas, in particular, has a good deal of Garonnais gravel. However, these gravel beds are lighter and thinner than those of Margaux and St-Julien.

Unlike Moulis, Listrac has a cooperative, which turns out roughly twenty-five per cent of the appellation's wine. Generalizations are difficult, but it is fair to say that the wines of Listrac, while robust, tend to have less finesse than those from Moulis. Indeed, a Listrac from a poor vintage or a poor producer can be distinctly rustic, probably because the terroir here is less uniform than in Moulis. Some producers report that it is difficult to ripen Cabernet Sauvignon here, and it is not unusual to pick the normally late-picked Petit Verdot before the Cabernet. Spring frost can also be a serious problem on these colder soils. However, the best wines can age very well.

Listrac gained its AC in 1957. There are 670 hectares of vineyards, and eighty-five growers, of whom fifty sell to the cooperative. The annual production averages just over four million bottles.

Château Baudan

*Tel: 0556 580740. **Website**: www.chateaubaudan.com. **Owner**: Alain Blasquez. 6 ha. 55% Cabernet Sauvignon, 42% Merlot, 3% Petit Verdot. **Production**: 25,000 bottles*

Alain Blasquez took over the family property in 1993 and replanted some of the vineyard. He decided from the outset to aim for high quality. The grapes are picked by hand and after fermentation they are aged for twenty months in one-third new oak. Most of his bottles go directly to restaurants, which is where I encountered the excellent, compact, solid 1996. The wines are relatively expensive.

Château Bibian

*Tel: 0556 580728. **Owner:** Alain Meyre. 24 ha. 65% Merlot, 20% Cabernet Sauvignon, 13% Petit Verdot,*
*2% Cabernet Franc. **Production:** 110,000 bottles. **Second wine:** Ch La Fleur-Bibian*

Bibian was founded in 1857 by Pierre Bibian, and it passed down through his descendants. When in 1983 Pierre-Henri Bibian, the mayor of Listrac, died without heirs, the estate was sold to a well-known footballer, Jean Tigana, who in Bordelais fashion appended his name to that of the property. In 1999, however, he in turn sold the property, and the purchaser was Alain Meyre, better known as the owner of Château Cap-Léon-Veyrin (*q.v.*). His daughter Nathalie makes the wine, and Michel Rolland offers his advice.

The parcels are scattered around the village of Listrac, mostly on clay-limestone soils but also on pockets of Pyrenees gravel. Fourteen hectares are planted with vines between forty and seventy years old; the remainder are a respectable twenty years of age. The harvest is both manual and mechanical. The wine is aged for twelve months in one-third new oak.

Bibian is a curious wine. The initial impression is of rich, rounded fruit, but then some rather fierce tannins kick in, and sometimes, as in 2002, there is some greenness. Yet they have a certain liveliness and good length (except in 2003), and I am inclined to give them the benefit of the doubt, especially since the prices are very reasonable. Moreover t

Château Cap-Léon-Veyrin

*Tel: 0556 580728. **Owner:** Alain Meyre. 23 ha. 57% Merlot, 40% Cabernet Sauvignon, 3% Petit Verdot.*
***Production:** 70,000 bottles. **Second wine:** Les Hauts de Veyrin*

Owned by the same family since 1810, this estate is run by Alain Meyre, aided by his son Julien, who looks after the vineyards, and his daughter Nathalie, who trained in Australia and helps to make the wines. Mme. Meyre owns a property in the Haut-Médoc called St-Julien, and in 1999 the Meyres bought the nearby Château Bibian (*q.v.*). Mme. Meyre also runs a bed and breakfast, so the family have plenty to keep them occupied. Their involvement in tourism also gives them an opportunity to sell wines directly, including many older vintages.

The vineyards are in two main blocks, principally on clay-limestone soils. They are ploughed, no herbicides are used, and the vines are green-harvested to control yields. Most of the vineyards are machine-harvested. After a moderate cold soak, fermentation takes place in stainless-steel tanks with both natural and cultivated yeasts. In 2004 the Meyres invested in micro-oxygenation apparatus. The wine is aged for twelve months in twenty-five per cent new oak.

The oldest vintage I have tasted, the 1996, was tannic and extracted, but in the 2000s a lighter touch has been applied. These are fairly aromatic wines, with scents of redcurrants and cherries; they are medium-bodied, quite lush, with tannins that vary from light to robust, and they have good length. They can be drunk young, but clearly have the potential to age in the medium term. The 2000 and 2004 are particularly good, and excellent value. There are smoky, plummy aromas on the 2003, which is richly fruity, indeed somewhat overripe, yet has a bizarre astringency on the finish.

Château Clarke

Tel: 0556 583800. Website: www.lcf-rothschild.com. Owner: Baron Benjamin de Rothschild. 53 ha. 70% Merlot, 30% Cabernet Sauvignon. Production: 300,000 bottles. Second wine: Les Granges des Domaines Edmond de Rothschild

Apparently, vines were cultivated here, among the woodlands of Listrac, in the twelfth century by the monks of Vertheuil. The property takes its present name from Irishman Toby Clarke who bought it in 1771. In 1820 it came into the possession of the St-Guirons family, who retained it until 1955, when it was sold and fell into neglect. It was bought in 1973 by Baron Edmond de Rothschild – a brave venture, as the entire property needed to be replanted, and the winery buildings all needed renovation or new construction. He also hired Emile Peynaud as a consultant. It would not be until 1978 that a first vintage was released. In 1997 Baron Edmond died, and the property is now run by his widow Nadine and their son Benjamin. Yann Buchwalter has been the technical director for many years, and Pascal Philippe looks after the vineyards not only of Clarke but of the neighbouring properties (Malmaison and Peyre-Labade) belonging to the family. Michel Rolland was taken on as a consultant in 1999.

It has proved a difficult property to manage. The Rothschilds may, after years of costly investment, have realized why the property had been abandoned. They commissioned a soil analysis, which studied 140 separate plots. New drainage had to be installed. The realization that Cabernet Sauvignon planted on SO4 rootstock was almost impossible to ripen required those vines to be removed and replaced by Merlot. In the early 1980s there had been about forty-five per cent Merlot and forty-two per cent Cabernet. Today the *encépagement* is very different, with Merlot in the clear majority. That is probably appropriate for these cold soils. Thus the investment made at Clarke (and the associated estates) has been colossal, and Baron Edmond must sometimes have wondered whether it would prove worthwhile.

The vineyards are a single block. The density is only 6,600 vines per hectare, as the vineyards were set up for mechanical harvesting. The soils have a good deal of clay, and Pascal Philippe compares them to those of St-Emilion.

Dramatic changes were made after Michel Rolland was hired. He made the switch from mechanical to manual harvesting. He had more Merlot planted and proposed the construction of a second-year *chai* so the wines could be aged for longer in barrel. The grapes are sorted before and after destemming, and lowered by gravity into the tanks. There they are cold-soaked under dry ice for about five days. In 2001 some wooden vats were purchased to add to the stainless-steel tanks. Fermentation takes place with natural yeasts. The wooden vats are equipped with mechanical *pigeage* and micro-oxygenation. Before 1998 hardly any of the wine went through malolactic fermentation in barriques; now all of it does so, in new oak. Before 1999 the wine was aged in wood for twelve months; now it is more likely to be sixteen or eighteen months. The proportion of new oak has been raised to eighty per cent, and there is less racking than in the past, but sometimes the barrels are micro-oyxgenated. Fining and filtration are not systematic.

Clearly, the style of the winemaking has changed beyond recognition over recent years. Is the wine better as a result? Rolland has undoubtedly brought more ripeness, oakiness, concentration, and extraction to the wine. It is lusher and more hedonistic than in the past, when it could be tough, even rustic. Conservatives may bemoan a lack of typicity, and it is true that the wine is now more international in style. It is also, in my view, more enjoyable. And it is by no means evident that the terroir of Clarke is so outstanding that it needs to be expressed at all costs.

In the 1990s there was another innovation: the production of a little white wine, Le Merle Blanc de Clarke, from Sauvignon Blanc and Sémillon, aged in thirty-five per cent new oak. The 2006 has light lime aromas, decent fruit and acidity, but it lacks some verve overall. There is also a rosé made from *saignée* juice, mostly Cabernet Franc.

In the 1980s Clarke was not a bad wine so much as an inconsistent wine. The 1981 was very perfumed; it had good fruit but the tannins were undoubtedly austere. Whether it ever came round I do not know. On the other hand, the 1985 was a delicious wine, quite oaky, fleshy, spicy, and balanced. There were stewed, liquorice aromas on the 1986, which tasted rather thick and chunky, but had some spiciness and even some finesse. The 1988 was rather dour, but the 1989 was sumptuous, oak-scented, with a firm tannic backbone and good length. The 1990 was plump, concentrated, and lively, but perhaps not as complex as the 1989. Two attempts to persuade me that the 1994 from magnum was irresistible failed. This was not an exciting wine. The 1995 was quite extracted, with dense, brambly fruit and a slight coarseness. The 1996 was light and lacking in complexity, and the 1997 forgettable. Rich aromas of blackcurrant and cherry marked the 1998; there was sweet fruit on the surface of the wine, but beneath there were some formidable tannins. The 2001 is perhaps too much of a good thing, with a lot of sweetness and oak on the nose; the wine is lush and spicy, a big, rich style with ample tannin. There are jammy aromas on the 2002, which is very ripe and fleshy, but excessively oaky in an assertive way, and with a long, chewy, peppery finish. The cool soils of Clarke proved an advantage in torrid 2003, and the wine shows richness, spice, and concentration, and although there is no elegance, it has decent length. The 2004 is dense but rather soupy and heavy-handed. The Clarke wines have certainly changed, but nowadays no one could complain about a lack of fruit.

Clos des Demoiselles

Tel: 0556 580243. Owner: Chanfreau family. 2.4 ha. 62% Merlot, 38% Cabernet Sauvignon. Production: 15,000 bottles
This tiny property, situated on a gravelly slope between Fonréaud and Lestage (*qq.v*) (both owned by the Chanfreaus), was bought in 2002, and this was also the first vintage. The must is fermented after a cold soak and aged in forty per cent new barriques. The 2002 had a rich, sweet, oaky nose, and the wine is certainly ripe and concentrated, with robust tannins balancing the rich, black-cherry fruit. The 2003 is more austere, but has some spice and zest on the finish. There are plum-compote aromas on the 2005, which is ripe and succulent, but marred by a rather dry finish.

Château Ducluzeau

Tel: 0556 731673. Owner: Mme. Jean-Eugène Borie. 5 ha. 90% Merlot, 10% Cabernet Sauvignon.
Production: 30,000 bottles
This small property belongs to the widow of Jean-Eugène Borie of Ducru-Beaucaillou. Until 1976 the crop was dispatched to the Listrac cooperative. The vines are planted on gravel soils to a high density and their average age is forty years. Merlot certainly seems to dominate this plush wine, with its moderate concentration and tannic structure. It always seems well balanced if not profound. I have enjoyed the 1989, 1990, and 1996, but have not tasted more recent vintages.

Château L'Ermitage

Tel: 0556 580225. Owner: Christian Thomas. 10 ha. 49% Merlot, 48% Cabernet Sauvignon,
3% Petit Verdot. Production: 70,000 bottles
When Roger Thomas bought this property in 1954, there were a mere three hectares under vine. It has been gradually expanded, and the vines are mostly planted on clay-limestone soils. They are picked by machine and also manually. The wine is aged for twelve to fifteen months in twenty-five per cent new barriques. The 1996 was a full-bodied wine, with blackberry-jam aromas, robust tannins, and hints of over-extraction, but overall it had a lot of density and personality. The 2000 and 2001 are much lighter and rather drab, while the 2002 is austere and rather green. Listrac's cold soils helped in 2003 to deliver a rich, solid wine with little charm but ample fruit.

Château Fonréaud

*Tel: 0556 580243. Website: www.chateau-fonreaud.com. **Owner:** Chanfreau family. 34 ha 32 ha.*
red: 55% Cabernet Sauvignon, 42% Merlot, 3% Petit Verdot. 2 ha white: 65% Sauvignon Blanc, 20% Sémillon,
*15% Muscadelle. **Production:** 220,000 bottles. **Second wine:** La Tourelle de Ch Fonréaud*

Fonréaud was bought in 1962 by Jean Chanfreau's grandfather on his return from North Africa; he also bought Château Lestage (*q.v.*). The flamboyant château is easily visible from the main road, and it was built in 1859 by the then-owner, Henri de Mauvezin. Fonréaud's distinction is that its vineyards reach the highest point in Listrac. The average age of the vines is thirty years, on soil that is essentially gravel over a limestone subsoil. The harvest is both mechanical and manual. A cold soak precedes the fermentation in cement tanks. The wine is aged for at least twelve months in one-third new oak, mostly Allier, but also in some American barrels.

In 1989 two hectares were planted with white grapes, which are used to produce Le Cygne de Château Fonréaud. It is aged in fifty per cent new oak with lees-stirring. The first vintage was 1992.

Le Cygne is one of the most successful of the new breed of Médoc whites. The 1996 was crisp and lemony; the 1998 was very aromatic, with a silky texture, a good deal of oak, and a slight lack of zest. The 2001 was very different, with ripe, melony aromas and flavours and moderate length. The more citric 2005 is delicious, ripe and intense, and long.

Fonréaud has some fine vineyards, so the wine ought to be excellent, but it rarely seems to rise to any great heights. The 1988, tasted recently, was a touch thin, and lacked concentration, weight, and length. The 1989 has a sweet, leafy, delicate nose; the wine is medium-bodied, a bit chunky, but with fair acidity and length. The 1995 was more solid, but there was ample fruit alongside the burly tannins. The 1996 was more vigorous, with dense blackberry aromas, a supple texture, and reasonable concentration and acidity. Excessive austerity and a tough texture marred the 1999. Although fairly light, the 2000 is ripe and supple and has an atypical charm. The 2002 is medium-bodied, but rather slack despite firm tannins and some astringency. At present the 2003 is dense and hard, and offers little pleasure. I prefer the robust and spicy 2004, with its ample fruit and length. The 2005 is unusually full-bodied and sumptuous.

Château Fourcas-Dumont

*Tel: 0556 580384. Website: www.chateau-fourcas-dumont.com. **Owner:** Jean-Jacques Lescoutra and Alain Miquau.*
*30 ha. 55% Merlot, 35% Cabernet Sauvignon, 10% Petit Verdot. **Production:** 200,000 bottles*

Until 1992 the crop from here was sold to the cooperative. The vineyards are cultivated following the Cousinié method, as at Château Lamarque (*see* Chapter Two). The young vines are picked by machine, but the juice is used only for the second wine. The main wine is aged in one-third new Allier oak for twelve months. I rather like Fourcas-Dumont, though it is far from exceptional. The 1995 was slightly hollow, even rustic, but the 1997 was succulent and fresh and a success for the vintage. The 1998 is robust and tannic, but there is no lack of fruit. Earthy aromas mark the 2000, and its supple fruitiness is at war with some very fierce tannins.

The owners also make a wine from another property integrated into the vineyards, Château Moulin de Bourg. Recent vintages have been fairly rich but rustic, and in some cases astringent.

Château Fourcas-Dupré

*Tel: 0556 580107. **Website:** www.chateaufourcasdupre.com. **Owner:** Patrice Pagès. 47 ha. 44% Merlot, 44% Cabernet Sauvignon, 10% Cabernet Franc, 2% Petit Verdot. **Production:** 280,000 bottles.*

Second wine: Ch Bellevue-Laffont

This important property used to be known as Cru Roullet, until in 1843 it was bought and renamed by Jean-Baptiste Dupré. He renovated the estate, also acquired what is now Château Saransot-Dupré, and died in the 1870s. The next owner was Yves Raymond. After phylloxera wrecked the vineyards, Raymond's widow sold Fourcas-Dupré as she preferred to live at Saransot, which was closer to the village. In 1967 the property was bought by Paul and Michel Delon, who began restoring the property and planting more vines. In 1970 the Delons decided to sell off some of their properties and offered Fourcas to their friend Guy Pagès, who had recently returned from North Africa. At that time there were thirteen hectares under vine, and Pagès revived the property, with advice from Emile Peynaud. In 1985 Patrice Pagès inherited the estate.

The vineyards lie on a *croupe* just north of the winery that rises to a height of forty-two metres (138 feet), over a clay subsoil. The lower parts of the *croupe* have more clay, and on the edge there is sand too. The average age of the vines is twenty-five years, and the vineyards are mostly machine-harvested. After a four-day cold soak, the must is fermented with selected yeasts. The wine used to be aged in twenty-five per cent new oak, but since 1997 the proportion has been increased to thirty-three per cent.

Pagès, who is welcoming, enthusiastic, and informative, admits that in the past this wine could be tough, especially when young. He has for some time been working to give the wine a more rounded, accessible profile. Since 2000 he has introduced some lees-stirring, though only in the new barrels, and these wines are not racked during that five-month period.

The 1975 was a good mouthful of wine despite some rather tough tannins. There was some uncomfortable austerity on the 1978 when young, but after fifteen years it had become more mellow on the nose, and turned into a rounded, reasonably concentrated wine, of no great stylishness but attractive fruit. The 1983 was fairly simple, but the 1985 aged well, a plump, spicy wine with some coffee tones. The 1986, tasted recently, had some attractive gamey aromas, but hadn't shed its youthful rusticity and thick tannins. The 1989 was supple and forward when young, but I have not tasted it in many years. There are sweet plum and blackcurrant aromas on the 1995, a mouth-filling wine with ample fruit and moderate length. The 1996 is much lighter, but it's bright, juicy, and accessible. The 1997 is pretty, with cherry aromas, an almost creamy texture, and light acidity; it's ready to drink. The 1998 has a slightly stewed character on the nose, and some hollowness on the mid-palate, resulting in a sound but unexciting wine. There are also some odd aromas on the 1999 – touches of rubber and that same stewed tone as the 1998 – but the palate is much fresher and the wine is holding up well. The 2000 is much better, though it's no heavyweight; it is a sleek, medium-bodied wine with reasonable concentration, moderate tannins, and quite good length. The 2001 is fresh and brisk but rather light; the 2002 has more sweet fruit but at present is not very expressive. The 2003 is fleshy and forward, but lacks stuffing and lift. The 2004 shows far more vigour and grip, and some fresh acidity on the finish. The 2005 is similar but has more charm, stylishness, and persistance.

Fourcas-Dupré is not a wine that rises to great heights, and there are vintages that seem too light, even dilute. At its best, it is a fruity, traditional claret with no lack of tannic backbone, and in good vintages it ages well. It is also reasonably priced.

Château Fourcas-Hosten

Tel: 0556 580115. Website: www.chateaufourcashosten.com. Owners: Laurent and Rénaud Momméja.
47 ha. 45% Merlot, 45% Cabernet Sauvignon, 10% Cabernet Franc. Production: 260,000 bottles.
Second wine: Les Cèdres d'Hosten

Until 1810 this estate was the property of M. Hosten, who then sold it to the St-Affrique family, who also owned Château Gressier Grand-Poujeaux in Moulis. They retained the property through numerous generations until its sale in 1971 to Peter Sichel – from a different branch of the family that owns Château d'Angludet and part of Château Palmer. Sichel lived in New York, and adapted the modest but charming chartreuse of Fourcas-Hosten, facing the Romanesque apse of Listrac's church, into a prettily decorated country house for family use. He entrusted the management and winemaking to his affable neighbour Patrice Pagès of Fourcas-Dupré, until in 2006 he sold the property to members of the Hermès company.

The two properties are of similar dimensions but the soil is different. The nineteen-hectare block behind the château is planted mostly with Merlot, as the soil is clay-limestone. A large block lies across the road from Fourcas-Dupré on a gravel *croupe*. The viticulture, harvesting, and vinification were similar to Fourcas-Dupré's.

It is odd that two neighbouring properties, with the same winemaker, can produce such different styles of wine. Hosten is more old-fashioned but ages extremely well. Pagès attributes this difference to the high proportion grown on clay-limestone, which is not present to nearly the same degree at Fourcas-Dupré.

In 1986, the 1970 had good depth of flavour but an astringent finish. In 2004, the 1971 had a rich, dense, meaty nose, but the wine was rather stringy, with some woody tones, high acidity, and a dry, minty finish – but it was by no means clapped out. The 1978 was charmless when young. Meaty, leathery tones mark the nose of the 1981, which still has sweet fruit, a lively, savoury character, and unusual elegance. The 1982 had earthy aromas, but was plump and silky on the palate, with supple tannins, and by 1990 seemed just about ready. By 2007 the 1989 had lush, truffley aromas, while the palate was sweet, charming, and delicate. The 1995 had dense blackberry aromas, but the wine is tannic and rather fierce, with little elegance. The 1996 is dour and seems to lack fruit. The 1998, though reserved on the nose, is full-bodied and concentrated, with good acidity and considerable complexity. There are already some baked, leathery aromas on the 1999, which is reasonably rich, quite forward, and has modest length. The 2000 is richer, but has a tannic backbone and quite good acidity and length. It should age well. The 2002 has a dense black-cherry nose; it's a medium-bodied wine, but has some succulence and power, and quite good length. The 2003 has some richness, but the tannins are dour and the finish bitter. The 2004 is supple and forward, and despite a firm tannic structure it lacks a little vigour and personality. The 2005 is initially supple, but becomes grainy on the mid-palate and then fades on the finish.

Château Fourcas-Loubaney

Tel: 0556 580383. Owner: François Marret. 48 ha. 60% Merlot, 35% Cabernet Sauvignon, 5% Petit Verdot.
Production: 190,000 bottles. Second wine: La Closerie de Fourcas-Loubaney

Before 1999 this estate was owned by an insurance company, which sold it to François Marret, the former head of a large Champagne group. Since 2000 the wines have been made by the personable Dutchwoman Marianne Lubberhuizen, whose features have, for good reason, been borrowed for some Bordeaux promotional posters. Denis Dubourdieu acts as the consultant oenologist.

Other wines are produced by the same team from vineyards that seem to have been integrated to some extent with those of Fourcas-Loubaney. These include the *cru bourgeois* Château Moulin de Laborde, where all the wines are vinified. Another label is Château La Bécade.

The vineyards are dispersed, but are mostly on gravel soils over clay-limestone. The grapes for Fourcas-Loubaney are picked by machine and the vinification is traditional. The wine is aged for at least twelve months in fifty per cent new oak. The process is similar for Moulin de Laborde, but the tanks are larger, and the wine can include some declassified lots of Loubaney. Lubberhuizen is aiming to produce a wine that is rounder and more forward than in the past.

The 1995 was svelte but tannic, a good wine with firm acidity and a certain solidity. The 1996 is similar, but a touch more elegant. There is far more aromatic complexity on the 2000, which has dense plum and liquorice aromas; it's a supple but concentrated wine with black-fruit flavours, some depth, and ample potential. It seems a very successful representative of the robust Listrac style. The 2001 has black cherries and spice on the nose, and plenty of grip and concentration on the palate, which has plump fruit, no excessive extraction, and quite good length. The 2002 is similar, more overtly oaky, but relatively closed. The 2003 is more chocolatey and dense, but there are no harsh tannins; it does, however, lack some length.

Château Lafon

Tel: 0556 580109. Owner: Jean-Pierre Théron. 15 ha. 55% Cabernet Sauvignon, 45% Merlot.
Production: 100,000 bottles. Second wine: Ch Les Hauts Marcieux

Théron is better known as the owner of Château de Portets (*q.v.*) in the Graves. He bought this estate in 1969, expanded it in 1973, and it is now run by his children. It lost its *cru bourgeois* status in 2003.

The soil is mostly gravel over a clay subsoil, but there is also a five-hectare parcel on more sandy soil. The grapes are picked by machine and by hand, and, after a traditional vinification, the wine is aged for twelve months, two-thirds in barrels, one-third in tanks. The only vintage I have tasted was the 2000, which had a cooked-fruit nose, but tasted of ripe cherries, had firm tannins and some power, and quite high acidity.

Château Lestage

Tel: 0556 580243. Website: www.chateau-fonreaud.com. Owner: Chanfreau family. 42 ha. 52% Merlot,
44% Cabernet Sauvignon, 2% Petit Verdot, 2% Cabernet Franc. Production: 250,000 bottles.
Second wine: La Dame de Coeur de Ch Lestage

Lestage is under the same ownership and management as Château Fonréaud (*q.v.*), and the vinification is similar. The vines are planted on exemplary gravel soils over a band of limestone. The wines, which used to be unoaked, have often struck me as dour and lacking in fruit. There was little to enjoy in the 1981 and 1982. The 1996 had a fine nose of blackcurrant and black cherry, with a touch of oak; the palate was lush, dense, rugged, and chocolatey, and the tannins were so firm that it was reasonable to wonder whether the wine would ever harmonize. The 2001 was significantly better, with a more toasty and elegant nose, ample lush fruit and stuffing, and no trace of rusticity. The 2002 has a similar aromatic sweetness, but this time, despite a supple attack, the tannic grip reasserts itself on the finish, which lacks charm. The 2003 is dilute and short. There's plenty of upfront fruit on the sturdy 2004, one of the best Lestage wines of recent years. The 2005 has aromas of plums and tobacco, and the tannins are kept in check, making this a very successful vintage here.

Château Liouner

Tel: 0556 580562. Owner: Pascal Bosq. 26 ha. 50% Cabernet Sauvignon, 41% Merlot, 9% Petit Verdot.
Production: 160,000 bottles. Second wine: Ch Cantegric

This used to be known as Château Renouil, until the Bosq family bought it in the 1920s and changed the name by rearranging the letters. Seventy per cent of the vines are planted on a gravel *croupe* near Fonréaud, the remainder on clay-limestone. The grapes are picked by machine. The wine is aged for twelve months in thirty per cent new barriques. The 2001 and 2002 were attractive wines, medium-bodied, fresh, with attractive fruit and light acidity, designed for medium-term drinking.

Château Mayne-Lalande

Tel: 0556 582763. Owner: Bernard Lartigue. 15 ha. 45% Cabernet Sauvignon, 45% Merlot, 5% Cabernet Franc, 5% Petit Verdot. Production: 110,000 bottles. Second wine: Ch Malbec-Lartigue

When Bernard Lartigue was young, his family practised polyculture and had just a single hectare of vines. He took over in 1975 and decided to focus exclusively on viticulture. At first he sold his crop to the cooperative, then began vinifying his wines from 1982. He keeps yields down to forty-five hl/ha for the *grand vin*. He picks as late as possible, but doesn't want overripe fruit. The grapes are picked in *cagettes* and sorted at the winery. The fermentation is classic except that in top years there is some *pigeage* as well as pumpovers. The wine is aged for twelve to sixteen months in one-third new oak, without racking or filtration. In outstanding years Lartigue produces a Grande Réserve called Cuvée Alice Jeanne, which is aged for around thirty-six months in new oak.

This has been a very good wine for some years. The 1989, when young, was plump and meaty, not exactly elegant, but with ripe tannins and good length. The 1995 tasted a touch overripe, while the 1996 went in the opposite direction and seemed austere and charmless. The 1997 was a little too extracted for this modest vintage. Far better is the 2001, with its plummy aromas, its excellent fruit, its robust but not tough tannins, and its persistent flavours. The 2002 was similar in aroma, with a touch more toastiness, while the palate has lush black-cherry fruit and firm tannins on the finish. Oak marks the adolescent 2004, which is weighty yet balanced, and has excellent length. The 2005 is the most complete Mayne-Lalande I have tasted.

Mayne-Lalande can't avoid, nor should it, the intrinsic chunkiness of Listrac, but it doesn't lack fruit and structure, and has enough acidity to give it persistence and vigour. Lartigue achieves this consistently high quality by ruthlessly declassifying up to half the crop in most vintages. He also produces, from five hectares of vines, a Moulis called Château Myon de l'Enclos.

Château Saransot-Dupré

Tel: 0556 580302. Website: www.saransot-dupre.com. Owner: Yves Raymond. 17 ha. 15 ha red: 58% Merlot, 21% Cabernet Sauvignon, 16% Cabernet Franc, 3% Petit Verdot, 2% Carmenère. 2 ha white: 60% Sémillon, 30% Sauvignon Blanc, 10% Muscadelle. Production: 120,000 bottles. Second wine: Ch Pérac

This property has been in the Raymond family since 1756. Most of the vines are on clay-limestone, with about one-fifth on gravel. In 1983 almost the entire vineyard was replanted. The harvest is both mechanical and manual. The wine is aged for eighteen months in thirty per cent new barriques. Like Château Fonréaud, Saransot-Dupré produces a modest quantity of white wine, from fairly old vines; eighty per cent is aged in barriques.

The 1989 was a fruity, easy-going wine, with little concentration but ample fruit. The 2001 has muted aromas, but it is ripe and concentrated, with sweet fruit balanced by robust tannins. There is some greenness on the nose of the 2002, and the palate too reflects some lack of ripeness, and is less accessible and more earthy than the 2001. The 2003 has baked aromas, and lacks acidity and vigour. The 2004, with its smoky, bacony aromas and assertive but not rustic tannins, is the estate's best wine in years. I prefer it to the easygoing and undemanding 2005..

Château Sémeillan-Mazeau

Tel: 0556 580112. Website: www.vignoble-jander.com. Owner: Jander family. 8 ha. 50% Cabernet Sauvignon, 50% Merlot. Production: 50,000 bottles

This has its origins in an ancient estate known as Château Sémeillan. In 1925 the owner, M. Hosten, died and the property was divided between his three daughters. The gravelly soils rest on a subsoil of clay-limestone, and the grapes are picked by hand. One-third of the wine is aged in tanks, the remainder in one-third new barriques for eight months. The only vintage I have tasted is the 2000, which has a slightly cheesy nose; it's medium-bodied, easy-going, and forward, with pleasant cherry fruit.

7. Margaux Part I

Despite the proliferation of properties, the châteaux of Margaux are surprisingly invisible. Driving through the region, you will be suitably impressed as you pass the nineteenth-century grandeur of Château Palmer, and you will glimpse on your left Prieuré-Lichine. Within the village of Margaux are the relatively modest mansions of Malescot-St-Exupéry and Ferrière, and that's about it. The two Labégorce châteaux and the two Rauzan complexes are set back from the main road, and the splendours of Château Margaux itself are hidden. As are the moated château of Issan, the boarding-school pomposity of Cantenac-Brown, the complex of buildings at Giscours or Lascombes. You will never find Brane-Cantenac, Tertre, or Angludet without directions.

Pauillac may be home to more First Growths than any other commune, but Margaux can boast that about one-third of all the classified growths, twenty-one of them, are within its boundaries. Margaux is quite a large area, about eight kilometres (five miles) from one end to the other and spread across a number of villages, with some 1,410 hectares of vineyards. In addition to the classified growths, there are twenty-one *crus bourgeois*. The average production amounts to some eight million bottles per year. The vineyards are divided among the following communes: Margaux (414 hectares), Soussans (219), Cantenac (520), Labarde (85), and Arsac (314).

THE CRUCIAL GRAVEL

The soils in Margaux are poorer than in the more northerly Pauillac and St-Estèphe, with more white gravel and sand and less clay. It is the soil – Quaternary-era gravel and stone deposits over Tertiary-era limestone – as much as the microclimate that enables the grapes to ripen between three and five days earlier than in Pauillac, which particularly benefits the late-ripening Cabernet Sauvignon. The Margaux soils tend not to be very deep, which is one reason why they warm up fast. Where there is a deep bed of gravel, the soil is ideal for Cabernet or Petit Verdot; but there are bands of clay and heavier soils where Merlot is favoured. Dominique Befve of Château Lascombes estimates the clay content in Pauillac at roughly five to six per cent, whereas in Margaux it is three to four per cent. Thus clay, and indeed limestone, are part of the Margaux terroir, even if less trumpeted than the fine gravelly soils. The disadvantage of the thin soils at Margaux is that they are easily susceptible to drought stress. That, in the view of Claire Villars of Ferrière, is why very hot years such as 1982 and 1990 did not deliver wines quite as spectacular as elsewhere in the eastern Médoc, and why 1983 and 1989 tended to be better than elsewhere.

Drainage can be a problem in Margaux, which is low-lying, at least compared to the alpine slopes of Pauillac or St-Estèphe. (The highest point, the peak of Margaux, is about thirty metres/ninety-eight feet, at Angludet.) The Syndicat has commissioned advice from a geologist in order to help out properties that can suffer from this predicament. The reason why drainage is an issue is, once again, the presence of clay. This clay appears in certain spots in thick bands dense enough to block the downward trajectory of vine root systems. What happens is that in wet weather the rain and moisture collect in pools over the clay bands, with the undesirable consequence that the roots can be swamped. Hence the importance of effective drainage. But, says John Kolasa at Rauzan-Ségla, parcels of vines are defined by roads and railway lines in Margaux, and they obstruct the passage of drainage channels, compounding the problem. Nonetheless, Kolasa found the drainage so poor when he took over running the property in the mid-1990s that he installed fourteen kilometres (nine miles) of new channels. Some châteaux, such as Kirwan, have also employed a tractor to cut through the clay band to a depth of sixty centimetres (two feet), so as to make space for the roots to continue their descent.

It is often thought that the gravel soils of Margaux are deep, but this is not so throughout the region. Paul Pontallier of Château Margaux notes:

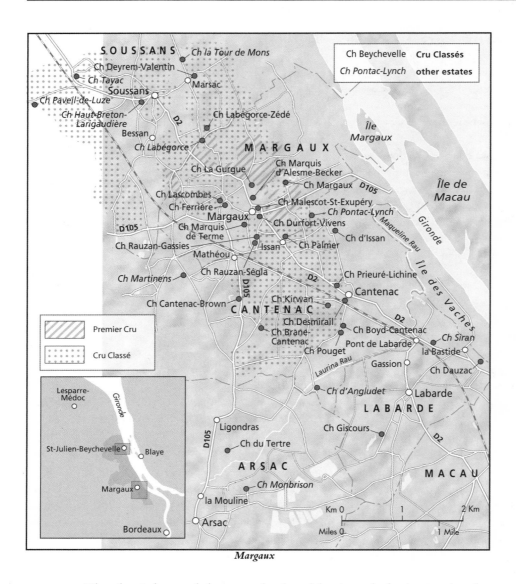

Margaux

Where there is deep gravel, the roots need to descend deep in search of moisture, as the soils are naturally well drained. But there is an element of clay in all gravel soils, and these ensure the roots will be able to find moisture, though maybe at six metres (nineteen feet) below the surface. However, there are sectors, and we have some in our vineyards too, where the soil is no more than a metre (three feet) deep, with limestone below. In those sectors the roots can't descend far, but they are nourished by the water absorbed by the limestone.

The soils are probably more diverse than in any other sub-region of the Médoc. Not only are there the bands of clay mentioned above, but there are also layers of limestone in some areas. The gravel itself, the defining soil type of Margaux, is also varied, with quartz pebbles in some spots, and infusions of sand in others. The commune of Cantenac may have the poorest soils of Margaux, giving wines with the greatest degree of finesse, while the commune of Margaux itself, having somewhat richer soils, often delivers more robust and structured wines that show great elegance in time. Farther south in Labarde the soils have more sand, yet the wines frequently exhibit more power. Soussans, in the north, is varied, as is Arsac.

Proximity to the estuary is, as elsewhere, a crucial factor since it encourages early ripening. It should not always be assumed that vineyards necessarily lie close to the château. Almost all properties, Château Margaux included, have parcels in various parts of the region, making generalizations about communes and their typicity rather unreliable.

Gonzague Lurton, president of the Margaux Syndicat, says the common perception that the wines of Margaux are "lighter" than those of the other communes is misleading. In his view, the wines have finesse but that does not mean they lack density; they are less powerful than some Médoc wines, but that does not make them lighter or less long-lived. Patrick Bongard of Prieuré-Lichine argues:

> *Margaux is such a large appellation that it is possible for many châteaux to make many different styles of wines here, which would not be the case in Pauillac. So perhaps this notion of Margaux as a "feminine" wine is misplaced.*

The boundaries of Margaux are in a state of flux. In the early 1990s Château d'Arsac, previously classified as Haut-Médoc, successfully petitioned to have some of its vineyards reclassified as AC Margaux. The Syndicat refused to consider the application, so Arsac took it to a higher authority, the Conseil d'Etat, which ruled in its favour in 1993. One consequence of this decision was to throw open for reconsideration the existing criteria and boundaries of the appellation. Since 1998 the INAO has been taking a fresh look at the delimitation of the area. When the institute finally issues its reports, they could prove contentious, since it is likely that some other Haut-Médoc parcels will be upgraded, and, more worryingly for existing Margaux proprietors, some parcels now legally accepted as Margaux could be downgraded to Haut-Médoc. That will no doubt lead to legal challenges.

"The difficulty", says Lurton, "is that there is no objective way to prove that one parcel has a terroir superior to its neighbours. The more you work at it, the less you understand."

Most observers of fine Bordeaux would agree that the growers of Margaux have made enormous progress in recent years. For historic reasons, which will be outlined further in the sections on individual châteaux, many classified growths underperformed from the 1960s to the late 1980s. Of the great regions of the Médoc, Margaux was almost always the most disappointing. Yes, properties such as Palmer and Margaux frequently made great wines, and there were *crus bourgeois* such as Angludet, Siran, and Labégorce-Zédé that were very reliable and often superior to many a classified growth – but these were the exceptions.

Nathalie Schÿler of Château Kirwan recalls:

> *Twenty years ago, yields were too high and all estates picked at one go. Here at Kirwan the harvest began when the train with our pickers arrived from Spain, and it was completed as fast as possible for financial reasons. So it's not surprising that many Margaux wines were harsh, vegetal, and acidic. Today, of course, it's entirely different. When he was president of the Syndicat, my father also introduced tastings among all the growers of Margaux to assess the new vintage. This was followed by a convivial dinner just in case anyone's feelings had been bruised by a poor result.*

These tastings have been perpetuated under Gonzague Lurton, who also instituted regular meetings and tastings among the classified growths, which soon made some of them realize that they were making wines clearly inferior to a number of *crus bourgeois*.

The year of 1992 was significant. It was then that the patriarchal Lucien Lurton, the owner of many properties, most of them in Margaux, decided to retire and hand over one estate or more to each of his many children. Almost overnight, a new generation – Denis at Desmirail, Henri at Brane-Cantenac, Gonzague at Durfort-Vivens, Marie-Laure at Tour de Bessan – was in place. They were aware that although their father's wines were often very good, they had the potential to be considerably better. They called a halt to machine-harvesting, lowered yields, and instituted other changes that would within a few years lead to a perceptible rise in quality. This was long overdue, as some of these properties were among the top vineyards of the Médoc.

Château d'Angludet

Cantenac. Tel: 0557 887141. Website: www.chateau-angludet.fr. Owner: Sichel family. 34 ha.
55% Cabernet Sauvignon, 35% Merlot, 10% Petit Verdot. Production: 190,000 bottles.
Second wine: La Ferme d'Angludet

This much admired property is of ancient origin, and there were already vineyards here in the seventeenth century. Under the ownership of Pierre Legras in the late eighteenth century, its wines sold for high prices. It was dismembered among four heirs in 1791, then reunited by an assiduous proprietor 100 years later. Its prices suggest that it was regarded as being of classified-growth quality. In 1953 a new proprietor began some much needed replanting, only to have his efforts largely wiped out by the frost of 1956. In 1961 Peter Sichel bought Angludet, partly as a holiday home for his large family. By that time there were only seven hectares of vines, but most of these he grubbed up and replanted. Today the average age of the vines is twenty-five years.

The vines are in a single block, mostly in the commune of Arsac, and they lie some three kilometres (two miles) away from the estuary. The soil varies: in part light gravel with sand, in part deep gravel with a clay subsoil. There were years when it was difficult to ripen Cabernet Sauvignon here, but careful attention to the viticulture in each plot has largely resolved this problem. Benjamin Sichel, who runs the property, has also planted some Petit Verdot to add complexity. Flowering can be a week later than by the river, but Sichel says the vines do tend to catch up. Angludet was a pioneer of ecological pest control in the Médoc, and has also practised green-harvesting since 1988. Sichel has also raised the trellising so as to increase the surface of foliage above the vines. All viticultural operations throughout the summer are designed to deliver fruit that ripens at the same time – or that's the ideal he strives for.

The grapes are picked by machine. Benjamin Sichel likes the flexibility it gives him, and attributes the success of his 1997 to his insistence on picking the Cabernet as late as possible. The vinification is classic, and since 1999 there has been no chaptalization. The wine is aged for twelve months in up to twenty-five per cent new oak; there is an eggwhite-fining, but filtration is not systematic. Angludet also produces a *clairet*, made by the *saignée* method.

The oldest Angludet I have tasted was the rounded yet spicy 1978, though I preferred the 1979. The 1980, a dim vintage, was still going strong when drunk at the château from magnums in 2000: the nose was sweet and cedary, the flavours lean and healthy if not especially rich or persistent – definitely ready to drink. The 1982 was lovely in 1990 but is now slightly past its best and rather light for the vintage. The 1983 was a great success here, not a blockbuster but a wine that developed delightful undergrowth aromas; it remains a touch austere on the palate, suggesting it still has a future. At ten years old the 1986 was going strong, plump-textured but with good extract and a chewy finish typical of the vintage. The 1987 and 1988 were uninspiring, but the 1989 was generous, spicy, and balanced. I have conflicting notes on the blackcurrant-scented 1990, finding it more forward than the 1989. The 1991 is good for the year, and preferable to the 1992 and 1993. The 1996 has steadily gained in complexity, a stylish wine with firm tannins but no excessive extraction, and good length. Charm and delicacy are the hallmarks of the 1997, which is fully mature. But the 1998, robust and even raw in its youth, has a way to go: the nose is intense and elegant, the palate firm and stylish. The 2001 has chocolatey aromas, and unusual opulence for Angludet, as well as spice, vigour, and grip. The 2002 is less aromatic, but has succulence and concentration, and should develop well. The 2003 is a touch jammy on the nose, rich and rounded but with rather fierce tannins. The 2004 is succulent and forward, yet has fine underlying acidity and length and should develop well.

Château d'Arsac

Arsac. Tel: 0556 588390. Website: www.chateau-arsac.com. Owner: Philippe Raoux. 112 ha.
60% Cabernet Sauvignon, 40% Merlot. Production: 700,000 bottles.
Second wines: Ruban Bleu d'Arsac, Baronne d'Arsac

You will be in for a surprise as you drive past this château in the hamlet of Le Comte just southwest of Arsac. The grounds are an open-air museum of modern sculpture, but, more startling, the stone trimming of the *chais* has been painted a bright cobalt blue, while the façade of the château itself is crossed by an immense beam that rests against the central turret and exceeds it in height.

The creator of this extravaganza is Philippe Raoux, who bought Château d'Arsac in 1986. The property is of twelfth-century origin, but the original château was destroyed during the Revolution. The present structure was built in 1830. By the nineteenth century there were 180 hectares under vine here, but from the 1930s onwards the property was gradually abandoned and ended up as a factory farm for poultry. When Raoux, who belongs to a Bordeaux négociant family, bought the property it was ruinous. He planted the abandoned vineyards in a single parcel behind the château, so the vines are no more than fifteen years old. Then he turned his attention to the château, hiring architect Patrick Hernandez, who gutted the interior and removed its ceilings, thus providing a soaring space traversed by vertiginous walkways. With its ultra-modern paintings and furnishings, it is used partly for receptions and partly as a home for Raoux and his family.

As has been mentioned in the introduction to this chapter, Raoux petitioned successfully to have part of his vineyard included within AC Margaux. Of the total area under vine, over one-third, forty hectares, is now within Margaux. Precisely why this should be so is puzzling, since even the château directors admit there is little in soil type or varietal mix to distinguish between the two sectors. All the vineyards are picked by machine. Micro-oxygenation is used during fermentation. The Margaux wine is aged in new barriques for twelve months; the Haut-Médoc, called Le Monteil d'Arsac, is aged for a similar period but in one-third new oak, including some American barrels.

In 2006 Raoux launched his Winemaker's Collection: each year a different winemaker will select some vines and vinify them separately. Michel Rolland is the first, Denis Dubourdieu the second of the winemakers to participate.

Vintages of Château d'Arsac I have tasted from the 1990s were very disappointing. The 2000 is a major step up, although the nose is far too oaky for my taste, while the palate has freshness and concentration if perhaps little depth or finesse. The 2001 has cappuccino aromas and, although the texture is lush, the finish is livelier than the 2000. The 2002 is dense and rather extracted, and was not showing well when tasted. However, the 2004 is juicy and vigorous, and has a long, lean finish. The only vintages of the Haut-Médoc I have encountered are the charming, zesty, but forward 2001, and the gutsy, gamey 2004. Given that this is a wine made, I imagine, for early consumption, it seems more balanced and enjoyable than the more ambitious Margaux.

Château La Bessane

Cantenac. Tel: 0557 880066. Website: www.chateaupaloumey.com. Owner: Martine Cazeneuve. 3 ha.
60% Petit Verdot, 20% Cabernet Sauvignon, 20% Merlot. Production: 14,000 bottles

The particularity of this little property, owned by the dynamic Martine Cazeneuve of Château Paloumey (*q.v.*), is the unusually high proportion of Petit Verdot. The wine is aged for up to fifteen months in one-third new barriques. The 2001 is excellent: still dense and oaky on the nose, but rich, rounded, and with ample grip. The 2003 is very promising, a touch jammy perhaps, but juicy and dense with a long, bright finish.

Château Boyd-Cantenac

Cantenac. Tel: 0557 889082. Website: www.boyd-cantenac.fr. Owner: Lucien Guillemet. Troisième cru. 17 ha.
60% Cabernet Sauvignon, 25% Merlot, 8% Cabernet Franc, 7% Petit Verdot. Production: 100,000 bottles.
Second wines: Jacques Boyd, Joséphine de Boyd

The property was founded in 1754 by Jacques Boyd, a Bordeaux merchant of Irish origin. In 1806 it was acquired by a rich relative, Englishman John Lewis Brown. Some of its vineyards were sold off in 1860. The Guillemet family acquired the estate in 1932, and Lucien Guillemet is the third generation to run the property. He had been the manager of Giscours until he dedicated himself to Boyd-Cantenac and Pouget (in his family for even longer) in 1996. M. Guillemet is not the most communicative of men, and when tasting the wines with him from his two properties, it took repeated questioning to be sure which bottle came from which estate.

The vines, mostly located on the Cantenac plateau, are about thirty-five years old, and no chemical fertilizers are used. The grapes are picked by hand and fermented in cement and steel tanks with makeshift temperature control; micro-oxygenation is used, despite Guillemet's lofty disdain for "*la vinification voodoo*". The wine is aged in up to sixty per cent new barriques for twelve to sixteen months and bottled without filtration. The *chais* are humidified but not air-conditioned. A peculiarity here is that the second wine is sold under a number of different labels, depending on the request of the négociant buying the wine. This seems a confusing practice for a classified growth.

The oldest Boyd-Cantenac I have tasted was the 1975, which was a touch musty. Vintages from the 1980s, including the 1982, were very disappointing, with the one exception of the 1986, which remained lively and vigorous and long. The 1990 was pleasant but lacked depth and complexity, and was forward for the vintage. The 1995 was mediocre, the 1997 savoury, intense, and with some attractive fruit marred by fierce acidity. The 1998 offers a big mouthful of succulent fruit, with robust tannins and little finesse. The 1999 showed the astringency that is quite common in these wines, and even the 2000 had this character. The 2001 was better, with quite rich fruit, light tannin, and brisk acidity on the finish. The 2002 seemed far better, with sweet blackcurrant aromas, and a lean but elegant palate. The 2003 is soft and lacks flair. Is a much needed improvement at last under way? It is perhaps too early to say.

Château Brane-Cantenac

Cantenac. Tel: 0557 888333. Website: www.brane-cantenac.com. Owner: Henri Lurton. Deuxième cru.
90 ha. 65% Cabernet Sauvignon, 30% Merlot, 5% Cabernet Franc. Production: 150,000 bottles.
Second wine: Baron de Brane

Founded in the eighteenth century by the Gorsse family, this estate was bought in 1833 by the Baron de Brane after he sold Mouton, and he renamed the property in 1838. He increased the renown and prices of the wines. In 1866 it was acquired by the Roy family, who were then the owners of Château d'Issan. The Lurtons claim that before World War I the wines fetched similar prices to the First Growths. In 1920 the property was bought by a consortium called the Société des Grands Crus de France. The next owners were the Berger family, who enlarged the estate. In 1925 it was bought by Léonce Récapet and his son-in-law François Lurton. Lucien Lurton inherited the estate in 1956, and when in 1992 Lurton unloaded his numerous properties on his equally numerous children, it was Henri who took over Brane-Cantenac. Despite his penchant for tweed jackets, his studious air, and the look of someone who hasn't seen daylight for quite some time, Henri Lurton is a trained oenologist with extensive southern-hemisphere experience.

This is a sizeable estate, divided into three substantial parcels. The largest consists of forty-five hectares, and this is the source of most of the *grand vin*. There are a further thirty hectares on the so-called Plateau de Brane, where the gravel is extremely deep and underlain by considerable bands of clay. The third parcel is in Soussans on gravelly sand, and its wine usually finds its way into the second label. Henri made some radical changes after he took over the estate. The soils are now ploughed, and only organic manure added. Much of the vineyard was replanted, bringing the average age to around twenty-five years, and he installed some new drainage channels. He also put an end to machine-harvesting. Yields are modest: forty-six hectolitres per hectare in 2000, thirty-six in 2001.

Lurton likes to pick late, but doesn't look for *surmaturité*, especially with Merlot. The grapes are selected in the vineyard and twice more at the winery. He has good things to say about his *sous-vide* concentrator, which he finds a useful way to avoid dilution caused by excessive dew or showers during harvest. Since 1997 the best lots have been vinified in wooden vats. He is increasingly devoted to them as, in his view, the oxygenation provided by the wooden containers gives the wine more roundness. He gives the must a cold soak with *pigeage*. He uses both selected and indigenous yeasts. Some of the wine undergoes malolactic fermentation in barriques, and remains on the fine lees for two months. Blending usually takes place in February after the harvest. Overall, the wine is aged for eighteen months (twelve for Baron de Brane) in fifty to sixty per cent new oak, then eggwhite-fined. Selection is extremely strict, reflecting the uneven quality of the vineyards; the proportion of wine consigned to the *grand vin* ranges from twenty-five to forty per cent.

I have not tasted any venerable vintages of Brane-Cantenac, but in 2006 *World of Fine Wine* reported on a vast tasting held in 1998. For these tasters the highlights were 1911, 1918, 1920, 1928, 1929, 1945, 1947, 1948, 1959, 1961, and 1966. My oldest vintage was the 1978, still in fine shape in 2003, with meaty aromas, and freshness and balance rather than power on the palate. The 1979 had charm but matured fast. When I tasted the 1982 blind in 1993 it tasted delicious and forward and I took it for a 1985. But it has held up well. Ten years later the nose was suffused with chocolate and cinnamon; on the palate it was full-bodied and spicy with a light raisiny tone. The liquorice-scented 1985 is now fading; it's elegant but lacking in flesh. The 1986 is splendid: again that aroma of liquorice as well as cedar, and a sumptuous and spicy palate, still fresh and delicious. The 1988 has leafy, blackcurranty aromas, a flavoursome but light wine for the vintage. The 1989 was forward and accessible in 2001, fresh and clean but not very exciting, despite delicate acidity on the finish. The 1990 is still quite oaky, a robust, concentrated wine with weight and complexity, and plenty of life ahead of it. The 1993 is dry and dull, the 1994 medium-bodied, with more evident ripeness on the nose than on the palate, which lacks finesse. The 1995 is evolving beautifully, with its smoky, coffee-tinged nose, and a graceful feel on the palate that is typically Margaux and pierces through the evident oakiness. The 1996 is even better, with the slight herbaceousness that marks many wines from this vintage, but a rich, juicy palate, supple tannins, and good concentration. The 1998 lacks grip and weight, has rather dry tannins, and little refinement. The 1999 has always been delicious, with a remarkably elegant bouquet and well-integrated oak; it has a silky texture, is concentrated and spicy yet harmonious and long. The 2000 has a lot of oak on the nose, considerable power and flesh, a suave texture, and good balance; it's not showing much subtlety but it is still very young. The 2001 is tightly structured, with a lot of force as well as finesse. When young, the 2002 seemed rather light and lacking in persistence, but recently it has developed more elegance and flair and has a fresh, lively finish. The 2003, initially chunky, now shows more flesh and suppleness, but it lacks length.

There are exceptions, but Brane-Cantenac tends to deliver wines of charm and fine texture rather than brute power, but they don't lack concentration and structure. Henri Lurton has certainly made the wines more consistent, and perhaps more sophisticated, but it should not be forgotten that some very fine wines were made by his father's team too.

Château Cantenac-Brown

Cantenac. Tel: 0557 888181. Website: www.cantenacbrown.com. **Owner:** *Simon Halabi. Troisième cru. 42 ha.*
65% Cabernet Sauvignon, 30% Merlot, 5% Cabernet Franc. **Production:** *180,000 bottles.*
Second wine: Brio du Ch Cantenac-Brown (Ch Canuet until 2001)

Cantenac-Brown is one of the most bizarre of Médoc châteaux, because it looks so institutional: more like a Scottish boarding school, or perhaps a Belgian town hall. The property takes its name from John Lewis Brown, the same English merchant who was for a while the owner of Boyd-Cantenac as well. The négociant firm of De Luze bought the estate in 1968, but soon sold it on. In 1989 it was purchased by an insurance company that two years later merged with AXA Millésimes. José Sanfins has been the director since 1989, giving the management continuity. It was he who reverted to manual harvesting as soon as he took over. In 2006 the property was sold to the London-based property developer Simon Habibi.

The vineyards are quite dispersed, and there are an additional eight hectares within the Bordeaux Supérieur appellation, which is sold under the Brown-Lamartine label. Within Margaux there are eight hectares at Soussans, three at Margaux, two near Château du Tertre, a few parcels near Brane, and sixteen hectares near the château. The average age of the vines is some thirty years. AXA invested in better drainage, and raised the trellising. Since 1990 green-harvesting has been the norm. The aim is riper fruit to offset the firm tannins that these vineyards deliver.

The grapes were carefully sorted at the winery, and every lot analysed for its polyphenol content. Fermentation took place with selected yeasts in stainless-steel tanks, and the wine aged for about fifteen months in fifty per cent new barriques.

I have tasted the 1976, 1982, 1984, and 1987, and have nothing nice to say about any of them. The 1988 was austere and closed for many years, but eight years have gone by since I last tasted it. The 1989 is quite mature in colour, and the nose has aromas of raisins and black olives. It's rich and lush, but also somewhat porty and lacking in refinement; it seems, dare I say it, slightly rustic. But the 1990 marks a distinct improvement. Over the years it has developed coffee aromas, and it shows a concentration and stylishness absent from earlier vintages. It's no heavyweight but it's very attractive and just about ready. The 1991 was good for the vintage, in a soft, accessible style. I have had one good and two poor bottles of the 1993, so can offer no assessment. The 1994 has a charming nose, but is a simple wine that lacks depth. The 1995 is very much better, with sweet ripe, blackcurrant aromas with a dash of chocolate and mint; the palate is concentrated and spicy, with a tight structure and good length. The 1996 is quite dry for the vintage, a somewhat lacklustre wine that doesn't fulfil the promise of its sweet blackcurrant nose. I prefer the rich, meaty 1998, with its cedary blackberry aromas, and its robust but not harsh tannins; the wine has good length and should improve with bottle-age. Blackberry aromas emerge again on the 1999; it's a wine that has evolved fast, agreeable but unremarkable and fully ready. The 2000 has been consistently fine from the start, with very ripe black fruits on the nose. The fruit quality is excellent, though perhaps there is a certain stolidity and lack of flair. The 2001 is lighter, lacking the weight, vigour, and complexity of the 2000; but it's well balanced and enjoyable. The 2002 is quite different: a lusher style than usual, with more evident oakiness, a chocolatey tone, and more toastiness and power than Cantenac-Brown usually displays. It should develop very well. The 2003 is a success for the vintage: appealingly juicy, balanced, and not over-tannic.

Although there are some very good wines under this label, there are also disappointments, and Cantenac-Brown seems significantly less consistent than most other classified growths. Perhaps the scattered vineyards don't always give a wine with a consistent profile – but this is mere speculation. Nonetheless there are other wines within this price band that set the pulses racing rather more.

Clos des Quatre Vents

Soussans. Tel: 0557 887131. Owner: Luc Thienpont. 2 ha. Production: 6,000 bottles

The varietal blend is missing above for the simple reason that Luc Thienpont isn't quite sure. The varieties are interplanted, though most of them are Cabernet Sauvignon. The vines, evidently, are very old, from fifty to eighty years, and some are planted on their own roots. They are located on the top of the plateau at Labégorce. The previous owner was an old man who never managed to make good wines, and eventually he sold the little property to Thienpont, who was running Labégorce-Zédé. Because Thienpont is unsure about what he's got in his vineyard, he picks the grapes as late as possible, hoping the fruit is properly ripe by then. Yields are low, a vertical press easily takes care of pressing after fermentation, and the wine is aged in 100 per cent new oak. The first vintage was 2000. Both 2001 and 2002 are first-rate: very rich, concentrated, flamboyant, chocolatey, and powerfully tannic. Yet the finish is sweet and long. Even the 2003 is robust and long, if not exceptional. Thienpont's wines are certainly atypical for Margaux, but the ancient vines clearly like to strut their stuff.

Château Dauzac

Labarde. Tel: 0557 883210. Website: www.andrelurton.com. **Owner:** *MAIF insurance group. Cinquième cru. 40 ha. 58%* *Cabernet Sauvignon, 37% Merlot, 5% Cabernet Franc.* **Production:** *240,000 bottles.* **Second wine:** *La Bastide Dauzac*

There were vineyards planted at Dauzac in the 1740s by Thomas Michel Lynch. Eight years after it was classified, it was purchased by the Bordeaux négociant Nathaniel Johnston, who also owned Ducru-Beaucaillou. It was here, incidentally, that "Bordeaux mixture" (*bouillie bordelaise*), the classic treatment against mildew, was invented by Ulysse Gayon and botanist Alexis Millardet in 1865. Shortly before World War I the property became neglected, and the Johnstons sold it in the 1930s. It was bought in 1954 by the Miailhe family, then revived in 1978 by a Champenois family that invested heavily, but then in 1989 sold Dauzac to the present proprietors. In 1992 MAIF took the somewhat surprising decision to ask André Lurton to manage the property – surprising because Lurton is better known for his expertise in white wine production.

Lurton, although a busy man, takes his responsibility here seriously. He tells me that whatever demands he made on his paymasters to improve quality, they readily acceded to. Philippe Roux is the resident winemaker.

In addition to the vines within AC Margaux, there are five hectares of Haut-Médoc sold as Château Labarde. Most of the Margaux vines face the château on a gravel *croupe*. Some parcels are up to seventy-five years old, but Lurton says they are not necessarily of exceptional quality because they were not planted on ideal rootstocks. There has been much replanting, so that the average age of the vines is around twenty years. The soils are precocious, thanks to the vineyards' proximity to the river, and Dauzac is often among the first to harvest. Parcels planted on sandier, lower-lying land between the château and the railway line usually end up in the second wine.

The winery is very well equipped. There are, since 2004, sorting tables before and after destemming; these are placed above the tanks, so that the grapes descend by gravity. The steel tanks are fitted with a patented system for breaking up the cap; this consists of wooden struts radiating from the centre of the tank. After *délestage*, the cap falls within the tank and is broken up by the struts. The wine is aged for twelve to fourteen months in around fifty per cent new barriques, before fining and bottling. Roughly half the crop is declassified into the second wine.

The older vintages I have tasted – 1979, 1982, 1986 – were easy-going wines, perfectly attractive and drinkable, but light and with little structure. Thus the 1986 was already beginning to fade by 1999. The 1989, tasted in 2001, was better: quite evolved in colour and aroma, but opulent on the palate yet with good underlying acidity – an enjoyable and still fresh wine but one with little complexity. The 1990 remained austere for a while, but by 2003 seemed fully mature, with a gamey, leathery nose, and an evolved funkiness on the palate. The 1993 was severe and over-extracted for the modest fruit. The 1995 was a rich, concentrated wine with the powerful tannins of the vintage, a dense, chocolatey tone, and quite good length. The 1997 is quite elegant and fully ready to drink, unlike the stylish 1998, which, despite a slight herbaceous tone, seems fully ripe, with abundant black fruits, a positive tannic structure to ensure a long life, and a long, firm finish. The 1999 has evolved into a lush, oaky wine with delicious fruit that is drinking well now but will certainly keep. The 2000 is a triumph, with rich, oaky aromas and a complex palate, with fleshiness, concentration, excellent fruit, and lovely bright acidity. The 2001 is more forward and less exciting, but it's hard not to be seduced by its flamboyant, blackcurranty aromas and balanced stylishness. It's outclassed by the excellent 2002, which seems classic Dauzac: sweet oak and blackcurrant on the nose, and a palate that is medium-bodied but graceful and elegant, with fine-grained tannins and good length. The 2003 is a supple, slightly green wine of moderate structure and length. The 2004 is full of charm, elegantly oaky, with tannins and acidity in perfect balance. It's less opulent than the sumptuous 2005, which is packed with fruit and yet very long.

Dauzac has been seriously underrated, perhaps because it is one of the least expensive classified growths. It can lack elegance, and sometimes the oak seems a touch too overbearing, but a good Dauzac has rich fruit, sufficient ripeness and stylishness, and good length. Some vintages, such as 1999 and 2003, may not prove that long-lived, but no matter: Dauzac gives great pleasure at between five and ten years of age.

Château Desmirail

Cantenac. Tel: 0557 883433. Website: www.chateau-desmirail.com. **Owner:** *Denis Lurton. Troisième cru.*
32 ha. 60% Cabernet Sauvignon, 39% Merlot, 1% Cabernet Franc. **Production:** *150,000 bottles.*
Second wines: Ch Fontarney and Initial de Desmirail

Just when we all thought Desmirail was lost forever, it was restored to us. The property takes its name from Jean Desmirail, a seventeenth-century lawyer who married into the Rauzan family. The estate passed through various hands, and in 1903 was bought by a banker, Robert Mendelssohn, the nephew of the composer Felix Mendelssohn. When World War I broke out it was confiscated by the state because of Mendelssohn's German origins and auctioned off. The new owner, an industrialist, sold off several parcels before selling what was left of the dismembered property. He sold the château itself to Château Marquis d'Alesme, which still occupies it. In 1957 Château Palmer bought the parcels of Desmirail in Cantenac, together with the rights to the name, while another sector of vines, in Arsac, was sold to François Lurton. Subsequently his son Lucien Lurton bought back the name of Desmirail from Palmer, and acquired some spacious buildings in Cantenac, so that the property would at least have a home once again. Over the years he gradually reconstituted the estate parcel by parcel, so that eventually about two-thirds of the original Third-Growth property was given new life. The first vintage of the reborn Desmirail was 1981. When Lucien Lurton dispersed his properties among his children, it was Denis who took over Desmirail. He hired Pierre Lafeuillade as winemaker, and installed sufficient tanks so that the whole crop could be vinified at the winery, whereas before part of it had been vinified at Brane-Cantenac.

The original parcels of Desmirail are nine hectares behind the cemetery at Cantenac and ten hectares at Soussans. There are also eleven hectares in Arsac not far from Château du Tertre, but these were not part of the original holdings. Lurton found that Cabernet Sauvignon was planted in spots to which it was not well suited, so much of it was replaced by Merlot. Today there is on average one-third Merlot in the blend.

Most of the wine is fermented in steel tanks, but in 1999 Denis Lurton bought four wooden vats, and intends to buy more, as he likes the expression they give to the new wine, especially the Merlot. Desmirail is equipped with a *sous-vide* concentrator, used in 1999 and 2004. There is a cold soak for up to five days for the ripest fruit. Then they add selected yeasts, on the grounds that the grapes are often very ripe and they don't want stuck fermentations. After malolactic fermentation in tanks (except for the press wine), the wine is aged for eighteen months in one-third new oak.

Lurton doesn't want an extracted style. He is aiming for structure and ageing potential, though not at the expense of elegance and perfume.

The oldest Desmirail I have encountered is the 1986, which is wonderfully aromatic, with sweet, leafy, mentholly tones; while the palate is medium-bodied, juicy, with integrated tannins, good length, but just a hint of dryness on the finish. The first Desmirail that made me sit up and take notice was the 1988, which was svelte and very polished, an elegant wine with impeccable balance. The 1990 was charming but seemed to lack stuffing; however, it too showed good balance. The 1994 was chunky and rather astringent, a wine short on elegance. The 1995 has a fleshy nose of black fruits, notably blackcurrant and plums; the palate isn't weighty, yet it has a certain charm. The 1997 had charm and delicacy, but needs to be drunk up. The powerful, opulent 1998 is typical of the vintage, with ripe but chewy tannins, good acidity and length, but perhaps a slight lack of succulence. The 1999 is equally typical of that vintage, with its more open nose, its charming cherry fruit, and a long, sweet finish. The 2000 is going from strength to strength, a luscious wine, supported by formidable tannins; it's unusually powerful for Margaux, but with splendid length and a great future. I have conflicting notes on the 2001, the first enthusiastic though wary of what seemed like excessive oakiness, the second (perhaps an unsatisfactory bottle) seemed tired and lacking in flair. The 2002 didn't show well after bottling, but has now come round, and has ample aromatic charm, while the palate is medium-bodied, airy and stylish, concentrated without being too extracted, with good acidity and structure. This wine, and the grand 2000 (though not the flabby 2003), show the stature of which the reconstituted Desmirail is capable.

Château Deyrem-Valentin

*Soussans. Tel: 0557 883570. **Owner:** Jean Sorge. 14 ha. 51% Cabernet Sauvignon, 45% Merlot, 2% Malbec,*
*2% Petit Verdot. **Production:** 80,000 bottles. **Second wine:** Ch Soussans*

This property, including the family house in Soussans, dates back to 1730. It has been in the Sorge family since they bought it at auction in 1928, and the courteous, modest Jean Sorge has run it and made the wine from 1972 onwards, though he is now assisted by his daughters. Of his fourteen hectares, 12.5 lie within AC Margaux between Soussans and Labégorce. There are some ten parcels in all, including 1.5 hectares of centenarian vines, and a plot sold to the Sorges in 1938 by Château Palmer.

The grapes are picked by hand, and sorted in the vineyard and winery. The must is fermented using indigenous yeasts, and no enzymes are added. Sorge is keen that the Margaux terroir should express itself, and doesn't want to mask it with too much extraction or manipulation. The wine is aged for twelve to eighteen months in thirty-five per cent new oak. Yet Sorge is quite keen on experimentation, and has planted some Carmenère. In 2002 he vinified separately a parcel of sixty-year-old vines within his AC Haut-Médoc vineyards; it is unusual in being almost pure Petit Verdot. It is bottled and released separately under the label of Château Valentin.

Deyrem-Valentin is an exemplary *cru bourgeois*, and I can't recall a vintage I didn't enjoy. The 1989 is still drinking well; the nose is sweet, delicate, and charming, while the palate shows ripe fruit, light tannin, and fine acidity, and a touch of meatiness to suggest it is close to its peak. The 1995 is excellent, with rich, full-bodied fruit, and fine acidity and concentration. The 1996 has a delicately herbaceous aroma, but with its fresh blackberry fruit is a pleasure to drink, a truly appetizing wine. The 1999 is in a similar mould to the 1995. The 2000 has aromas of blackcurrant and mint, while the palate is tight, concentrated, tannic, yet well balanced. The 2001 is excellent too, with ripe blackcurrant aromas and a light, savoury tone developing, while the palate has weight and concentration, without losing the fresh finish characteristic of Sorge's wines. The 2002 is balanced, spicy, and savoury, an attractive and elegant wine. The 2003 has light cherry aromas, but furry tannins and little length. The 2004 has finesse rather than opulence, and should be delicious in a few years.

Château Durfort-Vivens

*Margaux. Tel: 0557 883102. **Website:** www.durfort-vivens.com. **Owner:** Gonzague Lurton. Deuxième cru.*
*30 ha. 65% Cabernet Sauvignon, 23% Merlot, 12% Cabernet Franc. **Production:** 180,000 bottles.*
Second wine: Le Second de Durfort

Like Desmirail, Durfort-Vivens came close to being written out of the history books forever. The property was originally known as Château Durfort until a later owner, the Vicomte de Vivens, appended his name in 1824. In 1937 Durfort was sold to Château Margaux, and its vineyards were used essentially to supply grapes for its second wine. In 1962 Lucien Lurton began to claw back the Durfort property from the Ginestets. He acquired the rather ugly cellars at the southern entrance to the village, though he used them to store barrels rather than to make wine. The actual château, which stands across the road from the entrance to the *chais*, was retained by Bernard Ginestet, and shortly before his death it was acquired by Marojallia (*q.v.*).

It would not be until 1995 that Durfort became fully independent. Until then Gonzague Lurton, who took over in 1992, had been obliged to vinify half the crop at his brother's winery at Brane-Cantenac. This was unsatisfactory to both parties.

> *While my wine was macerating at Brane, Henri says to me that he needs the tank space for*
> *more of his crop. So I had to run off the wine much earlier than I wanted. So I went to see*
> *the bank manager and told him that this was no way to run a* deuxième cru.

Lurton must have been persuasive, as he soon built a new *cuvier*, and expanded it in 2001.

The average age of the vines is some twenty-five years, though there are parcels of very old vines that yield only around twenty-five hectolitres per hectare. Gonzague Lurton doesn't believe in conventional wisdom, and treats each viticultural or winemaking issue from a fresh stance. He is not keen on green-harvesting or leaf-pulling, both of which can retard the vigour of the vine. He accepts that these can be necessary remedial measures, but he doesn't want them to be seen as routine. Not that he seeks high yields; he just prefers to remove buds and follow other measures that will give him a crop of around forty hl/ha without recourse to practices that he believes can harm the life of the vine.

Grapes are picked by hand and sorted carefully in the vineyard and winery. The vinification takes place in cement and wooden vats, the latter acquired in 2002. Gonzague Lurton is delighted with them, since temperature control is scarcely necessary. Since 2002 malolactic fermentation takes place in barrel. The wine is aged in around forty per cent new oak for sixteen to eighteen months.

Gonzague Lurton is very clear about the style of wine he wants to make. He doesn't want opulent wines, preferring a combination of density and finesse.

There were some good wines made when Lucien Lurton was still running the property. The 1982 was stylish and attractive, if not that concentrated. The 1985 in 2000 was still fresh, almost crisp, with fine blackcurranty fruit despite the lack of concentration. The 1986 has become rather astringent, though the nose remains lovely, with cedar and tobacco aromas. The 1988 is rather light for the year, though it certainly doesn't lack charm and delicacy. The 1989 is very imposing, with a rich, smoky nose, and a palate that is almost voluptuous, with powerful, ripe tannins, good concentration and fine length. It seems more structured and gutsy than the 1990. The 1993 is a lightweight, and the 1994 veers in the opposite direction, being austere, almost bitter, and rather hollow. The medium-bodied but tight 1995 is a big step up, with its smoky bacon aromas, its rich tannins and fruit balanced by lively acidity and length. The 1996 is even better, with its cedary nose, its plump fruit, its fine acidity, and its tannic grip. The stylish 1997 is quite good for the vintage. There's an attractive perfume on the 1998, which is medium-bodied and elegant; it has developed an unusual succulence for Durfort, and is starting to drink well. The 1999 has sweet glacé-cherry aromas with a good dash of smoky oak, and over the years it has gained in weight and lushness, though not in complexity. The 2000 is odd: it seems a touch overoaked, overripe, and lacking in zest. Tasted in 2003 and again in 2005, there was something unsatisfactory about both bottles. I preferred the 2001. The 2002 is pure yet lacks complexity. The 2003 is quite rich and compact and well balanced, but has a light structure and lacks drive and complexity. The excellent 2004, with its purity of aroma, is, for Durfort, unusually rounded, spicy, and succulent.

Gonzague Lurton is a reserved man with a mind of his own. He thinks carefully about every aspect of wine production. As president of the Margaux Syndicat, he has a complete vision of the communes, their structure, their problems. Yet overall, his own wine remains somewhat disappointing, given its Second-Growth status. There is a certain austerity, a lack of succulence, that characterizes Durfort-Vivens. Perhaps it reflects the high proportion of Cabernet in the wine. This could be a stylistic choice on Lurton's part; flashiness is not part of his nature. Yet although there have been some excellent wines emerging under his stewardship, Durfort does not yet seem in the top tier of Margaux growths.

Château des Eyrins

Margaux. Tel: 0557 889503. Owner: Eric Grangerou. 9 ha. 75% Cabernet Sauvignon, 20% Merlot, 5% Cabernet Franc. Production: 15,000 bottles

M. Grangerou used to be the *maître de chai* at Château Margaux, and has been developing his own property. Of his nine hectares, only 2.5 fall within the Margaux appellation, the remainder being either AC Bordeaux or Haut-Médoc. The wine is much admired, but the only vintage I have tasted, the 2002, struck me as lacking in Margaux typicity. I don't like to use the term "Parkerized", but Eyrins, with its rich, oaky, liquorice-steeped aromas, its overripe flavours, its oak and coffee tones, seemed precisely in that mould.

Château Ferrière

Margaux. Tel: 0556 580237. Website: www.ferriere.com. Owner: Claire Villars. Troisième cru. 8 ha.
75% Cabernet Sauvignon, 20% Merlot, 5% Petit Verdot. Production: 50,000 bottles.
Second wine: Les Remparts de Ferrière

With only eight hectares under vine, Ferrière is the smallest classified growth of the Médoc, and is the same size as it was in 1855. It takes its name from Gabriel Ferrière, a *parlementaire* and merchant who owned the estate in the eighteenth century. The family were imprisoned during the Revolution, but Jean Ferrière survived to become mayor of Bordeaux in 1795. The estate remained in the family until 1914, when Henri Ferrière sold it to Armand Feuillerat, the owner of Château Marquis de Terme. His descendants leased the estate to Château Lascombes in 1952. The Merlaut family bought Ferrière in 1988, though the Lascombes' lease ended formally only in 1991. Bernadette Villars, the Merlaut daughter who also ran Chasse-Spleen, found the property in poor condition, and a new winery and *chai* had to be built. The first vintage of the reborn Ferrière was 1992. (The "Ferrière" produced at Lascombes was made in small quantities to maintain that estate's rights to the name, and the grapes did not come from the historic Ferrière vineyards but from lesser parcels at Lascombes.) After the death in 1992 of Mme. Villars and her husband, her brother (part of the Merlaut family of négociants) asked Bernadette's young daughter Claire whether she would take over. Although training for a career outside the world of wine, Claire responded, and has been running the property (and two others in her portfolio, La Gurgue (*q.v.*) in Margaux and Haut-Bages-Libéral (*q.v.*) in Pauillac) with flair and energy.

The vineyards are separated into a number of large parcels, mainly on deep gravel soils, mostly just south of Labégorce. There is a single hectare next to the château, and some other parcels on the plateau of Cantenac. Each parcel is monitored separately, and the vineyards are ploughed. She shares some of the viticultural views of her husband Gonzague Lurton at Durfort-Vivens, preferring to remove buds and shoots rather than green-harvest, though she does green-harvest when she considers it necessary. Yields are calculated in weight of bunches per vine, which can vary according to the age and vigour of each plant.

At first Ferrière was vinified in stainless-steel tanks but Claire Villars has been replacing them with small cement tanks, which she greatly prefers as she doesn't like the reductive effect of steel. She also has two wooden vats for the very best lots. If possible, she avoids temperature control, preferring the wine to find its own level. She employs *pigeage* as well as pumpovers. Fermentation takes place with natural yeasts. The *cuvaison* can be as long as four weeks, but temperatures never exceed 30°C (86°F). Malolactic fermentation takes place in new barriques, an affordable luxury given the small size of the property. The wine is then aged for sixteen to eighteen months in forty per cent new oak. Blending takes place quite early, usually in January. Racking is by gravity, and the wine is eggwhite-fined.

The oldest vintage I have encountered is the 1986, which I assume was produced at Lascombes. The nose was rich, minty, and cedary, and the wine was surprisingly plump, with integrated tannins, a dense texture, and fine length. The 1993 was a fine success in a difficult year: ripe, well balanced, with crisp tannins. The 1995 has an elegant, oaky nose, but I have sometimes detected a slight greenness and a lack of complexity. The 1996 seems better balanced, with a perfumed, cedary nose, ample rich, sweet fruit, and a sense of considerable potential. The 1997 is now ready, a wine of charm and suppleness. Ferrière avoided over-extraction in 1998, delivering a full-bodied, brambly wine with vigour, balance, and ripe tannins. The 1999 is somewhat atypical Margaux, but impressive nonetheless, with dense, black-fruits aromas; it is full-bodied, concentrated, structured, and a touch austere for the vintage. The 2000 is in a similar style, robust with firm tannins, and again a slight austerity. The 2001 shows a lot of oak on the nose but also has a floral character; it has the Ferrière robustness, yet there is something slack about the wine, which lacks some vigour. New oak is again present on the nose of the 2002, but there is greater elegance. There is no lack of concentration and structure, but again there is a certain austerity, though by 2005 it was beginning to reveal some Margaux succulence and charm. Despite a slack structure and lack of persistence, 2003 is reasonably successful at Ferrière, with blackberry aromas, and some spicy black-fruits flavours marred by a flat finish. Fortunately the medium-bodied, stylish 2004 sees a return to form, with plenty of complexity and length to promise a good future.

I admire Ferrière, and perhaps its robustness is part of its personality. However, the wine does often strike me as over-extracted, giving it power and density but at the expense of elegance. Claire Villars acknowledges that the wine has sometimes been overoaked, and I believe she is now making a conscious effort to rein in the extraction. It will be interesting to see how this property evolves.

Château La Galiane

Soussans. Tel: 0557 883527. **Owner:** *Christiane Renon. 5.7 ha. 45% Merlot, 35% Cabernet Sauvignon, 15% Cabernet Franc, 5% Petit Verdot.* **Production:** *30,000 bottles*

This small property is fortunate in that the average age of its vines is fifty-five years. No herbicides are used and the soil is ploughed. Mme. Renon is not keen on green-harvesting, and prefers to prune severely to control yields. The wine is fermented in cement tanks, and aged for twelve months in twenty per cent new oak. The 2000 is quite elegant on the nose with pretty blackcurrant fruit, while the palate is reasonably concentrated, delicate, and relatively forward. But the evolved, heavy-handed 2003 offers no joy. There's rawness to the 2004, but it has attractive red-fruits aromas and a youthful austerity that should flesh out in time. Given the modest price demanded for La Galiane, this is an estate that offers good value. The Renons also produce another Margaux called Château Charmant.

Château Giscours

Labarde. Tel: 0557 970909. **Website:** *www.chateau-giscours.fr.* **Owner:** *Eric Albada Jelgersma. Troisième cru. 80 ha. 53% Cabernet Sauvignon, 42% Merlot, 5% Cabernet Franc and Petit Verdot.* **Production:** *300,000 bottles.*

Second wine: Sirène de Giscours

This is one of the first estates the visitor glimpses arriving from Bordeaux on the southern fringes of Margaux. Although not easily visible from the road, there is a substantial complex of buildings at Giscours, the architecturally uniform winery buildings and, set apart, the grandiose and enormous château. There were vineyards here in the sixteenth century. The Marquis de St-Simon owned Giscours by the late eighteenth century, and the estate was confiscated during the Revolution and sold. The Comte de Pescatore, a Parisian banker, bought Giscours in 1845 and rebuilt the château a short time later. Under the management of Pierre Skawinski, whose reign at Giscours lasted almost half a century, the wines attained a very high reputation. Pescatore's nephew Guillaume inherited the property. In 1875 Giscours was bought by the Cruse family, who sold it again in 1913. By the mid-twentieth century the estate had become run-down. From 1947 to 1952 Nicolas Tari from Algeria began buying up the much diminished property, which was inherited by his polo-playing son Pierre. The Taris lived in high style, and I recall an idyllic Sunday afternoon in the park in the late 1980s, with the extensive family gathered close to the lake, itself an innovation by Nicolas Tari as a way of improving drainage and providing a landscape feature at the same time.

The Taris did much for Giscours, but in 1995 they decided to sell the property to the Dutch entrepreneur who is the present owner. He provided the new injection of cash and energy that the property badly needed. He also acquired Château du Tertre (*q.v.*). The winery buildings were restored, and measures set in place to improve quality. The numerous sub-labels used by the Taris for declassified wine were eliminated and replaced by a single label for the second wine. The elderly Taris had the right to occupy the château for the rest of their lifetimes, but after their deaths it continued to be occupied by Nicole Heeter-Tari, the owner of Château Nairac in Barsac. Legal action continued on both sides for many years, but in 2005 she finally vacated the mansion.

As well as extensive vineyards in Margaux, the Giscours estate includes some sixty hectares of neighbouring vines in the Haut-Médoc (Château du Thil). There was a scandal in 1999 when the winemakers were accused of adding Haut-Médoc wine to the second wine of Giscours, and of using oak chips, an illegal practice. Their motives were honourable – they wished to improve the quality of the second wine – but nonetheless the practice was unacceptable. A new team was brought in, notably Jacques Pelissié, who had worked at Cos d'Estournel for fifteen years. Alexander van Beek is the youthful general manager of both Giscours and Tertre.

Because of the size of the estate, the work involved in renovating it has been considerable. Over three years 200,000 unsatisfactory vines were replaced, some trees were removed to reduce the risk of frost, and ploughing was introduced. The vineyards are essentially spread over four *croupes* with a depth of gravel that varies from two to eight metres (seven to twenty-six feet); they have been subdivided into forty-three separate parcels. After harvest the grapes are sorted both in the vineyard and at the winery. Giscours is equipped with a *sous-vide* concentrator, but does not employ micro-oxygenation. Fermentation takes place with selected yeasts, and the wine is aged for around fifteen months in fifty per cent new oak.

Giscours apparently produced remarkable wines in celebrated vintages such as 1899 and 1929, but I have not tasted them. The 1970 Giscours is a splendid wine, with opulent blackcurrant aromas, while the palate is supple, with a certain meatiness, and good structure and length. The 1976 was good in the late 1980s, if rather four-square and lacking in finesse, but must be past its best now. The 1978 was rather austere and tannic after fifteen years, suggesting some lack of ripeness, but I have not tasted it more recently. The 1979 had a similar earthiness. The 1982 was delicious in its youth, and the 1983 is an exceptional Giscours, concentrated and chocolatey, yet with a freshness on the finish; it lacks some length and is now ready to drink. The 1984 was hard and charmless, and the 1985 rather loose and jammy. The 1990 was dense, almost chunky, but was balanced by its vigour. The 1993 was dilute and lacking in fruit, but the 1994, while lacking finesse, was a wine of surprising weight. The 1995 has gained in weight and power over the years, but lacks vivacity. The 1998 is somewhat dour, with rather harsh tannins. The 2000 is no blockbuster, but has a silky texture, lush, sweet black-cherry fruit and good tannic support without excessive extraction. The 2001, with its oaky blackcurrant perfume, has grandeur and weight, with powerful but not aggressive tannins, and excellent fruit. The 2002 has plummy, oaky aromas, a palate with depth, power, and complexity, and considerable finesse. The toasty 2003 is lush and moderately concentrated, with better acidity and more substance than many wines from this vintage. The 2004, in its sleekness and concentration, seems similar to the fine 2002.

I find it hard to focus on the stylistic identity of Giscours. In good years the wine has aromatic complexity, ample richness of fruit with fine tannic support, and well-judged oakiness. The elegance of Margaux is less evident, however. It is possible that changes and renovations in the vineyard, and changes in the winemaking team, have delayed the emergence of its typicity. I suspect the best is yet to come.

Château La Gurgue

Margaux. Tel: 0557 887665. Website: www.lagurgue.com. **Owner:** *Claire Villars. 10 ha.*
70% Cabernet Sauvignon, 30% Merlot. **Production:** *60,000 bottles*

This property, like Château Ferrière (*q.v.*), is managed by Claire Villars. It can trace its history back to the eighteenth century, when it was owned by the banker Peixotto; it has subsequently been owned by various mayors of Margaux. In 1979 it was acquired by the Merlaut family and run by Bernadette Villars until her death in 1992, when her daughter Claire took over. Bernadette Villars had found the vineyard in poor shape, and much of it had to be replanted. Although the average age of the vines is relatively young, the parcels are superbly located close to some classified growths, including Château Margaux. The wine is aged for twelve months in thirty per cent new oak.

This, like Ferrière, is a robust, quite oaky style of Margaux. Curiously, this is less marked in the suave and delicious 1995 than the spicy, tannic 1996, which still tasted youthful ten years on. Even the 1997 has some grip and concentration. The 1998 is a success here, with intense blackcurrany fruit both on the nose and the palate, a lush texture and considerable persistence. The 1999 is good for the vintage, with a black-coffee gloss on the nose, a good attack, and ample fruit with a fresh finish. I have not tasted the 2000 since it was bottled, but the 2001 is very impressive, rich and lush on nose and palate, with a compact structure that avoids excess thanks to the wine's fine acidity. The 2002 is robust and oaky on the nose, with dense, concentrated flavours but a vigorous finish. Although the 2003 is edgy and astringent, the 2004 is a great success, with dense plummy aromas and ample flesh on both nose and palate.

La Gurgue sells for reasonable prices and offers good value as one of Margaux's most consistent *crus bourgeois*. It may not be especially elegant, but it packs a punch without straying into over-extraction.

Château Haut-Breton-Larigaudière

Soussans. Tel: 0557 889417. Website: www.de-mour.com. Owner: Jacques de Schepper. 15 ha.
63% Cabernet Sauvignon, 31% Merlot, 4% Petit Verdot, 2% Cabernet Franc. Production: 90,000 bottles.
Second wine: Ch du Courneau

It's hard to miss this winery, which is located alongside the road that passes through Soussans. It has been owned by the de Schepper family since 1964. The wine receives a traditional vinification, and is aged for twelve to fifteen months in fifty per cent new barriques. The 1996 was excellent, with a strong blackcurrany tone on nose and palate, and rich, forward fruit that nonetheless did not lack structure. The 2000 is attractive and supple, though a touch light. The rather flat and dilute 2001 is a disappointment, and the 2004 seems lean and undernourished. Since 2000 there has been a special *cuvée* called Le Créateur, made from old Cabernet vines and aged in new oak for eighteen months, but I have never tasted it.

Château d'Issan

Cantenac. Tel: 0557 883591. Website: www.chateau-issan.com. Owner: Emmanuel Cruse. Troisième cru. 30 ha.
65% Cabernet Sauvignon, 35% Merlot. Production: 200,000 bottles. Second wine: Blason d'Issan

Like Agassac and Lamarque, Issan is a moated château. There are references to the property in twelfth-century documents, and among its illustrious owners was the Ségur family. It was the Chevalier d'Essenault (his name was later abbreviated to Issan) who razed the medieval castle and erected the present structure in the seventeenth century. The Foix de Candale family owned Issan until the Revolution, when it was confiscated. The Roy family, who owned the property from 1866 until 1920, constructed the existing *chais*. The wine was apparently a favourite of the Emperor Franz-Josef of Austria, though it's hard to say whether this is a recommendation. The present owners, the Cruse family, bought the property in 1945 and spent a fortune restoring its crumbling fabric, and since 1997 it has been run by the self-assured Emmanuel Cruse. As well as the Margaux vineyards, there are ten hectares of Bordeaux Supérieur (Moulin d'Issan) planted in 1985 on the *palus* between the château and the river. There are also eleven hectares of Haut-Médoc near Châteaux Giscours and Monbrison, under the label of Château de Candale.

The soils are quite mixed, but are primarily gravel and clay. Indeed there is a fairly high clay content, and since the vines lie quite close to the river, the Cruses had to renovate the drainage for the Margaux parcels. The soils are ploughed, and yields average fifty hectolitres per hectare. After Emmanuel Cruse took over from his father Lionel, he made some important improvements, building a new *chai* in 1999, increasing the number of small steel tanks to facilitate parcel selections, and, from 2002, buying more sorting tables. He also bought a *sous-vide* concentrator in 1998, but it is rarely used. The jobs of vineyard manager and cellarmaster have, since 1994, been combined in the person of Eric Pellon, who has supervised a programme of replanting and new drainage. As soon as the malolactic fermentation is completed, the new wine goes into oak, and blending follows in January. The wine is aged for around eighteen months in fifty per cent new barriques.

Most of the vintages I sampled from the 1980s were lean and rather light. The 1988 was underpowered for the vintage but the fruit was attractive, and the good acidity gave the wine some elegance. The 1989 was excellent, and is now displaying complex aromas of coffee, black fruits, and cigar-box, and an unusually voluptuous mouth-feel for a Margaux, without any absence of tannin and acidity. The 1990 too is ripe and generous with no hard edges and excellent length. The 1993 was dull and dry, but the 1995 is outstanding, with an intoxicating nose of blackcurrant, mint, and cloves; on the palate it is supple and open, not hugely concentrated, but stylish, with bright acidity and tannins, and a fresh, minty finish. It has more grip and staying power than the rather light 1996, which is nonetheless stylish. There are stewed characteristics on the 1998, which is rather flat and four-square, solid but dull. In its youth the 2000 seemed rather rough and chunky, but it has evolved well into a velvety, sumptuous, and concentrated wine with ripe tannins and excellent length. The run continues with very good wines in 2001 and 2002, compact in structure without being too dense. The 2001 is the tighter of the two, the stylish 2002 has more fluidity, acidity, and Margaux typicity. The gruff 2003 has some sweet fruit, yet lacks some acidity and zest.

Issan is one of the less appreciated Margaux growths, but in recent years the wines have been first-rate, with no flashiness or excesses: just pure aromas, delicious fruit, lively acidity, fine textures, and impressive length.

Château Kirwan

*Cantenac. Tel: 0557 887100. Website: www.chateau-kirwan.com. **Owner:** Schÿler family. Troisième cru.*
35 ha. 40% Cabernet Sauvignon, 30% Merlot, 20% Cabernet Franc, 10% Petit Verdot.
***Production:** 200,000 bottles. **Second wine:** Les Charmes de Kirwan*

The Schÿlers are a well-established family of négociants who run the firm of Schröder & Schÿler. In 1925 they bought Château Kirwan, principally as a country residence. And a very charming property it is too. Its original name was the Domaine de Lassalle. In the eighteenth century it was owned by John Collingwood, whose daughter married an Irish merchant named Mark Kirwan. In 1856 it was bought by a M. Godard, whose son Camille was to become mayor of Bordeaux. He asked Schröder & Schÿler to take care of distribution, and in 1925 the distributors became the owners. For many years the family didn't take much trouble with the wine, and there was no château-bottling until 1967; no new oak was used before 1978.

In the introductory comments to this chapter I have quoted Nathalie Schÿler's account of the slapdash harvesting practices of just a couple of decades ago. However, from 1990 the family decided it was worth taking Kirwan seriously, and began investing heavily. In 1992 they hired Michel Rolland as a consultant, making this his first venture on the Left Bank. He promptly insisted on lower yields and better selection, creating a second wine from 1993. He also studied the vineyards and instituted the monitoring of individual parcels, where some varieties were planted higgledy-piggledy. At Rolland's insistence the different varieties were tagged so as to ensure the harvesters picked only those that were fully ripe.

The extent and location of the vineyards have scarcely altered since 1855. Many are planted around the château on the plateau of Cantenac. Here the gravel soil is deep, nowhere more so than on the highest ground (twenty-one metres/sixty-nine feet). Toward Angludet there is more limestone in the soil, which is colder, and this is where much of the Merlot is planted. A peculiarity of Kirwan is the substantial percentage of both Cabernet Franc and Petit Verdot. Both make their contribution in very warm years such as 2000, when they ripened fully.

The grapes are sorted at the winery. There is more parcel selection than in the past, and the Schÿlers have bought a battery of smaller tanks to make this possible. A reverse-osmosis machine was used for the first time in 1999 for some of the Cabernet Sauvignon, but ultra-concentration is not their aim. Since 2002, fermentation takes place with indigenous yeasts. Malolactic fermentation takes place in tanks and in barriques, and the wine is aged for sixteen to eighteen months in up to forty per cent new oak.

There is no point commenting in detail on the vintages of the 1980s. The wine was pleasant enough, but it was fairly dilute and lacked excitement. It would have been hard to spot as a classified growth in a blind tasting. The 1990 is significantly better, with remarkable elegance on the nose. On the palate the wine, as before, lacked some concentration, but it had fruit, spiciness, length, and, above all, finesse. The 1993 was burly and rather dry, but the 1994 had some vibrancy and vigour, a good result for the vintage. With the 1995 the Rolland influence begins to make itself felt. When I tasted the wine blind, I noted chocolatey, oaky aromas, and even a hint of olives, and on the palate I found a supple texture, more concentration than in the past, and substantial ripe tannins. These characteristics were present in the elegant 1996 too, a very good and complex wine with persistence and depth that by 2007 was in its prime but by no means tiring. The 1997 was attractive when young, but is now fading gracefully. The 1998 is a sumptuous, fleshy wine, with toasty, smoky aromas, powerful fruit, and a spicy finish. My initial blind-tasting note recorded: "not very Margaux but complete and harmonious" and, having retasted the wine, I stand by that verdict. The 1999 has blackcurrant pastille aromas, and sweeter fruit, but by 2007 it had still to shed a certain stolidity.

The 2000 is voluptuous, with a splendid nose of blackcurrant, blackberry, oak, and woodsmoke; on the palate it is powerful and concentrated, but also complex and seductive; the tannins are massive but ripe, and this is a Kirwan built to last. The 2001 is similar, marked by new oak, weighty and concentrated, but lacking some elegance. The 2002 has vibrantly fruity aromas, and is lush and packed with fruit, but it has more flesh and roundness than the preceding two vintages. Fruit dominates tannin in the 2003, a serious effort that lacks the baked character of the vintage; the fruit is attractive even if the wine lacks some depth and length. The 2004 is rich and assertive, but less spectacular than the succulent and harmonious 2005.

Jonathan Nossiter's film *Mondovino* focused attention on the typicity of Kirwan. I share the view of those who maintain that Kirwan is not a copybook Margaux; it doesn't have the finesse, it doesn't soar. On the other hand, since Michel Rolland began advising the Schÿlers the quality has improved radically. Perhaps in the future, a middle way will be found. Rolland's association with the property ended in 2006.

Château Labégorce-Margaux

*Margaux. Tel: 0557 887132. Website: www.chateau-labegorce.fr. **Owner:** Perrodo family. 35 ha.*
*48% Cabernet Sauvignon, 40% Merlot, 10% Cabernet Franc, 2% Petit Verdot. **Production:** 240,000 bottles.*
Second wines: Tour de Laroze, Tour de Labégorce

In the mid-eighteenth century this property, which dates back to medieval times, belonged to the Gorsse family, whose name lives on in the place name. The imposing if rather chunky château was built by the architect Corcelles in the 1830s; ornate iron railings enclose its pert, formal gardens. The estate was sold in 1865 to a Bordeaux lawyer called Fortuné Beaucourt. It is not clear why the vineyards were never classified. In 1918 it was sold again, and once more in 1965. The modern era of Labégorce begins in 1989, when the property was bought by Hubert Perrodo, an oil tycoon from Brittany. In 2005 he bought the neighbouring property of Labégorce-Zédé. Perrodo also restored the ruinous Château de Labégorce de Gorsse, which stands between the two Labégorce wine estates. However, he died unexpectedly while on a skiing holiday in late 2006.

The vineyards are divided into three major parcels, the largest lying behind the buildings and just beyond the vineyards of Labégorce-Zédé. As they continue down toward the *palus*, the soil changes, with a gradually increasing clay content. There is a second parcel between the château and the D2 road, and other parcels on the other side of the road on deep gravel. Their neighbours to the south are Margaux and Lascombes. The average age of the vines is thirty years. The soil is ploughed and no chemical fertilizers are used. The harvest has been manual since 1991.

The grapes are sorted before and after destemming. After a brief cold soak, selected yeasts are added and fermentation begins in concrete tanks, with pumpovers and *délestage*. Some of the must is fermented in 400-litre barrels, and then blended into the rest of the wine. The Cabernet goes through malolactic fermentation in tanks, but the Merlot gets special treatment in new barriques. The winemakers have used micro-oxygenation in the past, but their enthusiasm has apparently waned. There is also some lees-stirring during the barrel-ageing, which continues for up to fifteen months in an average of thirty-five per cent new oak, with some American barrels.

The estate also cultivates almost four hectares of Haut-Médoc vineyards, which are of course vinified separately and released as Château La Mouline de Labégorce.

From the pre-Perrodo period I have tasted the 1976 and 1981, both rather lean wines. The 1990 was showing just a hint of maturity in 1997; the nose was ripe and charming, the fruit flavours upfront and lively. Forget the rather dilute and herbaceous 1994. The 1995 is a touch more extracted, but has a silky texture, and is marred only by rather assertive tannins. The 1996 is a medium-bodied wine, with attractive cherry fruit and a long but robust finish. The 1997 is drinking well but is fully ready. The 1998 is gamey on the nose, while the palate is medium-bodied with rather drab tannins. The 1999 is aromatic but lacks excitement and is quite forward. The 2000 is, as one would expect, much more opulent, with rich aromas of blackcurrants and plums; it's dense but opulent, lively and fresh. The 2001 has aromas of sour cherries and plums; the extraction of the preceding vintages is absent, and instead this medium-bodied wine shows more elegance. There are pretty cherry and raspberry aromas on the 2002, a supple, fresh wine that will come round soon. The 2003 is somewhat hollow, diffuse, and simple but it doesn't lack fruit and will be an enjoyable medium-term wine. The more stylish 2004 has more chewy tannins than usual, but they are well balanced by the wine's acidity and length. The 2005 is marked by gorgeous blackcurrant and cherry aromas, by the fleshiness of the palate, and by its excellent length.

Château Labégorce-Zédé

Soussans. Tel: 0557 887132. Website: www.chateau-labegorce.fr. Owner: Perrodo family. 36 ha.
50% Cabernet Sauvignon, 35% Merlot, 10% Cabernet Franc, 5% Petit Verdot. Production: 85,000 bottles.
Second wine: Domaine Zédé

The two Labégorce properties were once a single estate, and this portion was sold off in 1795. They may well be reunited again eventually, since in 2005 Hubert Perrodo, the late owner of Labégorce-Margaux, bought Zédé. This estate takes its name from Pierre Zédé, its owner in the mid-nineteenth century. In 1961 it was bought by Jean Battesti, who replanted part of the estate and did improve quality. Battesti sold the estate to the Thienpont family of Belgium in 1979. Luc Thienpont did a brilliant job here from the outset, but by the 2000s a general feeling that the family should focus on its more important properties on the Right Bank led to the sale.

When he arrived, Luc Thienpont knew, on his own admission, rather little about winemaking, and at first was heavily reliant on the good advice of Emile Peynaud (who considered the vineyards of classified-growth quality) and Jacques Boissenot. He learned fast.

Of the thirty-six hectares, twenty-seven are in AC Margaux, and twenty-two of those are next to the château. Grapes from lower soils near the river go into an AC Bordeaux called "Z de Zédé", which is Merlot-dominated. Various exchanges of parcels with Château Lascombes brought more coherence to the fragmented parcels of Margaux. These vineyards are on deep gravel soil but as they slope down toward the estuary the clay content increases. There are also some five hectares in Soussans, usually consigned to the second wine. The property is fortunate in possessing some very old vines; about one-third are between thirty and eighty years old. The oldest Cabernet Franc was planted in the 1940s, and some Petit Verdot is a century old. Luc Thienpont invested in new drainage and improved canopy management; new plantings were made at high density. No herbicides are used. Yields tend to be around fifty hl/ha.

The harvest is manual, and the vinification classic. "If on this terroir you can't make great wine without resorting to hi-tech innovations," Thienpont told me, "then you should give up being a winemaker." The wine is aged for about eighteen months in fifty per cent new oak.

I have tasted the 1982 at various points during its life, and it has always been a delicious, supple wine, with lovely blackberry fruit. Today it is showing some age, with a brick-red colour, cedary aromas, and a fine, ripe sweetness on the palate, dosed with spice. The 1990 remains thoroughly youthful, with a smoky, cedary nose, and a palate that is rich, tight, and concentrated, with fine acidity and length. The 1995 remains aromatically restrained, but has both sweet fruit and robust tannins on the palate. The 1996 has rich blackberry and cedar aromas; by 2007 it had become rounded and fully ready to drink. The 1999 has smoky, coffee aromas, with some black-cherry fruit, and although there is a core of sweet fruit, the tannins are firm. The toasty 2000 is bursting with blackcurrant fruit; there is no shortage of tannin, and the fruit is so ripe that the wine seems to lack a little acidity. Thienpont believes the 2001 will be longer-lived than the 2000, and he may well be right. It's certainly a wine of balance and vigour, with ample acidity cutting through the fairly dense fruit. The 2002 has a touch more charm, but does not lack fruit and concentration. The 2003 lacks some weight and stuffing; it's lush but the finish is dry and dour. The 2004 has everything going for it: well-judged oak, ripe tannins, and a long, vigorous finish. Despite its density and power, the 2005 has supple tannins and considerable finesse.

Overall, these wines reach greater heights than those of Labégorce-Margaux, and one can only hope they retain their stylishness and occasional brilliance under the new regime.

8. Margaux Part II

Château Lascombes

*Margaux. Tel: 0557 887066. Website: www.chateau-lascombes.com. **Owner:** Colony Capital. Deuxième cru.*
*84 ha. 50% Merlot, 45% Cabernet Sauvignon, 5% Petit Verdot. **Production:** 300,000 bottles.*
Second wine: Chevalier de Lascombes

This estate takes its name from the Chevalier Antoine de Lascombes, the owner in the seventeenth century. By 1855, a Mlle. Hue was the proprietor. In 1952 the wine merchant and writer Alexis Lichine headed a group of American investors who bought and transformed the property. It had shrunk by this time, and Lichine avidly collected parcels of vines, thus expanding the vineyards considerably. It appears that some well-connected *maîtres de chai* in Margaux alerted their friends to Lichine's hunger for vineyards, and some of them cannily sold him parcels at inflated prices. As a consequence, much of the expanded Lascombes estate was clearly not of Second-Growth quality, as the present managers readily concede. The brewers Bass Charrington had bought his wine company, and in 1971 Lichine sold them Lascombes as well. Unfortunately, good brewers are not necessarily good stewards of wine estates; yields climbed at Lascombes and quality declined. In 2000 the company sold Lascombes to a consortium that included Yves Vatelot of Château Reignac, Tony Ryan of Ryanair, and the controlling partner, Colony Capital, an American investment fund. (By 2007, however, the property was said to be once again on the market.)

To run the property, Colony hired Dominique Befve, who had previously worked at L'Evangile and Lafite. Michel Rolland was hired as consultant, as was Dr. Alain Raynaud, a man embedded in the traditions of Right Bank Bordeaux. It was not a popular appointment with the resident team at Lascombes. He did not last long, for reasons Befve is too discreet to reveal.

Befve knew there was much that needed doing at Lascombes. He instituted a close study of the vineyards, heightened the trellising, and reorganized the winery. There had been problems with brettanomyces in the *chai*, and Befve worked hard, and successfully, to eradicate it. To conduct the soil analysis, his team dug four holes per hectare; they also analysed the different rootstocks in use. They soon realized that one of the reasons that Lascombes had been underperforming was that soil type and variety were sometimes poorly matched. Thus there was Cabernet Sauvignon planted on clay soils where Merlot would have done better. Moreover, the density of plantation was low for Margaux: 6,400 vines per hectare. So Befve pulled out twelve hectares that he was convinced could never make great wine, and replanted them with Merlot at 10,000 vines per hectare. Missing vines were replaced; some Cabernet Franc near the château was grafted over to Cabernet Sauvignon. The net result of all this rejigging was a substantial increase in Merlot, but Befve insists this was to do with the nature of the terroir, rather than because of any tender feelings toward Merlot as a variety. Before 2001 there had been roughly thirty-five per cent Merlot; by now it is fifty per cent. Of the eighty-four hectares under vine, moreover, only fifty were deemed capable of producing the *grand vin*. It's hard to generalize about the soil at Lascombes, but overall it consists of *croupes* of gravel, quartz, and coarse sand on a clay base.

Alain Raynaud moved into action in 2001 by hiring more vineyard workers to perform operations that would reduce the yield to around thirty hectolitres per hectare. He also used reverse osmosis and bought more new oak barrels. The result was a powerful if atypical wine. Furthermore, the directors were obliged to increase the price dramatically. The *prix de sortie* in 1999 was 14.33 Euros, in 2000 it was 18.50; in 2001, it soared to 25.00. Almost all other estates moved their prices in the opposite direction, so Lascombes was out on a limb and the market was not impressed. A balance needs to be struck between making sensible investments and then recouping the outlay, but it was widely believed that Lascombes had got it wrong.

Nonetheless the improvements at Lascombes were permanent and beneficial. From 2001 harvesting was done in *cagettes*. The grapes are hoisted up to a platform above the tanks; here the fruit is sorted before and after destemming. Special lighting simulates natural light to make defective grapes easier to spot and remove. The fruit is crushed above the tanks, so there is no pumping. The must is cold-soaked for up to ten days. Then selected yeast is added and fermentation takes off; the *cuvaison* can last up to thirty days. From 2002 all malolactic fermentation takes place in barrels. Until 2001 the wine was aged in one-third new barriques; thereafter the proportion was increased to eighty-five per cent. The barrels are stored on special Oxoline racks that allow them to be rotated every few days so as to keep the fine lees in suspension. Befve prefers this to micro-oxygenation, as the stirring takes place in a reductive environment. This process continues for about five months. If any reductive aromas develop, subsequent rackings will dissipate them.

The older vintages of Lascombes that I have tasted have been a mixed bag, with a 1955 drying out by 1987, a 1962 dour and tired by 1993, but a 1979 perfumed and cedary in 1995, with a fine texture, remarkable freshness, and considerable elegance. The 1985 is quite rich, but lightly structured and not that concentrated. The 1986 has rich, leafy, cedary aromas, and on the palate has more backbone and concentration; it's holding up well. The 1988 has brambly aromas, but is loosely structured and a touch coarse. The 1990 is more lush, almost jammy, but has concentration and tannic backbone. The dour 1994 is forgettable, and the 1995 is disappointing for the vintage; it lacks flesh and weight and has only modest length. The 1996 has slightly vegetal aromas; it has some elegance, but insufficient depth and weight. Rough tannins still dominate the 1998, which has some fruit and fire but lacks finesse and finishes dry. The 1999 has light, floral aromas, but it's rather dilute and will evolve fast. I have mixed notes on the 2000, so perhaps I have been confronted by a couple of poor bottles. As for the controversial 2001, I quote my own note from a blind tasting in 2005: "rich new oak nose, powerful, imposing; very rich and concentrated, dense, powerful tannins, has real weight of fruit, not very Margaux but impressive, complex, and long". By 2007 it seemed jammy on the nose, but the impressive weight and spiciness remained, though it lacked length. The balance is somewhat rectified with the delicious 2002, which remains rather big and brash, but has a fine, silky texture and ripe, pure, direct fruit. Clumsy at first, the 2003 has settled down: it's rich and dense, with firm tannins giving structure and complexity. It also has more length than many wines from this year.

It is quite clear that the modern Lascombes is a considerable improvement on the Lascombes of old. Although the balance swung too far toward extraction in an attempt to correct the errors of the past, I am persuaded that Befve will find an appropriate middle ground. The 2004, on the basis of a barrel sample, had splendid tightness and concentration, suggesting that the new style of Lascombes will maintain those elements of richness and power, while aiming for the greater finesse that is a hallmark of great Margaux.

Château Malescot-St-Exupéry

Margaux. Tel: 0557 889720. Website: www.malescot.com. Owner: Jean-Luc Zuger. Troisième cru.
23.5 ha. 50% Cabernet Sauvignon, 35% Merlot, 10% Cabernet Franc, 5% Petit Verdot.
Production: 150,000 bottles. Second wine: La Dame de Malescot

Malescot dates back to the seventeenth century, and takes its name from Simon Malescot, whose descendants remained as proprietors until 1827. During the eighteenth century it was the largest wine property in the region, with 145 hectares. The purchaser in 1827 was Comte Jean-Baptiste de St-Exupéry. After his death, his widow put it on the market in 1853, and thereafter it had many owners. The château was built in 1870. The property grew in 1874, when it absorbed the neighbouring Château Dubigny, which in 1855 had also been classified as a Third Growth. It was bought by Bremen businessmen in 1900, which led to its confiscation during World War I. In 1919 Malescot was bought by a British wine merchant called W.H. Chaplin, which appointed two managers, Paul Zuger and Edmund Ritz. In 1955 Chaplin decided to sell, and Paul Zuger and his son Roger bought the estate. At this time the vineyards had dwindled to only seven hectares and the château was dilapidated. Since 1994 Roger's son Jean-Luc has been running the property, with advice from Michel Rolland until 2006.

The Zugers have expanded the property considerably. As well as the 23.5 hectares of vines in AC Margaux, they own 6.5 hectares of Bordeaux Supérieur (Domaine du Balardin). The Margaux vines are located near Château Margaux and Labégorce. The average age of the vines is thirty-five years. Zuger green-harvests to keep yields to around forty-five hl/ha, and claims he is one of the last in Margaux to pick. Thus in the precocious 2003 vintage, he began picking the Merlot only on September 25.

The grapes are brought to the winery in *cagettes*, where they are sorted before and after destemming. The grapes descend into cement and stainless-steel tanks by gravity. Zuger is an unapologetic believer in reverse-osmosis concentration, which he employs quite frequently. The must is fermented with indigenous yeasts, and the *cuvaison* can be prolonged to six weeks. Since 1998 Zuger has used entirely new oak to age the *grand vin*, and there is some lees-stirring at the beginning of the ageing period, which is usually sixteen to eighteen months. Rolland advises on the final blend shortly before bottling. Zuger aims to bottle at least eighty-five per cent as Malescot.

Zuger says the great vintages of Malescot were in the 1950s and 1960s, though I have not had the pleasure of tasting any of them. Thereafter they dipped in quality, but Zuger says he is working hard to restore quality to its former heights. Certainly in the 1980s the wines were disappointing, and I came across bottles that were funky or musty, which may have been the consequence of old or poor barrels. Even the 1982 is astringent and mediocre. The 1985 was soft, rounded, easy-going, with only modest concentration. The 1986 has been consistently tough and charmless, lacking in fruit. The 1988 is better, quite oaky, but a wine with panache and spiciness. The 1989 has toasty and minty aromas, but this is a fairly lean style and doesn't taste that ripe. The 1993 and 1994 were simple and rather dilute. The 1995 struck me as dull and over-extracted, with a soupy texture. But by 1998 the style had changed markedly: the aromas were more lush and generous, with evident sweet new oak; the palate was supple and juicy, and there were firm but not harsh tannins behind the black-fruits flavours. The 1999 had a similarly opulent nose, but was rather chunky and over-dense, without the usual charm of the vintage. The 2000 is lovely, with seductive blackcurrant aromas, a velvety texture, lush fruit with ample ripe tannin, an opulent but not overblown style, and good length. The 2001 also has a good deal of sweet new oak on the nose, with aromas of plums and mocha as well as blackcurrant; the palate is not too extracted, and this is graceful wine of impeccable balance and accessibility. The 2002 is similar, with much toasty new oak on the nose, fine texture, lots of flesh, and a spicy, vigorous finish. The 2003 is rounded but nonetheless austere, and the tannins are distinctly dry.

Like Kirwan, Malescot does bear the mark of Rolland. These are very dark wines, super-ripe, richly oaky, quite powerful in structure, and arguably lacking in Margaux typicity. Zuger insists he doesn't want to make wines that are heavy and that he is looking for freshness. I have to say that freshness is not the first word that springs to mind when reflecting on Malescot, but the wines are consistent in style and packed with fruit. More importantly, they are far superior to the insipid and sometimes faulty wines of the 1980s. Whatever the debate may be about their typicity, these are wines that will give a great deal of pleasure.

Château Margaux

Margaux. Tel: 0557 888383. Website: www.chateau-margaux.com. Owner: Corinne Mentzelopoulos. Premier cru.
78 ha. 66 ha red: 75% Cabernet Sauvignon, 20% Merlot, 5% Petit Verdot and Cabernet Franc. 12 ha white:
100% Sauvignon Blanc. Production: 380,000 bottles. Second wine: Pavillon Rouge de Ch Margaux

If one were to be offered a *premier cru* for Christmas, which would it be? I suspect most of us would choose Margaux, if only because it has the grandest château. (You could also drink it with pleasure every day, which is perhaps not the case with the noble Yquem.) Margaux, unlike most of the other *premiers*, physically lives up to its billing. The view of the tall neo-classical château never fails to thrill as one turns down the drive – only to be halted by the iron railings and directed politely to the car park near the *chais*.

The château dates from 1811, though it's thought there was once a medieval fortress on the site. The vineyards were developed by the d'Aulèdes family, who were the owners in the mid-seventeenth century. By the beginning of the following century, Margaux was already established as one of the most sought-after wines of the Médoc. The Fumel family maintained that reputation. The property was confiscated during the Revolution, and in 1802 purchased by the Marquis Douat de Colonilla, whom we have to thank for the present château. The estate frequently changed hands in the nineteenth century, and in the 1920s it was acquired by a consortium of shareholders, of whom the most important were the Ginestet family. By 1949 they had become the majority shareholders. But the difficult years of the early 1970s affected the fortunes of the Ginestets too (not to mention the quality of the wine). By 1975 they were badly in debt, with turnover failing to diminish that debt. Pierre Ginestet had no choice but to sell up. French interest was slight, so a Greek-born entrepreneur called André Mentzelopoulos, who had built up the substantial chain of Félix Potin grocery stores, secured the property in 1977 for what now seems like the bargain price of seventy-two million francs. Since the package included stocks of recent vintages, the new owner could subsidize his own purchase by selling off much of that wine.

Corinne Mentzelopoulos recalls:

> In the 1970s Margaux had been on the market for two years. These were very tough years for Bordeaux. My father went to see Pierre Ginestet and had lunch at the château, which had been unoccupied for three years, and after lunch they shook hands on a deal and that was it. He just fell in love with the place, and started spending money on it right away, before the boom of the 1980s. He also restored the château. He brought in Emile Peynaud, and by the time of the great years from 1982 onwards, my father was ready.

Sadly, André Mentzelopoulos did not have many years to enjoy his coup and his property. He died in 1980, and his widow Laure and his young daughter Corinne took over. In 1982 they built the temperature-controlled underground *chai* for the second-year barrels. Despite her inexperience, Corinne proved a quick study, soon getting to grips with the complexities of running a large and complex wine estate. One of her earliest and best decisions was to appoint Paul Pontallier as director. It was a courageous move because of his youth and relative inexperience. On the other hand, his educational background was impeccable — studies at Montpellier in viticulture and a doctorate on the barrel-ageing of red wines — and he was widely travelled. This was to prove an inspired choice. From 1983 owner and director have worked smoothly together to run and promote this exceptional estate. Moreover, Pontallier has also assembled a brilliant team to work with him. He too has chosen youth and energy over age and experience. When the vineyard manager Jean-Pierre Blanchard left in 2004, Pontallier chose as his replacement Julien Boiteau, who was in his mid-twenties.

Corinne Mentzelopoulos was such a visible figure internationally that it was always assumed she had a controlling interest in the property. It was known that the Agnellis of Fiat were shareholders, but after the death of Giovanni Agnelli in 2003 it emerged that the Italians owned seventy-five per cent of the company, since Giovanni Agnelli had bought a majority share in the Mentzelopoulos holding company. There was much speculation that Corinne would be unable to hang onto the château. This was to underestimate her business acumen, as she managed to raise the 350 million dollars required to buy the Agnelli share and gain complete control of Château Margaux. Wine-lovers, well aware of her personal commitment to the estate, breathed a sigh of relief.

About ninety per cent of the present vineyard holdings correspond to those of 1855. Three-quarters of the vineyards are on deep gravel and gravelly clay soils, which is ideal for Cabernet. Soils with more clay and limestone content are given over to Merlot. Not all the gravel is especially deep; one part of the property lies on thinner gravel close to the bedrock, yet gives excellent wines. Pontallier proudly claims that Château Margaux is a great terroir for Cabernet Sauvignon. Yes, the Merlot can be excellent too, as in 2001, but the Cabernet is even better. The average yield is around forty hl/ha, though in years such as 1995, 1996, and 2004 it can rise to fifty-five hl/ha.

When she first began managing Château Margaux, Corinne Mentzelopoulous was puzzled when her team spoke to her of the glorious terroir here.

> When I first came here in 1983 I didn't believe in terroir. Our team would show me a parcel and tell me that this particular patch of gravel always gave the best wine. How could that possibly be so, I wondered? But of course they were right. One year I woke up at the château and looked out of the window. The Gironde had flooded and there was water everywhere. I phoned the chef de culture in a panic. He told me not to worry. I soon discovered that every single vine and all the estate buildings were untouched by the water. Two, three centuries ago, those who created the estate simply knew the terrain and how to avoid such problems.

Discussing whether the wines of Bordeaux were becoming more standardized, Paul Pontallier told me:

> If certain well-known journalists reflect the taste of their readers, then it is not completely unreasonable to try to produce wines that will please those consumers. It's not a stupid approach. But it could be dangerous long-term. The quality and originality of our wine are still linked to our special terroir. Our job is to give the best possible expression to that terroir, not to cater to any one journalist's taste-buds.

> I have said that winemaking is the easy part at Margaux. But I don't want to sound complacent. We have our own research department here and we are constantly looking for ways to do better. I am not the only person on the Margaux team with a doctorate in oenology! We are always looking at new techniques.

Indeed, one of the valued members of Pontallier's team is Dr. Vincent Millet, whose job, I was told, is to question everything. Indeed, Château Margaux does not subscribe to many of the orthodoxies of modern Bordeaux viticulture. They are not at all keen on early deleafing, as that can cause the berries to shrivel up and give overripe flavours. Constant experimentation has aided their quest for ever-higher quality. For instance they have studied the oxygenation of the *marc* after fermentation. They concluded that it was important to protect the *marc* from oxygen at this stage, and believe this has improved the quality of the press wine. Just a detail, but one of hundreds that contribute to the overall quality and style of any wine.

The team experimented with reverse osmosis in 1999 and 2000, then compared the results with lots that had either been chaptalized or bled. They found the differences in the wine were negligible. Pontallier and Millet are utterly opposed to micro-oxygenation at Margaux, as they think it can increase micro-bacterial levels in the wine and dry it out. Thus all the techniques of modern vinification are assessed, primarily to see whether or not they can make any contribution to the wine of Margaux.

Pontallier believes strongly that the grapes should be sorted in the vineyard, and that highly trained pickers will do a better job than a sorting table. Nor, after more experiments, has he found any clear advantage in picking in *cagettes* as opposed to the larger *remorques* used at Margaux. There is no sorting at the winery, and after destemming and crushing, the must is pumped into a vat for fermentation. Thus none of the techniques now so much in vogue – ever-growing numbers of sorting tables, destemming by hand, no crushing, cold soaks – is employed at Margaux, yet the wine seems none the worse for it.

The wine is aged for eighteen to twenty-four months in new medium-toast barriques, with traditional racking. Many of the barrels are made by the estate's own cooper, but they also buy from five other coopers. Blending is done over the winter.

Production of Château Margaux is usually smaller than that of Pavillon Rouge, the second wine, which is excellent in its own right, especially in good years. Thus in 1999 only forty per cent of the crop was selected for Château Margaux, whereas in 1982 it was seventy per cent. Pavillon Rouge was first made in 1908. It differs from the *grand vin* in having considerably more Merlot, up to one-third, since much Merlot has been replanted in recent years. The vinification is identical for the two *cuvées*, but Pavillon Rouge is barrel-aged for a shorter period in about fifty per cent new oak.

There has been a white wine here since the 1920s; indeed the château has records of a Sauvignon made at Margaux in the nineteenth century. In the late 1960s a frost-prone site that had not been replanted after phylloxera was reserved for white grapes. Sauvignon was planted from 1968 to 1980. It has become more than a sideline, since there are twelve hectares planted. The grapes are whole-cluster-pressed, there is no skin contact, the must is fermented with selected yeasts, and the wine aged in one-third new barriques with lees-stirring. There is no malolactic, as acidity levels are not high in the first place, thanks to the high ripeness levels at which the grapes are picked. Pavillon Blanc is a powerful wine – fourteen degrees of alcohol is not unusual – but Margaux aims for a wine with complex aromas and freshness, which can evolve with bottle-age.

I am not entirely convinced by Pavillon Blanc, at least not at the price being asked for it. The 1980 was lemony, oaky, but had a rather rasping finish. The 1982 was quite catty and tart, though it had body and length. Vintages I have enjoyed include the plump, oaky 1983, the charmingly pungent 1987, the supple, peachy 1989, the spicy, highly concentrated 1990, the plump, silky, lightly honeyed 1993, the sleek, melony 1996, the very powerful 1999, which is slightly marred, though, by high alcohol, the citric, spicy 2001, the excellent 2002, the rich, sleek 2004, and the perfumed but full-bodied, boldly flavoured 2005.

The oldest vintage I have tasted is the legendary 1900. In 2007 it smelt agreeably of mushrooms and *café au lait*; the fruit was still sweet, pure, and intense, with no trace of astringency. The 1943 was fresh and silky but starting to fade. At forty years of age the 1949 was still glorious: very fragrant, perfectly balanced, and extremely long. The 1955 I found disappointing: the nose is exquisite and delicate, but the palate lacks weight and persistence. At thirty years of age, the nose of the 1959 was of violets, discreet but elegant, and the palate had intensity and delicacy rather than weight. The 1961 has remained youthful too, and the aromas are intense, spicy, and cedary; it may be a touch raisiny on the finish, but the fruit quality is delicious and the Margaux finesse is there in spades. Thereafter Margaux went through a bad patch.

The 1966 has a fine reputation, but the only time I have tasted it, it struck me as good but not exceptional: soft, plump, and rather light. My experience of the 1970 ranges from the fairly nasty to the acceptable if rather dry. The 1973 was lightweight, to put it mildly, and rather acidic. The 1975 is not one of Margaux's triumphs. It was made when the Ginestets were hitting rock bottom and it shows: it's lean but not harsh. The 1976 is better, but that's not saying much. The 1978 and 1979 were not bad wines, but they didn't have the fruit or finesse one expects from this estate.

The 1981, however, is a pleasant surprise, with a sweet, minty nose of startling intensity; perhaps the tannins are a touch dry, but the wine is rich, concentrated, spicy, and long. The 1982 has sweet, leafy aromas that never stray into portiness; on the palate it is sweet and sumptuous, concentrated and deep, yet with fine, lingering acidity on the finish. I was not always convinced by the celebrated 1983, but recent tastings have bowled me over: that vibrant, intense Margaux perfume now aromatized by a sumptuous hint of truffles, a cocktail of red fruits knitted together with stylish oak, and a palate of concentration and profundity, poised, harmonious, and delicious. The finish is remarkably lively and persistent.

The 1985 has classic blackcurrant aromas, with hints of black coffee and mint. It remains tannic and tight, especially for 1985, but has vigour and length and will continue to develop. The 1986 is more dense, despite its extreme concentration. The nose shows a light savoury tone, as well as intense blackcurrant aromas, while the palate has unusual power for Margaux and assertive tannins that suggest the wine is still far from its peak. The

1988 has cedary, blackcurranty aromas; it too is still concentrated and tight, perhaps lacking in Margaux charm, but it still tastes youthful. On the nose, the profound 1989 is both opulent and intensely pure, as is the palate, with its sweet, vibrant fruit and refreshing acidity; the balance is impossible to fault.

The 1990 is exquisite, with leafy, truffley aromas and finely integrated new oak; despite its depth, power, and concentration, it is laced through with lovely acidity, which gives it excellent length and impeccable finesse. I found the 1991 rather bitter when young, but have not tasted it recently. Delicate blackcurrant aromas mark the 1993, but the palate shows some hard edges and a lack of flesh. The 1994 is chewy and lacks elegance and charm, with a rather dour finish. The balance is back with the terrific 1995, with its elegant but forceful nose. This is still tannic, tight, and needs time, but it seems very complete and balanced.

The 1996 is a marvel of intensity and elegance. The aromas are lush, smoky, and thoroughly enticing – one's nose keeps dipping back into the glass for more stimulation. The wine is still tight and tannic, but creamy and highly concentrated, with formidable presence and length. I was pleasantly surprised by the quality of the 1997. Yes, it's svelte, supple, and quite forward for Château Margaux, but it's not shallow or simple. The 1998 has toasty aromas, with hints of blackcurrant and coffee; it's voluptuous for Margaux, with unusual power, tannic force, and length of flavour. The 1999 is very fragrant, while the palate is discreet and velvety, though backed by firm tannins, yet without any trace of over-extraction. The 2000 is formidable: the nose is voluptuous, with blackcurrant and plum aromas, but the palate packs a punch, with exceptional spice, weight, and depth. This is a remarkably complete and harmonious wine with tremendous length that promises a long and rewarding future. The 2001 is delicious, with slightly atypical cherry fruit; it's supple yet spicy, almost lush, with remarkable strength of flavour, but perhaps it lacks the length of the greatest vintages here. I love the purity and intensity of the 2002, sweet without being jammy, concentrated without seeming heavy, elegant and marvellously fresh. It has a great future. I was not expecting much from the 2003, but it's a good wine, with a rich, savoury, blackcurranty nose, a sweet, silky attack and fleshy texture, and, unlike so many 2003s, it is structured and doesn't lack acidity. However, a certain muscularity is imposed by the vintage. The 2004 is discreetly oaky on the nose, with ripe blackcurrant and cherry fruit; although inevitably tannic, it's also zesty and persistent, while a cask sample of the 2005 was simply sensational, with tremendous freshness as well as density.

No one tasting the remarkable series of vintages since 1982 would call Château Margaux "feminine". Yet even at its mightiest, there is a restraining elegance and grace to the wine. It's never brash, it's hardly ever burly, but equally it doesn't lack virility and strength. It's like a clipper in full sail drawing closer and gaining in amplitude as it moves deftly across the seas. One marvels at its beauty rather than at its power. Instead of femininity, I find perfume and purity, a crystalline note of the exquisite that is rare even among the great growths of the Médoc.

Marojallia

*Margaux. Tel: 0557 889697. Website: www.marojallia.com. **Owner:** Philippe Porcheron.*
*4 ha. 75% Cabernet Sauvignon, 25% Merlot. **Production:** 10,000 bottles. **Second wine:** Clos Margalaine*

Not Château Marojallia but plain Marojallia. This recent addition to the Margaux firmament is shining brightly. It began with a grower called Roger Rex, who was getting on in years and wondering what to do with his parcel of vines near Arsac. Apparently everyone was keen to get their hands on these vines, though it's not quite clear why Roger Rex decided to work together with Philippe Porcheron, who owned a property in Moulis. Porcheron then got in touch with Right Bank magician Jean-Luc Thunevin, who dispatched his wife Muriel Andraud to make the wine, which would be called Marojallia and make its debut with the 1999 vintage. Not only Michel Rolland but Riccardo Cotarella were called in as consultants. That makes an awful lot of interested parties in a very small parcel of vines – though it has subsequently been expanded with the acquisition of one hectare of ten-year-old vines at Soussans and half a hectare near the cellars.

When the wine was first released, much fuss was made of the exceedingly low yields of twenty hl/ha from which it had been made. A little detective work at the town hall, where harvest records must be deposited, soon revealed that, on the contrary, the yields were quite generous. Confronted by this apparent deception, Thunevin told me that whereas the yields for the whole parcel were indeed quite high, when you took into account the quantity of wine destined for the second label, the yields used to produce Marojallia were as low as had been stated. This is of course nonsense. When a classified growth claims to have yields of forty-five hl/ha, that figure is supposed to reflect the total yield, not the proportion used just for the *grand vin*. This is significant, because Thunevin and his associates were claiming that Marojallia was Margaux's first *vin de garage*, made from minuscule yields and aged entirely in new oak and bottled unfined and unfiltered. Thunevin likes to provoke and annoy, and he certainly succeeded. He also charges a very high price for the wine (80–120 Euros) despite its lack of track record, but I suppose he needs to pay the bills of his starry consultants.

Fuel was added to the flames when France's leading wine critic Michel Bettane described the 1999 as spectacular, and compared its qualities in some respects to those of the celebrated 1945 vintage. I have not tasted the 1999, but I have tasted the 2002, which is unquestionably a delicious wine, with lush, oaky aromas, a fleshy, even soft texture, sweet oak, and considerable charm. If it has a defect, it is that it lacks some persistence. The 2003, tasted shortly before bottling, was in the same mould but more massive, opaque in colour, dominated by new oak, and showing powerful but ripe tannins. The second wine isn't bad either.

So Marojallia is not all hype. The wine is good, if highly etxracted. I'm not sure it is recognizable as Margaux, but to many tasters and consumers that is of little importance. Meanwhile the Marojallia bandwagon rolls on. Much of the wine is sold by the Pavillon de Margaux, a pleasant little hotel with a wine boutique on the premises. Catherine Laurent, who owns the Pavillon, has joined forces with the Marojallia team to purchase the former Ginestet mansion, which stands opposite the entrance to the Durfort-Vivens winery. This has now been converted into a winery (for the 2005 vintage onwards) and, naturally, a luxurious bed and breakfast. In the meantime the burghers of Margaux, if their noses are out of joint, aren't letting on. They quietly ignore the interloper in their midst.

Château Marquis d'Alesme-Becker

Margaux. Tel: 0557 887027. Owner: Perrodo family. Troisième cru. 16 ha. 45% Merlot, 30% Cabernet Sauvignon, 15% Cabernet Franc, 10% Petit Verdot. Production: 90,000 bottles. Second wine: Marquis d'Alesme

This property is squatting, quite legitimately, in the former Château Desmirail, which was built in the 1840s. The estate, which dates back to the sixteenth century, was bought by M. Zuger's grandfather in 1938, and he is the uncle of Jean-Luc Zuger, who owns Malescot-St-Exupéry. Jean-Claude, a genial, ponytailed, chain-smoking gentleman, ran this estate from 1979. Until 1995 this was one of the smallest classified growths, but in that year he reclaimed six hectares that had formerly been leased to Malescot. I think he would agree that this property was not showing its full potential in recent years. But in 2000 he began making changes that would indeed result in higher quality. However, in 2006 he sold the vineyards, though not the mansion, to the late Hubert Perrodo, owner of Château Labégorce (*q.v.*).

The vineyards are divided into three principal blocks: 4.5 hectares near Château Margaux, four hectares opposite Labégorce, and 7.5 between Labégorce and Soussans. The grapes are picked by hand and since 2002 have been sorted at the winery. The vinification is traditional, and the wine is aged for twelve months in thirty-five per cent new oak, whereas until 1999 the proportion was a more modest eighteen per cent. The wine is fined but not filtered. There can be a good deal of Merlot in the blend; in 2003, for example, it was close to fifty-five per cent.

It is a wine I have rarely encountered, probably because Zuger sold most of his production to a single négociant. The 1986 was dour, the 1988 rugged even for that vintage, and I used the same term when I blind-tasted the 1995. The 1998 is dilute and lacks stuffing, a rather feeble effort. The 2002, however, has far more fruit and spice; it doesn't lack concentration and length, and should evolve well. The 2003 is initially fresh and delicate, but then firm tannins kick in to throw the wine off balance. The 2005 is not that concentrated and has rather dry tannins, but even in cask the richer, weightier 2006 shows the beneficial influence of the new owners.

Château Marquis de Terme

*Margaux. Tel: 0557 883001. Website: www.chateau-marquis-de-terme.com. **Owners:** Pierre-Louis and Philippe*
Sénéclauze. Quatrième cru. 38 ha. 55% Cabernet Sauvignon, 35% Merlot, 7% Petit Verdot, 3% Cabernet Franc.
***Production:** 180,000 bottles. **Second wine:** Les Gondats de Marquis de Terme*

In 1762 a young woman belonging to the Ledoulx d'Emplet family married François de Péguilhan, Marquis de Terme, who gave his distinguished name to this property. After the Revolution there were numerous owners, of which by far the most important was the Feuillerat family, who first managed and then acquired the estate over a period of 120 years. But by the 1930s they could no longer keep the property going, and it was offered for sale at auction. In 1935 it was bought by Pierre Sénéclauze, who was based in Algeria and exported its wines; the estate remains in his family, who also own a property in Bandol. For over thirty years Jean-Pierre Hugon has managed Marquis de Terme. A tall, relaxed man, Hugon does not deny that quality was not always optimal. In the 1970s yields were too high, and cellar hygiene was not perfect either. But over the years he has been able to make improvements, even expanding the property by twelve hectares, renovating the *cuvier*, and building a new *chai*.

The vineyards are dispersed, with only 5.5 hectares around the château, which stands close to the Rauzan properties. Here the soil is a shallow, fine gravel with a little clay. The majority of the vines, some nineteen hectares, lie on the plateau of Margaux with deep gravel over a clay subsoil. There are four hectares on gravel and black sand over sandstone at Les Gondats, a large parcel near Issan, and nine hectares on the plateau of Cantenac, where there is shallow gravel with a relatively high clay content. The average age of the vines is thirty years.

The grapes are picked by hand and sorted in the vineyard. The winery is equipped with a reverse-osmosis concentrator, though it is used only for specific lots. The must is fermented, malolactic fermentation too, in concrete vats of various sizes. Blending takes place in March, and the wine spends sixteen to eighteen months in up to fifty per cent new oak.

The oldest vintage I have tasted is the 1966, which was drying out by 1987. The 1978 had some sweet fruit, but there was worrying astringency on the finish. The 1982, which I tasted but once in 1987, is a success: a supple wine with rich fruit and good length – whether it is still going strong I cannot say. The 1986 was coarse and astringent, the 1988 slightly better but still essentially dour. Although the nose of the 1989 is rather stewed and porty, the palate shows good concentration, chewy tannins, and decent acidity. What it lacks is succulence. The 1994 was light and simple, but clean. There is some coarseness (and at one tasting some off-aromas) in the 1995, which lacks finesse and has a rather dry finish. The 1998 now has evolved aromas, a supple texture, and considerable vigour, though at the expense of flesh and weight.

With the 2000 there is a marked improvement, though it was scarcely a challenging vintage. Nonetheless this has rich, plummy aromas, some richness and concentration, quite good acidity, and the solidity that seems characteristic of this estate's wines. I found worrying, leathery, off-aromas with the 2001 on both occasions I have tasted it (once blind); the palate is better than the nose, with the tannins in balance, and there is even some elegance on the finish. The 2002 is remarkably good, with black cherries on the nose and a certain toastiness, while the palate is suave, rich, concentrated, and shows finesse. Tasted three times and with consistent notes, it suggests that there is a serious improvement under way at this estate. The 2003 is supple and fruity but hollow; drink soon.

Curiously, the brochure issued by Marquis de Terme remarks that the wine is not a classic Margaux:

> *Although it has the same elegance and complexity, it has its own characteristically powerful*
> *and assertive style.... Austere in their youth, Marquis de Terme wines only reveal their true*
> *style after several years in the bottle.*

I am not persuaded by this, and think it is essentially an excuse for insufficient ripeness, excessive extraction, and careless winemaking. Fortunately, it does seem that quality is improving.

Château Martinens

Cantenac. Tel: 0557 887137. Owner: Jean-Pierre Seynat-Dulos. 25 ha. 63% Merlot,
22% Cabernet Sauvignon, 10% Petit Verdot, 5% Cabernet Franc. Production: 45,000 bottles.
Second wines: Ch Guiney, Le Cadet de Martinens

This property, with its charming eighteenth-century château and parcels of very old vines near Cantenac-Brown, has been owned by the Dulos family since 1945. The soils are marked by quite a high clay content. The grapes are picked by machine and by hand. The wine used to be aged for twelve to fourteen months in a roughly equal blend of new barriques and tanks; today only barriques are used. The 2001 has red-fruits aromas and a slight greenness on the palate; it has some charm but is rather light, as is the 2004. The 2003 is supple and spicy but not built for long ageing.

Château Monbrison

Arsac. Tel: 0556 588004. Owner: Vonderheyden family. 21 ha. 50% Cabernet Sauvignon, 30% Merlot,
15% Cabernet Franc, 5% Petit Verdot. Production: 130,000 bottles. Second wine: Bouquet de Monbrison

Monbrison is a somewhat isolated property, not far from Château du Tertre. Part of it once belonged to Château Desmirail. In the 1920s it was bought by an American, Robert Meacham Davies. He married Kathleen Johnston, of the négociant family. Their daughter Elizabeth took over and replanted the vineyard. Today the property is run by her sons. Monbrison used to sell its production to négociant Maison Sichel. Then between 1974 and 1983 over half the vineyards were leased to Château Prieuré-Lichine and disappeared into the latter's wine. In the 1980s and early 1990s the property was run by Jean-Luc Vonderheyden but after his untimely death from leukaemia in 1992 his brother Laurent returned from the United States, where he was pursuing a career in television, and took over managing Monbrison. The third brother is Bruno. They share a passionate belief that quality derives from the vineyard, and that is where they focus most of their attention.

The entire property was replanted in 1963 and the average age of the vines is around forty years. There is a fine parcel of vines across from the château on a *croupe* that rises to around twenty-five metres (eighty-two feet). However, this is an inland area some five kilometres (three miles) from the estuary, and it is susceptible to frost. Of the twenty-one hectares belonging to Monbrison, only thirteen are AC Margaux.

The harvest is manual, in *cagettes*. The numerous lots are vinified separately, using indigenous yeasts. The wine is aged fourteen to twenty months in about fifty per cent new barriques, though the proportion of new wood varies according to the vintage. The wine is eggwhite-fined but bottled without filtration.

Monbrison has an excellent reputation, though I was not that impressed by the wines I tasted from 1983 and the early 1990s. However, the 1996 is an excellent wine, with sumptuous, oaky aromas and tremendous vigour, with a lively, almost peppery, finish. After that fine performance, the 1998 is surprisingly feeble, but the 2000 is a return to a more sumptuous and spicy style. The 2002 is excellent, with ripe Cabernet aromas and a stylish touch of oak. It's a medium-bodied wine with panache and good tannic backbone, which will make delicious medium-term drinking. The 2003 is agreeable but lacks weight and persistence, as does the rather tannic 2004. The 2005 is better balanced, with more freshness and zest than the two previous vintages.

Château Mongravey

Arsac. Tel: 0556 588451. Website: www.chateau-mongravey.fr. Owner: Régis Bernaleau.
10 ha. 56% Cabernet Sauvignon, 40% Merlot, 4% Cabernet Franc. Production: 40,000 bottles.
Second wine: Ch Cazauviel

Although this wine is aged in fifty per cent new oak, in 2002 it had sufficient flesh and concentration and tannin to carry the wood. The 2003 is as flat as a pancake, but the 2004 is splendid: a bold, lush wine, though not at the expense of freshness. The Bernaleau family also own Château de Braude (*q.v.*) in the Haut-Médoc.

Château Palmer

Cantenac. Tel: 0557 886178. Website: www.chateau-palmer.com. Owner: consortium of shareholders (see below).
Troisième cru. 52 ha. 47% Merlot, 47% Cabernet Sauvignon, 6% Petit Verdot.
Production: 250,000 bottles. **Second wine:** *Alter Ego*

If no one disputes that the finest property in Margaux is Château Margaux, it would also be widely accepted that the second in line is Palmer, which overall has performed better and more consistently than Second Growths such as Lascombes and Durfort-Vivens.

In the eighteenth century Palmer was known as Château de Gasq, after its then-proprietors, and takes its present name from the English general Charles Palmer, who bought the property in 1814 and trebled the area under vine. Before long Palmer owned over eighty hectares of vineyards, though many of them were on the *palus* and used to make *clairet*. Alas, he went bust in 1843 and the estate he had created was put on the market. A new era for Palmer began in 1853, when the estate was bought by a Parisian banking family called Péreire, who were great rivals of the Rothschilds. It was they who built the grandiose château, which was restored in 2005. They also replanted and expanded the vineyards, of which under thirty hectares remained when they bought Palmer. In 1938 the Péreires sold Palmer to a consortium of Bordeaux négociant houses: Sichel, Ginestet, and Mähler-Besse. The Miailhe family were also involved until the late 1970s. Today there are twenty-four shareholders, many of whom are distantly related to the Mähler-Besse family. Ginestet bowed out during the 1950s, and of the two remaining négociants, Sichel has the larger share.

Where many shareholders are involved, there is a risk that some of them, seeking to cash in on the success of the property, will want to sell up, thus opening the property as a whole to the possibility of takeover (as happened at Yquem). However, I am assured that the Palmer shareholders are a cohesive group with an active interest in the future of the estate and a willingness to invest in it, as in the case of the new *cuvier* built in 1994. They also make the final decision on setting the *prix de sortie*. Despite the close involvement of two négociant houses, the wine is sold on the *Place de Bordeaux* in the traditional way.

Today eighty per cent of the vines are on gravel soils around the château; the remainder are between the railway line and Château Brane-Cantenac on more sandy soil. There used to be some Cabernet Franc but they were unhappy with it, and it has been grubbed up. One peculiarity of Palmer is the high proportion of Merlot. Bertrand Bouteiller, who ran Palmer from the 1960s until 2004, pointed out that it used to be even higher, up to sixty per cent in the 1960s. He agreed this was excessive, but maintained that much of the terroir is well suited to Merlot, both on gravel and clay, each soil type giving a different expression to the variety.

The Palmer team has undertaken a detailed parcel analysis, allowing them to subdivide the vineyards into logical blocks during harvest. They have also measured the depth of the gravel bed, since the proximity of clay to the surface has implications for vineyard management in terms of water retention and the choice of rootstock. Bouteiller liked to control yields by severe pruning and the removal of secondary growth material, rather than rely on systematic green-harvesting. Yields tend to range from forty-five to forty-eight hl/ha. Bouteiller experimented with both higher and lower yields, and felt this average crop was about right. Exaggeratedly low yields, he maintained, gave such levels of concentration that the intrinsic finesse of Palmer can be masked.

The new *cuvier* was fitted with conical steel tanks, replacing the existing wooden vats. The volume of each tank was smaller, allowing a more detailed parcel vinification. The vinification is classic, though malolactic fermentation takes place in barriques, and the blend is made up progressively over the winter. There is no micro-oxygenation but they have experimented with concentrators. Palmer is aged for around twenty months in forty-five per cent new oak with a light toast. The team believed prolonged barrel-ageing gave the wine its remarkable aromatic complexity, as well as body and flesh.

Only about half the crop makes it into the *grand vin*. The second wine used to be the Réserve du Général, but in 1998 it was replaced by Alter Ego. Bouteiller, and his talented successor Thomas Duroux, insist that Alter

Ego is a different concept, not just a second wine for unsatisfactory lots. The idea was to produce a wine with more Merlot in the blend, aged for a shorter time in around twenty-five per cent new oak. Duroux conceives Alter Ego as another interpretation of the vineyard at his disposal. He describes Palmer as a classical painting, Alter Ego as a contemporary painting of the same subject. At harvest the team taste the fruit repeatedly to determine which block is appropriate for which wine. For Alter Ego they seek more upfront fruit, but with Margaux typicity. Anything that doesn't make the grade for either wine is sold off in bulk. Thus in 2000, forty-five per cent was released as Palmer, forty per cent as Alter Ego, and fifteen per cent was sold off.

In 2006, the stunning 1961 was still dense in colour, and the nose was slightly baked; but the wine had retained its power, concentration, and intense vibrancy. The 1962 is perfumed and leafy; though less dense than the 1961, it still has poise and remains light on its feet; despite a lightly candied finish, it's an exquisite wine. The 1964 had an ethereal nose at thirty years of age; it was light but elegant, with charm and delicacy rather than weight and structure. The 1966, tasted quite recently, had some worrying browning and a hint of Bovril on the nose; yet the palate was fresh, the fruit was delicious, and the wine had elegance and length. The 1970 is still going strong. The nose is very complex, with smoke, cedar, liquorice, and tobacco aromas, as well as ripe cherries; it's very rich and concentrated, and has tannic grip but not at the expense of its silky texture and red-fruits freshness. The 1971 is now a touch astringent, and the aromas suggest stewed cherries and tomatoes, while the palate, though still quite intense, is lean and high-toned. The 1975, tasted long ago, was very tannic and the fruit completely subdued. The 1976 was a trifle chunky but didn't have the baked character of so many wines from that vintage. It is almost certainly now past its best. The 1978 has tobacco and cedar aromas; the texture is supple but the wine is quite lean, though it filled out with aeration. The 1979 was delicious when young, the 1980 quite successful for the vintage. The 1982, tasted quite recently, had some baked aromas and flavours, though the wine was indisputably rich and concentrated and didn't lack acidity. The 1983 was far better, still very youthful in colour in 2006, very perfumed with a bouquet of cherries and red fruits. In the mouth this was everything one hopes for from Palmer: silky in texture, poised, harmonious, fine-grained in its tannins, elegant, and very long.

The 1985 is still quite oaky on the nose, though the easy-going palate suggests it is now ready to drink. It lacks grip, but there is good acidity and length, adding up to a thoroughly enjoyable wine. The 1986 shows the vintage character more than the Palmer terroir, with a slight earthiness and meatiness, and some forceful tannins. The 1987 was charming when young, but is likely to be faded by now. The 1988 is the opposite: a complex nose of tobacco, leather, and smoke, but still austere on the palate, with complex flavours and a somewhat dry finish. The 1989 is a triumph: very opulent, truffley, and fleshy on the nose, while the palate is spicy, concentrated, fresh, elegant, and impeccably balanced with no trace of heaviness. It's delicious now, but will age well. The 1990 has less power than the 1989 but perhaps more finesse. The bouquet is suffused with blackcurrant and cedarwood, the texture is silky and very stylish, and there's a refined gracefulness to the wine, which, unlike the 1989, is approaching its peak. The 1991 is good but perhaps lacks length. The 1992 lacks fruit, the 1993 has a dourness rarely encountered in Palmer and some edgy acidity. The 1994 seems stylish at first, but has a dry finish and lacks length.

The 1995 is very typical of the vintage: the nose is still inexpressive, while the palate is rich and velvety, with firm tannins to give it solidity, and a long, chewy finish. This still needs time. The 1996 has been impressive from the outset. The sweet, blackcurranty nose also has a slight savoury and herbaceous edge, which is not unattractive. It is no blockbuster, and the emphasis is on its elegant structure, its fine balance, its delicate acidity, and promising length. The 1997 is a pretty wine, but it lacks concentration and grip, though it has a pleasing peppery finish. The 1998 is intensely aromatic, with touches of milk chocolate and liquorice as well as oak, and it has evolved remarkably well into a classic Palmer, all silk and airiness, delicious fruit, and a persistent finish. The 1999 has perfumed aromas of plums and mint; the palate is fleshy, quite spicy, with blackcurrant and mint flavours, good grip and length; an accessible wine that will continue to give pleasure for many years. The 2000 has a discreet, toasty nose; on the palate it is reasonably concentrated, certainly ripe yet showing good acidity, and it is also a touch surly, being an adolescent wine that should not be touched for at least five years. The 2001 has oaky aromas of ripe cherries, and reasonable grip on the palate with attractive fruit in the foreground; it needs time. The 2002 is fabulous, with discreetly toasty aromas of blackcurrants and black cherries; on the palate there is admirable concentration, very ripe tannins, a silky texture, beguiling subtlety of flavour despite a mere hint of greenness, a sweet, chewy aftertaste, and impeccable length. It makes the 2003 seem rather obvious, with its sour plum flavours, its evident extract, its modest acidity, its rugged finish. The 2004 has polished red-fruits aromas with a hint of cloves; although only medium-bodied, it is very juicy and concentrated, with a long, elegant finish.

Like Château Margaux, Palmer needs a lot of time in bottle. It can be drunk fairly young, but once it closes up it can stay that way for many years. In a good vintage there is never any rush to drink Palmer. Even with its good dose of Merlot, it is a wine with structure and power as well as finesse, and it takes a while for its intensity and subtlety to emerge. That, I suppose, is where Alter Ego comes in. It is just about ready to broach on release, with its soft, plummy fruit, but there is always sufficient tannic backbone to avoid any suggestion of soupiness. It doesn't have the persistence and intensity of Palmer, and isn't meant to. Although it is wine that can, I suspect, be drunk over many years, its supple and seductive personality shows best within two or three years of bottling. The 2002 is disappointing, but the 2003 is attractive given the perils of the vintage, while the 2004 has enjoyably upfront fruit.

The long reign of Bertrand Bouteiller has given Palmer some rare continuity and consistency, which is not to say there have not been changes and improvements over the years. His replacement by Thomas Duroux seems an inspired choice, Duroux having been the winemaker at Ornellaia. He has experience, an international outlook, and a clear intelligence. Under his stewardship, Palmer will evolve, but is unlikely to deviate.

Château Paveil de Luze

*Soussans. Tel: 0557 883003. Website: www.chateaupaveildeluze.com. **Owner:** Baron Frédéric de Luze.*
*32 ha. 60% Cabernet Sauvignon, 35% Merlot, 5% Cabernet Franc. **Production:** 200,000 bottles.*
Second wine: L'Enclos de Banneret

The de Luzes are best known as Bordeaux négociants, but they have owned this fine property with its elegant chartreuse since 1862. When Geoffroy de Luze began looking after the property in 1973 there were only ten hectares planted. Over the years he gradually replanted abandoned parcels. He says that the vineyard today is almost identical to that which existed in the seventeenth century. Since 2004 the property has been run by his son Frédéric, who has refitted the vat room with smaller steel tanks to allow for more parcel selections. Most of the vines lie in one block between the château and the hamlet of Tayac. The soil is deep gravel, but one sector has more clay than the rest.

The grapes are picked by machine, with sorting before and after destemming. Since the late 1990s they have cold-soaked the grapes before fermentation. The wine is aged for twelve months in twenty-five per cent new barriques. In some vintages, such as 2003, they have practised some micro-oxygenation.

The wines are stylish rather than powerful, with good acidity and freshness, an abundance of blackcurrant and cherry fruit, and light tannins. They do not seem to have sufficient structure for very long ageing, but they are delicious, consistent, and sensibly priced wines for medium-term drinking: 1999, 2000, 2001, and 2002 can all be recommended.

Château Pontac-Lynch

Cantenac. Tel: 0557 883004. Owner: Marie-Christine Bondon. 10 ha. 40% Merlot, 35% Cabernet Sauvignon, 20%
Cabernet Franc, 5% Petit Verdot. Production: 70,000 bottles. Second wine: Ch Pontac-Faure

This property takes its name from two of its eighteenth-century proprietors. M. de Pontac owned it in 1720, and Comte Thomas Michel Lynch succeeded him. It was bought by Jean-Pierre Bondon in 1952, and today it is run by his granddaughter. The vineyards, which are hand-picked, are well located, enjoying as neighbours Margaux, Palmer, and Issan. The wine is aged for up to fifteen months in thirty per cent new barriques.

Rather confusingly, the wine appears in two forms. Much of the production is sold to the négociant Borie-Manoux, and released with a splendid dark blue and gold label with the crest, for some reason, of the Prince of Wales. However, Mlle. Bondon also releases her wine under a more classic white label. Nor are the wines identical: Mlle. Bondon's bottling has slightly more Cabernet Sauvignon. Most of the vintages I have tasted were from Borie-Manoux, and they have a rich, savoury nose, a reasonable weight of fruit, and forceful tannins. The 1999 and 2000 are good wines; the 2001, however, is distinctly light with some astringency. The only one of Mlle. Bondon's bottlings I have encountered is the 2003, which is a touch rustic.

Château Pouget

Cantenac. Tel: 0557 889082. Website: www.chateau-pouget.com. Owner: Lucien Guillemet. Quatrième cru.
10 ha. 60% Cabernet Sauvignon, 30% Merlot, 10% Cabernet Franc. Production: 50,000 bottles.
Second wine: Antoine Pouget

From 1650 onwards, Pouget belonged to various prominent Bordeaux families, and takes its name from François-Antoine Pouget, who became the owner in 1748. In 1906 it was bought by the forebears of the Guillemets, who would later buy Boyd-Cantenac (*q.v.*) as well. The château – or modest house, to be more accurate – was tacked onto the *chais* in the nineteenth century, and marble medallions in the pediment proudly cite Pouget's standing in various classifications. The vines are planted on sandy, gravelly soils. The average age of the vines is thirty-five years and, as at Boyd-Cantenac, there is no use of chemical fertilizers. The grapes are picked by hand and the wine is made in the same way as Boyd-Cantenac. Pouget is a joint exclusivity of two négociant houses, so it is not, it seems, available in all markets. Moreover, the house of Dubos has its own label for Pouget, which is a good way to confuse the consumer. It also appears, if I understand M. Guillemet correctly, that the second wines of Boyd-Cantenac and Pouget are interchangeable.

Pouget was vinified independently of Boyd-Cantenac only from 1983 onwards. Previously, it appears to have been a second wine of Boyd. I have tasted the 1986, 2000, 2001, and 2002, and not cared much for any of them. The 1986 was tannic but nonetheless quite stylish, though it was far from exciting. The 2000 is light and one-dimensional, the 2001 equally light though the fruit is sound enough. The 2002, despite a rich black-fruits nose, has an odd sweet-and-sour tone on the palate and lacks persistence. The 2003 is forward and short.

Château Prieuré-Lichine

Cantenac. Tel: 0557 883628. Owner: Ballande group. Quatrième cru. 70 ha. 68 ha red: 50% Cabernet Sauvignon,
45% Merlot, 5% Petit Verdot. 2 ha white: 80% Sauvignon Blanc, 20% Sémillon. Production: 300,000 bottles.
Second wine: La Cloître du Ch Prieuré-Lichine

As the name suggests, this property was a Benedictine priory. It was attached to the abbey at Vertheuil until the Revolution, when it was confiscated by the state. In 1952 it was bought by Alexis Lichine. Until that time the estate had been known as Prieuré-Cantenac, but Lichine, following an old Bordeaux tradition, changed the name in his own honour. During his tenure, Lichine expanded the property from seven hectares to sixty-five, though some of those vineyards were leased rather than owned. Lichine died in 1989 and was buried on the property. His son Sacha took over until the sale of the property to the present owner in 1999.

The new owner was the Ballande group, a family with extensive business interests in New Caledonia. Its various ventures in the wine trade (in Burgundy as well as Bordeaux) are overseen by a former négociant called Justin Onclin. Onclin made his name by buying and rapidly selling 1,000 cases of the then-unknown 1982 Château Bon Pasteur in Pomerol. Robert Parker rated the wine highly and the price soared, which benefited those who had bought the wine from Onclin, but not Onclin himself. Nevertheless he was given credit for his nous. Michel Rolland had been hired as a consultant in 1995, but in 2002 was replaced by Stéphane Derenoncourt. His initial contribution was to reduce yields, which had been high under Sacha Lichine, and to improve pruning and canopy management practices, such as increasing the foliage curtain. Patrick Bongard, formerly at Château Cissac, was hired as winemaker.

The buildings look unattractive from the D2, but the château here is a charming old house looking onto a courtyard. Visitors usually lunch and dine in the beamed eighteenth-century kitchens, which bear a striking resemblance to an old English pub. Some of the cellars back onto the courtyard, but the functional doors of the tanks are cleverly disguised by covering them with decorative metal chimney plates which, from a distance, make it appear that the courtyard is adorned with ancient brasses.

Alexis Lichine built up a large estate for Margaux, but it was divided into 125 parcels. The most important plot, some twenty-two hectares, is near the château and across the railway line from Kirwan. The other major parcel is at Arsac. In practice only fifty out of the seventy hectares are now used for the *grand vin*. Onclin found many missing vines, so from 1999 his team has embarked on a programme of complanting 50,000 new vines. Ploughing has also been introduced.

The grapes are picked in *cagettes*. Onclin has constructed two reception areas, with sorting tables before and after destemming in each. A reverse-osmosis machine is on hand. The grapes are usually given a cold soak, but it is not systematic; in 2004, for example, there was none, and instead twenty per cent of the must was bled off during fermentation. Derenoncourt is a pioneer of micro-oxygenation and doesn't hesitate to use it here, both during fermentation and during barrel-ageing. He also likes to stir the lees, but only in the case of the most concentrated wines. Malolactic fermentation takes place in new barriques, and the wine is aged in up to sixty per cent new oak. Micro-oxygenation continues until the spring, when the wine is racked for the first time; thereafter the *élevage* is classic. The final blend is made before bottling, and the wine is fined with eggwhite, but is usually unfiltered.

It was Sacha Lichine who decided it would be fun to produce a white wine here. Just under two hectares were planted from 1990 onwards, on gravelly soil at Arsac. The wine is barrel-fermented, but, as they are looking for freshness above all, Bongard ferments some of it in tanks. The wine is aged in fifty per cent new oak for eight months. The 2000 was far too heavy and lacked acidity, but the 2001 is persistent and stylish.

Twenty years ago I tasted some older wines from this property: a ripe, curranty 1964, a cigar-box-scented 1966, that was rounded and elegant, a sweet, fruity, stylish 1970, a rather loose and woody 1976, a delicious, charming but forward 1978, and a light but fresh 1979. Overall, these were very attractive if not very profound wines. The 1982 matured quite fast, and by 2000 seemed fully ready, with some oaky bite and a light chocolatey finish. The 1983 was formidable and stylish when young, but I have not tasted it since. Forget the 1984 and 1987. The 1988 was soft and rounded, its sweet fruit countered by rather high acidity; it was balanced but not especially long. The 1990 has a sweet, rich Cabernet nose, which was still bright and vibrant a decade on; it's not hugely concentrated, but it has charm, vigour, and a satisfying balance.

The 1995 has the firm tannins of the year, but there is powerful, opulent fruit here, making this a generous and concentrated wine with a long future. The aromas of the 1996 are sweet and intense; on the palate, it's fresh and refined, balanced but forward; it is drinking well now. The 1998 has rich plummy aromas and ample fruit, but the wine is marred by assertive acidity and some earthiness. The 1999 is rich and plump, but has vigour on the finish; a pleasurable mid-term wine. I rate the 2000 highly, but over and over my tasting notes contain the phrase "not very Margaux". This is unusual, as Prieuré-Lichine does have typicity and is rarely less than refined.

The 2000 is voluptuous but also assertive, with muscular tannins and rich, plump fruit. The 2001 is less formidable but more stylish, with a velvety texture, ample flesh and concentration, and a tannic backbone that should serve the wine well. The 2002 is remarkably flamboyant, and again the dreaded phrase "not very Margaux" turns up in my notes. It's dense, toasty, packed with fruit, it's splendid in every way, except that it would be hard to spot the wine as Margaux in a blind tasting. The 2003 has stewed aromas, but the tannins are kept in check and the wine is rounded and reasonably balanced. But I prefer the three preceding vintages, and the infant 2004.

There has been a radical shift in style at this property. In my tasting note on the *en primeur* 2004, I hazarded a guess as to the wine's identity: Malescot? Kirwan? It is no coincidence that I picked out the Rolland wines, for Prieuré in recent years has been in the same style. It is indisputable that the wine has gained in richness, ripeness, toastiness, and power, and that it is in many ways more complete and complex than in the past. But at the same time there is a loss of finesse, of typicity, though it's possible that both will re-emerge in time.

Château Rauzan-Gassies

Margaux. Tel: 0557 887188. Owner: Jean-Michel Quié. Deuxième cru. 30 ha. 65% Cabernet Sauvignon, 25% Merlot, 10% Cabernet Franc. Production: 120,000 bottles. Second wine: Chevalier de Rauzan-Gassies

In 1661 the merchant Pierre Desmesures de Rauzan bought the vineyards belonging to the Gassies family. He developed them, and would later establish the Pichon property in Pauillac. The Rauzans remained here until 1766, when the property was divided, Rauzan-Ségla being the other portion. At the time of the classification, the owner was a M. Viguerie, and there were many other proprietors thereafter. In 1946 the Quié family bought the estate (they also own Croizet-Bages (*q.v.*) in Pauillac). Since 1994 the properties have been run by Jean-Louis Camp, who has made painstaking efforts to improve quality, which had been truly mediocre before his arrival.

Sixty per cent of the vineyards are close to the château, in numerous parcels; the remainder close to Margaux and Kirwan, and opposite Labégorce. The soil is deep gravel, sandy gravel, and sand, and is ploughed every other year.

Most of the vineyards are picked by machine, which is surprising for a Second Growth. Camp insists that his vineyard team go through the vines carefully beforehand to prepare them by deleafing on one side, by cutting off secondary growths, and green-harvesting. As long as the vines are properly prepared in advance, says Camp, machine-picking can give better results than manual harvesting. After picking, the grapes are sorted and pumped, without crushing, into the tanks. He routinely bleeds the tanks by a good five per cent. The must is stabilized at low temperatures for about thirty-six hours with added enzymes to extract colour before fermentation, which takes place with pumpovers and *délestage*. Selected yeasts are added. Sometimes, and this is controversial, he will heat the *marc* toward the end of fermentation to gain more extraction. Some of the wine goes through malolactic in barrel, but most does so in tanks; it is of course the former that is presented to the *en primeur* tasters in the spring. There is no concentration, no micro-oxygenation. The wine is aged for twelve months in up to one-third new oak, fined in tanks with eggwhite, then filtered and bottled.

Of vintages before 2000, I have only negative notes on the 1985, 1986, 1994, 1995, 1997, and 1998. Dilution and greenness are the usual culprits. The 2000 is much better, with crunchy red fruits on the nose, while the palate has weight and some flesh, with a supple texture and attractive zest on the finish. Not great, but there is some elegance here. The 2001 is similar, with plump fruit, spice, and concentration, though not much complexity. The 2002 shows good blackcurrant fruit on the nose, nicely balanced tannin and acidity on the palate, some precision and elegance, and a toasty finish. The 2003 has plenty of upfront fruit and is not too extracted.

It is hard to avoid the impression that Jean-Louis Camp has been trying step by laborious step to improve quality, but that he is constrained by a less than enthusiastic absentee proprietor, who has established some loyal markets for his wines, and sees no reason for lavish expenditure to take them to a higher plane. But this, I readily admit, is speculation.

Château Rauzan-Ségla

Margaux. Tel: 0557 888210. Website: www.rauzan-segla.com. Owner: Wertheimer family. Deuxième cru.
51 ha. 54% Cabernet Sauvignon, 41% Merlot, 4% Petit Verdot, 1% Cabernet Franc.
Production: 220,000 bottles. Second wine: Ségla

When the Rauzan property was split up in 1766, two-thirds remained with the Rauzan daughter who had married Baron Ségla, who did not survive the Revolution. Thomas Jefferson had dropped by in 1790, placing an order for ten cases. The Rauzan family remained in possession of this part of the property until 1866. The new owner was Eugène Durand-Dassier, who invested in this prize possession. One of his daughters married into the Cruse family. After Frédéric Cruse died in 1950, the family put the estate on the market. (According to Edmund Penning-Rowsell, Rauzan-Ségla was the last important Bordeaux property to crush its grapes by foot. The practice ended in 1956.) In 1956 a purchaser was found. He invested heavily in the vineyards, adding more Merlot. But a few years later, in 1960, he sold it to a British company, John Holt Ltd, a subsidiary of Lonrho. The Holts were in the shipping business, and hired the Eschenauer négociant house to manage Rauzan and distribute its wines. Eschenauer clearly had a remarkable tolerance for mediocrity. In 1983 a new manager was appointed, Jacques Théo, and he made significant improvements, including a new *cuvier* and an additional *chai*. He also brought in Emile Peynaud as a consultant. Bravely, and perhaps perversely, he refused to release the 1987. Another British company, Brent Walker, bought Rauzan-Ségla in the late 1980s, allegedly for twenty-five million pounds sterling. Then in 1994 the Wertheimer family of New York, who own the Chanel business and had been scouring Bordeaux for a suitable First Growth such as Latour (unsuccessfully in their case), made do with this property. But it was a wise choice, as Rauzan had been ranked immediately behind Mouton in 1885, and it was evident its full potential was not being realized. They hired John Kolasa to run the property, as well as their other Bordeaux estate, Château Canon (*q.v.*).

One of the first decisions of the new team was to restore the historic spelling of the estate. From about 1900 onwards Rauzan had been spelt Rausan; from 1994 the original spelling was adopted again, rather to the annoyance of their neighbour Rauzan-Gassies. But there was more important work to be undertaken: some of the vineyard was badly affected by eutypiose and had to be replanted; at the same time the vine density was increased to 10,000 vines per hectare. New drainage channels radically improved the quality of certain blocks prone to being waterlogged. The Wertheimers funded the satellite mapping of the Margaux vineyards, a study that was then shared with the other members of the Syndicat.

About half the vineyards are around the château, but there are additional parcels near Margaux and Brane-Cantenac. Exchanges with Rauzan-Gassies have reduced the total number of individual parcels to a manageable thirty-five; in the 1930s there had been 240. Some Cabernet that never ripened properly has been replaced by Merlot, and some Petit Verdot has been added, using massal selections from Château Margaux and other properties.

The grapes are picked by hand and thoroughly sorted. Kolasa has installed many small tanks in the winery, permitting a better parcel selection. There are no hi-tech aids at Rauzan, as Kolasa worries that their systematic use is beginning to threaten the typicity of Bordeaux. If he feels some lots lack concentration, he will bleed those tanks, but never by more than fifteen per cent. Kolasa is careful not to extract too much during fermentation, and uses a high proportion of press wine (ten to thirteen per cent) if he feels the wine needs more stuffing. Blending is done in February, and the wine is aged for eighteen months in fifty per cent new oak. It is eggwhite-fined but not filtered.

A Belgian-bottled 1934 was at war, the remaining sweet fruit battling it out with the dryness of age, yet the wine's aromas were still charming and cedary. A curiosity, but far from moribund. A 1952 was similar, a bit tougher perhaps, concentrated but beginning to dry out at forty years of age. I have negative notes on the 1967, 1970, 1973, 1975, 1980, 1982, and 1983, but the 1961 was still in admirable shape in 1990, with a rich, plummy nose, a palate that was rounded and mellow but not tiring, and exceptional length. The 1985 had the charm of the vintage, forward, elegant, and balanced. The 1986 has a rich Cabernet nose, with little sign of maturity; the wine is boldly fruity with boisterous but not harsh tannins, and rude vigour on the finish. There is too much austerity on the 1988, I fear.

The 1989 is impressive in its concentration and has good acidity, but is rather stolid. I slightly prefer the tighter 1990, with its blackcurranty nose and its tannic density and length. The 1993 is acceptable but bland, but the 1994 is a great success, with its lush, oaky nose and its fine fruit and chocolatey finish. The 1995, which was chunky when young, is developing beautifully, and has acquired a velvety texture and an elegant, easy-going charm. The 1996 is more elegant, with high acidity and also some savoury tones, and, best of all, a fresh, persistent finish that bodes well. The 1997 is unexciting, and probably near its not-very-elevated peak. The assertive tannins that once dominated the 1998 have mellowed, and this is evolving into a sleek, concentrated wine with sweet blackberry fruit and a persistent finish. (By 2007 it was closing up again and becoming tougher.) There is suppleness and stylishness on the 1999; it's not a wine of great depth, but the fruit is very attractive. The new oak is very much present on the 2000, which has formidable fruit on the nose and palate, and a good deal of power, but its fine length helps to confer style and balance. The 2001 is admirable, with its stylish aroma of blackcurrant and blackberries and its well-judged oak; the wine is supple yet weighty. The 2002 is immensely perfumed, and the oak plays its supporting role in that, and the palate has more zest than the 2001. Again, the tannins are kept in check, and there is good length. The 2003 is rather candied, but it's supple and accessible and will be attractive for medium-term drinking. Tasting the 2004 and the yet-to-be-bottled 2005 in spring 2007, I found the former more satisfying, a supple, fleshy wine that nonetheless had tannins, structure, and length. The 2005 seemed to lack some personality, but it will probably recover its balance after bottling.

Kolasa and his team have done an excellent job at Rauzan-Ségla, delivering a wine that is true to its terroir. There is nothing exaggerated about it. There are certainly wines with more power and flashiness, but the emphasis here is on finesse, on drinkability. These are wines to give pleasure first and foremost. Kolasa is conscious that his replanting programme means that there are many young vines at Rauzan, which may account for an occasional lack of stuffing or density. It seems probable that Rauzan-Ségla will go from strength to strength.

Château Siran

*Labarde. Tel: 0557 883404. Website: www.chateausiran.com. **Owner:** William Alain Miailhe. 39 ha.*
46% Cabernet Sauvignon, 35% Merlot, 12% Petit Verdot, 7% Cabernet Franc.
*Production: 120,000 bottles. **Second wine:** S de Siran*

Siran has been in the hands of the Miailhe family and their forebears since 1858, and from 1988 the property has been run energetically by Brigitte Miailhe. The pretty pink buildings don't reflect the antiquity of the estate, which dates back, apparently, to the fifteenth century. Brigitte Miailhe points out that in 1855 Siran was owned by the Lautrec family, who, being Legitimists, would have nothing to do with Napoleon III. Hence their indifference to the classification.

Only twenty-four hectares fall within AC Margaux. Thirteen hectares produce a Bordeaux Supérieur called Château St-Jacques, and two hectares produce a Haut-Médoc, Bel Air de Siran. The average age of the vines is thirty years. There is often around fifty per cent of Merlot in the blend, yet Siran doesn't lack structure; no doubt the high proportion of Petit Verdot adds density and stuffing. Over time exchanges of parcels have been made with Siran's neighbours Dauzac and Giscours, and this, according to Brigitte Miailhe, means that at least one-third of the vineyards are of classified-growth quality. The grapes are picked by hand, and sorted before and after destemming. Yields range from forty-five to fifty hl/ha. After fermentation in stainless steel, the wine is aged for twelve months in barriques. Michel Rolland was the consultant here from 1995, and he favoured a substantial proportion of new oak, often around seventy per cent. It seems that the Miailhes felt Siran was becoming too muscular for its own good, and in 2004

Rolland was replaced by Denis Dubourdieu, who has reduced that proportion to between fifty and sixty per cent. Between twenty-five and forty per cent of the crop is declassified each year, and the young vines are also consigned to S de Siran.

That Siran can age was demonstrated by the 1949 in magnum, which was by no means perfect: the nose was slightly baked, and there was some woodiness on the palate, but there was also freshness and underlying sweetness. The 1966, tasted in 1988, showed considerable ripeness but was beginning to dry out. The 1978 had a leafy, minty nose, and the palate was fresh, lively, elegant, and long. The 1982 had more density and seemed, surprisingly, rather more evolved than the 1978. The 1986 is very robust but not inelegant and has a vigorous finish. The 1988 is quite mineral, but the wine overall is graceful and forward. The 1989 has evolved beautifully; by 2006 it showed leathery, meaty, truffley aromas, while the palate was full-bodied yet fresh and sweet and at the peak of its powers. The 1990 is more sleek and elegant, more Margaux-like with its acidity and length. The 1991 is ripe and balanced, the 1992 is light and should have been drunk, but the 1993 has assertive Cabernet aromas, and is compact and firm. The 1994 is good for the vintage, with a long, chewy finish. The 1995, not tasted for some years, was no blockbuster and showed considerable elegance as well as imposing tannins. The 1996 is becoming quite leathery on the nose, with some cedary tones, considerable freshness and acidity, and good length. The 1997 is fine for early drinking.

Black fruits dominate the nose of the 1998. Supple, lush, and fully ripe, it's an excellent and balanced example from this vintage. The 1999 shows sweet, ripe fruit on the nose, and has remarkable delicacy; despite its restrained style, it's well balanced and long. The 2000 has less obvious finesse, but the nose is splendidly rich, and the wine is full-bodied with ripe tannins and ample weight. The 2001 has a blackcurranty fragrance and simply delicious fruit; it will be ready well before the 2000. The 2002 is dense, rather extracted, and oaky – hard to read at present. The 2003 is broad, rich, and rather tough, and lacks some persistence. The fine 2004 is rich and fleshy, concentrated and weighty, with ample complexity and length.

Siran, then, is quite a muscular Margaux, and sometimes this outbalances any finesse there may be in the wine. But it is never shy and retiring, it never lacks fruit and structure, and can be elegant and persistent. Siran rarely fails to give pleasure, even though it is sometimes difficult to define the stylistic consistency of the wine.

Château Tayac

Soussans. Tel: 0557 883306. Website: www.chateautayac-margaux.com. **Owner:** *Favin family. 37 ha.*
60% Cabernet Sauvignon, 35% Merlot, 5% Petit Verdot. **Production:** *260,000 bottles.*
Second wines: Cuvée Larauza, Ch Grand Soussans

In the mid-nineteenth century the vineyards of Tayac were part of Château Desmirail, and it was only in 1891 that the present property was separated to form Château Tayac. It has now been in the Favin family for four generations. The vines are cultivated according to the Cousinié method (*see* Chapter Two) and are picked by machine as well as manually. The wine is aged for twelve months in thirty-five per cent new oak.

The only vintage that has been truly impressive was the 1996, with its powerful Cabernet aromas and its power on the palate, with weighty tannins and a long, chocolatey finish. I find the 1999 rather astringent, suggesting a lack of ripeness, and the 2000 quite stewed and bland, though sufficiently accessible to be drinkable now. The 2004 is also disappointing, rather astringent and marked by dry tannins.

Château du Tertre

*Arsac. Tel: 0557 970909. **Owner:** Eric Albada Jelgersma. Cinquième cru. 52 ha. 40% Cabernet Sauvignon,*
*35% Merlot, 20% Cabernet Franc, 5% Petit Verdot. **Production:** 200,000 bottles. **Second wine:** Les Hauts du Tertre*

This leading Arsac property has had a long history. Thomas, the brother of Michel de Montaigne, was an early proprietor in the 1590s, and in the late seventeenth century the Marquis de Ségur was the owner. In 1870 a Saxon called Heinrich Koenigswater owned Tertre, followed by Belgian wine merchants called De Wilde, and, from 1960, Philippe Capbern-Gasqueton, proprietor of Calon-Ségur. He found the estate in poor condition, renovated the vineyards, and produced some very good wines. The major revival in the fortunes of Château du Tertre came in 1997 when Eric Albada Jelgersma, already the new owner of Giscours (*q.v.*), added this estate to his portfolio. He soon got to work, building a new *cuvier* in 1999 and equipping it with temperature-controlled oak vats, and virtually rebuilt the run-down château, constructing a new wing in the same style as the existing château, as well as a pool and an orangery.

The vineyards occupy a *croupe*, one of the highest in Margaux at twenty-seven metres (eighty-nine feet), in a single parcel around the château, with a stream separating them from those of Giscours. The average age of the vines is thirty-five years. New plantings have been made to a higher density (8,500 vines per hectare), the trellising has been raised, and green-harvesting introduced. The grapes are picked by hand, and at the winery a conveyor belt moves them above the tanks to the crusher/destemmer. The *cuvier* is equipped with a reverse-osmosis machine. The must is fermented with pumpovers and *délestage*, using selected yeasts, then aged for fifteen months in up to sixty per cent new oak in the splendid two-storey *chais*.

Château du Tertre has had a fairly dim reputation, but there have been exceptions. An enthusiastic note from Michael Broadbent alerted me to the 1979, which I bought and drank with much pleasure until 1995, by which time the nose was ripe and cedary, while the palate showed beautiful balance, concentration, and finesse. I tasted a dreadful 1988 (poor bottle, probably) in 1997, but the 1990 had extremely ripe aromas, a lovely supple texture, a vanilla sheen to the fruit, and a long, elegant finish. The 1995 was quite oaky but didn't lack concentration and acidity. The 1998 has always had rather hard tannins; it's too rugged and earthy to give much pleasure. The 2000 has been very good from the outset, with sweet, blackcurrant aromas, an open palate of some opulence, yet balanced by a stylish finish. The 2001 matches it in elegance and charm, but has slightly less weight and structure; a fine wine for medium-term drinking. The 2002 shows a lot of new oak and Cabernet Franc perfume, and the fruit quality is super-ripe though not jammy, with an elegant and persistent finish. The 2003 is not too extracted, nor is it that concentrated, but it's an accessible wine to drink young. The 2004 has plenty of oak on the nose, but it's plump on the palate and a touch soft for a young wine.

There is no doubt that, since Albada bought the property, its wines have become much more consistent. Du Tertre delivers a concentrated but not massive wine, and elegance is always to the fore.

Château La Tour de Bessan

*Soussans. Tel: 0556 582201. **Website:** www.vignobles-marielaurelurton.com. **Owner:** Marie-Laure Lurton.*
*19 ha. 40% Cabernet Sauvignon, 36% Merlot, 24% Cabernet Franc. **Production:** 100,000 bottles.*
***Second wine:** Le Page de La Tour de Bessan*

Of the old castle of Bessan, only a ruinous tower remains as testimony to the property's medieval origin. In 1740 the owner was Jean-Baptiste, the elder son of the famous philosopher Montesquieu, and it remained in the family until the Revolution. The Clauzel family were the owners in the mid-twentieth century, and it was from them that Lucien Lurton bought the property in 1972. It was he who planted the vines. In 1992 he gave Villegorge (*q.v.*) and La Tour de Bessan to his daughter Marie-Laure.

The vines are in Soussans and Arsac, close to Château du Tertre and sharing the same *croupe*. Marie-Laure is steadily replanting the property and reducing the amount of Cabernet Franc. The grapes are picked by hand and fermented in steel tanks at her eye-catching, modern winery of rusted iron. (She explains that she commissioned this new winery principally in order to hide the existing winery from the 1930s that had been constructed from almost indestructible concrete.) The wine is aged for six to twelve months in about twenty per cent new oak.

I am not a huge fan of her Château de Villegorge, but I do like Tour de Bessan. Perhaps the Margaux terroir just gives a finer wine. The 2000 has a fleshy, savoury nose, while the palate is firm and concentrated, if still a tad austere. The 2001 is more delicate and lively, but doesn't lack supple fruit and ripe tannins. The nose of the 2002 is complex, with overtones of cloves as well as blackberries. Black fruits dominate the palate too; this is a generous mouthful of fruit. The 2003 is rich but has a very dry finish; the 2004 has more zest, as well as charming red-fruits aromas. Moreover, the wine is very reasonably priced and offers good value.

Château La Tour de Mons

*Soussans. Tel: 0557 883303. **Owner**: consortium of investors. 43 ha. 58% Merlot, 36% Cabernet Sauvignon, 6% Petit Verdot. **Production**: 280,000 bottles. **Second wine**: Ch Marquis de Mons*

This ancient property in Margaux dates back to the thirteenth century, when the Colomb family bought the now-ruinous château. In the sixteenth century it belonged to the Baron de La Brède. It takes its name from Pierre de Mons, who bought the estate in 1623. It remained in the Mons family after the Revolution; following the marriage of a Mons daughter, it passed into the Gastebois family, whose descendants sold the estate in 1995 to a group of financial institutions. The group appointed an agricultural researcher and authority on grey rot, Dominique Laux, to run the property. He invested substantially, digging new drainage and building a new *cuvier* and *chai*.

It is widely accepted that the terroir here is exceptional. It consists of a single parcel spread over various gravelly *croupes* just one kilometre (half a mile) away from the Gironde. There is a good deal of limestone in the subsoil, and some very stony blocks near the river that are planted with Cabernet Sauvignon. The oldest vines, Cabernet Sauvignon and Petit Verdot, were planted in 1934, although eight hectares have been planted since 1997. The grapes are picked by machine as well as manually. The vinification is entirely traditional, using selected yeasts. There is no chaptalization, but tanks are sometimes bled to increase concentration. The wine is aged for twelve months in thirty per cent new oak.

Overall, these are medium-bodied, supple wines, with fresh fruity and minty aromas. The 1995 was rather extracted when young, but may have settled down subsequently. The 1996 is more opulent, but doesn't lack tannic grip. The 1999 is still fairly tight and assertive, but the texture is supple and the wine should soon be broachable. The 2000 is more dense and concentrated, with a lot of weight and extract. The 2001 is reasonably concentrated but not that exciting, although it has more finesse than the 2002, which is fresh but rather light. The 2004 is pleasant but pinched and rather green and dilute. Good and dependable though the wines are, I can't help feeling they could be even better.

9. St-Julien

St-Julien is the most compact of the major appellations, tucked between Margaux and Cussac to the south, and Pauillac to the north. Its 910 hectares of vineyards represent about 5.5 per cent of the Médoc. What singles it out is that around eighty per cent of its vineyards belong to classified growths, of which there are eleven. There are only six *crus bourgeois*. St-Julien's annual production is approximately 5.5 million bottles.

The soil is essentially deep gravel on two extensive plateaux, blending quartz pebbles, sand, flint, and clay in varying proportions. Small streams, called *jalles*, function as drainage channels. This is a relatively precocious region, and the grapes ripen earlier than they do in Cussac to the south, or in Moulis to the west. The St-Julien vineyards often escape the hailstorms that can inflict such damage in the Médoc. The most elegant wines, and the highest rated in terms of reputation and price, lie alongside the estuary; those farther inland have body and richness, but perhaps not the finesse of the riverside vineyards such as Ducru-Beaucaillou.

Stylistically, St-Julien, as one might expect, is midway between Margaux and Pauillac. It may not have the finesse, the airiness of Margaux, nor does it often demonstrate the power and muscularity of Pauillac. But it borrows from both: forthright in its fruit expression, firmly structured, yet at the same time poised and elegant. Curiously, the broker Lawton, while singling out the St-Julien wines in 1815 as among the Médoc's finest, saw it the other way round: "They are not as robust as that of Rauzan at Margaux, not perhaps as delicate as those of Brane-Mouton at Pauillac. But they are generally more smooth and mellow."[1] Even though there are no First Growths in St-Julien, it has a clutch of properties that can sometimes rival the First Growths in quality and longevity.

Just as there is strife between Margaux and Arsac, so there is trouble brewing between the St-Julien growers and those in Cussac. By the early 2000s some Cussac growers, notably Hubert Bouteiller of Lanessan, were campaigning to have their properties officially attached to St-Julien. This would have the obvious advantages of conferring more status on their wines and allowing them to charge much higher prices than they can as Haut-Médoc. Not surprisingly, they are getting short shrift from the St-Julien estates.

The Cussac growers argue that there are a number of St-Julien estates – Beychevelle, Branaire-Ducru, Ducru-Beaucaillou – that have parcels of vines in Cussac, which they have owned since before the 1855

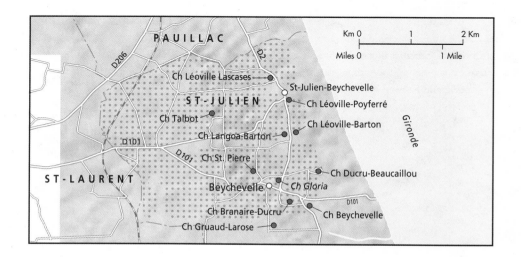

1 Quoted in Pijassou and Ters, *Gruaud-Larose*, Stock, Paris, 1997, 47

classification; thus it has been accepted that those Cussac vineyards are part of the brand, as it were, and can legally be integrated into the St-Julien wine. Bouteiller and others reason that if St-Julien growers can market their Cussac wines as St-Julien, why shouldn't they, the Cussac-based growers, be entitled to do the same? Pierre-Gilles d'Evry of Château Lamarque wryly notes that the *jalle* at Beychevelle is crossed by a bridge known locally as the Pont des Miracles, since Cussac wine is magically transformed into St-Julien wine as it passes north. This one is set to run and run.

Château Beychevelle

Tel: 0556 732070. Website: www.beychevelle.com. **Owner:** *Grands Millésimes de France. Quatrième cru.*
88 ha. 62% Cabernet Sauvignon, 31% Merlot, 5% Cabernet Franc, 2% Petit Verdot. **Production:** *500,000 bottles.*
Second wine: Amiral de Beychevelle

The name and the label derive from the sails lowered as boats on the estuary saluted the Duc d'Epernon, an Admiral of France, when he owned the château in the late sixteenth and early seventeenth centuries. Well, that's the official version. The more likely alternative is that the boats lowered their sails so as to escape detection and avoid paying the toll levied by the duke. The term "*baisse voile*" became transformed into Beychevelle. Epernon had acquired the estate in 1587, having married into the Foix-Candale family, one of the richest in France and previous owners of Beychevelle. The duke's son built the château, which was then reconstructed in 1757 by the Marquis de Brassier, who also owned other properties in the region.

Beychevelle was confiscated during the Revolution, and in 1825 was acquired by the négociant Pierre-François Guestier. After he died in 1874 it was sold to Armand Heine, a cousin of the great German poet. He extended the château, which is a striking building, with all kinds of baroque style embellishments, and the two façades – front and garden – are equally fine. Pavilions add heft at either end of the façade. Behind the château there are views from a balustraded terrace onto formal gardens and gravel walks, and, just beyond, the Gironde.

In 1890 a well-known banking family, the Achille-Foulds, acquired Beychevelle from their relative Heine, and it remained in their possession until 1986, when, after the death of Aymar Achille-Fould, Grands Millésimes de France, a subsidiary of the Garantie Mutuelle des Fonctionnaires insurance company, took a majority holding. Then in 1989 a forty per cent share was sold to the Japanese firm Suntory. In 1995 Philippe Blanc was hired as the manager of the property.

Of Beychevelle's eighty-eight hectares of vineyards, seventy-five are within AC St-Julien. The other thirteen are close to Château Beaumont (another GMF-owned property) in Cussac in the Haut-Médoc and their production is bottled as Les Brulières de Beychevelle. These Cussac vineyards are mostly Cabernet Sauvignon, but the soils are quite cold and the variety doesn't always ripen fully; so Blanc will be replacing some of it with Merlot. Blanc insists this is not part of some commercially inspired conspiracy. On the contrary, he points out, a plot of Merlot north of the château will be replaced by Cabernet. Apart from some exchanges made with Ducru-Beaucaillou, the vineyard area is not significantly different from the ownership pattern in 1855. The heart of the historic vineyard is the thirty hectares north of the château, between the D2 road and Château Ducru-Beaucaillou. There are other good parcels just south of Gruaud-Larose (six hectares) and among the Léoville vineyards (seven hectares). Blanc is introducing some changes in viticulture, heightening the trellising, and, from 2004, eliminating insecticides. Most of the vineyards are ploughed, and since 2004 the château has produced its own compost.

A sorting table was first installed in 1992, and more were added in 2003. Beychevelle has been equipped with a *sous-vide* concentrator since 1992. Fermentation takes place using selected yeasts in steel and cement tanks, and Blanc finds little difference in quality between the two. There is no cold soak, and the preferred means of extraction are pumpovers and *délestage*. Blending is completed early, in January. The wine is aged for fifteen to eighteen months in fifty per cent new barriques; a little American oak is used for the Amiral and Brulières. Selection has become more stringent since Blanc arrived, and about forty-five per cent of the wine is now declassified.

The 1929, tasted in 2005, looked healthy enough, but was a touch maderized and losing fruit; past its best. The 1961, thirty years on, was still severe and rather baked, with little aroma; a sound but solid wine that lacked excitement. The 1962 in 1991 was more supple and accessible, not a wine of depth or complexity, but attractive. The 1966 was delightful in 1995: it had a ripe, cedary nose, smoky and elegant, and the palate was fresh, spicy, and vigorous. The 1970 is still drinking well, with some mushroomy aromas, a light structure, and little complexity or personality; frail but still alive. Forget the 1972 and 1973; the 1976 was enjoyable when young but has faded. These were wines all cropped at around 70 hectolitres per hectare and aged in at most ten per cent new oak; and there was virtually no selection. The 1979 is well balanced but essentially simple; the 1980 good for the vintage but probably past its best. The 1981 is thin and astringent. The 1982, not tasted for some time, was chunky and fairly short. There is a similar absence of concentration and depth in the 1983. I prefer the 1985, which is still fragrant with raspberry and coffee aromas; it's not that concentrated but has supple tannins, and seems near its peak. The 1986 shows elegant cigar-box aromas, and is very stylish, concentrated, and spicy, and now probably at its peak. The 1988 is similar but in a more supple style, a wine of balance and considerable elegance. The 1989 is good too: rounded, forward, drinking well, with a lot of spice on the finish. The 1990 is lush and long. The 1991 now has gamey, smoky aromas, and although intense, is rather astringent and stringy. The 1994 is better than the disappointing 1993.

The 1995 is a pleasant, easy-going wine of considerable charm, but it lacks weight and complexity for the vintage. The 1996 has more vigour and acidity, but it's rather lean. The 1997 is supple and fleshy and ready to drink, while the 1998, which was charmless in its youth, has evolved into a graceful, perfumed wine with sweet fruit and a strength of flavour unusual for Beychevelle. The stylish 1999 is medium-bodied and fresh and ready to drink. By 2007 the 2000 had gathered weight to become a brambly, opulent wine. The 2001 is similar, lush, juicy, and open with fair acidity, a forward, fruity, even elegant style with good length – but scarcely profound. The 2002 is perfumed but rather pallid, with little evident structure. The 2003, despite a somewhat porty nose, is well made, tannic but with no excessive extraction; rounded and fleshy but lacking in finesse, it should give pleasure in the medium term. The 2004 has aromatic charm, ripe tannins, and ample freshness, but seems rather light for the vintage. There's an unusual power in the 2005, and a suave but spicy texture as well as fine ripeness of fruit; this could be the best Beychevelle in years.

There seems no question that Beychevelle is underperforming. Quality has certainly improved since Philippe Blanc took the helm. Older vintages were very prone to bottle variation, and in my notes above I have given preference to the most positive note. There is nothing wrong with Beychevelle. Today the wines are sound and well made, and sometimes very good indeed. But they just lack excitement and grip. The wine probably also suffers from having such strong competitors in St-Julien, and Philippe Blanc tells me he doubts the property is capable of making wines as good as those from his more illustrious neighbours, which seems an odd admission, and one open to challenge. The Beychevelle owners are corporate, and no doubt the directors keep a sharp eye on the bottom line. Fair enough, but that is not a formula that encourages the risk-taking sometimes required to make a great wine.

Château Branaire-Ducru

Tel: 0556 592586. Website: www.branaire.com. Owner: Patrick Maroteaux. Quatrième cru. 50 ha.
70% Cabernet Sauvignon, 22% Merlot, 5% Cabernet Franc, 3% Petit Verdot.
Production: 240,000 bottles. Second wine: Ch Duluc

Branaire is an ancient vineyard that once formed part of the Beychevelle domaine. After the death of the Duc d'Epernon, his vineyards were confiscated by the state in lieu of his debts, then divided in three, with Ducru and Branaire becoming detached. In 1680 it was bought by Jean-Baptiste Braneyre. His daughter married Pierre du Luc, and the property remained in the hands of their descendants for centuries. In 1824 they built the château, a rather austere Directoire building with a plain, pedimented façade and a shallow, though charmingly decorated, interior. It can scarcely compete with the splendours of Beychevelle facing it across the road. The name Ducru was appended to that of Branaire at this time. Gustave Ducru and his sister Zelie inherited the property in 1873, and after her death it passed to her three nephews, who sold the estate in 1919. Thereafter there were a number of owners, until in 1954 it was bought by Jean Tapie, whose daughter married into the Tari family of Giscours. Branaire was sold in 1988 to Patrick Maroteaux, whose family had prospered in the sugar business. Although the estate was in good condition, Maroteaux renovated the *chai* and undertook other improvements. He hired Philippe Dhalluin to manage the property and make its wine. A lot of credit goes to Dhalluin, who brought the wine to a high level of quality and consistency until his departure to Mouton-Rothschild in 2002.

The vineyards are dispersed. The warmest parcel is between the château and the road, whereas the very stony sites farther inland are cooler; a parcel near Lagrange is richer and more humid, so it is here that much of the Merlot is planted. Yields are kept low by planting green cover and by green-harvesting; and the age of the vines, thirty-five years on average, also keeps yields down naturally. In 2000 the yield for the entire vineyard was forty-seven hl/ha; for the *grand vin* it was thirty-two. Philippe Dhalluin was keen on massal selections and created a nursery at Branaire to propagate them. His successor, Jean-Dominique Videau, has maintained Dhalluin's approach, but perhaps places more stress on picking as late as possible, on the grounds that very ripe fruit yields up its colour and tannin without heavy extraction.

Maroteaux constructed the first gravity-fed winery in the region in 1991. It is impeccably equipped on three levels. Grapes are sorted in the vineyard and at the winery. Dhalluin and the rest of the team were very keen that Branaire should express the estate's terroir, so he avoided manipulations such as cold-soaking and concentrators. Selected yeasts are used only if the must is very rich in sugar. The vinification is classic. About five per cent of the press wine is usually added to the blend, which is done in early January. The wine is aged for eighteen months in fifty per cent new oak, with light to medium toast, as Videau doesn't want charred aromas or overt oakiness.

The second wine, Château Duluc, was another of Maroteaux's innovations; it is mostly composed of wine from young vines, and is aged in older barriques.

I have not tasted very old vintages from Branaire. In the 1960s the Tapies released wines blending the production from poor and good vintages, marketed as non-vintage wines. This bizarre policy came to an end in the early 1970s. I found the 1979 muscular when young, but the 1981 was delicious. The 1983 had good fruit but was a touch hollow, and lacked length. The black-fruited 1988 was quite austere and had a lot of acidity. The 1989 remains tight and rather pinched, but the fruit quality is interesting, with marked chocolatey tones. The 1990 is very ripe, with ample black-cherry fruit and ripe tannins, yet it seems to lack a little grip and distinction. The 1991 and 1992 were mediocre, but the 1993 has come round nicely, with some voluptuous fruit balanced by good acidity. The 1994 seems to combine a fairly light structure with a certain austerity, and it is not ageing gracefully. The 1995 is splendid and opulent, with very rich, concentrated, sweet fruit and good length. For elegance it can't match the 1996, which is fresh, silky, invigorating, and lively without any loss of intensity or length. The 1997 shows no dilution; indeed it has backbone as well as freshness behind the supple fruit. Dry tannins dominate the rigid 1998, a somewhat charmless wine, despite the high Merlot content, and one that lacks the usual Branaire elegance and flair. The 1999 sees a return to elegance, with spicy, blackcurrant aromas, and a palate that is concentrated and long but not extracted.

The 2000 Branaire is a great wine, with sumptuous aromas of black fruits and elegant oak. The texture is seamless, and the fruit quality voluptuous yet balanced by excellent acidity and vigour. The immensely stylish 2001 is lighter, but it's fresh and balanced, has supple tannins, and there is no lack of concentration or length. The 2002 is superb, with its smoky, toasty nose. As with the 1996 and 2000, it's the freshness that stands out, aided by a sleek texture, a fine balance of fruit and spice, and excellent length. The 2003 is a disappointment, with a rather soupy texture and a lack of zest, but the 2004 is a triumph, with rich berry aromas, considerable density and power, and fine length. Shortly before bottling, the 2005 seemed unusually extracted for Branaire.

Branaire-Ducru is still somewhat underrated. From the mid-1990s the wines have been extremely consistent, and, 2003 apart, there are no real disappointments. The wines are never blockbusters and may be less dramatic than some other top St-Juliens; but their balance, freshness, and complex fruit combine to ensure that Branaire is one of the most enjoyable St-Juliens, often drinkable young, but sufficiently balanced and structured to age well.

Château de la Bridane

Tel: 0556 599170. Website: www.vignobles-saintout.com. Owner: Bruno Saintout. 15 ha. 47% Cabernet Sauvignon, 36% Merlot, 13% Cabernet Franc, 4% Petit Verdot. Production: 50,000 bottles. Second wine: Ch Moulin de la Bridane
The Saintout family reconstituted this property in the 1960s. The grapes are machine-harvested, and the wine is aged for twelve months in thirty per cent new barriques. The wine can be good but it lacks consistency. The 1996 was full-bodied and fairly concentrated, and the plump, forward 1997 was good for the year. But the 2001 lacks finesse and has a blunt finish, and the 2002 is somewhat hollow and lacking in structure, though it's quite stylish.

Château Ducru-Beaucaillou

Tel: 0556 731673. Website: www.chateau-ducru-beaucaillou.com. Owner: Bruno Borie. Deuxième cru. 75 ha. 70% Cabernet Sauvignon, 30% Merlot. Production: 220,000 bottles. Second wine: La Croix de Beaucaillou
Like Branaire-Ducru, this was once part of the Beychevelle estate and was separated at the same time. It soon established a high reputation, and in the eighteenth century its wine sold for higher prices than Beychevelle. When the Revolution broke out, the Bergeron family owned the estate, and in 1795 it was bought by Bertrand Ducru, who expanded the vineyards and built the chartreuse-style château in the 1820s. In 1866 the négociant Nathaniel Johnston bought Ducru, and added the ungainly pavilions at either end of the chartreuse. In 1941 Ducru was bought by François Borie, who replanted the vines and renovated the property. After his death in 1953, the much liked and respected Jean-Eugène Borie took over. He too made improvements, hiring Emile Peynaud as a consultant, and commissioning the semi-underground cellars designed by Alain Triaud (the brother of the owner of Château St-Pierre). This construction was provoked in part by the realization that treatments employed in the former *chai* had resulted in the TCA contamination of the wine in 1988 and some years to follow (*see* Chapter Three). After Jean-Eugène Borie died in 1998, the family estates had to be divided among the heirs. François-Xavier took command of the Pauillac properties, and his brother Bruno took over Ducru in 2003.

The vineyards are divided into two principal sectors: stony, deep, gravelly soils on a limestone subsoil around the château and close to the river; and twenty hectares farther inland near Talbot, plus three hectares in Cussac.

René Lusseau has been the *maître de chai* since 1979. There is no cold soak and he doesn't ferment at temperatures higher than 28°C (82°F) for fear of over-extracting. The winery acquired a *sous-vide* concentrator in 1992, and has used it judiciously ever since. Lusseau believes malolactic fermentation in barrels is done more for the benefit of journalists than the wine, so at Ducru this process takes place in tanks. The wine is aged for eighteen months in a proportion of new oak that varies from fifty to eighty per cent, depending on the vintage.

Ducru has an exemplary reputation for its wines in years such as 1945, 1953, 1958, and 1961, none of which I have tasted. It crafted a beautiful wine in 1970, with a stylish Cabernet nose, and a rich, complex, structured palate with weight and length. The 1973 was soft, balanced, and forward, and is probably now past its best. The 1975 is a great success for the vintage. The nose is rich, cedary, and almost earthy, showing some maturity; it's very concentrated and powerful, with tannins that remained assertive for decades, and good acidity on the finish. The 1978 is classic, with a sweet, leafy, Cabernet nose, and a palate that is spicy, balanced, and long. This is surely one of the best wines from a vintage that was probably slightly overrated at the outset. The 1982 is fragrant and oaky, and still going strong. The wine is dense but not inaccessible, it has poise and minerality, and wonderful freshness and length. It is so well balanced it should keep effortlessly for years. I last tasted the 1983 in 1990, when it was hard and austere, but concentrated and long. Classic ripe Cabernet aromas still mark the excellent 1985, which is oaky, a touch lean and less opulent than the 1982, and has good length.

The 1986 was powerful and concentrated, but there were already signs of the taint that would seriously mar subsequent vintages. Musty, mushroomy aromas rang alarm bells on the 1989, which in other respects was a ripe, intense, complex wine. By 1990 the taint was horribly evident, giving astringency and a bitter finish. It still seemed present on the 1994, though perhaps its sour, bitter tones were a consequence of the difficult vintage. But the 1995 seemed entirely clean, with generous aromas of blackcurrant and blackberry, a sleek texture, and ripe tannins. The 1996 is classic St-Julien, with Cabernet aromas and finely integrated new oak; it's the reticence and fine acidity and balance that give the wine its distinction. The 1997 is good but lacks some grip. The 1999 is still quite closed, with ample fruit but firm tannins on the finish. The 2000 is retreating into a shell, with understated aromas, reasonable concentration, and appealing freshness, but at present a fruit expression that is somewhat muted. The 2003 is robust and assertive, but there is surprisingly good acidity that gives it some persistence.

Château du Glana

*Tel: 0556 590647. Website: www.chateau-du-glana.com. **Owner:** Jean-Paul Meffre. 43 ha. 67% Cabernet Sauvignon, 27% Merlot, 6% Cabernet Franc. **Production:** 180,000 bottles. **Second wines:** Ch Sirène, Pavillon du Glana*

When Gabriel Meffre bought this property in 1961, there were only three hectares of vines. He gradually bought up unplanted parcels from Lagrange, and before long the estate grew to seventy hectares. So it was divided into two entities: Glana and Lalande (*q.v.*). The vast *chais* were constructed in 1968, as Meffre intended to vinify both wines at Glana, but regulations required separate facilities, so Lalande is vinified elsewhere. Today the property is run by Jean-Paul's sons Ludovic and Julien, who are working hard, they say, to improve quality.

Many of the vineyards are close to Château Lagrange; the original three-hectare parcel is near the winery and once belonged to Château St-Pierre. The grapes are picked by machine and sorted at the winery. After a cold soak of three days, the must is fermented in tanks, which, the brothers concede, are too large to allow the parcel selection they would prefer. The wine is aged for twelve months in forty per cent new barriques, and eggwhite-fined.

The 1995 is a good wine, quite fleshy with lively tannins and a spicy finish. Recent vintages such as 2001 and 2002 are quite oaky on the nose, have good fruit but little complexity, and tend to lose some drive on the finish. The atypical 2003 is a burly, baggy brute. The 2004 is the best Glana in years, with elegant blackcurrant aromas, density balanced by fine acidity, and fairly good length.

Château Gloria

*Tel: 0556 590818. Website: www.chateaugloria.com. **Owner:** Françoise Triaud. 44 ha. 65% Cabernet Sauvignon,*
*25% Merlot, 5% Cabernet Franc, 5% Petit Verdot. **Production:** 250,000 bottles. **Second wine:** Ch Peymartin*

This property is well known because its founder, Henri Martin, painstakingly created it from scratch from 1939 onwards. On good terms with most of the proprietors of the local classified growths, he succeeded in buying parcels from many of them, and ended up with a dispersed estate but one with some exceptional soils. The age of the vines ranges from thirty to eighty years, giving an average of around forty-five years. After Martin died in 1991, the estate passed to his daughter Françoise, and her husband Jean-Louis runs both this property and Château St-Pierre (*q.v.*). The vinification of Gloria is the same as for St-Pierre, and the wine is aged for twelve months in up to forty per cent new oak. Since 1989 the winemaker has been Remi di Costanzo. Henri Martin never had any interest in applying for *cru bourgeois* status, and Triaud has maintained his approach.

Apart from a fruity but somewhat dull 1957, the oldest Gloria I have tasted is the 1971, which was a lovely, generous wine in its youth, but by 1990 was beginning to fade. The 1982 had a voluptuous, oaky nose, but the palate was quite austere though it didn't lack fruit. Gloria then disappeared from my personal radar for many years, but re-emerged with the 1996, with its leafy, savoury nose, and a palate that was reasonably concentrated but a touch dry. The 1999 was also pleasing aromatically, with its sweet oakiness, but the palate is quite tannic. There's a similar toughness on the 2000, though it's hard not to be beguiled by its aromas of mint, blackberry, and raspberry. It's a medium-bodied wine with not much depth or structure, but the tannins are fairly assertive. The 2001 has an oaky nose with a hint of marzipan; it's a supple wine, quite forward, but the tannins are somewhat obtrusive. Oak dominates the rather hard-edged 2002, which seems over-extracted, with a rather dry finish. The 2003 has hefty tannins but is more drinkable than most.

I find it hard to get excited by Gloria. It's a rather brusque wine, often perfumed, but equally often unbalanced by rather hard tannins. Somehow the fruit, which is undoubtedly present in the wine, doesn't get much of an opportunity to sing out. There's something surly about Gloria, with little of the finesse one would expect from a vineyard composed of off-cuts from the village's top properties.

Château Gruaud-Larose

*Tel: 0556 592700/0556 589009. Website: www.gruaud-larose.com. **Owner:** Taillan group. Deuxième cru.*
82 ha. 57% Cabernet Sauvignon, 31% Merlot, 7.5% Cabernet Franc, 3% Petit Verdot, 1.5% Malbec.
***Production:** 540,000 bottles. **Second wine:** Sarget de Gruaud-Larose*

As early as 1742 Bordeaux brokers such as Abraham Lawton were singing the praises of Stanislas Gruaud's wine. In 1778 his substantial estate was inherited by a relative, Joseph Sébastien de Larose, and the two surnames were first united in 1781. Larose died in 1795, but his heirs eventually put the estate up for auction in 1812. The successful bidder was a négociant company called Balguerie, Sarget. Intrigues within the company led to the property, which enjoyed a very high reputation, being divided in 1845 into Château Gruaud-Larose-Sarget and Château Gruaud-Larose-Faure. But the estate continued to be run as a single entity and the two wines were in fact identical. Désiré Cordier bought half the estate in 1917, and fortunately bought the other half in 1935, thus reuniting the property at long last. In 1985 Cordier sold the estate to the Suez banking group, which then sold it to the Alcatel Alsthom company in 1993. This new owner invested heavily in drainage and renovating the *cuvier*. But the head of the company eventually decided running a Second Growth in Bordeaux was a costly indulgence, so he sold the property to the Taillan group, the Merlaut family's négociant business. From the 1970s Georges Pauli had been running the wine production for all the Cordier estates, and he is still retained as general manager. Under Cordier, yields, by Pauli's own admission, were too high and there was insufficient selection. Pauli wanted to declassify between thirty and forty per cent of the crop, but his masters felt ten per cent was quite enough. New ownership has freed Pauli from some of these constraints.

The four-square yet elegant château was built in 1875, and it too was expensively restored by Alcatel. Just next to the château is a tower, from which there are fine views over the vineyards. These surround the buildings, on an often windy gravel *croupe* rising to twenty-one metres (sixty-nine feet), with calcareous marl below. There is a fair amount of clay in the subsoil, and patches of sandstone too. As the block slopes gently down to the *jalle* separating the estate from Lanessan, the clay content in the soil increases. Pauli and his team are still tinkering with the vineyard: an unsatisfactory clone of Cabernet Franc has been removed, and on the sandier soil at the northern end of the block they have increased the proportion of Merlot. The average age of the vines is an impressive forty years. The soil is ploughed, and since the 1970s has been composted with the active participation of neighbouring cattle. No herbicides or pesticides are used, and no chemical fertilizers.

One peculiarity of the vineyard is that it is divided into various blocks by stone-paved paths known as *pavés Napoléon* which were constructed during the First Empire. They provide natural drainage: rainwater runs off them into adjacent ditches, and they serve the secondary purpose of allowing tractors to move swiftly around the property.

During harvest, Pauli likes to sort as much as possible in the vineyard, where two teams inspect the grapes. The winery is equipped with a *sous-vide* concentrator, though Pauli prefers to bleed the tanks to eliminate any potential dilution. After a cold soak, most of the fermentation takes place with natural yeasts in cement tanks, but in 1996 they added a dozen wooden vats. Fermentation temperatures can rise as high as 33°C (91°F), and the *cuvaison* varies from twenty-one to thirty-five days depending on the vintage. The malolactic fermentation takes place in barriques, as Pauli is convinced this stabilizes the colour and harmonizes the tannins. The wine is aged for sixteen to eighteen months in forty per cent new oak. For the second year the barrels are moved to an impressive *chai* that resembles a Gothic crypt. The second wine, aged in older barrels, now accounts for roughly forty-five per cent of production.

A tasting held in Paris in 1991 gave me (and others) the opportunity to taste some venerable vintages, mostly from magnum. The 1929 was truly remarkable. Although brown on the rim, the colour was full, the nose sweet and intense and elegant; the palate silky, sweet, and mouth-filling, very concentrated with plenty of extract, astonishing vigour, and length. The 1934 had a light, cedary nose and some sweet fruit lingering, but it was clearly past its best. The great 1945, tasted again in 2002, was still ripe and youthful on the nose, while the palate was rich but with that same intensity of flavour, and a bright, fresh finish. The 1949 was leathery on the nose and drying out by the late 1980s. The 1952 was cedary and elegant on the nose; the palate showed delicious fruit and spiciness, and an elegant, minty finish, with a hint of astringency. At fifty years old, the 1957, admittedly from jeroboam, had very complex aromas of coffee, leather, and truffles, and fine acidity and finesse on the palate. The 1959 shows its age in the browning colour, but the nose is spectacular in its power and opulence. It has the burliness of many 1959s, but the power carries the wine through impressively to its long finish. The 1961 is immensely concentrated and has a remarkable sweetness of fruit; when lasted tasted in 1993, it was still brilliant, lively, and fresh, with extraordinary length. A 1962 from double magnum was muted and rather woody, though a second bottle was better, though not exceptional. The 1964, in 1992, was meaty and earthy – not disagreeable but more than ready to drink. The 1966, tasted frequently, is lovely, with a perfumed cigar-box nose, while the texture is lush and concentrated, adding up to beautifully harmonious wine.

I found the 1970 frail and faded in 1999, but perhaps it was an imperfect bottle. The 1973 was good for the vintage but probably past its best. The 1974 was mediocre. The 1975 is formidable, but with little overt fruit and finesse. The 1978 has evolved beautifully, with a rich, gamey, cedary nose, excellent concentration on the palate, and a density tempered by lingering acidity on the finish. For charm it was hard to beat the 1979, but that was some years ago. The 1980 and 1981 are forgettable, but not the magnificent 1982. The nose was so rich, fleshy, and chocolatey that I took it for Pomerol in a blind tasting, while in the mouth the wine was a monument of richness, spiciness, earthiness, and sheer power – not the most elegant of wines, but so intense and long it left one breathless. The 1983 was impressive too, with cigar-box aromas, and fine concentration and length, but not on the scale of the 1982. The 1985 was quite tannic, almost hard, which belied the sweet charm of the nose.

The 1986 has been good from the outset, and remains so. The aromas are of blackcurrant, smoke, and liquorice, and the palate is extremely concentrated; this is by no means ready to drink. The 1987 was attractive but is probably at its peak. The 1988 is robust, but the nose is discreet and very elegant, and there is no lack of fruit and acidity. Far sweeter is the lush 1989, with some jammy, tarry, tobacco notes on the nose; although plump and succulent, it lacks some grip and length. The 1990 was remarkably balanced and refined in 1995, but I have not tasted it since. The 1991 and 1994 are rather dour, the 1993 is now accessible, lightly charming, and gently structured; the 1992 is no more than an honourable effort and has an abrupt finish. The 1995 is extremely ripe with a supple texture. The charming, oaky 1996 seems better, its weight and concentration balanced by fine acidity. It's grippy yet sleek and should have a long future. The 1997 is supple and delicate, yet has good fruit. The 1998 has ripe but somewhat gamey aromas, a silky texture, robust tannins, and a slight rawness, but the weight of fruit should emerge victorious in time. Aromas of blackcurrant, raspberries, and toast dominate the 1999, which has a firm tannic backbone atypical of the vintage. With the 2000, Gruaud-Larose is in its element, delivering precisely the rich, voluptuous fruit one would hope for, and complex aromas of black fruits, toast, and woodsmoke; it's a wine of exceptional length. The 2001 is in a similar mould but has more immediate freshness. The 2002 teeters on the edge of overripeness but is not overtly jammy. It's bright and fruity, with a lot of flesh and quite good length. At present the 2001 seems better. The 2003 has candied aromas, some swagger, grip, and richness, but it is also distinctly earthy. Despite the splendour of the aromatic, well-balanced, concentrated and fresh 2004, it is outclassed by the magnificent 2005, with its immense bouquet, refreshed by a floral tone, and its power and vigour and exceptional length on the palate.

Gruaud-Larose is the most fruit-driven of St-Juliens, but at the same time it has astonishing weight and structure. In recent years it has been very consistent, with brightness and freshness balancing the richness of fruit. Furthermore it is reasonably priced and offers good value, especially since good vintages seem to age effortlessly for decades.

Château Lagrange

Tel: 0556 733838. Website: www.chateau-lagrange.com. Owner: Suntory. Troisième cru. 113 ha. 109 ha red: 66% Cabernet Sauvignon, 27% Merlot, 7% Petit Verdot. 4 ha white: 60% Sauvignon Blanc, 30% Sémillon, 10% Muscadelle. Production: 700,000 bottles. Second wine: Les Fiefs de Lagrange

Lagrange is an immense estate, quite far inland and bordering the classified growths of St Laurent. Its origins as a wine estate date back to the 1630s, when Marguerite de Vivien from the owning family married the Sire de Pauillac, Jean de Cours. It remained in the latter family until 1712, when Charles de Branne, a distant relative, inherited it. Another relative, Jean Cabarrus, bought the estate in 1796 and made substantial improvements to the vineyards, expanding them to 120 hectares. The politician Comte Duchâtel owned the estate from 1842 to 1875, and at this time it was the largest in the Médoc. The next proprietor was an eccentric Englishman who installed an aviary inside the château for his collection of exotic birds. Gradually the vineyards shrank. The owner from 1925 was Manuel Cendoya, but as economic conditions deteriorated, he began selling off various parcels. By the time Suntory bought it in 1983, there were only fifty-seven hectares under vine, and half of those vines were Merlot. Suntory spent a fortune on the property, investing the equivalent of some nineteen million pounds sterling in a complete renovation of the buildings. The château is a fairly standard neo-classical eighteenth-century mansion, with an incongruous neo-Romanesque tower attached to one end. Local wits joke that the tower was built so that the estate could claim, like all top Médoc growths, to have a view of the estuary.

Suntory hired Marcel Ducasse to run the property, which he did until his retirement in 2007. Under his direction the second wine was created and the vineyards were doubled in size. He also reduced the proportion of Merlot, which stood at an excessive fifty per cent. The presence of so many young vines was problematic, and until recently only about one-third of the crop made it into the *grand vin*. The vineyards are essentially planted on two *croupes*. The best parcel is just east of the château; along the drive to the property from the St

Laurent road are the oldest vines, but the soil is not exceptional. Although these old vines are pruned short and seem self-regulating in terms of yield, the younger vines are green-harvested.

The grapes are picked by hand and sorted in the vineyard. Ducasse would like to cull the grapes again after destemming, but the problem is the size of the estate and hence its enormous production. Lagrange has a *sous-vide* concentrator, but it is rarely used, most recently in 1999 and 2004. Chaptalization used to be common here, but there was none in 2002, so perhaps Lagrange is moving away from the practice. There is no cold soak, and fermentation takes place at fairly cool temperatures. Ducasse stresses that he does not want wines that are excessively tannic, and tells me that his model is Léoville-Barton, which always opts for finesse rather than extraction. The wines are aged in the immense but rather ugly *chais* built by Suntory. Blending takes place in January, and the wine spends sixteen to twenty months in sixty per cent new oak. The second wine is aged for twelve months in twenty-five per cent new oak. The *élevage* is entirely traditional.

There used to be a white wine at Lagrange, from a sandy parcel that ripens late and isn't ideal for red varieties. Ducasse replanted this parcel in 1992, and the first vintage of Les Arums de Lagrange was 1996. The wine is fermented and aged for ten months in new barriques. Production is limited, a mere 1,000 cases. The initial vintages were rather thin, but as the vines have aged, the wine has gained in weight and concentration.

Ducasse is mild-mannered, even self-effacing, but he is a man of strong opinions. He dislikes Cabernet Franc, for a start, so there is none at Lagrange. He does like Petit Verdot, but there have been vintages, such as 2000, when he found its wine too strong in flavour and didn't use it in the *grand vin*. As a consequence the 2000 contained seventy-six per cent Cabernet Sauvignon.

Because the selection for Lagrange is so severe, some excellent wine ends up in Les Fiefs de Lagrange, which is rightly admired as a consistent and fruity wine of exceptional value. Any wine not considered good enough for Les Fiefs is sold off in bulk. Lagrange is good value too. Whereas other properties vie with each other to obtain the highest possible *prix de sortie*, Ducasse and his Japanese bosses aim to price the wine attractively to encourage people to buy it. As a result, claims Ducasse, Lagrange has some of the lowest stock levels among the classified growths.

The vintages I tasted from the 1970s – 1970, 1978, and 1979 – were mediocre, with some greenness and dry finishes. The 1983 managed to be both light and tannic. The 1984 is light but still reasonably fresh after two decades. The 1985 is surprisingly tight and concentrated for this amenable vintage, with some chocolatey tones and good acidity. The 1986 has grown in amplitude over the years to become a very rich, dense wine with considerable persistence and elegance. The 1987 is a medium-bodied wine but there is no dilution; it's ready to drink. I have had mixed impressions of the 1988. Some bottles lack substance and optimal ripeness; others seem perfectly ripe, with bright, sweet flavours, and freshness on the finish. No doubts about the 1989, however. The nose is dense and complex, with aromas of blackcurrant, chocolate, and woodsmoke; the wine is still powerful and dense with hefty tannins. The 1990 is arguably even better, though the aromas are more truffley and leathery. The wine has terrific attack, less weight than 1989 but delicious fruit and considerable elegance. There's a St-Julien charm here that is less present on the 1989. The 1991 is very good for the vintage, perhaps a touch hollow, but there's no lack of fruit and concentration. The 1992 is austere but not dilute. The 1993 is rather slack and doesn't develop on the palate. The 1994 has a different problem: austerity and rather hard tannins, so not much pleasure here.

The 1995 is burly, unquestionably concentrated, but lacks some finesse and airiness. It's a wine that is working hard to make its impression, yet remains earthbound. The 1996 is leaner, with fine acidity supporting the blackcurrant fruit; it's far from fleshy but has great elegance. The 1997 is rather green, and there is something charmless about the robust and still austere 1998, although by late 2006 the long, sweet finish suggested the fruit was finally re-emerging. The 1999 is lush and juicy, with firm but not harsh tannins, finely integrated oak, and attractive length. With 2000, Lagrange gains an extra dimension. The splendid nose blends a good deal of new oak with voluptuous blackcurrant and plum fruit. This fruit is extremely ripe, with powerful tannic support that contributes to its length of flavour. The 2001 was rather stern when young, but now shows great opulence, lush, ripe tannins, powerful black-fruits flavours, and good balance. The 2002 is, perhaps, even better, having a greater purity of fruit and a livelier, fresher finish. Those qualities are precisely what is lacking from the rather jammy 2003, but it's evolving into a supple wine with modest tannins, surprising length, a spicy finish. The 2004 is nicely poised, reasonably concentrated, well balanced, and needs time to shed its youthful gawkiness.

I have the impression that in recent years the reticent, elegant Lagrange has acquired more flesh and weight, while rarely straying into over-extraction or jamminess. The wines also seem more tannic than before, despite Ducasse's protestations that this is not his aim. On the other hand, those tannins are not harsh and seem a natural part of the wines' structure.

Château Lalande

*Tel: 0556 590647. **Owner:** Jean-Paul Meffre. 31 ha. 50% Cabernet Sauvignon, 47% Merlot, 3% Cabernet Franc.*
*Production: 115,000 bottles. **Second wine:** Marquis de Lalande*

These vineyards lie in a single block of gravel and black sand close to Talbot and Lagrange, the properties that sold the vineyards to Meffre in 1964. The grapes are picked by machine and also by hand, and the vinification is the same as for Château Glana (*q.v.*). The wine is aged for twelve months in thirty per cent new oak, including some American barrels. It's an easy-drinking wine, with lush but elegant aromas, moderate concentration, good acidity, and little complexity.

Château Lalande-Borie

*Tel: 0556 731673. **Owner:** Bruno Borie. 18 ha. 65% Cabernet Sauvignon, 25% Merlot, 10% Cabernet Franc.*
Production: 100,000 bottles

The Bories bought this property, close to Talbot and Gruaud Larose, from Lagrange, and planted the vines in 1970. The soil is deep gravel that is well drained. The 1982 aged remarkably well, even though the wine was not especially concentrated; however, it retained its elegance and freshness. More recent vintages, such as 1999 and 2001, have struck me as lighter, more bland, easy-going but unmemorable. The 2003 has more stuffing.

Château Langoa-Barton

*Tel: 0556 590605. **Website:** www.leoville-barton.com. **Owner:** Anthony Barton. Troisième cru.*
*17 ha. 72% Cabernet Sauvignon, 20% Merlot, 8% Cabernet Franc. **Production:** 100,000 bottles.*
Second wine: Lady Langoa

Hugh Barton bought this property, with its lovely château of 1755, in 1821, and it has remained in the family ever since. It is run, and its wines vinified, in exactly the same way as Léoville-Barton (*q.v.*). It tends to be overshadowed by Léoville, but it should not be underestimated. Its high proportion of Cabernet Sauvignon gives the wine surprising backbone and tannic grip.

Anthony Barton poured me a glass of unidentified wine at lunch in 2000. The colour was still very deep, though with some signs of maturity. The nose was oaky, cedary, and very elegant, and that elegance was mirrored on the delicious palate. The wine was holding up beautifully, with no sign of decline other than unexceptional length. I guessed the wine was about twenty years old. But it was the 1949, which rather disposed of the idea that Langoa is for medium-term drinking. The wine was equally delicious in 2006. Its predecessor, the 1948, is very different; poured from magnum in 2006, it had sumptuous black-fruits aromas, a surprisingly thick texture and great concentration and length, and wasn't tiring in the slightest. The 1955 resembles the 1949 in its delicacy and ethereal nature; it may not be complex but it's elegant, balanced, and long. The 1961, from magnum, mirrors the 1948 in its almost inky blackcurrant aromas, its richness and intensity, and its remarkable youthfulness. A 1964 had become astringent by 1992, and in 2006 the 1966 seemed headed in the same direction but was still highly drinkable. The 1975 from magnum was successful for the vintage, with complex, tobacco aromas, and some richness, liveliness, and length that reined in the tannins. I did not care much for the 1976 and 1977, which both lacked fruit, but the 1978 is attractive, with lightly herbaceous aromas, modest concentration and fair acidity, and a touch of mocha on the finish. I tasted the 1982 in 2006, but it seemed stale and out of condition. The 1985 has all the ripeness and delicacy of that charming vintage, and the fruit quality is supple and lightly spicy. The 1986 today shows muted cedary aromas, the assertive tannins typical of the vintage, and a slight lack of drive on the finish. The 1988 is less successful than most, with a rasping, astringent quality and a lack of flesh. The 1989 is impeccable, with oak and liquorice aromas; there's a fine attack to the wine, which has finesse and vigour, a slight smokiness, and considerable complexity. However, the final impression is of more-ishness, the urge to grab the decanter and pour another glass. The 1990 is a touch leaner, but equally delicious, silky, and stylish, while delicately underpinned by ripe tannins. The trio from 1991 to 1993 are far from arresting; the 1994 is slightly more stylish and weighty.

With the 1995, Langoa is back on form, with its sleek, oaky nose, its fruit concentration, its robust tannins, and an unmistakable St-Julien gracefulness. For the first eight years there was an atypical muscularity to the 1995, but it is now beginning to drink well. The 1996 has ripe lead-pencil and blackcurrant aromas, the same stylishness as the 1995, with a shade more persistence and energy. The 1998 has evolved beautifully, with rich, plummy aromas, while the palate is rich yet rugged; the tannins are mitigated by the wine's inherent lift and vigour. The 1999 is more supple, spicy, plump, and a touch more forward. The formidable 2000 is both opulent and oaky on the nose, but the tannins are dominant now, and, by Langoa standards, this is somewhat burly and clearly needs time. The 2001 has more evident freshness and less weight, though it's quite a full-bodied wine with good length. There's remarkable intensity and purity of blackcurrant fruit on the 2002, and exceptional length; it's very tight and needs time to unwind. The 2003 is concentrated and dense, but with a worrying chewiness on the finish.

Langoa may not have quite the track record of its illustrious neighbour, but it is not always the case that Léoville delivers the superior wine.

Château Léoville-Barton

Tel: 0556 590605. Website: www.leoville-barton.com. **Owner:** *Anthony Barton. Troisième cru. 45 ha.*
72% Cabernet Sauvignon, 20% Merlot, 8% Cabernet Franc. **Production:** *250,000 bottles.*
Second wine: La Réserve Léoville-Barton

The fine chartreuse from the 1750s depicted on the label of Léoville-Barton is none other than Château Langoa-Barton (*q.v.*). There is no château at Léoville, but since the same family own both properties two contiguous châteaux might be surplus to requirements. The Léoville estate belonged in the eighteenth century to Alexandre de Gasq, and was bequeathed to four heirs, so the property was split up between various owners. Hugh Barton bought this part of the property in 1826, having already bought what was to be named Langoa-Barton in 1821. Since there were no *chais* or other structures connected to the Léoville vineyards, he made the wines next door at Langoa, which is still the case today. His ancestor Thomas Barton had come to Bordeaux from Ireland a century earlier, and Hugh maintained his Irish heritage by purchasing an estate there in 1835. Long after, in 1930, Anthony Barton was born there. Anthony's father was the older of two brothers, and thus inherited the Irish property, while his younger brother Ronald (1902–86) came to Bordeaux in 1924, and by 1929 was looking after the two St-Julien estates as well as the négociant business of Barton & Guestier.

Anthony Barton first came to Bordeaux himself in 1951, a vintage so awful that his Uncle Ronald told him that if there were one more like it, he would be obliged to sell up. Fortunately the négociant business provided sufficient income to allow Ronald to hang on. In 1983 he donated the properties to Anthony, who has run them ever since with his daughter Lilian. Anthony recalls:

> Uncle Ron was a very conservative figure in some ways. He had an old destemmer-crusher
> here, which was a ghastly machine, churning up the grapes. I suggested a more modern,

*gentler replacement, but he wouldn't hear of it. He would say that if it had been good enough
for great vintages such as 1945 and 1947, it was good enough still. Eventually I simply
declared that the machine had broken down irretrievably, so we had no choice but to replace it.*

Anthony Barton is, like a handful of other proprietors, opposed to green-harvesting, yet no one could accuse his wines of lacking ripeness. ("My Cabernet Franc vines have gained in ripeness", he told French reporters in 2003, "ever since I threatened to grub them up.") He must be fortunate in having a vineyard full of contented, well-balanced vines. The must is fermented in temperature-controlled wooden vats, where the wine remains for the malolactic fermentation too. Then *cuvaison* is usually around twenty-five days, with a maximum temperature of just above 30°C (86°F). The wine is aged in fifty per cent new barriques for some twenty months.

In this seemingly effortless way, the Bartons produce a delicious, well-structured, and highly consistent wine here. Ancient vintages can often prove disappointing, but the mediocre 1972 and 1977 vintages apart, venerable vintages of Léoville-Barton have been marvellous: luminous, sweet, intense, refined, long. I have enthusiastic notes from the late 1980s on the 1945, 1955, and 1970. The 1950 was still wonderfully perfumed in 2006, with great attack on the palate and an astonishing youthfulness, but the 1959 lacks a little lift and complexity. Even the 1975 was pretty good, with an elegant blackcurrant nose, though, admittedly, the palate was austere and a touch meagre in its fruit expression. Vintages from 1978 to 1981 were not at this level: they were good but not outstanding wines that lacked some complexity. The 1982, tasted from magnum in 2007, had a rich, lush, truffley nose, and a similar luxuriousness on the palate, though its opulence was far from heavy and the finish is bright and long. The 1983 has become plump and rounded, but hasn't lost its tannic structure; it's a wine that has retained its vivacity and length. The 1985 is enchanting, generous and oaky on the nose, lush and supple but with exceptional freshness and liveliness on the finish. It certainly has more immediate drinkability than the firmer and more assertive 1986, but the latter's richness and virility may give it the edge over the long term. The 1987 was very good if not enormously concentrated. There is something slightly herbaceous about the 1988; it's dense, peppery, concentrated and spicy, but it doesn't seem entirely ripe.

The 1989 shows a lot of oak and cedary aromas on the nose; it's voluptuous, even luxurious, yet sustained by good acidity. Although less accessible today than the 1989 Langoa, this may outpace it in the long term. The 1990 has leafy, cedary aromas, but there is masses of upfront fruit on the palate, as well as remarkable spiciness and freshness. The 1991 is significantly better than Langoa, but the 1992 tastes washed-out. The 1993 and 1994 are not bad, but neither are they exciting or that distinctive. There's great intensity on the nose of the 1995, which is awash in blackcurrant and mint aromas; the wine has a fine attack, but is medium-bodied without lacking concentration or backbone. It's bright, stylish, and long. The same is true of the more savoury yet more vigorous 1996. Ten years on, the 1997 has developed sweet, meaty aromas; it's supple, balanced, and fully ready to drink. The 1998 is rich and lush, but still chewy and rather closed; at present Langoa shows more overt fruit. It doesn't have the charm of the plumper 1999, but it will be interesting to compare the two in ten years' time. The sublime, sumptuous quality of the 2000 was evident from the outset, even though a battle was being waged between the blackcurrant aromas and the toasty new oak. It's a massive wine, for Léoville-Barton, super-ripe and almost burly, yet it has superb length as well.

The 2001 is weightier and more austere than Langoa, with a good deal of tannin that at present slightly overwhelms the fruit. The 2002 is wonderfully complex, with aromas of blackcurrants, plums, and crushed fruits; it's a powerful wine, tight and unevolved, and packed with fruit. Tasted blind with other St-Juliens, I took it for Gruaud-Larose because of its weight and power. The powerful 2003 does not have the finesse of Léoville-Barton at its best, but it's fleshy, rich, and has modest acidity. (In 2003, Anthony Barton remarked, there were two kinds of grapes: small and tiny.) The 2004 is delicious, with sweet blackcurrant aromas, and spicy succulence on the palate, which also shows excellent balance.

It's difficult for even the most hard-bitten wine writer not to feel well disposed toward this property: its château, its hospitable owners, its consistency, its sensible pricing. But many of my encounters with its wine have been in blind tastings, where its quality comes shining through.

Château Léoville-Las-Cases

*Tel: 0556 732526. Website: www.leoville-las-cases.com. **Owners:** Jean-Hubert Delon and Geneviève d'Alton.*
Deuxième cru. 97 ha. 65% Cabernet Sauvignon, 20% Merlot, 12% Cabernet Franc, 3% Petit Verdot.
***Production:** 550,000 bottles. **Second wine:** Clos du Marquis*

One of the most inspiring sights as you drive up the D2 toward Pauillac is the great lion-topped gateway guarding the entrance to the Clos Léoville-Las-Cases vineyard. It's a breathtaking combination of arrogance, confidence, and theatricality. It's a good introduction to the wine.

One of the four heirs to Alexandre de Gasq and his Léoville vineyards was the Marquis de Las-Cases. The marquis fled the country in 1794, and the state seized his property. Hugh Barton acquired roughly one-quarter, another quarter passed to a daughter (this was to become Poyferré), while the Las-Cases share remained by far the most important in terms of size. In 1900 the Marquis de Las-Cases found himself obliged to sell, and the estate passed into the hands of a consortium, including the Delon family. Over the years the Delons gradually accumulated a majority shareholding. From 1976 until his death in 2000, Michel Delon managed the property, and now it is owned by his son Jean-Hubert and daughter Geneviève.

Of all the classified growths, only Léoville-Las-Cases declined my repeated requests to visit the property in order to research this book. Although some years ago M. Delon assured me in person that my sins against him (*viz.* daring to turn up without an appointment during the *primeur* season) had been forgiven, that forgiveness has not extended to permission to visit the property and verify the information I have about it, let alone taste new vintages. This, however, is no personal vendetta. Léoville-Las-Cases is conspicuous by its absence from the splendid tome published by the Union des Grands Crus to mark the 150th anniversary of the 1855 *classement.* M. Delon prefers to be a loner, who dispenses his favours as he sees fit. So if there are any errors in the account that follows, it is not for want of trying to correct them.

This large property is divided into 125 different parcels, but the historic heart of the property is the fifty-hectare walled *clos* just south of Latour. Of all the vineyards of St-Julien, these are the closest to the estuary and to some of the greatest vineyards of Pauillac. So perhaps it is not surprising that in its richness and power Léoville-Las-Cases can be mistaken for a top Pauillac. The *clos* consists of some fifty hectares north of the village; there is another, much smaller, five-hectare *clos* just south of the village. Some seven hectares were purchased from Ronald Barton in the 1970s, and there are a further twenty hectares scattered around St-Julien.

The second wine is no recent innovation. The first vintage of Clos du Marquis was 1902. Of course much of the wine from the Clos finds its way into the *grand vin*, so the name is something of a misnomer. But its existence for so many decades, with the underlying assumption (not shared by most other properties at the time) that selection was essential in order to maintain quality, is part of the explanation for Las-Cases's imposing performance over such a long time span. Much of the wine that goes into the Clos du Marquis comes from the vineyards closer to Talbot, though of course young vines and declassified lots also enter the blend. But it is no dustbin, and lots of insufficient quality for the second wine are sold off in bulk. Before 1980 only about ten per cent of the wine was declassified; since then the portion can be as high as sixty per cent. Indeed, in 1990 the *grand vin* consisted of one-third of the crop, and the same was true in 2004.

If Michel Delon could not take credit for devising the second wine, he could claim to have been a pioneer of green-harvesting, beginning the practice in 1988. Delon renovated the *cuvier* some years earlier, but preserved the wooden vats for fermentation, although they are supplemented by steel and cement tanks. The three forms of container are all still in use. Reverse osmosis is used routinely, though the proportion of concentrated must varies. The vinification is traditional, and malolactic fermentation takes place in tanks. Blending is completed in the spring following the vintage. The *grand vin* is aged in sixty to 100 per cent new oak, Clos du Marquis in twenty per cent. Since 1985 the *chais* have been air-conditioned, and the wine is aged in them for around twenty months.

It is no secret that the Delons have long considered Las-Cases to be of First-Growth quality (many would agree with them) and that it should be priced accordingly. Some of the neighbours are not happy about this policy, since it suggests that Las-Cases is vastly superior to St-Julien's other classified growths. But the Delons have stuck to their guns and implemented their own idiosyncratic pricing and commercial policy, sometimes working through scores of négociants on the *Place de Bordeaux*, while, at other times, as with the 2002, refusing to release the wine *en primeur*.

Las-Cases is probably the richest and most powerful of the St-Julien wines, although Gruaud-Larose can match it for richness if not always for power. Some would argue that the emphasis on concentration has diminished the wine's typicity and elegance; others disagree. Certainly the very high price demanded for the wine raises the highest expectations from critics and consumers alike. At the same time, those prices have probably persuaded many admirers of the wine without bottomless pockets to look elsewhere for outstanding claret, preferring not to participate in the rivalries between growers that are a dispiriting feature of the Bordeaux market.

Clos du Marquis can be an excellent wine in good vintages. It is less oaky, less extracted than the *grand vin*, and possibly has more St-Julien typicity. I have much enjoyed vintages such as 1982, 1983 (slightly less so), 1988, 1995, 1996, 1997 (remarkably good for the vintage), and 1998.

Legendary vintages of Las-Cases include 1900 and 1928. I was poured the 1924 Las-Cases, blind, at a dinner in 1987 and confidently declared the vintage to be 1970. To redeem myself, I did identify (by pure luck) the estate, even if I was half a century out. The colour was still a healthy deep red, with some slight evolution, the nose fragrant and stylish and fairly mature, the palate still robust and spicy with lovely clean fruit and good length. The 1959, at twenty-five years of age, was still full, rich, and long. The 1961 is less perfumed than some wines from the vintage, but the concentration and density are remarkable; it's a wine of elegance and poise, yet there's a peppery vigour. The 1964 was figgy and rather simple and dry in 1992, but ten years later from magnum it was sumptuous, plump, and spicy, despite some leathery aromas. The 1967 is disappointing. There's a slight coarseness on some bottles from 1970, although the aromas have been exquisite. But tasted most recently in 1999, it was still elegant, though losing some richness and flesh.

The 1971, once robust and almost meaty, is now becoming attenuated and rather dry on the finish; not without interest but clearly in decline. The 1975 is certainly one of the top wines of this difficult vintage. The nose is smoky and complex but still reserved; the palate is massive and tannic, yet the wine isn't hard and there is an intense core of fruit. The 1976 in 1991 was robust and perhaps a touch dry, a good wine but one unlikely to have improved since. The 1978 is very impressive: velvety, concentrated, harmonious, spicy, and lively, with the tannins now entirely integrated. The 1979 is more evolved and less powerful than its predecessor. The nose is gorgeous: rich, earthy, truffley, yet fragrant and lively; even in 2005, the wine retained its freshness, its delicious fruit, its fine underlying acidity and length. The 1980 and 1984 were good but have both probably faded by now. The 1981 seemed to tire fast.

The 1982 is one of the top wines of that remarkable year. It offers a marvellous cocktail of sweet, ripe fruit and aromas of crushed berries. The palate is sumptuous and concentrated, with enormous depth and power, finely integrated new oak, and an amazingly persistent finish. Bordeaux doesn't get much better than this. The 1983 remains concentrated, sleek, and elegant, and now seems at its best. The 1985 has all the seductive opulence of the vintage: a big, sweet (but not jammy) and hedonistic wine, it has intense blackcurrant and chocolatey aromas and a classic structure. The 1986 was closed when young, and still closed when I last tasted it in 1998, but it will surely open up into a magnificent wine, concentrated, complex, and long.

I admire the 1988 because the temptation to over-extract was clearly resisted. Yes, the wine is structured and tannic, but there is elegance and spice and vigour too. The 1989 is sumptuous but burly, and, like the 1986, still rather closed. All the components are in place, but the wine remains inexpressive. The 1990 has more finesse, though not at the expense of opulence or concentration. It's a wine that seems very complete, with its complex aromas of blackcurrant, coffee, and oak, and its fruit expression, balance, and persistence. The 1992 is perhaps too extracted, going for concentration at all costs, and ending up as rather charmless; the 1994 is similar in its structure. The 1996 is classic, with elegant cedary aromas, yet has a lot of power and concentration on the palate, which, ten years on, still remains inexpressive. The 1997 is extremely good, and for the vintage quite exceptional, tight and elegant. Even better is the 1998, which is severe but doesn't lack fruit and length. The 1999 is, predictably, a touch more open, though here too there are firm tannins and structure. A run of fine vintages reaches its climax with the magnificent 2000, with its intense, blackcurranty nose, its sumptuous fruit and powerful structure, its huge tannins and striking length of flavour. However, the 2001 seems over-extracted, powerful but gawky and slightly bitter on the finish.

I don't know whether it is a profitable exercise to speculate whether Las-Cases is, as many claim, of First-Growth quality. There seems little doubt that if you drink Las-Cases from a great vintage alongside some First Growths it would hold its own. I also admire the wine for its sterling performance in difficult or lightweight vintages such as 1997. On the other hand, it offers a very rich, extracted style that may not be to everyone's taste. It is a wine that always impresses but less frequently delights. It is imposing, but is it too imposing? Does the hand reach for the bottle to pour a second glass? The fact is that Las-Cases is made for the long term. It needs a good deal of bottle-age for the precise fruit quality, the full complexity, and, dare I say it, the finesse to emerge.

Château Léoville-Poyferré

*Tel: 0556 590830. **Website:** www.leoville-poyferre.fr. **Owners:** Didier and Olivier Cuvelier. Deuxième cru.*
*80 ha. 65% Cabernet Sauvignon, 25% Merlot, 8% Petit Verdot, 2% Cabernet Franc. **Production:** 380,000 bottles.*
***Second wines:** Ch Moulin Riche, Pavillon des Connétables*

The history of the Léoville properties has been sketched in the entries for the other two estates. By marriage this one came into the hands of the wife of the Baron du Poyferré. In 1920 it was acquired by the Cuvelier family, and, with Le Crock (*q.v.*) in St-Estèphe, has been ably run by Didier Cuvelier since 1979. The family have invested considerably in the property and its buildings, constructing a new winery in the mid-1990s. There has also been a good deal of replanting, so the average age of the vines is still fairly youthful at twenty years. Cuvelier has been trying to diminish the proportion of Merlot and replace it with Cabernet on the finest parcels, as he wants Poyferré to be a structured, long-lived wine. Michel Rolland has been consulting since 1994.

The vineyards consist of a few large blocks of fine gravelly soil. The best lie on either side of the D2 road. The grapes are picked as late as possible, and sometimes reverse osmosis is used to remove up to ten per cent of the juice. Fermentation temperatures can be quite high. The wine is aged for eighteen to twenty months in seventy-five per cent new barriques. The blending begins in spring and continues progressively until the summer, by which time it is usually completed. The wine is eggwhite-fined and filtered. The overall result is a more opulent and hedonistic wine than the two other Léovilles, but one that has been steadily improving in quality.

The second wine is actually a separate property of twenty hectares, located two kilometres (one mile) inland on the way to Château Batailley. It too was bought in 1920, but has been extensively replanted, so the average age of the vineyard is fairly young. There is some interchange between the two properties. Unsatisfactory lots of Poyferré are blended into Moulin Riche, and the sector of the latter (about one-quarter) that gives exceptional wine is sometimes included in the *grand vin*. The major difference between the two wines is the much higher proportion of Merlot in Moulin Riche: up to sixty per cent. The youngest vines make their way into the third label, Pavillon des Connétables.

Poyferré was hugely admired in the late nineteenth century, and made classic wines in great vintages such as 1928 and 1929. A 1926, drunk from magnum in 1994, was browning and in decline, losing its fruit and teetering along. The 1955 was disappointing for the vintage, acidic and astringent. The 1959 is considerably better, but there is bottle variation; at its best it is mellow and attractive, but lacks persistence. The 1961 is probably as good as it is going to get: smoky bacon and cedar on the nose, while the palate is concentrated, smoky, bacony, quite elegant but unlikely to improve further. The 1964 remained sweet and spicy on the nose for decades; it has good acidity and vigour, not much flesh but considerable charm, and should be drunk soon. The 1970 is medium-bodied and rather soft and unexciting. The 1972 smelled of cabbage; enough said. The 1973 was good for the vintage, the 1974 both watery and dry. There are powerful tannins on the 1975, as one would expect; the wine is a bit coarse, but, when last tasted, did not lack fruit. The 1977 and 1980 are harsh and unpleasant. The 1981 had some charm but never had much persistence and may now be past its best.

The 1982 is delicious, with splendid aromas of cedar and coffee as well as sweet fruit. After twenty years, the wine, soft, plump, and voluptuous, seems ready to drink. The 1983 was stern and tannic and lacked length, but I have not tasted it for many years. The sweet, rich fruit of the 1986 is still somewhat masked by hefty tannins; this is made in a big, bold style and should improve further. The 1987 is not bad for the vintage. The 1989 has a sweet, smoky, toasty nose, with a touch of dill; it's voluptuous, very ripe, yet has considerable vigour and length. The well-structured 1990 seems a touch more elegant, but I have not tasted it recently. The 1993 is chunky but hollow and lacks finesse. The 1995 is going strong, with a rich, sweet, oaky nose of great elegance; the palate is rich, very concentrated, with bright acidity. I marginally prefer it to the leaner 1996, but the latter's supple tannins and zest should stand it in good stead. The 1997 is very enjoyable, but it lacks length. Muscularity marks the 1998, but the fruit seems fully ripe and there seems no reason why it shouldn't evolve very well. The 2000 is a more massive wine, hedonistic in its lush, oaky texture, and packed with blackcurrant and plum fruit. I prefer it to the similar 2001, which is broader, very chewy, and less precise. Oak dominates the 2002 at present; indeed the wine seems rather extracted; I certainly admire its swagger and vigour, and expect it will have a very good future. The 2003 was brutal when young, but has evolved into a rich if oaky wine with a good deal of energy, and the tannins no longer dominate the fruit. This is a striking success for the vintage. The 2004 has charming blackcurrant aromas, and remarkable power on the palate but not at the expense of vigour and balance. It comes close in quality to the superb 2005, very concentrated and tannic for St Julien, but with ample fruit and spice to the fore.

If Léoville-Barton is the most classic of the Léoville trio, and Las-Cases the most concentrated and majestic, then Poyferré is the most sensual and voluptuous. You pays your money (quite a lot of money, especially in the case of Las-Cases) and you takes your choice.

Château Moulin de la Rose

Tel: 0556 590845. **Owner:** *Guy Delon. 5 ha. 60% Cabernet Sauvignon, 30% Merlot, 5% Petit Verdot,*
5% Cabernet Franc. **Production:** *30,000 bottles*

Guy Delon also owns the excellent Château Ségur de Cabanac (*q.v.*) in St-Estèphe. His father bought this small estate in 1961, and the gruff, chain-smoking Guy took over in 1971. His son Jean-François is also involved. The vines are planted around the village of Beychevelle on gravel soils over a clay-limestone base, and are picked by hand. The wine is aged in one-third new barriques for twenty months. I have tasted only the 1996, but the wine has a very good reputation, and if it is as good as Ségur de Cabanac, then it will be very good indeed. Delon has a reputation for making burly wines, and the 1996 was certainly robustly tannic, though it had a more enticing nose of crushed red fruits.

Château St-Pierre

*Tel: 0556 590818. **Owner:** Françoise Triaud. Quatrième cru. 17 ha. 65% Cabernet Sauvignon, 25% Merlot, 10% Cabernet Franc. **Production:** 60,000 bottles*

Although Henri Martin was best known for creating Château Gloria (*q.v.*), this classified growth was also developed, though not created, by him. The estate dates back to the late seventeenth century, and in 1767 the Baron de St-Pierre became the owner. After he died in 1832, the property was divided between his daughters. One received half the vineyards, the *chais*, and the château; the other, who married M. de Luetkens of Château La Tour-Carnet, received the remaining vineyards. The division of the property did not impede its classification in 1855. The two halves passed through various hands and were usually marketed and labelled as St-Pierre-Sevaistre and St-Pierre-Bontemps Dubarry. Finally, in 1920, a négociant reunited the properties, though the *chais* were the property of a cooper called Alfred Martin. In 1981 his son Henri Martin bought the spacious château and its pretty park, and then the following year succeeded in buying some of the vineyards and reconstituting the property by making exchanges with neighbouring estates. So the vineyards of modern-day St-Pierre are quite scattered. Despite Martin's patient reconstruction, the total size of the vineyards is only half what it was in 1855.

Today the property is owned by his daughter Françoise and managed by her husband Jean-Louis Triaud. The winemaking team is the same as for Gloria. Triaud's brother Alain built the handsome modern *cuvier* in the village of Beychevelle across the road from the château.

The vineyards are old, as the latest plantings were over thirty years ago. Triaud says he is not obsessed by low yields. The harvest is manual, with sorting in the vineyard and again at the winery. Triaud uses a *sous-vide* concentrator if he feels any lots would benefit. Otherwise the vinification is classic, with selected yeasts. The wine is aged for twelve months in around fifty per cent new oak, with lees-stirring. Blending takes place progressively, and the final wine is eggwhite-fined and filtered.

Production is limited, and there is no second wine. Triaud explains that he likes to sell off a fair proportion of the crop in bulk as he can get good prices for the wine.

The oldest vintage I have tasted is the 1986, which is distinctly rustic. I much prefer the 1988, which has a rich, succulent nose of blackcurrant and cinnamon, while the texture is supple and plump with good concentration and length. The 1989 has an opulent, toasty nose and voluptuous fruit, with a touch of mint to keep it lively. The 1990 lacks some concentration, but is well balanced with ripe tannins and good acidity, adding up to an elegant wine. The 1992 is green, but the 1995 is complete and balanced, with sumptuous plum and blackberry fruit, and ripe tannins. I prefer it by some way to the 1996, which is a touch green and lacks length. There are firm blackcurrant aromas on the 1998, but the wine is rather light for the vintage, and lacks flesh and flair. The 1999 is surprisingly solid; perhaps it is going through a dumb phase. I have numerous notes on the 2000, but they are far from uniform. Most of them express a sense that although the aromas are very opulent, the wine is leaner than one would expect. The 2001 is also unsatisfactory, with very dry tannins on a couple of bottles sampled recently, and a certain rusticity one doesn't expect from St-Julien. The 2002 is also chewy, extracted, and rather dry, but richer and livelier overall than the two preceding vintages. The 2003 has filled out on the palate, its initially brutal tannins replaced by plump, concentrated fruit and enough acidity to give a long finish.

I understand that St-Pierre had some TCA problems in the early 1990s. I can't say I have detected this on the wines I have tasted, although the 1986 did seem somewhat tainted to me. I have had some excellent wines from this property, but also some disappointments, with a lack of stylistic consistency.

Château Talbot

*Tel: 0556 732150. Website: www.chateau-talbot.com. **Owners:** Nancy Bignon and Lorraine Rustmann.*
Quatrième cru. 107 ha. 102 ha red: 66% Cabernet Sauvignon, 26% Merlot, 5% Petit Verdot, 3% Cabernet Franc.
*5 ha white: 80% Sauvignon Blanc, 20% Sémillon. **Production:** 550,000 bottles. **Second wine:** Connétable de Talbot*

This very large property, neighbouring Gruaud-Larose but partly concealed by woodlands, was owned for many years by the Marquis d'Aux. In 1917 it was acquired by Désiré Cordier and run by his grandson Jean. After Jean died in 1993, the wines ceased to be tied commercially to the négociant firm of Cordier, and the property was run independently by his daughters and their husbands. Nancy Cordier is married to Jean-Paul Bignon, and Lorraine was married to Thierry Rustmann, who in recent years has bowed out of Talbot and dedicates himself instead to Château Sénéjac (*q.v.*) in the Haut-Médoc. The sisters made considerable investments, installing new drainage systems, a drying system to evaporate water from wet grapes at harvest, more manual work in the vineyards, and stricter selection at the winery. Since 1989 the *maître de chai* has been the genial Basque Ramon Sorajuria, who used to work at Latour, as did the long-term *chef de culture*, Christian Holstein.

Of the 108 hectares, all but six are AC St-Julien, the remainder being used for the white AC Bordeaux. The vineyards lie in a single parcel and rise to a height of twenty-three metres (seventy-five feet). About half the vineyard consists of deep gravel over sandstone bedrock, but the western fringes have thinner gravel and more sand, and give wines of less depth. The average age of the vines is around thirty-five years.

Picking is manual, and for Talbot the ideal is a late but rapid harvest. The grapes are sorted at the winery, using the aforementioned hot-air dryer. The must is sometimes concentrated by reverse osmosis. Fermentation takes place in both oak vats and stainless-steel tanks. The wine is aged for eighteen months in fifty per cent new oak, though only fifteen per cent for the second wine, which was introduced in 1979.

Talbot used to be quite well known for its white Caillou Blanc. In the past I found it very dull, but in the 1990s changes were made that have improved quality. The grapes are whole-cluster-pressed in a pneumatic press, and in the 1990s about half the wine was barrel-fermented; today it is all barrel-fermented in fifty per cent new oak, and aged for seven months with lees-stirring. About 30,000 bottles are produced.

I have had the rare pleasure of enjoying some old vintages of Talbot. The 1926 (from magnum in 1991) was browning, while the nose was elegant but mushroomy. The texture was silky, and there was not much concentration or weight, and the wine was clearly drying out. Not so the 1934, also from magnum and also browning, but the nose was sweet, leathery, and cedary; again, the texture was silky but there was far more ripe fruit, which was concentrated and mouth-filling, and the wine as a whole seemed perfectly balanced. The 1945, drunk from double magnum in 2000, showed only slight maturity of colour, while the nose was dense and smoky. Highly concentrated, the wine was minty and assertive, still powerful, with the merest hint of dry tannin. The 1949 appeared more evolved, with some vegetal and cedary aromas. The wine was happily dominated by its sweet, rich fruit; although youthful, there was some dryness on the finish. A magnum of 1953 in 2000 was silky, elegant, balanced, and charming; but the same wine from magnum in 2005 showed some sweaty aromas and astringency. In 1991, the 1955 was still great. Although browning, it was still full and bright; the nose was sweet and earthy, with cigar-box and tobacco tones. It's not especially elegant, but it is rich, rounded, and powerful, with a vigorous earthiness. The 1961 was not dissimilar, but it was more graceful, more pure, finely balanced, but perfectly tuned and very long.

In contrast, the 1970 seemed to lack fruit and concentration and was dominated by its acidity; it also lacked length. The 1978, last tasted at fifteen years of age, was evolving fast, with a sweet but mature cedary nose, with hints of cigar-box and cloves; it was supple and rather too sweet, with some evolved figgy flavours. The 1981 was lean and lively, with some elegance and good length; it seemed at its peak after about ten years. The 1982 has been delicious from the outset, and in 2000 was still splendid: the nose had become more leathery, but the wine was still sumptuous, ultra-ripe, and concentrated, with exceptional length. But the 1983 lacks generosity; the cedary aromas are attractive, but the palate is lean and pinched. The 1985 was typical of the vintage, soft and easy-going, with seductive fruit and modest length. The 1986 is less massive than most; it has intensity and elegance, but not much flesh or weight. I doubt the 1987, pleasant and supple in its youth, is still offering much fruit. The 1988 is disappointing, a mean and lean wine with all the austerity of the year but little underlying finesse.

Although the 1989 has always seemed forward, it was still going strong in 2001, with powerful oak and blackberry aromas, and a certain stylishness on the palate. However, both fruit and concentration were rather modest and the wine lacked force and distinction. The 1990 is better, with more spice and power, but it's also rather slack. The 1992 and 1993 are quite green, but the 1994 is somewhat riper, though it's still a lean wine that doesn't give huge pleasure. The 1995 has a fleshy Cabernet nose and is certainly ripe, but here too the palate disappoints, with a lack of weight and concentration, and only modest length. There is some greenness on the 1996, which the oakiness of the nose cannot disguise; for a fine vintage this is both bland and ungainly. There are charming blackberry aromas marking the 1998, which is a solid but forward wine, plump and accessible, but with little verve. However, the 1999 is remarkably fleshy and voluptuous, with excellent fruit and acidity. The 2000 is grand. Frequently tasted, it shows a rich, oaky, smoky, black-fruits nose, sumptuous fruit with fine concentration, a tight structure, persistent tannins, and a long, elegant finish. The 2001 is quite full-bodied, and now displays its aromatic cedary charms, and a structure that is discreet but balanced. The 2002 is reasonably concentrated, lightly tannic, and somewhat hollow; it lacks focus and distinction. The 2003 is rich but airy, not complex, but accessible and attractive, with sufficient acidity to keep it going for the rest of the decade.

In recent decades, Talbot, which has exceptional potential, has had moments of splendour, but overall the wine is disappointing, especially in top vintages when one expects a good deal. It is often compared with its neighbour Gruaud-Larose, and in my experience there is no doubt that the latter is usually superior. The 1980s seem a particularly lacklustre decade for Talbot. True, the wine is not that expensive, but there are so many other St-Juliens that seem greatly superior and more marked in personality. There is selection here – sometimes forty per cent of the wine goes under the second label – but the *grand vin* still doesn't taste like the cream of the crop. Ancient vintages show how magnificent this wine can be, but there is still a long way to go.

Château Terrey-Gros-Cailloux
Tel: 0556 731673. Owner: Bruno Borie. 14 ha. 70% Cabernet Sauvignon, 25% Merlot, 5% Petit Verdot.
Production: 100,000 bottles

I bought the 1976 vintage in 1983 and that was the last time I saw the wine until I tasted the 2001 and 2002 in 2005. The vineyards are dispersed, and some lie close to Beychevelle and Gruaud-Larose. The wine was aged for twelve months in twenty per cent new oak. Part of the production was sold under the name of Château Hortevie by the négociant firm of Nathaniel Johnston. The 1976 was robust and mouth-filling. The lively 2001 may not be complex, but it has admirable energy and freshness. The 2002 is more assertive, with a light, chocolatey tone and modest length. In 2005 the estate was bought by the Borie family of Ducru-Beaucaillou.

Château Teynac
Tel: 0556 599304. Owner: Philippe Pairault. 12 ha. 78% Cabernet Sauvignon, 20% Merlot, 2% Petit Verdot.
Production: 80,000 bottles. Second wines: Ch Les Ormes, Eléonore de Ch Teynac

This belonged to the mayor of St-Julien in the mid-nineteenth century, and enjoyed a good reputation. When Léon Sevaistre was owner of part of Château St-Pierre, the Teynac vineyards were incorporated into that estate, but were later separated and acquired by the Gauthier family, and subsequently purchased in 1989 by Philippe Pairault, a Parisian businessman. Nowadays the estate is conscientiously looked after: the soil is ploughed and the grapes picked in several passages. The first vintage of the new regime was 1993. The wine is aged for twelve to fourteen months in one-third new barriques. The 1999 had a stylish, oaky nose, though a more solid palate – good but not exceptional. The 2001 shows more spice but is somewhat hollow despite the solid fruit. The 2004 is distinctly dull, and the 2005 slight and somewhat dilute for the vintage.

10. Pauillac Part I

 Pauillac is the savage, beating heart of the Médoc. From here emerge many of the wines that set the standard for red Bordeaux, or, for that matter, red wine *tout court*. So important are these wines that many Bordeaux enthusiasts may have only the dimmest notion of where Pauillac actually lies, but they certainly know about the wines from Lafite, Latour, or Mouton.

It may be something of a caricature, and it is certainly a simplification, to characterize the wines of Margaux as exemplifying finesse or those of St-Julien as offering the ideal balance between power and elegance. For Pauillac, the defining terms are probably power and longevity. Connoisseurs with deep pockets can still discuss the respective merits of the 1865 and 1870 vintages.

Pauillac lies between St-Julien to the south and St-Estèphe to the north. The mighty gravel *croupes* of St-Julien – Ducru-Beaucaillou and the Léovilles – continue northwards into Pauillac. You can chuck a pebble from Léoville-Las-Cases into the vineyards of Latour. Just west of Latour are the vineyards of the two Pichon estates. The swathe of vineyards is interrupted by the port of Pauillac itself, and just west of the town is the plateau of Bages. Continue north toward the hamlet of Le Pouyalet, home to the other two First Growths: Lafite and Mouton. They are not as close to the estuary as Latour, but they occupy splendid gravel plateaux. Lafite marks the northernmost boundary, and the land sinks into shady meadows, kept green by the Jalle de Breuil and the efforts of the local cattle.

Continue westwards from the Pichons, Bages, and Mouton and you come to the Pauillac interior, with properties such as Batailley, Grand-Puy-Lacoste, and Duhart-Milon. The advantages of proximity to the estuary are the same as in St-Julien or Margaux. Latour, famously, scarcely ever suffers from frost, often enabling it to make great wine in years when others freeze, as in 1991.

The soil is similar to elsewhere in the Médoc, except that it generally has a higher clay content. The depth of the gravel is greater in the northern part of the zone. The subsoil can vary, but is often composed of *alios*, which is a hard sandstone band rich in iron. One peculiarity of Pauillac is that yields tend to be higher than elsewhere. It's not unusual for top estates here to have yields close to the legal maximum, whereas that would be the exception in Margaux. Yet few would complain about poor quality or dilution.

The Pauillac zone consists of 1,215 hectares of vineyards, which on average produce seven million bottles. There are about 100 growers, but some of them sell to the cooperative. There are eighteen classified growths and about sixteen *crus bourgeois*. Today the region exudes prosperity. Formerly neglected châteaux have been spruced up; some of them are floodlit, though for whose benefit it is hard to say, given the very few people around at night, other than Médocains. Some old-timers like to remind visitors that it was not always thus. May-Eliane de Lencquesaing recalls that in the 1950s there were buckets strategically placed on the upper floors of Pichon-Lalande to catch rainwater dripping through the holes in the roof. Back in the 1920s, when the harsh economic conditions of the interwar period were beginning, many vineyards disappeared altogether and were replaced by pinewoods. Near Château Lynch-Moussas there was a pheasant farm. A string of atrocious vintages marred the 1930s, as well as outbreaks of black rot that proved hard to treat. The war years, the German occupation, and the austere years of the 1950s continued difficult, but in the 1960s conditions at last began to improve. Vineyards began to expand once again and the region is now operating at full stretch.

The building of an oil refinery just north of the town was a controversial move. It was a blot on the landscape, but it provided a good deal of employment, and after its closure many former refinery workers were left on the dole, and there was an increase in light crime. Many visitors to the town are quite unaware of the presence of the shutdown refinery, and enjoy the quayside, its restaurants, bars, and wine shops. Yet the quayside has a desultory air, and never seems to offer much gaiety. The restaurants have improved, the recent introduction of speed bumps will make British visitors feel at home, but "chic" is not the word one would grasp for in describing the port. The modern Maison du Vin at the southern end of the quay provides information about wine estates,

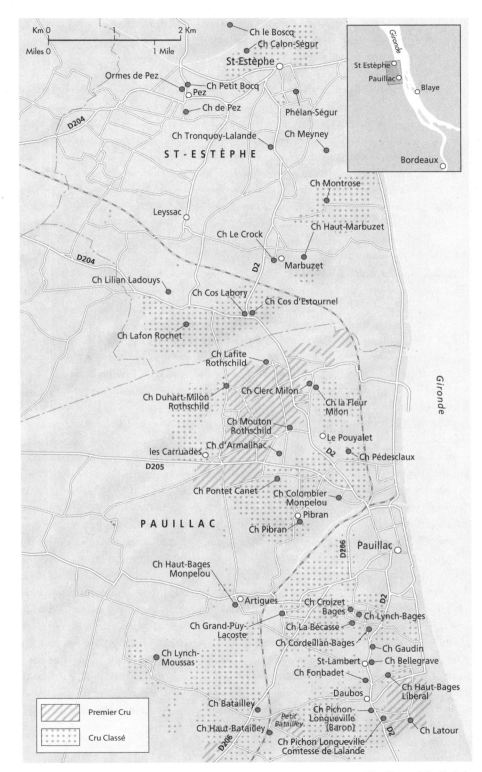

Pauillac and St–Estèphe

especially the growing number that are open to visitors. Well-heeled visitors can enjoy the luxurious hotel at Château Cordeillan-Bages and its superb restaurant.

There are not many *crus bourgeois* here. Jean-Michel Cazes explains:

> *Because there are so many classified growths, the* crus bourgeois *tended to be very small, and many of them suffered in the 1930s and either disappeared or joined the co-op. The story of Haut-Bages-Averous is typical. It belonged to the Averous family in the nineteenth century and was quite an important property. There is a story that about a hundred years ago Mlle. Averous routinely exchanged a barrique with the bishop of Lourdes, who provided holy water, which was poured into the hole into which new vines were planted after phylloxera. Haut-Bages-Averous used to have about twenty hectares. In the 1920s and 1930s financial problems forced sales of parcels to various neighbours. By 1973 the owner was left with three hectares virtually embedded within the Lynch-Bages vineyards, so he sold them to my family. The vineyards were in poor condition and had to be replanted.*

More recently, AXA Millésimes, which already owned the *cru bourgeois* Château Pibran, acquired Château La Tour-Pibran and integrated it into Pibran. And so another *cru bourgeois* vanished from the map.

Château d'Armailhac

Tel: 0556 732129. Website: www.bpdr.com. Owner: Baroness Philippine de Rothschild. Cinquième cru.

50 ha. 52% Cabernet Sauvignon, 26% Merlot, 20% Cabernet Franc, 2% Petit Verdot. **Production: 240,000 bottles**

In the early eighteenth century a rich merchant, Dominique d'Armailhacq, bought and expanded the vineyards here and acquired what was then called the château of Brane-Mouton. Thereafter he named the property Château Mouton-d'Armailhacq. It gets more complicated. The property was to remain rather obscure, perhaps because the vineyards were fragmented and also, it has been suggested, because the Bordeaux brokers did not rate the wine very highly. In 1838 Armailhacq's descendants expanded the property by buying land on the nearby Carruades plateau. The then-owner, Joseph Odet d'Armailhacq, got into financial difficulties and had to put the estate up for sale. The purchaser in 1844 was none other than his former wife, who found the money by selling the ten-hectare Carruades site, not yet planted, to Château Lafite, which retains it to this day. Her son Armand, who became well known as the author of a book on the Médoc, managed to expand the property to sixty-three hectares by 1855. When he died, his brother-in-law Comte Adrien de Ferrand inherited the property. By the early twentieth century it had become neglected. It was one of his descendants, Comte Roger, who sold the estate to Baron Philippe de Rothschild in 1933.

The baron allowed the elderly count to live in the château for the rest of his days; in exchange, he acquired not only the vineyards but a négociant business that he converted into La Baronnie, his own, soon-to-be-flourishing négociant house. It seems that one of his chief motives in buying Armailhacq was that it had a pleasant park, which Mouton had always lacked. (Indeed, Baron Philippe is buried here.) The château itself dated from the 1820s but had never been completed. Baron Philippe changed the name of the property to Château Mouton-Baron-Philippe. At the time of the purchase some of the vines were leased to Pontet-Canet next door, but that arrangement ceased in the late 1930s. Legally, Baron Philippe could have incorporated the Armailhacq vineyards into Mouton, but that might have damaged the quality, and reputation, of the then Second Growth. The vineyards needed renovation, but the baron was unable to undertake such an enterprise all at once, so the area under vine fell to thirty-two hectares, and did not expand until the 1960s.

After the baron's wife Pauline died in 1976, he decided to change the name once again to Château Baronne-Pauline, but permission was refused. Instead, he changed it to Château Mouton-Baronne-Philippe. After Baron

Philippe's death, his daughter Philippine changed it once again, and in 1991 the wine was reborn as Château d'Armailhac. Her principal argument for doing so was that too many customers were under the false impression that Mouton-Baronne-Philippe was Mouton's second wine.

Half the vineyards are located just south of the château; the rest lie west of the château and border those of Mouton. One peculiarity of the vineyards is the high proportion of Cabernet Franc. Philippe Dhalluin, who manages the Mouton group of properties, is no fan of this variety, but says it gives good results here because the vines are extremely old.

There are three main blocks. The first, some twenty-four hectares in extent, is called the Levantine and Obelisk Plateau, and is an eastward extension of the Carruades plateau. The soil here is light but very deep gravel which is ideal for the Cabernet varieties. As you move farther eastward along the plateau, the soil becomes sandier and thus less suited to the Cabernet Sauvignon that is planted on it. Near the park is a parcel of Cabernet Sauvignon from 1878, but Dhalluin says the soil is not ideal. The second block is the Pibran plateau (twenty hectares), where deep gravel lies over a subsoil of clay and limestone. Between Pibran and Pontet-Canet is a dip, where Merlot and Cabernet Franc are planted; some other Cabernet Franc near Pontet-Canet does not give particularly good fruit, so it will eventually be replaced with Merlot. The third block is the Béhéré Brow (eighteen hectares), where the gravel is some three metres (ten feet) deep; here the vines are mixed in with parcels belonging to Duhart-Milon and Pontet-Canet. Much Petit Verdot is planted here, but the vines are young. At the most westerly point of the property is a grove of plum trees, from which Baron Philippe produced his beloved Eau-de-Vie de Prunier.

Today much of Armailhac is ploughed and the grapes have been picked in *cagettes* since 2003. The must is fermented at up to 32°C (90°F) in stainless-steel tanks. Blending takes place after the malolactic fermentation is completed and before the wine goes into barriques, where it is aged for twelve to fourteen months in twenty-five per cent new oak as well as in older barrels from Mouton.

Armailhac is sometimes compared to its stablemate Clerc-Milon. Armailhac can be delicious when young, but in the long term it is usually Clerc-Milon that emerges as superior. But both properties are in a state of flux as improvements are made, so that may not always be the case.

I once tasted the 1941, but the nose was somewhat caramelized, and the wine was light and drying out. The 1961 and 1978 are said to be good, but I have not encountered them. The 1979, at ten years, lacked character, interest, and length. The 1981 was quite concentrated, but the finish was becoming dry and the overall impression was rather dull. The 1983 aged fast, with Bovril and liquorice aromas, and was distinctly frail on the palate. The 1988 had charming blackberry aromas, and was rich and well structured; it was not that elegant, but there was some complexity struggling to emerge. The 1989, tasted again in 2005, was rather odd: menthol and cough medicine on the nose, and still quite severe on the palate, giving a rather pinched impression. The 1990 is more opulent and oaky, with a silky texture, ripe tannins, and moderate length. The 1993 is not bad for the vintage: medium-bodied and forward. The 1994 has a sweet, oaky nose, but it's rather light and weedy.

The 1995 is on a much higher plane. The oaky nose is formidably ripe, with blackcurrant and chocolate tones. It's succulent but concentrated, with spiciness and charm and a discreet tannic grip. I slightly prefer it to the 1996. For all its lovely pure black-fruits nose, the 1996 is a very spicy wine, pungent and long, but seems less complex than the 1995. The 1997 is honourable for the vintage, a supple, juicy wine that is now ready to drink. The 1998, tasted at Mouton, was meaty on the nose and sumptuous on the palate, with robust tannins, spiciness and vigour, and fine length. The same wine, tasted blind a year later, had more tannin than fruit, and gave little pleasure. Which is the real 1998? There are savoury aromas on the 1999, which is a juicy, accessible wine, with concentration, charm, and length.

There is real weight on the classic 2000, with its spicy, oaky nose, its powerful tannins, and a power that Armailhac often lacks. The 2001 is unusually extracted and austere, and lacks some freshness and zest. I prefer the 2002, with its pure, intense blackcurrant aromas, with a slight floral character too, and its ripe, succulent, toasty palate and long, bold finish. The 2003 is somewhat disjointed, with a soft, rounded approach that leads to an invigorating and spicy finish. The 2004 is admirable, with fine blackcurrant fruit and unusual punch and persistence for the vintage.

Armailhac was erratic in the past, but it is clear that since 1995 it has gained immeasurably in richness, fruit expression, and complexity.

Château Batailley

*Tel: 0556 000070. **Owner:** Castéja family. Cinquième cru. 55 ha. 70% Cabernet Sauvignon, 25% Merlot, 3% Cabernet Franc, 2% Petit Verdot. **Production:** 360,000 bottles. **Second wine:** Pauillac-Borie*

The vineyards of Batailley, which lie about four kilometres (two and a half miles) inland, were laid out in the late eighteenth century by two sisters, who sold the estate in 1791 to a wine merchant called Jean-Guillaume Pécholier, and then it passed to the latter's son-in-law, Admiral de Bédout. After the admiral died in 1816, Batailley was put up for auction. The purchaser was a well-known négociant, Daniel Guestier, who expanded the estate and renovated its buildings. It remained in his family until 1866, when the estate was sold to a Parisian banker, Constant Halphen. But another family of négociants claimed the property in 1932, when it was bought by Marcel and François Borie. During World War II the brothers agreed to divide the property, as François had taken on Ducru-Beaucaillou, and they needed to sort out their holdings because of inheritance taxes. Château Haut-Batailley was the smaller offshoot. Marcel retained Batailley; François expanded the new Haut-Batailley by incorporating fifteen hectares that had been bought from Duhart-Milon back in the 1930s.

When Marcel Borie died in 1961, Batailley was inherited by his daughter Denise. She was married to Emile Castéja, the managing director of Borie-Manoux and the scion of an illustrious Médoc family. They moved into the château, which has retained its sober but charming nineteenth-century interior. I recall a contented hour spent with M. Castéja in his well-stocked library as he showed me some fascinating old books about Bordeaux, while his forthright wife made sure our lunch was served on time. Behind the château is a substantial park, which was laid out by Napoleon III's landscape gardener, Barillet-Deschamps. The Castéjas moved back to the city in 2001, and the château is no longer inhabited on a regular basis. In 2003 their son Philippe took over running the family properties as well as Borie-Manoux, and Denis Dubourdieu was taken on as the consultant oenologist.

The vineyards, which have an average age of forty years, are located across from the mansion in the direction of the Castéjas' other property of Château Lynch-Moussas (*q.v.*). The soil is relatively homogeneous, rising to twenty-five metres (eighty-two feet). The heart of the vineyard is a deep gravel bed over a subsoil of clay and sandstone. There are also parcels between Latour and the Pichons. Batailley retains a high proportion of Cabernet Sauvignon.

The must is fermented in mostly steel vats; the wooden vats in the *cuvier* are museum pieces. Apart from a brief cold soak and the use of selected yeasts, the vinification is entirely traditional. The charming *chai* dates from 1840 and is lit by iron candelabra. Here the wine is aged for eighteen months in roughly fifty per cent new oak. (In the late nineteenth century the area between the two *chais* was roofed over to form an airy shed, the perfect place for a party on a wet summer evening.)

It has to be admitted that under Emile Castéja the wines of Batailley (and Lynch-Moussas) were far from exciting. They were competent, correct, unmistakably claret. But they lacked concentration and dash. They tended to peak fairly early and were often best drunk within ten years. On the other hand, the wines were never expensive and prices remained stable. Batailley was not a wine for speculation. Philippe Castéja knows that Batailley should be better than it is, and is making changes, such as heightening the trellising and taking fresh technical advice.

The oldest vintage I have tasted is the 1959, in 1993. The colour was still healthy, the nose a touch farm-yardy, the palate rich but baked. The 1961 was deep in colour, with a fresh, sweet nose of mocha, cedar, and bacon; the wine is still dense, even chunky, but there is sufficient acidity to give it freshness and excellent length. The 1971 held up well, and after two decades had a ripe if piquant nose; it was light but still lively, a pleasant but not distinguished wine that had stayed on a plateau of accessibility for a long time. When young, both the 1979 and 1981 had sweet, curranty aromas and soft, generous fruit supported, in the case of the latter, by firm tannins. The 1982 was plump and easy-going from the start, with little complexity or depth, but attractively balanced. The 1983 lacks flair and is rather flat, a pleasant but undistinguished wine. The 1986, tasted recently, was a surprise: the nose was rich and savoury; the wine was rich, still a touch severe, yet there was freshness on the finish and a modicum of charm. The 1988 has some generous fruit, but it's loosely structured. The 1989 is ready: a velvety, supple wine that is ripe and harmonious but lacks some vigour.

Emile Castéja thought his 1992 was a success for the vintage, and he was right when the wine was young, although by 2000 the nose was mushroomy, and the fruit was fading. The 1993 is green and rather bitter. There is some rich, chocolatey, blackcurrant fruit on the nose of the 1994, which has sweetish fruit and some persistence. The 1995 is graceful but dilute, with a lame finish. The 1996 is far better, with stylish oak and considerable power and length, with no signs of tiring by 2007. Smoky, savoury, but rather dank aromas mark the 1998, which is supple but rather dilute, with an astringent finish. The 1999 is rather light yet lacks finesse. The 2000 certainly doesn't lack ripe, toasty aromas, but the wine itself is medium-bodied and slack in its structure, which makes it underwhelming for the vintage. There's greenness and some harsh tannins on the 2001, which is blunt and dull. The 2002 is better, with a fine Cabernet nose of considerable purity, and tight but juicy fruit on the palate, with firm tannins. The 2003 is supple, unremarkable, and has a short, dry finish.

For a classified growth, Batailley seems very inconsistent, but there are, fortunately, clear signs of improvement overall, with less dilution than in the past.

Château La Bécasse

*Tel: 0556 590714. **Owner:** Roland Fonteneau. 4.2 ha. 55% Cabernet Sauvignon, 36% Merlot,*
*9% Cabernet Franc. **Production:** 30,000 bottles*

Georges Fonteneau was the owner of Cru de la Bécasse in St-Julien and traded it for this property. The name refers to the woodcocks that he loved to hunt. Because of its small size, Bécasse did not qualify for *cru bourgeois* status in the past, and Fonteneau decided to bypass the 2003 reclassification as he had a sufficiently loyal customer base for promotion to confer no obvious benefit.

The vineyards are divided into twenty parcels scattered between Bages and the Pichons. Their average age is about thirty-five years. The vinification is classic, and Fonteneau progressively blends tanks during or just after the malolactic fermentation, and then adds a dose of press wine as he sees fit. The wine is aged for eighteen months in about one-third new barriques, with older barrels from Latour or Margaux. The wines are eggwhite-fined but not filtered. Except in years when he has a higher proportion of Merlot than he would like, Bécasse is a traditional Pauillac intended for ageing. The 1990 had lovely fruit and considerable complexity and elegance. The 1992 and 1993 were forgettable. The 2001 has splendid black-cherry aromas, ample richness and suppleness, and finishes long. In contrast the 2002 is lighter, rather austere, and lacks excitement and length.

Château Bellegrave

*St Lambert. Tel: 0556 590553. **Website:** www.chateau-bellegrave.com. **Owner:** Jean-Paul Meffre. 8 ha.*
*62% Cabernet Sauvignon, 31% Merlot, 7% Cabernet Franc. **Production:** 45,000 bottles.*
Second wine: Les Sieurs de Bellegrave

For most of the twentieth century this property, with its nineteenth-century château and park in the village of St Lambert, belonged to the Dutch Van der Voort family. Over the years parcels were sold off; its fifteen hectares of vines shrank to 1.5 hectares. The wine was rarely seen, and visits were discouraged. Then in 1987 the property was bought by Jean-Paul Meffre of Château du Glana (*q.v.*) in St-Julien, and today Bellegrave is run, like Glana, by his sons.

The vineyards are dispersed, but three hectares are in Artigues, not far from Grand-Puy-Lacoste. The remaining vines are scattered throughout the appellation. The Meffres practise *lutte raisonnée*. The grapes are transported in *cagettes* and sorted at the winery. After a three-day cold soak, fermentation takes place in steel tanks, and the wine is aged for twelve months in forty per cent new oak. The Meffres have introduced a second wine in order to elevate the quality of the first.

The only Van der Voort-era wine I tasted was the 1990, which was very attractive, with Pauillac typicity but more forward than a classic wine from that vintage. The 2001 has firm, blackcurrant aromas, and a good deal of density and power if not much elegance. The 2002 is similar, though more overtly oaky, and it appears to have slightly higher acidity and better length. Bellegrave hits its stride with the excellent, succulent 2004, suffused with black fruits and supple tannins.

Château Clerc-Milon

Tel: 0556 732129. Website: www.bpdr.com. Owner: Baroness Philippine de Rothschild. Cinquième cru.
32 ha. 46% Cabernet Sauvignon, 35% Merlot, 15% Cabernet Franc, 3% Petit Verdot, 1% Carmenère.
Production: 160,000 bottles

This was the third and last of the classified growths acquired by Baron Philippe de Rothschild. It is named after the gentleman who owned the property in 1855, and after the hamlet of Milon where some of the vineyards are located. After his death in 1863, his widow ran the property until it was sold and divided up in 1877. Thereafter it passed through various hands until, by the 1960s, under the name of Clerc-Milon-Mondon, it was owned by a local lawyer, Jacques Vialard. He died in 1970, bequeathing the estate to two sisters, Marie Vialard and Mme. Hedon. Baron Philippe made an offer – in retrospect a very low offer – for the estate, which they accepted. By this time the vineyards had dwindled to ten hectares and were in poor condition.

Although Clerc-Milon's reputation had dimmed through neglect, the baron clearly sensed its potential. He began buying up parcels that had been sold off by Mlle. Vialard. The result is that Clerc-Milon is extremely fragmented, with some 100 separate parcels, mostly on a plateau just north of Le Pouyalet, not far from the former refinery. The wine was made in a number of rented properties, an impractical arrangement that ended when in the 1990s new *chais* were built at the northern end of the Pauillac quays.

Not surprisingly, the soils are very varied. In some spots there is gravel over a clay subsoil; elsewhere the gravel is mixed with sand. There are small blocks of ungrafted vines, and the age of the vineyard ranges from truly venerable to relatively young. Not that long ago seventy per cent of the vines at Clerc-Milon were Cabernet Sauvignon. The proportion has been substantially diminished in favour of Merlot and Cabernet Franc. Philippe Dhalluin, who manages the property, is still not entirely happy with the varietal mix, and will gradually ensure that the higher-lying plots are planted with Cabernet, while the lower parcels with a higher clay content are planted with Merlot. Although the proportion of Merlot is quite high, Dhalluin observes that the soil gives a powerful rather than a supple wine. In 2004 Philippine de Rothschild snapped up a small property called La Fleur-Milon. Its vines were more or less encircled by those of Clerc-Milon, and indeed some of them had once formed part of Clerc's historic vineyards. The price was apparently high, but the Rothschilds couldn't resist the temptation to reconstitute more of the historic estate.

The vinification is classic, and the wine is aged for about sixteen months in one-third new barriques, with some older barrels from Mouton. The blend is made up quite early. In style Clerc-Milon is more robust than Armailhac. For many years it was a great bargain, but as the potential of the vineyards is being more fully realized, prices have risen. Clearly the baron's hunch was correct, and Philippe Dhalluin too believes that the wine has the potential for even higher quality once the vineyards have been restructured.

At twenty years old, the 1973 was still very much alive; perhaps a touch neutral in fruit expression, yet robust, with reasonable concentration and length. And at thirty years of age, the 1975, although aromatically reserved, had the earthy tannins of the vintage, but was drinking well. The 1981 was mediocre, but the 1982 has evolved well, with very dense, slightly baked, plummy aromas, and ultra-ripe chocolatey tones on the palate, which has admirable concentration. The elegant but slighter 1983 is fully ready. The 1986 is splendid, better balanced than the 1982, with lush blackcurranty aromas, a fine texture, perfectly integrated tannins, and a long, delicious finish. The 1988 has a finely perfumed cedary nose, and has retained its intensity and freshness; the tannins and oak are perfectly integrated and this is now drinking beautifully. I have not tasted the well-regarded 1989, but the 1990 has matured well: the nose is cedary, slightly dusty, and overall this is graceful rather than extracted, with fine intensity and length.

The nose of the 1993 suggests a rich, oaky wine, but the palate is leaner, with some astringency. The 1994 is much better, though not exactly elegant; its density gives it a somewhat rugged character. The 1995 has a savoury tone on the nose, and the dense, chewy severity of the vintage; but the wine is balanced and should evolve well. Aromatically, the 1996 used to be closed, but today the nose is resplendently plummy; it's supple but spicy, and silky in texture, but is marred by a slight astringency. There's unusual grip on the 1997, yet it is drinking well now and has a long, savoury finish. The 1998 remains austere, dense, and dour, with mouth-puckering tannins. The toasty 1999 is more immediately attractive and stylish, with its flavours of black fruits and chocolate, and its persistent finish. The 2000 is slightly disappointing for the vintage; it's exceedingly ripe but seems to lack some acidity and finesse. Cherries and blackberries mark the nose of the 2001, a solid wine, still rather closed and at present lacking in flair. The 2002 too is hefty and tannic, lacking some freshness and zest, though certainly packed with fruit. The 2003 is very oaky, concentrated, and tannic, and packs quite a punch. From cask, the rich 2005 and the pure and charming 2006 are revealing the potential of this property.

Clerc-Milon is evidently a *vin de garde*, without the immediate appeal of Armailhac when it is young. But it does repay cellaring, and with time the hefty tannins and youthful aggression calm down, allowing the fine core of fruit to surge through. Given the work now being done in the vineyards, the best is probably still to come.

Château Colombier-Monpelou

*Tel: 0556 590148. Owner: Bernard Jugla. 24 ha. 55% Cabernet Sauvignon, 35% Merlot, 5% Cabernet Franc, 5% Petit Verdot. **Production:** 180,000 bottles. **Second wine:** Ch Grand Canyon*

The businesslike Bernard Jugla thinks very highly of this property, which is of eighteenth-century origin, claiming that it missed out on classification in 1855 only because the Bordeaux brokers forgot about it. It passed through various hands and in 1934 was sold to Roger Seurin, from whom Jugla bought the estate in 1970. Seurin had no cellars, so he sold the crop to the cooperative. It was Jugla who built the existing *chais* in the 1970s. The vines lie just north of the town, alongside the road to Pontet-Canet; there are other parcels in Artigues, near Grand-Puy-Lacoste. The vineyards are quite precocious, says Jugla. The grapes are picked by machine as well as by hand. Since 1986 the must has been fermented in large steel tanks, and the wine is aged for fifteen months in forty per cent new oak.

The oldest vintage I have encountered was the 1975, tasted in 1997. There were aromas of plums and woodsmoke, but the wine overall was rather soft and flat, lacking personality and length. The 1989 developed a cigar-box nose, which was attractive; the wine was fresh and forward if not notably concentrated or complex. The 1994 showed some pleasant blackberry fruit, but it's a dull wine with little concentration. The 1995 was soft and dilute, the 1996 a pretty but lightweight wine with little evident structure. The 2000 is fragrant, but medium-bodied and simple, and a seriously disappointing effort given the vintage. Even more disappointing is the drab, dry 2001; less surprisingly, the 2003 is in a similar style. The 2005 is simple and easy-going, but hardly worthy of a great vintage.

Colombier-Monpelou is clearly underperforming. Given the location of its vineyards, the wine should surely be very good. But there seems little serious effort to make a wine that is structured and complex, and immediate gratification is not really enough for a wine rated in 2003 as one of Pauillac's top *crus bourgeois*.

Cave Coopérative: La Rose-Pauillac

Tel: 0556 592600. Website: www.la-rose-pauillac.com. 69 ha. 55% Cabernet Sauvignon, 40% Merlot, 3% Cabernet Franc, 2% Petit Verdot. Production: 550,000 bottles. Second wine: La Fleur-Pauillac

It must be a dispiriting job, running a cooperative that is in slow decline. The sixty members are, for the most part, owners of small plots of vines that are not worth vinifying and bottling on their own, even though some of those parcels are superbly located. The membership is shrinking, as some of the larger estates seek to snap up well-situated parcels that would complement their vineyards. The wines are vinified in temperature-controlled cement tanks, and aged for eighteen months in older barriques. Not all the wine is bottled, as some is sold off to négociants. As well as the La Rose-Pauillac label, there are other single-vineyard labels such as Château Haut-Milon (ten hectares with sixty-five per cent Merlot) and Château Haut de la Bécade (eight hectares).

The wine is inexpensive and better than one might expect, made in a fairly robust style with some concentration. Some vintages show a lot of herbaceousness, however.

Château Cordeillan-Bages

Tel: 0556 592424. Website: www.cordeillanbages.com. Owner: Jean-Michel Cazes. 2 ha. 80% Cabernet Sauvignon, 20% Merlot. Production: 12,000 bottles

The name has become synonymous with the Médoc's best hotel and restaurant, which is a handy sales outlet for this attractive wine. The seventeenth-century château on the edge of Bages was once called Château Bellevue-Cordeillan, and was quite an important property in the early twentieth century. By 1962 many of its vineyards had been sold off to, among other purchasers, the Cazes family. In 1985 they bought what was left of the estate, and replanted some parcels. The first vintage was in 1985. The wine is aged for twelve to fifteen months in fifty per cent new oak.

The style of the wine is quite voluptuous. The 1985 was a good start: soft, rich, spicy, and delicious, even if the wine did not have great depth. I have had a rustic 1989, possibly a poor bottle. The 1990 is better, with pure blackcurrant aromas and supple tannins. The 1994 is good for the vintage. Recent vintages have shown a marked blackcurrant character on the nose, ripe tannins, and reasonable freshness and length. But it's not a wine with much vigour and elegance.

Château Croizet-Bages

Tel: 0556 590162. Owner: Jean-Michel Quié. Cinquième cru. 28 ha. 58% Cabernet Sauvignon, 35% Merlot, 7% Cabernet Franc. Production: 180,000 bottles. Second wine: La Tourelle de Croizet-Bages

This property is under the same ownership as Rauzan-Gassies (*q.v.*) in Margaux. It takes its name from the two brothers who established the estate in the eighteenth century. In the early nineteenth century they sold it to Jean de Puytarac. He in turn sold it in 1853 to Julien Calvé. His descendants sold it in 1945 to Paul Quié, a wine merchant from northern France, whose son Jean-Michel inherited the estates after Paul Quié's death in 1968. The actual château has long been detached from the rest of the property, and the *chais* are located in Bages. Like Rauzan-Gassies, Croizet-Bages produced seriously disappointing wines until well into the 1990s. Possibly the assured outlets through the Quié sales network provided little incentive for improving quality. But eventually it was realized that Croizet-Bages was slipping ever further behind. In 1994 Jean-Louis Camp was hired to run the Quié properties, and he has made conscientious efforts to repair the damage.

The vineyards are well located on the Bages plateau in a single block, close to Grand-Puy-Lacoste and Lynch-Bages. The gravel is not especially deep here, often no more than one metre (three feet), but it lies over a belt of red sand that is usefully water-retentive, and below that is a further band of stony white sand that provides excellent drainage. The fact that much of the vineyard had to be replanted in the 1980s, leaving the average age of the vines lower than ideal, did not help with quality, nor did the fact that many vines had been planted on SO4 rootstocks. One of the changes Camp made in the vineyards was to reduce the proportion of Cabernet Franc, which had stood at twelve per cent, too much, Camp felt, for a well-structured Pauillac. There is also some ploughing in alternate years, which seems a rather odd approach. The trellising has been raised, which, Camp insists, has resulted in noticeably higher sugar levels. The density is also being increased, from 6,600 to 8,000 vines per hectare, whenever a parcel is replanted.

Croizet-Bages is still harvested by machine, which Camp stoutly defends. The vinification is the same as for Rauzan-Gassies. Until 1994, no new oak was used here, but today there is around twenty-five per cent. Camp has a fondness for a little American oak at the beginning of the *élevage*.

The oldest vintage I have tasted, the 1959, was already drying out in 1988. The 1979 did not have much depth but it was surprisingly perfumed and didn't lack fruit, though the finish was rather dry. The 1990 was lively and stylish but very light. The 1993 was feeble, the 1994 only slightly better. The 1995 showed a marked improvement, with attractive fruit and some richness, but it still lacked concentration and persistence. The nose of the 1998 is attractively sweet and gamey, but this medium-bodied wine is marred by rugged tannins. It's the 2000 that seems to signal this growth's return to the fold of rich, full-flavoured Pauillacs. The nose is splendid, fleshy, toasty, and succulent, while the palate delivers a lush, forward style with spice and vigour. The 2001 is reasonably ripe and concentrated but it's a touch flat and lacks excitement. The 2002 is oddly disappointing-with red-fruits aromas and a touch of herbaceousness; it's slightly coarse and flabby on the palate despite decent concentration. The confected 2003 is graceful but lacks persistence. Nonetheless the wines of the twenty-first century are significantly better than most of the preceding vintages. M. Camp's quiet persistence seems to be paying off.

Château Duhart-Milon

Tel: 0556 731818. Website: www.lafite.com. Owner: Domaines Barons de Rothschild. Quatrième cru.
67 ha. 70% Cabernet Sauvignon, 30% Merlot. Production: 400,000 bottles. Second wine: Moulin de Duhart

Not much is known about the M. Duhart who founded this property in the early eighteenth century. In the early nineteenth century the owner was a M. Mandavi, and after he died in the 1830s it was acquired by the Castéja family. By this time the vineyards consisted of forty hectares. They sold Duhart-Milon in 1937. Some fifteen hectares had been sold off to help form Château Haut-Batailley, and Duhart-Milon changed hands five times before the Rothschilds bought it in 1962. By this time the vineyards had dwindled to seventeen hectares and were in such poor condition that they had to be entirely replanted with proper drainage channels installed. Thus the average age of the vines is around twenty-five years.

The vineyards are located just southwest of Lafite at a lower elevation than the *premier cru*, and are farmed by the same team that runs Lafite. The vines have a more northerly exposition than is ideal, so the grapes tend to ripen about a week later than at Lafite.

The château was built in 1650 along the quay at Pauillac, but it was torn down and replaced in 1962 by a modern house still inhabited by André Cazes, former mayor of the town, and father of Jean-Michel Cazes. The winery is right in the middle of the town, and has recently been renovated with the installation of stainless-steel tanks that supplement the existing small cement tanks. The *grand vin* tends to have more Merlot than the *encépagement* suggests. The vinification is essentially the same as at Lafite. Various improvements were made in 2003, with the installation of vibrating sorting tables (before and after destemming) that supplement a sorting table in the vineyards. The wine is aged for eighteen months in between fifty and sixty per cent new barriques.

In style the wine is far removed from that of Lafite. It is more solid, even earthy, and richness is matched by sturdiness. It seems clear that the high proportion of Merlot is an attempt to give the wine more suppleness.

The 1976 had good fruit on the nose, but less so on the palate, and the finish was dry. The 1986 is dense and earthy, with tarry notes and a somewhat aggressive structure; two bottles tasted in 1999 were both faulty. The 1988 was very closed in 1997, an austere, extracted wine with little discernible finesse. The 1989 is far more open, with smoky, leathery aromas, the richness of fruit balanced by a fresh, lively structure. The 1990 is similar, with a great deal of overt ripeness, charm, and vigour. The 1994 is excellent for the vintage, with ripe blackcurrant fruit and a long, elegant finish. With the 1995, Duhart-Milon seems to be going at full throttle: there is a good deal of oak as well as black fruits on the nose, and the palate is opulent with supple tannins. This is a seriously good wine, marginally better than the graceful 1996, which has less weight but perhaps a touch more freshness. The 1998 is too rugged and austere, with the sweet fruit fighting a losing battle against a wall of tannin. The 2000 is a slight disappointment, smoky and almost jammy on the nose, but it has a rather slack, dull texture. The 2001 is promising, with blackcurrant and blackberries on the nose, and a concentrated, spicy palate. The 2002 is well balanced, with toasty aromas, ample fruit, but a rather broad structure and texture. The 2003 is lush if rather soft, and seems to be evolving fast.

Duhart has improved immeasurably since the 1980s; all it lacks is finesse.

Château La Fleur-Milon

*Tel: 0556 732129. Website: www.bpdr.com. **Owner:** Baroness Philippine de Rothschild. 13 ha.*
*65% Cabernet Sauvignon, 25% Merlot, 5% Cabernet Franc, 5% Petit Verdot. **Production:** 90,000 bottles.*
Second wine: Château Buisson-Milon

Although Mouton-Rothschild bought this entire property in 2004, the present intention is to maintain the estate as a separate entity. It seems probable that in the long term the best parcels, some of which have centenarian vines, will be integrated into Château Clerc-Milon. La Fleur-Milon was run for years with gusto by the Mirande family, and the wines were somewhat rustic but full of dense fruit and vivid spiciness.

Château La Fleur-Peyrabon

*St Sauveur. Tel: 0556 595710. **Owner:** Patrick Bernard. 5 ha. 70% Cabernet Sauvignon, 30% Merlot.*
***Production:** 30,000 bottles*

This is the wine from a section of Château Peyrabon (*q.v.*) in the Haut-Médoc that lies within AC Pauillac. The details of this property are given in Chapter Five. This Pauillac is aged for fourteen months in fifty per cent new oak. The wines made by Jacques Babeau before the sale of the property to Patrick Bernard were unexceptional, though there were good wines in 1990 and 1996. Bernard's wines are more oaky on the nose, and the fruit quality is more lush; the wine has considerable depth and firm tannins, though not a great deal of finesse. The 2000 was not demonstrably better than Peyrabon, the 2001 remains fresh and lively, and the 2002, although rather austere, does have more depth than the Haut-Médoc. Despite some richness of fruit, the 2003 is rather flat and lacking in zest. The 2004 has good acidity, but it's tannic and extracted, and needs time to settle down. The potential of the property is better demonstrated by the supple yet concentrated 2005, which is packed with fine black-cherry fruit.

Château Fonbadet

*St Lambert. Tel: 0556 590211. Website: www.chateaufonbadet.com. **Owner:** Pierre Peyronie. 20 ha.*
60% Cabernet Sauvignon, 20% Merlot, 15% Cabernet Franc, 5% Petit Verdot and Malbec.
***Production:** 100,000 bottles. **Second wine:** L'Harmonie de Fonbadet*

The château and its attractive little park stand in the centre of St Lambert. Pierre Peyronie's great-grandfather was the manager of Lafite, so he is steeped in the region and its traditions. Peyronie has been ceding responsibility to his able daughter Pascale, and since 2000 she has been adding her own imprint to the wines. The vineyards are very fragmented, with many parcels of very old vines, some near Mouton, others close to the town, plus four hectares behind the château, and four near Bages. Yields never exceed forty hectolitres per hectare, thanks to the age of the vines. Peyronie was reluctant to replant entire parcels, preferring to complant so as to maintain the average age of the vines.

Pascale Peyronie has lowered the fermentation temperature and is using more new oak, in an effort to produce wines that are more accessible when young. The vinification is traditional, using natural yeasts. She has retained the old vertical press and ages the wine for about eighteen months in thirty per cent new oak. The wine is eggwhite-fined and bottled without filtration.

Only about half the production is released under the château label. Many other labels (Padarnac, Tour du Roc-Milon, Haut-Pauillac, and others) are used for wine sold to négociants. Haut-Pauillac and Padarnac are individual five-hectare properties, but some labels seem to be different bottlings of the same wine.

At its best, Fonbadet is an excellent wine, although it is not always consistent. The 1990 was admirable, with an enticing and elegant nose, and considerable opulence and intensity. The 1995 was not quite at this level, but it was very true to the vintage, with firm tannins, considerable power, and unmistakable Pauillac typicity. The 1996 was astringent (perhaps a poor bottle), the 1997 distinctly light, the 1999 supple and forward and far from complex. Pascale Peyronie's wines are certainly more easy-going and less structured than those her father customarily made. Indeed, the 2000 is rather light for the vintage; the 2001 has abundant fruit but seems quite evolved. Better than either, however, is the oaky, mentholly 2002, which is fresh and elegant with well-integrated tannins. Although superficially opulent on nose and palate, the 2003 exhibits some green tannins and the finish is dry. The spicy, concentrated 2004 is elegant and persistent, and should age well. The rich and compact 2005 is the best Fonbadet I have tasted since the 1990.

Château Gaudin

St Lambert. Tel: 0556 592439. Owner: Linette Capdevielle. 11 ha. 85% Cabernet Sauvignon, 10% Merlot,
5% Cabernet Franc and Petit Verdot. **Production:** *80,000 bottles.* **Second wine:** *Ch Tastin*

Pierre Bibian owned this small property, and it is now run by his daughter, who is married to the cheerful M. Capdevielle. There are many old vines on the property, which has parcels near Pichon-Longueville and others near Lynch-Bages and Grand-Puy-Ducasse. No herbicides are used. The *encépagement* is remarkable for the exceptionally high proportion of Cabernet Sauvignon. The wine is fermented at up to 32°C (90°F), with a long *cuvaison*. The Capdevielles have always emphasized fruit rather than wood, and the use of new oak is minimal. Despite two visits to the property, I have succeeded in tasting only one vintage of the wine, the good if slightly rustic 1989. The proprietors rely on private sales to regular clients.

Château Grand-Puy-Ducasse

Tel: 0556 599822. **Owner:** *Crédit Agricole Grands Crus. Cinquième cru. 40 ha. 60% Cabernet Sauvignon,*
40% Merlot. **Production:** *160,000 bottles.* **Second wine:** *Prélude à Grand-Puy-Ducasse*

Grand-Puy is the name given to a plateau in the western part of the region. However, not all this estate's vineyards lie on the plateau. There are three main parcels: between Mouton and Pontet-Canet, near Batailley and Lynch-Moussas, and between Lynch-Bages and Grand-Puy-Lacoste. Arnaud Ducasse founded the property in the late seventeenth century, and successive generations expanded the property until by the time of the Revolution there were forty hectares under vine. In the 1820s Pierre Ducasse built the neo-classical château midway along the quays at Pauillac, replacing Arnaud's seventeenth-century mansion; today it serves as the winery and reception area for visitors. By the time of the 1855 classification, the estate was known as Château Artigues-Arnaud, which became the name of the second wine until recently. In 1932 the property came into the hands of a consortium, in which the Bouteiller family, then-owners of Château Pichon-Longueville, were the principal shareholders. Yet the estate was by now in severe decline, its vineyards neglected ("pitiful" is the term used by a Mestrezat brochure) and shrunk by 1949 to a mere ten hectares. In 1971 the firm of Mestrezat bought and revived Grand-Puy-Ducasse. In 2005 all the Mestrezat properties were sold to a group of investors under the umbrella organization of the bank Crédit Agricole.

The Mestrezat team turned their attention first to the vineyards. Additional parcels were bought, bringing the vineyards to thirty-six hectares. New plantings were at a high density of 10,000 vines per hectare. Mechanical harvesting was abandoned in 1991. The château, which until 1978 had served as Pauillac's Maison du Vin, was restored and given a scrub. In 1986 new stainless-steel tanks were installed, replacing the old cement tanks, and ten years later the *chai* was renovated and air-conditioned. For many years the good-humoured Bernard Monteau has supervised the winemaking, and Denis Dubourdieu has been consultant oenologist since 1998.

Yields tend to be quite high, and in 2001 the winery acquired a reverse-osmosis concentrator, which was used for some lots in 2004. The must is given a five-day cold soak before fermentation begins with selected yeasts. Monteau likes to get the wine into barrels fast, as there is no second-year *chai*. The wine is aged for twelve months in thirty per cent new oak.

These are not the most concentrated or powerful of Pauillac wines. Monteau admits he is looking for elegance, even at the expense of concentration. He also believes the wines have improved greatly since 1990, thanks to the return to manual harvesting and the introduction of greater selection. Nonetheless, this is a wine that tends to play safe. It is well made but rarely sets the pulses racing.

In the 1970s and 1980s the wines were sound but far from exceptional. The 1976 aged quite fast, the 1979 was elegantly fruity with quite good acidity; the 1983 was undernourished and woody. But the 1985 had the silkiness and lushness of the vintage. The 1986 was more tannic but lacked concentration. The 1988 is also true to the vintage, offering a tight tannic structure and some burliness which is atypical for the property. The 1993 is dense and muscular, but has a slightly hard finish. The 1995 is voluptuous, with lush fruit and a mineral edge. There's a solid, serious build to the 1998, which at the same time is supple and juicy and has no harsh tannins. The 2000 has power and weight, but fine acidity keeps it lively. The 2001 is perfectly sound, with ripe black-curranty aromas and a balanced but forward structure. The 2002 is reasonably concentrated but slightly herbaceous, its lack of flesh compensated for by brightness and vigour. The 2003 is a touch stewed but has sound fruit and concentration, if little finesse.

Château Grand-Puy-Lacoste

*Tel: 0556 590666. **Website:** www.domainesfxborie.com. **Owner:** Borie family. Cinquième cru. 55 ha. 70% Cabernet Sauvignon, 25% Merlot, 5% Cabernet Franc. **Production:** 300,000 bottles. **Second wine:** Lacoste-Borie*

Grand-Puy-Lacoste exemplifies everything a fine Pauillac should be: rich, virile, vigorous, concentrated, long-lived but elegant. Usually released at a reasonable price, it is a wine much loved by those who cannot afford the Pauillac superstars.

In the 1720s the plateau of Grand-Puy was owned by Bertrand Dejean, who was also the owner of Lynch-Bages. Some of the land was sold to Pierre Ducasse (*see* Grand-Puy-Ducasse). One of Dejean's descendants married François Lacoste, and their son Pierre-Frédéric seems to have transformed the estate into a substantial property that won classification in 1855. His daughter, the Comtesse de St-Léger, inherited the estate in 1868. In 1932, the then-proprietors sold Grand-Puy-Lacoste to Raymond Dupin, a well-to-do bachelor and *bon viveur*. He never lived at the château but he did entertain there, and acquired a legendary reputation for his hospitality. His love of good living did not extend to his own estate, which he rather neglected, as it was reduced to twenty-five hectares. Dupin was close to Jean-Eugène Borie of Ducru-Beaucaillou, and since he had no heirs, he asked Borie whether he would be interested in taking on the property. Negotiations took place around Dupin's lunch table, with numerous bottles of old vintages fuelling the discussion as the two owners good-humouredly set Grand-Puy-Lacoste against Ducru-Beaucaillou. In 1978 agreement was reached, and the Bories acquired a fifty per cent shareholding in the property and took over responsibility for the winemaking. In 1980 Dupin died, and the Bories became owners of the estate.

The château itself was built in the 1850s, but incorporates part of an older structure from the 1730s. It was handled roughly by occupying German soldiers during World War II, and Raymond Dupin never bothered to make it habitable. Today part of the mansion serves as a country home for Jean-Eugène's son François-Xavier, who has run the property, as well as Haut-Batailley (*q.v.*), for many years. Behind the house is a lovely English-style park, with flowering shrubs, slopes packed with daffodils in spring, and a long rectangular pool frequented by clans of ducks.

The park descends quite steeply from the château, illustrating the height of the various plateaux on which the best vineyards of Pauillac are located. Twenty-five metres (eighty-two feet) does not sound like much, nor is it. But viewed from this park it is easy to understand the importance of these *croupes*, their depth, their drainage. The Grand-Puy-Lacoste vineyards, which have not substantially altered since 1855, are located on two *croupes* of deep gravel: one stretches from the château to the road that leads to St Laurent; the other lies to the southwest, and borders Batailley and Lynch-Moussas. The average age of the vineyards is close to forty years, and in the oldest parcels any dead or missing vines are replaced by complantation. Borie is not a believer in systematic green-harvesting, and finds that the older vines tend to regulate themselves.

The Bories built a new *cuvier* alongside the château. When in 2003 Ducru-Beaucaillou became separated from Grand-Puy-Lacoste, as Bruno Borie took over the former and François-Xavier the latter, it became necessary to build new offices and a *chai* here, which was done without altering the outward appearance of the château. Since 1997 the grapes have been sorted in the vineyard, with one table per team of pickers. The winery is equipped with a *sous-vide* concentrator. Extraction is kept on the gentle side, with discreet rather than forceful pumpovers and no very prolonged *cuvaison*. If the wine needs more tannin or stuffing, they will adjust it by adding press wine. The wine is aged in up to sixty per cent new oak for fifteen to eighteen months, then eggwhite-fined in tanks.

Grand-Puy-Lacoste can age very well, and a 1955, though it offered delicate tea aromas, was richer than the nose suggested, and good acidity gave length without astringency. The 1970 seemed fairly mature twenty years later, with cedary aromas, ripe, almost minty fruit, and more elegance than weight. The 1972 is, in my experience, one of the very few drinkable wines from this vintage. The 1979 vintage was the first for which the Bories were entirely responsible; by 1997 the nose was firm and ripe, with hints of liquorice, while the wine was plump, reasonably concentrated, well-balanced, classic Pauillac though lacking some flair. The 1982 has always been delicious, voluptuous and oaky on the nose, and beautifully balanced, with rich, plummy fruit, ample depth, well-judged tannins, firm acidity, and fine length.

The 1988 is more discreet, more graceful, displaying elegant blackberry and vanilla aromas, a classic structure with some minerality, no excessive concentration, but fine length. The 1989 has a very good reputation but I have been unlucky with the bottles I have encountered, which have been austere. The 1990 is a resplendent wine, with sumptuous new oak and blackcurrant aromas. It's very concentrated but the tannins are supple, the texture lush, and if it seems to lack a little verve, no matter, as the fruit is so delicious. The 1993 is fairly dilute, and needs drinking up. The 1994 is considerably better, combining a lush fruitiness with firm tannins. The 1995 is plump and succulent, a rich, satisfying mouthful of fruit backed by solid tannins that should ensure a long life. But I prefer the 1996 for its ripe, blackcurranty nose, and for the freshness and lively acidity that balance the plump, concentrated fruit. The 1998 is an exemplary Pauillac, with plump fruit, ample weight and concentration, and dense but not harsh tannins. There's a leafy, elegant delicacy on the nose of the 1999, which is a charming, well-balanced wine with delicious fruit, an exemplary example of the accessible style of this vintage.

The 2000 is an enormous wine, with spicy, toasty aromas, a velvety texture, and a very rich, lush, chocolatey palate backed by big, ripe tannins; yet it's not too extracted, and has fine length and a brilliant finish. The 2001, surprisingly, is somewhat gawky, not lacking fruit on the nose or palate, but slightly extracted and unusually lacking in charm. The 2002 has an opulent nose of blackcurrant and liquorice, but doesn't quite deliver on the palate, for all its tightness and robust tannins; perhaps the finesse will emerge in time. The 2003 lacks acidity and zest.

Château Haut-Bages-Libéral

St Lambert. Tel: 0557 887665. Website: www.hautbagesliberal.com. Owner: Taillan group. Fifth Growth. 28 ha. 80%
Cabernet Sauvignon, 17% Merlot, 3% Petit Verdot. Production: 160,000 bottles. Second wine: La Chapelle de Bages
Not much is known of the origins of this property, but by 1855 the owner was a M. Libéral, the scion of a wine-broking family from Bordeaux. His name proved most convenient, as he found an enthusiastic market among the supporters of Liberal parties in Belgium and the Netherlands. Thereafter the estate passed through numerous owners, until in 1960 it was bought by a consortium that included members of the Cruse family. They replanted much of the vineyard, and incorporated some parcels into another of their properties, Château Pontet-Canet (*q.v.*). Indeed, from 1960 until 1973 the wine was vinified at Pontet-Canet. In 1983 the property was sold again, this time to the Bernard Taillan group, headed by Jacques Merlaut. He asked his daughter Bernadette Villars to run the estate, which she did until her death in 1992. Thereafter her daughter Claire Villars took on responsibility for Haut-Bages-Libéral, along with Ferrière and La Gurgue (*qq.v.*) in Margaux.

There is no château at the property. The winery and vineyards are located in St Lambert, just north of the Latour vineyards, with a smaller parcel on the Bages plateau. It is tempting to think that this proximity means that the Libéral vineyards are almost as good, but this is not the case. The soil is different. The Libéral *croupe* consists of stony gravel and sand over a subsoil of clay (much more so than at Latour) and limestone. The *croupe* lies three metres (ten feet) lower than that of Latour; nor is the natural drainage as efficient as at Latour. On the other hand, their location gives them excellent protection against frost. Only half the vineyards are near the winery; there are other parcels on the Bages plateau, and near the Pichons. Two-thirds of the vines are over thirty-five years old, and they are replaced individually by complantation.

A new *cuvier* was built in 2000, and it is connected to the old *chai* by a covered reception area. Claire Villars has converted that *chai* into another *cuvier*, this one equipped with small cement tanks, with which she is thoroughly pleased. The winery has a reverse-osmosis machine. Yields are quite generous, but that is often the case at Pauillac. The *cuvaison* can last for up to four weeks, and malolactic fermentation takes place both in tanks and in barriques. The wine is aged for eighteen months in up to fifty per cent new oak. Haut-Bages-Libéral is a burly, tannic wine, but in good vintages it is also packed with fruit. Its dense structure comes both from the high proportion of Cabernet Sauvignon and from the high clay content in the soil. There is a risk of over-extraction, and in the 1990s the wines were too hefty for some tastes, but recent vintages have been handled more gently, or so it seems.

I have not tasted really old vintages of this wine. The 1986 is still impressive: opaque in colour, a dense nose of woodsmoke, figs, and chocolate, and a rich, plump, full-bodied mouthful, still marked by youthful tannins. The 1988 is less explosive but it too is quite assertive, with firm acidity, little overt fruitiness, and good length. The higher Merlot content in the 1993 doesn't save it from a hard acidic structure and a lack of generosity. The 1994 is equally chunky, but has more concentration. The 1995 has a showy nose, with a strong black-fruits character, while the palate is robust and solid, but marred by slight astringency. There is some flesh on the 1997, which is no weakling, but the finish is rather short. The 1998 has dense plum and blackberry fruit and a fistful of tannin; it also has good length and lively acidity and the wine should open up in time. It runs neck and neck with the juicy, compact, muscular, oaky 1999. The spicy 2000 goes for broke, opaque in colour, aromatically powerful with lush, plummy fruit, and sumptuous fruit on the palate, perhaps rather low in acidity but nonetheless very long. The 2001 is more accessible, and the firm tannins do not mask the rich black-cherry fruit; but finesse is not a word that springs to mind. The 2002 is better, with its nose of black fruits and leather, its opulent texture and concentrated fruit backed by powerful tannins, and its long, chewy finish. The 2003 is a success here, with fleshy, oaky aromas, and a rich palate with weight and stuffing; though austere, the finish is long and spicy. The 2004 has excellent potential, with big, ripe tannins and good, rich fruit.

It's no use looking for purity and elegance with Haut-Bages-Libéral, but it's a serious and underrated Pauillac, with an almost dramatic degree of power and richness.

Château Haut-Bages-Monpelou

*Tel: 0556 000070. **Owner:** Castéja family. 15 ha. 70% Cabernet Sauvignon, 25% Merlot, 5% Cabernet Franc.*
***Production:** 50,000 bottles*

This property once formed part of Duhart-Milon and was integrated into that wine until 1948. When the Castéjas sold Duhart, they retained this portion of the vineyards, which they produced as a separate wine. It is aged for sixteen months in fifty per cent new barriques. Some vintages – 1999, 2000, 2001 – lack weight, concentration, and character. Others – 1998, 2002, 2003 – are richer but burly and lacking in finesse. The 1999, although marred by gamey aromas, is unusually lush and spicy, and still drinking well. Haut-Bages-Monpelou is not an expensive wine, but it does not, in my experience, reach any great heights. I believe even the Castéjas were somewhat surprised to be given *cru bourgeois supérieur* status in 2003.

Château Haut-Batailley

*Tel: 0556 590666. **Website:** www.domainesfxborie.com. **Owner:** Borie family. Cinquième cru. 22 ha.*
*65% Cabernet Sauvignon, 25% Merlot, 10% Cabernet Franc. **Production:** 120,000 bottles.*
***Second wine:** La Tour d'Aspic*

As has already been explained, Château Batailley was divided in the 1940s, and the smaller part went to François Borie, who then expanded the estate by incorporating fifteen hectares from Duhart-Milon. After Borie died in 1953, his daughter Françoise de Brest-Borie inherited the property. By chance I was present when she arrived with her sons at Grand-Puy-Lacoste to negotiate a renewal of the twenty-year lease which allows François-Xavier Borie to manage her property alongside Grand-Puy-Lacoste.

Some of the vineyards are planted close to the *chais*, a galleried structure not far from Batailley. They are near Petit Batailley, the block from which Latour usually produces Les Forts de Latour. The tower in the vineyards, after which the second wine is named, was constructed by the pious Averous sisters; it depicts the Virgin Mary trampling the satanic serpent underfoot. Another, earlier-ripening section lies on the Bages plateau. The winemaking is similar to that at Grand-Puy-Lacoste, though slightly less new oak is used as Haut-Batailley is a less structured wine. A pneumatic press replaced the horizontal presses as recently as 2005.

The 1966 is attractively rich but also a touch hollow and dry on the finish. The 1975 is surprisingly light and soft, with little of the earthy tannic structure so common in this vintage. The 1976 was good for the vintage but peaked early. The 1980 was remarkably good, with fine concentration and acidity and some complexity. The 1985 was simple and lacked length, the 1988 rather extracted and dour, the 1989 sweet and oaky on the nose, but quite astringent and seems already past its best. The 1990 has decent fruit but lacks weight and complexity. The 1994 isn't bad, though it's a tannic, chewy style. The 1995, however, is excellent, a rich, velvety, full-bodied wine, dense and spicy, and with sufficient structure to keep it going for many years. It seems better balanced than the coarser 1996. The powerful, spicy 1998 is still a battleground between sweet fruit and firm tannins, but this is a wine with force and presence, and I suspect the fruit will win in time. Although the nose of the 1999 is stylish, the palate surprises with an austerity that comes close to earthiness; it has richness and concentration but at present is still brooding and backward.

The 2000 is excellent. The aromas are richly oaky with voluptuous, plummy fruit, and the palate is sumptuous, with delicious fruit but not, perhaps, sufficient grip to sustain it beyond the medium term. The nose of the 2001 is more reserved, and the wine is ripe and dense; like the 2000, it is forward and accessible. The 2002 has more intensity and power, a lusher style than usual, with more tannin and weight than the 2000, making this a wine of fine potential. The 2003, initially slack and dull, has evolved into a rounded but fresh and balanced wine with good length.

There seems to be a real turnaround since 2000. Before then the wine was simply inconsistent: occasionally dilute and slack, sometimes extracted and astringent. But now the wine shows richer fruit and more complexity. Nor is there any excessive extraction. The wine, if not as powerful as some, is well balanced as a consequence.

11. Pauillac Part II

Château Lafite-Rothschild

*Tel: 0556 731818. Website: www.lafite.com. **Owner:** Rothschild family. Premier cru. 100 ha.*
*70% Cabernet Sauvignon, 25% Merlot, 3% Cabernet Franc, 2% Petit Verdot. **Production:** 480,000 bottles.*
Second wine: *Carruades de Ch Lafite*

Lafite appeared at the head of the First Growths in the 1855 classification. A century and a half later, choosing between the Pauillac First Growths is nothing other than an exercise in personal taste. For opulence choose Mouton, for power choose Latour. for elegance choose Lafite. (For maximum satisfaction, choose all three.)

The property lies at the northern end of the region, between Le Pouyalet and Cos d'Estournel across the border in St-Estèphe. From the D2 you glimpse the discreet turrets of the château on the far side of a pond against a backdrop of tall trees. The house is surprisingly modest. Only the main tower dates from the sixteenth century; the two-storey château itself is from the eighteenth century. The Second Empire furnishings, silk wallcoverings, family portraits, and memorabilia have been lovingly preserved. The present director, Baron Eric de Rothschild, comes here with his family for part of the holidays; at other times, the elegant salons of the house are used for entertaining. Those privileged enough to be invited to visit Lafite will also be shown the private cellars, where most vintages from the 1860s onwards are guarded in worthwhile quantities and formats; the oldest bottle is the legendary 1797.

Lafite certainly dates back to medieval times, though it is not certain that vines were planted here at that time. It is probable that vineyards were planted as a commercial proposition only in the early seventeenth century. When Jeanne Gasq was widowed and thus became owner of Lafite in 1670, she remarried, and chose well. Jacques de Ségur was already the proprietor of other estates in the region, and after his death in 1691 their son Alexandre inherited Lafite. Alexandre also married well, choosing Marie-Thérèse de Clauzel, the heiress to Château Latour, in 1695. Thus Alexandre and their son Nicolas-Alexandre, born in 1697, found themselves owning and running properties already producing some of the world's most sought-after wines. Mme. de Pompadour adored Lafite; across the Channel, Sir Robert Walpole bought the 1732 and 1733 in barrel. Nicolas-Alexandre was justifiably known as the *prince des vignes* or "prince of vines", controlling as he did Lafite, Latour, Calon, and other estates. Louis XV elevated him to the rank of marquis.

The two future First Growths were separated when Nicolas-Alexandre died in 1755, but Lafite remained in the family. When Comte Nicolas-Marie-Alexandre made a hash of his financial affairs, he fled the country and in 1784 was obliged to put Lafite on the market. It passed through various hands. When Revolution broke out, the owner was a relative of the Ségurs, Nicolas-Pierre de Pichard, a former president of the Bordeaux *parlement*. He did not survive to enjoy his estate; in 1794 he was guillotined. The state confiscated Lafite in 1797 and sold it to Jean de Witt, who had trouble coming up with the asking price. So the estate was back on the market. In 1800 it was sold to three Dutch wine merchants. Then in 1816 the Dutch consortium sold Lafite to the estranged wife of a financier called Vanleberghe. Mme. Lemaire – she had acquired a new surname after no fewer than two divorces from M. Vanleberghe – did not hold onto the property for long, selling it, it appeared, to a British banker, Sir Samuel Scott, in 1821. This turned out to be a smokescreen. Mme. Lemaire would have been obliged under French law to leave Lafite to her children in equal shares. This she had no wish to do, as she wanted her son Aimé-Eugène to inherit the lot. So she let it be known that she had sold the estate to Scott. The Scott bank functioned instead as the family accountant.

The property had been managed from 1797 by the Goudal family, the honour passing from father to son. It was they who made most of the commercial decisions, such as the purchase of the important parcel called the Carruades, which Emile Goudal considered the finest terroir in the Médoc. He went head-to-head with his counterpart at Mouton, and the Goudal offer was accepted from the owners of the parcel, Château Mouton d'Armailhacq, just half an hour before Mouton came through with an improved offer.

Cyril Ray quotes a wonderful letter from Goudal to Scott written on September 27, 1853. It illustrates that jockeying for position among the top growths is not a recent trend.

> *The sale of the Carruades to M. Rothschild would be very improper and could have for you the most disastrous consequences.... If M. Rothschild would buy the Carruades, which are appreciated by everybody as vineyards of the highest quality, which can do good to any wine it will be mixed with, M. Rothschild having great wealth will try to get Mouton made a First Growth. Do you realize the consequence this will have for you? Mouton as a First Growth could only depreciate Lafite...It would be better to sell the Carruades for 50,000 francs to a stranger than for 50,000 more than that to M. Rothschild.*[1]

Clearly Emile Goudal was not a man to tangle with.

When Aimé Lemaire died in 1866, Lafite was close to its present size, with some seventy-five hectares in production. His three surviving sisters decided to put the estate up for auction in 1868. It was then that Baron James de Rothschild strode onto the scene, paying the then-astronomical sum of five million francs for the vineyards, estate buildings, and stock of current vintages. The baron, who had not been known for his keen interest in wine, died just a few months later, before he had even had the opportunity to visit his property, which, it has to be said, was bought primarily as an investment. It passed to his three sons, and it has continued in the Rothschilds' hands ever since. The sole interruption was in 1942, when the property was expropriated by the Vichy government, which at least continued to run Lafite as a wine estate. This expropriation probably spared Lafite from being grabbed by Hermann Goering, who apparently had his rapacious eye on the property.

From 1974 onwards, the director has been Baron Eric, and the manager since the 1980s has been Charles Chevallier, who runs all the Lafite wine interests. Baron Eric is not the sole owner; through mysterious processes in Paris, one leading member of the family at a time is chosen to run and represent Lafite. The winemaker is Christophe Congé, and the vineyard manager is Régis Porfilet. Emile Peynaud used to be the consultant oenologist, and has been succeeded by Jacques Boissenot.

The Médocain word *fite* means a mound, and the vineyards do occupy a plateau that rises to twenty-seven metres (eighty-nine feet), making it one of the most elevated spots in Pauillac. The area under vine has never been larger. Chevallier explains that some parcels not previously planted are now in production, though principally for the second wine. Moreover, Lafite has been able to purchase small plots of vines embedded within their vineyards yet inconveniently belonging to other growers. Many of these are on the far side of the D2 and thus not of the best quality. Chevallier adds that, although the surface may have increased slightly, the volume of wine has not.

Two-thirds of the vineyards are in a single parcel surrounding the château on both sides of the D2. There is another portion intermingled with the vines of Duhart-Milon. Strangely, almost five hectares lie across the boundary in St-Estèphe, but they enjoy the right to the Pauillac appellation. Then there are the Carruades, divided into four parcels just south of the main Lafite vineyard, and there is also another block south of the Carruades. Rather confusingly, although Carruades lends its name to the second wine, some blocks within it give wine good enough for Lafite.

The soil is deep gravel, up to four metres (thirteen feet) in depth. This lies on a bed of marl, which itself lies on a band of limestone, which some believe explains the remarkable finesse of Lafite. The finest sector is the so-called plateau of Lafite just south of the *chais*. Here the gravel is exceptionally deep and the drainage impeccable. Where the land dips, Merlot is usually planted and drainage channels have had to be installed. Chevallier says

1 Ray, *Lafite,* Peter Davies, London, 1968, 46

that, despite the apparent homogeneity of the terroir, there are considerable variations in soil and exposure, so the winemakers try to vinify separately as many lots as they can, so as to analyse the differences between them. Lafite assigns the same vineyard workers to the same parcels, year in, year out. This means they have a deep familiarity with the vines; it also means that the vineyard manager knows exactly how well each of his team is working.

The density ranges from 7,500 to 8,800 vines per hectare. The average age of the vines is forty years, with the oldest vines about ninety years old. Replanting takes place at the rate of roughly one per cent each year. Virtually no chemical fertilizers are employed, and compost is the preferred method of enriching the soil. Green-harvesting is not systematic. It depends on the performance of each parcel and of course on climatic conditions and growth patterns each year. Cabernet Sauvignon will always be the dominant variety, but Chevallier is intrigued by Petit Verdot. They have a parcel planted in the 1930s, and have added another hectare in 1995, which is being vinified separately. He is more ambivalent about Cabernet Franc. He finds that it is either fabulous or useless, depending on the year. For most of the 1980s and early 1990s no Cabernet Franc was used in the *grand vin*, but it made its contribution in 1995 and 1996.

The Lafite microclimate also plays a crucial part in the wine. Charles Chevallier notes that the Lafite vines ripen about five to seven days earlier than those of Duhart-Milon, which are not that far away but have a more northerly exposure.

The climax of the viticultural year is, of course, the harvest. During the summer the vineyard workers tag all the vines less than ten years old, as well as any vines suffering from maladies. These are all picked separately. Then the harvest pauses as the team waits for optimal maturity for the remaining vines. Once the harvest proper begins, it is rapid, and usually completed within twelve days. Chevallier remarks:

> We have improved our knowledge of the maturation of our vines, which allows us to be much more exact in our harvesting dates. We have the capacity to hire 350 people to work fast, if that's what's required. We're looking for full maturity in our grapes but not for overmaturity. To determine the picking date we taste above all. I have all the analyses on my desk, but only give them a passing glance. Tasting is much more important.

The grapes are sorted in the vineyard, with one sorting table per team of pickers. At the winery there are two reception bays, so that selections can be made from the outset, if deemed necessary. The inventor of the *sous-vide* concentrator was a friend of Baron Eric, so Lafite bought the machine early on, trying it out in 1990 and 1991. "I think of it as a spare tyre," says Chevallier. "It's useful to have one in case you need it, but it's not essential to making a car function." It could theoretically be used in dry years too, but Lafite does not want super-concentration. Since Chevallier already aims for optimal ripeness, he has no wish to alter the balance of the wine so as to increase its alcohol or power. Lafite has experimented with all modern methods, but Chevallier remains sceptical about micro-oxygenation, specifically its long-term effects on a wine. He also believes that, after five years, there is no detectable difference between wines that undergo malolactic fermentation in oak, and those that go through it in tanks.

Lafite has its own cooperage. In a courtyard near the Duhart vineyards stacks of staves are left to dry for two years: one in the open, and the second sheltered beneath a roof but still exposed to the air. The barrels are used for Lafite, Duhart-Milon, Rieussec, and, in part, for L'Evangile (*qq.v.*).

Vinification takes place half in stainless-steel tanks, installed in 1988, and half in oak vats, though Chevallier finds that the container in which the must is fermented makes little difference to the final quality. Nonetheless the best lots are fermented in wood. He prefers to rely on indigenous yeasts, but sometimes uses selected yeasts just to begin the process. There is no cold soak, no *pigeage*. The *cuvier* is not computerized; all decisions on extraction and the length of the *cuvaison* are made on the basis of taste.

Blending begins after the first racking, in March. Then the wine continues its ageing for eighteen to twenty months in new barriques, though very little new oak is used for Carruades. There is no lees-stirring – Chevallier doesn't see the point of it. For the second year the barrels are moved to the profoundly still second-year concrete *chai* designed by the famous architect Ricardo Bofill, which was completed in 1988 and can house 2,200 barrels. The wine is eggwhite-fined and, if necessary, very lightly filtered before bottling.

Roughly one-third of the crop ends up in the *grand vin*, about forty per cent in Carruades de Lafite, and the rest is sold simply as Pauillac. The Moulin des Carruades label has been used from time to time. It used to be an exclusive bottling for the wine merchants Nicolas, and was revived as a second-wine label from 1974 to 1985. It is no longer in use.

The style of Lafite is more supple than that of its major rivals, and it is undeniably lighter in texture than Latour or Mouton. It is not the aim of the Lafite winemakers to outgun the other wines, but to surpass them in elegance, subtlety, and airiness. It is usually accessible more rapidly than the other two First Growths, yet it can age just as remarkably. Perhaps the wine is altering somewhat in style. Few wine critics are prepared to give the highest ratings to a wine that lacks concentration. Not that Lafite does lack concentration, but weight and density are not the priority here. Nonetheless the wine does seem to have gained in those respects, perhaps so that it does not show at a disadvantage during the *primeur* tastings. But Bordeaux connoisseurs know that it really doesn't matter greatly how the wines taste, in comparative terms, during their infancy. What's important is how the wines taste when they reach their successive stages of maturity.

Does Lafite age? Well, the 1870 was coming along nicely when I tasted it in 2002, although I admit to doubts about its authenticity. The colour had an extraordinary opacity I associate more with Napa Cabernet than nineteenth-century claret. The aromas were still dense and plummy, with a touch of mint. The wine was very rich and concentrated, silky in texture, seamless in its structure, still amazingly youthful, and with extraordinary length. This magnum was said to have come from Glamis Castle, been auctioned in London in 1970, and recorked in 1983. Other great nineteenth-century Lafites (none of which I have tasted) are the 1811, 1848, 1861, 1864, 1865, 1869, 1893, and 1899.

The 1928 from magnum was closer to my expectations of Lafite typicity. The nose was sweet, rich, delicate, charming, elegant; on the palate there was ample concentration and tannin, but it was still fresh and lively, with fine length. David Peppercorn recalls that its high volatile acidity and some secondary fermentation required the 1928 to be pasteurized. The 1929 from magnum had a rich nose with vigour and charm; concentrated and lively, it was still fresh and elegant and very long, despite a hint of dryness. It is a confirmation of how difficult this period was that the 1927, 1930, 1932, 1935, and 1936 were all declassified and sold as mere Pauillac. The 1949, consumed at the château in 1997, had marked brick tones. The nose was extremely delicate, with aromas of undergrowth, truffles, and coffee. The wine was clearly fading and ethereal, but it was exquisite nonetheless, with immense finesse and concentration, a taste of wild strawberries, and a delectable sweetness on the finish. A magnum tasted five years later was not quite at this level. A 1950 Carruades, tasted thirty years later, had a floral bouquet but was drying out. The 1953 is a classic Lafite which I have never tasted, but most bottles may be past their best. The 1955, tasted in 1987, was wonderful: the colour not deep but healthy, the nose rich and cedary and very intense, the palate rich and rounded, lightly tannic, of medium weight, and completed by a long, elegant finish. There was no suggestion of frailty with the marvellous 1959, with its rich Cabernet nose, sweet and black-curranty yet with the Lafite charm; the wine retained masses of fruit, a sumptuous texture, and what I can only describe as dignity and great persistence. The 1962 is very Lafite on the nose, with sweet, cedary, blackcurrant aromas and great elegance; on the palate it seemed fully mature in the 1990s, with ample fruit and a light tannic backbone.

Thereafter Lafite went through a disappointing patch until the mid-1970s, though I have been very impressed by the 1970. It's certainly mature in colour, the nose is classic, and the wine itself has power and depth, an overall harmoniousness, lovely Cabernet fruit, and impeccable balance. The 1978 has wonderful aromas of undergrowth, mushrooms, and truffles. It's medium-bodied, very refined, delicate rather than rich, but still graceful on the finish. The 1979, tasted recently from magnum, had a sweet, spicy, savoury nose, and the fruit had retained freshness and elegance, despite firm tannins, and showed fine length. The superb 1982 has an opulence, a plumminess, that is perhaps atypical of Lafite yet irresistible: such concentration, such supple tannins. The oft-tasted 1983 is a return to more typical Lafite form, with all the charm and finesse you could ask for. However, it is rather austere, and was still rather tight and tannic in 2005. There is something slightly strung-out about this wine. I first encountered the 1985 in 1995 when it was thrown into a blind tasting of Napa Cabernets as a ringer. It wasn't hard to spot. I noted: "rich pruney nose, ample fruit, cedary; rich, dense, quite tannic with good extract, Bordeaux-style, very good length". More recently, the wine was no longer pruney but the aromas were more heady, and it had gained in intensity, elegance, and length, adding up to an impeccable and delicious bottle.

When young, the outstanding 1986 had the character of the vintage, with a rich but reserved nose, a ripe but tannic attack, very apparent new oak, and an intense, almost redcurrant finish. The 1989's aromas are still dominated by oak, but there's great concentration and spiciness here; its long but surly finish suggests it still needs time. The 1990 is excellent, but perhaps slightly disappointing given the splendour of the vintage. It's rich and concentrated, but just a touch lean. The 1994 is very good for the year, with oaky cigar-box aromas and some rich, chocolatey fruit, but it doesn't have much finesse. But the 1995 is classic, smoky on the nose, and silky and sleek in texture. It's highly concentrated, almost peppery, has marked black-fruits flavours, power and complexity, and exceptional length. The 1996 is magnificent too, with a ravishing nose exuding intense blackcurrant fruit. The attack is discreet, it's very pure and poised, the oak well integrated; though not especially fleshy, it develops complexity and vigour on the palate. The 1997 is elegant and subtle, with good acidity, making it a success for the vintage. The perfumed 1998 is no blockbuster, but it's supple, fleshy, perhaps a touch extracted, but shows the Lafite finesse on the finish. The 1999 has exquisite cedary aromas and evident new oak, but it's very concentrated, the tannins are fine-grained, and although no blockbuster, it has wonderful elegance and length. I have not tasted the 2000, but it is widely regarded as a top wine of the vintage. The 2001 has blackcurrant and black-cherry aromas; it's lush and concentrated, with an imposing tannic structure, a lot of grip, and good but not exceptional length. I marginally prefer the 2002, with its flamboyant (for Lafite) blackcurrant aromas, its beautifully integrated new oak, its concentration without any sense of excessive mass, its balance, persistence, and complexity. From cask, the 2005 had discreet blackcurrant aromas, but the intensity on the palate was remarkable, as were its purity and length. The 2006, from cask, had aromatic purity and excellent concentration but was too tightly structured to reveal its eventual character.

It's my impression that the quality of Carruades has improved considerably. In the past, it could be a rather tough, charmless wine, but in the 1990s quality picked up, and I have good notes on the 1994, 1995, 1996, 2001, and 2002. There was some white wine produced at Lafite, almost certainly just for family consumption. Jean-Michel Cazes tells me he has drunk a 1937 white Lafite, but has no recollection of what it tasted like. The Belgian wine writer Jo Gryn tasted the first vintage, 1961, and declared it superb.

Château Latour

*Tel: 0556 731980. Website: www.chateau-latour.com. Owner: François Pinault. Premier cru. 66 ha.
80% Cabernet Sauvignon, 15% Merlot, 5% Petit Verdot and Cabernet Franc. Production: 350,000 bottles.
Second wine: Les Forts de Latour*

No other Médoc wine can match Latour for power, depth of flavour, and grandeur. Its personality is directly related to the location of its vineyards. The core of the estate is the forty-five-hectare L'Enclos, around the château and the *chais*, and very close to the estuary, with its moderating climate.

Detailed archival documentation is quite rare in the Médoc, so the development of its properties in medieval times is known only sketchily. Latour is the exception, and in 1974 Professor Charles Higounet published a detailed account of its history. Many now famous wine properties were no more than farms in the Middle Ages, but the *seigneurie* of Latour had fairly extensive vineyards as far back as the fourteenth and fifteenth centuries. A fort stood here in the fourteenth century to guard this stretch of the estuary. In the late sixteenth century Arnaud de Mullet reunited the estate's disparate holdings and transformed it into a more efficient single unit. After his death his son Denis inherited the estate, and then Denis's niece. It was in the early seventeenth century that the prominent dovecote was built here. In 1670 Latour was up for sale. The purchaser was François de Chavannes, who left it to his niece. It passed by marriage into the de Clauzel family.

By this time Latour was increasing its reputation for the excellence of its wine. By the early eighteenth century it was fetching the same prices as Lafite in northern Europe. It became particularly well known in England, which by 1780 was purchasing about eighty per cent of the production. As has been explained in the entry for Lafite, Marie-Thérèse de Clauzel, a descendant of François de Chavannes and heiress to Latour, married the owner of Lafite, Alexandre de Ségur, in 1695. So for some time the two properties were yoked together. It was after the death of Nicolas-Alexandre de Ségur in 1755 that they were properly separated. At this time the Latour vineyard did not exceed thirty hectares. By the time of the Revolution, the owners of the estate, which had now expanded to forty-seven hectares, were noblemen married to various Ségur daughters, and all were absentees. After the Revolution some shares were sold off, but in 1842 a company was formed to ensure that Latour remained in family hands, and this company bought back some of the shares that had been sold. The principal shareholders were the descendants of the Marquis de Beaumont and the Comte de la Pallu. In 1863 Latour introduced château-bottling for a portion of its production, but only in the early 1930s did the managers follow Mouton's example by bottling the entire crop at the property. Phylloxera was kept at bay for a surprisingly long time, and it was not until the 1920s that the entire vineyard was replanted on American rootstocks. Since the eighteenth-century and early-nineteenth-century owners had fine properties elsewhere, no one felt urged to build a fine château here, and it was only in 1864 that the present drab mansion was built.

As generation succeeded generation, the shareholders proliferated. By the 1950s there were sixty-eight of them, rewarded with six cases of wine rather than cash. It was inevitable that a growing number of shareholders would favour the sale of the property with its inevitable cash windfall. The Comte de Beaumont held out but was eventually outvoted. In 1962 fifty-three per cent of the shares were sold to the British company Pearsons; Harveys of Bristol took a twenty-five per cent share; the family retained what was left. The new owners entrusted the management of Latour to a wine broker, Jean-Paul Gardère, and to Henri Martin of Château Gloria. They expanded the vineyards and replanted the fallow parcel near Château Batailley known as Petit Batailley. Other parcels were acquired and planted; drainage channels were renovated. There was a great deal of work to be done, as half the vines were missing, effectively reducing the productive area to a mere twenty-five hectares. Pearsons bravely replanted individual vines, rather than grubbing up entire parcels, and this helped preserve the oldest vines. It took ten years to complete this process. Haut-Brion had pioneered the useof stainless-steel tanks in 1961, and Latour was swift to follow in 1964.

In the mid-1980s Jean-Paul Gardère began to ease himself into retirement, and his place was taken by Christian Le Sommer, a former winemaker at Yquem. Henri Martin left in 1987, leaving Le Sommer in control. It was a difficult period. By now Pearsons was part of the much larger Allied Lyons company, which had consolidated its grip by buying some shares held by the Beaumonts. But Allied Lyons as a whole was experiencing some difficulties and put the estate on the market in 1992. In June 1993 it was sold to a company called Artemis, which belonged to the industrialist François Pinault. Latour was back in French hands. For some years he retained the same management team, until the business graduate Frédéric Engerer was appointed as general manager. Le Sommer's days were clearly numbered, and he left in 1999. One Médoc proprietor drily noted that Engerer seemed very skilled at firing people. Also in 1999 Frédéric Ardouin – like Engerer, in his early thirties – took over as technical director. Latour in the early twenty-first century was in the hands of a young, very capable team.

In the early 2000s Pinault authorized an investment of about six million pounds sterling in a new winery. Engerer also initiated a detailed soil analysis of eighty different plots within L'Enclos, and parcels are now handled differently according to their specific character. In 2000 he told me:

> *The search for excellence is the very minimum one should expect from Latour. Even in the core of our main vineyard there is a mosaic of ages, varieties, soils, and clones. It's not nearly as homogeneous as it looks. We are defining the architecture of the winery to accommodate smaller vats, so that we can monitor parcels more efficiently. At present we have to blend Cabernet Franc and Petit Verdot because we have so little of each, but from 2001 they can be vinified separately.*

As has been mentioned, the core of the vineyards is the forty-five-hectare L'Enclos, which stretches from the boundary with St-Julien and Léoville-Las-Cases north to the lane near Haut-Bages-Libéral. The waters of the estuary flow just 300 metres (984 feet) away from the most easterly vine. The soil is quite varied. There is clayey gravel on a subsoil of marly sediment; the eastern and western slopes are composed of gravelly sands, with more small pebbles than in the main portion; in the northern sector the marly clay is hospitable to Merlot. Drainage is excellent, allowing Latour to succeed better than most in wet years, and clay bands quench the vines' thirst during even the driest spells, although in a few places where the gravel is exceptionally deep, the vines can be stressed. Northwest of the château is a separate parcel, which was planted from 1963 onwards by Pearsons; its wines usually go into Les Forts. The same is true of the fifteen-hectare Petit Batailley, and the four-hectare La Pinada, which are well inland from the main vineyards. These vines are planted on a gravel that is finer than that of L'Enclos, which has many quartz pebbles. No one at Latour disputes that although the outlying parcels can produce very good wine, it is the exceptional terroir of L'Enclos that has always produced the bulk of the *grand vin*. Apart from the qualities of the soil, L'Enclos has a warmer microclimate, so that flowering is early, and the grapes ripen earlier than elsewhere in Pauillac. Petit Batailley is only two kilometres (1.2 miles) away, but its grapes can ripen eight to ten days later. Early ripening has been a huge advantage in vintages such as 1964, when rain wrecked the vintage at most properties, but L'Enclos could be harvested before the weather turned. The microclimate also protects L'Enclos from frost. When in 1991 many properties lost seventy per cent of the crop, Latour lost only thirty per cent.

The average age of the Latour vineyard is now fifty years. It is still being modified. It has been decided that Cabernet Franc does not work well here, so from 2002 onwards it is being gradually replaced by Cabernet Sauvignon. Missing or dying vines are replaced by complantation, and the density throughout is 10,000 vines per hectare.

During the harvest the young vines are marked by a blue ribbon, then picked separately and relegated to Les Forts. Engerer has tightened the initial selection, so that only vines more than twenty-five years old are admitted into the *grand vin*. There are about 200 pickers, and the grapes are conveyed in *cagettes* to the winery, where they are sorted before and after destemming, although there is a prior sorting in the vineyards. Sixty-six new squat conical steel tanks allow numerous parcels to be vinified separately. Since 1997 Latour has owned a *sous-vide* concentrator, but the last time it was used was in 2001. The *cuvaison* is roughly four weeks, with automated pumpovers. Malolactic fermentation takes place in tanks, except for the press wine. By December the wine is in new wood, bought from ten different coopers, and the wine is aged for eighteen months. However, for lots certain to end up in the second wine, the proportion of new oak does not exceed fifty per cent. The first-year *chai* dates from the nineteenth century but was extended in 1988; the second-year *chai* is underground and exceptionally cool. Blending is completed by March. The wine is fined with eggwhite but since 1999 there has been no filtration. Before 1970 some bottle variation was possible, as only eight barriques, rather than the entire production, were blended at a time. And in the 1940s, a lack of staff meant that the wine was bottled at various times. Such inconsistencies are impossible now, but could have affected the experience of those older vintages.

Les Forts de Latour was created in 1966. Most of the wine comes from the outlying parcels, but it is also the destination for the young vines from throughout the estate. It used to be the policy at Latour to release Les Forts with considerable bottle-age, but this was discontinued after 1989. Since 1990 there has been a third wine, the Pauillac, that has helped maintain the quality of Les Forts. It is aged in no more than ten per cent new oak. In 1836 Cyrus Redding opined that:

> Latour's wine is distinguished from that of Château Lafite by its superior body and consistence, but it should be kept in wood at least a year more than the Lafite to attain proper maturity.... It is less fine than Lafite.

In style, Latour has scarcely changed. It still has power, fullness, immense depth; it is muscular but never coarse. Like all First Growths, it benefits from a good deal of bottle-age; indeed, there is never a rush to drink Latour. There were some disappointing vintages from the late 1970s onwards and in the early 1990s, when some wines were reported to have been tainted, though my tasting notes do not support this.

In 2003 I was privileged to taste some ancient vintages the night before the château auctioned them at Christie's. The bottles had come directly from the Latour cellars, so their provenance was as good as it gets. The 1881 was still amazingly fresh on the nose, which was rich and cedary. At first taste the wine was bright and youthful, with ripe tannins and no lack of vigour – yet it began to fade after a while. The 1890 was not quite at this level, although the colour was completely healthy. The nose was perfumed, with aromas of raspberry, mint, and cedar, but the wine was a touch lean and hard, though it didn't lack concentration. (Other legendary nineteenth-century vintages include the 1847, 1863, 1865, 1874, and the 1899.)

The 1909 was browning, and the nose slightly stewed, with hints of cinnamon too. This was clearly past its best, becoming attenuated, though it retained some sweetness of fruit and a length mostly sustained by rather high acidity. The 1917 had an odd nose of brine and nettles and Vicks; it was losing its fruit but still had some length. Although it was clearly past its best, it was nonetheless moving to experience a wine made, presumably, by old men and wives and widows, while the able-bodied men were in the trenches. The 1924 was magnificent, with astonishing depth of colour. The nose was a dense concoction of plums, smoke, and coffee, while the texture was almost thick; the tannins were extremely ripe, and the finish long. The 1928, 1929, and 1934 are acclaimed vintages at Latour, but I have not tasted them. The 1937 I tasted in 2003 smelt a touch musty, and although the palate was fresher, the tannins were fairly dry. The wine was still bright and lively, but one couldn't help wondering how long it would stay that way. The 1940 was remarkable for a wartime vintage, with a rich, meaty nose that was still massively fruity. Despite the wine's intensity and extract, it soon developed some astringency and declined in the glass.

The 1945 is a truly great wine. The nose is incredibly complex, with spice, liquorice, redcurrants, woodsmoke, and a certain meatiness, yet the palate was far more pure, bright yet supple, with fine acidity, remarkable elegance, and an impeccably balanced finish. The 1948 still looked bright and healthy in 1993; the nose was rich and weighty and cedary, and although the palate was somewhat chunky, there was so much ripe tannin, spice, and power that it was hard to think of that as a defect. The 1949 reminds me of Lafite in the same year. The nose, though very mature, is exquisite, with delicate cigar-box aromas, while the fruit is simply delicious, with wonderful elegance and balance, and a long finish that brings this supremely harmonious wine to a perfect landing. I was surprised by the firmness of the 1952, which is very rich, suave, and persistent. The 1955, tasted twice in 1987 and not since, was also very youthful in colour and aroma; it was sumptuous, rich, dashing, vigorous, balanced, and long. The 1959 is showing a touch more maturity, with firm but meaty aromas that are less refined than those of Margaux and Lafite, while the palate is medium-bodied and somewhat lacking in weight.

It is hard to imagine a Latour superior to the 1961, with its majestic fruit-cake and coffee nose, its immense concentration, its fire and spice, its invigorating acidity and exceptional length. The 1962 has held up brilliantly, with that rich, powerful, meaty nose so typical of Latour at full throttle; it's a slightly tamer version of the 1961. The 1964 developed in colour quite rapidly, but the nose has remained classic Latour, dense but sweet with excellent fruit; its defect is a certain burliness, but there is considerable bottle variation. The 1966, which I have not tasted, was widely regarded as the best of the vintage. I was pleasantly surprised by the 1967, with its rich, firm aromas and their classic elegance, and a palate that was sweetish and intense, perhaps not that complex but very enjoyable. I don't recall in which circumstances I drank the 1968, but it wasn't very pleasant: a stalky wine with a bitter finish. The 1970 was impenetrable when young, and only slightly less so thirty years on. Yet it was hard not to be bowled over by the astonishing intensity of blackcurrant fruit on the nose and palate, by the huge but not aggressive tannins, by the power, majesty, and profound structure of this still youthful wine. In 2007 the 1971 still had dense and cedary black-fruit aromas, and was drinking beautifully, although clearly at its peak.

The 1973 was good for the year, uncharacteristically open and accessible though it didn't lack tannin and reasonable length. The 1975 is reputedly one of the great successes of the vintage; others have found it very tough. I didn't care for the 1976, which had a coarseness rarely encountered with Latour, as well as a baked character and hard finish. The 1978, tasted recently, is splendid, with vivid blackcurrant and black-cherry aromas, while the palate is quite dramatic in its spice and power and persistence, all expressing some beautifully ripe fruit. The 1980, when fairly young, was not bad, but its sweet, cedary nose did not make up for its tannic austerity. The 1982 is formidable, a magnificent wine with a voluptuous quality; the tannins are massive but supple, the fruit quality lush and seductive, the finish tremendous. Shorter *cuvaisons* than usual, because of larger than expected crops, led to some relatively modest wines in the mid-1980s. The 1983 is a bit disappointing, with a slightly cooked character on nose and palate, and a lack of weight and complexity. But nonetheless it is quite stylish and long. The 1985 has the perfume and charm of the vintage; for Latour, it's medium-bodied, but has some spice and freshness and length. Many tasters found the 1986 disappointing when young, but when tasted in 2005 its aromas were floral and immensely stylish, and although it's not a big wine, it is intense and packed with flavours, with sleek tannins. In contrast, the 1988 in 2005 was showing hardly any evolution. The nose is rich and oaky with a marked graphite character; in the mouth there is very concentrated and bold blackcurranty fruit, some fresh acidity, and a shy sweetness.

The 1989 is closed and inky on the nose, and the palate massive and burly, with little evident finesse. At present it's a rather surly adolescent. The great 1990 has oak, blackcurrant, and iron on the nose; it's highly concentrated and forceful but suave and elegant too, and impeccably balanced. The 1994 is beginning to open up, with perky mocha aromas, and a concentrated yet gentle style of some complexity. The nose of the 1995 is blackcurranty but inexpressive, but this is a wine with huge extract, sumptuous texture, very ripe tannins, and excellent balance – give it time. The 1996 is more elegant and sleek, with more evident acidity though not at the expense of weight. The

1997 is fleshy and layered, with a supple texture supported by good underlying tannins. In the difficult 1998 vintage, Latour triumphed, delivering a wine of fully ripe blackcurrant fruit and fine concentration; it's a classic wine with vigour, balance, and length. There's an appealing herbaceous element on the nose of the 1999, a rounded, even creamy texture, and exceptional balance and length. Having blind-tasted the 2000 three times, I remained slightly disappointed by the wine. It has abundant richness on the nose and palate – that almost goes without saying – but there's an atypical softness that makes it a touch fatiguing. But it's early days. The 2003 is skilfully made, with ample upfront fruit and length.

Les Forts should not be overlooked. I have much admired and enjoyed the 1967, 1970 (exceptional), 1975, 1978, 1979, 1980 (surprisingly), 1982, 1989, 1990, 1994, 1995, 2002, and 2003.

Château Lynch-Bages

Tel: 0556 732400. Website: www.lynchbages.com. Owner: Cazes family. Cinquième cru. 100 ha. 95 ha red: 75% Cabernet Sauvignon, 15% Merlot, 10% Cabernet Franc. 5 ha white: 45% Sauvignon Blanc, 40% Sémillon, 15% Muscadelle. Production: 480,000 bottles. Second wine: Ch Haut-Bages-Averous

There was a wine estate on this spot in the early eighteenth century. Its owner, Bernard Dejean, also owned Grand-Puy-Ducasse. In 1728 he sold the property to Pierre Drouillard, who died in 1749. His sister had married Thomas Lynch in 1740, which is how the estate came into the hands of the well-known Lynch family. The first Lynch to come to Bordeaux was an Irish soldier called John Lynch. He married a Frenchwoman and stayed put, and his grandson Jean-Baptiste became mayor of Bordeaux in 1749. In 1824, some years before the death of John Lynch's son Michel, the property was sold to a Swiss merchant called Sébastien Jurine; it remained in his family until 1861. It passed through many hands after that, and in the 1920s belonged to a general called Félix de Vial. He lived elsewhere and hired a local insurance agent called Jean-Charles Cazes to manage the estate in 1933. So bad were conditions in that decade that the general leased the property to Cazes without charge, happy to have someone on the spot to take care of it. By 1939 the general found himself obliged to sell the estate, and was happy to let Cazes buy it, and offered him generous financial terms.

The new owner made many improvements to the estate, especially the vineyards, some of which needed replanting. He died at the age of ninety-five in 1972, but by then his son André had not only taken over the insurance agency but had been running Lynch-Bages since 1968. However, André Cazes, who was also mayor of Pauillac, was too busy to give his full attention to the wine estate, so he persuaded his son Jean-Michel, who had been living in Paris and working for IBM, to return to Pauillac in 1973. In the late 1970s, Jean-Michel hired a young man called Daniel Llose to make the wines, which he is still doing today. The Cazes family also own Château Ormes-de-Pez (*q.v.*) in St-Estèphe and Villa Bel-Air (*q.v.*) in the Graves. In the 1980s Jean-Michel helped create and then ran AXA Millésimes with its international portfolio of wine estates (enthusiastically aided by Daniel Llose, who was delighted to have the opportunity to make vintage port and Tokaj *aszú* as well as claret). At the same time he ran a thriving négociant business, established the Médoc's finest hotel and restaurant at Cordeillan-Bages, set up a wine school, founded a marvellous bakery in Bages, and heads the Commanderie du Bontemps, the Left Bank's major promotional organization. Despite the enormous demands on his time, Jean-Michel was indefatigable in maintaining contacts with all lovers of great Bordeaux, and no one has been a finer ambassador for the region and its wines.

When Jean-Michel Cazes arrived from Paris, he found the estate was not in good shape.

> *I arrived here just in time for the Bordeaux crisis and the oil crisis. It was also a time of major technical changes. We had very old equipment here, and no temperature control, so it wasn't possible to heat the* cuvier *and ensure the wines went through malo. All this forced us to renovate. The problem was this happened just when we had no money, as my father had bought out his brothers' shares in 1971.*

Nonetheless they persevered, and today no one disputes that Lynch-Bages delivers wines far superior to its status as a Fifth Growth. Its second wine, Haut-Bages-Averous, began life as an independent *cru bourgeois*, but since 1978 has been the second label, allowing a greater selection than before.

The château of Lynch-Bages is located on the plateau of Bages, right next door to the winery. Slightly hidden from view, it being the Cazes family home, this is a modest but comfortable country house, brightened by modern paintings. It was constructed in the 1820s by Sébastien Jurine. From the plateau itself you glimpse, beyond the town of Pauillac, the stately tankers sailing up and down the estuary.

The vineyards are in two main blocks. One is on the plateau of Bages; the other lies not far from Mouton, on either side of the road toward Batailley. Most of the vineyards are ploughed. During the harvest sorting tables are installed alongside each team of pickers, and there can be as many as four in operation at any one time. Yields can be on the generous side, but Llose points out that if your vineyard is healthy and complete, then there is no reason why you should not obtain good yields without any loss of quality. In Pauillac this certainly seems to be the case. Llose's viticultural goal is to have the healthiest possible grapes.

The winery has been very well equipped since 1980. It houses a concentrator, and Llose has experimented with micro-oxygenation, though he concluded that he couldn't detect any obvious benefits when using the technique. The *cuvaison* is around three weeks, with frequent *délestage*. The tanks are also equipped with programmable *pigeage* mechanisms. The wine is aged in at least fifty per cent new oak (seventy per cent in 2003 appears to have been the maximum) for around fifteen months, with a preference for medium-toast barrels.

Lynch-Bages also produces about 35,000 bottles of white wine. There were always some white grapes mixed in with the red vineyards. In 1978 these were vinified to provide some white wines for the Cazes family to drink at the beach. One day an inspector found the wine, and despite Jean-Michel's protestation that the wine was solely for personal consumption, he was fined. Moreover, he was fined four times for an array of offences: unauthorized planting, unauthorized production, non-declaration, and so forth. Then in 1987 he decided to plant a parcel near St Sauveur with white grapes. It had previously been left fallow as Cazes had no wish to produce a Haut-Médoc. After some limited skin contact, the wine is fermented and aged in up to fifty per cent new oak, and aged for six months with lees-stirring. The first vintage of Blanc de Lynch-Bages was 1990. It's a good wine, always quite oaky, especially on the nose, with varying degrees of citric fruit, and a creamy texture. I have particularly liked the 1999 and 2002.

The red Lynch-Bages is a much loved wine. And for good reason. It is richly fruity in an upfront style with no rough edges; it has great swagger, it's balanced, it's persuasive. It shows well when young, yet ages very well. It goes for immediacy rather than subtlety. The wine always has enough stuffing to support the substantial proportion of new oak. Unlike many of the top wines of Pauillac, relatively little is declassified into the second wine, yet the wine doesn't suffer from dilution or greenness. Perhaps this is because the high proportion of Cabernet Sauvignon always gives the wine backbone and strength, or because the vines are in such good shape that there are few unsatisfactory lots.

I have twice tasted the 1955, both English-bottled. One was drying out, the other vigorous and concentrated. The 1957 in 1985 still had massive fruit and some severity, with good length and a clean finish. The 1961, also in 1985, was still deep in colour, fruity and powerful on the nose, and tannic, balanced, and long. In 1994 the 1962 was remarkably good, with dense, chocolatey aromas, a rich, compact palate, deep and tannic but not harsh. The 1966 was rich and opulent but seemed at its peak in 1985. In 2006 the 1970 showed some maturity, but the nose was still sweet and minty, the palate rich, spicy, and very concentrated and long. The most recently tasted 1975 had some tough tannins and slight mustiness, but an earlier bottle, though tannic, had masses of fruit and a lingering aftertaste. The 1976 aged less well and combined a forward, fruity style with some astringency. When tasted long ago, the 1978 was sweet and rich and long. When tasted very recently, the 1979 was still impressive, with a sweet, ripe, oaky nose, a lot of spice and persistence, and marred only by rather high acidity. The 1981 was supple, spicy, and lively in the late 1980s.

The 1982 is a perfect vintage for this property. The sweet fruit and the oak are in perfect harmony, with some meatiness emerging by 2005; there is immense richness, a sumptuous texture, and an overall stylishness. The 1983 is excellent too, but not tasted for many years. The 1985 blends delectable fruitiness with the swagger and opulence of the Lynch-Bages style. It is very close in quality to the 1982. The 1986 has more overt tannin, as one would expect, and the aromas are more cedary and chocolatey; it has power and concentration if little finesse. The 1988 is also dense and chocolatey, a wine of extract and substance. The 1989 is more showy, with a sumptuous new-oak and liquorice nose, splendid fruit and intensity, and a long, peppery finish. The elegant 1990 is another brilliant wine, but it has more intensity, more mintiness, more overt acidity. The 1991 is a success for the vintage, with all the Lynch-Bages hallmarks but less length. The 1992 lacks grip and flair.

The 1993 is perhaps a touch too concentrated and powerful for the actual fruit quality, and the acidity is a bit edgy. The 1994 has a good deal of fruit, but it's austere. The 1995 is splendid, with its smoky, oaky aroma, its dense Cabernet fruit, its unusual minerality, and its fine length. There is more charm on the nose of the 1996, and an intensity and bright acidity that balance the rich, brooding, plummy fruit. There is still some rawness and surliness on the 1998, but there is massive fruit here backed by powerful, ripe tannins; the wine remains adolescent but should be grand in time. Jean-Michel Cazes is particularly proud of the 1999, but I have not tasted it since the *primeur* season, when it showed very well. The 2000 is entirely typical of the vintage and suits Lynch-Bages well, with its voluptuous, smoky, chocolate-mint nose; its opulence and flair are irresistible, and the only question mark is raised by its slightly low acidity. The 2001 is very similar, its fleshiness balanced by firm acidity and a flair that seems more pronounced than on the 2000. There's a slight jamminess on the nose of the 2002 that is atypical, but there's no lack of brawn and tannin on the palate. The outstanding 2003, in aroma and flavour, is powerful, opulent, and toasty, with enough spice and concentration to compensate for a slight lack of acidity.

Château Lynch-Moussas

Tel: 0556 000070. Owner: Castéja family. Cinquième cru. 55 ha. 75% Cabernet Sauvignon, 25% Merlot.
Production: 200,000 bottles. Second wine: Les Hauts de Lynch-Moussas

This originated as the property of Michael Lynch, brother of Comte Jean-Baptiste Lynch, who owned Lynch-Bages. By the time it was classified in 1855 it belonged to the Vasquez family. In 1919 the estate, in fairly moribund condition, was acquired by Jean Castéja. After his death in 1955, it was inherited by his widow. The property suffered from some neglect, since none of her heirs were keen to make the necessary investments while she remained the owner. The property declined to just a few hectares until Emile Castéja, who was already running Batailley (*q.v.*), took over the management in 1969. Thereafter almost the entire vineyard was replanted, and indeed restored, until it reached its present area of fifty-five hectares.

The vineyards are dispersed: one parcel near the château, another between Batailley and Grand-Puy-Lacoste, another just west of Pichon-Lalande. Gravel dominates, of course, but there is a substantial proportion of clay in the soil. The stately nineteenth-century château itself, almost surrounded by a handsome park, is the country home of Philippe Castéja, who has run the property since the retirement of his father Emile. As at Batailley, he has been keen to improve quality, and to this end he created the second wine in 2001.

The wine is made in essentially the same way as at Batailley. The 1961 looked fully mature but not tired in 1997, though the nose was somewhat stalky; there was still some richness and fruit and considerable vigour and length. The 1981 has a smoky nose; it's an old-fashioned claret, rather woody and dense, still holding up well and seemingly on a plateau of evolution. I had some positive notes on the 1988 in the 1990s, but by 2002 some dourness had set in and the wine lacked lift and finesse. The 1990 is hard, rather firm, and not very concentrated for this vintage. The 1993 is a bit green, but the nose is still vibrant and stylish, yet the structure is lean and rather acidic. The 1994 is dour, tannic, unexciting. The 1995 is marginally better, but has a similar chunkiness, and lacks finesse. The 1996 is very aromatic, with lush blackcurrant fruit; it's medium-bodied, quite forward, by no means complex, but enjoyable. The 1997 is thin and short. I reserve judgment on the 1998, as two of the three bottles

I have sampled were defective. The good bottle suggested the wine was light and superficial but well balanced. The 2000 lacks some weight and acidity – not a bad wine, but one expects better from this vintage. The 2001 is firm and spicy if only moderately concentrated. The 2002, however, is an excellent wine, showing much finer oak on the nose, and aromas of plums and coffee; the tannins are solid, but there's no lack of fruit and concentration. The 2003 has sweet, plummy aromas, and is lush if extracted on the palate. The 2004 showed extremely well during the *primeur* tastings, a view shared by many blind-tasters.

It is clear that this once mediocre property is being turned around and dragged swiftly into the modern era. Since the early 2000s the wine has shown much more fruit, richness, and even complexity, and a more overt oakiness too.

Château Mouton-Rothschild

Tel: 0556 732129. Website: www.bpdr.com. **Owner:** *Baroness Philippine de Rothschild. Premier cru. 82 ha.*
77 ha red: 77% Cabernet Sauvignon, 11% Merlot, 10% Cabernet Franc, 2% Petit Verdot. 5 ha white: 50% Sémillon,
48% Sauvignon Blanc, 2% Muscadelle. **Production:** *320,000 bottles.* **Second wine:** *Le Petit Mouton*

It was the firm conviction of Baron Philippe de Rothschild that Mouton was undeniably a First Growth, even if the 1855 *classement* failed to recognize the fact. Certainly its prices always matched those of the First Growths, suggesting that wine-lovers shared the baron's view. In a book about Bordeaux wines published in 1867, the author, Danflau, comments that, when the classification is revised, Mouton will surely be promoted. The baron doggedly pursued his campaign for Mouton's promotion, no easy task given the granitic character of the classification. In 1973 his perseverance paid off, and that well-known beer drinker Jacques Chirac, then minister of agriculture, signed the decree elevating Mouton to First-Growth status. The baron adopted the defiant motto: "*Premier je suis. Second je fus. Mouton ne change.*" ("First I am. Second I was. Mouton doesn't change.") Game, set, and match.

The name of the estate is derived from the word *motte*, which means mound, referring, of course, to the gravel *croupes*. The earliest proprietor of any importance was Joseph de Brane, who was the owner in the 1720s and who attached his name to that of the property. By the end of the eighteenth century the wine was fetching prices equivalent to those obtained by Pichon. By the time Brane put the estate up for sale in 1830, there were fifty hectares under vine and Joseph's grandson Hector had made Cabernet Sauvignon the principal grape in the vineyards. The new owner was a Parisian banker, Isaac Thuret, one of the first of many financiers to invest in the Médoc. It seems that Thuret did not make great efforts to maintain or improve quality, which may account for Mouton's disappointing ranking in 1855. By 1853, when Thuret put Mouton up for sale, the vineyards had shrunk to thirty-seven hectares. Perhaps the recent change of proprietor, the absence of a habitable château, and the condition of the vineyards influenced those who drew up the *classement*.

The purchaser was Baron Nathaniel de Rothschild, from the English branch of the banking dynasty. Although the baron never lived at Mouton, he did much to improve the vineyards and the quality of the wine. His son James inherited Mouton in 1870, and built the modest château, now called Le Petit Mouton and located, rather oddly, in the middle of the courtyard surrounded by *chais* and other buildings. James died young in 1881, but his widow Laura-Thérèse took over and ran the property until her death in 1920. She left the property to her elder son Henri, but he showed little interest, preferring to remain in Paris, and was happy to stand aside in favour of his brother Philippe, who was keen to manage the estate. It was not until 1947, however, that Philippe finally bought his siblings' shares and became the proprietor.

Baron Philippe was only twenty years old when he took over as manager of Mouton. His youth did not inhibit him from throwing himself with enthusiasm into his task, despite the fact that he was living there in primitive conditions, without running water or electricity. Two years later he took the radical step of bottling the entire 1924 vintage at the château, almost fifty years before the practice became compulsory in Bordeaux. He also commissioned the architect Charles Siclis to design and build the still impressive first-year *chai*, which was completed in 1926. In 1924 he had affronted tradition by commissioning a Cubist-style label for his wine from the artist Jean Carlu, initiating the series of artists' labels that was to become such a distinguishing feature of the marketing of Mouton. He also created a second wine (for declassified Armailhacq after 1933 as well as Mouton) which he called Mouton Cadet. The miserable vintages of the early 1930s were, he decided, not worthy of the Mouton name, so he needed a way to market the wines as a more basic product. Over the years Mouton Cadet was transformed into a brand that to this day gives some uninformed consumers the suggestion that Mouton-Rothschild and Mouton Cadet are somehow linked.

When war broke out, Mouton was expropriated and the baron was imprisoned, but managed to escape to Britain. His wife Elizabeth was less fortunate and died in a concentration camp in 1945. Ironically, the German Weinführer took good care of Mouton, which served as a military headquarters and continued to produce wine throughout the war. After the war Baron Philippe returned to Mouton, and in 1954 he remarried, choosing an American bride, Pauline Fairfax-Potter. She died in 1976, and the baron's grief was deep and prolonged.

Mouton won its place in the affections of consumers in large part because of the visibility of Baron Philippe. He not only inhabited the château, but developed it as a tourist destination, creating a superb museum of wine artefacts and opening the estate to guided tours. In the 1970s he also demonstrated to American consumers that he was no snobbish French aristocrat, when he created Opus One in Napa Valley as a joint venture with Robert Mondavi. Since he died in 1988, the estate has been vigorously managed by his daughter Philippine, a former actress whose flair and personal magnetism match her father's. She was striding into a room where a Mouton lunch in London was about to begin, when I heard her say to one of her importers: "Now who don't I know among our guests?" Thus speaks a born communicator. She also continues her father's strategy of developing joint ventures in other lands, such as Almaviva in Chile.

For decades the general manager here was Philippe Cottin, and Patrick Léon was the respected winemaker until his retirement in 2002. In 2003 Philippe Dhalluin, former director of Branaire-Ducru, was appointed technical director of all three estates.

There were fifty-one hectares under vine in 1945, and the property has been considerably expanded since then to its present eighty-two hectares. The average age of the vines across the estate is fifty years. The vineyards stretch westwards from the village of Le Pouyalet, lying south of the Lafite vineyards, although Mouton shares the Carruades plateau with Lafite. There are two principal blocks: the Grand Plateau, which lies west of the winery, and Carruades. The Grand Plateau has magnificent gravel soil that is fairly uniform in its structure. The gravel can be up to eight metres (twenty-six feet) deep and lies above a bed of larger stones mixed with sand rich in iron. Beneath this layer is a subsoil of clay, marl, and limestone. In the northern sector of the plateau there was, until recently, a 3.5-hectare block of 100-year-old Cabernet Franc, but it was uprooted in 2005, as the vines had degenerated and the wine, although good, was never as fine as the Cabernet Sauvignon all around it. This Cabernet Franc went into the *grand vin* only about once in every three years, whereas the Cabernet Sauvignon always qualified. Just north of this block is a parcel of even older Cabernet Sauvignon. (It is the Mouton policy not to use any vines under fifteen years of age in the *grand vin*.)

A slight dip separates the Grand Plateau from the Carruades, and this is where some Merlot is planted. Philippe Dhalluin describes Cabernet Sauvignon from the Carruades as more masculine and smoky than that from the Grand Plateau.

The white grapes for the wine called Aile d'Argent are planted on parcels with more sand than gravel, cooler soils better adapted to white wine. The grapes are picked by *tries successives*. There is a little skin contact. The first vintage was 1991. In true Mouton style, it is a very oaky wine, but one with flair and vigour. Of recent vintages I like the 2001 and 2002 best.

Many Médoc properties are now producing a little white wine (though few are as expensive as Aile d'Argent) but the real curiosity here is the cassis. In a remote western corner of the property blackcurrant bushes are planted like vines. The berries are cool-fermented, a slow process, and blended with a sugar syrup that has to be produced without caramelization. The brandy that is added is produced at Mouton and aged in barriques. The result is an intensely sweet cassis with about 240 grams of residual sugar. No more than 1,000 bottles are produced in any year.

Fertilizers are kept to the minimum, and compost is added every three years. The workers tend the same parcels, year in, year out, ensuring their familiarity with each vine. After a preliminary sorting, the grapes are transported in *cagettes* to the winery, where they are sorted again before and after destemming. In 2004 Mouton employed seventy sorters. The same grape reception procedure is followed for all three Mouton properties, though only in the case of Mouton do the grapes descend into the tanks by gravity. There have been experiments with concentrators, but they are not used systematically. The must is fermented in twenty-seven wooden vats with pumpovers. Indigenous yeasts are preferred whenever possible, though occasionally selected yeasts are used just to start the process. The vinification is straightforward, though the *marc* is pressed in vertical presses. About seventy per cent of the malolactic fermentation takes place in tanks and, once that process is complete, the blending begins.

The wine is aged in mostly new medium-toast oak sourced from eight coopers. The usual *élevage* is eighteen months, but the period can vary according to the structure of the wine. There is eggwhite-fining and a light filtration before bottling.

For many years Mouton was unpersuaded by the case for second wines. Philippe Cottin told me many years ago that having a second wine encourages the winemakers not to give their best efforts to the entire estate. Soon after he had a change of mind, and in 1993 Mouton released Le Second Vin, which has now been rejigged as Le Petit Mouton. Even so, the proportion of second wine is relatively low. In 2005, admittedly a great year, sixty-four per cent of the crop was released as Mouton, twenty per cent as Petit Mouton, and the rest was sold off.

Mouton has always been the richest, or at any rate the most fleshy, of the First Growths. It has an opulence more often associated with New World Cabernet, which is not to accuse Mouton of any lack of Pauillac typicity. But if, as a consumer, one is looking for voluptuousness, toastiness, exoticism, and weight, then Mouton will be your first choice. In recent years, however, the Mouton team has been making discreet alterations that should result in a wine with more finesse, more classicism. Despite their opulence, the wines can and do age very well. They have a slightly surprising tendency, given their youthful fleshi-ness, to close up for some years before re-emerging in all their sumptuous glory. Dhalluin admits he is trying to rein in the extraction by lowering fermentation temperatures (which could rise to 33°C/91°F in the past), by regulating the pumpovers more carefully, and by opting for barrels with a lighter toast, a policy initiated by Patrick Léon.

There were legendary vintages in the nineteenth century, and some of them are still said to be drinkable: 1869, 1874, 1878. The 1900 and 1926 are also said to be remarkable. The oldest Mouton I have tasted was the legendary 1945, drunk from magnum in 2002. It was in impeccable condition; it had a very rich, sweet, cedary nose, with tones of woodsmoke and tobacco. The wine was bright and intense, with immense richness but also fine acidity, finishing with tremendous vigour and persistence. The 1947 and 1949 have a comparable reputation, but I have not tasted them. The 1955 has remained quite youthful, and has a splendid nose of black fruits and cloves. It's a rich, spicy, complex wine with a bracing quality that contributes to its length. The 1959 is magnifi-cent, the colour healthy and bright, the nose cedary but infused with Cabernet richness. Indeed it is that intense Cabernet flavour that dominates the palate too, with its tight but stylish structure, its creamy texture, its vigour, and a certain restraint that keeps the wine on the right side of excessive fruitiness.

The 1961 is justly celebrated, with a bouquet that manages to be overpowering, voluptuous, and elegant at the same time, with its superb depth of Cabernet flavour, its splendid tight structure, its dash, and its amazing length. The 1962 is also very fine, but in a more feline way; it's ultra-refined for Mouton, yet rich and seductive and with exceptional length. However, the 1964 is a let-down, fragrant but very light in aroma, with a thinness rarely encountered at Mouton. The 1965 was way past its best by 1997. The 1966, drunk in 1987, had a lovely cigar-box nose, with a succulent, complex palate, but the same wine drunk at the château many years later proved more austere and tannic. The 1970 is healthy in colour, with a fragrant nose of cedar, graphite, and tea. When last tasted in 2006, it was still sweet and very concentrated; perhaps it had lost some flesh, but it was persistent and long. The 1971 is more forward than the 1970, with a fragrant cedar and chocolate nose; but there is some bottle variation.

The 1975 is not a great success here: the nose is dense and not very forthcoming, and there is some coarseness on the palate. There's no lack of fruit on the 1976, but the nose is rather sweaty, and there is a baked character to the fruit; by now this is probably past its best. The 1978 has the Mouton mellowness and vinosity, but there's something pallid about the wine, as though tasted through gauze. I have not tasted the 1979 for many years; it had some aromatic charm, but seemed rather light overall with a weak structure that is atypical of Mouton. The 1980 was light and loose, and is certainly past its best by now. There is some charm and elegance on the nose of the 1981; it was an enjoyable wine with decent Cabernet fruit, but it lacked structure and force and had a lean finish. With the 1982, Mouton is back on splendid form, with its rich, toasty, opulent aromas; its richness and body, its spice and force, a dash of flamboyance, and firm tannins balanced by surprising freshness.

I have always liked the 1983, though it has been overshadowed by the mighty 1982. It has a rich, cedary nose, with chocolate and raspberry tones. It's remarkably velvety and sumptuous, with fine acidity, suave tannins, and excellent length. The 1985, however, is a bit disappointing, with considerable evolution in colour and aroma; there is certainly concentration, power, and some freshness, but it doesn't have the persistence and complexity of a great Mouton. The 1986 has a fabulous reputation but I have never tasted it. The easy-going 1987 was attractive when young if not especially concentrated. There is a slight tarriness and gaminess to the 1988, which is not unattractive but somewhat atypical. Some bottles have been rather austere, but most recently there is ample ripe tannin, opulence, and spice.

The 1989, tasted recently from jeroboam, has sweet, opulent aromas with a touch of coffee; it's concentrated and tannic but lacks some weight as well as elegance. However, I don't detect the excessive woodiness that other tasters have found worrisome. Tasted in 2007, the 1990 is puzzling: intense and sensuous on the nose, it also has a stewed character; the palate too is oaky and elegant, but lacks some concentration, seems remarkably evolved, and although stylish is also rather pinched. The 1994 is too extracted for the fruit, and doesn't deliver on the opulent, oaky promise of the nose. Charred new oak dominates the 1995 but there is sweet blackcurrant fruit too; it's a massive and powerful wine, with a chocolatey finish and very good length. In its youth I found the 1996 too burly and inelegant, but by 2006 it had settled down: the nose showed Mouton's usual flamboyant oakiness as well as pure blackcurrant fruit, while on the palate the wine was super-rich but still tightly wound and persistent and truly exciting. The 1997 is lush but oddly hollow, with little overt fruitiness, and the wine tails off on the finish.

The 1998 is a triumph. The nose has all the opulence, oakiness, and currranty, chocolatey tones that typify Mouton, while the palate is dense and powerful without being tough. But this needs a lot of time to become pleasurable as well as impressive. The 1999 has a powerful, oaky, savoury nose; it's concentrated, inevitably, but also has the Mouton flamboyance and a welcome touch of fresh mint on the finish. An initial greenness on the 2000 now seems to have diminished in favour of the inherent sumptuousness of the wine. But at present it's all power and mass and tannin, at the expense of elegance and accessibility. Give it time. At this stage I prefer the 2001, which has similarly glossy new oak on the nose, but seems slightly better balanced, with good acidity to balance the weight and tannic structure. I find the 2002 almost too lush and new-oaky, easily taken, I would have thought, for a no-holds-barred Napa Cabernet. It's plump and voluptuous, but there's no elegance. I am no fan of the 2003s overall, but this is a vintage where Mouton appears to have succeeded, possibly because the character of the vintage suits the château style. The wine is a touch too massive and assertive, but it certainly isn't baked or flabby. From cask the 2005 was suave and luxurious. In 2006 one hundred persons sorted the crop, and only forty-four per cent of the wine entered the *grand vin*. Fifteen per cent was used for Petit Mouton and the remaining forty-one per cent was sold off. The result, from cask, was a balanced and complete wine of great concentration and succulence.

Mouton is a very great wine, but in some recent vintages it seems to be trying hard to prove it, strutting its stuff and not allowing the fruit to speak for itself. It is, in short, rather too extracted, which ends up giving a certain uniformity to the wine, smoothing over vintage variations. It's still a delicious wine, even if a bit overwhelming. Conversations with Philippe Dhalluin suggest that these excesses will be moderated in future.

Château Pédesclaux

Tel: 0556 592259. Website: www.chateau-pedesclaux.com. Owner: Jugla family. Cinquième cru. 12 ha.
50% Cabernet Sauvignon, 45% Merlot, 5% Cabernet Franc. Production: 120,000 bottles.
Second wine: Lucien de Pédesclaux

This property was established in 1825 by Urbain Pédesclaux, a Bordeaux wine broker who bought up parcels of land close to Grand-Puy-Lacoste and Armailhacq. In 1891 the property was sold to the Comte de Gastebois, and in 1950 it was bought by the Jugla family, who also own Château Colombier-Monpelou (*q.v.*). The Juglas had been renting the property since 1931, so they knew it well. Bernard Jugla ran Pédesclaux from 1965, but seemed singularly unambitious, offering a run-of-the-mill, moderately fruity, lightly structured wine that scarcely did justice to its origins. If he was passionate about wine, any wine, it certainly didn't show.

Then in 1997 he retired (though he still runs Colombier-Monpelou), and the next generation, Denis and Brigitte Jugla, took over. They are quite candid about the inadequacy of Pédesclaux over many decades, and seem determined to improve the wine as fast as possible. They initiated some major investments, such as a new *chai* and a modernized reception area for visitors. Bernard Jugla had modernized the *cuvier*, installing stainless-steel tanks in 1991. Denis has added sorting tables and a machine for *turbo-pigeage* which can be manoeuvred above each tank and is operated for two minutes every two hours during fermentation. The wine is now aged in fifty per cent new barriques for fifteen months and fined with albumen before filtration and bottling.

The Pédesclaux vineyards are in three main blocks: six hectares around the solid little château, which lies between Le Pouyalet and the river; another block just south of the château, and a parcel near the Pauillac fire station and Lynch-Bages. In addition the Juglas own a number of other properties in Pauillac and the Haut-Médoc.

The 1982 was an attractive wine, with a warm, spicy nose, reasonable concentration, balanced if lacking in weight, and lightly tannic. The 1983 had fruit but was very forward and lacking in persistence. The slightly baked 1989 was unexciting. The 1995 was soft and plump but not that concentrated, while the 1996 was perfectly drinkable but had little complexity or vigour. The major change comes with the 2000, with its intense aromas of black fruits and liquorice, its stylish freshness, its fine balance, its persistence of flavour. The 2002 is in the same mould, with aromas of plums, chocolate, and smoky oak, while the palate is rich, rounded, concentrated, and spicy. The supple 2003 is an honourable effort for the year.

Denis Jugla is still bedevilled by the wine's dreary reputation. It has improved beyond recognition, but it is difficult for him to obtain the higher prices he needs to justify and recoup the investments he has been making. The Bordeaux crisis could not have come at a worse time for Jugla, and the many others like him, who have revolutionized their wines.

Château Pibran

Tel: 0556 731717. **Owner:** *AXA Millésimes. 17 ha. 60% Cabernet Sauvignon, 30% Merlot, 5% Cabernet Franc, 5% Petit Verdot.* **Production:** *90,000 bottles.* **Second wine:** *Ch Tour-Pibran*

This property was acquired in 1941 by the Billa family, then sold to AXA in 1987. The vineyards were then replanted and the drainage renovated. Then in 2005 five hectares were grubbed up, as some Cabernet Sauvignon, planted near Armailhac, was going to be replaced by Merlot. By this time the château had been restored, and there were plans for a new *chai*. The vineyards are well located, with parcels near Mouton and Pontet-Canet, others closer to the château, and some behind Grand-Puy-Lacoste. In 2001 AXA bought the neighbouring Château Tour-Pibran, and incorporated its vineyards. The name Tour-Pibran survives only as the label of the second wine.

Jean-René Matignon of Château Pichon-Longueville (*q.v.*) is also responsible for the winemaking here. The *cuvaison* ranges from fifteen to twenty-five days, and the wine is aged for around twelve months in mostly one-year-old barriques.

I find Pibran a very satisfying wine. In its richness and weight it is typically Pauillac, and the technical skill and experience of the Pichon-Longueville team ensure that the wine is always well made and maximizes the potential of any vintage. The 1989 has a muted, spicy nose, with hints of milk chocolate; the wine is plump if not very structured, with good balance and a lively finish. The 1990 became slightly meaty on the nose, but it's a supple, concentrated wine with a long, tannic finish. The 1992 is remarkably good for the vintage, as is the 1994, with its silky texture and vigorous, tannic finish. The 1995 has a lot of punch and some lively acidity and should evolve well. The 1996 lacks some grip, but the nose is delightful, with aromas of blackberry and chocolate, and the wine overall is forward and enjoyable. Given the vintage, the 1997 is a serious effort, with good flesh and length. The 1999 is quite oaky and has developed savoury aromas, but it's reasonably fresh and has good acidity; although ready to drink, it should keep. There's surprising greenness on the 2001, despite some jammy aromas. The 2002 is better, with its lush, plummy, oaky nose; it's a full-bodied wine with Pauillac swagger but attractive acidity to balance the delicious fruit. The 2003 is less successful, with some baked aromas, and a sagging heaviness on the palate. The excellent 2004 resembles the 2002.

It has become academic to discuss Tour-Pibran, since it no longer exists as an independent property. The former owner, Jean-Jacques Gounel, made easy-going wines for relatively early consumption. The 1990 and 2000 were both good wines.

Château Pichon-Lalande

Tel: 0556 591940. **Website:** *www.pichon-lalande.com.* **Owner:** *Champagne Louis Roederer. Deuxième cru. 84 ha. 45% Cabernet Sauvignon, 35% Merlot, 12% Cabernet Franc, 8% Petit Verdot.* **Production:** *450,000 bottles.*
Second wine: *Réserve de la Comtesse*

The Pichon estate, along with Latour, dominates the southern part of Pauillac between St Lambert and the boundary with St-Julien. Before 1850 the two Pichons were a single estate. In the late sixteenth century it belonged to François de Pichon. His son Bernard, born in 1602, married Anne, the only daughter of the Baron de Longueville. Jacques de Pichon-Longueville, a future president of the Bordeaux *parlement*, married Thérèse de Rauzan in 1694. In the years that followed more vineyards were purchased, and there were exchanges with Latour. The estate must have been well managed, for by the mid-eighteenth century its wines were fetching prices comparable to Mouton's.

Jacques died in 1731, and was succeeded by a son of the same name, who begat Jean-Pierre, who begat Joseph. Joseph de Pichon-Longueville lived until 1850. Documents in the château archives from the revolutionary period refer to Citoyen Joseph, but he didn't escape imprisonment. He was clearly a survivor, and was either ninety or ninety-five when he died, depending on which documentary source is preferred. Of his seven children, only five were still alive at the time of his death. The property, including woods and fields as well as vines, was divided between them, but the eldest son died soon after, so his share was added to the portion going to the second son Raoul, and these twenty-eight hectares were the origin of Château Pichon-Longueville. The remaining three-fifths, including forty-two hectares of vines, was left to three daughters. One of the sisters, Sophie, an artist whose self-portrait hangs in the château, was disappointed in love and took herself to a nunnery, leaving her share of the property to her sister Virginie, Comtesse de Lalande.

At first the two parts of the estate were jointly managed, even though two châteaux had been constructed on either side of what is today the D2. Pichon-Lalande was built in the 1840s, and Raoul had Pichon-Longueville built in 1851. It was only after Raoul's death in 1860 that Virginie decided her property should be formally separated from Pichon-Longueville. Deaths in the family consolidated her ownership. By this time the estate was known, cumbersomely, as Château Pichon-Longueville, Comtesse de Lalande. Nobody can manage that mouthful, so the name is customarily abbreviated to Pichon-Lalande.

Virginie's niece Elisabeth inherited the property in 1882, and it remained in the family until 1926, when it was put up for sale. The Miailhes, a family entrenched in the Bordeaux wine business, were the purchasers. Edouard Miailhe ran the property until his death in 1959, when William-Alain Miailhe took over, but a serious family row led to his departure in 1972 (he still owns Château Siran). As a stopgap measure, Michel Delon of Léoville-Las-Cases briefly managed the estate from 1975 to 1978, even buying an additional five hectares of vines. Then in 1978 the Miailhe family co-ownership was split, and Edouard's daughter May-Eliane inherited most of the shares. She and her husband General Hervé de Lencquesaing bought out the other partners and restored the château. May-Eliane still runs the property with indefatigable energy and authority. After the general died, she asked his nephew, Comte Gildas d'Ollone, to help her run the commercial side of the business. Mme. de Lencquesaing added a Haut-Médoc property, Château Bernadotte (q.v.), to her portfolio in 1997, and more recently has acquired a property in South Africa, which she is developing. In her spare time, she is engrossed in the château archives, where, in her eightieth year, she is completing the history of the property. She has created, near the *chais*, a museum relating to wine, and guided visits and tastings are provided to tourists (by appointment). Mme. de Lencquesaing is an imposing figure, warm-hearted but imperious, proud of the fact that she is the latest in a long line of women to run the estate. She has done a superb job at Pichon-Lalande, everyone agrees, and, with her fluent English, acquired in Britain as a schoolgirl, is a fine ambassador for the wines of Bordeaux. In the early 1990s there was something of a bloodbath at Pichon-Lalande; there were tensions, firings, and ultimately the arrival of a new team under the leadership of a young Franco-Vietnamese oenologist, Thomas Dô-Chi-Nam. In 2006 Mme. de Lencquesaing succumbed to pressure from other shareholders and put the property on the market. The new owners, Champagne Roederer, made it clear that no radical changes would be made in the near future, and the management and winemaking team remains the same.

It is easy to suppose that the Pichon-Lalande vineyards lie around the château on the fine plateau overlooking the estuary. Not so: with the exception of one hectare just north of the château, these vineyards belong to Latour. The Pichon vineyards, some of which were acquired in the 1680s, lie in large parcels, both south of Pichon-Longueville to the St-Julien border (and just beyond), and west of the village of St Lambert. Curiously, nine hectares lie within St-Julien, and the estate has a special dispensation to allow its wine to be granted honorary citizenship of Pauillac. Before 1959, it was bottled separately as a St-Julien. Château Bernadotte, although it lies principally within the Haut-Médoc, also has some vines within the Pauillac appellation, which have been incorporated into Pichon-Lalande, though this wine is not used as yet for the *grand vin*. The average age of the vines is around forty years, the oldest having been planted in the 1930s.

The grapes are sorted in the vineyard and brought to the *cuvier*. This is equipped with thirty-three stainless-steel tanks, but the expansion of the vineyards has brought some cement tanks back into service. Pichon-Lalande invested in a *sous-vide* concentrator as long ago as 1991, but Mme. de Lencquesaing finds it slow and not very reliable. There is no cold soak, and fermentation is kick-started with selected yeasts. The wine is blended in late December. The main *chai* is a gorgeous structure, its columns encased in wood-panelling, and modern paintings and sculptures decorate the entrance. Above the *chai* is an extensive terrace, giving Mme. de Lencquesaing and her guests a wonderful view of the Latour vineyards between the château and the estuary. The wine is aged for eighteen months, half in new oak, half in one-year barrels. It is the high Merlot content that dissuades the team from using entirely new oak. The second wine is aged in roughly twenty-five per cent new oak. There is also a third wine called Les Gartieux de Pichon-Lalande.

The style of the wine is defined by the high proportion of Merlot, which has long been a feature of Pichon-Lalande. Above all, the wine is elegant and suave rather than powerful and dense. Fruit and oak are in such harmony that the wine is often accessible quite young, but the structure is deceptively subtle. Pichon-Lalande is beautifully balanced and ages very well.

In 1992 I was able to taste a range of old vintages before a London auction; the bottles had come directly from the château. The 1925 was very faded, in colour and aroma, and the fruit was slipping away. The 1931 was similar but had slightly more fruit, though the finish was acidic. The 1937, a better vintage, was orange-red, and there was some coarseness on the finish. The 1940 had more richness and sweetness and great charm, sustained by a long finish. Another wartime vintage, the 1942, had a sweet, cedary nose, a soft texture, and an elegant if frail finish. There was far more richness on the 1955, with its discreet grip and delicious fruit. There is sweetness, intensity, and great elegance on the nose of the 1957; it was an austere vintage and it still shows, being quite hard and tannic. The 1958 is loose and dried out, and barely alive. The 1964 is a pleasant surprise: the nose is cedary and ultra-refined; the wine is not weighty but still remarkably fresh and poised. The 1966 is very good: stylish and cedary on the nose, with no lack of plump, concentrated fruit, lovely weight and acidity, and good length. The 1967, however, is loose, astringent, and rather short. There is a lovely, intense perfume on the nose of the 1970; age has given the wine an elegant leanness and fine length.

There is considerably less finesse on the 1971, which has mature meat-extract and tea aromas; the palate is soft, lightly sweet, medium-bodied, and charming – but it's fully ready. In 2007, the 1975 was showing some frailty and delicate cedary aromas, but there were no dry tannins, and the wine was stylish and clearly at its peak. The 1976 is good for the vintage, slightly baked on the nose, rounded and supple, but not very long. There are firm, oaky aromas on the 1978, which is rich and hefty, concentrated and complex. The 1979 has delicate, black-currant aromas, its roundness and refinement backed by discreet tannins. The 1980, always austere, is almost certainly in decline, but the 1981 is a great success. The nose has sweetness and finesse; the wine is delicate but spicy, medium-bodied but very elegant. The 1982 has great opulence; it's fleshy, oaky, quite tannic, multi-layered and complex, and youthfully exuberant and long, a delicious and seductive wine that will age well.

The 1983 was very successful too. Tasted recently from jeroboam, the nose, once bacony, had become cedary and elegant; it's elegance that marks out the wine rather than richness, but the fruit quality is delicious, with a smoky, minty edge, and fine length. Also tasted recently from jeroboam, the 1984 is remarkably good for a mediocre vintage. But it won't improve. The 1985 is sumptuous, with smoky, cedary aromas, very ripe flavours, intense elegance, and impeccable length. There's unusual density on the 1986, but a lot of succulence and sweetness too. Although reputed to be a massive wine, in my experience the 1986 is already quite accessible though it will be long-lived. Oak, cedar, and spice mark the nose of the superlative 1988, which is shedding its austerity and becoming an opulent, concentrated, complex, and balanced wine.

The 1989 has a voluptuous nose of crushed black fruits and cedar; it's sumptuous, hedonistic wine, with a velvety texture, perhaps lacking a little backbone and acidity for the long haul, but drinking beautifully now. When young the 1990 had more exuberance, lively acidity, and generosity of fruit. But I have not tasted it in a decade. The 1991 is good for the vintage but has become rather tarry and is fading on the finish. The 1993 is better, with reasonable concentration, some smoky oak, no hint of unripeness, and reasonable length. The relative lushness of the 1994 may derive from the presence of one-third Merlot in the blend; yet the nose is elegant and classic, and the wine is stylish if not weighty. The 1995 is a classic vintage here, with fleshy, oaky aromas suffused with blackcurrant fruit; the wine is dense and concentrated with very ripe tannins, and has unusual power and length. Initially, the

1996 seemed unusually robust for this estate, very oaky, spicy, and assertive, with a long, vigorous finish. More recently it has closed up; it remains pure and intense on the nose, but oddly one-dimensional on the palate. But I'm convinced this is a very fine example of the vintage, and will re-emerge in due course.

The 1997 is very good if not that complex. There is a good deal of new oak on the perfumed 1998, which is soft and forward, a plump, luxurious wine that seems to lack some structure. The 1999 is developing beautifully, with very stylish, blackcurranty aromas, while the palate is tight and spicy, with delicious fruit; it may lack some depth, but it will drink well over the next ten years. The 2000 is almost bursting at the seams, with its very rich, toasty nose, its powerful tannins that don't quite obscure the highly concentrated fruit, and tremendous length. The 2001 is disappointing: a slight lack of fruit and flesh, rather harsh tannins, a hint of bitterness on the relatively short finish. The 2002 seems back on form, with smoky oak on the nose and unusual density and austerity, though it will need considerable time for the fruit to re-emerge. The 2003 is medium-bodied and easy-going, with more charm than weight. The 2004 is a triumph, sumptuous on the nose with perfectly integrated oak, while the palate shows finesse and balance, with surprisingly upfront fruit and exemplary length.

Château Pichon-Longueville

*Tel: 0556 731717. Website: www.chateaupichonlongueville.com. **Owner:** AXA Millésimes. Deuxième cru. 70 ha. 60% Cabernet Sauvignon, 35% Merlot, 4% Cabernet Franc, 1% Petit Verdot. **Production:** 400,000 bottles.*

Second wine: Les Tourelles de Longueville

The early history of the Pichon estates has been given in the entry for Château Pichon-Lalande (*see* above). Here we resume in 1850 when, on the death of Joseph de Pichon-Longueville, the estates were divided among his four children. His son Raoul inherited this property, and he built its reputation. After he died in 1860, his share passed to a cousin of the same name. It descended through various generations of the family until 1933, when it was sold to the Bouteiller family of Château Lanessan. Jean Bouteiller managed Pichon until his death in 1961. His son Bertrand inherited the estate, but being still very young and inexperienced, he delegated responsibility to various *maîtres de chai*, who allowed quality to slump. The problem was compounded by the reluctance of the shareholders to invest in this large property. There was no doubt that Pichon-Lalande was making much better wines during this period. Insiders are convinced that Pichon-Longueville has intrinsically better vineyards than its rival, yet in the 1970s its wines were often coarse.

With no light at the end of the tunnel the Bouteiller family resolved in 1987 to sell the estate. The purchaser was AXA Millésimes, a subsidiary of the immense French insurance company. It did not take long before its director, Jean-Michel Cazes, and his winemaker Daniel Llose set their mark on this prize property. The vineyard area had shrunk to thirty-three hectares, the *chais* were in poor condition, and the large neo-Renaissance château of 1851, though structurally sound, was in urgent need of renovation as it had been empty for half a century. New vineyards were acquired, notably a parcel near Batailley called Ste-Anne. All told, these purchases brought the total area under vine to sixty-eight hectares. The Bouteillers' practice of machine-harvesting was immediately halted. The property had always been known as Pichon-Baron, but Cazes insisted on renaming it Pichon-Longueville (nobody could remember the full name of Château Longueville au Baron de Pichon-Longueville). When some years ago I went into print with the term Pichon-Baron, Jean-Michel Cazes took me to task. I saw the error of my ways, but have to inform him that even today everyone still refers to Pichon-Baron.

Cazes's boldest stroke was to organize an architectural competition to commission a new winery. The various designs submitted are displayed at the winery, and the winning design is all around you. The Franco-American team of Patrick Dillon and Jean de Gastines devised a bold neo-baroque scheme that is not a pastiche, but a radical homage to the age of theatricality. Most of the new facilities, which were completed by 1991, were underground and would have been largely invisible had it not been for the monumental swags and curlicues above. Floodlit at night, and reflected in the large fish pool in front of the château itself, the design makes a startling if controversial impression. It is said that the neighbour across the road at Pichon-Lalande was none too pleased with this architectural triumphalism. But a decade on, it has worn well and the drive past the château has lost none of its drama.

The interior of the *cuvier* is startling too, a circular space with leaning columns supporting a central dome. Walkways above allow visitors to survey the winery without tripping over the cellar-hands. Aesthetic and practical considerations are beautifully united. Since the retirement of Jean-Michel Cazes from AXA Millésimes, the property has been run by Christian Seely, and Jean-René Matignon is in charge of the winemaking.

Seely admits that of the present seventy hectares, only forty are capable of producing truly great wine. These lie between the château and St-Julien, pushing westwards, with gravel on a subsoil of iron-rich clay and sand, and are mostly planted with Cabernet Sauvignon. Soils with more clay are reserved for Merlot. Despite the *encépagement* figures, the *grand vin* often has close to eighty per cent of Cabernet in the blend. The average age of the vines is thirty years, and yields are kept down to around forty-five hectolitres per hectare.

The vinification is straightforward, and the fact that each tank is computerized provides Matignon with a great deal of information about the state of each lot. Blending takes place in February, after malolactic fermentation in both tanks and barrels. The wine is aged for sixteen to eighteen months in a steadily increasing proportion of new oak. In 1987 the proportion was fifty per cent; today it is closer to eighty per cent. A greater proportion of the wine is declassified into Les Tourelles than was usually the case some years ago. The second wine is aged for up to fifteen months in twenty per cent new oak.

Pichon-Longueville is very robust in style, a muscular Pauillac with tremendous intensity and panache, and suffused with black fruits and ripe tannins. The oldest vintage I have drunk is the 1955, frequently. It has leathery, meaty aromas and good fruit, but lacks some persistence and weight. It is certainly showing its age. I have had more luck with the 1957, with its sweet, powerful nose, and a palate that is spicy, intense, and quite elegant. The 1961 was excellent in the 1990s; mature in colour, and with a leafy, cedary nose, but the palate was more youthful in its assertiveness, its almost porty fruit, its spice and complexity. The 1966, drunk recently at the château, had a slightly stalky nose; it is medium-bodied, a touch lean, and slightly tarry, but not entirely without freshness. I have had varying bottles of the 1978. The first was very good, the second more earthy and loosely structured, with noticeable acidity. In any case, a wine to drink up.

I have been lucky with the 1979, which had opulent Cabernet fruit on the nose, lively acidity, and good concentration, all adding up to a delicious glass of vigorous claret. I have had one decent bottle of the 1982, though it was marred by woody aromas. More recently broached bottles have been rather musty, and lack body, persistence, and finesse. The 1985 was not bad, with sumptuous, ripe aromas, and plenty of juicy and almost jammy fruit on the palate – not complex but reasonably long and enjoyable.

The 1986 is the first wine of the new regime. It was not made by the AXA team, but they were responsible for much of the *élevage* and the final blend. It has a lovely nose of cedarwood and chocolate, but the fruit quality is some-what neutral, and the tannins remain fierce. The 1987 is a bit green. It is with the 1988 that Pichon-Longueville is truly reborn. It has a dense and complex nose – mint, blackcurrant, truffle, tobacco, oak, chocolate – and this is matched by the palate, which has concentration, extract, and excellent length. In recent years the wine has relaxed its tannic grip and is drinking beautifully. The 1989 is marked by oaky, smoky, blackcurrant aromas; the palate is spicy and steeped in black fruits. It may be a touch too extracted, but the fruit is sufficiently rich to carry it. The 1990 is, by a whisker, even better. It's voluptuous on nose and palate, and has Mouton-ish tendencies, being succulent, choco-latey, and super-ripe. When last tasted in 1996, the 1991 was delicious and long, an excellent result for the vintage. The 1992, too, was very good for the year. The 1993 had an oaky, Cabernet nose of considerable sweetness; the wine was forward, easy-going, and not too extracted. The same is true of the 1994, which also had more vigour.

The 1995 is already evolving on the nose to reveal some smoky, gamey characters. The once-tight tannic structure is loosening up to show more voluptuous, truffley flavours. Good acidity and exceptional length promise a long future. The 1996 is a touch leaner and less fleshy, but it has other virtues such as bright acidity, assertive fruit, and excellent length. The 1997 was a bit short. The 1998 was thuggish in its youth but has developed into a rich, plump wine with swagger, its ample fruit backed by ripe tannin and considerable freshness. The

1999 is considerably less extracted, and by 2007 had evolved aromas of leather and tobacco, a plump texture, robust tannins, and considerable power for the vintage. The 2000 pulls out all the stops. There is ultra-ripe blackcurrant and plum fruit on the nose, while the palate is extremely voluptuous, yet supported by big, ripe tannins. This is a remarkable and hedonistic wine. The 2001 is classic Pauillac on the nose, with a touch of liquorice; the palate is tight and powerful, and starting to close up. But it will be splendid in ten years. The 2002 has a powerful, toasty nose, with plum and chocolate aromas; it's weighty and quite extracted and is also closing up. There are dense cherry and blackberry aromas and flavours on the 2003, which is powerful if austere; it should develop well. There's remarkable weight and power on the infant 2004, with impressive fruit and concentration.

Les Tourelles can be very good, and a good buy in good vintages. I have had particularly fine bottles from 1989, 1995, and 2000.

The pre-AXA era should not be written off entirely; there were some good wines made, but there is also an annoying inconsistency, even within the same vintage. Since 1988 the wine is back on form, but its density, oakiness, and a high degree of extraction mean that it can be quite tough and inaccessible when young. But then one does not and should not expect a Second-Growth Pauillac to give its all within the first few years.

Château Plantey

*Tel: 0556 593230. **Owner:** Claude Meffre. 26 ha. 50% Cabernet Sauvignon, 45% Merlot, 5% Cabernet Franc.*
*Production: 190,000 bottles. **Second wine:** Ch Artigues*

Gabriel Meffre from southern France bought this estate in 1958. He died in 1993, and it is now run by his son Claude, while his St-Julien properties (Glana and Lalande, *q.q.v.*) are run by Claude's older brother Jean-Paul. The vines lie in a single large block west of Pontet-Canet on good, gravelly soil with excellent drainage. Claude Meffre is an enthusiastic advocate of machine-harvesting. The fermentation is unexceptional, and the wine is aged for twelve months in older barriques. Meffre made a good wine in 1995, but other vintages I have tasted have been rather simple. The proportion of Merlot gives a rounded, even jammy wine, and there is little elegance.

Château Pontet-Canet

*Tel: 0556 590404. **Website:** www.pontet-canet.com. **Owner:** Alfred Tesseron. Cinquième cru. 79 ha.*
*62% Cabernet Sauvignon, 32% Merlot, 5% Cabernet Franc, 1% Petit Verdot. **Production:** 480,000 bottles.*
Second wine: Ch Les Hauts de Pontet

The property was founded by Jean-François de Pontet in 1725. He was governor-general of the Médoc and a secretary to King Louis XV. The property remained in his family through the Revolution, as did his other property of Langoa-Barton, which was sold by his descendant Bernard de Pontet to Hugh Barton in 1821. Pontet-Canet was far smaller than it is today, and in 1840 there were just twenty hectares under vine. In 1865 the estate passed into the hands of the powerful négociant Hermann Cruse. He made substantial improvements in the vineyard, getting rid of some hybrid vines, and built the impressive iron-beamed *cuvier*. The wine was aged and bottled at his Bordeaux cellars. For many years the Cruses sold the wine regularly to the French railways, so it became well known. However, there were various bottlings, including, bizarrely, a non-vintage version, and all of this militated against the château's reputation. In 1972 it became compulsory to château-bottle the wine, and the Cruses complied at the last moment.

After the wine scandal of 1973, the Cruses put Pontet-Canet up for sale. In 1975 it was bought by Guy Tesseron, a Cognac merchant, who also owned Lafon-Rochet (*q.v.*) in St-Estèphe. For some years two of his sons have managed these estates, and Pontet-Canet is under the care of Alfred Tesseron. He often entertains at the bulky nineteenth-century château, with its panelled rooms and old-fashioned comforts. At the winery he works closely with Jean-Michel Comme, who has been the estate's technical director since 1989, and since 1999 Michel Rolland has been consultant.

The vineyards are in two large blocks, divided into no fewer than ninety-two parcels. About fifty hectares surround the château, and another twenty-eight are on the other side of the D2 road, on slopes leading down toward the estuary. This latter block is where much of the Merlot is planted. The other block is a gently undulating plateau of Günzian gravel, rising to a height of almost thirty metres (ninety-eight feet), over a sub-soil of clay and limestone. The vineyards are looked after conscientiously. The soil is ploughed, and only organic compost and fertilizers are added. Green-harvesting has been practised since 1994. In 2003 Tesseron halted any use of herbicides. The harvest is equally painstaking, since the young vines are picked first.

All grapes are picked into *cagettes* and transported to the grand *cuvier* built by the Cruses. There were wooden fermentation vats here until 1985, then they were removed, and by 2000 had been replaced again in modern versions. There is a wooden platform above the tanks, where Tesseron has thrown parties for 400 guests, and during harvest the grapes arrive here for sorting. As early as 1987 Tesseron installed a sorting table here, making it one of the first in the Médoc. There are separate sorting tables for the top parcels and for the lesser parcels; after destemming the grapes are sorted again on a vibrating table. Then the grapes are lightly crushed and fall by gravity into the vats. Jean-Michel Comme believes strongly in the benefits of avoiding bruised skins, arguing that the fermentation takes place much more slowly, and that the extraction is gentler and the tannins more supple. Remarkably, he dislikes temperature control, even though this requires him and his team to monitor the vats more or less round the clock during the alcoholic fermentation.

The second wine, which was introduced in 1982, is usually fermented in steel tanks, though many of these will be replaced by small cement tanks. Natural yeasts have been used since 1989. Comme has experimented with micro-oxygenation since 2001, but has used it rarely, and only at the end of fermentation. The Merlot alone goes through its malolactic fermentation in barriques. The wine is aged in sixty per cent new oak for up to twenty months, then eggwhite-fined and lightly filtered. Selection is severe. In 1993 and 1997, for example, two-thirds of the wine was declassified. Les Hauts is aged for ten months in older barriques in a humid underground *chai*. Such *chais* are rare in the Médoc, and this one was constructed by the Cruses. Unfortunately the humidity is so high that it would wreck any new oak barrels, which is why only the second wine is matured here.

I am a great fan of Pontet-Canet. It is obvious from the location of the vineyards that the potential is enormous. The property was not that well cared for in the mid-nineteenth century, which may explain why it was ranked only as a Fifth Growth. It's a naturally powerful wine, and the winemakers can play with the proportion of Merlot to moderate its structure if necessary.

At fifty years of age, the 1947 was still lovely, with a sweet, intense, cedary nose of remarkable purity. The wine itself was rather pungent, a bit volatile, and clearly past its best, but it certainly didn't lack character. The 1959 has held up well, though I have encountered bottle variation. At its best, it retains a powerful, blackcurranty nose, while the palate is svelte, intense, concentrated, and spicy. The 1961 is still very impressive: the aromas are sweet, gamey, smoky, and so is the wine, which is also high-toned and assertive, though just beginning to lose some fruit. The 1975 was less impenetrable than many wines from this vintage, but the texture was loose and the wine was rather coarse. The 1978 managed to be both light-bodied and marked by hard tannins. I have not tasted the 1982 in many years, but in the past I found it lacking in concentration and interest, a rather feeble effort for the year. The 1985 is better, with its elegant, minty nose, its plump, lightly gamey fruitiness, and enjoyable length.

The 1986 was a bruiser that came out of its corner swinging; very dense and tannic, with scarcely perceptible fruit. There is better balance in the 1988, though this too is quite austere, with grippy tannins and little finesse. Excessive extraction also marks the 1989, with its chewy tannins and a certain charred tone. I prefer the 1990, which certainly doesn't lack tannin but is far less effortful, so that the bright, juicy, damsony fruit emerges clearly, as does the spicy, lively finish, which is very persistent. The 1992 is green and hard, but the 1993 has firm fruit, though it shows signs of over-extraction and bitterness. The 1994 is similar, a rather tough and charmless wine, but it has a certain muscularity, and a long, peppery finish. The 1995 was very tannic in its youth but its structure suggested that the fruit would triumph in the end, and this has turned out to be so. This is a splendid wine, with pure Cabernet fruit on the nose; it's rich and full-bodied, extracted but not harsh. The equally fine 1996 shows a good deal of new oak as well as blackcurrant fruit and chocolate mint on the nose; it's dense and concentrated, but also remarkably fresh and vigorous.

Alfred Tesseron is proud of the effort he made in 1997, but I can't say I have ever found the wine exceptional. The 1998 was very powerful in its youth, but the oak was well integrated; I have not tasted it recently. There are classic blackcurranty aromas on the 1999; it's still tight but it's also rounded, juicy, and remarkably youthful. The 2000 is a majestic effort, with plums as well as blackcurrant on the nose, and a massive structure. The fruit quality is voluptuous, and this has the force and virility of Pontet-Canet at its best. The 2001 is almost as good, a classic Pauillac, tight and sumptuous, with terrific balance, fine acidity, and exceptional length. The 2002 is spectacular, with amazing aromatic complexity, packed with blackberry, blackcurrant, and leathery fruit; the attack is plump and upfront, so there is no lack of overt fruit, but nonetheless the wine is imposing and powerful. The 2003, despite a rich, sweet, oaky nose, has startling power, drive, and concentration. The 2004 is a massive, opulent, chewy wine of great potential but even this powerful wine is outgunned by the resplendent, spicy, and focused 2005, which remains balanced despite its lavish oak and richness of fruit.

For the last ten years, Pontet-Canet has been producing superb wine. If one is in search of richness, power, tannin, and complexity, this wine has it all; what it lacks, perhaps, is some finesse, and there are also occasional signs of over-extraction. But this is not a wine to be broached young. It's a Pauillac on the grandest scale. It demands patience, and then rewards it.

Château St-Mambert

St Lambert. Tel: 0556 592272. **Owner:** *Mme. Josianne Reyes. 0.7 ha. 65% Cabernet Sauvignon, 25% Cabernet Franc, 10% Merlot.* **Production:** *4,000 bottles*

Driving into the courtyard of this property, you will see the cellars to the right, and some cattle to the left. This must be one of the last outposts of polyculture in Pauillac. The small vineyard lies between Haut-Bages-Libéral and the estuary. The vines are old – up to fifty years. Until 1993 the Reyes family sold their grapes to the cooperative. Because of the small volumes the varieties (note the high proportion of Cabernet Franc) have to be blended in the steel tanks, which means that the Merlot is likely to be overripe by the time the Cabernet is ready to be picked. The wine is no artisanal product, and the Reyes are prepared to spend money on new oak and good corks. I have not tasted the wines since the mid-1990s. The 1994 was very good for the vintage, with a lot of freshness, and the 1996 had vibrant, red-fruit aromas and was marginally better than the 1995.

Château La Tourette

St Laurent. Tel: 0556 594172. Website: www.larose-trintaudon.com. **Owner:** *Assurance Générale de France. 3 ha. 80% Cabernet Sauvignon, 20% Merlot.* **Production:** *22,000 bottles*

The huge vineyards of Larose-Trintaudon straddle the road from Pauillac to St Laurent. However, three hectares of vines managed to wander just across the frontier into Pauillac, close to parcels belonging to Pichon-Longueville and Lynch-Bages. The soil is a gravel *croupe* about four metres (thirteen feet) deep, over a clay sub-soil, which helps in dry vintages such as 1995 and 2003. Most of the vines were planted in 1966. These are vinified separately by the Larose-Trintaudon team and released as a Pauillac under the La Tourette label.

The grapes are picked at optimal ripeness, and at yields lower than those of the Haut-Médoc. Winemaker Franck Bijon likes a five-week *cuvaison*, so they don't go overboard with the pumpovers and high temperatures. Malolactic fermentation takes place in new barriques, in which the wine is also aged for twelve to fifteen months, with the toast of the barrels adapted to the vintage. The wine is given considerable bottle-age before release. La Tourette is a spicy wine with firm tannins, sometimes a touch too oaky on the nose, but generous in its fruit and reasonably persistent. The best recent vintages I have tasted were 1995 and 2000.

ABOVE: Château Haut-Selve, with its lofty new winery, is one of the growing number of properties in the Graves region seeking to make good wines at a fair price.

TOP RIGHT: Modern sculpture and an austere but beautiful exterior mark the new winery at Château Haut-Selve in the Graves.

PREVIOUS PAGE Anthony Barton is Irish by birth, but both Châteaux Langoa-Barton and Léoville-Barton have been owned by his family since the early 19th century. The property is as beautiful as the wines.

BOTTOM RIGHT: In contrast, Château Bellefont-Belcier in St Emilion has retained its circular vat room, which is both practical and beautiful, with easy access from above to each fermentation tank.

PREVIOUS PAGE: In 2005 the owners and directors of the classified growths of the Médoc, Graves, and Sauternes gather by the walls of Yquem to celebrate the 150th anniversary of the classification.

LEFT: Château Pape-Clément, one of a handful of properties now surrounded by the suburbs of Bordeaux. Since this photo was taken, owner Bernard Magrez has planted more vines, renewed the cellars, and opened a wine boutique.

ABOVE: But the *chartreuse* of Château La Lagune, built in the 1730s, is as typical of the first heyday of Bordeaux wines as its winery is typical of the modern era.

LEFT: The ideal modern winery: here at Château La Lagune the vat room offers space, hygiene, practicality, and the ability to vinify wines by gravity without the need to pump the juice.

TOP LEFT: Are the grapes ready for harvesting? The best way to find out, as Christian Moueix demonstrates at Château Pétrus in Pomerol, is to taste them.

BOTTOM LEFT: Jean-Michel Cazes is known not only as the proprietor of the outstanding Château Lynch-Bages in Pauillac, but as Bordeaux's finest ambassador and communicator with

ABOVE: The dynamic duo of Florence and Daniel Cathiard have not only restored the fortunes of Château Smith-Haut-Lafitte in Pessac-Léognan, but have created Bordeaux's leading wine spa and resort.

OVERLEAF: After decades of wrangling and law suits, Alain Vauthier won full control of St Emilion's illustrious Château Ausone in 1995. Since then the wine has been spectacular.

12. St-Estèphe

There is no mistaking the boundary between Pauillac and St-Estèphe. As you drive northwards through Pauillac, just after you pass Château Lafite the road climbs toward the fantastical mock-Chinese façade of Cos d'Estournel. You are now in St-Estèphe. Nowhere else in the Médoc is the contrast so marked between one region and another. It not that the first plateau of St-Estèphe is especially high; rather, the boundary, the Jalle de Breuil, is on low, marshy land, well below the gravel *croupes* where vines are planted.

This is the least prestigious of the major Médoc ACs. There are only five classified growths, none of them a First Growth. Many of its wines used to be dismissed for their rusticity, and not without reason. In the past St-Estèphe produced some of the Médoc's toughest wines. There is exceptional terroir here, but principally along the band of *croupes* overlooking the estuary. Farther inland, the soils are dominated by their clay content, rather like the Haut-Médoc which borders St-Estèphe to the west and north.

The explanation for the region's mixed reputation is not mysterious. In the past much more Cabernet Sauvignon was planted than is the case today. Cabernet thrives on gravel soils near the estuary; farther inland, on cool clay over a limestone subsoil, it does not always ripen. Around Cos d'Estournel, the soil is not unlike that of Pauillac, as there is a fractured subsoil of limestone and of the hard sandstone called *alios* that is commonly found in Pauillac and points south, but rare elsewhere in St-Estèphe. This gives excellent drainage. In the northern and western parts of the region there are also sandier soils that give lighter wines that can be stylish if not that structured.

In recent years there has been a significant shift toward Merlot, and in most cases this is probably the right decision. Those clay soils are far better adapted to Merlot than Cabernet. At the hamlet of Marbuzet, which is not far from the estuary, there are pockets of heavy gravel soils over a clay subsoil, and here too the terroir is said to be better suited to Merlot. The problem is that Merlot, especially, can be very productive on these soils, so green-harvesting is often essential. The rough proportions occupied by each variety are as follows: fifty per cent Cabernet Sauvignon, forty per cent Merlot, seven per cent Cabernet Franc, three per cent Petit Verdot and Malbec. Where once the wines from many *crus bourgeois* were as tough as boots and took decades to become drinkable (and in some cases never did), today those wines are more likely to be fleshy, solid, and rich. Few wines from here attain a high degree of finesse, but they can be perfumed, robust, and long-lived.

The water-retentive clay soils and subsoils favour the region in very dry years. In 2003, for example, when most of the vines of the Médoc and Graves were suffering from hydric stress and sunburn, those at St-Estèphe were relatively untroubled. The vines stayed healthy and productive because the roots had access to reserves of water. Conversely, should it rain just before harvest, the clay will retain the moisture and there is a risk of dilution in the juice. In wet or cool years, St-Estèphe generally performs less well than the other regions. In wet years the drainage can be inadequate and the vines can become waterlogged and swollen; in cool years, the Cabernet in particular may struggle to ripen. When he was still the owner of Château de Pez, Robert Duisson told me: "The problem with St-Estèphe is that too much Merlot in the blend can dilute the wine, while too much Cabernet hardens it."

Gaëtan Lagneaux of Château Petit-Bocq explains further:

> It's hard to find parcels of good Cabernet Sauvignon here, as small growers tended to plant it
> on frost-prone soils in the west of St-Estèphe, rather than on the gravel soils to the east.
> That's because Cabernet buds later and is less likely to suffer from frost.

To encourage Cabernet to ripen on cold soils, Lagneaux prunes early in November, so as to stimulate growth after the winter, and he also leaf-thins as late as possible.

Jean-Louis Charmolüe of Château Montrose also attributes the toughness that used to afflict the wines to astringent tannins that were the consequence of picking too early, before the Cabernet especially was fully ripe. In the past destemming was not universal and *cuvaisons* were longer than they are today; both these factors could contribute to the rugged and astringent character of certain wines and vintages.

There are some 1,255 hectares under vine in St-Estèphe, of which just over 250 are owned by the classified growths. *Crus bourgeois* dominate the scene, and account for fifty-nine per cent of production. There is a cooperative here, to which about eighty growers dispatch their grapes, and the total annual production of the region averages eight million bottles.

However, St-Estèphe is in a state of flux. Whereas the regions to the south are fairly stable, even though châteaux change hands from time to time, here there are possibilities to enlarge properties because of the decline of the cooperative. Every five years, the cooperative gives its members the opportunity to withdraw should they wish to do so; then it clams up until another five years have elapsed. It opened its doors in 1994, 1999, and 2004, and this allowed ambitious growers to acquire parcels of vines, often of high quality, from growers wishing to leave the cooperative or exchange their vines for cash.

This has helped make St-Estèphe a surprisingly dynamic region, with many new properties that have yet to establish a reputation but are already producing wines of high quality. They, as well as the established estates, are mentioned in the entries that follow.

Château Andron Blanquet

*Tel: 0556 593022. **Owner:** Bernard Audoy. 16 ha. 60% Cabernet Sauvignon, 25% Merlot,*
*15% Cabernet Franc. **Production:** 100,000 bottles. **Second wine:** Ch St-Roch*

In 1971 the owner of this property decided to move out of the region and put it up for sale. It was purchased by the Audoy family, already owners of Cos-Labory (*q.v.*), which is located close by. The soil is Günzian gravel over a limestone subsoil, and the average age of the vines is twenty-five years. The grapes are picked by machine as well as manually. After fermentation in cement tanks, the wine is aged for twelve to fifteen months in thirty per cent new oak. Prices are reasonable.

In the 1990s this was a humdrum wine. Even the 1990 was a touch herbaceous, light, and dour. The 1993 and 1997 were simple and light. The 1995 and 1996 had more weight. The plump 1996, especially, with its aromas of black fruits and olives, was a good wine that is drinking well now. The 1998 is full-bodied and not too austere, but lacks some personality. There is a rustic edge to the 2000, which lacks complexity and is a dull effort for the year. The 2001 has more delicacy, more elegance, though at the expense of grip and stuffing. The 2002 has considerably more richness than the preceding two, with black-fruits flavours and moderate acidity and length. The 2003 has unusual concentration and power and should evolve well, but the rather cooked and flat 2005 is a disappointment.

Château Beau-Site

*Tel: 0556 000070. **Owner:** Castéja family. 35 ha. 70% Cabernet Sauvignon, 30% Merlot.*
Production: 220,000 bottles

Beau-Site has a fine location on stony soils close to Château Calon-Ségur. I have been told (this is a familiar story among Médoc *crus bourgeois*) that the property was highly regarded in the mid-nineteenth century but the owner couldn't be bothered to submit samples to the brokers charged with the classification in 1855, so the estate was overlooked. It was acquired by the Castéjas when the previous owner ran out of money, and after the 1956 frost the whole estate was replanted. The château is a recent structure. During the early 1990s only about one-third of the wine was aged in barriques, but today about seventy-five per cent of the wine is aged in forty per cent new oak for up to eighteen months.

Beau-Site first grabbed my attention with the 1990 vintage (the 1979 having been light and uninspired). It wasn't a profound wine, but it was rich and ripe on the nose, and the palate was lively, lightly tannic, and quite long. The 1993 was dilute, the 1998 juicy but robust. The 1999 is a lightweight, and the 2001 a disappointment for the vintage, reasonably concentrated but lacking complexity. The 2002 is far better, with its rich, oaky aromas, its robust tannins and ripe fruit nicely balanced by some freshness and elegance. More opulent, more solid, and perhaps less elegant, is the perfumed 2000. The 2003 is powerful with hefty tannins but little finesse. Although a touch light, the 2004 is forward, attractive, and balanced.

Beau-Site is not a great wine, but it has gained considerably in weight and richness and sophistication, and it sells for reasonable prices.

Château Bel Air

Tel: 0556 582103. **Owner:** *Jean-François Braquessac. 5 ha. 75% Cabernet Sauvignon, 20% Merlot, 3% Petit Verdot, 2% Cabernet Franc.* **Production:** *35,000 bottles.* **Second wine:** *Ch Bel Air Coutelin*

This small property is fortunate enough to possess some parcels of vines up to ninety years old. The grapes are picked by hand and the wine is aged in one- and two-year-old barriques for twelve months. It's a typical St-Estèphe with dense, sometimes earthy aromas, medium-bodied structure, and firm, occasionally dry tannins. I have enjoyed the 1996 and 1999.

Château Le Boscq

Tel: 0556 355300. **Website:** *www.dourthe.com.* **Owner:** *L'Union Française de Gestion. 18 ha. 60% Merlot, 23% Cabernet Sauvignon, 10% Petit Verdot, 7% Cabernet Franc.* **Production:** *130,000 bottles.*
Second wine: Héritage de Le Boscq

This fine eighteenth-century property, with its vines and lawns sloping down toward the Gironde, was built for Thomas Barton on a stony *croupe* of deep gravel over clay bands. Despite the institutional ownership, the property is managed and commercialized by the négociant company CVBG. It took over the estate in 1995 just days before the vintage was due to begin, threw out the old rotting wooden vats, and replaced them two days before harvesting began. A new *cuvier* was completed in 1997. Thomas Frugier makes the wines, and Michel Rolland acts as a consultant. The creation of a second wine was one of the CVBG innovations.

The vineyards are in a single block. They are planted with green cover and ploughed, with herbicides used only beneath the oldest and most fragile vines, which are fifty-five years old. Yields tend to be around forty-five hectolitres per hectare. So the aim is clearly to make a rich and serious wine. The one concession to commercial considerations has been to maintain a high proportion of Merlot, so as to give a wine that can be drunk fairly young. On the other hand, the ample proportion of Petit Verdot is there to give the wine some spice and fire.

Reverse osmosis is sometimes employed if the potential alcohol is considered rather low. After a cold soak of three to five days, fermentation begins with natural yeasts, with micro-oxygenation used toward the end of the *cuvaison*. The *marc* is pressed in vertical and pneumatic presses. About half the wine goes through malolactic in new oak, and the wine is aged in fifty per cent new oak for around fourteen months.

Older vintages were sound but not that exciting. I have drunk balanced but loosely structured wines from 1983 and 1990. There was a discernible improvement in the 1995, which had more density and depth, and the 1996 was very impressive. There were pure blackcurrant aromas, and a good deal of richness backed by ripe tannins. The 1997 had fruit and vigour in a tricky vintage. The 1998 had a dense blackberry nose and lush Merlot fruit. In 1999 Le Boscq produced a lightweight, but the 2000 was back on form, with ample fruit and spice, and reasonable length. The 2001 was more solid, less harmonious, less interesting, and I preferred the livelier 2002 with its ample plum and black-cherry fruit. The splendid 2003 has sumptuous black fruits on both nose and palate, but its mighty tannins are balanced by fresh acidity. Merlot certainly dominates the nose of the sleek, enjoyable 2004, which is balanced and accessible.

This has become a very dependable modern-style wine, well made, packed with fruit, not lacking in structure, and sensibly priced.

Château Calon-Ségur

*Tel: 0556 593008. **Owner:** Mme. Denise Capbern-Gasqueton. Troisième cru. 55 ha. 65% Cabernet Sauvignon, 20% Merlot, 15% Cabernet Franc. **Production:** 300,000 bottles. **Second wine:** Marquis de Calon*

This property, just south of the village of St-Estèphe, is the most northerly classified growth in the Médoc, and one of the oldest. It can trace its history back to the Middle Ages, though not as a wine estate. In the seventeenth century the estate belonged to the de Gasq family, and a century later, when vines were planted, to Marquis Nicolas-Alexandre de Ségur, who also owned Lafite and Latour. The heart on the wine label is an apparent reference to the fact that the marquis felt his heart was most completely engaged here. The first part of the château's name may be derived from the Latin word *calonis*, which refers to a boat used for transporting timber up and down the estuary. However, it may refer to Monseigneur de Calon, a bishop in the twelfth century. After Ségur died in 1755, his son inherited but eventually got into financial difficulties and had to sell up in 1798. The new owner was Etienne-Théodore Dumoulin. His son, of the same name, helped develop Montrose and built its château. In 1824 he sold Calon to the Lestapis family, who owned it for seventy years before selling it to the Capbern-Gasqueton family, who remain the owners.

For many years the property was run by Philippe Capbern-Gasqueton, and since his death in 1995 it has been managed by his widow. She is not the most communicative of proprietors and it took a certain doggedness merely to obtain permission to visit Calon-Ségur. To some of my questions her response was "I don't think that's of any importance."

It is very easy to pass by the property and not realize it is there. The vineyards are mostly walled, and apart from one carved name-stone embedded in a post, there is no indication of the name of the property. The château is a low-slung, rather forbidding chartreuse with an unadorned pediment and blank-windowed pavilions. But the interior is said to be richly furnished.

Most of the vineyard lies in a single block, and is identical to that classified in 1855. Another block is located near Montrose. On the north side, the Chanel de Calon drains directly into the Gironde. The soil is varied, with much gravel near the château, sand and clay elsewhere, over a limestone subsoil. The average age of the vines is around forty years, but the density is rather low for the Médoc and new plantings are at 8,000 vines per hectare. The soil is ploughed. From mid-August, berries are picked from various parcels and analysed, so as to help the winemaking team determine the harvesting dates. They are anxious to avoid overripeness.

This is not a hi-tech winery. Should the must lack concentration, the tanks are bled. Since 1994 about a quarter of the wine undergoes malolactic fermentation in barriques. The blend is made up early, and the wine is aged in a splendid eighteenth-century *chai* with stone arcades. It spends at least eighteen months in fifty per cent new oak, though the second wine is aged in older barriques.

Great wines were made in celebrated vintages such as 1928, 1945, 1947, 1953, and 1962, but there have also been disappointments, especially in the 1960s and 1970s, when the density of the vineyards was reduced and the wines were kept too long in barrel. More recently there have been some excellent wines, but I don't find the same consistency as at Montrose or Cos d'Estournel.

The oldest Calon I have tasted was the 1945, bottled in London. Though a brownish red colour, and rather meaty on the nose, it was still, in 1994, a rich, concentrated, high-toned wine with a sweet mocha finish. It was a delicious and very satisfying old wine. The 1959 was rather woody and hot, with a baked character I found rather rustic. The 1982, tasted recently, had a rich, cedary nose that was quite beguiling; the palate was spicy and concentrated, but surprisingly high in alcohol, with some astringency on the finish. There's real complexity on the nose of the 1988, a cocktail of blackcurrant, nutmeg, and menthol. It's a powerful and balanced wine, with no hard edges despite the ample tannins.

Both the 1989 and 1990 are somewhat jammy, especially on the nose. They were chewy and rather austere when young, but may have become more supple and complex with age. The 1994 has a sweet, upfront vanilla nose; it's vibrant but not very concentrated, and the finish is rather dry. The 1995 is a big, burly, brooding wine, still closed and tannic; perhaps more fruit will emerge in time, but the finish is a bit dry. There is a fine balance on the 1999, which is only moderately rich, but has some grip and complexity. The 2000 is excellent, though very oaky on the nose; it's rich and lush and forceful, with complexity, freshness, extract, and length. There is fruit and weight in the 2001, but it also seems earthy and grippy, and I find little finesse here. The 2003 is burly and hefty, rather aggressive and tannic, but does not have enormous length.

Château Capbern-Gasqueton

Tel: 0556 593008. Owner: Mme. Denise Capbern-Gasqueton. 41 ha. 50% Cabernet Sauvignon, 35% Merlot, 15% Cabernet Franc. Production: 120,000 bottles. Second wine: Ch Grand-Village Capbern

This estate, under the same ownership as Calon-Ségur (*q.v.*), has a finely located vineyard close to the river as well as another near Calon. Taking the river road from Pauillac, the property lies on the left just before the turn left up to the village of St-Estèphe. There is more Merlot than at Calon-Ségur. The wine is aged for eighteen months in thirty per cent new barriques. I don't know where this wine ends up, as the only vintage I have ever seen was the forward, supple, strawberry-tinged 1985.

Château Chambert-Marbuzet

Marbuzet. Tel: 0556 593054. Owner: Henri Dubosq. 7 ha. 70% Cabernet Sauvignon, 30% Merlot. Production: 50,000 bottles

This property, on the Houissant plateau opposite Montrose, was bought by Henri Dubosq's father Hervé in 1962. The soil is gravel over clay-limestone. The grapes are picked by hand and the vinification is classic apart from some micro-oxygenation. The wine is aged for up to fourteen months in one-third new wood. The aim is to produce a lighter wine than the Dubosq flagship, Haut-Marbuzet (*q.v.*), emphasizing fruit rather than concentration.

The 1988 is a remarkable wine, especially since it was not oak-aged. Its aromas are leathery and meaty, and the wine is rich, spicy, and fresh. The 1995 is very good too, lush and elegant on the nose; the tannins are ripe and, though the wine lacks a little verve, it has good fruit and length. The 1996 is quite jammy, as is the lighter 1997. There are somewhat confected blackcurrant and raspberry aromas on the 2000 but the palate is quite rich and supple, with good acidity. Although the wine is not intended for long ageing, it does, rather to Dubosq's surprise, age rather well.

Château Clauzet

Leyssac. Tel: 0556 593416. Website: www.chateauclauzet.com. Owner: Baron Maurice Velge. 28 ha. 55% Cabernet Sauvignon, 40% Merlot, 3% Petit Verdot, 2% Cabernet Franc. Production: 160,000 bottles

From 1997 the new owner, a Belgian, began acquiring parcels from various sources and in various locations. At the same time he bought Château de Côme (*q.v.*). As technical director for the estates he hired José Bueno, who had worked for twenty-three years at Clerc-Milon and Armailhac. Their first vintage was 1998, but the first with which they were pleased is 1999.

The best parcels are fairly close to the river. No herbicides are used and the soil is ploughed. The average age of the vines is estimated at forty years, and yields are restricted to no more than forty hl/ha. The grapes are picked in *cagettes*, sorted in the vineyard and at the winery, and fermented in cement tanks with both natural and selected yeasts. Bueno told me he does not use micro-oxygenation, but the Clauzet press pack suggests otherwise. The wine is aged for fourteen to twenty months in fifty per cent new oak, with racking from barrel to barrel.

Velge is clearly pulling out all the stops to make a good wine, and he seems to be succeeding. The 2000 is plump and fleshy, but there's welcome spice to balance the fruit and tannin. The 2001 is supple and concentrated with good acidity and no lack of underlying tannin. The 2002 is more opulent, with very ripe tannins, but it is surprisingly forward. The 2003 is weighty and dense, but it's strangely flat-footed and lacking in zest. There is some aromatic complexity on the 2005, which is rich and plummy though somewhat extracted.

Château de Côme

Tel: 0556 593416. Website: www.chateauclauzet.com. Owner: Baron Maurice Velge. 7 ha.
50% Cabernet Sauvignon, 50% Merlot. Production: 35,000 bottles

Under the same ownership and management as Château Clauzet (*q.v.*), the soils at Côme are dominated by clay and limestone. The viticulture and vinification are the same as at Clauzet, though yields are slightly higher, and less new oak is used. The 2005 is supple and balanced but lacks some concentration.

Château La Commanderie

Tel: 0556 593230. Owner: Claude Meffre. 8.5 ha. 50% Merlot, 45% Cabernet Sauvignon,
5% Cabernet Franc. Production: 60,000 bottles

Meffre is also the owner of Château Plantey (*q.v.*) in Pauillac. His father Gabriel Meffre bought the property in 1956. The vineyards are in two main parcels: one near Montrose, the other on a *croupe* near Cos d'Estournel. As at Plantey, the vines are harvested by machine. Vinification is traditional, and eighty per cent of the wine is aged in thirty per cent new barriques, the rest in tanks. The 2000 and 2002 are bright, breezy wines, fresh but not complex or especially concentrated. The 2003 is surprisingly green and has a dry finish.

Cave Coopérative: Marquis de St-Estèphe

Tel: 0556 733530. Website: www.marquis-saint-estephe.fr. 100 ha. 59% Cabernet Sauvignon, 40% Merlot,
1% others. Production: 700,000 bottles

This cooperative, founded in 1934, is housed in one of the ugliest buildings in the Médoc. Like so many French cooperatives, this one is shrinking fast as members leave either to vinify their own wines or to sell to one of the many eager buyers looking for vines in St-Estèphe. The *maître de chai*, Christian Marange, is insisting on better selection in an attempt to improve quality.

There are various bottlings. La Mission du Marquis is an unoaked wine. Marquis de St-Estèphe Prestige, which until 1999 was known as Tradition du Marquis, is aged in one-third new oak, including a little American oak. In 2000 the cooperative acquired Château Léo de Prades, a fifteen-hectare property with some old vines and planted with seventy per cent Cabernet Sauvignon. This is vinified separately and aged for twelve months in eighty per cent new oak. In 2002 the cooperative merged with another cooperative, La Chatellenie de Vertheuil.

Quality is middling. The Mission is fresh but simple; the oaked *cuvées* are rather raw and tannic and lack finesse. The wines are inexpensive.

Château Cos d'Estournel

Tel: 0556 731550. Website: www.cosestournel.com. Owner: Michel Reybier. Deuxième cru. 64 ha.
58% Cabernet Sauvignon, 38% Merlot, 2% Petit Verdot, 2% Cabernet Franc. Production: 360,000 bottles.
Second wine: Les Pagodes de Cos

This estate couldn't have asked for a better marketing tool than the design of its *chais*. This is the first building one sees on entering St-Estèphe from Pauillac, and it's hard not to be charmed by all this chinoiserie and the (genuine) carved doors from Zanzibar. It's commonly supposed that the building is the château, but there is no mansion as such at Cos d'Estournel (the owners lived sumptuously off-site) and this delightful building is none other than the winery.

There probably were vines on this fine gravel plateau in the eighteenth century, but Cos d'Estournel took its modern form after 1811, when Louis d'Estournel developed the estate and expanded its vineyards. He commissioned the design of the *chais* to remind him of the time he had spent as a trader in the Far East. In 1852 the property was sold to English bankers, who continued to invest in the estate. At this time the wine sold for prices higher than almost all Second Growths. In 1889 the Charmolüe family, which would also acquire Montrose a few years later, bought Cos, before selling it in 1917 to Fernand Ginestet. His daughter Arlette married into the Prats family, which is how, in 1971, it came into the hands of Bruno Prats, who became an internationally known ambassador for the wine. He too invested substantially in the property and restructured the vineyards. However in 1998, for complex family reasons, Prats decided to sell Cos, and the new owners were the Taillan group (owners of Gruaud-Larose and many other properties) and some Argentinian investors. This arrangement lasted only two years, and in 2000 the property was sold to Michel Reybier, a French food manufacturer based in Geneva. After the departure of Bruno Prats his son Jean-Guillaume stayed on as general manager of the property. Since 2004 the technical director has been Dominique Arangoits, who in his time has made wine in Tokaj too.

Some would argue that Cos d'Estournel is closer in style to Pauillac than St-Estèphe. It is certainly true that the vineyards share a long boundary with Château Lafite. The soil is very gravelly and there is less clay than at most St-Estèphe properties. The drainage is excellent and it is the sand mixed in with the gravel that helps retain water to keep hydric stress at bay in hot summers. However, there is a high proportion of Merlot planted, which is not the case at most Pauillac properties (Pichon-Lalande and Pontet-Canet being exceptions). The vineyards hug the château, except for a parcel belonging to its neighbour Cos-Labory. Cabernet Sauvignon is planted on the higher reaches of the *croupe*, Merlot lower down. The average age of the vines is thirty-five years, and some parcels are over seventy years old. Yields range from forty to forty-five hl/ha and are considerably lower than they were when Bruno Prats was still running the property. Jean-Guillaume Prats confirms that in the 1970s there was no economic incentive to lower yields, since this was not a factor that could influence the price you obtained for your wine. That is no longer the case.

The winery is well equipped. A new *cuvier* was built in 1984, and in 1990 the *chais* were air-conditioned. Then in 2004 smaller tanks were being added to the battery to allow more separate lots to be vinified. Prats was also starting work on an underground *chai* that would allow his team to work by gravity in the winery and reduce pumping. There are two concentrators – *sous-vide* and reverse osmosis – and the estate has not been shy about using them. Only the Merlot is cold-soaked before fermentation, which takes place with natural yeasts, and the winemakers favour a lengthy post-fermentation maceration. The different grape varieties are blended before the wine goes into barriques. The proportion of new oak used has varied considerably. The 1982 and 1985 were aged in entirely new oak, lighter vintages such as 1984 and 1987 in thirty-five per cent, more powerful vintages such as 1988 and 1989 in ninety per cent. In the 2000s it has ranged from sixty to eighty per cent. The wine is aged for eighteen months, and stays *sur lie* without racking until July. Cos is fined in the barrel, but is no longer filtered before bottling.

Cos d'Estournel is always a rich wine, with a more sumptuous character than the other top growths of St-Estèphe. But it often has a good deal of elegance, and there is nothing rustic or rugged about the wine. There is ample depth of colour and aroma, and its spice and vigour are completed by a degree of polish that adds up to a very satisfying and sophisticated glass of wine. The power of the tannins is sometimes concealed by the fleshy appeal of the Merlot, but this is a wine that can and does age well. Perhaps, when young, Cos can be a touch too concentrated, impressing rather than pleasing, but that is a quibble.

I have not tasted very old vintages of Cos. David Peppercorn has been enthusiastic about the 1869, 1870, 1926, 1928, 1929, 1947, 1953, and 1961. The oldest I have tasted has been the delicious 1970, which now shows a fine, elegant, cappuccino nose, a plump texture, a welcome touch of spice and tannin, and excellent length. The 1971, tasted again in 2005, had delicate, cedary aromas that were bright and stylish, but there was some austerity on the palate, which was impressive but lacked a little freshness. The 1978, tasted some time ago, had ripe, sweet aromas, but was rather one-dimensional and marred by jarring acidity. The 1981 is excellent for the vintage. It developed a sweet, cedary, liquorice nose, a silky texture, and a seductive quality, such was the charm and balance of the wine. The 1982 has a dense, plummy nose, a touch baked on some bottles, and the palate is still rich, dense, and tannic, with fine depth and length, if not enormous elegance. Tasted in 1996, the 1983 had a worryingly mature nose, with hints of tea, but the palate was better: silky in texture, quite sweet, with some tannic grip and reasonable length. The 1985 is very attractive, with cherries and cedar on the nose, and a palate that is still quite tight and rich, but perhaps it lacks staying power.

When young, the 1986 was a brute, highly extracted, dense and brooding. Tasted more recently, it is still burly, with rich chocolate and plum aromas, but the fruit is at last beginning to emerge. The 1987 is good for the vintage, though it's quite earthy. The 1988 is developing nicely, with dense, plummy aromas, its richness of fruit balanced by tannin and quite marked acidity. Far richer is the 1989, which has recently opened up on the nose to display aromas of plums, blackberries, and cloves; on the palate there is considerable density and opulence, and a slight mushroomy character. Some bottles have been distinctly better than others. The 1990 is more flamboyant, with a good deal of smoky new oak in evidence. It's a wine that is very powerful, concentrated, and assertive, with the fruit leaping from the glass, but it still needs time.

Even though it has more Merlot than usual (about forty per cent), the 1993 is hard and austere, giving little pleasure. In contrast the 1994 is a success for the vintage: classic blackcurrant and oak aromas, and striking concentration on the admittedly oaky palate. Even when young, the 1995 was striking and accessible. It is now in its prime, with a rich, oaky, cherry-compote nose and a firm and concentrated structure, with grip and length. The 1996 has always been open, with pure Cabernet fruit, freshness, grace, and intensity, all underpinned by ripe tannins. The nose of the 1997 is a touch gamey, but the palate is more rounded, with spiciness, elegance, and a touch of coffee on the finish. The 2000 is a triumph, aromatically reserved, but gorgeously fruity, with a voluptuous texture, and power, complexity, and a fine elegance. New oak dominates the 2001, and despite the initial opulence and grandeur, there's a fine, tannic backbone to give structure and complexity. The succulent 2002 is toasty, chocolatey, and luxurious, and the tannins are surprisingly supple. The 2003 is, for my taste, impressive if somewhat overwhelming in its concentration and tannins; it's unquestionably a splendid effort, but how drinkable will it turn out to be?

Château Cos-Labory

Tel: 0556 593022. **Owner:** *Bernard Audoy.* **Cinquème cru.** *18 ha. 55% Cabernet Sauvignon, 35% Merlot,*
10% Cabernet Franc. **Production:** *120,000 bottles.* **Second wine:** *Le Charme-Labory*

This medium-sized property, with its vines well situated on the Cos plateau, has always been overshadowed by its mighty neighbour, Cos d'Estournel. In the mid-nineteenth century they had the same owner, the British banker Charles Martyns. In the 1930s it was owned by an Argentinian family, who appointed one of their relatives, George Weber, to manage the estate. His daughter Cécile married François Audoy, and he bought the estate in 1959. Today the property, as well as Château Andron-Blanquet, is run by oenologist Bernard Audoy. In 1999 he constructed a new *cuvier* and filled it with squat stainless-steel tanks. Audoy has bought a concentrator but has not switched it on since 2001. As well as the vines near Cos d'Estournel, there is a parcel behind Lafon-Rochet, but the ground is lower and richer, so Merlot has been planted here. Cos-Labory is always dominated by Cabernet Sauvignon, and the Cabernet Franc is often reserved for the second wine.

The vinification is traditional, though Audoy uses selected yeasts. The wine is filtered and blended before it goes into barriques, where it is aged in a semi-subterranean *chai*. The wine spends twelve to sixteen months in an average of forty per cent new oak, with variations according to the strength of the vintage.

Cos-Labory has often been disappointing. It is inconsistent, producing some very good wines in unexpected vintages, and failing to deliver in some great years. There seems to be no reason, given the location of the vineyards and average age of the vines (around thirty-five years), why the wine should not be very good.

The oldest vintage I have drunk is the 1971, which twenty years on had a light, leafy nose quite reminiscent of Pinot Noir, a soft texture, an easy-going quality, and a suggestion that it was already past its best. The 1976 was a bit musty and dull. The 1986 was far better, with its chocolate-mint and cloves aromas, and a palate that developed quite fast to show succulence, good acidity, and reasonable concentration. The 1988, which one might expect to be austere, is very good here, with finely tuned blackcurrant aromas, an opulent texture, and layers of rich if extracted fruit, with good length. The 1990, which was aged in fifty per cent new oak, has lasted well. It has rich aromas of chocolate and black olive; the palate is rich, spicy, almost dense, with flavours of black fruit and black olives. The 1993 is green, bitter, and short. Two of three bottles of 1994 I have tasted have been musty, and the third was slightly bitter. The 1995 is dense and chunky, with ample fruit but also a certain rusticity; but it may yet open up. There are baked, tobacco aromas on the 1996, by 2007 a good wine with concentration, vigour, and a black-olive tone if little finesse. The 1997 has grip, rather too much so for the fruit. The 1998 has few admirers, but I am one of them, as I enjoy the wine's rugged exuberance, its structure, vigour, and length. Cherries and tobacco dominate the nose of the 2000, which is supple and concentrated, and a good if not exceptional result for the vintage. By 2007 the 2001 was very evolved, and the palate was drab and chunky. The 2002 is forward but stylish, with ample fruit and oak, but perhaps lacks some vigour. The 2003 has rich, cherry-compote aromas, but the palate is soft and somewhat flabby and it's hard to see it ageing well. In contrast, the 2004 has concentration and presence; the tannins are supple, the finish is fresh.

Château Coutelin-Merville

Tel: 0556 593210. **Owner:** *Bernard Estager. 23 ha. 46% Merlot, 25% Cabernet Franc, 25% Cabernet Sauvignon, 4% Petit Verdot.* **Production:** *180,000 bottles.* **Second wine:** *Ch Merville*

This property has belonged to the Estager family since 1902, and used to be integrated into Château Hanteillan in the Haut-Médoc, which they owned until 1973. The vineyards are in a single block, and the wine is aged for twelve months in twenty-five per cent new oak. The two vintages I have tasted, 1998 and 2001, have attractive fruit but little grip and complexity, and a slightly dry, rustic finish. Both are outgunned by the burly but sumptuous and very concentrated 2003. Older vintages have a reputation for robustness and longevity.

Château Le Crock

Marbuzet. Tel: 0556 590830. Website: www.cuvelier-bordeaux.com. **Owner:** *Cuvelier family. 32.5 ha. 55% Cabernet Sauvignon, 40% Merlot, 3% Petit Verdot, 2% Cabernet Franc.* **Production:** *160,000 bottles.* **Second wine:** *La Croix-St-Estèphe*

This rather grand château and park of the 1820s is just north of Cos d'Estournel in the hamlet of Marbuzet. It has been owned since 1903 by the Cuvelier family of Château Léoville-Poyferré (q.v.). In 1993 Didier Cuvelier renovated the winemaking facilities and believes the wines have become less rustic as a consequence – though, for my part, I have never found Le Crock guilty of rusticity. Michel Rolland is the consultant oenologist.

Cuvelier is keen on the lesser varieties here in St-Estèphe. He finds that Cabernet Franc gives interesting aromas and softens the wine, while Petit Verdot gives colour, structure, and aroma. He is clearly tempted to remove some of the Merlot and replace it with more Petit Verdot. About half the vineyards, and the better half, are on gravelly soils that adjoin Montrose; the other parcels near Cos-Labory and Marbuzet have a good deal of clay, so the Merlot is mostly planted here. The soils are vigorous, so pruning is severe to control the yields.

The grapes are picked in *cagettes* and sorted at the winery. The must is fermented with natural yeasts in cement and steel vats, and the wine is aged in twenty-five per cent new barriques for eighteen months.

The 1979 was a good wine, with succulent blackcurrant aromas and a rounded, well-balanced palate with just a trace of dilution; but it is probably past its best now. The 1985 was firmer, medium-bodied and elegant, with a gentle finish. The 1986 was quite forward and, although stylish, was not that concentrated or long. There is no sign that the 1989 is tiring: it has an evolved nose of tobacco and liquorice, and the palate has sweetness, charm, and intensity. The 1994, with its black-fruits flavours, was tannic but balanced for the vintage. The 1995 and 1996 both have more elegance, though they too are robust. The 1997 is quite rich and doesn't lack grip or length, but the 1998 is slack and disappointing. The 1999 too is rather disappointing, lacking concentration. With the 2001 there is more density, more tannin, more depth, with a core of blackcurrant fruit, but the wine has freshness too. The 2002 is similar but brighter, with livelier acidity and a spicy finish. The 2003 is rich and dense, but the tannins are too chunky to keep it in balance. The 2004 has rough tannins and seems a bit rustic, but the 2005 has body, force, and concentration – not elegant but as persuasive as a half-nelson.

Le Crock is not among the most prestigious of the St-Estèphe *crus bourgeois*, but I have always liked the wine. It's solid, rarely lacks fruit and substance, gives reliable pleasure, and keeps well.

Château Domeyne

Tel: 0556 597229. **Owner:** *Roger Franchini. 7 ha. 60% Cabernet Sauvignon, 35% Merlot, 5% Cabernet Franc.*
Production: *55,000 bottles*

This small property was bought in 1978 by Roger Franchini, who also owns the nine-hectare Château Haut-Vignoble du Parc in the Haut-Médoc. The soils are gravelly and the grapes are picked by hand. The wine is aged for eighteen months in forty per cent new barriques. The wines are lean and rather simple, with aromas and flavours of red rather than black fruits, which suggests the grapes are not picked at optimal ripeness. But these wines are clean, fresh, and inexpensive.

Château Haut-Beauséjour

Tel: 0556 593026. **Owner:** *Champagne Louis Roederer. 20 ha. 52% Merlot, 43% Cabernet Sauvignon,*
5% Petit Verdot. **Production:** *120,000 bottles*

Like Château de Pez (*q.v.*), this property was bought by the Champagne house of Roederer in 1992. It reunited two properties: Picard (since sold to Mähler-Besse) and Beauséjour. The remaining property was subsequently renamed. The first vintage was supposed to be 1992, but the château was unhappy with the quality, so it was not released. Roederer made improvements to the vineyards, some of which are over fifty years old, introduced selective harvesting, and renovated the winery. The grapes are picked by hand, and aged twelve to fifteen months in one-third new barriques. The winemaking team is the same as for Château de Pez.

The 1994 was unremarkable but perfectly acceptable. The 1995 had considerably more concentration and a richer mid-palate, and showed more overt oak influence. The 1996 was medium-bodied but vigorous and quite stylish. The 1998 is quite light, with delicate cherry aromas and a supple texture. In 2001 Haut-Beauséjour produced an oak-scented wine that is ripe, concentrated, and balanced. The medium-bodied 2002 had a porty tone on the nose that was rather odd; it has St-Estèphe robustness, and fair acidity and length.

On present showing this is a well-crafted, medium-bodied wine, Merlot contributing the supple texture, Cabernet the acidity and structure. It can be drunk soon after release but should keep for up to eight years.

Château Haut-Coteau

St-Corbian. Tel: 0556 593984. Website: www.chateauhautcoteau.com. **Owner:** *Bernard Brousseau. 7 ha.*
65% Cabernet Sauvignon, 30% Merlot, 5% Petit Verdot. **Production:** *50,000 bottles*

This property has been in the hands of the Brousseau family since 1908, but until 1988 the fruit was sold to the cooperative. There are three main parcels of vineyards in the northern part of the region between Calon-Ségur and Sociando-Mallet. The soils vary but are mostly sandy gravel over clay-limestone with good drainage. The wine is aged for twelve months in one-third new barriques. These are fairly light, sleek, medium-bodied wines with light tannins. Other than the rather cheesy 1999, recent vintages have been attractive. But these are essentially simple wines for short-term drinking. The Brousseaus also produce a Haut-Médoc.

Château Haut–Marbuzet

Marbuzet. Tel: 0556 593054. Owner: Henri Dubosq. 58 ha. 50% Merlot, 40% Cabernet Sauvignon,
10% Cabernet Franc. **Production:** *350,000 bottles.* **Second wine:** *Ch MacCarthy*

In a region where reserve is the norm, Henri Dubosq is an outgoing, exuberant man of remarkable energy and wit. He also makes terrific wine. The history of Haut-Marbuzet is long and complex. In 1825 there existed a property called Domaine de Marbuzet, which was owned by the MacCarthys, a family of Irish descent. In 1848 the property was sold and divided up into various portions, of which the seven-hectare Haut-Marbuzet was one. In 1952 Henri's father Hervé bought this estate and revived it, rather to the irritation of the Ginestet family who owned the neighbouring Château Marbuzet. At the time the négociants were offering such low prices for wine that Hervé Dubosq sold his bottles from door to door. Eventually he prospered and the Dubosqs began buying up some of the other parcels that had been sold in 1848. By 1996 the original Domaine de Marbuzet had been essentially reunited. Château Marbuzet had never been part of the domaine and remained the property of the Prats family (Arlette Ginestet had married into the Prats family) of Cos d'Estournel. By 1973 Henri formally took over from his father, though he had been involved in the winemaking since his teens. In addition to Haut-Marbuzet, there were two additional Dubosq properties: Chambert-Marbuzet and Tour de Marbuzet (*qq.v.*).

There is a good deal of clay in the soil which accounts for the high proportion of Merlot. Dubosq picks late, as he wants very ripe grapes. During fermentation, the wine is bled if more concentration is required. After a fairly long *cuvaison*, the wine is aged in barriques for around eighteen months. In the 1960s only fifty per cent new oak was used, but since the early 1970s Dubosq adopted the somewhat outrageous policy of using only new oak. The final blend is made about four months before bottling, and the wine is returned to barrel. There is no fining or filtration.

Dubosq admits that when he started using new oak he was deliberately imposing a style on the wine. It was a strategy that worked well. The wine was sweet and intense (and oaky), and tasted delicious soon after release. The American market in particular adored Haut-Marbuzet. So Dubosq has seen no reason to alter a winning formula, though he says that today he uses new oak more for its texture and svelteness than for the flavour it gives the wine. "I used to be considered a great revolutionary in Bordeaux, but now the press cites me as an example of a great Bordeaux classic," he says with a laugh. "No doubt in another ten years I will be revered as an ultra-conservative respecter of tradition."

The fact that the wines are so attractive and so delicious, despite what would seem to be excessive oaking, is a tribute to Dubosq's understanding of his terroir and of course to his skills as a winemaker. Nor do their initial charm, lushness, and spiciness fade fast. This is a wine that can age well. It fetches prices comparable to some of the more modest classified growths but few would dispute that Haut-Marbuzet is playing in their league.

Thirty years on the 1975 is still in good shape. The nose is, it's true, rather charred, and there is quite high acidity on the palate, but there are none of the harsh tannins that mar so many 1975s, and the wine finishes with elegance and length. The 1979 still had plenty of stuffing ten years on, with ample tannin and good length. The 1983 was very fruity, even a touch jammy, in its youth. The 1986 had a firm vanilla nose, and excellent vigour, with rich peppery fruit. When young the 1988 was dominated by aromas of new oak, and the fruit was immensely vivid and spicy. I didn't care for the 1993 and 1994, which had an atypical cloying quality, and only modest length. There is more density on the 1995, but the fruit is ripe and sweet. There are slightly cooked aromas on the 1996, which is robust and tannic but vigorous. The new oak glosses over the density of fruit in the 1998. It's rich, plump, and powerful, but it's quite a chewy wine. The 1999 is very complete: rich, spicy aromas and juicy, concentrated fruit backed by powerful tannins, adding up to a harmonious wine with fine length. Dubosq prefers it to his 2000, and so do I. But it's a close-run thing, as the 2000 has gorgeous aromas of blackcurrant, blackberry, and toasty oak, while on the palate there is lush, concentrated fruit, but perhaps rather less vigour than the 1999. The 2001 has less body, but it's svelte and stylish, with marked oakiness on the finish. The 2002 is even better, with its lean, intense, oaky aromas, its tight structure and good acidity, and a more subtle fruit expression and structure than is usually found in Haut-Marbuzet. The new oak is a bit overbearing on the full-bodied 2003, but the wine is very young. The 2004 is gorgeous: full-bodied, lush, and concentrated, its weight and power balanced by fine acidity.

Now in his sixties, Dubosq seems to have lost none of his energy and still conveys an almost boyish excitement when reporting on his winemaking activities. Today he is assisted by his son Bruno.

Château La Haye

*Leyssac. Tel: 0556 593218. Website: www.chateaulahaye.com. **Owner:** Georges Lécallier. 11 ha.*
*50% Cabernet Sauvignon, 42% Merlot, 8% Cabernet Franc. **Production:** 75,000 bottles.*
Second wine: Fief de La Haye

This estate was the property of the Ste-Affrique family for four centuries, and was bought in 1989 by food executive Georges Lécallier. Since then he has bought more vineyards and renovated the cellars. Three hectares are located in front of the sixteenth-century château, and there are other parcels near Montrose, de Pez, and Phélan-Ségur. Yields do not exceed fifty hl/ha and the harvest is manual, with careful sorting at the winery before vinification in steel tanks. The wine is aged for eighteen months in thirty per cent new oak. The wines have perfumed, blackcurrant aromas, and on the palate they are supple, accessible young, but lacking some grip and vigour. Lécallier wants wines that are rounded, and these deliver that for a reasonable price. They are not designed for long ageing. Of recent vintages I like the 2001 best.

Château Laffitte-Carcasset

*Tel: 0556 593432. **Owner:** Constance de Padirac. 27 ha. 70% Cabernet Sauvignon, 29% Merlot, 1% Petit Verdot.*
*Production: 190,000 bottles. **Second wine:** Ch La Vicomtesse*

The estate and château, in the northern sector of the appellation, date back to the eighteenth century. Today it is machine-harvested, and seventy per cent of the wine is aged in barriques, of which one-third are new, for fourteen months. This is a cherry-scented wine, medium-bodied, rounded, enjoyable, but not that structured or long.

Château Lafon-Rochet

*Tel: 0556 593206. Website: www.lafon-rochet.com. **Owner:** Michel Tesseron. Quatrième cru. 45 ha.*
*55% Cabernet Sauvignon, 40% Merlot, 5% Cabernet Franc. **Production:** 250,000 bottles.*
Second wine: Les Pelerins de Lafon-Rochet

The estate is named after Pierre de Lafon. He acquired the property in 1658 by wedding Antoinette de Guillemotte, who brought the vines to the marriage as her dowry. It passed through their descendants until 1820, when it was sold to M. Lafon de Camarsac. His family retained it for about thirty years, during which period it was classified, and thereafter it had numerous owners. In 1959 it was bought by Guy Tesseron, a Cognac merchant, who would later buy Pontet-Canet (*q.v.*). The property was in poor condition by this time; much of the vineyard had to be replanted and the château, a pastiche chartreuse, was built in 1964. Tesseron planted a very high proportion of Cabernet Sauvignon, but this turned out to be an error given the structure of the soils; over the past decades the balance has been corrected in favour of more Merlot. For some years Lafon-Rochet has been ably managed by Guy's son Michel, who has improved quality and, as a diversion, painted the château a rather startling mustard-yellow. He is known for his caustic wit, but when it comes to improving his wine, Michel Tesseron is utterly serious.

The vineyards lie very close to Pauillac, with Lafite on one side and Cos d'Estournel on the other; there are forty-one parcels in all, with varying soils. Cabernet is planted on gravel soils, and Merlot on the clay parcels close to Pauillac. Only organic fertilizers are used. In 1987 the old wooden vats were replaced by stainless-steel tanks. More recently sorting tables were installed for use before and after destemming. In 2000 a new air-conditioned *chai* was built, and smaller tanks are being acquired to allow for more parcel selections. The vinification is traditional, and the wine is aged in fifty per cent new oak for sixteen to eighteen months. The wine is eggwhite-fined and filtered before bottling. The second wine, introduced in 1986, used to be called No. 2, but has been renamed Les Pelerins.

The style of the wine has been changing. In the past, the high proportion of Cabernet gave the wines a certain toughness, but today the *grand vin* tends to be dominated by Merlot.

The 1961 was quite evolved by 1987. The nose was especially complex, with aromas of undergrowth, coffee, and truffles; the wine was medium-bodied, high-toned, and concentrated, but beginning to lose some fruit. The 1975 had a rather stale nose, and combined a looseness of structure with a good deal of tannin. In 1982 the Cabernet contributed considerable elegance; it's not enormously concentrated and is a touch austere, but that slight leanness gives it elegance. However, it is not a top 1982. The 1985 is very perfumed, with aromas of coffee, woodsmoke, nutmeg, and oak. The wine is rounded and spicy but has retained a good deal of freshness to enliven the delicious fruit. It is unlikely to improve further. The 1986 is very dense and powerful; it has developed leafy tobacco aromas, but remains assertive, with fruit that now seems to be slipping away. The 1987 had little to recommend it, but the 1988 is a success. Although the nose is dense and subdued, this is a plump, rich, structured wine that has firm tannins, but not at the expense of fruit and length. The 1989 has a more baked nose of blackcurrant and cinnamon; chunky and austere when young, it has evolved well and now shows plump fruit and attractive spiciness.

The 1990 is disappointing for the vintage, a rather light wine that lacks fruit and vigour. The 1993 tasted rather green and tough when young, but has improved with age, developing into a more creamy wine with attractive fruit. The 1994 has a lot of tannin, which comes as a shock after the charm of the nose; but it's fresh and reasonably concentrated. The 1995 was hard work when young, the lush fruit obscured by powerful tannins. But by 2007 it had developed spicy, gamey aromas and a more supple texture, and lovely blackberry fruit, though the finish remains a bit brutal. When young, the 1996 seemed forward but balanced. The 1997 was a serious effort, a wine of considerable density that should still keep well. Black fruits and a light leafiness dominate the aromas of the 1998, which is a full-bodied wine with swagger and pep, though marred by rather dry tannins. There's a good deal of sweet oak on the 1999, which is ripe and compact with a long, chewy finish.

The 2000 has gamey aromas, but it's a very extracted wine without, perhaps, the concentration to sustain it. In 2005 it was still very burly, and it will be interesting to see how it develops. The 2001 is impressive, with black-cherry and plum aromas, powerful but not harsh tannins, a certain solidity that precludes finesse, but it's a persuasive package overall, and better, in my view, than the 2000. I am not sure what happened in 2002, which is fresh and forward, but rather slack and lacking in grip. Yields were quite high in a year when most properties had a short crop, so perhaps the vines were overcropped. At any rate, it doesn't seem to be a wine with much of a future. The 2003 has a sweet, oaky nose, opulent fruit and dark chocolate tones, and when tasted blind it seemed reminiscent of a Napa Cabernet.

There is a nagging inconsistency to Lafon-Rochet, but at its best it is a virile, full-bodied wine that packs a punch but is stuffed with fruit and oak, and ages well.

Château Lavillotte

*Tel: 0556 733210. **Owner:** Jacques Pédro. 12 ha. 72% Cabernet Sauvignon, 25% Merlot, 3% Petit Verdot.*
***Production:** 60,000 bottles. **Second wine:** Ch Aillan*

The Pédro family bought this property in 1962, when it was in derelict condition and in need of replanting. (At the same time they acquired two Haut-Médoc estates, Domaine de la Ronceray and Château Le Meynieu (*q.v.*), where all three wines are made.) The wine enjoys a long *cuvaison*, and is aged in forty per cent new barriques. Lavillotte is reasonably fresh but lacks flesh and in some vintages (1981, 2002, 2003) it can have some astringency and invariably lacks length. The 2001 is the best of recent vintages.

Château Lilian Ladouys

*Tel: 0556 597196. Website: www.chateau-lilian-ladouys.com. **Owner**: Martin Bouygues. 45 ha.*
*58% Cabernet Sauvignon, 37% Merlot, 5% Cabernet Franc. **Production**: 280,000 bottles.*
Second wine: La Devise de Lilian

Few properties in Bordeaux have a more twisted and nebulous recent history than Lilian Ladouys. There was a property on this spot, close to Lafon-Rochet, in the sixteenth century, and it was owned in the eighteenth by the Barre family, which retained it for 150 years. By the early twentieth century there were sixty hectares under vine, but after World War I the estate was broken up and vanished from the map. Then in 1985 a certain Christian Thiéblot, who had apparently made money in the computer business, arrived and started reconstituting the estate by purchasing numerous small parcels, often from growers who were leaving the cooperative. In 1989 Thiéblot renovated the turreted château, named it in part after his wife Lilian, and constructed a modern winery. He hired an excellent team, including consultant oenologist Georges Pauli, to help create the new wine. At first everything went well and there was wide acclaim for the early vintages. But with 170 separate parcels to cultivate, and some lean years in the early 1990s, Thiéblot soon found himself in difficulties and departed.

The former manager of the property, François Peyran, pointed out that Thiéblot was not all he claimed to be. Although giving the impression that he was using his own fortune to build up the estate, he was in fact working on behalf of a Parisian bank that remains the owner. Thiéblot's departure was clearly not regretted by those who had employed him. But without its dynamic front man, Lilian Ladouys lost its lustre and was put on the market. Potential buyers, however, were deterred by the extreme fragmentation of the property. Then in 2006, Martin Bouygues, the new owner of Château Montrose (*q.v.*), added this estate to his St-Estèphe portfolio.

With so many parcels, the soils are very varied, but Peyran estimates that about sixty per cent of the property is on gravel, twenty-three per cent on clay-limestone, and the remainder on sandy clay to the north of St-Estèphe. The average age of the vines is some forty years, and yields do not exceed fifty hl/ha. At harvest the grapes are sorted in the vineyard and at the winery. After a cold soak, the must is fermented at fairly high temperatures, using natural yeasts. Malolactic fermentation takes place in new barriques, and the wine is aged in one-third new oak for twelve to fifteen months. There is an eggwhite-fining and light filtration before bottling.

The first vintage, the 1989, is still going strong. The colour remains youthful, the nose is dense and imbued with menthol and coffee aromas, while the wine remains very concentrated, spicy, and meaty, with good length. The 1990 has aged slightly less well. The aromas of cedar and tobacco are quite mature, but there's a certain hollowness on the palate, as well as slight astringency and a blunt finish. Oak rather dominated the 1993, but it was an impressive wine for the vintage. The 1994 was too extracted and dry. The 1995, as so often at this property, was very oaky when young, but I have not tasted it recently. The 1996 was more reserved on the nose, but the wine was stylish and concentrated when young. Excessive oak marred the 1997. The 1998 has remained youthful, with an inky, black-fruits nose, and a palate that is sweet but medium-bodied. There are blackberry and chocolate aromas on the 1999, which lacks some concentration. It's an accessible wine but it lacks the grip and character of the 1998. The 2000 is full-bodied and there is good underlying acidity and ripe tannins beneath the lush fruit. The stylish 2001 is very promising, with black fruits and oak on the nose; it's plump, concentrated, and lively, and the extraction is held in check. The 2002 is more rounded and supple but has reasonable freshness; what it lacks is some complexity and length. The 2003 is predictably dense but has freshness, vigour, and length as well as mass and weight. Despite attractive black-cherry aromas, the 2004 is fluid and a bit slack, but it doesn't lack fruit and acidity. A surprising blandness marks the 2005, which is undernourished for the vintage.

Lilian Ladouys, once trendy, is a wine that has passed out of fashion. This is regrettable, as it remains well made and pleasurable, if not especially complex. The excessive new oak aromas and flavours have been reined in, and the wine is more reliable, if less flashy, than when the enterprise began.

Château Marbuzet

*Tel: 0556 731550. Website: www.cosestournel.com. **Owner:** Michel Reybier. 11 ha. 60% Merlot,*
*40% Cabernet Sauvignon. **Production:** 60,000 bottles*

In the great French tradition, this château was constructed to house a pretty singer from the Grand Théâtre in Bordeaux. Her lover owned Château Le Crock at the time, and Château Marbuzet was handily around the corner. In 1918 the property, *sans* singer, was bought by Fernand Ginestet of Cos d'Estournel (*q.v.*), and after 1971, when Bruno Prats took over running Cos d'Estournel, Marbuzet was part of the package. Until 1995 this was the second wine of Cos. After it was replaced by Les Pagodes, Château Marbuzet became an independent label. The 2000 is especially good, medium-bodied but with a great deal of elegance. The 2001 is leaner and lacks some flesh, as does the chewy 2004. Despite some raisiny aromas, the blackberry-scented 2003 is an imposing mouthful of concentrated fruit.

Château Meyney

*Tel: 0556 599822. **Owner:** Crédit Agricole Grands Crus. 51 ha. 70% Cabernet Sauvignon, 24% Merlot,*
*4% Cabernet Franc, 2% Petit Verdot. **Production:** 360,000 bottles. **Second wine:** Prieur de Meyney*

The date 1662 appears over the portal that leads into this chartreuse, and that was the year when this convent was founded. Despite its monastic origins, it appears that the property was never inhabited by nuns. Nonetheless, the property was confiscated in 1789, and acquired in 1919 by Désiré Cordier. Like the other Cordier/Mestrezat properties, this was sold in 2005 to a consortium of investors under the umbrella of the Crédit Agricole bank. Georges Pauli stayed on as consultant, and the long-term *maître de chai*, Denis Rataud, here since 1989, remains in place.

The vineyard is in a single block that slopes gently down toward the estuary. There is more gravel at the top of the slope, but beneath the stones a large and unusual band of iron-rich blue clay contributes power and structure to the wine. Cabernet rightly dominates the blend, given the soils, but the Merlot here is valued, especially a three-hectare parcel planted in 1924. The soil is ploughed and no herbicides or insecticides are used. The *cuvaison* often lasts thirty days, and the temperature can rise to 33°C (91°F). Temperature control was installed as recently as 1998, and the *chais* were air-conditioned in 2002. Meyney acquired a concentrator in 2000 and Rataud prefers it to chaptalization as long as the crop is healthy. Since 1993 malolactic has taken place in barrique. The wine is aged for up to eighteen months in twenty per cent new oak, then eggwhite-fined and filtered.

The 1964 was still attractive thirty years later, with a sweet Cabernet nose and supple texture, its sweet fruit supported by some backbone. The 1978 evolved in a similar way, with ripe tannin, spice, and moderate length. The 1980 had good fruit for the vintage, but is almost certainly past its best. The 1981 was dry and charmless. The 1983 had some plump fruit but was distinctly tannic. The 1985 was always an attractive Meyney, with ripe aromas, ample ripe fruit, and discreet tannins. The 1986 was more earthy, though there was rich fruit and the texture was sleek. There were broad shoulders on the 1988, which was surprisingly soft and lush despite its generous tannins. The 1990 was perfectly sound and made all the right noises, yet it was not an exciting wine for the vintage. The 1987 and 1991 were of little interest; the 1994 had more richness but also considerable austerity.

The 1995 is, and always has been, reserved on the nose, while the fruit is rounded, even plump, yet the wine seems blunt and lacking in flair. The 1996 is more stylish, with a core of dense fruit. The 1997 is acceptable but unexciting. The 2002 is very good, with rich, ripe fruit, ample acidity, good concentration, and considerable vigour. The 2003, tasted young, struck me as rather coarse. The 2004 is rather burly, despite ample fleshy black-cherry fruit; there's little finesse here.

When I stand in the Meyney vineyards, with the river glistening below, I can't help thinking that this estate ought to be making exceptionally good wine, with elegance from the gravel gleaming on the surface, and power from the clay below. Meyney has always been sound, robust, four-square, dependable, but it has been almost painfully lacking in excitement and flair. It turns up to work regularly, does the job, and then goes home again without having said anything interesting.

Château Montrose

*Tel: 0556 593012. Website: www.chateau-montrose.com. **Owner:** Martin Bouygues. Deuxième cru. 95 ha.*
*65% Cabernet Sauvignon, 25% Merlot, 8% Cabernet Franc, 2% Petit Verdot. **Production:** 320,000 bottles.*
Second wine: La Dame de Montrose

It is a tribute to the quality of the terroir at Montrose that the estate was classified as a Second Growth just a few decades after the property was created. In 1815 there was no such place as Montrose. However, the owner of Calon-Ségur, Etienne-Théodore Dumoulin, had bought this land in 1778, and his son suspected there was a fine gravel terroir beneath the scrub and woodlands. He cleared the land, drained and planted it at enormous expense, and called it Montrose, a reference to the flowering shrubs that once flourished here. He began building the château in 1815, and ten years later there were a few hectares of vines. By 1855 there were fifty hectares in production. (Henri Dubosq points out that the peasants at Marbuzet nearby also suspected their land was exceptional, but they were too poor to afford the kind of investment Dumoulin had made at Montrose.)

Dumoulin died in 1861 and five years later his heirs sold the estate to Matthieu Dolfus from Alsace. He expanded the vineyards further to their present surface. In 1889 the property was sold to Jean Hostein, and in 1896 it was sold to his son-in-law Louis Charmolüe. It was inherited by his grandson Jean-Louis Charmolüe. He began running Montrose in 1960 before handing over to a younger team consisting of manager Philippe de Laguarigue and *maître de chai* Laurent Savovitch-Vuk. In 2006 the estate was sold to French construction tycoon Martin Bouygues. The property has the air of a small village of disparate buildings, new and traditional, as well as the château itself.

The vineyards lie in one block between the château and the Gironde, some 800 metres (half a mile) away. The soil is composed of gravel and large stones about two metres (6.6 feet) in depth, and ferrous sands. Below is a band of clay and limestone. It is possible that the iron content in the soil is partly responsible for the pronounced tannins of the wine. The average age of the vines is forty years, and the vineyard is partially ploughed. Yields rarely exceed fifty hl/ha, and the Merlot, as elsewhere in St-Estèphe, needs to be green-harvested to keep its growth in check.

In 2000 Montrose constructed a new *cuvier* and replaced its old wooden vats with squat, temperature-controlled steel tanks. During harvest, two sorting tables are employed simultaneously to feed the destemmer. The must is pumped into the tanks. There is no cold soak, and selected yeasts are used only at the very beginning of fermentation. The extraction techniques include pumpovers and *délestage*, and no use is made of concentrators or micro-oxygenation. Blending begins in February, and is usually completed by June, with the addition of about seven per cent press wine – but of course this can vary. The wine is aged for eighteen months in about fifty-five per cent new oak, though in weighty vintages such as 2003 it can be as high as sixty-five per cent. The wine is eggwhite-fined but not filtered.

The style of Montrose has changed over the years. Until the 1980s it could be tannic and austere, requiring many years in bottle for the fruit to emerge. However, it was usually worth the wait. Perhaps the introduction of the second wine in 1984 helped change the style. Montrose remains robust and concentrated, but is far more accessible young than used to be the case. Another characteristic of Montrose is that, like Latour, it often produces very good wines in difficult vintages. M. Charmolüe took some delight in demonstrating this to me many years ago by presenting pairs of vintages at the château for comparison.

At thirty-five years of age, the 1952 was just past its best: the sweet, cedary nose faded with aeration, and the wine, though still supple and attractive, was a touch dilute and dry. No such problems with the glorious 1955 in 1987, sweet and earthy on the nose, with sweet, rounded fruit on the palate, subdued tannins, and alluring elegance and length. It was better than the 1959, which was rather coarse and hollow, with a dry, tannic finish – possibly a poor bottle. The 1962 was holding up well, a medium-bodied wine of charm rather than intensity. The 1964 was a success for the vintage, with tannins that did soften with time. By 2006, the 1970 had developed intense leafy, cedary aromas, but the undeniably sweet fruit was being gnawed at by dry tannins and the inescapable overall impression was of a wine now in decline. The 1973, 1974, and 1977 were good for the vintages, but must be past their best.

Not surprisingly, the 1975 was immensely solid and earthy; it was rather lean and hard and had everything except fruit. In 1990 the 1976 was more opulent, though the aromas were quite stewed and leathery; there was ample fruit and intensity if not much complexity, but there were hints of dryness on the finish.

The 1979 was quite impressive in a meaty sort of way in the 1990s, but now seems to be drying out. There have been some woody, dour aromas on recently broached bottles, and a diminishing amount of fruit. The 1981 was typical Montrose: rich, austere, tannic, spicy, yet vigorous and long. Curiously, the splendid 1982 was never a tannic blockbuster, and by 2001 the nose was dense and cedary, with tobacco tones. For Montrose, it was sumptuous and very concentrated, spicy too, with good acidity and length. The 1984 was light but quite stylish when young, but is easily outclassed by the sweet, charming 1985, with its red-meat aromas, its ripe, rounded textures and very ripe fruit. The 1986 is taking its time. It was tannic on release and still is, though there is no harshness, and the wine has a chocolatey, mineral finish. Dourness made the 1987 unappealing. There was oak and menthol on the nose of the 1988, and the plummy fruit was balanced by assertive tannins; for the vintage, it seemed relatively forward. The 1989 has remained quite tightly packed, with immense concentration and spice. The celebrated 1990 is, if anything, even more massive, with opulent oak on the nose, and a plump texture that becomes explosive as the powerful tannins kick in; the length of flavour is formidable. The 1993 has good blackberry fruit; there's not much charm but the wine seems quite structured. The 1994 is chunky but rich and compact, with a sweet, persistent finish. There is a cocktail of aromas on the fine 1995: damsons, chocolate, oak, and mint. It's full-bodied and robust, with a firm, mineral finish. When last tasted in 2000, the 1996 still seemed unformed. There was fine Cabernet fruit and oak on the nose, but the palate was austere, highly concentrated, and tight, but it seems very complete. The 2000 has super-ripe oaky aromas, but the palate is very backward, highly concentrated and pungent, but for now the tannins rather overwhelm the undoubtedly rich fruit. The toasty 2001 is rugged and earthy now, and somewhat lacking in elegance, but needs some years to emerge from its shell. The 2002 is a tad disappointing, with ample lush fruit but an underlying hollowness and lack of freshness. Perhaps a poor bottle. The 2003 is an amiable monster: very rich and powerful, with splendid plummy fruit, ample ripeness and persistence, and better length than most wines from this torrid year.

Château Les Ormes-de-Pez

Pez. Tel: 0556 732400. Website: www.ormesdepez.com. **Owner:** *Jean-Michel Cazes and family. 33 ha.*

55% Cabernet Sauvignon, 35% Merlot, 10% Cabernet Franc. **Production:** *190,000 bottles*

This fine property, of eighteenth-century origin, has belonged to the Cazes family since 1940. The vineyards are quite widely spread. About one-third is near the house on gravel and clay; another third is just west of the cooperative on gravel and sand; and the rest, near Tronquoy-Lalande, is pure gravel. Six hectares were lost to frost in 1985 and had to be replanted, so the average age of the vines is only around twenty-five years. The vinification is traditional. The wine is aged in barriques for fifteen months, in about forty per cent new oak. Until 2000 only about ten per cent new oak was used, but the proportion has been increased. The eighteenth-century *chai* was renovated in 1993.

Ormes-de-Pez is a generously flavoured wine, usually full-bodied and invariably satisfying. It is not especially subtle and rarely complex, but it has ample fruit and ages well. Most of all it has drinkability, and doesn't try too hard to impress.

The 1959 was certainly fading by 2004, and the brick-red colour was not encouraging, but the nose was very attractive, leafy and cedary with cappuccino tones; the wine lacks weight and complexity but still has a sweet finish. The 1962 was similar, especially aromatically, but it was more stylish and showed more freshness and charm. The 1970 had a sweet blackcurrant nose and masses of flavour in the 1980s, but I have not tasted it recently. The 1975 is a pleasant surprise, a wine that is rich and supple, with reasonable concentration and no tough tannins. The 1979 is a medium-bodied wine that evolved fast. There are some mature leathery aromas on the 1982, which is still a delicious wine, concentrated but supple, with fine acidity. The 1985, recently drunk from double magnum, had smoky cherry-pie aromas, and had retained its sweet seductive charm. The 1986 was tough and brooding when young but I have not tasted it in many years. The 1984 and 1987 lacked substance. With 1988, the estate presented a different face, as this was earthy and tannic, even at ten years of age, and there was a distinct lack of fruit.

The 1989 is back on form, with cedar, bacon, and blackcurrant on the nose; the wine is still rich, dense, and chocolatey, with a long, spicy finish. The 1990 is impressive too: the nose reminds me of glacé cherries as well as woodsmoke, and there is richness as well as freshness on the palate. The liquorice-scented 1991 was good for the vintage, if on the chunky side. The 1994 had charm, liveliness, stylishness, and persistence, with a peppery finish. The 1995 is solid and dense and less succulent than usual. The 1996 is better. The aromas are a complex blend of blackcurrant, vanilla, and mint; it's the acidity, the lively tannins, and the overall stylishness that are striking. The 1997 is good for the year, the 1998 pleasant enough but less fleshy than expected. In contrast, the 1999 seems very complete, rather closed on the nose, but juicy and accessible, yet not without structure. The 2000 has closed up, and the lush fruit and fresh acidity are, no doubt temporarily, in retreat. The 2001 has charm. It's fresh and airy rather than complex, but it's highly drinkable. The 2002 shows great promise, with lovely ripe cherry fruit, good acidity, and considerable elegance. The 2003 is a forward wine with unexpected charm and silkiness.

Château Petit Bocq

*Pez. Tel: 0556 593569. Website: www.chateau-petit-bocq.com. **Owner:** Dr. Gaëtan Lagneaux. 15.5 ha. 55% Merlot, 43% Cabernet Sauvignon, 2% Cabernet Franc. **Production:** 100,000 bottles*

This fine property is an excellent example of the "new" St-Estèphe. The vineyards (only two hectares, near Marbuzet) were assembled in 1971 by the Souquet family, and the first vintage was 1972. In 1993, Francis Souquet, the vineyard manager at Ducru-Beaucaillou, sold the property to a Belgian doctor called Gaëtan Lagneaux. His family already owned a holiday home at St-Seurin, but Lagneaux was keen to make wine and had been keeping an eye out for a small property. Once he had acquired Petit Bocq, he kept buying parcels as they came onto the market, and has accumulated eighty of them, mostly from former members of the cooperative. He also bought some ruinous buildings at Pez, which he converted into a serviceable winery. At first Lagneaux had a local grower tend the vines on his behalf, but he soon realized that he couldn't be a commuting wine producer, and settled in St-Estèphe full-time.

Most of the vineyards are on gravel or gravelly clay, though about ten per cent are on sandy soils. The average age of the various parcels is quite high, but until 1999 there was too much Merlot, resulting in up to eighty per cent Merlot in the final blend. Green-harvesting keeps yields modest. The grapes are sorted three times: in the vineyard, and before and after destemming. Lagneaux is a strong believer in a week-long cold soak under dry ice, the idea being to obtain softer tannins and more forward wines. Thereafter the wine is fermented in steel tanks with selected yeasts, pumpovers, and *pigeage*. About half the wine undergoes its malolactic fermentation in barriques. Petit Bocq is aged for twelve months in forty per cent new oak, and eggwhite-fined but not filtered.

There is no second wine, but there is a small production of rosé made by bleeding the tanks. The 1995 is oaky but has the concentration and robustness of the vintage. The 1996 is more elegant but less complex by a long way. There is too much oak for the fruit in the 1997, which is otherwise a supple wine that's ready to drink. There are stylish, blackcurranty aromas on the 1998, but the wine is over-extracted and lacks finesse. The 1999 has well-integrated oak on the nose, and with some bottle-age it has become more supple, with lush black-fruit flavours. There is a big step up in quality from 2000 onwards, and the 2000 itself is delicious despite a pronounced oakiness. The Cabernet Sauvignon seems much more evident on the 2002, there is much more finesse overall, and the fruit quality is dense without being too extracted or dour. Extraction is rather too evident in 2003, and the wine lacks persistence. The 2004 has admirable savoury black-fruits aromas, a delicious succulence, and big ripe tannins backing the weight of fruit. The 2004 has admirable savoury, black-fruits aromas, a delicious succulence, and big, ripe tannins backing the weight of fruit. Petit Bocq has become a fine, if forceful, wine that combines plump fruit with a firm structure.

Château La Peyre

Tel: 0556 593251. Owner: René Rabiller. Cru artisan. 5 ha. 50% Cabernet Sauvignon, 50% Merlot.
Production: 30,000 bottles. Second wine: Ch Clos du Moulin

This small estate, composed of parcels scattered around the region, sold its crop to the cooperative until the mid-1990s. The only vintages I have tasted, the 2000 and 2001, were very enjoyable, with black-cherry and plum aromas, plump Merlot-ish fruit but good tannic backbone.

Château de Pez

Pez. Tel: 0556 593026. Owner: Champagne Louis Roederer. 26 ha. 45% Cabernet Sauvignon, 43% Merlot,
9% Cabernet Franc, 3% Petit Verdot. Production: 150,000 bottles. Second wine: Ch La Salle de Pez

It was a member of the celebrated Pontac family, Jean de Pontac, who acquired the property in 1585, though it is unlikely that vines were planted by him at this time. It passed through many hands until it was acquired by the Dousson family in 1955. Robert Dousson made excellent wines here and the property became well known and well respected in the 1970s and 1980s. However in 1995 he sold the estate to Roederer, the Champagne house which also acquired Haut-Beauséjour (*q.v.*). The director of the estate is the highly articulate Philippe Moureau.

The vineyard is in a single block around the château. Günzian gravel overlays a clay-limestone subsoil. The *encépagement* has altered over the years. Under Dousson there was seventy per cent Cabernet Sauvignon. He was wary about Merlot, which he felt was too generous in its yields. The Roederer team have not only increased the proportion of Merlot, but raised the trellising to increase the surface of foliage, so as to speed up maturation. The soil is ploughed and they aim for yields of no more than fifty hl/ha.

Since 1995 the grapes have been sorted in the vineyard and the winery. The wooden vats used by Dousson have been retained, but are now equipped with cooling apparatus and some smaller tanks have been added to allow for more separate vinifications. The wine is aged for twelve to sixteen months in forty per cent new oak, and twenty-five per cent of the wine undergoes malolactic fermentation in new barrels. Racking usually ceases after six months of ageing. The wine is unfiltered. There has inevitably been a change in style since Roederer bought this estate. Dousson made elegant, occasionally austere wines that needed bottle-age for their fruit to emerge. There was some bottle variation, and unclean tones in some wines suggested winery hygiene was not always ideal. Under Roederer, with the higher proportion of Merlot, the wine has become more supple, more user-friendly.

In 1970 Dousson vinified all the varieties separately and aged a single barrique from each; each barrique was bottled separately. It was just a curiosity, but it gave those who encountered a bottle an opportunity to taste, as I did in 1986, pure Petit Verdot from Pez. It was still soft and ripe, with fine fruit and spice. The commercially released 1970, tasted in 1993, had a chocolatey nose; the wine was chunky and dense, undeniably concentrated but lacking elegance. The 1971 in 1994 had a sweet nose, and the wine seemed at its peak, still vibrant, with just a touch of dryness on the finish. The 1980 was good for the vintage, and fully ready within ten years. I tasted the 1982 frequently and the good bottles were soft, plummy, and had reasonable length. The 1986, tasted twice, was coarse and dour. However, the 1988 had robust blackberry aromas, and was a ripe, succulent wine, spicy and high-toned, and with good length. Rather surprisingly, the 1994 was a fairly lush but structured wine.

The first vintage aged, if not vinified, by Roederer, was the 1995; it had a spicy Cabernet nose, and was rather fat and forward, but none the worse for that. There are discreet black-cherry aromas on the 1996, and the wine, though fruity, is rather hollow. The 1998 is a pleasant surprise, stylish and delicate, with some youthful zest that allows the fruit to glide along the palate. The 1999 has developed well, with sweet, lush aromas, and it's rich and concentrated on the palate with integrated tannins. There is more overt oakiness on the 2000, with its exuberant aromas of blackcurrant and chocolate-mint; this is a rich, full-bodied wine with well-judged extraction and a reasonable degree of elegance. The 2001 is similar but fresher, with less complexity but more charm. Particularly harmonious and stylish is the 2002, which resembles the 2000 aromatically, but has a touch more intensity. But the slack 2003 is seriously disappointing.

Château Phélan-Ségur

*Tel: 0556 597400. Website: www.phelansegur.com. **Owner:** Thierry Gardinier. 90 ha. 49% Cabernet Sauvignon,
49% Merlot, 2% Cabernet Franc. **Production:** 550,000 bottles. **Second wine:** Frank Phélan*

This handsome château, the centrepiece of a building complex much expanded by recent construction, stands on the edge of the village of St-Estèphe. The property was assembled in the early nineteenth century by Bernard Phélan, of Irish descent, and by the 1860s this was the largest wine estate in St-Estèphe. His son Frank built the château but had no heirs, so the estate was sold in 1883 to the Delon family. The Delons made very good wine here, but ran into some family difficulties and, after the death of Roger Delon in 1984, the estate was put on the market by Guy Delon, who still owns properties in the Médoc. Xavier Gardinier, then head of Champagne Lanson, got to hear about this, and moved fast. Within three days he had viewed the property and made his offer, before other prospective purchasers could get a look in. Since 1993 his son Thierry has been running the estate.

The Gardiniers got off to a bad start, through no fault of their own. They began to commercialize the preceding vintages, but customers expressed dissatisfaction with the 1983, which was clearly tainted. The villain turned out to be an insecticide that left a residue which found its way into the bottled wine. What was worse, the 1984 and 1985 were equally tainted. The Gardiniers recalled the 1983 and halted distribution of the 1984 and 1985. The loss of income must have been staggering, though later recouped in part by legal action against the manufacturers of the product, but it was essential to retain the confidence of the market. The Gardiniers also invested in a new winery in 1988 and renovated the château.

Only eight hectares of vines are near the château, and the main sector, some forty hectares, lies near Montrose. There are twenty-five more hectares near Calon-Ségur. In 2002 the estate was expanded further when Gardinier bought Château Houissant, a twenty-five-hectare property high on the plateau just inland from Montrose. Winemaker Alain Coculet asserts that this substantial addition will not alter the character of Phélan-Ségur. There is always the possibility of declassification, especially for young vines. In 1986 the Gardiniers introduced the second wine, Frank Phélan, and there is also a third wine called Croix Bonis. By the late 1990s only about half the crop was used for the *grand vin*. The oldest vines are some sixty-five years old, and the average age is around twenty-five years. Thierry Gardinier aims for an average yield of fifty hl/ha, which is achieved by green-harvesting. Phélan-Ségur was one of the first Médoc châteaux to install a sorting table in 1987. From 1993 onwards parcel selection became stricter, which has also improved the quality of the wine.

Thierry Gardinier finds his reverse-osmosis machine a useful tool. The must is fermented with selected yeasts. Gardinier doesn't want excessive extraction, as he is seeking to produce an elegant wine; any lack of grip can be adjusted by the addition of press wine. The wine is aged for about sixteen months in fifty per cent new barriques, mostly from the local cooper Berger.

Gardinier is emphatic about the style of wine he wants to produce:

> I want to keep making claret, and I certainly don't want a style imposed on my wines by the
> press or anyone else. I can easily make wines that will appeal to Parkerites by lowering yields,
> but then I will have a small quantity of wine that only collectors can afford. Volume is
> important for Bordeaux. And reducing my volumes and increasing my prices would mean that
> I would risk losing customers. I want to make wines that will be drunk to the dregs at dinner.

The 1961 was still in fine form in 1996, with a mellow, earthy nose, and lush fruit sustained by robust tannins and a long, elegant finish. The 1982 had slightly baked aromas, and the wine was chunky and rather clumsy. The 1988 was a rigid wine when young, but by 2006 it had gained in briskness and liveliness, if not in complexity. The 1989 is a great success, with its sweet, elegant, minty nose, a soft, silky texture, and charm rather than weight. The 1990 is concentrated and slightly austere, but finely balanced. The 1991 was elegant and lively but was fully ready some years ago. The 1992 was a bit feeble, but the 1993 was a success for the vintage, tannic but also supple, balanced, and reasonably long. The 1994 was balanced but lighter.

There is real complexity on the 1995. The aromas are opulent and quite oaky, almost gamey, with a touch of mocha; it's juicy and full-bodied, with a lively finish. The 1996 at first lacked some zest and was somewhat four-square, but it has evolved well and is now charming and stylish. The 1997 is light but balanced and fully ready to drink. The firmness of the vintage is apparent on the 1998, which is in a classic style but lacks a little finesse. Perhaps there is a touch too much oak on the 1999, which comes over as somewhat lean, even under-nourished. The 2000 has elegant blackberry aromas. It's a rich, harmonious wine, backed by ripe tannins and good acidity. The nose is similar on the 2001, with a touch more oak evident; it's typical Phélan in its discretion and elegance, but it doesn't lack concentration and spice. The 2002 has more weight and succulence, with more density than usual, and considerable persistence. The 2003 is a richer, more brawny wine, but the texture is velvety and there are no harsh tannins, making it exceptional for the vintage. The 2004 is a return to typicity, elegant, fresh, and supple. Despite some invigoratingly spicy aromas, the 2005 is a slight disappointment; it's in the usual style and doesn't lack grip, but perhaps this great vintage should have made greater demands.

Not everyone likes the Phélan style, as Thierry Gardinier is the first to admit. It is not a wine that's weighty or fleshy, and what seems to be a lack of fruit can give a certain austerity when the wine is young. Phélan is a wine for the dining table, not the tasting bench.

Château Picard

Tel: 0556 560430. Website: www.mahler-besse.com. Owner: Mähler-Besse. 8 ha. 85% Cabernet Sauvignon, 15% Merlot. Production: 60,000 bottles. Second wine: Les Ailes de Picard

When in 1995 Roederer bought the vineyards that were to become Haut-Beauséjour, it decided to dispose of Picard, apparently because the density of planting differed from that at its other St-Estèphe properties. In 1997 it found a purchaser in this distinguished Bordeaux négociant. The vineyards are dispersed and have an unusually high proportion of Cabernet Sauvignon. The grapes are picked by hand and aged for up to fourteen months in thirty per cent new barriques.

The 1996 was austere and tight. The 1998 is light on the nose, but it's quite a rich wine, robust initially, though the finish is weak. The 2001 has a sweet, oaky nose of some charm, but this is a medium-bodied wine with attractive fruit and light acidity, but little depth and persistence. Although the attack of the 2004 is rich and positive, the wine becomes leaner on the palate, and seems somewhat undernourished.

Château Pomys

Tel: 0556 593226. Website: www.chateaupomys.com. Owner: François Arnaud. 12 ha. 60% Cabernet Sauvignon, 30% Merlot, 10% Cabernet Franc. Production: 100,000 bottles

This property has passed through the hands of all the leading families of the region: d'Estournel, Charmolüe, and Ginestet. Unfortunately, as the property changed owners, the vineyards became scattered. In 1951 the Arnaud family bought an estate that had shrunk to four hectares; they restored it and acquired more vineyards. In 1988 the Arnauds bought the château itself and converted it into a hotel. The family also own Château St-Estèphe (*q.v.*).

The main vines are in a single parcel near Marbuzet. The average age of the vines is twenty-five years, and they are picked by hand. The wine is aged for twelve months in up to thirty per cent new oak, and the aim is to make a wine that is enjoyable young.

The 1970 had aged well after twenty years, with cloves on the nose; it was ripe and gentle and fully ready. There were tobacco and leather aromas on the 1975, but the palate was dry. The 1976 was better, but still had an inherent burliness. There is firm Cabernet fruit evident in the 1986, but it's a tough wine. The best Pomys I have tasted is the 1995, which has more spice, complexity, and length. Recent vintages have been disappointing. The 1999 is supple and upfront, with no depth or structure. There's some greenness on the 2000, and a similar greenness and some dilution on the 2001, which finishes short, as does the unappealing 2003.

Château St-Estèphe

*Tel: 0556 593226. Website: www.chateaupomys.com. **Owner:** François Arnaud. 12 ha. 55% Cabernet Sauvignon, 35% Merlot, 5% Cabernet Franc, 5% Petit Verdot and Malbec. **Production:** 100,000 bottles.*

Second wine: Ch Tour-Coutelin

This property is under the same ownership and management as Château Pomys (*q.v.*), but the wines are slightly cheaper. The vineyards are dispersed throughout the appellation, with a major parcel near Le Crock, but overall there is more clay than at Pomys. The vinification and ageing are identical at both properties. The wines lack succulence and complexity, and some green, sharp flavours suggest that the grapes are picked too early.

Château Ségur de Cabanac

*Tel: 0556 597010. **Owner:** Guy Delon. 7 ha. 68% Cabernet Sauvignon, 32% Merlot. **Production:** 45,000 bottles*

It must be galling for Guy Delon to look up the slope to Phélan-Ségur and recall that this splendid château used to be in his family. Nonetheless, Delon is left with a property in St-Julien (Château Moulin de la Rose, *q.v.*) as well as Ségur de Cabanac, which he assembled from 1984 onwards by buying twelve parcels from former cooperative members. He built a winery down by the port of St-Estèphe. The chain-smoking Delon has a voice as gravelly as his vineyards, which are well located near Calon-Ségur, Meyney, and Phélan-Ségur. The vinification is traditional, mostly relying on natural yeasts. The wine is aged for eighteen to twenty months in one-third new barrels, all from the local Berger cooperage.

The 1995 was austere and lacked fruit. The 2000 had a reserved nose with a whiff of tobacco (or perhaps I picked up the scent from M. Delon's brimming ashtray); it's lush and full-bodied, with delicious blackcurrant fruit backed by firm tannins. The 2001 is possibly even better, with very ripe fruit and more apparent acidity and zest than the 2000. These are not the cheapest wines among the *crus bourgeois*, but recent vintages have been concentrated and serious.

Château Sérilhan

*Pez. Tel: 0556 593883. Website: www.chateau-serilhan.com. **Owner:** Didier Marcelis. 20 ha. 54% Cabernet Sauvignon, 34% Merlot, 6% Cabernet Franc, 6% Petit Verdot. **Production:** 120,000 bottles. Second wine: Ch Moutinot*

This property was quietly cultivated by the Marcelis family for many years, and most of the fruit was dispatched to the cooperative. In the late 1980s the estate was expanded when it was merged with Château Moutinot, a seven-hectare property on sandier soils. In 1998 Jean Marcelis began ageing some of the wine in barriques. But in 2002 he told his son Didier that, unless he was prepared to take over running the estate, it would have to be sold. Didier Marcelis, however, was in his late forties, enjoying a high-flying career in hi-tech industries far from the Médoc. However, he did return to St-Estèphe, bringing with him a devotion to management-speak and a fiancée with skills in wine marketing. He wanted Sérilhan to be a wine that would appeal to modern tastes. He hired Olivier Douga and Philippe Lespy as consultants, and they proposed some radical changes: Marcelis began ploughing the soil, used only organic fertilizers, and heightened the canopy. He also bought some additional parcels to integrate into Sérilhan, and planted a little Petit Verdot.

The grapes are sorted twice, and fermented in cement and steel tanks. In 2003 Marcelis experimented with the dry-ice technique practised by Gaëtan Lagneaux at Château Petit Bocq (*q.v.*). He also introduced mechanical *pigeage*. The wine is aged for twelve months in forty per cent new barriques, and he is experimenting with lees-stirring to give the wine more fat. The aim is to make an opulent, modern-style wine that will appeal to international consumers.

The 2000 and 2001, aged in ten per cent new oak, are old-style Sérilhan, medium-bodied, attractive, and forward, but lacking structure and length. There is a major change with the 2002, with its dense, spicy, liquorice nose; it's rich and juicy, with bright acidity and fair length. The 2003 is rich but more heavy-handed. The 2005, however, vindicates Marcelis's efforts: it's pungent and powerful, but the fruit shines through.

Château Tour de Marbuzet

Tel: 0556 593054. Owner: Henri Dubosq. 5 ha. 40% Merlot, 40% Cabernet Sauvignon, 20% Cabernet Franc.
Production: 35,000 bottles

This small property, was integrated into Cos d'Estournel when the Ginestets owned it. In 1932 it was sold, and in 1981 it was bought by Henri Dubosq. The vineyards are close to Château Pomys on gravel soils over clay-limestone. The vinification is traditional, and the wine is aged for fourteen months in twenty-five per cent new barriques. This is intended as a lighter wine for restaurants, and it enjoys a strong following in Jersey.

The 1998 has sweet, meaty aromas, and is a supple, balanced, medium-bodied wine that is now ready. The 2000 has a slightly confected nose, suggesting blackcurrant pastilles; it's quite tannic but has ample fruit and acidity, and considerable length. The 2001 has charming red-fruits aromas and flavours, and is refreshed by quite high acidity that gives a lingering finish.

Château Tour de Pez

Tel: 0556 593160. Owner: Philippe Bouchara. 30 ha. 45% Cabernet Sauvignon, 40% Merlot, 10% Cabernet Franc,
5% Petit Verdot. Production: 200,000 bottles. Second wine: "T" de Tour de Pez

This historic estate belonged in the seventeenth century to the abbey of nearby Vertheuil, and was given its current name in 1931. When Bouchara bought this property in 1989, it was in ruinous condition, and there were only eleven hectares under vine. The whole crop was sold to the cooperative. Today the purchase of additional parcels has expanded the domaine to thirty hectares, located all over St-Estèphe. Half the soils are gravel, half clay-limestone, and yields are kept below fifty hl/ha.

The harvest is manual and the grapes are sorted in the vineyard and the winery, which was modernized by Bouchara. Vinification is traditional, and the wine is aged for fourteen months in forty per cent new barriques. The second wine is aged in ten per cent new oak, but there is an additional wine made in much larger quantities. This is Château Les Hauts de Pez, which is produced essentially from young Merlot vines, and aged in older barrels.

Tour de Pez made a light but elegant 1991. The 1996 is dull and soupy, the 1997 simple and fairly short. There is much more substance in the 1998, with its sweet, oaky nose, its juicy blackberry fruit and moderate length. The 1999 is fresher and livelier, not a profound wine but well balanced and enjoyable. The 2000 is not markedly better, but has some rich cherry fruit and ample vigour and length. The 2001 has fruity aromas but lacks depth and length. Although austere in its youth, the 2004 shows promise, though it's far from exciting.

These are well-made, middle-of-the-road wines, fruity and easy to drink, with reasonable liveliness and depth. They are perhaps a touch overpriced for the quality.

Château Tour des Termes

St-Corbian. Tel: 0556 593289. Website: www.chateautourdestermes.com. Owner: Jean Anney. 16 ha. 50% Merlot,
50% Cabernet Sauvignon. Production: 130,000 bottles. Second wine: Les Aubarèdes du Ch Tour des Termes

The Anney family own a group of properties in St-Estèphe and the Haut-Médoc. Jean Anney is the proprietor, and his son Christophe has been making the wines for some years. This estate, which they have owned since 1939, consists of two major parcels: eight hectares on clay-limestone soils near the château, and seven on a gravel *croupe* in front of Château de Pez.

Most of the vines are machine-harvested, and since 2001 it has been possible to concentrate the must by reverse osmosis. Selected yeasts are used just to kick-start the fermentation, which takes place in steel tanks with pumpovers and *délestage*. The Merlot undergoes malolactic fermentation in new barriques, and the blended wine is aged for twelve to fifteen months in fifty per cent new oak. It is eggwhite-fined and bottled without filtration.

Since 1994 Christophe Anney has produced 2,000 bottles of a Cuvée Prestige from forty-year-old vines at Pez, almost all Merlot, and aged entirely in new oak. For Anney, the production of this bottling is a chance for him to experiment and try out new ideas without affecting the quality of the regular wine.

Overall, these are rich, ripe wines, vivid and direct, and very enjoyable. The 1996 had a good deal of swagger, with brambly aromas and considerable force of flavour. The 1997 was dilute but the well-balanced 1998 is a success. The 2000 has delicious black-fruits flavours and good length generated by fine acidity. The medium-bodied 2001 lacks a little excitement but it too is well balanced and has some backbone and acidity. The 2002 has more density and solidity, but it doesn't lack freshness and length. The only prestige bottling I have tasted is the 2003 from cask, which was extremely oaky, with a hefty structure and immense concentration. It was certainly more successful than the rather jammy, grippy regular 2003. The 2004 has sweet fruit, a supple texture underpinned by firm tannins, and finishes fresh and long.

Château Tronquoy-Lalande

Tel: 0556 593024. Owner: Martin Bouygues. 17 ha. 45% Merlot, 45% Cabernet Sauvignon, 10% Petit Verdot. Production: 120,000 bottles. Second wine: Ch Tronquoy de Ste-Anne

This château, a dignified chartreuse set in a wooded park, is visible from far around; from 1969 onwards it was the home of the widowed Mme. Texier-Castéja. The vineyards surround the château on exceptional gravel soils. The vines have an average age of thirty-five years, and the grapes are picked by hand. The must is vinified in cement tanks, then aged in thirty-five per cent new barriques for twelve months, followed by a further twelve months in tanks. The wines used to be deep-coloured, dense, but rather hard, and took many years in bottle to come round. Mme. Castéja worked closely with the négociant Dourthe, whose oenologists moderated the winemaking to produce a more supple and approachable wine. The acquisition of a pneumatic press also helped.

I recall the 1986, with its firm, cedary nose, unmistakably Médoc, though the wine itself had dry tannins, lacked concentration, and was rather dull. Yet the 1996 is going strong, with discreet blackberry aromas and a fine balance of acidity and tannin. The 1999 is over-tannic and charmless. The 2002 lacks aroma, but is juicy, supple, and concentrated, still though with a rustic edge and some dryness on the finish. The 2003 is jammy and fatiguing. Now that the estate is under the same ownership as Montrose, it will be interesting to see whether the property's potential will be developed further.

Château Valrose

Tel: 0557 345151. Owner: Edonia. 5 ha. 50% Merlot, 45% Cabernet Sauvignon, 5% Cabernet Franc. Production: 25,000 bottles

In 2000 Edonia, a wine company with holdings across Europe, bought this small property, with some parcels of old vines near Lafon-Rochet and Le Crock. Its best wine is called Cuvée Aliénor, made mostly from Merlot. The blackberry-scented 2003, which is much superior to the 2002, has weight and an appealing rude vigour.

13. Pessac-Léognan Part I

In medieval times, the main swathe of Bordeaux's vineyards lay around the city itself and up to ten kilometres (six miles) to its south. This region became known as the Graves de Bordeaux. Farther south, around Langon, the vineyards were mostly dedicated to sweet white wines; by the eighteenth century this area would become prized for its botrytized sweet wines, of which the benchmark was and remains Yquem. Gradually the area south of La Brède became planted too, until vineyards stretched from the city to just south of Langon.

As the city grew, the structure of the region began to change. In the nineteenth century there were some fifty estates in the commune of Pessac, and 100 in Mérignac, just west of the city. In 1875 the area under vine in the northern Graves was 5,000 hectares. The great majority of these vineyards vanished as rising land prices offered owners quick profits; urban expansion demanded more and more building land for houses and commercial developments. By the 1970s there were only 500 hectares left in the northern Graves, where all the most prestigious properties were located.

Their proprietors, especially those who owned classified growths, grew increasingly worried as their region continued to shrink. Foremost among these was André Lurton. Lurton, whose primary property was Château Bonnet in the Entre-Deux-Mers, had ploughed his profits back into vineyard land. His brother Lucien was doing the same thing, principally in Margaux, but André focused on the northern Graves. He started buying up renowned but often derelict properties. Convinced of their potential to produce great wines, he restored them both physically and in terms of their reputation.

In the 1930s the Graves appellation had been created. A classification followed in 1959 from a list of 130 candidates. Without exception all the classified properties were north of La Brède. As was usually the case in Bordeaux, it was the city's brokers who determined the classification, using price as well as intrinsic quality as criteria. Rather confusingly, some châteaux were classified for their white wine but not their reds – or vice versa. The classified properties were: Haut-Brion, Bouscaut, Carbonnieux, Domaine de Chevalier, Couhins, Couhins-Lurton, Fieuzal, Haut-Bailly, La Mission Haut-Brion, La Tour Haut-Brion, Latour-Martillac, Laville Haut-Brion, Malartic-Lagravière, Olivier, Pape-Clément, and Smith-Haut-Lafitte. From these sixteen châteaux, there were eight classified whites and thirteen classified reds.

THE NORTH BREAKS AWAY

The fact that every classified estate lay in the north did not improve relations between the northern and southern Graves. Not only did the north have quality on its side, but it had the political influence of the owners of the top properties. In the south there were no counterparts to the powerful figures of André Lurton, Antony Perrin, and the Dillon family. In 1964 the northern estates founded their own syndicat, which united around sixty properties in the north, leaving over 500 in the south outside the fold. In effect there were now two Graves syndicats, always a recipe for confusion and strife.

André Lurton was elected president of the Syndicat de Hautes Graves in 1974 and he and some other proprietors began pressing for a new AC for the north. Naturally the southern Graves opposed the idea. Much time and energy were spent on lawsuits and tribunals. Lurton insisted, as he does today, that the new AC he was proposing was not a way of regrouping the classified growths. Had there been some classified growths in the southern Graves, his views on the boundaries of the new AC would have been the same. In 1980 a formal application was made to the INAO for the creation of an AC Pessac-Léognan. In 1984 estates were allowed to use the two district names of Pessac and Léognan on the labels, and after years of dithering, an official decree created the new appellation in 1987. One of the factors that had convinced the INAO that a new AC made sense was that the wines from the north fetched consistently higher prices than those from the south, and in Bordeaux that counted for a good deal. A new Syndicat de Pessac-Léognan replaced the Hautes Graves group-

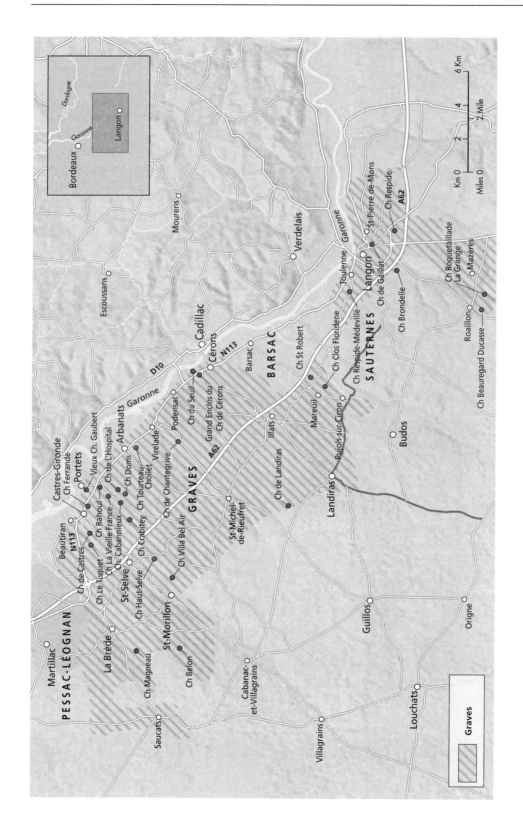

Dordogne

Garonne

Bordeaux

Langon

6 Km

4

2 Mile

2

Km 0

Miles 0

Mourens

St-Pierre-de-Mons

Ch Respide

A62

Verdelais

Toulenne

Garonne

Langon

Ch de Gaillat

Ch Roquetaillade

La Grange

Mazères

Ch Brondelle

Escoussans

Cadillac

Cérons

N113

BARSAC

Ch St Robert

Ch Clos Floridene

Ch Respide-Médeville

SAUTERNES

Roaillon

Ch Beauregard Ducasse

D10

Barsac

Pujols-sur-Ciron

Arbanats

Garonne

Ch du Seuil

Grand Enclos du

Ch de Cérons

Mareuil

Budos

Podensac

Castres-Gironde

Vieux Ch. Gaubert

Ch de L'Hospital

Ch Doms

Virelade

Illats

A62

Ch Ferrande

Portets

Ch Tourteau

Cholet

Ch de Chantegrive

Ch de Landiras

GRAVES

Beautiran

N113

Ch Rahoul

Ch Crabitey

St-Michel-

de-Rieufret

Ch de Castres

Ch La Vieille France

Ch Cabannieux

Ch Villa Bel Air

Landiras

Ch Le Tuquet

St-Selve

Ch Haut-Selve

St-Morillon

Guillos

Origne

Martillac

PESSAC-LÉOGNAN

La Brède

Ch Magneau

Ch Belon

Louchats

Saucats

Cabanac-

et-Villagrains

Graves

Villagrains

ing, and Lurton continued as its president, finally stepping down in February 2005 after thirty-one years as the undisputed leader of the appellation. The southern Graves was mollified by the creation of a Maison du Vin at Podensac, largely financed, I have been told, by the northern estates as a way of offering a consolation prize.

The 1987 decree did more than lay out the geographical boundaries of the new region. It also stipulated a higher density of vine plantings – 6,500 per hectare rather than the 5,000 usually found farther south. This posed problems for properties, such as Château de France, that had significant parcels of old vines planted at 5,000 vines per hectare. The deadline for conversion to at least 6,500 vines per hectare is 2010, but there is considerable pressure to obtain a postponement from the INAO to 2025. The decree also required white vineyards to contain at least twenty-five per cent Sauvignon Blanc. Lurton explains: "You can't make great white wines from Sémillon alone, which is why a minimum proportion of Sauvignon is required." (Not everyone would agree.)

The new AC was a triumph for Lurton and his associates:

> It was a recognition of quality. At about this time there was a blind tasting of wines from all over the Graves. Professor Ribéreau-Gayon was there and could identify which wines came from the north and which from the rest of the Graves. Pierre Guignard, of Château Roquetaillade-La-Grange in the south, then pointed out that the wines from the north, including many classified growths, were in a slightly larger bottle, which nobody had spotted before, so he insisted the results were discounted.

Despite the cumbersome name of the new appellation, it soon proved successful. It also gave the northern proprietors additional political muscle in the fight that preoccupied them all: the struggle against relentless urban expansion. It was not just that the historic vineyards close to the city of Bordeaux needed the protection of the new Syndicat. Even within the heart of the region some of the finest vineyard land was under threat. Celebrated vineyards such as those of Château Branon in Léognan itself had been mostly built over. Former nineteenth-century vineyards of exceptional quality were now pine forests. The superlative gravel beds of the region were greatly in demand by housing developers, who could line the driveways of suburban mansions with the pretty little stones. The Syndicat would help those proprietors keen to expand their properties by planting on historic vineyard sites that had long been abandoned. Urban expansion was not the only villain in the piece. Other factors, such as phylloxera, the loss of important markets after World War I, and the economic crises of the 1930s had all contributed to the conversion of some of the region's finest *croupes* into woodland.

No sooner had the new AC come into being than plans were developed for a "Technopole" close to Léognan. This was a proposed 1,400-hectare science park. No doubt this was a splendid concept, but the land that would have been appropriated would have included some of the top historic vineyard sites in the Graves. André Lurton rose to the challenge. He relishes telling the story of how the proposal, which had powerful political backing, was eventually defeated, but the details of suit and countersuit, of judgment and appeal, are far too lengthy and complex to present here. Suffice it to say that the Technopole that exists today occupies a mere forty hectares and the vineyards have been saved from the bulldozers.

REVIVAL AND REBIRTH

Because it was evident that AC Pessac-Léognan really did include the finest sites of the Graves, the region could play the quality card and maintain good prices for its wines. This in turn encouraged the investment that had been lacking in the past. New wineries and *chais* were built at Domaine de Chevalier, at Fieuzal, and more recently at Haut-Bailly, Rochemorin, and Malartic-Lagravière. Properties of enormous potential that had underperformed for decades – Malartic-Lagravière is an obvious example – were turned around thanks to copious investment and a passionate desire on the part of new owners to strive for quality.

Because the area of potential vineyard – delimited but unplanted – in Pessac-Léognan is so great, it has been possible for new estates to come into being by reviving historic vineyards. Properties such as Chevalier and Olivier have recovered excellent parcels, once part of their estates but abandoned, for economic reasons, long ago. The Garcins at Haut-Bergey revived Château Branon. Francis Boutemy created Clos Marsalette and Haut-Lagrange more or less from scratch. Vineyards planted in the early 1990s now form Château Le Thil Comte Clary. The Gonet family re-created, or rather revived, wine estates at Château Haut-Bacalan and Château d'Eck. Even close to the city centre, in suburban Mérignac, a new vineyard was planted at Château Luchey-Halde, on a former military base.

The revival of which André Lurton, Antony Perrin, and others had dreamed is actually taking place, and the area under vine has grown to 1,500 hectares and is set to expand further, market conditions permitting. The region won the right to plant an additional forty hectares each year. By 2000 the number of properties in Pessac-Léognan stood at sixty, and annual production at around seven million bottles.

WHITE HEIGHTS

But the success story is less than complete when it comes to white wines. The Graves as a whole is a region where white as well as red wines of excellent quality can be produced. There have always been a handful of white Graves that have fetched prices that often exceeded those of the red wines from the same estates: Haut-Brion, Laville Haut-Brion, Domaine de Chevalier, and Fieuzal. Although less prestigious, white wines from Lurton properties such as La Louvière and Couhins-Lurton can rise to great heights. There are properties, such as Larrivet-Haut-Brion, where in my view the white wine is consistently better than the red.

Yet the market has failed to be totally convinced by the merits of white Pessac-Léognan. One does hear optimistic reports from retailers as well as producers of growing sales of white wines from some properties, but it is also evident, when visiting certain properties, that the proportion of white wine has been shrinking. In 2001 the area planted with white grapes diminished for the first time, though André Lurton dismisses the shrinkage as insignificant. Philippe Lacoste of Château Ferran explains:

> *Small producers have difficulties with white wines. Haut-Brion and Chevalier can charge*
> *even more for their whites than the reds, because they have a long-standing reputation for*
> *them. But small properties have to charge less, even though the wine is more labour-intensive*
> *to produce.*

It is also the case that white grapes cannot be planted just anywhere. Professor Denis Dubourdieu, who advises many estates at Pessac-Léognan, says that white vines should be planted only on soils with a subsoil of clay and limestone. Thus it is entirely right for Haut-Bailly to be a red-only estate, because its soils will always deliver better red than white wines. The Lurton group of properties has about sixty hectares of white grapes planted, and the Perrin group has about the same. Between them these two families account for about half the white wine production of Pessac-Léognan.

Sauvignon Blanc remains important, and at a few properties, such as La Garde and Couhins-Lurton, the white wine is made entirely from that variety. That used to be the case at Smith-Haut-Lafitte, until some years ago a proportion of the Sauvignon Blanc was replaced by Sauvignon Gris. This sub-variety is becoming increasingly widely planted throughout the Graves. It needs to be planted on soils slightly cooler than those for Sauvignon Blanc.

Sémillon retains a strong following, but its vigour needs to be curbed. Its drawback is that young Sémillon, unlike young Sauvignon, can be over-productive, and shows at its best only when the vines are old and the yields are low. I find that a proportion of Sémillon in a white Graves can, when the wine is mature, give an alluring toastiness to the aromas that I have sometimes identified, incorrectly, as oak influence. I find this particularly marked in old vintages of white Chevalier. Parcels of old-vine Sémillon survive at Latour-Martillac, Bouscaut, and Laville Haut-Brion, and undoubtedly contribute to the quality and character of those wines.

The balance of red varieties is also changing. As in the Médoc, much Cabernet Sauvignon is being replaced by Merlot. There are certainly some terroirs within Pessac-Léognan, notably at Martillac, that are better adapted to Merlot than Cabernet, thanks to large bands of clay within or beneath the soil. At Château La Garde, where Merlot has been planted on gravel as well as clay, they have found that gravel gives elegance but not much power, while clay gives more abundant fruit and concentration but at the expense of finesse. But such logical reasoning does not fully account for the diminution of Cabernet, even at very fine estates such as Domaine de Chevalier and Haut-Bergey. The explanation is not mysterious: Merlot ripens earlier and is less prone to diseases such as eutypiose. But it would be a shame, to put it mildly, if Merlot were to replace Cabernet on the greatest gravel *croupes* of the region.

The soil structure is more complex than it may appear. Material eroded from the Pyrenees was conveyed by rivers and glaciers that deposited alluvial soils, gravel, quartz pebbles, and other debris on what is today the prime vineyard land of the Left Bank. But it did not do so all at once. There were five or six waves of glacial deposits. Over the centuries, streams tunnelled valleys into the landscape, exposing the well-drained *croupes* on which vines would later be planted and providing a conduit for moisture filtering down through the soils. The most recent glacial deposits are found closer to the Garonne. Thus there are different bands of *croupes*. Olivier shares the same general soil type as Smith-Haut-Lafitte and Carbonnieux; while Chevalier, Fieuzal, and Malartic-Lagravière are first cousins in terms of their soil structure. The *croupes* vary enormously in depth. The most shallow may have only thirty centimetres (one foot) of gravel before the subsoil is reached; in other places the gravel bed can be many metres deep. Moreover, "gravel", as in the Médoc, is a catch-all term for a huge range of stone types. Farther south, into the present-day Graves region, the gravel tends to be mixed with higher proportions of sand, clay, and limestone.

It is very difficult to pin down the influence of this diversity of soils on the quality and character of the wines produced from them. My own tastings suggest that red wines from Martillac develop a smokiness less frequently encountered around Léognan. Olivier Bernard of Domaine de Chevalier suggests that the explanation may lie in the fact that Martillac has colder soils and picks later than Léognan. This may also explain why in the nineteenth century the reputation of Martillac lagged behind Léognan. The estates close to the city invariably ripen up to ten days earlier than those around Léognan. Haut-Brion, in 1989 and 2003, issued press releases to announce it was harvesting its white grapes at an unprecedentedly early date. Such precocity is unsurprising: cities enjoy a microclimate that is always somewhat warmer than their rural fringes.

Overall, the creation of Pessac-Léognan has been a success story. The fact that many wine-lovers have only a remote idea of where it is, and that not even wine professionals can recall which estates are classified for which colour, is not that important. Prices have remained relatively high and relatively stable, with fewer of the greed-driven zigzags that bedevil the commercialization of the great Médocs. The supremacy of Haut-Brion within the region will always give it a cachet that the southern Graves can never attain. In general, quality is high; I find few rustic or clumsy wines here.

The Graves equivalent is not set in stone. It was the intention of the Syndicat to review it in due course, although there was no pressure from the existing classified growths for a revaluation. On the other hand, there are some Pessac-Léognan properties – Haut-Bergey, Larrivet-Haut-Brion, La Louvière, Carmes Haut-Brion – that might be in line for promotion. Brown, de France, and La Garde could also be candidates, as well as some properties in the southern Graves – Chantegrive and Clos Floridène being prime examples. However, with the *cru bourgeois* and St-Emilion classifications floundering in the courts in early 2007, it would be safe to bet that there will be no revised classification embarked upon here.

The following are the various communes and the area under vine within each: Pessac (86 hectares), Léognan (725), Mérignac (21), Talence (28), Gradignan (9), Villenave d'Ornon (70), Canéjan (46), Cadaujac (55), St Médard d'Eyrans (107), and Martillac (340).

Château Bardins

Cadaujac. Tel: 0556 307801. Owner: Stella Puel. 9.4 ha. 9 ha red: 30% Merlot, 30% Cabernet Sauvignon,
30% Cabernet Franc, 10% Malbec and Petit Verdot. 0.4 ha white: 33% each Sauvignon Blanc, Sémillon, and Muscadelle.
Production: 55,000 bottles (of which 1,500 white). Second wine: Ch Bardey

This old property lies quite close to the motorway, and shares a plot of land with its neighbour Bouscaut. A fourteenth-century mill on the property testifies to its long history, though the château itself is from the nineteenth century. Since 1903 it has belonged to the Bernardy de Sigoyer family, into which Stella Puel was born in 1964. Her husband is a doctor, so she alone runs the property. Not that long ago there were only three hectares of vines, so there were additional plantings in the 1980s and in 2000. But the old vines are old indeed: some Malbec and Petit Verdot from the 1940s, and 0.4 hectares of white vines from 1960. The soil is gravelly on a subsoil of clay-limestone, and the harvest is manual.

The wine is aged in twenty-five per cent new oak for twelve months, before fining, filtration, and bottling. The white wine is pressed directly without skin contact, then barrel-fermented in about fifteen per cent new oak and aged for some nine months.

Mme. Puel loves to welcome visitors to her property. There is a small museum, a cosy tasting room, and a selection of older vintages for sale as well as current releases. So it's a shame that the quality of the wines is not more exciting than it is. The old-vine white has a slight minerality but not much complexity or length. The red is frankly light. I suspect Mme. Puel knows full well that her wine could be very much better than it actually is. A 1989 tasted in 2005 was fully ready, but silky and balanced and attractive. The 2004, with its freshness and bite, seems the best of recent vintages. She has recently hired Arnaud Dessis, Francis Boutemy's right-hand man at Haut-Lagrange, to assist her, so it is likely that within the next few years we will see further improvements in quality at this hospitable estate.

Château Baret

Villenave d'Ornon. Tel: 0556 000070. Owner: Ballande family. 22 ha. 19.5 ha red: 53% Merlot,
40% Cabernet Sauvignon, 7% Cabernet Franc. 2.5 ha white: 70% Sauvignon Blanc, 30% Sémillon.
Production: 135,000 bottles (of which 15,000 white). Second wine: Ch de Camparian

This grandiose château and its vineyards lie just south of the Bordeaux ring road. It has been the summer home of the Ballande family since the nineteenth century. The Ballandes have numerous business interests in New Caledonia and own Prieuré-Lichine (*q.v.*). But Baret is a personal property, not part of the business portfolio. This explains why it is run by Philippe Castéja of the négociant house Borie-Manoux, as he is married to the daughter of the late André Ballande.

The vineyards are essentially in a single parcel, though in three distinct sectors. The soil is pure gravel with bands of clay and stones beneath. The average age of the vineyards is twenty-five years, with some parcels that are fifty years old. The harvest is manual. The white wine sees some skin contact, then is barrel-fermented in thirty-five per cent new oak, and aged on the fine lees for ten months. The red goes through a cold soak before fermentation; it is aged for fourteen months in thirty per cent new oak, including some American barrels.

The white wine is attractive, with considerable weight. The somewhat atypical and opulent 2003 has more melony aromas and a creamy texture. The reds are variable in quality. The 1996 has bacon aromas; it's concentrated but a touch austere. The 1999 is lightweight. The 2001 is rounded, lightly tannic, and forward, and outclassed by the very good 2002, which has grip, some Graves earthiness, and a long, fresh finish. The 2003 is spicy and accessible.

Baret is modestly priced, and Castéja, aided by the counsels of Denis Dubourdieu, seems keen to keep the quality on an upward curve.

Château Bouscaut

Cadaujac. Tel: 0557 831220. Website: www.chateau-bouscaut.com. Owner: Sophie Lurton. Cru classé. 47 ha.
40 ha red: 55% Merlot, 40% Cabernet Sauvignon, 5% Malbec. 7 ha white: 50% Sauvignon Blanc, 50% Sémillon.
Production: 120,000 bottles (of which 20,000 white). Second wine: La Flamme de Bouscaut

Bouscaut is the largest estate in Cadaujac, and since 1929 has incorporated the vineyards of Château Valoux. Some wines are still released under the Valoux label and that of another property Bouscaut has owned since 1999, the twelve-hectare Château Lamothe-Bouscaut. The château itself looks quite old but it's a replica: the original structure burned down in the 1960s and was rebuilt according to the original plans. In the 1970s the property was owned by an American consortium, which sold it in 1979 to Lucien Lurton. From 1984 to 1992 the wines were made by Lucien's son Louis, who now runs Haut-Nouchet and Doisy-Dubroca in Barsac. In 1992 Lucien handed over his many estates to his equally numerous children, but there was an awkward transition period at Bouscaut as his daughter Sophie bought out her brother Louis. Sophie secured control in 1995, and since then has run the property with her easy-going but professionally trained husband Laurent Cogombles. They have been aided technically by the splendid circular winery built by Louis Lurton in 1990.

The soil is essentially gravelly but over a limestone base, and there are sectors with more clay and sand. The vineyards are in one block that is traversed by a road. It's a mature estate, with an average vine age of forty years. There are even some treasured Sémillon vines, 3,000 in all, from the nineteenth century that still give excellent fruit. Cogombles has been steadily making improvements in the vineyard, heightening the trellising, planting green cover, and decreasing radically the use of fertilizers. Since 2003 the grapes have been picked in *cagettes* with double sorting at the winery. But not all is picked by hand; usually the younger vines and the very ripest Cabernet Sauvignon are machine-harvested. There is no precise formula, and Cogombles likes the flexibility that a harvesting machine gives him.

The red grapes are fermented with pumpovers and *délestage*. Malolactic fermentation takes place in tanks and in barriques. The wine is blended in January, then aged in forty-five per cent new oak for eighteen months. There is a very cautious use of micro-oxygenation and a conscientious effort to avoid excessive extraction, as this has never been the style at Bouscaut.

The white grapes are harvested solely by hand, with two passages through the vineyards, so as to focus on the ripest fruit. There is occasional skin contact, but it's not systematic, and the wine is fermented with indigenous yeasts and aged for ten months in barriques. Only the Sémillon sees a proportion of new oak, fifty per cent in the early 2000s, but Cogombles plans to reduce the proportion slightly in future.

I have been following the wines of Bouscaut for two decades, and they remain something of a puzzle. The red often has an underlying austerity, as though the tannins are not always fully ripe. It is rarely a fleshy wine, the emphasis being on finesse and delicacy. The oak is always quite present, especially on the nose, but overall it seems well judged and is rarely obtrusive. Vintages I have enjoyed include the 1983, the concentrated and classic 1990, the sleek and supple 1998 with its fine tannins, the firm, spicy, well-structured 2001, and the dense, cherry-scented, persistent 2002. Less successful have been the slightly hard and herbaceous 1985, the meagre, earthy 1986, the rather austere 1989, the dense and even impenetrable 2000, and the simple yet grippy 2003, with its abrupt finish. What is not easily discernible at Bouscaut is a clear stylistic imprint.

The white, in general, is lean and citric, and in some vintages the acidity is very marked, almost to the point of discomfort. I have tasted most of the white vintages of the 1980s and didn't much care for any of them, though 1987 was always surprisingly good and is still drinking well. In the 1990s I detect a bit more richness with the 1996 and 1997 vintages, though in 1996 that richness is undercut by a lean edge; but there was a return to a tarter, greener style in 1998. The 1999 was still amazingly fierce when last tasted in 2001, and the 2000 lacks vigour and personality. The 2002 is very good indeed, certainly citric but not green, with strong herbal tones; its raciness gives a long and vigorous oaky finish. The 2003 is juicy and reasonably fresh and will be attractive over the next few years. The 2004 has light herbaceous aromas, but is more rounded and overtly fruity on the palate, with a toasty finish and reasonable length.

Bouscaut is a wine that rarely wins lavish praise from wine critics. The owners have sought to turn this to their advantage, ostentatiously revelling in their low Parker scores, but I am not sure this is a wise approach. There is indeed something lacking in the Bouscaut wines; they are clearly not as good as the terroir would seem to suggest they should be. I suspect that Laurent Cogombles is aware of this and thinking hard about how to make Bouscaut more complete, more complex, more rewarding. It will be interesting to see how the property evolves over the next decade.

Château Branon

Léognan. Tel: 0556 640522. Owner: Sylviane Garcin-Cathiard. 6 ha. 5 ha red: 50% Cabernet Sauvignon, 50% Merlot. 1 ha white: 100% Sauvignon Blanc. Production: 8,000 bottles

Since 1996 this remarkable little property has been under the same ownership as Château Haut-Bergey (*q.v.*), on the other side of Léognan. The château itself and its cellars are a burnt-out wreck, and half the historic vineyards have been concreted out of existence and replaced by a bland housing estate called, ironically, the "Résidence de Branon". Thus a highly regarded property has in effect been vandalized. The remaining vineyards, on a shelf around the buildings, are evidence that this was once a remarkable terroir: the vines emerge from a sea of pebbles. Yet Mme. Garcin's daughter Hélène points out that even this small vineyard has thirteen different soil types. They are modifying the grape mix, and have planted some Petit Verdot. At present only two out of the five hectares of red vines are used for Branon, but when the remaining three hectares have gained in maturity they too will enter the blend. The white wine is blended with that of Haut-Bergey. The red is vinified at Haut-Bergey in wooden vats. The 2001 and 2002 are remarkably powerful (and expensive) wines, sumptuous and oaky, spicy, tannic, perhaps a touch viscous. The 2003 seems marginally less successful, being considerably more assertive and extracted. The 2004 is in a similar style, with aromas of smoke, oak, and liquorice, and a sumptuous texture, very marked by oak, yet with a lively finish; nonetheless it seems quite extracted and lacks finesse. The 2005, just before bottling, seemed similar. Branon demands bottle-age to shed its youthful aggression, but I am not entirely convinced that this *garagiste* style is appropriate for the terroir.

Château Brown

Léognan. Tel: 0556 870810. Website: www.chateau-brown.com. Owners: Yvon Mau and the Dirkzwager company. 28 ha. 23 ha red: 60% Cabernet Sauvignon, 35% Merlot, 5% Petit Verdot. 5 ha white: 70% Sauvignon Blanc, 30% Sémillon. Production: 130,000 bottles. Second wine: Colombier de Ch Brown

Not the most inspiring name for a fine wine, but it is derived from the name of the eighteenth-century owner, John Lewis Brown (who also owned Cantenac-Brown in Margaux). In the nineteenth century this was a very important estate, with 100 hectares of vineyards. Like so many properties it went into a decline in the course of the twentieth century, and most of the vineyards were converted into orchards, while other parcels succumbed to urbanization. The surviving vineyards are in a single parcel on a *croupe* shared with Château Olivier. The property was revived by Jean-Claude Bonnel, who completely renovated it. He died in 1992. Two years later the estate was acquired by Bernard Barthe, a cereal merchant based in Madrid. Although essentially an absentee landlord, Barthe invested substantially in the property, building air-conditioned *chais* and improving the vineyards and drainage. Under Bonnel, chemical fertilizers and herbicides had been employed, and Barthe put a stop to that. After ten years, he decided to sell up, and the property was bought by the Mau family, of the Yvon Mau négociant house, and their partners, the Dirkzwager company.

Jean-Christophe Mau, who administers the property, has continued the restructuring of the sandy-gravelly vineyards that was begun by Bernard Barthe. Less satisfactory frost-prone sites lower down are being abandoned in favour of higher-lying parcels. Some of the older sectors, planted in 1975 to a fairly low density, are being grubbed up, as Mau gradually converts the vineyards to a higher density. Claude Bourguignon, better known in Burgundy than in Bordeaux, is the viticultural consultant, and Mau has engaged Stéphane Derenoncourt as consultant oenologist for the red wine.

The harvest is manual, in *cagettes*, and Mau reports that the average yield over ten years is a modest forty-four hectolitres per hectare. There is preliminary sorting in the vineyard and two sorting tables at the winery. Under Bonnel the wines spent no more than six months in barriques. Today the wine undergoes malolactic fermentation partly in barriques, and is then aged in thirty-five per cent new oak for fourteen months. Under Barthe there was no systematic skin contact for the whites, and Mau too is very wary of the technique, though he employs very brief skin contact under the protection of dry ice.

The white wine became very reliable in the 1990s, with floral and oaky aromas, and ample spiciness and length. The 2003 is reasonably balanced for the vintage, with white peach and apricot aromas, and a predictable plumpness on the palate. The 2005 is far better, an aromatic confection of lemons and mandarins, a medium-bodied palate with freshness and gracefulness, probably best drunk relatively young. The robust 2006 shows promise.

The few vintages of the red wine that I tasted up to 1990 were uniformly dull and earthy. By the late 1990s the red was solid, spicy, and long, with an occasional herbaceousness that Mau attributes to relatively early harvesting. Nonetheless the 1998 is delicious, with an elegant acidic structure, and the 1999 rich, toasty, and forward. The blackcurrant-scented 2000 is more chunky, and has weight rather than elegance. The 2001 has developed meaty, savoury aromas, and its weight and spiciness are balanced by a fresh finish. It is more exciting than the good but not outstanding 2002. The 2003 is plump and opulent, but lacks length. It's out-classed by the lovely 2004, with its cedary aromas, its supple texture underpinned by firm tannins, and its refreshing Graves typicity.

Château Le Bruilleau

St Médard d'Eyrans. Tel: 0556 727045. Owners: Serge and Nadine Bédicheau. 10 ha. 8 ha red:
50% Cabernet Sauvignon, 50% Merlot. 2 ha white: 80% Sémillon, 20% Sauvignon Blanc.
Production: 50,000 bottles

This property lies at the southern edge of Pessac-Léognan, a stone's throw from the northerly Graves vineyards of La Brède. Its owner is Mme. Bédicheau, who is the fourth-generation proprietor. She and her husband took over the estate about twenty years ago, and began bottling the wine in 1984. At that time there were only 5.5 hectares of vineyards, but over time more parcels were acquired. So the estate consists of a number of small plots grouped around the cellars on very diverse soils. The white vines are exceptionally old, with an average age of forty years. The vineyards are worked by a team from a nearby centre for the handicapped.

The white grapes are destemmed, given some skin contact, pressed in a pneumatic press and settled, and then forty per cent of the must is barrel-fermented in fifty per cent new oak, while the rest of the must is vinified in tanks. The oak regime for the white wine was introduced in 2002. The red grapes are given a cold soak for up to six days, then fermented in steel tanks. Until 1997 only a small proportion of the red wine was barrel-aged, but by the 2000s the crop was being aged for twelve months in twenty-five per cent new oak.

The 1990, produced almost entirely from Merlot and unoaked, was surprisingly drinkable fifteen years later, with ripe fruit aromas, a good deal of flesh and reasonable concentration, all supported by ripe tannins – a very enjoyable wine with good length if little complexity. In the 2000s the wine shows some herbaceousness, even in a year such as 2000. The wines have a certain robustness but little elegance. The white from the atypical 2003 vintage tasted both overripe and phenolic – a wine to consume soon.

Château Cantelys

Martillac. Tel: 0557 831122. Owners: Daniel and Florence Cathiard. 30 ha. 20 ha red: 60% Cabernet Sauvignon,
40% Merlot. 10 ha white: 50% Sémillon, 50% Sauvignon Blanc. Production: 170,000 bottles

One would have thought that Daniel and Florence Cathiard had enough on their plate when they acquired Smith-Haut-Lafitte (*q.v.*) and transformed the property beyond recognition. Nonetheless in 1994 they leased the nearby estate of Cantelys, with its well-located vineyards near Rochemorin. The drawback is that they are susceptible to frost, so some woodland was cleared to improve ventilation and wind machines were installed. The wines are made at Smith in much the same way as Smith, with the white aged in fifty per cent new oak.

The red 1996 was remarkably good, with forthright but ripe tannins and good length; the wine was no blockbuster but highly enjoyable. The 2000 is more dense, with aromas of menthol and liquorice; it's chewy and structured, with good length if little elegance. The white has been consistently good since 1994, ripe and nutty, with ample fruit and body; it lacks the grandeur of Smith, but then the terroir is not as fine. Cantelys is sensibly priced and offers very good value. These are not wines for long ageing.

Château Carbonnieux

Léognan. Tel: 0557 965620. Website: www.carbonnieux.com. Owner: Antony Perrin. Cru classé. 90 ha.
47 ha red: 60% Cabernet Sauvignon, 30% Merlot, 7% Cabernet Franc, 2% Malbec, 1% Petit Verdot and Carmenère.
43 ha white: 65% Sauvignon Blanc, 35% Sémillon. Production: 500,000 bottles. Second wine: Ch Tour-Léognan

This property dates back to the twelfth century, and medieval traces are incorporated into the essentially seventeenth-century château, which forms an attractive architectural ensemble on the plateau between Léognan and Cadaujac. Vines were first planted, it seems, by Benedictine monks in the eighteenth century. When Thomas Jefferson paid a visit here during his grand tour of the Bordelais vineyards in 1787, the monks were still in charge, although they were evicted once revolution broke out. The modern era of Carbonnieux dates from 1956, when Marc Perrin, a *pied noir*, bought the property. The vineyard was in dire shape after the frost that year, and the château had been empty for half a century. Today Carbonnieux is run by his genial son Antony, and his two sons Eric and Philibert. Antony Perrin is a familiar and welcome presence at events both formal and informal on the Bordeaux wine scene.

It's a very large estate, planted on a gravelly *croupe* in three main sectors, since the soil is far from uniform, and there are sandy patches and a good deal of clay subsoil. The land is slightly tilted to the northwest, and the natural drainage is good. Cabernet Sauvignon and Sémillon are planted on the higher parts of the *croupe*, Merlot and Sauvignon Blanc lower down on heavier soils where there is more clay. What singles out Carbonnieux, even in Pessac-Léognan, is the very high proportion of white vines, roughly half the total. The average age of the vines is around thirty years, and the entire vineyard is picked manually.

Carbonnieux is run along sound commercial lines. It produces substantial volumes of wine (although yields rarely exceed fifty hl/ha) at a fair price. Its wines may rarely figure among the greatest wines of Bordeaux, but they are consistent and very reliable. This should not be taken to imply that the Perrins are indifferent to quality. They were among the first producers to adopt the then-novel theories of white wine vinification espoused by Denis Dubourdieu, who has been a consultant here since 1988. New cellars were built in 1989, and sorting tables were introduced a year later. The white wines used to be fermented in tanks before being transferred to barriques, but today the entire crop is barrel-fermented in twenty-five per cent new oak, where it is aged for around ten months.

The Perrins have experimented with all the modish techniques for red wine vinification but are not greatly impressed by most of them. Although they own a reverse-osmosis machine, it has hardly ever been used. In the mid-1990s they tried malolactic fermentation in barriques, but decided any marginal improvement in quality did not justify the amount of labour involved. The wine is aged for sixteen to eighteen months in around forty per cent new oak, with traditional racking.

The wines are drinkable young, though they will and do age. Antony Perrin argues that the proportion of Sémillon in the white gives it considerable ageing potential. I am not entirely convinced. Even the 1988, the first vintage overseen by Dubourdieu, seems to have lost much of the vigour and stylishness that characterized it when young. The 1995, 1996, and 1998 are holding up well, with waxy aromas, a touch of honey in the case of the 1996; they remain citric, vigorous, and long. By 1999, white Carbonnieux had become a weightier, silkier wine, with a power it lacked in the past. It's hard to resist the flowery, elegant aromas of the 2001, a fine wine with pungency and fresh acidity. The 2002 too is a terrific wine, spicy and vigorous, with flavours of ripe grape-fruit. The 2003 initially seemed heavy, but has now developed freshness and a long, nutty finish. Pear-drop aromas mark the 2004, which is rich and opulent, but also vibrant and long, making this one of the best Carbonnieux whites in years.

Red Carbonnieux is sometimes perceived as a relatively lightweight Pessac-Léognan, but it does age well. In 2007 the 1966 from magnum was very evolved, with smoky, leathery aromas, but it was still full-bodied and intense, though the finish was somewhat dry. The eminently drinkable 1985, twenty years on, retains some intensity and charm. The 1990 is even better: leafy and minty on the nose, while on the palate it is still silky, concentrated, and balanced. The 1995 has great charm, with its sweet, leafy aromas, but it's quite light. I prefer the more imposing 1996, with its tobacco and meat aromas, its gentle gaminess, and its impressive length. The 1997 has long been ready to drink, but the 1998 is going strong, with aromas of blackcurrants, cherries, and a whiff of cut grass; it's sleek and concentrated, though a touch dry on the finish. The 2000 is stylish and bright, but lacks some concentration. I prefer the more robust 2001, with its well-integrated oak and fine underlying acidity. The 2002 has delightful aromas of cherries and raspberries and a touch of oak, but doesn't deliver as solidly on the palate, which seems to lack grip and complexity. The 2003 is aromatic but quite hard and chewy on the palate.

Château Les Carmes Haut-Brion

Pessac. Tel: 0556 932340. Website: www.les-carmes-haut-brion.com. Owner: Didier Furt. 4.7 ha. 55% Merlot, 30% Cabernet Franc, 15% Cabernet Sauvignon. Production: 24,000 bottles. Second wine: Le Clos des Carmes

This small red wine estate is hidden behind high walls near the centre of Pessac. It has been here for centuries. From 1584 to 1789 it belonged to the Carmelite order, from which it took its name. The story goes that because the monks had always prayed for the Pontacs of nearby Haut-Brion, they were rewarded with this vineyard. The property was confiscated during the Revolution and later bought by Léon Colin, whose descendants ran the négociant firm of Chantecaille and built the grandiose château. Didier Furt married into the family, and has been running the property since 1987. Since the Chantecaille company vinified and aged the wine in their cellars in Bordeaux, there were no such facilities in Pessac. Furt built both, though this was scarcely a major undertaking, given the small size of the property.

The soil is less gravelly than at Haut-Brion, and the gravel is often mixed with sand. About one metre (three feet) beneath the gravel is a layer of clay, which in turn covers a layer of hard limestone. The vineyard is gently sloping, so the drainage is excellent. The historic vineyard lies in one parcel, no more than a powerful golf stroke away from Haut-Brion itself. Furt planted an additional hectare on a slope just below the château. Although some parcels are now being replanted, the average age of the vineyard remains around forty years, with the fruit from the youngest vines going into the second wine. Furt is particularly proud of the old Cabernet Franc here. He admits that since 2000 he has focused much more on the viticulture, ploughing the rows and eliminating the use of herbicides. He believes the consequence has been better maturation of the grapes. Furt also introduced some new oak and better selection in the form of a second wine.

The wine is aged eighteen months in fifty per cent new oak, eggwhite-fined, and bottled with minimal or no filtration. These are not especially long-lived wines, says Furt, who believes they are usually approachable after three to five years. In my limited experience, I find the wines can age considerably longer. The 1990 has charm but lacks some weight and complexity. The 1991 was good, with typical Graves earthiness and spice. The 1996 is still very much alive, silky, harmonious, and balanced, with more flesh than usual. The sleek 1998 was also successful, with lush, blackcurrant fruit on the nose and palate, and an attractive oakiness. Both the 2001 and 2002 are very stylish, with some spicy oakiness on the nose, and elegant tannins. I marginally prefer the 2002. The 2003 is built on a mightier scale, with less finesse than the preceding two vintages, but with impressive weight, power, and spice. Pronounced tannins dominate the floral, sleek 2004.

Domaine de Chevalier

*Léognan. Tel: 0556 641616. Website: www.domainedechevalier.com. **Owner:** Olivier Bernard and family. Cru classé. 40 ha. 35 ha red: 64% Cabernet Sauvignon, 30% Merlot, 3% Cabernet Franc, 3% Petit Verdot. 5 ha white: 70% Sauvignon Blanc, 30% Sémillon. **Production:** 200,000 bottles. **Second wine:** L'Esprit de Chevalier*

Keep heading west from Léognan and the last vineyard you come to is Domaine de Chevalier. The vines stretch in a lightly undulating mass from the road to the modest château and less modest winery. Just beyond the buildings, and fringing the vineyards themselves, are the dark pinewoods of the Landes, stretching from here to the wild Atlantic shore. This is marginal land for vines, and the wind machines and smudge-pots in the vineyards show that spring frosts are a significant risk. Vines seem to have first been planted here in the 1770s, when the estate was known as Domaine de Chivaley, but the estate began to win recognition after the Ricard family bought it in 1865. The Ricards were coopers, who gradually acquired a number of properties in what is today Pessac-Léognan. Jean Ricard expanded what was a very small property to a more viable fifteen hectares. His descendants continued to develop the estate, changing its name to Chevalier in the late nineteenth century, and in 1940 Jean Ricard inherited the property. Eight years later it came into the hands of Claude Ricard, who was only twenty-one at the time. Claude Ricard was planning a career as a classical pianist, but gave that up in order to take up the reins at Chevalier. He proved an exemplary steward, installing drainage in 1962 and developing a policy of selective harvesting normally reserved for sweet wines such as Sauternes.

By the mid-1980s, when I had the pleasure of lunching at Chevalier with the urbane and charming Ricard and his other guests – flamenco musicians on this occasion rather than wine professionals – Ricard was no longer the owner. In 1983, that perennial French problem of squabbling heirs made the sale of Chevalier inevitable. The purchaser was the Bernard family, better known for the brandy they produced than for wine. Olivier Bernard, at the age of twenty-three, was installed as co-director of the domaine. Remarkably, Claude Ricard stayed in place and the two men worked amicably together until in 1988 Ricard gracefully bowed out. In the more than twenty years that have passed, the fiercely proud Olivier Bernard has enhanced the reputation of Chevalier even further, but has done nothing to change the wines' character. Chevalier remains Chevalier.

One striking feature of the vineyards is that the vines are planted to a density of 10,000 vines per hectare, which is still rare south of Bordeaux. Domaine de Chevalier is not organic, but close: the soil is ploughed, no herbicides are used, and any fertilizers used are organic. The soil is gravelly black sand of up to one metre (three feet) in depth, over a rich subsoil of clay mixed with sandstone. Average yields range from thirty to forty hl/ha. Despite the seeming homogeneity of the vineyard, there can be striking variations in maturation – as much as fifteen days even within the same parcel. This explains why the white-grape harvest can be spread over three weeks, with teams of harvesters combing through the same parcel up to five times. Defective bunches are removed; only fully ripe bunches are picked. To the best of my knowledge, no other Bordeaux estate, other than in Sauternes, practises this degree of selective harvesting for a dry wine. Such exacting procedures are very labour-intensive and, inevitably, costly. In 1991, a difficult year, the pickers spent 1,100 hours per hectare harvesting grapes.

In the 1990s Olivier Bernard built a superb circular winery equipped with stainless-steel tanks. When the grapes, red or white, arrive at the winery, they are sorted, and since 1999 the reds have been sorted again after destemming. There is no skin contact for the white grapes, which are pressed directly. Bernard likes their fermentation to start at around 18°C (64°F), so he chills the newly filled barrels in a cold chamber. There can be as many as 120 barrels, each of which is handled individually when it comes to chaptalization and other operations. Fermentation begins slowly with natural yeasts, and there is no malolactic fermentation. In the 1980s the wine would have spent only around five weeks on the lees, but today it remains in contact with the lees with *bâtonnage* for around twelve months. The risk of this procedure is that the wine can become too plump and broad, but the naturally high acidity of the Chevalier white means that in practice that is rarely a problem. And when the risk is high, as in 2003, the wine is taken off the lees much earlier.

White Chevalier remains in oak for around eighteen months, far longer than most other white Bordeaux. The purpose is to give the wines weight, structure, and texture, not woody flavours. The barrels are only lightly toasted and the proportion of new oak doesn't exceed thirty per cent (although in the early 1990s the proportion was a bit higher). The barrels are often soaked in hot water before leaving the cooperage so as to eliminate any bitterness lurking in the staves.

For some years Chevalier has employed two distinguished consultants: Professor Denis Dubourdieu, and Stéphane Derenoncourt, who has encouraged non-Bordelais practices such as *pigeage*. Walkways above the steel tanks facilitate manual punching down, which, Bernard is convinced, breaks up and moistens the floating cap more evenly than any other method. Another feature of the red wine, since 1996, is that the must is routinely concentrated to reduce the volume by up to ten per cent. Because of the expansion of the vineyard in 1989, and the replanting of various parcels, the average age of the red vines is only around twenty years. There is no pumping of the must into the tanks. The fermentation is quite prolonged, and after pressing the wine is aged for eighteen months in around fifty per cent new oak, with about thirty per cent of the malolactic taking place in new barrels. There is usually a light fining and filtration before bottling.

Less than half the production finds its way into the *grand vin*, the rest being released under the second label of L'Esprit de Chevalier. This too is explained by the relative youth of the vineyards. The white Esprit gives a very good facsimile of the Chevalier style at a reasonable price.

If the white wine is universally acclaimed as one of the great dry white wines of the world, the red is often underrated. The high proportion of Cabernet, the marginal and youthful vineyards that require ruthless attention to ensure the grapes ripen fully, mean that red Chevalier is rarely a big, powerful wine. In its youth it is delicate and fine, sometimes austere, yet it somehow takes on weight and flesh as it ages. When I tasted, blind, a half-bottle of deeply coloured red at the château, I placed it in the 1970s. It was 1955. Any notion that red Chevalier is light or insubstantial is groundless.

The white remains astonishing. It has twice been my privilege to participate in vertical tastings of this wine: first in London in 1988, and more recently at the château, where twenty-six vintages were tasted blind. Just one elderly wine was unsatisfactory: the somewhat oxidized 1981. The other twenty-five were at the very least good, and most were exceptional, even from tricky vintages. Nor was there any rupture or stylistic change in the 1980s, when the château was changing hands. In their youth the wines can be racy and citric, but it's after fifteen or twenty years that white Chevalier really comes into its own. The minerality remains, but the aromas evolve. There are stone-fruit aromas, a toastiness and smokiness that aren't oak-derived, sometimes a nuttiness, a harmonious balance between fruit and the ever-present acidity, and an extraordinary length of flavour. Their purity and stylistic consistency are abundant proof that, here at least, it is the terroir that is speaking.

The oldest red Chevalier I have tasted is the 1935, very mature in colour, yet still rich and concentrated. The 1955, drunk when fifty years old from a half-bottle, was astonishingly deep in colour, and had savoury, tobacco aromas that were reflected on the palate too. The 1959 is a great Chevalier, concentrated and dense, even if a touch baked. The 1970 is classic, with sweet, elegant, cedary aromas, and little sign of age on the palate, which retains its freshness. Perhaps it lacks some power, but Chevalier is not about power — it's about finesse. The 1978 in 2000 seemed lacking in fruit and vigour, but aeration revived the wine. The 1979 is a success for the vintage, leafy on the nose, but richer and more elegant on the palate. The 1983 is now becoming quite delicate, with its raspberry and blackcurrant aromas and a touch of smokiness; it's lean, with fine acidity, perhaps lacking a little flesh and weight, but extremely attractive now. There are atypically meaty aromas on the 1985, which is robust and spicy, with a touch of coffee on the finish. By 2007 the aromas of the 1986 are lifted and elegant, and the palate is equally delicate, while still fully alive. The 1989 is holding up well, with a rich nose of tobacco and cloves, while the palate is still tight and youthful, with fine acidity and length. The wines of the early 1990s were uncharacteristically slight for Chevalier, but the estate was back on form with the delicious 1995, with its sweet, intense, tobacco nose and its tight but complex finish. The 1998 is quite sumptuous, perhaps lacking a little freshness but supple and lightly spicy, with a savoury finish. The 2000 has a ripe, fleshy, smoky nose; it's supple but some spiciness brightens the rather soft texture, and it has persistence. The 2001 is extremely stylish, unusually powerful for Chevalier, with toasty, blackcurrant aromas, while the palate is lush, succulent, and concentrated. The 2002 is improving in bottle, and is now delicious, tangy, spicy, and elegant. The 2003 is predictably lush, at the expense of acidity and persistence, but it's better balanced and considerably more stylish than most Graves that year.

The oldest white I have encountered, the 1941, was still honeyed and rich fifty-five years later, though the fruit was beginning to fade into a dry, walnutty finish. I rated the 1958, 1964, and 1966 highly when I last tasted them, but that was long ago in 1988. The 1970, tasted in 2005, had a fabulous nose that I have come to recognize as an old white Chevalier cocktail: wax, honey, toast, dried apricot, apples. But the palate was showing some angularity and edginess that suggested it was beginning its decline. The 1975 has never tasted particularly ripe, and I was unimpressed by the 1976. The highly concentrated 1978 is a classic Chevalier, with pungency and vigour, but the 1979 is distinctly lighter in style, though still balanced and fresh. The 1982 was exceedingly acidic in its youth (having been made from second-crop grapes that sprouted after a May frost wiped out most of the first-growth bunches), but had become smoky and spicy by 2005. The 1983 was incredibly austere when young, and is still not that expressive; but it's refined and lively, with lemony aromas and a very fresh finish. The 1984 is astonishingly good, with a great attack, flavours of grapefruit, apricot, and sherbet, and showing perfect balance and length. Tangy, toasty aromas mark the 1985, which is fresh and nutty, with a good mineral finish. The 1986 is equally good, with a waxy nose of apricots and pears; there is firm acidity on the palate, a measure of stylish oak, and a scattering of white pepper on the finish. The 1987 is lush, supple, and succulent, but perhaps has less precision than the other good vintages of the 1980s. The 1988 has force and power, but is blunter and less fresh than some other vintages, with weight rather than elegance. The 1989 has power too, and a strong, robust, mineral character, verging on bitterness, such is the intensity of the extract.

The 1990 is classic white Chevalier, more evolved on the peachy nose than on the palate, which remains fresh, luminous, and elegant, with a mineral, stony finish. The 1991, which gave the harvesters such trouble, has a powerful, toasty nose of lanolin and white peaches, and a distinct toastiness on the palate too; yet it lacks some excitement. The 1992 is leaner, sherbetty, quite acidic, and still youthful, though it is a shade lighter than a typical Chevalier; though by 2007 it had become more sumptuous and intense. The 1994, with its very stylish aromas of apricots and pears, is still lean, zesty, and tight, with finesse rather than exuberance. The 1995 has been great from the outset and remains so: mineral on the nose rather than fruit-driven, and almost austere in its concentration and power, without sacrificing any of its intrinsic elegance. The 1996, in 2007, had pear aromas and tremendous intensity on the palate. The 1998 seems forward, without the expected weight and density. By 2007 the 1999 was lush, creamy, and nutty on the finish. The 2000 has gone into a shell, seeming tight and unevolved and thus hard to assess. Both 2001 and 2002 are brilliant, with stone-fruits flavours, forceful minerality, and pronounced but ripe acidity. I find it hard to choose between them, but suspect the 2002 will pull ahead over the long haul. The peachy, opulent 2003 is good for the vintage, but clearly outranked by the other brilliant vintages of the early 2000s. The 2004 shows enormous promise, and Olivier Bernard is convinced it is the best white he has ever made. It combines great aromatic power with richness and vigour on the palate. The highly elegant 2005 is its equal, however, concentrated and sumptuous and with extraordinary length.

Clos Marsalette

Martillac. Tel: 0674 798847. **Owner:** *Francis Boutemy. 6.6 ha. 6 ha red: 50% Cabernet Sauvignon, 50% Merlot.*
0.6 ha white: 60% Sémillon, 40% Sauvignon Blanc. **Production:** *38,000 bottles*

Like Château Haut-Lagrange (*q.v.*), this is run by Francis Boutemy and his team. However the ownership structure is different. Clos Marsalette is a domaine created by Boutemy in conjunction with Stephan von Neipperg of Canon-La-Gaffelière and one other partner. It was Boutemy who found the land in the 1990s, but he lacked the means to develop the property on his own. The vineyards lie near La Garde and Haut-Nouchet and are mostly in a single block. Until 2002 the wines were made at Haut-Lagrange; thereafter they were vinified in a cellar at the property. As at Haut-Lagrange, the winemaking is relatively unconventional. Thirty per cent of the white wine is aged in new oak, while the rest remains in vats until blending and bottling. The red wine is partly vinified in wooden vats with *pigeage*, and is then aged in sixty per cent new barriques, with *bâtonnage*. Overall, the red wines are more opulent and seductive than those from Lagrange; the 2000 and 2002 are particularly successful. I find the white wines less persuasive.

Château Couhins

Villenave d'Ornon. Tel: 0556 307761. Website: www.chateau-couhins.fr. Cru classé for white only. **Owner:** *INRA*
(French national agricultural research centre). 24 ha. 17 ha red: 50% Merlot, 40% Cabernet Sauvignon,
10% Cabernet Franc. 7 ha white: 84% Sauvignon Blanc, 15% Sémillon, 1% Sauvignon Gris.
Production: *30,000 bottles (white)*

Couhins is located next door to Couhins-Lurton (*q.v.*), and was the same property until it was divided in 1968. Since then this property has been owned by INRA, which has conducted experiments into lyre-training and other techniques. In 1968 there were fewer than two hectares in production, but INRA has planted considerably more since then, and may yet plant five more. The soil is quite varied with a fine gravel *croupe* in front of the château, as well as clay-limestone slopes.

In 1981 wine was made from Couhins grapes for the first time since the division of the property. But it was only sold internally to INRA employees. The Couhins directors were not forbidden to sell the wine to other customers, but made no effort whatsoever to promote it, since they had no wish to set up a commercial structure. With the arrival of a new director and winemaker in 1999, the strategy has been gradually altered. Dominique Forget has decided not to offer the red wine to the general public, but from 2004 the white has been sold through the *Place de Bordeaux*. He feels that since in the past the estate was well known for its white wine, it is here that he should focus his efforts.

The soil is quite precocious, so harvest tends to be early. In the admittedly atypical 2003, Couhins was picking its white grapes from August 13 onwards. They are harvested in *cagettes*, then chilled overnight or given skin contact or pressed directly – it all depends on the vintage conditions. Seventy per cent of the wine is fermented in tanks, the remainder in one-year-old barriques. This is in contrast to the vinification in the 1990s, when the crop was aged entirely in new oak. Both the tank and barrel lots are aged nine months with *bâtonnage*. There also used to be two *cuvées*: a Prestige and a regular bottling. The former is being dropped.

The red is aged for twelve months in thirty per cent new oak, and Forget is experimenting with micro-oxygenation. The 1998 and 2000 red are tannic, even rustic, with little charm or interest. The white is a good, straightforward wine, grassy on the nose, and with lively acidity on the palate, and hints of grapefruit pith on the finish. Both the 2004 and 2005 seem correct but one-dimensional.

Château Couhins-Lurton

Villenave d'Ornon. Tel: 0557 255858. Website: www.andrelurton.com. Cru classé for white only. **Owner:** *André Lurton.*
25 ha. 18 ha red: 77% Merlot, 23% Cabernet Sauvignon. 7 ha white: 100% Sauvignon Blanc.
Production: *45,000 bottles.* **Second wine:** *Ch Cantebau*

This property belonged until the 1960s to the Gasqueton family, the owners of Calon-Ségur. But they wanted to be rid of the property and were proposing to grub up the vines. Michel Delon of Léoville-Las-Cases got to hear about this and mentioned it to André Lurton. Lurton offered to lease the property, and the Gasquetons accepted his proposal. He recalls that the wines were in need of considerable attention. Nonetheless he started to produce a white wine here in 1967. The following year the property was divided. Lurton renamed his portion Couhins-Lurton, while the other part continued to be known as Château Couhins. In 1992 Lurton was able to buy the château itself, though it was not until 2003 that he got round to renovating it. He also constructed a terrace behind the house, with a view onto the adjacent woodland and the pool he built. The wine had always been made at La Louvière (*q.v.*), but since the renovation he has been able to vinify the wines here. The vineyards, like those of Couhins, are closer to the Garonne than most in the region.

The Sauvignon vines are planted to a density of 6,500 to 8,000 vines per hectare. They are picked in *cagettes*, with careful sorting at the winery. There is no skin contact. Since 1982 Couhins-Lurton has been fermented in fifty per cent new barriques and aged for around ten months. Since 2003, the white wine has been offered with a screwcap closure, as has La Louvière. In 2006 an oddity was produced: a late-harvest Sauvignon with a potential alcohol of twenty degrees.

The red wine is an innovation, though Lurton points out that in the nineteenth century ninety-five per cent of the vineyard here was planted to red vines. The red Couhins-Lurton comes from vines planted about two kilometres (1.2 miles) away, near Rochemorin on a gravelly site. They have been in production since 1994, but until 2002 the crop was blended with the wines of Château Coucheroy. The proportion of Merlot is unusually high. The wine is aged for twelve months in fifty per cent new oak and is eggwhite-fined before bottling.

The white wine is remarkable in being pure Sauvignon, yet with a fine capacity to age. The 1967 in 2000 was still spicy and lemony on the nose, while the palate was rich, full-bodied, and slightly nutty. The 1981 had faded by the late 1980s, but the 1985, 1987, and 1988 were all rich and vigorous in their youth, though I have not tasted them since the early 1990s. The 1990, at fifteen years of age, was a tremendous wine: the aromas are rich, waxy, and honeyed, while on the palate the fruit is rich and plump, with a nutty, zesty finish. The 1993 was also going strong in 2005 but the wine lacks the complexity and drama of the 1990. The Couhins-Lurton style – aromas of oak and citrus, with hazelnut nuances, and a blend of firm, elegant acidity and rich citric fruit – is evident on the splendid wines from 1995, 1996, 1997, 1998 (particularly fine), 1999, 2000 (still austere in 2005), 2001, and the assertive and first-rate 2002. The 2003 is quite powerful and tight for the vintage, but the oak gives some oily aromas and the wine lacks the invigorating acidity of earlier vintages. The 2004 is a distinguished wine, with complex lemon, pear, and oak aromas, and a concentrated and stylish structure.

The first vintage of red, the 2002, shows sweet cherry aromas. The high proportion of Merlot is evident on the sleek, supple palate, which is softer than, say, La Louvière. It seems to be a wine for relatively early drinking, but with the wines of André Lurton, one is always ready to be surprised. The 2003 too is supple, fleshy, and forward. The 2004 is oaky yet fragrant, with a sleek texture and firm tannins; raw now, it needs a few years to harmonise.

Château de Cruzeau

*St Médard d'Eyrans. Tel: 0557 255858. Website: www.andrelurton.com. **Owner:** André Lurton. 97 ha.*
70 ha red: 55% Cabernet Sauvignon, 43% Merlot, 2% Cabernet Franc. 27 ha white: 100% Sauvignon Blanc.
***Production:** 275,000 bottles*

André Lurton bought this large property in 1973, and the following year was felling woodland and replanting the vineyards in their entirety. There were substantial vineyards here by the late eighteenth century, planted on a single *croupe* with deep gravelly soil. The density ranges from 6,500 to 8,000 vines per hectare, and the reds are machine-harvested, whereas the whites are picked by hand. Until 1992 the wine was produced at La Louvière, but new cellars have been built to enable vinification to take place here, under the watchful eye of the director, Jean-Marc Comte. The red wines are fermented with *délestage* and aged twelve months in barriques of which twenty per cent are new. The white used to be aged partly in tanks, but since the late 1990s the entire crop has been aged in twenty-five per cent new barriques.

Although the white is pure Sauvignon, it has considerable weight, and a discreet waxiness as it ages. The wine is fresh and balanced, and intended to be drunk young, though it can be aged for quite a few years in good vintages such as 2004. The red is medium-bodied, discreet in its structure. It doesn't lack tannin, and sometimes has a delicate herbaceousness. Like the white, it is best enjoyed at three to five years old.

Château d'Eck

*Martillac. Tel: 0557 892157. **Owner:** Michel Gonet. 5 ha. 70% Merlot, 25% Cabernet Sauvignon, 5% Petit Verdot.*
***Production:** 15,000 bottles. **Second wine:** Ch Lantique*

As you drive down the autoroute from Bordeaux toward Langon, you soon pass the façade of a thirteenth-century castle on the right. This was once a residence of the bishops of Bordeaux, but has often changed hands. It takes its name from the Catholic theologian, Monseigneur Eck, who was a fierce opponent of Martin Luther. In 1999 the property was bought by Champagne producer Michel Gonet, who planted the vineyards. The wine is made at another of his properties, Haut-Bacalan (*q.v.*), and the first vintage was 2002. After manual harvesting, the grapes are sorted twice, and then vinified in conical steel vats. The wine is aged for fourteen months in new wood, with micro-oxygenation. The oak is quite evident on the rather charred aromas of the 2002, but this is a fleshy, easy-going wine, best enjoyed young. So is the spicy but rather stewed 2003. The wine is likely to gain in depth and structure as the vines age.

Château d'Eyran

*St Médard d'Eyrans. Tel: 0556 655159. Website: www.chateaudeyran.com. **Owner:** De Sèze family. 17 ha.*
*50% Cabernet Sauvignon, 45% Merlot, 5% Petit Verdot. **Production:** 80,000 bottles. **Second wine:** Ch Haut L'Artigue*

This château, on the edge of the village, was once a medieval fortress, but was rebuilt in the seventeenth century around a central courtyard. In 1796 it was bought by a well-known local family, the De Sèzes, whose descendants still live here. The vines were grubbed up between the world wars, and replanted from 1984 onwards. The estate is run by Stéphane Savigneux, who married into the family. The vineyards are not far from the Garonne, so the gravel is mixed with sand in places, and there is a base below of clay-limestone. The grapes are hand-picked, and the wine is fermented in fibreglass tanks before being aged for twelve months in thirty-five per cent new barriques.

The 1996 has retained considerable freshness, but it's not a wine with great depth of flavour. The 2000 has more concentration and grip, even to the point of austerity, and it could do with a bit more flesh on its bones. The 2002, with its light, cherry nose, is in the same mould. The 2001 is perhaps more slight, but also has a charm and delicacy missing in the other vintages. Château d'Eyran is not an expensive wine, but it shows a certain rusticity.

Château Ferran

Martillac. Tel: 0556 726273. Website: www.chateauferran.com. Owner: Hervé Béraud-Sudreau. 22 ha. 18 ha red:
67% Merlot, 30% Cabernet Sauvignon, 3% Cabernet Franc. 4 ha white: 55% Sémillon, 45% Sauvignon Blanc.
Production: 350,000 bottles

This property takes its name from the owner in the seventeenth century, Robert de Ferrand. It has belonged to the Béraud-Sudreau family since the late nineteenth century. Ferran has never been an exclusively viticultural estate, and to this day other farming activities are pursued in addition to grape-farming. M. Béraud-Sudreau has five daughters, which makes for very jolly family lunches, and one of them is married to the urbane Philippe Lacoste, who has been running the property since 1999. Although his previous career had nothing to do with wine, his father was a well-known Bordeaux *courtier*. Professor Denis Dubourdieu has been taken on as the consultant oenologist here.

The vineyards are in a number of parcels, the largest of which is a ten-hectare block between the château itself and Latour-Martillac, on a mix of gravel and clay-limestone. Harvesting is manual. As for the white wine, the Sauvignon receives some skin contact before pressing; both varieties are fermented and aged in thirty per cent new oak for ten months. The new oak barrels tend to be reserved for the Sémillon. The red is also aged in thirty per cent new barriques, for around twelve months.

Vintages of red Ferran from the 1990s that I have encountered have been unimpressive, but from 2000 there has been a significant improvement. The 2000 itself is powerful but fresh despite its robustness. There's a cedary, herbaceous tone in the 2001, but it's a wine with that refreshing Graves minerality and bite. The 2002 is less structured than 2000 but perhaps more elegant and spicy. The 2003 is rather slack and should be drunk soon. The 2002 white is very attractive, with lightly grassy aromas and flavours of ripe grapefruit. The 2003 is rich and silky but less complex and long. The 2004 has spicy, oaky aromas and ample and lively apricot fruit. Overall, Ferran offers very good value.

Château de Fieuzal

Léognan. Tel: 0556 647786. Website: www.fieuzal.com. Owner: Lochlann Quinn. Cru classé for red only. 48 ha.
40 ha red: 48% Cabernet Sauvignon, 48% Merlot, 2.5% Cabernet Franc, 1.5% Petit Verdot. 8 ha white: 50% Sémillon,
*50% Sauvignon Blanc. **Production: 250,000 bottles. Second wine: Abeille de Fieuzal***

Once the property of the La Rochefoucauld family, Fieuzal was owned in the early nineteenth century by the family from which it takes its name, and from 1851 by the Griffon family. Alfred Griffon had useful connections to the papal authorities, which helped secure good sales of the wine to the Vatican. In the twentieth century Fieuzal passed through various hands. In 1974 it was bought from the Bocké family by Georges Négrevergne, whose son-in-law Gérard Gribelin was installed as director; he worked energetically and successfully to improve quality. In 1994 the estate was sold to a French bank, though Gribelin stayed on to run the property. An Irish chapter opened in 2001, when Fieuzal was sold for the equivalent of thirty-six million pounds sterling to the banker Lochlann Quinn, who recently built a house adjacent to the stylish winery. Under Gribelin the winemaker was the esteemed Michel Dupuy; since 1999 Jean-Luc Marchive has been directing the property, having previously worked at Château L'Evangile.

The soil here is very fine, principally white pebbles on gravel and sand, with some clay. The average age of the red vines is around thirty years, and Fieuzal is particularly proud of a parcel of Petit Verdot dating from 1908. The soil is ploughed, and the grapes picked in *cagettes*. After sorting and destemming the must is fermented, then aged in varying amounts of new oak depending on the vintage. In 2000 the proportion was sixty-five per cent, but it had been reduced to thirty-five per cent by 2004. Marchive has been experimenting with different kinds of oak, and has introduced some larger barrels of 400 and 500 litres.

The white wine is more expensive than the red, as yields tend to be lower, production is limited, and demand is high, even though historically this estate produced only red wine. It was only from 1985 that the entire crop was barrel-fermented. There is no skin contact, and the new wine is usually in barrel ten hours after it has been picked. There is no malolactic fermentation, and the wine is aged for up to eighteen months in fifty per cent new oak, although the proportion was higher under Gribelin.

White Fieuzal is one of Bordeaux's best. The first modern-style white, the 1985, was still going strong a decade later, a fresh, creamy wine with a long, spicy finish. The 1986, 1987, 1988, 1990, and 1991 were all excellent within five years of the vintage, but I have not tasted them more recently. The 1995 is a delicious wine, with fine acidity and impeccable balance. The 1998 seems dominated by Sémillon, with a rich and supple palate, and an elegant oakiness. The 1999 is very similar, though with a touch more force. The 2002 is outstanding, with oak and lime on the nose, while the palate exudes very ripe fruit, balanced by almost racy acidity; this is a very stylish wine. There is broad, creamy fruit on the 2003, but the wine has less vigour than most from Fieuzal. I have twice tasted the 2004, which seemed oddly flabby.

The oldest red I have tasted is the 1964; encountered thirty years later, it had brooding, mushroomy aromas and rich, earthy flavours, and little sign of old age. The 1985 was still seductive in 2005, with a savoury, black-curranty nose, its elegant Cabernet flavour and silky texture in complete harmony. I have conflicting notes on the 1986, but the 1987, though a touch overoaked, was very good for the vintage. The 1988 is classic Graves: delicately herbaceous, tobacco aromas, and an elegant, savoury character on the palate. The 1990 has more intensity, though the oak is too dominant; nonetheless this is a dense, assertive wine of elegance in harness with power. The 1992 was stringy and acidic, and the 1994 a touch astringent. The 1996 has evolved beautifully, losing its youthful chunkiness to exhibit sweet, cedary aromas and a tight, lean, oaky structure. The 1997 shows unusual robustness and spice for the year. The vintages from 1998 to 2000 were supple in texture, but showed forceful tannins in their youth. The 2000 has a ripe, fleshy nose that's also quite smoky; although medium-bodied and supple, the wine is concentrated, with a spiciness that brightens the rather soft texture. The 2001 has firm, ripe tannins but seems to lack a little vigour, and is outshone by the excellent 2002, with its black-cherry aromas, silky texture, fine tannins, and integrated acidity. In 2003 the Fieuzal team avoided excessive extraction and the wine, despite a somewhat confected nose, seems attractive and balanced, for medium-term drinking. The medium-bodied 2004 has waxy, red-fruits aromas and is concentrated and persistent.

The style of Fieuzal is consistently more weighty than many other Pessac-Léognans, with a marked black-fruits character on the nose, and robust tannins and oakiness. Both red and white Fieuzal age very well. I suspect that under Marchive the wine will gain in finesse without losing its richness and density.

Château de France

*Léognan. Tel: 0556 647539. Website: www.chateau-de-france.com. **Owner:** Bernard Thomassin. 38.5 ha.*
36 ha red: 60% Cabernet Sauvignon, 40% Merlot. 2.5 ha white: 70% Sauvignon Blanc, 30% Sémillon.
***Production:** 220,000 bottles. **Second wine:** Ch Coquillas*

These vineyards, in one of the best sectors of Léognan, were developed by a Bordeaux parliamentarian called Taffard in the eighteenth century. In 1862 the property was bought by Jean-Henri Lacoste, who built the gawky yellow château, which lords it over the surrounding countryside. In the twentieth century the estate passed through numerous hands. When Bernard Thomassin purchased Château de France in 1971, he found the property badly neglected and needing a good deal of work in the vineyard. In 1993 he constructed a rather ugly new *chai*.

The vineyards lie just north of Fieuzal, mostly in a single parcel of Pyrenees gravel that surrounds the château. The soil is very gravelly but quite diverse, and in winter three different soil types are clearly visible from the château terrace. Compost is added to enrich the soil, which is light and poor in organic matter. A further four hectares lie alongside the road to Gradignan. The Thomassins have the right to plant a further seven hectares on a *croupe* near Château Le Sartre, so the property may expand. One-third of the red vines are over thirty years old, but the average age is considerably less. There are also some parcels that were planted at a density of 5,000 vines per hectare, which will need to be increased to meet the AC requirements. Since 1995 the grapes have been picked by hand.

White wines were produced only from 1988 onwards. The Sauvignon grapes receive some skin contact. Like the Sémillon, the Sauvignon is barrel-fermented, and aged for about seven months with *bâtonnage* in fifty per cent new oak. There is no malolactic fermentation.

The reds, after sorting and destemming, are fermented in steel tanks that Thomassin installed here in the early 1970s. There is a cold soak for up to four days before fermentation begins. No concentrator is used, so the tanks are bled if the must lacks concentration. The wine is aged in up to fifty per cent new barriques for about twelve months, with racking from barrel to barrel. The wine is eggwhite-fined and lightly filtered.

The oldest white I have tasted, other than the very modest 1991, is the plump 1998. I prefer the highly drinkable 1999, with its aromas of apricot and quince, and a fresh, sherbetty tone on the palate. The 2002 is more citric, with grapefruity flavours and considerable piquancy; not a complex wine, but refreshing and assertive. The 2003 has similar flavours but the finish is short; the flowery but powerful and spicy 2004 shows great promise. The 2005 shows mor elegance than power.

As for the reds, the 1990, when young, had a strong black-cherry character. The 1996, while not hugely concentrated, combined richness with elegance, and has good underlying acidity and a very discreet herbaceousness. The 1997 is astringent now, but the 1998 has gained in complexity over the years, though it remains a wine that is solid rather than graceful. The 2001 has ripe, plummy aromas, and ample fruit and spice on the palate. The 2002 has an aroma of sour cherries, and some greenness on the palate. I prefer the 2001. Dilution, a rather soupy texture, and a whack of tannin add up to an unbalanced 2003. The 2004 is juicy and forward but well balanced.

Château de France is a somewhat underrated wine. It is not one of the region's superstars, but quality is dependable and the price moderate. It's not surprising that it features on restaurant wine lists throughout Bordeaux.

Château La Garde

Martillac. Tel: 0556 355300. Website: www.cvbg.com. Owner: Dourthe. 59 ha. 57 ha red: 60% Cabernet Sauvignon, 40% Merlot. 2 ha white: 50% Sauvignon Gris, 50% Sémillon. Production: 240,000 bottles.

Second wine: La Terrasse de la Garde

From 1926 until 1990 this property, which borders Latour-Martillac, Rochemorin, and Haut-Nouchet, was owned by the négociant house of Eschenauer, which also owned Smith-Haut-Lafitte and Rauzan-Ségla. Under its stewardship the quality never rose above acceptable: there was no selection, no temperature control, no new wood. In 1990 ownership passed into the hands of another négociant, Dourthe-Kressmann, which is now part of the CVBG group. Since 2002 the winemaker has been Caroline Debelmas, with Michel Rolland as consultant oenologist for the red wines, and Christophe Ollivier as consultant for the whites. The château itself is a small but charming chartreuse dating from 1739. Under Eschenauer it was used for storage, but has now been restored; moreover, a new underground *chai* has been constructed.

CVBG has undertaken some vineyard expansion and replanting, so the average age of the vines is only around twenty years. Density is up to 8,700 vines per hectare, and trellising is quite high so as to increase the wall of foliage. There are three principal stony *croupes* that adjoin, and individual treatment is given to each of twenty-five parcels. The soil is predominantly gravelly but there is a vein of clay on which the Merlot and some Petit Verdot have been planted; the Petit Verdot came into production in 2006.

The harvest is manual and can take as long as three weeks, given the varying pace of maturation within the vineyards. The red winemaking is sophisticated. The cold soak takes place under a blanket of dry ice. The grapes are destemmed but not crushed. La Garde has acquired a destemming machine called an *égreneur* (see Chapter Three), which separates those less-ripe grapes that will be consigned to the second wine. There is some *pigeage* during fermentation with a device that hauls up the juice from the bottom of the tanks and breaks the cap. Some lots are micro-oxygenated toward the end of fermentation. The wine is aged for twelve to fifteen months in thirty-five per cent new oak, with micro-oxygenation in barrel as an alternative to racking. There is usually an eggwhite-fining before filtration.

The white wine, of which only about 10,000 bottles are made, is unusual in that it contains a high proportion of Sauvignon Gris grapes that add richness and weight to the blend. The must is barrel-fermented, and aged for ten months in twenty-five per cent new oak with *bâtonnage*. After the malolactic fermentation, the lees are separated from the juice and stirred for a month in tank in order, the theory goes, to liberate proteins and other compounds. Then those lees are redistributed to the barrels that would most benefit from the richness they would impart. Stirring is done by rolling the barrels.

La Garde is a hotbed of experimentation, with Caroline Debelmas using 400-litre barrels for micro-vinifications in order to compare grapes from ploughed versus green-covered soils, and to compare varying periods of cold soak, and so forth.

My first experience of the white wine was the spicy, elegant, oaky 1990 Réserve (a category abandoned some years ago). The 1998 was rich and full-bodied, the 2003 predictably rich but with an odd sweet-and-sour tone. But the 2004 is outstanding, with aromas of apricots and apples, a supple texture, good concentration and acidity, and a bracing austerity that should soften with time.

As for the reds, the 1990 Réserve was plump and lush – a fine wine if not markedly Graves in character; the 1992 Réserve was excellent for that difficult vintage. The 1998 got off to an awkward start, with chunky tannins, but has now mellowed into an elegant and concentrated wine that has kept its freshness and length. The 2000 is suave, savoury, quite extracted, and still youthful. In 2007 the 2001 was sound but lacklustre, but the 2002 is delicious, with all the charm of Graves at its most ingratiating, yet with firm underlying tannins. The 2003 is heavy and somewhat stewed, and should be drunk soon. The 2004 lacks some substance, but it's lean and elegant, with charming cherry aromas.

Château Gazin-Rocquencourt

Léognan. Tel: 0556 647508. **Owner:** *Alfred-Alexandre Bonnie. 22 ha. 55% Cabernet Sauvignon, 45% Merlot.*
Production: *80,000 bottles.* **Second wines:** *Ch Gazin-Michotte, Les Granges de Gazin*

The family of Jean-Marie Michotte, a Bordeaux doctor, bought this property on the outskirts of Léognan in 1966, when it was in a parlous state. Originally known simply as Château Gazin, the second part of the name was added in 1995. Having an absentee proprietor did little to maintain quality here, so the purchase of the estate, which enjoyed a fine reputation a century ago, by the owner of Château Malartic-Lagravière (*q.v.*) in 2006 has to be a welcome development. The Malartic team had already been responsible for the vinification of the 2005 vintage. After the purchase, Bonnie began constructing a new winery and replanting dormant parcels to a higher density; later the old vines will be restructured. By 2007 only 15 hectares were in production, but this area will gradually increase and production will rise to around 100,000 bottles.

Under Michotte, the grapes were machine-harvested, the vinification was highly interventionist, and only part of the crop was aged in barrels. Not surprisingly the wines were mediocre, lacking in fruit, concentration, and vigour. No doubt, Bonnie's wealth and professionalism will help to turn things around. The revived Gazin will be aged in 40 per cent new barriques for fifteen to twenty months. The dense and chewy 2005 shows the hand of the new team, though it remains somewhat rustic, while the infant 2006 seems to have more purity of fruit.

Domaine de Grandmaison

Léognan. Tel: 0556 647537. Website: www.domaine-de-grandmaison.fr. Owner: Jean Bouquier. 19 ha.
16 ha red: 50% Cabernet Sauvignon, 50% Merlot. 3 ha white: 65% Sauvignon Blanc, 20% Sémillon,
15% Sauvignon Gris. Production: 120,000 bottles

François Bouquier came from the Auvergne and bought this property in 1939. Today it is run by his grandson, also called François, who is given some kindly advice by his courteous father Jean. The main parcel of Grandmaison is close to Carbonnieux, and there is also a three-hectare block near Olivier. The entire property was replanted by Jean Bouquier from 1970 onwards. The soil is varied, with a good deal of clay-limestone as well as gravel and sandy gravel; however the vineyards do not lie on one of the appellation's prestigious *croupes*.

The grapes are hand-picked by a Roma clan that has been harvesting here for decades. The bunches are sorted at the winery. Yeasts are added to the tanks, as the Bouquiers like the fermentation to begin rapidly so as to avoid any risk of oxidation. The tanks are bled to increase concentration, and the wine is aged for twelve months in one-third new barriques.

As for the white wine, the Sémillon is fermented in new barriques with *bâtonnage*, while the Sauvignon remains in tanks. The two components are blended after about five months, and bottled in the spring. The white is attractive, with fresh grassy and floral aromas, and a lean, lively palate. Not a great wine, but eminently drinkable and well balanced. The crisp, delicious 2005 rises to greater heights.

Jean Bouquier generously opened a bottle of his 1955. At fifty years old, this wine showed a slight leafiness on the nose, while on the palate it was supple, even fleshy, with no trace of oxidation; the texture was sleek, the tannins ripe, and there was no indication that the wine was tiring at all. It was remarkable, given that Grandmaison does not claim to be an exceptional terroir. Jean Bouquier attributes the wine's quality and longevity to the old vines still flourishing a year before the destructive frost of 1956, to the absence of clones, and to low yields. As for more recent vintages, I found the 1996 somewhat astringent and coarse, the 1998 assertive and concentrated with a sweet, ripe finish, the 2001 rather dry and dour, the 2002 much more charming, with freshness and a light tannic backbone. Even better is the bright yet fleshy 2004.

Prices are very reasonable for the quality, and Grandmaison is an admirable wine for medium-term enjoyment.

Château Haut-Bacalan

Pessac. Tel: 0557 892157. Owner: Michel Gonet. 7 ha. 80% Merlot, 20% Cabernet Sauvignon.
Production: 30,000 bottles

The Champenois Gonet family, who bought Château d'Eck (*q.v.*) in the late 1990s, also bought this property, which had to be entirely replanted, so that the first vintage was 2001. The estate is run by Gonet's son Charles-Henri. The vineyard, which lies not far from the autoroute from Bordeaux to Toulouse, once belonged to Montesquieu, but by the 1930s there were no longer any vines here. The soil is gravelly, so it is surprising that the Gonets planted so much Merlot. The grapes are selected carefully, yeasts are added to the must, and vinification takes place in conical steel vats. Despite the youth of the vines, the wine is aged in eighty per cent new French and American oak for some fourteen months, with the aid of micro-oxygenation.

I tasted the wines in the Gonets' drawing room, with the active participation of their small son, which probably didn't enhance my powers of concentration. I find the 2001, 2002, and 2003 far too oaky and dense, with a thick texture, evident extraction, but also a certain hollowness and lack of length. The 2004 is less extracted, but still rather overripe and one-dimensional.

Château Haut-Bailly

*Léognan. Tel: 0556 647511. Website: www.chateau-haut-bailly.com. **Owner**: Robert Wilmers. Cru classé.*
*28 ha. 65% Cabernet Sauvignon, 25% Merlot, 10% Cabernet Franc. **Production**: 160,000 bottles.*
Second wine: La Parde de Haut-Bailly

There are few wines from Bordeaux that inspire the same affection as Haut-Bailly. And with good reason. For typicity, consistency, harmony, stylishness, and value, Haut-Bailly is hard to beat.

The property, which lies between Léognan and the vineyards of La Louvière on a very visible *croupe*, was created in the 1630s by a Parisian banker called Firmin Le Bailly, in partnership with a wine merchant called Nicolas de Leuvarde. Firmin's son was obliged to sell the estate, which passed through various hands, until in 1872 it was acquired by the engineer Alcide Henri Bellot des Minières, who built the château and developed the vineyards further. When phylloxera struck, he was opposed to the use of American rootstocks, which explains why there is still a three-hectare parcel of ungrafted vines. The present administrator, Véronique Sanders, likes to point out that from the 1870s to the 1920s Haut-Bailly was selling for the same price as many *premiers crus*.

After Bellot des Minières died in 1906, his daughters inherited the property, but they sold it in 1918 to Frantz Malvezin. Once again it was inherited by daughters, who promptly sold the estate in 1923. There followed a period of instability and some neglect. Then in 1955 a Belgian wine merchant, Daniel Sanders, bought Haut-Bailly and replanted much of the property. Only ten hectares were under vine, as many parcels had been abandoned and turned into grazing land, which he realized was a waste of an outstanding terroir. In 1979 his courteous and dignified son Jean took over. He continued to restore the property, which by 1988 was once more at its original size.

Jean Sanders had a few years in which to enjoy the fruits of his labours, until his sisters decided they wanted their share of the property. He had no option other than to sell, but he was fortunate in his buyer: a banker from New York State called Robert Wilmers, whose passion for the property and its wine was genuine. He invested heavily, expanding the *chais* and quadrupling the number of tanks in the *cuvier*, thus allowing more detailed parcel selections to be made. He retained the services of Jean Sanders as administrator, and when Jean retired in 2000, the mantle passed to his able daughter Véronique. By this time Denis Dubourdieu was already working as a consultant to the estate, and Jean-Bernard Delmas, formerly of Château Haut-Brion, later joined the advisory team. In 2003 Gabriel Vialard, who had made a great contribution to the revival of Smith-Haut-Lafitte, was brought in as technical director.

From the château there is a good view over the vineyard. This is a wonderful terroir for Cabernet Sauvignon, but the team is less keen on Cabernet Franc. So, as old Cabernet Franc vines die off, they are being replaced with Cabernet Sauvignon. The average age of the vineyard is some thirty-five years, boosted by the plot of very old ungrafted vines, which includes some Carmenère. The density is 10,000 vines per hectare, still very much the exception in Pessac-Léognan.

As well as embarking on an ambitious building programme, Robert Wilmers initiated a two-year study of the soil. This showed that the soils here are complex indeed, and that the subsoil is largely composed of petrified fossils. Merlot is planted, as it should be, on the heavier soils. "We were surprised to learn", says Véronique Sanders, "that the roots don't descend very deep into the soil. This means we have problems in very dry years." No herbicides are used, the soil is ploughed, and, of course, the grapes are picked by hand.

Until 1959 the wine was made in wooden vats, which, on the advice of Emile Peynaud, were replaced by cement tanks. These function well, and have even been added to by Véronique Sanders. At the *cuvier* the grapes are sorted twice, given a three-day cold soak, then almost always fermented with indigenous yeasts. Malolactic fermentation takes place in tanks, and then the wine is blended and aged in fifty per cent new barriques for fourteen to fifteen months. There is less racking than in the past.

Only red wine is produced, though in the eighteenth century there were white vines too, but by the 1950s they had vanished.

A second wine, Domaine de la Parde, was introduced in 1967, then revived in 1979 under its present name. In the late 1980s and early 1990s a third wine was also made in some years to maintain the quality of the Haut-Parde, and today that third wine is produced systematically.

The château administrators look back with awe at vintages such as 1900, 1918, 1921, 1928, 1929, 1945, 1947, 1955, 1959, 1961, and 1964. The oldest Haut-Bailly I have tasted is the 1970. At over twenty years old, the aromas were cedary, while on the palate richness was balanced by charm. The 1976 smells enticing: leaf and mint, with hints of undergrowth; in 2005 the wine (from magnum) was still alive, silky and spicy, yet showing little weight or complexity, and the finish is somewhat dry. The 1978, tasted in the mid-1990s, struck me as quintessential Haut-Bailly in that it was not exceptionally concentrated or obviously structured. Instead, I scribbled: "rounded, ripe, velvety, lovely fruit, elegant, discreet, harmonious, perfect now". The 1979 was in the same mould; in 1988 I thought it just ready to drink, but in 1999 it was showing no sign of fatigue.

The 1981 was reasonably stylish but had a disconcerting earthiness. I found the 1982 generous and voluptuous, though the Sanders never thought this was a great year at Haut-Bailly. They were right to value the 1983 more highly. It has a seamless texture and the balance is completely harmonious. The 1985 took a while to unfold, but by 2007 it had become truly elegant, supple in texture but tight in structure. Although it can certainly be drunk with pleasure now, there need be no rush to empty the cellar. The 1986 has atypical liquorice aromas; on the palate it is now amazingly silky, with the firm tannins of the year without being overbearing. The 1988 had the toughness, even aggression, of the vintage when young, but retains its firm core of fruit. The 1989 has more power and density, undoubtedly impressive though perhaps not the most elegant Haut-Bailly. I prefer the 1990, which has been consistently delicious, full of charm and silkiness, and now approaching maturity, with lovely cedary aromas, and a palate that fuses opulence and elegance, and finishes very long indeed.

The 1994 has more charm than many wines from this vintage, though there is a certain neutrality to the fruit quality. At ten years of age, the 1995 was still very youthful. This is a wine for the long haul, austere and tight but not tough, but also with complexity and persistence. The 1996 has minty, even gently herbaceous, aromas; it is graceful and concentrated, but is rather leaner than one expects from Haut-Bailly. The 1997 is a success for the vintage. The 1998, which has forty-three per cent Merlot, has taken a while to open up, but is now showing its true splendour: it has a perfumed and sumptuous oaky nose, fruit intensity, robust tannins, fine balance, and a fresh, spicy finish. The 1999 is stylish and floral on the nose, medium-bodied yet tightly structured, a soft-spoken but eloquent wine that's beginning to drink nicely.

The 2000 has exquisite, pure blackcurrant aromas; the texture is supple, the fruit concentrated, the ripe tannins balanced by good acidity, and the finish is long – what more could one want? The 2001 has bold but elegant oaky aromas and a supple texture, fine black-fruits flavours, less structure than the 2000, and some welcome acidity on the finish. The 2002 is seductively fruity on the nose with the oak beautifully integrated; in the mouth the wine shows engaging blackcurrant and mint flavours with a touch of Graves earthiness. The 2003 is atypical, with slightly jammy aromas and mocha overtones; surprisingly, the wine lacks density; it seems hollow despite its grippy tannins. But the 2004 sees a return to Haut-Bailly's purity and elegance, and is gaining weight as it evolves.

There are few properties in Bordeaux that offer greater consistency than Haut-Bailly. That, and its reasonable price, makes it easy to understand why the wine is such a firm favourite among discerning consumers.

Château Haut-Bergey

*Léognan. Tel: 0556 640522. Website: www.chateau-haut-bergey.com. **Owner:** Sylviane Garcin-Cathiard.*
25 ha. 23 ha red: 60% Cabernet Sauvignon, 40% Merlot. 2 ha white: 80% Sauvignon Blanc, 20% Sémillon.
***Production:** 90,000 bottles. **Second wine:** Etoile de Bergey*

The property dates from the fifteenth century, and the original château once stood across the road from the hulking neo-Gothic structure erected here in the nineteenth century. In the 1770s there were 100 hectares of vineyards, but in subsequent years the property shrank. Its revival dates from 1991, when Mme. Garcin-Cathiard bought the estate, which lies between the town and Domaine de Chevalier. She may have caught the bug for vineyard purchases from her brother Daniel Cathiard of Smith-Haut-Lafitte, and has since acquired more properties in Pessac-Léognan and on the Right Bank, as well as in Argentina. It is very much a family business, with her husband, a lawyer, increasingly involved, and her energetic daughter Hélène Garcin-Lévêque now the public face of the group.

At first the Garcins relied heavily on advice from consultants Michel Rolland and Christophe Ollivier, but since 2001 have dispensed with such services, and entrust the winemaking to Véronique Sancet. The year 2001 also saw the complete renovation of the *chais* and château. In addition, they have undertaken an exhaustive geological analysis of the soil to ensure that the harvesting and vinification are perfectly adapted to the specificity of the wine from each parcel. As Hélène sees it, the idea is to express the hidden minerality of the wines, rather than rely on the easier charms of their aromatic qualities.

The vineyards are quite dispersed, with parcels near Chevalier, others behind the winery, and others across the road in patches now surrounded by housing. The average age of the holdings is thirty-five years, and there are parcels of very old vines, though the white vines date from 1989. Yields are low: about thirty hl/ha for the red wines, thirty-five for the white. The estate is not organic but does practise *lutte raisonnée*. For the white wine the model is a burgundian style. Hence the emphasis on seeking minerality rather than perfume, on lengthy fermentations and lees-stirring. There is no malolactic fermentation and the wine is aged in about one-third new oak for twelve months, although the Sauvignon is aged in one-year-old barriques. It has taken a while for the white wine of Haut-Bergey to show its true potential. Vintages such as 1998 were rather heavy-handed, oaky, and even dull, while 1999 was more lively and citric yet lacked complexity and structure. So, for that matter, did the 2000. The 2002 is markedly better, with clear minerality on the nose, a silky texture, good concentration, and ample vigour. The 2003, predictably, is more opulent and peachy, even soft, but it is certainly packed with fruit and will give considerable pleasure in the short term. The 2004, with its lemon-sherbet nose, seems a return to the style and fine quality of 2002, although with greater power.

The red is given a modern vinification, with a cold soak, natural yeasts, some bleeding of the tanks to increase concentration if necessary (the reverse-osmosis machine, the Garcins say, is used only as a last resort), and, on an equally pragmatic basis, some micro-oxygenation toward the end of fermentation. Most of the malolactic fermentation takes place in barrels, and the wine is aged in forty to sixty per cent new barriques for around fifteen months, before eggwhite-fining and bottling.

As with the whites, the reds of the 1990s were often unbalanced, but there was a distinct improvement with the 1998 vintage, with its intense aromas of oak and mint, and remarkable youthful vigour on the palate – a wine that has steadily gained in complexity with bottle-age. The same is true of the sleek 1999, with its elegant black-cherry aromas, silky texture, and good length. The 2000 is in a similar mould but with more richness and power. The 2001 is beginning to unfurl, and in 2005 its tannins had become more supple and were balanced by good acidity. The 2002, tasted in 2005, was still oaky and inexpressive. In 2003 excessive extraction was clearly avoided, and the result is a medium-bodied, spicy, chocolatey wine with considerable length. The 2004 and 2005 show great promise, although the latter is quite extracted.

14. Pessac-Léognan Part II

Château Haut-Brion

*Pessac. Tel: 0556 002930. Website: www.haut-brion.com. **Owner:** Dillon family. Cru classé for red only. 46 ha.*
43.2 ha red: 45% Cabernet Sauvignon, 37% Merlot, 18% Cabernet Franc. 2.7 ha white: 60% Sémillon, 40% Sauvignon
*Blanc. **Production:** 160,000 bottles. **Second wines:** Ch Bahans Haut-Brion, Les Plantiers de Haut-Brion (white)*

This was the first red Bordeaux to achieve name recognition outside France, astonishing England's wine fanciers long before Lafite or Margaux landed at its ports. Much admired in England in the seventeenth century, Haut-Brion had been a leading property for at least a century by then. Although Pepys's celebrated diary entry of 1663 sang the praises of "Ho Bryan" and its "good and most particular taste", there are earlier references to the wine in the cellar books of Charles II from 1660. In the seventeenth century the Pontac family owned a number of estates, of which Haut-Brion was the most lustrous, fetching considerably higher prices than the most renowned properties of the Médoc.

It was Jean de Pontac's good fortune to marry an heiress who brought the estate with her as part of her dowry in 1525. Jean's father Renaud de Pontac was a rich merchant and mayor of Bordeaux. After Jean's marriage to Jeanne de Bellon, he consolidated the estate, buying additional parcels, building the château in the 1550s, and living to the alarming age of 101. Their descendants, Arnaud de Pontac and his son François-Auguste, decided to exploit the growing renown of their wine in London by opening a tavern called The Pontack's Head. It remained open for over a century, selling Haut-Brion at a very high price.

François-Auguste had no sons, and the property passed through the female line to the Fumel family. The property was divided in 1749, but the Fumels, who also owned Château Margaux, received the major share. Joseph Fumel invested heavily in the estate. Later in the century Thomas Jefferson dropped in during his tour of Bordeaux's top estates and admired its terroir. The Fumels didn't make it through the Revolution, and Joseph lost his head in 1794. Nonetheless the property was recovered by the family, but swiftly sold in 1801 to the French foreign minister Talleyrand. He kept Haut-Brion for only three years before selling it to a banker. There were more changes in ownership, and a reported decline in the quality of the wine by the time it was put up for auction in 1836. The purchaser was a Parisian banker called Joseph-Eugène Larrieu, who also managed to acquire the smaller section of the property that had been separated almost a century earlier. It remained in the Larrieu family until 1923. During their tenure the second wine, Bahans Haut-Brion, was created, and represented roughly fifteen per cent of production. Rather confusingly, it would come to be offered in both vintage and non-vintage versions, a practice that ceased as recently as 1982.

During the 1920s the property was owned by André Gilbert, who, according to wine writer Clive Coates, maintained quality at a high level but could not weather the economic difficulties of the 1930s, and the property was once again offered for sale. At this point the modern era of Haut-Brion begins, as the purchaser in 1935 was the American banker Clarence Dillon, whose descendants are still at the helm in the form of his granddaughter Joan Dillon (the Duchesse de Mouchy) and her son by a previous marriage, Prince Robert of Luxembourg, who is in his mid-forties. Of crucial importance has been the contribution of the Delmas family as administrators of the estate. Georges Delmas was hired in 1921, succeeded in 1960 by the revered Jean-Bernard, and he in turn, in 2004, by his son Jean-Philippe.

It was Jean-Bernard Delmas who created the remarkable *cuvier*, equipped with stainless-steel tanks of his own design, in 1961, making Haut-Brion the first major estate in Bordeaux to vinify in stainless steel. Further renovations and extensions took place over the years, and in 1983 the Dillons consolidated their holdings by acquiring the prestigious neighbouring property of La Mission Haut-Brion.

Although it's hard to perceive, the vineyards are considerably elevated, at a height of up to twenty-seven metres (eighty-nine feet). There is plenty of deep and occasionally stony Günzian gravel as well as parcels with a higher clay content. Most of the vineyard lies grouped around the château, the remainder being on the other side of the main road. Jean-Bernard Delmas attached enormous importance to the selection of appropriate rootstocks and clones, and from 1970 onwards conducted research under the auspices of INRA. There were no fewer than eighty-four micro-vinifications to establish which rootstocks and clones performed best on this terroir. The criteria for evaluation included colour, sugar levels, acidity, phenols, and yield. The study established that ten per cent of the clones performed best in all conditions here, eighty per cent showed significant variations from year to year, and the remaining ten per cent were unacceptable. This immense labour has also made its contribution to the quality of the plant material in the vineyards. The long-term aim has been to lower the yield not by green-harvesting but by ensuring the vines (based on the correct choice of rootstock and clone) are healthy and balanced.

The average age of the vineyards is now over thirty-five years, the oldest parcels dating from the 1930s. The average density is 8,000 vines per hectare. The white vines are planted on a hillock across the road from the château on very deep gravel over a clay subsoil. Two-thirds of these vines were replanted in 1977, so the average age is some twenty-eight years. Each parcel of vines is tended by the same team of workers, giving them deep familiarity with each vine and its requirements. There is some ploughing of the soil, but also a discreet use of herbicides. All vines are harvested by hand. The harvest is always precocious, especially for the white grapes, since proximity to the city gives a warmer microclimate than more rural sectors of Pessac-Léognan.

Pascal Baratié is the *chef de culture* here. It's a vitally important job, especially given the atypical microclimate. He calculates yields by weight per vine. Merlot has larger bunches, so he looks for fewer bunches on Merlot than on Cabernet vines. Leaves are removed in early July, but only on one side of the row to minimize the risk of sunburn. Rows that require green-harvesting are operated on in the latter half of July.

The white grapes are picked as late as possible in *cagettes*, sorted, then pressed in whole bunches in a pneumatic press. There is no skin contact. Fermentation takes place in Allier barrels with indigenous yeasts. There is no malolactic fermentation and no lees-stirring, although it's not a firm rule; in 1998, for instance, some barrels were stirred. The ageing continues for ten to twelve months. In the past 100 per cent new oak was used, but this has now been moderated to forty to forty-five per cent.

The red grapes are sorted in the vineyard. At the winery they are destemmed, lightly crushed, then pumped into tanks. The custom-designed tanks are double-deckers, the lower storey reserved for the malolactic fermentation, the new wine descending by gravity into the lower tanks. In addition, the tanks are squat in design so as to provide as much contact between the cap and the juice as possible. Not all the tanks date from their invention in 1961; more vats, on the same principle, were installed in 1991. Pumpovers are computerized. Indigenous yeasts are relied upon, except in very tricky vintages such as the rainy 1992. The temperature is allowed to rise as high as 33°C (91°F), and the *cuvaison* usually lasts for eighteen to twenty-one days. The vinification remains classic, with no cold soak and no extended maceration.

Blending takes place fairly early, so that the specific quality of the various lots is not obscured by oak influence. The wine used to be aged for eighteen months in 100 per cent new oak, but the new oak has been reduced to about thirty-five per cent. Lots destined for the second wine are aged in about twenty-five per cent new oak. Haut-Brion has its own cooperage, with a barrel-maker from Séguin-Moreau fashioning the casks used for the château's wines. This allows the winemakers to have greater control over the toasting, which is usually medium-minus. Eggwhite-fining takes place after the wine has been in barrel for about a year.

Haut-Brion is, as one would expect, quintessential Graves. It doesn't have the overt power and structure of the Médoc First Growths. Instead it offers exquisite aromatic complexity, subtlety, a supple earthiness, nuance, and elegance, as well as a softer and more accessible texture. It's a wine that can age well, though rarely with the longevity of the Médoc growths. But it can come close.

Some years ago I drank a 1970 wine called Passion de Haut-Brion. No one knew what it was, other than that the label clearly suggested a connection with Haut-Brion. I later learned that the wine came from a parcel behind La Mission that was rented by Haut-Brion and bottled separately, as many of the bottles were sent to the vines' owner, a doctor from Cannes. Whether the vinification was separate, or whether the wine was actually Haut-Brion with a private label I have not been able to establish. It is no longer produced.

The white wine was often overoaked in the 1980s and early 1990s. Vintages such as 1983, 1985, 1988, and 1992 are magnificent, with tremendous concentration and depth and a beautifully creamy texture, but the aromas in particular were often overpowered by the wood. Nor did this diminish with age. The 1988, drunk once more in 2002, was still pungently oaky. Recent vintages have, in my view, been far better balanced. The brilliant 1999, for example, seems tighter, more intense, with fine acidity balancing the hints of peach and dried fruit. The 1998 is fatter, more overtly oaky, but has a dash of citric acidity and the minerality of the wine comes through clearly. The only recent vintage I have tasted is the infant 2006, a flamboyant wine with great intensity and length.

The oldest red Haut-Brion I have tasted is the 1928, still amazingly deep in colour seventy-five years later. The aromas were ravishing and succulent, but there was a hint of astringency on the palate which intensified with aeration. But the intensity and length were deeply impressive. A magnum of 1929, tasted on the same occasion, was almost opaque in colour, with an aroma of coffee grounds (as with the 1928) and cigar ash; but there was some *pétillance* on the palate from secondary fermentation, though the wine had kept its freshness and spiciness. Even finer was the 1934, again from magnum, which had similar qualities to the older vintages but was healthier, tighter, and had impressive length and vigour.

I last tasted the 1947 and 1957 in 1985. The 1947 had plummy, heady aromas, and the highly concentrated palate showed sweet fruit alongside a rather dry texture. The 1957 was lighter but brighter, lacking depth but very much alive, with cedary aromas and a sweetness on the finish. The 1966 is quintessential Haut-Brion in its luxurious texture, its depth of flavour combined with an absence of tannic assertiveness (which is not to say it lacks tannin). The 1967 is very good for the vintage, stylish and ripe, but it has aged faster than the 1966. The 1968 is surprisingly fresh for a dreadful year, but should have been drunk up. The 1970 has become quite meaty on the nose but retains its fine blackcurrant fruit; it's plump and weighty, highly concentrated, and was still alive and kicking in 2006.

The 1971 and 1973 were relatively light and evolved quite rapidly; they seemed ready to drink by 1985. The 1978 was impressive in its youth. As it aged, it became more discreet, elegant, and high-toned; it has raciness rather than power. The 1981 was poised and elegant in its youth, but I have not tasted it recently. The 1982 is predictably voluptuous, with masses of fruit but perhaps not the finesse of Haut-Brion at its most classic. The 1983 was superb in its youth, tannic but beautifully balanced and long. The 1985 was always forward and attractive; it's delicate and graceful yet slightly disappointing. The supple, stylish 1987 is a success for the year. The 1988 has developed a leafy character on the nose, and though reasonably tannic and concentrated, it lacks some vigour.

The 1989 is magnificent: a fabulously complex nose of cedar and woodsmoke, and on the palate it's fleshy, opulent, burly, and pungent, but finishes sweet and long. This is red Graves at its imperial best. The 1990 is just as good, but the opulence of the 1989 is replaced by intensity. The 1993 has Graves earthiness, but remains tight and rather unyielding. I like it better than the 1994, which has a fragrant, oaky nose but is rather raw. Elegance and precision are the hallmarks of the 1996, but it still seems surprisingly closed, with distinct underlying tannins. The graphite-scented 1998 is deceptive: fleshy, medium-bodied, not especially powerful, but delicious and elegant and long. The 1999 is wonderfully suave, a forward wine yet with considerable reserves of tannin. It should age well. The superb 2000 is close to overripe, but has tremendous spice, vitality, and power without being over-extracted. The 2002 is a sumptuous wine, with spice, vigour, and fluffy tannins; it exhibits considerable depth and power without being in the least overbearing. Oak and black fruits dominate the nose of the 2003, which, despite an indisputable lack of zest and freshness, nonetheless has ample fruit and tannic structure. The 2004 is immensely stylish and perfumed, yet it has evident grip and minerality. Early cask tastings suggest the 2006 will be a full-bodied, concentrated wine with a succulent core of fruit and good if not exceptional length.

Château Haut-Gardère

Léognan. Tel: 0556 647786. Owner: Lochlann Quinn. 50 ha. 39 ha red: 60% Cabernet Sauvignon, 40% Merlot.
11 ha white: 50% Sauvignon Blanc, 50% Sémillon. **Production: 60,000 bottles.**
Second wine: Le Reflet de Haut-Gardère

Haut-Gardère, which lies across the road from Fieuzal (*q.v.*), was an important property in the nineteenth century, and, in terms of its surface, still is. At one time the Ricard family (of Domaine de Chevalier) owned the estate, and its wines sold for high prices. After the onslaught of phylloxera and other crises, Haut-Gardère went into a decline and pinewoods grew where vines had once ruled. In the 1970s it was bought by Jacques Lésineau, and then sold to Fieuzal in 1995. The estate has its own winery, but the property is looked after, and the wine vinified, by the Fieuzal team. The soil does not differ greatly from that of its neighbour.

Not being a classified growth, its wines are offered at prices roughly half those of Fieuzal. Its actual production is rather low, as much of the wine is sold off in bulk. The white is aged in a good deal of new oak for ten to twelve months; the red for rather longer. My experience of the wine is limited. The white wines from 1995, 2001, and 2005 were all very attractive, with peach and citrus aromas, and considerable freshness and length. The 1989 red was rather dull, but the 2001 and even better 2004 are ripe, concentrated, and spicy, with some attractive austerity and good length. This is clearly a property that deserves to be better known.

Château Haut-Lagrange

Léognan. Tel: 0556 640993. Website: www.hautlagrange.com. Owner: Francis Boutemy. 20 ha.
18 ha red: 55% Cabernet Sauvignon, 45% Merlot. 2 ha white: 50% Sauvignon Blanc, 45% Sémillon,
5% Sauvignon Gris. **Production: 110,000 bottles**

Francis Boutemy should have been running Château Larrivet-Haut-Brion (*q.v.*), but on the death of his grandmother there were too many heirs clutching shares, so the property had to be sold. Boutemy knew, however, that the neighbouring property was for sale, and in 1989 he bought it. In the meantime he remained at Larrivet until 1997 as its general manager. This gave him time to prepare the soil and plant the vines at Haut-Lagrange. Although he was starting from scratch, Boutemy knew that there had been vineyards here from the 1760s until the early twentieth century, and André Lurton found a classification from the 1840s that ranked the wine highly. So Boutemy had a hunch he could make very good wine here. But it would take time: the soil had been saturated in copper, and the location was prone to frost. He found that although the topsoil is a fine layer of gravel and sand, just below is a band of impermeable sandstone. By mechanical means he was able to claw down and break up the sandstone band without disturbing the topsoil excessively. By 2005 he was on his fourteenth vintage and toying with converting the estate to biodynamism.

Francis Boutemy is a thoughtful man, who considers carefully every aspect of wine production. For example, the grapes used to be picked by selective harvesting, with teams going through the rows more than once. Then he realized he liked a blend of very ripe and slightly underripe grapes in his wine, presumably to give better acidity. Nor does he believe in very low yields. He has picked at thirty-five hectolitres per hectare and found the results unsatisfactorily solid.

The red wine is vinified in cement tanks. A quarter of the wine is then aged in new barriques, while the remainder stays in tanks. After eighteen months the two components are blended. He clearly does not care for overly oaky wines, and indeed the red Haut-Lagrange is stylish and balanced, expressing the purity and varietal character of the fruit as well as the terroir.

Hardly any of the white wine is aged in oak. It is mostly aged in tanks with lees-stirring for about one year. Boutemy insists that, although the wine can seem awkward and inexpressive for a year after bottling, it ages very well, better than if it had been vinified in barriques. The sole function of oak-ageing for his whites is to give the wine some additional roundness.

I am not entirely convinced by these wines. The white is certainly good. At its best, it has a citric zest, a liveliness combined with good concentration and impressive length. The best white I have encountered was the 1998, which by 2005 had developed toasty aromas of exotic fruit, which Boutemy plausibly attributes to the Sémillon component, since there is virtually no oak to impart those characters. The 2003 is simple but broad, the 2004 has bruised-apple aromas and a candied slackness that is not to my taste. The reds show good primary fruit of blackcurrants and blackberries; although medium-bodied, they are quite tannic. Perhaps oak would have given the wines more complexity; for while they are soundly made and, in the case of 2002, quite classic in their Graves typicity, they do lack some excitement.

Boutemy knows that he is following an unfashionable path, but is undeterred. Now at his side is a young winemaker called Arnaud Dessis, who worked in St-Emilion at Canon-La-Gaffelière. Perhaps he will contribute a touch more flesh to the wines.

Château Haut-Nouchet

Martillac. Tel: 0556 726974. **Owner:** *Louis Lurton. 38 ha. 28 ha red: 70% Cabernet Sauvignon, 30% Merlot.*
10 ha white: 70% Sauvignon Blanc, 30% Sémillon. **Production:** *100,000 bottles.*
Second wines: *Dom du Milan, Grande Réserve de Haut-Nouchet*

The estate was first planted in the 1830s, but by the 1960s the vineyards were derelict and the land destined for housing. Lucien Lurton rode to the rescue in 1973, buying the property, which is now run by his son Louis. Once based at Château Bouscaut, he fell out with some of his siblings and took himself off to Martillac. As the property had been entirely replanted, the first year of production at the property was 1986, and in 1992 he converted the estate to organic viticulture. The white vines are planted on gravelly soils near La Garde and Latour-Martillac; the reds on deep gravel and sandy gravel, between the château and Château de Cruzeau. Compost is added to the soil, and green cover is left between the rows for seven months of the year. I have the impression that M. Lurton is none too popular with his neighbours, who consider the levels of diseases such as mildew and black rot in his vineyards unacceptably high, whereas M. Lurton believes they are part and parcel of the organic approach.

The harvest is manual, with a very strict selection in the vineyards; indeed the yields rarely exceed thirty-five hl/ha. Since 2000 Haut-Nouchet has used a vertical press for the whites, and there is some skin contact if the grapes are healthy. The wine is aged in 400-litre barrels, of which one-third are new, for eight months with lees-stirring. Partial malolactic fermentation gives it greater richness.

The reds are destemmed and crushed, and descend by gravity into the stainless-steel tanks. After a cold soak, fermentation begins naturally with indigenous yeasts. There is, surprisingly, no computerized temperature control, although tanks can be chilled by the old method of pouring cold water down the sides. The wine is aged twelve months in one-third new oak, fined with eggwhite but bottled without filtration.

Louis Lurton is emphatic that he dislikes oakiness in wine and make-up on women, which are presumably related. He also admits to some rather strange experiments, such as allowing a sixty-day *cuvaison* for some lots in 1996 in order to extract as slowly as possible from very thick skins.

My experience of the white wines is limited. The 1987 was stylish but too tart. The 2002 has some grassy aromas and flavours and reasonable weight, yet seems one-dimensional, with an abrupt finish. The 1996 red is attractive: it has smoky, cedary aromas of some charm, and a light airiness on the palate, which is attractive despite the lack of weight. The 1998 has rather hard tannins, the 1999 is balanced but slight. There's a similar thinness on the 2001 and the 2003, which is also quite earthy. I find these wines, and their self-confident maker, very puzzling.

Château Haut-Vigneau

Martillac. Tel: 0557 965620. Website: www.carbonnieux.com. **Owner:** *Eric Perrin. 20 ha. 70% Cabernet Sauvignon, 30% Merlot.* **Production:** *120,000 bottles*

The vineyards of this property were abandoned long ago, and then replanted in the early 1990s by Eric Perrin, the son of Antony Perrin of Carbonnieux (*q.v.*). There are two principal parcels: one, and the new winery, is next door to Carbonnieux along the road to Cadaujac; the other is next to Château Lafont-Menaut (*q.v.*). The vines are unavoidably young. Half the wine is aged in barriques, half in tanks. The wines are well made, with good acidity and reasonable concentration, but they are undemanding, and as yet lack personality.

Château Lafargue

Martillac. Tel: 0556 727230. Website: www.chateau-lafargue.com. **Owner:** *Jean-Pierre Leymarie. 24 ha. 22 ha red: 40% Cabernet Sauvignon, 40% Merlot, 15% Cabernet Franc, 2.5% Malbec, 2.5% Petit Verdot. 2 ha white: 70% Sauvignon Blanc, 30% Sauvignon Gris.* **Production:** *150,000 bottles*

Not far from the autoroute to Bordeaux are the rambling winery buildings of Château Lafargue. This is a family property dating back many generations. The present owner, M. Leymarie, was born in the house, as was his mother. In her day the property was polycultural, but he studied at the wine college at Château La Tour-Blanche before taking over the property in 1983. At that time there were only three hectares. M. Leymarie didn't need to purchase vineyards; he simply converted land that lay within the AC boundaries but was being used for other agricultural purposes. The vineyards are fragmented, with some near the house and winery, others near La Garde. In addition he leases some vines. This means that the soils are very varied. Parts of the vineyards are machine-picked.

M. Leymarie is a fan of Sauvignon Gris, admiring its combination of power and aroma. After a period of skin contact, the white, which is known as Cuvée Alexandre, is barrique-fermented and aged for about ten months. The red is cold-soaked under the protection of dry ice, and fermented with micro-oxygenation. His Cuvée Prestige is aged entirely in new oak; the regular wine in twenty-five per cent new oak, with additional micro-oxygenation in barrels.

Older vintages such as 1990 and 1996 were quite rustic, but this character is more subdued in the vintages of the 2000s. These are straightforward wines, well crafted, reasonably concentrated, though they lack some personality and finesse. The lightly toasty 2003 white has vigour and is thoroughly enjoyable, and the 2004 is creamy and, despite the very evident oak, has elegance and length. The 2005 is simpler and lighter.

Château Lafont-Menaut

Martillac. Tel: 0557 965620. Website: www.carbonnieux.com. **Owner:** *Philibert Perrin. 10 ha. 7 ha red: 60% Cabernet Sauvignon, 40% Merlot. 3 ha white: 70% Sauvignon Blanc, 30% Sémillon.* **Production:** *90,000 bottles*

In the eighteenth century this property formed part of Château Rochemorin, which lies close by. Purchased by Antony Perrin and his son Philibert, the estate was entirely replanted in the early 1990s, so the vines, which are manually harvested, are still young. The soils are well-drained gravel over clay. The white is aged half in older barriques, half in tanks, both portions remaining on the fine lees. The red is aged for twelve months in thirty-five per cent new oak. These wines are the least expensive of those from the Perrin stable. They're clean, straightforward, with some charm and zest and without pretensions to profundity. As such, they offer good value, and recent vintages such as the 2004 red and 2005 white have been highly successful.

Château Larrivet-Haut-Brion

*Léognan. Tel: 0556 647551. **Owners:** Philippe and Christine Gervoson. 56 ha. 48 ha red: 55% Merlot,*
42% Cabernet Sauvignon, 3% Cabernet Franc. 8 ha white: 50% Sauvignon Blanc, 50% Sémillon.
***Production:** 300,000 bottles. **Second wine:** Les Hauts de Larrivet or Les Demoiselles de Larrivet (same wine)*

This property thrived in the nineteenth century, but was slowly dismembered over the following decades, until its purchase in 1941 by Jacques Guillemaud. In the 1930s the estate was renamed Haut-Brion-Larrivet, which incurred the displeasure of the Dillons at Haut-Brion, whereupon the name was changed to its present form. Mme. Guillemaud died in 1986, and her grandson Francis Boutemy inherited what was left of the property. But family problems made it impossible for Boutemy to hang onto Larrivet, so he was obliged to sell the estate and went to pitch his tent at Haut-Lagrange (*q.v.*). However, he stayed on to manage the property for some years. The present owners are the Gervosons, known to every family in France as the producers of the Bonne Maman range of jams. The energetic Christine Gervoson seems to be the force behind the estate, and she hired Michel Rolland as a consultant in 1996.

The vineyards have been considerably expanded over the past decade, so many of the vines are still young. To add diversity to the red wine, the Gervosons planted two hectares of Cabernet Franc (not yet in production), and are contemplating adding some Malbec and Petit Verdot. The vineyards stretch on a long band from Haut-Bailly to the frontiers of Smith-Haut-Lafitte, yet the soils are quite varied. But essentially they are gravel over a sandstone subsoil. Treatments are kept to the minimum and no herbicides are used. Yields are low, especially for the white wine, which never exceeds forty hl/ha. The vines are picked by hand, but Philippe Gervoson is wondering whether to introduce some machine-harvesting. His wife is against it, which must make for some interesting discussions over the Bonne Maman at breakfast.

The whites are whole-cluster-pressed and since 1987 have been barrique-fermented; from 2000 only new oak barrels have been used, and the wine is aged for twelve months. Over the years the proportion of new oak used for the red wine has risen from thirty to fifty per cent. The vinification is entirely traditional, with no recourse to modern technology. The Gervosons have experimented with micro-oxygenation but were not altogether happy with the results.

Overall I find the whites better than the reds. They were dull and muted in the 1980s and early 1990s, but the 1995 and 1998 saw a marked improvement. The 2001 seems the first vintage that truly reflects the modern style of Larrivet: it shows spicy, oaky aromas, and then a fine attack on the palate, which has concentration and complexity, and flavours that embrace apricots, almond tarts, white peaches, and melons. The 2002 and 2004 are similar in structure and quality. The 2003 is creamy, oaky, and opulent, but let down by low acidity that brings the wine to a fairly abrupt halt. I prefer the 2004, but this too had a leaden character; it's soft-centred and had only moderate length. From cask the 2005 was far more complex and vigorous. These white wines seem to age well, though they are extremely enjoyable in their perky adolescence.

As for the red, the 1987 and 1990 were sound and very much Cabernet-dominated. The 1996 seemed raw and astringent, and the 1998 has developed meaty aromas and has lost some focus on the palate. The 2000 is ripe and stylish on the nose, reasonably concentrated, and by 2007 was still showing considerable austerity. The 2001 seems a touch undernourished, and I also find this slight herbaceousness on the 2002, which tastes of red berries rather than cherries or blackcurrants. At present the 2003 is rich and plump, but the fruit is still at war with heavy tannins. Enticing red-fruits aromas mark the 2004, but there are some pungent tannins on the palate that give the wine some rusticity. The red wine doesn't seem at quite the same qualitative level as some of Larrivet's illustrious neighbours, but the white has become very reliable.

Château Latour-Martillac

*Martillac. Tel: 0557 977111. Website: www.latour-martillac.com. **Owner:** Kressmann family. Cru classé. 45 ha.*
36 ha red: 60% Cabernet Sauvignon, 35% Merlot, 5% Petit Verdot. 9 ha white: 55% Sémillon, 40% Sauvignon Blanc,
*5% Muscadelle. **Production:** 190,000 bottles. **Second wine:** Lagrave-Martillac*

I first visited this estate in late August 1989 only to find, unexpectedly, that the harvest was already in full swing. Nonetheless I was hospitably received by the Kressmanns, who even extracted a bottle of 1949 white from the cellar for lunch. The Kressmanns are a well-known négociant family, now subsumed into the very large CVBG firm. They had been closely associated with the estate since the 1870s and in 1929 Alfred Kressmann bought the property and entrusted his son Jean with the winemaking. He was still at the property forty years later. Today the estate is owned by his numerous children, and run by two of Bordeaux's gentlemen, Tristan and Loïc Kressmann. Since 1989 Michel Rolland has been the consultant oenologist for the red wines, and Denis Dubourdieu keeps an eye on the whites. The winemaker since 1990 has been Valérie Vialard, whose husband Gabriel fulfils a similar role at Haut-Bailly.

Most of the vineyards are on a plateau and close to the château. The white vines are, on average, older than the reds, and a plot of Sémillon planted in 1884 struggles on. The Petit Verdot is a recent addition, and first entered the blend in 2000. All grapes are picked by hand, and, since 2002, the reds are sorted both before and after destemming. The whites are given skin contact only when the fruit is entirely healthy, and the grapes are whole-cluster-pressed and then fermented in barriques, of which up to forty per cent are new. The wine stays on its lees with stirring for around fifteen months.

Most of the red grapes are fermented in steel tanks, but in 1999 the Kressmanns purchased two wooden vats which are reserved for the oldest vines. Occasionally, as in 2001 and 2004, they have rented a reverse-osmosis machine to concentrate a few lots. The wine is aged in forty per cent new oak for some sixteen months, eggwhite-fined, lightly filtered, and bottled.

Latour-Martillac is always sensibly priced, but often offers better quality than some more expensive Pessac-Léognan wines. The terroir is excellent, as that distant tasting of the white 1949 confirms. Even with four decades behind it, the aromas were wonderfully honeyed, while the palate was fat and spicy, with a nutty aftertaste and good length. The 1982 white, made in a year probably better suited to reds, was still citric and lively in 1989. These whites do show some oakiness on the nose, though it is rarely obtrusive. The 1987 was plump yet elegant, the 1989 had the same surprising acidity as the 1982, but I have not tasted it recently. The 1993 was more austere, the 1994 disappointingly dour. The 1996 showed a fine balance between citrus fruit and oak, and the 1998 was a splendid wine from the outset, and remains so, with waxy aromas, a rich, creamy texture, and considerable complexity. I have very positive notes on all subsequent vintages, other than the lacklustre 2003. Latour-Martillac has weight without heaviness, and never lacks acidity and length.

As for the reds, my notes on the 1975, 1979, and 1981 are none too flattering, but from 1985 I find the wine delicious. It's very Graves, with that lovely ethereal earthiness typical of the region, and the smoky aromas often encountered in the Martillac zone. The 1982 was delicious young, and is still gorgeous today, with sweet tobacco and cigar-box aromas, and a palate that remains bright and elegant – an irresistibly drinkable wine. In 2007, the 1986 made a very similar impression. If the 1989 is a touch flabby, the 1990 has no lack of tannic backbone and spicy, truffley fruit. There were some disappointments in the difficult vintages of the early 1990s, but the wine was back on form by 1998, showing a silky texture, discreet oakiness, and even minerality. The vintages from 2000 to 2002 have a smokiness and succulence very typical of the property, although the latter is somewhat light. The 2003 is sound, perhaps a touch earthy, and lacks zest. The 2004 and 2005 are graceful, fresh, and enchanting.

Latour-Martillac is a copybook Graves, never heavy-handed, nearly always beguiling in its fruit, and velvety in texture. In good vintages these wines, white and red, offer a great deal of pleasure in the glass.

Château Laville Haut-Brion

Pessac. Tel: 0556 002930. Website: www.haut-brion.com. Owner: Dillon family. Cru classé. 3.7 ha. 70% Sémillon,
27% Sauvignon Blanc, 3% Muscadelle. Production: 10,000 bottles

This celebrated wine emanates from La Mission Haut-Brion (*q.v.*), but has such a strong identity of its own that it requires its own entry. In the nineteenth century it belonged to the Boucasse family, then was sold in 1912 to Léopold Bibonne, who sold it on in 1931 to Frédéric Woltner of La Mission. When La Mission was acquired by Haut-Brion in 1983, Laville joined the Dillon group of estates. The vines lie across the road from Haut-Brion on south-facing slopes close to the university, and the clay content is relatively high. No particular distinction is made between the two principal grape varieties in terms of siting. Indeed one parcel is a field blend, so that the Sémillon vines have to be flagged to help the pickers identify them during harvest. The average age of the vines is somewhat older than those of white Haut-Brion, and the oldest parcels were planted in 1934. Yields range from thirty to forty hl/ha, and the grapes are sorted in the vineyard.

Since the late 1980s the grapes have been whole-cluster-pressed in a pneumatic press. At that time the fermentation was begun in tanks, but since the early 1990s the whole crop has been barrel-fermented with natural yeasts. There is no malolactic fermentation. The wine is aged in at least fifty per cent new oak for about fifteen months, with some lees-stirring.

As recently as 1980 there was a special Crème de Tête bottling, but this has been discontinued. (Haut-Brion has no records from Laville before 1983, so is unable to supply information about precisely how this bottling was defined.) In the early 1990s I had the opportunity to taste a number of vintages from the 1960s through to the early 1980s. Wines such as the 1967, 1968, 1979, and 1981 all seemed rather similar, with a waxy, lanolin nose, rounded textures, and good balance and length. What the wines lacked, however, was fruit definition. They seemed reined-in and inexpressive, perhaps a consequence of the high sulphur levels that were common at that time. However, the 1964 Crème de Tête was certainly an exception, with its honeyed, biscuity nose, its opulent, nutty, almost viscous palate, and its fine length. The same was true of the remarkable 1975, with its powerful hazelnut nose, and its soft, creamy texture allied to exceptional length. I have good but not ecstatic notes on the peachy, silky, yet slack 1982 (still youthful in 2007), and the nutty, concentrated, but not exactly fruity 1983.

The Dillon purchase clearly had a positive effect on the wines, and this may also account for the quality of the 1983. Every vintage I have tasted subsequently has been at the least extremely good, and sometimes, as in 1985, 1989, 1995, 1999, and 2002, sensationally good. The opulent 2003 tastes of tropical fruit. The 2004 is seamless, powerful and very long. The 2006 seems in the same mould, though outclassed in that year by Haut-Brion. Laville at its best has a rich but stylish nose, with a marked oaky sheen, while the palate combines opulence (of texture and flavour) with powerful concentration, nutty extract, bracing austerity and minerality, and exceptional length. This is one of the world's great dry white wines.

Château Lespault

Martillac. Tel: 0556 727121. Owner: S.C. Bolleau Lespault. 7 ha. 6 ha red: 70% Merlot, 25% Cabernet Sauvignon,
5% Malbec. 1 ha white: 100% Sauvignon Blanc. Production: 35,000 bottles

This estate, which shares a *croupe* with Domaine de la Solitude, has been leased since 1973 by the Kressmann family of Latour-Martillac. The red wines are fleshy, easy-going, and supple, with ample black-cherry fruit but a fairly light structure. The barrel-aged white is attractive but simple.

Château La Louvière

Léognan. Tel: 0557 255858. Website: www.andrelurton.com. Owner: André Lurton. 48 ha.
35 ha red: 64% Cabernet Sauvignon, 34% Merlot, 2% Petit Verdot. 13 ha white: 85% Sauvignon Blanc, 15% Sémillon.
Production: 350,000 bottles. Second wine: "L" de La Louvière

La Louvière is the flagship estate among the many Pessac-Léognan properties owned by André Lurton. Its imposing neo-classical château was built in the 1790s by Jean-Bernard Mareilhac, a former mayor of Bordeaux. Behind the château and the park is an avenue of plane trees that once stretched all the way to Château Olivier. From 1618 until the Revolution the property was owned by Carthusian monks. After it was bought in 1791 by Mareilhac, it remained in his family until 1911. Lurton bought the property in 1965, but it was only over the past ten years that he was able to turn his attention from the badly neglected vineyards and *chais* to the château itself, painstakingly restoring its grand interior. His costly efforts have been repeatedly frustrated by the depredations of thieves. However, not even the burliest malefactor has managed to extract the enormous Napoleonic granite bathtub that is the centrepiece of M. Lurton's bathroom.

All the vineyards surround the mansion, and border those of Carbonnieux and Haut-Bailly; the oldest are now some forty years old. The Sémillon tends to be planted on reddish soils, the Sauvignon on cooler sites. Site selection has been carefully considered, as there are considerable variations in soil and elevation. There is more ploughing and green-harvesting than in the past. The grapes are now all picked by hand, which was not the case fifteen years ago for the red vines.

The white grapes are usually whole-cluster-pressed, without skin contact. Fermentation begins in tanks, and continues in barriques, which were first introduced here in 1984. The wine used to be aged for around ten months in entirely new oak, but this has now been sensibly reduced to around forty-five per cent. White La Louvière is a wine that frequently demonstrates the remarkable ageing potential of white Graves, despite the preponderance of Sauvignon Blanc. The red is given a classic vinification, and aged for some twelve months in sixty per cent new oak.

In 1988 I was able to taste some older vintages of the white wine. A half-bottle of the 1966 had mellow apricot aromas, and was still a big mouthful of wine, though beginning to lose its fruit. A half of 1975 showed more honeyed fragrance and an elegant balanced palate. The 1981 was sound but perhaps not entirely clean. In 2005 the 1990 was still going strong, with aromas of quince and apricot, and a long, nutty finish – now at its peak. The 1993, once gawky, settled down to show honeyed, smoky aromas, while still fresh and citric on the palate. The 1997 is serious but remains austere. The assertive, creamy 1998 has been consistently good, as has the concentrated, oaky 1999. The grapefruity 2000 remains austere, and has a long life ahead of it. The 2002 is in a more toasty style, but has good depth of fruit and acidity. The 2003 is concentrated and spicy, but tails off on the finish. The 2004 has aromas of oak, citrus, and pear drops, and with its richness and vibrancy is the best white La Louvière for many years. There can be no doubt that the white is of classified-growth quality.

The reds, at their best, are rich, meaty, and solid. Their defects are a certain lack of charm and an occasional excess of tannin; they also need some bottle-age to shed some youthful astringency. The 1978, austere when young, had, by 2000, developed a spicy Marmite and coffee nose, and was showing surprising lushness and less surprising concentration on the palate. The 1983 also developed well. By 2005, the 1986 had become an imposing wine, dense and chocolatey, but the tannins remained somewhat dusty and dry. The 1988, while meaty on the nose, had a lean elegance, though perhaps at the expense of complexity. The 1989 had evolved well; its initial astringency had diminished, leaving a fleshy, stylish wine with forceful acidity. The 1990 was plump yet tannic in its youth, but I have not tasted it since. The vintages of the mid-1990s were a bit tough and raw, but the 1998 was excellent. The 1999 was chunky for the vintage, with good concentration and assertive tannins. There was a welcome refinement to the 2000, with its lead-pencil aroma, its sleek texture, its discreet tannins, and fine length. The 2001 was similar, and refreshed by its long, suave finish. The 2002 had hints of tobacco on the nose, firm, chewy tannins, and a persistent finish. The 2003 is predictably robust but not over-extracted; there's a sweet intensity on the nose, and more length than many wines from this vintage. There are aromas of redcurrants and raspberries on the 2004, but the palate is less expressive; robustly structured, it clearly needs a few more years in bottle.

It is hard to say whether it is the terroir or the winemaking that makes red La Louvière a somewhat severe wine, though it does tend to mellow with age. The Lurton team produce fleshier, more immediately appealing wines at some of their other Pessac-Léognan estates, so it's likely that the soil, which has a good deal of clay-limestone in certain sectors, may give the wine its imprint.

Château Luchey-Halde

*Mérignac. Tel: 0556 459719. Website: www.luchey-halde.com. **Owner:** Mérignac agricultural college.*
22 ha. 18 ha red: 55% Cabernet Sauvignon, 35% Merlot, 5% Cabernet Franc, 5% Petit Verdot.
*4 ha white: 55% Sauvignon Blanc, 45% Sémillon. **Production:** 120,000 bottles. **Second wine:** Les Haldes de Luchey*

In a remarkable renaissance, Luchey-Halde is a vineyard that has been resurrected on its once-abandoned site close to the city. Formerly known as the Domaine de Luchey, it became derelict after World War I and the property was used as a military sports ground. This saved the land from suburban development, and when in 2000 the military base became surplus to requirements and an agricultural college was established in its place, its new director, Jean Magne, decided to replant the vineyard, using the students as a source of inexpensive labour. Soil studies confirmed that the site was worth reviving: the analysis revealed three *croupes* with deep gravel, interspersed with thin strata of clay. The first vines were planted in 2000, and the first vintage was 2002. No herbicides are used, and the soil is ploughed; the grapes are picked by hand.

The new winery is well equipped, with sorting before and after destemming, and crushing directly over the vats to avoid pumping. After a three-day cold soak, cultivated yeasts are added and fermentation is conducted in conical steel vats, often with an extended maceration. The marc is pressed in modern vertical presses, and some of the malolactic fermentation takes place in new oak barrels. The wine is aged in one-third new oak for twelve months, with a little lees-stirring to soften the tannins.

The 2003 was the first vintage for the white wine, which was fermented in entirely new oak, but this proportion will diminish in future vintages. The white does not actually taste overoaked, but it is short on acidity. The 2004 is also supple and broad, but has more spiciness and a sherbet tone, though its length is only moderate. The 2005 is delicious, with ripe grapefruity aromas, and fine concentration and spiciness on the palate. The 2002 red has sweet, oaky blackcurrant and plum aromas, but the palate, which is somewhat hollow, lets it down. This is scarcely surprising given the youth of the vines. The 2003 is light and easy-going, but an attractive wine for early drinking. The 2004 has more elegance and charm, with distinctive red-fruits aromas; it lacks a little weight, but has reasonable structure and length.

Château Malartic-Lagravière

*Léognan. Tel: 0556 647508. Website: www.malartic-lagraviere.com. **Owner:** Alfred-Alexandre Bonnie. Cru classé.*
53 ha. 46 ha red: 45% Cabernet Sauvignon, 45% Merlot, 8% Cabernet Franc, 2% Petit Verdot.
*7 ha white: 80% Sauvignon Blanc, 20% Sémillon. **Production:** 280,000 bottles. **Second wine:** Sillage de Malartic*

Pierre de Malartic, who bought this estate in 1803, was the nephew of Comte Hippolyte de Maurès de Malartic, an admiral whose occupation is commemorated by the ship on the label. At the time the property was known as Domaine de Lagravière, and when in 1860 it was bought by Mme. Arnaud Ricard, she honoured her predecessors by appending the Malartic name. Malartic remained in the family for generations, and one of Mme. Ricard's descendants, Jacques Marly-Ridoret, became the owner in 1947. He was an old man when I first visited the property in the late 1980s, and the winemaking was in the hands of his son Bruno, who had trained as an accountant and was hauled back to Léognan to run the estate, apparently with some reluctance on his part.

The wine at this time was undistinguished. The white was usually picked at a potential alcohol of eleven degrees to preserve acidity, and was routinely chaptalized. The wine certainly had acidity; it didn't always have sufficient ripeness. Moreover, yields were high. Jacques Marly, the present proprietor M. Bonnie told me, was a deeply religious man who believed that everything was a gift from God, including his ten children and the very copious crops from his vines. In 1990 Jacques Marly decided to retire, and the property was sold to Laurent-Perrier, Bruno staying on as winemaker. But the Champagne house was soon spreading itself too thinly, and the quality of the wine did not significantly improve. In 1997 the company put Malartic on the market, and it was bought by Alfred-Alexandre Bonnie, a courteous Belgian businessman, who had had his eye out for a Bordeaux property since 1994. He found that although Laurent-Perrier had invested in the vineyards, not much else had been touched. "I found the property", he told me, "in a state of suspended animation."

Bonnie did not waste time. Although Bruno Marly stayed on for a while, he was eventually replaced as winemaker by the personable and competent Philippe Garcia. As consultants he hired Denis Dubourdieu (who left in 2000) for the white and Michel Rolland for the red. Although the Marly family had been large, and the Bonnie clan was relatively small, the Bonnies decided the château was on the small side. So they built a duplicate alongside it, with a roofed-in gap in between as a kind of atrium. More importantly, Bonnie more or less reconstructed the winery and cellars, hiring as architect Bernard Mazières, who had undertaken similar works at Margaux and Yquem. This was ready by 1999.

The vineyards occupy a kind of plateau adjacent to the buildings. The soil is stony gravel, up to eight metres (twenty-six feet) deep in places, with much clay and iron-rich sandstone in the subsoil. Bonnie also bought additional land within the appellation, allowing him to grub up unsatisfactory parcels of the original Malartic vineyards and replace them by replanting parcels nearby (to a high density of 10,000 vines per hectare). He also increased the proportion of Merlot. Whereas the white wine under the Marlys had been pure Sauvignon, there is now a significant proportion of Sémillon, often up to thirty per cent, in the blend. Yields are usually kept to between forty and forty-five hl/ha.

The white grapes are picked in *cagettes*, and sorted twice at the winery. Skin contact is the exception rather than the rule, and native yeasts are preferred. After pressing, the must is barrel-fermented, and aged in fifty per cent new oak for ten to fifteen months.

The red grapes are destemmed and lightly crushed into metal bins that are then hoisted and tipped into the vats without pumping. After a long cold soak, fermentation begins with native yeasts. If required, pumpovers continue day and night, with a special night shift to supervise the latter. Malartic is equipped with a reverse-osmosis concentrator, which is sometimes used for parcels of over-vigorous young vines. Trials have been conducted with micro-oxygenation, but it has not been adopted as systematic. *Pigeage* is also used, by means of a mechanical device that can be moved on rails from vat to vat. Most of the vats are conical stainless-steel tanks, but Bonnie has also acquired ten wooden vats which are used for the best lots. The *marc* is then pressed in an automated vertical press, which works much faster than the hand-operated version. The wine is aged for fifteen to twenty-two months in sixty per cent new oak, with traditional racking.

The white wines made by the Marlys were not always second-rate. Some indeed were one-dimensional, and marred by detectable burn from maximal chaptalization. I have tasted almost every vintage from 1980 onwards, and there were good wines in years such as 1983 and 1987. But there is no doubt that the intelligent investments made by Bonnie led to a dramatic improvement from 1998 onwards. The Marly wines were always citric in their aromas. Under Bonnie (and Garcia), the nose became more complex: the citric element remained, but was supplemented by riper apricot, honey, and oak aromas. On the palate, the wines have become broader and plumper, while retaining a good acidic backbone. I have very positive notes on all vintages since 1998. The only disquieting element is a hint of overripeness, notably in 1999, 2001, and 2002. The 2004 is excellent, and the 2005 outstanding, with dramatic passion fruit and citrus aromas, and a flamboyance on the palate that is balanced by fine acidity.

The reds under the Marlys were a mixed bunch. The 1967 was still leafy and attractive twenty years on, though fully ready to drink. The 1985 had elegance and charm. The 1990 was quite good, though disappointing for the vintage; the 1996 had bold, upfront fruit, though little elegance. As with the whites, the elegant 1998 marked a turning point, showing an intensity of blackcurrant fruit, a discreet minerality, and a long, graceful finish. Very Graves, in short. The momentum has been maintained, with very ripe fruit, supple tannins, a welcome accessibility, but clearly sufficient structure to age well. Only the rather austere 2003 breaks the run of superb wines.

The wines are considerably more expensive than they used to be, especially the whites, but there is no doubt that Bonnie and his team have raised the wines to a much higher level, and are intent on improving further. In 2006 he introduced a rosé wine for the first time.

Château de Malleprat

*Martillac. Tel: 0556 727116. Owner: Jean-Claude Cots. 15 ha. 12 ha red: 60% Merlot, 20% Cabernet Sauvignon, 20% Cabernet Franc. 3 ha white: 60% Sémillon, 40% Sauvignon Blanc. **Production:** 80,000 bottles*

The Cots family bought this property in 1947, but the vines were leased out as the family were more interested in breeding racehorses. In 1990 Jean-Claude Cots took back the vineyards, but the crop was sold off, and it is only since 2001 that Malleprat has produced and marketed its own wines. The vineyards, on a gravelly *croupe* over a clay-limestone subsoil, are not far from the Bordeaux–Toulouse autoroute.

The grapes are picked manually. The white wine begins its fermentation in tanks with cultivated yeasts, and completes it in barriques. The Sémillon component is aged in one-third new oak; the Sauvignon is aged in older barrels. The red wine is aged for twelve to fourteen months in thirty per cent new oak.

The red is a modest wine, showing some signs of dilution. The white is quite herbal, with a grapefruity tang. Although the wines are far from exceptional, with the exception of the assertive and stylish 2004 white, they are inexpensive.

Château Mancedre

*Léognan. Tel: 0557 743052. Owner: Jean Trocard. 7 ha. 50% Cabernet Sauvignon, 50% Merlot. **Production:** 30,000 bottles*

The Trocards are wine producers in Fronsac, but have long had a property here, some of which was sold to Fieuzal. But Jean Trocard decided to halt the sell-offs and in 1992 replanted the remaining parcels, which are scattered around the commune of Léognan; there will eventually be ten hectares under vine. Trocard finds he has to practise severe green-harvesting to curb the vigour of his young vines, and average yields have been kept very low. The wine is aged in fifty per cent new oak for twelve months. The wines are well made in a modern style, with ripe, toasty, and smoky aromas, and considerable concentration and power. The 1999 is the most stylish of recent vintages, the 2001 the richest and most spicy.

Domaine de Merlet

*Léognan. Tel: 0556 640237. Owner: Tauzin family. 4 ha. 75% Cabernet Sauvignon, 25% Merlot. **Production:** 20,000 bottles*

The modest eighteenth-century house and cellars facing Haut-Bailly belong to the tiny Domaine de Merlet, which is owned by brothers Yves and Jean-Joel Tauzin and their sister. The vineyards, in a single parcel near the house, were abandoned after phylloxera, and replanted only in 1989. The Tauzins are essentially hobby winemakers, but Yves Tauzin has professional experience, working as he does at Fieuzal. The wine is aged in fifteen per cent new oak for twelve months, but there is a parcel selection called Cuvée Spéciale, which is aged entirely in new oak. The 1999 is an attractive wine with red-fruits aromas and fair concentration, though it doesn't have much weight and persistence. I preferred it to the 2002 Cuvée Spéciale, which lacks depth and substance, as does the regular 2002, which is fairly herbaceous and superficial.

Château Mirebeau

Martillac. Tel: 0556 625366. Website: www.chateau-mirebeau.com. Owner: Cyril Dubrey. 4.5 ha. 70% Merlot,
25% Cabernet Sauvignon, 5% Cabernet Franc. Production: 25,000 bottles

This charming little property, surrounded by the houses of Martillac, used to belong to Alexandre Dumas. In the 1950s its owner, M. Hortala, left it to his daughters. One of them promptly sold half the land to a housing developer. In 1996, Cyril Dubrey, whose family own Château d'Ardennes in Illats, bought the rest of the property. Half the vines are planted on a plateau next to the house; then the land drops, and a further two hectares are planted on a terrace below. The soils are different, with much clay in the higher sector, more sand and limestone below. The peculiarity of the property is the high proportion of Merlot, which is not a recent development as some of the Merlot vines are sixty years old.

Dubrey likes very ripe grapes, so picks late. The vinification is modern, with a long cold soak, fermentation with natural yeasts, and *délestage*. Malolactic fermentation takes place in tanks, then the wine is aged twelve to sixteen months in fifty per cent new oak, although from 1996 to 2000 Dubrey used entirely new oak. The wines have smoky, toasty aromas and are solid and rich, with ample plummy fruit. On the palate the wine is quite powerful, but lacks a little flair and persistence.

Château La Mission Haut-Brion

Pessac. Tel: 0556 002930. Website: www.haut-brion.com. Owner: Dillon family. Cru classé. 21 ha.
48% Cabernet Sauvignon, 45% Merlot, 7% Cabernet Franc. (For the white, see Château Laville Haut-Brion.)
Production: 100,000 bottles. Second wine: Ch La Chapelle de la Mission Haut-Brion

The La Mission château and vineyards lie across the road from Haut-Brion, and the vineyards are to some extent intermingled. In the sixteenth century the estate belonged to the Lestonnacs, and in 1664 Mme. de Lestonnac bequeathed the property to the Lazarite fathers, who maintained its quality and reputation. During the Revolution the estate was confiscated and sold. In 1821 a shipowning family from New Orleans, the Chiapellas, bought La Mission, but later in the century it passed through various hands. In 1919 the Woltner family became the owners, until in 1983 they sold the property to their neighbours, the Dillons. Today the property is managed and vinified by the same team.

Despite the proximity to Haut-Brion, there are significant differences between the two properties. The La Mission vineyards are less undulating, and the soil slightly richer, stony with a subsoil of chalky sand, which supports a higher density of 10,000 vines per hectare. The average age of the vines is just over twenty years. Green-harvesting is a touch more severe at La Mission, perhaps reflecting the greater vigour of the vines. The major difference, of course, is in the style of the wines. La Mission is more robust, more virile, more overtly tannic than Haut-Brion, and it doesn't easily match the finesse of the First Growth. This is despite the fact that there is a fair amount of Merlot in the wine, as much of the Cabernet Sauvignon ends up in the second wine. It often excels in difficult vintages. The winemaking, however, is essentially the same, with ageing (since 1983) in new oak, except in certain vintages such as 2003, when it seemed wiser to diminish the proportion to seventy per cent. From 2006 onwards the crop from five hectares of vines of the neighbouring Château La Tour Haut-Brion have been incorporated into La Mission and the second wine.

Celebrated past vintages include 1878, 1921, 1928, 1929, 1937, 1945, 1947, 1949, 1955, 1959, and 1961. At over sixty years of age, the wartime 1943 still had a dense colour, but was aromatically weary; despite a slight maderization on the palate, the attack was still sweet and there was good acidity on the finish. In 2006 the 1945 was still stupendous: bright and clear in colour, intense and truffley on the nose and unmistakably Graves; there was a good attack on the palate, tremendous concentration, a sweet core of fruit refreshed by fine acidity, and a robust finish. The 1962 is now dried and faded, but the 1964 is better than expected, despite its mature brick-red colour. The nose shows mint and truffle and a whiff of iodine; it's medium-bodied, concentrated, still sweet and long, and although clearly at its best, will still keep. I have not tasted the 1966 in twenty years; back then it seemed lacking in generosity and complexity. The 1970, tasted twice in the 1980s, seemed far from harmonious but by 2000 the same wine had developed cedar and tea aromas, and a silky texture, yet seemed to be entering a premature old age before it had achieved a peak of flavour and complexity. The 1971 was a delicious wine, ripe, lush, and cedary, with hints of charcoal and chocolate on the finish when twenty years old.

The 1973 aged fast; but the 1975 remains vibrant. It has leafy, floral aromas, with hints of coffee and woodsmoke, and although the palate is lean, it has tremendous incisiveness and vigour. The 1976 showed a bit more breed and persistence than most wines from this torrid year. The 1981 seemed raw and stalky, but perhaps was a poor bottle. The 1982 in 2006 was still opaque, and the aromas utterly typical of the Graves in their mulchy sweetness and tobacco tones; the palate was lush, sweet, and smoky, with very rich fruit balanced by a long, chewy finish. The 1983 in 2007 was pungent and forceful, with plenty in reserve. When young the 1984 was a robust effort, but it is probably past its best now. The aromas of the 1985 were still fresh in 2007, but there were hints of tobacco, cedar, and toast; the attack was sweet and intense, and the grip on the finish and the balanced elegance of the wine suggest it will not tire for many years. When young, the 1987 was attractive and sweet. It was interesting to compare the 1989 and 1990 in 2007. The 1989 was more evolved in colour, and more sensuous in its aromas of undergrowth and truffles and coffee; it has purity of fruit and firm tannins, and although persistent lacks a little finesse and complexity. I marginally prefer the 1990, which shows delightful sweetness of fruit backed by firm, almost earthy tannins, and has slightly better length than the 1989. But both are superb wines. The 1994 is stylish and intense for the vintage, with remarkable length. The 1995 now shows a lot of oak on the nose, while the palate is spicy and concentrated, with some chewy tannins. La Mission did well in 1997, though it is outgunned by the 1998. When young, power dominated the fruit; by 2006 it had developed elegant cedary aromas, while on the palate it was lean and fresh, although underpinned by firm tannins, and the finish was lingering. The 1999 is aromatically complex, with hints of raspberry as well as blackcurrant, and there is sweet fruit behind the pronounced tannins − a wine that clearly still needs a lot of time. The beguiling 2000 is sumptuous and powerful, marked by new oak aromas and very ripe tannins that give a long, chewy finish. I find the 2002, although perfumed, somewhat disappointing, as the tannins seem rather coarse and the wine lacking in overall finesse; but perhaps it will settle down with more bottle-age. The 2003, tasted shortly before bottling, is grippy and austere, with a bitter-chocolate finish. The 2004 is unusually fragrant and refined, but has a fine tannic backbone. Early tastings of the 2006 suggest a wine that's no blockbuster, but one with grip, balance, and elegance.

Château Olivier

Léognan. Tel: 0556 647331. Website: www.chateau-olivier.com. **Owner:** *Jean-Jacques de Bethmann. Cru classé.*
55 ha. 46 ha red: 50% Merlot, 45% Cabernet Sauvignon, 5% Cabernet Franc. 9 ha white: 50% Sauvignon Blanc,
50% Sémillon. **Production:** *350,000 bottles.* **Second wine:** *Seigneurie d'Olivier*

Unlike most châteaux in Bordeaux, Olivier is a real castle, screened from the road by dense woodland and standing in a fine park on the outskirts of Léognan. The Black Prince, it's said, stayed here while on a hunting spree in the 1360s. The estate, which includes substantial woodlands, was bought at auction by the Bethmann family in 1886. The Bethmanns were of Alsatian origin but have been in Bordeaux for over two centuries, making a fortune in shipping goods to and from the West Indies. The genial Jean-Jacques de Bethmann has been running the estate since 1981. For the previous eighty years its vineyards had been leased to the Bordeaux négociant house of Eschenauer, which failed to exploit its potential.

Most of the vineyards are located in front of the moated château, with white grapes planted on land with more clay content. Denis Dubourdieu has been the consultant here for some years, and may have been responsible for planting much more Merlot here, whereas in the early 1990s two-thirds of the red vines were Cabernet Sauvignon.

Until fairly recently Olivier produced rather dull wines, especially the unoaked whites and reds made by Eschenauer. M. de Bethmann surely realized that his wines were underperforming, and a few years ago hired the young Laurent Lebrun to manage the property. Lebrun had worked in Australia and had a wider perspective than the Bordeaux region alone. He commissioned Dubourdieu to undertake a detailed study of the soil types at Olivier. This involved 200 soil analyses. Much of the property now planted with woodland is actually classified within the AC Pessac-Léognan, so Lebrun was particularly keen to see whether any of those sectors showed promise as potential vineyards.

The analysis identified eleven separate soil types at Olivier. The least interesting were clay soils on which white vines had been planted; these were among the parcels grubbed up in the 2000s. To the delight of Bethmann and Lebrun, Dubourdieu was able to identify a sector of the northeastern corner of the estate which had perfect gravel soils compacted with sand and clay. Such a soil would deliver exactly the right amount of moisture to any vines planted there. The famous map compiled by Belleyme in the 1760s showed that this sector, called Bel-Air, had indeed once been planted with vines. Lebrun pulled out some rows in less interesting corners of the property, and planted Cabernet Sauvignon here in 2004. There will soon be six hectares of new vines. Dubourdieu has also located an area with a limestone base that could prove ideal for Sauvignon Blanc.

At the same time a new winery was built. The Eschenauer-era winery had very large tanks that were poorly suited to separate vinification of individual parcels. By 2002 they had been replaced by small, conical stainless-steel tanks. Lebrun now has the facilities for pumpovers, *pigeage*, or *délestage*, depending on what he believes is appropriate for any specific vintage.

About one-third of the white grapes are given skin contact before pressing in a pneumatic press. The must is settled, and selected yeasts added. Fermentation begins in tank, and is completed in barriques in which the wine is aged for nine months, with lees-stirring. There is no malolactic fermentation. The red wine is aged for twelve months in barriques, of which one-third are new. In 2002 some 500-litre barrels were purchased. These, Lebrun explains, lessen the risk of reduction for the red wine and allow the wine to be aged on its lees with less frequent racking.

Bethmann has always been against super-concentrated wines. The winery is equipped with a reverse-osmosis concentrator, but it has been used only rarely. Nor is there any recourse to micro-oxygenation. The effect of Lebrun's reforms has been a very rapid enhancement of quality at Olivier. The white wines in particular have improved beyond recognition.

The oldest white I have tasted is the 1978, with its honeyed, lanolin aromas. It was remarkably fresh, with ample sweet fruit on the finish. None of the vintages I tasted from the 1980s come close in quality. The apricotty 1993 was a success, as was the weightier, concentrated 1998. The 1999 is fresh and balanced, but it's the 2001 that marks a real change for the better, with its well-judged oak, and a beguiling sweet-and-sour tone on the palate. The 2002 is more citric, and perhaps more elegant, having a long, lean finish. The 2003 is good and not too heavy, though it seems oakier and more melony than other vintages. The 2004 shows great promise, being both powerful and silky, with good length. It is matched by the powerful, mineral, tangy 2005.

My experience of the reds is limited. The 1990 was quite rich and earthy, and just the right side of astringency. The 1993 lacked some concentration, but had charming tobacco aromas, and a good core of fruit. The 1996 is quite lush and spicy, and balanced by good acidity. The 1998 has developed nicely, with delicate savoury aromas, a supple texture, and bright accessible fruit. The 1999 is soft and rather light. The 2001 is very much in the new Olivier style, showing great delicacy and charm and moderate tannins. The 2003 is rich and not too extracted, and its evident tannins are reined in; but it remains a modest wine. The 2004, however, has an intense blackcurrant nose, and sleek elegance as well as concentration.

The renaissance of Olivier has been less well publicized than that, say, of Malartic-Lagravière, but the days when one could look down one's nose at its wines are well and truly over.

Château Le Pape

*Léognan. Tel: 0556 641090. Website: www.chateaulepape.com. **Owner:** Patrick Monjanel. 6 ha. 70% Merlot, 30% Cabernet Sauvignon. **Production:** 30,000 bottles*

This small property was bought by Monjanel's father in the 1960s, but he was a busy négociant with little spare time, so he leased his vines to Antony Perrin of Carbonnieux. In 1998 Patrick Monjanel, a doctor, decided to take back the property when the lease expired. Apparently there was a house here in the twelfth century, he explains, though the present château is a chartreuse from the eighteenth century. He speculates that the name may be derived from its possible ownership by Pope Clement V.

The vineyard is in one single gravelly parcel, not far from Carbonnieux and La Louvière. In 2003 Monjanel bought two hectares of woodland within AC Pessac-Léognan, cleared the land, and intends to plant it in 2006. Monjanel thinks there is rather too much Merlot on the property, and will be increasing the proportion of Cabernet.

The vineyards are prone to hail attacks, so Monjanel has installed a highly unusual form of protection (*see* Chapter Two). The grapes are sorted at the winery, fermented in temperature-controlled cement tanks, then aged for eight months in one-third new oak (though the proportion used to be higher). Monjanel's initial vintage, 1998, was a touch rustic, but ever since 2000 the wines have been excellent, with dense black-cherry and blackberry aromas, and considerable power and impressive concentration. All recent vintages have shown fine tannic structure which should ensure a long life, yet there is no lack of flesh and succulence.

Château Pape-Clément

*Pessac. Tel: 0556 415312. Website: www.bernard-magrez.com. **Owner:** Bernard Magrez. Cru classé for red only. 32.5 ha. 30 ha red: 60% Cabernet Sauvignon, 40% Merlot. 2.5 ha white: 45% Sauvignon Blanc, 45% Sémillon, 10% Muscadelle. **Production:** 120,000 bottles. **Second wine:** Le Clémentin de Pape-Clément*

When, in 1299, the nobleman Bertrand de Goth was appointed bishop of Bordeaux, his brother offered him his estate in Pessac. In 1305 Bertrand was elected to the papacy, taking the name Clement V. Subsequently the town of Pessac named this estate after him and it remained an ecclesiastical property until the Revolution. The wine was always highly regarded, and in the 1860s a French wine expert called Danflau rated it as the finest wine of the Graves after Haut-Brion. In 1939, when it seemed likely that the vineyards, which had been devastated by hail in 1937, would be grubbed up and replaced by commercial or housing development, Pape-Clément was acquired by Léo Montagne. A Montagne daughter later married an ambitious négociant called Bernard Magrez, who had created a company called William Pitters, best known for North African wines and for spirits, and for Malésan, Bordeaux's best-selling generic brand. Magrez also bought a few properties, notably in the Côtes de Blaye. But Pape-Clément was his prize possession, and even today, when he has sold William Pitters to finance his acquisition of over thirty properties throughout Bordeaux and the rest of the wine world, it remains his finest jewel.

There are three different soils at Pape-Clément, according to the quantity of pebbles, sand, and clay blended with the gravel. Where there is clay, Merlot is planted. Although the vineyards are not far from Haut-Brion, the vintage here sometimes begins a week later. Since 2001 the estate's team has undertaken a detailed soil analysis, to help them identify the best parcels.

Magrez is a forceful personality, sparing no expense in the quest for quality. Yields are extremely low, with an average over recent years of thirty-one hl/ha. The crop is destemmed by hand, even though it requires no fewer than 120 sorters to accomplish this. The perfect grapes are then placed in boxes and tipped into the tanks by hand. Here, since 2001, they undergo a cold soak under dry ice, which allows the winemakers to reduce the amount of sulphur dioxide. Fermentation takes place with indigenous yeasts. There is no micro-oxygenation during fermentation, though occasionally some is employed during the *élevage*. The best lots are fermented in wooden vats, with *pigeage* as well as pumpovers. The *cuvaison* is sometimes as long as thirty days; malolactic fermentation takes place in barrels. The amount of new oak has varied; in 1990 it was seventy per cent, then it decreased, but since 2000 it has been between eighty and ninety per cent. The lees are stirred twice weekly, and the wine is aged for up to eighteen months, then bottled without fining or filtration.

There has long been a tradition of white wine production here, but on a tiny scale. In the 1940s a third of a hectare produced the white wine, which was never sold commercially. More vines were planted by Magrez in 1988. He did not want to affect the existing red vineyards, so the new vines were planted in the park alongside the nineteenth-century baronial-style château. The wine is made as carefully as the red, with harvesting by *tries successives* and careful sorting in the vineyard and at the winery. After whole-cluster-pressing the juice goes straight into barrel for fermentation, with each picking kept separate. There is no malolactic. The wine is aged for around eleven months in sixty per cent new oak, and about half is declassified.

The oldest vintage of white I have tasted was the 1990, which had aromas of melon and lanolin; its roundness was countered by ample acidity and some toastiness from the oak. But it wasn't a wine of enormous depth. The 1998 is excellent, though with pronounced oakiness on the nose; but the fruit is splendid, the texture creamy, the finish spicy and persistent. The 1999 has a similar texture and oakiness, but less grip. More recently, the 2002 was superb, with aromas of pears and oak, while the palate was extremely complex, with hints of exotic fruits and mandarins and an attractive herbal component. The 2004 is more citric, while the palate is lively and vivid, exhibiting exceedingly ripe fruit and a bracing minerality.

But Pape-Clément's reputation rests on its red wine. It went through a dull patch for the two decades preceding Magrez's acquisition. Already in 1985 the improvement in quality came shining through, with delicious but lively blackcurrant fruit, and fine concentration and length. The 1986 has evolved beautifully and now shows a silky elegance and great intensity. The 1987 is quite sweet and smoky, but without the structure and weight of the preceding vintages. The 1988 remains austere, still dominated by oak and tannin. The 1989 was excellent young, but I have not tasted it recently. Perhaps the 1990 is almost too concentrated: it has tremendous power, but one is too aware of the structure at the expense of the fruit. The 1994 is chunky and almost bitter. The 1995 has appealing lushness and weight, with a long, spicy finish. In contrast, the 1996 has less power but more charm, vigour, and persistence. The 1997 is a triumph for the vintage, with gorgeous sweet truffley aromas and remarkable freshness on the palate; but it is ready for drinking. By 2007 the 1998 was drinking beautifully: intense, oaky, but elegant on the nose, and equally refined on the palate, with a sweetness of fruit that's by no means cloying. The 1999 is slightly herbaceous and rather lean. The 2000 is predictably bold, smoky, dense, and oaky on the nose, but highly concentrated, sleek and elegant on the palate, and still showing lovely primary fruit; it's powerful, long, and complete. The 2001 has superb aromas of blackcurrants and raspberries, but by 2007 had closed up on the palate, and showed more weight than finesse. The stylish 2002 was initially very muscular, but has settled down into an opulent, toasty wine, with spice and lively acidity to balance the plump fruit. The 2003 is jammy and cooked; it has power and concentration, but the finish is dry. The 2004 is far better, no powerhouse but a wine with refinement and considerable complexity.

Pape-Clément, whether red or white, is an expensive wine, but by and large its cost is justified. Not everybody likes the style. It is far from discreet, and the wine when young, and sometimes when mature, can seem rather too oaky. But it does have aromatic complexity, a palate with richness and force, and a lingering finish. It does sometimes seem that the winemaking style, reflecting the personalities of Magrez and Rolland, is more evident than the specificity of the terroir. Nonetheless Pape-Clément is securely in the top ranks of Pessac-Léognan, which wasn't the case thirty years ago.

Château Picque-Caillou

Mérignac. Tel: 0556 473798. Owners: Paulin and Isabelle Calvet. 20 ha. 19 ha red: 45% Cabernet Sauvignon,
45% Merlot, 10% Cabernet Franc. 1 ha white: 50% Sauvignon Blanc, 50% Sémillon.
Production: 100,000 bottles. Second wine: Picque-Caillou La Réserve

This suburban property, with its château dating from 1758, has managed to fend off the developers, but has not been able to prevent a new road being constructed in 2005 that effectively cuts the vineyards in two, with the loss of half a hectare of vines.

In the nineteenth century Picque-Caillou was owned by the Vanderlinden family. In 1949 it was bought by Etienne Denis, the grandfather of Isabelle Calvet. Other business interests meant that he was under no pressure to accept tempting offers from housing developers. Paulin Calvet, whose day job is in Libourne with Moueix, has been running the property since 1993, when he began restructuring the vineyards, which had been somewhat neglected. The soil is stony, with deep gravel, but there is also a good deal of sand. This has advantages in cooler years, as the soil heats up fast and helps the grapes to ripen. But there are drawbacks too. In wet years, the rain filters down to the roots fast, and can swell the grapes. And in torrid 2003, some vines failed to survive the onslaught of heat.

The Calvets also own a five-hectare property nearby called Château Chênevert. Its grapes are vinified separately, yet in effect the production is considered as part of Picque-Caillou, although some of the wine is bottled under the Chênevert label.

The grapes are picked by hand. The red is fermented with cultivated yeasts, and aged for twelve months in twenty-five per cent new oak. The small quantity of white begins its fermentation in tanks, but is then transferred to barriques, where the lees are stirred, and the wine is aged for up to eight months in fifty per cent new oak.

Overall, these are not very exciting wines, especially before 2000. The 1985 red was soft and charming, and the 1996 had Graves typicity and fine black-fruits flavours. The 2000 has more complexity and weight than the preceding two vintages, and the 2002 is a good if solid wine with supple tannins and a lively finish. The same is true of the 2003, a surprising success for the vintage. But they do seem to lack personality. The whites vary in quality. Vintages such as 2001 and 2003 exhibit lively citric fruit; other years, such as 2002, seem rather slack and dull. Yet the wines seem to be improving, and the arrival of a new manager, Jean Seroin, in 2004 should help maintain that momentum. Indeed the white 2004 showed more complexity, with pear and toasted almonds on the nose, and masses of ripe fruit balanced by refreshing acidity. The 2005 too showed more density and complexity than previous vintages.

Château Pont St-Martin

Léognan. Tel: 0556 641715. Website: www.chateaupontsaintmartin.com. Owner: Bernard Fontaine. 3.2 ha.
80% Merlot, 20% Cabernet Sauvignon. Production: 15,000 bottles

In 1999 Bernard Fontaine bought this charming eighteenth-century house just across from Malartic-Lagravière. He also acquired a parcel of fifteen-year-old vines close to Larrivet-Haut-Brion, on deep gravel with some sand and a band of clay. Fontaine comes from a family of Bordelais origins and has always appreciated fine claret, so he was keen to make wine here. His first vintage was in 2000. He acknowledges that there is too much Merlot at present, so is looking out for other plots that would redress the balance. Yields are very low, at roughly thirty-five hl/ha.

The grapes are destemmed but not crushed, and in 2003 Fontaine used the cold-soak technique for the first time, plus some micro-oxygenation during fermentation. The first three vintages were aged mostly in tanks, with the remainder in new oak. But from 2003, the whole crop is barrel-aged for twelve months in fifty per cent new oak.

It's clear that M. Fontaine is still finding his way. The 2000 vintage was green and tart, but the 2002 is a huge step up, with aromas of plums and blackcurrant, and a lush texture balanced by good acidity and length. The 2003 is a bit of a bruiser, but doesn't lack persistence for the vintage. This is a property worth watching.

Château Poumey

Gradignan. Tel: 0556 415312. Website: www.bernard-magrez.com. Owner: Municipality of Gradignan. 8.4 ha.

8 ha red: 60% Cabernet Sauvignon, 40% Merlot. 0.4 ha white: 100% Sauvignon Blanc. **Production:** *65,000 bottles*

Bernard Magrez has leased this property from the town of Gradignan since 1995. In 1988 the town acquired the estate to save from extinction the last vineyard within its boundaries. He has replanted much of the vineyard, so the vines are still young. The wine is made at Pape-Clément (*q.v.*), and given the full treatment: double sorting, tipping into the tanks by gravity, a long *cuvaison*, and ageing in eighty per cent new oak. I found the 2001 rich but somewhat cooked and lacking in zest. The 2002 was far better, with blackcurrant and blackberry aromas; the texture was supple yet spicy, and despite considerable density the finish was fresh. The 2003 is wildly overoaked on the nose, but better balanced on the palate, which is certainly opulent. I have never encountered the white wine.

Since 2000 this property has also been the source of a *micro-cuvée* called Sérénité, made from very low-yielding vines, hand-destemmed, cold-soaked, and fermented in small wooden vats with manual *pigeage*. The only vintage I have tasted, the 2002, had rich, smoky aromas, with oak and coffee tones; the palate was chewy, oaky, and extracted. Impressive, certainly, but scarcely recognizable as Graves.

Château de Quantin

St Médard d'Eyrans. Tel: 0557 255858. Website: www.andrelurton.com. Owner: André Lurton.

32 ha. 22 ha red: 50% Cabernet Sauvignon, 50% Merlot. 10 ha white: 100% Sauvignon Blanc.

Production: *150,000 bottles*

This abandoned property was revived and replanted in 1985 by André Lurton. There are no buildings and the machine-harvested must is vinified at Château de Cruzeau (*q.v.*). The vineyards are in a single block, with varied soils and perceptible slopes. Lurton's team produce a red wine that is usually Merlot-dominated, and easy to drink young; little of it is oak-aged. The white too is mostly unoaked. The wine, which I have rarely encountered, is probably the most commercial of Lurton's offerings from the Graves.

Château Roche-Lalande

Martillac. Tel: 0556 675151. **Owner:** *José Rodrigues-Lalande. 10 ha. 55% Merlot, 40% Cabernet Sauvignon,*

5% Cabernet Franc. **Second wine:** *Campeador*

This property, not far from Smith-Haut-Lafitte, is under the same ambitious ownership as Château de Castres (*q.v.*) in the Graves. Its first vintage was in 2004, when the wine was aged for six months in new oak.

Château Rochemorin

Martillac. Tel: 0557 255858. Website: www.andrelurton.com. Owner: André Lurton. 60 ha.

53 ha red: 60% Cabernet Sauvignon, 40% Merlot. 7 ha white: 85% Sauvignon Blanc, 15% Sémillon.

Production: *400,000 bottles.* **Second wine:** *Ch Coucheroy*

This historic property was owned by the Montesquieu family for many centuries, but reached the end of the line in 1919 when it was sold and its vines were replaced by trees. André Lurton bought the estate in 1973. The buildings consisted of a fortified farm in rather ramshackle condition, and the extensive vineyard was replanted by Lurton in a single parcel. These vineyards are of high quality, being located on the highest *croupe* in Martillac, with a southerly exposure; the soils are varied but mostly stony.

Until 2004 the wines were made at La Louvière (*q.v.*), but this changed after the construction of a modern gravity-fed winery of considerable architectural distinction. It is visible from afar, as the main entrance is capped by a witches' hat tower made of dark glass, with a lattice of stainless steel imposed over it and jutting out horizontally. From this tower there is an observation platform with impressive views. Lurton and his winemaker here, Laurent Bouthonnier, are very proud of their state-of-the-art grape sorter, called the Tribaie (*see* Chapter Three).

The red grapes are picked by machine, and aged for twelve months in thirty per cent new barriques. The white is aged in twenty-five per cent new oak. The oldest white Rochemorin I have tasted is the 1986, and the Sauvignon-dominated style has remained fairly consistent ever since. It's a well-made wine with reasonable concentration of flavour, a light spiciness that seems to be oak-derived, a welcome tangy bite on the finish, and good length. It rarely attains great heights, but it's always enjoyable. The 2004 and 2005 are particularly good.

The red, in my view, is somewhat underrated. Though not the most prestigious wine in the Lurton stable, it can age extremely well. The 1990, tasted in 2005, had a splendid nose of tobacco and liquorice, and there was a fine attack followed by ample concentration, acidity, and length. The 1996 is remarkably full-bodied, even extracted, an assertive wine with good acidic backbone that should keep well. The 1998 is robust but undeniably ripe, the 2001 more four-square with a slightly dry finish, and the 2002 rich and juicy, with a fine underpinning of tannin and acidity. The 2003 is baked and hollow.

The second wine, Coucheroy, omnipresent on Bordeaux brasserie wine lists, is equally reliable and extremely good value.

Château de Rouillac

Canéjan. Tel: 0557 124353. Website: www.lafragette.com. Owner: Lafragette family. 19 ha.
17.5 ha red: 60% Cabernet Sauvignon, 40% Merlot. 1.5 ha white: 34% Sauvignon Blanc, 33% Sauvignon Gris,
33% Sémillon. Production: 50,000 bottles. Second wine: Moulin de Rouillac

Canéjan is one of the least known communes in Pessac-Léognan, but the chartreuse at Rouillac once belonged to the renowned Baron Haussmann, who created the boulevards of modern Paris. However, he lost the property at the gaming tables, and it passed through various owners until it was bought by the Lafragette family in 1996. Like the other Lafragette properties, notably Loudenne (*q.v.*) in the Médoc, it is run by young Florence Lafragette with great energy and enthusiasm. When she took over, the vineyards on fine gravelly soils had been badly neglected. Although some parcels had been replanted in the 1960s, only eight hectares remained by 1996. Michel Rolland was hired as a consultant, and in 2005 Matthieu Bordes was hired as vineyard manager and winemaker. The white vines are young, having been planted by the Lafragettes to replace Cabernet Sauvignon that had been planted in a spot where it never ripened.

The red grapes are picked in *cagettes*, and fermented in both steel and wooden vats. The wine is aged for around fifteen months in thirty per cent new oak. The first vintage of the white wine was 2003; it is barrel-fermented and aged for eight months in thirty-five per cent new oak, with lees-stirring.

The Lafragettes managed to hit the ground running, and even an early vintage such as 1998 is a rich, succulent wine, with black fruits on the nose, and fairly good length. The 2000, 2001, and 2002 are in a similar style, but with some hints of menthol on the nose, and considerable density, even chewiness, on the palate. These are not especially elegant wines, but they pack a punch and seem built to last. I didn't care for the 2003 white, with its broad, peach-syrup character, but the flamboyant 2004 is a complete contrast, with toasty pear aromas, and a plumpness and oakiness that are not at the expense of vibrancy, minerality, and length.

Château Le Sartre

Léognan. Tel: 0557 565620. Owner: Marie-Josée Lariche. 35 ha. 27.5 ha red: 65% Cabernet Sauvignon,
33% Merlot, 2% Cabernet Franc. 7.5 ha white: 73% Sauvignon Blanc, 27% Sémillon.
Production: 180,000 bottles. Second wine: Ch Bois-Martin

Antony Perrin of Château Carbonnieux (*q.v.*) bought this property in 1981, and formal ownership was transferred to his sister in 2005. Its frost-prone vineyards are located near Domaine de Chevalier and Fieuzal, but the soils are light and quite sandy; the absence of clay subsoil keeps the wines relatively light in texture. The grapes are picked by hand and sorted twice at the winery. From 2004 onwards, major efforts have been made to reduce yields, impose stricter selection, and raise the quality of the wines.

The Sauvignon is given some skin contact before being fermented and aged, as is the Sémillon, in thirty per cent new oak with lees-stirring. The red grapes are destemmed but not crushed, and then fermented at fairly low temperatures, with a *cuvaison* of up to five weeks. It is aged in thirty-five per cent new barrels for twelve months.

The white was rather neutral for most of the 1990s, but I detect more richness and stylishness since 1998. The wines' aromas have also become oakier, though not excessively so. Aromas and flavours can range from lemon to white peach, and the tight, piquant 2002 and 2004 seem excellent expressions of this style. The 2005 is even more exuberant; it's not complex but it's highly enjoyable.

The red lacks some flesh, although there have been exceptions, such as the robust, plump 1990. The 1996 was excellent, a sleek wine with balance and vigour, with blackcurrant flavours and a dash of chocolate on the finish. The 1998 is rather lean and stretched. The 2001 has charming red-fruits aromas and a floral character too; but the wine is lean and lacks complexity. The 2002 has an attractive texture and fresh acidity, but lacks grip and succulence. The 2004 is stylish if not profound, with some youthful austerity that gives some welcome grip. Once a rather dull wine, Sartre has grown in sophistication over recent vintages.

Château Seguin

Canéjan. Tel: 0556 750243. Website: www.chateau-seguin.com. **Owners:** *Denis Darriet and Moise Ohana. 30 ha.*
54% Cabernet Sauvignon, 46% Merlot. **Production:** *200,000 bottles.* **Second wine:** *L'Angelot de Seguin*

By the time this once-substantial property was bought in 1987 by surveyor Denis Darriet and his Paris-based business partner Moise Ohana, the vineyards were run-down. Since 1988 they have been gradually replanted. The process was completed only in 2004. The vineyards are divided into two parcels of equal size, one near the cellars, where there is a stony gravel *croupe.* The soil is ploughed and green cover is widely planted to reduce vigour. The yield, even in a copious vintage such as 2004, is kept to forty-five hl/ha.

An experienced consultant oenologist, Serge Charritte, monitors the winemaking process. The grapes are picked by hand, sorted, and mounted on a conveyor belt so that they can be crushed directly above the vats, thus avoiding pumping. After a cold soak, fermentation takes place with pumpovers or *pigeage.* The *cuvaison* can be as long as thirty days, and micro-oxygenation is used toward the end of the process. The wine is aged for fourteen months in fifty per cent new oak.

The oldest vintage I have tasted was the 1999, and I find this and the subsequent vintages rather forced, with dense textures and dogged concentration, and an overall lack of finesse. Yet the fruit quality, except in the somewhat stewed, cherry-compote flavours of the 2003, seems good.

Sérénité

See *Château Poumey*

Château Smith-Haut-Lafitte

Martillac. Tel: 0557 831122. Website: www.smith-haut-lafitte.com. **Owners:** *Daniel and Florence Cathiard.*
Cru classé for red only. 55 ha. 45 ha red: 55% Cabernet Sauvignon, 33% Merlot, 10% Cabernet Franc, 2% Petit Verdot.
10 ha white: 90% Sauvignon Blanc, 5% Sauvignon Gris, 5% Sémillon. **Production:** *200,000 bottles.*
Second wine: *Les Hauts de Smith*

This large property takes its name – or one of them – from George Smith, who was its owner around 1720. It passed through many owners until it was leased by the Bordeaux négociant house of Eschenauer in 1902. Eschenauer looked after the property well, yet the wine, though always correct, was never exciting. The firm bought the property in 1958, but started making wines of some complexity only from the mid-1980s onwards. Then in 1991 the estate was bought for a substantial sum by the Cathiards. Daniel Cathiard had made a fortune by developing a chain of sports shops; his wife Florence was a senior advertising executive, and her skills too would be crucial in transforming the reputation of this fairly obscure estate. They were also virtuosi on the ski slopes, having represented France at international events, and they channelled that energy into Smith-Haut-Lafitte.

Other rich owners have made dramatic improvements to their estates – such as Alfred-Alexandre Bonnie at Malartic-Lagravière – but they all pale into insignificance compared to the Cathiards. They rebuilt the château, which is set well apart from the winery buildings, and made it their principal home; and they renovated the winery and built a new *chai*. But that was just the beginning. By the end of the 1990s they had located a disused mineral spring on the property, which became the foundation of a spa, the Sources de Caudalie. This cleverly exploited the concept of using winemaking residue (such as grape skins) as part of a beauty and health regime. To accommodate would-be visitors to the spa, they constructed a large and luxurious faux-rustic hotel set around a lake. Moreover, they created two restaurants, one for everyday dining, the other as a temple of gastronomy, and soon won themselves a Michelin star. To Florence Cathiard's chagrin, the spa, and its widely distributed line of beauty products, both run by one of their daughters, has proved more profitable than the wine estate.

Although some of their more traditional neighbours in Pessac-Léognan may have looked askance at the creation of a modern resort in their midst, there is no doubt that the Cathiards have done a huge amount for the Graves, bringing visitors to a region most tourists merely sped through on their way south.

Yet none of this was achieved at the expense of what was clearly the Cathiards' primary goal: transforming Smith-Haut-Lafitte into a truly fine wine. They enrolled the best consultants: Michel Rolland and, from 2000, Stéphane Derenoncourt. They chose highly skilled winemakers: Gabriel Vialard (now at Haut-Bailly), and from 2003 Fabien Tietgen, who had previously been the vineyard manager. Smith is in a state of constant evolution, as Daniel Cathiard is always open to experimentation and trying out new techniques such as barrel-fermentation. Cathiard also created his own cooperage on the property in 1995.

The vineyards occupy a large plateau fringed by woodlands. The soil is deep gravel, with plenty of quartz pebbles and glacial sand in the mix. The farming is not organic, but the soil is ploughed and no herbicides are used. Since 1996 the estate has produced its own compost. Yields rarely exceed forty hl/ha and all grapes are picked by hand.

In the Eschenauer days the white wine was pure Sauvignon Blanc, but the Cathiards have added some Sauvignon Gris, which they like for its floral aromas. They are not looking for a racy, acidic style, but for very ripe fruit. Tietgen observes: "If you pick Sauvignon too early you get varietal character, but only that. But we want Sauvignon that has power and density as well." Skin contact is considered only when the grapes are exceptionally healthy. The grapes are thoroughly sorted, pressed in pneumatic presses, and then the wine is barrel-fermented and aged with lees-stirring for twelve months.

The red grapes are very carefully sorted, twice before destemming, and then twice more. There is minimal crushing in order to slow down the fermentation process; only natural yeasts are used. The wines used to be fermented in steel tanks, but in 1998 they were replaced with wooden vats to permit *pigeage*. Pumpovers are also used during fermentation. In recent years some lots have been fermented in barriques, which is a very costly method given that part of the barrel must be left empty so as to accommodate the gases released during fermentation. The wine is aged for sixteen to eighteen months in barriques, of which up to eighty per cent are new.

The pre-Cathiard white wines varied from bland and characterless to spicy and vigorous. Most of the vintages had a herbaceous tone that was not necessarily disagreeable. After 1991 the improvement was swift. The wines were more oaky, but also more stylish. The fruit was clearly riper and less grassy, but there was never any suggestion of flabbiness or overripeness. In the 2000s the wines seemed to gain even further in complexity, with toast, apricot, and honeyed aromas. All vintages since 1993 have been of excellent quality, with the possible exception of the 1997 and 2003, which are marginally less successful. Since 1995 Smith-Haut-Lafitte has been producing some of the most succulent, consistent, and enjoyable white wines of Bordeaux.

The oldest red Smith I have tasted is the 1878, recorked in 1988. The colour was reddish-brown, and although there were caramel notes on the nose, there was no oxidation. There were toffee flavours, yet the wine remained delicate, concentrated, and in remarkable health for its age. The 1961, tasted three times, is now showing some age, with a sweet, leafy nose, remarkably sweet, intense fruit, and quite good length. It is by no means over the hill, but seems unlikely to improve further. The 1966 was charming in 1988 but is sure to be flagging now. The various vintages from the 1980s that I have tasted were uniformly dilute and charmless; they were greatly inferior to the white wines. However, the 1990 has always been remarkably good, and is now showing cedary aromas, dense fruit, and a spicy finish. Although 1993 was not an easy vintage, Smith produced a classic Graves, medium-bodied, elegant rather than fleshy, a wine of charm and balance rather than power. The 1994 is similar. The 1995 is surprisingly lush and forward. The 1996 is classic Graves, with delightfully savoury, oaky aromas, and the palate is elegant and graceful. The 1997 is successful for the vintage, and ready to drink. The 1998 is unusually succulent and opulent for the Graves, with delicious fruit; yet it has the structure to allow the wine to evolve for years to come. The 1999 is lighter but nonetheless has elegance. The vintages of the 2000s have all produced superb wines, perhaps a touch too oaky in their youth, but very well balanced, with tannin, acidity, and fruit all in harness. The 2003 is atypical with its plumpness and powerful tannins, but it too is a rich, well-made wine. Very ripe fruit and sweet oak mark the nose of the 2004, a supple, charming wine, but with sufficient tannin and structure to ensure a good life ahead. The 2005, for all its richness and concentration, is unmistakably Graves, and manages to be both weighty and delicious.

Domaine de la Solitude

Martillac. Tel: 0556 727474. Website: www.domainedelasolitude.com. **Owner:** *Soeurs de la Ste-Famille. 30 ha.*
23 ha red: 45% Cabernet Sauvignon, 40% Merlot, 15% Cabernet Franc. 7 ha white: 70% Sauvignon Blanc,
30% Sémillon. **Production:** *100,000 bottles.* **Second wine:** *Prieuré La Solitude*

This monastic order, founded in 1920, is now the headquarters of a group of convents with 2,000 members. Their vineyards, on the western edges of Martillac close to Rochemorin on well-drained gravelly sand, were replanted in the 1970s but were poorly managed, and were machine-picked for many years. In 1993 the sisters leased their vineyards to Olivier Bernard of Domaine de Chevalier for a period of forty years. Bernard is free to manage the vineyards and sell the wines as he thinks fit. His first action was to stop the use of herbicides. He also reverted to harvesting in *cagettes*, introduced ploughing, and acquired modern presses.

The white wine is fermented and aged in barriques for nine months with *bâtonnage*, but the proportion of new oak is kept low at fifteen per cent. There is no malolactic fermentation. The red wine is fermented with manual *pigeage*, then aged for twelve months in twenty-five per cent new barriques.

The whites in 2001 and 2002 are very good, with peachy aromas, and a slight exoticism on the palate – not an elegant style, but a good mouthful of wine with ample acidity. The 2004 shows a touch more complexity. It has taken a while to improve the reds, and there were disappointing wines in 1996 and 1999. But the 2001 and 2002 are much better, with black-fruits aromas, ample concentration, solid tannins, and quite good length. The 2004 may be lighter, but has a silky elegance. But it seems that Bernard's team is still wrestling with the terroir and seeking to unearth its potential finesse.

Château Le Thil Comte Clary

Léognan. Tel: 0556 300102. Website: www.chateau-le-thil.com. Owners: Jean de Laitre and Guillaume de Tastes.
17.5 ha. 14.5 ha red: 70% Merlot, 30% Cabernet Sauvignon. 3 ha white: 50% Sauvignon Blanc, 50% Sémillon.
Production: 120,000 bottles. Second wine: Les Reflets du Ch Le Thil

This property, buried in the woods not far from Carbonnieux, has a complicated history. Until the 1950s it was known as Château Le Désert. The vineyards were not well looked after, and after they were inherited by a branch of the de Laitre family in the 1970s, they were leased to the Perrins of Carbonnieux, who subsequently bought them in 2002. So Le Thil was left with a fine house and park (by the landscape gardener who designed the Jardin Public in Bordeaux), but no vines. The estate included twenty hectares within AC Pessac-Léognan that had not been planted. The de Laitre family elders persuaded two brothers, Jean and Arnaud, to revive viticulture here, even though neither of them knew much about grape-farming; indeed Jean was immersed in medical studies in Paris. However they began planting the vineyards in 1990 and continued until 1996, then planted a further six hectares in 2002. By this time Arnaud de Laitre had bowed out, leaving Jean in charge. He added "Comte Clary" to the name to avoid confusion with another Château Le Thil in the Premières Côtes. The Clarys were a notable family to which the de Laitres were related, and a certain Désirée Clary had married the future king of Sweden in 1818. In 2007 co-owner Guillaume de Tastes became the director of the estate.

The soil here is atypical, being mostly clay-limestone rather than gravel. This proved an advantage in 2003, when even the youngest vines survived the heat. This also explains the high proportion of Merlot among the red vines. All the grapes are picked by hand. The first vintage of red was 1992, the first of white 1993.

The Sauvignon component of the white wine is fermented and aged *sur lie* in tanks, while the Sémillon is fermented and aged in new barriques. After nine months the two components are blended. The red is traditionally vinified, and aged for twelve months in thirty per cent new oak; fining and filtration are rare.

The white wine is delicious: perhaps a touch austere in 2001, but the 2002 had melon and citrus aromas, and a keen and lively attack, with good length and a lemony finish. The 2003 is super-ripe, but livelier than many whites from this vintage. The 2004 seems oddly one-dimensional and lacklustre. The red is medium-bodied, rather subdued on the nose, and has a good tannic backbone and fresh cherry fruit on the palate. The 1996 and 1998 are both very good, and I prefer them to the rather charmless 2000. The 2001 is fleshy and quite forward, but the 2002 is livelier if a touch overripe. No doubt as the vines continue to age the wines will gain in depth and personality.

Château La Tour Haut-Brion

Pessac. Tel: 0556 002930. Website: www.haut-brion.com. Owner: Dillon family. Cru classé. 5 ha.
42% Cabernet Sauvignon, 23% Merlot, 35% Cabernet Franc. Production: 30,000 bottles

Already well known in the sixteenth century, when it was owned by the noble Rostaing family, this small estate would later pass through many changes of ownership. It was the Cayrou brothers, owners in the mid-nineteenth century, who devised its current name. In 1935 the estate was bought by the Woltner family, and thence came into the possession of the Dillons. The vineyards are next door to La Mission Haut-Brion, and the soils are similar; indeed, until 1983 La Tour Haut-Brion was the second wine of La Mission. It was made in a more powerful, beefier style than the post-1983 version. Today the wine is aged for twenty months in thirty per cent new barriques.

The 1990 was a lovely wine with captivating charm, perhaps less opulent than some other Graves of that vintage, but it had delightful freshness and firm tannins. The 1994 was good for the year, perhaps a touch hollow, but with fine acidity on the finish. The 1998 is a great success, with savoury tobacco aromas and rich, spicy fruit on the palate. The 1999, surprisingly, is a touch severe, though it has fresh acidity on the finish. The chewy 2000 is extremely ripe, yet maintains some elegance and vigour. Tasting the 2002 alongside the same vintage from Haut-Brion and La Mission, it was easy to see why the estate is the least highly regarded of the three. The aromas of blackberries and oak were almost overwhelming in their charm, and on the palate the wine was ripe, concentrated, supple, and with plenty of spice. It was beautifully made and delicious, but considerably more forward than the other two. Unlike them, it seemed to be giving its all. It was fine wine, but without the class of Haut-Brion and without the powerful complexity of La Mission. La Tour is certainly able to age well, but it is so enticing when young that there seems little point consigning it to long-term cellaring. However, in 2006 the Dillons decided to incorporate its vines with those of La Mission Haut-Brion, so 2005 was the last vintage here.

Château Trigant

*Villenave d'Ornon. Tel: 0556 758249. Website: www.chateau-trigant.com. **Owner:** Gabriel Sèze and family.*
*3.5 ha. 60% Cabernet Sauvignon, 40% Merlot. **Production:** 20,000 bottles.*
***Second wine:** Cuvée Lartigue-Ch-Trigant*

Hidden from view just off the road from Cadaujac to Bordeaux is this eighteenth-century chartreuse, which was built for a Bordeaux lawyer named Philippe Trigant. The Sèze family bought the property in 1860, but they abandoned the vineyards during the crisis of the 1930s. In 1990 their successors began replanting the vines, and the first commercial vintage was in 1996. The vines lie in a single parcel entirely surrounded by houses, blocks of flats, and a sports stadium. The soil is gravel over a clay subsoil. The vineyards are ploughed, deleafed by hand, and picked in *cagettes*. The must is given a cold soak before fermentation, and the wine is aged in one-third new barriques for twelve months. I find these wines rather chunky and austere, and of modest quality. But they are inexpensive.

15. The Southern Graves

The somewhat melancholy history of the division in 1987 of the Graves region into two ACs has already been given in the introduction to Pessac-Léognan. Ever since, the properties of the southern Graves have felt at a disadvantage, lacking the marketing muscle of their neighbours to the north, and of course hampered further by the absence of a single classified growth among them.

Yet it has to be acknowledged that in 1987 no great injustice was done. Of course there are some excellent properties within the Graves, but very few with the track record of most Pessac-Léognan estates. Certainly estates such as Brondelle, Chantegrive, Vieux-Château-Gaubert, and Clos Floridène produce wines that are better than some of the more lacklustre Pessac-Léognan estates. But what is there in the Graves to match Haut-Brion or Chevalier, or for that matter Smith-Haut-Lafitte or Haut-Bailly?

That should not imply that the wines of the Graves are second-rate. There are some good terroirs here, but they rarely produce wines with the longevity of the best *croupes* farther north. But structure, power, and longevity are not the sole criteria for enjoyment. For everyday drinking, it is hard to beat the Graves. Red and white, they are among the most appetizing wines of Bordeaux, fresh, sometimes even light, but with an earthy grip that gives them interest on the palate without being too demanding.

At the same time, there are too many wines that are underperforming: white wines that are dull and lacking in zest, and reds that are dilute or astringent. One explanation is that many Graves properties are caught in a vicious circle. Unable to charge high prices for their wines, they cannot afford the investments that would result in an improvement in quality. Many wines in the Graves are sold directly from the cellar door, and must therefore cater to a clientele unwilling to pay high or even realistic prices, and seeking wines that are ready or will soon be ready to drink. Such factors encourage growers to steer a middle course of adequacy at best, mediocrity at worst.

In addition, there are no cooperatives in the Graves, and never have been. The Bordeaux négociants took their place, buying from growers to supply their brands. After the crisis of the early 1970s, however, many négociants either lost interest or could no longer offer prices acceptable to the growers, who had to find other ways to sell their wines. A well-run cooperative, had there been one, might have mopped up wine from the smaller properties, thus relieving growers of the obligation to vinify their own production, and do it badly. Growers have also been caught in the fluctuating tides of taste. Historically, the southern Graves was white wine country. Three decades ago, more white than red was grown here. Then the market for inexpensive white Bordeaux, even with Graves on the label, sagged about fifteen years ago, and many red wines are produced from soils that are not well suited to red vines. Merlot has been replacing much Cabernet Sauvignon, both because it is easier to grow and because some Cabernet has been planted in spots where it ripens only with difficulty.

The more forward-looking growers concede that it is better to regard Pessac-Léognan as a model than as a rival unjustly favoured by fortune. Dominique Haverlan of Vieux-Château-Gaubert, and the president of the Syndicat, argues that since the Pessac-Léognan wines are quite (or very) expensive, they should not be seen as a threat to the Graves. Instead they set standards to emulate. In the 1970s and 1980s scarcely anybody in the southern Graves barrel-fermented white wine. When Peter Vinding-Diers at Rahoul started doing so in the early 1980s, many other producers thought he was mad. Today barrel-fermentation is the norm at any estate with pretensions to producing a white wine of quality.

As the name makes very clear, Graves is a region dominated by gravel soils, although in the south there is a good deal of limestone, better suited to white than red wine. But are some gravel soils more equal than others? Clearly they are, though Haverlan, for one, argues that the quality of the gravel deposits is just as fine in the south as in Pessac-Léognan. However, the *croupes* are less extensive, and most of them are located near the river and consist of geologically recent deposits. He believes that the absence of *vins de garde* in the Graves has more to do with human effort and resources than with the nature and quality of the soils. Not everyone agrees.

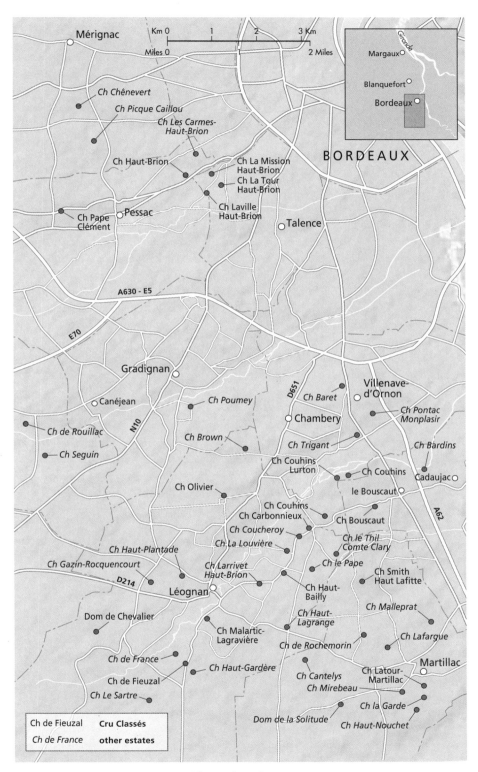

Mérignac

Ch Chênevert

Ch Picque Caillou

Ch Les Carmes-
Haut-Brion

Ch Haut-Brion

Ch La Mission
Haut-Brion

Ch La Tour
Haut-Brion

BORDEAUX

Ch Pape
Clément

Pessac

Ch Laville
Haut-Brion

Talence

A630 - E5

E70

Gradignan

Canéjean

Ch Poumey

Ch Baret

Villenave-
d'Ornon

Ch Pontac
Monplasir

Chambery

Ch de Rouillac

Ch Brown

Ch Trigant

Ch Bardins

Ch Seguin

Ch Couhins
Lurton

Ch Couhins

Cadaujac

Ch Olivier

le Bouscaut

Ch Couhins
Ch Carbonnieux

Ch Coucheroy

Ch Bouscaut

Ch La Louvière

Ch le Thil
Comte Clary

Ch Haut-Plantade

Ch le Pape

Ch Gazin-Rocquencourt

Ch Larrivet
Haut-Brion

Ch Smith
Haut Lafitte

D214

Léognan

Ch Haut-
Bailly

Ch Malleprat

Dom de Chevalier

Ch Haut-
Lagrange

Ch Lafargue

Ch Malartic-
Lagravière

Ch de Rochemorin

Ch de France

Martillac

Ch Haut-Gardère

Ch Cantelys

Ch Latour-
Martillac

Ch de Fieuzal

Ch Mirebeau

Ch Le Sartre

Ch la Garde

Dom de la Solitude

Ch Haut-Nouchet

Ch de Fieuzal — **Cru Classés**
Ch de France — other estates

Km 0   1   2   3 Km
Miles 0   1   2 Miles

Margaux

Gironde

Blanquefort

Bordeaux

N10

D651

A62

The Southern Graves

Michel Garat of Château St-Robert is not convinced that the Graves can make wines as long-lived as those from Pessac-Léognan. Many red wines from gravel soils are light in texture and body. There is nothing wrong with light red wines, but it is difficult to avoid an impression of thinness. Gravel soils are very sensitive to yields: overcrop them, and the resulting wine will indeed be thin and characterless. Growers are tempted to improve these poor soils by adding fertilizers. Garat believes the absence of clay from many soils leads to a lack of flesh in the red wines. For him, the strength of the Graves lies in the production of the equivalent of good *crus bourgeois* in the Médoc: well balanced, fresh, drinkable wines at a reasonable price.

EXPANDING VINEYARDS, SHRINKING GROWERS

Perhaps the Graves region has grown too large. Historically, there were the estates of what is today Pessac-Léognan, and the sweet wine regions such as Sauternes and Barsac. In the second half of the nineteenth century, the two regions were joined up as the vineyards expanded southwards. By the end of the century there were some 5,000 hectares under vine. The economic crisis of the 1930s had a devastating effect on these vineyards, which shrank by 1935 to 1,500 hectares. Replanting after the 1956 frost and subsequent periods of expansion meant that by 2000 there were once again 5,000 hectares of vineyards. But they were not necessarily in the best locations.

The number of growers is shrinking, and quite rapidly. In 1993, there were 420 producers declaring a crop. By 2004 there were only 327. But that should not be seen as a sign of economic stagnation. Many of the properties that have disappeared are no longer economically viable, being six hectares or less. Today the average holding is twelve hectares. Thus over the past decade many properties have expanded by purchasing parcels from retiring growers. Quality-conscious owners seeking to expand are now able to snap up excellent parcels of old vines in good locations. So in the long term the disappearance of the smallest estates is likely to lead to an improvement in quality across the board.

It is very difficult to get an accurate picture of the quality of the Graves' numerous terroirs. There is too much local chauvinism, and every grower seeks to promote the excellence of the land where his or her vines are planted. Some communes have relatively homogeneous soils, such as Arbanats; others, such as Portets, are much more diverse. Pujols, it is widely agreed, is an excellent terroir for white wines (and could, if permitted, make exceptional sweet wines too) thanks to its limestone subsoil and late-ripening microclimate. Climatic differences within the Graves are between riverside vineyards and those farther inland, rather than between Portets, for example, and Langon much farther south.

The vineyards are divided between the various communes as follows: Ayguemorte (twelve hectares), Beautiran (115), Portets (600), La Brède (140), Arbanats (150), St Selve (100), Virelade (75), Podensac (314), Cérons (342), Illats (325), St Michel de Rieufret (16), Landiras (200), Pujols (206), St Pardon-de-Conques (94), Toulenne (56), Langon (306), St Pierre-de-Mons (287), Guillos (17), Budos (138), Léogeats (10), Roaillan (32), Mazères (205), and Isle-St-Georges (88).

WHITES – AND GRAVES SUPERIEURES

About sixty-five per cent of the annual production of around sixteen million bottles is of red wine. Of the remaining third of white wine, about one-third is sweet Graves Supérieures. Until the late 1990s Graves Supérieures could theoretically be vinified dry. Even though in practice it was invariably lightly sweet, some négociants produced the wine by blending dry Supérieures with cheap sweet wine. Dominique Haverlan pressed successfully for a change in the rules, requiring a minimum residual sugar of eighteen grams per litre and forbidding the use of mechanical harvesting. About ninety per cent of Graves Supérieures is sold in bulk, and most of that goes to the Netherlands to satisfy the demand for nondescript sweet white wines. For growers it is good news as the bulk price is higher than for dry white wine. Most Graves Supérieures is pretty bland, but there are some good examples around, and the typical balance would be thirteen degrees of alcohol and forty to fifty grams of residual sugar.

The two principal white varieties, as elsewhere in Bordeaux, are Sauvignon Blanc and Sémillon. There is also some Muscadelle, but many growers are happy to do without this fragile, difficult variety, though it can add aromatic charm to the wine. André Lurton believes Sauvignon Blanc is popular because it is less prone to botrytis than Sémillon. A touch, or even a good deal, of botrytis is no problem when you are making a sweet wine, but it is undesirable in dry white wines. He rejects the argument that Sémillon gives the wines more longevity, and there are certainly wines either exclusively or predominantly from Sauvignon Blanc (such as Couhins-Lurton, Smith-Haut-Lafitte, and Malartic-Lagravière) which age very well. Moreover the trend toward fresh white wines to drink very young is more easily satisfied by Sauvignon, especially for unoaked versions. Some growers prefer Sémillon not because of its flavour or personality but because the vine itself can live to a ripe old age, whereas Sauvignon vines often need to be replanted after about thirty years.

Some winemakers believe Sémillon has been underrated as a dry wine grape. Peter Vinding-Diers, who derided Sauvignon Blanc as grassy and one-dimensional, used to say that the problem with Sémillon was not the grape as such but the fact that most producers had no idea how to vinify it. He argued that setting the lees and cool fermentation were essential to bring out its inherent finesse. Sémillon does give large crops, if allowed to do so, and this too may account for some of its appeal. As will become clear, very good wines are made from both Sauvignon and Sémillon.

A newcomer to the region is Sauvignon Gris, a variant of Sauvignon Blanc. The skin is pink, so it is not a variety that can withstand a long maceration. In character, it is less citric than Sauvignon Blanc, but has more floral and, some would say, complex aromas. Its drawback is that it is more susceptible to rot than Sauvignon Blanc. It has been adopted with some enthusiasm at Pessac-Léognan estates such as Rouillac and Smith-Haut-Lafitte, but also in the Graves at Châteaux l'Hospital, L'Avocat, Landiras, Haut-Selve, Rahoul, and elsewhere.

White grapes need to be picked at the right moment. Sean Allison of Château du Seuil believes many growers pick their white grapes when it is too hot, and the wines inevitably acquire an unappealing oxidative tone. Denis Dubourdieu, while hardly defending those who pick in torrid conditions, argues that if you have a great terroir, the exact harvest date is not that important:

> A great terroir for whites is one that allows the grapes to develop slowly, so even if you have to wait a few days the fruit won't vanish and the acidity will diminish only very slowly. If you have a limestone subsoil and cold nights, as at Pujols, you have no need to worry about overmaturity and flabbiness.

The Graves is particularly susceptible to the economic crisis that is now afflicting Bordeaux. The great wines of Pessac-Léognan will usually find a market, if the price is not too extortionate, but the Graves makes an abundance of easy-going wine that few feel compelled to buy. Although the Maison du Vin tries hard to promote the wines, the region lacks internationally known properties that can act as flagships for the area. Bulk prices for Graves remain perilously low and some growers will find it difficult to weather the crisis. Michel Garat notes that this too can affect quality:

> With bulk prices low, many growers are tempted to crop as much as possible. That results in green wines that damage the reputation of the region as a whole. Much Chardonnay from the south of France may be boring but at least it's ripe.

I can confirm that a fair proportion of inexpensive Graves does taste unripe.

Nor is it always the case that improving quality is rewarded financially. Françoise Lévêque of Chantegrive says she has a dependable market for her basic white Graves. But the wine that has made the reputation of the estate, Cuvée Caroline, barely pays its way, given that it has to be cropped at much lower levels and aged in expensive oak. "For a white wine region to be taken seriously," says Dubourdieu, "you need ageability." He believes that although the quality of white wine in Graves is patchy, there is a real opportunity for the growers to succeed, since the production of prestigious white wine in Pessac-Léognan is marginal.

Nonetheless the crisis is real. At Château La Vieille France I was told:

> As well as our Graves vineyards, we have ten hectares of Bordeaux Supérieur intended for everyday drinking. But the days when workers drank a couple of litres of wine each day have long gone. So we have to focus more on our Graves wines, but we're constrained by the prices buyers are prepared to pay. If we invest heavily to improve quality further, that has to be reflected in the price of the wine, and we risk losing our markets.

Jean-Noël Belloc of the excellent Château Brondelle was happy to report that his 2002s flew out of the cellars. "But I have to be careful about how much I produce. The prices of the best Graves are approaching those of some Pessac-Léognans, and there is a limit to how much we can sell at that price."

Some estates are eager to see the whole issue of classification reopened. As has been mentioned in the chapter on Pessac-Léognan, there are certainly some strong candidates for promotion in the Graves, and were they eventually to be classified it would strengthen the profile of the region. But at present there is too much opposition from vested interests, especially among the existing classified growths, which have nothing to gain from the swelling of their ranks, however worthy the beneficiaries.

Château d'Archambeau

Illats. Tel: 0556 625146. Owner: Jean-Philippe Dubourdieu. 28 ha. 19 ha red: 50% Cabernet Sauvignon, 50% Merlot. 9 ha white: 55% Sémillon, 40% Sauvignon Blanc, 5% Muscadelle. Production: 180,000 bottles.

Second wine: Ch Mourlet

Dubourdieu's machine-harvested vineyards are planted in a single block on a fine slope, with clay-limestone below. He used to age his white wines in barriques, but the négociants who were his regular clients told him his wines were becoming too expensive, so he threw out the barrels and aged his wines in tanks alone. He established a new image for his wines, as fruity and easy to drink. Unfortunately this robbed them of much of their character, so in 2004 he started ageing some of the white in older barriques, as he has always done for his red wine. Dubourdieu's wife Corinne is the daughter of Roger Biarnès, who retired in 2002, leaving her the Sauternes Second Growth of Château Suau, and a property in Podensac that will be labelled as Moulin de Julien.

Signs of improvement in the white wine are not yet apparent, and the 2003, like its predecessors, was simple and reasonably fresh but with no distinguishing characteristics. The red is dilute, fresh, and rather bland, though the 2000 was a lusher wine with more concentration than usual.

Château d'Ardennes

Illats. Tel: 0556 625366. Website: www.chateau-ardennes.com. Owner: Cyril Dubrey. 64 ha. 44 ha red: 45% Merlot, 42% Cabernet Sauvignon, 10% Cabernet Franc, 3% Petit Verdot. 20 ha white: 70% Sémillon, 25% Sauvignon Blanc, 5% Muscadelle. Production: 450,000 bottles. Second wine: Ch La Tuilerie

The Dubrey family, who also own Château Mirebeau (*q.v.*) in Pessac-Léognan, acquired this large and ancient property in 1968. Two-thirds of the vineyards are on gravel soils, the remainder on clay-limestone. The white wine is unoaked, the red is aged in forty per cent new barriques. My experience of the wine is too limited to offer a judgment, but I enjoyed the ripe, full-bodied 1996 red.

Château L'Avocat

Cérons. Tel: 0556 271156. Website: www.chateauduseuil.com. Owners: Robert and Susan Watts. 8 ha.
5 ha red: 50% Cabernet Sauvignon, 45% Merlot, 5% Cabernet Franc. 3 ha white: 70% Sémillon, 20% Sauvignon Blanc,
10% Sauvignon Gris. Production: 40,000 bottles

Under the same ownership and management as Château du Seuil (*q.v.*), L'Avocat was bought in 2002. The property was well known in the interwar years, and in the 1990s the wine was sold exclusively to the Philippe de Rothschild négociant business in the Médoc. During that period the vineyards were overcropped, but that has been rectified and the average yield is forty-five hectolitres per hectare. There are some parcels of very old red vines. The harvest is manual and the wine is vinified at Seuil. The red grapes are cold-soaked for five days, then fermented with pumpovers, *pigeage*, and *délestage*. Malolactic fermentation takes place in barriques, and the wine is aged for up to sixteen months in around thirty per cent new oak.

The white wine is picked at different times, to balance early and late pickings. The Sémillon is aged for eight months in up to seventy per cent new oak, while the Sauvignon stays in tanks on the fine lees. The barrels are rotated so that the lees can be stirred without aeration. The 2003 has aromas of oak and pears; it's a plump wine tasting of peaches, melons, and pears, with fair acidity but not much length. The 2004 is far livelier, with oaky aromas, a graceful structure, and considerable stylishness. The 2002 red has dense aromas of chocolate and plums, and is quite full-bodied, with reasonable persistence.

Château Beauregard-Ducasse

Mazères. Tel: 0556 761897. Owner: Jacques Perromat. 45 ha. 36 ha red: 50% Merlot, 45% Cabernet Sauvignon,
5% Petit Verdot. 9 ha white: 50% Sémillon, 50% Sauvignon Blanc. Production: 200,000 bottles.
Second wines: Ch Ducasse, Ch Lagupeau

Mazères is in the southern Graves, not far from Langon, and the vineyards here are quite distinctive. Perromat's best site is a twenty-hectare gravelly *croupe* that is the most southerly in Bordeaux and probably the highest in the Graves, at 112 metres (367 feet). The site is also quite windy, which helps keep rot at bay.

Perromat started off in 1981 with just two hectares belonging to his wife's family, then gradually rented and bought other parcels. The soils are essentially gravel and sand over a clay subsoil with high iron content. Herbicides are used only immediately beneath the rows, and the grapes are picked by hand. The Petit Verdot is a recent addition, and entered the wine from 2003 onwards.

Part of the white crop is given skin contact for a few hours, then the must is chilled for a few days before fermentation in stainless steel. The wine is bottled young after a few months on the lees. There is a special *cuvée* called Albertine Peyri, which is mostly fermented and aged in new oak for up to eight months, with lees-stirring. Given this treatment, it is surprising to me that the Peyri, while oaky on the nose, is an assertively citric wine that can be rather tart and grapefruity.

The red, like the white, is fermented with selected yeasts. The barriques in which the white is fermented are then used for part of the red wine for twelve months. Since 1990 there has been a special *cuvée* for red too: Albert Duran is aged in one- and two-year-old barrels for twelve months. Duran is attractively cherry-scented, but the wine is a touch rustic, with tannins that are too assertive for the fruit. Jacques Perromat points out that the Cabernet in Duran needs a few years to soften up, but a 1990, tasted in 2005, although endowed with a charming cigar-box nose, was still quite tannic. I am not persuaded that the wine improves significantly from long cellaring.

Château Belon

St Morillon. Tel: 0671 918133. Owner: Laurent Depiot. 32 ha. 20 ha red: 40% Cabernet Sauvignon, 40% Merlot,
20% Cabernet Franc. 12 ha white: 60% Sémillon, 30% Sauvignon Blanc, 10% Muscadelle.
Production: 200,000 bottles. Second wine: Ch des Trois Tours

Lost in rural obscurity Belon is undergoing, if slowly, a radical transformation. When I first came here in 1993, the vineyards were machine-harvested, other than the very old vines, and barriques were largely absent. Depiot's father began working the estate in 1972, when there were only six hectares of vines. Laurent, with international experience in Napa Valley and Tuscany, took over in 1998, and brought with him a whole new approach. His father produced easy-drinking wines for the traditional French market. In 1993 they were unimpressive, to put it mildly. Depiot admits the wines lacked fruit and structure.

The most important changes are in the vineyards. "When I was growing up, my father would use fertilizers and herbicides, crop at ninety hl/ha, and never bleed the tanks. That's what everyone did at that time." This is being reversed, although herbicides are still used beneath the rows. Depiot wants to bring out the best in the vineyards, which include a gravelly *croupe* where there is some venerable Cabernet Sauvignon, clay soils with more Merlot, and parcels of red sand over deep clay-limestone, which is excellent for Cabernet Franc. The vineyards are still machine-harvested but at night. The red is now aged for sixteen months in fifty per cent new oak.

The Depiots also own another property, the fifteen-hectare Château Gravette, half planted with red grapes, half white. The terroir has less potential than Belon, as there is more clay.

At present the Belon wines remain rather dilute and lacking in interest, and it will be a few years before Laurent Depiot's changes become apparent.

Château Le Bonnat

St Selve. Tel: 0557 940920. Owner: Laubade et Domaines Associés. 25 ha. 22 ha red: 50% Merlot,
46% Cabernet Sauvignon, 4% Cabernet Franc. 3 ha white: 95% Sémillon, 5% Sauvignon Blanc. Production: 165,000 bottles

From 1987 to 1997 the wines were made by the same team responsible for Fieuzal. Since 1997 Le Bonnat has been owned and managed by a Cognac-based company called LEDA that is also the proprietor of the more important Château Haut-Selve (*q.v.*). The vines are fairly old and picked by hand. The white is aged nine months in barriques, the red for twelve months in forty per cent new oak. The white is commercial in the sense that it is quite weighty, well made, and has modest acidity. The red is solid, with black-fruits aromas and considerable density and weight on the palate. Both red and white lack some lift and verve.

Château Brondelle

Langon. Tel: 0556 623814. Website: www.chateaubrondelle.com. Owners: Jean-Noël Belloc and Philippe Rochet.
40 ha. 25 ha red: 60% Cabernet Sauvignon, 40% Merlot. 15 ha white: 50% Sémillon, 45% Sauvignon Blanc,
5% Muscadelle. Production: 150,000 bottles. Second wine: Ch La Croix St-Pey

Purchased by Rolland Belloc in 1968, Brondelle, which already had vineyards in the early nineteenth century, has slowly evolved from a polycultural farm to one of the southern Graves' leading wine estates. Belloc and Rochet are brothers-in-law: Rochet looks after the vineyards, Belloc makes the wines. A new winery was built in 1999, and it is now being adapted so that Belloc can work by gravity and ferment the red wines with *pigeage*.

This is a complex estate, since not all the vineyards are in the Graves appellation. The property also includes four hectares of Bordeaux Rouge, six of Bordeaux Supérieur (Château Bras d'Argent), and three in Sauternes (Château Les Tuileries). Belloc also makes a small quantity of unoaked Graves Supérieures from Sémillon.

The owners are no fans of systematic green-harvesting but prefer to let nature take its course – though bunch-thinning is certainly employed as a last resort. For white wines they are looking for a yield of around fifty hl/ha. In the third and fourth year, they remove all the bunches from the young vines in order to give those plants more strength, a procedure I have not heard of elsewhere. In most years the grapes are picked by hand, but in 2003, because of the heat, Belloc did use a machine to bring in the crop quickly. For whites, he likes skin contact. The regular white Graves is unoaked. From older vines he makes Cuvée Anais, which excludes Muscadelle. This is aged for eight months in sixty per cent new barriques.

The normal bottling of red Graves is aged for twelve months in older barrels, including a little American oak. More serious is the Cuvée Damien, which is aged entirely in new oak and bottled without filtration. Since 2003 there has also been some Petit Verdot in the blend. Belloc thinks he used to pick the reds too early, and is now trying to pick at optimal ripeness.

The Brondelle whites are excellent. The unoaked white is copybook modern Graves: it has aromas of apples and pears, with some floral notes; the palate is delicate but concentrated, stylish with lively acidity but no greenness. In Cuvée Anais the oak is well integrated, the texture is plumper but not heavy, and the wine retains a citric character and considerable minerality. It ages moderately well, but seems at its best within five years. I find the Graves Supérieures unexciting.

For my taste Cuvée Damien has been overoaked. In the southern Graves the wines rarely have the structure and body to withstand so much new oak. The ripe blackcurrancy fruit aromas are often obscured by this powerful oaky overlay. The actual fruit quality is very good, with flavours of cherries, blackcurrants, and blackberries; the texture is robust and fleshy, and it has a firm tannic undertow and quite good length. My favourite vintages since 1996 are 1998, 2000, and 2002.

The Brondelle wines are very good and offer excellent value, and since Belloc is a thoughtful winemaker, always open to new ideas and to his consultants' suggestions, there is every reason to think they will improve even further. At present the whites are more exciting than the reds, but the reds are beginning to catch up.

Château Cabannieux

Portets. Tel: 0556 672201. Website: www.chateaucabannieux.com. **Owner:** *Régine Dudignac. 22 ha.*
16 ha red: 60% Merlot, 35% Cabernet Sauvignon, 5% Cabernet Franc. 6 ha white: 80% Sémillon,
20% Sauvignon Blanc. **Production:** *90,000 bottles*

The kindly Mme. Dudignac, who comes from an old négociant family, the Barrières, receives visitors, as she has done for years, in her cluttered drawing room, which is festooned with dozens of decorative spittoons. Her husband used to make the wines, but in 2000 their son Hugo took over that responsibility.

The vineyards are in a single block, and occupy the highest ground in Portets, which, at thirty-two metres (105 feet), is not saying much. Nonetheless that elevation means the vines are well ventilated and protected from rot. The soil is deep gravel over a subsoil of clay. The Dudignacs are not keen on Cabernet Franc, but since the vines are very old, they don't have the heart to grub them up – or not yet.

The white vines are picked by hand. The wine used to be essentially unoaked, but nowadays a quarter of the crop is aged in new oak with lees-stirring for three to six months. The red grapes are machine-harvested (except for the oldest and youngest vines), often at night to conserve acidity, and fermented in cement tanks, then aged for up to eighteen months in twenty per cent new oak.

I have a soft spot for the wines of Cabannieux. They are not great wines and never have been. But they are very traditional, very Graves, inexpensive, and in most vintages give modest but genuine pleasure. The white has melony aromas and the oak is well integrated. The fruit is reasonably concentrated, always has some acidic bite but remains just about on the right side of greenness. They can age: a 1997 in 2005 had become nutty in aroma and had retained its acidity and freshness, but was fully ready to drink.

The reds have some spice: there are hints of clove as well as black cherries on the nose. The 2000 was quite aggressive and tannic, but other vintages have been more overtly fruity, with a light earthiness and supple tannins. The 1995 was drinking well in 2005, but I see no point in keeping it any longer. Despite Mme. Dudignac's insistence that her wines can age well, they seem at their best within about eight years.

Château de Castres

Castres. Tel: 0556 675151. Owner: José Rodrigues-Lalande. 30 ha. 28 ha red: 55% Merlot, 40% Cabernet Sauvignon,
5% Cabernet Franc. 2 ha white: 55% Sémillon, 40% Sauvignon Blanc, 5% Muscadelle.
Production: 180,000 bottles. Second wine: Ch Tour de Castres

This property dates from the seventeenth century and was once one of the largest estates in the Graves. In the early twentieth century it was bought by a German chemist who manufactured *bouillie bordelaise*. Rodrigues-Lalande bought the estate in 1996 and set about renovating it. He is an oenologist, a former student of Denis Dubourdieu's, and an expert on yeasts and aromas. His wife makes an ideal partner, since she is an accountant specializing in the wine business. Rodrigues-Lalande acquired vineyards in Portets and St Selve from his father-in-law, and has also planted some vines here and nearby at Beautiran. He has been clearing woodland around the château, exposing the site of the historic vineyards which he will eventually replant.

He has analysed his vineyards closely, so that each parcel is handled separately. They are all ploughed, he cultivates his vines according to *lutte raisonnée*, and he has been experimenting with biodynamism. Although the vineyards are essentially picked by hand, he has been experimenting with machine-harvesting at night, using dry ice to protect the fruit. He has not reached a firm conclusion, but suspects that machine-harvesting will be better suited to his vineyards.

Rodrigues-Lalande is an articulate man with forceful opinions. He states that as far as white wines are concerned, he wants wines that are "gastronomically versatile", that can be drunk throughout a meal. He is not that interested in aromatic wines, and wants length of flavour – though I don't see that one is obliged to choose one or the other. Until recently his white wines were aged in sixty per cent new oak, but he is now reducing the proportion to thirty per cent. These are excellent wines, and they don't lack aroma. The 2003 was suffused with peach, mango, and honey; the 2002 was more classic with lime aromas. These are rich, ripe wines, well balanced with ample acidity and length.

The red grapes are given a cold soak in conical steel tanks, then fermented with locally selected yeasts, though he plans to use indigenous yeasts in the future. The fermenting wine is micro-oxygenated, then aged for fourteen months in thirty per cent new oak. He fines with eggs from his own chickens (how many does he have, I wonder?) before giving the wine a light filtration. He wants his reds to be silky and accessible young, since no one these days waits twelve years to open a bottle of wine. The wines are indeed supple, rich, and savoury, but I suspect the micro-oxygenation has been used with a heavy hand, as they also seem prematurely evolved. However, the 2002 is excellent, with smoky tobacco aromas, excellent ripeness and concentration, and integrated tannins.

These are definitely wines to look out for. He also makes a Bordeaux Supérieur called Château Lalande-Poitevan, and Château Roche-Lalande at Pessac-Léognan.

Château de Chantegrive

Podensac. Tel: 0556 271738. Website: www.chantegrive.com. Owners: Henri and Françoise Lévêque. 95 ha.
50 ha red: 50% Merlot, 50% Cabernet Sauvignon. 45 ha white: 50% Sauvignon Blanc, 50% Sémillon.
Production: 600,000 bottles. Second wine: Benjamin de Chantegrive

Thirty-five years ago, wine broker Henri Lévêque set out to prove his hunch that the good terroirs of the Graves could produce first-rate wine. He created this substantial domaine more or less from scratch, aided by his wife and his daughter Hélène, who look after the estate today. As the vineyards are dispersed around Podensac, Illats, Cérons, and Virelade, the soil is varied, but is essentially deep gravel over a band of white sand with quartz pebbles, and a limestone subsoil. The soil is ploughed, no herbicides are used, and the harvest is manual.

Until 1988 their white was unoaked, but then the négociant Calvet asked them to try their hand at barrique-aged wine. That was the genesis of their flagship white, Cuvée Caroline. This is made from vines with an average age of thirty years, and aged in fifty per cent new barriques. The production now outstrips that of the regular white Chantegrive. There is also a small production of sweet Cérons (*see* Chapter Thirty-One) in certain vintages.

The red wine is aged in fifty per cent new barriques for fifteen months. There used to be a Cuvée Edouard from the oldest vines, but by 1995 it was discontinued, since the entire vineyard was now reaching a respectable age. The winery is equipped with a reverse-osmosis machine, to cope not only with wet years but with over-productive young vines.

The regular white Chantegrive is a lively, citric wine, with fairly sharp, grassy flavours. The oak is very apparent on the Cuvée Caroline, which often smells of pears. It has a plump, creamy texture, an occasional sherbet tone, and good persistence of flavour. It's not hard to understand its appeal. The 2005 was the equal of many a top Pessac-Léognan. The red is somewhat underrated. I like its savoury, black-fruits aromas, its robust but ripe tannins, its vigour and length. It benefits from some bottle-age, whereas the whites can be drunk on release. The slightly earthy but balanced and spicy 2000 is an excellent example of the Chantegrive red.

Clos Bourgelat

Cérons. Tel: 0556 270173. **Owner:** *Dominique Lafosse. 15 ha. 7 ha red: 51% Merlot, 49% Cabernet Sauvignon and Cabernet Franc. 8 ha white: 83% Sémillon, 15% Sauvignon Blanc, 2% Muscadelle.* **Production:** *65,000 bottles*

Lafosse is the very model of the conscientious, independent wine producer. From vineyards in Cérons, Illats, and Podensac, he is able to produce a wide range of wines, and with his affability and immediately recognizable moustache, he presides over his tasting room with panache, cultivating the regular customers and passing trade that are essential to his economic survival.

He makes an unoaked white wine, as well as one called Caprice that is barrel-fermented and aged for six months in new oak. His red wine is aged in barriques, few of them new. When climatic conditions permit, he likes to make some sweet Cérons; if the weather is unfavourable, then he makes white Graves from the same vines.

The white is fresh and citric, but has no complexity. I prefer it to the rather oily Caprice, in which the oak is not well integrated. The red is light and straightforward. As well as the attractive if lightweight Cérons, he also makes a small quantity of Sauternes called Vignobles de Sanches.

I might wish that the wines had more concentration and complexity, but Lafosse knows his market, which is price-conscious and not so demanding.

Château Crabitey

Portets. Tel: 0556 671864. **Website:** *www.vignobles-seillon.com.* **Owner:** *Association Amis de la Chartreuse de Seillon. 27 ha. 25 ha red: 60% Merlot, 40% Cabernet Sauvignon. 2 ha white: 50% Sauvignon Blanc, 50% Sémillon.* **Production:** *100,000 bottles.* **Second wine:** *Ch Puycastaing*

On the Portets plateau stands an ugly complex of buildings that until the early 1990s was a religious orphanage, founded in 1882 and vacated in 1992. In 1985 the nuns hired Jean-Ralph de Butler (who is remotely related to British wine writer Oz Clarke) to run the attached wine estate. This he did, expanding the vineyards and building a *chai* in 2001. Since 1998 the property has been run by his son Arnaud de Butler.

The vineyards are on deep gravel soils in two principal blocks, one on the plateau opposite Cabannieux, the other close by. The average age of the vines is twenty-five years. The soil is ploughed. The best wine is the *grand vin*, which is seventy per cent Cabernet Sauvignon. It is given a cold soak, and the *cuvaison* can extend for twenty-five days. The wine is aged for twelve months in one-third new barriques and bottled without filtration.

Until de Butler is happy with the vineyards, there is no Crabitey white, and the white appears as a second wine. The red *grand vin* is superb, with a truly opulent nose of blackberries, blackcurrants, and chocolate. It is tight, concentrated, minty, and sleek, and should age very well. The 2002 has the edge on the 2001, but both are excellent, as is the more lush 2005. This is a new star in the Graves.

Château Doms

Portets. Tel: 0556 672021. **Owner:** *Hélène Durand. 22 ha. 17 ha red: 70% Merlot, 30% Cabernet Sauvignon.*
5 ha white: 70% Sémillon, 30% Sauvignon Blanc. **Production:** *80,000 bottles*

Hélène Durand is a pharmacist by training, but she gave up her career in 1998 to take control of the family estate. The château is a charming chartreuse that the family believe probably had its origins as a religious community-turned-hunting lodge. The stony, well-drained vineyards lie mostly in a single block around the house. (There are also six hectares of Bordeaux Supérieur, all planted with Merlot.) The white vines are picked by hand, the reds by machine.

The white must is given skin contact and is unoaked. The red is cold-soaked for five days, then fermented in steel and cement vats. The regular Château Doms is unoaked, but there is also a Cuvée Amélie, which is the same wine but aged around twelve months in one-third new barriques. Compared to other wines of this area, they are quite expensive.

The 2003 white is atypically honeyed and heavy 2003. The 2006 has more freshness and minerality. The regular 2001 red is quite solid and spicy, with attractive fruit if not great length. The 2000 Amélie tastes stewed, but the 2001 is more stylish and complex. The 2003 is predictably more chunky and earthy.

Château Ferrande

Castres. Tel: 0556 670586. **Owner:** *Castel Frères. 86 ha. 80 ha red: 60% Cabernet Sauvignon, 40% Merlot.*
6 ha white: 50% Sémillon, 50% Sauvignon Blanc. **Production:** *420,000 bottles.* **Second wine:** *Ch Guillon*

This enormous property has grown quite speedily. In 1976 the Castel family, a powerful force in the international wine business, rented the estate, and bought it outright in 1992. At that time there were forty-four hectares under vine; that surface has subsequently doubled. The soil is gravel, and very stony clay mixed with sand. The average age of the vines is now around thirty years. The soil is ploughed, and no herbicides are employed. The white grapes are picked by hand, the reds by machine.

The white wine is unoaked and does not go through malolactic fermentation. It develops aromas that led me to believe it had been barrel-aged, but that is not so. Indeed, I was informed that barrel-fermentation "is too much work". The red is aged in twenty per cent new oak, but rotates with lots that are ageing in tanks.

The white is surprisingly rich, and seems dominated by Sémillon. It has some weight, honeyed tones on the nose and palate, and ample fruit. The red is sound, with fragrant cherry and blackberry aromas, a certain richness and density, modest tannins, and moderate length. It is certainly a pleasant wine to drink but lacks character and flair. The winemaking team seem somewhat complacent, arguing that if their clients are happy, why change? But at the same time there are indications that improvements are being made, even in such details as higher density for new plantings.

Château La Fleur Jonquet

Portets. Tel: 0556 170818. **Owner:** *Laurence Lataste. 7 ha. 6 ha red: 80% Merlot, 15% Cabernet Sauvignon,*
5% Cabernet Franc. 1 ha white: 50% Sémillon, 50% Sauvignon Blanc. **Production:** *35,000 bottles.*
Second wine: *"J" de Jonquet*

This small property possesses some very old vines. The white grapes are always picked by hand, the reds usually by machine. The white is aged in one-third new barriques for up to ten months; the red up to twelve months in twenty-five per cent new oak. The only wine I have tasted is the fragrant, spicy 2002 red.

Clos Floridène

Pujols. Tel: 0556 170818. Website: www.denisdubourdieu.com. Owners: Denis and Florence Dubourdieu.
30 ha. 17 ha red: 80% Cabernet Sauvignon, 20% Merlot. 13 ha white: 50% Sémillon, 40% Sauvignon Blanc,
10% Muscadelle. Production: 160,000 bottles. Second wine: Ch Montalivet

For many years, Professor Denis Dubourdieu has been Bordeaux's leading authority on white wine vinification, as well as on wine aroma. He puts his ideas and skills into practice at the various properties belonging to his family, including the Barsac estate of Doisy-Daëne and his wife's property at Château Reynon (*qq.v.*), where this wine is vinified.

Floridène, which has vineyards in Illats and Pujols, is named after his wife and himself in a charming viticultural pact. It was established from 1982 onwards. The soil is akin to that at neighbouring Barsac: clay and sand over a band of limestone. The Sémillon vines are considerably older than the Sauvignon, which was first planted in 1982. Only the Sémillon component sees new oak (about thirty per cent), while the Sauvignon is aged in older barrels. Pujols is late-ripening, and the wines tend to have a lot of aroma and a mineral structure that allows them to age well.

The white wine has been excellent from the outset, but has gained in complexity since the late 1990s, with enticing scents of dried apricots and pears. The palate is intense and spicy, sometimes sumptuous; this is a wine with extract and some power and benefits from bottle-age. The red, with its strong Cabernet aroma and flavours, is less remarkable than the white. Nonetheless, the graceful 2002 slips down the throat with silky ease, while the 2004 has more substance.

Château de Gaillat

Langon. Tel: 0556 635077. Owner: Hélène Bertrand-Coste. 7.5 ha. 70% Cabernet Sauvignon, 20% Merlot,
10% Malbec. Production: 80,000 bottles. Second wine: Ch de Carrelasse

The wine merchant Pierre Coste is one of the personalities of the Graves, and his droll daughter Hélène, who owns this very odd estate, is in the same mould. The property used to be known as Domaine de Gaillat, but she had to change the name after her Canadian clients were under the misapprehension that a "domaine" wine was not château-bottled. The vineyards are entirely surrounded by Langon's suburbs, which allows Mme. Bertrand-Coste to refer to her estate as "the Haut-Brion of Langon". It produced white wine until 1968, when the whole property was replanted with red grapes only. Her father had rather eccentrically laid out the vineyard in wide rows with high-trained vines. It turns out, she tells me, that you can make excellent wines from such vines, as long as you keep yields very low at around thirty-five hl/ha. That, however, proved uneconomic, so in 1996 she planted additional rows between the existing ones. Now the yield is a more commercially acceptable fifty hl/ha.

The soil is clay and limestone. She plants green cover and ploughs between the rows, practising *lutte raisonnée*. About one-third of the wine is oak-aged to give it some gentle oxidation. She believes her wine needs about five years to open up after bottling.

Since 1996, she has also owned a small 1.5-hectare property at St Pierre-de-Mons with the impossible name of Courrèges Seguès de Château Gaillat. Here there is more gravel, and the same high proportion of Cabernet Sauvignon, at around seventy per cent. Half the wine is barrique-aged. It sells for higher prices than Gaillat.

I recall some pleasant vintages of Gaillat from the 1990s: medium-bodied but juicy and lively. But from 1999 onwards they have become rather strange, with gamey, mentholly aromas and bitter flavours that Mme. Bertrand-Coste believes are related to the soil. But since they are apparent in the wines of both properties, I suspect they are related to something unwholesome in the cellars.

Château du Grand Bos

Castres. Tel: 0556 673920. Owner: André Vincent. 13 ha. 12 ha red: 45% Merlot, 45% Cabernet Sauvignon,
8% Petit Verdot, 1% Malbec, 1% Cabernet Franc. 1 ha white: 63% Sémillon, 35% Sauvignon Blanc, 2% Muscadelle.
Production: 75,000 bottles. Second wine: Ch Plégat-La-Gravière

André Vincent used to be the proprietor of Château La Haye in St-Estèphe, and has owned this estate since 1989. Most of the vineyard had to be replanted by Vincent. The château is a fine chartreuse dating from 1771, lording it over a courtyard flanked by *chais*. The vineyards have deep, pebbly soil over a band of limestone, and are picked manually. The white is aged in fifty to 100 per cent new barriques on the fine lees with stirring. The red is aged in forty per cent new barriques.

The production of white is minuscule and I have never tasted it. The red is delicious, with smoky, black-cherry aromas, and a supple but concentrated palate, with spiciness and plenty of grip. The 2000 is exceptional, the 2001 and 2002 close behind.

Grand Enclos du Château de Cérons

Cérons. Tel: 0556 270153. Owner: Giorgio Cavanna. 26 ha. 16 ha red: 50% Merlot, 50% Cabernet Sauvignon.
10 ha white: 70% Sémillon, 21% Sauvignon Blanc, 9% Sauvignon Gris. Production: 100,000 bottles.
Second wine: Ch Lamouroux

Long ago this fine property formed part of the ancient domaine of the Marquis de Calvimont, who owned the château at Cérons. When the N113 road was built in the mid-nineteenth century, the two parts of the property were separated. Thereafter Calvimont sold the property in three lots, and in 1875 the Lataste family bought this portion. Under Olivier Lataste, who inherited the property in 1985, some good wines were made, sweet as well as dry. But in 2000 he sold the estate to Giorgio Cavanna, co-owner of the famous Chianti property of Castello di Ama. Patrick Léon, the former winemaker at Mouton, had been a consultant at Ama, and his son Bertrand knew that Cavanna was looking for a Bordeaux estate, and also knew that the Grand Enclos was on the market. Cavanna bought it and installed Bertrand Léon as manager. At the same time he bought Château Mondorion in St-Emilion. Cavanna didn't stint on new investments: a new *cuvier* was built and equipped with conical steel tanks, while in the vineyard the trellising was raised and missing vines replaced. The soil is ploughed and vines cultivated according to *lutte raisonnée*. Green-harvesting is used to reduce yields.

Behind the château is the *enclos*, a ten-hectare walled vineyard; the remaining vines are on the plateau of Podensac in three main parcels. The grapes are picked in *cagettes*, with sorting in the vineyard and the winery. There is no skin contact for the white, sixty per cent of which is barrique-fermented with stirring, then aged in forty per cent new oak for up to twelve months. The remaining forty per cent is fermented in tanks and aged there on the lees. Then the two batches are blended.

The red is vinified with natural yeasts, then aged for twelve to fourteen months in around fifty per cent new oak. For the second wine, no new oak is used. There is also a production of Cérons made entirely from Sémillon.

Under Lataste the white was a rich, spicy wine, with melony aromas and flavours and sufficient acidity to keep it balanced. Under Cavanna, the wine has retained its spicy, piquant aromas, but the palate has put on weight. For my taste the wine is now too lush and lacks some finesse, but many consumers will certainly enjoy this style. The 2004 is the best of recent vintages. The red is quite aromatic, with red fruits on the 2001, blackcurrants on the 2002. The palate is a touch simple, even bland, with moderate length. There is room for improvement here, and perhaps this terroir is better suited to white than red wines.

Château des Gravières

*Portets. Tel: 0556 671570. **Owners:** Thierry and Denis Labuzan. 45 ha. 43 ha red: 80% Merlot,*
20% Cabernet Sauvignon. 2 ha white: 80% Sémillon, 15% Sauvignon Blanc, 5% Muscadelle.
***Production:** 310,000 bottles. **Second wine:** Ch Lamouroux*

The brothers took over running this substantial family property in 1991. Denis looks after the vineyards; Thierry makes the wine. At present there is no white wine production, as the vines were entirely replanted after the 2003 vintage, so the next vintage will be in 2007.

Not all the vineyards are at Portets, though that is where the oldest vines are located; there are also some large parcels in Arbanats and elsewhere. The grapes are picked by machine. The red is given a brief cold soak, then fermented with some micro-oxygenation. The wine is aged in oak for about twelve months, and about twenty-five per cent is aged in American oak, but for a shorter period, around six months. From 2001 onwards, the proportion of new oak was increased from twenty-five to thirty-three per cent.

The labelling is slightly confusing. The principal wine is called Prestige; the regular Gravières is essentially the second wine. There was no Prestige in 2002 because of hail damage. There is also a Bordeaux Supérieur made from vines planted on the *palus* near the river.

The only white I have tasted is the atypical 2003. The red Prestige is a fresh wine with light acidity and tannin, and a good base of fruit. I find a significant jump in quality from the straightforward 2000 to the more concentrated, spicy 2001. The 2003s, regular and Prestige, are perfectly drinkable but exhibit the defects of the vintage. The Labuzans are ambitious professionals, and the wine seems likely to continue to improve.

Château Haut-Selve

*St Selve. Tel: 0557 940920. **Website:** www.vignobles-lesgourgues.com. **Owner:** Laubade et Domaines Associés.*
42 ha. 31 ha red: 50% Merlot, 50% Cabernet Sauvignon. 11 ha white: 50% Sémillon, 35% Sauvignon Blanc,
*15% Sauvignon Gris. **Production:** 320,000 bottles*

The LEDA company is based in Armagnac, but is also the owner of Château Le Bonnat (*q.v.*) in the Graves, Château Cadillac in Fronsac, and Château Peyros in Madiran. In 1992 it uprooted sixty hectares of vines in Fronsac, which gave it plantation rights which it decided to use in the Graves. The following year it found this property, which had been well known in the eighteenth century but abandoned in the early twentieth century; they cleared it of pinewoods and replanted it entirely. There are two major parcels, both on fine gravel soils: twenty-seven hectares near the winery, and fifteen in Castres. The vines are young, of course, but the vineyards are well drained, and they are cultivated according to the principles of *lutte raisonnée*.

The well-equipped winery, designed by Sylvain Dubuisson, is an impressive pink granite slab, adorned, somewhat incongruously, by large nude bronzes. The grapes are hand-picked. Almost all the white is given skin contact, then aged for ten months in thirty per cent new barriques with lees-stirring. A small proportion is retained in tanks to give the blend more freshness. The red is given a classic vinification with selected yeasts, then aged for around twelve months in twenty per cent new oak.

The LEDA wine estates are run by Arnaud Lesgourgues, and the wines are made by Patrick Soyé. They have plans to expand the range here in 2006, by producing an unoaked white and a Merlot-dominated red, using micro-oxygenation and some American oak. These will clearly be modern-style, fruit-driven wines for early consumption.

The Haut-Selve white is lightly oaky, with some freshness and delicacy, a light grassiness, and ample fruit. It is correct rather than exciting, and the best vintage I have encountered is the 2002. In 2004 the property also produced a pure Sauvignon Blanc, but both bottles I tasted were defective. The red has plummy aromas and a light liquorice tone; these are straightforward, rounded wines, sturdy but lacking in verve. The 2003 is rich and suave but has a dour finish.

Château de L'Hospital

*Portets. Tel: 0556 731780. Website: www.lafragette.com. **Owner:** Lafragette family. 20 ha. 17 ha red: 85% Merlot,*
15% Cabernet Sauvignon. 3 ha white: 80% Sémillon, 20% Sauvignon Blanc and Sauvignon Gris.
***Production:** 90,000 bottles. **Second wine:** Ch Thibault-Ducasse*

This estate had a Swiss owner, Marcel Disch, until it was bought by Jean-Paul Lafragette in 1998. He is also the owner of Châteaux Loudenne and de Rouillac (*qq.v.*), and his daughter Florence manages all three properties. Half the vineyards are on the plateau of Portets; the remainder are in a ten-hectare *clos* near the château on a well-drained, stony slope. The château is on the other side of the Bordeaux road, and was commissioned in 1787 from the famous architect Victor Louis by the then-owner, Michel de l'Hospital. It is still inhabited by the elderly widow of a previous owner, and awaits restoration.

Given that much of the soil is deep gravel, it is puzzling to note the proportion of Merlot, but Florence Lafragette is convinced that the soil is better suited to Merlot than Cabernet. The grapes are hand-picked in *cagettes*. The white goes through skin contact for a day, and is then fermented in fifty per cent new barriques, and aged for eight months. The red is given a classic vinification, then aged for twelve to fourteen months in one-third new oak.

The winery is a hotbed of experimentation, trying out different sizes of barrels and ageing some wines on double lees. Nonetheless Florence Lafragette says the aim here is to make wines that will give pleasure rather than to produce very structured *vins de garde*.

The 2001 white was quite rich and honeyed, with considerable freshness to balance the weight; the 2003 is succulent but soft-centred while the fresh 2004 was more exotic in its aromas and was delicately oaky. The red is consistently good, but not that concentrated. Instead it offers cherry aromas and a pronounced whiff of new oak; it is medium-bodied and fresh, with spice and tannin, and a light structure.

Château de Landiras

*Landiras. Tel: 0556 624075. Website: www.chateau-landiras.com. **Owners:** Canadian and Swiss investors.*
19 ha. 14.5 ha red: 50% Merlot, 50% Cabernet Sauvignon. 4.5 ha white: 75% Sémillon, 25% Sauvignon Gris.
***Production:** 80,000 bottles. **Second wine:** Dom La Grave*

Landiras is right on the edge of the Landes, and the few vineyards in the commune are surrounded by pinewoods. It's a picturesque spot, with the vestiges of a ruined fourteenth-century castle as well as the rather four-square château. After the Danish winemaker Peter Vinding-Diers left Rahoul (*q.v.*), he bought this property in 1988. At that time there was just one hectare of vines, the historic vineyards having been destroyed by the 1956 frost. He replanted more and by 1995 there were fourteen hectares under vine. Vinding-Diers was a specialist in white wines, and after the market for white Bordeaux slumped in the mid-1990s, he lost control of the property and moved elsewhere. Frequent bouts of frost didn't help either. In 2002 it was acquired by Hélène Lévêque of Château de Chantegrive (*q.v.*), who fronted an international group of investors. For her, the appeal of Landiras was its terroir of fine white gravel and the high-density plantings. The new owners grafted over eight hectares of white grapes to red. By 2005, however, she was no longer involved, and in 2007 the property was sold once again.

Returning to Landiras is a melancholy experience. When Peter and Suzie Vinding-Diers and their sons were living here, life at Landiras was a perpetual party. Today the château stands empty. Worse, it seems that all the decisions made by Vinding-Diers in the interests of high quality, and justly appreciated by Hélène Lévêque, are precisely the features that the new management found most troubling. Pasquier planned new plantings at a lower density that would have allowed him to experiment with machine-harvesting. This ill-considered scheme soon floundered, and in March 2007 the property was again sold, to a local hotel owner.

With so many changes of management and philosophy in recent years, it makes little sense to comment on the style of the wines, which are unlikely to resemble those made by Vinding-Diers. The wines I have tasted from the 2000s have been dull, with the exception of a spicy, well-balanced 2001 white. It will be a few years before the consequences of the changes now taking place will be evident in the glass.

Château Léhoul

Langon. Tel: 0556 631774. **Owner:** *Eric Fonta. 9.5 ha. 6.5 ha red: 50% Merlot, 48% Cabernet Sauvignon,*
2% Cabernet Franc and Malbec. 3 ha white: 50% Sémillon, 50% Sauvignon Blanc. **Production:** *50,000 bottles.*

Second wine: Le Cadet de Léhoul

The dishevelled, assertive Eric Fonta makes a range of wines from his property just outside Langon. No chemical fertilizers are used, the vines are green-harvested, and they are picked by hand. The Sauvignon Blanc is used mostly for the dry white, the Sémillon for the Graves Supérieures. Of the dry whites, one is unoaked, the other aged for seven months in new barriques. There are also two red wines. Léhoul is aged for twelve months in older barrels. Plénitude is a parcel selection cropped at thirty-five hl/ha, and fermented with micro-oxygenation. After malolactic fermentation in new oak, the wine stays in oak for up to eighteen months, and is bottled without fining or filtration. And there are usually two Graves Supérieures. Le Cadet is made from grapes picked at a potential alcohol of up to sixteen degrees; Léhoul is made from much riper grapes to give about eighty grams of residual sugar, and this wine is aged in barriques.

The 2004 dry whites, oaked and unoaked, have grassy aromas but taste a touch overripe, though they are indeed vinified dry. The 2006 unoaked white is fresher. The regular red has freshness and charm, and a delightful nose of crushed red fruits and summer pudding. Plénitude pulls out all the stops, with evident blackcurrant, cherry pie, and new oak aromas. On the palate the wine is rich and concentrated, distinctly tannic but not harsh, and has quite good length.

Château Magneau

La Brède. Tel: 0556 202057. Website: www.chateau-magneau.com. **Owner:** *Henri Ardurats. 41 ha.*
16 ha red: 50% Merlot, 45% Cabernet Sauvignon, 5% Cabernet Franc. 25 ha white: 45% Sauvignon Blanc,
45% Semillon, 10% Muscadelle. **Production:** *220,000 bottles.* **Second wine:** *Ch Guirauton*

This is very much a family enterprise, and Henri Ardurats is assisted by his two sons. The Ardurats family have been here since the eighteenth century. It's a large property, with three large parcels in La Brède and a seven-hectare block at St Morillon. The soil varies but is mostly pebbles and gravel, with some clay-limestone. Some of the red grapes are picked by machine, but all the whites are picked by hand.

There are two whites. The basic one is unoaked, but the Cuvée Julien, first made in 1988, is produced from sixty per cent Sémillon, and aged for nine months in sixty per cent new medium-toast barriques. The lees are stirred and the wine is bottled without filtration.

For the red wine, a small proportion of stems is retained, and the must is fermented at high temperatures, before being aged for twelve months in thirty per cent new oak.

The basic white is inexpensive but very attractive, with aromas of white peach. It's not a wine of great complexity, but it has abundant fruit and good acidity. The Cuvée Julien is, of course, quite different, with toasty oak and apple-compote aromas. The 2001 and 2006 are lean and oaky, the 2002 and 2004 more opulent, with apricot flavours and a touch of white pepper.

Although Magneau is best known for its white wines, the red is equally good, with aromas of black cherries and tobacco, sometimes with smoky, minty tones too. The texture is supple, there is ample fruit and spiciness, and balance and freshness rather than complexity. But it is typical Graves, with no trace of heaviness or over-extraction. Curiously, no red wine was released in 2001. The Ardurats considered they already had too much stock, so they sold it all in bulk.

Château de Malle

See *Chapter Thirty*

Château Pessan

Portets. Tel: 0556 623686. Website: www.chateau-de-malle.fr. Owners: Comtes de Bournazel. 9 ha. 50% Merlot,
50% Cabernet Sauvignon. Production: 6,000 bottles

This property was bought in 1999 by the Bournazel brothers of Château de Malle in Sauternes. The vineyard, of fine gravel over clay and limestone, is close to the centre of the village. The harvest is manual, and the wine is aged in one-year-old barriques. The first vintage, 2002, was somewhat sharp and herbaceous.

Château de Portets

Portets. Tel: 0556 671230. Website: www.chateau-de-portets.com. Owner: Jean-Pierre Théron. 25 ha.
22 ha red: 55% Merlot, 45% Cabernet Sauvignon. 3 ha white: 60% Sémillon, 30% Sauvignon Blanc, 10% Muscadelle.
Production: 150,000 bottles. Second wine: Les Quinze Barons du Ch de Portets

This fine property stands on a terrace overlooking the Garonne on the site of a former Roman villa. In 1587 it was bought by Guillaume de Gasq, Baron de Portets. In the splendid courtyard a plaque commemorates Napoleon's rest-stop here en route to Bordeaux from Spain in 1808. The château was badly treated during the German occupation during World War II, but was bought and restored by the father of Jean-Pierre Théron, who had returned from North Africa to France in 1956. Jean-Pierre Théron is now handing over the management of the estate to his daughter Marie-Hélène Yung-Théron, who makes the wines, and his son Jean-Pierre, who looks after the commercial side. Since 1998 the well-known Médoc winemaker, Georges Pauli, has been working as their consultant.

Since the vineyards are on gravel soils fairly close to the river, they are usually free of frost. (The estate also includes seventeen hectares of Bordeaux Supérieur vineyards on alluvial soils even closer to the Garonne.) The average age of the vines is thirty years for the red, thirty-five for the white. Green-harvesting is the exception rather than the rule. Most of the grapes are picked by machine, though the oldest vines are harvested by hand.

The white wine is given some skin contact before being fermented in new oak and aged for nine months with lees-stirring. Nonetheless the Thérons say they are not aiming for overt oakiness. Since 2004 the reds have been cold-soaked, then fermented in cement tanks for up to thirty days. The wine is aged in one-third new barriques for twelve months. However, about one-fifth of the red wine remains in tanks for the *élevage*.

The Thérons are very proud of their wine, and believe their estate should be seen as one of the flagship properties of the Graves. Yet the wines, which I have been tasting over a period of fifteen years, do not match the splendour and antiquity of the site. The white is often both overoaked and green, although the 2002 is riper and more vigorous than most. The 2003 is very ripe but a touch flat. The reds have a cherry and tobacco nose that has Graves typicity, but on the palate they lack ripeness and flesh and can have assertive tannins.

Château Rahoul

Portets. Tel: 0557 977333. Website: www.thienot.com. Owner: Alain Thiénot. 40.5 ha. 37.5 ha red: 70% Merlot,
30% Cabernet Sauvignon. 3 ha white: 90% Sémillon, 10% Sauvignon Blanc and Sauvignon Gris.
Production: 130,000 bottles. Second wine: Ch La Garance

This estate is named after the Chevalier Guillaume de Rahoul, who was the owner in the mid-seventeenth century. It remained in his family until the Revolution, when the guillotine intervened. There were numerous owners thereafter, until in 1971 a Briton called David Robson bought the estate and replanted some vines. A group including Australian wine entrepreneur Len Evans bought him out, and they took on Peter Vinding-Diers, a Danish expert on yeasts, as their winemaker. In 1983 Rahoul was sold to another Dane, Lothar Dahl. Vinding-Diers shocked the locals by barrel-fermenting white wine, and he also insisted on using pure Sémillon. Three years later the Champagne producer Alain Thiénot bought Rahoul. He and Vinding-Diers did not see eye-to-eye, and it was not long before the latter packed his bags and moved to Château de Landiras (*q.v.*). Thiénot remains the owner, and Laurent Fedou is the long-term winemaker.

The historic Rahoul vineyards, about twenty hectares, surround the charming neo-classical château and border the main road from Bordeaux to Langon. There are also parcels in other communes, including some vines in Cérons that used to be white but were grafted over to Merlot. The wines bottled as Rahoul tend to come from the Portets vineyards. Although Thiénot told me in the 1980s that he planned to increase the production of white, the opposite has happened, and for perfectly sound commercial reasons.

The vines are all picked by hand, and from 2002 stricter sorting was introduced at the winery, a spotlessly clean, modern structure. For the white wine, only the Sauvignon Blanc undergoes skin contact. The wine is barrel-fermented, then aged for eight months in fifty per cent new barriques.

The red wine is made in an overtly fruity style, reflecting the high proportion of Merlot. It is fermented in stainless-steel tanks with selected yeasts, then aged for eighteen months in one-third new barriques.

The whites made by Vinding-Diers were very Sémillon in their texture and creaminess, but they rarely lacked acidity and vigour. The wines from the 2000s are more citric, soundly made but lacking in excitement, although both 2004 and 2005 are more precise, elegant, and complex than their predecessors. The reds are robust and plummy but I have detected off-aromas and flavours in the 2001 and 2002. The 2001 is weightier and better balanced than the 2002.

Château de Respide

*Roaillan. Tel: 0556 632424. Website: www.chateau-de-respide.com. **Owner:** Franck Bonnet. 37 ha.*
25 ha red: 60% Merlot, 37% Cabernet Sauvignon, 3% Petit Verdot. 12 ha white: 50% Sémillon, 50% Sauvignon Blanc.
***Production:** 230,000 bottles. **Second wine:** Ch La Carrade*

This vast nineteenth-century edifice outside Langon is easily recognizable, as its chimney stacks all have the ironwork letter "R" stapled to them. When the family could no longer afford to maintain the château, it was sold and converted into flats, while the family retain the vineyards. These are divided in two by the autoroute. They are machine-harvested, although the vines are carefully prepared beforehand to ensure the grapes are healthy and as even as possible in their maturation.

After some skin contact, the white grapes are partly fermented in tanks, partly in new 300-litre barrels. The Cuvée Callipyge is aged for eight months in oak, with lees-stirring. The red wine goes through a classic vinification in stainless-steel tanks, and is then aged in older barrels. The red Cuvée Callipyge, which is a parcel selection, is aged in fifty per cent new oak, including some American barrels.

The 2002 white is piquant and grapefruity and has reasonable concentration and length. The 2004 has more of a stone-fruits character and some intensity on the palate; the 2004 Callipyge is broader, juicier, but less elegant. The regular red is medium-bodied and quite lively; the 2000 in particular was extremely bright and fresh. Bonnet says that he likes red wines that are fleshy and rounded, but I find Cuvée Callipyge rather tannic and overoaked. Of recent vintages I like the dense, chocolatey 2001 and the sleek, concentrated 2005 best. The wines are very reasonably priced.

Château Respide-Médeville

*Toulenne. Tel: 0556 762844. Website: www.respide-medeville.com. **Owner:** Christian Médeville. 15 ha.*
11 ha red: 50% Merlot, 50% Cabernet Sauvignon. 4 ha white: 60% Sémillon, 37% Sauvignon Blanc, 3% Muscadelle.
***Production:** 70,000 bottles. **Second wine:** La Dame de Respide*

These vineyards are quite high up on a gravelly-clay slope just north of Langon in the suburb of Toulenne. The property was rented by Christian Médeville until 1980, when he bought it. He replanted large sections, though some old white vines have survived. Yields are low, and the harvest is manual.

The white wine is partly vinified and aged in tanks; the Sémillon is mostly fermented and aged for twelve months in twenty per cent new barriques with lees-stirring. Then the two components are blended. The red is aged for twelve months in up to fifty per cent new oak.

In the 1980s the white wine was quite angular and acidic. In the 2000s the wine is riper but lacks personality and flair, with the exception of the bright, racy 2004. The red is better, with aromas of blackcurrants and plums; it's plump and supple, with light tannin and acidity, and moderate length. The 1996 had become leafy by 2005, but had retained some vigour and solid fruit, showing that the wine, though accessible young, does keep.

Château Roquetaillade-La-Grange

Mazères. Tel: 0556 761423. Owner: Guignard family. 75 ha. 48 ha red: 50% Cabernet Sauvignon, 37% Merlot, 10% Cabernet Franc, 3% Malbec. 27 ha white: 50% Sémillon, 40% Sauvignon Blanc, 10% Muscadelle.
Production: 300,000 bottles. Second wine: Ch de Carolle

The extended Guignard family own a number of properties in the Graves and Sauternais. Pierre Guignard acquired this large estate in 1962, and today it is run by his sons Dominique and Bruno, the latter being the winemaker. The vineyards used to belong to the fine fourteenth-century fortress next door, but were sold off to Guignard. They are in three large parcels of more or less equal size not far from the château. Mazères is one of the highest parts of the Graves, and at some points the vines grow at over 100 metres (328 feet). In recent years the vineyards have been restructured to make sure the right variety is adapted to the right soil. Thus the best gravel *croupes* are now being replanted with Cabernet Sauvignon. Picking is by machine.

The white is protected by dry ice during and after the harvest. This allows Guignard to use less sulphur dioxide during the skin-contact period. Selected yeasts are added, and part of the wine is vinified in tanks, and part in oak for six months. The red is cold-soaked under dry ice for up to five days. It is fermented with natural yeasts if at all possible, and the *marc* is pressed in vertical presses. It is then aged in oak for fourteen months, with a proportion of American barrels, and very little new oak.

The white is quite aromatic, fresh, grassy, sometimes floral. It's a clean, simple wine to be drunk young. The red has always had aromas very typical of the Graves: plums, tobacco, woodsmoke, and liquorice. On the palate it doesn't lack fruit, but it is rather chunky, lacks finesse, and sometimes has a rather hard finish.

Château St-Robert

Pujols. Tel: 0556 632766. Website: www.saint-robert.com Owner: Crédit Foncier. 40 ha. 33 ha red: 49% Merlot, 33% Cabernet Franc, 18% Cabernet Sauvignon. 7 ha white: 50% Sauvignon Blanc, 50% Sémillon.
Production: 225,000 bottles

The large French bank Crédit Foncier owns a number of properties in the Graves and Pomerol. This fine property, which was first planted in the seventeenth century, is perhaps less well known than Bastor-Lamontagne or Beauregard (*qq.v.*), which belong to the same bank. It is located just on the other side of the autoroute from Climens. The soil is siliceous gravel on a limestone subsoil, with some sandy areas as well; it's a cold terroir and susceptible to frost. Indeed, there were damaging frosts in 1985 and 1986 that made a good deal of replanting necessary. The vines are picked by hand.

There is a simple unoaked white, from sixty per cent Sémillon aged on the fine lees. More complex is the Cuvée Poncet-Deville, first produced in 1990, which is made from sixty per cent Sauvignon Blanc. It is essentially a parcel selection, since winemaker Philippe Aubertin and director Michel Garat know which blocks will give the most structured white wines. The grapes are picked over a ten-day period, given skin contact, and aged in twenty-five per cent new barriques for ten months. The wine has proved a commercial success and is now made in greater volumes than the unoaked wine.

There is also a red Cuvée Poncet-Deville, aged for sixteen months in twenty-five per cent new oak, and a pretty, strawberry-scented rosé.

The unoaked white is a simple, citric wine that's lively, fresh, and intended to be drunk young. The oaked *cuvée* is considerably more complex, with aromas of white peach and apples, sometimes of pineapple. It's a wine with good attack, medium body, considerable stylishness, and quite good length. It can be drunk young, but will age easily for five years.

The basic red is pleasantly herbaceous and best drunk young. The Cuvée Poncet-Deville is very different, with its rich, oaky, minty aromas; it's a medium-bodied wine, not too extracted, with supple tannins and moderate acidity. It does age, but the 1996 from magnum was fully ready in 2005. The 2000 had developed a slight savoury tone by 2006, and was both lush and lively.

Château du Seuil

*Cérons. Tel: 0556 271156. Website: www.chateauduseuil.com. **Owners:** Robert and Susan Watts. 15 ha.*
10 ha red: 60% Cabernet Sauvignon, 40% Merlot. 5 ha white: 60% Sémillon, 40% Sauvignon Blanc.
***Production:** 80,000 bottles*

In 1988 this property with its pretty eighteenth-century château was bought by Robert and Susan Watts from Wales. At that time there were only three hectares of vines, so the estate has been steadily expanded as parcels of vines come on the market. In 2001 the next generation arrived: the Watts's daughter Nicola and her husband Sean Allison, a self-taught winemaker from New Zealand. They brought with them the curiosity and enthusiasm of outsiders, and a willingness to experiment.

The vineyards are green-harvested to keep yields at around forty-five hl/ha, and grapes are picked by hand and sorted at the winery. Numerous lots are vinified separately, using a blend of natural and selected yeasts. The Sauvignon Blanc is aged in tanks on the fine lees, while the Sémillon is aged for eight months in about seventy per cent new oak. The barrels are rotated so that the lees can be stirred without aerating the wine. The white is ripe and melony, sometimes with leesy aromas, and has an oaky finish. A richer, plump Cuvée Héritage was made in 2004, but it's a rather sombre wine that lacks a little lift.

The red must is given a five-day cold soak, and part of the crop is fermented in 400-litre barrels; rather than pump over such small volumes, Allison rolls the barrels to aid extraction. The regular red wine is aged in thirty per cent new oak, but the top bottling, Héritage, is given the full *garagiste* treatment. All wine destined for Héritage is barrel-fermented, and undergoes malolactic fermentation in new barriques, with *bâtonnage*. Then the wine is aged for a further eighteen months in another set of new barrels.

The regular red is very fragrant, with aromas of blackcurrants and blackberries, and with age it develops a meaty, leathery nose typical of the Graves. The Héritage is impressive in its way, if you have a taste for oakiness, power, and tannin. It's very concentrated but it doesn't taste like Graves. The price is high and the production limited.

The property owns ten hectares outside the AC Graves. Seuil also produces some Cérons from Sémillon, and the Allisons run a second property nearby, Château L'Avocat (*q.v.*).

Château Toumilon

*St Pierre-de-Mons. Tel: 0556 630724. Website: www.chateau-toumilon.com. **Owner:** Mme. Jean Sévenet. 16 ha.*
11 ha red: 50% Cabernet Sauvignon, 35% Merlot, 15% Cabernet Franc. 5 ha white: 50% Sémillon,
*50% Sauvignon Blanc. **Production:** 110,000 bottles. **Second wine:** Ch Cabanes*

This property has been owned by the Sévenet family since the eighteenth century. The soil is peppered with the large stones called *galets*, and has good drainage. The grapes are picked by hand. The white wine is unoaked, and the red aged mostly in tanks and in some barriques. The white is fragrant and has some charm; there's not much concentration but it's a very drinkable style. The 2005 has more richness and weight. The 2002 red is rather herbaceous.

Château Tourteau–Chollet

*Arbanats. Tel: 0556 674778. **Owner:** Maxime Bontoux. 54 ha. 49 ha red: 52% Cabernet Sauvignon, 45% Merlot,*
*3% Petit Verdot. 5 ha white: 100% Sauvignon Blanc. **Production:** 350,000 bottles. **Second wine:** Ch Chollet*

A royal notary, Etienne Tourteau, founded this property in the eighteenth century. In 1973 it was bought by the Mestrezat company, and sold in 2001 to a former accountant, Maxime Bontoux. He had prepared himself for his new career by working as a cellar rat at Château Malescasse in the Médoc. Mestrezat had not been that focused on quality at this property, and Bontoux was determined to raise standards. He hired Georges Pauli, the former director of the Cordier estates, as a consultant.

The vineyards lie inland on a single block of sandy gravel. Bontoux has increased the density of plantings and reduced the use of insecticides by employing *confusion sexuelle*. Most of the property is picked by machine.

Under Mestrezat the white wine was aged in tanks for four months, then bottled. Bontoux gives the white grapes up to thirty-six hours of skin contact, and ages two-thirds of the wine in tanks. The remainder is barrel-fermented in twenty per cent new oak and aged three months on the fine lees. The two lots are blended and bottled in March.

Bontoux has introduced proper temperature control for the steel fermentation vats. The reds are fermented with selected yeasts, with a *cuvaison* of about twenty-five days. Mestrezat never oaked the red, but Bontoux uses both barriques and 350-litre barrels. He does rotate lots between barrels and tanks, but the wine will spend at least six months in oak during its *élevage*. The wine bottled as Château Chollet is unoaked, and Bontoux likes to think of it as a different expression of his vineyards rather than as a second wine.

Overall, the wines are well made in a commercial style and are intended for early consumption. They are given considerable bottle-age before release so that they are drinkable immediately. The red is sound if unexciting, the white grassy, melony, and very attractive.

Château Le Tuquet

*Beautiran. Tel: 0556 202123. **Owner:** Paul Ragon. 56 ha. 45 ha red: 50% Merlot, 40% Cabernet Sauvignon,*
*10% Cabernet Franc. 11 ha white: 60% Sémillon, 40% Sauvignon Blanc. **Production:** 360,000 bottles.*
Second wines: Ch de Bellefont, Ch Rocher du Tuquet

This fine property is grouped around its early-eighteenth-century château. It belonged to a négociant for many years until bought by Paul Ragon in 1963. The gravelly vineyards are in a single block. The average age of the vines is thirty-five years, and they are picked by machine, except for some whites.

The large cellars are well maintained and equipped with steel tanks. Two white wines are produced from the same must: one unoaked, the second fermented and aged in new oak for twelve months. The red undergoes a classic vinification and is aged for twelve months in one-third new barriques.

The unoaked white wine is decent if unexciting, although the 2004, with its stone-fruits character, is much more concentrated and stylish than usual. Paul Ragon confesses he doesn't much like the oaked version, and neither do I. The red is another matter. It's a quintessential Graves, with aromas of tobacco, cloves, black fruits, and coffee. It has body and concentration, supple tannins, sound acidity, and moderate length. It has freshness and eminent drinkability. Well made and inexpensive, it is a wine that has given me great pleasure over the years. The 1990 drank beautifully for a decade, but that is usually pushing it for Tuquet. The rich 1998 was at its peak in 2005.

Vieux–Château–Gaubert

*Portets. Tel: 0556 671863. **Owner:** Dominique Haverlan. 34 ha. 28 ha red: 60% Merlot, 40% Cabernet Sauvignon.*
*6 ha white: 60% Sémillon, 40% Sauvignon Blanc. **Production:** 250,000 bottles.*
Second wine: Benjamin de Vieux-Ch-Gaubert

The estate had been owned by the Gaubert family since the eighteenth century. After the last Gaubert died here in 1987, the property was bought by Dominique Haverlan, who comes from a local wine family. The château and *chais* were in a ruinous condition, and Haverlan is still restoring them. Most of the vineyards, gradually accumulated by

Haverlan, are on the plateau of Portets, and the woods around the château have been cleared and replanted. There are also some blocks at Beautiran. Newer plantings are at a density of 8,000 vines per hectare. Those parcels and the white vines are picked by hand, the remainder by machine. The soil is warm, with very little clay; this keeps acidity fairly low, which, in Haverlan's view, suits barrique-aged white wines. (He is currently developing another property, the ten-hectare Château Pontet-Caillou near Domaine de Chevalier. Its first vintage was 2006.)

The whites are given some skin contact and fermented with selected yeasts in sixty per cent new oak, then aged for seven months with lees-stirring. The reds are cold-soaked, and the tanks are bled if greater concentration is needed. The wine is aged for twelve months in forty per cent new barriques. Haverlan gives his wines considerable bottle-age before release. Thus in 2005 the current release was 2001.

These are among the best wines of the Graves. The white has fine aromas of pears, lime, and oak, and the right balance of richness, oakiness, and a lively, often piquant, acidity. They have considerable complexity, and the 2001, 2002, and 2004 are all excellent. The red has aromas of cherries and plums, developing mushroom and tea tones with age. Black fruits dominate the palate, which is concentrated, has ripe tannins and gently earthy flavours, and enough acidity to give the wine persistence. By 2007, the supple 2000 was fully ready to drink.

Château La Vieille France

Portets. Tel: 0556 671911. Website: www.chateau-la-vieille-france.fr. Owner: Dugoua family. 25 ha.
21 ha red: 50% Merlot, 45% Cabernet Sauvignon, 5% Petit Verdot. 4 ha white: 80% Sémillon, 20% Sauvignon Blanc.
Production: 150,000 bottles. Second wine: Ch Cadet La Vieille France

This property on the plateau of Portets has been in the Dugoua family for four centuries. Brothers Bertrand and François Dugoua took over from their father Michel in 2000, having both worked at the estate since 1990. However, the financial difficulties that afflict so many estates in Bordeaux forced François to seek work elsewhere, leaving Bertrand to run the property on his own. The vineyards are scattered over many parcels, and the dominant soil is gravel over clay-limestone. Since 1998 the vines have been picked by hand.

The white wine has been barrel-fermented since 1994, and aged in fifty per cent new oak for nine months, with lees-stirring. The red must is sometimes given a cold soak, and fermented with micro-oxygenation. The wine is aged for twelve to fourteen months in one-third new barriques.

The white has melon and lanolin aromas, with plenty of ripe fruit, a touch of oak, and quite good acidity. I find the whites better than the reds. Dugoua admits that his reds are never that concentrated or powerful, but even so they lack some flesh and complexity.

He also produces a Bordeaux Supérieur called Château Galley, from ten hectares of vines closer to the Garonne.

Château Villa Bel-Air

St Morillon. Tel: 0556 202935. Website: www.villabelair.com. Owner: Jean-Michel Cazes. 44 ha.
32 ha red: 50% Merlot, 40% Merlot, 10% Cabernet Sauvignon. 12 ha white: 50% Sauvignon Blanc, 50% Sémillon.
Production: 250,000 bottles

The vineyards here occupy a gentle slope, surrounded by woodlands, just outside St Morillon. When Jean-Michel Cazes bought the estate in 1986 from the Mauriac family, there were no vines, so everything here is recently planted.

The white wine is aged in barriques, of which twenty to thirty-five per cent are new. However, in 2003 Cazes decided to preserve freshness by fermenting a third of the wine in tanks, while raising to fifty per cent the amount of new oak in the barrel-fermented portion. The red wine is aged in twenty per cent new barriques.

The white wine is quite lush in texture, but always retains some citric freshness; though not complex, it is boldly flavoured and persistent. The red is a medium-bodied wine with no pretensions to depth or grandeur. It is sleek and straightforward, stylish, sometimes charming, and extremely drinkable. The 2001 is particularly attractive, as is the white of that year, and the 2002 has abundant charm.

The Right Bank

16. Introduction

After the expansive vistas of the Médoc and Graves, the vineyards of the Right Bank of Bordeaux are a return to a more domestic scale of cultivation. On the Left Bank estates of anything from twenty to eighty hectares are common; on the Right Bank they are very much the exception. Across the Gironde and, even further to the east, across the Dordogne, polyculture survived well into the twentieth century. Farmers grew grapes as part of a broader agricultural operation that would have included cereals and cattle. This tradition still continues in some of the more tangential areas of Bordeaux, such as the Côtes, where woods and pastures dominate the landscape, framing scattered vineyards.

The Left Bank has been the natural home of Cabernet Sauvignon, and still is, even if Merlot is now making ever-greater inroads. On the Right Bank, Merlot has always been at home, very much dominating St-Emilion and Pomerol and their satellites. Malbec too, rather despised in the Médoc, has its outposts and defenders in St-Emilion and the Côtes, though it is far from significant. Proprietors, even super-rich new proprietors, often like to explain that they have chosen to buy estates on the Right Bank rather than the Left because they are *plus familiale*, more family-oriented. And it's true that the new proprietors of the Right Bank tend to be tycoons seeking a change of life, rather than corporations looking for a prestigious long-term investment. Few newcomers fancy a squire's life in the austere Médoc, but many a new owner has been drawn to the bucolic charms of Entre-Deux-Mers or St-Emilion.

Unlike the Médoc, the Right Bank has been hospitable to would-be winemakers of slender means. No one without a considerable fortune can contemplate buying good vineyards in the Médoc or Graves, but a few hectares in the Premières Côtes or the St-Emilion satellites are, or have been, within financial reach. Many of the so-called *garagiste* operations started up because the only way to vinify the production of a hectare or so of vines was to return to artisanal procedures.

The proliferation of small estates in the Right Bank – there are quite a few St-Emilions and Pomerols that consist of no more than a single hectare – also poses commercial problems. The hedonistic wines from these areas are in demand, but the consumer is spoilt for choice. The top growths fetch high prices, but there are countless wines for which demand is slight. This is now beginning to include many *garagiste* wines, many of which are too recent to have acquired any reputation at all. A vintage such as 2005 should be a golden opportunity for less established wines. In a year when the potential for fine wine was uniform across the region, less prestigious areas such as Fronsac, the St-Emilion satellites, and the various Côtes offer terrific value, but it is yet to be seen whether the canny consumer will make the most of it.

The situation is even less rosy in vast areas such as Blaye and Entre-Deux-Mers. Constrained by low prices, many growers have been reluctant or unable to make the investments that would significantly improve their wines. Certain rich proprietors, such as the Vatelots at Reignac, and some dedicated, motivated, and skilful growers such as the Courselles at Thieuley, have certainly demonstrated the potential for fine wine in the Entre-Deux-Mers. But much of the wine from here, and from the various Côtes, is of indifferent quality, not necessarily bad, but simply without distinction and personality. Whether there is a future for such wine is far from evident. It is here that the crisis of Bordeaux production strikes hardest. Vineyard expansion in the 1980s and 1990s led to the planting of vines in areas better suited to other types of agriculture. It seems inevitable that many of these vineyards, producing wines for which there is no market – or no profitable market – will eventually disappear.

At the same time that the marginal areas are struggling to survive, there has been a stunning improvement in quality throughout the Right Bank, an improvement more marked than that in prestigious regions such as the Graves. St-Emilion has surely never made better wine than it does today. Perhaps this is because the revision of the classification every ten years encourages producers to strive to do better, or perhaps the considerable investment by passionate amateurs is bearing fruit. The best properties of the Côtes de Castillon, Fronsac, and Côtes de Bourg are also making wines of excellent quality, offered, moreover, at very attractive prices.

Some attribute the rise in quality to the influence of the *garagistes*. It seems probable that the term *garagiste* came into being as a reference to the fact that the early vintages of Jean-Luc Thunevin's Valandraud were vinified in his garage in St-Emilion. The movement, if one can call it that, was a phenomenon of the 1990s and seems to have abated. The early *garagistes* were revolutionary in seeking to overturn one of Bordeaux's most cherished beliefs, since they argued that it was possible to make excellent wine from essentially undistinguished terroir. But this was only possible if certain measures were taken, such as reducing yields to scarcely economic levels. Thus a fine estate would normally aim for yields of around forty or forty-five hectolitres per hectare. The *garagiste* would aim for fifteen to twenty hl/ha. The juice could be concentrated further by bleeding or passing it through a concentrator, though few *garagistes* could afford such expensive technology. It should also be recalled that the pioneering *garagistes* such as Thunevin took immense pains in the vineyard, not only reducing yields but eliminating any less than perfect fruit; it was this, says his friend Alain Vauthier of Ausone, that allowed him to make an exceptional wine in the dismal 1992 vintage. Similarly, in 1999 the *vignerons* at Rol Valentin spent 1,000 hours removing hail-damaged berries from the vines. Such costly attention to detail is only possible when you are cultivating a small area of vines.

A *vin de garage* will usually be aged in new oak, and its accessibility enhanced by techniques such as cold-soaking, barrel-fermentation, malolactic fermentation in barrels, and extended lees-ageing. Such wines can undoubtedly be very impressive and have won great praise from some wine writers. They received rapturous welcome for such wines from Robert Parker, who is always happy to champion those whom he perceives as foes of an entrenched Bordeaux wine establishment. High scores and very limited production allowed their producers to obtain very high prices. However, their continuing success was almost entirely dependent on high scores, as few, if any, had any track record to fall back on; one mediocre score and they were at risk of vanishing from the radar screen. Their critics, moreover, argued that their celebrity is undeserved because their longevity is uncertain, and one of the criteria of a great Bordeaux is surely its capacity to age and evolve. The veteran wine merchant Jacques Merlaut told me some years ago: "I have no interest in *vins de garage*. Their prices are silly and they distort the market. I'm not interested in wines that are made with collectors in mind." The négociant Pierre Lawton was dismissive too: "The whole idea was modelled on Napa cult wines such as Screaming Eagle, which nobody could buy and nobody ever drinks. It's a caricature of wine." Many Médoc proprietors were scathing, observing that anyone can make a decent wine from a mere hectare by using extreme methods; producing 20,000 cases to the highest standards is a very different matter.

There has in my view been much misunderstanding of the concept of *vins de garage*. True *garage* wines include Valandraud in the 1990s and Jonathan Maltus's Laforge, and perhaps Marojallia in Margaux. These wines came, mostly, from mediocre soils, but were given a no-holds-barred treatment in the winery. On the other hand, St-Emilions such as La Gomerie or La Mondotte, while very opulent and expensive and limited in production, are not *vins de garage*. They come, as does Le Pin in Pomerol, from exceptional terroir, and only their limited production and intense demand have led to their winning a cult status that has been confused with *garagiste* triumphalism. Other wines often thought of as *garagiste* include Rol Valentin and Gracia. These are borderline cases, since their *terroir* is very good if not the finest. Other wines often referred to, falsely, as *vins de garage* are no more than *super-cuvées* from large estates, picked at very low yields and vinified according to *garagiste* orthodoxy. These include Haut-Condissas from Rollan de By in the Médoc, Péby-Faugères from Faugères, and Magrez-Fombrauge from Fombrauge. Indeed, Bernard Magrez is the high priest of *micro-cuvées*, producing examples from almost all his proliferating estates. This practice he defends not as a commercial enterprise by artificially creating scarcity, but, as he told me, "as a way of showing the potential of certain terroirs". Well, maybe, although in my view the exaggerated winemaking easily obliterates any specificity of terroir. More convincingly Thunevin brushes off his critics by justly observing: "After all, it's not as though we are stopping the First Growths from making great wine!"

Such wines worked commercially for a while because they were limited in number and attracted the eye of influential critics such as Robert Parker and Michel Bettane. Collectors snapped them up as high-scoring rarities. By 2000 the number of *garagiste* wines had risen sharply, and their appeal became diluted. Vintages such as 2000, 2001, 2004, and 2005, when most Right Bank estates made excellent wines, also lessened the differential in quality between many large estates and the *garagistes*. The latter still exist, of course, but are of dwindling importance. Nonetheless, they are to be saluted for having shaken up a fairly complacent industry and persuading some underperforming estates to raise their game.

The American merchant Jeffrey Davies, who has lived in Bordeaux for many years, has put a new spin on *garagisme* by encouraging growers in some of the least promising Right Bank areas to produce super-concentrated, richly oaky wines that he then sells, sometimes on an exclusivity basis, to his clients. Often sold at modest prices under the bland Bordeaux or Bordeaux Supérieur appellations, because they are not entitled to anything grander, they can offer very good value. Some of these wines are excellent; others are exaggerated caricatures.

However patchy the performance of *garagiste* wines, there can be no doubt that they extended the potential of wine quality from some unpromising terroirs at the very time that the marginal areas are most under threat, with bureaucrats rightly demanding that tracts of mediocre vineyards be grubbed up to rid the market of large quantities of unsaleable wine. If the Left Bank remains a bastion of conservatism, and none the worse for it, the Right Bank is constantly pushing at the boundaries, in terms of viticulture, winemaking, and marketing. Bordeaux is lucky to have them both.

17. St-Emilion I

In mid-September the small medieval town of St-Emilion celebrates its *nuit du patrimoine*, its heritage night. The members of its winemaking guild, the Jurade, parade in their scarlet robes through the steep lane, descending to the monolithic church to induct new members into their order. Merchants, oenologists, and wine writers gather in a medieval hall nearby to taste and reward the best of the *crus classés* in a blind tasting. After a solid lunch, the Jurade's senior members climb the steps of the Romanesque tower, a trumpeter in tow, and proclaim the *ban de vendange*, the date when harvesting may commence. At night, while boisterous visitors file out of overflowing restaurants, the sky explodes with a twenty-minute display of ever-more-lavish fireworks. The privileged gather on the terrace of the village's finest restaurant, the Plaisance, for the best view. St-Emilion is *en fête*, and few towns in France do it better.

It's not hard to see why tens of thousands of visitors, French and international, are drawn to this town. It's a UNESCO World Heritage site, thanks to its largely unspoilt character and its medieval monuments. St-Emilion's celebrity has led to some depopulation, as its shrinking number of inhabitants move out to make room for more boutiques, wine shops, bars, and restaurants. If the town is becoming petrified by its fame, the same is far from true of its vineyards, which stretch in all directions from the hub of the old town. The wealth and renown of these estates have sustained the prosperity of St-Emilion itself.

The zone of production was delimited in 1936, when St-Emilion received its AC. To the north the Barbanne stream separates it from the so-called satellite appellations of St-Georges and Montagne. To the south, after a precipitous descent from the plateau on which the town is located, the vineyards on the flatlands of the Dordogne valley stretch almost to the banks of the river. To the west lie Libourne and the appellation of Pomerol, and to the east the wilder terrain of the Côtes de Castillon. Nine communes are included within the appellation: St-Emilion itself, a part of Libourne, the hillside villages of St-Etienne-de-Lisse, St-Christophe-des-Bardes, St-Hippolyte, and St-Laurent-des-Combes, and the plains communities of St-Sulpice-de-Faleyrens, Vignonet, and St-Pey-d'Armens. These boundaries may strike visitors as somewhat bizarre, since the vineyards of the plateau have nothing in common with those down on the river plain. Instead of being drawn up on the basis of topographical consistency, as one might expect, the St-Emilion appellation matches the ancient medieval boundaries of the town and its environs, which makes little sense from a viticultural point of view.

There are 5,400 hectares under vine, representing some six per cent of the Bordeaux region. Vine density is typically around 5,500 vines per hectare, far less packed than in the Médoc. It used to be higher, and the oldest vines at Ausone, for example, are planted at a density of 7,000 or 8,000 vines per hectare. Alain Vauthier of Ausone, advised by the soil expert Claude Bourguignon, believes strongly in even higher densities, and recent plantings have been at 12,000 per hectare. He can leave no more than five bunches per vine, and during the summer never thins out entire bunches but instructs his vineyard workers just to remove parts of bunches instead. The result of high-density plantings is, he argues, better flavour and higher yields. The costs are high, special *enjambeur* tractors need to be bought, and the vineyard workers need to be highly trained, which may explain why few estates have followed his example.

Merlot has long been the dominant variety. Today it accounts for some seventy per cent of plantings, followed by Cabernet Franc at twenty-five per cent, and five per cent of Cabernet Sauvignon. In the 1970s the INAO, aware of Merlot's susceptibility to rot, encouraged growers to plant Cabernet Sauvignon, which everyone now recognizes was a mistake, as the variety is ill at ease on clay soils and often fails to ripen. Cabernet Sauvignon needs warmer gravelly soils, such as at Figeac or down on the plains of the Dordogne valley. Very little Malbec is planted, though it survives here and there, as at Bélair. In St-Emilion it is known as Noir de Pressac, or plain Pressac. This is because a former owner of Château de Pressac came from the Cahors region and allegedly planted its principal grape at his property.

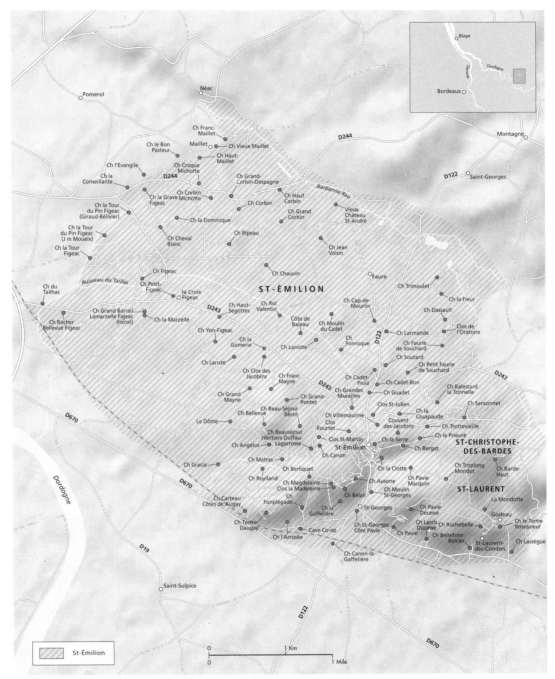

St-Emilion

Alain Vauthier points out that Cabernet Franc (or Bouchet, as it is known locally) is the region's traditional variety, dominating St-Emilion before phylloxera. Merlot gained ground when the vineyards were replanted because it is easier to cultivate, and the trend intensified after the frost of 1956. For his part, Vauthier has planted nothing but Cabernet Franc at Ausone since 1982. Its proportion in the total vineyard has declined because it is harder to cultivate than the more easy-going Merlot. It needs clay in the soil and doesn't do well on the sandier soils of the plain. It also ripens about one week later than Merlot, though it can attain equally high sugar levels. The main drawback of Cabernet Franc, however, is the poor quality of most commercially available clones. Growers need access to the best massal selections if they are to improve their wines by planting more Cabernet Franc.

The average rainfall in St-Emilion is about 800 millimetres (31.5 inches), but has been as low as 450 (17.7 inches; in 1989) and as high as 1,160 (45.6 inches; in 1960). Production varies, of course, but the average figure is around thirty-two million bottles. In contrast to the Médoc and Graves, it remains a region of relatively small estates. In 1998, out of St-Emilion's 840 properties, over half were smaller than five hectares, and only sixteen exceeded thirty hectares.

St-Emilion traces its viticultural history back to Roman times, when Decimus Magnus Ausonius lived here. He was born in Bordeaux in the early fourth century and, after a career as a teacher and administrator, retired to his native region in AD 383 and died twelve years later. His name lives on in Château Ausone. Traces of Roman viticulture remain at Beau-Séjour-Bécot. Shallow trenches carved into the limestone are still extant; these were filled with earth, in which fruit trees that in turn supported vines were planted.

The town itself is named after Aemilianus, the head of a local religious community. He died in 787 and the vast monolithic church within the old town was subsequently dug out around his venerated cell. The town we know today was an eleventh-century creation that rapidly prospered. St-Emilion became known as a religious centre after a Benedictine monastery and other ecclesiastical institutions were founded here. It grew in importance after 1199, when it was granted an independent charter. It was at that time that the original Jurade was founded, as a civil body set up to administer the region and maintain its citizens' rights. One of its roles was to announce the date of the grape harvest. It also awarded a seal of approval to wines that met its standards, and was empowered to destroy barrels deemed of poor quality.

The port of Libourne was an English creation of the late thirteenth century that facilitated the distribution of wines from its hinterland. This commercial progress was undermined by the Hundred Years War, and the Libournais remained a backwater until the eighteenth century, when a revival of trade with northern Europe stimulated demand for its wines. Even so, the wines of Fronsac were more highly esteemed than those of St-Emilion. The anticlericalism of the years of Revolution greatly damaged the local economy, and the wine industry. But by the mid-century St-Emilion was recovering. Vineyards expanded twofold. During the course of the nineteenth century, some of the most famous properties of the plateau were establishing a sound reputation for their wines. But few properties could challenge, in terms of size or quality, the great estates of the Médoc. Moreover, the great négociant houses of Bordeaux continued to perceive the Libournais as a backwater. Nobody even thought of assessing Libournais wines when the classification of 1855 was under consideration.

Yet in 1884 St-Emilion became the first region in France to set up a Syndicat Viticole to protect and regulate its interests. In 1931, responding to the economic crisis afflicting Bordeaux, it set up its cooperative, and in 1936 it became an *appellation contrôlée*. The Jurade, which had been abolished during the Revolution, was revived in 1948 as a promotional organization. It has been highly successful in fostering the appreciation of St-Emilion's wines worldwide.

St-Emilion is very much marked by its soil. On the plateau, the dominant soil type is loam and clay over weathered limestone. There are considerable variations in the depth of the topsoil and its composition. The unifying characteristic is, however, the thick band of limestone of which the plateau itself is composed. Beneath many of the châteaux are extensive limestone quarries. Visitors to Canon, Bélair, and Franc-Mayne, among others, are often shown these immense underground caverns. Some are empty, others are used for storing bottles or barrels, and at Bélair the winery itself is located underground.

There are also microclimatic variations between, for example, the areas close to the town and those at St-Etienne-de-Lisse. During the hot September of 2005, my car thermometer registered 5°C (41°F) at 8.30 in the morning at St-Etienne. Vineyards in these outlying regions can ripen from seven to twelve days later than those near St-Emilion itself. Proprietors in these corners of the appellation may claim, rightly, that their soils are outstanding, but microclimatic factors can make a considerable difference. In difficult years, late maturation can be a distinct disadvantage. The same is true of St-Christophe-des-Bardes, where the clay content is quite high, and maturation is slower than on the plateau. There are even climatic variations on the main plateau of St-Emilion. Alain Vauthier at Ausone points out that Canon, Bélair, Ausone, and Magdelaine often harvest a week earlier than Pavie and Troplong-Mondot.

The more westerly parts of the plateau have an entirely different soil structure. Around Figeac and Cheval Blanc the soil is more gravelly. It is for this reason that the proportion of Cabernet Franc is far higher in this sector. The deep clay-limestone soils of the plateau have the advantage of being water-retentive, an undeniable advantage in very dry years such as 2005. On the other hand, they pose practical problems. As Gérard Perse of Pavie points out: "When it rains the clay turns into mud, making it almost impossible to get into the vineyards. And when it's very dry, the clay turns into cement, which also makes it very difficult to work the soil."

Because limestone retains water, it is often supposed that vine roots descend through the rock in search of water deposits. This may be the case in some regions, but not here. The plateau limestone is not porous or especially fissured. What happens is that the roots descend through the topsoil, and when they reach the rock they are obliged to strike out horizontally. Should the vines be stressed, capillary action sucks up moisture from the rock from a depth of up to six metres (nineteen feet eight inches). The topsoil also varies considerably in depth. At Ausone it is scarcely fifty centimetres (twenty inches) in depth; elsewhere it is more profound.

Similar to the plateau soils are those of the slopes or *coteaux* leading down to the Dordogne valley; these are the soils on which much of Pavie and Larcis-Ducasse are located. Quite different, however, are the more gravelly soils to the west, around Figeac, La Dominique, and Cheval Blanc. To the north the soils are marked by *sables anciens* (weathered wind-blown sand, unlike the alluvial sands of the plain), silt, and sandy gravel, especially around the hamlet of Corbin. These northerly areas are not considered among the best, although surprisingly fine and long-lived wines do sometimes emerge from them.

Finally, there is the Dordogne valley. Here the alluvial sandy soils have nothing in common with those of the other sectors. Indeed, the vineyards closest to the river are classified only as Bordeaux AC. Nonetheless there are pockets of interesting soil down on this river plain. In the communes of Vignonet and St-Sulpice there are areas of gravel that can give good wine. The success of wines such as Monbousquet or Teyssier shows that very good, if not great, wines can be made here. But even Jean-Luc Thunevin, who has made some good wines from the plain, admits that he can never produce a wine to match the best from the plateau.

A good deal of mediocre wine is produced in St-Emilion. This is inevitable in an area of this size. However standards are steadily rising, and there can be little doubt that the region's exemplary classification system is at least partly responsible for this amelioration. The first St-Emilion classification was established in 1955. The estates were divided into four tiers. The first two consist of the *premiers crus*. In 1955 there were twelve of them, of which two – Cheval Blanc and Ausone – enjoyed superior status, being defined as *premier cru* (A), whereas the other *premiers* were classified (B). The next tier consisted of sixty-three *grands crus classés*. There followed a large number of *grands crus*, a fairly amorphous group. The remainder were obliged to label their wines as basic and unadorned St-Emilion.

What makes the St-Emilion classification special is that it is required to be revised every ten years. The 1966 classification consisted of thirteen *premiers* and fifty-five *grands crus classés*. For the 2006 classification every classified property was required to submit a dossier should it wish to be re-included; no estate is permitted to coast on its reputation. Before 1996 the jury was composed mostly of brokers, but in 2006 the panel included the head of the CIVB, Christian Delpeuch, the leading wine broker Max Lestapis, a wine lawyer, and at least five others. Their deliberations were conducted with the utmost discretion.

The criteria for classification include the quality of the wine (assessed by a tasting of recent vintages), the quality of the terroir, and the renown, pricing, and presentation of the wine. These last criteria are somewhat controversial. Nicolas de Bailliencourt of Gazin in Pomerol, and thus an outsider, remarks that the inclusion of price as a factor encourages aspiring estates to keep increasing their prices. The *premiers* (A) obtain very high prices for their wines. On grounds of terroir and track record, Figeac applied for promotion from (B) to (A) in 2006, but was rejected on the grounds that Figeac keeps its prices well below those charged by the (A)s. This seems to encourage price speculation and to punish moderation.

The classification process has always been taken very seriously, and estates have been demoted as well as promoted. Châteaux Sansonnet and Grand-Corbin-Despagne were demoted from *grand cru classé* to *grand cru* in 1996, and their present owners don't deny that the jury was right in its judgment. Loss of status also had considerable commercial consequences. François Despagne of Grand-Corbin-Despagne (who took over the property only after its demotion) recalls how former clients deserted the property, while négociants offered to buy up existing stock at ridiculously low prices. The numerous demotions in 2006 penalized those proprietors, whose wines would in future inevitably be of far less interest to the trade, and sales are likely to plummet. There was criticism in 2006 of the demotion of properties that had recently been bought by ambitious proprietors, who were punished for the deficiencies of the previous owners' wines.

Promotion allows estates to charge higher prices for their wines, which now come with the seal of approval. Dominique Decoster, who acquired Château Fleur-Cardinale in 2001, argued that the investments and efforts he had made, together with the critical acclaim its wines had received, amounted to a strong case for promotion. He was successful. On the other hand, the owner of another worthy contender told me she held out little hope for promotion since she did not sell her wines through the *Place de Bordeaux*, and the négociants on the panel took a dim view of properties that commercialized their wines independently.

In the Médoc there is no obstacle to a château incorporating newly purchased vines into its production. Thus when Mouton-Rothschild bought La Fleur-Milon in 2004, it could in theory have blended in the production from that *cru bourgeois* into its *grand vin*. In St-Emilion the rules are stricter, and newly purchased parcels must be vinified separately for ten years, so as to give the jury a chance to assess the wine's worth before permission is granted to incorporate it into the château's existing production. It was for failing to observe this rule that Château Beau-Séjour-Bécot was demoted from *premier* status in 1986, though it won back its status ten years later.

It is indisputable that the existence of a well-regulated classification system, for all its faults, has been a positive force. It gained credibility in 2006 by having the courage to demote a surprisingly large number of properties. It has encouraged a near-universal desire to produce ever-better wine. Very few of the *grands crus classés* are producing second-rate wine, even if there are quite a few *grands crus* that make wine at the same level.

However, perhaps emboldened by the success of those who had successfully challenged (and destroyed) the 2003 *cru bourgeois* classification in the Médoc, four demoted properties in 2006 – Cadet-Bon, La Marzelle, Tour du Pin Figeac, and Guadet – went to court, saying procedures had not been followed and not all the properties had been visited. On March 30, 2007 a judge ruled in their favour and the *classement* was suspended, a ruling confirmed after an appeal on April 13. By implication, so were previous classifications; this meant that officially Ausone is now a mere *grand cru*. Many leading figures in St Emilion, including Syndicat president Hubert de Boüard, were furious, believing that a force for good in the region had been overturned by a handful of proprietors acting out of spite. Nicolas Thienpont, the manager of the demoted Bellevue, accepted that decision, pointing out that you had to apply to be classified – it was not an obligation, and properties such as La Mondotte and Tertre-Roteboeuf do not apply – and if you did so, then you should accept the rules. Guy Pétrus Lignac and Guy Richard, owners of two of the properties that took the Syndicat to court, told me they had no intention of destroying the classification; they merely wanted it frozen for a while, and were keen to have the matter settled amicably. No doubt the lawyers will sort it out in due course, but since the final outcome of this outburst of litigation is highly uncertain, I have decided to retain the current classification in this book.

Winemaking styles are varied, of course, and St-Emilion (and Pomerol too) have for some years been hotbeds of experimentation and innovation. The vast concentrating machines that glower from the corners of many Médoc wineries are relatively rare on the Right Bank, if only because the smaller size of most estates makes the acquisition of concentrators too costly. On the other hand, Right Bank winemakers have been in the vanguard of those employing micro-oxygenation (*see* Chapter Three). The trend toward ever-later harvesting is certainly marked in St-Emilion and Pomerol, encouraged by oenologists such as Michel Rolland and his associate Jean-Philippe Fort. However, it is far from universal, and some winemakers are sceptical about the cult of phenolic maturity at all costs, and pick relatively earlier in order to preserve the freshness of their wine. Stephan von Neipperg of Canon-La-Gaffelière argues that in cooler soils, where acidity levels are higher, it is sensible to aim for optimal ripeness, even for some overripeness. In general, St-Emilion is less avant-garde than some suggest. There are many estates where the vinification and ageing processes remain entirely traditional.

The rise and gentle decline of the *garagiste* movement has been discussed in the introduction to this section. If it starts to fade away, few will regret its passing. The appeal of a well-made St-Emilion is so immediate, and repays the drinker with such generosity, that there seems little reason to go for extremes. Yields are rarely excessive here and in a good vintage the wines find their own balance of succulence, flesh, tannin, and freshness. Little seems to be gained by aiming for hyper-concentration, and that trend seems to be shuffling away. Super-extracted wines such as the controversial Pavie stand out not because they are diverting winemakers from the true path, but because they are so atypical of what a great St-Emilion should be. They may have other virtues, but few winemakers seem tempted to move stylistically in their direction.

Château Angélus

Tel: 0557 247139. Website: www.chateau-angelus.com. Owner: Hubert de Boüard de Laforest.
Premier grand cru classé (B). 23 ha. 50% Merlot, 47% Cabernet Franc, 3% Cabernet Sauvignon.
Production: 80,000 bottles. Second wine: Le Carillon de l'Angélus

The sonorous name supposedly derives from that of a particular parcel where devout *vignerons* could hear the Angelus bell tolling from all the town's churches. The estate was bought by the present owner's great-grandfather in 1921. He also owned Château Mazerat, and after World War II his sons united the two properties under its present name. The next generation took over in the form of the dynamic Hubert de Boüard in 1985. He admits that in the 1970s and early 1980s the property had been underperforming, and he worked hard to reinvigorate the estate.

In 1979 three hectares of vines were acquired from Beau-Séjour-Bécot, and Hubert is convinced that this acquisition of *premier cru* terroir made a substantial contribution to the improvement in quality that in 1996 led to Angélus's promotion to *premier cru classé*.

The vineyards lie on slopes that lead down from the hill topped by Château Bellevue; they continue their descent beyond the château itself. Three hectares at the foot of the slope were not classified as *premier cru* in 1996, so their production is incorporated into the second wine. De Boüard is particularly proud of his Cabernet Franc. These vines are up to sixty-five years old. The vineyards are often planted to a rather higher density than is usual here. The vines are cultivated according to the principles of *lutte raisonnée*, meaning that chemical treatments are practised only when there seems no other sensible choice.

The vineyards are by no means uniform. Some are exceptional, with the classic clay-limestone of the *côtes*. But lower down, the land is flatter and the soil has less clay but more sand. De Boüard agrees that much of this lower-lying soil would not be considered outstanding were it planted with Merlot, but he says its warm, well-drained soils suit Cabernet Franc perfectly.

There was a clear change of direction when Hubert de Boüard took over from his father. Indeed, there seems to have been considerable generational conflict between them. In his father's time there wasn't a single oak barrel in the winery. Practices such as green-harvesting, eliminating the use of fertilizers, and raising the height of the trellis were seen as radical measures twenty years ago. Frequent visits to Burgundy in the 1980s – an adventurous expedition for a Bordelais – led to an enthusiasm for ageing wines on the fine lees. De Boüard has of course been vindicated.

In 2001 twin vibrating tables were installed at the reception area, and after manual destemming the grapes are lifted by conveyor belt to just above the tanks, where they are crushed and then tumble into the vats by gravity. De Boüard remains quite conservative in his winemaking techniques. He occasionally gives the fruit a cold soak, but not systematically. He is not keen on reverse osmosis, and rarely employs micro-oxygenation, though he did so in 1999. *Pigeage* too is not systematic. Until 2001 all the tanks were stainless steel, but he has since introduced some concrete tanks, in which about half the crop is now vinified. If the must requires greater concentration, he will bleed the tanks.

The wine goes into barriques as early as possible, a technique he borrowed from Dominique Lafon in Burgundy, whom he visited in 1981. It stays in oak for up to twenty-two months, and the proportion of new oak varies from eighty-five to 100 per cent. Although the wine remains on its lees without racking until June, De Boüard does not use modish techniques such as lees-stirring or *cliquage*. He says reduction is rarely a problem if you have selected impeccable grapes.

The oldest L'Angélus (the name was changed to Angélus pure and simple in 1990) I have encountered is the 1961, tasted in 1996 from a half-bottle and still showing brilliantly, with sweet, intense aromas and spicy, concentrated fruit on the palate, with a touch of gaminess that didn't impair the wine's freshness. The 1964 was mellow and rounded by 1988, but surely at its peak. The 1981, tasted in 2005, was still going strong, a lush but spicy wine with little subtlety but delicious fruit. The 1986 was still rather closed in the mid-1990s, but it had a sleek texture, ripe tannins, some complexity, and good length. The 1989 is splendid, sweet and oaky on the nose with a whiff of mint and seaweed; it's full-bodied, concentrated, and stylish with a very long, chocolatey finish.

The 1992 was attractive when young, but may be past its best. The 1993 is very much in the modern Angélus style, with ample sweet new oak on the nose, and a palate that, even twelve years on, is still very dense and tannic. It's difficult not to admire the richness and extract, but it's quite a fatiguing wine. However, it's very typical of the estate, which places as much emphasis on power as elegance. The 1994, also tasted recently, is slightly more evolved, with light leafy, mushroomy aromas skating over the black-cherry fruit. On the palate it remains tight and tannic, with quite pronounced acidity. The 1995 has none of the awkward edges of the 1994. There's summer pudding and mint on the nose, and the palate is dense and chunky, with ample tannin but not much charm.

The 1996 has complex, oaky aromas of plum compote and mushrooms; although the palate is very concentrated and the tannins are chewy, there's a good deal of spice and truffle to add complexity. For a light year the 1997 shows well, let down only by its lack of persistence. The plum-scented 1998 is Angélus to the maximum, almost impenetrable in its youth, but by 2007 the tannins had integrated and the wine had become delicious and elegant, with superb length. In 1999 the vineyards suffered from hail damage, but the small amount of wine produced is concentrated and of good quality, with a little more flesh and succulence than is usual.

It's hard to resist the explosive 2000. There's much new oak on the nose, of course, but also touches of tobacco and damsons that add complexity; the immense richness and concentration are tempered by the lilting lift and persistence contributed by the Cabernet Franc. The 2001 is very similar, sumptuous and massive, and still a bit of a bruiser with very chewy tannins. The 2002 is still rather raw and too closed to judge; but it seems typical of the estate, and has some fresh acidity on the finish. There can be few finer 2003s from the Libournais than Angélus, which has power without extraction and unusual vigour and spiciness for this difficult vintage. The 2004 resembles the 2001 but is less extracted: it's a sumptuous wine of remarkable depth and power, without being overblown. The astonishing 2005 has aromas of black fruits and black pudding, immense power, and an exotic, peppery, dramatic character that is remarkable even for Angélus.

When it finally sheds its youthful toughness and austerity, Angélus can be a great wine, but it is not going to be to every taste. For myself, I find it somewhat effortful and over-extracted.

Château L'Apolline

St-Sulpice-de-Faleyrens. Tel: 0557 512680. Owner: Philippe Genevey. Grand cru. 2.8 ha. 66%
Merlot, 34% Cabernet Franc. Production: 18,000 bottles

Philippe Genevey, the winemaker at La Marzelle, bought this property, then known as Brégnet, in 1996. The vines, with an average age of thirty-five years, are planted on warm sand and gravel soils. The wine is aged in fifty per cent new barriques. The only vintage I have tasted is the oddly balanced 2003, which has little structure or length and some strange bubble-gum flavours.

Château Armens

St-Pey-d'Armens. Tel: 0557 560506. Website: www.malet-roquefort.com. Owner: Alexandre de Malet Roquefort.
Grand cru. 18 ha. 70% Merlot, 20% Cabernet Sauvignon, 10% Cabernet Franc. Production: 100,000 bottles.
Second wine: La Fleur du Ch Armens

The Malet Roqueforts are the owners of La Gaffelière. While Léo de Malet Roquefort looks after that *premier cru*, his son Alexandre has been developing this property in the southwestern part of the region, with advice from Michel Rolland. The vines are mostly planted on an outcrop of clay-limestone, though Alexandre admits only about half the soil is exceptional. The wine is aged for eighteen months in about eighty per cent new oak. Although Armens does not have a great deal of body, it is made in quite an extracted style. Of recent vintages I prefer the 2002, though the 2004 shows promise.

Château L'Arrosée

St-Emilion. Tel: 0557 246944. Website: www.chateaularrosee.com. Owner: Roger Caille. Grand cru classé.
9 ha. 60% Merlot, 20% Cabernet Franc, 20% Cabernet Sauvignon. Production: 35,000 bottles.
Second wine: Ch l'Armont

This estate, named after an underground spring on the property, is located on the slopes that descend towards the cooperative. For many years it was owned by François Rodhain, but had been underperforming. Roger Caille, who founded express transport services for banks, retired in 2002 and bought L'Arrosée, which he runs jointly with his media-savvy son Jean-Philippe. Gilles Pauquet was the consultant under Rodhain and the new owners retain his services. Alain Vauthier of Ausone had told Caille that L'Arrosée's wines had once been among the finest in St-Emilion, and this vote of confidence helped persuade Caille to buy the estate.

The winery had been built by Rodhain in the late 1950s, when he withdrew from the cooperative, but Caille decided to raze it and rebuild on the same spot. The new *chais*, which are tunnelled into the hillside, are in the form of an E-shaped Tuscan villa and cut quite a dash.

Most of the vines had been planted in the early 1970s, but many were missing, so Caille's team has been replacing them individually. The major part of the vineyards is on the *côtes*, surrounded by Magdelaine and Berliquet, but there is also a sector on less favourable sand and clay soil on flat land behind the cooperative.

The winemaking now pulls out all the stops. The grapes are carefully sorted using a machine invented by the Cailles. It resembles a small airport baggage carousel, allowing the bunches to be more carefully inspected before being consigned to the destemmer. From there they are taken by conveyor belt to the crusher over a battery of small cement tanks. There is *pigeage* as well as pumpovers during fermentation, and the wine is aged in entirely new oak for sixteen to eighteen months and blended shortly before bottling. The second wine, an innovation in 2002, comes from an adjoining parcel of vines that is only *grand cru*.

In 2005 I was able to taste six vintages from 1989 to 2000, and I found them all seriously disappointing, with dilute fruit and dry, coarse tannins. The 2001, which was completed but not harvested by the new team, is cleanly made, fresh and simple, but modest for the vintage. The 2002 shows more aromatic complexity, better concentration, and an attractive stylishness. The 2003 has sweet, fleshy aromas, and lush fruit, with some bite and freshness. The super-ripe, weighty 2004 is similar and is easily the best wine from here in years.

Château Ausone

St-Emilion. Tel: 0557 242457. Website: www.chateau-ausone.com. **Owner:** *Alain Vauthier. Premier grand cru classé (A).*
7 ha. 55% Cabernet Franc, 45% Merlot. **Production:** *25,000 bottles.* **Second wine:** *Chapelle d'Ausone*

You can see the steep-roofed nineteenth-century château as you approach the town from the south. Part of the property lies perched high up on the limestone plateau, the remainder on the clay-limestone slopes beneath it. At the foot of this southeast-facing slope, the soil is sandier than in the higher sectors. You can easily imagine why the Roman poet Ausonius might have chosen to build his villa here, although there is no historical evidence that he ever did so.

Although Ausone is the smallest of Bordeaux's First Growths, its reputation has long been stellar, despite the occasional dull patch. Its history is long and complicated. In the sixteenth century it belonged to the Lescours family, and by the early eighteenth century was in the hands of the Chatonnets, who intermarried with the Cantenat family in 1718. However, in 1891 a niece of the Cantenats, whose surname was Challon, married Edouard Dubois, and the couple changed their name to Dubois-Challon. By this time Ausone was already widely recognized as one of the top wines of Bordeaux. In 1916 they bought Bélair. The couple had two children, Jean and Cecile. Cecile married a Vauthier, from whom two generations down the line Alain Vauthier is descended. In 1958 Jean Dubois-Challon, at the age of sixty-three, married a far younger woman. They had no children, and after Jean's death in 1974 his share of the property should have passed to the father of Alain Vauthier, but Jean's widow Heylette claimed the right to run Ausone, and, having hired the very young Pascal Delbeck to run Bélair, was keen to install him at Ausone too. From 1974 to 1995 the two parts of the family, the Dubois-Challons and the Vauthiers, were at loggerheads. During this period, when the long-term ownership of Ausone was in doubt, no significant investments were made.

There is much uncertainty about one important question: who was making the wine during this period? I am indebted to Michel Bettane for helping to clarify the position. It seems that Alain Vauthier, from about 1976 onwards, was the winemaker. As a protégé of Mme. Dubois-Challon and as the *régisseur* of Bélair, Pascal Delbeck had a say, and for many years the two men worked amicably together. But then their views began to diverge. Hence the interminable battles, which often ended up in court, over such matters as the harvesting date. Whatever the outcome, and it usually favoured Vauthier, Delbeck had no role as winemaker; he was never the *régisseur* at Ausone. It may have suited Mme. Dubois-Challon to give the impression that Delbeck was more deeply involved than was the case, but it was Vauthier who made the crucial decisions.

In 1995 this period of uncertainty ended when Alain Vauthier took over the estate. What precipitated the change was that Mme. Dubois-Challon was tempted to sell Ausone to François Pinault, who already owned Château Latour. Alain Vauthier and his sister insisted they had the first right of refusal on any proposed sale and took Mme. Dubois-Challon to court. Their action was successful, but she retained the right to live in the château for the rest of her days. She died in 2003, and builders moved in to renovate the château, which was becoming dilapidated.

Alain Vauthier does more than manage Ausone. He and his family control close to 100 hectares in the region (*see also* Châteaux Moulin-St-Georges and de Fonbel). At Ausone he is assisted by Pauline Vauthier, one of his three daughters, and by cellarmaster Philippe Baillarguet. Vauthier's forte, or one of them, is vineyard management. Few vineyards are as impeccably maintained as Ausone's, which are also noteworthy for the atypically high proportion of Cabernet Franc. They form a kind of amphitheatre, being both very sunny and sheltered and, incidentally, usually frost-free. Vauthier likes to deleaf very early so as to ensure the bunches remain small; the last thing he wants is swollen berries. He green-harvests and removes leaves systematically and removes the wings from the bunches to improve their aeration. He has installed new drainage, reconstructed some of the stone terraces, introduced integrated pest management and *lutte raisonnée*, and harvests by repeated passages through the vineyard. He also employs some biodynamic treatments, though he does not want to be tied down to any dogmatic system. Density is quite high for St-Emilion, at between 6,500 and 7,500 vines per hectare. The most recent plantings have been at 12,000 vines per hectare, which, he is convinced, gives better flavour at slightly higher yields. An average age of some fifty years has been maintained. Because in some older parcels Merlot and Cabernet Franc are co-planted within the same row, he tags the vines individually to help the pickers identify which is which. Out of sheer curiosity Vauthier planted a little Petit Verdot, but he wasn't happy with the results and the vines have gone; but he remains tempted to try a few rows of Carmenère.

Because the property is small, most grape selection is done in the vineyard, although there is also a vibrating table at the winery. The must undergoes a cold soak under dry ice for four to six days; then the grapes are gently heated until natural yeasts kick-start the fermentation. This takes place in open-top wooden vats, which are kept for nine years. The *cuvaison* is often five weeks, with frequent pumpovers and some *délestage*. The new wine undergoes malolactic fermentation in new oak barrels and, after racking, the blend is assembled. Ausone is aged in new barriques in the disused quarries beneath the house for up to twenty-one months. There is no filtration, and fining trials are conducted each vintage to ensure the wine is fined to exactly the right degree.

In the 1950s and 1960s yields were much higher and the *cuvaison* quite short, although the wine would have spent more time in barrel. Some vintages from this period were quite light. Under Delbeck, up to one-third of the stems were retained during fermentation, and there was no malolactic fermentation in barriques; the *élevage* was shorter than it is today, about sixteen months, but he too used only new oak.

In the past, Vauthier explains, the grapes would have been picked at 11.5 to twelve degrees of potential alcohol, as was common throughout Bordeaux. Chaptalization was unavoidable. Significantly lower yields, as well as some exceptional recent vintages, have allowed Vauthier to dispense with chaptalization since 2000. He is not afraid of high must weights, and recalls great wines such as 1990 Tertre-Roteboeuf, which had fifteen degrees of potential alcohol. In 2005 some Merlot was picked at fifteen degrees, and he had no concern about the balance of the final wine, but intended to be very careful to ensure fermentation temperatures did not exceed 28°C (82°F).

Selection is quite severe. Because all the vineyards are treated identically, even the second wine, first introduced in 1997, is of high quality. Each year some wine that doesn't make the grade for either Ausone or Chapelle is sold off in bulk.

Alain Vauthier likes to stay on top of his game:

> *My aim is to do the least possible work by having exemplary vineyard and winery material. My bottling line is three years old. In two years I'll replace it because there will be technical improvements that will make a difference, even a small one, to the quality of the wine. I welcome these improvements.*

Nonetheless Ausone is undoubtedly a hand-crafted wine.

Michel Rolland is the consultant here but that is to overstate his role. Vauthier says he never asks Rolland to come to Ausone to taste grapes or wines. But he sometimes brings some wines to Rolland and his team just to hear their views. He likes Rolland because he finds him stimulating.

The 1947 is the oldest Ausone I have tasted. (David Peppercorn[1] has written eloquently of the many nineteenth-century vintages he was able to taste in 1988.) It was sweet and cedary and refined some twenty years ago, but I have not encountered it since. The 1952 was drying out by 1999, with Bovril and menthol aromas; there was still ample concentration and power, but the fruit was fading. A Cruse bottling of the 1953 was cedary and elegant in 1985. The 1964 and 1976 were aromatic in a farmyardy way in 1985, but both lacked backbone and are unlikely to have improved. In 2000, the 1981 showed slightly coarse, woody aromas, was still tight and vigorous on the palate, although the finish was rather dry.

The 1982 is a gorgeous wine. Over the years it has gained in weight and spiciness and is now in its prime. The nose is voluptuous with coffee overtones, but the palate remains very youthful, with plump fruit, tremendous concentration, and a long, peppery finish. The 1983, in contrast, is quite evolved, with some gamey, liquorice aromas, rather dry

---

1 Peppercorn, *Bordeaux*, Faber, London, 1991, 397-8

tannins, and considerable astringency. More surprisingly, the self-effacing 1985, as Vauthier acknowledges, is a disappointment. It's quite svelte and elegant, but lacks the usual concentration. The 1986, tasted ten years on, had oaky, truffley aromas, but the wine was marred by some vegetal tones and chunky tannins, despite its impressive length. Far better is the 1989, with its sweet, elegant, toasty aromas, rich, supple texture, elegance, and long, toasty finish. The 1990, tasted in 2006, was disappointing: delicate and truffley on the nose and fresh on the palate, yet lacking in complexity and distinction.

The 1995 was monumental in the late 1990s, dense and brambly, highly concentrated, with a long, tannic finish. The 1996 has a sweet, oaky, minty nose; the wine has developed a light savoury tone, with more pronounced red-fruits flavours than most vintages here. (There are, however, some bottle variations with the 1996 vintage.) The 1998 shows Ausone at its magnificent best, with its rich blackberry nose, its savoury tones, and its perfectly integrated new oak. It's a sumptuous, velvety wine, highly concentrated but balanced by fine acidity, which gives great elegance. I prefer it to the 2000, which has more charred, smoky aromas; but the palate is so dense it shows signs of excessive extraction, and doesn't seem to have the finesse of 1998. Nor, I suspect, is it as good as the stupendous 2001. The nose offers a superb cocktail of fruits – plums and blackberries mostly – with hints of oriental spices; the palate is sleek and opulent and not too dense, the tannins are chewy but they don't dominate the fruit.

The 2002 is inevitably in a lighter style, but the nose is very elegant, with aromas of cherries, raspberries, and mint; the texture is velvety and there is ample freshness, spice, and length. With massive concentration and spiciness, the 2003, one of the outstanding wines of the vintage, is a return to the blockbuster style of 2000, yet it doesn't lack freshness or length. It's too early to assess the 2004, but from cask I was dazzled by its exquisite perfume, and by its fine structure, good acidity, and exemplary length. The 2005, tasted young from cask, is as good as anything from this superb vintage.

Château Balestard-La-Tonnelle

*St-Emilion. **Tel:** 0557 746206. **Website:** www.vignoblescapdemourlin.com. **Owner:** Jacques Capdemourlin.*
*Grand cru classé. 10.6 ha. 70% Merlot, 25% Cabernet Franc, 5% Cabernet Sauvignon. **Production:** 60,000 bottles.*
Second wine: Chanoine de Balestard

The Capdemourlins have been a prominent family in St-Emilion since at least 1617. Their major contribution was the re-founding of the Jurade in 1948 by brothers Jean and Roger. Roger's son Jacques, an elder statesman of the St-Emilion establishment, is a grave figure with a kindly if slightly schoolmasterly manner. Balestard came into his hands through his maternal grandfather, who bought the estate in 1923. Its antiquity is evident from the poem by François Villon, reproduced on the label, which refers to the *divin nectar* of Balestard. Jacques Capdemourlin has run the property since 1973, with increasing help from his son Thierry.

The vines are fairly old, and the usual measures – leaf removal and green-harvesting – are practised to reduce yields. The grapes are hand-picked, then sorted repeatedly at the winery. In 2005 the Capdemourlins introduced a brief cold soak under dry ice, followed by fermentation in cement and steel tanks, usually with natural yeasts. The wine is aged in fifty per cent new oak for about fifteen months. There is no systematic racking.

It's asking too much to expect a 1975 to show charm, but the 1975 Balestard was an honourable effort. Flavoury and concentrated in the 1990s, it has now become raw and stringy. The aromas of the 1982 are now ripe and elegant, but this is a fairly light wine, svelte but lacking fruit and persistence. Although the nose of the 1985 is ripe and fleshy, the wine is surprisingly lean, with some astringency. The only vintage of the 1990s I have tasted is the elegant, supple 1996, not a complex wine but balanced and lively. The 2000, although medium-bodied, has robust fruit, lively acidity, and an easy-going attractiveness; but it's far from outstanding. The 2001 is far better. The nose shows complexity, with aromas of plums, cherries, and chocolate; the palate is supple yet concentrated, firm but fleshy, and fine acidity gives length and finesse. The 2002 is lean, with rather pinched acidity given the slender fruit. There are aromas of black cherry and coffee on the 2003, which is rich, rounded, and concentrated, but a bit of a bruiser. The 2004 is a bold, plummy, tannic wine with considerable power, freshness, and length.

Château Barde-Haute

St-Christophe-des-Bardes. Tel: 0557 247821. **Owner:** *Sylviane Garcin-Cathiard. Grand cru. 17 ha. 90% Merlot,*
10% Cabernet Franc. **Production:** *65,000 bottles.* **Second wine:** *Le Vallon de Barde-Haute*

This property was bought and completely overhauled in 2000 by Mme. Garcin-Cathiard, who also owns
Haut-Bergey in Léognan and Clos l'Eglise in Pomerol (*qq.v.*). Her energetic daughter Hélène now lives here,
and her husband Patrice makes the wine. At first Michel Rolland acted as consultant oenologist, but he has
since been replaced by Alain Raynaud of Quinault.

Most of the vines are in a single parcel of sloping land adjoining the house and winery, though there are
other smaller parcels near Fombrauge. The topsoil is a thin layer of clay over a solid limestone base. As the
vineyards lie within a shallow amphitheatre not far from Troplong-Mondot and Trottevieille, there are varying
expositions. The Garcin-Cathiards replanted much of the vineyard and installed new drainage. Although this
reduced the average age of the vineyards, there are nonetheless some very old parcels of Cabernet Franc that
give exceptional quality.

The winery operates by gravity, and, after a cold soak, fermentation takes place in a variety of tanks. A *pied de
cuve* of selected yeasts is used to get the process going, and thereafter indigenous yeasts usually take over.
Pumpovers, *pigeage*, and occasional *délestage* are employed; although the winery is equipped with micro-oxygenation,
its use is rare. The *marc* is pressed with a vertical press, and the wine aged for sixteen months in eighty per cent new
oak. There is some lees-stirring during the *élevage*, as Hélène says the wine can be quite hard without it.

I have no experience of older vintages. The 2001 is exceptional and complete, with rich, plummy aromas,
sumptuous fruit, fine concentration and tannins, and a long, fresh finish. The 2002 is stylish, delicate, and fresh.
I am less keen on the 2003, with its cherry-compote aromas, hollow palate, and dry finish. The 2004 shows
great promise, though the style is quite flashy, with very oaky aromas, super-ripe flavours, and a plump texture
fortunately balanced by quite good acidity. Shortly before bottling, the impressive 2005 had lush, chocolatey
aromas, great richness and concentration, and an underlying freshness.

Château Beau-Séjour-Bécot

St-Emilion. Tel: 0557 744687. **Website:** *www.beausejour-becot.com.* **Owners:** *Gérard and Dominique Bécot.*
Premier grand cru classé (B). 16.5 ha. 70% Merlot, 24% Cabernet Franc, 6% Cabernet Sauvignon.
Production: *85,000 bottles.* **Second wine:** *La Tournelle de Beau-Séjour-Bécot*

Surviving trenches carved into the limestone confirm that the Romans cultivated vines here. In medieval times
the estate belonged to the monks of the nearby foundation of St-Martin-de-Mazerat, then to the lords of
Camarsac. In 1722 one of their descendants, Jeanne de Gères, married into the Carles de Figeac family,
bringing the estate as her dowry. It was renamed Beau-Séjour in 1787. Thereafter it passed through various
hands, and in 1924 Dr. Jean Fagouet bought the property and enlarged it to ten hectares. Michel Bécot owned
the nearby Château La Carte, and in 1969 he bought Beau-Séjour. Ten years later he expanded the property by
acquiring 4.5 hectares on the Trois Moulins plateau close by. Since Michel Bécot's retirement in 1985, the
property has been run by his sons Gérard and Dominique.

The property was demoted to *grand cru classé* in 1986 on the grounds that some of the vineyards of
Château La Carte had been incorporated into Beau-Séjour and they were not worthy of *premier cru* status.
The Bécots agreed not to use the La Carte grapes in the *grand vin*, and in 1996 the property was restored
to its former position.

Although the topsoil is very thin, the vines, according to Gérard Bécot, never experience hydric stress. The
limestone plateau on which the vines are planted distributes the reserves of water evenly, nourishing the plants.
The Bécots usually practise double leaf removal and green-harvest twice. After picking in *cagettes*, the fruit is
carefully sorted, then fermented in stainless-steel tanks with natural yeasts. Although Jean-Philippe Fort, the
consultant oenologist, is an enthusiast for micro-oxygenation, the practice is by no means systematic. Since

1992 the malolactic fermentation has taken place in new barriques, and the wine is aged for up to eighteen months in eighty-five per cent new oak. Blending takes place late.

The 1982 was very marked by Merlot aromas, and in its youth was soft, sweet, and generous, with good balance. I have not tasted it recently. The 1988 has aged well: it has a fine attack, and although not very complex or fleshy, has a good deal of spice, vigour, and length. The 1990 has always been delicious. The nose is very complex, with menthol, liquorice, and cedar shading the succulence of the fruit. It's not a wine with great weight, but it has intensity, charm and length. The 1993 was austere and unexciting in its youth, and the 1995 seemed both overripe and over-tannic, but it has doubtless evolved. The 1996 is a great success, with plums and blackcurrants on the nose, ample concentration, and a lively, spicy aftertaste. Although the 1998 remains closed on the nose, it's a sumptuous wine with a gorgeous suave texture, perked up by its light acidity; it's undeniably delicious and well balanced.

The sumptuous 2000 walks a tightrope between lushness and overripeness, but is not jammy. With a firm tannic backbone, quite good acidity, and superb length, this has more finesse than many 2000 St-Emilions. The elegant 2001 shows black cherries and almonds on the nose, and is surprisingly supple and accessible. The robust 2003 shows no overripe characters. There is ample new oak and flesh on the nose, and although the tannins are chunky, there is a core of sweet fruit and decent acidity. Although verging on overripeness, the highly impressive 2004 shows a similar hedonistic style, but has sufficient vigour to balance its weight and concentration.

Château Beauséjour Duffau-Lagarrosse

St-Emilion. Tel: 0557 247161. Owner: Jean Duffau-Lagarrosse. Premier grand cru classé (B). 7.5 ha. 70% Merlot, 20% Cabernet Franc, 10% Cabernet Sauvignon. Production: 36,000 bottles. Second wine: Croix de Beauséjour

This estate has been in the Duffau-Lagarrosse family since 1847. The Beauséjour estate was divided in 1869, and the other portion is now known as Beau-Séjour-Bécot. The vineyards are in a single parcel, with half on the plateau, the remainder on southwest-facing slopes. The average age of the vines is close to forty years. Practices such as debudding, leaf removal, and green-harvesting vary according to the needs of each parcel. The grapes are sorted in the vineyard rather than at the winery. After a cold soak, fermentation takes place with indigenous yeasts by preference. The *marc* is pressed in a vertical press, and after the malolactic fermentation the wine is aged in two-thirds new barriques for eighteen months.

My experience of Beauséjour Duffau-Lagarrosse has been mixed. The 1970, tasted in 1983, was already austere, dry, and short. On the other hand, the 1982 was delicious in 1995, with a seductively rich nose, sweet, supple fruit, and a lively finish. In 2007 the 1983 still had fresh cherry aromas; although one-dimensional on the palate, it shows no sign of fatigue. I found a slight herbaceous aroma on the 1986, and some hollowness on the palate, despite good fruit and acidity. The 1989, tasted in 2005 from magnum, was enticingly ripe on the nose, with super-ripe flavours supported by a firm tannic backbone.

After ten years, the 1995 is showing well, with complex aromas of plums, black cherries, wax, and woodsmoke; it's a weighty, even dense wine, balanced by ripe tannins and good acidity, exhibiting both power and persistence. I have never been able to work up much enthusiasm for the hollow, slack 1996, nor for the dilute 1997. Despite a slight lingering austerity, the 1999 is concentrated and firm but vigorous. Red fruits and toast dominate the nose of the excellent 2000, although it's made in an atypically lush and slightly heavy style. The aromas of the 2001 are elegant and graceful, smelling of very ripe cherries; perhaps the palate lacks some vigour, but this is nonetheless a rich, supple, and concentrated wine. The 2003 is robust and a touch baked, but it has grip and assertiveness; what it lacks is finesse. It is unclear how this wine will evolve. Tasted blind in 2007, the 2004 showed remarkably well, with spicy, oaky aromas, a sleek texture, ample concentration and pungency, and fine potential.

Château Bélair

St-Emilion. Tel: 0557 247094. Website: www.chateaubelair.com. Owner: Pascal Delbeck. Premier grand cru classé (B).
12.5 ha. 80% Merlot, 20% Cabernet Franc. Production: 48,000 bottles. Second wine: Ch Haut Roque Blanquant

In 1916 this finely located property was bought by Edouard Dubois-Challon, the owner of Ausone. After his daughter-in-law, Mme. Heylette Dubois-Challon, took over in 1974, she hired as her winemaker Pascal Delbeck, who was then only nineteen years old. He repaid this confidence in his winemaking skills with intense devotion. After her death in February 2003 at the age of eighty-four, he inherited all her properties. This would turn out to be a mixed blessing, as crippling French inheritance taxes threatened to force the sale of the property. Fortunately, Delbeck seems to have clung on, though he described his position as being like that of a spider hanging by a single thread. In 2006 the firm of J.P. Moueix took a minority share in the property.

Delbeck is a man of many talents. His winery is a showcase for his skills as an inventor. He cultivates the vineyards in a manner akin to biodynamism, but without adopting its theology. In his spare time he produces and sells grainy salt flavoured with red wine, and, being of partly Belgian ancestry, dreams of adding brewing to his portfolio.

In the fourteenth century, when Aquitaine was English, the owner was Sir Robert de Knolles (or Knollys). After the Hundred Years War the family remained in France and changed their name to Canolle. They continued as owners through and after the Revolution, acquiring the title of marquis along the way. Remarkably, the first vintage to be bottled here was 1802. It was the descendants of the Canolles who sold the property to Edouard Dubois-Challon. The château is an attractive, rambling structure of sixteenth-century origin that was largely rebuilt after a fire in the eighteenth century.

The location of the vineyards could hardly be bettered, as its neighbours include Magdelaine, La Gaffelière, Ausone, and Canon. Just over half of the vineyards are on the limestone plateau behind the château; the remainder on clay-limestone slopes. The Cabernet Franc has been planted on soils with higher silt and sand content. Up on the plateau are some centenarian vines, with Petit Verdot and Malbec mixed in, and the average age of the vines is forty years. Delbeck is keen to avoid overripeness so he only removes leaves on one side of the row. Traversing the vineyards it soon becomes clear that the vines are far from manicured, as they are, for example, at Ausone. There are varying numbers of bunches, and some clustering of bunches. Delbeck explains that in the case of young vines, he likes a good number of bunches, but doesn't use the crop for the *grand vin*. Old vines, he adds, can be very productive and still ripen the crop fully, but that is rarely the case with young vines. Yields are moderate, and the twenty-year average is thirty-nine hectolitres per hectare.

Delbeck is very attentive to environmental issues, although he does not claim to be fully organic. There are spots where the vines are quite tightly packed, and here he will use herbicides beneath the rows. Nonetheless this is very much the exception. No insecticides are used, and he employs homeopathic treatments that resemble biodynamic tinctures. He uses no anti-botrytis sprays, as they can inhibit natural yeast activity, so he uses other forms of treatment. And in the winery there is some use of solar energy.

The winery is located in lofty caverns tunnelled into the limestone. Delbeck claims to have been the first winemaker in Bordeaux to install a sorting table, which, he admits, he copied from the Domaine de la Romanée-Conti in Burgundy. The grapes are lightly crushed over the squat steel tanks. *Pigeage* is carried out by robotic machines of his own devising. More Delbeck innovations regulate the pumpovers, when the wine falls by gravity into tanks, which are then hoisted up and redistributed into the fermentation vats, again by gravity. After malolactic fermentation in small vats, the wine is aged in about seventy per cent new oak, although in practice the wine destined for the *grand vin* sees only new oak. The barrel staves are air-dried for three years at the estate. The final wine is fined with eggwhite from organically reared hens.

Bélair is a strange wine. It can be exquisite in some vintages; in others, unremarkable. It is certainly a wine of the old school. There is little sign of overripeness or super-concentration, nor of toasty aromas. It is restrained to the point of self-effacement. If the rich fleshiness of Ausone is seen by some as the epitome of great St-Emilion, that leaves little room for the more discreet charms of Bélair. Yet it is a wine that can age remarkably well.

The oldest Bélair I have tasted is the 1961 at almost forty years of age. There was a slight portiness on the nose, which was nonetheless spicy, vigorous, and elegant. Initial richness on the palate soon gave way to a dry finish, suggesting that this bottle had not held up well. I have not tasted the 1975 since 1985, when it was too tough and tannic to give much pleasure. I was served the 1976 blind in 2005, and relished its stylish nose of cherry pies and almonds; the palate was rich but silky, with fine acidity, and a hint of raisins on the finish. I was astonished to discover the vintage, as most 1976s are stewed and fell apart long ago. Delbeck explains that since most bunches were overripe, he deliberately picked some green bunches and co-fermented them with the very ripe grapes. His aim was to give the wine some freshness, and he certainly succeeded.

The 1978 aged quite fast, and by 1993 was showing some astringency, though I have not tasted it since. The 1980 is poor. Served the 1982 blind in 2005, I identified it as 1985 since it lacked the opulence of most 1982s. Nonetheless it is a very fine wine, perfumed and with ample rich fruit and a touch of menthol; although intense and elegant, it is also quite lean and pungent, and seems rather one-dimensional. I have drunk the 1983 frequently and it has never provoked much excitement. The nose is delicate and cedary if not that complex; on the palate there is some elegance and silkiness, and a savoury finish. The 1986 is quite evolved, with some leathery, gamey aromas; it has more body and overt tannins than many other vintages. I prefer it to the charming but rather thin 1988. The 1989, last tasted ten years ago from magnum, had a classic cedary nose, but lacked some personality on the palate, although stylish and quite concentrated.

The 1990 is surprisingly lean, with aromas that already seem quite evolved, with leather and menthol tones. On the palate it has concentration and some bite, but lacks persistence. The 1992 and 1994 were disappointing by the late 1990s. Bélair is back on form with the excellent 1995, with its fragrant, smoky nose. It's typical Bélair on the palate: there is no great weight, but it's sweet and silky, very ripe yet stylish and balanced. In its youth the 1996 had a charming nose, but seemed dilute and forward on the palate. The 2000 is far better, but again in a most discreet style. The nose is rich, with scents of blackberries, cherries, and marzipan, but the palate lacks some flesh and tautness. The 2001 is supple but seems underpowered, with firm tannins but only modest length. The 2003 lacks the excesses of many wines from this year; it is medium-bodied and lacks some flair, but has delicacy and charm. The 2004 has a welcome lightness of touch but it lacks flair and vigour, and seems rather slack.

Château Bellefont-Belcier

*St-Laurent-des-Combes. Tel: 0557 247216. Website: www.bellefont-belcier.com. **Owners:** Alain Laguillaumie, Jacques Berrebi, Dominique Hébrard. Grand cru classé. 13 ha. 70% Merlot, 20% Cabernet Franc, 10% Cabernet Sauvignon. **Production:** 55,000 bottles. **Second wine:** Marquis de Bellefont*

This property takes its name from Louis-François de Belcier, who owned it in the seventeenth century. In the early 1990s the proprietor was a doctor who sold the wine to private clients. In 1994 two investors, Alain Laguillaumie and Jacques Berrebi, bought the property. Initially they hired Louis Mitjaville as winemaker, and from 1999 to 2003 the wines were made by Marc Dworkin. In 2003 Dominique Hébrard was hired to run the estate and was also made a partner. The energetic Hébrard was at a loose end after his family ceased to be involved in the management of Cheval Blanc, and this is one of a number of projects that now absorb his time. The efforts of all involved were rewarded when in 2006 the property was promoted to *grand cru classé*.

The vineyards are complex, since they are planted on the plateau, on the south-facing slopes beneath it, and on flatter land near the château. The neighbours are prestigious: Larcis-Ducasse, Tertre-Rôteboeuf, Pavie-Decesse, Troplong-Mondot, and La Mondotte. The vines on the slopes form a kind of amphitheatre benefiting from slight variations in exposure; the new owners also invested in some terracing. Density is quite high at up to 7,200 vines per hectare.

The *cuvier* is one of the most unusual in Bordeaux. A semicircle of tall cement tanks is ranged beneath a circular wooden gallery, which also serves as the reception area after the grapes are harvested into *cagettes*. After double sorting, wagons convey the destemmed fruit to the crusher above the tanks. There is a cold soak, and after fermentation the residue is pressed in a vertical press. The wine is aged for fourteen to eighteen months in about seventy-five per cent new oak. Blending takes place quite late.

The vintages since 2001 have yielded excellent wines in a distinctly modern style. There are aromas of coffee, and a slight gaminess. On the palate the wines are plump, rounded, quite forward, and accessible. The 2002 is particularly successful. There does seem to be a slight change of style in 2004, when Hébrard made his debut. The nose has pure blackberry aromas, and there is both more concentration and more finesse on the palate, as well as a hard-to-define exotic quality to the fruit. Despite its opulence and richness, the resplendent 2005 has ample bite and acidity.

Château Bellevue

*St-Emilion. Tel: 0557 247423. **Owner:** Pradel de Lavaud and de Coninck families. Grand cru. 6 ha. 80% Merlot, 19% Cabernet Franc, 1% Cabernet Sauvignon. **Production:** 24,000 bottles*

You just have to glance at Bellevue's location to sense its potential. A lane winds up the slope from Angélus, passing through woodland, and emerges onto the plateau, close to Beau-Séjour-Bécot. Here stands the château and a fine park, a rarity in St-Emilion. It's an ancient property, which belonged to the Lacaze family from 1642 until 1938. In more recent times it has been owned by two Libournais families. Unfortunately the property was neglected and its vineyards overcropped. By the late 1990s the owners realized that Bellevue's wines lagged behind most other *grands crus classés*. To turn things around, they hired Nicolas Thienpont, the manager of Pavie-Macquin, and consultant Stéphane Derenoncourt to run the property. But they were unable to save it from demotion in 2006.

The average age of the vines is some forty years. Although there is already much Cabernet Franc planted, Thienpont is keen to plant more. Today the soils are ploughed and the viticulture is organic. Leaf removal and green-harvesting keep yields low: just thirty hl/ha in 2000. After treble sorting, the grapes go into the cement vats without crushing. Thienpont employs some micro-oxygenation to fix the colour and plump up the wine. The *marc* is pressed in a vertical press. The wine is aged on its fine lees for eighteen to twenty months with stirring and some *cliquage*. The proportion of new oak is high at eighty per cent. Blending is completed late, and Thienpont finds quality consistent throughout the vineyards, which, he believes, all have the potential to produce the *grand vin*.

Thienpont and Derenencourt made an immediate impact on the quality and style of the wines. The 1999 was light and fruity, whereas the 2000 was darker, denser, more exotic. But eyebrows were raised when prices doubled in 2000, an ambitious strategy for a property only just beginning its renaissance. Nonetheless the 2001 is a splendid wine, sweet and opulent on the nose; rich, sumptuous, and compact, it exhibits firm tannins without any toughness. The 2004 is rich and concentrated but lacks panache, and has a chewy, oaky finish.

Château Bellevue-Mondotte

*St-Emilion. Tel: 0557 554343. **Website:** www.vignoblesperse.com. **Owner:** Gérard Perse. Grand cru. 2.5 ha. 90% Merlot, 5% Cabernet Franc, 5% Cabernet Sauvignon. **Production:** 5,000 bottles*

The three parcels that make up the vineyards of this small property, which Perse bought in 2001, are intermingled with those of Pavie-Decesse up on the limestone plateau. The average age of the vines is forty-five years. Yields are exaggeratedly low at around fifteen hl/ha, and the winemaking is the same as for Perse's principal property, Pavie. With very small quantities produced, Perse admits it's a collector's wine, and he makes it *"parce que on s'amuse"* ("because it amuses me"). The only vintage I have tasted was the 2004 after a year in barrel; the colour was opaque, the nose tarry, and the palate highly concentrated, rich, plump, and lush, with hefty tannins but rather low acidity. It's undeniably impressive; how drinkable it is, is another matter.

Château Bellisle Mondotte

St-Laurent-des-Combes. Tel: 0557 512047. Owner: Escure family. Grand cru. 4.5 ha. 100% Merlot.
Production: 20,000 bottles

This estate near Tertre-Rôteboeuf is leased by Jean-Marie Bouldy, the owner of Bellegrave in Pomerol. The wine is fermented in concrete vats and aged in fifty per cent new oak. The 1998 is a pleasant wine with blackberry aromas; but it's one-dimensional and doesn't have much concentration or length. Aromatically, the 2001 is rather confected, and the palate has an earthy quality and some rusticity.

Château Bergat

St-Emilion. Tel: 0556 000070. Owner: Castéja family. Grand cru classé. 4 ha. 50% Merlot, 40% Cabernet Franc,
10% Cabernet Sauvignon. Production: 12,000 bottles

This property is not well known, both because of its modest production, and because it is overshadowed by Trottevieille, the *premier cru* in the portfolio of Borie-Manoux, the négociant house owned by the Castéja family. Bergat was rented by them from 1950, then bought outright in 1990. The vines are old and well located. Some are on the plateau near Trottevieille, and a large parcel is close to the town in the Fongaban valley. Vinification is entirely traditional, and the consultant oenologists, as at Trottevieille, are Gilles Pauquet and Denis Dubourdieu. Yet until 2004 the wine was disappointing. Even the 2000 is a touch herbaceous, with flavours of redcurrants and sour cherries. I prefer the richer 2001. The 2002 is rather hard and lacks charm, while the 2003 is fruity and attractive but lacks depth. There seems a marked leap in quality with the 2004, which has smoky, black-fruits aromas, and ample flesh, ripe tannins, and spiciness, all leading to a long, stylish finish.

Château Berliquet

St-Emilion. Tel: 0557 247048. Owner: Vicomte Patrick de Lesquen. Grand cru classé. 9 ha. 72% Merlot,
20% Cabernet Franc, 8% Cabernet Sauvignon. Production: 45,000 bottles. Second wine: Les Ailes de Berliquet

Berliquet doesn't lack good neighbours. Magdelaine, Canon, the Beauséjours, and Angélus, First Growths all, are close by. The loquacious Patrick de Lesquen is descended from the ancient St-Emilion family, the de Carles, who once owned considerable tracts of the region, including what is now Figeac. Berliquet, he explains, was highly reputed in the 1820s. When his mother inherited it in the 1950s from the last Comte de Carles, the vines were in dreadful shape. So she joined the cooperative, although the wine was always handled separately. Patrick de Lesquen's father died in 1967, and his mother three years later, so he, an investment banker based in Paris, returned to take over the property. In 1978 he reached an agreement with the cooperative to restore the *chai* at Berliquet, so the wine could be vinified on the spot. This stratagem made it possible for the wine to be promoted to *grand cru classé* in 1986. Ten years later he left the cooperative, and took on Patrick Valette as his consultant. Valette is better known for his winemaking activities in Chile, but has his own property in Bordeaux as well as some clients in the region.

The vineyard is a single parcel but not uniform in its terroir. About one-third is up on the limestone plateau, half is on the clay-limestone slopes descending from it, and the rest is on sandy clay soil lower down. Lesquen sees this diversity as an advantage, giving him and Valette a large palette of components. The vines are quite old, and exceptionally well ventilated. Valette introduced green-harvesting and leaf removal, sorting in both the vineyard and the winery, malolactic fermentation in new oak for the *grand vin*, and the creation of a second wine.

The wine undergoes a cold soak before fermentation with indigenous yeasts (except in 1999, when there was hail damage). If there is any dilution, the tanks are bled. The wines are aged in former quarries, where the barrels, of which sixty per cent are new, repose for sixteen months. Lesquen is insistent that he does not want a Parkerized style of wine. Although, he says, he respects other producers who think differently, he wants to retain Berliquet's typicity.

The only pre-Valette wine I have encountered is the 1995, which was a graceful, medium-bodied wine of considerable charm in its youth. Despite some chewy tannins, the 1997 has remarkably good fruit for a tricky year, and Lesquen observes that Berliquet often produces good wines in difficult vintages. The 1999 had to be picked earlier than was ideal because of hail damage; moreover, it is pure Merlot. It's a very attractive wine, nicely scented, and with ample bright fruit and charm, though admittedly little weight. The nose of the 2000 shows a good deal of oak, but no lack of cherry and raspberry fruit. It's a very complete wine, with fine concentration and length. The 2001 is even better, with oaky, chocolatey aromas, and on the palate great richness and vigour. The 2002 suffers by comparison, being broad and fleshy yet slightly hollow and lacking in persistence. The 2003 is very good, though not especially complex or long. The 2004 has flesh but it's easy-going, yet lacks flair, complexity, and structure. The 2005 is distinctly superior, rich and rounded on the palate, with a lively, minty finish.

Château Boutisse

*St-Christophe-des-Bardes. Tel: 0557 554890. Website: www.milhade.fr. **Owner:** Milhade family. Grand cru.*
*24 ha. 85% Merlot, 10% Cabernet Franc, 5% Cabernet Sauvignon. **Production:** 200,000 bottles.*
Second wine: Baron de Boutisse

The Milhades are an important Libournais family of négociants and property owners. They bought Boutisse in 1996. The vines are in a single parcel on undulating slopes up on the plateau; lower down the soil has a higher silt content. The St-Christophe area can be late-ripening, so the Milhades may switch to earlier-ripening rootstocks. Cabernet Sauvignon struggles to ripen here, and may eventually be replaced by Carmenère.

The fruit is picked in *cagettes*, sorted at the winery, then fermented in steel tanks. The Milhades buy their own wood and air-dry it; then craft the barrels at their own cooperage. Boutisse is aged for twelve to eighteen months in fifty per cent new oak. It's not a particularly exciting wine, but it is reasonably priced. The 1998 has charming aromas of wild strawberries, but it's sound rather than thrilling. The 2000 has a rather stewed nose, and perhaps too much grip given the modest fruit. The 2001 is plumper and more full-bodied, balanced by quite good acidity, and the ripe red-fruit flavours shine through on the finish. The 2003 is too jammy for my taste, but the 2004 from cask is silky and lively.

Château Les Cabannes

*St-Sulpice-de-Faleyrens. Tel: 0557 246286. **Owner:** Peter Kjellberg. Grand cru. 5 ha. 75% Merlot,*
*25% Cabernet Franc. **Production:** 25,000 bottles*

Peter Kjellberg, a tall, wiry Canadian, caught the wine bug young, studied oenology at Bordeaux University, and worked for ten years in Canon-Fronsac. Then in 1997 he bought three hectares in St-Sulpice. Today he has two more, plus two hectares of AC Bordeaux on more alluvial soil. The soil is sandy gravel, with parcels of clay subsoil that required new drainage. Only part of the wine is barrique-aged. It tends to be pure Merlot, which gives better results here than Cabernet Franc, and Kjellberg will reduce the latter. The wine is fresh, pretty, medium-bodied, with some easy-going charm. Kjellberg has the sense not to extract more than this modest terroir can give. Judging from the 1998 and 2000 vintages, the wine ages reasonably well despite its lack of evident structure.

Château Cadet-Bon

*St-Emilion. Tel: 0557 744320. Website: www.cadet-bon.com. **Owner:** Guy Richard. Grand cru.*
*6.5 ha. 70% Merlot, 30% Cabernet Franc. **Production:** 20,000 bottles*

Bernard Gans, who also owned Curé-Bon, bought this estate in 1992, saw it promoted to *grand cru classé* in 1996, and sold it to Guy Richard in 2001. Richard's origins are in grape-farming in the Cognac region, but he made his money as a supermarket entrepreneur, and retired early to return to his first passion. To bring his knowledge up to date, he studied oenology at Bordeaux University. In 2004 he hired Stéphane Derenoncourt as a consultant, and in 2005 embarked on a complete renovation of the estate buildings.

Only 4.6 hectares of the estate were classified as *grand cru classé*, so the remainder is used for Vieux Moulin du Cadet, which is vinified separately. The vines are in a single parcel between the house and the town, across the road. Since 2004 the soils have been ploughed and the use of herbicides has been stopped. Pruning has been altered from *guyot simple* to *guyot double*, a sensible if costly option to attain better quality. At the winery there are three sorting tables, and the grapes are not crushed. There is only a brief cold soak before fermentation in steel tanks. Part of the wine undergoes malolactic fermentation in barriques. Cadet-Bon is aged in one-third new oak for fifteen months in air-conditioned *chais*, with some *cliquage*.

My experience of this wine has been decidedly mixed. The 1994 was a severe disappointment in 2000, with a flat, bitter finish. In contrast, the 1996, when young, had a dense, damsony nose, and proved to be a big, swaggering wine with robust tannins – a touch rustic, but vigorous. The 1997 was light and simple but lacked distinction. The 2000 shows some opulence on the nose, while the palate is lush, with ample ripe tannins if little finesse. The 2001 has ample fruit and supple tannins, and more backbone than complexity. The 2002 has reduced aromas, and is slightly jammy and lacking in grip. The 2003 is overripe and has a hot, short finish. Clearly the first vintage by which the revived Cadet-Bon can be judged will be the 2004, which is concentrated and opulent, with ripe black fruits backed by sturdy tannins and finishing with balance and length. It seems regrettable that Richard's dedication was rewarded with demotion to *grand cru* in 2006.

Château Cadet-Piola

St-Emilion. Tel: 0557 744769. Website: www.chateaucadetpiola.com. **Owner:** *Alain Jabiol. Grand cru classé.*
7 ha. 51% Merlot, 28% Cabernet Sauvignon, 18% Cabernet Franc, 3% Malbec. **Production:** *35,000 bottles.*
Second wine: Chevaliers de Malte

This estate, named after a former mayor of Libourne, lies north of the town in a single parcel on sloping terrain. The vineyards used to be larger, but in the 1990s four hectares were sold to Larmande. The soil is clay-limestone over a layer of rock that, unusually for St-Emilion, is fairly porous. There is a good deal of Cabernet Sauvignon planted, and it apparently does ripen here. But the Jabiols are tempted to increase the proportion of Merlot, to give a wine that is easier to appreciate young.

The Jabiols bought the property in the early 1960s. The winemaker is Alain Jabiol's daughter Amélie, advised by consultant Gilles Pauquet. After a cold soak, the must is fermented with selected yeasts. Although there is both pumping over and *délestage*, the Jabiols are not seeking to make a very extracted wine. They use a vertical press, which is gentle enough to allow most of the press wine to be blended back. The wine is aged for up to eighteen months in one-third new oak, with some lees-stirring early on. The blend is made up late, and eggwhite-fined before bottling.

Cadet-Piola may not be the most fashionable of St-Emilions, but it's a wine I much enjoy. A bottle cuts a fine dash on the dinner table, thanks to the charming old label, in the fleshy, frivolous style of Boucher, depicting a youth brandishing a bottle while seducing a young woman who is not wearing all her clothes.

The 1994 is now at its peak, a well-balanced, medium-bodied wine with more fruit and length than many 1994s. The 1995 is eminently drinkable, gently oaky on the palate, the tannins integrated, and the finish fresh. The 1996 is rather dull, and the dense, chunky 1998 remains somewhat austere and surly, but the 2000, with its firm, plummy aromas, has more lushness and weight. The 2001 is similar, but has a touch more lift. The 2002 is inevitably leaner, but has stylish redcurrant and strawberry flavours, and much finesse. The 2004 is aromatic and reasonably concentrated but rather severe and lacks lift and personality.

The Jabiols also own Château de Pasquette, a *grand cru* located near Fonplégade but lower down the slope on rather sandy soils.

Château de Candale

*St-Laurent-des-Combes. Tel: 0557 744311. **Owner:** Stephen Adams. Grand cru. 11 ha. 80% Merlot,*
*20% Cabernet Franc. **Production:** 36,000 bottles. **Second wine:** Ch Roc de Candale*

Since 2002, this small estate has been under the same ownership and management as Fonplégade (*q.v.*). The vineyards are located on light clay-limestone soil near Tertre-Rôteboeuf. After thorough sorting, the fruit is fermented in wooden vats following a five-day cold soak. The *cuvaison* can be as protracted as forty-five days. Malolactic fermentation takes place in new oak, with lees-stirring during the *élevage*. The 2002 has attractive aromas of cherry and oak; there is plenty of plump fruit on the palate with chewy tannins and a vigorous finish. The 2004, tasted from cask after twelve months, has slightly overripe aromas, and shows a sweet red-fruits character and good acidity.

Château Canon

*St-Emilion. Tel: 0557 552345. **Website:** www.chateau-canon.com. **Owner:** Wertheimer family.*
*Premier grand cru classé (B). 18 ha. 75% Merlot, 25% Cabernet Franc. **Production:** 70,000 bottles.*
Second wine: Clos Canon

This substantial estate on the plateau close to the town owes its name to an eighteenth-century owner, Jacques Kanon, who bought and restored the property in 1760 before selling it to a local merchant, Raymond Fontémoing, in 1770. The Fontémoings retained Canon until 1857, when it was sold. In 1919 it came into the hands of the Fournier family. Under their stewardship its wines achieved a very high reputation. But the Fourniers encountered family problems that eventually obliged them to put their estates on the market. In 1996 it was bought by the Wertheimers of New York, owners of the Chanel group and Rauzan-Ségla in Margaux.

There was considerable surprise at the low price for which the Wertheimers had secured Canon. But, as they knew perfectly well, it was not the bargain it seemed. There were, as the Fourniers had made clear, severe problems that would require considerable investment to sort out. One of the most vexatious problems was TCA contamination within the winery. The new owners installed John Kolasa, who was already running Rauzan-Ségla, as Canon's new director. He soon ripped out all the old tanks in the winery and burnt all existing barrels in the *chai*. Now deprived of older barrels in which to age a portion of the new wine, Kolasa purchased second-fill barrels from Sociando-Mallet to make up the shortfall.

A potentially more dangerous problem was the subsidence within the quarries beneath the property. Pockets of clay within the limestone band were gradually disappearing, making the rock more susceptible to subsidence. Concrete pillars were swiftly constructed to support the roofs, which in turn supported the château and winery. Moreover, the quarries were malodorous, as they seemed to have served as Canon's drainage system. The caverns were cleaned up and new drainage installed.

Nor were the vineyards in good shape. Many vines were virused and needed to be replanted, and there were thousands of missing vines. This replanting affected one-third of the vineyards and inevitably reduced the vines' average age. To get his hands on some older vines, Kolasa bought Curé-Bon from Bernard Gans and, in a masterstroke, persuaded INAO to promote 3.5 hectares of the best parcels to *premier grand cru classé* status, allowing Canon to blend them into its *grand vin*. (A lesser parcel near Ripeau was not promoted, and a parcel near the petrol station on the road to Libourne was sold to Jonathan Maltus of Teyssier.)

When all the vines are in production, the vineyard area at Canon will rise to twenty-two hectares. There used to be some Cabernet Sauvignon, but Kolasa was not happy with it, and ripped it out. Although the majority of the vineyards are on the plateau, there are also some parcels on the slopes near Angélus and near Tertre Daugay.

The grapes are picked into *cagettes* with initial sorting in the vineyard, followed, since 2002, by further sorting at the winery. After light crushing, the grapes are forklifted up over the wooden vats, into which they fall by gravity. They are fermented with pumpovers and occasional *pigeage*. The best lots go through their malolactic fermentation in barrels, and the wine is aged in fifty to sixty-five per cent new oak for eighteen months. After the *élevage* the wine is eggwhite-fined but not filtered.

I have not tasted the celebrated postwar vintages. The 1971 in 2007 was gamey on the nose but still tight and concentrated; but fully ready to drink. In 2005 the 1975 had fragrant but rather herbaceous aromas, and lacked flesh and persistence. The 1979, tasted less recently, was a stern, charmless wine that clearly lacked ripeness. The 1980 in 2005 had some greenness on the nose, as well as some glacé cherry aromas; the acidity was harsh and the wine seemed well past its modest best. As for the 1982, two out of the three bottles I have come across were faulty. This is a shame, as the third was an impressive wine of profound concentration that still seemed quite youthful. The 1988 is also excellent, and its firm tannins don't obscure the sumptuous blackberry fruit. The 1989 seems more forward, with its sweet, leafy, cedary nose, and rounded, spicy fruit. I was disappointed by the 1990 in 1994 but have not tasted it since.

By 1995 there had been a complete change of gear. There was ample new oak on the nose, and the palate was sweet, sleek, almost brash, but with ripe tannins and good length. The 1996 seems a touch extracted, imposing but lacking some charm; but it's rich, concentrated, serious, harmonious, and long. The 1998 has developed a sweet, truffley, almost tarry nose, while the palate is rich and concentrated. The 1999 shows some austerity and a skeletal structure, but it's not unripe and fine acidity gives it good length. There is far more power on the mighty 2000, with its dense, oaky nose, intense black-cherry fruit, hints of bitter chocolate, and impressive length. The 2001 is very similar, though with a touch more freshness and perfume, and may well be better balanced. The 2002 comes across as a relative lightweight, but it's fresh and elegant. The 2003 is fleshy, supple, and surprisingly forward given its youth. Although medium-bodied and fresh, the 2004 has firm, chewy tannins and, at present, a distinct austerity that make it hard to assess its true potential.

The typicity of Canon still eludes me. The wines of the past decade have been hit and miss, with some fluctuations in style. This is hardly surprising, given the radical restructuring of the vineyards. Almost half the wine goes into Clos Canon, yet the *grand vin* has still to find its true form. Nonetheless, once written off as mediocre by some wine experts and connoisseurs, Canon is clearly back on track and can only improve further.

Château Canon-La-Gaffelière

St-Emilion. Tel: 0557 247133. Website: www.neipperg.com. Owner: von Neipperg family. Grand cru classé.
19.5 ha. 55% Merlot, 40% Cabernet Franc, 5% Cabernet Sauvignon. Production: 90,000 bottles.
Second wine: Neipperg Selection

This fine property, at the foot of the slope that descends southwards from the town, has been revived by Stephan von Neipperg. The dapper Neipperg, sporting a well-trimmed moustache and discreet cravat, is a well-known figure wherever fine wine is drunk. His appearance and charming manner seem reminiscent of a Parisian boulevardier, but his origins lie among the dark forests of Württemberg, where his family has lived since medieval times. The Neippergs are still landowners with extensive vineyards and forests. As one of many children, there was little to detain Graf Stephan in rural Württemberg, so he went to Paris to study politics and administration, and then spent a year in Montpellier in the early 1980s studying viticulture.

His father, Joseph-Hubert von Neipperg, had bought Canon-La-Gaffelière long before, in 1971. In the nineteenth century the estate had been known as La Gaffelière-Boitard. It had been owned from 1953 to 1969 by Pierre Meyrat, mayor of St-Emilion. Graf von Neipperg never lived here, but installed a *régisseur*. As a fluent French speaker, it seemed logical for Stephan himself to run the property. After a year in St-Emilion to familiarize himself with the region, he agreed in 1985 to move there permanently. His father had bought the stock at Canon-La-Gaffelière, so Stephan knew that great wines had been made here in the 1950s and 1960s. But from 1964 onwards, quality had declined: too much chemical fertilizer had been routinely employed and yields had been far too high. The 1956 frost had killed off many vines, so the vineyard was young, although five hectares of old Cabernet Franc had survived. Graf Stephan recognized the potential.

He renovated the buildings, replaced the large steel tanks with smaller wooden vats, and assembled a good team, including the young Stéphane Derenoncourt, who was winemaker here until his growing fame led him to set up his own consultancy. The first vintage with which Neipperg was truly satisfied was 1988. Renovating the winery was relatively simple; restoring the abused vineyards would take longer. There were three hectares on the slopes near La Gaffelière and Magdelaine. The venerable Cabernet Franc was planted between the slopes and the railway line. Lower down was a ten-hectare parcel on sandier soils that were too vigorous unless their productivity was ruthlessly curbed. No herbicides are used, and any fertilizers are organic. Neipperg prefers to control yields by very tight pruning, and regards green-harvesting as a last resort.

During harvest, there is scrupulous sorting in the vineyard and winery. The grapes ascend by conveyor belt to a platform over the tanks. Crushing is minimal, as Neipperg wants to prolong the fermentation. Since 1996 there has been some *pigeage* for a brief period. Neipperg is keen on micro-oxygenation, though its use is never formulaic. He was an early practitioner of malolactic fermentation in barriques, and doesn't worry if the process is protracted. The wine is aged for fourteen to eighteen months in fifty to seventy per cent new oak on the fine lees with some *cliquage*. Neipperg's guiding principle is simply to follow the wine, rather than impose winemaking practices on it. He is in no rush to accelerate its evolution. Similarly, although he fines with eggwhite, there is no rule about filtration.

Older vintages – between 1971 and 1987 – that I have tasted were unremarkable. The wines matured fast, were dilute, and lacked persistence. The 1988 is considerably better, with more succulence, spice, vigour, and length. The 1990 is more lush and velvety, and the perfumed nose has considerable charm; this is a lovely, stylish wine that will continue to age well. The 1992 was rather green, and the 1993 took a few years to find its feet, but matured into a surprisingly plump and harmonious wine. Despite numerous tastings, I have never found much pleasure in the over-extracted 1994. Far superior is the 1995, which is voluptuous if very oaky, and even in 2005 still seemed tight and youthful. The 1996 is a success, with vibrant black fruits on the nose, ample concentration, and a silky texture. The 1997 may be a touch extracted for the vintage, but it's a solid and full-bodied wine with plenty of life ahead.

Canon-La-Gaffelière certainly delivers the goods with its sumptuous 1998. Plums and woodsmoke mark the nose; there is splendid concentration, simply delicious fruit, and beautifully ripe acidity. The 1999 is another exercise in the super-ripe but not jammy Neipperg style, with no harsh tannins and a stylish finish. The 2000 is very marked by new oak, and although the palate is plump and concentrated and backed by chewy tannins, it has less persistence than the 1998. The 2001 had a surly youth, but by 2007 it was exhibiting luscious, almost candied aromas, a supple texture, ripe tannins, and fine freshness and length. At present the 2002 seems to have more flair, vigour, charm, and finesse. Despite the dangerously ultra-ripe aromas on the 2003, the wine is a success, with some spice and impressive length. The richly fruity 2004 has sweet, toasty aromas, and a palate that's broad and opulent if a touch extracted. Yet it has freshness too, as does the beautifully elegant as well as succulent 2005.

Stephan von Neipperg enjoys the challenge of taking an underperforming property and turning it around. This he has done triumphantly at Canon-La-Gaffelière and at his other St-Emilion properties of Clos de l'Oratoire and La Mondotte (*qq.v*), not to mention Château d'Aiguilhe in the Côtes de Castillon and his estate in Bulgaria. It's a remarkable achievement for a man still in early middle age, and he is clearly not done yet.

Château Cantin

*St-Christophe-des-Bardes. Tel: 0557 246573. Website: www.chateau-cantin.com. **Owner:** Jean Leprince (négociants). Grand cru. 30 ha. 65% Merlot, 25% Cabernet Franc, 10% Cabernet Sauvignon. **Production:** 150,000 bottles. Second wine: Vieux Ch des Combes*

This former Benedictine monastery was acquired after the Revolution by the Baron de Mauvezin and remained in the family until the early twentieth century, when it was bought by Alphonse Bisch and the Chamson family. New owners in the 1960s renovated the vineyards, yet Cantin did not gain much of a reputation. In 1999 it was acquired by the négociant house of Jean Leprince, which invested heavily in the large property and its buildings. Bernard Crebassa was installed as director, and he admits his dissatisfaction with vintages such as 2000 and 2002.

The extensive vineyards slope down toward a lake constructed in the 1960s. The soils are clay-limestone and sandy limestone. The best sectors are on the higher ground, and these are used for the *grand vin*. Before 1999 there was no ploughing and no selection, policies that Crebassa has reversed. Today the grapes are picked manually. After sorting the fruit is tipped into the vats without pumping. The *marc* is pressed in a modern vertical press. The wine is aged from twelve to eighteen months in one-third new oak.

Vintages such as 1989 and 1999 are quite hard and astringent. The 2000 shows black-cherry fruit and liquorice on the nose, yet the palate is lean and lacks flesh. The 2001 is significantly better, with more weight and concentration, even if the tannins are somewhat chunky. I was not shown the 2002, and the 2003 is a touch jammy on the nose, less so on the palate, which is juicy and concentrated. Crebassa would readily agree that it is still early days for the revived Cantin.

Château Cap de Mourlin

St-Emilion. Tel: 0557 746206. Website: www.vignoblescapdemourlin.com. Owner: Jacques Capdemourlin.
Grand cru classé. 14 ha. 65% Merlot, 25% Cabernet Franc, 10% Cabernet Sauvignon. Production: 70,000 bottles

This is an ancient property: there are records of wine being sold in 1647. Many years ago the property was divided between two brothers; each released the wine under the identical label, with just the Christian name of each proprietor to distinguish between the two bottlings. In 1982 the property was reunited under the present owner, who also owns Balestard-La-Tonnelle (*q.v.*) and other estates.

The vines, located north of the village, have a respectable average age of thirty-five years. The soil is clay-limestone over a subsoil of sand and *alios*. Vinification, since 2005, has begun with a cold soak under dry ice, followed by fermentation in squat steel tanks, usually with natural yeasts. The wine is aged in fifty per cent new oak for fifteen months, without systematic racking and with some lees-stirring.

By 2007 the 1995 had developed delicate, leafy aromas, and was still fresh; it's a straightforward wine, not that complex, and now at its peak. The 1996 seems better, with rich, oaky aromas encircling plum and blackcurrant fruit; the palate is fleshy and opulent. The 1998 is rich but chunky and lacks some elegance and persistence. The 2000 is a classic St-Emilion, with scents of plums and black cherries, while the palate is lush, full-bodied, and powerful. The 2001 is even better, with its sweet, stylish nose, a velvety texture, and a firm, spicy structure. The 2002 is more austere and clearly less ripe, with some edgy acidity and a lack of charm. The 2003 has a fresh, juicy attack, but the firm tannins give a rather austere finish. The 2004 is a medium-bodied wine with appealing fruitiness, and some pronounced tannins on the finish.

Château Carteau Côtes Daugay

St-Emilion. Tel: 0557 247394. Owner: Jacques Bertrand. Grand cru. 16 ha. 65% Merlot, 30% Cabernet Franc,
5% Cabernet Sauvignon. Production: 90,000 bottles. Second wine: Ch Vieux Lescours

Jacques Bertrand is a former president of the St-Emilion Syndicat, and is gradually handing over his property to his children Anne-Marie, Catherine, and Bruno. The Côtes Daugay refer to the slopes below Tertre Daugay, although the Bertrand vineyards are much lower down, on clay-limestone and sandy gravel soils. Vinification remains traditional and the wine is aged for fifteen months in fifty per cent new oak. The 2001 has attractive aromas of black cherries and chocolate, but the wine is fairly light for the vintage. The 2002 is also quite perfumed, and the palate is fresh, supple, and accessible. The 2003 has confected red-fruits aromas; it's a medium-bodied, easy-going wine with pleasant fruit but it's marred by a dry, short finish.

Carteau is attractive and reliable, and far from expensive, but it doesn't set the pulses racing.

Château Le Castelot

*St-Sulpice-de-Faleyrens. Tel: 0557 514186. Website: www.j-janoueix-bordeaux.com. **Owner**: Jean-François Janoueix.*
*Grand cru. 9 ha. 70% Merlot, 20% Cabernet Franc, 10% Cabernet Sauvignon. **Production**: 35,000 bottles*

This property, along the main road from Libourne to Bergerac, was bought by the ebullient Jean-François Janoueix in 1978. The château dates from the late sixteenth century, and Henri IV took shelter here in 1578. The wine ages in thirty per cent new barriques. I have limited experience of the wine. The 1990 was tannic and rather harsh, with rich fruit but little finesse. The 2003 is lacklustre.

Château Chauvin

*St-Emilion. Tel: 0557 247625. Website: www.chateauchauvin.com. **Owners**: Béatrice Ondet and Marie-France Février.*
*Grand cru classé. 15 ha. 75% Merlot, 20% Cabernet Franc, 5% Cabernet Sauvignon. **Production**: 60,000 bottles.*
Second wine: La Borderie de Chauvin

Located in the northwest sector, near Pomerol, Chauvin was bought in 1891 by Victor Ondet, a master dyer from Libourne. His descendants are two sisters. Marie-France Février, a former anaesthetist, looks after the vineyards, and Béatrice Ondet, a former pharmacist, is the winemaker. With very different personalities and a fair degree of combativeness between them, they make an engaging double act.

Although the vineyards are fragmented, they surround the house on sandy soil over a clay subsoil, with traces of clinker. Over one-third of the vines are over fifty years old. In 1998 the sisters bought a 2.3-hectare parcel across from the house. Here too the vines, in a field blend that included some Malbec, were very old. When they bought the parcel, it was classified only as *grand cru*, but after the sisters had demonstrated to INAO the quality of the wine they vinified separately from it, permission was granted to incorporate its wine into Chauvin.

The vines are cultivated according to *lutte raisonnée* principles. The grapes are sorted repeatedly, cold-soaked, then fermented in small steel tanks, with pumpovers and *pigeage*. Only natural yeasts are used. Although Béatrice Ondet does use some micro-oxygenation, it is not systematic. The wine is aged in a proportion of new oak that varies from thirty-five to sixty per cent. There is no systematic fining or filtration.

The 1990 is lush but lacks some flair and concentration. The 1995 is more impressive, with its voluptuous nose, its sleek and sophisticated stylishness, and its persistent oaky finish. The 1998 is similar but more explosively and meatily aromatic, and with more lushness and savoury character. The 1999 is a surprise for a vintage often outgunned by 1998 and 2000: it's plump and juicy, with a silky texture, luscious fruit, and good length, and with more finesse than the assertive but more foursquare 2000. The 2001 has dense aromas, with a trace of liquorice; the palate is both sumptuous and chewy, but bright acidity and delicious fruit keep it lively. The 2002, with its aromas of sour cherry and redcurrants, is leaner and lacks some complexity, though it is spicy and concentrated. The 2003 is drab. The fleshy 2004 has similar aromas, and a palate that's fresh and silky; it's a wine of rude vigour rather than elegance, but has fruit and personality. Chauvin doesn't enjoy quite the reputation it should. The sisters are conscientious stewards of their property and make splendid wines.

Château Cheval Blanc

*St-Emilion. Tel: 0557 555555. Website: www.chateau-cheval-blanc.com. **Owners**: Bernard Arnault and*
*Albert Frère. Premier grand cru classé (A). 37 ha. 58% Cabernet Franc, 42% Merlot. **Production**: 120,000 bottles.*
Second wine: Le Petit Cheval

Compared to other great Bordeaux estates, Cheval Blanc is a newcomer. The land was originally part of Figeac, but it seems the vineyard was created in the 1830s. It was only in 1853 that the name of Cheval Blanc was first used. By 1870 the property had attained its present dimensions, other than a parcel exchanged with La Dominique in the 1970s. The estate was sold in 1998 to its present owners. Although Arnault controls the luxury-goods group LVMH, Cheval Blanc is a personal acquisition on his part.

The sale brought no great upheaval at the estate. For decades the manager had been Jacques Hébrard, who had married into the family; he retired in 1989 and was succeeded by his son Dominique. In 1991 Pierre Lurton was hired as director, and Dominique Hébrard left to pursue a future at other Libournais properties. Gilles Pauquet stayed on as consultant oenologist, but his services have been supplemented by those of Denis Dubourdieu.

The terroir at Cheval Blanc is highly distinctive. It lies in the westerly part of the region, a stone's throw from Pomerol, and technical director Kees Van Leeuwen says the soil resembles that at Trotanoy. There are three soil types at Cheval Blanc: forty per cent consists of gravel over a clay subsoil, forty per cent is deep gravel, and the remainder is sand over clay. This adds up to a precocious terroir. The Cabernet Franc for which Cheval Blanc is so noted and which gives the wine its structure has been there essentially from the outset. Lurton points out that without its presence in the blend, the warm microclimate of Cheval Blanc would result in an opulent but overripe Merlot-based wine.

The Merlot is planted in various sectors, as a clay *croupe* traverses the property. There is a tiny amount of Cabernet Sauvignon and Malbec in the vineyards, but they are never included in the *grand vin*. The average age of the vines is some forty years, with some Cabernet Franc dating from 1920. Density is high, at up to 8,000 vines per hectare. The vineyards are ploughed, no chemical herbicides are used, and the use of fertilizers is minimal. Pruning is severe and green-harvesting reduces the crop further to five or six bunches per vine. Low yields are aided by the low vigour of the stony soil.

The grapes are sorted before and after destemming. The winery operates essentially by gravity, although Lurton wonders whether such gentle handling makes much sense when the must is about to be pumped over during fermentation. There is no cold soak as such, but there is a brief pre-fermentation maceration at 20°C (68°F). The must is vinified in steel and cement tanks. A pneumatic press extracts more juice from the *marc*, and around twelve per cent of press wine goes into the blend. The press wine and some other lots go through malolactic fermentation in barriques, but this is not systematic. Blending takes place over the winter, and the wine is aged overall for fourteen to eighteen months in new oak from five coopers, with regular racking. The final wine is eggwhite-fined but unfiltered.

The second wine, Petit Cheval, was introduced in 1988. It is aged for twelve months in fifty per cent new oak. On average just over half the crop is released as Cheval Blanc.

Two ancient vintages came my way in the mid-1980s. The 1924, with its piercing fragrance and soft, elegant texture, was a lovely old wine by no means on its last legs; and the 1928, browning and a touch volatile, still retained sweet fruit on the palate, a rounded texture, and a long, elegant finish. Ten years ago the 1943 was losing its fruit, and there was some oxidation on the nose, yet the wine still had intensity and vinosity. The 1945 was bedevilled by high volatile acidity and was actually pasteurized to keep it under control. The remedy worked, and this vintage, drunk twice recently, is magnificent. The nose is intense, with aromas of mint, coffee, and meat extract; the intensity carries over onto the silky palate, which has lingering sweetness and a bright finish.

The 1947 is a legendary Cheval Blanc. I have tasted the 1946 and 1948 but, as luck would have it, the 1947 has eluded me. And with a current auction price of around 50,000 pounds sterling per case, it will continue to do so. The 1946, however, turned out to be remarkably good when tasted blind from magnum. The nose was intensely elegant and delicate, yet the palate was assertive, with powerful tannins and great concentration, a velvety texture, and splendid length. The 1948, tasted blind alongside the 1946, had begun to fade. There was a certain leafiness on the nose, with tobacco aromas; the palate had a delicate, leafy charm, but with aeration it began to unknit. I last tasted the 1949 twenty years ago, when it put in a schizoid performance, with a weird, almost cabbagey nose, but a palate that was rich, earthy, and strong, with terrific intensity on the finish. The 1950, tasted at the same time, was aromatic but attenuated, and despite some sweet fruit the finish was dry.

The 1955 was splendid in the 1980s and by 2002 had lost none of its fruit or stylishness. The nose was rich and cedary, with some chocolatey tones; while the palate was immensely concentrated, simply bursting with fruit yet with fine acidity and a firm finish. In the late 1980s the 1959 was still going strong: reserved on the nose, but sweet, rich, and finely balanced. The 1961 in 2002 did not look especially mature, and the nose was still tight, with a slight gaminess; it was a rich, voluptuous wine, with great concentration and some earthy tannins. The 1964 (in magnum) was in fine form in 2002, with a lively, cedary, chocolatey nose, and remarkable vigour and brightness – perhaps not the most complex Cheval Blanc, but still fresh and giving great pleasure.

The 1970s were not an outstanding period for Cheval Blanc. By the late 1980s the 1970 was distinctly evolved, with cedary aromas and some earthiness on the palate. Also disappointing is the 1971, which, in 2002, was medium-bodied and fading. The 1975, drunk from double magnum in 2007, had an intensely perfumed nose, but was still austere, though surprisingly spicy and pungent. I enjoyed the 1978 in 1993 but have not tasted it since. The 1979 was harsh and dry even in its youth, and the 1980 seemed to have better fruit. The 1981 has a splendid nose with smoky oak and hints of cloves, but the palate, while elegant, is somewhat lean and there are astringent notes.

In a blind tasting ten years ago I took the 1982 for a great Pomerol – not such a stupid guess when one considers the proximity of Pomerol to Cheval Blanc. Ten years later it had retained that Pomerol sensuousness, with a seductively voluptuous nose, a gorgeous velvety texture, and a discreet tannic backbone supporting the luxurious fruit, yet with fine acidity giving exceptional length. I have numerous ecstatic notes on the 1982 and 1985, with aromas of truffle, spice, and coffee, and a sumptuous fleshy palate with succulence and spice. I marginally prefer the 1985 for it sheer sexiness. I have had varied luck with the 1989, which on one occasion seemed lean and past its best, on others seemed dense and lacking in Cheval Blanc's customary elegance. Fortunately the 1990 is back on tremendous form. When young the nose seemed overripe, but more recently it has recovered its poise and charm, while the fruit quality is lush yet exquisite.

The 1994 lacks body and seemed raw when young, but the 1995 is a great wine, intensely fragrant and refined, with a similar delicacy and silkiness on the palate, which retains a wonderful freshness and spiciness through to the long finish. Although discreetly fragrant, the 1996 pales in comparison with its predecessor, and I find its damsony fruit in conflict with a slight astringency. The 1997 is surprisingly burly. The 1998 is magnificent, with a sumptuous nose of plums and chocolate, but always with that intense perfume so typical of Cheval Blanc, and, despite the fruit concentration, there is exemplary freshness and acidity and an underlying elegance. Tasted shortly before bottling, the 1999 was excellent, with sweet toasty aromas. Merlot dominated in that vintage, giving a more supple and overtly fruity wine than is usual at Cheval Blanc.

In 2000 the fruit, especially the Cabernet Franc, was even riper than in 1998. So the aromas were super-ripe, and, despite the wine's richness and concentration, the texture was slightly soupy and lacking some zest. The 2001 had unusual plum aromas, and the oak was quite marked, while the palate seems understated though balanced and compact; the wine had probably not recovered from recent bottling. The 2002 vintage may not have a great reputation, but the Cheval Blanc is lovely: with rich, sweet, black-cherry aromas, a plumpness balanced by spice, good acidity, and an overall stylishness. The 2003 is disappointing, with uncharacteristically baked aromas, a fair amount of tannin and some astringency. Cheval Blanc is back on form with the 2004. The nose is already complex, with toasty aromas of ripe plums and blackberries, while the palate shows a seamless texture, and a lively quality that cuts the evident richness and concentration. From cask, both the 2005 and 2006 are marked by perfume, concentration, and finesse; the former was considerably more impressive.

At a recent dinner party organized in Bordeaux by some leading young winemakers, our host, who had better remain nameless, opined that Cheval Blanc was vastly overrated. That I do not share this heretical view should be apparent from my comments above, but I do concede that Cheval Blanc often does not show well young. I am not sure why. Perhaps it is the high proportion of Cabernet Franc that imposes its structure and tannins on the wine. At *primeur* tastings, in particular, when colleagues all around me are swooning, I sometimes find myself wondering what the fuss is about. Five or ten years later I start swooning myself. A great Cheval Blanc is about perfume and texture. It can be opulent and powerful, but not always. It can have an intense delicacy that miraculously does not impair the wine's ability to age majestically. For me Cheval Blanc is the most mysterious of the First Growths, the wine I find hardest to pin down. Yet at its best, it is incomparable.

18. St-Emilion II

Clos Badon Thunevin

St-Sulpice-de-Faleyrens. Tel: 0557 550913. Website: www.thunevin.com. Owner: Jean-Luc Thunevin.
Grand cru. 6.5 ha. 70% Merlot, 30% Cabernet Franc. Production: 12,000 bottles

This property was bought by local négociant Jean-Luc Thunevin, the creator of Valandraud, in 1998. It lies on sandy and gravelly soil on the flatter land below Pavie. Some of the vines are planted at a density of 8,000 vines per hectare. It is aged in new oak for eighteen months. Thunevin says the wine is always good but never great or especially concentrated, because of the soil. The 2001 was decidedly overripe as well as tannic, and thus rather fatiguing. The 2002 is better balanced, though the nose is dominated by smoky oak; the palate is quite savoury yet lacks some substance.

Clos de ia Cure

St-Etienne-de-Lisse. Tel: 0557 247718. Owner: Pierre Bouyer. Grand cru. 6.5 ha. 75% Merlot,
15% Cabernet Sauvignon, 10% Cabernet Franc. Production: 35,000 bottles

This estate is under the same ownership as Château Milon (q.v.). Clos de la Cure is located on higher ground, not far from Fleur Cardinale and Pressac. The vineyards, some of which date back to the 1920s, are cultivated and the grapes vinified in the same way as at Milon, but with a slightly higher proportion of new oak: around forty per cent. I find these wines somewhat rustic and austere. Of vintages from 1999 onwards, the 2000 is rather green and light, the 2003 is hefty and lacks elegance, and the 2002 is hard. The best of recent vintages is the 2001, which has rich black-fruits aromas, and ample fruit if not much zest.

Clos Fourtet

St-Emilion. Tel: 0557 247090. Website: www.closfourtet.com. Owner: Philippe Cuvelier. Premier grand cru classé (B).
19 ha. 85% Merlot, 10% Cabernet Sauvignon, 5% Cabernet Franc. Production: 80,000 bottles.
Second wine: La Closerie de Fourtet

This fine property with its late-eighteenth-century château could hardly be closer to the town. For many decades it was owned by négociant families, and its wine sometimes slipped from view. Then in 2000 it was sold to Philippe Cuvelier, a good-humoured, boisterous businessman based in northern France. He does not claim to be a great wine expert, but from the outset he was determined to improve the reputation of Clos Fourtet. He retained the services of its winemaker since 1991, the witty and assured Tony Ballu. Cuvelier's son Matthieu is also increasingly involved in running the estate.

From 1917 until the 1940s Clos Fourtet was owned by the Ginestet family. In 1948 the Ginestets gave the estate to François Lurton in exchange for the Lurtons' share of Château Margaux, thus strengthening the Ginestets' hold on the First Growth. Rather to Cuvelier's chagrin, Ginestet took all the stock of old vintages of Clos Fourtet away with him. In the 1980s the estate was run by Pierre Lurton, who in 1991 became director of Cheval Blanc. Cuvelier's purchase meant that for the first time since 1917, the château was, after extensive renovations, once again inhabited.

Most of the vineyards lie, of course, on the limestone plateau, with just a thin topsoil of clay over the rock. Five hectares are situated farther north near Cadet-Piola, but little of that wine is used for the *grand vin*. Ballu points out that this sector has been part of Clos Fourtet since the eighteenth century. The vineyards overall are fairly young, as two-thirds of the property was replanted in 2001. Green-harvesting has been practised here since 1992, and Ballu likes to see eight bunches remaining on each vine. He also removes the "wings" from the side of each bunch, to give the remaining juice more eventual concentration. No herbicides have been used since 2002.

The grapes are picked into *cagettes* and thoroughly sorted. There is no crushing and the grapes descend into the steel and wooden vats by gravity. After a moderate cold soak, fermentation is usually sparked off by the indigenous yeasts. Ballu favours manual *pigeage*, and the *cuvaison* can last thirty days. The *marc* is pressed in a vertical press, and after malolactic fermentation in barriques, the wine is aged in eighty per cent new oak for fifteen to eighteen months. Under the Lurtons the wine was aged in entirely new oak, but Ballu has reduced the proportion, and may reduce it further yet. There is no micro-oxygenation during the *cuvaison*, but if there is any reduction during the *élevage*, he will employ it then. The barrels are stored in the former quarries beneath the vineyards. Apparently ventilation is good enough for this to be done without risk from excessive humidity.

I encountered the 1945 Clos Fourtet in a blind tasting in 1995. It showed sweet flowery aromas, and intense ripeness, pungency, and strength; not the most subtle of wines but one with character and force. I have tasted the 1947 twice recently, and it is magnificent. The nose is sumptuous, with marked meat and coffee aromas, as well as intense ripe fruit; the richness and intensity are mirrored on the palate, together with tones of mint and spice and exceptional length. The 1952 was still going strong in 2005, with plump fruit and cinnamon on the nose, as well as some woody tones; the acidity is a bit high, giving the wine a lean structure, and it remains tight and long. Thereafter no Clos Fourtet came my way until the dim, dry 1980. The 1982 showed initial generosity on nose and palate, with a crushed-fruits character; with bottle-age its depth and concentration mellowed out into a leaner, more high-toned style. There are blackberry scents on the 1985, but the wine, though sleek, lacks grip and complexity.

The 1988 has retained its youth. The cherry-pie nose is restrained, and the palate quite sweet and concentrated, with ample oak and enticing freshness and balance. The 1989 has evolved well. The nose is complex, with aromas of leaves, mint, rubber tyres, and coffee; it's not especially concentrated, but the tannins are fine and it's elegant rather than fleshy. The 1990 is more succulent, being a plump, supple wine with delicious fruit and ripe tannins. By 2007 the 1995 had lush cherry aromas but the palate, although supple, was surprisingly feeble and lacking in structure. The 1997 is lush, plump, and chewy, an honourable effort for the vintage. The 1998 has been sumptuous from the outset, its fruit framed by tannins and by acidity that give the wine vigour and elegance. The medium-bodied 1999 has atypical redcurrant aromas, and a lean, edgy palate. The 2000 has always had gorgeous aromas of blackberries, ripe cherries, and plums, and it's rich and rounded, with quite powerful tannins. Yet it's not as long as one would expect, adding up to a very good but not exceptional 2000.

The 2001 is rather closed and inexpressive, but there's considerable power and extract here, with the fruit blasting its way through to a strong, chewy finish. The 2002 is very successful; although quite tannic and austere, no astringency ruffles the elegant fruitiness. I prefer it to the slightly baked 2003, which is reasonably harmonious but has only modest acidity. By 2007, the 2004 was still a bit raw, despite its upfront fruit; the tannins still overwhelm the fruit on the rather dour finish, but it seems probable that the fruit will emerge victorious in time.

Although very good wines were made here in the 1980s and 1990s, there seems to be a greater consistency in the present century. As the vines become more mature, there is no reason why Clos Fourtet shouldn't take its place among the very best growths of St-Emilion.

In addition to the second wine, there is an alternative bottling of the same wine under the name of Marcialis de Fourtet, which is a Lurton exclusivity; the name has been retained so as to avoid confusing the long-term Lurton clientele.

Clos des Jacobins

St-Emilion. Tel: 0557 247014. Owner: Bernard Decoster. Grand cru classé. 8.5 ha. 75% Merlot, 23% Cabernet Franc,
2% Cabernet Sauvignon. Production: 40,000 bottles. Second wine: Prieuré des Jacobins

Driving from St-Emilion toward Libourne, you soon pass Clos des Jacobins on the left. It's an old property renowned since the eighteenth century, when the Laveau family were the owners. In 1964 it joined the group of estates owned by the Cordier négociant house. In 2001 it was bought, together with Château La Commanderie (*q.v.*), by the *parfumier* Gérald Frydman. He brought in Hubert de Boüard of Angélus as a consultant, and under his advice restructured the vineyards and put in new drainage; they installed a row of wooden fermenters and adopted a more modern vinification than under Cordier. Yields were sharply reduced, and far more new oak was used to age the wines. However, by late 2004 Frydman was experiencing some financial difficulties, and sold both properties to the present owner, the cousin of Dominique Decoster of Fleur Cardinale. Bernard Decoster has entrusted the management of both properties to his son Thibault and Thibault's wife Magali. Both are young, eager, and highly committed. Hubert de Boüard has stayed on as consultant.

The vines are on clay-limestone and sandy limestone soils in a single parcel near Grand-Mayne, apart from 0.6 hectares close to Angélus. The average age of the vines is thirty years, and some sectors are eighty years old. That average age would be greater had not Frydman replanted three hectares in 2001. The use of fertilizers has been stopped, and the vines are cultivated according to *lutte raisonnée*, with herbicides used only beneath the rows.

After harvesting in *cagettes*, the fruit is sorted, cold-soaked under dry ice, and fermented with pumpovers and *pigeage*. Malolactic fermentation takes place in new oak, where the wine remains for eighteen months. However, Decoster may reduce the proportion to eighty per cent in future. The wine is left on the fine lees for as long as possible to minimize the rackings. After eggwhite-fining, Clos des Jacobins is bottled without filtration.

Vintages from the Cordier years – 1985, 1990, 1992, 1995, 1998 – were always well made and attractive, but lacked grip, structure, and excitement. Already by 2000 there was a clear improvement; this is a stylish wine with impressive fruit and fine potential. With the 2001 the influence of Hubert de Boüard was making itself felt, with more opulent, plummy aromas and flavours, greater concentration, and fine length. The nose of the 2002 is a touch confected and forced, but has considerable richness and ripeness. The 2003 is overdone, with jammy aromas and little finesse. The 2004 has spicy red-fruits aromas, and is a medium-bodied, supple wine that has gained in zest and persistence since bottling. The tannic 2005 is splendid, with a joyous fruitiness and a sumptuous character not previously seen at Clos des Jacobins.

These are early days for the revived Clos des Jacobins. But already the determination of the new owners and the advice of de Boüard are making an impact.

Clos la Madeleine

St-Emilion. Tel: 0557 553803. Website: www.closmadeleine.com. Owner: SOGEFI investment group.
Grand cru. 2.2 ha. 75% Merlot, 25% Cabernet Franc. Production: 8,000 bottles

This small property enjoys a spectacular location on south-facing slopes adjacent to Bélair. It was owned by the Pistouley family until 1992, when it changed hands. New fermentation tanks were installed and the wine was aged in fifty per cent new barriques. Yet in 1996 the Clos was demoted from *grand cru classé*. The wine continues to disappoint. The 1995 was light and fresh, but lacked any complexity. Nor was the 1998, another fine vintage, much better, showing a slight meatiness on the nose, and a soft, dull palate. In contrast, the 2000 is properly voluptuous on the nose, and although the wine is not that concentrated, it is fresh, enjoyable, and forward. There are light, smoky, cherry aromas on the 2002, which has the merit of typicity; it is medium-bodied and quite lively. Initial tastings of the 2005 suggested another easy-going wine that lacks concentration. Although not especially rich or weighty, the 2006 seemed fresh and balanced from cask.

Clos de l'Oratoire

*St-Emilion. Tel: 0557 247133. Website: www.neipperg.com. **Owner:** Graf von Neipperg. Grand cru classé.*

*10 ha. 90% Merlot, 5% Cabernet Sauvignon, 5% Cabernet Franc. **Production:** 50,000 bottles*

Like Canon-La-Gaffelière (*q.v.*), this property is owned and run by Stephan von Neipperg. The wines are actually made at Peyreau nearby, but in a different cellar. Until the 1960s Oratoire formed part of Peyreau, but the better section was separated in the 1960s and, unlike Peyreau, soon made wine good enough to deserve promotion in 1969. The Neippergs bought both properties in 1991. The vines lie on a gentle slope of clay-limestone, with more sand at the foot of the incline. The harvest is manual, in *cagettes*, and the grapes are sorted before and after destemming. They are fermented in wooden vats with *pigeage*, mirroring the process followed at Canon-La-Gaffelière. The wine is aged in eighty per cent new oak for about eighteen months. There is neither fining nor filtration.

Clos de l'Oratoire is marked by its very high proportion of Merlot. It is also the fruit of a fairly cold soil that does not always shine in cooler years. But when all goes well, this is an exuberant, fleshy, fruity wine with a sensuous appeal. The oldest vintage I have tasted was the 1993, which was lively if not exciting. The 1994 is rather dense and extracted, and I don't see it improving with further ageing. With the 1995, Clos de l'Oratoire hit its stride, being aromatically lush and charming, with a plump texture supporting the plummy fruit. The 1996 is close in quality, though a touch extracted and dense. The 1997 is suffused in oak, and although rich and concentrated, seems rather thick and fatiguing. The 1998 absorbs the new oak far better, and the palate is lush and very marked by Merlot, although there are firm tannins on the finish. The 1999 is equally lush on the nose, and is also forward, with plump, sweet fruit, and ample concentration and vigour.

The 2000 is oaky on the nose, with an odd dill tone too; although only medium-bodied, this is still quite tight and spicy, with plums and pepper on the finish. The 2001 comes close to overripeness; the nose is plump and seductive, the palate luscious and rounded, yet with fair acidity. There is slight greenness on the nose of the 2002, though the palate is more fleshy; but it can't match the charm and opulence of the 2001. The 2003, which has super-ripe aromas, is evolving fast, showing very attractive fruit but little structure or length. In its lushness, the 2004 resembles the 2001, but has even more weight and density; it seemed forward in 2007 but has the stuffing to age well. The super-ripe 2005 may not be that complex or subtle, but it has delicious fruit and impeccable length.

Clos St Julien

*St-Emilion. Tel: 0557 247205. **Owner:** Catherine Papon-Nouvelle. Grand cru. 1.2 ha. 50% Merlot,*

*50% Cabernet Franc. **Production:** 3,500 bottles*

Blink and you'll miss it, as you drive out of the town toward Montagne and pass this tiny property on your right opposite the Gendarmerie. Mme. Papon-Nouvelle took over the family properties in 1998, and made a clean break with the practices of her father. He had machine-harvested, and made substantial quantities of wine, whereas her approach was more quality-oriented. The once dilapidated *chai* has been restored, and the 2005 was the first vintage vinified here in half a century.

The soil thinly covers the limestone rock below. After careful selection, the wine is aged in new oak on the lees but without stirring. Mme. Papon-Nouvelle finds that the Cabernet Franc needs more time to open out than the Merlot. Her aim as winemaker is to retain as much fruit as possible, so she is loath to intervene unless she considers it absolutely necessary.

The 2002 already showed the results of the pains she is taking. Although rather too oaky on the nose, there was ample blackcurrant and blackberry fruit, while the palate was almost overwhelming in its intensity and ripeness. The 2003 is in a similar, rather overwrought style, but has even more density and extract, resulting in a rather heavy wine that lacks vigour.

Clos St-Martin

*St-Emilion. Tel: 0557 247109. Website: www.vignoblesreiffers.com. **Owner:** Sophie Fourcade and family. Grand cru classé.*

*1.3 ha. 70% Merlot, 20% Cabernet Franc, 10% Cabernet Sauvignon. **Production:** 6,000 bottles*

Sophie Fourcade is part of the Reiffers family, who have owned properties here since the seventeenth century. Côte de Baleau (*q.v.*) is the headquarters. She has been making the wines since 1997. Clos St-Martin has been in the family since 1850, and consists of a single parcel close to the cemetery and Canon. The vines are on a southwest-facing clay-limestone slope, and their average age is thirty-five years. The difficulty of working such a small property, she explains, is that you can't blend different parcels, so everything needs to be good. Michel Rolland is the consultant oenologist, so the vinification reflects his style. After a cold soak, the must is fermented with some micro-oxygenation. Malolactic fermentation takes place in barriques, and the wine is aged in new oak and blended late.

In a blind tasting in 1998, the 1995 vintage delivered a powerful, lively, peppery wine of great individuality that seemed destined for a long evolution. The 2000 seems overripe with a good deal of sweet oak; the palate is better balanced, yet doesn't have the expected opulence. The 2001 is another blockbuster, with smoky, gamey aromas, and a supple texture almost undermined by massive though ripe tannins. The 2002 is almost as dense, a tight, tannic, powerful wine that will need years to reach its peak. the 2003 is chunky and blunt, while the extracted 2004 has sufficient fruit concentration to ensure a long future. Overall Clos St-Martin packs a punch. On the verge of excess, its wines are nonetheless persuasive in their fruit and structure.

Château La Clotte

*St-Emilion. Tel: 0557 246685. Website: www.chateaulaclotte.com. **Owner:** Nelly Moulierac. Grand cru classé.*

*4 ha. 80% Merlot, 15% Cabernet Franc, 5% Cabernet Sauvignon. **Production:** 15,000 bottles*

This delightful little estate dates its modern history back to 1912, when it was acquired by the Chailleau family. In the early 1960s it was leased to J.P. Moueix, but in 1990 Nelly Moulierac, *née* Chailleau, took the management back into her own hands. At first she was advised by Stéphane Derenoncourt, but from 2002 she felt confident enough, as she puts it, to fly with her own wings.

The vines are located in the small Fongaban valley close to the town, with the major parcel on the clay-limestone slopes opposite Pavie-Macquin, and a smaller parcel on the plateau behind the house. There are different expositions and soil types, but in general the soil is quite deep and the vines never suffer from hydric stress. The vines are old too, with an average age of forty years. The soil is ploughed, and the vines are deleafed and green-harvested.

The winery is within the tunnels beneath the limestone plateau. The entire crop is vinified in three cement tanks. Thus there is no practical possibility for a second wine, forcing her to ensure the quality is uniformly high. After sorting, there is a cold soak and a lengthy *cuvaison*, with pumpovers, *pigeage*, and some *délestage*. The high ripeness in recent vintages has persuaded her to give up relying on indigenous yeasts, as she fears stuck fermentations. The wine is aged for sixteen months in fifty per cent new barriques with a little lees-stirring.

Nelly Moulierac recalls that La Clotte was a perfumed wine in the past and she wants it to stay that way. She doesn't want aromas or flavours derived from overripeness, nor is she aiming for super-concentration. Her first vintage, 1990, was a bit earthy and drab when young, but I have not tasted it recently. The 1996 was supple and rounded but had a slightly dry finish. Sweet truffley aromas mark the 1998, which is medium-bodied, supple, and balanced. The 2000 has a sweet, minty, oaky nose; it's unusually fresh and stylish for the vintage, with a supple texture and a light, chocolatey finish. The 2001 is better, with smoky, black-fruits aromas; it's a rich, juicy wine that is also spicy and has considerable charm. The 2002 comes close, with similar aromas, a lighter structure, and a fine texture. The 2003 is unusually fleshy and blackcurranty on the nose, while the palate oozes ripe fruit and tannins, wrapped up in a fairly long, charming finish. There are stylish blackberry and plum aromas on the 2004, a plump wine with some swagger and delightful vibrancy. The 2005 is similar but with even better vigour and length.

La Clotte is an underrated wine that sells for a very fair price. Were it not for its limited production and a name that does no favours in Anglo-Saxon markets, it would surely be better known and appreciated.

Château La Clusière

*St-Emilion. Tel: 0557 554343. Website: www.vignoblesperse.com. **Owner:** Gérard Perse. Grand cru classé.*
*2.8 ha. 100% Merlot. **Production:** 3,000 bottles*

This small estate had vines alongside those of Pavie on a rich clay soil. Its wine was aged for up to twenty months in new barriques. The 1995 was a very opulent wine, reasonably concentrated, but somehow lacking in grip. The 1999 was jammy, the 2000 a touch over-extracted and overoaked, though it had a welcome fresh finish. The best Clusière I have tasted is the dense, fleshy, and highly concentrated 2001, a hedonistic wine with a long, chocolatey finish. However, La Clusière no longer exists as an independent *cru*, as from 2002 onwards its crop has been incorporated with that of Pavie.

Château La Commanderie

*St-Emilion. Tel: 0557 247014. **Owner:** Bernard Decoster. Grand cru. 6 ha. 80% Merlot,*
*20% Cabernet Franc. **Production:** 35,000 bottles*

Like Clos des Jacobins (*q.v.*), this property belonged to Gérald Frydman until its purchase in 2004 by Bernard Decoster. Both properties are managed by the same team. The vineyards are mostly clustered in various parcels near the house; the remaining one-third are near La Dominique and Figeac. The soils are reasonably uniform in all sectors, being gravel and sand with a high iron content. The viticulture and vinification resemble that at Clos des Jacobins, except that the wine is fermented in cement tanks and aged in fifty per cent new oak (although in 2001 de Boüard used all new oak). The wines do not have the structure of Clos des Jacobins, but the 2001 and 2002 are both concentrated and balanced by firm acidity which gives good length. There are marked aromas of black cherries and plums and, in 2004, liquorice too. Some vintages, such as 2001 and 2004, are a touch jammy, but may settle down with bottle-age. The 2003 is lean and undernourished, and lacks personality and persistence.

Château La Confession

*Libourne. Tel: 0557 259119. **Owner:** Jean-Philippe Janoueix. Grand cru. 3 ha. 52% Cabernet Franc, 48% Merlot.*
***Production:** 10,000 bottles. **Second wine:** Ch Barreau*

In 2001 Jean-Philippe Janoueix added this small property to his portfolio of estates. Being located close to Libourne, it is warmer and more precocious than other sectors of St-Emilion. Much of the Cabernet Franc, which dominates the vineyards, was planted before the frost of 1956 and survived it. Jean-Philippe Janoueix has pioneered the use of elongated barrels called "*cigares*" which, he maintains, give more lees contact. The barrels are entirely new, and there is just a single racking before the summer. The formula may be rather *garagiste* but the wine is excellent, with the emphasis on super-concentration and a rich oakiness. This shows at its best in the 2001, when even the second wine was of fine quality. The 2003 is less satisfactory: heavier, slightly soft and stewed, with no lack of power and alcohol but at the expense of finesse.

Cave Coopérative: Union des Producteurs de St-Emilion

*St-Emilion. Tel: 0557 247071. 900 ha. **Production:** 4,500,000 bottles*

The cooperative is the eyesore just south of the town below Fonplégade and Arrosée. It was founded in 1931, and today has 220 members. Until the 1980s the cooperative mostly supplied bulk wines to merchants and bottled wines to supermarkets. From the late 1990s there was a change in strategy, as the cooperative opted to produce higher-quality wines. This was reinforced by the appointment in 2000 of Alain Naulet as president. He promoted the virtues of lower yields, an alien concept at most cooperatives, and launched some high-quality, limited-production bottlings.

In 2003, at a cost of 10 million pounds sterling, the co-op added a new winery of enormous sophistication. Its 141 steel tanks are all equipped with micro-oxygenation stations. It is no use having state-of-the-art equipment if the base wine is mediocre, so Naulet and his team have encouraged the members to lower yields by green-harvesting. By 2005, over half the membership had signed up to the stricter regime, in exchange for financial benefits to compensate them for the lower volumes. All eight presses are vertical presses, larger than the basket presses still frequently seen in Libournais cellars, but vertical presses for all that. Moreover the entire winery is gravity-operated, with a system of hoists that can move tanks of must over any of the tanks, and then move the tanks, after fermentation, over the presses. Thus there is no pumping. The top wines, insist the directors, are made in the same way as classified growths, aged on the fine lees with *bâtonnage*. Of the 5,000 barriques in the cellars, about five per cent are of American oak.

There are some fifty wines that bear a château name, each vinified separately. In addition there are the following bottlings:

Royal St-Emilion A brand created in 1933. Seventy-five per cent Merlot, fifteen per cent Cabernet Franc, ten per cent Cabernet Sauvignon. Aged in both tanks and older barrels.

Côtes Rocheuses A brand created in 1945 from *grand cru* sites. Sixty per cent Merlot, thirty per cent Cabernet Franc, ten per cent Cabernet Sauvignon. Aged twelve months in one-year-old barriques.

Pagus Novertas A *grand cru*, from seventy-five per cent Merlot, thirteen per cent Cabernet Franc, twelve per cent Cabernet Sauvignon. Aged in older barriques. Production: 250,000 bottles.

Galius A *grand cru*, from seventy-five per cent Merlot, twenty per cent Cabernet Franc, five per cent Cabernet Sauvignon. Part of this wine goes through malolactic fermentation in new oak. Aged for twelve months in fifty per cent new barriques. Production: up to 150,000 bottles.

Aurélius The latest addition to the range, a *grand cru* selected from specific parcels at thirty properties. Eighty-five per cent Merlot, fifteen per cent Cabernet Franc. Aged fourteen months in new barriques and eggwhite-fined. Production: 50,000 bottles.

Quality is remarkably high. I have not tasted all the château wines, but both Grangey and Haut-Nauve are very good indeed, supple, even lush, yet well balanced and drinkable in the short to medium term. Pagus Novertas is supple and easy-going, a firm and fruity wine that is balanced but lacks personality. Galius has sweet, oaky aromas, but can be a touch bland. Aurélius, on the other hand, is delicious, super-ripe to be sure, but in 2000 and 2001 it was opulent and silky, and showed good concentration and stylish acidity.

Château Corbin

*St-Emilion. Tel: 0557 252030. **Owners**: Anabelle Cruse Bardinet and sisters. Grand cru classé. 13 ha. 80% Merlot, 20% Cabernet Franc. **Production**: 65,000 bottles. **Second wine**: XX de Corbin*

This property with its fine mid-nineteenth-century mansion has been owned by the Cruse family since 1924. In the late 1990s there were family disputes, as most of the shareholders wished to sell up. As a consequence, investment ceased and the estate became neglected. Finally Anabelle Bardinet and her sisters bought out the other shareholders, and she moved into the house with her family and set about restoring the buildings. Fortunately the vineyards were in decent shape.

The vineyards are on a gradually sloping single parcel around the château. The principal soil type is sand over clay, although across the road, near Grand Corbin-Despagne, there is more clay. The sandy sector gives more elegance, the clay sector more structure, and she is happy with the resulting blend. There are minimal treatments in the vineyards. The fruit is carefully sorted and given a four-day cold soak before fermentation with natural yeasts. The wine is aged in forty per cent new oak for sixteen months.

I once tasted blind the 1947, but it had lost its fruit. The 1990 was quite a good wine, aromatic, with ripe tannins if modest concentration. The 1995, tasted young, was rounded and forward, with lively acidity and moderate length. The 1998 is lacklustre, dilute, and somewhat green. The 2000 is easy-going, certainly ripe and supple, but lacking some concentration, although its charm and freshness are welcome. The 2001, with aromas that reminded me of cherry clafoutis, is richer than the 2000, with more opulence and oakiness without any loss of freshness. The 2002 is supple and forward and has put on some weight recently, making it both accessible and spicy. The 2003 has ample fruit and light tannin and does not suffer from over-extraction. The nose of the 2004 is a touch jammy, but the palate has appealing succulence and concentration, but at the expense of some lift and freshness. The 2005, tasted shortly before bottling, was plump and weighty, but seemed a touch extracted.

Château Corbin Michotte

St-Emilion. Tel: 0557 516488. Owner: Jean-Noël Boidron. Grand cru classé. 7 ha. 65% Merlot, 30% Cabernet Franc, 5% Cabernet Sauvignon. Production: 35,000 bottles. Second wine: Ch Les Abeilles

Jean-Noël Boidron owns a number of properties in the St-Emilion satellite appellations, and Corbin Michotte has been in his family since 1953. The property lies close to Pomerol, not far from Gazin and Pétrus. Consequently the soil is gravelly sand, with a good deal of iron content. The vines, which are in a single parcel, can easily suffer from hydric stress. The soil is ploughed, and there is no use of herbicides or insecticides, but Boidron does treat for diseases such as mildew and oïdium. Instead of green-harvesting, he goes through the vines at *véraison* to remove damaged or underripe bunches.

After careful sorting, the bunches are conveyed into the cement tanks without pumping. The wine is aged in sixty per cent new oak, usually for fifteen months, with blending completed toward the end of the *élevage*. Although a selection is usually made for the second wine, it is not systematic.

The 1993 was a bit dilute and had a dry finish, but the 1995 was very attractive and lush, with well-integrated oak and considerable charm. The 1996 is a touch lighter, more discreet in its aromas, but the wine has freshness, delicacy, and elegance. The 1999, rather surprisingly, has quite jammy aromas, but this is not reflected on the palate, which is sleek and quite concentrated, with firm, ripe tannins. The 2000 is fresh and vibrant on the nose; it's a medium-bodied wine that is clean, fruity, and forward. The 2001 has more opulence and complexity, and is balanced by good acidity that gives it considerable stylishness. The 2003 is simple and lacks flesh and weight. Energy and drive characterize the 2004, which has tangy, oaky aromas of red fruits, a good deal of spice and concentration, and an appealing freshness on the finish.

Château Côte de Baleau

St-Emilion. Tel: 0557 247109. Website: www.vignoblesreiffers.com. Owner: Sophie Fourcade and family. Grand cru. 9 ha. 70% Merlot, 20% Cabernet Franc, 10% Cabernet Sauvignon. Production: 45,000 bottles

Like Clos St Martin (*q.v.*), this is owned by the Reiffers family, and Sophie Fourcade has made the wines since 1997, with advice from Michel Rolland. In addition to the nine hectares used for the château wine, an additional eight hectares, on more sandy soil and with younger vines, is used to produce a second *grand cru*, Roche Blanche. Côte de Baleau is aged in sixty per cent new oak for up to eighteen months. I have tasted only the 2001 and 2004, but both were plump, fleshy wines with immediate appeal if rather light acidity.

Château La Couspaude

St-Emilion. Tel: 0557 401576. Website: www.la-couspaude.com. Owner: Jean-Claude Aubert. Grand cru classé. 7 ha. 70% Merlot, 20% Cabernet Franc, 10% Cabernet Sauvignon. Production: 40,000 bottles.
Second wine: Junior de La Couspaude

This fine property has been owned by the forebears of Jean-Claude Aubert since 1908. It was in that year that a cooper named Jean-Prosper Robin, already the owner of Sansonnet, bought La Couspaude. His granddaughter married into the Aubert family in 1963. One of her sons, Jean-Claude, runs not only this estate but six other Right Bank properties that amount to 250 hectares in various appellations. He is advised by Michel Rolland. The fine eighteenth-century house is just east of the village on the way to Trottevieille, and Aubert has turned its courtyard into an open-air sculpture museum, while the spacious interior of the chartreuse is used to receive groups of visitors in a welcoming atmosphere.

La Couspaude was declassified in 1986, then regained its status in 1996. The walled vineyards are in a single parcel, on thin clay over soft limestone. Vineyard operations such as debudding, deleafing, and green-harvesting can vary according to the climatic conditions of each year.

After harvesting in *cagettes*, the fruit is sorted thoroughly, with another *table de tri* above the vats. After a cold soak at 8°C (46°F) under dry ice, fermentation begins in wooden vats, with pumpovers and manual *pigeage*, and a couple of *délestages*. Aubert keeps the vats only for three years at La Couspaude; he then dispatches them to his various other properties. After a very long *cuvaison*, the wine goes through malolactic fermentation in new medium-toast barrels. The wine is aged for fourteen to eighteen months in a labyrinth of caves he tunnelled into the rock in the 1980s. The proportion of new oak varies from seventy-five to 100 per cent. He blends after the first racking, and although there is an eggwhite-fining before bottling, there is no filtration.

This is a thoroughly modern-style wine, but a very successful and consistent example of the approach. The 1989 was supple and enjoyable by 2000, with a sweet oakiness and quite good length. The 1990 is more sumptuous, and has now developed delicate oak and coffee aromas; it's rich and velvety, yet still youthful, stylish, and long. The 1994 lacks depth and complexity, but is pleasant and accessible. The 1996, ten years on, had oaky, smoky aromas, a rich, silky palate and more elegance than power. The 1997 is more than acceptable given the vintage. The 2000 is a full-throttled wine, with rich plum and chocolate aromas, a rich juiciness on the palate, and is let down only by a slight lack of acidity. Not so the 2001, which is opulent and very rich, with splendid fruit and a minty aftertaste, built to last but already enjoyable. With its lush, toasty aromas, the 2002 is clearly heavily oaked, but the richness of fruit and concentration manage to support the oak well. The 2003 is just the right side of jammy; it's a robust wine with powerful but not harsh tannins, and there is sufficient acidity to assure it a fairly long life. The 2004 is a touch overripe, and made in a burly, oaky style that would be fatiguing were it not for the dash of acidity on the finish.

Couvent des Jacobins

St-Emilion. Tel: 0557 247066. Owner: Joinaud-Borde family. Grand cru classé. 11 ha. 75% Merlot, 25% Cabernet Franc. Production: 40,000 bottles. Second wine: Le Menut des Jacobins

Although this estate's vineyards are dispersed, the winery is within the village, near the top of the Rue Guadet. The buildings were once a medieval monastery, but the monks departed in the 1750s. In 1902 Jean Jean bought the property and it passed to his descendant Rose Noëlle Jounard; in 1956 she married Alain Borde, and the now elderly couple still oversee the property, which is managed by Denis Pomarède, with advice from Denis Dubourdieu. The house is the former priory, which was restored in the mid-eighteenth century for the Guadet family. The former bakery, with its medieval windows and Renaissance chimney, is now the tasting room.

The vineyards are in three sectors: one between Angélus and Grand-Mayne on the slopes; the second on a *croupe* closer to Libourne, where the soil is sand over blue clay; and the third near Laroze. The average age of the vines is forty-five years. The soil is ploughed and no herbicides are used. The fruit is fermented in cement tanks with selected yeasts. The wine is aged in fifty per cent new oak for twelve to fifteen months in air-conditioned, humidified cellars, with very late blending and no filtration. After bottling, the wines repose in the quarries beneath the house.

These are quite old-fashioned and structured wines, with firm tannins. The 1996 certainly had grip, and the palate was lush and dense if not particularly expressive. The 2000 has more muscle than charm, with a rich, oaky nose and sour-cherry aromas; the palate, though rather austere, has good length. The 2001 is fresher, with more zest and elegance, although here too there is ample ripe tannin and persistence. The 2002 has a light minty nose, and is leaner than the preceding vintages, with redcurrant flavours, higher acidity, and a slightly dry finish. The stewed, dry 2003 is forgettable. There are ripe black-cherry aromas on the nose of the 2004, a medium-bodied wine with considerable intensity that's a touch angular now, but has freshness and length. The 2005 is plump and concentrated, but doesn't quite deliver the vintage's potential.

Château Curé-Bon

St-Emilion. Grand cru classé. 4.5 ha. See Château Canon

This small property, with its dispersed parcels, was sold to Canon in 2000 and its best vineyards were absorbed into the *premier grand cru classé*. Having tasted various vintages from 1979 to 1997, I cannot say I have ever been impressed by the wine, which in most years was robust, even chunky, and often charmless, although the 1997 was quite good for the vintage.

Château Dassault

St-Emilion. Tel: 0557 551000. Website: www.chateaudassault.com. Owner: Laurent Dassault.
Grand cru classé. 24 ha. 70% Merlot, 25% Cabernet Franc, 5% Cabernet Sauvignon.
Production: 115,000 bottles. Second wine: D de Dassault

As a plane flew over the vineyards, Laurence Brun looked up and said, "That's probably one of ours." That is because the property belongs to a family that made its fortune as aircraft manufacturers. When Marcel Dassault bought what was then called Château Couperie in 1955, the property was badly run down. For many years André Vergriette managed the property, and in 1995 was succeeded by his daughter Laurence Brun, who is advised by Michel Rolland and his team. Dassault is a very attractive property, one of the few in St-Emilion with a sizeable park, its lawns lapped by the vineyards. Yet looks are not everything, and the property, in the appellation's northern sector, required a great deal of attention, both in its buildings and in the vineyard. The improvements continue, and in recent years Laurence Brun has focused her efforts on raising the trellising and improving the drainage. If Dassault has a drawback as a vineyard, it is that the water table is high.

The soil is varied. A clay band traverses the property; elsewhere, especially on lower-lying sectors, there is more sand. The pride of Dassault is a two-hectare parcel of very old Merlot and Cabernet Franc planted together as a field blend.

The grapes are harvested in *cagettes*, and thoroughly sorted. Until 2001 vinification took place in large steel tanks, but Laurence Brun has now installed some small cement tanks, thus facilitating parcel selections. There is occasional but not systematic use of micro-oxygenation and *pigeage*. The wine is aged in seventy per cent new oak for fourteen to eighteen months, although sometimes, as in 2000, it sees entirely new oak. Blending is late.

A 1961 tasted recently gave a glimpse of the potential of the terroir. Its aromas were lean and redcurranty, rather surprisingly, but the palate retained sweetness and weight, with firm but not hard tannins and good acidity on the finish. Vintages tasted before Laurence Brun took over – 1988, 1992, 1993, and 1994 – were all disappointing, with dilution, ungainliness, and dry finishes. There is a clear improvement after 1995, which shows more fruit and richness and overall stylishness. The 1996 has charm, a nicely balanced juicy wine for drinking soon. The 1997 shows a touch too much new oak, but has freshness and delicacy. With the 1998, Dassault comes into its own. The nose is lush, ripe, and oaky, yet the wine is not too extracted, and there is an invigorating spiciness alongside the firm tannins. The 1999 is a fine success, its robust tannins balanced by good acidity, and it is already drinking well. A sweet, vibrant oakiness marks the nose of the 2000, a rich, chewy, concentrated wine that perhaps lacks a little finesse. The nose of the 2001 has great charm, yet the wine, although fresh and balanced, lacks presence, force, and complexity. The 2002 shows toasty, chocolatey aromas, a rich, svelte texture with some spiciness and length, a more convincing performance overall than the 2001. The 2003 combines overripe fruit with chewy, brawny textures and a lot of alcohol. There are rich, oaky aromas on the 2004, but the wine seems overworked and extracted, giving a very chewy, tannic finish.

Dassault is a very good wine that never quite attains greatness. It is hard not to feel that a lighter touch on the pedal of extraction, and a more restrained use of new oak, would result in a more harmonious wine.

Château Destieux

St-Hippolyte. Tel: 0557 247744. Website: www.vignobles-dauriac.com. Owner: Christian Dauriac. Grand cru classé.
8 ha. 70% Merlot, 15% Cabernet Franc, 15% Cabernet Sauvignon. Production: 30,000 bottles.
Second wine: Reflets de Destieux

Christian Dauriac, whose day job is running a medical laboratory, is an original. He has his own ideas about how to make and market wine, and adheres to them even if they may strike most people as relentlessly uncommercial. He also owns Château Montlisse in St-Emilion and La Clémence in Pomerol (*qq.v.*). Without any doubt he is obsessed by wine. When he was young he was a classmate of Michel Rolland's; the two have remained good friends, and Dauriac's approach to winemaking is clearly influenced by that of Rolland.

The property, which he bought in 1971, consists of a single parcel of old vines around the house, which is perched quite high up at around 100 metres (328 feet) in an isolated spot. The vineyards are gently sloping and have been divided into twenty-three blocks. Rigorous bunch-thinning keeps yields below forty hectolitres per hectare.

Dauriac has divided the vineyard into eight principal parcels, each vinified separately in its own wooden vat with *pigeage*. Moreover, each of these vats is made by a different cooper. Dauriac likes to conclude the vinification with a hot post-fermentation maceration. His almost excessive attention to detail is apparent with the *élevage* in new oak. He has acquired special Sylvain barrels with twice the usual number of staves, as he thinks they are perfectly adapted to his Cabernet Franc. Other batches are aged in Radoux Blend barrels, the most expensive in Bordeaux, with staves sourced from thirty-two different forests. This, he feels, gives the wine more complexity. Even more singular is his policy of requiring his coopers to taste the wine with him from the vat, and then asking them to make and toast the barrels one day before the juice is run off, the idea being to adapt each barrel to the wine.

It used to be Christian Dauriac's eccentric policy to only sell ten per cent of any year's production in each year. This allowed him to stockpile large quantities of older vintages, which he made available as mature wines to his clients. However, he has been modifying this costly strategy.

Destieux fully deserved its promotion to *grand cru classé* in 2006. (I judged the finals of the Coupe des Grands Crus, when Destieux triumphed. Most of the jury, myself included, considered Destieux the obvious winner.) The aromas are quite oaky, yet oak is not the dominant component, as it is complemented by a range of red-fruit flavours and nuances of woodsmoke. On the palate the wines are invariably rich and concentrated, with a dense but sleek texture, a lot of spice and, sometimes, alcohol. I particularly admire the 1998 and 2002, and the spicy, powerful 2004 and majestic 2005 are superb. What is impossible to determine is whether the wines would be any less satisfying were they made in a more conventional manner.

Le Dôme

St-Emilion. Tel: 0557 846422. Website: www.teyssier.fr. Owner: Jonathan Maltus. Grand cru. 2.8 ha.
75% Cabernet Franc, 25% Merlot. Production: 10,000 bottles

Le Dôme emanates from vines planted in 1956 and 1970 between Angélus and Grand-Mayne that Jonathan Maltus bought in 1996. The originality of the wine is that it contains around seventy-five per cent Cabernet Franc. Maltus reduces the crop severely by pruning to around four bunches per vine. The vinification is sophisticated, with multiple sorting at the winery, a cold soak, no pumping, *pigeage* as well as pumpovers, and fairly high fermentation temperatures. The wine goes through its malolactic fermentation in new barrels, and is then aged for up to eighteen months in the same barrels. Any sub-standard lots are dispatched into the Teyssier blend.

The first vintage, the 1996, has held up well. Despite the very low yields, this is not an overwhelming wine. The aromas are elegant, zesty, and attractively herbaceous and smoky; the palate is lean and intense, with a good deal of spiciness and a distinct edginess. The 1997, in contrast, struck me as severely overoaked. Le Dôme came into its own in the great 1998 vintage. The Cabernet Franc was marked when the wine was young, but now seems subsumed in the super-ripe opulence of the wine; yet it retains its freshness and liveliness. The 1999, inevitably, is a bit lighter, and has developed some lush, gamey aromas, and it remains a rich, spicy wine with ample fruit. In 2000 the Cabernet Franc contributed that slight herbaceousness that sometimes marks the wine, but the texture was wonderfully sleek, and fine acidity and suave tannins balance the extreme concentration. The 2001 is similar but has the vigour of that year combined with the luxurious fruit and texture of the Le Dôme style; the aromas are evolving, with nuances of coffee and red meat, which are more alluring than they sound. The blackberry-scented 2002 is very successful, being rich and supple, with considerable concentration and above all a fine balance that ushers in a lengthy finish. The 2004, tasted from cask after twelve months, had an opulent blackberry and leather nose, while the palate had a silky texture, and surprising finesse and acidity alongside the considerable concentration and tannins.

Château La Dominique

*St-Emilion. Tel: 0556 352379. Website: www.vignobles-fayat.com. **Owner:** Clément Fayat. Grand cru classé. 23 ha. 86% Merlot, 12% Cabernet Franc, 2% Cabernet Sauvignon. **Production:** 70,000 bottles. **Second wine:** St Paul de Dominique*
This estate takes its name from the Caribbean island where in the eighteenth century the founder made his fortune. It was already well known in the nineteenth century, when its vineyards overlapped with those of Cheval Blanc. In the 1890s the owner exchanged some parcels with Cheval Blanc to rationalize the holdings of both estates.

La Dominique was owned by the De Bailliencourt family of Gazin in Pomerol from 1933 until 1969, when motorway construction tycoon Clément Fayat, who today also owns properties in the Médoc and Pomerol, bought it. For some reason he did nothing with the property for some five years and hardly sold any of its wine. In the mid-1970s, with advice from Michel Rolland, Fayat took a more active interest. Drainage was improved, some replanting undertaken, and the *cuvier* was equipped with stainless-steel tanks. In the mid-1990s the property was expanded when some adjoining parcels were bought and integrated into the existing estate. In 2006 Clément Fayat enlisted Jean-Luc Thunevin to manage La Dominique as well as his other properties.

The vineyards lie in a band alongside those of Cheval Blanc. Of the twenty-three hectares, only eighteen are classified. The best parcels are those close to Cheval Blanc and L'Evangile. The soil varies. About one-quarter of the vineyards lie on deep gravel, the remainder on sandy gravel over a clay subsoil.

The wine is fermented at fairly high temperatures with some use of micro-oxygenation. In 2005 La Dominique experimented with some barrel-fermentation. Malolactic fermentation takes place mostly in new oak, followed by ageing in seventy per cent new oak, with *bâtonnage*.

The oldest vintage I have tasted is the 1982 at twenty years old. It was curious, combining ultra-ripe fruit with a rather lean, cedary aftertaste. Yet it added up to very good and satisfying wine. The 1989 shows more complexity, with aromas of marzipan and truffles; it's supple, suave, and fresh, with a stylish if tannic finish. The 1989 is slightly less well balanced; despite some intensity and length, it finishes rather dry. The 1994 is rather raw. Far better is the elegant, truffley 1995, which is not over-concentrated but has ample chewy fruit and a persistent, spicy aftertaste. The 1996, when young, was lighter but quite elegant, yet there was something hollow about it, and the upfront 1997 seemed better balanced and more complete. There are evolved, leafy aromas on the reserved 1998, which is a sumptuous, full-bodied wine with firm tannins.

The 2000 is a slight disappointment. It's a rich, oaky, damsony wine with a silky texture and good underlying acidity and tannins, yet it seems forward and essentially unexciting. The 2001 is better, with plummy, oaky aromas that nonetheless have finesse, while the palate has sweetness, stylishness, and charm. The 2002 has developed aromatic elegance and charm; for the vintage it is full-bodied, concentrated, and has good acidity to balance its slight austerity. The 2003 is earthy and rather drab. The 2005 is plump and exuberant, with ample acidity and spice on the finish.

La Dominique can be an excellent wine but it remains inconsistent and often lacks elegance. Its intrinsic personality remains elusive.

Château Faugères

*St-Etienne-de-Lisse. Tel: 0557 403499. Website: www.chateau-faugeres.com. **Owner:** Silvio W. Denz. Grand cru. 49 ha. 85% Merlot, 10% Cabernet Franc, 5% Cabernet Sauvignon. **Production:** 180,000 bottles. **Second wine:** Haut-Faugères*

Faugères lies at the eastern edge of the appellation, and indeed some of its vineyards fall within the Côtes de Castillon and are vinified and released as Cap de Faugères. A well known film-maker, Péby Guisez, inherited the property in 1987. It had been in his family since 1823. The wine had never made much of an impact, but he, aided by his wife Corinne, started turning the property around. However, he died suddenly in 1997, and Corinne kept going, more determined than ever to put Faugères on the map. Although by the early 2000s she was still in her prime, it had become clear that her two daughters had no interest in following her, so in 2005 she sold Faugères to a Swiss *parfumier*, Silvio Denz. Denz, with homes in London as well as Switzerland, and a number of business interests including an art gallery in France, had been looking for a property for some years, and found Faugères with the help of Stephan von Neipperg of Canon-La-Gaffelière.

Denz has retained the services of long-term winemaker Alain Dourthe, and of Michel Rolland, who acted as Corinne Guisez's consultant oenologist. In addition he has asked von Neipperg to act as an adviser. The suave and rich Denz has ambitious plans. He swiftly expanded the property's vineyards. And although the existing winery of 1992 is modern and well equipped, he has commissioned a more innovative building by Swiss architect Mario Botta, who built the remarkable Petra winery in Tuscany.

The vines were cultivated according to the Cousinié method (*see* Chapter Two), but Denz plans to go further by eliminating all chemical treatments. Since 1993 the vineyards have been green-harvested, but this is not done systematically, as much depends on the individual conditions within each parcel. After sorting and a moderate cold soak, the grapes are fermented in conical steel vats. Bleeding is often used to improve concentration, and in 2004 about one-quarter of the juice was removed in this way. Micro-oxygenation during fermentation was introduced in 1997. The wine is aged for fifteen months in fifty per cent new oak.

In 1998 Corinne Guisez decided to make a parcel selection from eight hectares of Merlot that face due south. This sector is quite hilly, so there are many varied expositions. To compensate for the loss of volume she bought an additional seven hectares. This new wine she named Péby-Faugères in honour of her late husband, and about 12,000 bottles are produced. Yields were pushed lower than for the regular wine, and the must was vinified in wooden as well as steel vats, with *pigeage*. Denz introduced manual destemming and changed the fermentation method: half the crop is now barrel-fermented. The wine undergoes malolactic fermentation in barrels, and is aged in new oak for eighteen months and bottled unfiltered. Denz has changed the wine's name to Cuvée Spéciale Péby.

Faugères is a consistently good wine, with ample upfront fruit on the nose and palate. There is always a balance between firm but not excessive extraction, acidity, and firm tannins. Of recent vintages perhaps the 2002 is rather forced, but it is a good wine nonetheless, as is the aromatic and beautifully balanced 2004. I am less convinced by Péby-Faugères, which is a bit of a show wine: super-ripe and oaky on the nose, while the palate is highly concentrated, sometimes jammy, and often overpowering. It's an impressive wine, but usually the regular Faugères seems better balanced and simply more drinkable. In 2006, however, Péby from cask seemed considerably richer and weightier than the regular Faugères.

It is clear that Silvio Denz is keen to push quality even further. From 2004 he introduced a second wine, which should mean that the regular Faugères is of even higher quality. In 2006 he planted, in equal proportions, Sémillon, Sauvignon Blanc, and Sauvignon Gris, from which he will produce 5,000 bottles of white Bordeaux in due course. This will be a fascinating estate to follow over the next few years.

Château Faurie de Souchard

*St-Emilion. Tel: 0557 744380. Website: www.chateau-faurie-de-souchard.net. **Owner:** Françoise Sciard. Grand cru.*
*11 ha. 65% Merlot, 26% Cabernet Franc, 9% Cabernet Sauvignon. **Production:** 55,000 bottles.*
Second wine: Ch Souchard

The vines of this long-established property are just north of the town in a single block. It has been owned by the Jabiol family, to which Françoise Sciard belongs, since 1933. After a classic vinification in cement tanks, the wine is aged for about eighteen months in thirty-five per cent new oak. I have good bottles from the 1996 and 1997 vintages, robust wines with ample tannin supporting good fruit wrapped in an elegant structure. The 2000 is a slight disappointment, an attractive and well-balanced wine that lacks a little distinction. The 2001 is aromatically complex, but the palate is less than harmonious, with rather edgy acidity and dry tannins. Subsequent vintages have been disappointing, medium-bodied but very tannic; the 2004 is the best of an uninspiring bunch. In 2006 the property was demoted from *grand cru classé*. Stéphane Derenoncourt has been hired as a consultant to improve quality, which the owners admit has been lacklustre.

Le Fer de Cheval Noir

*St-Emilion. Tel: 0556 560430. Website: www.mahler-besse.com. **Owner:** Mähler-Besse. Grand cru. 4 ha.*
*100% Merlot. **Production:** 6,000 bottles*

The Bordeaux négociant has since 1937 produced a St-Emilion brand called Cheval Noir. Le Fer is a *garagiste* wine from a parcel cropped at yields below thirty hl/ha and picked by successive forays through the vines to select only the ripest bunches. Sometimes the wine is concentrated further by bleeding the tanks. It is aged entirely in new oak for eighteen months. The 1998 had all the lushness one could wish for, not to mention a good deal of oakiness, but it somehow lacked complexity and excitement. In 2001, a sumptuous attack of rich, sweet fruit led to a rather bitter, inelegant finish. The only subsequent vintage I have tasted is the infant 2006, which is fleshy, not too extracted, but somewhat lacking in personality.

Château de Ferrand

*St-Hippolyte. Tel: 0557 744711. Website: www.chateauferrand.com. **Owner:** Baron Bich family. Grand cru. 30 ha.*
*70% Merlot, 20% Cabernet Franc, 10% Cabernet Sauvignon. **Production:** 165,000 bottles. **Second wine:** Ch St Poly*

This substantial estate includes the hamlet next to the church of St-Hippolyte, where the workers are housed. The fine château, which consists of two pavilions linked by a windowed gallery, dates from the seventeenth century and was built by the original owner, the Marquis de Mons de Dunes. Ferrand remained in his family until 1978, when it was bought by Baron Bich, the creator of the celebrated Bic pens. He died in 1994 and today the property is owned by his six children. However, none of them lives in the château and they plan to convert it into a luxury hotel.

The thirty hectares of vines are in a single parcel on a clay-limestone plateau; the soil varies in depth from eighty centimetres (thirty-one inches) to three metres (nine feet ten inches). Green cover is planted and no herbicides are used. The harvest is manual and the self-confident estate director Thomas Guibert has installed an automated vibrating table that shakes down the berries without surveillance.

After a brief but very cold soak, the fruit is fermented in cement tanks with indigenous yeasts. Although Ferrand is equipped with micro-oxygenation, it is rarely used. The wine is aged in fifty per cent new oak with minimal racking, and any reduction is resolved by *cliquage*. Some lees are kept apart at very low temperatures for two months, and if after analysis they are shown to be entirely healthy, they are added to the barrels. Guibert blends as late as possible. One particularity of the estate is that the wines are aged for a few years before release. Thus in 2005 the youngest vintage on sale was 2000.

Despite all the efforts made to ensure the health of the wines, I find, having tasted six vintages from 1995 to 2003, many of them affected by bizarre aromas, both cooked and metallic. On the palate these are medium-bodied wines, straightforward, reasonably balanced, but lacking in personality. Prices, however, are modest.

Château Figeac

*St-Emilion. Tel: 0557 744574. Website: www.chateau-figeac.com. **Owner:** Thierry Manoncourt.*
Premier grand cru classé (B). 40 ha. 35% Cabernet Franc, 35% Cabernet Sauvignon, 30% Merlot.
***Production:** 150,000 bottles. **Second wine:** Grangeneuve de Figeac*

The slender, elegant figure of Thierry Manoncourt is familiar to all who attend tastings and other events associated with St-Emilion. As well as being a man of great charm and courtesy, qualities shared by his wife Marie-France, he is a repository of knowledge about St-Emilion and its past. He inherited Figeac in 1947 and still lives in the stately château. Although still alert and active, Manoncourt has since 1988 left the daily management of Figeac to his genial son-in-law Comte Eric d'Aramon.

Before the Revolution Figeac was the property of the well-known Vital Carles family. At one point the estate consisted of about 200 hectares, though not of course all under vine. During the early nineteenth century the estate was broken up, which explains the large number of properties nearby with "Figeac" as part of their name. Parts of La Conseillante and Cheval Blanc were formerly part of the Figeac vineyards. The Manoncourts' ancestors acquired Figeac itself in 1892. It must be one of the most habitable of St-Emilion châteaux, as the house is attached to a large park. A stream traverses the property, making adjacent areas too damp for viticulture, so these lands are given over to pasture, shrubberies, and the Manoncourts' vegetable patch.

The Manoncourts certainly don't feel the loss of these few hectares of land, as they own forty hectares of some of the region's most remarkable vineyards. They are essentially in a single parcel, other than two hectares that lie alongside the road to Libourne. Three gravelly *croupes* run from north to south, and there are sandier sectors to the west and east of them. These *croupes* give Figeac its specificity. The gravel soil, with little or no clay beneath, is perfectly suited to the Cabernet varieties, which explains why they are dominant at Figeac, although Eric d'Aramon says he would like to see a little more Merlot planted. The family has also bought a 1.5-hectare parcel, historically once part of the estate and subsequently detached, and Manoncourt has requested authorization from INAO to incorporate it into Figeac itself.

The harvest tends to be late here, as one would expect with so much Cabernet. The must is fermented with natural yeasts in wooden and steel vats. As well as pumpovers, there is some *pigeage* and *délestage* to ensure good extraction. Aramon and his consultant Gilles Pauquet conducted some trials with micro-oxygenation but were not happy with the results. The *marc* is pressed in vertical presses. For some decades the wine has been aged in entirely new oak for eighteen to twenty months.

In its youth Figeac does not always show well, at least when tasted alongside its Merlot-dominated neighbours. And in some vintages there is some agreement among tasters that, good though Figeac is, it could be even better. One owner of a First Growth, who had better remain anonymous, told me that he believed the terroir of Figeac was even finer than that of Cheval Blanc, but the wine was sometimes let down by the winemaking.

Any doubts about Figeac's stature tend to be resolved when one has the rare opportunity to taste mature vintages. A magnificent 1950, still grand and pungent, sparked spontaneous standing ovation at a St Emilion dinner in 2007. Thierry Mamoncourt was there to relish the moment. A 1959, tasted from magnum in 2005, was exquisite, and even the colour showed little sign of age. The nose suggested red fruits tinged with woodsmoke, while the palate was sweet, intense, and delicious, still youthful and elegant, and with perfect balance and length. Even a torrid vintage such as 1976 was holding up well when tasted twice in 2001: cedary on the nose and far from baked, it was a supple, spicy, moderately concentrated wine with a fine texture. Oak still marks the intense and fragrant nose of the 1978, but the palate is sweet, minty, and almost racy. I have differing experiences of the 1982 (bottle variation?), but at its best this is a sumptuous wine, although a slight lack of lift suggests it may be close to its peak. The 1983, rather surprisingly, has shown consistently well over two decades. The nose – pungent, mentholly, leafy, sweet, and spicy with whiffs of nutmeg and clove – is exceptionally complex. The wine has an attractive spiciness, concentration, and freshness, and a long, almost peppery finish. The 1984 is forgettable, but the 1986 has always shown well despite what at first seems a lack of weight. By 2006 it had developed sweet smoky aromas that were enchanting, while the flavours included nuances of cedar and tobacco. Its freshness and length remain exemplary.

The 1988 is ageing beautifully, with ripe, cedary, almost raisiny aromas, while the palate is rich and concentrated, with fine elegance and length. The 1989 has developed some truffley aromas, and a sweet meatiness on the palate balanced by fine acidity. The 1990 had been a disappointment, with, at one tasting, a succession of musty bottles. When I mentioned this recently to Eric d'Aramon, he admitted that there had been a problem with TCA contamination in that vintage which had affected certain batches of the wine; however, the problem had been solved. Tastings in 2005 and 2007 were more reassuring, revealing intense leafy raspberry aromas, ample spice and vigour on the palate, and delicious fruit. The 1994 has flesh and charm on the nose, but a slightly chunkiness on the palate, though it does not lack vigour. The powerful 1995 has been superb from the outset. The nose is wonderfully elegant, with some delicate mushroomy nuances; the fruit is almost sweet, but there is a firm tannic backbone supporting it, and intensity on the very long finish.

I found some unsatisfactory bottles of the 1996 in the late 1990s, but bottles tasted more recently have been impeccable, with a sweet, intense leafiness on the nose, and a tight, elegant structure giving some grandeur to a sweet oakiness. The 1998 is splendid, if perhaps less typically Figeac, in the sense that it had ultra-ripe aromas, and a palate that was plump and dense; but it also had remarkable length. The 1999 seems quite marked by the Cabernet, with some blackcurrany aromas, and a robust palate in tandem with fine acidity. Cask tastings of the 2000 showed promise, but the one time I have tasted it since bottling it has shown poorly, and I can only hope this was an atypical bottle. There is surprising grip on the 2001, and despite the stylish red-fruits nose, its oakiness, burliness, and broad texture initially suggested more effortful extraction than usual. But by 2006 it was showing much more balance and finesse. The 2002 certainly needs more time: it's a lean wine with high acidity and a certain lack of weight; yet the tannins seem ripe and there is reasonable length. The young vines suffered in 2003, which yielded a hefty wine without the usual finesse and persistence. No doubts, however, about the superb 2004, with its aromas of blackberries and blackcurrants, its fresh attack, its nimble delicacy, its fine balance and poise, and its good acidity and length. Tasted blind among its peers in 2007, it stood out thanks to its impeccable elegance.

Château La Fleur

St-Emilion. Tel: 0557 551000. Owner: Laurent Dassault. Grand cru. 6.3 ha. 92% Merlot, 8% Cabernet Franc.
Production: 20,000 bottles

In 2002 this property was bought by Laurent Dassault of Château Dassault. It is conveniently close to Dassault. In 1898 the property was known as Cru Mérissac, then in 1929 it became La Fleur Mérissac, and was given its present name in 1949. Dassault bought the estate from Lily Lacoste, who had previously entrusted the running of the property to the Moueix company. The young Romain Depoins has been installed as *maître de chai*.

The vineyards are on clay with limestone and silt; being on a slope, new drainage was put in to keep the roots clear of excess water. Viticulture and vinification are similar to those at Dassault, and the wine is aged in eighty-five per cent new oak for up to eighteen months.

The only vintage I have tasted from the Moueix era, the 1982, was quite sweet and attractive but rather loose and lacking in length. The first Dassault vintage, the 2002, is the opposite extreme, with rather jammy fruit and a lot of oak on the nose, which is overwhelming. On the palate too the wine is rather confected and overripe, which, combined with the oakiness, makes for a fatiguing glass of wine. Far better balanced is the lush but spicy 2004. From cask, the 2006 had oaky, black-cherry aromas, but very dense tannins.

Château Fleur Cardinale

St-Etienne-de-Lisse. Tel: 0557 401405. Website: www.chateau-fleurcardinale.com. **Owner:** *Dominique Decoster.*
Grand cru classé. 18 ha. 70% Merlot, 20% Cabernet Franc, 10% Cabernet Sauvignon. **Production:** *60,000 bottles.*
Second wine: Ch Bois-Cardinal

This property lies in a lofty and chilly sector, where the vines ripen late. It used to belong to the Asséo family, whose scion Stéphane decamped some years ago to Paso Robles in California, where he established his own estate. Fleur Cardinale was bought by porcelain manufacturer Dominique Decoster in 2001. He had sold his business in 1998 but his wife Florence insisted that since he was only in his early fifties, he was too young to retire. He and Florence now devote themselves full-time to their new vocation. He built a new winery and commissioned a soil analysis to enable him to understand his property better. Despite the recent acquisition of the property by Decoster, he was swiftly rewarded with promotion to *grand cru classé* in 2006.

Although most of the vineyards are on slopes close to the best sectors of Valandraud, there are also four hectares elsewhere. The soil is moisture-retentive reddish clay-limestone and the expositions are so varied that there can be significant differences in maturation between different sectors. Indeed, in 2006 the vintage took four weeks to complete. Decoster finds that his vines are self-regulating in terms of yields, which rarely exceed thirty-five hl/ha. Nonetheless he removes buds and thins bunches, presumably to increase fruit concentration.

After harvesting in *cagettes*, the fruit is sorted before and after destemming, then conveyed on a belt to a platform for crushing above the vats. A cold soak of around five days is followed by fermentation, with mechanical *pigeage* and *délestage*. The wine is aged in new oak for just over a year, and is usually bottled without fining or filtration.

I have tasted a few vintages from the Asséo years; they were unexceptional and marked by fairly hard tannins. The 1999 seemed the best balanced. The Decosters' first vintage, the 2001, was successful, with sweet, ripe, oaky aromas, and plenty of plump fruit and spice on the palate, although the oak was very pronounced. The 2002 also suffers from a touch too much extraction and oak, although the fruit itself is ripe and rounded. The 2003 is distinctly overripe, with aromas of cherry compote, yet there is no lack of vigour on the finish. The 2004 has remarkable power and concentration, but not at the expense of balance and length, and the 2005 is even better; it seemed extracted just before bottling, but had sufficient weight of fruit to carry the tannins.

Château La Fleur Morange

St-Pey-d'Armens. Tel: 0557 471090. **Owner:** *Jean-François Julien. Grand cru. 3.5 ha. 70% Merlot,*
30% Cabernet Franc. **Production:** *15,000 bottles*

Jean-François Julien is a carpenter by trade whose wife comes from a family of growers who sold their grapes to the cooperative. Julien bought some vineyards of his own, but exchanged them with other growers in order to build up a small property composed of very old vines, including some centenarian Merlot. The average age of his holdings is an impressive sixty years. His first vintage was in 1999. In 2000 he built a small but well-equipped winery. In 2003 he also planted some vines: Cabernet Franc and Merlot in alternate rows.

His approach is *garagiste*. Yields are exaggeratedly low, with the *grand vin* cropped at twenty hl/ha, and his other wines at thirty hl/ha. He picks as late as possible, claiming that his soils preserve freshness in the grapes in any case. Sorting at the winery is obsessive, with fifty workers destemming by hand. There is no crushing and the fruit is given a cold soak under dry ice. Fermentation begins with selected yeasts in conical steel vats with manual *pigeage* as well as regular pumpovers, although since 2004 he has replaced *pigeage* with *délestage*, which he believes gives better fruit quality. The press wine, processed with a vertical press, is aged in new oak, as is the free-run, for eighteen to twenty-four months. To rack the wines, he hoists the barrels into the attic so he can work with gravity.

As well as La Fleur Morange, he makes a wine called Avalone, from young vines planted from massal selections from his oldest vines. The destemming is mechanical, and the wine is aged for twelve months in eighty per cent new oak. A third *cuvée*, Mathilde, is intended to be drunk young, and thus is aged for a mere six months in sixty per cent new oak. He makes 4,000 bottles each of the *grand vin* and Avalone, and 6,000 of Mathilde.

It is not difficult to see why La Fleur Morange has made an impression in certain circles. The colour is opaque, the nose is dominated by aromas of prunes, plums, and chocolate; the palate is undeniably rich, soupy in vintages such as 2000, massive in years such as 2001, tannic and super-concentrated in 2002, and simply overwhelming in 2003. I find it difficult to imagine anyone taking great pleasure from more than a glass. Tasted from cask after twelve months, I found the 2004 the best of the range, being less exaggerated in aroma and flavour than preceding vintages, with an alcohol level of 14.2 degrees that was not discernible, and a sumptuous velvety texture and good length. It is hard to say whether this represents a new and better-balanced style for the wine, or whether it is a one-off.

The 2003 Avalone is in a similar style to its hefty stable-mate La Fleur Morange, but far more accessible. Although the 2004 Mathilde also shows signs of overripeness and has a slight boiled-sweet tone, it is an attractive wine precisely because it is rounded and easy-going and isn't struggling to make an impression.

Château Fombrauge

St-Christophe-des-Bardes. **Tel:** *0557 247712.* **Website:** *www.fombrauge.com.* **Owner:** *Bernard Magrez. Grand cru.*
52 ha. 51 ha red: 77% Merlot, 14% Cabernet Franc, 9% Cabernet Sauvignon. 1 ha white: 41% Sauvignon Blanc,
33% Sémillon, 21% Sauvignon Gris, 5% Muscadelle. **Production:** *160,000 bottles.*
Second wine: Le Cadran de Fombrauge

This large estate has a long history, and its chartreuse dates back to 1679. In the mid-eighteenth century it belonged to a *parlementaire* called Dumas de Fombrauge, who was also a progressive viticulturalist. The property declined in the early twentieth century. In 1936 it was owned by industrialists from Lille called Bygodt. In 1988 Fombrauge was bought by the Danish firm of Hans Just. Then in 1999 Bernard Magrez acquired the property. He told me he enjoys acquiring underperforming properties and turning them around. He retained the services of Ugo Arguti, who had been the director since the early 1980s, and Michel Rolland also turned his attention to Fombrauge.

There are three major soil types at Fombrauge. The main sector is on relatively deep clay-limestone around the chartreuse; a further twenty hectares are located on the slopes on iron-rich soil. In addition, there are vines on south-facing slopes not far from Pavie. Pruning has been converted to *guyot double*, and the trellising heightened in 2005. *Lutte raisonnée* is the guiding principle in the vineyards. There is leaf removal on both sides of the rows, and green-harvesting reduces the bunches to between six and eight per vine. Magrez insists on further heavy selection at the winery, so that only about half the crop ends up as *grand vin*.

After harvesting in *cagettes*, there is rigorous sorting, with as many as fifty workers scanning the grapes after destemming. There is no crushing and the fruit goes into wagons which are then lifted over the wooden vats, so that fruit enters them without pumping. There is a long cold soak at no more than 12°C (54°F). Fermentation takes place with natural yeasts and the *cuvaison* can last six weeks. The cap is punched down manually every six hours, day and night. Malolactic fermentation takes place in new oak, and the wine is aged in fifty per cent new oak for eighteen months. After a late blending, the wine is eggwhite-fined and bottled without filtration.

There is a special *cuvée* of around 5,000 bottles called Magrez Fombrauge, drawing on grapes from three different parcels, amounting to three hectares in all. These bunches are thinned to give a very low yield: twenty-four hl/ha in 2004, seventeen in 2003. The grapes are picked as late as possible, destemmed by hand but not crushed, and vinified in small wooden vats, then aged twenty-four months in new oak. The usual blend is ninety per cent Merlot, with ten per cent Cabernet Franc.

Finally, there is since 2003 a very small production (3,000 bottles) of white Bordeaux Sec from one hectare. This is fermented in new oak and aged for up to ten months with frequent *bâtonnage*.

The pre-Magrez wines were not necessarily poor, but they were inconsistent. The 1990 has sweaty aromas and is dry (on the basis of two bottles), but the 1995 is a good wine, quite rich and concentrated with good acidity and well-judged oak. The 1998 was disappointing, being stringy and astringent. The 1999 is a marked improvement and is still sleek, concentrated, and attractive. Although there is lush black-cherry fruit on the nose of the 2000, the palate is soupy and still very tannic. I slightly prefer the sumptuous 2001, but this too has a firm tannic grip that has yet to relax. The 2002 shows the delicacy and charm of the vintage, and is well balanced and enjoyable. The 2003 is simply porty and massive, an ungainly wine with low acidity and modest length. The 2004 is much better balanced though undoubtedly opulent. When I indicated to Ugo Arguti that I find many of the wines too overbearing and alcoholic, he admitted that they go all out for phenolic maturity even at the cost of high alcohol.

The Magrez Fombrauge is in the same style, but even more extreme. The 2001 has 15.5 degrees and tastes like it. What such a wine has to do with Bordeaux I cannot imagine. I was once poured this wine at lunch with Bernard Magrez and found it hard to disguise the fact that I found it undrinkable. M. Magrez, with whom one does not like to cross swords, conceded that it was not a wine for everyone, but insisted that there was a market for this style. That may be so, but I do rather wish winemaking styles were not determined by the sage of Baltimore, whose own long experience of the wines of Bordeaux should by now have included a realization that wines more reminiscent of Zinfandel or Barossa Shiraz have no business being produced in Bordeaux.

The 2003 white Fombrauge had a hefty nose of pears and oak, and was a touch heavy and fat on the palate. The 2006s are far better, and the Magrez Fombrauge has powerful stone-fruits flavours and good acidity and length.

Château de Fonbel

*St-Emilion. Tel: 0557 242457. Website: www.chateau-ausone.com. **Owner:** Alain Vauthier. Grand cru.*
*19 ha. 80% Merlot, 15% Cabernet Sauvignon, 5% Petit Verdot. **Production:** 120,000 bottles*

Since 1971 Fonbel has been owned by Alain Vauthier of Ausone. The vineyards occupy various parcels on flatter land below Ausone on a soil of clay with sand and gravel. Vauthier acknowledges that the terroir is not particularly interesting, but the wine is sold at a fairly low price. The wine is fermented in stainless-steel tanks, then aged for twelve months in thirty per cent new oak.

The 2001 has rich, ripe aromas with some charm; the flavours are opulent but there is a fine thread of acidity that balances the wine nicely and gives a positive finish. The 2002 is something of a disappointment, with light, smoky aromas and a supple texture, but not much flesh, substance, or length. The 2003 is a touch jammy, but reasonably fresh and forward.

Château Fonplégade

*St-Emilion. Tel: 0557 744311. **Owner:** Stephen Adams. Grand cru classé. 18 ha. 91% Merlot, 7% Cabernet Franc,*
*2% Cabernet Sauvignon. **Production:** 50,000 bottles. **Second wine:** Fleur de Fonplégade*

The mid-nineteenth-century château lords it over the slopes that descend from the plateau around Château Magdelaine toward the St-Emilion cooperative. From 1953 onwards it was owned by the négociant house of Armand Moueix. Christian Moueix became involved in the winemaking from 2000 onwards, but eventually the family was obliged to put it on the market, and in 2004 it was acquired by an American investor.

The south-facing vineyards are principally on the slopes around the château, but there are also parcels on the plateau above, and on more silty soil on flatter land below. The new management swiftly made changes to vineyards that, in their view, were not that well planted although their average age is some forty years. Density is being increased to 8,000 vines per hectare, which is high for St-Emilion. In the winery the cement tanks have been replaced by wooden vats. After being picked into *cagettes*, the grapes are carefully sorted and only lightly crushed above the tanks. After a five-day cold soak, selected yeasts are added, and fermentation begins. There is no concentrator but the tanks can be bled of up to forty per cent of the must. Extraction is by *pigeage* and micro-oxygenation *sous marc*. After pressing in modern vertical presses, malolactic fermentation takes place in barriques, and the wine is aged in 100 per cent new oak (only thirty-five per cent new oak was used by Moueix) for twenty to twenty-four months, the lees agitated by being rolled on racks. There is no fining or filtration.

This modern vinification is a far cry from the more traditional methods practised by Moueix. However, Moueix rarely made wines of much character or interest. I recall good wines from 1982 and 1986, and indifferent and frequently dilute ones from 1979, 1983, 1985, 1995, 1996, 1998, and 1999. There were certainly signs of improvement in 2000, which has a nose of cherries and bacon, and a supple, juicy palate with some concentration and freshness. There was a falling back in 2001, which has smoky, oaky aromas, but is slack and easy-going on the palate. It is far too early to judge the success of the new regime, but the 2004 shows great promise, with a rich, juicy, concentrated palate, supple tannins, and a fresh, stylish finish. The 2005 is similar, but with an added layer of voluptuousness, concentration, and vibrancy.

Château Fonroque

St-Emilion. Tel: 0557 510048. Website: www.chateaufonroque.com. Owner: Alain Moueix. Grand cru classé.
17.5 ha. 88% Merlot, 12% Cabernet Franc. Production: 85,000 bottles. Second wine: Ch Cartier

The Moueix family have been associated with Fonroque since 1931, when it was acquired by the family of Armand Moueix. A century before, it had been in the hands of another celebrated Libournais family, the Malet Roqueforts of La Gaffelière. In the 1990s the wines were made by the firm of J.P. Moueix, and in 2001 it was taken over by Alain Moueix, who also runs properties in Pomerol and South Africa. Fonroque has become a testing ground for some of his ideas.

He began by organizing a close study of the soil. Although the vineyard is in a single block just north of the village, the soils are varied, with limestone in the highest sector, heavier clay-limestone on the slopes, and more silt and clay lower down. He installed new drainage, replanted some rows with massal selections, planted green cover in alternate rows, and initiated green-harvesting. Yields need to be low here, he discovered, to ensure that the grapes ripen fully; otherwise Fonroque can be an austere wine. His predecessors had never used herbicides, but he went further: Fonroque became organic in 2002 and biodynamic in 2005.

After sorting at the winery, the grapes are fermented with natural yeasts in cement vats. Moueix uses vertical presses and there is no pumping at racking. There is also some micro-oxygenation after fermentation. Malolactic fermentation can be slow as, he explains, the low pH of organic wines can be an inhibiting factor. The wine is aged for sixteen months in forty per cent new oak. After the *élevage*, he either fines or filters, but never does both.

There have been some very good wines made here in the past. This comes as no great surprise, since Jean-Claude Berrouet of J.P. Moueix supervised the winemaking. The 1982 was a sweet, luscious wine with plenty of backbone, but I last tasted it many years ago. The 1983 was good but far from exceptional, but the 1990, tasted recently, was excellent. The nose was complex, with scents of mocha and smoke, while the rich palate was balanced by a refreshing piquancy. The 1998 has leafy aromas and a whiff of liquorice, but the palate is chunky and the finish rather dour. The 2000 also has more grip than fruit and finishes a bit short. Because of hail damage, no Fonroque was released in 1999. There is complexity on the 2001, which has a rich, black-cherry nose, while the palate is rich, plump, and concentrated, with liquorice tones on the finish. The 2002 is similar but firmer and less succulent; although a touch hollow, it has some elegance. The 2003 is very aromatic, with exuberant blackcurrant and raspberry fruit, but the palate is rather assertive; although spicy, it seems quite extracted and punishing now. The 2004 is slightly disappointing, medium-bodied yet dense, and with a rather dour finish. Tasted just before bottling, the 2005 seemed rather tough and ungainly, but it's early days.

Alain Moueix acknowledges that Fonroque does not show that well when young, and my experience of the wine tends to confirm this. However, in good ripe years it is certainly worth waiting for.

Château Franc Grâce-Dieu

St-Emilion. Tel: 0557 246618. Owner: Daniel Fournier. Grand cru. 8 ha. 60% Merlot, 40% Cabernet Franc.
Production: 40,000 bottles. Second wine: Ch Franc-Guadet

This property is notable for its high proportion of Cabernet Franc. The harvest is manual, and after sorting the must is fermented in steel tanks and then aged in fifty per cent new barriques. The 2002 is light and gentle, but the 2004 is supple but lively, if not especially structured.

Château Franc-Mayne

St-Emilion. Tel: 0557 246261. Website: www.chateaufrancmayne.com. Owners: Hervé and Griet Laviale. Grand cru classé. 7 ha. 90% Merlot, 10% Cabernet Franc. Production: 30,000 bottles. Second wine: Les Cèdres de Franc-Mayne

Franc-Mayne, which enjoys a fine location on the plateau has had a hectic history. In the nineteenth century it belonged to the Baron de Cordes, and changed hands in 1903, when a Libourne merchant called Theillasoubre bought the estate. His descendants owned it until 1984, when it was bought by the insurance company AXA. In 1996 it sold it to a consortium headed by Belgian wine merchant Georgy Fourcroy. Some years later, in 2005, he put the property on the market. The new owners also own Vieux Maillet in Pomerol and Château de Lussac in Lussac-St-Emilion (*qq.v.*). The château, which is of seventeenth-century origin, was converted into a small hotel in the 1980s, and the Laviales have no plans to change that. The winemaker for their properties is the young, energetic Laurence Ters, with Michel Rolland acting as consultant oenologist.

The neighbours are Beau-Séjour-Bécot and Grand-Mayne, from which the vines are separated by a walled lane once used by pilgrims on their way to Santiago. The wine is aged for up to eighteen months in barriques, and the proportion of new oak varies from sixty-five to 100 per cent.

The 1996 had plenty of upfront fruit but little complexity or distinction. The 1998 is supple and easy-going, but rather drab overall. The 2000 was ripe but lumpy, with a soft texture and a lack of zest. The 2001 has more richness and depth; while sound and undoubtedly ripe, it lacks some finesse. The 2002 is a touch lean, with cherry and redcurrant aromas, but it's balanced and elegant. The 2003 is rather tough and coarse, even though it is not that extracted. More appealing is the overt juiciness of the 2004; it's is fruity and balanced, with a long, fresh finish. The 2005, ripe and minty on the nose, is lush and full-bodied, with a rather soft texture, yet with fine length.

Château La Gaffelière

St-Emilion. Tel: 0557 247215. Website: www.chateau-la-gaffeliere.com. Owner: Comte Léo de Malet Roquefort.
Premier grand cru classé (B). 22 ha. 80% Merlot, 10% Cabernet Franc, 10% Cabernet Sauvignon.
Production: 95,000 bottles. Second wine: Clos La Gaffelière

The Malet Roqueforts have been in town since the sixteenth century, making them one of St-Emilion's oldest families. The property is named after the medieval hospice where lepers ("*gaffets*") were cared for. The château, close to the southern exit from the village, is easy to spot, with its gabled roof in neo-Gothic style, although the building is of late medieval origin. Adjoining the château is a walled park dominated by an ancient cedar. In 2003 the hospitable Malet Roqueforts entertained an international gathering of journalists, merchants and friends during Vinexpo. A storm gathered and almost destroyed the marquee, which collapsed onto thousands of Riedel glasses as the startled guests ran for cover. There were no serious injuries and, although the guests were denied their banquet, they settled happily for bread and cheese and bottles from the Comte's cellar.

La Gaffelière once enjoyed a reputation as one of St-Emilion's very finest wines, but few would make that claim today. The present owner, the bluff and very likeable Comte Léo, is said to take as much pleasure in hunting as in winemaking. He, and his vigorous son Alexandre, seem aware that they need to be making more of an effort to validate the estate and its wine. Michel Rolland, who advised the estate in the 1990s, is no longer on the scene, as he and the Malet Roqueforts seem to have disagreed on stylistic issues. Since 2004 Stéphane Derenoncourt has been involved as their consultant oenologist.

In 2001 the family commissioned a detailed soil analysis, and as a consequence there has been some replanting and some changes in row orientation to north–south. The vineyards fall into three distinct sectors. Seven hectares lie on the slopes in a single, beautifully located parcel below Bélair and Ausone; three are planted on west-facing slopes above Moulin St Georges; and there are nine hectares planted on flatter, more alluvial land across the road from Pavie. The particularity of La Gaffelière is the balance between the power of the wines from the slopes and the elegance of those from the lower parcels.

After the grapes have been sorted at the winery, they are fermented in steel tanks with indigenous yeasts. As well as pumpovers, there is some *pigeage*, and, in some recent vintages, micro-oxygenation. The wine is aged in fifty per cent new oak for around fifteen months and eggwhite-fined before bottling.

The estate's great potential was more than apparent at a recent dinner when the 1961 was served. In colour the wine had scarcely evolved, while the nose was very rich, minty, and stylish. It remains rich, sumptuous, and powerful. By 2007 the meaty 1970 was showing its age. The aromas of the 1982 are mellow and lightly cedary, but the wine lacks body and richness; it has charm but little verve. I have enjoyed the 1985 and 1986 at about ten years old, but have not tasted them recently. They had good fruit and reasonable richness, but little depth or complexity. The 1989 is rather hollow. With the 1990 the emphasis is again on charm and silkiness rather than weight and complexity. It is hard to know whether its slightly lacklustre performance is a consequence of a terroir that seems less exceptional than that of many other First Growths, or whether it is due to a lack of rigour in the vineyard and winery.

The 1995, however, is developing well, with sweet, oaky aromas and considerable density. Oak also marks the 1996, but there is no lack of rich, damsony fruit; the texture is supple and the finish persistent. In 2000 the fruit is, if anything, slightly overripe, while the palate is still dominated by big, chewy tannins. On the one occasion I have tasted the 2001 it struck me as dour and lacklustre. The 2002 is more successful, a touch lean, as one would expect, but nonetheless a wine with stuffing. The 2003 is very juicy and concentrated, but let down by a lack of acidity; still, it will drink well for quite a few years. The 2004 is lush and very concentrated, though it sags slightly on the mid-palate and lacks some bite and finesse; nonetheless its ample fruit and firm tannins suggest it has a long future.

Vintages before 1964 were usually labelled Château La Gaffelière-Naudes.

Château Gaillard

St-Hippolyte. Tel: 0557 247244. **Owner:** *Catherine Papon-Nouvel. Grand cru. 20 ha. 70% Merlot, 30% Cabernet Franc.* **Production:** *100,000 bottles*

Mme. Papon-Nouvel is perhaps better known for her microscopic Clos St Julien (*q.v.*), but Gaillard is the family's bread-and-butter wine. The property has been owned by the family since 1792, and is located on flat land that can suffer, rather inconveniently, from both drought and flooding. Yields are quite generous, the harvest is manual, the must is sometimes concentrated by reverse osmosis, and the wine is aged in thirty per cent new oak. It's an easy-going wine of no great character, but in recent vintages it has been consistent and balanced.

Château La Gomerie

St-Emilion. Tel: 0557 744687. **Website:** *www.beausejour-becot.com.* **Owners:** *Gérard and Dominique Bécot. Grand cru. 2.5 ha. 100% Merlot.* **Production:** *12,000 bottles.* **Second wine:** *Mademoiselle La Gomerie*

You pass La Gomerie on the left after a kilometre (0.6 miles) as you drive from St-Emilion toward Libourne. It is sometimes derided as a *vin de garage* but this does the wine a serious injustice. It came into being after, in effect, a series of unplanned incidents. In the mid-1990s the Bécot brothers of Beau-Séjour were hoping to purchase another property and came across good vineyards in Fronsac. The day before they were due to sign for its purchase they heard that the small property of La Gomerie, on the site of a former priory, was for sale. Their interest was engaged by the fact that 0.7 hectares of this property touched Beau-Séjour which they hoped could be incorporated into the First Growth.

In 1995 the Bécots had to make do with the existing winery, and fermented the must in its cement tanks after sorting the grapes, and aged the wine in new oak. The American wine critic Stephen Tanzer heard about this new wine, and later so did Robert Parker. The Americans scored it highly. Because of these high scores and the limited production, the Bécots released the 1995 Gomerie at a slightly higher price than the First Growth. It sold. The brothers abandoned their plan of absorbing the 0.7-hectare parcel into Beau-Séjour.

The fact is that La Gomerie is on fine soil, sandy on the surface but with clay and the iron clinker called *crasse de fer*. Yields are strictly reduced by the usual methods in the vineyard. The soil is more precocious than on the plateau at Beau-Séjour, so La Gomerie is always picked first. The grapes are fermented in steel tanks of a squat form that allows for *pigeage* as well as pumpovers. Malolactic fermentation takes place in new oak, and the wine is aged for twenty months in top-quality barrels. After the first racking, the wine remains on the fine lees without racking and with some stirring. Fining or filtration are very much the exception.

I have tasted every vintage since 2000 and rate them all very highly. There is a sweet oakiness on the wines that could be cloying if that were all there were to it, but that is not the case. The fruit is always succulent and concentrated, with fine acidity, a lovely texture, and an underlying finesse. The 2001 is the best La Gomerie I have encountered, but even in 2003 the Bécots succeeded brilliantly. From cask, the 2006 seems graceful and supple, with just the lightness of touch needed in this difficult year.

Château Gontey

St-Emilion. Tel: 0557 422980. Owner: Marc Pasquet. Grand cru. 2.4 ha. 80% Merlot, 20% Cabernet Franc.
Production: 12,000 bottles

Marc Pasquet is better known as the owner of the leading Blaye estate, Mondésir-Gazin (*q.v.*). In 1997 he was able to acquire this property just east of Libourne. The terroir may not be exceptional, but the vines are old. The wine is aged in fifty per cent new oak for twelve months. The 1998 was rich on the attack, but also quite hard-edged. The 2001 is better: supple and juicy, but with bright acidity, and good freshness and balance.

Château La Grâce Dieu

St-Emilion. Tel: 0557 247110. Owners: Pauty family. Grand cru. 13 ha. 80% Merlot, 10% Cabernet Franc,
10% Cabernet Sauvignon. Production: 65,000 bottles

This estate, owned by two sisters, lies midway between St-Emilion and Libourne, on soils of clay-limestone and sand over a clay subsoil. There are some parcels close to the main road, and others near Laroze, Beau-Séjour-Bécot, and Grand-Pontet. Half the wine is aged in fifty per cent new barriques for about fifteen months, while the other half remains in tanks. Fining is not systematic, but the wine is filtered before bottling. La Grâce Dieu is a sound wine, with vibrant fruit aromas, light tannic grip, and sufficient acidity to give some modest length. Relatively inexpensive, it offers good value.

Château La Grâce Dieu Les Menuts

St-Emilion. Tel: 0557 247310. Website: www.lagracedieulesmenuts.com. Owner: Odile Audier. Grand cru. 13.5 ha.
70% Merlot, 25% Cabernet Franc, 5% Cabernet Sauvignon. Production: 75,000 bottles.
Second wine: Vieux Domaine des Menuts

This estate, which has been in the same family for five generations, is composed of parcels scattered around the appellation. There are clay-limestone sectors near La Couspaude and Trottevieille, parcels with more clay near Chauvin and La Dominique, and further parcels near Figeac. The average age of the vines is forty years, and they are cultivated by *lutte raisonnée*. The wine is aged in thirty-five to fifty per cent new oak for twelve months, with an occasional resort to micro-oxygenation. Given the location and age of the vines, one would expect more concentration and complexity than the wine actually offers. The 2001 is supple and attractive though simple. The 2002 is fragrant and has some aromatic charm; it's medium-bodied, quite supple and forward, but showing a slight rusticity on the finish. Since 2003 there has been a more conscientious effort to restrict yields, so quality may rise. Madame Odier also owns Château Haut Troquart La Grâce Dieu (*q.v.*).

Château Gracia

St-Emilion. Tel: 0557 247035. Owner: Michel Gracia. Grand cru. 2.6 ha. 80% Merlot, 15% Cabernet Franc, 5% Cabernet Sauvignon. Production: 8,000 bottles. Second wine: Les Angelots de Gracia

If you are exploring the medieval core of St-Emilion and encounter a flurry of reversing pick-up trucks, barrels glimpsed behind half-open doors, and yelled instructions from an ebullient gentleman with tufts of grey hair springing from his pate, chances are you have stumbled across Château Gracia. This is one of the few wineries rather inconveniently located right in the village. Michel Gracia is by profession a building contractor, employed at Cheval Blanc, Pétrus, and other top estates. This, he explained to me, enabled him to quiz the likes of Christian Moueix and Stephan von Neipperg about their properties and their plans. So, although not primarily in the wine business, he soon got to know a great deal about it.

In 1994 Michel inherited 1.3 hectares near Barde-Haut on good clay-limestone soils and the medieval house where he makes his wine. At first he sent his grapes to the cooperative, but, with encouragement from Alain Vauthier of Ausone and négociant Jean-Luc Thunevin, he decided to vinify his own wines from 1997 onwards.

His approach is frankly *garagiste*. The vines are cultivated by *lutte raisonnée*. He aims for a yield of no more than around twenty hl/ha. After careful selection in the vineyard, Gracia takes his grapes to his *chai lilliputien* in the village. Fermentation takes place in a variety of containers, and in 2004 he experimented with some barrel-fermentation. The wine is aged entirely in new oak, although he may reduce the proportion to around eighty per cent. There is minimal racking, and all lots are kept separately until blended at the last moment.

Gracia is always modifying his approach on pragmatic grounds. As well as reducing the amount of new oak, he has started to increase his yields slightly, as he fears that exaggeratedly low yields could unbalance the wine. Thus in 2005 he picked at a generous thirty-six hl/ha, but then bled the tanks to end up with the equivalent of twenty-eight.

In 2001 he bought a further 1.3 hectares on sandier soil over *crasse de fer* near Angélus. This parcel is planted with eighty per cent Merlot, and the rest with Cabernet Franc. He soon realized that the wine he made here was so different from Gracia that it was a mistake to blend them. So he produces a separate wine called Les Angelots de Gracia. It is not so much a second wine as a different wine, styled to be accessible fairly young. His original idea was to exchange the parcel for something closer in structure to Gracia, but having made the wine he realized he liked it so much that he resolved to keep it.

In 2005 Gracia bought a parcel of 0.3 hectare in the Fongaban valley near Pavie-Macquin. This he planted in 2006 to a density, rare in St-Emilion, of 10,000 vines per hectare. It's a fairly cool site on clay-limestone soil.

Michel Gracia's enthusiasm has persuaded his daughters Marina and Caroline to follow in his footsteps. Caroline, with experience at wineries in Clare Valley and Margaret River, is bringing a fresh perspective to the winemaking here. There are also plans to build a gravity-fed winery, but it will take all his engineering skills to accomplish that in the narrow lanes of the village.

The opaque 2000 Gracia shows a hint of overripe plums on the nose. The palate is predictably rich and sumptuous, but there is some spice and freshness here too, and the oak is well integrated. Even though the wine is not exactly zesty, like many 2000s, it nonetheless has very good length. The 2001 is very similar, perhaps with a little more overt power and weight and a touch less elegance. Tasted from cask after 12 months, the 2004 was splendid, with opulent cherry and raspberry-coulis flavours, and a fine vein of acidity enlivening the palate. The 2004 Angelots, also tasted from cask, has an airiness not encountered in Gracia, and fine acidity on the finish.

It is hard to generalize about Gracia, as the wine is constantly being fine-tuned from year to year. Although unquestionably a *vin de garage*, it is not a parody wine. In my admittedly limited experience, it has balance and freshness as well as lushness and exuberance.

19. St-Emilion Part III

Château Grand-Barrail-Lamarzelle-Figeac
St-Emilion. Tel: 0556 355300. Owner: Union Française de Gestion. Grand cru. 15 ha. 80% Merlot,
20% Cabernet Franc. Production: 80,000 bottles

This underperforming property was demoted from *grand cru classé* in 1996. In 2005 the owner, Louis Parent, sold the property to the present owners, who promptly leased it to the négociant firm CVBG, which also runs Belgrave in the Médoc and La Garde in Pessac-Léognan. The CVBG team blended the 2004, but the first vintage for which it will be wholly responsible will be 2005. It moved fast to impose sustainable viticulture on the vineyards, restored manual harvesting, and renovated the winery. The same sophisticated destemming system installed at Château La Garde in Pessac-Léognan has also been introduced here. The wine is aged in twenty per cent new oak.

The château itself, built in 1903, has for some years been a luxury hotel and restaurant, owned and run separately from the vineyards.

Château Grand Corbin
St-Emilion. Tel: 0557 247062. Website: www.grand-corbin.com. Owner: Giraud family. Grand cru classé.
15 ha. 68% Merlot, 27% Cabernet Franc, 5% Cabernet Sauvignon. Production: 90,000 bottles.
Second wine: Ch Tour du Pin Franc

This property lies close to the other Corbin properties on mostly sandy soil over clay with iron strata. The wine is aged in one-third new oak. Although the wine was promoted in the 2006 classification, my experience of it leaves me unenthusiastic. The 1998 is dilute with drab tannins, leading to a dry finish. There's more solidity and fruit in 2000, but the wine lacks length. The 2003 is dull, while the 2004 is supple and straightforward with little evident structure. The 2005 is certainly better, with more concentration, but still lacks complexity.

Château Grand Corbin-Despagne
St-Emilion. Tel: 0557 510838. Website: www.grand-corbin-despagne.com. Owner: François Despagne.
Grand cru classé. 27 ha. 75% Merlot, 24% Cabernet Franc, 1% Cabernet Sauvignon.
Production: 125,000 bottles. Second wine: Ch Petit Corbin-Despagne

The Despagnes have been a prominent Libournais family since the seventeenth century. They acquired this estate in 1812. It lies in the Corbin sector, not far from Pomerol. Once classified as a *grand cru classé*, it lost that status in 1996, then won it back in 2006. The present owner is a trained oenologist who conducted research into yeasts with Denis Dubourdieu. He took over running this property with the aim of restoring Grand Corbin-Despagne to its former renown. He does not dispute that the estate's demotion was a fair recognition that quality had slipped, mostly as a consequence of overcropping.

François Despagne initiated soil analyses of some fifty-three parcels, so as to adapt the viticulture to the specificity of each parcel. Closer to the château there is a good deal of sand in the soil; toward Pomerol, more clay. Because of this diversity, no viticultural practices are systematic. Thus he may plant green cover to restrict growth on richer soils, and plough between the rows on poorer soils. Nor is pruning systematic; much depends on variety, density, soil, and vigour. He is rigorous, however, about reducing yields to no more than forty hectolitres per hectare. Despagne also renovated the winery in 1998. He has also acquired Château Ampélia (*q.v.*) in the Côtes de Castillon.

Despagne uses no herbicides and the viticulture is essentially, though not formally, organic. The average age of the vines approaches forty years, and the oldest parcel is ninety-five years old. Despagne is against the fashion for picking as late as possible, as he is keen to retain freshness in the wine. In the winery he first installed a *table de tri* in 1996, and now has a battery of them. After a cold soak, the wine is fermented with natural yeasts in steel and concrete vats. Extraction methods – pumpovers, *pigeage*, *délestage*, micro-oxygenation –

vary according to the structure and requirements of each lot. The *marc* is pressed in vertical presses, and there is partial malolactic fermentation in barriques. The wine is aged for up to eighteen months in thirty-five to fifty per cent new oak in air-conditioned cellars. There is no systematic fining or filtration.

François Despagne stresses that the style of his wine favours elegance over power, because that is appropriate to the property's terroir. Older vintages do confirm the estate's potential. The 1947 is still youthful, rich, and fleshy, with spiciness, vigour, and elegance. The 1961 is dominated by the concentration of the vintage, with powerful, smoky, gamey aromas, and considerable power and richness. But vintages I tasted from the mid-1990s illustrated the decline of the property: the 1993, 1995, and 1997 were loose, simple, and dull. There was a clear improvement in 1998, a suave, spicy wine with ripe tannins. The 1999 had a kind of severe elegance on the nose, but was a lacklustre wine with a slight astringency. Far superior is the 2000, with its aromas of plums and cloves, and a vivid, plump fruitiness on the palate, with fine complexity and length. The 2001 is a touch austere and lean, but may fill out with time. The 2002, too, seems a touch too extracted and oaky for the slender fruit. The 2003, predictably, is more dense and tannic, but has ample plummy, minty fruit on the nose, and a palate of some intensity and power. The lively 2004, which has plums and a touch of tar on the nose, is far more succulent, though the tannins are putting up a formidable fight. There's a similar weight and swagger on the 2005, but it also has spice and vigour and shows great promise.

Château Grand Destieu

St-Sulpice-de-Faleyrens. Tel: 0557 846422. Website: www.teyssier.fr. Owner: Jonathan Maltus. Grand cru.
6 ha. 74% Merlot, 26% Cabernet Franc. Production: 24,000 bottles

Jonathan Maltus of Château Teyssier (*q.v.*) bought this property in 2003. It is located near Monbousquet on soil that is sandy with some iron. Maltus prunes severely to reduce the yield to forty hl/ha to counter the soil's inherent lightness. After sorting, the grapes are fermented with *pigeage*. The wine is aged for twelve months in oak. The 2004 was still in barrel when I tasted it: it is firm and oaky on the nose, and the palate balanced ample tannins with freshness and some lushness. The 2005, in extreme youth, seemed more stylish.

Château Grand Faurie La Rose

St-Emilion. Tel: 0557 247141. Owner: La Mondiale insurance company. Grand cru. 6.5 ha. 75% Merlot,
15% Cabernet Franc, 10% Cabernet Sauvignon. Production: 36,000 bottles

In 2005 this small property changed hands, and was bought by the insurance company that owns Château Larmande (*q.v.*). Larmande owns 2.5 hectares of vines that are not classified, so these have now been integrated into Grand Faurie La Rose. The wine is aged in forty per cent new oak. The only vintages I have encountered are very recent. On the nose there are delicate cherry aromas, and in some vintages (2002, 2003) a hint of coarse oak. On the palate the wines are plump and supple, moderately tannic, and quite long. Soundly made, they are enjoyable wines for medium-term drinking. The best of these vintages has been 2001.

Château Grand Lartigue

St-Emilion. Tel: 0556 674778. Owner: Maxime Bontoux. Grand cru. 6 ha. 90% Merlot, 10% Cabernet Franc.
Production: 30,000 bottles. Second wine: Ch Queyron Lartigue

In 2001 Maxime Bontoux, who owns the large Graves property Château Tourteau-Chollet (*q.v.*), bought this estate, which is located on sandy soil on the plain. It required renovation as it had been more or less abandoned for some years. The celebrated winemaker Georges Pauli advises Bontoux in the Graves, and here too. Their first vintage was 2002. I once tasted the 1986, which was uncomfortably austere in its youth. Bontoux's 2002 is extremely ripe on the nose, while the palate is supple and easy-going.

Château Grand–Mayne

St-Emilion. Tel: 0557 744189. Website: www.grand-mayne.com. Owner: Marie-Françoise Nony.
Grand cru classé. 17 ha. 75% Merlot, 15% Cabernet Franc, 10% Cabernet Sauvignon. Production: 75,000 bottles.
Second wine: Les Plantes du Mayne

The vineyards surround a fine château dating from the late fifteenth century, though with many later additions. From the late eighteenth century to the mid-nineteenth century it was owned by the Laveau family, and thereafter by numerous owners, until in 1934 it was bought by the wine merchant Jean Nony. His son Jean-Pierre took over the property in 1977, but died young in 2001. Today Grand Mayne is run by his charming widow Marie-Françoise and one of their sons, Jean-Antoine. A second son, Damien, has been studying wine law and one day may join his brother.

Although the vineyard is in one block, there are various sectors. Behind the house a fairly steep slope of chalky clay rises to fifty-five metres (180 feet), where it meets the vineyards of Beau-Séjour-Bécot. This is all planted with Merlot, and gives very powerful wines that provide the final blend with its backbone. On a more gentle slope between the house and Laroze and Clos des Jacobins there is more clay, although it becomes sandier as one moves down the slope. On this lower sector much of the Cabernet Franc and Cabernet Sauvignon are planted. There is also a parcel on clay-limestone near Franc-Mayne. Leaf removal and quite severe green-harvesting bring yields down to around thirty-five hl/ha.

The Nonys first installed a sorting table in 1993 and added a second one in 2002. The vats are both wooden and stainless steel, and equipped for manual *pigeage*. The Merlot goes through malolactic fermentation in barrels, whereas the Cabernets remain in tanks. The wine is aged for up to eighteen months in a proportion of new oak that varies from sixty per cent (2003, 2004) to 100 per cent (1996, 1998). The blend is made up late and bottled without fining or filtration. The second wine comes primarily from a twenty-hectare parcel of Merlot that is classified only as *grand cru*.

The oldest Grand-Mayne I have tasted is the splendid 1989, with its powerful and intense aromas, its lovely fruit and remarkable freshness. However, the Nonys prefer the 1990, which I have not tasted. The nose of the delicious 1995, once voluptuous, is now more subtly fragrant with some coffee tones, but the palate has retained its vigour, spiciness, and sweet, firm finish. The 1996 has a similar fragrance but is tougher on the palate. Despite marked oak on the nose, the 1997 is a fine success, with ample fruit and no sign that it is flagging. The 1998 has all the opulence and complexity one could hope for. The nose, once very perfumed and scented with black fruits, is showing secondary aromas of mushrooms and truffles. The palate is sumptuous, still tight, but the fruit quality is irresistible and the finish persistent.

The 1999 is ninety per cent Merlot, but has no trace of heaviness. The nose is rich, oaky, and stylish, while the palate is velvety yet lively and fresh. Blind-tasted soon after bottling, the 2000 was brisk and charming, but seemed to lack some complexity. The 2001 had more overt fruit and offers a seductive, lush, forward style of considerable charm and no trace of over-extraction. There are black cherries on the nose of the 2002, which is fairly rich but more fluid than preceding vintages, with quite sharp acidity and a slight lack of substance. The 2003 also lacks some weight, though the nose has charm; it's a supple wine to drink fairly soon. The 2004 is rich and plump with very robust tannins and, in 2007, a seeming lack of vigour.

Grand-Mayne hardly ever disappoints. It's a consistently fine St-Emilion, with flesh and succulence and considerable complexity; above all, the fruit quality is irresistibly lush and ingratiating.

Château Grand-Pontet

*St-Emilion. Tel: 0557 744688. **Owner:** Sylvie Pourquet. Grand cru classé. 14 ha. 75% Merlot, 15% Cabernet Franc, 10% Cabernet Sauvignon. **Production:** 55,000 bottles. **Second wine:** Dauphin de Grand-Pontet*

The Bordeaux merchant Barton & Guestier owned Grand-Pontet from 1965 until 1980, when the Pourquet and Bécot families pooled their resources to buy it. Today it is owned and run by the sister of the Bécot brothers. Pascal Lucin has made the wines since 2000, with Michel Rolland as a consultant.

The location, in a single parcel, is excellent: its neighbours are the Beau-Séjours, Canon, and Clos Fourtet. No chemicals are used, and any fertilizers added are natural. There are three soil types on the property: clay-limestone below a thin topsoil; grey and blue *marne*; and sandy clay. Recent improvements have included some new drainage, and planting to a higher density of around 7,000 vines per hectare.

Because of the variations in soil, the harvest can take up to three weeks. There is thorough sorting both in the vineyard and winery. The grapes are not crushed but are cold-soaked under dry ice for five days. Fermentation takes place in steel tanks, and there has been no chaptalization since 2000. Lucin is very careful, he says, not to over-extract, as the wine tends to be powerful. He does not want any rusticity in the wine and wants to preserve its natural acidity. One hundred per cent new wood was used in 2000, but only fifty per cent in 2004.

The 1990 was terrific after fifteen years, with a complex nose of cherries, leather, and marzipan; the palate is concentrated and tannic but the texture is supple, and there is ample spice and vigour. The 1995 is less evolved, with blackberry and plum fruit, and the palate is a touch lighter than the 1990. The impeccable 1998 shows the power that this terroir can deliver; in 2007 the wine was still sumptuous, concentrated, spicy, and long. The 2000, after bottling, was almost impenetrable and seemed rather extracted; I preferred the 2001, which has sweet fruit as well as a long, chewy finish. The 2002 has surprisingly meaty aromas, and brawny, hefty tannins that are now softening up. Although the 2003 is relatively forward and has baked and bacony aromas, it doesn't lack lush, upfront fruit and a good whack of alcohol. Although the 2004 is supple and doesn't seem very structured, it has sumptuous black-cherry fruit, a lively aftertaste, and good length.

The terroir here is surely exceptional, and it is a pity both that the property is not better known and appreciated, and that the wine, for all Pascal Lucin's efforts, is often a bit too extracted to exhibit finesse as well as power.

Château Les Grandes Murailles

*St-Emilion. Tel: 0557 247109. **Website:** www.vignoblesreiffers.com. **Owner:** Sophie Fourcade and family. Grand cru classé. 2 ha. 100% Merlot. **Production:** 7,000 bottles*

Sophie Fourcade looks after two other family properties: Côte de Baleau and Clos St-Martin (*qq.v.*). Grandes Murailles is the best known, thanks to the lofty ruin from which it takes its name. This isolated Gothic wall is all that remains of a Dominican convent that was mostly destroyed during the wars of religion. It stands alongside the village's upper roundabout, and countless tourists walk past it every day, unaware that the ruin is uninsurable.

When she started vinifying here in 1997, Sophie Fourcade found that the shallow soil was exhausted and thus the wines lacked power. She has made considerable efforts to restore the vines to their former vigour and to complant missing vines. After a cold soak, the must is fermented in steel tanks, with some micro-oxygenation. The barrels are stored in the quarry beneath the vineyard, where the temperature is constant and the wines evolve slowly in 100 per cent new oak. Michel Rolland assists with the blending.

The 2000 is massive, with dense aromas of oak and liquorice; it is made in a very extracted style and lacks some finesse. It has a long, chewy finish, but is somewhat fatiguing. The 2001 is similar, with a nose that suggests not only black cherries but tobacco and brine. The palate is solid and chocolatey, but rather leaden and one-dimensional. The supple, spicy 2003 is balanced but lacks persistence. The 2004 has more zest, and although not hugely concentrated, has spice and balance and length. Les Grandes Murailles is undoubtedly impressive, but for my taste it is rather effortful.

Château La Grangère

St-Christophe-des-Bardes. Tel: 0557 744307. Owner: Patrice Bigou. Grand cru. 7 ha. 75% Merlot,
20% Cabernet Sauvignon, 5% Cabernet Franc. Production: 25,000 bottles. Second wine: L'Etrier de La Grangère

La Grangère enjoys a delightfully rural setting. The house is no château, but a low-slung building that was once a staging post for pilgrims to Santiago. There's a pond in front of the house, a stream that trickles through the property, and fairly steep slopes all around. The estate was assembled by a Belgian called Louis Parent from 1996 onwards, but in 2001 he sold it. The purchasers were a show-jumping champion called Pierre Durand and his wife, a former auctioneer with a diploma in oenology. She looked after the property, with advice from Denis Dubourdieu. In 2006 the property was sold after the couple divorced.

The vines are located on clay-limestone slopes below Château Laroque, as well as on flatter land below. The wine is fermented with selected yeasts in cement and steel tanks, then aged in thirty per cent new oak for twelve to fifteen months. The 1998 had a sweet vanilla nose, but the tannins are rather raw, and despite some richness on the palate, it's rather charmless. The 2001 has more purity of fruit but lacks some grip and concentration. The 2002 is a bit of a lightweight, a pleasant wine for medium-term drinking. The 2003 lacks substance and has a dry finish, but the juicy, vigorous 2006 from cask shows promise.

Château La Grave Figeac

St-Emilion. Tel: 0557 741174. Website: www.chateau-la-grave-figeac.fr. Owner: Jean-Pierre Clauzel. Grand cru.
6.5 ha. 66% Merlot, 34% Cabernet Franc. Production: 35,000 bottles. Second wine: Ch Pavillon-Figeac

I know little about this property, which sells most of its wines to private customers, but it is certainly well located, close to both Cheval Blanc and La Conseillante in Pomerol. It was bought by Jean-Pierre Clauzel in 1993. After fermentation in concrete tanks, the wine ages for a year in fifty per cent new barriques. A 2000 tasted recently was impressive, with rich, smoky black-cherry aromas, a good attack and excellent freshness, and good fruit backed by firm tannins. The 1996 was very different: dour and lacking in fruit.

Château Guadet

St-Emilion. Tel: 0557 744004. Website: www.gaudet.com. Owner: Guy-Pétrus Lignac. Grand cru.
5.5 ha. 75% Merlot, 25% Cabernet Franc. Production: 22,000 bottles

This property, assembled in 1844, takes its name from the local revolutionary Elie Guadet. The vineyards are located just outside the village along the road to Montagne, with another parcel near Soutard. Near the top of the rue Guadet within the old village a plain door leads into the house and winery. Robert Lignac owned and ran the property until he retired, aged eighty, in 2000. In that year, his son Guy-Pétrus, who had enjoyed a career in industry, returned to St-Emilion to run the property. The Lignacs are closely related to the Loubat and Lacoste families who were the owners of Château Pétrus, which explains his unusual Christian name. In 2006 the name of the property was changed from Guadet-St Julien.

The vines are cultivated without the use of herbicides and are green-harvested. After sorting, the must is fermented with natural yeasts in cement tanks, with pumpovers and *pigeage*. The *marc* is pressed in a vertical press, and the wine aged for eighteen months in between thirty-five and sixty per cent new oak.

M. Lignac retains stocks of old vintages up to forty years old, which he sells gradually to his private customers. Although these are wines that can age well, this is not true of all vintages. The 1959 in 1986 was browning and clearly past its best, with a mouth-puckering finish. A 1962, drunk recently, was much fresher in appearance, and its charming and delicate nose of red fruits had by no means faded. However, the palate was austere. My one encounter with the 2000 was not rewarding, as I found it slightly green and dilute. The 2001 is much better, a supple, graceful wine with concentration but no excessive extraction, and an elegant finish. That elegance is also present on the 2002, a lighter wine that is nonetheless vinous and quite complex. The 2003 is a success, silky and ripe but not jammy, with restrained oakiness and moderate acidity. The 2004 is medium-bodied and lively but lacks some flesh and complexity; but it's a forward wine with much immediate appeal.

Château Haut-Brisson

Vignonet. Tel: 0557 846957. **Owner:** *Peter Kwok. Grand cru. 13 ha. 70% Merlot, 25% Cabernet Sauvignon,*
5% Cabernet Franc. **Production:** *60,000 bottles.* **Second wine:** *Ch Haut-Brisson La Grave*

This property was bought in 1997 by a Chinese investor, who hired Patrick Moulinet as manager and wine-maker. Before 1997, according to Moulinet, the wine had been good but far from outstanding, and his mission was to improve quality. Although the vineyards are on the plain, they are mostly on gravel soils. Moulinet eschews herbicides and fertilizers, has installed *guyot double* pruning, and green-harvests to reduce yields.

The fruit fermented, after a week-long cold soak, in conical steel tanks, employing natural yeasts only. Sometimes Moulinet uses micro-oxygenation, but not systematically. The wine is, rather daringly, aged in entirely new oak for around eighteen months, with few rackings, and bottled without fining or filtration.

The only old vintage I have come across is the 1983, which was loosely structured and dry. I have had mixed impressions of the 1999, sweetly fruity and balanced at the estate, gamey and drab at a blind tasting. The 2000 has evolved fast, and although quite tannic, the texture is soft and close to flabby. The powerful 2001 seems riper, with fine concentration, and packed with sweet fruit on the mid-palate. The damsony 2002 is more easy-going, with little complexity and a tannic finish. The 2003 lacks elegance; it's too assertive and dry and lacks persistence. The first-rate 2004 resembles the 2001 but has more vigour.

Château Haut-Corbin

St-Emilion. Tel: 0557 970282. **Website:** *www.hautcorbin.com.* **Owner:** *SMABTP insurance company. Grand cru classé. 6 ha. 65% Merlot,*
25% Cabernet Sauvignon, 10% Cabernet Franc. **Production:** *30,000 bottles*

Located in the northern sector of St-Emilion, Haut-Corbin is very close to Pomerol. The vineyards are on sandy clay soils with some *crasse de fer*. Since 1985 the property has been under the same ownership and management as Cantemerle in the Haut-Médoc. The wine is aged in one-third new oak for twelve months. The 1990 was fleshy yet spicy; the 1995 was ripe and chocolatey, with ample lush, upfront fruit that seemed very much on the surface. The 1996 was dour, lacking vigour and length. The nose of the 2000 was stylish and oaky, but despite a sleek texture the wine finished hard and fairly short. The 2001 is better, with more weight and density; a solid wine, it is also slightly dull. The 2003 lacks vigour. The 2004 mirrors the 2001, although the tannins seem more surly.

Château Haut La Grace Dieu

St-Laurent-des-Combes. Tel: 0557 247303. **Owners:** *Jean-Christophe and Jean-Philippe Saby.*
Grand cru. 2 ha. 100% Merlot. **Production:** *5,000 bottles*

The Saby brothers own the much larger Château Rozier (*q.v.*), but this limited-production wine, first made in 1998, is their showcase bottling. The vines are on a slope near Tertre-Roteboeuf, and there is another small parcel near Chauvin. It is aged entirely in new oak. The 2002 suffers from some rusticity and rough tannins, but the 2000 and 2001 are excellent, with lush, plummy aromas, a plump texture, ample concentration, and quite good length. The 2003 lacks vigour and finishes rather flat, but is certainly an honourable effort.

Château Haut-Rocher

St-Etienne-de-Lisse. Tel: 0557 401809. **Website:** *www.vins-jean-de-monteil.com.* **Owner:** *Jean de Monteil. Grand cru. 9 ha. 65% Merlot, 20% Cabernet Franc, 12% Cabernet Sauvignon, 3% Malbec.* **Production:** *40,000 bottles*

The de Monteils have been in St-Emilion since 1761, and the present owner, Jean de Monteil, is very much a hands-on proprietor. The vineyards are on clay-limestone soils, facing southeast. Most of them are in a single block, with five hectares on slopes and two near Château Faugères, plus a fine hillside close to Château de Pressac. They are cultivated according to the principles of *lutte raisonnée*. The harvest is both manual and mechanical. The wine is fermented in steel and cement tanks, and since 1999 de Monteil has practised some micro-oxygenation to give the wine greater softness. It is aged for twelve to fifteen months in one-third new oak.

Haut-Rocher has a good reputation but I have found recent vintages rather disappointing, a touch light and lacking in energy and grip. The 2002 is an easy-drinking wine that's balanced but not very exciting. The 2003 has a strange glacé-cherry nose, with ripe fruit on the palate but a sweetish finish.

De Monteil also makes a wine called Pavillon du Haut-Rocher, a basic St-Emilion from a two-hectare vineyard that is not *grand cru*. It is aged in older barrels and in tanks.

Château Haut-Sarpe

St-Christophe-des-Bardes. Tel: 0557 514186. Website: www.j-janoueix-bordeaux.com.
Owner: Jean-François Janoueix. Grand cru classé. 21 ha. 70% Merlot, 30% Cabernet Franc.
Production: 120,000 bottles. Second wine: Ch Vieux Sarpe

This splendid late-nineteenth-century château lies to the east of the village. Until 1930 the estate, which adjoins Trottevieille, was owned by the Baron du Foussat de Bogeron. Then it was bought by Joseph Janoueix. Like the Moueix family, the Janoueix had come from the Corrèze and established a successful négociant business, which exists to this day. And also like the Moueix, they were not slow to snap up interesting properties throughout the Libournais.

Haut-Sarpe is the family headquarters, and the mansion is still inhabited by the nonagenarian but spry widow of Joseph Janoueix. Close to the house is a small hamlet owned by the family. This comes to life during the harvest. The Janoueix family have evolved a harvesting tradition by inviting friends and customers to pick the grapes. They come in droves from all over Europe. In return for their labours, the Janoueix family organizes a prolonged party at Haut-Sarpe. The centrepiece of the hamlet is the Glou Glou nightclub, which throws open its doors after copious dinners. Various generations of the Janoueix family and their guests and friends can be observed bopping away into the small hours.

Once the Janoueix circle of acquaintance has picked the grapes, they are fermented in cement tanks, and aged in fifty to seventy per cent new oak. My experience of the wines is not that extensive, since my visit coincided with harvest and I spent too much time in the Glou Glou, where the Janoueix family were, quite rightly, more intent on partying than on attempting a serious tasting.

The 1996 is an excellent and elegant wine, with well-integrated tannins and acidity and good length. The 1998 is prettily aromatic, but lacks depth and complexity. I was disappointed by the 2000, which seemed light for the vintage, while the 2001 (thrice tasted) has wet, asphalt aromas, and a superficial richness that can't disguise its hollowness and lack of length. The 2003 is surprisingly soft and lacks structure; it's an attractively fruity wine, but should be drunk young. The two bottles of the 2004 I have tasted were both musty and tired. A third was clean but modest in its concentration and structure. The 2005 shows more vigour and ripeness, and is easily the best Haut-Sarpe I have encountered.

Château Haut Troquart La Grâce Dieu

St-Emilion. Tel: 0557 247310. Owner: Odile Audier. Grand cru. 3 ha. 80% Merlot, 15% Cabernet Franc,
5% Cabernet Sauvignon. Production: 5,000 bottles

Mme. Audier of Château La Grâce Dieu Les Menuts (*q.v.*) bought this small estate in 1997. The vines are planted close to the latter on soils of clay with sand. The must is fermented in cement tanks and then aged in sixty per cent new barriques for twelve months. The only vintage I have tasted, the 2000, is a good wine, quite rich and well balanced. The label depicting the village from across the vineyards is especially charming.

Château Jean Faure

*St-Emilion. Tel: 0557 519459. Owner: Olivier Decelle. Grand cru. 18 ha. 54% Cabernet Franc, 40% Merlot, 6% Malbec. **Production:** 75,000 bottles*

Olivier Decelle made his money in the frozen food business, and has since bought a number of properties in the Médoc, Fronsac, and Roussillon. Jean Faure, which he bought in 2004, represents another challenge, as this *grand cru classé* was demoted in 1986.

The property has scarcely altered in centuries, according to Decelle, and is located in a long band just east of La Dominique, and there is a parcel near L'Evangile. It was bought by Marcel Loubat in 1921. In 1946 his granddaughter married Michel de Wilde, but a subsequent divorce led to problems. As a consequence, the property was badly neglected by the time Decelle arrived, although the vines themselves were in decent shape and have an average age of forty years. He commissioned the soil expert Claude Bourguignon to assess the vineyards, and they set up a plan to improve the drainage, for a start. This was essential, says Decelle, as otherwise there is an underground pond lying over the clay subsoil.

The grapes are now harvested in *cagettes*, and sorted on no fewer than five sorting tables. The destemmer is particularly sophisticated since it is programmed to discard grapes that don't attain the highest quality. The fruit is only lightly crushed. It is fermented in cement tanks with natural yeasts. Primary extraction is by *pigeage*. Jean Faure is unusual in that only half the crop is aged in oak, all of which is new; the other half remains in tanks. The total *élevage* is some sixteen months.

The 2004 is very perfumed, with elegant aromas of violets and blackberries. On the palate the wine is imposing and concentrated, with a light touch of oak and a fine balance. The Cabernet Franc was certainly leaving its signature. The 2005 seems richer and more opulent. Certainly, Olivier Decelle, with advice from Michel Rolland, is keen to produce a wine worthy of its terroir, and, no doubt, regain its former status in due course.

Château Laforge

*St-Emilion. Tel: 0557 846422. Website: www.teyssier.fr. Owner: Jonathan Maltus. Grand cru. 4.5 ha. 90% Merlot, 10% Cabernet Franc. **Production:** 18,000 bottles*

Château Laforge, which Jonathan Maltus began assembling in 1998, is brazenly *garagiste*, since some of the parcels are not on exceptional soils. Since its inception, some of the vines used for Laforge have been separated off to form the basis of new wines. By 2005 there were 4.5 hectares in two principal locations. The wine is quite different from his Le Dôme (*q.v.*). It is ninety per cent Merlot, for a start. It is cropped to equally low levels, resulting in a yield of around thirty hl/ha. The vinification is similar to that for Le Dôme, though with more use of micro-oxygenation and lees-stirring; however the proportion of new oak is fifty per cent.

Laforge has a less individual personality than Le Dôme. In the 1998 the oak is very much to the fore, but the dominant impression is one of plumpness, roundness, and a chewy, tannic finish. There is more elegance in 1999, with its sweet, smoky aromas, its fine acidity, its balance and length. In the 2000, the oak is more stylish; there is power and concentration but also a long finish. Like the 2000, the 2001 is built to last, and is decidedly tannic and dense without being over-extracted. The 2004 from cask is also stylish; despite the body and concentration, there is no excessive extraction, and the opulence of fruit is countered by the tannic grip. But Laforge, while impressive and packing a punch, lacks the individuality of Le Dôme.

Château Laniote

*St-Emilion. Tel: 0557 247080. Website: www.laniote.com. **Owner:** Arnaud de la Filolie. Grand cru classé.*
*5 ha. 75% Merlot, 20% Cabernet Franc, 5% Cabernet Sauvignon. **Production:** 25,000 bottles.*
Second wine: Chapelle de Laniotte

This small but well-tended property, in a single parcel near Fonroque, has been in the family since 1921 but has descended through the female line. So perhaps it is appropriate that it is Florence de la Filolie who makes the wines. Her husband looks after the vineyards, and also entertains visitors. This he does with panache, and one can see his eyes light up as the next batch of Japanese wine-lovers is disgorged from the minibus. He shows videos, makes little jokes (especially about his wife), bursts into song, and praises his wines.

The soil is essentially clay-limestone, although some sectors are sandier. De la Filolie ploughs and sows green cover, and green-harvests in summer. After sorting, the fruit is pumped into cement tanks for fermentation, which is sparked off by selected yeasts. There is some micro-oxygenation toward the end of the vinification. The wine is then aged for twelve months in forty per cent new oak.

In the mid-1990s the wines were tannic and chunky, but the tannins are more evidently in check in the luscious 1998, a lovely and concentrated wine with good length. The 2000 is almost as good, with flavours of cherries and blackberries, and ample acidity to give both length and finesse. I was disappointed by the 2001, and the 2002 shows some astringency and a blunt finish despite ample initial fruitiness. The 2003 is rounded and fleshy. In 2007 tannin dominated the otherwise plump 2004, but there seems to be sufficient fruit to ensure a good future. The 2005 is far superior, with more lushness and concentration, and length.

Château Larcis-Ducasse

*St-Emilion. Tel: 0557 247084. Website: www.larcis-ducasse.com. **Owner:** Jacques-Olivier Gratiot. Grand cru classé.*
*11 ha. 75% Merlot, 20% Cabernet Franc, 5% Cabernet Sauvignon. **Production:** 35,000 bottles*

Well located on the southern slopes of the plateau near Pavie, Larcis-Ducasse was acquired by the Raba family in the nineteenth century, and has passed down through the female line to its present owner. M. Gratiot lives in Paris, and that may partly explain the estate's lacklustre performance in the 1990s. A few years ago, however, there were some major changes: Nicolas Thienpont, a member of a Belgian wine family thoroughly implanted on the Right Bank, became the general manager, supplementing his similar role at Pavie-Macquin, and Stéphane Derenoncourt was hired as the consultant oenologist. In 2005 they converted the estate to organic viticulture.

One glance at the property, which has scarcely altered in over a century, makes it clear that it should be capable of producing outstanding wines. The vineyards, which enjoy an average age of forty years, are very well exposed and face south. The slopes are partly terraced, and about one hectare is located up on the plateau next to Pavie-Decesse. The soil is varied, with limestone on the plateau, and sand at the foot of the slope.

The winemaking is supervised by the knowledgeable *maître de chai*, Philippe Dubois. The grapes are thoroughly sorted but not crushed, and the must descends by gravity into the cement tanks. There is no cold soak, but Dubois uses some micro-oxygenation to help stabilize the colour and plump up the wine. The yeasts are usually but not invariably indigenous. Malolactic fermentation takes places in barriques. In the 1990s only about twenty per cent new oak was used to age the wine, but by 2003 that proportion had increased to sixty per cent. The wine stays in barrel for eighteen months, without racking; instead it stays on the fine lees with stirring.

Thienpont believes the entire estate has the potential to form part of the *grand vin*, and indeed there is no second wine here. He describes Larcis-Ducasse as a wine that is never that powerful, but always has elegance. The volume produced has been reduced in a further attempt to increase quality.

Of the handful of vintages I have tasted from the 1980s, the best was the 1988, with its perfumed, oaky nose, its spice and elegance, its gentle persistence of flavour. The 1989 was good too, in a plumper style with light tannin, and an impression of slight laziness given the vintage. The 1993, tasted recently, was rather drab, and the aromas excessively woody. The 1996 was pleasant enough, with sweet tobacco aromas, but it lacks richness and depth. Tasted soon after bottling, the 2001 was rich and full-bodied yet oddly hollow; there was little flavour or texture development on the palate. The 2002 is good, despite a very light vegetal whiff; it is rich yet airy, not weighty but well made and stylish. The 2003 is a success, with lush, spicy flavours, firm tannins, and modest acidity that leads to a sweet finish. When I tasted the 2004 in 2007 it was dull and flat and hot, and I suspect this was a duff bottle. In its infancy the 2005 shows an elegance and balance largely lacking in the past.

Château Larmande

St-Emilion. Tel: 0557 247141. Website: www.chateau-larmande.com. **Owner:** *La Mondiale insurance group.*
Grand cru classé. 25 ha. 65% Merlot, 30% Cabernet Franc, 5% Cabernet Sauvignon. **Production:** *120,000 bottles.*
Second wine: Le Cadet de Larmande

In the early twentieth century Larmande was owned by a member of the Capdemourlin family. Indeed, Château Cap de Mourlin is just next door. She married Fernand Méneret, and their descendants remained proprietors until 1990, when Jean Méneret sold Larmande to the La Mondiale insurance company. The firm invested a good deal in restoring the property, and in 2000 appointed Claire Thomas-Chenard to manage it.

Of its twenty-five hectares, nineteen are a single parcel, and two are classified only as *grand cru* and thus are used as the basis for Cadet de Larmande. On higher ground the soil is clay-limestone, lower down there is sand over clay. The vineyards are ploughed, and are being converted to *guyot double*.

The *cuvier* is unusual, since in 2003 the large, round steel tanks were replaced by square ones, essentially to save space. After a cold soak for five days, selected yeasts are added just to start the fermentation; as well as pumpovers, there is some experimental manual *pigeage*. The wine is aged for twelve to fifteen months in sixty per cent new oak with very little racking, and fining has been dispensed with since 2002.

The location of Larmande suggests its wine should be very good indeed, although Claire Thomas-Chenard says its style is fruity and elegant rather than powerful. It is indeed often very good, yet never reaches the greatest heights. I recall an excellent 1983, a fruity, peppery, but not especially complex 1990, a charmless 1993, and an austere yet stylish 1994, marred by rather edgy acidity. There was a similar severity in 1995, but also a good deal of sweet oak and ample fruit, yet the wine still seemed lacking in verve. The 1996 may have less weight but it has more vigour. There are smoky, leathery aromas on the 1998, yet the wine lacks generosity and has a rustic edge. The 2000 gives a better idea of the estate's potential. The nose remains dense but the palate is plump, robust, and persistent, with flavours of black fruits and chocolate. It's not an elegant wine but it has strength and muscle. The 2001 may turn out to be superior, thanks to its swagger and spice and energy, although the fruit profile resembles that of the 2000. The 2002 has a very slight vegetal aroma, and is more slender than preceding vintages, but it has considerable purity. The 2003 was too massive and hollow when young, but seems to be filling out into a plump, full-bodied wine with chewy tannins and moderate length. The blunt tannins of the 2004 are balanced by good acidity and a tight structure; although it shows little complexity. The 2005 has spicy red-fruits aromas, but is light compared to most other wines from this year.

Château Laroque

St-Christophe-des-Bardes. Tel: 0557 247728. Website: www.chateau-laroque.com. **Owner:** *Beaumartin family.*
Grand cru classé. 61 ha. 87% Merlot, 11% Cabernet Franc, 2% Cabernet Sauvignon. **Production:** *150,000 bottles.*
Second wine: Ch Les Tours de Laroque

Laroque is one of the most dramatic of St-Emilion châteaux. Its origins as an eleventh-century fortress are still visible in the medieval tower, but the main part of the building is a glorious slab of window-filled masonry constructed in the eighteenth century. Behind the main block are some less felicitous neo-Gothic additions. Opposite the main gates stands a splendid avenue of ancient cedars; sadly, it was much damaged during the storm of December 1999.

The vineyards were first laid out, it seems, in the eighteenth century by the Marquis de Rochefort-Lavie, and it remained in that family until 1935, when it was bought by the present owners. At that time there were no longer any vineyards, and the estate was replanted from the 1960s onwards. Today Laroque is co-owned by three branches of the Beaumartin family, but the château is uninhabited.

Although the vineyards are enormous (for St-Emilion) only twenty-seven hectares are used for Laroque; the remainder are classified only as *grand cru* and are sold as Château Peymouton. Until 1996 the whole estate was only *grand cru*, but the best parcels were promoted in that year. They lie on a plateau of clay-limestone with rather shallow soil and varied expositions. The highest and best sectors are quite close to Troplong-Mondot, and there are other classified parcels west of the château. Buds and bunches are thinned, and leaves removed in summer. Some of the vineyards have alternating rows of green cover; others are ploughed.

Bruno Sainson has been the respected director of the property since 1982. The grapes are picked by hand, twice sorted, crushed, and pumped into cement tanks. Sainson does not believe that a cold soak makes much difference to the final wine. He favours the use of natural yeasts if at all possible, but is not dogmatic about it. Since 1999 he has applied some micro-oxygenation toward the end of fermentation. The tanks are quite large, but instead of going to the expense of completely reorganizing the winery, he has raised the floor level of most tanks to give smaller volumes. The wine is aged in fifty per cent new oak (only fifteen per cent for Peymouton).

Sainson does not make wine to a recipe. He likes to start blending in January, but if he feels uneasy about making up his mind at that stage, he has no qualms about blending later. I found the 1988 rather austere and bitter, but more recent vintages have been excellent. The 1998 has a sweet nose tinged with liquorice; the palate is clearly concentrated and rich, but it remains tight and youthful, with a long but solid finish. The 1999 is slightly bizarre aromatically with tobacco and balsamic tones, but the palate has an intensity reminiscent of the 1998, though it could use more flesh and weight. The 2000 is delicious. There are aromas of ripe black fruits, mint, and violets, while the palate is classic, with its spicy cherry fruit, firm tannins, and a fresh, lively finish conferred by good acidity.

The 2001 is in the same mould, but even better, with a tad more lushness, extract, and power. The 2002 is leaner, but there is no astringency or meanness here; it will make very attractive medium-term drinking. The 2003 was fine when young, but by 2007 had lost fruit and grip, and the tannins were dour. The 2004, with its graphite and black-fruits aromas and firm tannins, is nonetheless understated and lacking in excitement.

Although Bruno Sainson says he is aiming to make wines that have elegance rather than weight, I find the style dense, even inky, and tight, but redeemed by freshness and vigour. Clearly Laroque fully earned its promotion in 1996.

Château Laroze

St-Emilion. Tel: 0557 247979. Website: www.laroze.com. Owner: Guy Meslin. Grand cru classé. 27 ha. 68% Merlot, 26% Cabernet Franc, 6% Cabernet Sauvignon. Production: 110,000 bottles. Second wine: Lafleur-Laroze

This substantial property lies in a single block, divided only by a road, next to Grand-Mayne. It was owned during the nineteenth century by the Gurchy family, who created the property by amalgamating two others. A descendant married a Dr. Meslin, whose grandson has been the present owner since 1990. The Meslins are from Libourne, where they made their money as rope merchants. Guy Meslin has invested heavily to modernize the property; he has also put in extensive drainage in cooperation with his neighbours and has improved the vineyards.

The soil consists of sand over between one and two metres (three and six feet) of clay. The sand means that ripening is relatively early, which suits Cabernet Franc, which represents a quarter of the plantings. Meslin is always among the first to pick, as not only are the soils precocious, but he is keen to avoid overripeness. Density is around 5,555 vines per hectare, but newer plantings are at 6,100 and 8,300 vines per hectare. He uses no fertilizers or herbicides and ploughs the soil. In the 1990s he toyed with biodynamism, but attacks of mildew persuaded him to back off.

The grapes are sorted rigorously. Fermentation takes place in a variety of containers, with frequent pumpovers and *délestage*. Meslin recently abandoned the use of natural yeasts, as he finds they can result in high volatile acidity. He is equipped with a vertical press, and after partial malolactic fermentation in new barriques the wine is aged without racking for twelve to fourteen months in about sixty per cent new oak. He uses *cliquage* and lees-stirring to counter any reduction. In recent years Meslin has diminished his use of sulphur dioxide, which he believes hardens the wine; he reports that his wines have become darker and more structured as a result. There is fining or filtration, but never both.

The second wine is an innovation since 2000, and now represents about twenty per cent of production.

I once tasted the 1961, which had a sweet, lush nose with some figgy aromas; but some initial richness on the palate gave way to an astringent finish. The 1989 is typical of the vintage, with opulent aromas and a lush but robust structure, with welcome acidity and length. The 1990 is less successful, with more backbone than the fruit requires, and a slightly coarse finish. Both the 1995 and 1996 seemed rather rustic when young, and the 1996 still has an extracted, charmless finish. The smoky aromas on the 1998 are very attractive, and the wine shows elegance and freshness and should keep well. Since 2000 Laroze seems far more consistent. The oak is well integrated into the 2000, which also has delicate damsony aromas and much spice on the finish. The 2001 is similar but has more opulence, and the aromas are more savoury, almost balsamic; yet there is nothing over-bearing about the wine. The 2002 is quite concentrated and tannic, but a touch hollow and dry. The plummy 2003 has welcome concentration and length, while the 2004 is a return to a more classic style. The aromas are oaky, the palate is supple, and there is freshness and complexity on the long finish. The 2005 is more exciting, though, with black fruits and liquorice aromas, fine concentration, and a long, chocolatey finish.

Château Lassègue

*St-Hippolyte. Tel: 0557 241949. Website: www.chateau-lassegue.com. **Owner:** Jess Jackson. 24 ha. 60% Merlot, 35% Cabernet Franc, 5% Cabernet Sauvignon. **Production:** 80,000 bottles*

This property, with its seventeenth-century chartreuse, was bought in 2003 from the Freylon family by Jess Jackson, who has built up a colossal wine business in California. He runs Lassègue in partnership with one of his senior winemakers, Pierre Seillan. The sloping vineyards are on nine soil types, and efforts are made to keep yields to no more than thirty-five hl/ha. The wine is aged in eighty per cent new oak, and the style is bold and lush. Seillan didn't remove leaves in 2003 so the wine turned out well, although the suave, powerful 2004 and 2005 are even better. Grapes from the lower sector are consigned to the Château Vignot label, and these wines are also good, if less structured.

Château Louvie

*St-Laurent-des-Combes. Tel: 0607 285380. **Owner:** Christian Veyry. 3 ha. 80% Merlot, 20% Cabernet Franc. **Production:** 20,000 bottles*

Christian Veyry is a wine consultant who worked side by side with Michel Rolland, developing his own clientele with the blessing of Rolland. He owns a few small vineyards, based on the family property. Louvie lies both on alluvial soil below St-Laurent, and at the foot of slopes closer to St-Emilion itself. The soil is essentially sand, with some decomposed clay and limestone. The vines are, on average, thirty-five years old. The 2000, 2002, and 2003 are sound wines, medium-bodied, supple, quite oaky, with moderate length. The rather green 2002 is the weakest of this trio.

Château Magdelaine

*St-Emilion. Tel: 0557 517896. **Owner**: Ets J.P. Moueix. Premier grand cru classé (B). 11 ha. 95% Merlot,*
*5% Cabernet Franc. **Production**: 50,000 bottles. **Second wine**: Les Songes de Magdelaine*

Magdelaine is one of the most beautifully situated of the First Growths. Its neighbours on the plateau, where two-thirds of its vines are planted, are Canon and Bélair, while the remaining one-third lie on south-facing slopes in the form of a horseshoe embracing Fonplégade below.

The estate was owned for two centuries by the Chatonnet family until in 1952 it was bought by Jean-Pierre Moueix. Magdelaine has by far the highest proportion of Merlot of all the First Growths; the small amount of Cabernet Franc is planted on sandier soil lower down the slope. The oldest vines at Magdelaine are planted to a density of up to 9,000 per hectare, which is unusual for St-Emilion. On the plateau there is rarely more than twenty centimetres (eight inches) of sandy topsoil over the limestone, whereas there is more clay in the slopes. As far as I know, it is the only St-Emilion property where the vineyards are worked by a horse-drawn plough.

Following the usual Moueix policy, the vines are normally picked quite rapidly, then sorted. Only indigenous yeasts are used, and there is no chaptalization. The wine is aged for about eighteen months in a proportion of new barriques that varies from thirty to fifty per cent. Blending is late, and the wine is bottled unfiltered.

I have been able to taste some old vintages of Magdelaine, mostly in the late 1980s but also in the late 1990s. The 1945 had a lovely cedary nose, elegant despite a raisiny tone; on the palate the attack was sweet and intense, but then a baked character undermined the fruit, leaving a long but somewhat dry finish. A 1955 had lost its fruit, but perhaps was an atypical bottle, as the 1959, from the same Belgian-bottled source, was magnificent, with a fleshy, oaky, chocolatey nose; the wine was highly concentrated and plump, with an extremely long and peppery finish. The 1964 looked mature and the nose was evolved, with aromas of iodine, mint and smoke; but there was no shortage of fruit on the palate, which was utterly alive after twenty-five years. The 1970 had a slight herbaceous aroma, but on the palate there was intensity and quite high acidity, but also a lack of flesh and dimension – stylish but not exceptional.

After fifteen years the 1976 was tired, with a hot finish; the 1980 was evolved and supple, but is now likely to be past its best. The 1981 is elegant but quite light, with some herbaceousness, and may well be fading by now. The 1982 was gorgeous in the 1990s, with seductive cedary aromas, and a palate of unexpected elegance, given the very ripe character of the year, and intensity; in all, an exquisite wine in perfect harmony, and with exemplary length. In the late 1980s the 1983 was austere and reserved, but had plenty of power and concentration. I have not tasted it recently. At the time I preferred the 1985, with its intense blackcurrant aromas, its excellent attack, and its forthright charm. Ten years on, the 1986, though elegant and oaky on the nose, was rather coarse on the palate, though it had impressive length. The 1987 was modest but well made and balanced, but is probably past its best.

The 1989 remains very youthful in colour and aroma. It's medium-bodied and no blockbuster; what it may lack in weight and power, it makes up for in finesse and persistence. By 2007 the 1990 was pure refined and gentle. With the 1995 a lushness of fruit had yet to harmonize with some rather blunt, even hard, tannins; since none of that rawness was apparent when the wine was still in cask, I would surmise that it is going through a closed stage. The 2000 comes close to overripeness, but there is also a great deal of freshness and vigour on the nose; it's opulent and very concentrated, but with enough acidity to keep it lively. It should have a brilliant future. New oak is apparent on the nose of the 2001, but here too the palate is dominated by freshness and vigour. The 2004 is superb, with exquisite smoky damson aromas, and a lushness on the palate that's underpinned by robust tannins and firm acidity, adding up to a wine of terrific finesse. The 2005, tasted in its infancy from cask, shows a similar freshness, a silky texture, and great stylishness. The 2006, also tasted from cask, has red-fruits aromas and the palate seems similar though with rather less flesh.

Magdelaine shows the imprint of Christian Moueix and his winemaker Jean-Claude Berrouet. It's never flashy or particularly dense; instead, the emphasis is on elegance and intensity, which is rather surprising when one recalls that the wine is almost pure Merlot. When young, Magdelaine can hold back. It needs a decade for a good vintage to reveal all its complexity and stylishness. The second wine was introduced only in 2004.

Château Mangot

St-Etienne-de-Lisses. Tel: 0557 401823. Website: www.chateaumangot.fr. Owners: Jean-Guy and Anne-Marie Todeschini. Grand cru. 34 ha. 84% Merlot, 10% Cabernet Franc, 6% Cabernet Sauvignon.
Production: 160,000 bottles. Second wine: Ch Bardoulet

In 1953 Jean Petit bought the Château de Lisse, which had six hectares of vines. Thirty years later Jean-Guy Todeschini, who was married to a Petit daughter, bought the adjoining property of Château Mangot, with twenty-three hectares under vine. A century ago the two properties had been one and the same, and now they were again united. The vineyards lie below Château de Pressac and adjacent to Faugères.

Todeschini has divided the vineyard into twenty-one sectors, based on soil types and exposition. The highest parcels are on the St-Etienne plateau near Fleur Cardinale. The grapes are partially picked by machine. After destemming, they are sorted, lightly crushed, then pumped into steel tanks for a cold soak. Todeschini sometimes employs micro-oxygenation during fermentation. The wine is aged for twelve to sixteen months in forty-five per cent new oak, with different wood sources adapted to wines from different parcels.

Since 1996 Mangot has also produced a late-picked parcel selection of Merlot called Quintessence. These vines are almost fifty years old, and yields are around thirty hl/ha. This wine is made with *pigeage*, and then aged for sixteen months in new barriques; some lots, indeed, are barrel-fermented. No more than 12,000 bottles are produced, and they are sold at twice the price of Mangot. A third *cuvée*, called Château de Lisse, is made exclusively from some lower parcels; it sees less new oak, and is intended for early drinking.

The 2000 Mangot, despite a firm nose of plums and liquorice, has rather sharp acidity and seemed lacking in ripeness and flesh. The 2000 Quintessence is considerably better, with more obvious oakiness on the nose, and better concentration and length. In 2001 the difference between the two wines is less marked. The Mangot has more flesh and complexity than the 2000, and although the Quintessence is more powerful and extracted, the nose is rather jammy, and the tannins quite brutal. Indeed, the 2001 Mangot is better balanced than its pricier cousin. In the 2003, both bottlings are marred by cooked aromas and rather dry tannins. Again, the Mangot seems better balanced, being less extreme in extraction and alcohol. In St-Emilion, going for extremes – of ripeness, concentration, alcohol – is not necessarily the right decision.

Château Marquey

St-Emilion. Tel: 0557 246261. Owners: Hervé and Griet Laviale. Grand cru. 3 ha. 75% Merlot,
25% Cabernet Franc. Production: 15,000 bottles

When Georgy Fourcroy, former owner of Château Franc-Mayne, sold the latter in 2005, he also sold this small property, with its vineyards on flatter sandy soil below Pavie. Fourcroy aged the wine in twenty-five per cent new oak. The only vintage I have tasted, the 2001, had rich, meaty aromas, a rounded palate, and slightly austere tannins. But it had personality.

Château La Marzelle

St-Emilion. Tel: 0557 551055. Website: www.lamarzelle.com. Owner: Jean-Jacques Sioen. Grand cru.
17 ha. 84% Merlot, 16% Cabernet Franc. Production: 70,000 bottles

The cellars of La Marzelle are located behind the imposing bulk of the Hotel Grand-Barrail midway between St-Emilion and Libourne. It has a complicated history. Until 1956 La Marzelle was united with what are now two other properties just south of Figeac, Grand-Barrail and La Marzelle-Figeac. Then in 1956 the château of Grand-Barrail became detached from the estate and in 1972 was converted into a hotel. In 1996 Châteaux Grand-Barrail and La Marzelle-Figeac were demoted to *grand cru*. A year later all three properties were put on the market, and La Marzelle was bought by a new Belgian owner, Jean-Jacques Sioen. In 2003 he bought a further four hectares that had formed part of Grand-Barrail, but these vines were, of course, mere *grand cru* and could not be blended in with La Marzelle.

There are three soil types. Near Figeac there is gravel. Elsewhere there is brown soil over clay, where Merlot is planted; and ancient sandy soils, where Cabernet Franc and some young Merlot are growing. The manager of La Marzelle, Philippe Genevey, has expended much effort on the vineyards, which were designed for machine-harvesting and have had to be re-adapted. Herbicide use was stopped in 1998 and there is much planting of green cover to restore more organic material to the once-abused soil.

The grapes are picked by hand, sorted, and then lightly crushed over the tanks to avoid pumping. After a cold soak, the must is fermented in both wooden and steel tanks, usually with natural yeasts. Genevey corrects any deficiencies by bleeding the tanks, and also uses *pigeage*. The length of *cuvaison* varies greatly, but has been as long as sixty days. The length of barrel-ageing depends on the wine's structure. Wine from young vines may stay in oak for only eight months; wine from old vines can be oaked for as long as eighteen months. Genevey started by using sixty per cent new oak, but has now reduced the proportion to around one-third. The wine is bottled without filtration.

The four hectares acquired in 2003 are vinified separately and bottled as Prieuré La Marzelle. After the demotion of La Marzelle in 2006, there is no reason why the two wines should not be blended.

The 2000 La Marzelle is very oaky on the nose, while the palate is rich and boldly flavoured; the tannins are properly integrated and the wine has reasonable length. I slightly prefer it to the lusher and slightly jammy 2001, which also seems more one-dimensional. The 2002 is plump and fruit-forward; although not persistent, it is balanced and enjoyable. The 2003 is at the other end of the spectrum, being baked and confected, and manages to be simultaneously meagre and aggressive. The 2004 is a step above previous vintages, with its succulent fruit, ripe tannins, and long, fresh finish. The 2005 is sleek and charming, but lacks some weight.

Château Matras

St-Emilion. Tel: 0557 515239. Owner: Véronique Gaboriaud-Bernard. Grand cru classé. 8 ha. 34% Merlot,
33% Cabernet Franc, 33% Cabernet Sauvignon. Production: 35,000 bottles. Second wine: L'Hermitage de Matras

Matras is well located on sheltered southern slopes of St-Emilion, not far from Angélus and Tertre Daugay. The soil is silty limestone, as well as clay-limestone in some sectors. The peculiarity of the property is the high proportion of Cabernet Franc and Cabernet Sauvignon, which is highly unusual in this sector. The wine is aged in fifty per cent new oak for up to eighteen months.

I have positive notes on the 1995 and 1996, which were both marked by their vigour and stylishness. The 2000, however, seemed to lack both, having a rather flat texture. In contrast, the 2001 has more meaty aromas, more weight and concentration, and a strong, chewy finish. The 2003 is jammy and flabby. The 2004 is excellent, with smoky, oaky aromas, a sleek texture, fine concentration and a long, compact finish.

Château Milon

St-Christophe-des-Bardes. Tel: 0557 247718. Owner: Pierre Bouyer. Grand cru. 6.5 ha. 75% Merlot,
15% Cabernet Sauvignon, 10% Cabernet Franc. Production: 35,000 bottles

Like Clos de la Cure (*q.v.*), this property belongs to the Bouyer family. Pierre Bouyer runs Clos de la Cure and Milon, but another 6.5 hectares that once formed part of Milon have been carved off and put into the hands of his sister. Her share of the estate is bottled as Château Les Giraudelles de Milon, but Pierre vinifies both wines. Only organic fertilizers are used, no herbicides are employed, and since 1995 the soil has been ploughed.

The estate is partly machine-harvested. After a light crushing, the grapes are cold-soaked for about five days. Selected yeasts are added only when Bouyer considers there is a risk of stuck fermentation. Vinification takes place in cement tanks, with both automatic *pigeage* and micro-oxygenation. The wine is aged for twelve months in one-third new oak with minimal racking and with *cliquage* to neutralize any reduction.

Aromatically, the wine is marked by blackberries and black cherries. There is a slight rusticity on the palate, as the tannins are fairly tough and can be hard-edged. Of recent vintages the 2000 and 2001 are the best, while both the 2002 and 2003 are disappointing.

Château Monbousquet

*St-Sulpice-de-Faleyrens. Tel: 0557 554343. Website: www.vignoblesperse.com **Owner:** Gérard Perse. Grand cru classé. 31 ha. 30 ha red: 70% Merlot, 20% Cabernet Franc, 10% Cabernet Sauvignon. 1 ha white: 60% Sauvignon Blanc, 30% Sauvignon Gris, 5% Muscadelle, 5% Sémillon. **Production:** 90,000 bottles. **Second wine:** Angélique de Monbousquet*

This fine mansion and its vineyards were bought by supermarket tycoon Gérard Perse in 1993. It was to be the first of many purchases in the Libournais, and the château has become the Perse family home. The estate's history dates back to 1540, when François de Lescours was the owner; the house was built in 1684 by Jacques de Gères, and until the late nineteenth century was in the hands of various noble families. In 1945 it was bought by Daniel Querre, in whose family it remained until the sale to Perse. In 2006 Monbousquet was promoted to *grand cru classé*.

Being on the flat alluvial soil of St-Sulpice, the soil is far from exceptional. It is sandy clay to the north, and farther south essentially gravel, which has the advantage of being warm and precocious. The Cabernets are planted on the most gravelly sectors, which are well drained. The average age of the vines is a substantial forty years. Yields are rigorously reduced to no more than thirty hl/ha.

In 1997 Perse began to produce a white wine from an unusual blend of grape varieties, which he had planted on fallow land. The first vintage came from a poor harvest, and only 300 bottles were produced. It was not at all bad, however. The nose was firm and oaky, and the wine showed plump fruit and decent concentration. The 2001 is floral and exotic on the nose, and the palate almost Alsatian in its flowery character; perhaps a touch overripe, it is nonetheless a seductive mouthful of fruit.

The red wine is vinified in stainless steel, then aged in new barriques for eighteen months, before being bottled without fining or filtration. The only pre-Perse wine I have tasted is the 1975, which had surprising charm and fruit. Other reports suggest that the wines made in the decade or more before Perse bought Monbousquet were decidedly mediocre. The first Perse vintage, 1993, is remarkably good, since it had to be vinified without temperature control as the *cuvier* had not yet been renovated. It is supple, plummy, and concentrated even if the finish is blunt. The 1995 was voluptuous and fleshy, though I detected a slight earthiness too; but it was balanced, long, and very enjoyable. Thereafter I have mostly tasted Monbousquet during its *élevage*, when it was invariably very marked by new oak. The 2004, tasted after twelve months in wood, was opaque in colour, rich and sweet on the nose with blackcurranty fruit, and was extracted and powerful; the fruit was undoubtedly impressive if a touch overpowering. Perse makes no secret of the fact that he, and Michel Rolland, go all out for maximum concentration, and compensate for the deficiencies of the terroir by determined winemaking.

Château Mondorion

*St-Sulpice-de-Faleyrens. Tel: 0557 247611. **Owner:** Giorgio Cavanna. Grand cru. 11 ha. 76% Merlot, 24% Cabernet Franc. **Production:** 42,000 bottles. **Second wine:** Etoile de Mondorion*

In 2000 this property was bought, and given its present name, by Giorgio Cavanna, co-owner of the renowned Castello di Ama estate in Tuscany. He also purchased Grand Enclos du Château de Cérons (*q.v.*) in the Graves jointly with Patrick Léon and other shareholders. Mondorion lies close to Monbousquet on sandy and gravelly soils. The average age of the vines is some thirty-five years. The grapes are picked in *cagettes*, sorted and destemmed, then fermented in concrete tanks. The wine is aged for twelve months in around fifty per cent new oak, and bottled without filtration.

The 2000 and 2001 were disappointing: attractive aromas were let down by earthy, chunky tannins and a dull coarseness. The 2002 was considerably richer and more harmonious, suggesting that the preceding vintages were the result of teething problems. The 2003 is also good, with rich, flamboyant aromas, including cloves, and a juiciness and welcome persistence on the palate.

La Mondotte

St-Emilion. Tel: 0557 247133. Website: www.neipperg.com. Owner: Von Neipperg family. Grand cru.
4.5 ha. 80% Merlot, 20% Cabernet Franc. Production: 12,000 bottles

It's either luck or genius, but somehow Stephan von Neipperg transformed this lacklustre wine almost overnight into a St-Emilion superstar. The property was bought by his father in 1971. Stephan von Neipperg wanted to incorporate Château La Mondotte, as it then was, into Canon-La-Gaffelière, but La Mondotte was not a *grand cru classé*; moreover it was in a different sector, with Troplong-Mondot and Pavie-Decesse for neighbours. The wine was vinified with no great care and aged in older barriques. Then in 1996 it was reborn as La Mondotte pure and simple, and its success was immediate. The 1995 had been released with a *prix de sortie* of 35 francs; the 1996 came out at a brazen 180 francs.

What happened? Neipperg knew that to make the most of the terroir he needed a separate cellar on the small property. This he constructed, and to recoup the cost he and his then-winemaker Stéphane Derenoncourt knew they needed to make something special. Clearly they both had a hunch that the terroir was capable of this. For a start the vines had an average age of forty-five years. Then the soil, although the property was on the plateau, had a good deal of clay. The limestone here is fractured and the roots can descend in search of moisture and nutrients. Yields were curbed, though some of the oldest vines never gave more than twenty-five hl/ha. The yield at La Mondotte is generally between twenty-five and thirty hl/ha. The vineyard work is meticulous, even more so since the property was converted to biodynamism in 2000.

The grapes are sorted at the winery, destemmed, sorted again, and then descend as whole bunches into conical wooden vats for fermentation. Neipperg opts for a slow fermentation with *pigeage*, and the malolactic fermentation is unrushed, as at Canon-La-Gaffelière. The wine is aged for eighteen months in new barriques, with about half the *élevage* on the fine lees. La Mondotte is neither fined nor filtered.

In character the wine is very different from the elegant Canon-La-Gaffelière and the fruity, opulent Clos de l'Oratoire. It has immense richness and power, verging on overripeness at times. Even in a tricky vintage such as 1997 La Mondotte is imposing. Behind its lush nose are subtle aromas of sour cherries, eau-de-vie, and mint; there is an invigorating spiciness on the palate that enlivens the wine's extreme concentration, and it has good acidity and length. The 2001 is brilliant, with smoky, black-cherry aromas, and its concentration of flavour is finely matched by an underlying restraint and finesse. The 2004 is very rich but has a distinct flamboyance and no overripeness, with, again, fine underlying acidity. The 2005 is similar but even more intense and persistent, but the 2006 from cask seemed dangerously overripe.

Stephan von Neipperg admits that La Mondotte is a very big wine, but has not gone for power for the sake of it. "La Mondotte is different from Canon-La-Gaffelière because the soil is different. If we attempted the same level of maturity at Canon-La-Gaffelière we would end up with soft, heavy wines."

Château Montlisse

St-Etienne-de-Lisse. Tel: 0557 247744. Website: www.vignobles-dauriac.com. Owner: Christian Dauriac. Grand cru.
7 ha. 85% Merlot, 8% Cabernet Franc, 7% Cabernet Sauvignon. Production: 30,000 bottles

The single-minded approach of Christian Dauriac has already been described in the entry for Château Destieux (*q.v.*). Montlisse is a more recent creation, produced from vineyards detached from Destieux, and the début vintage was 1998. It is the least qualitative of his properties, with sloping clay-limestone vineyards next to Fleur Cardinale. But yields are kept low, below forty hl/ha, and the winemaking is meticulous. The wine is aged in fifty per cent new oak in a *chai* hung with grotesque hunting trophies, including a bison.

The 1998 is fairly rich but the oak is not fully integrated; the wine still tastes youthful, with a pronounced red-fruits character and a surprising lack of flesh. The 2002 is in the same style, with cherry and redcurrant aromas, and a lean, intense palate that is quite assertive. This leanness may be a consequence of Montlisse's cold soil, which ripens late and sometimes with difficulty.

Château La Mouleyre

St-Etienne-de-Lisse. Tel: 0557 845316. Website: www.vignobles-bardet.fr. Owner: Philippe Bardet.
Grand cru. 12 ha. 88% Merlot, 12% Cabernet Franc. Production: 60,000 bottles

Bardet, who also owns Château Val d'Or (*q.v.*), bought this property in 1996, but most of it had to be replanted since the vines were in poor shape. Thus he considers the first satisfactory vintage was 2002. The 2001 was rounded and fleshy but lacked vigour and was a rather dull wine. The 2002 is indeed better, with light cherry aromas, and a dash more acidity than the 2001; but it too sags in the middle and lacks verve.

Château Moulin du Cadet

St-Emilion. Tel: 0557 550050. Owner: Isabelle Blois Moueix. Grand cru classé. 5 ha. 100% Merlot.
Production: 20,000 bottles

This rather obscure *grand cru classé* has since 2002 been run by Alain Moueix, brother of the owner and proprietor of the neighbouring Château Fonroque. He has taken over from other members of the family, who had been running the estate since 1989. His most radical move was to convert the estate to biodynamism. The soil is essentially limestone, with sandier sectors where the terrain dips. The wine is aged for eighteen months in fifty per cent new oak. The oldest vintage I have encountered is the full-bodied, robust 1995, which is packed with fruit. The 2002 is rich, full-bodied, rounded, yet accessible and long. The 2003 is rather dilute and feeble. The 2004 is sound but very tannic and lacks persistence. Despite rather low acidity, the 2005 is mouth-filling and concentrated and shows great promise.

Château Moulin-St-Georges

St-Emilion. Tel: 0557 247457. Owner: Alain Vauthier. Grand cru. 7 ha. 70% Merlot, 15% Cabernet Franc,
15% Cabernet Sauvignon. Production: 35,000 bottles

Moulin-St-Georges has been owned by the Vauthier family (of Ausone) since 1921. The estate lies just across the road from Ausone, close to La Gaffelière, but the terroir is very different, lacking Ausone's elevation and soils. There is also a parcel that lies near La Clotte in the Fongaban valley. What once made the property unusual was the significant proportion of Petit Verdot, which Vauthier planted in 1990 in collaboration with the Chambre d'Agriculture. But the rootstock proved to be poor, so Vauthier decided to pull it out. In addition, it only gave good wine one year out of three.

The wine, which is fermented in steel tanks, is made by the Ausone team, and spends eighteen months in new barriques. The 2000 is now opening up aromatically to show a good deal of cherry and raspberry fruit; on the palate the wine remains dense and assertive but with a welcome spiciness and persistence. On the 2002 the oak is well integrated, giving the wine more elegance and silkiness than the robust 2000; but there is a similar boldness of flavour, spiciness, and length.

Château Pas de l'Ane

St-Christophe-des-Bardes. Tel: 0557 746255. Owners: Arnaud Delaire and partners. Grand cru. 2.5 ha.
60% Merlot, 40% Cabernet Franc. Production: 10,000 bottles. Second wine: Ch Haut St Brice

Delaire and his associates are co-owners of some important properties in the satellites of St-Emilion, notably Château Branda (*q.v.*). They also own this small property near Laroque. The soil is varied, and a sector with more silty soil is the source of the second wine. The wine is aged for eighteen months in new oak, and neither fined nor filtered. The 2003 is rich and oaky yet there is a certain fluidity and lack of grip in this admittedly atypical year. An early cask tasting suggested the 2006 had more richness than zest, and was somewhat over-extracted.

Château Patris

*St-Emilion Tel: 0557 555160. **Owner:** Michel Querre. Grand cru. 8.5 ha. 90% Merlot, 5% Cabernet Franc, 5% Cabernet Sauvignon. **Production:** 50,000 bottles. **Second wine:** Le Filius de Ch Patris*

Michel Querre is a dynamic négociant who also owns a number of properties in the Libournais. Patris has been in his family since 1967. The vineyards lie on a gentle slope below Angélus and on both sides of the main road to Libourne. They are planted on sandy soil over a clay-limestone subsoil. Querre green-harvests and keeps the yield to around forty hl/ha; he does not want exaggeratedly low yields as he wants to offer the wine at a reasonable price. Since 1999 Marie-Hélène Schaaper has been the winemaker at all his properties.

The grapes are picked in *cagettes* and repeatedly sorted. Most of the vinification takes place in steel tanks, but there are also a few wooden vats that are equipped for *pigeage*. Toward the end of fermentation the wine is micro-oxygenated, a system that, according to Querre, gave very good results in 1999 when a hailstorm required him to pick earlier than he wanted to. The wine is aged in fifty per cent new oak, with some ageing on the fine lees. There is no fining, and only occasional filtration.

The 1998 was delicious, truly voluptuous and concentrated yet with fine acidity. There are no vegetal tones on the 1999, but it's a rather solid wine, reasonably fresh but lacking some flair. The 2001's rich blackberry nose leads one to expect a lush mouthful of wine, but the palate is modest: supple but lacking in body and persistence. The 2003 has no cooked aromas, but is light and unexciting, and the 2004 lacks vigour and length.

Château Pavie

*St-Emilion Tel: 0557 554343. **Website:** www.vignobles-perse.com. **Owner:** Gérard Perse. Premier grand cru classé (B). 42 ha. 60% Merlot, 30% Cabernet Franc, 10% Cabernet Sauvignon. **Production:** 90,000 bottles*

No wine in St-Emilion excites more passions than Pavie. Robert Parker has always been an extravagant admirer of Pavie since Perse bought the property; British tasters often find the wine wildly over-extracted. There is no right or wrong response. This is no more than a question of taste, and the *ad hominem* arguments that have marred the debate about Pavie should have no place in any discussion about a bottle of wine.

Pavie was expanded to its present dimensions in the 1880s by the then-owner, Ferdinand Bouffard. After World War I Bouffard sold the property to Albert Porte, who in turn sold it to Alexandre Valette in 1943. The wines from the 1940s and 1950s enjoyed a very high reputation. There were, however, some subsequent vintages widely regarded as disappointing. Eventually Pavie was put on the market, and the purchaser in 1998 was a wine-loving supermarket tycoon called Gérard Perse, who was already the owner of Monbousquet. He had always admired Pavie and jumped at the opportunity to buy it.

Those who visit Pavie are immediately struck by the winery and *chai* sprawled along the slope leading up to the plateau. It is natural to infer that the Pavie vineyards are located on this slope, and indeed some of them are. But Pavie is a very large property. To visit its various sectors by car with Gérard Perse took the best part of an hour. The vineyards fall into three sectors: below the *chai*, on gravelly soil; on the steep slope behind the *chai*, where clay dominates; and on the plateau, where his neighbours include Troplong-Mondot. This third sector is the most complicated, since the plateau is not uniform; there are different expositions and small side valleys. Pavie's oldest parcel lies in one of these west-facing side valleys, where some eighty-year-old Cabernet Franc and Cabernet Sauvignon are planted. It won't be around for much longer, as there are many missing vines and the mortality rate is high. However, Pavie has many old vines, and their average age is around forty-five years.

In 2001 Pavie expanded. Perse had requested INAO to allow him to incorporate two other properties he owned, La Clusière and Pavie-Decesse (*qq.v.*), into Pavie. INAO agreed to the inclusion of La Clusière, but only allowed 6.5 hectares of Pavie-Decesse to be incorporated, as the other 3.5 lay across the border in the commune of St-Laurent-des-Combes. INAO argued that there had never been a *premier grand cru classé* vineyard outside the commune of St-Emilion itself, and they did not want to set a precedent. To compensate for the expansion of Pavie in 2001, Perse declassified six hectares from a site called Simard, which was on sandy soils that were clearly not of First Growth quality.

Perse says that much of Pavie is late-ripening, which is the main reason why he is ruthless about green-harvesting. Yields in 2004, for example, were twenty-eight hl/ha, a level that few estates would regard as economic, especially in an abundant vintage. Before he bought the property, yields, he claimed, had been closer to sixty hl/ha, and many vines were missing. This stark crop reduction does, of course, have economic consequences, and the production of Pavie has more or less halved since the Valette family owned it.

The winery buildings were either renovated or rebuilt by Perse. The old *chai*, he decided, was too cold and humid for ideal *élevage*. After sorting, the grapes are taken by conveyor belt to a platform above the tanks, where they are destemmed and crushed. A cold soak follows for at least four days. The must is fermented in oak vats, and is sometimes bled by as much as thirty per cent of the juice, so as to concentrate the wine even further. However, there are no must concentrators at Pavie. Both pumpovers and *pigeage* aid extraction. The new wine is decanted, still warm, into new oak barrels, where it undergoes malolactic fermentation and is then aged. The first six months of the *élevage* are spent on the fine lees. The total ageing is usually twenty-four months, and in the case of the 2003, twenty-eight months. There is no fining or filtration. Perse is convinced that the wine's longevity and aromatic complexity derive, in large part, from lees-ageing, and he racks only when he considers it absolutely necessary.

Perse is very clear about the style of wine he wishes to make. He told me: "I want to make *vins de garde* with plenty of tannin. We have adapted the viticulture to give the result we want: removing leaves so there is no risk of rot should it rain, low yields, and picking at perfect maturity. All these measures ensure we can make good wine in difficult vintages too." Perse is a free spirit. He does not have to report to directors or shareholders, and can follow his own taste. Those who ascribe the excesses of Pavie to Rolland are largely wrong: Perse calls the shots for his own wines.

Not everyone shares his view that ultra-concentration is the right path to follow. One of his fellow First-Growth proprietors told me that at the kinds of yields Perse aims for, the typicity of Pavie in terms of its terroir becomes obliterated. Perse would certainly not agree.

Such perfectionism, which I imagine is how Perse perceives his approach, comes at a cost. Pavie is very expensive, but Perse is unapologetic. "To make great wine is very costly. At Pavie and Pavie-Decesse we have made enormous investments at the wineries, and have large teams in the vineyards. We also produce only half as much wine as Pavie used to. As for the *prix de sortie*, well, it's a function of the market. Of course the quality has to be there, but it's in the context of a commercial environment. I am certainly keen for my wines to be considered at the very top level, so they are released at a high price."

Pavie wins high scores, but its price seems to deter buyers. In December 2005 the London-based wine broker Farr Vintners offered substantial discounts on two Perse wines from 2001. Monbousquet was reduced from £460 to £250 in bond, and Pavie from £950 to £650. The offer indicated that the wines came directly from the château. Since Farr does not carry much stock, it is clear that Perse was unloading some of his own stock. The implication must be that the wines, despite their high scores, were too high-priced on release to find sufficient customers.

The oldest Pavie that has come my way was a 1952 in 1999. It had slightly baked aromas, with coffee and cedary tones, but the nose was certainly intense; the palate was rich and plump and spicy, but on the finish there was some astringency and dryness. A 1964, tasted recently, was voluptuous on the nose, and the palate married a creamy texture with a slight earthiness that was not disagreeable; however, it was a very good rather than a stellar wine. After twelve years the colour of the 1975 had developed brick tones, the nose was meaty, and the palate was tough and unyielding. The 1982 was fleshy and harmonious by the mid-1990s, with spice, elegance, and length. I also liked the 1983, although the nose was slightly herbaceous; its supple, rich palate was enlivened by good acidity. The 1985, by the late 1990s, had developed meaty aromas, and the wine itself was dense and chunky, and seemed rather over-extracted. I slightly preferred the stylish 1986, which was well structured, although less overtly rich.

The 1988, tasted recently, looked mature, and tasted a touch stewed and clumsy; it lacked finesse and persistence. The 1989 is far better, with elegant truffley aromas verging on gaminess; the palate was dense and concentrated yet fresh and lively. The 1990 has tasted good from the outset and is still going strong, a velvety, concentrated, peppery wine with a long, complex finish. In its youth the 1995 was voluptuous but backed by ripe tannins and fine oak. The 1996 is a disappointment, lacking grip and vigour; it has some charm but little weight.

The 1998 was the first Perse vintage. My most recent note (2005) reads: "Very rich, very oaky nose, vanilla, cloves, soy. Very rich, dense, tannic, oaky, oddly hollow in its fruit expression, modest acidity, lacks freshness and vigour, too powerful." The Perse style was born. The 1999 is a more modest version of the 1998. The 2000 was undoubtedly impressive, with massive fruit on the nose; the tannins were chewy but ripe, the wine had power and persistence if little elegance, and it didn't lack length. The 2001 had similar qualities, but to excess; the wine smelt and tasted distinctly overripe, and despite the sumptuous texture and fruit, and the concentration and power, it was worryingly alcoholic on the finish. I have never tasted the 2003 that aroused so much excitement, but if its hallmark is indeed portiness, then I doubt it would appeal to me.

I tasted the 2004 blind in April 2005 alongside most of the other St-Emilion First Growths. It was not hard to identify the wine as Pavie, thanks to its super-ripe aromas, its huge tannins, its rather soupy texture, and bitter-chocolate finish. Tasting the wine later with Gérard Perse, where he found complexity I found a monolith. Tasted blind with its peers in 2007, it was, again, easy to spot Pavie, with its tarry aromas, its lashings of new oak, its power and chewiness; it has length, certainly, but no elegance.

Perse says he makes the kinds of wines he likes to drink. That is fair enough. But he must have a more robust constitution than I do. It should be obvious by now that in the great debate over his wines I am among those who do not much care for them, and find them overwhelming. They are built to impress – and do impress – but they are very hard to drink with great pleasure. In his own publicity material, Gérard Perse refers to "the famous Perse method, which consists of pushing to extremes the quest for excellence". There lies the problem: a high degree of vanity combined with an assumption that going to extremes is a formula for achieving excellence.

Château Pavie-Decesse

St-Emilion. Tel: 0557 554343. Website: www.vignobles-perse.com. Owner: Gérard Perse. Grand cru classé.
3.5 ha. 90% Merlot, 10% Cabernet Franc. Production: 6,000 bottles

Ferdinand Bouffard assembled the Pavie estate in the 1880s. At the century's end he separated some parcels and named them Pavie-Decesse. After World War I he sold this property to M. Marzelle. After Marzelle's death in 1970, the estate was run by Jean-Paul Valette, who eventually acquired it in 1990, only to sell it in 1997 to Gérard Perse. As has been mentioned in the entry for Pavie, much of Pavie-Decesse was incorporated into Pavie in 2001, leaving just a few hectares. The vines themselves are above those of Pavie, and their average age is over forty years.

Perse adopts the same approach to Pavie-Decesse as to the *premier grand cru classé*. Michel Rolland is his consultant and the vinification techniques are similar, with very low yields, fermentation in wooden vats, and long ageing in new oak. One major difference is the much lower proportion of Cabernet in the blend.

Some of the vintages just before the sale to Perse were not bad at all. The 1995 was sweet and elegant on the nose, and there was an appealing juiciness to the wine, which had reasonable concentration and length. The 1996 was less intense but perhaps more stylish and better balanced. The 1997 is very good if a touch extracted; nonetheless it had richness and concentration. The 1998 is delicious, with a brightness that I find lacking in its big brother Pavie; its sweet and concentrated fruit is finely balanced by ripe tannin and acidity. The 2000, like Pavie, is undoubtedly impressive. Although super-ripe and assertively oaky, with flavours of plums and choco-late, there is sufficient acidity to prevent the wine from being overbearing. The 2001, on the other hand, is over the top, with its jammy, oaky nose, its massive fruitiness, plumpness, and succulence, and absence of finesse. The opaque 2004 has lush blackberry and plum aromas and is compact and immensely rich on the palate, showing super-ripe Merlot; but the concentration is admirable, and is far more appealing than the 2004 Pavie.

20. St-Emilion Part IV

Château Pavie-Macquin

St-Emilion. Tel: 0557 247423. **Owner:** *Corre-Macquin family. Premier grand cru classé (B). 15 ha. 70% Merlot,*
25% Cabernet Franc, 5% Cabernet Sauvignon. **Production:** *60,000 bottles.* **Second wine:** *Les Chênes de Macquin*

Albert Macquin made his fortune by grafting vines onto American rootstocks after the phylloxera epidemic. He bought this well-located property, which today is owned by his descendants. As absentee proprietors, they rather neglected the property and various consultants were called in. In 1990 Stéphane Derenoncourt converted part of the estate to biodynamism. But in 1993 there was widespread mildew and Pavie-Macquin lost two-thirds of its crop; the manager took early retirement and that was the end of the biodynamic era here. The following year, Nicolas Thienpont was hired to run the estate. Since 1997 the vineyards have been cultivated according to the principles of *lutte raisonnée*. In practice Pavie-Macquin is an organic estate, although Thienpont doesn't seek certification, as he wants to retain the possibility of applying treatments should he ever feel they are necessary.

Thienpont is a member of a well-known Belgian family of wine merchants, many of whose members have settled in Bordeaux. It's a cousinage: Alexandre runs Vieux-Château-Certan, Jacques owns Le Pin, and, until a few years ago, Luc ran Château Labégorce-Zédé in Margaux and now owns Clos des Quatre Vents in Margaux. Nicolas Thienpont has some properties of his own in the Côte de Francs.

Most of the vines lie on the limestone plateau near Pavie, yielding a wine quite powerful in style. A solitary tree stands on that plateau, one of two trees that appears on the Pavie-Macquin label, along with a noose, to remind the drinker that miscreants used to be hanged here. Soil structure would have been of little interest to the condemned, but the soils here are fairly homogeneous, though their depth varies. The deepest sector is near the winery, and from here the wines can be massive. The vines are green-harvested to a maximum of eight bunches, and Thienpont likes to pick very late if conditions permit. Even in 2003 he waited until September 20 before beginning.

The whole bunches drop into the tanks by gravity. Most of the fermentation vats are wooden, supplemented by some concrete tanks. A streak of whimsy (which seems remote from Nicolas Thienpont's character) has intruded and most of the tanks carry girls' names of an old-fashioned sort: Cunégonde, Berthe, and Eliane, among others.

There is no cold soak at Pavie-Macquin, but Thienpont favours micro-oxygenation *sous marc* to fix the colour and give the wines more body. In addition there is *pigeage* and *délestage*. Malolactic fermentation takes place in barriques, and the wine is aged on the fine lees for sixteen to twenty months in eighty per cent new oak, with no racking for at least six months, sometimes more. The lees are stirred, and if there is any reduction, *cliquage* is employed. The blend is made up late.

The only venerable Pavie-Macquin I have tasted is the 1937, which was very acidic and dry – no pleasure there after half a century. I found the 1990 and 1992 charmless, but from 1995 onwards quality has been very high. The 1995 itself has an elegant if oaky nose, a voluptuous texture, soft, ripe tannins, and excellent length. The 1996 has smoky, oaky aromas, and like the 1995 is very well balanced, with every element in place, though it is less fleshy than the 1995. The 1999 has a light structure but clear and sustained fruit. The 1998, tasted recently, had a pronounced mintiness on the nose and palate, an excellent attack, a tight structure, and impressive length. Pavie-Macquin was untouched by the hailstorm in 1999, so the wine that year remains impeccable: very oaky with some coffee tones, concentrated and juicy, with ample tannins and extract without being overbearing. The 2000 is more sumptuous and generous, though there is a slight confected tone, but that may well diminish with further age. My notes on the 2001, 2002, and 2003 are in the same vein. The 2004 is magnificent, and when tasted blind alongside the *premiers crus*, it showed at the same level, with intense aromas, wonderfully ripe tannins, abundant fleshy fruit, and ample lift and elegance.

Few St-Emilions, over the past decade at any rate, offer the same consistency as Pavie-Macquin. Despite the use of micro-oxygenation, there is no indication that the wines lack structure or vigour or will not age very well. Its promotion to the ranks of the Firsts in 2006 was a welcome recognition of its performance.

Château Petit-Faurie-de-Soutard

St-Emilion. Tel: 0557 746206. Website: www.vignoblescapdemourlin.com. Owner: Jacques Capdemourlin.
Grand cru. 8 ha. 65% Merlot, 30% Cabernet Franc, 5% Cabernet Sauvignon. Production: 45,000 bottles

Like Balestard-La-Tonnelle and Cap de Mourlin (*qq.v.*), this property belongs to Jacques Capdemourlin. It has come into the family via his wife. The estate used to be part of Soutard, but became detached in 1850. The vines are in a single parcel next to Balestard, with clay-limestone slopes leading to sandier soils lower down. The average age of the vines is thirty years. The vinification and ageing are the same as for Balestard.

The only time I tasted the 1995, it was dour and rustic; perhaps a poor bottle. Certainly since 2000 the wine has been reliable. The 2000 has considerable aromatic charm; it's medium-bodied, supple, even silky, with reasonable acidity and fruit; it's well made but not very exciting. The 2001 is better, with both more flesh and elegance, and a lively, peppery finish. The 2002 is a bit green though far from worryingly unripe. The chewy 2003 doesn't have the balance of the best vintages, and the tannins are ungainly. The 2004 is rich and solid, with hints of plums and coffee on the palate; it has good length if no great finesse.

Château Petit Gravet Aîné

St-Emilion. Tel: 0557 241234. Owner: Catherine Papon-Nouvelle. Grand cru. 2.5 ha. 80% Cabernet Franc,
20% Merlot. Production: 1,800 bottles

Another tiny property belonging to the owner of Clos St Julien (*q.v.*). This lies on deep sandy soils near Canon-La-Gaffelière. Its peculiarity is the very high proportion of Cabernet Franc. The wine is fermented with some micro-oxygenation, and then aged in new oak for eighteen months. A slight herbaceousness on the nose of the 2002 is not mirrored on the palate, which is juicy, chocolatey, and forceful. I prefer it to the 2003, which clearly suffered on these soils, delivering a lightly aromatic wine with a dry, grippy finish.

Château Peyreau

St-Emilion. Tel: 0557 247133. Website: www.neipperg.com. Owner: Von Neipperg family. Grand cru. 13 ha.
70% Merlot, 25% Cabernet Franc, 5% Cabernet Sauvignon. Production: 55,000 bottles

This rather run-down mid-nineteenth-century château and park lie in the northeastern sector of St-Emilion next door to Neipperg's Clos de l'Oratoire. The soil is sandy clay. The vines are picked by hand and sorted twice, and the wine is aged in second-use barriques for twelve to eighteen months. The idea is to produce a supple wine for fairly early drinking. I have never tasted it.

Château Pipeau

St-Laurent-des-Combes. Tel: 0557 247295. Website: www.chateaupipeau.com. Owners: Richard Mestreguilhem and
Dominique Lauret. Grand cru. 35 ha. 80% Merlot, 10% Cabernet Franc, 10% Cabernet Sauvignon.
Production: 190,000 bottles

Although the winery is based in the village of St-Laurent, the vineyards are dispersed, with parcels on sandy soil in St-Laurent, on slopes at St-Hippolyte, and on gravelly soil on the plain. Only part of the vineyards are picked by hand. After sorting, the grapes are fermented in large steel tanks. The *marc* is pressed in vertical presses, and the wine aged in seventy per cent new oak for twelve to fourteen months, although the small amount of Cabernet Sauvignon is often kept in tanks. It is Pipeau's policy to give the wines some bottle-age before release, as Mestreguilhem says they can be rather closed when young.

The 1986 was a bit rustic, though there was nonetheless some attractive blackberry fruit. The vintages between 1999 and 2003 share a common style, with bright cherry aromas that are appealing. It's on the palate that Pipeau seems unbalanced, with too much oak and grip for a wine that seems intrinsically light. The result is a wine that is overworked and rather dry on the finish. This is regrettable as the fruit quality seems fine: it's the cellar treatment that undermines it.

Château Pontet-Fumet

Vignonet. Tel: 0557 845316. Website: www.vignobles-bardet.fr. Owner: Philippe Bardet. Grand cru. 12 ha.
72% Merlot, 21% Cabernet Franc, 7% Cabernet Sauvignon. Production: 60,000 bottles

This estate was assembled by Philippe Bardet's father in 1962. As at all Bardet's properties in St-Emilion and the Côtes de Castillon, the grapes are harvested by machine. The soil is very gravelly. The wine is aged in fifty per cent new barriques. In style, Pontet-Fumet is marked by somewhat overripe black-fruits aromas, and the palate is soft, even a touch blowsy, adding up to an easy-going wine with some vanilla tones and modest length. The 2001 is marginally the best of recent vintages.

Château de Pressac

St-Etienne-de-Lisse. Tel: 0557 401802. Owner: Jean-François Quenin. Grand cru. 36 ha. 70% Merlot,
15% Cabernet Franc, 13% Cabernet Sauvignon, 2% Carmenère and Malbec. Production: 130,000 bottles.
Second wine: Ch Tour de Pressac

Situated quite high up on a knoll, with fine views over undulating vineyards from its park, Pressac is an imposing château, which closer up reveals itself to be a nineteenth-century pastiche of a Renaissance manor. Parts of the ensemble are medieval – some walls and a machicolated gateway. In the 1920s the Pouey family were the owners. After a son took over in the 1970s, the property became neglected, and his own heirs were uninterested in the estate. It went onto the market, and in 1997 Quenin, a former executive with the electronic-goods retailer Darty, bought it.

He soon found there was much to be done. The vineyards, for a start, were not in great shape, and among the old vines forty per cent of the plants were missing. The property is right at the end of the St-Emilion escarpment, with vines at various elevations. They are divided into roughly equal sections, with one-third on the St-Etienne plateau, one-third on the slopes at its end, and the remainder on flatter land at the foot of the slope. It was this third section that required the most attention, as the vines suffered badly from water coursing down the slopes, so Quenin had to undertake enormous and costly works to divert springs and protect the vines from regular soakings. The slopes also needed attention, and Quenin replanted much of this section along terraces that were expensive to construct and maintain. In all, well over half the property has been replanted since 1998. Quenin profited from the exercise by planting a little Malbec and Carmenère. Malbec had originally been planted here in the 1730s, when a native of Cahors bought the property and planted some Malbec, which became known as Noir de Pressac. The Carmenère is just for fun and out of curiosity.

Quenin also renovated the *cuvier* in 1999, removing some of the largest steel tanks and replacing them with smaller temperature-controlled cement tanks. Before his arrival, the property had been machine-harvested. He put a stop to this. Now the grapes are sorted twice and crushed over the tanks. There is some mechanical *pigeage* during fermentation. The wine is aged for twelve months in sixty-five per cent new oak. Quenin doesn't like the drying effect of air-conditioning, so he has devised a system whereby a thermostat can open the windows and switch on extractor fans when interior conditions require it. However, he took the precaution of installing air-conditioning for use during very hot spells.

Pressac is a solid rather than an elegant wine. The best of recent vintages has been the 2001, which has smoky, leathery aromas, a rich, rounded palate, and reasonable balance; all it lacks is some flair and vigour on the finish. The 2002 is tighter and lacks some weight, while by 2007 the 2003 was showing surprising freshness and intensity of fruit. The 2005 is finely composed, with no rough edges and a long finish. From cask, the 2006 seems very successful, with considerable weight and persistence. Quenin knows he is working with a difficult terroir, especially in cooler years, but seems determined to restore the estate's reputation.

Château Le Prieuré

St-Emilion. Tel: 0557 516458. Owner: Guichard family. Grand cru classé. 6 ha. 90% Merlot, 10% Cabernet Franc.
Production: 30,000 bottles. Second wine: Les Délices de Prieuré

In 1832 a certain Pierre Brisson bought this property, then known as Cru des Cordeliers. His grandson Joseph renamed it Le Prieuré at the end of the nineteenth century. In 1919 Joseph's daughter Madeleine married Louis Guichard, and the estate has remained in the Guichard family ever since. By the 1980s, Baron Olivier Guichard, a Gaullist minister, was running this property as well as Vray Croix de Gay in Pomerol and Siaurac in Lalande de Pomerol. He did much to modernize the estates and in 2001 hired the oenologist Yannick Reyrel, who had been the right-hand man of Jean-Claude Berrouet at Moueix, to make the wines. In 2006 Stéphane Derenoncourt was taken on as a consultant.

Baron Guichard died in 2004, and the properties were inherited by his three daughters. One of them, Aline, is married to Paul Goldschmidt, who now manages the estates on behalf of the sisters.

Although the property is not very large, it is somewhat dispersed, with parcels on the limestone plateau not far from Trottevieille, on clay slopes near the winery, and near Troplong-Mondot and La Clotte in the Fongaban valley. After a major replanting programme began in 1998, at least one-third of the vines were replaced. Yields had been quite high in the 1990s, but have now been reduced to a maximum of forty hectolitres per hectare. The regime is *lutte raisonnée*, so there is no use of insecticides and the soil is ploughed.

The *cuvier* was renovated in 1999. After sorting, the grapes are fermented traditionally in concrete tanks. The *marc* is pressed in a vertical press, and the wine is aged in one-third new oak in an underground cellar for twelve to sixteen months.

Le Prieuré wines from top years such as 1982 and 1990 struck me as simple and easy-going rather than complex, and not really of *grand cru classé* standards. Quality has certainly improved, and since 2001 the wines have gained in concentration and elegance. When young they are a touch austere, but that is no bad thing. Goldschmidt says he does not want to sacrifice longevity for primary attraction; he could use micro-oxygenation and lees-stirring to obtain softer, more opulent wines, but does not want to do so. Quality is now very good, and the 2004 shows fleshiness, zest, and some complexity, while the 2005 is similar but with more panache and persistence.

Château Prieuré-Lescours

St-Sulpice-de-Faleyrens. Tel: 0557 550913. Website: www.thunevin.com. Owner: Jean-Luc Thunevin. Grand cru.
6 ha. 70% Merlot, 30% Cabernet Franc. Production: 25,000 bottles

This small property is located on sandy and gravelly soils on the plains. Jean-Luc Thunevin bought it in 2001 and constructed a new winery, equipping it with steel and wooden vats. The wine is rather ambitiously aged in eighty per cent new oak. The only vintage I have tasted is the 2002, which had a glacé-cherry nose marked by a lot of smoky oak; but the palate was lean, rather hollow, and lacked character, although the wine was certainly drinkable.

Château Quinault

Libourne. Tel: 0557 741952. Website: www.chateau-quinault.com. Owner: Dr. Alain Raynaud. Grand cru.
15 ha. 75% Merlot, 10% Cabernet Franc, 10% Cabernet Sauvignon, 5% Malbec. Production: 60,000 bottles.
Second wine: Ch La Fleur Quinault

Dr. Alain Raynaud is a man of multiple activities. Although a medical doctor, he comes from a well-established wine family, and his sister owns Croix de Gay in Pomerol and other properties. He bought Quinault in 1997. He is a man who enjoys the limelight, and has served as president of the Union des Grands Crus de Bordeaux and is co-founder and president of the Cercle du Rive Droite, a promotional organization for quality-conscious properties of the Right Bank. He has also been a confidant of Robert Parker and for a while was a business associate of Gérard Perse of Pavie and Monbousquet. When I arrived at Pavie for an appointment in 2000, I was surprised to find the door opened by Dr. Raynaud, who also sat through my entire interview with Perse, as though he were his minder. Today Perse is happy to fly solo. More recently, in 2001, Raynaud was appointed as a consultant to Château Lascombes in Margaux, but the appointment was short-lived.

Raynaud was derided by some when he purchased this property in 1997, as its location in a single block on alluvial soil near the Libourne cemetery was hardly propitious. However, he tells me the site is of an ancient origin as a vineyard. Being within the town, the vineyard was attractive to property developers; when former owner Henri Maleret wanted to sell up in 1997, Raynaud snapped it up. He invested considerably to make the best wine he could from this doubtful terroir. Raynaud was assailed for the high prices he charged, which he justified by pointing to the high scores he often obtained from the American wine press. Quinault had never been renowned before 1997 because it had been machine-harvested and the wine never went near an oak barrel. (Nonetheless the British wine merchant Freddy Price, impressed by the old vines at Quinault, bought the wine every year, and his customers were apparently happy with it.)

It was also Raynaud who planted Cabernet Sauvignon here. He concedes that Merlot alone makes a soft, low-acidity wine on this sandy, gravelly soil, and he wanted to give the wine more structure. Quinault is lucky to have some parcels of old vines, planted in 1930, 1947, and 1961. The vineyard's proximity to Libourne and to the Dordogne means that it is rarely affected by frost. Only organic fertilizers are used here, and pest control is by organic means.

Alain Raynaud claims to have invented the system of double sorting of grapes – before and after destemming – and has since supplemented it at Quinault with two vibrating tables. In hot years such as 2005, any fruit picked in the afternoon is stored overnight in refrigerated trucks. Vinification begins with a long, cold soak under dry ice. Fermentation begins with indigenous yeasts, and in 2002 Raynaud also began barrel-fermenting some lots; he claims other estates such as Smith-Haut-Lafitte copied the idea from him in 2003. After pressing in vertical presses, the wine is aged in fifty to eighty per cent new barriques. Part of the wine is racked; other barrels are left on the lees on Oxoline racks, on which the barrels are rolled rather than stirred. Almost half the wine is aged for twelve months, so that he can reuse the barrels the following vintage; the remainder spends an additional four months in oak.

Dr. Raynaud's media-savvy approach is evident in the tasting room, which is adorned by rather inept mural portraits of the great and good such as Robert Parker and James Suckling. I am not clear how many points a critic must award Quinault in order to qualify for inclusion.

In 2002 he launched a special *cuvée* of 4,000 bottles called Absolut de Quinault from lots fermented in barrels. In the United States the wine is sold as Oriel L'Exception and L'Exception, since a vodka company objected to the use of the word Absolut. A number of us compared the regular 2002 with Oriel and there was no consensus about whether there was any significant difference between the two. My own view is that nuances distinguishing them were too slight to be important.

The 1998 is a good wine, though the nose is rather jammy. The palate is richly fruity, with plenty of spiciness and oak; but by 2005 it seemed fully ready with little in reserve. The 2001 was in the same mould though smokier and less overtly jammy on the nose; but the ripeness was very evident on the super-suave palate, which lacked a little verve. The 2002 has plum and vanilla aromas, and no lack of richness or concentration; it has more persistence than many wines from this year. Conditions in 2006 seem to have suited Quinault well, as the wine from cask was fleshy and generous.

Château La Révérence

St-Emilion. Tel: 0557 511861. **Owner:** *Emeric Petit. Grand cru. 3 ha. 70% Merlot, 30% Cabernet Franc.*
Production: *10,000 bottles*

Emeric Petit is the owner of the excellent Château Tournefeuille in Lalande de Pomerol, and in 2003 he bought the former Clos Jean Voisin and changed its name, as under the previous owner the wine was not much esteemed. The vines lie in a single parcel near Chauvin. Part of the crop is fermented in 400-litre barrels, and the wine is aged in sixty per cent new oak. The atypical 2003 is the only vintage I have tasted from bottle. Plummy on the nose, it was quite sweet and jammy, yet had a rather tannic finish. It will need another couple of vintages before the quality and style can be properly assessed, but the little estate is in good hands.

Château Ripeau

St-Emilion. Tel: 0557 744141. **Owner:** *Françoise de Wilde. Grand cru classé. 15.5 ha. 62% Merlot,*
30% Cabernet Franc, 8% Cabernet Sauvignon. **Production:** *55,000 bottles.* **Second wine:** *Garennes de Ripeau*

This attractive property has been run for almost thirty years by the elegant Mme. de Wilde, aided increasingly by her daughter and her nephew Louis. The château interior is a throwback to an earlier age of pleasure, as it once belonged to the director of the Monaco Opera, Raoul Guinzburg, who left much of his art collection here when he sold the property to Marcel Loubat (whose brother owned Pétrus) in 1917.

The vineyards are in a single parcel on fairly sandy soils, just east of La Dominique and Cheval Blanc. They are cultivated by *lutte raisonnée*. The wine is aged for twelve to fifteen months in fifty per cent new oak, and since 1999 there has been some ageing on the fine lees.

There seems to be some inconsistency here. Some wines have been distinctly disappointing, such as 1996 and 2002, whereas others have been very enjoyable. The 2000 has an excellent aromatic balance of black fruits and oak, and the palate is dense and concentrated, with a long, positive finish. The 2001 is similar, but the 2003 is supple and forward. The 2004 has a plump texture with considerable fruit concentration, but overall it lacks some flair. In 2004 there was a change of consultant oenologist, when Michel Rolland replaced Gilles Pauquet, so there may be further stylistic changes here.

Château Rochebelle

St-Laurent-des-Combes. Tel: 0557 513071. **Owner:** *Philippe Faniest. Grand cru. 3 ha. 85% Merlot,*
15% Cabernet Franc. **Production:** *12,000 bottles*

One of the most popular tourist attractions in St-Emilion is the miniature train that trundles through the lanes and vineyards. Philippe Faniest is its creator and owner, so it comes as no surprise that when the train stops to allow the tourists to visit a tasting room, the halt is at Rochebelle. Despite this rampant commercialism, the wines are very good. He shrewdly takes advice both from Michel Rolland and from Jean-Claude Berrouet, the winemaker at Moueix, even though the two men often have very different ideas.

The vineyards are well located, close to Troplong-Mondot, Tertre-Rôteboeuf, and Pavie-Decesse. Some vines are on the limestone plateau, but the majority are on the clay-limestone slopes. At *véraison*, Faniest goes through the vines, tagging those that are well behind in their development; then two weeks before harvest he goes through the vines again, removing any pink and green berries. After sorting, the fruit is crushed over the tanks, and there is no pumping. Fermentation takes place in cement tanks with micro-oxygenation. The wines are aged for up to eighteen months in the quarries beneath his house; he uses only new oak.

Faniest says the terroir is uniform, so there is no second wine here. He likes to offer his clientele older vintages such as, in 2005, 1989 and 1990. Nor does he inflate the prices of these mature wines. On the nose cherry fruit is evident beneath the overt oakiness. On the palate the wine is lush and concentrated, massive in vintages such as 1998, more delicate and spicy in years such as 2002. This is not the most complex of St-Emilions, but its opulence and plumpness are hard to resist. And clearly the wines age well. The 2001 is outstanding.

Château Rol Valentin

*St-Emilion. Tel: 0557 744351. Website: www.rolvalentin.com. **Owner:** Eric Prissette. Grand cru. 7.5 ha.*
*85% Merlot, 15% Cabernet Franc. **Production:** 25,000 bottles. **Second wine:** Les Valentines*

This property first attracted attention when it was acquired in 1994 by Eric Prissette, a well-known football player for the Lille team. Despite the stereotype of his original calling, he turns out to be friendly and highly articulate. The vines are in the northwest sector of St-Emilion. The original part of the estate was on two hectares on sandy soil near the winery; in 1999 he purchased 5.5 hectares more on clay-limestone soils in the chillier sector of St-Etienne-de-Lisse, which gives more powerful wines.

The viticulture is close to organic, though not certified, and the soil is ploughed. There is scrupulous green-harvesting but no formula to determine the number of bunches per vine, and each plant is handled separately. Prissette says he and his team are constantly observing the vines from April onwards, and try to react rapidly to any problem or imbalance that may arise. By the time the harvest begins, just about everything left on the vine is ready for picking. Nonetheless there is sorting both in the vineyard and at the winery.

Prissette's first vintage was 1994, and from 1998 onwards the wines have been made by Stéphane Derenoncourt. (Some years ago I accompanied Derenoncourt to Rol Valentin and observed as he and the *maître de chai* scrupulously tasted and noted every barrel.) In 1997 the cement tanks were replaced by small open-top wooden fermenters. Derenoncourt favoured wooden vats, as he believes the wood integration is earlier and more satisfactory, and the wine is less shocked by oak by the time it goes into barriques for malolactic fermentation. The wine is aged in new oak for fourteen to sixteen months, and stays on the fine lees until June. There is no micro-oxygenation.

Rol Valentin has a reputation as a *garagiste* wine, but with the expansion of the vineyards that would now be a misnomer. These are admirable wines, sumptuous and oaky in vintages such as 2000 and 2003, more perfumed and delicate in years such as 2002. Despite an occasional hint of overripeness, the wines are true to their vintage. Thus in 2002 the wine had cranberry flavours and fairly high acidity, whereas the 2003 was more plump and upfront. The 1999 was particularly successful for the vintage. My only quibble is that sometimes Rol Valentin lacks a little length.

The second wine is not produced systematically, and in most years Prissette bleeds the tanks to produce a rosé called Cupidon.

Château Rolland-Maillet

*St-Emilion. Tel: 0557 512305. **Owner:** Michel Rolland. Grand cru. 3.3 ha. 75% Merlot,*
*25% Cabernet Franc. **Production:** 12,000 bottles*

This is a lesser wine from the Rolland stable. The vines are in the Corbin sector on clay-silt and gravelly silt soils, and the wine is aged for twelve to fifteen months in barrels previously used for his Pomerol, Bon Pasteur. The only vintage I have encountered is the 2003, which is medium-bodied, supple, forward, reasonably fresh, and clean, if with no pronounced personality.

Château La Rose-Côtes-Rol

*St-Emilion. Tel: 0557 247128. **Owner:** Yves Mirande. Grand cru. 10 ha. 74% Merlot, 15% Cabernet Franc,*
*10% Cabernet Sauvignon, 1% Malbec. **Production:** 50,000 bottles. **Second wine:** Ch Tour de Lagarde*

This property, owned by the Mirande family since 1951, is now run by Pierre Mirande. Most of the vines are on sandy and clay soils near the winery, which is not far from Cap de Mourlin and Larmande, and the remainder are near Fombrauge. Only the oldest vines are picked by hand. The grapes are destemmed, then sorted, and fermented in cement tanks. Seventy-five per cent of the wine is aged in twenty-five per cent new barriques; the rest stays in tanks. This is a lean, rather pinched wine, lacking in succulence. The 2000 is the best of recent vintages but that is not saying a great deal.

Château Roylland

St-Emilion. Tel: 0557 744311. Owner: Stephen Adams. Grand cru. 10.5 ha. 90% Merlot, 10% Cabernet Franc.
Production: 50,000 bottles. Second wine: Ch Rocheyron

This property is based at the foot of the slopes in the southwest sector of St-Emilion, but half the vineyards are some distance away on the plateau of St-Christophe-des-Bardes, while the remainder are near Angélus. The grapes are harvested by *tries successives* and sorted twice at the winery, before being fermented in cement and steel tanks. The wine is aged in thirty-five per cent new barriques for between twelve and eighteen months. I recall a slightly bland but plump and fruity 1990, but recent vintages have been less satisfactory. The 1999 is rather soft and soupy; the 2002 is medium-bodied but has worryingly dry tannins, as does the more rasping 2003. The 2004, however, shows more promise from cask; it may lack some grip and concentration but it has some finesse. Roylland's sale in 2007 to the quality-conscious Stephen Adams suggests future vintages should see some improvement.

Château Rozier

St-Laurent-des-Combes. Tel: 0557 247303. Website: www.vignobles-saby.com. Owners: Jean-Christophe and Jean-Philippe Saby. Grand cru. 24 ha. 80% Merlot, 20% Cabernet Franc. Production: 110,000 bottles.
Second wine: Cuvée Terre Rouge

The Saby brothers are the ninth generation of their family here, and they also own properties in the St-Emilion satellites and in Fronsac. Rozier is not a particularly coherent property. There are six hectares of vines in St-Laurent, eight more near the cooperative, and other parcels in St-Sulpice, Corbin, and St-Hippolyte. Inevitably soil types vary considerably. All principal parcels are vinified separately. A two-hectare block near Tertre-Rôtebouef is the source of a separate wine called Château Haut La Grâce Dieu.

The Sabys did experiment for a while with cold soaks and micro-oxygenation, but abandoned both in favour of a more classic fermentation in cement tanks. Since 1998 the wine has been aged in thirty-five per cent new barriques for twelve months. This is not a very exciting wine, though it is inexpensive. The 2000 is light and earthy, the 2001 has more weight but lacks flair, and the 2002 has some charm but is essentially simple. The 2003 is pleasantly fruity but rather short. In contrast the 2005 seems extracted and rather rustic.

Château St-Georges-Côte-Pavie

St-Emilion. Tel: 0557 554890. Owner: Jacques Masson. Grand cru classé. 5.5 ha. 80% Merlot,
20% Cabernet Franc. Production: 50,000 bottles. Second wine: Côte Madeleine

As its name suggests, this well-situated property is close to Pavie, and across the road from La Gaffelière. There is also a small 0.5-hectare parcel on the plateau near Ausone. The owner never made much of an effort with this wine, and in 2004 decided to entrust the running of the property and the sales of its wines to the Milhade négociant house. Xavier Milhade, now advised by Rhône winemaker Jean-Luc Colombo, moved swiftly to heighten the trellising, to green-harvest in summer, and to pick later than in the past. At the winery the grapes are sorted twice and fermented in steel tanks. The *marc* is pressed in a vertical press, and the wine aged in fifty per cent new oak for up to eighteen months, with traditional racking. It is too early to assess the changes. In 2007 the 1998 was pleasantly fruity, but rather dilute and dry for the vintage. The 2003 is plummy and robust but simple and lacking in length. The oaky 2004 shows more aromatic richness, and there's good fruit on the palate, although overall it lacks excitement. The 2005 is lush, concentrated, and powerful, and sets a new standard for this estate.

Milhade intends to produce a second wine here as a further measure to improve quality, but its name was undecided at the time of writing.

Sanctus du Château La Bienfaisance

St-Christophe-des-Bardes. Tel: 0557 246583. Website: www.chateaulabienfaisance.com. Owners: Patrick Baseden and Aurelio Montes. Grand cru. 4.3 ha. 70% Merlot, 30% Cabernet Franc. Production: 12,000 bottles

From this fifteen-hectare property Patrick Baseden and his cousin Aurelio Montes, one of Chile's top wine producers, have sequestered a few hectares on clay-limestone and gravel soils from which they are making this frankly *garagiste* wine, with advice from Stéphane Derenoncourt. The first vintage was 1998. The wine is aged in new oak for twenty months. The 2002 is rich and tannic though a touc blousy, while the 2004 is opulent but somewhat over-extracted.

Château Sansonnet

St-Emilion. Tel: 0557 556060. Website: www.edoniawines.com. Owner: François d'Aulan. Grand cru. 7 ha. 90% Merlot, 10% Cabernet Franc. Production: 30,000 bottles. Second wine: Ch Lasalle

When Sansonnet was demoted from *grand cru classé* in 1996, no one was surprised. Quality had apparently slipped badly. In 1999 the owners since 1892, the Robin family, sold the property to François d'Aulan, who used to own the Champagne house Piper-Heidsieck and still has important wine interests in Tokaj and Argentina. At first Sansonnet was run by Jean-Michel Arcaute of Château Clinet, but in 2003 Arcaute merged his company with d'Aulan's to form a new company called Edonia.

The new owners had to make significant investments from the outset, especially in the vineyards. They enjoyed a good and lofty location on the plateau, on degraded limestone soil not far from Trottevieille and Haut-Sarpe, but many vines were missing. Some vines were replanted and the trellis was heightened. Ploughing was introduced for the first time, with green cover on alternate rows. The vines are green-harvested, as the Robins' use of fertilizers meant the soil was too vigorous.

The grapes are harvested in *cagettes* and thoroughly sorted. The must is fermented in steel tanks, with micro-oxygenation, pumpovers, and *délestage*. After the alcoholic fermentation, there is a prolonged maceration at temperatures of up to 35°C (95°F). The wine is aged for fifteen months in one-third new oak, with some *cliquage*.

The wines are sound but lack concentration, despite the efforts of the new owners. The 2001 evolved fast; it's a solid wine but now ready to drink. The 2002 is tart and assertive; although the nose is lush and smoky, the palate is lean. The 2003 has reasonable freshness but little persistence or grip. The 2004 and 2005 lacks concentration, vigour and persistence. These are frankly commercial wines.

Château La Serre

St-Emilion. Tel: 0557 247138. Owner: Luc d'Arfeuille. Grand cru classé. 6.5 ha. 80% Merlot, 20% Cabernet Franc. Production: 35,000 bottles. Second wine: Les Menuts de La Serre

The courteous Luc d'Arfeuille (cousin of the owner of La Pointe in Pomerol) inherited this property from his father, who had acquired it over fifty years ago. The vineyards lie in a single block close to those of Trottevieille and Pavie-Macquin on the limestone plateau.

The viticulture is conscientious, with removal of buds and leaves, and green-harvesting. After sorting, the grapes are cold-soaked before being fermented in concrete vats, which in 2003 replaced the winery's stainless-steel tanks. In the same year d'Arfeuille also switched to a vertical press. The wine is aged for fifteen months in forty-five per cent new oak, with less racking than in the past. Blending is completed late during the *élevage*.

La Serre, judging by the 1995 and 2000 vintages, used to be a bland and rather uninteresting wine, but there has been a marked improvement since 2001, with much more aromatic complexity and density. Red fruits dominate the nose and palate, and the finish is lively and generous. The 2003 is a touch baked, but reasonably concentrated and spicy; not a wine for the long haul. The 2004 is rich and plump but lacks some finesse, and already seemed very accessible by 2007.

Château Soutard

*St-Emilion. Tel: 0557 247141. **Owner**: La Mondiale. Grand cru classé. 22 ha. 70% Merlot, 30% Cabernet Franc.
Production: 120,000 bottles. **Second wine**: Clos de la Tonnelle*

This important property just north of the village, with its grand eighteenth-century château, was long owned by the de Ligneris family. Francois de Ligneris, who ran the property from 1981 until its sale in 2006, is also the proprietor of the deservedly popular wine bar in St-Emilion, L'Envers de Décor. There used to be a TCA problem at Soutard but all woodwork in the *chai* was removed and the problem solved.

François de Ligneris had a long-standing feud with the Syndicat and refused to accept an appointment for my visit made through its office. Unfortunately my own attempts to make an appointment, at his suggestion, both by email and in person over a five-month period (since I became a habitué of his wine bar), failed. Since I do not like to rely on secondary sources, I would rather say little about his vineyards or vinification for fear of misleading the reader. The proportion of new oak has varied from vintage to vintage, and there is no fining or filtration. By 2006 the estate was on the market, and was eventually sold to the La Mondiale company, which also owns Larmande nearby.

As for the wines, the 1923 was past its best (but only just) in 2005, and the 1947, despite some leanness and austerity, was still fresh and vigorous in 2002. I bought some bottles of the 1970 long ago, but they were always lacking in generosity. The 1986 was chunky and inelegant, but I have a positive note on the 1988, which was lively and stylish. The 1997 was surprisingly fruity and structured given the vintage. In 2007 the 1998 was quite closed on the nose; the palate had reasonable fruit and tannin but was hollow and unimpressive. A sample of the 2005 tasted shortly before bottling was so stewed and weird that I have to hope it was unrepresentative.

Château Tauzinat L'Hermitage

*St-Christophe-des-Bardes. Tel: 0557 255045. **Owner**: Catherine Moueix. Grand cru. 9 ha. 85% Merlot,
15% Cabernet Franc. **Production**: 40,000 bottles. **Second wine**: Ch Le Grand Treuil*

Catherine Moueix is better known as the owner of Taillefer (*q.v.*) in Pomerol, but this property has been in her family since 1953. It's an old estate that dates back to the seventeenth century and the vineyards are in two sectors: one near Fombrauge, the other near Fonroque. The wine is aged in one-third new oak for twelve months. The 2001 is ripe, balanced, and forward, but the 2003 is distressingly flat, chunky, and short. The 2004 is pleasant but slight, with a clear lack of concentration. Catherine Moueix is making efforts to improve quality here, but they are not yet in evidence.

Château Tertre Daugay

*St-Emilion. Tel: 0557 247215. **Website**: www.chateau-tertre-daugay.com. **Owner**: Comte Léo de Roquefort Malet.
Grand cru. 16 ha. 70% Merlot, 30% Cabernet Franc. **Production**: 65,000 bottles. **Second wine**: Ch de Roquefort*

The major Libourne–Bergerac road skirts the southern edge of St-Emilion, and Tertre Daugay is the property on the first hillock on the left. That makes it the most westerly estate on the escarpment, with three hectares of vines on the plateau itself, and the remainder on various sides of the hill and thus enjoying different expositions. The lowest sector is down by the railway line on sandier soils. The Cabernet Franc, for instance, is planted on north-facing slopes. In previous centuries there was a tower here that was a lookout point for spotting aggressors well before their arrival; tunnels apparently connect the buildings to the village.

Comte Léo de Roquefort Malet, the owner of La Gaffelière, bought this property at auction in 1978. He had to replant much of the property, as the vineyards were in poor shape. Although some sixty-year-old vines remain, the average age is only twenty years. The soil is clay-limestone with some clay-silt. At present only about fourteen of the sixteen hectares are in production.

The grapes are sorted before and after destemming, and there is no crushing. Fermentation usually takes place in steel tanks with natural yeasts. There is some *pigeage* for the Cabernet Franc. In some vintages, the winemakers use micro-oxygenation toward the end of fermentation. The wine is aged for sixteen months in up to sixty per cent new oak. Stéphane Derenoncourt is the consultant oenologist, so it is no surprise that the wine stays on the fine lees with *cliquage* until it is racked in May.

My experience of the wine is limited, though I recall a good 1947 tasted recently. The nose was sweet, cedary, and elegant. The palate was rich and firm, but the tannins were rather dry. The 1990 is holding up well, with complex aromas of liquorice, coffee, and tobacco; it's medium-bodied, not ultra-concentrated, but there is some intensity on the finish. The 2000 and 2001 are somewhat disappointing, given the quality of the vintages. They are fresh, attractive, even stylish wines, but without much weight or complexity. The 2002 is true to vintage character: quite high acidity, a strong red-fruits character, and a lively finish. The 2003 is successful for the vintage, with ample plump fruit, slightly extracted tannins, but more vigour than many wines from this year. There's promise on the nose of the 2004, with its smoky, plummy aromas, but the wine is slack for all its solidity, and it lacks freshness. Tertre Daugay is not quite in the top ranks of classified growths in St-Emilion, but I was surprised by its demotion in 2006.

Château Tertre-Rôteboeuf

St-Laurent-des-Combes. Tel: 0557 744211. Website: www.tertre-roteboeuf.com. **Owner:** *François Mitjaville.*
Grand cru. 6 ha. 85% Merlot, 15% Cabernet Franc. **Production:** *30,000 bottles*

The elegant, silver-haired François Mitjaville is a man with a mind of his own. His forebears had been wine producers, but more recently the family business had been in road transport. Château de Tertre, as it was then known, belonged to his wife's family, and when his father-in-law died in 1960, some cousins decided to run the property but did not make a good job of it. Mitjaville was keen to switch from corporate life to a more individualistic existence and was tempted to exchange his desk for a pair of secateurs. In 1975 he went to Figeac to learn the ropes and then in 1978 took over the estate. His first task was to restore the vineyards, which, on the slopes above St-Laurent, had always been subject to erosion. Ten years later he would buy Château Roc de Cambes (*q.v.*) in the Côtes de Bourg.

From the outset his strategy was to opt for high quality at high prices. A man of philosophical bent, Mitjaville wanted to adapt the viticulture to the terroir. Because the soil at the property was homogenous, he decided to make just one wine, with no selection. This forced him to ensure the quality of the grapes was impeccable every year. The south- and southeast-facing vineyards lie in a single block in an amphitheatre behind the charming old house. He was a pioneer of the planting of green cover to control erosion and reduce vigour, and he also championed the notion of very late harvesting.

One glance at the vineyards is sufficient to show that Mitjaville has no truck with fashion or conventional wisdom. The overwhelming majority of Libournais vineyards are pruned according to the *guyot* system, whether *simple* or *double*. Not here. The Tertre-Rôteboeuf vines are trained on low cordons, but with higher trellising. Mitjaville claims that low-cordon training used to be traditional here. The advantage is that the grapes benefit from their proximity to the soil and its natural heat. This way he achieves even maturation and small bunches. Although he is not dogmatic on the subject, he is no fan of leaf removal, as he doesn't want any raisining of the fruit. Nor is there any green-harvesting, though he does remove any berries that are clearly rotten. It does not bother him at all that some vines will give a substantial crop, others a low crop. He says he does not want to impose a style on his vines, but wants the vintage character and terroir to speak out clearly. Merely fruity wines do not interest him; nor does power, although his wines can certainly be robust. He is looking, he says, for a *paysage aromatique*.

The vinification is fairly straightforward. He is opposed to a cold soak, which contributes little to the final quality, but likes a hot fermentation in cement tanks with some micro-oxygenation, which he claims helps aroma retention. The wine is aged in new oak for at least eighteen months. He does not like to be hailed as a great wine-maker, though his wines suggest otherwise. "The winemaker can't take credit for the quality," he remarks, "as the vines, not the winemaker, create quality. But the winemaker has to take responsibility if he messes it up!"

Some critics have claimed that the wines, while undoubtedly impressive in their youth, do not age well. That has not been my experience. Admittedly, my knowledge of Tertre-Rôteboeuf is patchy. The 1982, twelve years on, was still sweet, fleshy, and elegant on the nose; although rounded, it remained tannic, even earthy, with attractive spiciness and length. At the same age the 1983 was similar, but had more pronounced cedary tones and more austerity. By 2000 it was certainly ready, with a delicate nose, a compact structure, well-judged tannins, and reasonable length. The 1985, tasted recently, was superb: oaky but dense and discreet on the nose, with remarkable richness and power. The 1996 is stylish rather than powerful, with prominent oakiness aromas, but a smoky, elegant palate with considerable persistence. The stylish 2001 is packed with fruit, with aromas and flavours of olives and plums; the oak is well integrated, and the wine's power is balanced by its sleek texture. The 2004, from cask at twelve months, also had a black-olive and black-cherry aromatic profile, and density and persistence on the palate.

Château Teyssier

Vignonet. Tel: 0557 846422. Website: www.teyssier.fr. Owner: Jonathan Maltus. Grand cru. 20 ha. 70% Merlot, 30% Cabernet Franc. Production: 110,000 bottles

Teyssier, located in the unpromising flatlands of Vignonet, has become in less than a decade the headquarters for a burgeoning group of properties, developed or created by the tireless Jonathan Maltus. In 1991 he sold off a successful engineering company he had created some years earlier. Then he took himself off to Cahors to learn how to make wine, and helped friends there sell their wines onto the British market. In 1994 he decided to try his luck in Bordeaux, and bought twelve hectares of vines in St-Emilion and the Bordeaux appellation. Since then he has been buying up further parcels with the intention of expanding his St-Emilion holdings at Teyssier to twenty-five hectares (in St-Sulpice as well as Vignonet) and reducing the Bordeaux sectors to close to zero. From the start he retained the services of consultant Gilles Pauquet.

Maltus is fully aware that the sandy terroir at Teyssier will never be capable of making great wine. So under the château label he releases a fruity, well-crafted, easy-going St-Emilion for medium-term drinking. It is aged for twelve months in barriques. But Maltus was more ambitious, and well aware that the Teyssier vineyards alone would not allow him to make a good living. Inspired by the commercial and critical success of the *garagistes*, he decided to emulate them. The result was a pair of wines: Le Dôme and Laforge (*qq.v.*).

In 2000 Maltus completed a new winery, and equipped it with some new wooden vats for fermenting the top wines. He also expanded his range, by adding a sumptuous white from the Entre-Deux-Mers (*see* Clos Nardian). In 2003 he bought Château Destieu-Berger. A year later he bought 1.3 hectares of eighty-year-old vines from the town hall. Fonroque had had first refusal on this parcel, but Alain Moueix declined to purchase it, leaving the coast clear for Maltus. This parcel is planted with seventy per cent Merlot, thirty per cent Cabernet Franc, on thin clay over limestone. Pruning is as rigorous as for his other top wines, and this *cuvée*, Les Astéries, differs from the others in that its Cabernet Franc is barrel-fermented. But only 300 cases are currently produced. Despite a price tag of 100 Euros, the first vintage sold out fast.

A new addition to the range in 2005 was Le Carré, made from one hectare of vines close to Clos Fourtet. When Canon acquired Curé-Bon and incorporated some of its vineyards into its own, it was obliged to sell off some that were not considered worthy of inclusion. Le Carré is one of those parcels. It is made in the same way as the other top wines from Maltus, with some *cliquage*. About 400 cases are made.

Maltus helps finance his complex operations by producing a rosé for Berry Bros in London, and some other basic wines, such as a white Teyssier. It is hard to keep up with his numerous winemaking enterprises.

Jonathan Maltus admits that he was very fortunate in forging an alliance early on with Hew Blair of Justerini & Brooks, who bought the entire production of Le Dôme and much of Laforge, which fetch very high prices. Although Maltus is well known in British and American wine circles, he is virtually unknown in St-Emilion itself, where he is referred to as "the businessman", which, as he himself wryly remarks, is the "ultimate put-down". However, while many St-Emilion growers are bemoaning the current state of the market and wondering how on earth to sell their wine profitably, Maltus merrily bypasses the traditional commercial structure and seems to be thriving.

Little needs to be said about Teyssier itself. It is a ripe, fleshy, accessible wine of some charm that does what it sets out to do: provide an easy-drinking wine that requires little or no cellaring. The 2000 was particularly successful. The first vintage of Les Astéries, the 2004, tasted from cask, was closed on the nose, but powerful and tight on the palate, with robust tannins and good length.

The Maltus wines overall are a fine blend of intuition, intelligence, and manipulation. It is clear that the market, the final destination for his wines, is never far from Maltus's mind. In commercially troubled times, that is surely no bad thing.

Château Tour de Corbin-Despagne
St-Emilion. Tel: 0557 746218. Owner: Nicolas Despagne. 5 ha. 90% Merlot, 10% Cabernet Franc.
Production: 6,000 bottles

The Despagne family own Château Maison Blanche (*q.v.*) in Montagne-St-Emilion as well as a few other properties in the region. Although this wine is entitled only to the lowly St-Emilion appellation, it is in fact composed of parcels that are rated *grand cru* and *grand cru classé*. But since the wine is vinified at Maison Blanche, it cannot be labelled with those grander appellations. Nicolas Despagne is a rigorously non-interventionist winemaker, and the vinification of this wine is the same as for Maison Blanche, except that it is aged entirely in new barriques. The wine is not often seen, since most of the production is sold by the négociant André Quancard under the name of Graviers-Figeac. The only vintage I have tasted, the 2000, was excellent if a touch too oaky, a dense, weighty wine with firm black-cherry fruit and fine potential.

Château La Tour Figeac
St-Emilion. Tel: 0557 517762. Website: www.latourfigeac.com. Owner: Otto-Maximilian Rettenmaier. Grand cru classé.
14.5 ha. 65% Merlot, 35% Cabernet Franc. Production: 60,000 bottles. Second wine: L'Esquisse de la Tour Figeac

In 1879 this property was separated from Figeac and two years later divided between two families; the other property was named La Tour du Pin Figeac. Soon after Graf von Neipperg bought Canon-La-Gaffelière, his friend Herr Rettenmaier decided to buy La Tour Figeac from the then-owner, François Rapin. Twenty-one years later, in 1994, his genial son Otto took over running the property. For many years the Rettenmaiers had no access to the château itself, as the widow of the previous owner had the right to live out her days there; although she was already sixty-seven in 1973, she breathed her last only in 2002. In 2004 the house was renovated.

Since 1997 La Tour Figeac has been cultivated biodynamically, though it is not certified as such, and Stéphane Derenoncourt has been the consultant winemaker. However, Rettenmaier is thinking of abandoning a strict adherence to biodynamic principles, as there have been problems in some vintages with grey rot. The vineyards lie near Figeac and Cheval Blanc on gravelly and sandy clay soil that warms up fast and ripens the grapes early. There is a substantial proportion of Cabernet Franc planted, and not surprisingly these vines are near Cheval Blanc. The vines are ploughed and manure is added in conformity with biodynamic principles.

In 1999 open-top wooden fermenters were installed to allow mechanical *pigeage*. Conveyor belts carry the grapes up and over the vats, so there is no pumping. Vinification takes pace with indigenous yeasts. The wine is aged for thirteen to eighteen months in about sixty per cent new barriques (though this was reduced to one-third in 2003), with some micro-oxygenation. There is no systematic fining or filtration.

I have enjoyed many excellent bottles from this estate. True, a 1959 was drying out by 1985, but the 1982 was still lively and delicious in the mid-1990s, with dense, chocolatey fruit. The 1985 was also excellent in 2000, less dense than the 1982 but more elegant and showing excellent balance. The 1986 was stylish, concentrated, and spicy after ten years. The 1995 had a slightly herbaceous nose and was rather austere, but it nonetheless had freshness and length. The 1996 had plenty of upfront fruit but lacked structure; I preferred the medium-bodied but charming 1997.

The 1998 has always been magnificently sensuous. The sumptuous, plummy, truffley nose is irresistible, and the opulence carries over onto the silky, chocolatey palate, that nonetheless has freshness and length. The 2000 is similar, though more overtly oaky on the nose; it's rich and juicy, and so are the tannins, and acidity gives the wine persistence. Two wines poured blind by Otto Rettenmaier to divert and perplex some journalists over dinner turned out to be pure varietal bottlings (not for sale, of course) of Merlot and Cabernet Franc from the 2000 vintage. Eventually someone cracked the code: the Merlot was simply explosive, with aromas of liquorice and blackberries; the Cabernet Franc was highly concentrated but fresher. Was the final blend superior to its components? I am not sure. The super-ripe 2001 also has truffley aromas; the tannins are robust but not harsh, and the finish long and lush. Derenoncourt worked hard not to over-extract in 2003, and the wine, while rich and supple, is both forceful in its tannins yet lacking in verve. The splendid 2004 is similar to the 2000 in its lushness, oakiness, succulence, power, and length. Despite an alcoholic strength of 14.5 degrees, the 2005 is so voluptuous that one is unaware of its strength, and it has a very long and fresh finish.

La Tour Figeac is a hedonist's wine, with a lushness often reminiscent of fine Pomerol. Quite why it should be so much more overtly opulent than Figeac and Cheval Blanc, I do not know, but it rarely fails to give deep pleasure, rather like being cosseted in velvet.

Château La Tour du Pin Figeac (Giraud-Bélivier)

St-Emilion. Tel: 0557 510610. Website: www.vins.giraud-belivier.com. Owner: André Giraud. Grand cru. 11 ha.
75% Merlot, 25% Cabernet Franc. Production: 65,000 bottles. Second wine: Tournelles du Pin Figeac

This portion of the Tour du Pin Figeac estate, which has been in the Bélivier and Giraud families since 1923, lies on similar soil to the Moueix property, with vines close to both Cheval Blanc and La Tour Figeac. The house stands just across from the main drive that leads to Cheval Blanc. After a manual harvest, the grapes are sorted and there is usually a cold soak before fermentation begins in cement tanks. One-third of the wine stays in tanks, the remainder in barriques, of which one-third are new; the two components are rotated so that all the wine spends twelve months in oak.

The 1999 is dilute and dull. The 2000 had attractive black-cherry aromas, but was rather dilute for the vintage – pleasant but far from exceptional. The 2001 is also aromatic, with aromas of crushed berries, but the wine does not taste fully ripe and is fairly short. The 2004 is medium-bodied and fresh, but it's bland and lacking in structure.

The Girauds are also the owners of Château Le Caillou (q.v.) in Pomerol.

Château La Tour du Pin Figeac (Moueix)

St-Emilion. Tel: 0557 555555. Owners: Bernard Arnault and Albert Frère. Grand cru. 9 ha. 80% Merlot,
20% Cabernet Franc. Production: 48,000 bottles

To perplex the consumer, two properties share the cumbersome name of La Tour du Pin Figeac. The formerly united property once formed part of Figeac, but by the end of the nineteenth century it was owned by two sisters. In 1923 one of them sold her portion to a M. Bélivier, from whom it descended to the present owners, the Girauds. Some years later the other sister sold her portion to someone who subsequently sold it on to Jean-Marie Moueix, the son of Armand Moueix, in 1947. In 2006 this latter proportion was sold to its neighbour Cheval Blanc.

The property lies close to Cheval Blanc on sandy gravel soil over a subsoil of blue clay. The wine is aged in thirty-five per cent new oak for twelve to fifteen months. It is not an especially exciting wine. The 1995 was quite rich and concentrated, with ripe tannins, but it was rather bland and lacking in flair. The 1996 was a disappointment, despite the promise of delicate and charming aromas. The 2000 had more panache, but the texture was somewhat soupy and there was little zest or complexity. The 2001 is better, with a nose of crushed red fruits, and an open but stylish palate, with a light tannic grip.

Château Trianon

*St-Emilion. Tel: 0557 253446. Website: www.chateau-trianon.com. **Owners:** Dominique Hébrard, Jacques Berrebi, and Alain Laguillaumie. Grand cru. 10 ha. 80% Merlot, 10% Cabernet Franc, 5% Cabernet Sauvignon, 5% Carmenère. **Production:** 32,000 bottles. **Second wine:** Le Petit Trianon*

After Dominique Hébrard left his administrative post at Cheval Blanc after its acquisition by Bernard Arnault and Albert Frère, he decided he needed a challenge, and found it in this estate, which he bought late in 2000. In 2004 his partners at Château Bellefont-Belcier (*q.v.*) became co-proprietors at Trianon too. For the previous three decades a merchant had sold almost all its wine to Scandinavia, so it was little known internationally. The property was not in good condition, so Hébrard made huge investments in new drainage, soil analysis, trellising, and replanting to a high density of 9,000 vines per hectare.

Eight hectares are located on sandy soils over clay in the southwest sector of the region, not that far from Libourne. Hébrard bought two more hectares in St-Sulpice on gravelly soils over clay. What singles out the Trianon vineyards is the presence of forty-five-year-old Carmenère vines. Hébrard does not aim for exaggeratedly low yields, as he doesn't want any flavours of *surmaturité*.

After harvesting in *cagettes*, the grapes are repeatedly sorted, and cold-soaked in squat steel tanks at no more than 10°C (50°F). Jacques Lurton, with his extensive experience of winemaking in Chile, offered advice on how the Carmenère should be handled. The wine is given prolonged ageing in fifty per cent new oak, although some of the wine from the youngest vines remains in tanks. There is eggwhite-fining before bottling.

Hébrard knows that the Trianon terroir is never going to yield big, powerful wines, so he does not aim for excessive extraction, and seeks instead to produce fruity wines that can be drunk with pleasure relatively young. And that by and large is what he delivers. The oak is quite noticeable on the nose, but there are also blackberry and blackcurrant aromas; on the palate the wine is medium-bodied, nicely textured, quite lively, and with a moderate tannic backbone. Of vintages since 2001, I particularly like the generous 2002 and the flamboyant 2004.

Château Trimoulet

*St-Emilion. Tel: 0557 247056. Website: www.chateautrimoulet.com. **Owner:** Michel Jean. Grand cru. 16 ha. 60% Merlot, 40% Cabernet Franc. **Production:** 80,000 bottles. **Second wine:** Emilius de Ch Trimoulet*

This property has been in the same family for two centuries, and the vines are in the northern sector of St-Emilion on clay-silt and sandy soils that can be frost-prone. The grapes are picked by machine as well as by hand. Most but not all of the wine is aged in barriques for twelve months, and no more than half the oak is new. Before the 1950s, says M. Jean, the grapes were not destemmed and the wine was undrinkable for twenty years; nor was its drinkability enhanced by the crushing of the grapes in a kind of mangle. Now the wine is at the opposite extreme, being pretty but lacking in structure and length.

Château Troplong-Mondot

*St-Emilion. Tel: 0557 553205. Website: www.chateau-troplong-mondot.com. **Owner:** Christine Valette. Premier grand cru classé (B). 30 ha. 90% Merlot, 5% Cabernet Franc, 5% Cabernet Sauvignon. **Production:** 130,000 bottles. **Second wine:** Mondot*

Troplong-Mondot is easy to spot, as its vineyards, and the charming château, lie just below the water tower east of the village. In the eighteenth century the property belonged to the Abbé de Sèze, who built the house in 1745. In 1850 Raymond Troplong took over the estate and created the vineyards that still flourish today. In 1868 his nephew Edouard inherited the estate, which he sold in 1921 to the Belgian wine dealer Georges Thienpont. But in 1936 Thienpont sold it to a Parisian wine merchant, Alexandre Valette, whose great-granddaughter Christine has owned the property since 1980. Very much present at Troplong-Mondot, she and her family live in the house, which is crammed with books and paintings.

Christine Valette admits that when she took over she knew nothing about wine production. Michel Rolland was already acting as a consultant, so she simply retained his services. One of the first decisions was to put a stop to machine-harvesting. Rolland's influence is evident in the late harvesting of the crop, and in the very low yields he has insisted on ever since 1990. His guidance and skill surely contributed to Troplong's promotion to the First Growths in 2006.

About two-thirds of the vines slope down from the house in the direction of the village; the remainder glide southwards toward the plain. The soil is clay-limestone, although one sector near Trottevieille is very close to the bedrock; the average age of the vines is thirty-five years.

The winemaking is essentially traditional. After double sorting at the winery, the must is fermented in steel tanks, with little recourse to either cold-soaking or micro-oxygenation. The wine is aged in seventy-five per cent new oak, although the exact proportion does vary, for between twelve and twenty-four months, all depending on the wine's structure and character. The *chai* is one of St-Emilion's most elegant, being lit by numerous tiny chandeliers, while the entrance hall is flanked by glass-panelled wooden bays for bottles. These design features are all the inspiration of her husband Xavier Pariente, a dealer in eighteenth-century decorative arts, as is the exquisite interior of the château.

Ten years ago I drank the 1929, a remarkable wine. The colour was still healthy and bright although there were signs of maturity. The nose was complex, with blackcurrant fruit mingling with mushroom and cedar aromas, while the palate remained fresh and intense and long. The 1975, even after fifteen years, gave little pleasure, however, having that vintage's austerity and assertive tannins. There is also some austerity on the 1988 but it is balanced by its elegance and richness of fruit. The 1989 is aromatically opulent and seductive but fresh, and this is all mirrored on the palate, adding up to a glorious wine. The 1990 also shows hints of tobacco and truffles, while the palate is super-ripe and very intense. Even at fifteen years of age it remained youthful and required considerable aeration.

The 1992, although far from remarkable, is exceptionally good for the sodden vintage, with rich, plump fruit and ample length. The 1994, when young, seemed rather too extracted, but may have softened since. The 1995 shows Troplong-Mondot at its glorious best: rich, to be sure, but intense, poised, and very stylish. When young, the 1996 was rather one-dimensional and raw, but this too may have improved with more age. The 1997 is well made and persistent for the vintage, but is probably not for long keeping. The superb 1998 has a gloriously opulent nose, lush and oaky and very seductive; the texture is velvety, the fruit highly concentrated and spicy yet backed by tannic grip, the finish sweet yet lively. I prefer it to the rather heavy 2000, but I have only tasted this latter vintage once since bottling.

The 2001 is highly concentrated and big-shouldered, with plums and mulberries on the nose, a juiciness on the palate countered by big, ripe tannins, and ample acidity on the finish. This may well prove the equal of the 1998. I admire the 2002, subdued and oaky on the nose but with stylish cherry fruit, while the palate is a model of decorous restraint. There is surprising elegance on the discreet nose of the 2003, but the palate seems rather chunky and tough. The weighty 2004, tasted from cask at twelve months, gives every sign of being one of the top St-Emilion wines of the vintage, an impression confirmed when blind-tasted in 2007.

Troplong-Mondot is a much admired wine, and it is easy to see why. At its best it has a seductive Merlot-derived lushness without teetering over the edge into jamminess; and there is always an underlying elegance that charms and refreshes.

Château Trottevieille

St-Emilion. Tel: 0556 000070. Owner: Castéja family. Premier grand cru classé (B). 10 ha. 55% Merlot,
35% Cabernet Franc, 10% Cabernet Sauvignon. Production: 60,000 bottles.
Second wine: La Vieille Dame de Trottevieille

The Castéja family, who own the négociant house of Borie-Manoux, are also, since 1949, proprietors of a clutch of properties throughout Bordeaux. According to Philippe Castéja, the name of Trottevieille derives from an old woman who ran an inn nearby, as she was always scurrying about attending to her clients. She lives on too in the second wine, which was introduced only in 2000.

The property, with its charming old chartreuse, is located on a slight eminence just east of the village. The vines are in a single and exceptionally well-exposed parcel of reddish clay over limestone, with Pavie and Troplong-Mondot for neighbours. A parcel of pre-phylloxera Cabernet Franc vines survives, and in 2004 a very small quantity of wine from this sector was bottled separately, just for the fun of it. Because the Cabernet Franc vines form part of a field blend, they need to be tagged so that they can be picked separately. Yields throughout the property are now quite low, and even in 2000 were only thirty-five hl/ha. Castéja is clearly determined to improve quality at what had been one of the least impressive *premiers grands crus classés*, and has hired Denis Dubourdieu as well as Gilles Pauquet as consultants.

After picking in *cagettes*, there is thorough sorting, and then the grapes are crushed. After a cold soak, fermentation begins with indigenous yeasts in small cement tanks. The *marc* is pressed in a vertical press, and the wine is aged in new oak for sixteen to eighteen months.

The oldest Trottevieille to come my way has been the 1962, which thirty years later was still lively and sweet and balanced, though it was not especially rich. The 1979 had a similarly gentle structure, and no lack of sweet, supple fruit. In 2007 the 1982 was still suave and full of life, if not very persistent. The 1986 at ten years was rather stewed and astringent, but perhaps I was unlucky with this particular bottle. There is considerable charm on the 1989, with its delicate truffley aromas, its modest richness, and graceful structure. But it is outclassed by the 1990, with its black-cherry fruit, its drive and length. The chunky 1994 had fruit but little finesse; when young the 1995 was a seductive wine with appealing freshness, good though not great. The 1996 struck me as rather light and dilute, despite attractive aromas of plums and cherries. The 1999 also smells of plums, and delivers a solid wine, robust for the vintage, reasonably fresh but lacking in finesse.

The 2000 has a plump, opulent nose, and considerable brashness, density and power, yet does not lack freshness. The 2001 is less overtly tannic but has more finesse, its lush fruit harmoniously balanced by a lively finish. The 2002 is leaner, as one would expect, but its aromas of raspberries and redcurrants have charm; the wine does not lack concentration and the high acidity is well integrated. The 2003 is a touch charred, but there are sweet, almost candied, new oak aromas, and no harshness on the palate, which is supple but lacks grip. The tightly structured 2004 shows in full the new determination to raise the game at Trottevieille: it's concentrated, balanced, and complex, with a graceful quality allied to a very long, fresh finish.

Château du Val d'Or

Vignonet. Tel: 0557 845316. Website: www.vignobles-bardet.fr. Owner: Philippe Bardet. Grand cru. 12 ha.
82% Merlot, 12% Cabernet Franc, 6% Cabernet Sauvignon. Production: 70,000 bottles

This property, on gravelly soils not far from the Dordogne, has been bottled since the late 1940s. Like all Philippe Bardet's properties, this is machine-picked, using his innovative Tribaie harvester (*see* Chapter Three). After a prolonged *cuvaison* in steel and cement tanks, the wine is aged in oak for about eighteen months, although some of the wine remains in tanks, and the two components are later blended. Val d'Or is a simple, fruity wine, with aromas of ripe cherries (sometimes cherry jam), and the texture is supple and plump. This is essentially a commercial wine for drinking soon after release, as most vintages lack acidity and length.

Château de Valandraud

St-Emilion. Tel: 0557 550913. Website: www.thunevin.com. Owner: Jean-Luc Thunevin. Grand cru. 10 ha.
9 ha red: 66% Merlot, 33% Cabernet Franc, 1% Malbec. 1 ha white: 50% Sémillon, 50% Sauvignon Blanc.
Production: 40,000 bottles. Second wine: Virginie de Valandraud (red), No 2 de Valandraud (white)

Enter Jean-Luc Thunevin. Few men have done so much to cause a revolution within Bordeaux; he inspires admiration in many, disdain in others. It was the prestigious but flexible region of St-Emilion that permitted this Algerian-born former bank official to become an entrepreneur, with a small group of wine estates, a thriving négociant business, a wine bar, and who knows what else besides. He came here only in 1984, and started a wine bar (not the present one), but he soon sold it and established a wine shop with, from 1988 onwards, his négociant offices above.

From 1990 he began buying some parcels of vines, a section near Pavie-Macquin and a larger block near the river at St-Sulpice. In 1991, when he had 1.8 hectares, he made his first vintage of Valandraud; only 1,200 bottles were produced in this frost-ravaged year. The name is an invention, incorporating his wife's maiden name of Andraud. Indeed, Murielle Andraud is very much involved in the Thunevin winemaking business. He made the wine in a garage adjoining his house, and this is one of many explanations of the origin of the term *vin de garage*. Thunevin points out that this used to be where the Bécot family made wine in the 1940s, so he was merely continuing a long tradition. Today Thunevin has a number of wineries to give him more flexibility; since all his properties are *grand cru*, he can use them interchangeably.

His first vintage was truly artisanal. He both destemmed and crushed the grapes by hand, since he couldn't afford a destemmer in those days. Nor could he afford a pump for pumpovers, so he did some *pigeage* instead. In these early years he was greatly helped by advice from Alain Vauthier of Ausone, who remains a close friend. From the start he let the wine go through malolactic fermentation in barrels, and was thus one of the pioneers of this now common technique.

The 1992 vintage was poor, yet Thunevin made a good wine from his two parcels. Vauthier recalls how Thunevin spent long days in the vineyards, removing leaves to improve aeration, and reducing the crop to just under thirty hl/ha. Hardly anybody else in the appellation was taking such pains, and his efforts clearly paid off. He also created the second wine in this year. Critics recognized the quality of the wine, especially given the vintage.

He made another good wine in another tricky year, 1993, and in 1994 bought another parcel, on gravelly soil on the plain, where Merlot was planted. In this year he pitched the price of his 9,600 bottles high, which annoyed some, but attracted even more attention. The breakthrough came the following year. He aged the wine in 200 per cent new oak; that is, racking after the first year into a brand-new set of barrels. The wine attracted high scores, and became much sought-after. At an unusual *en primeur* auction at Christie's in London, it fetched a higher price than 1995 Mouton-Rothschild.

Valandraud had also become a controversial wine. Its super-concentration and flamboyant oakiness clearly appealed to American tasters and consumers, but more conservative British tasters were less impressed. It was, some suggested, all make-up and no substance; nor, since the majority of the grapes came from undistinguished sites, would the wine age. I have no experience of older Valandrauds, but Alain Vauthier assures me the 1992 is still drinking well.

By the mid- to late 1990s Valandraud was no longer an artisanal wine. The wineries are simple but well equipped, with vats of various types, including wood, and pumpovers, *pigeage*, *délestage*, and micro-oxygenation are all employed to extract richness. There is no fining or filtration.

Jean-Luc Thunevin has a sure sense of his market, and is an adept businessman. From the mid-1990s Valandraud was as expensive as many First Growths (if not more so), and by 1998 was priced at similar levels to the very top growths of St-Emilion and Pomerol. In recent years prices have dropped considerably, but that is a reflection of the global market rather than any falling off in the perceived quality of the wine.

For all his shrewdness and roguish iconoclasm, the intelligent Thunevin is a genuinely gifted wine producer, and fully aware of the importance of terroir, even if Valandraud is hailed by those arguing against the concept as the shining example of a great wine emanating from a modest site. Nonetheless it is significant that in 1999 Thunevin bought an additional 5.5 hectares high on the plateau at St-Etienne-de-Lisse, not far from Fleur Cardinale and Pressac. This was the former Château Bel-Air-Ouÿ, which has now been incorporated into Valandraud. It is not an easy site, as it ripens late; indeed, in 1999 and 2000 he believes he picked too early here, and did not use those grapes for Valandraud. At the same time he found that some of the parcels near the river were no longer delivering top grapes; this puzzled him, as these very blocks were the principal source of the acclaimed 1995.

At the former Bel-Air-Ouÿ, new plantings of the Cabernet varieties are to a density of 10,000 vines per hectare. There is another Valandraud plot, all Merlot, near Laroque. All this gives Thunevin maximum flexibility; with the second wine, Virginie, the third wine, 3 de Valandraud, and two other labels to play with, he can juggle his fruit sources.

Another innovation from the indefatigable Thunevin since 2003 has been a white No 1 Blanc de Valandraud, from vines near Bel-Air-Ouÿ. These vines are picked by *tries successives* – there were four of them in 2004 – and in September 2005 he bought an adjoining parcel of sixty-year-old Sémillon, which proves that white grapes are no novelty in St-Emilion. When I visited the parcel during the 2005 harvest, I noticed plastic bottles tied to the vines and partly filled with beer and honey, in an attempt to lure bees and wasps away from the bunches. It seemed at least partly successful. One-third of the crop is aged in tanks, the remainder is fermented and aged in new oak, with lees-stirring. Thunevin insists he dislikes the taste of new oak in a white wine. The wine is very expensive, naturally, but there is a second wine at a more affordable price.

The 2004 white is impressive, with floral as well as oaky aromas. It's a strongly flavoured, spicy wine with considerable force and bite, firm acidity, and no overt oakiness. I have not tasted red Valandraud from the 1990s. The comments of other tasters suggest that 1995 and 1998 were first-rate, while the 1994 and 1996 were not that exceptional. I tasted the 2000 from cask, and it was very ripe, very tannic, but the overriding impression was of sumptuous, slightly jammy fruit. I was disappointed by the 2001, which had sweet, oaky aromas, and was fleshy and succulent on the palate, yet lacked precision. Despite some cooked aromas in 2003, the palate is better, with high concentration, good acidity, and no raisiny character.

Château Vieux Fortin

St-Emilion. Tel: 0557 254997. Owner: Claude Sellan. Grand cru. 5.5 ha. 60% Merlot, 40% Cabernet Franc.
Production: 30,000 bottles

Claude Sellan is a relative newcomer to St-Emilion, having bought this small property in 1993, though his cultural roots have always been in the Libournais. The vineyards are close to Ripeau and La Dominique on clay-limestone soils that retain water well, so there is never any hydric stress. The oldest vines, Cabernet Franc, date from 1935, and the youngest were planted in 1989.

Sellan picks the grapes into *cagettes*, sorts, destems, cold-soaks, then vinifies in steel tanks, with up to twenty per cent of the must being bled off. The wine is aged in new oak for at least twenty months, with traditional racking, and is bottled unfiltered. His policy is to age the wines for a few years before release, so the eventual price is fairly high. The 1995 has a lush, chocolatey nose, but is more forward and less concentrated on the palate – a balanced, stylish wine now ready to drink. The 1998 is powerful and robust, with plenty of spicy oak and good length. It's not elegant but it has presence and personality. The 2001 is a glorious wine, very ripe but with a stylish savoury undertow; the tannins are very ripe, the texture succulent, the fruit delicious, the finish invigorating.

Château du Vieux-Guinot

St-Pey-d'Armens. Tel: 0557 561023. Website: www.vignoblesrollet.com. Owner: Jean-Pierre Rollet.
Grand cru. 12 ha. 70% Merlot, 15% Cabernet Franc, 15% Cabernet Sauvignon. Production: 50,000 bottles.
Second wine: La Chartreuse du Vieux-Guinot

The amiable M. Rollet comes from a family that has been grape-farming here for almost three centuries. He also owns Château Fourney and, in the Côtes de Castillon, Château Grand Tertre (*q.v.*). The soil here is essentially clay, and the vineyards are machine-harvested. Fermentation takes place in enamel and cement tanks, with some micro-oxygenation. The wine is aged in about thirty per cent new oak for twelve months, with *cliquage* as well as rackings. The aim is to produce an accessible wine that is not too demanding on the palate.

Since 2003 Rollet has also made a special *cuvée* called Osage from four parcels, all Merlot, spread over two hectares. Yields are lower, and, unlike Vieux-Guinot, the wine goes though malolactic fermentation in barrels, and is aged in new oak. Production is limited to 2,500 bottles.

Some vintages, such as 1993 and 1998, suffer from dilution and a rather dry finish. The 2001 is distinctly better, with more muscle and freshness too, though not much complexity. I prefer it to the debut of Osage, admittedly from the tricky 2003 vintage, which seems overoaked and marked by rather brutal tannins and a dry finish.

Château Villemaurine

St-Emilion. Tel: 0556 580862. Owner: Justin Onclin. Grand cru. 7 ha. 85% Merlot, 15% Cabernet Sauvignon.
Production: 40,000 bottles

Apart from attending a grand dinner in the former quarries beneath the winery, at which an Austrian colleague caught a chill so severe he had to return home, my acquaintance with this property is minimal. The vines are old, and the location close to the village is excellent. The wine is aged in fifty per cent new oak, and bottled without filtration. Since 1970 the vineyards have been leased by the négociant house Robert Giraud. My few tastings of the wine left me seriously disappointed, even in excellent vintages such as 2000 and 2001. More recently, the 2004 was insubstantial and dominated by rugged tannins. An early cask sample of 2006 struck me as flabby and lifeless. The property was bought by Justin Onclin, owner of Branas Grand Poujeaux (*q.v.*) in Moulis, in early 2006, nine months before Villemaurine lost its classified status. The Giraud lease will expire in 2008.

Château Yon-Figeac

St-Emilion. Tel: 0557 244059. Website: www.fr.yon-figeac.com. Owner: Alain Chateau. Grand cru. 25 ha. 85% Merlot,
10% Cabernet Franc, 5% Petit Verdot. Production: 130,000 bottles. Second wine: Ch Yon St Martin

Bernard Germain manages, leases, and owns a number of properties on the Right Bank, and owns a clutch of superb estates in the Loire. Yon-Figeac, which he acquired in 1985, was run for many years by his son Philippe, then sold in 2005 to paper magnate Alain Château, who also acquired some Loire properties from the Germain family.

The vineyard is in a single block not far from Figeac. Despite its name, Yon-Figeac never formed part of its grander neighbour. The soil is quite sandy but rich in iron. As at other Germain properties, the wines are aged in 400-litre barrels; although new oak is used, the wood influence is less marked than it would be were conventional barriques used.

Yon-Figeac has never been an exciting wine. My scores, often in blind tastings, have been utterly consistent, regardless of vintage. Yon-Figeac is a good wine, but with a lean and one-dimensional character that robs it of complexity. The 1997, admittedly from a modest vintage, was bland and rather weedy. The 1998 seems the best of recent vintages, having a robust fruitiness, and the 2000 has considerable charm. The 2001 has rich, fleshy, oaky aromas, but the palate shows more vigour than weight, and a tangy redcurrant finish. The 2002 is successful for the vintage, with plump blackberry aromas and a palate that balances suppleness and spiciness. The 2003 is far less successful, with beef-extract aromas and a dry finish. The 2004 is light and shows little complexity, but has enough acidity and tannin to give it grip and length.

21. Pomerol Part I

 "There is no there there," famously wrote Gertrude Stein. Many first-time visitors to Pomerol may well share that reaction. True, there is a noble neo-Gothic spire rising above a village that scarcely exists. There are no other landmarks and few great châteaux to enliven the landscape. At first glance, and at second, Pomerol is a sea of vines. Most visitors would have driven past Pétrus without noticing it until Christian Moueix smartened it up. Celebrated growths such as Le Pin and Lafleur and L'Eglise-Clinet are simply modest houses and cellars without any distinguishing characteristics. Even though Pomerol is now world-famous, most proprietors are happy to maintain this aura of genteel shabbiness. There is simply no point in offering anything – a sign, a tasting room, a car park – that might delude visitors into supposing it's worth stopping at a property where all the wine is usually sold shortly after the harvest. There are a few exceptions: Gazin, L'Evangile, Trotanoy, and Vieux-Château-Certan have some architectural merit, though on a modest scale. The one grandiose château, Sales, is concealed in woodlands.

Another surprise is quite how small Pomerol is. With only 780 hectares under vine, it is smaller even than St-Julien, and measures four kilometres by three (2.5 miles by 1.9). It is bordered to the north by the Barbanne stream, a tributary of the Isle; to the east by St-Emilion, and to the south and west by the town of Libourne, with a few properties well within the city limits. In 2003 there were 150 declared producers, and there is no cooperative. Almost all wines are estate-bottled and in an average year account for 4.3 million bottles. Merlot dominates, as throughout the Libournais, with about eighty per cent of plantings; the remaining surface is taken by fifteen per cent of Cabernet Franc and five per cent of Cabernet Sauvignon. Pomerol became an AC in 1936.

Much nonsense has been talked about the terroir of Pomerol, confusing the appellation as a whole with the clay plateau where most top vineyards are located. This makes it difficult to pin down the authentic character of Pomerol. I look for a distinctly sensuous character, in aroma and texture, combined with a firm but not rigid structure. Where there is power, it is usually discreet; where there is tannin, it does not obscure the fruit. But although this may characterize the wines from the plateau, it is less likely to apply to wines produced in the sectors closer to Libourne.

The fact is that the Pomerol soils are very varied, and in some locations there is a good deal of sand and gravel. The soil at Château de Sales, for instance, has virtually nothing in common with that at Pétrus. Pomerol benefited from the same gravel deposits as the Médoc, so the celebrated plateau is largely composed of gravel beds with varying degrees of clay and the iron deposits known as *crasse de fer*.

The unsurprising consequence of the mix of outstanding and mediocre soils (essentially sandy) is that quality too is variable. As well as the giants of the plateau, there are some truly mediocre wines grown on lightweight soils. There are still many growers with a hectare or two of vines who, in the absence of a cooperative, produce a few thousand bottles of usually overpriced wines in artisanal conditions. Although some of the world's great wines emanate from Pomerol, many of its wines are of little interest. Nor is there any classification to help the consumer. The best guide to quality tends to be price; the wines most sought-after tend to be the most expensive. On the other hand, many growers cynically but understandably exploit the renown of Pomerol to sell their wines at exaggerated prices.

The Romans were here, and two important roads crossed the region. No one is sure of the origin of the name of Pomerol, but Nicolas de Bailliencourt of Gazin says some attribute it to the Latin word "*poma*", which means a fruit with seeds. Pomerol must have received a boost after the British founded Libourne in the thirteenth century. It also benefited from being located along one of the pilgrimage routes. The Knights of Malta and St John established hostels and/or hospitals on the site of modern-day La Commanderie and Gazin. The Gazin hospital was mentioned in documents from 1288. By the late fifteenth century the pilgrimage route was in decline, but the Knights remained in place, maintaining farms and vineyards, often restoring them after the ravages of the Hundred Years War. They were still in Pomerol at the outbreak of the French Revolution.

The Right Bank: Pomerol

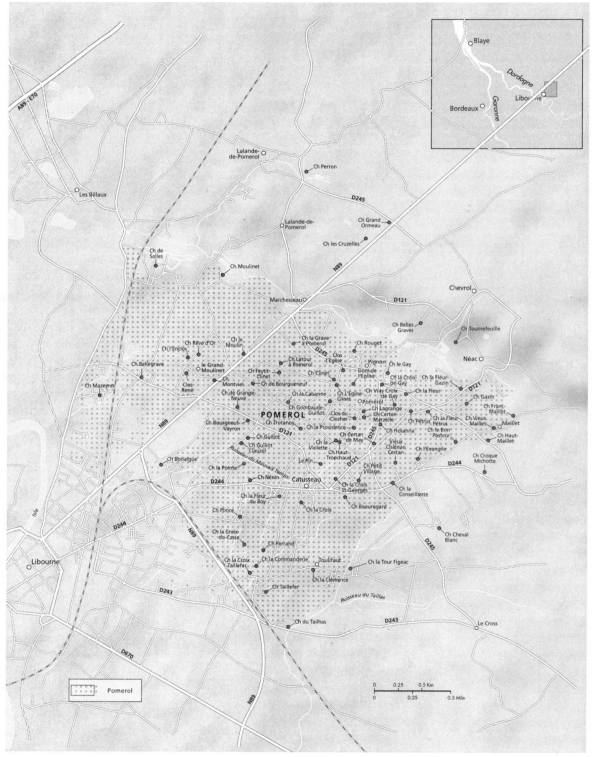

Pomerol

It is not entirely clear how well developed the vineyards were by this time. Cabernet Franc, under the name of Bidure or Vidure, had already been planted by the sixteenth century. Merlot, it seems, was a relative latecomer, having been adopted by a Libournais négociant called Louis-Léonard Fontémoing, who was the owner of what is today Château Rouget. Until around 1760 his vineyards had been planted with white grapes, but something persuaded him that Merlot was the ideal grape for this area. By the late eighteenth century, a substantial proportion of Pomerol's land was dedicated to wine production. Wine commerce was of course greatly aided by easy access to the Dordogne and Gironde rivers from Libourne.

White vines remained popular well into the nineteenth century. Bailliencourt believes that it was the dominance of the Dutch merchants and proprietors that maintained white wine production, since the crop was easy to sell in northern Europe. It was only in 1936 that white vines were banned from Pomerol. By the late nineteenth century a handful of estates had become well known: Vieux-Château-Certan, Pétrus, Trotanoy, among others. But the picture remained mixed: there was still a good deal of polyculture here. Victorian connoisseurs focused on the great growths of the Left Bank, and even Professor Saintsbury found no room to report on the wines of Pomerol. Today there is recognition that some magnificent wines were made in Pomerol in the great vintages of the 1920s, 1940s, and 1950s, yet they were never valued on release in the way that the top growths of the Médoc or St-Emilion were.

It was the foresight, skill, and canniness of a single wine merchant that helped raise the reputation of Pomerol in the latter half of the twentieth century. Jean-Pierre Moueix came, like many other modern Bordeaux dynasties, from the rugged and poor Corrèze region. Unable to gain a footing in Bordeaux itself, where the established négociants ruled the roost, he implanted himself in the Libournais. At first he simply traded in the wines in their traditional markets such as Belgium. Then he began buying properties or leasing them. His son Christian has continued the process. It would be an exaggeration to say that without the astute purchasing, winemaking, and promotional activities of Etablissements Jean-Pierre Moueix Pomerol would be an undervalued wine. But it certainly helped put Pomerol on the international map, and has set standards of excellence and brilliance that others eagerly try to emulate.

Although modern Pomerol is closely associated with Merlot, some proprietors point out that it took a dominant role relatively recently. It was after the devastating frost of 1956 that many growers decided to replace the lower-yielding Cabernet Franc with the early-ripening Merlot. At Lafleur, Jacques Guinaudeau has a vineyard composed in equal measure of Merlot and Cabernet Franc. He remarks that while Merlot performs superbly on clay soils, on the other sectors of Pomerol Cabernet Franc can give better acidity, structure, and longevity. Alexandre Thienpont of Vieux-Château-Certan finds Merlot too one-dimensional to be of real interest without a dose of Cabernet Franc. Dany Rolland believes that the Cabernet varieties were planted in Pomerol because Merlot often suffers from *coulure* during flowering. For Denis Durantou of L'Eglise-Clinet, the role of Cabernet Franc is to counter the tendency of Merlot to be harvested at very high sugar levels, with the danger that the resulting wine can be opulent but flat.

I have already mentioned that the soils of Pomerol are very varied. The clay *bouttonière* ("buttonhole") on which much of Pétrus lies is, in terms of area, atypical of Pomerol as a whole. Much of the plateau of Pomerol is composed of gravel layered over sandy clay (marl). The gravel is Günzian in origin, as in much of the Médoc; gravel in lower sectors close to Libourne is from the Mindel glaciation. The celebrated buttonhole is simply a band of blue clay that, after various geological upheavals, has pushed through the gravel overlay.

Promotional literature, and some growers, make much of the presence of *crasse de fer* in the soils. This is essentially the presence of iron, either in the form of clinkers, or in bands of sand tinted by iron. Catherine Moueix of Taillefer claims that *crasse de fer* contributes aromas of truffles and violets to the wine. Alexandre Thienpont points out that *crasse de fer* has positive consequences, since it reduces vigour. Denis Durantou believes that because a layer of *crasse de fer* is impermeable, it inhibits roots from descending into the soil. In his view a soil rich in *crasse de fer* can never be a great terroir. He is a consultant at Moulinet, where there is a ferruginous band about one metre (three feet) below the surface, and he has been attempting to smash this band by mechanical means to improve permeability. Kees van Leeuwen, the technical director of Cheval Blanc and a distinguished viticulturalist, seriously doubts that the presence of iron has any direct impact on the quality of the wine. He echoes the great soil expert Enjalbert, who declined to make a case for the influence, positive or negative, of *crasse de fer*.

The complex nature of the Pomerol soils may be hard to assess in terms of their impact on the aromas or flavours of the wines. More easily discernible is their influence on the precocity of the vines and the structure of the wines. Dany Rolland believes that however important the geological composition of the soil may be, it is the capacity of these soils to respond to climatic changes that is an intrinsic part of the terroir of Pomerol. The clay plateau, which Pétrus shares in part with estates such as La Conseillante, L'Evangile, Lafleur, Gazin, Trotanoy, and Vieux-Château-Certan (and perhaps some sectors of Le Gay and Clinet), is more moisture-retentive than other sectors, an advantage in dry years. The wines from here always have body and considerable power. Walking through the vineyards of the plateau with Nicolas de Bailliencourt of Gazin, it was easy to see the heavy clay soils close to the surface, while on the fringes of the plateau (defined most generously at around twenty hectares) stony gravel is easily visible. And a similar walk through La Conseillante also revealed enormous differences in soil within very short distances. So the plateau is very far from uniform.

Nothing better exemplifies the complexity of the Pomerol terroir than the vineyards of Lafleur, which consist of 4.5 hectares in a single block of amazingly diverse soil types. It is unlikely that anybody other than the owner, Jacques Guinaudeau, begins to understand the possible significance and contribution of these varied soils.

Denis Durantou, moreover, discerns not just one buttonhole but two. The first takes in Vieux-Château-Certan, parts of La Conseillante, L'Evangile, Hosanna, Lafleur, and Pétrus. The second takes in parts of his own property of L'Eglise-Clinet, Clos l'Eglise, La Cabanne, Trotanoy, and Nénin. It is impossible for the outsider to assess how accurate or significant these essentially geological divisions and definitions are, but they are at any rate worth reporting, although proprietors are understandably anxious to proclaim the excellence of their soils.

Nearer the church the presence of sandy gravel is greater, and the proportion of sand and of fine-grained gravel increases as the land slopes down toward the N89 road that links Libourne with Périgeux; a short distance farther west the vineyards are traversed by the railway line and end at the northern suburbs of Libourne. Here the vineyards benefit from earlier ripening, but the wines tend to have less power, complexity, and staying power. These vineyards are often derided for their high sand content, which gives the wines a certain fruitiness but at the expense of structure, longevity, and depth; yet there are properties, such as Clos René and L'Enclos, that also contain a good deal of gravel, which gives wines of more finesse.

The southernmost sector of Pomerol, just beyond the hamlet of Catusseau, is not well thought of, although some properties here, such as Le Plince and Taillefer, can produce perfectly good wines. Just north of Catusseau are some of Pomerol's finest gravelly soils. Here one finds properties such as Le Pin, Beauregard, and Petit-Village. Another lesser sector is close to the hamlet of Maillet, which borders three other appellations: St-Emilion, Montagne-St-Emilion, and Lalande de Pomerol. The road through the hamlet is in fact the boundary between Pomerol and St-Emilion, leading to the legally recognized anomaly that certain vineyards within St-Emilion belonging to Pomerol properties in Maillet are granted honorary citizenship of Pomerol. There is a fair amount of clay in the soil. The best-known property based in Maillet is the Rollands' Le Bon Pasteur.

While St-Emilion has benefited from a rigorous classification system, Pomerol has always got by without one. Nicolas de Bailliencourt believes that it was the opposition of some small growers, unwilling to have the inferiority of their wines officially recognized, that left Pomerol without a classification. One could argue that in Pomerol it is the market alone that rates the wines, but given the limited production and availability of many of them, prices have often been distorted. Le Pin may be a great wine, but it is hard to see why it should fetch prices many times higher than those obtained by, say, La Conseillante or Vieux-Château-Certan.

There is little to unite the properties of Pomerol, other than their appellation, so proprietors rarely work together to promote their wines. The Moueix and Janoueix families own numerous properties, but they follow their own path, being merchants and distributors as well as proprietors. L'Evangile forms part of the Lafite-Rothschild group, and Petit-Village belongs to the AXA Millésimes group. They too stand to one side. Nor is it hard to understand why the prestigious properties feel they have little to gain from promoting their wines alongside those of the lesser properties.

If there are still too many truly mediocre properties that let down the good name of Pomerol, they do not seem to have tarnished the lustre of the region as a whole. Some may be bought up by more ambitious proprietors, others will continue to sell their wines for modest prices to undemanding customers. The manager of one estate told me he was astonished, when attending the *label* tastings that authorize wines to bear the Pomerol *appellation contrôlée*, to learn that not a single wine from the less than stellar 2002 vintage had failed the test. He told me:

> *What disturbs me about this is that the system allows the mediocre wines to profit from the reputation of Pomerol's best wines. When the results were announced, applause broke out. Everyone knows that there are some poor wines from Pomerol, and everybody colludes with it.*

There is little to be said about viticulture or vinification that is specific to Pomerol and its wines. There are certainly two schools of thought when it comes to harvest dates. Michel Rolland has many clients in this, his native, region, and they usually follow his advice to pick as late as possible in order to produce the rich, fleshy styles that Pomerol has come to be associated with. On the other hand, the Moueix team is often among the first to pick, hoping to attain the maximum freshness and vibrancy in the wines; yet no one would claim that the Moueix wines show unripeness. Robert Parker gives a succinct presentation of the two philosophies in one of his recent books.[1] Parker makes no secret of where his sympathies lie, and indeed his closeness to Rolland for two decades suggests that the two men share a similar palate. Nothing wrong with this, but there should be room for more than one approach to viticulture and winemaking. There is no need to choose between Trotanoy and Pétrus on the one hand, and those who follow the counsels of Rolland on the other. We can enjoy both.

The small dimensions of many properties allow a style of vinification that in many cases is essentially *garagiste*, with a minute attention to detail. I also suspect that in few other regions of Bordeaux have so many estates invested in modern vertical presses in an attempt to ensure the handling of the pomace is as gentle as possible. Indeed, Jean-Claude Berrouet, the long-term winemaker at the Moueix properties, helped to design the modern version of this most traditional of presses.

Château Beau Soleil

Tel: 0556 702011. Owner: Thierry Rustmann. 3.5 ha. 90% Merlot, 10% Cabernet Franc.
Production: 18,000 bottles. Second wine: Petit Soleil

I was surprised to see Thierry Rustmann strolling toward the town hall in Pomerol, since I know him as the energetic owner of Château Sénéjac (*q.v.*) in the Médoc. A few days later, when I arrived at this small property in the southwest corner of Pomerol, he was there to greet me. This is a rare example of an individual proprietor from the Left Bank crossing the Dordogne. Strictly speaking, Rustmann is not the owner of the property, but in 2005 took a twenty-five-year lease from Anne-Marie Audy-Arcaute. As winemaker he has installed Aurélie Carreau. Jean-Michel Arcaute had made the wines here until his untimely death in 2001.

This is not the best sector of Pomerol, and the soil is a fine sandy gravel, with some *crasse de fer* and, Rustmann believes, some clay below, as the vines suffered no stress during the dry 2005 summer. Rustmann picks by selective harvesting in *cagettes*. After sorting, the grapes are cold-soaked, then fermented in steel tanks with selected yeasts. The wine is aged in seventy per cent new oak for at least fifteen months, and the portion aged in new wood also goes through malolactic fermentation in new barrels.

---

1 Parker, *Bordeaux,* Dorling Kindersley, London, 2003, 623–4

Of course it is far too early to see what Rustmann and Carreau have coaxed from Beau Soleil. However, I have good notes on some previous vintages. The 2001 has fragrance and charm, and considerable richness balanced by good acidity; but it does lack structure. The 2002 has more plummy aromas, and is quite a rich, solid wine for the vintage. The aromas of the 2003 are not cooked, but it's an unruly wine with grippy tannins and modest acidity. The stylish 2004 has aromas of black cherries and cloves, a plump, velvety texture, and a persistent finish.

Château Beauregard

Tel: 0557 511336. Website: www.chateau-beauregard.com. Owner: Crédit Foncier. 17.5 ha. 70% Merlot, 30% Cabernet Franc. Production: 80,000 bottles. Second wine: Benjamin de Beauregard

Beauregard is one of the few architecturally distinguished mansions of Pomerol, having been constructed soon after the French Revolution by a rich St-Emilion merchant named Berthoumieu. The Guggenheim family based a Long Island mansion, built in 1920, on the chartreuse of Beauregard. When I first visited Beauregard in the early 1980s, I was kindly welcomed (as a mere wine-lover with no professional attachments) by the proprietor, M. Clauzel. In 1991 he sold the property to the Crédit Foncier bank, which also owns Château St-Robert in the Graves and Château Bastor-Lamontagne in Sauternes (*q.q.v.*). However, M. Clauzel's widow still lives in the château, enjoying its charming terrace and park. Crédit Foncier installed Vincent Priou as the director here, and he has supervised an extensive programme of renovations, with much replanting, new drainage, better vine selections, and so forth.

The property has also been expanded by six hectares since 1991. There used to be some Malbec and Cabernet Sauvignon in the vineyards, but both have been replaced by either Merlot or by massal selections of Cabernet Franc. Beauregard has a fairly high proportion of the latter, and Priou is tempted to increase it further, as it seems to thrive on the clay-gravel soils that dominate the property, which lies just east of Catusseau, close to both Petit-Village and the St-Emilion border. The average age of the vines is some thirty-five years, and the vineyards are cultivated by *lutte raisonnée*. Green-harvesting was introduced back in 1992.

After sorting, the fruit is destemmed, lightly crushed, and cold-soaked at moderate temperatures. Fermentation begins in steel tanks with natural yeasts (though Priou admits that he would use selected yeasts in a vintage when he believed it would give better results). The vinification is traditional, with no mechanical concentration, no *pigeage* or *délestage*, no micro-oxygenation. Priou has replaced the pneumatic press with a modern vertical press. The wine is given a lengthy ageing, up to twenty-four months, in barrels, of which sixty per cent are new. Priou believes the wines gain in complexity after long barrel-ageing, but he tastes frequently to make sure the wines don't dry out. The wines are neither fined nor filtered.

The oldest Beauregard I have tasted is the 1978, which was so dour I suspect I experienced a faulty bottle. The 1985, tasted in 1990, was gorgeous; despite its surprising softness, it was concentrated and deep. I imagined it would keep well, but have had no opportunity to test the hunch. The 1990 was easy-going and lacked grip, making it disappointing for the vintage. I did not care for the 1994 or 1997, but the 1996 is evolving well, with some attractive cedary aromas and a touch of tobacco; but it's solid rather than elegant.

The 1998 is delicious, with splendid aromas of ripe cherries and vanilla; by 2005 the wine was supple, concentrated, and spicy, with no undue extraction and excellent length. The 1999 is not quite at this level, but it's a very good wine with some lushness and stylishness, and the oak is well integrated. The powerful, backward 2000 is dense and oaky with a touch of liquorice, and shows good acidity and length. The 2001 is lively and vigorous Pomerol, but possibly marred by excessive new oak despite the concentrated fruit. The 2002 has aromatic complexity, with blackcurrants and raspberries on the nose; it is true to the vintage, being medium-bodied with some grip and freshness, but may soon be at its best. I prefer it to the 2003, which has rather jammy aromas, little depth of fruit, some fairly dry tannins, and only modest length. The 2004 has piquant red-fruits aromas of cherries and cranberries; it's solid and firmly tannic yet has charm and balance.

Beauregard has always been somewhat underrated, perhaps because of its corporate ownership and its relatively light style. Yet it is a very reliable wine, well balanced and stylish.

Château Bel-Air

*Pomerol. Tel: 0557 510245. Website: www.belair-beausejour.com. **Owner:** Mme. Jacques Melet. 13 ha. 95% Merlot, 5% Cabernet Franc. **Production:** 75,000 bottles. **Second wine:** L'Ermitage de Bel-Air*

The Bel-Air vineyards are divided into roughly equal sectors on either side of the N89 road. The hospitable Melet family, who also own Château Beauséjour (*q.v.*) in Fronsac, have been the proprietors since 1914. The sandy gravel soils are ploughed and the crop green-harvested. After a manual harvest the bunches are sorted repeatedly and given a brief cold soak. The must is fermented in cement tanks, with some bleeding if there is any lack of concentration. The wine is aged for about twelve months in one-third new oak with regular rackings, although about one-third of the crop stays in tanks. There is an eggwhite-fining but no filtration.

My experience of this wine is very limited. The 2001 is disappointing, with some vegetal tones behind the plummy fruit; the wine doesn't lack concentration, but the finish is leathery and lacks finesse. The 2004, tasted from cask, seems better balanced with more density and succulence.

Château Bellegrave

*Tel: 0557 512047. **Owner:** Jean-Marie Bouldy. 8 ha. 75% Merlot, 25% Cabernet Franc. **Production:** 45,000 bottles*

The vineyards of this family property lie near the winery in the southwest sector of Pomerol, close to the railway line. The soil has deep gravel and, says Bouldy, about twenty per cent clay content. The average age of the vines is thirty-five years and the viticulture is close to organic. Bouldy is emphatic that he is not seeking overripeness; in this he reflects the view of his friend Jean-Claude Berrouet of Moueix. The fruit is picked by hand and sorted at the winery. Fermentation takes place in temperature-controlled cement vats, and the wine is aged for at least eighteen months in thirty per cent new barriques.

Although no one would claim that Bellegrave is located in a top sector of the region, the somewhat atypical soil does seem to make a difference, as Bouldy invariably delivers a sound and sometimes excellent wine. Of the two vintages from the 1980s I have encountered I much preferred the spicy, vigorous 1986 to the rather charmless 1989. The 2000 and 2001 are both excellent. There's ample ripe, succulent fruit on the nose of the 2000, while the wine itself is full-bodied and gutsy, without being coarse. The 2001 is discreetly oaky on the nose, and its balance is impeccable. It has fine cherry fruit, vigour and piquancy, a supple texture, and good acidity. It will give great pleasure over the next eight years or so. The 2002 has a strong red-fruits character and plenty of zest and fine length, if little complexity. I find it hard to like the baked 2003, with its short finish. The excellent 2004 is stylish, forceful and oaky, rich and concentrated, with black-fruits flavours and bright acidity. The youthful 2005 is surprisingly open and supple, but it doesn't lack tannic structure and it finishes with welcome freshness.

Bellegrave may not be the most majestic of Pomerols, but it is consistently well made and balanced. It is frequently underrated. Jean-Marie Bouldy and his consultant Christian Veyry know what they are doing.

Château Le Bon Pasteur

*Maillet. Tel: 0557 515243. Website: www.rollandcollection.com. **Owner:** Rolland family. 7 ha. 80% Merlot, 20% Cabernet Franc. **Production:** 30,000 bottles*

This has been a Rolland family property since the 1920s. Some seven hectares, as well as the winery, are located in Maillet, literally across the road from St-Emilion. There are also some parcels on stonier soil near Gazin and L'Evangile. Needless to say, the viticultural practices follow the Rolland model: the soils are ploughed, *lutte raisonnée* is the governing principle, and the vines are deleafed and green-harvested in most years. The terroir may not be outstanding, but the vines are old and tended with care.

The grapes are sorted twice, then destemmed but not crushed. Le Bon Pasteur was one of the first Pomerol estates to be equipped with temperature-controlled steel tanks. The Merlot is punched down and given a lengthy maceration. The pomace is pressed in a modern vertical press. Malolactic fermentation takes place in new barriques, and the proportion of new oak for the *élevage* is between eighty and 100 per cent. There is some lees-stirring, but the ageing is essentially traditional. Fining was abandoned in the mid-1990s and filtration is not systematic.

It is hardly surprising that Le Bon Pasteur is a rich, fleshy, oaky wine of considerable concentration and power. The 1985, 1988, and 1989, all tasted long ago, were very good, and the 1990 exceptional in its extract and length. No Le Bon Pasteur was released in 1991; instead it was bottled as a generic Pomerol. The decision was the correct one, as the wine was modest and rather dry. The 1997, although rather oaky, was very good for the vintage. The 1999 has evolved well aromatically, with toasty, leafy aromas, but I find the wine too extracted. Voluptuousness marks the 2000, with its toasty blackberry and coffee aromas, a plump palate, robust tannins, a chocolatey tone, and moderate acidity – *très* Rolland. The 2001, in a very similar style, is marginally better, in its vigour and spiciness, but the tannins are quite assertive. Le Bon Pasteur is a major success in 2002, with no hint of greenness; the aromas are rich in blackberry fruit, the oak well integrated, and the palate has ample flesh and weight. The 2003 has some jammy aromas, but the palate is more satisfactory, showing better balance and upfront fruitiness than many 2003 Pomerols. The 2004 may be one-dimensional, but it's rich, fleshy, and reasonably concentrated, with enough acidity to keep it lively and drive it to a fine finish. The 2005 is voluptuous and very concentrated, a wine for sensualists.

Le Bon Pasteur is a wine that seems to develop quite rapidly. At five or eight years of age it is already so attractive that it is not clear that further ageing will confer much benefit. But as I have not tasted vintages of the wine with a good deal of bottle-age, it is hard to be certain.

Château Bonalgue

Tel: 0557 516217. **Owner:** *Pierre Bourotte. 6.5 ha. 90% Merlot, 10% Cabernet Franc.*
Production: *38,000 bottles.* **Second wine:** *Ch Burgrave*

The Bourottes family, like the Moeuix and Janoueix, originated in the Corrèze region and came to the Libournais in 1926. Pierre took over running both Bonalgue and their other property of Clos du Clocher (*q.v.*) in 1969, and is now assisted by his son Jean-Baptiste and, since 2004, by winemaker Lucas Leclercq. The Bourottes also own various other properties in other Libournais appellations.

The usually precocious Bonalgue vineyards lie just northeast of Libourne, mostly on the eastern side of the N89, but with one block across the road. The soil is described as sandy-clay gravel, with *crasse de fer* and a gravelly subsoil – which seems to cover most possibilities. Parcels at a lower elevation are the source of the second wine.

After sorting and a short cold soak, the must is fermented in cement tanks at fairly low temperatures. The Bourottes have tried micro-oxygenation but are not keen on the technique. Malolactic fermentation takes place in both tanks and barrels, and the wine is aged for around fifteen months in fifty per cent new oak, mostly from the Darnajou cooperage.

Bonalgue is a sound if not spectacular Pomerol, always well made and stylish though it rarely scales great heights. The 1990, though, has evolved beautifully, displaying smoky, truffley aromas, while the palate is still juicy and lively, with ample tannic backbone and persistence. The 1998 has more overt fleshiness and an attractive sheen of sweet oak; it's plump and concentrated, but there is sufficient acidity to keep the wine lively. The 1999 is ripe, stylish, and smoky on the nose, while the palate has zest, freshness, and no dilution.

There's a hint of overripeness on the 2000; consequently it also lacks some vigour and length. It's a decent wine, but scarcely exceptional for the vintage. The 2001 is more stylish; it doesn't have much complexity or weight but is well made, has a good attack and fair length of flavour. The 2002 is undemanding and fresh, but a touch hollow and dilute. The 2003 is quite baked on the nose, and a touch volatile, while the palate is both confected and fiercely tannic. It is easily outclassed by the richer, more structured, and immensely enjoyable 2004.

Château Bourgneuf-Vayron

*Tel: 0557 514203. **Owner:** Xavier Vayron. 9 ha. 90% Merlot, 10% Cabernet Franc. **Production:** 42,000 bottles*

This estate has been in the Vayron family for generations, and was originally known simply as Château Bourgneuf; the name was changed to avoid confusion with other properties with a similar name. Despite his laid-back manner, Xavier Vayron has a clear notion of the style of wine he wishes to produce – one that is well structured and capable of ageing. His wife Dominique is a talented artist, and her work often appears on promotional literature, such as the logo for the Cercle du Rive Droite.

The vineyards, which have scarcely altered in extent since the nineteenth century, are located in a single parcel close to both Trotanoy and La Cabanne. Near Trotanoy the soil is rich in clay, giving very ripe grapes. The average age of the vineyards is some forty years. Some younger parcels are planted on grey sandy soils of less distinction.

The grapes are sorted twice at the winery, then fermented in cement tanks. A modern vertical press crushes the *marc*, and the wine is aged in thirty per cent new oak for around sixteen months, with usually no more than a single racking. Vayron is opposed to the use of concentrators, micro-oxygenation, and excessive new oak, and dismisses any technique that could artificially alter the structure of the wine.

The oldest vintage I have tasted is the 1985, which was aged entirely in tanks. Nonetheless the wine at twenty years old was delicious, with complex leafy, smoky aromas; although not especially full-bodied, it had silkiness and great purity and length. The 1990 is a triumph, with little evolution in colour and considerable lushness on the nose; it's rich, sumptuous wine of a velvety texture, enlivened by fine acidity, which in turn confers excellent length. The 1998 still has plenty in reserve; it's supple and ripe with firm underlying tannins, delicious fruit, and a lively finish. It will age beautifully. So will the splendidly fruity 2000, which is harmonious and finely balanced, though less lively than the succulent, spicy 2001. The 2002 is a disappointment, showing a slight greenness and dill character, culminating in an austere finish. The 2003 is not cooked, but even manages to show some elegance, though it is essentially one-dimensional. The 2004 seems gawky, with chewy tannins and little finesse despite abundant fruit, but it may need time to settle down.

Xavier Vayron succeeds in producing a wine that is certainly drinkable young with considerable pleasure, but that always seems to have sufficient reserves to age extremely well.

Château de Bourgueneuf

See *Château L'Ecuyer*

Château La Cabanne

*Maillet. **Tel:** 0557 510409. **Website:** www.estager.com. **Owner:** Estager family. 10 ha. 92% Merlot, 8% Cabernet Franc. **Production:** 50,000 bottles. **Second wine:** Dom de Compostelle*

The Estagers, like so many well-known Libournais families, hail from Corrèze. They arrived here in 1912, but only started to acquire wine estates from 1934 onwards. La Cabanne was bought in 1952 and run from 1966 onwards by Jean-Pierre Estager. He died in 2001 and the business is now in the hands of his widow Michèle and their children.

The La Cabanne vineyards are at the geographical centre of Pomerol, just west of the church, with most of them grouped around the château. The soils are blue clay with *crasse de fer* beneath a layer of gravel. After sorting and a cold soak, the grapes are fermented with the aid of both pumpovers and *pigeage*. The wine is aged for eighteen months in fifty per cent new oak, and eggwhite-fined and filtered only when considered necessary.

The wines are decidedly tannic, though whether this is a terroir characteristic or a consequence of the vinification it is hard to say. There is little in the latter to suggest over-extraction. Nonetheless there is a slight rusticity in La Cabanne, and in some vintages, such as 1996, this seriously impairs the quality of the wine. Vintages I have enjoyed include 1989, 1994, and 2001. The 2000 is aromatically complex, with blackcurrant and blackberry tones, and a certain floral character; but the palate is marked by robust tannins. The 2001 is better, though it shows a slight earthiness. The 2002 is more than acceptable for the vintage, and the 2003 has surprising power and lushness, if little finesse or persistence. There are odd jelly-baby aromas on the 2004, which has good acidity but modest concentration, and little length or depth of flavour.

La Cabanne is by no means a mediocre Pomerol, for all of its lack of stylishness. Nonetheless, it is difficult not to feel that, given the location of its vineyards and the dominance of user-friendly Merlot, the wines ought to be better than they are.

Château Le Caillou

Maillet. Tel: 0557 510610. Website: www.vins-giraud-belivier.com. Owner: André Giraud. 7 ha. 75% Merlot,
25% Cabernet Franc. Production: 40,000 bottles. Second wines: Ch La Fleur Lacombe and Dom de Lacombe

The Giraud family also own one of the two St-Emilion estates known as Château La Tour du Pin Figeac (q.v.). Lucien Giraud bought out the other owners of Le Caillou, the Belivier family, in 1975; since 1981 the properties have been run by André Giraud, who also makes the wines, with advice from Gilles Pauquet. Most of the vineyards are on the western side of the N89 near Moulinet on sandy gravel soils; the remainder are close to Gazin.

Fermentation takes place in cement tanks, sometimes, but not always, with indigenous yeasts. One-third of the wine is aged in tanks, the remainder in one-third new barriques. The two lots are rotated, so that all the wine spends around twelve months in oak. These are simple, slack wines, sometimes with decent fruit on the attack (as in 2000), but lacking persistence. The 2000 is the best of recent vintages; the 2001 is surprisingly green; the 2002 is pleasant but fades fast. Curious wine-gum aromas mark the 2004, which has good fruit but sags on the mid-palate and lacks some freshness. The 2005 is slight.

Château Cantelauze

Maillet. Tel: 0557 516488. Owner: Jean-Noël Boidron. 1.5 ha. 90% Merlot, 10% Cabernet Franc.
Production: 4,500 bottles

Jean-Noël Boidron owns Corbin Michotte (q.v.) in St-Emilion and substantial properties in the St-Emilion satellites. This tiny property was assembled from various tiny parcels in 1989. They are scattered, and have for neighbours properties and locations as diverse as Trotanoy, Grange-Neuve, and Rouget. Most of the soils are deep gravel with sand; the average age of the vines is twenty years. The wine is aged in eighty per cent new oak. Although the property is little known, the wine is excellent, and I have very positive notes on 1999, 2001, and 2002. Oak certainly marks the nose, perhaps to excess, but the wine is more beguiling on the palate, with ripe fruit, considerable elegance, and concentration without excessive extraction. The 2004 was very individual, fresh and lively, bright and brisk, with little complexity but attractive upfront fruit. The label is rather bizarre, being based on the illuminated manuscripts that are one of M. Boidron's personal enthusiasms.

Château Certan-Giraud

This seven-hectare property no longer exists under this name, though bottles are still to be found with this label. The owners since 1956 were the Giraud family. In 1999 they sold up. Most of the vineyards were acquired by Christian Moueix, who renamed one portion of the property Hosanna and another Certan-Marzelle (qq.v.). The remaining vines were sold to the Delon family, who incorporated them into Nénin. The only pre-Moueix vintage I have tasted was the 1995, which was not especially concentrated, and had hard edges and rather coarse tannins; and the easy-going, charming, but dilute 1998.

Château Certan-Marzelle

Tel: 0557 517896. **Owner:** *Ets J.P. Moueix. 3.3 ha. 100% Merlot.* **Production:** *12,000 bottles*

This small property formed part of Château Certan-Giraud, until it was acquired and renamed by Christian Moueix in 1998. In 2000 the vineyard was expanded when a parcel of Château Lagrange was incorporated. Although the vineyards are near the village, they are on fairly light sandy soils. The wine is aged in fifty per cent new barriques for eighteen months. The first Moueix vintage, 1998, had rich plummy aromas, but the wine, though full and tannic, lacked some finesse. The 2001 is considerably better, with bright, fresh cherry aromas, and a palate of some complexity, with plenty of upfront fruit, ripe tannins and acidic backbone, and good length.

Château Certan-de-May

Tel: 0557 514153. **Owner:** *Odette Barreau-Badar. 5 ha. 70% Merlot, 25% Cabernet Franc, 5% Cabernet Sauvignon.* **Production:** *20,000 bottles*

This property lies just next to the better-known Vieux-Château-Certan, and has long been in its shadow. The full name of the property is Certan-de-May-de-Certan, which is such a mouthful that it is always known by its abbreviated version. Once part of Vieux-Château-Certan, Certan-de-May became detached in 1858. Its owners were the de May family, a noble clan of Scottish origin that had settled in the region centuries earlier. After the family died out in 1925, the estate was bought by André Badar, the father of the present owner, Mme. Barreau-Badar. She is elderly and frail, but still very much present; the property is run on a daily basis by her articulate son Jean-Luc.

The five hectares of vineyards lie in a single parcel of varied clay-gravel soils just north of the house in the direction of the church. Jean-Luc Barreau estimates their average age at fifty years. Viticulture is according to the principles of *lutte raisonnée*, and yields are low. Barreau is careful to avoid overripeness. After the manual harvest, the grapes are sorted, destemmed, and fermented in steel tanks with automatic pumpovers. Natural yeasts are favoured but not systematic. After malolactic fermentation in barriques, the wine is aged in seventy per cent new oak for eighteen months, with a short period of *bâtonnage*.

Because, I suspect, of the superlative quality of its neighbour Vieux-Château-Certan, Certan-de-May has been underrated. In my experience this is a very good, and often excellent wine. I tasted a number of vintages from the 1980s, and the 1985 was gorgeously luxurious, with delicious fruit, ripe underlying tannins, and fine balance and length. The 1989, however, was somewhat disappointing: a pleasant wine but lacking in grip and complexity. The 1994 is unexciting, but the 1998 is immensely appealing. The nose is oaky, but has lush cherry fruit and enormous charm. The palate is rich and velvety, with delicious fruit balanced by exceptional vigour. The 1999 is not quite at this level, but it has a similar silkiness, with firm underlying tannin to give it structure. The length is admirable too. The 2001 is a slight disappointment, a graceful wine somewhat unbalanced by tannins that are too present; but it's solid, chocolatey, and persistent. The 2002 is no blockbuster, being a medium-bodied wine of some elegance, charm, and freshness. The 2004 has more hedonistic appeal, with its opulence and spiciness, and a long, toasty finish. Both the 2005 and 2006 were delicious and elegant from cask.

La Clémence

Tel: 0557 247744. **Website:** *www.vignobles-dauriac.com.* **Owners:** *Christian and Anne-Marie Dauriac. 3 ha. 85% Merlot, 15% Cabernet Franc.* **Production:** *10,000 bottles*

Dr. Christian Dauriac is also the owner of Château Destieux (*q.v.*) in St-Emilion, and in my account of that property I described his fanatical attention to detail. The same qualities are applied to La Clémence, a property he assembled in 1996. By the time he had completed his shopping spree he had acquired six parcels on six different soil types, ranging from blue clay to sandy gravel. His neighbours were numerous: La Fleur-Pétrus, Trotanoy, Vieux-Château-Certan, Taillefer, and Figeac, the latter being close to where the Cabernet Franc is planted. The average age of the vines is an admirable forty-five years.

Dauriac built a beautiful new winery very close to La Tour Figeac. It was first used in 2002, the wine having been previously made at Le Bon Pasteur. The new winery features a semicircular row of wooden vats, each containing the wine from a different parcel. Facing the vats is a semicircular row of barrels. The two sectors of the winery are separated by a glass wall, allowing each side to be either heated or chilled. The compact design allows all pumping to be eliminated.

Dauriac works closely with Michel Rolland, and likes his wine to be as rich as possible. All wings of grape bunches are removed in early August to ensure the most even ripening and best aeration. He picks as late as possible, and yields are very low, averaging sixteen hectolitres per hectare. It is hardly surprising, then, that the wine is very expensive.

The wines are destemmed. In most years a machine is employed, but in 2002 there was considerable rot, and Dauriac decided instead to employ 125 people to destem by hand. Rather than crushing the grapes, Dauriac treads them by foot to release some juice; and once fermentation begins, there is manual *pigeage*. Malolactic fermentation and ageing take place in 100 per cent new oak, press wine included. The contents of each vat are aged in barrels from a different cooper. Instead of racking, Dauriac uses *bâtonnage* and *cliquage*. The wine is aged for at least eighteen months.

It comes as no surprise that the style of La Clémence is lush, oaky, super-ripe, and opulent. It exemplifies the Rolland style of winemaking but is an outstanding example of that approach. Even in a mediocre year such as 1997, Dauriac made a splendid wine, highly concentrated, but also spicy, harmonious, and elegant, with no trace of over-extraction. The 1998 is even better, as one would expect, with exquisite aromas of blackcurrants and violets; the tannins are beautifully integrated, the texture is suave, and there is opulence but not at the expense of stylishness. The 2001 is sumptuous, highly concentrated, and long. The 2002 is one of Pomerol's top wines of that vintage, complex on the nose, and with a palate that is sumptuous, powerful, complex, and spicy. Early tastings of the 2006 suggest that Dauriac has again produced a wine of concentration and power but not at the expense of fruit.

La Clémence is an admirable hand-crafted wine but customers are required to pay a good deal for it. Some may well feel that the hand of the winemaker (and the cooper) count for more here than the mosaic of terroirs from which the wine is sourced.

Château Clinet

Tel: 0557 255000. **Website:** *www.chateauclinet.com.* **Owner:** *Jean-Louis Laborde. 9 ha. 85% Merlot,* *10% Cabernet Sauvignon, 5% Cabernet Franc.* **Production:** *45,000 bottles.* **Second wine:** *Fleur de Clinet*

The history of this well-known property is quite complicated. It was established in the nineteenth century by the Arnaud family. A century later, in the 1980s, the owner was the merchant Georges Audy. (It has been said that at this time the vineyards were picked by machine, but I am assured this was not the case.) In the mid-1980s the property was taken over by Jean-Michel Arcaute, who had married Audy's daughter. In 1987 he took on Michel Rolland as a consultant, and the wines were made in an opulent style with a good deal of new oak. In 1991 Clinet was sold to the GAN insurance company, but Arcaute stayed on as winemaker, and in 1998 it was sold again to Jean-Louis Laborde. Arcaute died in an accident in 2001. Laborde owns two substantial properties in the Tokaj region of Hungary, and a property in the Central African Republic said to be the size of a small European country. Since 2003 the property has been run by Jean-Louis's son Ronan, who supervised the completion of a new winery here in 2004.

The vineyards are in two main sectors: on the slopes near the winery, with excellent parcels near the church, and on the plateau near Pétrus and Lafleur. The soils are gravel mixed with clay, over a subsoil containing *crasse de fer*. The average age of the vineyards was around forty years, but in 2005 two hectares of old virused vines were replanted. In recent years the trellising has been heightened, and the estate converted to *lutte raisonnée*.

The grapes are scrupulously sorted at the winery. (In 2005 a refrigerated lorry was rented to chill down the grapes before processing.) Ronan Laborde has experimented with hand-destemming, but is as yet uncertain about the value of the procedure, though the wines do seem softer. Crushing takes place over the tanks. A five-day cold soak follows under dry ice at 8°C (46°F). Whenever possible, fermentation is activated with natural yeasts. Until 1997 the wine was fermented in concrete tanks; these were then replaced by stainless-steel tanks; in 2001 wooden vats began to be introduced. The first vintage in which the entire crop was fermented in wood was 2004. Extraction is by all means available: pumpovers, *pigeage*, and *délestage* Another innovation has been a modern vertical press, installed in 2001. Malolactic fermentation and *élevage* took place in entirely new oak until 2004, when the proportion of new oak was reduced to two-thirds. Stacked on Oxoline racks, the wine remains on the fine lees, with racking and *cliquage* applied when necessary. There is no fining and only the lightest filtration.

My experience of older vintages of Clinet is patchy. The 1985 was seductive on the nose, with blackberry and coffee aromas; but there was some austerity and over-extraction on the palate. The plump, silky 1987 was a great success for the vintage. The 1989 and 1990 are renowned vintages here, but I have not tasted them. I did taste various vintages from cask in the 1990s, but they were clearly unfinished wines that are not worth commenting on. In 1999 Clinet delivered an unusually powerful wine, rich, broad, and sumptuous, with tannins KO-ing any finesse when the wine was young. The 2000 is so lush as to come close to blandness, but I last tasted the wine shortly before bottling.

I have conflicting notes on the pure-Merlot 2001, the most negative discerning soupy, even porty tones. Most recently, however, there are enticing black-cherry aromas, with the oak well integrated; the opulent texture is balanced by some inherent freshness and by chewy but not tough tannins. The 2002 is fragrant and toasty, less complex than the preceding vintages, but it is juicy and spicy and likely to give considerable pleasure in the medium term. Clinet did well in the difficult 2003 vintage. Despite a light boiled-sweets character on the nose and a slight raisined quality on the palate, it's a succulent, spicy wine with ripeness but little overripeness, and well-integrated oak. The nose of the 2004 is dominated by oak, as is its chewy, powerful texture, which has yet to reveal its core of fruit. Early tastings of the 2005 from cask show enormous promise: a wine that's velvety, spicy, seamless, and balanced.

The second wine, Fleur de Clinet, is relatively recent, having been inaugurated in 1997, but today it represents about forty per cent of the total production.

Clos Beauregard

Toulifaut. Tel: 0557 515258. **Owner:** *Jean-Michel Moueix. 5 ha. 70% Merlot, 20% Cabernet Franc, 10% Cabernet Sauvignon.* **Production:** *36,000 bottles.* **Second wine:** *Clos Toulifaut*

As the name suggests, this small estate once formed part of Beauregard, but was sold off in 1935 to Antoine Moueix, the grandfather of the present owner. Its vineyards are located in the mediocre southernmost sector of Pomerol on sandy and gravel soils; but the vines are old. The wine is aged in one-third new barriques for fifteen to eighteen months. The 2001 and 2002 are quite fragrant and cherry-scented, but the wines are rather light, with a lean structure and little length.

Clos du Clocher

Catusseau. Tel: 0557 516217. **Owner:** *Pierre Bourotte. 5.7 ha. 75% Merlot, 25% Cabernet Franc.* **Production:** *30,000 bottles.* **Second wine:** *Château Monregard La Croix*

This property was created in 1931 by Jean-Baptiste Audy, when he assembled various parcels. Today the estate is owned by Audy's grandson Pierre Bourotte and his son Jean-Baptiste, who also run Château Bonalgue (*q.v.*). The vines are in two major parcels, over four hectares being on gravelly clay soil just south of the church and close to Trotanoy, where some vines are fifty years old; the remainder are in Catusseau and used for the second wine. The vinification is almost identical to that at Bonalgue.

My notes, mostly unenthusiastic, on older vintages of Clos du Clocher are too far in the past to be relevant today. The 1998 is a lovely wine, with its sweet, elegant, raspberry-coulis nose, made complex by whiffs of smoke and truffle. It's a medium-bodied yet concentrated and velvety wine that glides along beautifully to a persistent finish. The smoky, oaky aromas are equally present on the 1999, which is in a leaner style, more forward than the 1998, and already drinking well. There are similar aromas on the 2000, which, however, remains rather closed. The nose of the 2001 is perhaps too dominated by oak at present; it's a fleshy yet tannic wine, with tones of coffee and leather. The 2002 has surprisingly lush black-fruits aromas, and ample fruit on a medium-bodied frame – successful for the year. So is the 2003, which has smoky, plummy aromas with a touch of cloves; the palate is lush and rounded but not raisiny or short. The excellent 2004 resembles the 2002 but has a more robust structure.

Clos du Clocher is a very good wine, often underrated, and its smoky aromas do seem to be a hallmark in most vintages. Overall, it has more spice and fire and complexity than Bonalgue.

Clos l'Eglise

Tel: 0557 517025. Website: www.vignoblesgarcin.com. Owner: Sylviane Garcin-Cathiard. 6 ha. 70% Merlot, 30% Cabernet Franc. Production: 28,000 bottles. Second wine: Esprit de l'Eglise

In the eighteenth century this property was much larger than it is today, but family divisions led to a split, the other half becoming L'Eglise-Clinet in the 1940s. Until 1997 the Clos was owned by the Moreau family who now own Le Plince, but for family reasons they were obliged to sell it. Although the property had been managed for the Moreaus by the Moueix team, the wines rarely stood out. The purchaser was Sylviane Garcin-Cathiard, sister of Daniel Cathiard, and in her own right the collector of a number of fine properties, including Haut-Bergey in Pessac-Léognan and Barde-Haut in St-Emilion (qq.v.). The consultant services of Michel Rolland were initially retained, but discontinued in 2002. Today the property is managed by Madame Garcin-Cathiard's daughter Hélène and her husband Patrice.

The house stands across the lane from L'Eglise-Clinet in downtown Pomerol. Its vineyards, essentially in a single block, are at Pomerol's highest point, which is not saying a great deal. The soils are clay and gravel with *crasse de fer*. Some Cabernet Franc survives from before the frost of 1956, but on average the vineyards are thirty years old, and planted to a fairly high density. The Garcins removed the remaining Cabernet Sauvignon vines.

After sorting, the grapes are taken by conveyor belt above the wooden vats, into which they drop by gravity. After a cold soak, they are fermented with natural yeasts and regular *pigeage*. The *marc* is pressed in a vertical press, and the wine aged in the air-conditioned *chai* for sixteen to eighteen months in new barriques.

The 1991 and 1992 were disappointing, but then so were the vintages. The 2001, however, is very impressive, despite a hint of overripeness on the nose; there's not much finesse here, but with so much fruit and power and spice, it is churlish to complain. The 2002 has stylish, plummy aromas, and an unexpectedly suave, concentrated, structured palate. It is harder to work up much enthusiasm for the slack, jammy 2003, with its dry tannins and lack of length. The 2004 is very tannic and powerful but has masses of sweet fruit but perhaps at the expense of freshness; tasted blind alongside the second wine, I found the greater elegance of the latter more appealing. The 2005 has super-ripe aromas while the palate is dense and formidable, and possibly too extracted.

Clos des Litanies

Catusseau. Tel: 0557 514186. Website: www.j-janoueix-bordeaux.com. Owner: J. Janoueix family. 0.8 ha. 100% Merlot. Production: 5,000 bottles

This minute property lies just south of Beauregard. The soil is sandy, but the subsoil is rich in iron. The wine is aged in new oak for fifteen to eighteen months, and eggwhite-fined before bottling. The 2003 is a pretty wine, with cherry aromas mingled with oak; despite the low acidity, it shows some freshness and charm, but should be drunk fairly soon.

Clos René

*Tel: 0557 510141. **Owner:** Jean-Marie Garde. 18 ha. 70% Merlot, 20% Cabernet Franc, 10% Malbec.*

***Production:** 80,000 bottles*

This is a large property, with vineyards in various parcels west of the N89. The soils are gravel and sand over a subsoil of *crasse de fer*. For many years the property was owned and run by Pierre Lasserre, who lived into his nineties and eventually handed over to his grandson, the present owner.

The grapes are picked manually and fermented in a mixture of cement and steel tanks. The *marc* is pressed in a modern vertical press, and the wine aged for fifteen months in twenty-five per cent new barriques.

No one would claim that the soils here are exceptional, though some of the gravelly parcels are of good quality. Nonetheless in some vintages Clos René can age well. Over lunch M. Garde generously poured his 1975. There was a slight mustiness that may have been cork-derived, but the wine retained sweet fruit and some density and length – not great, but still very drinkable. Vintages in the late 1980s and the 1990s were lacklustre, in my experience. The 1989 had plenty of grip and extract but was distinctly austere. The 1990 was ripe and supple but unremarkable; the 1994 chunky and rather rustic. The 1995 has some light truffley aromas, ample red fruits on the palate, and is still going strong. The 1998 has charm rather than weight, and is attractive and balanced but far from exceptional. The 2000 too is supple and pleasant but lacks grip and weight; enjoyable but lacking in concentration. The 2001 is better, with a fragrant cherry and raspberry nose; there is some richness and elegance on the palate, with better acidity and persistence than the 2000. The 2003 is forgettable, and ageing fast, but the satisfying, juicy 2004 has more solidity and concentration.

There is no second wine at Clos René, but for some markets M. Garde uses a different label, Château Moulinet-Lasserre. Originally this was a separate property, subsequently incorporated into Clos René, but today it's the same wine.

Château Clos de Salles

*Tel: 0557 510607. **Owner:** Jean de Coninck. 1.3 ha. 60% Merlot, 30% Cabernet Franc,*
*10% Cabernet Sauvignon. **Production:** 6,000 bottles*

This small property between Château de Sales and Château Mazeyres was bought by Libourne wine merchant Jean de Coninck in 1998, and is run by his son-in-law Ivan Merlet. The vineyard is cultivated by *lutte raisonnée*. The wine is aged for about eighteen months, racked from barrel to barrel, and eggwhite-fined before bottling. The only vintage I have encountered, the 2004, was extremely ripe, concentrated, and vigorous, with fine-grained tannins and a long, stylish finish.

Clos de la Vieille Eglise

*Tel: 0557 555790. **Owner:** Jean-Louis Trocard. 1.5 ha. 90% Merlot, 10% Cabernet Franc. **Production:** 7,000 bottles*

This tiny estate, located north of the village on clay and gravel soils near the cemetery and Rouget, is little known. The average age of the vines is about forty years, and the wine is aged in seventy per cent new barriques. The 2001 was impressive, if quite oaky and somewhat herbaceous on the nose. The texture is silky and supple, with light tannins to give some structure, and overall the wine seemed balanced and stylish if not especially complex. The 2002 was very good too, with ample flesh and spiciness and length. The 2004 is even better, rich, suave, and concentrated, with power and solidity and good length.

Château La Commanderie de Mazeyres

*Tel: 0557 257115. Website: www.vignobles.fayat.com. **Owner:** Clément Fayat. 9.5 ha. 55% Merlot,*
*45% Cabernet Franc. **Production:** 50,000 bottles. **Second wine:** Ch Closerie Mazeyres*

This estate apparently dates back to medieval times, and once formed part of its neighbour Château Mazeyres, though no one seems to know when it became detached. In 2000 it was bought by Clément Fayat, already the owner of La Dominique (*q.v.*) in St-Emilion and other properties in Bordeaux. Previously, the property had not been well maintained, and the entire production was sold in bulk. Fayat and his consultant Michel Rolland swiftly introduced changes, such as higher trellising and conversion to *guyot double*.

The vineyards are in a single block, but a new bypass around Libourne has chewed up a third of a hectare. The soils are mixed: gravelly sand dominates, but just under one-third of the property is on deep gravel. The oldest vines are Cabernet Franc, and the average age of the entire vineyard is around forty years. The harvest is manual, and after sorting the grapes are crushed over the wooden fermentation vats. As well as regular pumpovers, the must undergoes *pigeage* and some micro-oxygenation. Malolactic fermentation takes place in new barrels, and the wine as a whole is aged for fifteen to eighteen months in up to seventy per cent new oak, with lees-stirring. If necessary the wine is eggwhite-fined but it is unfiltered. At present more of the second wine is produced than of the *grand vin*.

Of the vintages since 2000, the 2001 seems the best. The 2000 has some bright cherry aromas, but the wine lacks concentration and structure. It's a rather feeble performance, but then the vineyards were in poor shape. The 2001 has similar aromas and an attractive herbal character; sweet oak shows through on the palate, which has charm rather than weight. The 2002 has charm too, and delicacy; there has been no attempt to over-extract in this lighter vintage, and although the wine is fairly simple, it is very drinkable. The 2003 seems overoaked, but has decent acidity. The 2004 is more forceful and aromatic; the 2005 is richly fruity, but has a chunky finish.

The wine is carefully made, though initial vintages have had to struggle with the deficiencies of some of the terroir and the unreformed state of the vines. It seems probable that in the future this will be an enjoyable, medium-bodied Pomerol with good balance.

Château La Conseillante

*Tel: 0557 511532. Website: www.la-conseillante.com. **Owner:** Nicolas family. 12 ha. 80% Merlot,*
*20% Cabernet Franc. **Production:** 50,000 bottles*

This fine property takes its name from Catherine Conseillan, a Libournais businesswoman who bought the estate in the 1730s and renamed it. She built the château itself in about 1750. Despite the middling reputation of Pomerol's wine in the eighteenth century, hers fetched high prices. After she died in 1777 the property passed to her niece. It was in 1871 that the Nicolas family acquired La Conseillante, and the present owners are Bernard Nicolas, a doctor, his sister Marie-France d'Arfeuille, and other family members. Since 2004 the self-confident Jean-Michel Laporte has directed the property, and Gilles Pauquet acts as the consultant.

The vineyards, the boundaries of which have scarcely altered in two centuries, lie east of Catusseau and south of Vieux-Château-Certan. The border with St-Emilion is close by, and Cheval Blanc is only a short distance away. The soil is by no means uniform. About sixty per cent of the vines are planted on blue clay, and the remainder, close to Beauregard and Cheval Blanc, on sandy gravel over a subsoil rich in *crasse de fer*. But it's more complex than this suggests, and a walk through the vineyards reveals stony parcels near Vieux-Château-Certan and Pétrus. The density is around 6,000 vines per hectare, but more recent plantings are at 7,500 vines per hectare with higher trellising. Some parcels are now being converted to *guyot double*. The average age of the vines is forty years. Yields are kept to around forty hl/ha, and *lutte raisonnée* is the guiding principle here.

The vinification blends traditional and modern techniques. La Conseillante has purchased an *égreneur* destemmer (*see* Chapter Three) and the grapes undergo four sortings. Since 2002 the must has been cold-soaked for six days. There is no concentrator, no micro-oxygenation. Fermentation takes place in steel tanks, and in 2001 the pneumatic press was traded in for a modern vertical press. Malolactic fermentation takes place in tanks, and the wine is aged for eighteen months in a proportion of new oak that varies from two-thirds to total. Thus the 2003 was aged in eighty per cent new oak, the 2005 in entirely new oak. The wine is racked regularly, eggwhite-fined, but not filtered.

The oldest Conseillante I have tasted is the 1955, which at over forty years old was still attractive. The colour was mature, and the nose sweet and spicy, with some tobacco tones, which were discernible on the palate too. The wine was concentrated, with firm tannins, and an intense sweetness slightly marred by some dryness on the finish. The 1970 is exquisite: scarcely any evolution in the moderate colour; a nose dominated by sweet oak; the palate silky, with fine acidity and incomparable finesse, with no sign of fatigue in 2006. The 1975, tasted recently, was a puzzle: there were attractive smoky aromas, and the palate was medium-bodied and sleek, but the tannins were dry to the point of bitterness. Yet with aeration the bitterness vanished and the wine became much more harmonious.

The 1980 was attractive young but is probably now past its best. The 1985 is sensational, especially in its aromas, which are lush and generous, with notes of game, liquorice, and coffee as well as sweet black fruits; the palate is equally sumptuous, yet with splendid concentration. The balance seems well nigh perfect, and the persistence of flavour is irreproachable. The 1989, tasted recently from magnum, is on the same high level. The nose is rich, ripe, and truffley, with a touch of liquorice; the palate is rich, velvety, and succulent, and the delicious fruit is still fresh and persistent with a delightful acidity and excellent length. This is a wine that is complete in every respect. The 1990 is very similar. Perhaps it has a slight edge over the 1989 with its exquisite aromas and its intense purity of flavour, which is by no means at the expense of complexity. Both wines are gorgeous now, but should keep effortlessly for many years.

The 1996 is rather slight, but not the magnificent and impeccably balanced 1998, which goes from strength to strength every time I taste it. In 2006 the nose was fleshy and oaky, with aromas of black cherries and mint; the palate has concentration and lushness, of course, but it's the charm and freshness that are most striking. It's accessible now but built to last. The 2000 has seductive oaky aromas, but plums and vanilla penetrate the sheen of new barriques; it's luxurious and silky, dense but persistent. Yet the 2001 is even finer, with a touch more exuberance; I find blackberries rather than plums on the nose, plus a dash of mint. It's a wine that's highly concentrated yet not at the expense of its plump fruitiness and an invigorating spiciness. The length is astonishing too. The 2002 has similar properties, more overt charm, but is on a lower key, without the power and weight of the preceding two vintages, and the oakiness does rather jut out. The 2003 is kicked out of balance by the austere tannins, and it is hard to see the wine ever becoming harmonious. The powerful 2004 has an explosive nose of black cherries and liquorice, while the flavours, fine-grained tannins, and structure of the wine seem similar to those of 2001. The 2005 and 2006, tasted early from cask, seem to confirm La Conseillante's growing reputation.

It should be apparent that in most vintages I have tasted over the past two decades, La Conseillante has scarcely put a foot wrong. It's a quintessential Pomerol, offering vinous hedonism while rarely straying into overripeness or lack of finesse.

Château La Croix

*Catusseau. Tel: 0557 514186. Website: www.j-janoueix-bordeaux.com. **Owner:** J. Janoueix family. 10 ha. 60% Merlot, 20% Cabernet Franc, 20% Cabernet Sauvignon. **Production:** 60,000 bottles. **Second wine:** Ch La Gabachot*

This fine property, with its neo-classical eighteenth-century mansion, was for a long time the property of the ubiquitous de Sèze family, but since 1960 it has been owned by the equally ubiquitous Janoueix family. Like many properties in Pomerol with the word "Croix" in the title, its name alludes to the stone cross left as a pilgrimage marker by the Knights Hospitaller of St John. The château is in Catusseau, and the vineyards are in a single block on sandy gravel soil, with a subsoil rich in iron. Leaves are removed in summer, and there are usually two green-harvestings. The wine is fermented in cement tanks with a *cuvaison* of up to five weeks. It is aged in about sixty per cent new oak.

The 2000 is magnificent, with vibrant aromas of blackcurrant and blueberry; the plump texture is allied to a brightness of fruit, even a slight but appealing herbaceous edge. I have conflicting notes on the 2001, one entirely positive, noting the wine's tightness, concentration, and vigour; the other finding some hollowness and absence of finesse. The 2003 is an honourable effort; the wine certainly has some baked characteristics but it doesn't lack fruit or length. Despite its overt oakiness, the juicy 2005 shows promise.

Château La Croix du Casse

*Tel: 0556 000070. **Owner:** Philippe Castéja. 9 ha. 90% Merlot, 10% Cabernet Franc. **Production:** 55,000 bottles. **Second wine:** Les Chemins de la Croix du Casse*

This estate is noted on the eighteenth-century maps by Belleyme, so it would appear that there have been vines planted here since 1775 at least. The property is located in the southern sector of the region, not far from Nénin. In the late 1980s it was owned by Georges Audy, until acquired by the Castéja family in the early 2000s. The 1982 was rich, but tannic and quite rustic, the 2004 was mediocre, but the 2005, Castéja's first vintage has richer fruit but abrasive tannins.

Château La Croix de Gay

*Tel: 0557 511905. Website: www.chateaulacroixdegay.com. **Owner:** Chantal Lebreton. 7 ha. 95% Merlot, 5% Cabernet Franc. **Production:** 40,000 bottles. **Second wines:** Le Commandeur and Vieux-Ch-Groupey*

This property has been in the Raynaud family for six generations. Dr. Alain Raynaud owns Quinault in St-Emilion, and La Croix de Gay is run by his sister. The vineyards are composed of numerous parcels, so the soil is very varied. The location of the best blocks is highly favourable, with sectors near Vieux-Château-Certan, Beauregard, and Trotanoy. The vinification is traditional and the wine is aged for eighteen months in seventy per cent new oak.

Another wine, essentially a prestige *cuvée*, is made from the same property. This is Château La Fleur-de-Gay (*q.v.*). One wonders whether La Croix de Gay might not be more impressive were the three hectares used for La Fleur-de-Gay reincorporated into the wine.

The oldest vintage I have drunk is the 1985, with its lovely, ripe aromas; it's a medium-bodied wine but doesn't lack intensity, acidity, and tannin. It's far from spectacular and is not among the great 1985s, but it's a very pleasurable wine that is by no means past its peak. The 1989, tasted some years ago, was disappointing, even dull, with some earthiness on nose and palate. The 1990 is better, but comes close to overripeness, which may not be to everyone's taste. The 1994 is medium-bodied, quite elegant, a touch lean, but still very much alive. The 1996 is surprisingly assertive, with a lot of spice and force and firm acidity on the finish; it's very good but seems atypical for the property.

The 1999 is evolving slowly but well, with opulent oaky aromas. On the palate there is succulence and charm, but there is no lack of tannin, and the wine remains fresh. In spring 2007, the 2001 was still excellent, with a good deal of ripe plum and cherries on the nose, a fleshy texture, good grip and concentration, and a long, chewy finish. This clearly has a fine future. The 2002 seems a touch underripe, with aromas of sour cherries and redcurrants, and a certain dourness on the palate. The black-fruits aromas of the 2004 are a bit jammy, and the palate is rather dense and heavy; but although there's not much zest, it doesn't lack fruit.

Overall, Croix de Gay seems to lack some consistency, but the wine can be very good and the prices are far from exorbitant.

Château La Croix-St-Georges

*Catusseau. Tel: 0557 514186. Website: www.j-janoueix-bordeaux.com. **Owner:** J. Janoueix family. 4 ha.*
*90% Merlot, 10% Cabernet Franc. **Production:** 18,000 bottles*

One of many Janoueix properties on the Right Bank, this has been managed since 1999 by Jean-Philippe Janoueix, the most ambitious member of this extended family. The soil is a mix of clay and gravel, and the vines are close to those of Petit-Village and Vieux-Château-Certan. The must is fermented in wooden vats with *pigeage*, and the wine aged for around twenty months in barrels of peculiar design. Jean-Philippe Janoueix stipulates an oblong shape akin to a robusto cigar, hence the name of the barrel: *cigare*. I was invited to compare the same wine in a regular barrique and in the customized version. I found the latter had more sweetness of fruit, though I was at a loss to explain why. I have not tasted the wine in bottle.

Château La Croix-Taillefer

*Tel: 0557 250865. **Owner:** Rivière family. 5.5 ha. 90% Merlot, 8% Cabernet Franc, 2% Cabernet Sauvignon.*
***Production:** 28,000 bottles. **Second wine:** Ch La Loubière*

Romain Rivière is an oenologist, and has taken over the running of the estate from his father Claude, who bought the property in 1978. Most the vines are near Taillefer, and there is another parcel near Plince. They share a sandy and gravelly soil that heats up fast in summer. In 2005 Rivière converted the estate to organic viticulture.

After sorting, the grapes are sorted, crushed, then pumped into steel tanks. Temperature control was installed as recently as 1999, and cold-soaking initiated in 2001. After a warm post-fermentation maceration, the wine is aged in up to eighty per cent new oak, though Rivière favours 400-litre barrels rather than traditional barriques. This allows him to prolong the ageing to eighteen months without overoaking the wine.

In 2001 Rivière began producing a *vin de garage*, Cuvée Romulus, from a single hectare of pure Merlot, cropped to very low yields. This is aged in new oak for twenty-eight months and 4,500 bottles are produced.

The 2001 shows the influence of new oak on the nose, though there are floral and raspberry aromas too; the wine is bright and tight, with precise tannins and acidity. The 2001 Romulus is markedly more oaky, lush, and juicy, and has more weight and persistence than the regular bottling. The 2002 is a touch green with rather tough tannins; the Romulus, in contrast, seemed a bit cooked and overoaked. Both 2003s are rather dull and dour.

Château La Croix-Toulifaut

*Tel: 0557 514186. Website: www.j-janoueix-bordeaux.com. **Owner:** Jean Janoueix. 1.8 ha. 85% Merlot,*
*15% Cabernet Franc. **Production:** 9,000 bottles*

This small property is located on sandy soils in southern Pomerol, close to Beauregard. The wine is fermented in cement tanks, undergoes malolactic fermentation in new oak, and is aged for eighteen months. The Janoueix family themselves describe this wine as "feminine" and it is clearly not one of the more high-powered wines of the appellation. The 1997 was attractive and supple if not particularly concentrated. The 2001 struck me as initially sleek and fleshy, but the mid-palate was quite tannic and severe. There is no over-extraction on the 2003, which is forward and easy-going, silky but not for long ageing.

Château L'Ecuyer

*Tel: 0557 511861. Website: www.chateau-tournefeuille.com. **Owner:** François Petit. 4.5 ha. 90% Merlot,*
*10% Cabernet Franc. **Production:** 10,000 bottles*

Until 2004 this property was known as Château de Bourgueneuf. After it was bought by François Petit, the owner of Château Tournefeuille (*q.v.*) in Lalande de Pomerol, it was renamed to avoid confusion with other similarly named properties. The property is somewhat dispersed, with parcels near La Cabanne and Bourgneuf-Vayron, and another near Rouget. Petit's son Emeric runs L'Ecuyer, and has begun replacing some of the Cabernet Franc with Merlot. The wine is vinified in fifty per cent new 400-litre barrels.

Under the previous owner, Jean-Michel Meyer, the wine was unimpressive, though I drank a robust yet well-balanced 1990 on two occasions. The Petits are well aware of the unrealized potential of the property and it will be interesting to see what they make of it. The 2004 is very rich, and although the finish is rather dour now, it has spice and complexity and should evolve well. The 2005 is even better: intense, stylish and long.

Château du Domaine de l'Eglise

*Tel: 0556 000070. **Owner:** Castéja family. 7 ha. 95% Merlot, 5% Cabernet Franc. **Production:** 30,000 bottles*

Records pertaining to this property apparently date back to the late sixteenth century. It was sold in 1793 and remained under the same ownership until the Castéja family, owners of Trottevieille in St-Emilion, bought it in 1973. The vines lie near the Pomerol church on stony and clay soils. The wine is aged in about sixty per cent new oak. Over the past few years Denis Dubourdieu has acted as a consultant to the Castéjas.

Both the 1989 and 1990 were unimpressive, lacking concentration and richness. The 2000 was in the same mould, though it did show plenty of ripeness and vigour and reasonable length. There is a marked improvement in 2001, which has spicy oak on the nose, while the palate is packed with fruit, adding up to a stylish and delicious whole. The 2004 is equally fine, with a similar personality, and the surprisingly lively 2005 seemed very promising from cask.

Château L'Eglise-Clinet

*Tel: 0557 259659. Website: www.durantou.com. **Owner:** Denis Durantou. 6 ha. 75% Merlot, 20% Cabernet Franc,*
*5% Malbec. **Production:** 20,000 bottles*

This property was assembled in 1882 by an ancestor of the present owner, Denis Durantou, who took over running the estate in 1983. (Previously it had been made on a sharecropping basis by Pierre Lasserre of Clos René.) Durantou is slim and youthful despite the greying hair, and after just a few minutes of conversation it becomes clear that his is a lively and sharp mind. He thinks hard about what he does and why he does it. The family house and the cellars adjoin the Pomerol cemetery, and the vines lie behind and opposite the house. Three-quarters of them are close to the cemetery and church. There are two basic soil types: clay, which gives the wine its power, and gravel, which imparts finesse. Durantou is keen on Cabernet Franc, and always includes it in the blend for the floral dimension it gives to the wine. The average age of the vines is an impressive forty years, as some parcels survived the 1956 frost.

Durantou rejects many techniques popular with other Libournais winemakers. He does not pick in *cagettes*, preferring larger containers; he selects the fruit in the vineyard rather than in the winery; he does not like to harvest late as he actively seeks tannin and acidity, there is no cold soak or must concentration or micro-oxygenation, no malolactic fermentation in barriques. In short the winemaking is highly traditional.

When I visited his neighbour Clos l'Eglise during harvest in 2005, Patrice Lévêque remarked, with some puzzlement, on the absence of sorting tables at L'Eglise-Clinet. Durantou is unapologetic. He does not believe the few leaves and insects removed from a sorting table would make any significant difference to the quality of the final wine. He prefers to go through his vines before harvesting to remove any unsatisfactory bunches; the worse the climatic conditions, the closer to the picking date will this *trie* be.

The must is fermented in small squat steel tanks that are wider than their height. This increases the contact of juice with the cap. The wine is aged in roughly seventy per cent new oak for up to eighteen months. The result is a firm, well-structured wine with a distinct personality, a wine far removed from the broad, supple, evidently oaky wines that often attract critical acclaim. Andrew Jefford quotes Durantou: "We are lucky enough to be able to create wines here that will, in time, constitute *des pépites de goût* ['nuggets of taste']. Not just something nice to drink, but something that will serve us as reference points in our sensorial education, something almost shocking; something unforgettable."[2]

Durantou also makes a wine called La Petite Eglise, sometimes described, incorrectly but understandably, as a second wine. It is sourced from his youngest vines, and he also buys in fruit from his neighbours. It invariably comes from the same parcels each year, so it has a separate identity, since the gravelly sandy parcels give a less structured wine that he ages in only forty per cent new oak. It is produced as a brand by his négociant company.

The oldest L'Eglise-Clinet I have tasted is the 1962, which at thirty years of age still had a fresh colour, and the nose was sweet and ripe. The wine was clearly just past its best, being a touch flat, but it was enjoyable and rounded, if not especially persistent. The 1979 could not decide whether lush fruit or tannic structure should have the upper hand; and the finish was dry. The 1984 was vigorous and flavoury, but had little depth. The 1989 is magnificent. Rich and sumptuous on the nose, it was still surprisingly closed, despite its opulence, when drunk from magnum in 2001. A few years later it had begun to open up, with aromas of mocha and truffles; the texture was seductive, the fruit intense, and there was an understated elegance on the finish. The 1990 and 1995 are said to be excellent but I have not tasted them. The 1999 was splendid for the vintage, a big, creamy mouthful of wine with power and ripe tannins, as well as the acidic backbone Durantou likes and that gives the wine its length. The 2002 is a triumph for the vintage, with spicy, oaky aromas, fine concentration and density, yet no lack of sweet fruit on the mid-palate, and with fine-grained tannins on the finish. Even in 2003 Durantou managed to make a wine that was sumptuous and dense without any slackness. Nor are the tannins tough, and there is spice and complexity on the finish. The luxurious 2004 is gorgeous: rich and seamless, discreet yet complex and long.

Château L'Enclos

Tel: 0557 510462. Website: www.chateau-lenclos.com. Owners: Marc and St-Martin families. 9 ha. 82% Merlot, 17% Cabernet Franc, 1% Malbec. Production: 45,000 bottles

The same family have owned this property for about three centuries, and one of the owners, Catherine Marc, married the genial Hugues Weydert, who has run the estate since 1989, with advice from Gilles Pauquet and Denis Dubourdieu. Welcoming me into the house for our tasting, he remarked, "Sit down. The cat's friendly and the dog's already eaten. So you'll be fine." And I was.

The vineyards mostly lie west of the N89 in five large parcels just south of Château de Sales; there are also a few parcels closer to the heart of Pomerol, not far from Clinet and Trotanoy. The dominant soil is siliceous sand over gravel. Production expanded slightly when Weydert planted the asparagus patch next to the house with vines. No herbicides are used.

L'Enclos is equipped with a *sous-vide* concentrator. "It's like an umbrella," notes Weydert, "useful when it rains." The must is fermented in cement tanks, and aged in one-third new barriques for twelve months, with a little *cliquage*. The wine is eggwhite-fined and lightly filtered.

M. Weydert brought up a dusty bottle from the cellar, and poured the wine without disclosing the vintage. It was showing some age, with meaty, gamey aromas beginning to mask the floral delicacy of the nose. The palate, however, was rich, sweet, and lush; though lacking depth of flavour, the wine was concentrated and still fresh and long. It was the 1961. The 1979 had not fared as well; ten years ago it had leafy aromas, and a touch of oxidation; although concentrated, it was showing some astringency and dryness. The 1982 was a disappointment, being light and lacking in vigour. The 1985 was also rather insubstantial for a great year, but at least it had charm and sweet blackberry fruit. The 1989 was surprisingly dilute. I seem to have missed out on all vintages of the 1990s, but the 2001 was impressive, with more weight than most wines from this property. It had rich black-cherry fruit, and ample spice, concentration, and vigour, with a firm tannic backbone and a long, minty finish. The 2002 seemed a touch green when first tasted, but in 2005 it didn't seem unripe; although it lacks some flesh, it is attractive and balanced. Sweet, generous aromas on the 2003 show promise, but the palate is more charred, with some astringency and a rather flat finish. The 2004 is a touch confected, a supple, reasonably concentrated wine that lacks some personality and zest.

L'Enclos does seem to be an inconsistent wine, though my experience of it is far from complete. It does demonstrate that despite a terroir that many regard as unexceptional, it can, when conditions are favourable, produce wines of power, depth, and longevity.

Château L'Evangile

Tel: 0557 554555. Website: www.lafite.com. Owner: Domaine Barons de Rothschild. 14 ha. 70% Merlot, 30% Cabernet Franc. Production: 60,000 bottles. Second wine: Blason de L'Evangile

Despite the involvement of the Rothschild family at L'Evangile since 1990, it took them many years to establish a grip on the property. The château was built by the Chaperon family in the nineteenth century, and the Ducasse family, from which the Rothschilds acquired the estate, were their descendants. The then Mme. Ducasse sold seventy per cent of the property to the noble Parisians but they were, one imagines, somewhat perplexed to find that the redoubtable lady had no intention of relinquishing any of her control over L'Evangile. She did agree to the introduction of a second wine from 1990 onwards, but that was it. The frustrated Eric de Rothschild and Charles Chevalier, the general manager of the Rothschild wine estates, were unable to initiate any other changes, nor to make the investments they considered necessary to improve quality.

However, in 1999, Mme. Ducasse, by then well into her eighties, sold her remaining shares to the Rothschilds, though she continued to inhabit the château. But now Eric de Rothschild was *co-gérant* and the old lady had to loosen her grip. Dominique Befve came from Lafite to run the property, but left soon after to take over the management of Lascombes in Margaux. He took the decision to raze the existing winery, which was too small, and replace it with the existing building, which was completed in 2004. Mme. Ducasse died in April 2000 and the long-awaited changes were put into practice. Jean-Pascal Vazart arrived in 2001 to replace Befve as winemaker. Some locals dislike the new winery, which they consider too Médocain in design, although the interior, with its circular *chai*, is undeniably impressive.

The vineyards are divided into twenty-six parcels. Some lie on fairly deep soil near Cheval Blanc, while behind the château the vineyards are planted on heavy clay; southwest of the château the soil is different again, being gravel over clay. There are other parcels near Gazin. Some lie on sandy soils, but these wines are never included in the *grand vin*.

Since 2001 the grapes have been picked in *cagettes*, and are then sorted at the winery. Conveyor belts take the fruit above the cement tanks, where they are crushed. Some but not all lots are cold-soaked. Both natural and selected yeasts are used for the fermentation, which is conventional. The Rothschilds age the wine for eighteen months in 100 per cent new oak, whereas the Ducasses had used rather less. The blend must be carefully assembled from the different parcels, and this is done progressively. The wine is rarely fined but is lightly filtered.

The difficulties of the last years of the Ducasse ownership should not be seen as implying that the wines themselves were unsatisfactory. The 1966 was still healthy in colour in 2005, and showed elegant raspberry aromas; the wine was beginning to dry out but retained some sweet fruit and length. The 1982 was rich and meaty when young, as was the 1983. The 1985 was leaner, but very elegant. Tasted recently, the 1986 displayed evolved, leafy aromas, but considerable freshness in the mouth. The 1989 remains opulent, rich, and supple, though there are sufficient earthy tannins to ensure a long life. The 1993 was a disappointment, but I enjoyed the concentrated, chocolatey, and persistent 1994 in its youth. I have not tasted the vintages of the late 1990s, but the 2001 is a stunning wine, with aromas of damsons and vanilla, while the palate is velvety and sumptuous and fleshy, yet with a fine vein of acidity that gives the wine elegance and harmony. The 2005 is very similar, and the 2004 is not far behind, though it shows more severity and considerable power.

At L'Evangile, as at La Conseillante and other fine Pomerol estates, the magnificence of the terroir shines out despite changes in management and winemakers. At its best L'Evangile has all the opulence one could wish for, backed by tannic robustness and elegant acidity. It is a magical combination.

Château Ferrand

*Tel: 0557 512167. **Owner:** Henry Gasparoux. 12 ha. 50% Merlot, 50% Cabernet Franc.*
***Production:** 65,000 bottles. **Second wine:** Ch Vieux Ferrand*

It was the father of the present owner, a wine merchant, who developed the property from 1934 onwards, while Henry Gasparoux pursued a career as a chemistry professor. Since his retirement in 2002, he has devoted himself full-time to the estate. The vineyards are in a single block in southern Pomerol, hardly its most exceptional terroir. Much of the soil is sandy, with some gravel, blue clay, and *crasse de fer* in the subsoil. Ferrand is notable for its high proportion of Cabernet Franc, though Gasparoux intends to reduce it to around forty per cent.

The Gasparoux approach is frankly commercial. Yields are fairly high, at fifty hl/ha; deleafing and much of the harvesting is mechanical; chaptalization has been quite common. Gasparoux, wary of extracting too much tannins for the style of wine he prefers, favours a relatively short *cuvaison*. When he feels the wine needs further extraction, he will make use of the automatic *pigeage* apparatus. The wine is aged for fifteen months in mostly Darnajou barriques.

My experience of Ferrand is limited. The 1979 was austere and drying out after a decade. The 2000 is well made, with some liquorice aromas and a certain aromatic charm; the palate is plump, the tannins supple, and there is little finesse, but the fruit is sound. Though the 2000 is far from great, it will offer attractive if undemanding medium-term drinking. The 2004 is quite marked by the Cabernet Franc, which contributes some luscious blackcurrant aromas and a firm structure. There is no dilution here, there is freshness and length, and the wine overall shows considerable promise. Ferrand is certainly not a great Pomerol, but among the more commercial offerings from the appellation it appears to offer decent quality at a fair price.

Gasparoux also owns another property, Haut-Ferrand, which has been assembled from various parcels from 1970 onwards. Some of the vines are on the north part of the plateau near Croix de Gay, and there are parcels farther south near Beauregard. Gasparoux believes the terroir is inherently superior to that of Ferrand. Although the two wines are vinified in much the same way, Haut-Ferrand is aged in a slightly higher proportion of new oak. The 1999 has quite a dramatic nose, with black fruits and touches of tar and smoke; the palate is sturdy, perhaps a touch rustic, but it has richness and grip. The 2004 is similar but has greater complexity, though it does lack a little length. The 2005 has decent fruit but lacks excitement, finesse, and length.

Château Feytit-Clinet

Tel: 0557 255127. Owner: Jérémy Chasseuil. 6 ha. 90% Merlot, 10% Cabernet Franc. Production: 28,000 bottles.
Second wine: Les Colombiers de Feytit-Clinet

I drove past this property several times without realizing it was a wine estate. It was hard to believe that such dilapidated buildings could be the source of a fine wine. But this is Pomerol, not the Médoc, and no value is placed on showy architecture. The main reason for its shabbiness is that for many years the wine was a J.P. Moueix exclusivity; the company farmed the vineyards and took care of vinification, but had no interest in sprucing up the buildings. However, in 2000 Jérémy Chasseuil wrested back control of his family property, and has been devoting his energies, and financial resources, to improving the wine.

The vineyards surround the house, which is located between Clinet and RN89. The soil is gravelly with sand. Chasseuil has been swift to improve viticultural standards: he has converted the pruning to *guyot double*, heightened the trellising, and reduced yields to around forty hl/ha. After sorting the must is cold-soaked for five days, and then fermented in cement tanks, primarily using indigenous yeasts. Pressing takes place in a modern vertical press, and most of the wine goes through its malolactic fermentation in barrels. Feytit-Clinet is aged for fifteen months in up to eighty per cent new oak, with some lees-stirring. There is no fining and no systematic filtration.

Chasseuil has transformed Feytit-Clinet into a sumptuous, modern-style Pomerol, clearly marked by new oak, and with tannins that are dense but not tough. The only older vintage I have tasted is the 1978, which was flavoury but thin. The 2000 is lush and oaky, with fair concentration and hefty tannins, but flawed by a lack of acidity and length. The 2001 is considerably better, with smoky, oaky, plummy aromas; the fruit is powerful, the tannins firm but ripe, and there is no lack of juiciness or length. The 2002 is exceptional, coming close to the 2001 in quality and structure but perhaps lacking some of that vintage's vigour. In 2003 Chasseuil vinified fruit from vines that had lost their leaves separately to assess whether they were suitable for blending into the *grand vin*. It's a predictably super-ripe wine, but not jammy, with chocolatey flavours and dense tannins; it seems slightly hollow but has ample fruit and moderate length – an honourable result for this very tricky vintage. The outstanding 2004 has vibrant black-cherry aromas, while the palate is medium-bodied, with sound fruit underpinned by firm tannins.

Château La Fleur-de-Gay

Tel: 0557 511905. Website: www.chateaulacroixdegay.com. Owner: Chantal Lebreton. 3 ha. 100% Merlot.
Production: 8,000 bottles

This is a special *cuvée* produced from three hectares of Merlot that form part of Croix de Gay (*q.v.*). These vines lie close to Pétrus and Lafleur on clay-gravel soils. They have an average age of forty-five years, and the wine is aged for eighteen months in new barriques. The first vintage was in 1982. The aromas are inevitably marked by new oak. The 1988 is soft, sleek, and slightly sweet. I much prefer the meatier 1989, with its hint of liquorice, its sumptuous mouth-feel, and deliciously spicy fruit. When young, the 1990 seemed a touch too extracted, with some bitterness on the finish, but it may well have settled down. There is more elegance and a finer balance in the 1995, though perhaps it's rather one-dimensional. The 1998 is truly sumptuous: very rich, chocolatey, lightly savoury, as supple as velvet, and already drinking well, though it will keep. The 2004 is exemplary and harmonious, and built to last.

ABOVE: Luscious, ripe, freshly harvested Merlot grapes arrive at the winery to begin their processing and fermentation.

RIGHT: Painstaking grape sorting by hand has become routine at most quality-conscious properties. Here the Merlot berries at Château Cheval Blanc are treated like caviar.

PREVIOUS PAGE TOP: Château Pavie, and Château Pavie-Decesse behind it, dominate one of the finest slopes of St Emilion, with the ancient town in the distance. Both are owned by Gérard Perse.

PREVIOUS PAGE BOTTOM: Pomerol's sole landmark is the 19th-century church. Besides the church, this world-famous wine region consists of a few, mostly shabby houses and 780 hectares of priceless vineyards.

OVERLEAF: Winemaker and adminstrator Pierre Lurton is the only man in Bordeaux who has ever run two first growths simultaneously: Cheval Blanc in St Emilion and Yquem in Sauternes.

ABOVE: The ebullient Jean-Luc Thunevin, who in the early 1990s took St Emilion by the scruff of the neck, shook it up, and became a leading winemaker, merchant, blogger, and wine-bar owner.

LEFT: The owner of Château Canon La Gaffelière in St Emilion, Count Stephan von Neipperg (right), confers with his gifted consultant oenologist, Stéphane Derenoncourt.

ABOVE AND LEFT: Tradition, promotion, and showmanship all combine as the members of the St Emilion Jurade parade through the streets and mount the ancient tower to proclaim the new vintage.

OVERLEAF: This unappetizing bunch of grapes at Château Haut-Bergeron has been attacked by botrytis (noble rot) and will soon be harvested and transformed into the sweet, luscious wine of Sauternes.

ABOVE: Priceless old bottles repose in the cellars of Château Margaux. Only a privileged few are ever likely to taste these ancient and often historic wines.

RIGHT: More recent vintages from Margaux and all the other top estates of Bordeaux can be found at L'Intendant, a wine shop in central Bordeaux that has turned a confined space into a browser's paradise.

LEFT: One role of the traditional négociant is to maintain stocks of fine old vintages, growing in complexity as well as in value. Mähler-Besse in Bordeaux still has thousands of cases of mature vintages slumbering in its cellars.

OVERLEAF TOP: The beautiful Renaissance mansion of Château de Carles produces one of the top wines from Fronsac.

OVERLEAF BOTTOM: The broad waters of the Gironde estuary help to deter frost from attacking the renowned vineyards of Château Latour.

22. Pomerol II

Château La Fleur-Pétrus

*Tel: 0557 517896. **Owner:** Ets J.P. Moueix. 12 ha. 80% Merlot, 20% Cabernet Franc. **Production:** 50,000 bottles*

This property has been in existence since at least the 1870s, and during the early twentieth century was owned by the Pineau family, succeeded in the 1940s by the Garets. In 1953 it was bought by the Moueix family, but had to be entirely replanted after it was destroyed by the frost of 1956. In 1995 its vineyards were expanded after the Moueix family bought four hectares that had belonged to Le Gay; these vineyards were old but not in outstanding shape, so many of them had to be replanted. This means that the newly constituted La Fleur-Pétrus is probably not performing at its full potential quite yet. Some of the vineyards slope down to the woodlands near the boundary with Lalande de Pomerol, but the best parcels are on higher ground close to Pétrus. However, the soil is entirely different from its more illustrious neighbour, being very stony gravel with marl rather than clay.

As with the other Moueix properties, the winemaking is entirely traditional and without frills, and the wine is aged in thirty-five per cent new oak. The 1983 was still youthful at ten years of age, showing splendid fruit and concentration on both nose and palate. (More recent reports suggest it is now over the hill.) The 1985 was sweet and lively when young, but I have not tasted it for many years. The 1989, tasted quite recently, was surprisingly youthful and even austere, a wine of considerable force and with a bracing finish. The 1993 is fresh and a good result for the vintage, as is the stylish and well-focused 1994. The 1999 is outstanding, with pungent and ripe oaky aromas, robust but ripe tannins, and the welcome severity of youth. I have not tasted the renowned 2000, but if it is as good as, or better than, the 2001 then it is excellent indeed. The 2001 has sumptuous black-fruits aromas, including blackcurrant, and the gorgeous texture on the palate is beautifully balanced by the wine's spice and vigour, which give it a long, elegant finish, supported by good acidity. I found the 2002 both dour and rather light, and suspect the bottle was not as it should have been. No such qualms about 2005 and 2006, tasted young from cask. If the former is ultra-elegant, the latter has more power without any loss of opulence.

Château Franc-Maillet

*Tel: 0557 519675. **Website:** www.vignobles-arpin.com. **Owner:** Gérard Arpin. 6 ha. 80% Merlot, 20% Cabernet Franc. **Production:** 35,000 bottles. **Second wine:** Ch La Fleur Maillet*

This property lies in the hamlet of Maillet, so close to the St-Emilion border that some vines belonging to the estate but technically within St-Emilion have been authorized to be blended in with the Pomerol lots. The property was bought by Jean-Baptiste Arpin in 1919. At that time there was just a single hectare, but succeeding generations have slowly expanded the property. Since 1999 Gérard Arpin, who did much to modernize the estate, has been joined at the helm by his son Gaël.

The vineyards are dispersed, with some parcels at Maillet, others near Nénin and L'Evangile. However, gravel and sand seem to be the dominant soil types. The Arpins are firm believers in debudding and green-harvesting to keep yields at a reasonable level. Although the grapes are picked by hand, the Arpins own a harvesting machine that is presently housed at their property in Lalande de Pomerol, and Gaël Arpin is honest enough to say they would consider using it at Franc-Maillet if they felt that circumstances demanded it.

After sorting, the grapes are cold-soaked for a few days, then fermented with selected yeasts in steel or metal tanks. After the alcoholic fermentation is finished, the Arpins like to macerate for a week more at fairly high temperatures to complete the extraction. They also micro-oxygenate the wine during this period. The wine is aged for twelve months in around fifty per cent new oak, although until 1994 no barrels at all were used.

In 1997 Gérard Arpin began producing a special Cuvée Jean-Baptiste from ninety per cent Merlot, which has evolved into a parcel selection from the oldest vines. The merchant and winemaker Jean-Luc Thunevin took on the wine as an exclusivity in 2001, but today Thunevin markets only half the production of around 4,000 bottles. The wine, aged in new oak, is produced only in top vintages.

The only old vintage I have encountered is the 1982, which was eminently forgettable and unrecognizable as Pomerol. Fast-forward to 1999, when the Arpins produced a supple, lush, and satisfying wine with a firm tannic backbone that didn't suppress the plummy fruit. The 2001 has strident black-fruits aromas of blackberry and blackcurrant; the texture is supple and the fruit upfront. The 2003 is perfectly drinkable, though soft and easy-going and faltering on the finish. The 2004 is quite different, a voluptuous, concentrated wine with a powerful but not overbearing tannic structure that bodes well for its future.

Franc-Maillet is a steadily improving Pomerol; the price is reasonable and it can offer good value.

Château La Ganne

Tel: 0557 511824. Website: www.chateaulaganne.com **Owner:** *Michel Dubois. 4 ha. 80% Merlot, 20% Cabernet Franc.*
Production: *16,000 bottles.* **Second wine:** *Vieux Ch Brun*

The vineyards of this obscure property are planted on sandy and gravelly soil near Moulinet and Mazeyres that gives light wines. They are aged for eighteen months in one-third new oak. I have tasted the 2000, 2001, 2002, and 2004, and find the wines slack, green, and lacking in fruit. The 2005 is better yet lacks distinction.

Château Le Gay

Tel: 0557 255645. Website: www.montviel.com. **Owner:** *Catherine Péré-Vergé. 10 ha. 89% Merlot, 11% Cabernet Franc.* **Production:** *24,000 bottles.* **Second wine:** *Manoir de Gay*

Until 2002 this fine property belonged to the venerable Marie Robin, one of two sisters who had owned Le Gay for sixty years; she simplified her life by selling the whole crop to J.P. Moueix. In 2002 she sold the estate to a wealthy glassware producer called Catherine Péré-Vergé, who already owned the less prestigious Montviel (*q.v.*) at Pomerol. Mme. Péré-Vergé apparently spent around 16 million pounds sterling on the vineyards, and then spent further sums building a new winery, with the fermentation tanks located in a kind of atrium that separates the two *chais*. At the same time the modest house was converted into a reception centre for visitors (by appointment only). She also hired Michel Rolland as her consultant oenologist.

She supplemented the existing vineyards by planting 3.4 hectares near Lafleur that were within the AC but had never been planted, and these came into production for the first time in 2006. These vines, on deep gravel soil, were planted to a density, unusually for Pomerol, of 9,000 vines per hectare. There are also vines near La Fleur-Pétrus on clay-gravel, which is probably Le Gay's finest terroir, and parcels between the winery and Rouget. The vines are up to sixty years old, and are given minimal treatments: no herbicides are used. The yield is restricted to about thirty-five hectolitres per hectare.

As one might expect, the vinification is in the modern style. The grapes are picked in *cagettes*, sorted at least three times, and after crushing conveyed into the tanks without pumping. There follows a cold soak under dry ice for up to one week. Extraction is obtained primarily by *pigeage*, and usually there is some micro-oxygenation after the alcoholic fermentation. The *marc* is pressed in a modern vertical press. Malolactic fermentation takes place in barrels, and the wine is aged for sixteen to twenty months in new oak with minimal racking and some lees-stirring; *cliquage* is used as an alternative to racking. There is no systematic fining or filtration.

The few vintages I tasted during the Moueix years were good but not sensational. The 1985 is surprisingly austere, and even after fifteen years there was some astringency. The 2001 is a mighty wine, with aromas and flavours of black fruits and plums; there is no lack of extraction and the wine is far from elegant, but it has density and persistence. I find the 2002 jammy and fatiguing; perhaps it will shed some of that disconcerting sweetness with more bottle-age. The 2005, however, is irresistible, with its elegant oaky aromas, its weight and power, and its long finish.

I find the set-up at Le Gay somewhat disconcerting. Devotees of Jonathan Nossiter's film *Mondovino* will recall the scene in the Le Gay winery when Michel Rolland gives orders for micro-oxygenation to begin, while Mme. Péré-Vergé looks on and admits she doesn't really know what's going on. Of course she is the proprietor, not a winemaker, so it is probably wise of her to leave the oenology to more qualified folk. But when, during my own visit, I asked the *maître de chai* a few slightly technical questions, he replied that he merely followed instructions. In my experience, cellarmasters are usually only too eager to claim some of the limelight (after all, they do all the hard work) and explain what they are up to. Great wines are made when all parts of the team – from vineyard management to winemaking to commercial direction – work in harmony, and that did not seem to be the case at Le Gay. Perhaps I swung past on a bad day.

Château Gazin

Tel: 0557 510705. Website: www.gazin.com. Owner: Nicolas de Bailliencourt dit Courcol. 24 ha. 90% Merlot, 7% Cabernet Sauvignon, 3% Cabernet Franc. Production: 110,000 bottles. Second wine: L'Hospitalet de Gazin

Gazin is quite unlike most other Pomerol properties. For a start, there is a real château: nothing palatial, but a comfortable early-nineteenth-century house. It is also a very large estate by Pomerol standards, with vineyards in a single block. Because Gazin is made in sizeable quantities, the wine is, I suspect, somewhat underrated.

Nicolas de Bailliencourt dit Courcol, one of Bordeaux's true gentlemen, believes that the property stands on the site of a hostel and hospital established for pilgrims by the Knights of St John, which explains the presence of a cross on the label. The owning family is considerably more ancient than Gazin, as they trace their origins back to the thirteenth century, when the name "Courcol" (short neck) was given to them by King Philippe Auguste in 1214 as a tribute for their heroism in battle. The name Gazin first turns up in records in 1741, when the property was being developed by the Bayonne family. At that time the property also included what is today Rouget. Pierre Bayonne, who built the château, died in 1828 and his widow subsequently married his former partner David Fabre. After the latter's death in 1874 the property went through various owners until in 1917 it was bought by Louis Soualle, the great-grandfather of the present owner.

Soualle died in 1946 and his son-in-law Edouard de Bailliencourt took over. The postwar period was difficult for the Gazin estate. Louis Soualle had also owned La Dominique, but in 1970 Edouard's son Etienne, in order to retain complete control of Gazin, had to sell the property. He also sold 4.5 hectares to his neighbours at Pétrus, and for the same reason. In 1988 Nicolas de Bailliencourt took over the management of the much reduced family property. He has taken on Christian Veyry as his consultant oenologist.

My visits to Gazin invariably include a stroll through the vineyards. There is something moving about walking up the gentle slope from the château to the plateau, where the Gazin vines are separated from those of Pétrus by an alley. How Nicolas de Bailliencourt must wish it were possible to reclaim those exceptional vineyards sold to his neighbour! Not all the Gazin vines are on the plateau, but about seventeen out of the twenty-four hectares are indeed in this exceptional spot close both to Pétrus and L'Evangile. The soils are clay and gravel, and the slight decline from plateau to château ensures good drainage. De Bailliencourt admits that the presence of Cabernet Sauvignon here is something of an anomaly. In the 1980s it often failed to ripen, and he is now replacing some of it with Cabernet Franc. On the other hand, he is not happy with most of the selections of Cabernet Franc on the market, and is not convinced that the parcels planted with the variety are on a terroir best suited to it.

Because until quite recently the wine was commercialized by J.P. Moueix, the Bailliencourts did not have complete control over how the property was run. Indeed, during the early 1980s the vineyards were machine-picked, Gazin being probably the last of the major Pomerol estates to be harvested in this way.

The winemaking is conventional. Indigenous yeasts are usually relied upon, except in super-ripe years such as 2005 when the winemaking team is worried about the possibility of stuck fermentations. Fermentation takes place in both cement and steel tanks. The wine is aged for eighteen months in fifty per cent new barriques, and blended in the early summer following the vintage.

I tasted the 1955 in 2002 and was pleasantly surprised by how fresh and stylish this venerable wine still was. Its aromas were of sweet raspberries, and the palate was silky and lean. Although no blockbuster, it still had delicious fruit. The 1976, at ten years old, was a success for the year, with plenty of flesh and length; it is probably past its best by now. The 1979, drunk in 2006, was unexpectedly delicious; there was some meatiness on the nose, but it was far from gamey; the palate was rich and plump, with some very light tannic support. It was clearly fully ready to drink but by no means tiring. The 1980 was attractive when young, but soon faded on the palate. The 1986 was chunky and lacking in fruit. The 1987 exudes a faint charm, but the wine is essentially dilute and probably long past its best.

The 1988 is a great success. Drunk twice in recent years, it has lean, cedary aromas of great elegance; the palate shows charm rather than weight, but the wine remains fresh and long, with a lively, peppery finish. I have consistently ecstatic notes on the 1989, which is as voluptuous and concentrated as a great Pomerol should be. It has now developed some alluring truffley aromas and seems ready to drink, though it will hold for many years. Almost as fine is the 1990, a vibrant wine of considerable force and concentration. Less opulent than the 1989, it is silkier and perhaps more elegant. The 1992 is easy-going but lacks excitement, and the 1993 is simple and rather dry.

I have drunk the 1994 on many occasions, rarely with much enthusiasm. Although not that concentrated, it has retained its tannic grip, which is fortunately balanced by sound if unexciting fruit. The 1995 is a return to form, with sumptuous fruit on the nose and palate, and a silky texture; as a wine it seems very complete and balanced. The 1996 has blossomed over the years into a highly concentrated wine with elegant blackcurrant aromas and a light tarriness, an intense elegance and delicacy, and a vigorous, spicy finish. When young the 1997 had some charm, but more recently some greenness is emerging.

The 1998 is still far from mature. Last tasted in 2005, its aromas were still muted. But the fruit is simply delicious, with a plump red-fruits character, a stylishness that comes from well-judged extraction, and a fine long finish. The 1999 is certainly very good, but doesn't have the flair and elegance of its splendid predecessor. The 2000 has an exemplary balance between power, tannic structure, and sweet blackberry fruit, but the 2001 seems just as good, with sumptuous but intense savoury aromas, ample plummy, chocolatey fruit, and tannins that are chewy without being clumsy. The 2002 is clean and pure but somewhat underpowered, a wine of charm for medium-term drinking. The 2003 has lush black-fruits aromas and similar flavours, but the wine remains rather dense and I find it hard to predict its future; it certainly seems better balanced than many Pomerols of this vintage.

The 2004 is very perfumed, a confection of raspberries and vanilla, but it's rather solid and inelegant on the palate. The 2005, just before bottling, also seemed unusually robust and extracted for Gazin, and will need many years to harmonize.

Although it would be overdoing it to place Gazin within the very top ranks within Pomerol, I can't help noting how much pleasure the wine has given me over the years, even during supposedly problematic periods in its history. The great merit of Gazin is that it always seems to retain freshness and elegance without sacrificing any of the structure and density required of a Pomerol built to last.

Château Grand-Beauséjour

Tel: 0557 845588. Website: www.vignobles-mouty.com. Owner: Daniel Mouty. 1 ha. 100% Merlot.
Production: 6,000 bottles

This micro-property, on deep gravelly soil, adjoins Beauregard and was bought in 1998 by the present owner. Since 2003 the wine has been fermented in new 400-litre barrels with regular pigeage. Clearly only the small scale of the enterprise makes possible this costly and labour-intensive form of vinification. The wine is aged for sixteen months in new Alliers oak; it is then eggwhite-fined but bottled without filtration. The 2001 and 2002 were conventionally vinified, and none the worse for it. Both wines show stylish new oak on the nose, have exemplary concentration and density, yet show a lighter touch than many vins de garage, leading to a vigorous finish. The 2004 is fine indeed, with aromas of plums and woodsmoke, while the palate is plump, concentrated, and succulent, despite some rather dry tannins. A property to watch.

Château Grand-Moulinet

Tel: 0557 512868. Owner: Patrick Fourreau. 3 ha. 90% Merlot, 10% Cabernet Franc.
Production: 20,000 bottles

The vineyards of Grand-Moulinet adjoin those of its better-known neighbour, Moulinet. The soil is sandy gravel and no one would claim that this is an exceptional terroir. Nonetheless Fourreau ages the wine entirely in new oak for twelve months. Both the 2001 and 2003 strike me as too extracted. That is excusable in 2003, but the more favourable 2001 vintage still resulted in coarse tannins and a lack of finesse. The 2004 and 2005 are slack and, frankly, dull.

Château Grange-Neuve

Tel: 0557 512303. Owners: Yves and Jean-Marie Gros. 7.5 ha. 95% Merlot, 5% Cabernet Franc.
Production: 30,000 bottles. Second wine: La Fleur des Ormes

A visit to Grange-Neuve was a welcome reminder that Pomerol is not all about powerful négociant companies and new wealth. The Gros family, father and son, received me in their modest farmhouse kitchen, and instead of presenting me with a tasting of recent vintages in expensive stemware, they simply uncorked a bottle of their 1990 and put it on the table.

The Gros family have owned the property since 1887. Some of the vines are near the house, others are close to Château de Sales, and a third block is near Trotanoy. The average age of the vines is a respectable forty years; green cover is planted to reduce vigour. After a brief cold soak, the wine is fermented in cement tanks, usually with natural yeasts (though not in 2003). It is then aged for twelve to eighteen months in one-third new oak.

The 1990 was, admittedly, slightly sweaty on the nose and the colour showed some signs of age. On the palate, however, it was rich and opulent, with some characteristics of a mature wine: a leafy tone, and some gaminess on the finish. The 1998 is medium-bodied and rather soft, and lacks the concentration and presence of the 1990. The 2001, on the other hand, is extremely good, a plump, accessible wine with good acidity and some charm and exemplary length. More extraction is evident in 2004, although the red-fruits aromas are attractive, and there is ample if burly fruit. Grange-Neuve may, like its owners, be slightly old-fashioned, but on its own terms it is a perfectly acceptable wine.

Château La Grave à Pomerol

Tel: 0557 517896. Owner: Ets J.P. Moueix. 9 ha. 90% Merlot, 10% Cabernet Franc. Production: 45,000 bottles.
Second wine: Dom Trigant-de-Boisset

This property used to be known as La Grave-Trigant-de-Boisset, so it was not surprising that after Christian Moueix acquired it in 1971, he eventually (in 1986) changed its name to this more succinct version. At the same time there were changes in vineyard holdings, as some of its best parcels were incorporated into La Fleur-Pétrus and Le Gay. This explains why decades ago this was clearly one of the leading wines of Pomerol, whereas today it is one of the lightest and most accessible wines in the Moueix portfolio, from vineyards close to the N89 in the northern part of the appellation.

That is why the old vintages I tasted from magnum in 2002 bear no relation to the style of the wines produced today. Those vintages – 1921, 1928, 1929 – were simply magnificent, immensely luxurious, spicy, complete, and persistent. The next vintage I encountered was the 1982, a sweet, medium-bodied, spicy wine that was elegant and balanced but didn't seem particularly structured. The 1986 was rich and soft but rather chunky. The 1998 has succulent plummy aromas, but it's a relative lightweight, conforming to the easy-going style presumably sought by Moueix. The same is true of the graceful 2001, a supple, undemonstrative wine, ripe and with good acidity, yet essentially unambitious. The 2005 is similar, well made and stylish but lacking complexity.

Château Guillot

Tel: 0557 511895. **Owner:** *Aimé Luquot. 5 ha. 77% Merlot, 23% Cabernet Franc.* **Production:** *25,000 bottles.*

Since 1937 this property, located near the church and close to Trotanoy and La Fleur-Pétrus, has been owned by the Libourne négociant family Luquot. Here on the plateau the soil is deep gravel over clay, with *crasse de fer*. The wine is aged in forty per cent new barriques. The 1990 and 2001 were pleasant, medium-bodied wines, quite succulent but lacking in flair. Despite some richness, the 1999 remains hollow and a touch rustic. In the more difficult 2002 vintage, Guillot delivered a rather green wine with a rasping finish. The 2004 is riper and more concentrated, but has an earthy finish.

Château Guillot Clauzel

Tel: 0557 511409. **Owner:** *Etienne Clauzel. 1.7 ha. 80% Merlot, 20% Cabernet Franc.* **Production:** *7,000 bottles.*
Second wine: *Ch Graves Guillot*

The vineyards here are very old and well located, close to Nénin and Trotanoy, but the property does not have a particularly good reputation. The only vintage I have encountered, the 2004, is fleshy, with firm tannins but modest acidity and a rather blunt, coarse finish.

Château Haut-Ferrand

See *Château Ferrand*

Château Haut-Maillet

Tel: 0557 510409. **Website:** *www.estager.com.* **Owner:** *Delteil family. 5 ha. 79% Merlot, 21% Cabernet Franc.*
Production: *30,000 bottles*

Maillet is a hamlet in the easternmost sector of Pomerol, and Haut-Maillet is one of a clutch of properties based there. For many years it has been leased by the Estager family, the owners of La Cabanne (*q.v.*). The vineyards are dispersed and there are parcels close to L'Evangile and Gazin, mostly on sandy and gravelly soils. The grapes are picked partly by machine, partly by hand. After sorting, the fruit is given a short cold soak. Fermentation takes place in steel and cement tanks with pumpovers and *pigeage*. The wine ages for fifteen months in twenty-five per cent new barriques, followed by eggwhite-fining if necessary.

I have often tasted the 2001. The cherry aromas are very ripe and close to jammy; however, on the palate it's a medium-bodied wine with good acidity and light tannins. It lacks depth and complexity but is certainly a pleasant mouthful. Rather surprisingly, I prefer the 2002, which has more charm and spice. The 2004 is a disappointment: a touch underripe, fresh but simple, with a short finish.

Château Hosanna

Tel: 0557 517896. **Owner:** *Christian Moueix. 4.5 ha. 70% Merlot, 30% Cabernet Franc.* **Production:** *20,000 bottles*
After the firm of Moueix purchased Château Certan-Giraud in 1998 it renamed one sector as Certan-Marzelle, and sold off some parcels to Nénin. Christian Moueix separated the best vineyards, renaming them Hosanna in 1999. They are wonderfully located, close to Lafleur, La Fleur-Pétrus, and Certan-de-May; the soil is essentially gravelly over subsoils of siliceous clay and *crasse de fer*. The Moueix team felt that part of the reason why Certan-Giraud underperformed was because of poor drainage, and this problem has been rectified. The wine is aged for eighteen months in fifty per cent new oak. Hosanna is magnificent; it is also very expensive. The 2000 has all the opulence and concentration one might expect, but what is particularly impressive is its superb balance and stunning length. The 2001 is similar, but marginally less expressive, bold, and structured than the 2000. Tasted from cask, the 2005 and 2006, although very good, did not have quite the same degree of elegance as many other Pomerols from the Moueix stable.

Château des Jacobins

*Tel: 0557 512047. **Owner:** Jean-Marie Bouldy. 1 ha. 60% Merlot, 40% Cabernet Franc. **Production:** 6,000 bottles*

For many years Jean-Marie Bouldy, who owns the better-known Bellegrave (*q.v.*), leased this small property near Taillefer. Then in 2000 he was able to buy it. The only vintage I have tasted is the 2001, with its fruit-packed aromas of cherries and blackcurrants, its fine, ripe attack, its concentration and liveliness. Although not complex, it is an enjoyable and well-made wine.

Château Lafleur

*Tel: 0557 844403. **Owner:** Jacques Guinaudeau. 4.5 ha. 50% Merlot, 50% Cabernet Franc.*
*Production: 18,000 bottles. **Second wine:** Les Pensées de Lafleur*

Like many of the most renowned properties in Pomerol, the buildings of Lafleur are so nondescript that few passers-by would ever imagine that one of Bordeaux's greatest wines emerges from such a modest structure. There were vineyards here in the early nineteenth century, but the property established its reputation only after it was purchased in 1872 by Henri Greloud. He already owned Le Gay, and was quick to recognize the potential of his new property. He built the house and cellars here, and an identical structure 200 metres (660 feet) away in what is today La Fleur-Pétrus. The latter house has been given a smart coat of paint; Lafleur remains its happy, shabby self. The market recognized the quality of Lafleur, which Greloud had named, but the property declined after it was inherited by Charles Greloud, who showed little interest in it.

In 1915 he sold it to his cousin André Robin, who was already married to a Greloud daughter. After his death in 1947, his daughters Thérèse and Marie inherited both Lafleur and Le Gay. The sisters were inseparable and spent the following decades sharing the same bedroom at Le Gay, as they had done since girlhood. Although they maintained the two properties well, they made no changes. Jean-Claude Berrouet of Moueix supervised the winemaking, and was entirely responsible for the 1983 and 1984 vintages. In 1984 Thérèse died, and the following year Marie leased the property to her second cousins, the Guinaudeaus. Jacques Guinaudeau was already the owner of Château Grand Village north of Fronsac, so he was perfectly capable of maintaining the reputation of Lafleur. His first vintage there was 1985.

Marie died in 2001, and Jacques Guinaudeau seized the opportunity to gain control of Lafleur. He was, of course, not the only would-be purchaser, and neither did he have great financial resources at his disposal. But in 2002 he was victorious. He immediately brought the vineyards up to date, replacing missing vines and improving trellising and drainage. Observant visitors to the property in the early 2000s noticed that the vineyards had been discreetly expanded. The Robins' chicken run, which lay close to the entrance to the *chai*, is no more, and has been replaced by a row of vines, which express the terroir better than chickens.

Lafleur is magnificently located, enjoying as neighbours La Fleur-Pétrus, Pétrus, Vieux-Château-Certan, Hosanna, La Fleur-de-Gay, and Vraiy Croix de Gay. Even though it is a small property, it has complex soils. To the northwest rises a hillock with brown gravelly soil and, one metre (three feet) beneath the surface, a band of clay just ten centimetres (four inches) thick. To the south the soil is sandy gravel over gravelly clay, while to the east the soil is brown sandy gravel over sandy clay; this eastern sector is close to Pétrus and gives wines with power but less finesse. In the centre of the property is the deepest soil, from which Pensées, the second wine, often comes.

Lafleur is notable for the very high proportion of Cabernet Franc in its vineyards; much of it is planted near Vieux-Château-Certan, which also has a good deal of the variety. There is no secret to explain the exceptional quality of this wine: it boils down to old vines, very stony soils, and very low yields. Moreover, the small dimensions of the property mean that Guinaudeau's team can treat each vine individually.

The vineyards are picked selectively, adopting the Sauternais method of *tries successives*. Thus whatever is picked is at optimal maturity. The fruit is first sorted in the vineyard, and again at the winery. Until the late 1980s the bunches were not destemmed, but today destemming is systematic. Most of the must is fermented in steel tanks, but Guinaudeau vinifies the finest lots in small cement tanks. There is no technological wizardry here. In 1991 malolactic fermentation in barriques was practised for the first time, for the practical reason that the frost-punished vines hadn't delivered enough wine to fill a tank. The wine is aged for eighteen months in fifty per cent new oak, all from Darnajou, and Guinaudeau blends progressively over the first winter. The wine is racked every three months, though without any pumping. It is fined before bottling. Selection is ultra-strict. As well as producing a second wine here, Guinaudeau always sells off in bulk any wine with which he is unhappy. In 1987 and 1991, no Lafleur was released.

Lafleur is admired for its complexity, which surely derives from the multiplicity of soil types as well as from the strong presence of Cabernet Franc. The oldest vintage I have tasted is the 1948, which seemed either past its best or slightly faulty, since woody tones were very marked, even though there was some underlying sweetness of fruit. But the 1955 and 1959, which I drank recently from magnum, were sensational, with an intensity of voluptuous aroma, immense concentration and weight, and very good length.

In contrast, the 1980 was falling apart by the end of the decade. The 1982, when young, was slightly baked on the nose, but the palate was fresher, with fine fruit concentration, substantial tannins, and excellent structure and length. The 1985 is a broad-shouldered wine, with sweet cedary aromas and a touch of menthol; this is an immensely concentrated wine with almost excessive density, and great depth. It is often said that Lafleur needs more time than most to deliver its full potential, and the mighty 1985 certainly seems in this category.

I have not tasted any vintages from the 1990s, but the 2001 has pure cherry aromas, an elegant use of oak, and impeccable balance; it's far from being massive but it is spicy, complex, and long. The 2003 is one of the better Pomerols from this vintage. Yes, there is a slight aroma of boiled sweets, and a certain chunkiness on the palate, but it's also spicy and concentrated and doesn't sag on the finish. But the 2004 is clearly the better wine, with an unusual floral perfume that is beguiling. It's a wine of considerable grandeur, opulent but bright fruit, and it's perfectly balanced with a long, complex finish.

The continuing success of this great wine has not gone to Guinaudeau's head. His flowing moustache suggests a flamboyant nature, but the wine he makes is classic. The tiny production means that he cannot open the doors of the winery to all and sundry, but those who are admitted are privileged to share in his passion, his thoughtfulness, and, in limited quantities, his wine.

Château Lafleur-Gazin

Tel: 0557 517896. **Owner:** *Mme. Delfour-Borderie. 8 ha. 80% Merlot, 20% Cabernet Franc.* **Production:** *35,000 bottles*
The name says it all: these vineyards lie between Lafleur and Gazin. Although the property still belongs to the Delfour-Borderie family, it has been managed since 1976 by the J.P. Moueix company. Along with La Grave à Pomerol this is one of the lightest wines in the Moueix range. The Merlot is planted on gravelly soils, while the Cabernet Franc grows on lighter, sandier soils. As always, the Moueix team is careful not to over-extract, and the wine is aged in no more than twenty-five per cent new oak.

The only older vintage I have tried was the seductive and fleshy 1982. More recently, the 2001 is in a more delicate and discreet style, with lean, red-fruits aromas and a rounded palate supported by firm acidity. Given its location, though, one might expect a richer and more complex wine.

Château Lafleur du Roy

Tel: 0557 517457. **Owner:** *Laurent Dubost. 4 ha. 85% Merlot, 10% Cabernet Franc, 5% Cabernet Sauvignon.*
Production: *20,000 bottles*
Based just south of the village of Catusseau, this little-known property has vineyards on sandy gravel soils. The 2001 had stewed-cherry aromas and a medium-bodied palate; it was forward and easy-going, with little complexity. The 2004 has attractive cherry-cordial aromas, but is rather confected, soupy, and bland.

Château Lagrange

*Tel: 0557 517896. **Owner:** Ets J.P. Moueix. 4.7 ha. 95% Merlot, 5% Cabernet Franc. **Production:** 20,000 bottles*

The soils here are gravel over clay and the vines are on the plateau next to Le Gay, so there is fine potential. The property was bought by Moueix in 1953. The wine is aged for up to eighteen months in fifty per cent new oak. In 2000 one block of Lagrange was incorporated into Certan-Marzelle. Apart from the burly but powerful 1985, I have been unimpressed by this wine. The 1982 was flaccid and short, the 1983 meagre and charmless, and the 1993 light and simple. I have not encountered any recent vintages, as the wine is never shown at the usual Moueix tastings.

Château Latour-à-Pomerol

*Tel: 0557 517896. **Owner:** Foyer de Charité Châteauneuf de Galaure. 8 ha. 90% Merlot, 10% Cabernet Franc. **Production:** 45,000 bottles*

This property, most of which lies near the church on gravelly clay soils, belonged to Lily Lacoste, the co-owner of Pétrus. However, it has been managed since 1962 by J.P. Moueix. Lily Lacoste gave the estate to a charitable foundation but the property is still run by Moueix. There is a second parcel of vines near the RN89, which is clearly on lighter, sandier soil; how much of this wine enters the final blend I cannot say. The wine is aged for eighteen months in one-third new oak.

The 1961, drunk from magnum in 2002, was a superb wine, with gorgeously plummy aromas; despite the wine's extreme concentration, the texture was plump and luxurious, and the finish showed extraordinary vigour. The 1979 was a great success for the vintage, with a sweet, pungent nose, a succulent Merlot fruitiness, and a chewy but not harsh finish. The 1982, which I last tasted in 1991 from magnum, was in a similar mould to the 1961, grapey, ripe, opulent, silky, and complex. The 1983 had a sweet, blackcurranty nose of great finesse, but by the late 1980s the wine seemed forward and lacking in vigour. I didn't care for the rather dour 1988, but the 1992 is surprisingly successful, being a wine of spiciness, charm, and some ripeness. The 2001 is wonderfully stylish, the cherry and blackcurrant aromas in harmony with the delicate oak; the palate is plump and concentrated without being overblown. Its excellent balance suggests the wine should age impeccably. The 2005 showed immense promise from cask.

Château Mazeyres

*Tel: 0557 510048. **Website:** www.mazeyres.com. **Owner:** Caisse de Retraite de la Société Générale. 22 ha. 80% Merlot, 20% Cabernet Franc. **Production:** 110,000 bottles. **Second wine:** Le Seuil de Mazeyres*

This large property lies in the northern part of Libourne, the château itself surrounded by a shady park. It was owned by the Querre family for many decades, but they were compelled for family reasons to sell the estate in 1988. It was then acquired by the Société Générale pension fund, which financed the construction of new cellars and also expanded the property by buying nine adjacent hectares. In 1992 Alain Moueix was appointed director and has made his home here. Moueix is a studious and reserved man, but has made a reputation for himself not only at Mazeyres but more recently at Fonroque in St-Emilion and at various properties in South Africa.

The soils here are sandy gravel with some clay, and the consequence is wines of elegance rather than power. Only half the vines are around the château; the remainder are on sandy clay near Nénin and Plince; a small sector is near Bonalgue. Fonroque is farmed according to biodynamic principles, but at Mazeyres Moueix has opted for the less radical *lutte raisonnée*.

The harvest is manual and the grapes are sorted twice. Fermentation takes place in a battery of small stainless-steel tanks, with occasional use of indigenous yeasts and micro-oxygenation. The wine is aged for twelve to eighteen months in forty per cent new barriques, with some *sur lie* ageing and racking from barrel to barrel. The wine is unfiltered. Selection remains severe, and about half the production ends up in the second wine.

The 1990 and 1994 were medium-bodied, attractive wines of no great distinction, but the 1995 had more density, and some weight and elegance. The 1999 is sleek and stylish, with a red-fruits character that gives it freshness and some delicacy. The 2000 is surprisingly tannic; it is not the most exciting expression of this vintage. The 2001 is very much better, with black-fruits aromas; the palate has weight and depth without sacrificing any poise and finesse. The 2002 reflects the difficulties of the vintage; it has ample upfront fruit, but then an edgy acidity and some hard tannins kick in. Although the aromas of the 2003 are somewhat baked, the palate is attractive, with suppleness, a gentle fruitiness, and a fine texture. The supple, silky 2004 is better, with its overt fruitiness, but although attractive it lacks excitement.

Mazeyres is a middle-rank Pomerol, well made, balanced, and satisfying. It suffers slightly from the deficiencies of its terroir, but it's an honest wine that reflects the different vintages admirably.

Château Montviel

Tel: 0032 6988 0118. Website: www.montviel.com. Owner: Catherine Péré-Vergé. 5 ha. 80% Merlot, 20% Cabernet Franc. Production: 24,000 bottles. Second wine: La Rose Montviel

Madame Péré-Vergé is better known as the owner of Le Gay (*q.v.*), but she acquired Montviel earlier, in 1985. She restored the entire property and also hired Michel Rolland as her adviser. The vineyards are mostly near Clos René on the western side of the N89, but she sold off some of those parcels in favour of retaining others near Clinet and Feytit-Clinet, which are on a more interesting terroir. The vinification is similar to that at Le Gay, and the wine is aged for sixteen months in sixty per cent new oak.

The 2000 has confected aromas and flavours, with clear signs of overripeness and a rather flat finish. The 2001 was far better, but here too there was some soupiness of texture alongside the plummy, voluptuous aromas and fruit. But it finished more strongly and may well improve with age. The 2002 is slack and rather dull. The 2003 is jammy and overripe, with solid tannins and a rather dry finish. The 2004, tasted from cask, shows more promise. The 2005 is a seductive wine, supple and silky, elegant and long.

Château Le Moulin

Tel: 0557 555160. Website: www.querre.com. Owner: Michel Querre. 2.4 ha. 80% Merlot, 20% Cabernet Franc. Production: 9,000 bottles. Second wine: Le Petit Moulin

Wine merchant Michel Querre is the owner of several properties in St-Emilion. The lovely nineteenth-century house and mill called Le Moulin de Lavaud, set in a small park, have been his home since 1969. Although just inside the Pomerol appellation, the vines from which Le Moulin are produced straddle the N89 in six parcels. He bought them in 1989, taking over a property previously known as Vieux-Château-Cloquet, but his first vintage was only in 1997. He made the first two vintages himself, but since 1999 Marie-Hélène Schaaper, who is his winemaker at Château Patris (*q.v.*) in St-Emilion, also took on Le Moulin.

The soil is sandy gravel, and Querre is well aware that he can never produce a wine like those that emanate from the plateau. So he keeps yields very low to compensate for the unexceptional terroir and picks as late as possible. After numerous sortings, the grapes are taken by conveyor belt to the crusher located above the wooden vats. Since 2003 there has been a cold soak for a few days. There is some manual *pigeage*, and Querre and Schaaper have been experimenting with fermentation in 400-litre barrels. The initial vintages were aged entirely in new oak, but Querre has cut back and now uses some one-year barrels too.

The 1997 shows the weakness of the vintage. There are some vegetal aromas, and although the palate is sweet, oaky, and concentrated, the wine overall lacks some grip and complexity. It is ready to drink. The 1998 is more lavish, with the new oak well integrated, the tannins firm but ripe, and the length exceptional. The 1999 has bright fruit but seems a bit underpowered and the finish is rather dry.

There is some overripeness on the nose of the 2000, but it is less marked on the palate, which shows good acidity and considerable finesse, adding up to an attractive wine that, if not profound, is balanced and very enjoyable. The 2001 has more aromatic purity, with scents of raspberries and blackcurrants, and it seems tighter and better structured than its predecessor; it also has more in reserve, and should age well. The 2002 is good for the vintage, with generous, oaky aromas, ripe fruit, and plenty of flesh and weight, although there is a slight caramel tone. The 2003 has sweet, toasty aromas, but the palate is rather baked, with dark-chocolate tones and a very chewy finish. The 2004 is delicious, plummy, opulent, and juicy, with a firm tannic backbone and good length.

Le Moulin is an ambitious wine, making the most from a modest terroir. Stylistically, it sometimes seems a bit out of control, with excursions into overripeness and overoaking. Nonetheless it offers ample fruit and some complexity, and it's true to vintage, suggesting that this is a wine to look out for in top years.

Château Moulinet

Tel: 0557 512368. Owner: Marie-Josée Moueix. 18 ha. 70% Merlot, 20% Cabernet Sauvignon, 10% Cabernet Franc.
Production: 80,000 bottles. Second wine: Clos Ste Anne

This large property on the Libourne side of the N89 was acquired by the négociant Armand Moueix in 1971. The terroir here, essentially sandy gravel in a single block, is not exceptional, and Mme. Moueix-Guillot, who runs the estate, is now making sterling efforts to maximize quality. A new winery was constructed in 2002 and Denis Durantou of L'Eglise-Clinet hired as a consultant. Vinification is conventional, and the wine is aged in thirty-five per cent new barriques for twelve months with regular racking. Some bottles are labelled Réserve de la Proprieté, but the wine is identical to the normal bottling.

Moulinet has always been a lighter style of Pomerol, and not always a good example of that style. The oldest vintage I have tasted, the 1964, still had sweet, blackcurranty aromas almost forty years later, but the palate soon crumbled to reveal brutal tannins and an astringent finish. The 1979 was not especially clean on the nose, and was both hollow and astringent. The 1989 was pleasant, with an elegant, cedary nose and a slightly neutral fruit quality; it had a lively finish but was hardly outstanding. Some rusticity was apparent on both occasions that I drank the 1998, which was decidedly modest for the year. Nor was the 2001 a great success: the aromas were confected, and there was again a certain rusticity from coarse tannins and raw acidity. The 2002 was much the same. However, over the next few years the investments here should make their mark, so it is too soon to write off Moulinet despite its lacklustre performance over many decades.

Château Nénin

Tel: 0556 732526. Owner: Jean-Hubert Delon. 32 ha. 70% Merlot, 30% Cabernet Franc. Production: 110,000 bottles.
Second wine: St Roch de Nénin until 1997; thereafter Fugue de Nénin

The revival of Nénin by the Delon family has been one of the most ambitious projects undertaken in Pomerol in some years. The Delons bought the estate in 1987 from their cousins the Despujol family, and the following year bought a four-hectare parcel belonging to the dismembered Certan-Giraud; this was incorporated into Nénin. Delon also replanted eight hectares of vines with massal selections from Léoville-Las-Cases. He made substantial investments, improving drainage, replacing missing vines, and heightening the trellising. A new *chai* was completed in 2004. Since 2000, the director here has been Jérôme Depoizier.

Inevitably the soils are varied. The former Certan-Giraud vines, adjoining Hosanna, are of fine quality, but much of the sector around the winery on the edge of Catusseau is less distinguished. Here the soil is sand and gravel, whereas farther north gravel dominates. Much of the sandy area is used for Merlot, which gives good results here, especially since some of the vines are now sixty years old. Debudding and green-harvesting are practised so as to keep yields down to around thirty-five hl/ha. The fruit is no longer picked mechanically, as was the case for most of the 1980s. Fermentation, alcoholic and malolactic, takes place in conical steel tanks. The wine is aged for twelve to fifteen months in about twenty-five per cent new oak.

Until recently Nénin has not enjoyed a particularly good reputation, but older classic vintages do demonstrate the potential of the property. The 1947, drunk from magnum in 2002, had a curious nose of burnt logs, but the wine was concentrated and full-bodied, with ripe tannins and a hint of austerity. The 1955 at thirty years of age was impressive aromatically, with plenty of sweet fruit, but the palate was somewhat forbidding and dry. After thirty-five years, the 1961 still had massive fruit, with cedary, chocolatey aromas, distinct assertiveness on the palate, and surprising acidity and a raisiny character. The 1987 and 1988 were stalky and dour. The 1990 was disappointingly hollow and light. Although rather hard, the 1993 was a good effort for the year. I found the 1996 earthy and hollow, the 1997 supple and easy-going but essentially simple.

There was considerable richness on the 1998, even a certain chunkiness, but it lacked excitement, finesse, and charm. Despite the low yields of recent years, I find the 2000 and 2002 both rather disappointing. Aromatically there is plenty of attractive black-cherry fruit, but neither wine shows much complexity, vigour, or length. However, the 2004 has more opulence and concentration, though it too lacks some complexity and finesse. This lack of spark is rather strange, given the excellence of the other Delon wines and the major investments and efforts made here over recent years.

Château La Patache
Tel: 0557 553803. **Owner:** *La Diligence investment group. 3.5 ha. 75% Merlot, 25% Cabernet Franc.*
Production: *17,000 bottles*

La Patache lies on the western side of the N89 on sandy gravel soils, and the vineyards mostly surround the winery. However, there are other parcels near Clinet and Rouget. In 1991 the run-down property was acquired by a group of investors, who have gradually increased quality. The vines are fairly young, and yields are kept to around forty hl/ha to increase concentration. After the grapes are sorted, crushing takes place directly over the cement tanks. A cold soak follows, then selected yeasts and enzymes are added to provoke the fermentation, and there is both pumping over and *délestage*. The wine is aged in one-third new oak, but the period in oak varies according to the vintage. Neither fining nor filtration is practised systematically.

Despite the estate's lack of renown, the wines are good. The 2000 doesn't lack richness and ripeness; it is lush without being jammy, and has only moderate acidity. The 2001 has similar plummy and chocolatey aromas, but the fruit is more opulent but not at the expense of stylishness and length.

Château Petit-Village
Tel: 0557 512108. **Website:** *www.petit-village.com.* **Owner:** *AXA Millésimes. 11 ha. 75% Merlot,*
17% Cabernet Sauvignon, 8% Cabernet Franc. **Production:** *55,000 bottles.* **Second wine:** *Le Jardin de Petit Village*

For almost a century Petit-Village has been a colonial outpost governed by the Médoc. Fernand Ginestet bought the property in 1919, and in 1971 it was inherited by Bruno Prats of Cos d'Estournel. By all accounts, he rarely visited Petit-Village and in 1989 sold it to AXA Millésimes, making it its sole wine estate on the Right Bank. In 2002 Gérard Perse made a more than generous offer, about 3 million pounds sterling per hectare, for the property. AXA had never put Petit-Village on the market, but found it hard to turn down such a profitable deal. However, Perse withdrew his offer and Petit-Village remains in AXA's hands.

The vineyards lie in a single triangular plot just east of the Catusseau roundabout, and thus not that far from Figeac, Cheval Blanc, and Vieux-Château-Certan. Since the 1950s the property has had a high proportion of Cabernet Sauvignon, no doubt a Médocain influence. The soil is gravelly and stony, and the average age of the vines is now thirty-five years. They are planted to a fairly high density of 7,500 vines per hectare.

The vinification is straightforward. It takes place with selected yeasts in cement tanks. Petit-Village is equipped with micro-oxygenation but it is hardly ever used. The *marc* is pressed in a modern vertical press. Malolactic fermentation takes place in barriques, in which the wine remains for fifteen months. The AXA team, directed by Daniel Llose with Serge Ley as the on-the-spot winemaker, used seventy per cent new oak until 1995, then increased it to 100 per cent, before reverting to around seventy per cent from 2004 onwards.

Michel Rolland acts as the consultant oenologist. His wife Dany tells me that in the past the vines were overcropped, presumably because Ginestet and Prats were used to the Médoc's higher yields. The oldest vintage I have encountered is the 1942. Despite its evolved colour, the nose was smoky and cedary, with aromas of raspberry coulis; the palate was medium-bodied, sleek and delicate, with some dryness but overall the elderly wine was holding up well. The 1948 is considerably better, retaining some spice and opulence on the nose. The 1960, tasted in 1994, had elegant, cedary aromas, and its plush fruit was backed by light tannins. The 1961, after almost forty years, showed a lovely sweet, truffley nose, with aromas of cedar and damp earth; on the palate it was surprisingly lean but still elegant, concentrated, and spicy, with a long finish.

Despite a slightly dour finish, the 1975 in 2005 had little harshness: the colour was still dense, and the flavours still youthful with good acidity. The 1982 was a seductive wine, ultra-ripe but elegant too. Almost as good was the 1985, which had ripe aromas with a slight animal nuance; rich and rounded, it seemed ready to drink by 1995. The 1986 had opulent aromas, but lacked the concentration of 1985. A light gaminess marked the nose of the 1989, but ten years on the wine was still dense, chocolatey, and youthful. The 1990 has been delicious from the outset, voluptuous in aroma and flavour, svelte, fleshy, and elegant. The 1992 lacked some vigour but was pleasant enough, and the 1994 has some austerity behind the dense fruit.

The 1995 is still youthful, with sumptuous oaky aromas, and freshness as well as weight. For some reason the 1996 has been consistently disappointing, with a slight vegetal tone and a slack structure. Yet the 1997 was quite good for the vintage. For some years the 1998 was rather tough and drab, but by 2007 it had recovered its balance. It's robust but it's also harmonious and has attractive blackberry fruit. As does the 1999, a lush, still youthful wine with light acidity and robust tannins.

There's slightly jammy fruit and a good deal of oak on the nose of the 2000, a plump, concentrated wine with hefty black-fruits flavours and a long, sumptuous finish. The 2001 is tannic and dense, still dominated by new oak, and with a slight austerity that is unusual in this vintage. The 2002 is discreet in aroma and flavour, with modest blackberry fruit and somewhat raw tannins; it seems a bit overworked but may yet settle down. There are confected aromas on the 2003, a wine that lacks weight and structure. The 2004 is delicate and supple, elegant rather than complex, but very satisfying, and sustained by its long, fresh finish. The 2005 is potentially superb.

My experience of Petit-Village over the years has been better than its reputation. Under AXA there seems to have been some stylistic hesitancy, as if Llose and his team have not been quite certain how to deal with the property. With a good deal of Cabernet Sauvignon in the blend, there is always a possibility that the wine will be too tannic for its own good, and some recent vintages strike me as excessively oaky. It's clearly a wine that benefits from more bottle-age than most Pomerols. Petit-Village remains a work in progress, and perhaps in future years it will shed its occasional Médocain austerity.

Château Pétrus

Tel: 0557 517896. Owner: Jean-François Moueix. 11.5 ha. 95% Merlot, 5% Cabernet Franc.
Production: 30,000 bottles

What can one say about a wine that is a monument as well as a drink? For many, the name Pétrus conjures up Bordeaux at its most splendid, most rarefied, and most luxurious. It is the quintessential expression of a certain type of Pomerol, though by no means typical of Pomerol as a whole. Its vineyards are dominated by clay soils that give it power and longevity, as opposed to the elegance and poise of, say, Vieux-Château-Certan. We can rejoice in both styles, but Pétrus remains very much *sui generis*.

The property was first mentioned in 1837, when it belonged to the Arnaud family, who remained its owner until just after World War I. (I am indebted for much of this historical account to Clive Coates.) By this time its reputation was already well established and its prices matched those obtained by second growths in the Médoc. Mme. Edmond Loubat bought up parcels of Pétrus progressively from 1925 onwards, and twenty years later she was the sole owner. She had no doubts about the quality of the wine and demanded high prices for it. The estate was then inherited in 1961 by her nieces, Mme. Lily Lacoste and Mme. Lignac, but the two ladies did not get on. The present owners became involved with the property in 1943, when Jean-Pierre Moueix became its sole agent. Shortly before her death, Mme. Loubat gave a share in Pétrus to Moueix to ensure that he remained involved in its management. In 1969 Moueix bought a majority share from Mme. Lignac, though the extent of his shareholding remained a secret until the late 1990s. Also in 1969 Moueix took advantage of the fact that Gazin felt compelled to sell some vines, purchasing four hectares of superb clay soil on the plateau. In 2002 the buildings were given a face-lift and expanded. By 2005 Lily Lacoste was ninety-eight years old, and there was a great deal of controversy, which I am not able to shed much light on, about poor advice some claimed she had been given involving the sale of her remaining shares in Pétrus and the disposal of Latour-à-Pomerol (*q.v.*) to a charitable institution. Fortunately Pétrus remains in the safest of hands.

Pétrus is renowned for its famous "buttonhole" of clay. It's a rich blueish clay that lies over a subsoil of gravel and, beneath that, a layer of hard iron-rich *crasse de fer*. Pétrus is not alone in having vines on this twenty-hectare sector of the plateau, but it is probably the only estate with vines almost entirely on the buttonhole. There is just one hectare on gravelly soil. The Pétrus vineyards are flanked by those of La Conseillante, L'Evangile, La Fleur-Pétrus, and Vieux-Château-Certan. By walking through the vineyards one can see that they are gently sloping, and this aids drainage, which can be problematic on dense clay soils. Their advantage is that they retain water and thus resist hydric stress. Patrolling the vines just as the harvest was beginning in 2005, I could detect no signs of stress despite the very dry summer. Until the mid-1960s Cabernet Franc accounted for twenty per cent of the vines, but the Moueix family was convinced that the cold soils here were much better suited to Merlot. The small amount of Cabernet Franc that remains is hardly ever included in the final blend. Thus Pétrus is one of the very few great wines of Bordeaux that is monovarietal.

The average age of the vines is around forty-five years. Christian Moueix is not a fan of complantation, preferring to replant entire blocks in one go rather than replace individual vines. He maintains that the existing root system in an old vineyard makes it difficult for young vines to establish their own. Although some clones were planted in the 1980s, more recently only massal selections have gone into the ground. Christian Moueix was a pioneer of green-harvesting, which he first practised in 1973. No effort or expense is spared to preserve the integrity of the fruit. He has gone so far as to rent helicopters to dry out the vines during rainy spells at harvest.

Moueix – and this applies to almost all the properties owned or run by the house – does not favour late harvesting, and he is often criticized for picking too early. He also begins picking at Pétrus after a boisterous lunch at which both the harvesters and the Moueix family and employees are present. By the afternoon any dew will have evaporated, thus avoiding any risk of dilution, however slight. In 2005 I was present when he began picking young vines at Trotanoy and Pétrus at least a week before other properties commenced. Christian Moueix and wine-maker Jean-Claude Berrouet are adamant that their primary concern is to maintain freshness in the wine, and to avoid any hint of pruney, raisiny, jammy aromas and flavours that can arise from late harvesting. Whatever the motivation, no one could claim that the Moueix wines are green or underripe.

The grapes are sorted twice, destemmed, and then fermented in cement tanks. In 2005 two double-decker stainless-steel tanks were added so as to allow more parcel selections. In general indigenous yeasts are used, but Berrouet has no qualms about using cultivated yeasts should he consider it necessary or preferable. Vinification is classic, with pumpovers; there is no recourse to adding enzymes or *délestage* or micro-oxygenation. The malolactic fermentation takes place in the tanks, and the *marc* is pressed in a vertical press. The press wine is kept apart until January, when its quality is assessed, and up to seven per cent may be blended in. Blending takes place in March. The wine spends two years in new oak, although in lighter or more difficult years, such as 1997, 2002, and 2003, considerably less new wood is used. The wine is racked every three months, eggwhite-fined, and filtered only if necessary.

Pétrus is a sumptuous wine, but it is not, usually, a blockbuster. The emphasis is on resplendent fruit and texture rather than power or weight for their own sake. There is tannin and concentration, of course, but they are at the service of the wine rather than its primary features. In some ways Pétrus has become an old-fashioned wine, with its early harvesting and traditional vinification. The proprietor of some other outstanding Right Bank estates once told me he didn't consider Pétrus among the truly great wines of Bordeaux. This, in my view, represents a clash of styles rather than an objective assessment.

The oldest vintages I have tasted were a quartet of magnums, sampled in 2002: 1900 (Belgian-bottled), 1921, 1928, and 1929. With wines of this age, even in magnum, everything depends on a variety of factors, of which storage and cork condition are probably the most important. All I can say is that all four were superb. The 1900 had voluptuous aromas, immense concentration and spiciness, and astonishing freshness, vigour, and length. The 1921 was a touch more evolved in colour, but rich and sumptuous on both nose and palate; tremendous length gave the wine an elegant lift. The 1928 was, marginally, the weakest of the quartet, as despite an intense, minty, blackcurranty nose, the palate was a touch raw and the finish dry. Yet an hour later the wine seemed more harmonious. The 1929 was truly great, with opulent, plump fruit on the nose; the wine stood out because of its vigour, its fine acidity, and almost peppery finish.

Sadly, there follows a gap in my tasting notes, although the following vintages were also drunk in 2002, from bottles rather than magnum. The 1964 had power and spice on the nose; its sheer power dominated the palate, which was somewhat chunky and over-assertive, although with aeration some balance was restored and it also developed better length. The 1970 was decidedly austere, with hefty oakiness on the nose and assertive tannins on the palate, though balanced by fine acidity. I preferred the 1971, less massive but more elegant, with a silky texture and a persistent finish. The 1975 has a slight dryness on the finish, but it's a minor flaw; the nose is dense, ripe, and fleshy, while the palate is rich and spicy, with ample vigour and length.

The 1981 is lighter in style, but has an invigorating elegance and balance; the nose is a beguiling blend of cherries and blackcurrants, while the tannins are supple and the finish long. The 1982 is a great wine, with a slight mintiness on the nose that saves the rich plummy aromas from being too overwhelming; there is great concentration on the palate, ample bite and extract, and remarkable elegance and stupendous length. The 1985 seemed a touch light in 1990, but subsequent tastings reveal a very great wine: very rich, very powerful, but also with plenty of spice and vigour and overt fruit, and no trace of excessive extraction. In 2005 it seemed far more youthful than in 1990. The 1989 is another remarkable wine: aromatically voluptuous, of course, but also airy and elegant; fine acidity balances the powerful tannins and gives a long, bright finish.

I have yet to taste any Pétrus vintages of the 1990s. I have no reason to question the assessments of others that 1990, 1995, 1998, and 2000 are very great vintages here. Aromatically, the 2001 was still dumb in 2005, but on the palate it was dense and imposing, with ample force and vigour; yet in terms of fruit expression it was very muted. The 2005, tasted from cask in 2006, had aromas of black cherries and discreet oak. The palate is sumptuous and spicy, but it was very dominated by the tannins. (Since by July 2006 the as yet unbottled wine was trading for 20,000 pounds sterling a case, it is unlikely I will ever taste it again.) In its infancy, the 2006 was more aromatically floral, but had the hallmark power of Pétrus, while being at the same time vigorous and complex and long.

Château Pierhem

*Tel: 0557 745318. **Website**: www.pejanoueix.com. **Owner**: Pierre-Emmanuel Janoueix. 1.8 ha. 70% Merlot, 30% Cabernet Franc. **Production**: 12,000 bottles. **Second wine**: Ch Grands Sillons Gabachot*

This small property was bought in 1964 by Pierre Janoueix, another branch of the better-known J. Janoueix family that owns so many Libournais properties. In 2000 his son Pierre-Emmanuel took over and renamed it, as the previous name of Grands Sillons Gabachot was clearly too much of a mouthful. The vines, which are on average about forty years old, lie near Catusseau on sandy and gravelly soils, and are cultivated according to the principles of *lutte raisonnée*. After a cold soak there is a lengthy *cuvaison* of up to five weeks, and the wine is aged in new oak for fifteen months.

The 2001 is pleasant and supple, not that weighty or concentrated, and a touch rustic. The same is true of the 2002, which shows some greenness on the nose; but it's fresh and quite elegant. Both vintages seem styled for early or medium-term drinking. The 2004 is disappointing: earthy and chunky.

Le Pin

*Tel: 0557 513399. **Owner:** Jacques Thienpont. 2.3 ha. 88% Merlot, 12% Cabernet Franc. **Production:** 9,000 bottles*

Just outside the village of Catusseau stands a singularly ugly little house shaded by a tall pine tree. This is Le Pin. From 1924 until 1979 the house and a single hectare of vines were owned by a Mme. Loubie, who sold the wine as a generic Pomerol. After her death the little property was eyed by the Thienpont family, owners of Vieux-Château-Certan nearby, with a view to incorporating its vines into the latter estate. They decided the price was too high, but Jacques Thienpont, his father, and his uncle, suspecting the soil here was truly exceptional, bought it on their own account. Eventually Jacques became the sole proprietor.

Meanwhile, just across a ditch from Le Pin was a vegetable patch that belonged to a widow. Jacques had his eye on this too. He paid court to the old lady, hoping to induce her to sell; eventually, his persistence paid off. He bought it, and began planting it in 1984.

The vineyards are located on one of the highest parts of the Pomerol plateau. The soil is gravelly, with some sand and clay on an iron-rich base. The drainage is exceptional. Yields are kept to around thirty hl/ha, as the vines are not very old. Despite the small size of the property, Thienpont is surprised by the variations in bunch size and in maturation dates that he encounters each year.

I visited Le Pin during the 2000 harvest. Picking was taking place in perfect conditions. Later in the day I returned, and found Jacques Thienpont hosing down the cellar. The grapes were safely in the vats and his day's work was done. The vinification is conventional, except that in years when the acidity is a bit low, he will return a batch of stems to the vats. Should the must lack concentration, he will bleed the tanks. Malolactic fermentation takes place in barriques "because I had nowhere else to put the wine", he explains. The wine is aged for eighteen to twenty-four months in new oak and bottled without filtration.

Jacques Thienpont is a modest man with an engaging smile. I sometimes think that smile may be an understandable tendency to wonder at his amazing good fortune in producing a wine that is easy to make and sells for vast sums. But Le Pin was not an instant hit. The 1979 vintage, his first, was sold cheaply. Robert Parker did taste the 1982, and a French wine writer became very excited by Le Pin in the mid-1980s. René Gabriel, the wine buyer for the Swiss Mövenpick chain, encountered the wine at a blind tasting in 1987 and was hugely impressed. So gradually word spread that something exciting was happening near that pine tree. Prices rose fast on the secondary market, as collectors rushed to buy up the best vintages.

Since the Thienponts are wine merchants in their native Belgium, Jacques in effect sells his wine to himself, as well as to a handful of other négociants who were his original customers. Prices are, frankly, silly, but that is thanks to the frenzy induced by high scores and by the wine's scarcity. In 1996 the celebrated 1982 sold at auction for 23,100 pounds sterling for a case; and in 2005 the 2000, which I tasted, alas, only as grape juice, sold for 4,600 pounds sterling per case.

In style the wine is rich, hedonistic, and exotic. Sometimes it has a mocha character, especially on the nose. It's lush, being almost entirely from Merlot, but it's no blockbuster. Alexandre Thienpont of Vieux-Château-Certan just down the road observes that Le Pin is quite burgundian, because of the gravelly soils. There is some truth in this. In 2005, for instance, the wine tasted from barrel was no monument of opulence. Instead it was a perfumed, floral wine with great aromatic elegance; it was super-ripe, of course, but there was also an underlying delicacy and liveliness. The only older vintage I have drunk is the 1985, which, in a horizontal tasting of 1985 Pomerols conducted in 1998, I rated very highly for its lush, upfront, smoky character, and its finely integrated oak. In 2007 the 1999 and 2001, from magnum, had resplendent red-fruits aromas, lovely intensity, and sprightliness, and a long finish; the 2001 is marginally superior. Thienpont prefers it to the 2000, and sold off the entire crop in 2003.

The adulation with which Le Pin is usually regarded is not universal. There are respected figures who question whether Le Pin has the capacity to age and who suggest the 1982 and 1985 are past their best. Parker certainly rejects the suggestion. I can't comment, and it may be that such remarks reflect irritation with a relative newcomer.

Château Plince

Tel: 0557 516877. Website: www.chateauplince.com. Owner: Michel Moreau. 9 ha. 70% Merlot, 30% Cabernet Franc.
Production: 50,000 bottles. Second wine: Pavillon Plince

Plince has been owned by the Moreau family for a few generations; they were also proprietors of Clos l'Eglise, which they were obliged to sell in 1997. The vines are in a single parcel on sandy soil between Catusseau and the RN89. The Cabernet Sauvignon vines were pulled out in 2005. The terrain is flat and sandy. This is one of the few Pomerol properties that is picked by machine, which Michel Moreau justifies on the grounds that the quality is just as good. Once in the winery, the grapes are destemmed, then sorted. The tanks are equipped with micro-oxygenation, which is hardly ever used. The wine is aged in one-third new oak for eighteen months.

The 1989 was rather good, a lush, plump wine with some spiciness and length. The 1998, tasted in 2005, was grubby, a slack wine with coarse tannins; but this may have been a poor bottle. The 2000 has subdued aromas of blackberries and raspberries; it's supple, quite forward, with little complexity. The 2001 is significantly better, being richer and more sumptuous, with a suave texture and good length.

Château Plincette

Tel: 0557 510409. Website: www.estager.com. Owner: (leased by) Estager family. 2 ha. 83% Merlot,
17% Cabernet Franc. Production: 12,000 bottles

This small property, south of Nénin, is leased by the Estager family of La Cabanne (q.v.). This is not one of the best sectors of Pomerol, and the soil is sandy and gravelly. After manual picking and sorting, the grapes are vinified with pumpovers and *pigeage*, and the wine is aged for fifteen months in twenty-five per cent new oak. The only vintage I have tasted (twice) is the 2001, which has lush, ripe, oaky aromas, plenty of upfront fruit, well-integrated oak, and plenty of freshness and vigour. None of this vigour appears in the 2004, which is bland and slightly green.

Château La Pointe

Tel: 0557 510211. Website: www.chateaulapointe.com. Owner: d'Arfeuille family. 22 ha. 80% Merlot,
15% Cabernet Franc, 5% Cabernet Sauvignon. Production: 150,000 bottles. Second wine: Ch La Pointe Riffat

The d'Arfeuille family own and run two important estates: La Serre (q.v.) in St-Emilion and La Pointe. Stéphane d'Arfeuille is a cousin of Luc d'Arfeuille of La Serre. The vines stand in one block north of the Libourne to Catusseau road. Its boundaries have scarcely altered in over 150 years.

The soil is sandy yet varied: there are areas of clay traversed by bands of sand and gravel. There is a cold soak for five days, and then fermentation begins with selected yeasts in cement tanks, with a post-maceration fermentation and micro-oxygenation. The *marc* is pressed in a modern vertical press. The wine is aged for fifteen to eighteen months in one-third new oak; there is no systematic fining or filtration. The present winemaker is the self-confident Emilie Faniest, the daughter of the owner of Rochebelle in St-Emilion.

The oldest La Pointe I have tasted is the 1947. Despite a very mature colour in 2002, the wine retained almost burgundian aromas of raspberries. It was medium-bodied yet intense, with fine acidity behind the lovely fruit, and a note of chocolate on the finish. The 1983, tasted in 1990, was quite earthy and hard-edged, though it had ample concentration. The 1985 showed a good deal of aromatic charm, but was somewhat grippy in its tannins and structure. I found the 1989 soft and dull, but the 1990 is much better: pleasantly if atypically herbal on the nose, but sweet, soft, ripe, and delicious on the palate, with more charm than weight. The 1998 was extremely impressive from cask, and represented one of the bargains of the vintage, but I have not tasted it from bottle.

The 2000 was certainly opulent, but seemed too rounded and almost bland when young. The 2001 is excellent, with plummy aromas enlivened by a floral tone, and no lack of concentration or grip on the lush palate. The 2003 avoided over-extraction and emerged as a supple, fleshy wine, with light acidity and modest length, probably best drunk young. Blind tastings of the 2004 and 2005 were quite impressive, and La Pointe, which is not especially expensive, is probably underrated.

Domaine de la Pointe

Tel: 0557 745076. **Owner:** *Max Silvestrini. 1.2 ha. 85% Merlot, 15% Cabernet Franc.* **Production:** *6,000 bottles*

Max Silvestrini is better known as the owner of Château Chéreau (*q.v.*) in Lussac-St-Emilion, but he also owns this property, with some old vines planted on a small *croupe* of gravelly clay. Silvestrini admits the wine is never that structured, but the only vintage I have tasted, the 2003, was dilute and lacked interest. This hardly compensated for its relatively low price.

Château Pomeaux

Tel: 0557 519888. **Website:** *www.pomeaux.com.* **Owner:** *Ted Powers. 3.8 ha. 100% Merlot.* **Production:** *18,000 bottles.*
Second wine: *Ch La Fleur Pomeaux*

The set-up here is complicated. Pomeaux used to be known as Vieux Taillefer, until it was bought by Ted Powers in 1998 and renamed, as Vieux Taillefer did not enjoy a particularly good reputation. However, Powers, an American businessman, lives in Hong Kong, so he employs Wine & Vineyards, a company that specializes in managing properties owned by ambitious absentee landlords. The winemaker is Frank Juggelmann, with advice from Michel Rolland.

The vineyards are south of Catusseau, close to La Tour Figeac in particular. The soil is sandy but rich in *crasse de fer*. The winemaking is sophisticated. After a cold soak, fermentation takes place in wooden and steel vats with *pigeage*. To increase the concentration of a wine that is not naturally virile, up to forty per cent of the must is bled off during fermentation. The *marc* is pressed in a new vertical press. Malolactic fermentation takes place in new oak, in which the wine remains for up to twenty-four months. Juggelmann favours a light toast to avoid excessively pronounced oakiness. Wine & Vineyards gives the wines considerable bottle-age before release. Thus in 2005 the current release was the 2000.

The 1998, the first vintage under the new regime, has oaky aromas that are a touch stewed; overall the wine, although rich and rounded, has a rather flat texture and a dry finish. I prefer the 1999. The 2000 is the best of the initial trio, with aromas of blackcurrants and strawberries enlivened by a dash of spice, while the palate is rich with no rough edges; it's a wine with concentration, vigour, and style, and avoids the imbalances of the 1998 and 1999. Although lacking in elegance, the toasty 2004 is rich and amply fruity, with firm tannins to give it structure and persistence.

Pomeaux is clearly a wine that is worked very hard in order for the winemaking and *élevage* to triumph over the unremarkable terroir.

Château Prieurs de la Commanderie

Tel: 0557 513136. **Website:** *www.vignobles.fayat.com.* **Owner:** *Clément Fayat. 3.5 ha. 75% Merlot,*
15% Cabernet Franc, 10% Cabernet Sauvignon. **Production:** *15,000 bottles*

Clément Fayat is a building magnate and collector of wine estates. This property, which he assembled in 1984 from numerous blocks, is in the northwest, not far from L'Enclos and Clos René. The soil is essentially deep gravel and sand over a clay subsoil. The vines are quite old – forty years on average – and the vinification is classic other than an occasional recourse to micro-oxygenation. The wine is aged in up to fifty per cent new barriques for fifteen to eighteen months. Michel Rolland acts as the consultant oenologist.

I find this a very modest wine. The 2001 is medium-bodied, rather light, yet quite tannic, so that it has a disappointingly rustic edge. The 2002 has a certain prettiness and delicacy; it's a charming lightweight to drink young. The 2003 is similar, but at least it avoids the pitfalls of over-extraction and dense tannins.

Château Providence

Tel: 0557 517896. Owner: J.P. Moueix. 2.7 ha. 98% Merlot, 2% Cabernet Franc. Production: 12,000 bottles.
Second wine: Les Chemins de la Providence

Christian Moueix has gradually crept up on this small property located between Certan-de-May and the church property. It used to be owned by a M. Dupuy; in 2002 Moueix bought a share in the property and then in 2005 gained full control. Before Moueix entered the picture La Providence did not have much of a reputation. I admired the infant 2005 in cask for its aromatic purity, its sleek texture, its stylishness and persistence. The 2006, also from cask, has more power but also tremendous vigour and finesse.

Château La Renaissance

Tel: 0557 510607. Owner: François de Lavaux. 3 ha. 85% Merlot, 15% Cabernet Franc. Production: 24,000 bottles

This rarely encountered wine (other than in the Benelux countries and Switzerland) is made from young vines grown in the northwest sector, not far from L'Enclos. One-third of the wine is aged in new oak, the rest remaining in tanks. The 2000 was dumb on the nose, lacked personality (let alone typicity) and finished with dry tannins. The 2004 is richer, with considerable concentration and power.

Château La Rose Figeac

Tel: 0557 746218. Website: www.chateaumaisonblanche.com. Owner: Despagne family. 5.5 ha. 95% Merlot,
5% Cabernet Franc. Production: 24,000 bottles. Second wine: Les Sables de la Rose Figeac

As the name suggests, this property could, in terms of its terroir, equally well be in St-Emilion. It is located between Figeac and Taillefer and next to La Tour Figeac, which used to belong to Despagne's grandfather. The Despagnes are an extensive family with estates in St-Emilion and the satellites. This estate came into their possession after Nicolas Despagne's mother inherited it in the 1970s.

There are two distinct soil types here. One hectare is farther north on gravel soils, the rest on sand near Taillefer. The soil is ploughed and no chemical fertilizers are used. Nicolas Despagne is anti-interventionist, so the wine is vinified without selected yeasts, without enzymes, chaptalization, or acidification. Nor, for that matter, is there any systematic temperature control. The wine is aged in new barriques.

I have inconsistent notes on the 2001 vintage. One bottle, sampled in 2004, was a bit rough and rustic; the same wine, a year later, had gained in weight and roundness, and also showed some vivacity and length. The 2002 has aromas of sour cherries and vanilla, but shows little concentration, weight, or length. The 2004 is super-ripe and lacks some freshness.

Château Rouget

Tel: 0557 510585. Website: www.chateau-rouget.com. Owner: Jean-Pierre Labruyère. 18 ha. 85% Merlot,
15% Cabernet Franc. Production: 120,000 bottles. Second wine: Vieux Ch des Templiers

Rouget never had much of a reputation before its purchase by Jean-Pierre Labruyère in 1992. He invested substantially, restoring the vineyards, replanting some parcels and removing the existing Cabernet Sauvignon, and building a new winery. From 1994 the manager of the property (Labruyère being Mâcon-based) has been Antoine Ribeiro and Michel Rolland has been giving his advice since 1997.

By Pomerol standards, this is quite a large property. Twelve hectares are around the house. There are 3.5 hectares on less favourable terroir on the other side of the RN89 near Clos René; and two more between Trotanoy and Petit-Village. The soil around the château is clay and gravel, with the former dominating the lower sectors; here drainage has been installed. Although the soil mix inevitably varies, there is hardly any sand on the property. Rouget believes in very low yields: thirty-two hl/ha on average, twenty-two in the sparse 2002 vintage.

As is common at properties advised by Rolland, harvesting is delayed until the last possible moment to ensure maximum ripeness. The grapes are sorted twice, crushed over the tanks to avoid pumping the fruit, and then a five-day cold soak follows. Fermentation takes place in either steel or wooden vats with indigenous yeasts; there is both pumping over and *pigeage* during the fermentation, and although the *cuvier* is equipped with micro-oxygenation, it is rarely employed. Malolactic fermentation takes place in barriques in the air-conditioned *chai*, and the wine stays in fifty per cent new oak for fifteen to eighteen months. There is no systematic fining or filtration. About half the production is declassified into the second wine.

The 2001 is still dominated by smoky oak, although it shows elegance too; it's a weighty, tannic wine with considerable concentration, exotic flavours of plums and cloves, and a long, dense finish. It needs time. The 2002 is unusually powerful for the vintage, and no one could describe it as lightweight. If anything it's a bit too charged and extracted, but there's no denying the opulence and density of fruit. The 2003 has a sweet, spicy nose that is close to jammy; it's rather overripe and pruney and lacks acidity, but it has reasonable length. The nose of the 2004 is similar but the palate is livelier; there's little complexity here, but it delivers straightforward fruitiness and some finesse. The 2005 is super-ripe and sleek, but does lack length.

Rouget is now a rich, modern-style Pomerol, aiming for power and density; it's impressive, but there is no lightness of touch here.

Château St-Pierre

*Tel: 0557 511729. **Owner:** M. de Lavaux. 3 ha. 75% Merlot, 25% Cabernet Franc.*
Production: 20,000 bottles

This small property is located close to the Pomerol church on gravelly soil over a subsoil of sandy clay. Half the wine is aged in tanks, the remainder in barrels, of which only a small proportion is new. The only vintage I have tasted is the 2000, which had aromas of boiled sweets, and was light and simple on the palate. M. de Lavaux also owns an even smaller property, the Clos du Vieux-Plateau-Certan, which is bottled separately. The location is admirable, being surrounded by Vieux-Château-Certan, Pétrus, La Conseillante, and Petit-Village, but production is minute and prices very high. I have not tasted it.

Château de Sales

*Tel: 0557 510492. **Website:** www.chateau-de-sales.com. **Owner:** Bruno de Lambert. 47 ha. 70% Merlot,*
*15% Cabernet Franc, 15% Cabernet Sauvignon. **Production:** 300,000 bottles. **Second wine:** Ch Chantalouette*

This is by far the largest property in Pomerol, dominated by one of the region's few architecturally worthwhile buildings: a château from the late sixteenth century, currently inhabited by the owner's stepmother. Bruno de Lambert and his family live in a kind of annexe. His family has owned the property since the mid-fifteenth century. Little has changed, in terms of the boundaries of the vineyards, since then, although a few hectares were lost when the railway was built.

The vineyards, in one large block, occupy the northwestern corner of Pomerol. This is not the most prestigious sector, but Bruno de Lambert discerns several beneficial consequences. For instance, the warm, sandy soils give precocious maturation, and thus this is one of the few spots in Pomerol where Cabernet Sauvignon stands a good chance of ripening. Its inclusion gives his wine more grip. Viticulture is essentially *lutte raisonnée*, and the soil is ploughed. De Lambert is not a great fan of green-harvesting, and prefers to debud rigorously. Nor does he like to pick very late, with the exception of the tardy Cabernet Sauvignon. From 1979 to 1996 he picked by machine, but then stopped for the unusual reason that the *confusion sexuelle* sachets attached to the vines ended up tumbling into the machine and thus the vats. Nonetheless, he is thinking of returning to partial machine-harvesting in the future.

De Sales is equipped with a reverse-osmosis machine, as the sandy soils absorb rain rapidly and can swell the grapes with water. But de Lambert has hardly ever used the machine, except in 2004. The wine is fermented in cement tanks, usually with indigenous yeasts, though he used selected yeasts to kick-start the process in 1990 and 2005. The vinification is entirely traditional, but the *élevage* is unusual. For twelve months he ages half the wine in tanks, half in barriques, with rotation between the two; then all the wine goes into tanks for a further six months. The idea is to retain freshness. Little new oak is used, and the wine is eggwhite-fined and occasionally filtered.

De Sales is inevitably a light style of Pomerol, so it makes no sense to compare it with a Conseillante or Trotanoy. When it succeeds, it does so with balance, finesse, bright fruit, and charm. The 1973 was light and short, the 1975 rather jammy and not well balanced. But the 1979 delivered the goods: in 2005, the aromas were leafy and charming, while the palate was silky, although the fruit had become rather frail. The 1983 had similar virtues, and although the acidity seemed quite high, it was balanced by the sweetness of the fruit. The 1986 had more firmness and tannin, but was accessible even when relatively young; I have not tasted it recently. The 1989 was a soft, rounded, juicy wine, but it lacked grip and excitement.

The 1995 is a disappointment: light for the vintage, and with rather dry tannins, adding up to a worryingly austere wine. There is little going on in the 1996, which lacks concentration and weight. The fruity 1998 has aromas of black cherries enlivened by notes of black pepper; the wine is dense and quite full-bodied, and it remains youthful. I tasted the 2000 just before bottling, and found it lacked bite and vigour. In contrast the 2001 is excellent, unusually broad and voluptuous for de Sales, but with sufficient spice and acidity to keep it lively. The 2002 has some odd, stewed aromas, and on the palate it is easy-going, with a light liquorice tone, and though attractive and charming, it lacks some flesh. The 2003 is not that fresh and lacks persistence; nonetheless it is a pleasant, fruity wine for drinking soon. The 2004 shows promise, with its bright cherry fruit, light tannin, and good acidity.

Château du Tailhas

Tel: 0557 512602. Website: www.tailhas.com. Owner: Luc Nebout. 10.5 ha. 80% Merlot, 10% Cabernet Franc, 10% Cabernet Sauvignon. Production: 65,000 bottles. Second wine: Ch la Garenne

This estate has been owned by the Nebout family since 1932, and it lies close to the St-Emilion border in the southernmost sector of Pomerol. The vineyards are in a single block on a mixture of silt and sand mixed with gravel. This is not a terroir likely to result in powerful wines, so Luc Nebout aims for finesse instead. The wine is fermented in steel and cement tanks, then aged in fifty per cent new oak for six months, and in tanks for twelve months, with rotation between the various lots. The 1990, fifteen years on, had a light, leathery nose and no lack of sweet, generous fruit; a wine of little depth but considerable charm. The 1999 is in a similar style but lighter, and kept lively by a peppery aftertaste. The 2001 is disappointing for the vintage, with light balsamic aromas, and a broad but slack structure marked by coarse tannins. The 2002 has a light, fruity, cherry nose, but it is easy-going and simple, though refreshed by fair acidity – a modest wine to drink young. The 2004 has wine-gum aromas, and the same easy-going style as earlier vintages, but also a hint of greenness.

Tailhas is not an outstanding Pomerol, but it offers accessibility and drinkability at a very modest price.

Château Taillefer

Tel: 0557 255045. Website: www.chateautaillefer.com. Owner: Catherine Moueix. 12 ha. 75% Merlot, 25% Cabernet Franc. Production: 50,000 bottles. Second wine: Ch Fontmarty

Ancient maps suggest that this property has been in existence for some centuries, its boundaries scarcely altered in 200 years. In 1923 it was bought by Antoine Moueix. The property passed down to Jean-Michel and Bernard Moueix, and after the latter died in 1996, his widow Catherine took over running the property. In 2001 she hired Denis Dubourdieu to act as a consultant.

Most of the vineyards, which lie close to the imposing if inelegant château, are on sand and gravel soils, but there is another parcel not far from Figeac. *Lutte raisonnée* is practised in the vineyards, and at Dubourdieu's suggestion the vines are now pruned according to the *guyot double* system. In 2005 the use of insecticides was halted. Sometimes compost is added to the soil, but no fertilizers. Catherine Moueix prefers to reduce vigour by planting green cover than by green-harvesting. One interesting feature of her administration is that at harvest she requires her vineyard workers to toil in the winery, and vice versa, so that all her employees are familiar with the entire production process.

The vinification is traditional, and then the wines are taken down to the *chai* beneath the château. After malolactic fermentation in barrel, the wine is aged for twelve to fifteen months in one-third new oak, with regular rackings.

I had tasted the 2000 only *en primeur*, so was looking forward to tasting the wine in bottle when I visited the château. Alas, it was corked, and there was no replacement bottle. The 2001 has a rich plum and vanilla nose; the wine is lush and plump, almost forward, with a good deal of tannin though not a great deal of acidity. The 2002 is more muted aromatically, but the palate is supple and juicy, with soft tannins; the wine doesn't lack concentration but shows little zest. The 2003 wasn't picked until mid-September and the gamble paid off, resulting in an opulent wine, concentrated and tannic, with unusual vigour and length for the vintage. The 2004 has toasty plum, and liquorice aromas; it's a robust, chewy wine that lacks fluidity and vigour, but may become more harmonious with time. The 2005 is similar but has more bite and finesse.

Château Tour Maillet

*Tel: 0557 746163. **Owner:** Jean-Claude Lagardère. 2.2 ha. 100% Merlot. **Production:** 13,000 bottles*

This wine is a newcomer to the list of Pomerols, as until 1999 it was sold in bulk. In the late 1990s, however, Lagardĕre built a *chai* so that he could barrel-age the wine. The vines are planted on sandy gravel soil in a single parcel next to Bon Pasteur. The must is cold-soaked under dry ice for a few days before being fermented with selected yeasts in stainless-steel tanks. Lagardère practises micro-oxygenation *sous marc*. Until now the wine has been aged for twelve to sixteen months in fifty per cent new oak, but the proportion of new oak may be reduced in the future.

Both the 2000 and 2001 are excellent, with lush black-fruits aromas, ample richness, and firm tannins, yet without excessive extraction. Both are accessible but balanced, and should age well. I marginally prefer the 2000. The 2003 is supple and fruity though a touch hollow. New oak marks the 2004, an excellent wine, broad and succulent, with black-olive as well as black-cherry flavours, and fine persistence. Tour Maillet is a modern-style Pomerol that is worth keeping an eye on.

Château Trotanoy

*Tel: 0557 517896. **Owner:** Ets J.P. Moueix. 7 ha. 90% Merlot, 10% Cabernet Franc. **Production:** 40,000 bottles*

This wonderful property, already renowned in the late eighteenth century, was bought by Jean-Pierre Moueix in 1953. It is located on the western edge of the plateau, with a good deal of gravel on the top of the incline, and more clay in the lower sectors. The gravelly soils retain warmth, and this protected the vines during the frost of 1956, which left Trotanoy relatively unscathed. Many of those vines are still in production today. This is usually the first of Moueix's Pomerol estates to be harvested.

The grapes are sorted before and after destemming, then pumped into cement tanks. Until the mid-1980s a proportion of the stems was usually retained during fermentation. The wine is aged for about twenty months in fifty per cent new oak.

Trotanoy is unquestionably one of the greatest wines of Pomerol, and produced some highly esteemed wines in the 1960s and 1970s. What it may lack in power, it more than makes up for in perfume, flesh, and finesse. I recall the 1970, tasted in the late 1980s, as one of the loveliest Pomerols ever to come my way. It wasn't just the splendid fruit that impressed but the immense stylishness of the wine, its impeccable balance and superb length. Yet the same wine, tasted in the 1990s from magnum, seemed surprisingly austere. Which was the real Trotanoy? I like to think the earlier bottle.

In 1982, too, all the wine's components were in harmony: the oak, the very ripe fruit, the elegance and balance, the persistence of flavour. In comparison the 1985 seemed a bit lacklustre, failing to scale any great heights, though a perfectly good wine. In its youth the 1990 was silky and lean, and although reticent in flavour, immensely elegant and long. The 1993 was good for the year, a juicy, forward, spicy wine with a good dose of oak. The 1994 is better, though when young it had a slight rawness and chunkiness that robbed it of Trotanoy's customary elegance. The 2001 is glorious, with a gorgeous texture and immense opulence, yet all achieved without a hint of heaviness or clumsiness. The 2005, admittedly tasted in its infancy from cask, was sensational, with great purity of fruit, rich without any trace of flab, and amazingly long. And the 2006, also tasted from cask, seemed equally fine and the epitome of elegance. When Trotanoy is on form, which is most of the time, it is one of the supreme red wines of Bordeaux.

Château de Valois

*Tel: 0557 511977. **Owner:** Frédéric Leydet. 8 ha. 80% Merlot, 20% Cabernet Franc. **Production:** 45,000 bottles.*
Second wine: Ch La Croix St-Vincent

This property once formed part of the Figeac estate but became detached in 1862, when it was bought by Leydet's ancestors. It was given its present name in 1886. The vineyards are scattered among seven parcels, of which the best are on the plateau. The remainder are on different soil in southern Pomerol (a grander Pomerol proprietor once told me he thought the terroir here simply "awful"). The grapes are machine-picked, vinified in stainless steel, and aged for up to fifteen months in one-third new oak. Racking is kept to the minimum, as since 1999 the wines have been partially aged on the fine lees. I recall a light but characterless 1995, and a far more solid and hefty 2001, which had some power but little elegance. The 2004 is quite fragrant; although overtly fruity, it also has earthy tannins and seems too lean overall.

Vieux-Château-Certan

*Tel: 0557 511733. **Website:** www.vieuxchateaucertan.com. **Owner:** Alexandre Thienpont. 14 ha. 60% Merlot,*
*30% Cabernet Franc, 10% Cabernet Sauvignon. **Production:** 60,000 bottles. **Second wine:** La Gravette de Certan*

Of all the Bordeaux properties owned or managed by the extensive Thienpont clan, VCC (as it is often known) is surely the jewel in the crown. It has been run since 1985 by the diffident Alexandre Thienpont, who combines shyness with articulacy and high intelligence. He says that although the property dates back to the sixteenth century, little is known about its distant past, other than that it once formed part of a much larger property. From the mid-eighteenth century it was owned by the de May family, until bought in 1858 by a Parisian banker called de Bousquet, who gave the estate its present name. Georges Thienpont of Belgium acquired the property in 1924.

The vineyards are mostly in a single block, adjoining those of Pétrus, La Conseillante, and L'Evangile. The highest point of the Pomerol plateau lies just where the VCC vines meet those of Pétrus. Thus VCC shares some of Pétrus's celebrated buttonhole of clay. The other vines are on the other side of the St-Emilion road. What makes the vineyards unusual is that Merlot represents only sixty per cent of plantings, the choice of variety being dictated by the soil types found on the property. Thus the Merlot is planted on clay, the Cabernet Franc on strata of gravel with clay, as well as on pure gravel near the château, and the Cabernet Sauvignon on red gravel. The average age of the vines is some forty years.

Thienpont is fanatical about intelligent vineyard work, even adjusting the height of the trellising according to the climatic conditions each summer. He prunes to ensure that no vine delivers more than one kilo of fruit. The vineyard workers go through the vineyards very carefully before the harvest, removing any bunches or parts of bunches that show signs of uneven maturation or other problems. The grapes are then sorted in the vineyard during the harvest, but there is no *table de trie* at the winery, a piece of equipment Thienpont dismisses as "folklore".

The best fruit, from older vines, is vinified in wooden vats; the remainder in stainless steel. There is no gadgetry at VCC, and the vinification is entirely classic. Blending is progressive, after repeatedly blind-tasting the various lots. Thienpont points out that the best individual lots are not necessarily going to form the best possible wine; complementarity and balance are the most important criteria. The wine is aged for eighteen to twenty-two months in 100 per cent new oak with regular racking. The wine is eggwhite-fined but not filtered.

The high proportion of Cabernet makes it a very distinctive Pomerol, one with elegance rather than power. It must also be a challenge to produce, since the grower must ensure that the Cabernets ripen as fully as possible.

I have not tasted any venerable vintages. It is said that the 1970s, compared to the 1940s and 1950s, were a poor patch here, because of high yields and an absence of selection. Certainly the 1978 was mature and elegant by 1998 but rather lean; there were attractive cedary and peppery tones on the nose, but the palate was too gentle for anything of great interest to emerge. The 1981 was a charming wine that may now be past its best. I have not tasted the 1982 since the later 1980s, but then it was a lovely yet understated wine, elegant yet without the hedonistic quality of so many 1982 Pomerols. The 1985 is gloriously perfumed, with plummy aromas from the Merlot and a cedary character from the Cabernets; it's very concentrated, the texture is taut and sleek, and the wine is a long way from its peak.

The 1988, last tasted in 2001, was surprisingly meaty in aroma, and less elegant than usual on the palate, which was dense, concentrated, and long. The 1990 is classic, with generous blackcurrant and cedar aromas, and a richness of fruit on the palate balanced by a long, spicy finish. The 1994 is good for the vintage, refined yet marked by a hint of bitterness on the finish.

Elegance is the hallmark of the lovely 1996. It doesn't have the power of the 1998 but its intensity and restraint, its spiciness and finesse, are remarkably attractive. The 1998 is more sumptuous, with rich red fruits on the nose, even a hint of orange peel, while the palate is dense, concentrated, and chocolatey. The 1999 has charm and elegance, but also considerable opulence and structure. The 2000 is very rich and weighty, but seems quite low in acidity. Alexandre Thienpont prefers the 2001, which is certainly a wonderful wine, and so do I. Initially reticent on the nose, it is now showing a toasty black-fruits character, while the palate is delectable, fresh, yet unusually powerful. The 2002 is sleek, well structured, yet graceful. I have not tasted the 2003, but Thienpont is not excited by it, finding it rather baked. The 2004 has no Cabernet Sauvignon, yet there is no lack of freshness and finesse; the aromas are smoky and infused with red fruits, while the palate is rich, mineral, and concentrated. The 2005 has, from cask, tremendous elegance and concentration, backbone and length.

Château Vieux Maillet

Tel: 0557 745680. **Website:** *www.chateauvieuxmaillet.com.* **Owners:** *Hervé and Griet Laviale. 4.6 ha. 90% Merlot, 10% Cabernet Franc.* **Production:** *20,000 bottles*

Another property in the hamlet of Maillet, this has passed through various hands recently. In 1994 it was bought by Baudouin and Isabelle Motte, who then sold it to the present owners in 2003. The Laviales have also bought and restored the Château de Lussac in Lussac-St-Emilion and, more recently, Franc-Mayne in St-Emilion (*qq.v.*). They have hired Jean-Philippe Fort as their consultant oenologist.

The vines are in various parcels around Maillet, the soils being sandy clay with *crasse de fer*. The Cabernet Franc ripens about two weeks later than the Merlot. The wine used to be aged in ninety per cent new oak, but the Laviales decided this was excessive and reduced the proportion of new wood to one-third.

Vieux Maillet made a very good wine in 1998, an upfront blend of voluptuous aromas, rich, plump fruit, and good acidity. The 2000 is slightly disappointing: rich and supple, yet lacking some stuffing and vigour. The 2001 was more imposing, with an elegant, oaky nose, plenty of plump fruit, and a long, chocolatey finish; but by 2007 it was developing some meaty, funky, fruit-cake tones. Despite some hollowness, the 2003 is good for the vintage, but not for long ageing. The 2004 is richly fruity on nose and palate, yet has a fine attack, chewy but not harsh tannins, and fine structure and length.

Château La Violette

Tel: 0557 255645. **Owner:** *Catherine Péré-Vergé. 2 ha. 100% Merlot.* **Production:** *8,000 bottles*

This small property, well located between Le Pin and Trotanoy, languished in obscurity under the ownership of the Servant-Dumas family until 2006, when it was bought by the owner of Le Gay (*q.v.*). Michel Rolland supervised the winemaking. In an orgy of publicity-grabbing measures, the grapes were hand-destemmed and fermentation took place in new barrels. Early tastings of the 2006 suggest it will be an excellent wine with considerable power and pungency.

Château Vray Croix de Gay

Tel: 0557 516458. **Website:** *www.baronneguichard.com.* **Owner:** *Guichard family. 3.2 ha. 89% Merlot, 11% Cabernet Franc.* **Production:** *18,000 bottles.* **Second wine:** *L'Enchanteur de la Vray Croix de Gay*

This property was bought by Baron Louis Guichard in 1949. The Guichard family also own Le Prieuré (*q.v.*) in St-Emilion, under which entry the complex story of the family and its estates is recounted. Although the vineyard area is small, it is nonetheless divided into three plots, which border La Fleur-Pétrus, Le Gay, Le Pin, Rouget, and Trotanoy. The soil in general is clay and gravel. The vineyards are ploughed, leaf-thinned, and green-harvested. Recent replantings mean that the proportion of Cabernet Franc is set to increase. After picking the grapes are sorted twice. At present vinification takes place at Château Siaurac (*q.v.*) in Lalande de Pomerol. The wine is fermented in concrete tanks, usually with natural yeasts, though selected yeasts were used in 2005 to avoid a blocked fermentation. The *marc* is pressed in a vertical press, and the wine aged in one-third new barriques for twelve to sixteen months.

I have always liked this wine. The 1990 was delicious, yet had plenty of tannic support and the acidity to give it good length. The 2000 was a bit light for the vintage, but zesty and spicy and very enjoyable. The 2001 has a vibrant, oaky nose with lovely fruit and a chocolatey tone; the palate is immensely ripe and opulent, with flavours of plums and blackberries. The 2002 is relatively forward and lacks some complexity, but it's an attractive and balanced wine for medium-term drinking. There is a touch of boiled sweets and gumdrops on the nose of the 2003, but it's not jammy; the tannins are not harsh and the finish is pleasantly sweet – a good result for the vintage. The 2004 has exquisite oaky aromas and admirable concentration and spiciness, while the luxurious 2005 has both explosive fruitiness and powerful tannins that bode well.

23. The Satellites of Pomerol and St-Emilion

The appellations of Lalande de Pomerol, Lussac-St-Emilion, Montagne-St-Emilion, St-Georges-St-Emilion, and Puisseguin-St-Emilion don't much like the term "satellites" being applied to them. On the other hand they benefit from the hyphenated association with two prestigious regions of Bordeaux. Moreover, the clay-limestone soils of the St-Emilion satellites do not differ greatly from those of St-Emilion. However, the topography is different. The satellites are hillier, though there are plateau sectors as well, and the greater distance from the Dordogne River gives a somewhat cooler microclimate and thus later ripening. In short, the satellites are not quite as favoured as St-Emilion itself. There used to be an appellation called Parsac-St-Emilion, but in 1973 this was absorbed into Montagne-St-Emilion.

In the distant past the four St-Emilion satellites were part of the broader St-Emilion appellation. However in 1921 a legal ruling defined the present boundaries of St-Emilion. Respected growers such as Louis Rapin, from whom the large Despagne family is descended, fought the ruling, claiming, with some justification, that some parts of the new St-Emilion region had until recently been planted as wheatfields. He lost his battle, but secured the right for the satellites to precede the St-Emilion name with the name of their commune. There was a certain injustice here, as sectors of the newly defined St-Emilion district – notably those close to the Dordogne on alluvial soils – were clearly inferior in terms of their quality to the best clay-limestone slopes of the satellites. But medieval boundaries took precedence over geological precision, and the situation persists to this day and is unlikely ever to change. Jacques Capdemourlin, a leading grower both in St-Emilion and in Montagne, is convinced it would be a mistake for the satellites to campaign to rejoin St-Emilion itself. He believes that this would lead to a significant increase in volume which would itself result in lower prices that would damage all producers.

The soils with a high proportion of limestone – in particular the starfish limestone or *calcaire à astéries*, which is commonly found on the eastern sectors of the St-Emilion plateau – are those with the highest potential for quality. This soil type is found in all four satellites, but is less common in Lussac. I have asked many growers and winemakers whether, in a blind tasting, they would be able to differentiate one satellite from another; they all admitted that it would be extremely difficult.

Machine-picking is quite common, but far from ubiquitous. Since the wines, other than top *cuvées*, rarely command high prices, many producers feel an economic incentive to keep costs down. However, many estates are resolutely picked by hand. Others are run more pragmatically, with old vines picked by hand, and the remainder by machine.

This is a very large area, with almost 4,000 hectares of vineyards in the St-Emilion satellites and over 1,000 in Lalande de Pomerol. Taken together, they represent an area roughly equivalent to the whole of St-Emilion. Even though quality can be very good indeed, this adds up to a very large quantity of wine to sell. Many estates have made dramatic improvements in quality over the past decade; others still churn out substantial quantities of dilute and coarse wines. Is there still a market for the latter? It seems doubtful, given the current crisis in Bordeaux.

LALANDE DE POMEROL

North of Pomerol, on the far side of the Barbanne River, lies this fairly large region of 1,100 hectares, farmed by 180 growers. It was probably first developed in medieval times, when the Knights Hospitallers founded staging posts on the pilgrimage route to Santiago de Compostella. A fine Romanesque church remains at Lalande. One of the two communes, Néac, used to have its own AC (Néac-Pomerol), and the wines of Lalande were sold as Pomerol, but this came to a halt after a ruling in 1922. In 1954 INAO created the new AC by joining the two communes and changing the name of the region. Pomerol growers were none too happy with the link made to their prestigious region.

The soils are varied. In the eastern sector, around Néac, there is clay and clay-gravel; to the north gravel dominates, and as you move to the west, around Lalande itself, there is more sand as well as gravel. The two communes are separated by the RN89 that links Libourne and Périgueux. Néac is the hillier of the two

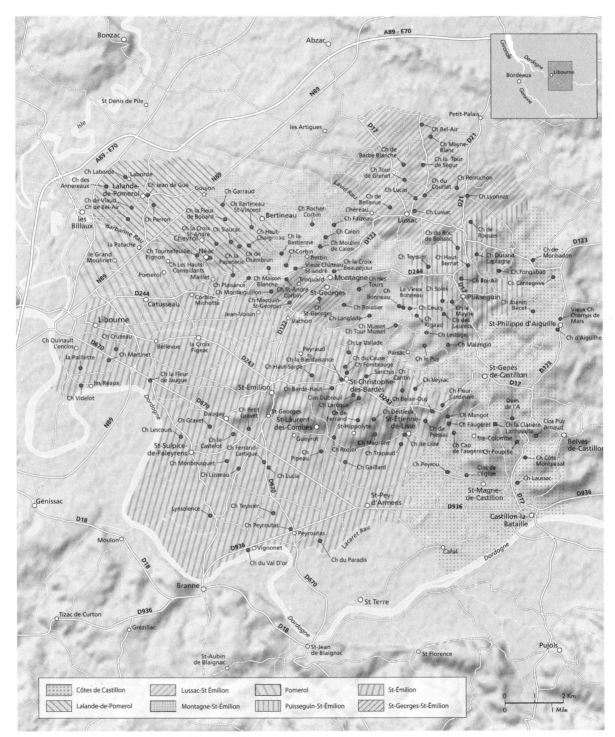

Bonzac

Abzac

A89 - E70

St Denis de Pile

les Artigues

Petit-Palais

Ch Bel-Air

Ch de Barbe Blanche

Ch Mayne-Blanc

Ch la Tour de Ségur

Ch Tour de Grenet

Ch du Courlat

Ch Perruchon

Ch Laborde

Laborde

Ch des Annereaux

Lalande-de-Pomerol

Ch Jean de Gué

Goujon

Ch Garraud

Ch de Viaud

Ch de Bel-Air

Ch Bertineau St-Vincent

Bertineau

Ch Rocher-Corbin

Ch de Bellevue

Ch Lucas

Ch Lussac

Ch Lyonnat

les Billaux

Ch la Fleur de Boüard

Chéreau

Lussac

Ch du Roc de Boissac

Ch de Roques

Ch la Croix St-André

Chevrol

Ch Siaurac

Ch Haut-Chaigneau

Ch Faizeau

Ch Calon

Ch Teyssier

Ch Haut-Bernat

Ch Durand Laplagne

Ch de Monbadon

D123

Barbanne Rau

la Patache

Ch Tournefeuille

Néac

Ch la Papeterie

Ch de Chambrun

Ch la Bastienne

ChCorbin

Ch Moulins de Calon

Ch Bel-Air

Ch Fongaban

Ch Cantegrive

le Grand Moulinet

Pignon

Ch Les Hauts-Conseillants

Maillet

Berlin

Vieux Château St-andré

Ch la Croix-Beauséjour

Ch des Tours

Puisseguin

Ch Joanin Bécot

Vieux Ch Champs de Mars

Pomerol

Ch Plaisance

Ch Maison Blanche

Troquard

Ch St-André Corbin

St-Georges

La Vieux Bonneau

Ch Soleil

Ch Bel-Air

Ch Coucy

St-Philippe d'Aiguilhe

Corbin-Michotte

Ch Montaiguillon

Ch Macquin St-Georges

Ch Bonneau

Ch Roudier

Montagne

Ch le Mayne

Ch des Laurets

Ch Rigaud

Ch d'Aiguilhe

Catusseau

Libourne

Jean-Voisin

Vachon

St-Georges

Ch Langlade

Ch Musset

Ch Tour Musset

Ch Lestage

Ch Malangin

St-Genès de-Castillon

Ch Cruzeau

la Croix Figeac

Peyraud

Ch la Vallade

Parsac

Ch le Puy

Ch Veyrac

Ch Fleur-Cardinale

D123

Ch Quinault L'enclos

Ch Martinet

Bellevue

Ch la Bienfaisance

Ch du Cause

Ch Fombrauge

Dom de l'A

la Paillette

Ch Haut-Sarpe

Sanctus

Ch Cantin

Ch Mangot

Clos Puy Arnaud

les Reaux

Ch la Fleur de Jaugue

St-Émilion

Ch Barde-Haut

Clos Dubreuil

St-Christophe des-Bardes

Ch Belair-Ou

Ch Destieux

Ch de Pressac

Ch Faugères

Ch la Clarière Laithwaite

Belvès-de-Castillon

Ch Videlot

Daugay

Ch Petit Gravet

St-Georges

Ch Laroque

St-Étienne-de-Lisse

Ste-Colombe

Ch Poupille

Ch Gravet

Ch Lescours

St-Laurent-des-Combes

Ch de Ferrand

St-Hippolyte

Ch Cap de Faugères

Ch Côte Montpezat

Gueyrot

Ch le Castelot

Ch Ferrand-Lartigue

Ch Rozier

Ch Maurens

Ch de Lisse

Ch Peyrou

Clos de l'Église

Ch Laussac

St-Sulpice-de-Faleyrens

Ch Monbousquet

Ch Pipeau

Ch Trapaud

St-Magne-de-Castillon

Ch Lusseau

Ch Lucia

Ch Gaillard

D936

Castillon-la-Bataille

Génissac

Lynsolence

Ch Teyssier

St-Pey-d'Armens

Catol

Dordogne

D18

Moulon

Ch Peyroutas

Peyroutas

Lacaret Rau

D936

Vignonet

Ch du Paradis

Ch du Val D'or

Branne

St Terre

Tizac de Curton

Grézillac

St-Aubin de Blaignac

St-Jean de Blaignac

St Florence

Pujols

Satellites of St-Emilion and Côtes de Castillon

Côtes de Castillon

Lussac-St Émilion

Pomerol

St-Émilion

Lalande-de-Pomerol

Montagne-St-Émilion

Puisseguin-St-Émilion

St-Georges-St-Émilion

2 Km

1 Mile

picked immediately after the Merlot had been brought in, and was often unripe. It is also more susceptible to disease and less long-lived than Merlot, so it is probable – unless global warming confounds forecasts – that it will decline.

Yields are higher than in Pomerol, and are usually between forty-seven and fifty-three hectolitres per hectare. Many of the vineyards are machine-picked, and much of the crop is sold in bulk. Nonetheless it is evident that some sectors are capable of producing rich, robust wines, and an increasing number of estates are aiming for better quality. If the wines had a lacklustre, rustic reputation in the past, this was probably the consequence of excessive yields and insufficient ripeness. The best producers have demonstrated that there is no intrinsic reason why the region should not make very good wines. The appellation has also benefited from the investments of successful outsiders such as Hubert de Boüard and Denis Durantou.

Château L'Ancien

Lalande. Tel: 0557 555858. Website: www.vln.fr. Owner: Nony family. 4 ha. 100% Merlot. Production: 8,000 bottles
This property is under the same ownership and management as the much larger Château Garraud (*q.v.*). As at Garraud, the wines are made by Vincent Duret. The first vintage here was 1997. The soils are deep gravel and clay-gravel, and the vines have an average age of forty years. Yields are low at around thirty hl/ha, and the grapes are picked by hand. Because the volumes are small, Duret has been able to experiment with barrel-fermentation, using both 225-litre and 400-litre barrels. The wine is aged for eighteen months in entirely new oak. The only vintage I have tasted, the 2003, had boiled-sweets aromas, but was rich, rounded, concentrated, and lightly spicy; the oak was well integrated and overall the wine showed some elegance.

Château de Bel Air

Lalande. Tel: 0557 744311. Owner: Stephen Adams. 15 ha. 75% Merlot, 15% Cabernet Franc,
5% Cabernet Sauvignon, 5% Malbec. Production: 72,000 bottles
These vineyards lie on an elevated site overlooking the Barbanne River. In the past it enjoyed a high reputation, but had become run-down in recent years. In 2005 it was bought by the American investor who acquired Fonplégade (*q.v.*) in St-Emilion in 2004, so it is safe to assume that quality will leap upwards. I have yet to taste the wine.

Château Bertineau St Vincent

Néac. Tel: 0557 512305. Owner: Rolland family. 5 ha. 75% Merlot, 25% Cabernet Franc. Production: 18,000 bottles
This property belongs to the celebrated oenologists Michel and Dany Rolland. The vines are over thirty years old, and are picked by hand. The grapes are sorted, then crushed over the tanks, so that no pumping is required. The wine is aged up to fifteen months in oak. The 2001 was a very good wine, with cherry fruit on the nose and palate, a lively texture, moderate tannins, and a clean finish. The 2003, however, is overripe and confected, with a dour finish.

Château La Borderie-Mondésir

Lalande. Tel: 0557 490610. Website: www.vignoblesrousseau.com. Owner: Laurent Rousseau. 2.2 ha. 95% Merlot,
5% Cabernet Sauvignon. Production: 5,000 bottles
The Rousseau family own a number of properties in the satellites. Here the vines, planted on gravelly soils, are over forty years old, and give wines of considerable concentration. The Cuvée Excellence, first made in 1999, comes from the oldest parcels, and is aged entirely in new barriques.

The 1999 has some charm and elegance on the nose, but is more rustic and tough on the palate. The 2001 is far better, with black-cherry fruit, a plumpness that comes close to opulence, and some spice and vigour. The 2002 seems rather extracted and the finish is quite dry; and the 2003 is baked and dense. The 2004 shows a lighter touch; it's supple, not too concentrated, yet there is some extraction evident on the finish.

I am not convinced the Cuvée Excellence is better. The 2000 is burly, concentrated, and oaky, with richness but little finesse. The 2001 is overdone, with some rubber-tyre aromas and a chunkiness on the palate that obscures the richness of fruit. The 2002 is fresher, but not significantly better than the regular bottling. The 2003 is extreme: not baked, but bitter on the finish, with fierce tannins. The 2004 has plummy aromas, and is plump, concentrated, and chocolatey on the palate.

Château de Chambrun
Néac. Tel: 0557 259119. Owner: Jean-Philippe Janoueix. 1.7 ha. 97% Merlot, 3% Cabernet Franc.
Production: 9,000 bottles

Jean-Philippe is the most dynamic member of this wine-producing family, developing and running properties in St-Emilion, Pomerol, and here in Néac. He bought this property on the Néac plateau in 1994, and has established it as one of the region's leading estates. Michel Rolland acts as a consultant. There is a good deal of clay as well as gravel in the soil, so the wine tends to be robust. After destemming by hand, the grapes are fermented in cement tanks, with pumpovers and *délestage*. Chambrun is aged in new oak for eighteen months. The 2000, with its sweet, minty nose, was a delicious wine, rich and rounded, but also with some depth and bite and a lively finish. The 2003 is extremely powerful, with fifteen degrees of alcohol, and the nose is dominated by new oak; the palate is lush, with ample cherry fruit, and more swagger than finesse, yet the high alcohol is not discernible.

Château Les Cruzelles
Lalande. Tel: 0557 259659. Owner: Christian Pichon. 10 ha. 50% Merlot, 50% Cabernet Franc.
Production: 15,000 bottles

Denis Durantou is the admired owner of the superb Pomerol estate L'Eglise-Clinet. He leased Les Cruzelles in 2000, and the house is just visible from L'Eglise-Clinet. He had to replant four hectares, so the vineyards, which are in a single parcel, are not yet in full production. The soil is clay and gravel, similar, says Durantou, to the Pomerol plateau. The high proportion of Cabernet Franc is highly unusual for this Merlot-dominated region. He also produces a wine from purchased fruit called La Chenade; it comes from vines planted in soils of gravelly sand, and is aged in one-third new oak.

The 2001 is a weighty, tannic wine, with rich plummy aromas - robust rather than elegant. The 2002 seems even better and unusually concentrated and structured for this tricky vintage; fine acidity kicks in on the mid-palate, giving the wine freshness and length. The 2003 is solid, with some grip but little charm. I prefer the predecessors. La Chenade is a much more slight and easy-going wine, with delicate cherry aromas. The 1998 is the best of the recent vintages I have tasted.

Enclos de Viaud
Lalande. Tel: 0557 553803. Owner: group of investors. 3.6 ha. 80% Merlot, 20% Cabernet Franc.
Production: 20,000 bottles

Enclos de Viaud has since 1991 been owned by a consortium of investors under the umbrella of the Société Générale bank; it also owns La Patache (*q.v.*) in Pomerol. The vinification is almost identical to that at La Patache. About half the wine is aged in one-third new oak; the rest is tank-aged. The only vintage I have tasted is the chewy 2001, which is rich and concentrated and has a rude charm and reasonable length.

La Fleur de Boüard
Tel: 0557 252513. Website: www.lafleurdebouard.com. Owner: Hubert de Boüard de Laforest. 20 ha. 85% Merlot,
10% Cabernet Franc, 5% Cabernet Sauvignon. Production: 80,000 bottles. Second wine: Ch La Fleur St-Georges

This property belonged to an insurance company until 1998, when it was bought by Hubert de Boüard of Angélus (*q.v.*). Michel Rolland is the oenological consultant. De Boüard was fortunate in that the vineyards had been well cared for. Some eleven hectares are on sandy clay over gravel, but the best sector is in Lalande in a single 8.5-hectare block with deep, stony gravel and some clay. De Boüard and his estate director Philippe Nunes have undertaken some improvements, heightening the trellising and replanting some vines to a density of 8,500 per hectare, making this block the most densely planted of any in the region. Yields vary from thirty to forty-five hl/ha. Hubert de Boüard admits that although about half the vineyards are on superb terroir, the rest is far from outstanding. Although the wine isn't as fine as a great Pomerol, he believes it is better than about half of the Pomerols produced.

After manual harvesting and sorting, fermentation takes place in stainless-steel tanks, but the malolactic fermentation proceeds in barriques. The wine is aged for eighteen to twenty-four months in seventy-five per cent new oak in the air-conditioned *chai*. There is no systematic racking, and no fining or filtration.

In addition there is a special *cuvée* called Le Plus, first made in 2000 from forty-year-old vines, almost entirely Merlot, grown on the stoniest soils. Yields are reduced to a fairly extreme twenty hl/ha. The grapes are destemmed by hand, then fermented in wooden vats with *pigeage*; some of the must is vinified in very squat steel tanks. The wine is aged for thirty-three months in 100 per cent new oak. Production is very limited, and only about 3,500 bottles are released.

La Fleur de Boüard is impressive. The 2000 has remained very closed on the nose, but is rich and full-bodied, with flavours of plums and chocolate, and some spicy overtones. It's a bit of a bruiser but more accessible than the very concentrated, tannic 2001. The 2002 has sweet, plummy, oaky aromas, and is concentrated and weighty for the vintage; it is a bit extracted – which de Boüard wine isn't? – without being over-dense. The 2003 has very toasty aromas, while the palate is decidedly chewy, yet seems slightly hollow; like so many wines of the vintage, it lacks acidity.

The 2001 Le Plus has a massive oaky presence on the nose; it's very rich and highly concentrated, but has sufficient freshness to keep it lively and balanced. It supports the long barrel-ageing in new wood with surprising success. In contrast, the 2002 seems overworked: very toasty on the nose, but entirely dominated by oak on the palate and lacking some zest.

The wines are among the most expensive of any from the satellites, but they are undoubtedly impressive.

Château Garraud

Néac. Tel: 0557 555858. Website: www.vln.fr. Owner: Nony family. 19 ha. 95% Merlot, 5% Cabernet Franc.
Production: 90,000 bottles. Second wine: Graves de Goujon

Léon Nony, a Libourne-based négociant, bought this property in 1939, and today it is run by his grandson Jean-Marc. Until the mid-1980s most of the wine was sold in bulk. Since 1994 Vincent Duret has been running the estate and making its wines. The *chai* and the eighteenth-century hunting lodge are rather austere neo-classical buildings, but behind them are more modern installations, including ultra-modern offices and workers' housing.

The soils are very varied, ranging from deep gravel to sand and including a parcel of pure clay over *crasse de fer*. The major portion of the vineyards lies close to Montagne-St-Emilion. The vines are on average some forty years old. Some of the vineyards are picked by hand, but Duret favours machine-harvesting if the grapes are healthy. Fermentation takes place in steel tanks, with occasional use of micro-oxygenation, although Duret is not very keen on the practice. The wine is aged for twelve months in forty per cent new oak, and, depending on the vintage, some lots are kept in tanks and blended in with the oaked lots. The same team also vinify Châteaux Treytins and L'Ancien (*qq.v.*).

The 2001 is generously fruity on the nose; the wine is rich and full-bodied, but has a leathery finish. The 2002 is more discreet aromatically, but very pure; it's sleek and stylish, with moderate concentration and firm tannins on the finish. Overall, it lacks the energy of the 2001. The aromas of the 2003 are a touch confected, and the palate, which shows attractive cherry fruit, is rather hollow. In general these are well-made and reliable commercial wines.

Château Grand Ormeau

Lalande. Tel: 0557 253020. Owner: Jean-Claude Beton. 14 ha. 64% Merlot, 18% Cabernet Franc,
18% Cabernet Sauvignon. Production: 80,000 bottles. Second wine: Chevalier d'Haurange

It was Robert Parker who first brought this wine to my (and others') attention almost twenty years ago at a tasting in London. However, two years later Grand Ormeau was sold. The purchaser, Jean-Claude Beton, was the founder of the Orangina company, perhaps not the most encouraging qualification. He built a new winery, and bought five more hectares near Néac. The soils are varied, but are mostly gravel and sand over a subsoil of clay and *crasse de fer*. Some parcels are exceptionally stony. The high proportion of Cabernet Sauvignon is unusual, and the estate's wine-maker André Femenia, who has been here since 1990, was told it wouldn't fare well here; but he finds that with improved drainage, short pruning, and low yields, it does ripen and adds a good deal of structure. The vineyards are ploughed, with some rows planted with green cover to reduce vigour.

The younger vines, destined for the second wine, are machine-harvested, while vines over twenty years old are picked by hand. After a brief cold soak, the grapes are crushed over the tanks. The must is fermented in squat steel tanks and wooden vats. Femenia favours indigenous yeasts, but in super-ripe years such as 2005 will choose selected yeasts. The wine used to be aged for twelve months in sixty per cent new oak, but this has now been reduced to one-third, though it is unclear whether this is an economy measure or a reaction to perceived overoaking.

There is also, since 2001, a *garagiste* wine called Cuvée Madeleine, from three hectares of older vines cropped at thirty-five hl/ha. The grapes receive a longer cold soak, and are fermented in wooden vats with *pigeage*. The wine used to be aged for eighteen months entirely in new oak, but for this *cuvée* the proportion of new wood is also being reduced, in this case to forty per cent. There is no fining or filtration. The production is around 10,000 bottles.

The wine Parker presented was the 1982, and it was immensely fruity. I later bought a bottle and the second encounter with it was more disappointing, with some vegetal aromas and astringency. Perhaps I had a bottle that was out of condition. It hardly matters now, since these are not wines that one cellars for two decades. More recently, I have enjoyed the successful 2002, despite a whack of vanilla on the overoaked nose; the texture is rich and rounded, and the tannins are ripe. The nose of the 2003 is a bit overpowering – too much oak, again – but there's an appealing juiciness on the palate, though its fruitiness is slightly marred by a rather dry finish. The 2004 is excellent: plummy and opulent on the nose, and surprisingly powerful on the palate, yet balanced by good acidity and firm tannins.

As for Cuvée Madeleine, I did not find the 2002 superior to the regular bottling; indeed, the oak was too overwhelming, and overall it seemed heavy-handed. Aromatically, the 2003 is overpowering, with jammy fruit and sweet oak; this overripe style is too fatiguing for my taste. The 2004 is in the same mould, though less extreme.

Château La Gravière
Néac. Tel: 0557 255645. Website: www.montviel.com. Owner: Catherine Péré-Vergé. 7 ha. 80% Merlot,
20% Cabernet Franc. Production: 35,000 bottles. Second wine: Ch Moulin-La Gravière

This small estate, a stone's throw from Château Rouget in Pomerol, was bought in 1985 by Catherine Péré-Vergé, the owner of Le Gay (*q.v.*) in Pomerol. A few years ago she bought a further five hectares which is mostly used for the second wine. La Gravière is aged in fifty per cent new oak; Moulin-La Gravière is less concentrated and has a far larger production of 30,000 bottles. Much of the wine is sold to the group of restaurants controlled by Alain Ducasse, as Mme. Péré-Vergé is a shareholder. The only vintage I have tasted, the 2005, has smoky, oaky aromas and considerable density; but it lacks some lift on the finish.

Château Haut-Chaigneau
Néac. Tel: 0557 513131. Owner: André Chatonnet. 28 ha. 70% Merlot, 15% Cabernet Franc,
15% Cabernet Sauvignon. Production: 160,000 bottles. Second wine: Ch Tour St-André

André Chatonnet created this property from 1977 onwards, and today it is one of the most impressive in the region. He is aided by his son Pascal, an oenological consultant and the leading authority on TCA taint (and what to do about it). The soil here is silty clay with some *crasse de fer*, with other parcels of gravelly clay. The average age of the vines is an impressive forty years. The vineyards have been machine-picked since 1982. After sorting, the grapes are vinified in steel tanks. The wine is aged for twelve to fifteen months in fifty per cent new barriques, with blending toward the end of the *élevage*. Fining is not systematic and there is no filtration.

In 1996 the Chatonnets first made a special bottling they call Château La Sergue. The grapes are grown on a five-hectare parcel on silty sand on the plateau near the village of Chevrol. There is more Merlot in this wine, the yields are lower than for Haut-Chaigneau, harvesting is manual, and fermentation takes place in wooden vats. The wine is aged for fourteen to sixteen months in 100 per cent new oak. Only about 18,000 bottles are produced.

The 1998 Haut-Chaigneau is still youthful, with a sweet, toasty nose of plums and coffee. The palate is juicy and concentrated, and backed by good acidity and firm tannins. The 2001 is even better, with black fruits on the nose and palate, and the oak is well integrated, giving a long, sweet finish.

The 1998 La Sergue is more lush thanks to the high proportion of Merlot, and there's no doubting its ripeness and opulence; despite a touch of overripeness, there is liquorice and spice on the palate, and the finish is long. In 2001, I marginally prefer the Haut-Chaigneau, which has more zest than the tarry La Sergue. Nonetheless, these are among the best and most dependable wines of Lalande de Pomerol.

Château Haut-Surget

Néac. Tel: 0557 512868. Owner: Patrick Fourreau. 35 ha. 70% Merlot, 15% Cabernet Franc, 15% Cabernet Sauvignon. Production: 200,000 bottles. Second wine: Ch Lafleur Vauzelle

This substantial property, with vineyards divided between Néac and Lalande, has been in the Fourreau family for five generations. About half the grapes are picked by machine. They are fermented in cement tanks with selected yeasts, followed by a lengthy post-fermentation maceration. There is occasional micro-oxygenation *sous marc*. Fourreau likes the wine to go into barrels after malolactic fermentation in as clean a condition as possible, so that he can minimize the racking. The wine is aged for twelve months in forty per cent new oak, of which one-fifth is American oak.

In 2000 Fourreau introduced an old-vine selection, mostly Merlot, that he called La Grande Sélection. This receives an even longer *cuvaison*, usually around six weeks, and is aged for up to eighteen months in new oak. It is made only in top vintages, and some 10,000 bottles are released.

My experience of these wines is limited. The 2003 had rich black-cherry aromas; the palate was certainly dense, with firm and furry tannins, yet the wine had grip and was far from flabby. The 2000 Grande Sélection is dominated aromatically by new oak, but this is a very ripe and concentrated wine, yet with some freshness.

Château Les Hauts-Conseillants

Néac. Tel: 0557 516217. Owner: Pierre Bourotte. 10 ha. 75% Merlot, 17% Cabernet Franc, 8% Cabernet Sauvignon. Production: 60,000 bottles. Second wine: Ch Les Hautes Tuileries

Pierre Bourotte and his son Jean-Baptiste are the owners of the excellent Pomerol estates of Bonalgue and Clos du Clocher (*qq.v.*). This property is spread over both Néac and Lalande communes, although two-thirds of the vineyards are near the village of Chevrol. Thus both principal soil types are represented. The Bourottes keep yields to reasonable levels, and harvest by hand. After double sorting, the wine is fermented in steel tanks with a lengthy *cuvaison*, then aged for eighteen months in forty per cent new oak. Jean-Philippe Fort is the oenological consultant.

These are very good wines, although the 2003, despite its dense, plummy aromas, is a brute, with rough tannins and a dry finish. However the 2001 is exemplary, well balanced and lively. The 2002 displays fine blackcurrant aromas; it's supple and forward wine with good acidity and freshness.

Château Jean de Gué

Musset. Tel: 0557 401576. Website: www.la-couspaude.com. Owner: Jean-Claude Aubert. 10 ha. 75% Merlot, 20% Cabernet Franc, 5% Cabernet Sauvignon. Production: 55,000 bottles. Second wine: Dom de Musset

Jean-Claude Aubert owns La Couspaude (*q.v.*) in St-Emilion, and numerous other properties. He bought the former Domaine de Musset in 1983 and promptly changed its name. Seven of the ten hectares are on gravel soil, three on more sandy soil. The grapes are picked by hand, and fermented in wooden vats with *pigeage*. Aubert, who is advised by Michel Rolland, favours a submerged-cap fermentation here, sometimes with micro-oxygenation. Thus Aubert used it in 2004 but not in 2005. Most of the wine is aged in fifty per cent new oak; a small part of the crop is aged in wooden or steel vats. Rather confusingly, some labels bear the term Cuvée Prestige but this is in fact the regular bottling.

Aubert likes to pick at the edge of overripeness, and it shows on these wines, which are weighty and solid, with super-ripe aromas. The 2001 is particularly impressive. The silky 2002 shows very high ripeness for the vintage, but is less opulent on the palate, with ample acidity giving good length. The 2003 is more jammy and charred on the nose. It's robust but not earthy, with ample fruit and a slightly bitter finish. Both 2004 and 2005 are very successful, with sweet, oaky aromas, robust tannins countered by fine freshness, and an accessible but structured style.

Château Laborde

Lalande. Tel: 0557 743052. Website: www.roy-trocard.com. Owner: Jean-Marie Trocard. 21 ha. 80% Merlot, 10% Cabernet Franc, 10% Cabernet Sauvignon. Production: 180,000 bottles

The Trocards are a family with deep roots here and in Fronsac. Jean Trocard claims to be the fifteenth generation of his family to grow vines here; the succession has passed through the female line. The soil here is sandy gravel with a subsoil of *crasse de fer*. It's not a heavy soil so Trocard finds it gives elegant rather than powerful wines. The vineyards are cultivated according to *lutte raisonnée*. About half the grapes are picked by hand. The must is fermented in cement and steel tanks, using both indigenous and selected yeasts, depending on the vintage. About eighty per cent of the wine is aged in tanks, the remainder in oak. Since 2004 Trocard has left the wine on its fine lees during the *élevage* so as to give it more weight. There is no systematic fining or filtration.

There is also a special *cuvée* called 1628, this being the date when the Trocards' ancestors acquired this property. This is aged in one-third new oak. It is a surprisingly lean wine, even in a vintage such as 2001. Even the 2003 shows astringency, and the 2002 is decidedly green.

Château Pavillon Bel-Air

Néac. Tel: 0557 511336. Owner: Crédit Foncier. 8 ha. 60% Merlot, 40% Cabernet Franc. Production: 40,000 bottles

This is owned by the bank that also owns Beauregard in Pomerol and Bastor-Lamontagne in Sauternes (*qq.v.*). The Beauregard team looks after this estate, which was acquired in 2003. Most of the vines are on the plateau of Néac on clay-gravel soil with a mostly clay subsoil. The gravel component aids the ripening, which is precocious here. The grapes are picked manually, sorted, gently crushed, then fermented in concrete tanks. The wine is aged for twelve to sixteen months in one-third new barriques, then eggwhite-fined before bottling. There is also a superior bottling called Le Chapelain, drawn from two plots of old vines in Lalande, one planted with Cabernet Franc, the other with Merlot. This is aged for eighteen months in fifty per cent new barriques.

It is too early to assess the quality of the wine here, as the atypical 2003 was the first vintage. The regular bottling has a jammy nose, with nuances of woodsmoke and coffee; on the palate it's supple, sweet, and forward, with some spiciness. Le Chapelain has a curious jelly-baby nose; by 2007 it seemed supple and fully ready, a pleasant wine but lacking in bite and length.

Château Perron

Lalande. Tel: 0557 513597. Owner: Bertrand Massonie. 15 ha. 80% Merlot, 10% Cabernet Franc, 10% Cabernet Sauvignon. Production: 100,000 bottles. Second wine: Ch Pierrefitte

The wine merchant Jean Massonie bought this attractive house and property in the 1950s. It was then run by his genial son Michel-Pierre, who in turn handed the reins to his son Bertrand in 2001. About two-thirds of the vineyards lie in a single parcel around the house on a remarkably uniform soil of large stones over clay and gravel. Harvesting is both manual and mechanical. The vinification is modern: after a lengthy cold soak, the must is fermented in cement tanks, with micro-oxygenation *sous marc*. Temperature control was installed only in the late 1990s. Indigenous yeasts are favoured, except in super-ripe years such as 2005. The wine is aged for twelve months in twenty-five per cent new oak. Bertrand tastes each year with the six coopers from whom he orders barrels, and after a blind tasting he eliminates one of them and selects a replacement. Jean-Philippe Fort acts as the Massonies' oenological consultant.

In 1997 a new wine was created, Cuvée La Fleur, sourced from a five-hectare block, though further selection follows after fermentation. This wine is aged in at least eighty per cent new oak for twelve months, without racking.

Perron is a consistently good wine. The 1982 was still going strong in 2005, with truffle aromas and surprising freshness; it's not hugely concentrated or weighty, yet it is perfectly balanced. A similar lack of concentration is evident in more recent vintages. This is not a criticism. Concentration of flavour is certainly a positive attribute, but it should not be regarded as a cult. We need wines not produced from exaggeratedly low yields, wines that are a pleasure to drink yet affordable. Perron fits nicely into that category. The 2001 has aromas of black cherries; red fruits such as strawberries and cherries mark the 2002. Both wines are supple, approachable, and finely balanced. The 2003 is more baked and chocolatey, but there are no harsh tannins and no lack of length, despite the wine's low acidity. The 2005 is exemplary, fleshy and concentrated, yet balanced and accessible, with a long, fresh finish.

Where La Fleur differs from Perron is not so much in concentration as in complexity. The 1998 has an oaky nose with aromas of cherries and vanilla, a sleek texture, charm, and freshness. The 2000 is a disappointment, lacking some acidity and grip, and 2001 seems rather dilute and fades on the finish. The 2002 is very oaky, but has surprising complexity, with good acidity and a rather tannic finish. The 2003 is a success for the year, plump, concentrated, and suave. The 2005 is succulent and concentrated but fresh and long.

I am not sure that La Fleur is notably superior in quality to the basic wine. It certainly shows more oak influence, but seems to be trying hard, whereas the regular wine has an immediate drinkability and vigour, thanks to ripe fruit and confident winemaking.

Château Sergant

Lalande. Tel: 0557 554890. Website: www.milhade.com. **Owner:** *Milhade family. 18 ha. 75% Merlot, 20% Cabernet Sauvignon, 5% Cabernet Franc.* **Production:** *100,000 bottles*

The Milhade family are négociants based in Galgon. They also own numerous properties in the Libournais, and they are working hard to improve the quality of their wines. The Sergant vines are on light gravel and sand soils in the northwest of the region. The grapes are picked mechanically and by hand. Half the wine is aged in one-third new barriques, half in tank. The 2002 is very fragrant, and it is supple, sleek, and easy-going on the palate. The 2003 is more baked and chunky, with obtrusive tannins and little finesse; but it has plenty of fruit. Curiously, the Milhades still offer vintages from the 1960s for sale, confirming that the wines of that time were made in a different style.

Château La Sergue

See *Ch Haut-Chaigneau*

Château Siaurac

Néac. Tel: 0557 516458. Website: www.baronneguichard.com. **Owner:** *Guichard family. 59 ha. 80% Merlot, 20% Cabernet Franc.* **Production:** *200,000 bottles.* **Second wine:** *Plaisir de Siaurac*

The Guichards have been here since 1919, and on the maternal line, the family have been in place since 1832. The rather complex details of the family's ownership and management of their various properties are given in the entry for their St-Emilion property of Le Prieuré (*q.v.*). Benjamin Brisson built the fine château and laid out its park in the 1850s, and one of his descendants married Baron Louis Guichard in 1919.

At the time of writing, the vineyards occupy about forty hectares but they are being expanded. They consist of adjoining parcels on varied soils: there is a block on gravelly soil near the Néac church, another near La Fleur de Boüard, others near the château. The soil is ploughed, and there is no use of insecticides. The old vines are picked by hand, the remainder by machine. After a four-day cold soak, fermentation follows in concrete tanks, using indigenous yeasts in all but the ripest years such as 2005. The *marc* is pressed in vertical presses. The wine is aged for twelve months in twenty per cent new barriques, although about one-fifth of the wine stays in tanks.

The second wine is a pure Merlot, mostly aged in tanks. In 2005 a rosé was introduced for the first time. In 1982 I encountered an English bottling of the 1970 – forgettable. The 2001 has discreet plummy oakiness on the nose; it's a wine with some concentration and weight, balanced and long if not exactly zesty. The 2002 has more red-fruits aromas and less grip but it's supple, balanced, and enjoyable. The 2003 is more dense and tannic, but lacks finesse. The 2004 has fragrant cherry aromas, and surprising density and assertiveness on the palate, although the balance is superior to that of the 2003. The 2005 resembles the 2001. Overall, these are well-made, enjoyable wines, and I suspect the Guichards are keen to make them even better.

Château Tournefeuille

Néac. Tel: 0557 511861. Website: www.chateau-tournefeuille.com. **Owner:** *François Petit. 15 ha. 70% Merlot, 30% Cabernet Franc.* **Production:** *75,000 bottles.* **Second wine:** *Ch Rosalcy*

François Petit comes from an agricultural background, but his enthusiasm for wine was that of the amateur. In 1998 he decided to acquire a wine estate while he still had the energy to develop it, and he bought Tournefeuille. His son Emeric caught the wine bug fast, studied at Bordeaux University, and now runs this and the other family properties.

Tournefeuille is splendidly situated, with half the vineyards on the clay plateau next to the church, the other half on the slopes descending toward the Barbanne River. Much of the Cabernet Franc is planted at the foot of the slope, but it doesn't ripen easily and is never used for the main wine. Yields rarely exceed forty hl/ha, and the harvest is manual. Fermentation takes place in small cement tanks, usually but not systematically with natural yeasts. A small part of the crop is fermented in 400-litre barrels, which François Petit believes give more supple tannins. The wine is aged for twelve to fourteen months in one-third new oak.

The 2000 has attractive cherry aromas, but it's light for the vintage, with slightly rustic tannins. Tournefeuille hit its stride with the 2001, which is far more generous in its fruit, giving a fleshy wine with some backbone and freshness. The 2002 is a touch lighter but has elegance, freshness, and a long, spicy finish. The 2003 has no stewed character, and the clay soils seem to have preserved the wine's fruit and lushness and the tannins, while chewy, are not hard. In just a few years Tournefeuille has become one of the appellation's best wines.

Château Treytins

Néac. Tel: 0557 555858. Website: www.vln.fr. **Owner:** *Nony family. 11 ha. 55% Cabernet Franc, 45% Merlot.* **Production:** *50,000 bottles*

Like the larger Château Garraud (*q.v.*), this property belongs to the Nony family and is run by Vincent Duret. Clay and gravel dominate the well-drained soils. The grapes are picked by hand and by machine. The wine is aged partly in older barrels and partly in tanks. The only vintage I have tasted is the very ripe but rather confected 2003, which has modest length and a rather dry finish. The high proportion of Cabernet Franc is unusual here, and I wonder what effect it has on the wine in more conventional vintages.

Three more hectares fall within the Montagne-St-Emilion appellation and are vinified and labelled separately. The wine is made in exactly the same way, but the grape mix is very different: eighty-five per cent Merlot and fifteen per cent Cabernet Franc. The 2002 lacks concentration and vigour, while the glossy 2003 has boiled-sweets aromas, ripe, easy-going fruit, and modest length.

Château de Viaud

Lalande. Tel: 0556 504280. Owner: Philippe Raoux. 21 ha. 65% Merlot, 31% Cabernet Franc, 4% Cabernet Sauvignon. Production: 100,000 bottles. Second wine: Ch du Grand Chambellan

In the eighteenth century there were already documented references to Viaud's wines. The estate was bought in 2002 by the art-loving Philippe Raoux, who is best known for his revitalization of Château d'Arsac (*q.v.*) in Margaux. About three-quarters of the vineyards are in a single block on gravelly soil over a clay subsoil; lower sectors are more sandy. The soil is ploughed and the grapes are picked by hand.

After sorting and a cold soak, the wines are fermented with selected yeasts in stainless-steel tanks, with occasional use of micro-oxygenation. The wine is aged for twelve months in fifty per cent new barriques, and the final blend is made up late. Before bottling, the wine is eggwhite-fined and filtered.

This is a remarkably consistent wine. Having tasted all vintages from 2000 to 2005, I find there is little to choose between them in terms of quality (2003 perhaps trails slightly), though they do of course reflect vintage variations. The oak aromas are quite pronounced, but the wood is better integrated on the palate, which always has bright ripe fruit, fair acidity, and good balance and length. However, the stern 2005 seems unusually extracted.

Château Vieux Rivière

Néac. Tel: 0557 250865. Owner: Rivière family. 5 ha. 88% Merlot, 6% Cabernet Franc, 6% Cabernet Sauvignon. Production: 32,000 bottles

Romain Rivière is the young oenologist who also runs Croix-Taillefer (*q.v.*) in Pomerol. This vineyard on the Néac plateau is planted on clay-gravel soil, and picked by hand. In 2003 he produced for the first time a special *cuvée* called Bonne Rive, from vines cropped at very low levels and aged twenty-eight months in new oak. The 2003 tasted unpleasantly jammy.

There are some other properties in Lalande de Pomerol that are worth keeping an eye on.

Château Bel Air Edmund Penning-Rowsell was an admirer of this wine some decades ago. I have never tasted it, but the estate has been purchased by the same reclusive but deep-pocketed American investor who owns Fonplégade (*q.v.*) in St-Emilion.

Château de la Commanderie The wines are apparently of little interest (though I have not tasted them) but other growers inform me that the terroir is of the highest quality.

Château St-Jean-de-Lavaud This tiny 1.1-hectare property has been owned since 2003 by the Laviale family, who also own Franc-Mayne in St-Emilion and Château de Lussac (*qq.v.*). Laurence Ters is the winemaker, with advice from Jean-Philippe Fort. I have not tasted the wine. Only 8,000 bottles are produced.

LUSSAC-ST-EMILION

This is the most northerly of the satellites. In medieval times the Cistercian abbey of Faize maintained the vineyards, and the abbot bore the title of Baron de Lussac. Much of the wine was dispatched to the ecclesiastical establishments of Bordeaux, which helped establish its reputation.

Its 1,440 hectares are, overall, planted with sixty-five per cent Merlot, twenty per cent Cabernet Franc, and fifteen per cent Cabernet Sauvignon. The soils are very varied, with clay-gravel and silt in the valleys, clay-sand on the plateau over on the west side, dense clay to the east, and clay-limestone on many slopes. Inevitably the geological facts on the ground are less clear-cut. The more northerly parts of Lussac have richer and thus more fertile soils, often with a good deal of gravel, than those farther south. These are not always well suited to viticulture. Late ripening can also be a problem in some years. André Chatenoud of Château de Bellevue notes that the region is traversed by bands of limestone, and many of the best estates are located on these bands. The limestone's contribution to the wine is to preserve good levels of acidity.

There are over 100 growers. The cooperative controls forty per cent of the total production, which stands at around ten million bottles.

Château de Barbe-Blanche

Tel: 0557 745652. Website: www.andrelurton.com. Owner: André Lurton. 28 ha. 70% Merlot, 20% Cabernet Franc, 10% Cabernet Sauvignon. Production: 170,000 bottles. Second wine: Ch Tour de Ségur

This attractive property belonged to André Magnon until 2000, when André Lurton (owner of La Louvière and Bonnet (*qq.v.*) and countless other properties) purchased a half-share and took over its management. He installed Sébastien Ravilly as director. He had his work cut out for him, as the vineyards were not in the best shape; many missing vines had to be replaced and Ravilly complanted the equivalent of one hectare. The trellis was also heightened.

Fifteen hectares lie on the plateau that stretches out behind the house; this is on a very thin layer of clay over limestone; the remaining vineyards are close by. The plateau is at a height of eighty metres (260 feet), so it is often refreshed by winds that help keep the vines healthy. Some of the soil is ploughed; in other sectors green cover has been planted. No herbicides are used. The grapes are picked mechanically. The wine is aged in one-third new barriques for twelve to eighteen months, with limited rackings. Ravilly says the style he is trying to establish is one with finesse and concentration.

Rather confusingly, the standard *cuvée* is labelled Réserve. The wines from the late 1990s were mediocre, being both dilute and hard. Already in 2000 there were signs of improvement, with more concentration, but it remains a rather solid wine. The 2001 is better, with lush black-cherry aromas and flavours; it's a touch too burly for the fruit. The 2002 has more freshness but less complexity and should be drunk fairly young. The 2003 has impressive weight but the tannins are hefty and there is little finesse here. I prefer the youthful 2004, although the oak is now very marked on the nose.

Château Bel-Air

Tel: 0557 746040. Owner: Jean-Noël Roi. 21 ha. 70% Merlot, 15% Cabernet Franc, 15% Cabernet Sauvignon. Production: 150,000 bottles

This property, with vineyards in a single block, has been owned by the Roi family for over a century. The soil here is very gravelly. The grapes are picked by machine. Half the wine is aged in tanks, the other half in one-third new barriques. In 1998 Roi introduced the Cuvée Jean-Gabriel, made from the oldest vines and aged in new oak. My experience of this wine is very limited: a rather grubby 1988 and a light but appealing 1997.

Château de Bellevue

Tel: 0557 831804. Website: www.chateau-de-bellevue.com. Owner: André Chatenoud. 12 ha. 95% Merlot, 5% Cabernet Franc. Production: 60,000 bottles. Second wine: Ch Moulin-Brûlé Bellevue

André Chatenoud, whose father bought this property in 1971, is a trained oenologist who has worked at Stag's Leap Wine Cellars in Napa and at Brown Brothers in Victoria. The vineyards, mostly in one block, are planted eighty metres (260 feet) up on Lussac's limestone plateau, beneath which are three hectares of cellars in former quarries. The average age of the vines is forty years, and some of the Cabernet Franc is eighty years old. Bellevue has been organic since 2002. The grapes are hand-picked and sorted twice. The must is fermented with natural yeasts, and Chatenoud says the wines are naturally high in tannin, so he must take care not to over-extract. He uses gentle vertical presses. Most of the wine is aged in twenty per cent new oak for twelve months, and it is fined but not filtered.

Chatenoud likes to innovate, and in 2004 he produced a new screwcapped wine called Les Griottes, an unoaked Merlot intended to be drunk young. He has also planted some Carmenère, but only enough for a single barrique. He says the variety used to be quite widely planted but then disappeared, which is why it was omitted from the current AC regulations.

Given the experience and sophistication of André Chatenoud, I find the wines rather disappointing. They are sound and consistent but they lack excitement. The 1995, ten years on, had attractive strawberry aromas, and some plump fruit on the palate; but there's little finesse here. Similarly, the 1998 has red-fruits aromas, but it's rather tannic and rustic. The 1999 is ungainly, surprisingly cooked and fairly short. Although the 2000 is chunky and lacks acidity, the 2001 is significantly better, with spice and red fruits on the nose, and ample fruit and freshness on the palate. The 2002 is meagre, but the 2003 is successful, with weight and concentration and supple tannins. The 2004 Griottes is vividly aromatic, but there's some greenness on the palate.

Château Chéreau

Tel: 0557 745076. Owner: Max Silvestrini. 22 ha. 70% Merlot, 15% Cabernet Franc, 15% Cabernet Sauvignon.
Production: 120,000 bottles

Max Silvestrini is the president of the Lussac syndicat. When his father bought this property in 1958, there was just a single hectare under vine. Max Silvestrini took over in 1982, after pursuing an earlier career as a chemist. He is now beginning to hand control of his properties (Vieux Moulins in Montagne and Domaine de la Pointe in Pomerol (*qq.v.*)) to his son and daughter.

The vineyards are in various sectors. Ten hectares are planted on thin soil on the limestone plateau, another five are near Montagne on deeper soil. Almost all the vineyards are picked by machine. Fermentation takes place in steel tanks, and the wine is aged in older barrels, except for the Cuvée L'Egerie, which sees some new oak. Having tasted most vintages from 1996 to 2003, I find the wines fresh and straightforward but lacking in stuffing and personality. Even the 2002 Cuvée L'Egerie lacks the fruit to withstand the barrel-ageing without developing astringency.

Cooperative: Producteurs Réunis

Puisseguin. Tel: 0557 555040. Website: www.producteurs-reunis.com. 860 ha. 71% Merlot, 16% Cabernet Franc,
13% Cabernet Sauvignon. Production: 5 million bottles

Although based in Puisseguin-St-Emilion, the cooperative vinifies fruit from Lussac too. Indeed forty per cent of all Lussac is made here, and twenty per cent of all Puisseguin. It was founded in 1937 and now handles the crop of 139 growers. Since 2000 the technical director has been Benjamin Masson from the Loire, and in 2006 the thirty-year-old Masson became managing director, with technical advice from consultant Jean-Philippe Fort. Quality control is always a problem at cooperatives, whose members may resent what they see as excessive interference by the technocrats. Here, each parcel of vines is visited by a technician at least three times per year; when the grapes are delivered, they are assessed for quality and placed into one of three categories.

The principal brand here is Roc de Lussac (also Roc de Puisseguin), vinified with the aid of micro-oxygenation. About fifteen per cent of the wine is barrique-aged. For Lussac, there is also a Cuvée Renaissance from vines yielding under forty hl/ha; this is aged in new oak for twelve months and sold at a remarkably low price. In 2001 the cooperative launched a wine called L'Intemporel for its sixteen top parcels; these are picked by hand at yields of twenty-five hl/ha, cold-soaked for three days, fermented with frequent *délestages* for up to four weeks. This wine too is aged in new oak, and only 28,000 bottles are made.

The Roc wines are solid and not very aromatic, but they certainly don't lack fruit and reasonable concentration. They are fine value. In 2001 I marginally prefer the Puisseguin. The 2001 Cuvée Renaissance is rich and full-bodied, and the oak is well integrated; a lush style, it is probably at its best. I prefer it to L'Intemporel, which I find excessively toasty and worked over, culminating in a rather dry finish.

Château du Courlat

Chevrol. Tel: 0557 516217. Owner: Pierre Bourotte. 17 ha. 90% Merlot, 10% Cabernet Franc.
Production: 110,000 bottles. Second wine: Ch Les Echevins

The Bourottes own estates in Pomerol, as well as Les Hauts-Conseillants (*q.v.*) in Lalande de Pomerol. Here their vines are planted on clay and limestone slopes, and picked by hand. Jean-Philippe Fort acts as consultant at Hauts-Conseillants; here they use the services of Christian Veyry. The oldest Merlot grapes are reserved for Cuvée Jean-Baptiste, and this wine is aged for up to twenty months in one-third new barriques; some 25,000 bottles are produced, and only in top vintages.

The only wines I have tasted are Cuvée Jean-Baptiste. The 2001 is first-rate, with ripe, fleshy, raspberry fruit on the nose, a silky texture, ample concentration and fruit, and a long finish. The 2002 shows the limitations of the vintage, but it's bright, lightly oaky, and well balanced. The 2003 has plum and mint aromas, but the palate is too hefty and thick, with little lift and persistence.

Château La Croix de l'Espérance

Tel: 0556 263838. Website: www.bernard-magrez.com. Owner: Bernard Magrez. 7 ha. 100% Merlot.
Production: 20,000 bottles

In 2002 Bernard Magrez bought this small property to add to his burgeoning collection of wine estates. The soil is clay-limestone, and Magrez's team keeps yields down to around forty hl/ha by green-harvesting. The harvest is manual with successive forays into the vineyards to pick only the ripest fruit. The grapes are sorted before and after destemming. Fermentation takes place in small wooden vats with *pigeage*. Malolactic fermentation takes place in new barriques, and the wine is aged for eighteen months in mostly new oak. The only vintage I have tasted is the 2002, which had ample upfront fruit and tannin and a hint of greenness.

Château La Grande Clotte

Tel: 0557 512305. Owner: Malaterre family. 8.4 ha. 7 ha red: 80% Merlot, 20% Cabernet Franc.
1.4 ha white: 60% Sauvignon Gris and Sauvignon Blanc, 25% Sémillon, 15% Muscadelle.
Production: 40,000 bottles (of which 5,000 white)

Michel and Dany Rolland rent this property. The red wine is unoaked and straightforward. It is the white that the Rollands are particularly proud of. It is barrel-fermented and the wine is aged in new oak with lees-stirring. As the grapes, which were planted in 1992, grow on clay-limestone soils, the resulting wine is quite structured. It is bottled without fining or filtration. The red is fairly light, leafy, and lively, simple but highly drinkable. Of recent vintages, the 2001 seems the best. The white is delicious. The 2002 has peachy aromas behind the oak; it's plump, mouth-filling, ever so slightly phenolic, and has a creamy finish. The 2004 is fresher, more mineral, and has a bracing finish, while the excellent 2006 is more floral.

Château Lucas

Tel: 0556 746021. Owner: Frédéric Vauthier. 19 ha. 50% Merlot, 50% Cabernet Franc. Production: 100,000 bottles.
Second wine: Ch Rouzaud

When Lussac was part of the domaine of the abbey of Faize, this property was said to have been given to the Vauthier family (or their ancestors) in the sixteenth century as a gift for services rendered. The house itself certainly dates from that period. Polyculture was practised here until the 1930s, when grape-growing became more important. Frédéric Vauthier is the half-brother of Alain Vauthier of Ausone.

The vines lie on the limestone plateau of Lussac at a height of some eighty metres (260 feet). The grape mix is unusual, and Vauthier explains that in the 1940s Merlot cuttings were not readily available, so they planted Cabernet Franc instead. Presumably he must be happy with it, as this atypical *encépagement* remains. He follows the principles of *lutte raisonnée*. The harvest is usually manual, but not always; thus in 2002 Vauthier preferred to use a machine.

The basic wine is an inexpensive bottling that is intended to be easy to drink. Lengthy macerations are avoided to retain the fruit, and there is some micro-oxygenation *sous marc*. Since 2000 up to one-fifth of this wine has been oak-aged. It represents about half the production. Some forty per cent is made up of Grand de Lucas Cuvée Prestige, cropped at forty hl/ha and aged in older barriques. Some of the wine stays in tanks, but is then rotated with the barrel-aged lots.

Since 1998 there has been a third *cuvée*, L'Esprit de Lucas, not made every year, and never representing more than ten per cent of production. The grapes chosen for L'Esprit are given a prolonged cold soak, then aged for up to twenty months in new oak.

With so much selection in the vineyard and winery, it is not surprising that the basic wine is uninspired. I have tasted only the 1995, 1996, and 2003, but they were quite dilute and simple, and rather dry. Alas, Grand de Lucas is not much better. The 1996 is quite rich but charmless; the 1999 has lovely blackberry aromas, but the palate is quite hollow and lean. The 2000 is not bad, but rather light for the vintage, with some astringency. The 2002 is sleek and light, but it's quite lively and spicy.

L'Esprit is extremely oaky, especially on the nose, and Vauthier concedes 100 per cent new oak may be over-doing it. The 1998 begins well, with plump fruit on the palate, but then it fades into a lean finish. The 2000, while quite stylish on the nose, has a good attack, but also ends with a dry finish. The 2001 is similar, and lacks flesh. Surprisingly, the 2002 is very good, especially for the vintage; with ample cherry fruit, it is a sinewy wine of some concentration, moderate acidity, and a sweet finish.

The Lucas vines are well located, so it is a shame that the wines are not better. I suspect that slightly later harvesting might make a significant difference, but that's just speculation.

Château de Lussac

Tel: 0557 745658. Website: www.chateaudelussac.com. Owners: Hervé and Griet Laviale. 23 ha. 80% Merlot, 20% Cabernet Franc. Production: 80,000 bottles. Second wine: Le Libertin de Lussac

This was the first purchase by Hervé Laviale and his wife Griet, and later they added Vieux Maillet in Pomerol and Franc-Mayne in St-Emilion (*qq.v.*) to their portfolio. They bought the château in 2000 and immediately began restoring it as a home. They also renovated the *chai* and constructed a new semicircular *cuvier*. The winemaker is Laurence Ters, as at their other properties, and the consultant is Jean-Philippe Fort.

The vineyards lie behind and alongside the château on the edge of the village. The soil is cold, so they have to pick as late as possible. Indiscreet neighbours suggest that only about one-third of the vineyard is of outstanding quality, a claim I cannot verify. The harvest is mechanical and at the winery a Tribaie system (*see* Chapter Three) sorts the grapes, followed by hand-sorting. After a cold soak, the grapes are fermented with natural yeasts in steel tanks. The wine is aged in about one-third new oak, and in 2005 Ters began experimenting with an *élevage* on the fine lees.

Whatever the reservations of the neighbours, the 2001 and 2003 were very good wines. The 2001 had muted chocolatey aromas, and was rich and quite powerful without losing approachability. The 2003 showed a bit more spice and density, and there is no over-extraction.

Château Lyonnat

Tel: 0557 554890. Website: www.milhade.com. Owner: Milhade family. 52 ha. 70% Merlot, 15% Cabernet Franc, 15% Cabernet Sauvignon. Production: 280,000 bottles. Second wine: Ch La Rose Perruchon

This well-known property is now going through a complete overhaul. The Milhade family are both merchants and proprietors, and some kind of family split led, in 2005, to Gérard Milhade and his wife Brigitte taking over the running of Lyonnat. They have renovated the dilapidated château with a view to making it a family home. They also made an imaginative choice of consultant oenologist in Jean-Luc Colombo from the Rhône. Milhade admits that in the past his family did not take a close enough interest in Lyonnat. The vineyard was mostly planted in 1962 in more or less one parcel. The soil is excellent: thin red sandy clay over limestone. The grapes are mostly picked by machine. The must is fermented in cement tanks with selected yeasts, with some use of micro-oxygenation, especially for some young-vine lots. The wine is aged in one-third new oak, using barrels made from their own supply of oak.

In top years the Milhades produce La Réserve de la Famille from three hectares of hand-picked old vines. This wine is given a longer maceration than the regular bottling, and aged in fifty per cent new barriques. Only 15,000 bottles are produced.

Older vintages of Lyonnat that I have tasted were both light and dry. Only the 1989 and 1998 rose above mediocrity. More recently, the 2000 was excellent, with ample plummy fruit on the nose, and no lack of spice and vigour as well as fruit. The 2001 is similar in structure and quality. The 2002 is a bit lighter but has elegance and balance that make up for any lack of flesh. I prefer the 2003, which has sweet cherry fruit on the nose, and surprising freshness on the palate, which is rich and full-bodied.

The 2000 Lyonnat is surpassed by the Réserve, which has more toastiness, succulence, and persistence. The 2001 is similar, but perhaps has a bit more dash; the tannins are more imposing but they are balanced and somehow tamed by lively acidity. The 2003 is a touch overripe but not obtrusively jammy; it is juicy and has a sweet finish.

Gérard Milhade knows that Lyonnat ought to be one of the satellites' best properties, and in recent vintages quality has radically improved.

Château Mayne-Blanc

Tel: 0557 746056. **Owner:** *Jean Boncheau. 17 ha. 80% Merlot, 20% Cabernet Franc.* **Production:** *80,000 bottles*
Mayne-Blanc is in northern Lussac, where the soil is deep heavy clay, an advantage in dry years such as 2003 and 2005, less so in wetter years. Most of the vines were planted in 1961, and by the end of the decade the Boncheaus were bottling some of the crop, although even today they sell half the production in bulk, retaining the best for themselves. Only the grapes for their top wine, L'Essentiel, are picked by hand, and Jean Boncheau's son Charles is very keen on machine-harvesting.

The Cuvée Tradition is aged in older barrels. Their Cuvée St Vincent is produced from vines over thirty-five years old, and aged in mostly new oak. L'Essentiel is made from very low-yielding vines, and aged eighteen months in new oak. Only 4,000 bottles are made.

The grapes are sorted before fermentation with selected yeasts in cement tanks, which have been temperature-controlled since 1997. The wine stays in tanks over the first winter, and only then goes into barrel.

The Cuvée Tradition is a perfectly sound wine, judging by three diverse vintages, 1996, 2001, and 2003. They are fleshy and attractive and clearly intended to be drunk fairly young. At ten years old, the 1989 St Vincent was marred by some farmyardy aromas, but it was plump and oaky until the rather skinny finish. The 1997 is good, with no excessive oakiness to impede the clear fruit expression. The 2001 lacked complexity though it was certainly an attractive wine; the 2003 has more overt oakiness and is quite tannic and structured. I preferred the St Vincent to L'Essentiel in 2003, as the latter seemed too extracted, with a dense, savoury tone that was disconcerting in a young wine.

These are wines that are soundly made and that, L'Essentiel apart, offer good value. The Boncheaus sell directly to a loyal following of private clients.

Château du Moulin Noir

Tel: 0557 880764. **Owner:** *Alain Tessanier. 6.5 ha. 60% Merlot, 30% Cabernet Franc, 10% Cabernet Sauvignon.*
Production: *45,000 bottles*
The Tessanier family, based in Macau in the Haut-Médoc, bought this property in 1990. The wine is aged for twelve to sixteen months in one-third new oak, as well as in tanks. The only vintages I have tasted were a row from 1994 to 1997, all of which seemed rather dilute and rustic, with the slight exception of the 1996. There is an additional vineyard, under the same name, in the Montagne appellation, and this is vinified and labelled separately.

Vieux-Château-Chambeau

Tel: 0557 746255. **Owners:** *Arnaud Delaire, Yves Blanc, and Guy Benjamin. 28 ha. 70% Merlot, 20% Cabernet Franc, 10% Cabernet Sauvignon.* **Production:** *180,000 bottles (both wines)*
In 1998 the enterprising winemaker Arnaud Delaire of Château Branda (*q.v.*) in Puisseguin bought this large property, together with his partners. Today the grapes are picked by machine and by hand, and fermented in steel tanks. The wine is aged for twelve months in one-third new barrels with some *cliquage*. Another wine from

a different sector of the property is released under the label of Château Tour des Agasseaux. I have tasted only the wines from the four vintages before Delaire's purchase, and, to put it politely, there was considerable room for improvement. From Tour des Agasseaux I have tasted only the 2002, which was pinched and slightly astringent.

Another property worth mentioning:

La Croix de Peyrolie This is a *garagiste* venture between Bernard Magrez, Michel Rolland, and the actress Carole Bouquet. In 2005 she sold up. The 1.3-hectare property is planted solely with Merlot, which is fermented in wooden vats with manual *pigeage*, before being aged twenty months in barriques. I have not tasted it.

MONTAGNE-ST-EMILION

Montagne is a fairly coherent region that lies just north of St-Emilion, from which it is separated by the Barbanne River. It was expanded in 1973 when the neighbouring satellite of Parsac fused with Montagne. On the other side of the St-Emilion frontier lies the clutch of properties with Corbin in their name. Another section of the region borders the Côtes de Castillon. There are some 1,064 hectares of vines cultivated by over 200 growers, giving an average production of eleven million bottles. In general the soils are clay-limestone, with vines planted on slopes with varying expositions. However, there are sectors with some clay and silty sand. The terrain rises to a height of 114 metres (374 feet) alongside the picturesque Moulins de Calon. As elsewhere in the satellites, Merlot accounts for about seventy per cent of plantings. In general the level of quality here is high and relatively homogeneous.

Château Beauséjour
*Tel: 0557 746210. Website: www.chateau-beausejour.com. **Owner:** Pierre Bernault. 12 ha. 70% Merlot, 30% Cabernet Franc. **Production:** 50,000 bottles*

This interesting property has had a chequered history. A local quarry owner bought the estate in the 1850s. He owned other properties too, but they were gradually sold off as the family began to experience financial difficulties. In the 1990s his descendants sold Beauséjour to a group of investors. They in turn hired Bernard Germain and his team (owners of various properties in Blaye and Bourg, as well as in the Loire). Germain put the property on the market in 2004 and found a buyer in Bernault, a former Microsoft executive.

On moving in he found an indifferent and overcropped 2004 vintage in the cellar and decided to make a fresh start. He took on Stéphane Derenoncourt as his consultant and plans, with his advice, to convert the vineyards to biodynamic viticulture. The pride and joy of Beauséjour is a five-hectare parcel near the church that already under the Germains was vinified separately and released as Clos l'Eglise. In addition there is a three-hectare parcel of Merlot and Cabernet Franc that was planted in 1901, and Bernault plans to bottle this wine separately too. Indeed, the average age of the vines here is an impressive fifty-five years. The vineyards are all picked by hand.

The sorting at the winery is extremely strict. Even in 2005, Bernault discarded fifteen per cent of the crop. The must is fermented in cement tanks, with temperature control installed as recently as 2005. The *marc* is pressed in vertical presses. Germain used to age the wines in 400-litre barrels, but Bernault has been phasing them out in favour of conventional barriques. The wine is aged for at least sixteen months and blended late.

I twice tasted the 2000 Clos l'Eglise, which by 2005 was showing rather confected, glacé-cherry aromas; the wine was supple, medium-bodied, but, though reasonably concentrated, had lost some stuffing since first tasted in 2002. Bernault had not, at time of writing, bottled his own wines, but a barrel sample of the 2005 wine from the 1901 vines was wonderfully ripe and generous. This is a property to keep an eye on.

Château Calon

Tel: 0557 516488. Owner: Jean-Noël Boidron. 38 ha. 36.5 ha red: 70% Merlot, 15% Cabernet Franc, 12% Cabernet Sauvignon, 3% Malbec. 1.5 ha white: 40% Sauvignon Gris, 25% Sauvignon Blanc, 25% Muscadelle, 10% Sémillon. Production: 200,000 bottles. Second wine: Ch Fonguillon

The Boidrons own numerous properties in St-Emilion and the satellites; this is easily the largest and it has been in his family, he says, for centuries. The vineyards are divided into about sixty parcels, providing many soil types and styles of wine to work with. There are substantial parcels of sixty-year-old vines. The soil is ploughed, and no herbicides or insecticides are used. Vinification takes place in cement tanks relying on indigenous yeasts. The wine is aged in both tanks and barrels, and then blended. Boidron likes to offer older vintages for sale.

He also makes a small amount of white wine (AC Bordeaux) called Mayne d'Olivet, from vines planted high up on clay-limestone soil near the Calon windmills. The wine is barrel-fermented and aged for at least twelve months. The 1999 is a rich, broad, peachy wine, quite fat on the palate but with some freshness and length. The 1999 Calon is straightforwardly fruity, a balanced wine with light tannin that is enjoyable if unremarkable.

Château de la Couronne

Tel: 0557 746662. Owner: Thomas Thiou. 11 ha. 100% Merlot. Production: 62,000 bottles. Second wine: Ch La Rousselerie

Thiou, a self-taught winemaker, bought this property in 1994, but admits he wasn't really happy with the quality until the early 2000s. He prefers a non-interventionist approach, and is happy if the malolactic fermentation continues until the late spring. He does not rack his wines, nor does he stir their lees. From a three-hectare parcel called Reclos de la Couronne he has, since 1998, made a special *cuvée*, which is aged for sixteen months in new oak, and bottled without fining or filtration.

The 2002 is a solid wine, rather tannic and blunt, lacking some finesse. But it doesn't lack fruit. The 2003 Reclos has overripe aromas, and some liquorice tones; it is very rich and powerful, but a hint of sweetness on the palate is distinctly fatiguing. Not so in 2005, when the wine was rich, oaky, and concentrated, a vindication of this terroir.

Château Faizeau

Tel: 0557 246894. Website: www.chateau-faizeau.com. Owner: Chantal Lebreton. 12 ha. 100% Merlot. Production: 60,000 bottles. Second wine: Ch Chants de Faizeau

Chantal Lebreton, the owner of Croix de Gay (*q.v.*) in Pomerol, used to run Faizeau jointly with her brother Dr. Alain Raynaud until she bought him out in 2000. She takes oenological advice from Christian Veyry. The vines are in a single parcel on a gentle clay-limestone slope with some sandy sectors. Most of the vines are very old, with some dating from 1911, and the average age of those used for Faizeau is over fifty years. For many years she has planted green cover to reduce vigour, and also ploughs the soil. She debuds and green-harvests to bring down the yields.

The grapes are picked by hand and sorted twice. The wine is aged for eighteen to twenty-four months in up to fifty per cent new oak. Rather confusingly, Faizeau is all labelled as Sélection Vieilles Vignes. Juice from younger vines goes into the second wine.

I did not greatly care for the 1995, with its glossy, varnishy nose and flavours. The 2000, however, is very good: closed on the nose, but sleek and fruity, with an attractive zesty earthiness. The 2001 is similar but less concentrated. The 2002 shows a good deal of black-cherry fruit on the nose; it's a robust, spicy wine that lacks a little zest, but has ample fruit and length. The rich 2004 has excellent balance and should age well. Faizeau is reliable and sensibly priced.

Château Maison Blanche

Tel: 0557 746218. Owner: Despagne family. 32 ha. 50% Merlot, 50% Cabernet Franc and Cabernet Sauvignon. Production: 120,000 bottles. Second wine: Les Piliers de Maison Blanche

This is the impressive headquarters of one branch of the Despagne family, the other being at Grand-Corbin-

Despagne (*q.v.*) in St-Emilion. Although the present château is a substantial nineteenth-century house, the property is far more ancient, and Gallo-Roman tombs and pottery have been found in the grounds. The Despagnes have been in the region for centuries, but Maison-Blanche was bought by Nicolas Despagne's maternal grandfather, Louis Rapin, in 1938. The ponytailed Nicolas took over running the family properties (other than those controlled by his brother François at Grand-Corbin-Despagne) in 2000. His father Gérard had been typical of his times, opting for high yields and a generous use of chemical treatments.

Nicolas Despagne turned this approach on its head. He began ploughing the soil and eliminated all chemical treatments. He has now applied for organic certification, and has been experimenting with biodynamism with a three-hectare parcel. He does not practise deleafing or green-harvesting in a systematic way, although he will remove bunches toward the end of the growing season in order to improve aeration.

In the winery he is non-interventionist too, making no use of selected yeasts or enzymes or tartaric acid or sugar. He eschews cold soaks and other modish practices. He does not even see the need for systematic temperature control, preferring to decant any warm wine into a cistern where it can cool off for a while before being returned to its fermentation vat. He likes the notion that plants retain and express the history of the year, so he is more than content if wines offer a true reflection of their vintage.

The vineyards, with an average of forty-five years, are mostly in a single block around the château on clay-limestone soils. Despagne considers these soils particularly well suited to Cabernet Franc and Cabernet Sauvignon. The best parcels are picked by hand, the rest by machine. Since 1998 the entire crop has been aged for twelve to eighteen months in fifteen per cent new barriques. The *chai* is deliberately not air-conditioned, as he wants the wines to breathe naturally and has no problem with slight fluctuations in temperature.

In 1985 Gérard Despagne decided to honour his father-in-law by creating a special Cuvée Louis Rapin from the oldest vines. It is aged in new oak for up to twenty-four months. Only 3,000 bottles are produced.

These are wines of consistently good quality. The 1998 has more charm than weight, with a supple texture and integrated tannins. The 2000 is better, with rich, oaky aromas; although quite dense and chewy on the palate, there is sufficient acidity to keep the wine lively. The 2001 is similar though still surprisingly austere in 2006. There are oak and liquorice aromas on the 2003, which is powerful and full-bodied, and has a long, chewy finish. The only Cuvée Louis Rapin I have tasted is the 2001, which is similar to the regular bottling, but more tightly wound, with more richness and power; the wine has good acidity and balance, and should evolve well.

Château Messile Aubert

*Tel: 0557 401576. Website: www.la-couspaude.com. Owner: Jean-Claude Aubert. 10 ha. 70% Merlot,
20% Cabernet Franc, 10% Cabernet Sauvignon. Production: 50,000 bottles. Second wine: Dom du Roudier*

Aubert is the proprietor of the St-Emilion estate of La Couspaude (*q.v.*), but has owned this property since 1978. Until 2003 it was known as Château Vieux Messile Cassat. The soils are clay-limestone, and the grapes are picked by hand in *cagettes*. He adopts a submerged-cap fermentation in steel vats for part of the crop, but some lots are fermented in wooden vats with *pigeage*. There is an occasional use of micro-oxygenation. The wine is aged in fifty per cent new barriques. These are quite powerful wines, with forceful oak and cherry aromas. They are concentrated and have some tannic grip, resulting in wines that need some bottle-age to become expressive. The 2003 has softened with time; it is slightly confected and ready to drink. The 2001, 2002 and 2004 are nicely balanced, the latter being exceptionally good though oakey.

Château Montaiguillon

*Tel: 0557 746234. Website: www.montaiguillon.com. Owner: Chantal Amart Ternault. 28 ha. 60% Merlot,
20% Cabernet Franc, 20% Cabernet Sauvignon. Production: 160,000 bottles. Second wine: Ch du Haut-Plateau*

This large and well-known estate was bought by Mme. Ternault's grandfather in 1949. Well located on south- and southwest-facing slopes overlooking the Barbanne valley, the vineyards are in a single parcel on clay-limestone soils, and the average age of the vines is forty years. Mme. Ternault is keen on the high proportion of Cabernets, as she feels they give the wine more structure and length. She practises deleafing and green-harvesting, and insists she treats her vines just as if they were in St-Emilion itself, as her customers expect high quality. The grapes are picked by hand and by machine.

Since 2004 the practice has been to sort the fruit twice at the winery, then ferment in steel and cement tanks. The wine is aged for twelve months in one-third new oak; it is eggwhite-fined but unfiltered. In the owner's view the wines reach their peak at between seven and ten years.

I encountered the wine quite frequently from the 1979 vintage onwards, and was never excited by it. It often showed some earthiness and a dry finish. The best of these older vintages was the 1990. The style has not changed greatly in the early twenty-first century. Although the wines are attractively perfumed and have some aromatic charm, they are only modestly fruity, quite tannic, and dry on the finish. They are not that expensive, but don't reach any great heights.

Château La Papeterie

Tel: 0557 510409. Website: www.estager.com. Owner: Estager family. 10 ha. 70% Merlot, 30% Cabernet Franc.
Production: 60,000 bottles. Second wine: Ch Guede Leyrat

The Estager family own La Cabanne (*q.v.*) in Pomerol and various other estates. La Papeterie is an attractive property with a late-eighteenth-century house, its name referring to a paper-mill that used to stand here. The vines are in a single block close to the spot where four appellations meet: Montagne, Lalande de Pomerol, St-Emilion, and Pomerol. The grapes are machine-picked, sorted, cold-soaked, and after fermentation the wine is aged for fifteen months in thirty per cent new barriques. The only vintage I have tasted is the 1995, which at ten years of age had slightly gamey aromas, and a rather dour, charmless palate.

Château Roc de Calon

Tel: 0557 746399. Owner: Bernard Laydis. 24 ha. 78% Merlot, 21% Cabernet Franc, 1% Cabernet Sauvignon.
Production: 110,000 bottles

This property was established in 1922, and the enthusiastic Bernard Laydis has run it from 1988 onwards. The vineyards are mostly in a single block, and machine-picked. Although the regular wine is unoaked, about a third of the crop is used for the Cuvée Prestige, made from the oldest vines and aged in one-third new oak. In 2004 Laydis introduced a wine punningly called Deylis, aged in tanks and in high-toast American oak, the intention being to produce a lively, flavoury wine to drink young. The regular wine is very good, with the emphasis on upfront fruit and freshness. The 2001 lacks a little flesh but is sleek and enjoyable, while the 2003 is rich, juicy, and tannic. The Cuvée Prestige has more finesse, and the oak is kept well in check. The 2001 had a light savoury tone and delicious black fruits on the palate; the 2000 was more suave but lacked the thrust of the 2001. The 2002 is lean, delicate, and poised. The 2003 is quite perfumed, while the palate is supple and rounded, and has reasonable length. The 2005 is broad and rather flabby.

Château Roudier

Tel: 0557 746206. Website: www.vignoblescapdemourlin.com. Owner: Jacques Capdemourlin. 30 ha. 65% Merlot,
25% Cabernet Franc, 10% Cabernet Sauvignon. Production: 160,000 bottles

Although the avuncular Jacques Capdemourlin is associated with his three St-Emilion estates, he is nonetheless proud of Roudier and its wines. It's an old property that dates from the seventeenth century. The vines are well exposed, being on south-facing slopes. On the higher slopes the soil is clay-limestone, with more silt on lower sectors. The harvest is manual. The wine is aged in tanks and, occasionally, some barriques as well.

In 1997 Capdemourlin introduced a special *cuvée* called L'As de Roudier. This selection is aged for fifteen to eighteen months in one-third new oak, with malolactic fermentation in barriques. Production never exceeds

15,000 bottles, and it is made only in top years.

Thanks to the Capdemourlins' generosity, I recently tasted the 1959. The colour was certainly evolved, the aromas smoky, leafy, and savoury. The wine was still concentrated and tannic, yet there was no rusticity. Capdemourlin is fairly certain that this was vinified with the stems, which may account for its longevity; however, it may have been tough work drinking it in its youth. The 1998, tasted twice, is a severe disappointment: dilute, simple, and dull. The 1999 has some red-fruits aromas; it's a pleasant and balanced wine that is fully ready to drink. The leathery 2000 has little structure or complexity, and is also ready to drink. The 2001, with its cherry aromas, is more expressive and complex than the 2000, with firm tannins on the finish. The 2002 is rather odd, since there is a certain sweetness harnessed to some hard tannins. The 2003 is rugged and a touch jammy, but it has ample ripe fruit and should develop well. From cask, the 2004 showed great promise, with fine cherry fruit.

If the regular Roudier is disappointing, that may be because the cream of the crop goes into L'As. The 2000 has some elegance and a long, fresh finish. The 2001 is on the same level, but the 2002 is light, confected, and lacks persistence. The 2003 is very successful, with sweet cherry fruit, considerable power, and some force on the finish.

Château Teyssier

Tel: 0556 355300. Owner: Durand-Teyssier family. 22 ha. 86% Merlot, 12% Cabernet Sauvignon, 2% Cabernet Franc.
Production: 90,000 bottles

Since 1993 this property has been managed by the négociant house CVBG. The wine is aged for eighteen months in fifty per cent new oak. I found the 1998 rustic, and the 2003 is stewed and heavy-handed.

Château Vieux Moulins de Chéreau

Tel: 0557 745076. Owner: Max Silvestrini. 5.5 ha. 80% Merlot, 10% Cabernet Franc, 10% Cabernet Sauvignon.
Production: 30,000 bottles

Silvestrini's main property is Château Chéreau (*q.v.*) in Lussac-St-Emilion. Here the vines are on deep soil with much clay. The vines are mostly machine-picked, and the wine is unoaked. The only vintage I have tasted, the 2003, was very light and lacking in personality.

PUISSEGUIN-ST-EMILION

The town of Puisseguin is said to take its name from one of Charlemagne's military commanders called Seguin, who settled here. "Puy" means hill. The terroir is more uniform than that of Lussac, being almost entirely clay-limestone. Its southern slopes border the Côtes de Castillon. The wines have a good deal of tannin, so less skilled producers turn out rather rustic wines. There are 725 hectares under vine, cultivated by 130 growers, of whom about fifty supply the Producteurs Réunis cooperative (*see under* Lussac). The average production is about five million bottles.

Château Branda

Tel: 0557 746255. Owners: Arnaud Delaire, Yves Blanc, and Guy Benjamin. 10 ha. 70% Merlot, 20% Cabernet Franc, 10% Cabernet Sauvignon. Production: 65,000 bottles

Delaire's first career was in property development. In 1998 he teamed up with his father-in-law and with a Parisian friend to buy and renovate this property in northern Puisseguin. Delaire is quite ambitious, and takes advice from both Michel Rolland and Pascal Chatonnet. He keeps yields low, but picks by machine as well as by hand. Malolactic fermentation takes place in barriques, and the wine is aged for fifteen to eighteen months in fifty per cent new oak, with some *cliquage*.

The 2002 is a touch confected, and the oak overwhelms the modest fruit. I prefer the sweeter but riper 2003, which is supple and spicy and absorbs the oak more successfully. The 2004 is packed with black cherry fruit but lacks complexity.

The same team also owns and manages Vieux-Château-Chambeau (*q.v.*) in Lussac.

Château Haut-St-Clair

*Tel: 0557 746682. **Owner:** Yannick Le Menn. 4.5 ha. 65% Merlot, 25% Cabernet Franc, 10% Cabernet Sauvignon.*
***Production:** 30,000 bottles. **Second wine:** Cuvée Moulin-St-Clair*

These vineyards are located both on clay-limestone slopes and on the plateau above. These are cold soils and the vines ripen fairly late. They are picked by machine and by hand. The wine is aged for eight to twelve months in one-third new oak. The 2002 has a firm, oaky nose, ample richness, and a lush texture with no sharp edges. The 2003 has good fruit but has more earthy aromas and less length. The wines are inexpensive and offer good value.

Château des Laurets

*Tel: 0557 746340. **Owner:** Baron Benjamin de Rothschild. 86 ha. 75% Merlot, 14% Cabernet Franc,*
*11% Cabernet Sauvignon. **Production:** 300,000 bottles*

This enormous property has had a complex history. For 250 years it was owned by the same family, who constructed the immense château in the 1860s. Eventually the property was sold to a group of Quebecois investors, who also own Tour de Mons in Margaux. They modernized the *cuvier* and expanded the vineyards from the seventy hectares then planted. Since they sold most of the wine in bulk, the estate never enjoyed much renown. In 2003 they sold Laurets to Benjamin de Rothschild, the owner of Château Clarke (*q.v.*) and a member of a branch of the Rothschilds that seems to enjoy a challenge. Since his team – director Fabrice Bandieras and consultant Jean-Philippe Fort – had no influence on the 2002 and 2003 vintages, they were released under the name Château Tour des Laurets, which was suppressed from 2004 onwards.

The vineyards are planted on south-facing slopes in more or less a single block. However, they are divided almost equally between the Puisseguin and Montagne appellations. It is likely that the wine made from the latter will be labelled Château de Malengin. Until 2003 the vineyards were picked by machine. This is being partially phased out. Fermentation takes place in steel tanks after a cold soak; the *cuvaison* is prolonged, and there is some micro-oygenation *sous marc*. The very best parcels are vinified in wooden vats. At present one-third of the wine is aged in one-third new barriques for twelve to fifteen months, with a little American oak. The bulk of the wine remains in tanks.

It is likely that as the Rothschild team get to grips with this extensive vineyard there will be further changes in the winemaking and marketing. Production is also expected to rise to about 500,000 bottles. The only wine from the estate I have come across was the 2003 Tour des Laurets, which was too jammy and alcoholic for my taste.

La Mauriane

*Tel: 0557 746806. **Website:** www.lamauriane.com. **Owner:** Pierre Taïx. 3.5 ha. 80% Merlot, 20% Cabernet Franc.*
***Production:** 15,000 bottles*

If there is a Young Turk in the satellites, then it is probably Pierre Taïx. He began working at his family property of Château Rigaud (which he still runs; *q.v.*), but by 1997 was having serious differences with his more conventional father. So they agreed that he could carve out a few hectares, which were renamed La Mauriane, and follow his own ideas. The average age of the vines is forty-five years, and one parcel is eighty years old. The harvest is manual, and after a short cold soak the must is fermented in steel tanks with natural yeasts. Because the must tends to be rich in tannin, Taïx tries to be very careful about extraction. The *marc* is pressed in a vertical press, and the wine is aged in barrels of various sizes, eighty per cent of them new; the Cabernet Franc is always aged in 500-litre barrels. There is just a single racking.

The results are impressive. These are deeply coloured wines with rich aromas that are perhaps too marked by new oak. Very ripe years also show aromas of black cherries, liquorice, and blackcurrant. The 1998 is on the edge of over-extraction, with heavy-handed oak and a slightly dry texture, but it's redeemed by a long, sweet finish. The 2002 is rich, opulent, and concentrated, and has good acidity. I marginally prefer the more dense and exotic 2001, with its tight structure and long, tannic finish. Oak dominates the 2002 and gives it a more austere character, but there's no lack of rich fruit. The 2003 betrays its vintage. It's a rather brutal wine, with ultra-ripe aromas and flavours, extreme concentration, and powerful tannins.

These are wines that live dangerously, and if occasionally they stray into excess, they are nonetheless a welcome change from the numerous lean and undernourished wines that still dominate the satellites.

Château Rigaud

Tel: 0557 746806. Website: www.lamauriane.com **Owner:** *Pierre Taïx. 8 ha. 80% Merlot, 20% Cabernet Franc.*
Production: 50,000 bottles

This has been the property of the Taïx family since 1840. Although Pierre Taïx established his own winemaking style at La Mauriane (*q.v.*), he continues to run Rigaud. In 2002 he began converting the estate to organic viticulture, and is experimenting with biodynamic preparations, all aimed at creating the most extensive possible root system for the vines. The viticulture and vinification are essentially the same as for La Mauriane, but there is considerably less oak-ageing, and the Cabernet Franc remains in tanks.

Although not as concentrated and dramatic as La Mauriane, Rigaud is a very good wine, especially given its modest price. Less overtly oaky on the nose than La Mauriane, it is instead more perfumed. It's medium-bodied, yet doesn't lack tannin and structure. Of recent vintages only the 2002 is a shade disappointing. Both the vigorous 2001 and the lush 2003 are very successful.

Other properties to watch include:

Château Fonbagan This, like Rigaud and La Mauriane (*qq.v.*), is vinified by Pierre Taïx. The only vintage I have come across, the 2001, was not on the same level of quality as the wines from the other two properties.

Château Haut-Bernat Under the same ownership as Côte Montpezat (*q.v.*) in Côtes de Castillon, this 5.5-hectare vineyard makes robust, vigorous, all-Merlot wine.

Château Pierdon is another wine from the Pierre Taïx stable. Produced from four hectares, it is mostly Merlot and aged in mostly new oak. Only about 15,000 bottles are made.

Château Soleil is located close to Château des Laurets. In 2005 the fourteen-hectare property was bought by Stephan von Neipperg of Canon-La-Gaffelière (*q.v.*). He is very enthusiastic about its potential, but it will be a while before tastings can confirm it.

ST-GEORGES-ST-EMILION

This small satellite appellation can claim to be both one of the best and one of the most homogeneous in terroir. All the vineyards are on well-drained slopes, although the limestone bedrock retains moisture too. Thus the vines rarely suffer from either an excess or a deficit of water. Rather confusingly, the twenty-two growers have the right to declare the wines as Montagne, which it borders, rather than St-Georges. Roughly 170 hectares are declared as St-Georges, and a further fifty as Montagne. But this can fluctuate. It's an attractive region too, with some fine châteaux and a good Romanesque church.

Château Belair St-Georges

Tel: 0557 746540. **Owner:** *Nadine Pocci. 10 ha. 80% Merlot, 10% Cabernet Franc, 10% Cabernet Sauvignon.*
Production: 60,000 bottles. **Second wine:** *Ch Belair Montaiguillon*

Nadine Pocci is the sister of Yannick Le Menn, an oenologist who owns Château Haut-St-Clair (*q.v.*) in Puisseguin. He makes these wines too. The vineyards are in a single parcel around the house; they are mostly on south-facing clay-limestone slopes. Only the Cabernets are picked by machine. The wines are aged for ten to twelve months in one-third new oak. All the wine is labelled Réserve du Château.

These are easy-going wines of little depth. They have attractive cherry fruit and ample freshness but there is little complexity. The best of recent vintages has been the 2001.

Château Calon

Tel: 0557 516488. Owner: Jean-Noël Boidron. 8 ha. 80% Merlot, 10% Cabernet Franc, 10% Cabernet Sauvignon.
Production: 40,000 bottles

Calon makes a second appearance in this chapter, since this property owned by Jean-Noël Boidron lies in two appellations, both Montagne and St-Georges. The winemaking is similar for both, except that the St-Georges is aged in fifty per cent new barriques, The 1999 is an attractive wine, with sweet, ripe cherry and coffee aromas; it's sleek, with supple tannins and considerable elegance. Oak is more evident on the 2002, which also has ample fruit but perhaps less vigour than the 1999.

Château Macquin

Tel: 0557 746466. Owner: Denis Corre-Macquin. 31 ha. 80% Merlot, 10% Cabernet Franc,
10% Cabernet Sauvignon. Production: 160,000 bottles. Second wine: Ch Bellonne

Albert Macquin was a nurseryman who founded Pavie-Macquin in St-Emilion and various other properties, including this one. The present owner is his descendant. In all Albert Macquin owned eighty hectares. He and his estate managers kept complete records of weather conditions and other developments, and these are perfectly preserved here at Macquin. He died in 1912 and in 1949 his various properties were separated among his heirs. Denis Corre-Macquin has run Macquin since 1978. When he took over, the property was in poor shape and, with the exception of nine hectares of Merlot planted in 1947, all the vineyards have been replanted.

The vineyards, on south-facing slopes, are low-lying, so there is a risk of frost. The soil is rich and high in clay content, making it somewhat atypical of the appellation. The grapes are machine-harvested, and sorted twice at the winery. The wine is fermented with selected yeasts and some micro-oxygenation, and then aged in one-third new oak, with *cliquage*. Some of the crop is kept in tanks, and then blended with the oaked lots.

Both the 2002 and 2003 are very good wines, with rich cherry and blackberry fruit on the nose. They have both succulence and energy, with ripe tannins to give structure. The plump, vigorous 2003 is particularly good for the vintage.

Château St-André-Corbin

Tel: 0557 247303. Website: www.vignobles-saby.com. Owners: Jean-Christophe and Jean-Philippe Saby.
19 ha. 75% Merlot, 25% Cabernet Franc. Production: 80,000 bottles

For eighteen years this property, the second largest in St-Georges, was leased by J.P. Moueix. In 2003 it reverted to the owners, the Saby family, who own Château Rozier (*q.v.*) in St-Emilion. The vineyards here are in a single block, on clay-limestone slopes facing south and southwest. The harvest is manual, and the wine is aged in one-third new oak. The 2003 has aromas of black fruits and woodsmoke, while the palate is lush and full-bodied, with powerful but not harsh tannins. The 2005 is similar, but has more lift and length.

Château St-Georges

Tel: 0557 746211. Website: www.chateau-saint-georges.com. Owner: Georges Desbois. 45 ha. 80% Merlot,
10% Cabernet Franc, 10% Cabernet Sauvignon. Production: 320,000 bottles. Second wine: Ch Puy St-Georges

This lovely château was designed by the celebrated Bordelais architect Victor Louis in the early 1770s. In Roman times there was a villa on this spot, and it was later replaced by a medieval castle. The owner at the time the château was constructed was M. de Bouchereau, the Baron de St-Georges. The property often changed hands in the nineteenth century and was almost abandoned after phylloxera wrecked the vineyards. In 1890 the present owner's grandfather Pétrus Desbois bought it. His day job was running a fashion house with show-rooms in Berlin, and the château was essentially his retirement home. His son renovated the estate, and I recall being graciously received by him in 1984, when I was lured here by the architecture as much as the wine.

He died in 1994 and the current owner took over. This large vineyard is in a single walled block on clay-limestone soils around the buildings. The vines face south and southwest, so both exposure and drainage are exemplary. Since 1984 the grapes have been machine-harvested, and for some reason Georges Desbois is rather defensive about the practice. After sorting, the must is fermented in steel tanks with selected yeasts. The wine is aged for fifteen months in one-third new oak, with regular racking (though a brochure from the early 1990s rather alarmingly refers to the wine being aged for twenty-four months in new Limousin oak).

There is a special *cuvée* called Trilogie, first produced in 1995. It is apparently pure old-vine Merlot, aged in barrels for eighteen months. The château brochure makes no reference to it, and neither did Georges Desbois in the course of my visit.

The only older vintage I have tasted is the 1979, which even after ten years was quite tannic and austere, and not exactly a mouthful of pleasure. The 1998 has delicate oaky aromas, but is neutral on the palate and simply dull. The 2002 is fresher, with good cherry fruit; there's little depth but it's stylish and quite long.

Château Tour du Pas St-Georges

Tel: 0557 247094. Owner: Pascal Delbeck. 15 ha. 50% Merlot, 30% Cabernet Franc, 10% Cabernet Sauvignon, 10% Carmenère, Petit Verdot, and Malbec. Production: 80,000 bottles.
Second wine: Les Sabliers du Ch Tour du Pas St-Georges

Like Château Bélair in St-Emilion, this was the property of Mme. Dubois-Challon, until she bequeathed it to Pascal Delbeck, who had made the wine since 1979. Its vineyards are in a single south-facing block; although essentially clay-limestone, there is more sand and clay lower down the slope. Delbeck is an inveterate experimenter, which explains the small blocks of unusual varieties, all massal selections from the Bélair vineyards. The viticulture is *lutte raisonnée*, and there are some experiments with biodynamic treatments.

The harvest is manual, and fermentation takes place with natural yeasts. Two-thirds of the wine is aged in oak, of which half is new; one-third of the wine stays in tanks. In top vintages Delbeck makes a wine called Cuvée Eugénie from a parcel of 100 per cent Merlot; it is aged in fifty per cent new oak. Only 6,000 bottles are made.

Like Bélair, Tour du Pas St-Georges is an old-fashioned wine, in the sense that it offers restraint over flashiness, balance over concentration. The 1985, tasted recently, is fragrant, quite intense, yet still fresh and delicate and made with a light touch; it is certainly at its peak. The 1995 is more concentrated, and has curious aromas of cherries, mint, and peanuts; there is little complexity but the wine has an attractive piquancy. The 1996 has cedary aromas, but it's a rather simple wine with slight astringency. There are sweet, lush black-cherry aromas on the 2001, while the palate is rich with firm tannins and reasonable concentration. The 2000 Eugénie has more overt ripeness and richness on the nose, but the palate and flavours echo those of the regular wine.

Château Vieux Guillou

Tel: 0557 746209. Owner: Yannick Menguy. 13 ha. 68% Merlot, 24% Cabernet Franc, 6% Cabernet Sauvignon, 2% Malbec. Production: 65,000 bottles

Menguy's great-grandfather was the mayor of St-Georges (not exactly a vast conurbation), and his father Jean-Paul the president of the syndicat. Menguy maintains good stocks, enabling him to sell only wines that he considers ready to drink. Thus in 2005 the vintages on sale were 1998 and 1999. He had no hesitation about bottling no wine at all in dim vintages such as 1993 and 1997.

The vineyards are divided into varied parcels. The average age of the vines is fifty years, with some rows dating from the 1880s. Menguy follows the principles of *lutte raisonnée*, and likes to pick at maximum ripeness. Harvesting is both mechanical and manual. At present fermentation takes place in cement and steel tanks, but Menguy is thinking of buying some wooden vats. The wines are unoaked but bottled only, without fining or filtration, some four years after the harvest.

Despite this unorthodox approach, these are good wines, with sour-cherry aromas, ample solidity of fruit, and good freshness and balance.

24. Côtes de Castillon and Côtes de Francs

 In 2005 and 2006 a proposal was made to make the AC system more rational in parts of Bordeaux. It was suggested that the five Côtes appellations – Castillon, Francs, Bourg, Blaye, and Premières Côtes – should band together under a single Côtes de Bordeaux appellation, plus the regional name. Thus Côtes de Castillon would be changed to Castillon: Appellation Côtes de Bordeaux Contrôlée. This may well make sense from a marketing viewpoint, but most of these appellations have little in common other than their locations in hilly sectors of Bordeaux. Castillon and Francs do share a common border. Indeed, Francs is no more than the nail on the thumb of Castillon. Many miles to the northwest Blaye and Bourg also share a frontier. But whereas Castillon and Francs are eastern extensions of St-Emilion, Blaye and Bourg are riverside regions directly across the estuary from the Médoc.

The Premières Côtes group the communes that line the Garonne from the sweet wine regions of Loupiac and Ste-Croix-du-Mont to the suburbs of Bordeaux. The vineyards, though, are on the slopes and plateau above the river. They are geographically quite separate from Bourg and Blaye, and from Castillon and Francs.

It makes sense to group Castillon and Francs together in the same chapter, and to give Bourg and Blaye the same treatment. The Premières Côtes, however, will be considered together in Chapter Twenty-Seven, which will include the areas covered by neighbouring appellations such as Entre-Deux-Mers and Bordeaux Supérieur.

Castillon and Francs are now offering some wines of exceptional quality and value. There are a number of reasons for this. Their colder soils cope well with the very hot, dry years of the early twenty-first century. Some of the terroir, with its classic clay-limestone mix, is of high quality and intrinsically superior to the flatter, riverside sectors of St-Emilion. Then there is the human element. A number of proprietors from St-Emilion and elsewhere, wishing to expand their holdings, have often turned to these Côtes, and applied similar standards of viticulture and winemaking to their vineyards. With substantial resources behind them, these colonists could afford to take risks in pursuit of quality that smallholders were unable or unwilling to attempt. They have demonstrated that the Côtes can produce excellent wines and are setting an example which encourages other, less visionary growers to raise their game. There are still many dull, grimly tannic, and rustic wines emerging from Castillon and Francs, but their numbers are shrinking.

As in other outlying regions of Bordeaux, low prices discouraged growers from investing in measures that would improve quality, and a vicious circle began to spin, a circle gradually being broken by growers with a more global vision of wine quality and marketing.

COTES DE CASTILLON

It was at Castillon that the famous battle took place in 1453 that brought the Hundred Years' War to an end, and with it the life of the British commander Talbot. This large region of around 3,000 hectares is essentially the easterly extension of the St-Emilion plateau. It became an AC only in 1989, having previously been sold as Bordeaux Supérieur: Côtes de Castillon. Before 1931 the region had been known, not very precisely, as the St-Emilionnais. The wines were rugged, and mostly used by négociants to beef up their blends. Of the 366 growers, about 150 are members of the cooperative: Les Chais des Francs et Gardegan vinifies about fifteen per cent of the crop. The grape mix across the region is seventy per cent Merlot, twenty per cent Cabernet Franc, and ten per cent Cabernet Sauvignon. Minimum vine density is 5,000 vines per hectare, although there are still parcels of older vines at a considerably lower density. Yields range from fifty-five to sixty hectolitres per hectare at most properties, delivering about twenty-four million bottles each year. These yields, notably higher than those of St-Emilion, can also undermine quality. The most important communes are St-Magne-de-Castillon with 975 hectares of vines, Belvès (312), Gardegan-et-Tourtirac (350), St-Genès-de-Castillon (275), St-Philippe-d'Aiguilhe (283), Les Salles de Castillon (295), Castillon (140), Ste-Colombe (247), and Monbadon (238). St-Philippe has a high reputation, being renowned for wines of elegance as well as power; the vines from Les Salles are on soil with a higher clay content and thus the wines tend to be heavier. Ste-Colombe has a fine terroir, but the vineyards of St-Magne are mostly on the flat, silty plain on soils that are rather too fertile.

The Castillon vineyards not surprisingly vary greatly in soil structure and quality. As in St-Emilion, the least interesting vineyards are on alluvial soils near the Dordogne River, which flows through the town of Castillon itself. Behind the town, however, the clay-limestone hills soon rise up, and here the best sites are located. Marl and sandstone also make their appearance on certain slopes. At its highest point the Côtes reach an elevation of 119 metres (390 feet) in St-Philippe-d'Aiguilhe. Exposition varies considerably in this undulating terrain, and the most favoured sites face south and southeast. Location matters here, and there can be a difference of two weeks in maturation between the warmer soils of the river plain and the hillsides.

It's a wilder area than St-Emilion, still reflecting its polycultural past, offering a patchwork of woodlands and meadows and farmland as well as vines. Other less welcome echoes of that past are the state of some of the vineyards. Driving through the Côtes shortly before the 2005 harvest, I was surprised, even shocked, to see many overgrown vineyards planted to a low density and carrying more fruit than would be compatible with decent quality. Anyone tending vines like that in St-Emilion would probably be run out of town by his or her neighbours. I am also told, though this is very difficult to verify, that there are many parcels planted with poor clones and rootstocks. One can only hope that the commercial success of the best estates will dissuade growers from indulging in practices primarily directed at producing the maximum quantity with no regard as to quality.

On the other hand, growers do have to battle with a climate clearly less favourable than in St-Emilion. Stephan von Neipperg, one of the first "outsiders" to invest here, notes:

> I am convinced the terroir here is underestimated because it is later ripening than St-Emilion. Growers prefer lighter, precocious soils because they are easier and more reliable. But now with techniques such as leaf removal, you can get earlier ripening in Castillon. But the wines always have higher acidity than St-Emilion, so you need to have good ripeness to balance it.

François Despagne, another St-Emilion grower who has a property here, finds that his vines tend to ripen about five days later than at St-Emilion. On the other hand, there are sectors of St-Emilion such as St-Christophe-des-Bardes that ripen at about the same time. Indeed, ripeness for Despagne is hardly problematic. "You can get very high sugars here," he told me. "Fifteen per cent alcohol is not difficult to attain, though I certainly don't want my wines to have that kind of strength."

Domaine de l'A

Ste-Colombe. Tel: 0557 246029. Website: www.vigneronsconsultants.com. Owner: Stéphane Derenoncourt. 8 ha. 60% Merlot, 25% Cabernet Sauvignon, 15% Cabernet Franc. Production: 35,000 bottles.
Second wine: B de l'A

Stéphane Derenoncourt is one of Bordeaux's best-known consultants, and his team advises estates in other countries too. In 1999, when he founded this property, he was less well known, although his advocacy of micro-oxygenation and his superb winemaking efforts at the estates of Stephan von Neipperg had certainly attracted wide attention.

The vines he bought were planted to a very low density of around 3,000 per hectare. Interplanting of rows and other measures have increased the density to around 8,000 per hectare. He showed his confidence in Cabernet Franc by planting massal selections from Vieux-Château-Certan and L'Eglise-Clinet. From the beginning the vines have been cultivated according to biodynamic principles. Yields were well below the average, as low as twenty hl/ha in his first vintage, though about double subsequently. The juice is fermented in small wooden vats and aged in new barriques, with no racking until the summer. The second wine is handled differently, being pure Merlot that spends just a short period in barrels before being aged further in tanks with micro-oxygenation. Being his own master here, Derenoncourt is in no rush to complete malolactic fermentation, which can be delayed until well into the spring in his cold *chai*.

I visited the *chai* in late 2000 and tasted the initial vintage, which at that stage seemed rather extracted. From barrel, the 2005 is highly promising, with rich, plump fruit, a supple texture and lively acidity, and no trace of over-extraction. Given the difficulties of the vintage, the 2006, tasted from cask, is a resounding success.

Château d'Aiguilhe

St-Philippe-d'Aiguilhe. Tel: 0557 247133. Website: www.neipperg.com. **Owner:** *Comte Stephan von Neipperg. 50 ha. 80% Merlot, 20% Cabernet Franc.* **Production:** *200,000 bottles.*

Second wine: Seigneurs d'Aiguilhe

Stephan von Neipperg, best known for having transformed the wines of Canon-La-Gaffelière and La Mondotte in St-Emilion, has a good eye for an opportunity. His aristocratic antennae were probably first sent a-quiver after glimpsing the ruinous fourteenth-century English-built fortress in this sector of St-Philippe. In the eighteenth century the owners were the Leberthon family, who sold it to Etienne Marineau shortly before the Revolution. It remained in their hands until 1920. Neipperg bought Aiguilhe in 1989, but it was run-down. Much of the vineyard has since been replanted, although the oldest vines have been preserved. He was not happy with the Cabernet Sauvignon, which has now been grubbed up. Although it is already a large property in a region where the average wine estate is nine hectares, he plans to expand to about seventy-five hectares by buying neighbouring properties as they come on the market. He has spent a small fortune in restoring the existing buildings, other than the medieval fortress, and constructed a new circular winery.

The vines, which are cultivated organically, are planted on various plateaux that slope gently southwards. The soils vary, with clay-limestone and clay-silt. The harvest is manual. Since the reception area is above the wooden and steel tanks, no pumping is necessary. Neipperg says he has to be careful not to over-extract as the wine is endowed with robust tannins. Thus he prefers *pigeage* to pumpovers. The wine is aged for twelve months in just under fifty per cent new oak, and bottled without fining or filtration.

This has long been a leading Castillon wine. The 1996 had ample black-cherry fruit, substance and body without excessive tannin, and a long, balanced finish. The 1997, predictably, was much lighter. The 2000 has a rich, ripe, savoury nose, and a lush palate; fairly low acidity suggests it is now at its peak. I marginally prefer the sumptuous 2001, which has spice and charm as well as excellent fruit and well-judged oak. The 2003 has baked, plummy aromas, and jammy flavours I find fatiguing. The 2004 is more balanced, with aromas of great charm, and flavours reminiscent of the 2001. The blackberry-scented 2005 is splendid, oozing with fruit and spiciness.

Château d'Aiguilhe-Querre

St-Philippe-d'Aiguilhe. Tel: 0557 252252. Website: www.aiguilhe-querre.com.

Owner: *Emmanuel Querre. 2.4 ha. 80% Merlot, 20% Cabernet Franc.* **Production:** *8,000 bottles*

Michel Querre is a well-known Libournais négociant and the owner of Le Moulin (*q.v.*) in Pomerol. His son Emanuel looks after this small property, which made its debut in 2000. Until 2003 it was even tinier, with only 1.2 hectares under vine. The vines lie on the clay-limestone plateau of St-Philippe, an excellent sector of the Côtes. Yields average thirty hl/ha. The harvest is manual, and after sorting the must is fermented in wooden tanks with *pigeage*. The wine is aged for eighteen months in sixty per cent new barriques.

This is quite a burly wine, with considerable muscle. It's short on elegance but then few would turn first to Castillon in search of finesse. I find the 2002 a touch over-extracted, though the aromas are a splendid amalgam of oak, blackcurrant, and blackberry. The 2003 is both rather baked and overoaked for my taste; it's opulent but marked by low acidity. Still, a fair effort for the vintage. The 2004 has more aromatic delicacy, yet there's no lack of body, backbone, and balance. The 2005, tasted from cask, was very plump and full-bodied.

Château d'Ampélia

St-Philippe-d'Aiguilhe. Tel: 0557 251994. Website: www.grand-corbin-despagne.com.
Owner: François Despagne. 5 ha. 95% Merlot, 5% Cabernet Franc. Production: 25,000 bottles.
Second wine: La Dame d'Ampélia

François Despagne, who owns Grand Corbin-Despagne (*q.v.*) in St-Emilion, bought this property in 1999, and the first vintage was 2000. The vineyards lie close to Château d'Aiguilhe on the plateau on clay-limestone soils over a rocky subsoil. The farming follows the principles of *lutte raisonnée*. The grapes are picked manually and given a cold soak before being fermented in steel and cement tanks. A vertical press is maintained, and the wine goes through malolactic fermentation in barriques. It is aged for twelve to eighteen months in one-third new oak.

This is a wine that closely reflects its vintage. Thus in 2002 there were crunchy red-fruits aromas, and the wine was medium-bodied yet supple, though rather earthy on the finish. The 2003 has more menthol and spice aromas, and considerable power, concentration, and length of flavour. The 2004 has splendid blackberry aromas, but the palate is surprisingly dense, with rather jagged tannins and acidity.

Château La Brande

Belvès. Tel: 0557 401823. Website: www.chateaumangot.fr. Owners: Jean-Guy and
Anne-Marie Todeschini. 23 ha. 70% Merlot, 22% Cabernet Franc, 8% Cabernet Sauvignon.
Production: 170,000 bottles. Second wine: Ch Briand

M. Todeschini co-owns Château Mangot (*q.v.*) in St-Emilion, but also runs this substantial property. The vines have an average age of thirty-five years, and are cultivated by *lutte raisonnée*. Some of the vineyards are picked by machine. The wine is aged in one-third new oak, with eggwhite-fining. The 2002 was rather blunt and lacking in persistence, but the 2003, despite its plum-jam nose, has attractive fruit, and vigorous though not harsh tannins.

Château Bréhat

Ste-Magne-de-Castillon. Tel: 0557 401809. Website: www.vins-jean-de-monteil.com.
Owner: Jean de Monteil. 5 ha. 65% Merlot, 20% Cabernet Franc, 15% Cabernet Sauvignon.
Production: 30,000 bottles. Second wine: Clos Lucas

Jean de Monteil, the owner of Château Haut-Rocher (*q.v.*) in St-Emilion, runs this property on similar viticultural principles. The vines are at the foot of the slopes, on clay, silt, and sand soils over a limestone base. The fruit is machine-picked, and aged mostly in tanks; about one-third is aged in older barriques for six months, and the two components are rotated. The only vintage I have come across, the 2001, had muted cherry and mint aromas; a supple approach on the palate led to fairly aggressive tannins, but there was ample fruit and concentration.

Château Cap-de-Faugères

Ste-Colombe. Tel: 0557 403499. Website: www.chateau-faugeres.com. Owner: Silvio W. Denz. 31 ha. 85% Merlot,
10% Cabernet Franc, 5% Cabernet Sauvignon. Production: 100,000 bottles

Faugères, on the eastern fringes of St-Emilion, falls within two ACs, a sizeable chunk of the property lying within the Côtes de Castillon. Like Château Faugères (*q.v.*), this property was bought in 2005 by Swiss businessman Silvio Denz.

The vines are picked by hand. After a cold soak, the must is fermented in conical steel vats and the wine is aged in older barrels, with some micro-oxygenation.

I have usually found this an exemplary wine. The 1998 was disappointingly light, with pretty strawberry aromas but little substance. But all the vintages from 2000 to 2003 have been fleshy, concentrated, and well balanced; they are not wines of any great pretensions, but the fruit is appealing, the structure shows a light touch without being feeble, and, with the one exception of the 2003, the wines have persistence of flavour too. The 2004 shows more structure and grip than previous vintages, without sacrificing any fruit and stylishness.

Clos Louie

Tel: 0557 744663. Owner: Pascal Lucin Douteau. 0.9 ha. Merlot, Cabernet Franc,
Cabernet Sauvignon, Carmenère, Malbec. Production: 4,000 bottles

This *garagiste* property is owned by the *maître de chai* at Château Grand-Pontet in St-Emilion, and its crop was sold to the cooperative until 2003. Most of the vines are 150 years old and thus pre-phylloxera, which explains the presence of some uncommon grape varieties. Not surprisingly, yields are very low, around twenty-five hl/ha. The vinification is meticulous, with double sorting and whole-cluster fermentation with *pigeage*. I have not tasted the wine, but it sounds fascinating. It is also expensive.

Clos Puy-Arnaud

Belvès. Tel: 0557 479033. Owner: Thierry Valette. 12.5 ha. 60% Merlot, 25% Cabernet Franc,
7% Cabernet Sauvignon, 5% Malbec, 3% Carmenère. Production: 50,000 bottles.
Second wine: Ch Pervenche-Puy-Arnaud

The Valette family owned Pavie before its sale to Gérard Perse in 1998, and its younger members have forged new careers both in France and abroad. Thierry Valette bought this property in 1999 and worked hard to restore the vineyards. He also decided to plant some Carmenère. He hired Stéphane Derenoncourt as his consultant oenologist, but as they were good friends he replaced him in 2005 with Derenoncourt's assistant Anne Calderoni. By 2005 the estate was cultivated organically and in part biodynamically. Not all the vines are in Belvès; some 3.5 hectares are within St-Genès.

Yields are very low, at about thirty hl/ha. Valette opts for non-interventionist winemaking, avoiding crushing and pumping, using indigenous yeasts, and eschewing cold soaks. He ferments the Cabernet Sauvignon in cement tanks, usually with some micro-oxygenation, while the Merlot and Cabernet Franc are fermented in wooden vats with *pigeage*. The wine is aged in thirty-five per cent new oak, some of which is Hungarian, for twelve to eighteen months. The second wine is mostly Merlot and comes from different parcels than those used for Clos Puy-Arnaud. It is often better than the first wines from many other estates in the region.

Valette made a good wine in 2002, with ripe, almost candied aromas, attractive fruit, some finesse, and a slight slackness of structure. The 2003 is stylish, with sweet oaky aromas, intensity and freshness on the palate, and supple tannins. The 2004 is even better, rich and plummy on the nose, splendidly ripe and concentrated on the palate, with fine-grained tannins and good length.

Château Côte Montpezat

Belvès. Tel: 0557 560555. Website: www.cote-montpezat.com. Owner: Dominique Bessineau. 30 ha.
70% Merlot, 20% Cabernet Franc, 10% Cabernet Sauvignon. Production: 180,000 bottles.
Second wine: Ch de Brousse

Plastics industrialist Dominique Bessineau bought this property in 1989. Two-thirds of the vineyards are on south-facing clay slopes near the winery, while the remainder are on the thin soils of the plateau.

At present the grapes are harvested manually, but director Jean-François Lalle does not rule out machine-picking, at least on the plateau, in future. The grapes are sorted, then given a lengthy *cuvaison* in steel tanks. Lalle put a halt to micro-oxygenation after 2002, as he felt the ripeness of the fruit made it unnecessary. Half the wine is aged in oak (100 per cent new in 2005), while the other half stays in tanks. A small proportion of American oak is used. There is just a single racking, so *cliquage* is used to oxygenate the wine. There is no fining or filtration.

The *cuvée* called Compostelle is exactly the same wine as the regular bottling under a different label. And in 2004 Lalle introduced Le Canon de Côte Montpezat, a wine with higher Merlot content intended for earlier drinking.

Côte Montpezat is a lean, fresh style of wine, well made but a touch hollow and lacking in personality. In some vintages such as 2002 and 2003 the tannins are somewhat obtrusive, but the 2005 reaches greater heights, with more density and concentration and no lack of zest.

Château La Fourquerie

Gardegan-et-Tourtirac. Tel: 0557 561020. Website: www.vignobles-rollet.com. Owner: Jean-Pierre Rollet. 6 ha. 85% Merlot, 15% Cabernet Franc and Cabernet Sauvignon. Production: 36,000 bottles.

Second wine: Dom de la Grande Côte

The affable Jean-Pierre Rollet owns properties in St-Emilion and in neighbouring appellations. This is one of two he owns in Castillon, the other being Grand Tertre (*q.v.*). La Fourquerie has been in his family since 1934. The vines are picked both by hand and by machine. Some of the wine is aged for twelve months in barriques, the balance remaining in tanks. The only vintage I have tasted is the easy-going, fresh, but essentially simple 2000.

Château Grand Tertre

Gardegan-et-Tourtirac. Tel: 0557 561020. Website: www.vignobles-rollet.com. Owner: Jean-Pierre Rollet. 13 ha. 85% Merlot, 15% Cabernet Franc and Cabernet Sauvignon. Production: 80,000 bottles

Since 1980 Grand Tertre has been under the same ownership as La Fourquerie (*q.v.*). The grapes, which are machine-picked, are vinified with minimal oak-ageing. The 2001 had delicate cherry aromas, and was fairly rich, adding up to a well-made but unexceptional wine.

Château La Grande Maye

Belvès. Tel: 0557 479392. Owner: Paul Valade. 12 ha. 75% Merlot, 20% Cabernet Franc, 5% Cabernet Sauvignon. Production: 90,000 bottles

The average age of the vines here is a respectable thirty years, and the wine is aged in thirty per cent new oak for twelve months. The 2001 and 2002 were wines of some vibrancy, with juiciness and concentration, and a firm but not astringent tannic structure.

Château Joanin-Bécot

St-Philippe-d'Aiguilhe. Tel: 0557 744687. Website: www.beausejour-becot.com. Owner: Bécot family. 5 ha. 75% Merlot, 25% Cabernet Franc. Production: 40,000 bottles. Second wine: Le Secret de Joanin

The Bécot brothers, owners of Beau-Sejour-Bécot and La Gomerie in St-Emilion (*qq.v.*), bought this property in 2001, entrusting its management to Gérard's daughter Juliette. The vines are in one of the best corners of the appellation, and despite some recent replanting the average age of the vines is thirty years. Moreover the density is high for Castillon at 6,250 vines per hectare. The vinification is supervised by the oenologist Jean-Philippe Fort, a leading modernist. Sorting is rigorous, followed by a five-day cold soak, and fermentation takes place with *pigeage* in squat steel tanks, with some micro-oxygenation. The wine is aged in around sixty-five per cent new barriques for sixteen to eighteen months.

This is a rich and oaky style of wine. I found the 2001 overoaked and rather slack in structure, though it certainly doesn't lack fruit. The 2002 is bright but somewhat soupy. The 2003 is a big, bold wine, with powerful aromas of plums and chocolate; the concentration and power are evident on the palate, and the tannins are chewy. (The 14.8 degrees of alcohol are not apparent, thanks to the weight of fruit.) The 2004 is more satisfying, with rich, succulent aromas, a discreet presence of oak, the opulence of fruit nicely balanced by bright acidity. Clearly Joanin-Bécot is going from strength to strength.

Château Lagrave Aubert

St-Magne-de-Castillon. Tel: 0557 401576. Website: www.la-couspaude.com. Owner: Jean-Claude Aubert. 20 ha. 75% Merlot, 20% Cabernet Franc, 5% Cabernet Sauvignon. Production: 50,000 bottles.
Second wine: Ch Labesse

Jean-Claude Aubert owns a number of properties throughout the Libournais, and this is his outpost in the Côtes de Castillon. The vines, on gravelly and sandy soils, are picked by hand. The wine is fermented in cement vats and aged in oak. The only vintage I have tasted is the 2003, a rich and supple wine with good depth of black-cherry fruit, no excessive extraction, and quite good length.

Château Lamartine

St-Philippe-d'Aiguilhe. Tel: 0557 406046. Owners: Gilbert and Jérôme Gourraud. 17.7 ha. 17.5 ha red: 70% Merlot, 15% Cabernet Franc, 15% Cabernet Sauvignon. 0.2 ha white: 50% Sauvignon Blanc, 50% Muscadelle. Production: 120,000 bottles

There are two *cuvées* here. Of the regular wine, the only vintage I have tasted is the light, simple 2002. The 2001 Cuvée Excellence has some sweet oak on the nose, and is a medium-bodied wine with reasonable concentration, and a long if slightly earthy finish.

Château de Laussac

St-Magne-de-Castillon. Tel: 0557 401376. Owner: Alexandra Roché. 28 ha. 75% Merlot, 25% Cabernet Franc. Production: 90,000 bottles. Second wine: Ch La Rose-Laussac

This estate used to belong to Alain Raynaud of Château Quinault in St-Emilion, but it recently changed hands. The only vintage I have tasted was the 2002, which had ripe raspberry aromas, and was a rich, juicy wine with some tannic backbone.

Château Lideyre

Gardegan-et-Tourtirac. Tel: 0557 845316. Website: www.vignobles-bardet.fr. Owner: Philippe Bardet. 3.7 ha. 62% Merlot, 38% Cabernet Franc. Production: 24,000 bottles

This small property has been in the hands of the Bardet family since 1979. The vines are located on deep clay-limestone soils on the plateau. The grapes are picked by machine and the wine is unoaked. The only wine I have encountered is the 2000 Cuvée Alice, which had stewed aromas and cherry fruit obscured by rather grim tannins.

Philippe Bardet also owns three other properties in the appellation: the nineteen-hectare Château Lardit in Ste-Colombe; the nineteen-hectare Château Picoron (here the 2000 was rather coarse and hard-edged); and the thirty-five-hectare Château Rocher Lideyre.

Château Moulin de Clotte

Les Salles de Castillon. Tel: 0557 406094. Owner: Dominique Chupin. 8 ha. 60% Merlot, 30% Cabernet Franc, 10% Cabernet Sauvignon. Production: 60,000 bottles

The regular wine here is aged in tanks only for about eighteen months. The Cuvée Dominique is made from the oldest vines. There is a higher proportion of Merlot in the blend, and the wine is aged for twelve months in barriques. The 2001 Cuvée Dominique had ripe but slightly cooked aromas, and although the wine had plenty of fruit, it was also somewhat dilute and lacked length.

Château Peyrou

St-Magne-de-Castillon. Tel: 0557 247205. Owner: Catherine Papon-Nouvel. 4.5 ha. 80% Merlot,
10% Cabernet Franc, 10% Cabernet Sauvignon. Production: 25,000 bottles

Although she comes from an established wine-producing family, Catherine Papon-Nouvel, who also owns Clos St Julien (*q.v.*) in St-Emilion, bought this property in 1989 in order to have an estate for which she alone was responsible. The vines border those of St-Etienne-de-Lisse in St-Emilion, and she claims there is no significant difference in terroir between the two appellations at this spot. However, there is a fourfold difference in price, and her limited means required her to stay within the Castillon borders. The vines, which are from forty to seventy years old, are in a single parcel below those of Château de Pressac in St-Emilion. The soil is clay with some sand. Harvesting is manual.

It was only in 1998 that Mme. Papon-Nouvel felt able to make the investments that would bring quality to a level with which she was happy. It was in that year that she began systematic green-harvesting and acquired some new oak barrels. Fermentation takes place with indigenous yeasts, and some micro-oxygenation *sous marc*. The wine is aged in around fifteen per cent new oak for twelve months.

This is a consistently good and polished wine, deeply coloured, with rich and sometimes smoky blackberry aromas. The 1998, 2001, 2002, and 2003 share a rich, rounded palate, with firm tannins, black-fruits flavours, and ample freshness and length.

In 2002 Catherine Papon-Nouvel bought four more hectares in Ste-Colombe. The vines were in poor shape and had been abused by over-enthusiastic use of fertilizers. She plans to make an unoaked wine from this site, but at the time of writing its name had not yet been chosen.

Château de Pitray

Gardegan-et-Tourtirac. Tel: 0557 406338. Website: www.pitray.com. Owner: Alix de Pitray,
Comtesse de Boigne. 31 ha. 70% Merlot, 30% Cabernet Franc. Production: 210,000 bottles

This ancient property is located high on the clay-limestone plateau. An earlier generation of the family built the handsome neo-Renaissance château here in 1868. The grapes are picked by machine, cold-soaked, then fermented with indigenous yeasts. The regular bottling is aged solely in tanks for about eighteen months, while the Premier Vin, which accounts for roughly one-quarter of production, is aged in one-third new barriques.

The 2001 Premier Vin showed great aromatic power, with aromas of plums and chocolate; it's a robust wine, dense and forceful, that should age well. The 2002 Premier Vin has sweet oaky aromas, a supple texture, with lush fruit countered by assertive tannins; but there is some freshness here. These may not be the finest wines of the appellation, but they are inexpensive and offer good value.

Château Roc de Joanin

St-Philippe-d'Aiguilhe. Tel: 0557 247128. Owner: Yves Mirande. 4.6 ha. 70% Merlot,
15% Cabernet Franc, 15% Cabernet Sauvignon. Production: 35,000 bottles.
Second wine: Douceur de Joanin

The Mirande family, proprietors of Château La Rose-Côtes-Rol (*q.v.*) in St-Emilion, also own this small property located high on the plateau. The vines are quite old, and Roc de Joanin sometimes contains more Merlot than the *encépagement* suggests, as the Cabernet Sauvignon in particular struggles to ripen here. The wine is aged for twelve months in twenty-five per cent new oak. The second wine comes from higher-yielding vines, and is unoaked and intended to be drunk young.

The 2002 Roc de Joanin was quite stylish, but marred by edgy acidity and rather dry tannins. The 2003 was more robust, but also more fruity and generous.

Château Roque le Mayne

*St-Magne-de-Castillon. Tel: 0557 401732. Website: www.vignobles-meynard.com. **Owner:** Jean-François Meynard.*
*16 ha. 80% Merlot, 15% Cabernet Sauvignon, 5% Malbec. **Production:** 60,000 bottles*

Only the best sectors of this property, on south-facing clay-limestone slopes, are used for Roque le Mayne, the rest being consigned to another wine called Château La Bourrée. The harvest is manual, and Meynard favours bleeding the tanks by around fifteen per cent to increase concentration. There is no crushing, and the wine is fermented in squat steel tanks with *pigeage* and micro-oxygenation. The wine is aged for around fourteen months in one-third new barriques, with some lees-stirring. La Bourrée comes from sandier soils lower down and these vines are machine-harvested. It offers a lighter, fruitier style at a lower price.

Roque le Mayne is a sound wine, with discreet cherry aromas. The 2001 is rich and concentrated, but light acidity and tannin suggest it may not age that well. The 2003 is a touch extracted and chocolatey, with firm tannins, but the texture is surprisingly soft. The 2004 was ungainly before bottling, with a supple texture fighting some rather sharp acidity.

Château Tifayne

See Château Lalande de Tifayne (Côte de Francs)

Château Veyry

***Castillon. Tel:** 0557 740956. **Owner:** Christian Veyry. 4 ha. 90% Merlot, 10% Cabernet Franc. **Production:** 60,000 bottles*

Christian Veyry owns Château Louvie (*q.v.*) in St-Emilion but is better known as a consultant far and wide in the Libournais; in Fronsac he has cornered the market on most of the top properties. He was trained by Michel Rolland but applies his own ideas. This is an estate he assembled from scratch from 1997 onwards. At present the vines are on chalky clay soils on steep south-facing slopes. The density ranges from 5,000 to 7,000 vines per hectare, and yields rarely exceed thirty-five hl/ha.

The grapes are harvested by hand and Veyry works hard to ensure there is no overripe fruit. The vinification is traditional, but Veyry uses a good deal of micro-oxygenation during the *élevage*, which takes place in one-third new barriques for eighteen months. There is no fining.

The 2001 exhibits rich, plummy aromas with some chocolatey tones; the flavours are sweet but not jammy, and there is good acidity. The 2002 has similar aromas, but is more supple and lighter in body than the 2001; it has both freshness and finesse. The plump 2003 is more effortful and muscular, but the fruit quality is fine and the wine does not lack length. The 2004 is unusually powerful and structured, with plummy fruit and a good deal of spice. Overall these are concentrated and sophisticated wines, but they are at the top end of the price range for the appellation.

Vieux-Château-Champs-de-Mars

*Les Salles de Castillon. Tel: 0557 406349. **Owner:** Régis Moro. 17 ha. 80% Merlot,*
*10% Cabernet Franc, 10% Cabernet Sauvignon. **Production:** 60,000 bottles.*
Second wine: Ch Puy-Landry

Régis Moro bought this property in 1984. The average age of the vines is some forty years, and there are parcels of centenarian vines. To keep yields down, Moro prunes short, but does not green-harvest. Only the oldest vines are picked by hand. Fermentation takes place with indigenous yeasts. Barriques were first introduced in 1989, and today the wine is aged in one-third new oak, without racking. Jean-Philippe Fort is the consultant oenologist, so there is some micro-oxygenation and lees-stirring during the *élevage*. Fort blends shortly before bottling, and there is no fining or filtration.

The oldest vines are used for Cuvée Johanna, which rarely includes any Cabernet Sauvignon. This wine is fermented with *pigeage* in wooden vats and given an extended maceration before being aged in new oak for eighteen months. The 1989 is still remarkably youthful and flavoury; it's opulent, vigorous, and long. It seemed better than the fresh but rather light 2000. However, the 2000 Johanna is far denser, and the fruit is submerged at present; this is a sumptuous wine, tight and unyielding now, but with fine potential. The regular 2002 has sweet cherry aromas, and it's juicy, fresh, and attractive, perky rather than complex. Clearly the creation of the high-priced Cuvée Johanna has altered the style of the regular wine, emphasizing freshness and drinkability rather than power and richness.

Other wines with a good reputation, but which I have never visited and rarely tasted, include **Arthus**, **de Belcier**, **Clos Les Lunelles**, **Fontbaude**, **Poupille**, and **Robin**.

COTES DE FRANCS

This region with just over 500 hectares of vines is simply the northern extension of the Côtes de Castillon, and lies sixty kilometres (thirty-seven miles) east of the city of Bordeaux. The name Francs is apparently derived from a fort established here by Clovis, king of the Franks, in 507. Until 1921 the Côtes de Francs formed part of the St-Emilion satellites but then lost its right to the link with St-Emilion. Although the Côtes de Castillon did not object to fusing with its neighbour, the Côtes de Francs growers decided in 1967 to form their own appellation.

There is no significant different in terroir or microclimate between these two Côtes. Francs is quite high, with vineyards at 105 to 127 metres (344 to 417 feet), and rainfall is slightly lower than in Castillon. Many of the vineyards face east or southeast rather than due south. Overall, summers tend to be hotter and drier, and winters somewhat colder. The best soils tend to be on the plateaux, on asteriated and other types of limestone with clay, and subsoils of sand, gravel, and quartz. At lower elevations the soils are sandier and more alluvial.

Curiously, the Côtes de Francs used to be best known for its sweet wines, as white vines in lower locations are often attacked by botrytis. But after World War II sweet wine production diminished, as the very low yields required for high-quality botrytis wines were no longer economical. Only about twenty hectares of white vines remain, with sixty per cent Sémillon, thirty per cent Sauvignon Blanc and Sauvignon Gris, and ten per cent Muscadelle. Cabernet plays a more important role here than in other Libournais appellations. The average red-vine plantings for the appellation are fifty per cent Merlot, twenty-five per cent Cabernet Franc, twenty-four per cent Cabernet Sauvignon, and one per cent Malbec. The region is spread over three communes: St-Cibard (161 hectares), Tayac (154), and Francs itself (150). Of the three, Tayac tends to be the most precocious, thanks to more silt in the soil. There are some fifty-five growers who produce their own wine, as well as thirty-three who sell to cooperatives. Production in 2001 consisted of 3.8 million bottles of red wine, 62,000 of white, and 8,000 of sweet wine.

The grapes ripen relatively late, though some growers point out that they mature no later than sectors of St-Emilion such as St-Christophe-des-Bardes. The wines can be quite tough and are less approachable than those from Castillon, but this may have more to do with the high proportion of Cabernet than with climatic factors. Indeed some growers try to diminish that proportion in their vineyards. On the other hand, a grower such as Régis Moro is a great believer in the variety, though remarking that it ripens only on the best sites.

As in the Côtes de Castillon, the presence of newcomers has led to a rise in quality. Nicolas Thienpont alone is responsible for vinifying about ten per cent of the total crop. Yet the region languishes in obscurity, and its wines, whatever their quality, struggle to make an impression in a crowded marketplace. There are still too many rustic wines emerging from here, and even though they tend to be inexpensive, there is little demand for this style of wine even at a bargain price. Thanks to the local syndicat, I tasted numerous wines from here, but the majority, I regret to say, were of insufficient quality or character to merit inclusion.

Château Les Charmes-Godard

*St-Cibard. Tel: 0557 560747. Website: www.nicolas-thienpont.com. Owner: Nicolas Thienpont. 14.5 ha. 13 ha red: 70%
Merlot, 30% Cabernet Franc. 1.5 ha white: 65% Sémillon, 20% Sauvignon Gris,
15% Muscadelle. Production: 60,000 bottles*

The Thienponts have been proprietors in the region since 1946, but in those days they were general
farmers rather than wine producers. In 1983 Nicolas Thienpont began to look after the family properties,
and focused on wine production. This estate was bought by Nicolas and two of his brothers in 1988.

Thienpont also owns a nine-hectare property called Château Laclaverie, but since 2005 its crop,
which is machine-harvested, has been merged with that from Charmes-Godard. The red wine is
unoaked. It bears the label of both properties for marketing reasons, but the wine is identical.

Thienpont is particularly proud of his white wine, a barrel-fermented blend from vines that are on
average forty years old. After some skin contact, the wine is fermented and aged for eight months in one-
third new oak with lees-stirring. Thienpont is right to be proud. The 2001 had very ripe honey and
peach aromas, with pronounced oakiness; the wine was rich and broad yet had a firm acidic grip, an
invigorating dryness, and remarkable freshness. The 2003 is lush but short. The 2004 is leaner than the
2001, but it has attractive white-peach flavours and considerable length. The 2006 resembles the 2001.

Château Franc-Cardinal

*Tayac. Tel: 0557 406339. Owner: Philip Holzberg. 10 ha. 80% Merlot, 18% Cabernet Franc,
2% Malbec. Production: 60,000 bottles*

Philip Holzberg used to run wine bars in his native Canada and always dreamed of having his own vineyard
in France. After a false start in Beaune, he began searching in Bordeaux and bought this property, then named
Domaine du Cardinal, in 2001. The vines, planted on clay and silt, had been well cared for, but the whole
crop had been sold in bulk. Holzberg is very selective about the grapes that go into his wine, and in 2002 he
rejected twenty-five per cent of the crop. The wine is aged both in barrels and in tanks. The 2002 is delicate,
medium-bodied with little grip, but reasonably fresh.

Château de Francs

*Francs. Tel: 0557 406591. Owners: Hubert de Boüard and Dominique Hébrard (lessees). 35 ha.
34.5 ha red: 90% Merlot, 10% Cabernet Franc. 0.5 ha white: 100% Sauvignon Blanc.
Production: 200,000 bottles*

These two major players in St-Emilion teamed up in 1985 to rent this substantial vineyard. The château was
an episcopal residence in the eighteenth century. In 2003 the dilapidated buildings were bought by Belgian
partners, though de Boüard and Hébrard remain in control of the vines and winemaking. The vineyards are
in three main blocks, all on slopes at an elevation of around 100 metres (328 feet). The soil is rich in white
limestone, but as a terroir it is colder than St-Emilion, which is why the proportion of Merlot is so high.
Systematic green-harvesting accelerates ripening.

Until 1998 there was a conventional second wine, but it was then replaced by a top *cuvée* called Les
Cerisiers. The grapes for Les Cerisiers are picked by hand, unlike the regular bottling, but manager Eric de
Loynes is so pleased with the results given by new harvesting machines he tried out in 2005 that in future all
the fruit may be mechanically harvested.

After sorting, the grapes are given a cold soak, and some ten per cent of the juice is bled off. The must is
fermented with cultivated yeasts in steel tanks, with a prolonged *cuvaison* and occasional micro-oxygenation
sous marc. The regular wine is aged in twenty per cent new oak; Les Cerisiers in fifty per cent new wood.
There is also a minuscule production of barrel-fermented white wine, which I have not tasted.

The 2000 is now cedary, silky, and mature. The 2002 has lush, fruity aromas, but the wine, although quite rich, lacks some vigour. The 2003 has sweet, ripe cherry aromas and flavours, but it's not that concentrated and the acidity is modest. The 2004 is decidedly rustic. Perhaps it suffers from the removal of the best fruit for Les Cerisiers, which in 2003 and 2004 is a big, robust wine, with black fruits on the nose, and considerable weight.

Château de Garonneau

St-Cibard. Tel: 0557 406074. Owner: Roussille family. 24 ha. 60% Merlot, 30% Cabernet Sauvignon, 10% Cabernet Franc. Production: 180,000 bottles

The star attraction here is the oak-aged Cuvée Magnis des Nauves. The 2002 had fairly rich but discreet aromas, while the palate was quite rich, juicy, and accessible.

Château Godard

Francs. Tel: 0557 406594. Owner: Franck Richard. 9 ha. 8.5 ha red: 78% Merlot, 17% Cabernet Sauvignon, 5% Cabernet Franc. 0.5 ha white: 80% Sémillon, 20% Sauvignon Blanc. Production: 70,000 bottles

The bulk of the grapes Franck Richard grows go to the Puisseguin-St-Emilion cooperative, but from a two-hectare parcel he makes a red wine called Cru Godard that has a higher proportion of Cabernet and is oak-aged for twelve months. The 2002 has delicate, charming cherry aromas, some richness backed by firm tannins, and good acidity. Richard also produces a little sweet wine, harvested by successive forays into the vineyards, and fermented and aged for twenty months in oak barrels.

Château Lalande de Tifayne

Tel: 0557 406129. Owner: Renaud Limbosch. 5 ha. 65% Merlot, 20% Cabernet Sauvignon, 15% Cabernet Franc. Production: 20,000 bottles

This small property was bought by the present owner, a Belgian, in 1997. The vines are cultivated by *lutte raisonnée*, and the harvest is both manual and mechanical. Limbosch also owns seven hectares of vines in the northern Côtes de Castillon, at Monbadon, and the wine from there, which has a higher Merlot content than the Côtes de Francs, is sold as Château Tifayne.

There is also an oaked Côtes de Castillon known as Roc de Tifayne, aged for eighteen months in twenty-five per cent new French and American barrels.

The 2003 Lalande de Tifayne has light cherry aromas, fair concentration, and firm tannins. The weighty 2002 Roc de Tifayne strikes me as overripe, both on the nose and on the palate, and there are dry tannins on the finish.

Château Marsau

Francs. Tel: 0557 443049. Owner: Jean-Marie Chadronnier. 15 ha. 100% Merlot. Production: 70,000 bottles. Second wine: Prélude de Marsau

Jean-Marie Chadronnier's day job is running the important négociant house of CVBG; Marsau has been his personal property since 1994. Michel Rolland acts as his consultant oenologist, which may help to explain the high proportion of Merlot here. Of the fifteen hectares under vine, four lie on the far side of a lane alongside the property and thus fall within the Bergerac appellation. The soil is essentially clay-limestone, with sand in some sectors. The vines are fairly young, and green-harvesting is employed to curb their vigour.

The grapes are picked by hand. Marsau is equipped with a refrigerated tunnel that allows the winemaker to chill the fruit before fermentation if that is deemed advantageous. Fermentation usually takes place with natural yeasts and some micro-oxygenation. The *marc* is pressed in a vertical press. After partial malolactic fermentation in barriques, the wine is aged in one-third new oak, with *cliquage*.

Marsau is a rich, plummy wine, and the character of the Merlot certainly shows through. The 2002 is admirably concentrated and spicy, yet the tannins remain supple so the fruit can shine through. The 2003 is lively for the vintage, with aromas of black cherries and liquorice, and a good deal of spice on the palate. The 2004 is sumptuous and powerful.

Château Nardou

*Tayac. Tel: 0557 406960. **Owner:** Florent Dubard. 15 ha. 80% Merlot, 10% Cabernet Sauvignon, 10% Cabernet Franc. **Production:** 100,000 bottles. **Second wine:** Cuvée de Bois Meney*

Before Dubard bought this property in 1998, its fruit had been delivered to the cooperative. The vines lie in a single parcel on sandy and stony soil on clay-limestone slopes. Dubard practises *lutte raisonnée* and reduces yields by green-harvesting. The fruit is machine-picked. The wine is aged for twelve months in one-third new barriques with lees-stirring.

Cherry aromas and a touch of spice characterize the nose, while the palate is reasonably concentrated, with firm but not harsh tannins, plenty of overt fruitiness and a modest finish. Of the vintages from 2000 to 2004, I prefer the 2000 and 2001, and the 2004 shows good potential.

Château Pelan Bellevue

*Francs. Tel: 0557 406349. **Owner:** Régis Moro. 25 ha. 45% Merlot, 40% Cabernet Sauvignon, 15% Cabernet Franc. **Production:** 80,000 bottles*

Régis Moro also owns Vieux-Château-Champs-de-Mars (*q.v.*) in Castillon, and is an enthusiast for the Cabernet varieties. He bought this property in 1994, and since 2005 it has been cultivated organically. Viticultural practices are the same as for the Castillon estate. The wine is fermented in cement tanks with natural yeasts, and aged for twelve months in older oak barrels, with some *cliquage*. Blending takes place shortly before bottling, without fining or filtration.

In 1997 Moro inaugurated a special *cuvée* called simply Pelan, a highly unusual wine composed of eighty per cent Cabernet Sauvignon. It is fermented in wooden vats, with *pigeage* and extended maceration. It is then aged for eighteen months in new barriques, with some lees-stirring. Pelan now represents about twenty per cent of production.

The regular 2000 has much aromatic charm, with a nose of cherries and tobacco; it is extremely ripe and reasonably concentrated. The 2003 has mighty and opulent fruit but the finish is tannic and lacks some finesse. The only Pelan I have tasted, the 2000, struck me as over-extracted, with dark chocolate flavours, brutal tannins, and an overall impenetrability.

Château La Prade

*St-Cibard. Tel: 0557 560747. **Website:** www.nicolas-thienpont.com. **Owner:** Nicolas Thienpont. 4.5 ha. 90% Merlot, 10% Cabernet Franc. **Production:** 12,000 bottles*

Nicolas Thienpont and his brothers bought this property in 2000 from Patrick Valette. It is located just north of their principal property, Puygueraud (*q.v.*), on the limestone plateau. The vines are old, and the soil is ploughed. The grapes are not crushed, and are fermented in cement tanks with *délestage*, then aged for twelve to sixteen months in eighty per cent new barriques, with lees-stirring and *cliquage* if necessary.

The 2000 is extracted and austere. Far better is the oaky, slightly confected, but lush and plump 2001, which has plenty of grip on the finish. There is a slight but not unpleasant herbaceousness on the nose of the 2002, and the wine overall shows more freshness and a lighter touch than the 2001. The 2003 is plump and accessible, a big mouthful, but the texture is decidedly soft and it should be drunk young.

Château du Prévot

Francs. Tel: 0557 843852. Owner: G.F.A. Cedefranc. 9 ha. 70% Merlot, 20% Cabernet Franc,
10% Cabernet Sauvignon. Production: 60,000 bottles

The vines here are fairly young. Two *cuvées* are produced, the better being Le Prévot. The 2002 of the latter was supple, reasonably concentrated, and though sound and balanced, was unexciting.

Château Puyanché

Francs. Tel: 0557 406577. Owner: Joseph Arbo. 19 ha. 16 ha red: 70% Merlot,
30% Cabernet Sauvignon. 3 ha white: 55% Sauvignon Blanc, 45% Sémillon. Production: 40,000 bottles

The red wine is unoaked and lacks character. Of more interest are the whites. The dry white is aged in one-third new barriques with lees-stirring. The 2003 had rich peachy aromas, ample fruit, discreet oak, and decent acidity. Arbo also makes a *moelleux* from eighty-five per cent Sémillon. In 2002 this was only lightly sweet; it had a silky texture and fair acidity but was far from complex.

Château Puyfromage

St-Cibard. Tel: 0556 395904. Website: www.puyfromage.com. Owner: Philippe Marque. 45 ha.
60% Merlot, 25% Cabernet Sauvignon, 15% Cabernet Franc. Production: 300,000 bottles

Encumbered by a somewhat unfortunate name, this large property has been in the family for three generations. The château occupies a commanding hilltop position, and the vineyards are dispersed along its slopes on clay-limestone soils. Five of its forty-five hectares are within the Côtes de Castillon.

This is an unashamedly commercial estate, cropping by machine at close to maximum yields, employing micro-oxygenation after fermentation, and ageing the wine in tanks only. The 2003 and 2004 are decent and solid wines with ample fruit but little personality. Part of the production is sold under a different label, Vieux-Château-du-Colombier, but the wine is identical.

Château Puygueraud

St-Cibard. Tel: 0557 560747. Website: www.nicolas-thienpont.com. Owner: Nicolas Thienpont. 35 ha. 65% Merlot,
30% Cabernet Franc, 5% Malbec. Production: 200,000 bottles. Second wine: Ch Lauriol

This is the most important of the Thienpont properties in the Côtes de Francs, and its charming sixteenth-century château is still inhabited by the widow of George [sic] Thienpont, who bought it in 1946. However, the estate was run as a mixed farm and the vineyards were not planted until 1979. In 1983, George's son Nicolas took over running the property. Nicolas Thienpont has made his reputation by vastly improving the quality of wines at the properties he manages in St-Emilion. There he is working with great terroir; here in the Côtes de Francs the challenge is greater.

After harvesting (manually for the *grand vin* only) the grapes are vinified as whole clusters in steel tanks, with occasional micro-oxygenation. The wine is aged for sixteen to eighteen months in forty per cent new barriques, with lees-stirring and *cliquage*. In outstanding vintages a prestige wine called Cuvée George, named after the founder, who died in 1997, is made from equal proportions of Malbec, Merlot, and Cabernet Franc. Only 6,000 bottles are produced.

The 1998 had robust black-cherry and liquorice aromas, and a dense, tannic palate with sufficient acidity to give it good length. The 2001 is similar, but less sturdy and with more charm and overt fruitiness. The nose of the 2003 is rather baked, but it's an enjoyably plump, supple, forward wine. The only Cuvée George I have tasted is the 2003, with its firm, oaky aromas, its grippy structure, its impressive concentration, and its rather austere finish. It may become more supple and accessible with time, but I am not sure. The second wine, Château Lauriol, is sometimes slightly herbaceous, but also has attractive, upfront fruit. It is sold at a bargain price.

25. Fronsac and Canon-Fronsac

These two regions – for all practical purposes a single zone – used to be one of the most prestigious in all Bordeaux. In the 1630s Cardinal Richelieu owned estates here, and his descendants made wines that found favour at the French court. According to historian Henri Enjalbert, in the eighteenth century these were the most prized wines of the entire Libournais, and were even cited in an early Christie's auction catalogue. They continued to sell for high prices in the nineteenth century. The presence of some very splendid riverside mansions is explained by the fact that after phylloxera had destroyed many of the hillside vines, growers planted on the richer *palus* soils which, being subject to river floods, were immune to the louse. These proprietors grew rich and some flaunted their wealth. Unfortunately the *palus* wines were usually mediocre, which undermined the region's reputation.

To refer to this glorious past to a Fronsac grower today would probably prompt a wry, downturned smile. Few regions have been as badly affected by the economic crisis afflicting Bordeaux in the early twenty-first century. By 2005, according to the négociant Gérard Milhade, the wines were fetching the lowest prices of any Bordeaux AC. Ironically, this has nothing to do with the quality of the wine. Of course there are mediocre wines on the market, but the best wines – fleshy, Merlot-based, rich, succulent, and often elegant too – are excellent. Some special *cuvées* fetch high prices, but in general the wines are not expensive.

It doesn't help, I suppose, that one region is home to two ACs with little discernible difference between them. The actual difference is geographical, not geological. Canon-Fronsac lies between the villages of Fronsac and St-Michel-de-Fronsac, and the hills just to the north of them. The region is flanked by the broad flow of the Dordogne on one side and the meandering of the Isle on the other. It was in 1925 that some growers formed two syndicats: Côtes de Fronsac and Côtes de Canon-Fronsac. The latter became AC Canon-Fronsac in 1964, and in 1976 a decree replaced the Côtes de Fronsac with AC Fronsac. As there is no difference at all in the regulations governing the two ACs, this makes no sense from a marketing viewpoint. (However, a promotional organization called Expression de Fronsac was formed in 1987 and made no distinction between the two ACs.) In theory, Canon-Fronsac is supposed to be rather better in quality, or potential quality, than the larger Fronsac appellation.

With gently rolling hills, sudden, steep valleys, and expansive views over the two river valleys, this is a region of great charm. On the slopes and plateau the basic soil type is known as *molasses du Fronsadais*, essentially limestone but mixed with clay and sandstone. The higher the elevation – eighty-eight metres (289 feet) is the maximum – the greater the proportion of limestone; and the farther north you go, the higher the sand content. All agrees that it adds up to a fine terroir for grape-growing. The elevation means that frost damage is rare, and the profusion of slopes ensures good drainage.

Exposition is important too, as in all undulating regions. Canon-Fronsac has many south-facing slopes, which of course tend to give the ripest grapes. Clay is also an important factor that influences the style of the wines. Its depth over the limestone bedrock varies greatly, from forty centimetres (sixteen inches) to three metres (nearly ten feet). Different soil structures combined with the varied topography mean that each vineyard, each slope, tends to differ from its neighbours. This may require differing viticultural approaches for parcels within the same estate. This can be positive in that it can result in wines of greater complexity.

In the past some wrong decisions were taken which undermined the potential of Fronsac's wines. For instance, INAO in the 1960s required a proportion of Cabernet Sauvignon to be planted, even though experience and common sense demonstrated that Merlot and Cabernet Franc were far more appropriate. Clearly, estates with a high proportion of Cabernet Franc or Sauvignon require warmer vintages for those grapes to have a better chance of ripening fully. (Michel Ponty, owner of Grand Renouil, goes so far as to say that even Cabernet Franc ripens properly in only one year out of five, so he has only Merlot in his vineyards.) In the 1970s and 1980s some growers rejigged their vineyards to a lower density so as to aid mechanization. In the 1990s some growers and winemakers became over-ambitious. I recall tasting dozens of 1998 wines in their infancy and was dismayed by the number of soupy, lush, low-acidity wines. On the other hand, there are still wines that have been unable to shed their rusticity.

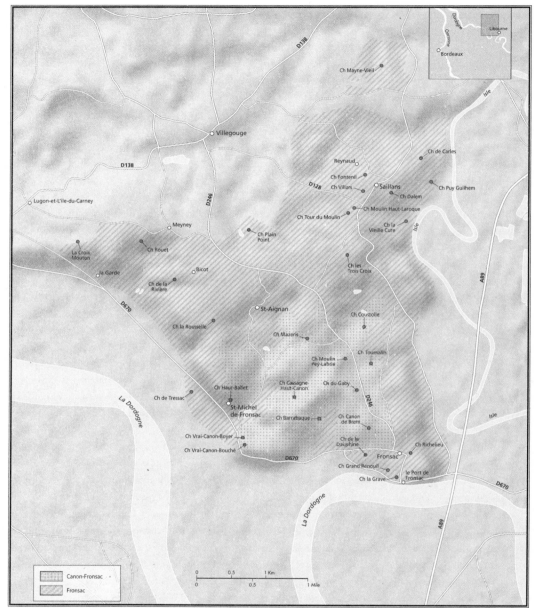

Fronsac

An estate manager who directs properties on the Left and Right banks told me:

*Many estates tried to ape Pomerol. They thought they could sell their wines
en primeur, which didn't make much sense given that the wines were not that
expensive in the first place. They began to practise micro-oxygenation, malolactic
fermentation in barriques, and used lots of new oak. All this costs money, so
prices have risen, and the growers are finding there just isn't a market for this
type of wine – at least not from Fronsac.*

On the other hand, this change in direction probably stemmed from a desire to correct the errors of the past. Jean-Noël Hervé of Moulin Haut Laroque, one of the best estates, acknowledges the limestone soils can give wines high in tannin:

> But the rusticity one used to find in our wines had more to do with poor winemaking than with terroir. In the past winemakers didn't destem, so that added astringency to the wines. So did the use of old barrels. Clay sectors also delay maturation, but growers often picked too early, and that, too, gave harsh tannins. It's true that after some years in bottle, some of them turned out well, but they were far from enjoyable young, and today it is no longer acceptable to produce wines that demand long ageing. Another factor was machine-harvesting. Machines are much more delicate these days, but in the past they handled the vines roughly and a lot of vegetal matter would go into the vats. So all these factors needed to be corrected.

The total area for both appellations is around 1,130 hectares, of which 300 lie within Canon-Fronsac. Six communes fall within the two ACs: Fronsac (425 hectares), La Rivière (144), Saillans (243), St-Aignan (190), St-Germain-la-Rivière (42), and St-Michel-de-Fronsac (250). Overall, the *encépagement* is seventy-eight per cent Merlot, thirteen per cent Cabernet Franc, seven per cent Cabernet Sauvignon, and two per cent Malbec. The minimum density is 5,000 vines per hectare, and the usual method of pruning is *guyot double*. There are about 170 estates, of which forty supply the cooperative at Lugon.

Château Barrabaque

Fronsac. AC Canon-Fronsac. Tel: 0557 550909. Owner: Bernard Noël. 9 ha. 70% Merlot, 25% Cabernet Franc, 5% Cabernet Sauvignon. Production: 60,000 bottles. Second wine: B de Barrabaque

This estate, owned by the Noël family since 1936, is now managed by Mme. Nicole Noël. Although Barrabaque is located in Canon-Fronsac, 1.5 hectares lie within Fronsac, and these vines provide the basic wine, the Cuvée Tradition. The vineyards, on slopes overlooking the Dordogne, are on chalky and sandy clay soils and are picked by hand. Some micro-oxygenation *sous marc* is applied after fermentation, and the wine is aged for twelve months in older barrels. The Cuvée Prestige is entirely made from old vines from Canon-Fronsac, and aged for at least fifteen months in thirty per cent new barriques.

The 2000 and 2001 are both very good, with highly ripe aromas enlivened by a good dose of new oak, while some tannins and spiciness add complexity to the fleshy fruit. The 1998 Prestige was very harmonious with the oak and fruit nicely in balance, and the firm 2005 is similar.

Château Beauséjour

Fronsac. AC Fronsac. Tel: 0557 510245. Website: www.belair-beausejour.com. Owner: Jacques Melet. 21 ha. 80% Merlot, 15% Cabernet Sauvignon, 5% Cabernet Franc. Production: 120,000 bottles. Second wine: Ch Faure-Beauséjour

The Melet family headquarters is at Château Bel-Air (*q.v.*) in Pomerol, but since 1870 they have also owned this substantial property in Fronsac. The average age of the vines is thirty-five years, and they are harvested manually. Christian Veyry is the consultant oenologist. After repeated sortings and a brief cold soak, the must is fermented and aged in steel and cement tanks. In practice most vintages are pure Merlot, as is the special *cuvée*, first made in 2002, called B de Beauséjour, a selection from the oldest vines, aged in one-third new barriques. About 15,000 bottles are produced.

The 2002 is fairly rich and nicely textured. The 2002 B de Beauséjour has a dense, damsony nose, and considerably more richness than the regular bottling; it's full-bodied and assertive and should develop well.

Château Bellevue

St-Michel-de-Fronsac. AC Fronsac. Tel: 0557 249410. Owner: Olivier Decelle. 9 ha. 100% Merlot. Production: 28,000 bottles

Bellevue is another recent acquisition by Olivier Decelle, who also owns Haut-Ballet (*q.v.*) in Canon-Fronsac. His first vintage was 2002. The soil is clay-limestone, and the vinification is essentially the same as for Haut-Ballet, but thirty per cent of the wine is aged in concrete vats; of the remaining seventy per cent, half is aged in new oak, the remainder in one-year-old barrels. Judging by the 2002 and 2003, this is a lighter, sharper, simpler wine than Haut-Ballet, but it is also less expensive.

Château Canon de Brem

Fronsac. AC Canon-Fronsac. Tel: 0557 740661. Website: www.chateau-dauphine.com.
Owner: Jean Halley. 8 ha. 80% Merlot, 20% Cabernet Franc. Production: 30,000 bottles

For the history of this property, see Château de La Dauphine below. J.P. Moueix owned the property from 1984 until 2000, when Christian Moueix sold it to Jean Halley. He had labelled and sold wine from one part of the vineyards as Château Canon-Moueix, but after 2000 this wine was incorporated into Canon de Brem. Its vineyards are on south-facing slopes in a single parcel above La Dauphine, with just a lane separating the two properties. The soils are clay-limestone with some white clay. The density is 6,600 vines per hectare and the soils are ploughed. The grapes are picked into *cagettes*, sorted, then crushed above the tanks. After fermentation, the *marc* is pressed in modern vertical presses. The blend is made up early, with advice from Denis Dubourdieu, and the wine is then aged for twelve months in thirty per cent new barriques.

My experience of older vintages is limited to the 1983 and 1985, both of which seemed rather dour and graceless when tasted in the late 1980s. The 2001 has developed well: very Merlot on the nose, it has richness, spice, and freshness, with a lively finish. The 2002 went in the opposite direction, being light and lacking in structure. The 2003 is medium-bodied and supple, but low acidity gives the wine a soupy texture and an abrupt finish. The 2004 is a great improvement, with rich, plump fruit, good concentration, and considerable freshness.

The new owners soon discovered that, despite its quality, Canon de Brem was hard to sell, and from 2006 they decided to discontinue independent production and to incorporate the crop into the production of La Dauphine and its second wine. Thus 2005 was the last vintage.

Château Canon-St-Michel

Fronsac. AC Canon-Fronsac. Tel: 0557 512853. Owner: Jean-Yves Millaire. 5 ha. 60% Merlot,
25% Cabernet Sauvignon, 10% Cabernet Franc, 5% Malbec. Production: 20,000 bottles.
Second wine: Ch Canon-Garnier

Charming aromas of raspberries and cherries lifted the 1999, but the palate was considerably tougher than the nose led one to expect. The 2001 is very much better, with an opulent generosity of fruit on the nose, rich in blackcurrant and cherry aromas, and with ample upfront fruit on the palate, which is concentrated and vigorous. The 2002, in contrast, is distinctly green and lean. The 2003 was still inexpressive in 2006, with a rather flat texture and evident extraction.

Château de Carles

Saillans. AC Fronsac. Tel: 0145 033360. Website: www.haut-carles.com. Owner: Constance Droulers.
20 ha. 90% Merlot, 10% Cabernet Franc. Production: 80,000 bottles

The estate's name, it's said, echoes that of Charlemagne, who had an encampment here. The fine fifteenth-century château is the centrepiece of what used to be one of Fronsac's most important properties. However, during the nineteenth century parts of the estate were sold off. Guillaume Chastenet, the great-grandfather of Constance Droulers, bought the property in 1900 and one of his contributions was to decorate parts of the interior with North African tiles. His son Jacques, who was a writer, historian, and member of the Académie Française, turned over the management of the estate to the négociant house of Labegue. Mme. Droulers and her husband Stéphane took over in 1979, and found the vineyards and winery in poor condition. They dispensed with the services of Labegue in 1982, and began to run the property themselves. Their first vintage was 1983.

Nonetheless the couple remain absentee landlords, living in Paris where Stéphane Droulers is an investment banker. So they have hired Christian Veyry as, in effect, technical director of the estate. He has supervised substantial recent investments, such as the new air-conditioned *chai* of 1998 and the new *cuvier* of 2002.

The harvest is manual, the grapes are sorted thoroughly, but there is no cold soak. The construction of the winery along a slope allows gravity to be exploited and pumping avoided. Fermentation takes place in squat, stainless-steel tanks. The wine goes through malolactic fermentation in barriques. The very best fruit, representing about one-quarter of production, is reserved for the special *cuvée* called Haut de Carles, and this is aged in two-thirds new barriques for eighteen months. It was first made in 1994. There is no systematic fining or filtration.

Despite his laid-back manner, Stéphane Droulers is keen to produce an excellent wine, and to sell it for good prices. The oldest vintage I have tasted is the 1999, which has rich, oaky aromas with a whiff of smoke; undoubtedly firm and concentrated, it remains austere and somewhat extracted. The 2000 is fleshy and oaky, with aromas of strawberry jam; it is supple, forward, and persistent. I prefer the opaque 2001, with its sweet, plummy nose, its silky texture, its light chocolatey tone, and long finish. As one would expect, Haut de Carles shows more overt oakiness and greater concentration and flamboyance. Yet it's a well-balanced wine, never over-extracted, marked by firm but ripe tannins, and long on the finish. The 2002, 2003, and 2004 are all excellent, marking it as one of Fronsac's top wines. From cask, the seamless and ripe 2006 seemed one of the best Fronsacs from a tricky vintage.

Château de Carlmagnus

Fronsac. AC Fronsac. Tel: 0557 512468. Owner: Arnaud Roux-Oulié. 2.2 ha. 100% Merlot.
Production: 12,000 bottles

This small property was bought by Arnaud Roux-Oulié, who owns other Right Bank properties, in 1998. It was originally known as Carolus, but he changed the name to avoid confusion with another estate of that name; the new name maintained the allusion to Charlemagne. The vines are on clay-limestone slopes, facing due south. The *cuvaison* is prolonged, and the wine is aged in new oak. The only vintage I have drunk is the 1998, still youthful in 2005, with fleshy, black-fruits aromas. It's weighty, rich, and supple, with good acidity on the finish.

Château Cassagne-Haut-Canon

St-Michel-de-Fronsac. AC Canon-Fronsac. Tel: 0557 516398. Owner: Jean-Jacques Dubois. 13 ha.
70% Merlot, 20% Cabernet Franc, 10% Cabernet Sauvignon. Production: 80,000 bottles

The vineyards, high on a *croupe*, lie on very stony soils over fossil limestone. The harvest is manual, the juice fermented in cement tanks, and then the wine is aged for twelve months in older barrels and bottled without filtration. The 1998 was medium-bodied, but quite fleshy, with rather obtrusive tannins and a slightly dry, rustic finish. The 1999 is fairly rich and rounded, with some grip and structure, but not excessive extraction. The 2000 is lusher, with supple forward fruitiness, initially, but then some firm tannins kick in.

In 1985 Dubois launched a special *cuvée* called La Truffière, which now accounts for about half the production.

The 2001 was excellent, although it had a slightly confected, cherry nose; broad and concentrated, it had moderate acidity and firm tannins. The 2003 is broader, yet has grippy tannins that lead to a bitter finish.

Château Chadenne

St-Aignan. AC Fronsac. Tel: 0557 249310. Owner: Philippe Jean. 5 ha. 92% Merlot,
8% Cabernet Sauvignon. Production: 40,000 bottles

Philippe Jean made some money in the packaging industry before purchasing Chadenne in 1999. His first vintage was 2000. The vines are on the St-Aignan plateau on chalky clay soils, and their average age is thirty years. The harvest is manual. The wine is aged for eighteen months in fifty per cent new oak, and made under the guidance of Christian Veyry. The 2002 was a disappointment, with its glossy, oaky, cherry-scented nose, its soft texture at odds with rather sharp acidity, and dry tannins. The 2003 is marginally more successful, but here too the texture is rather flat and dull. However, the 2005 is riper and more accessible.

Château Coustolle

Fronsac. AC Canon-Fronsac. Tel: 0557 513125. Website: www.chateau-coustolle.com.
Owner: Alain Roux. 20 ha. 60% Merlot, 35% Cabernet Franc, 5% Cabernet Sauvignon.
Production: 120,000 bottles

Although the vineyards are cultivated by *lutte raisonnée*, they are mostly machine-harvested. After fermentation in cement tanks, the wine is aged in fifty per cent new barriques. There are two special bottlings. La Horse is aged in eighty per cent new barriques and only 8,000 bottles are produced. St-Jacques comes from a 2.5-hectare parcel, is hand-picked, and aged entirely in new oak.

I have tasted only the regular bottling. The 2000 had slightly herbaceous aromas, and did not seem fully ripe. The 2001 is slightly better, with more tannin and lively acidity; but it lacks character. The 2003 has dense black-fruits aromas; it's rich, juicy, and plump, but also rather heavy, with an austere finish.

Château La Croix Canon

Fronsac. AC Canon-Fronsac. Tel: 0557 740661. Website: www.chateau-dauphine.com.
Owner: Jean Halley. 12 ha. 80% Merlot, 20% Cabernet Franc. Production: 60,000 bottles

One of the three Moueix estates bought by Jean Halley in 2000 (*see* La Dauphine for full details), this was originally known as Château Bodet until bought and renamed by Christian Moueix in 1995. Halley sees La Croix Canon as essentially a second wine, as it has less structure than those from his other properties, even though some of the vines are over 100 years old. A proportion of American oak is used to age the wine. I have not tasted the wines under the Halley regime, but the 1999, tasted in 2006, was pleasant and accessible, with light acidity and moderate length.

Château Dalem

Saillans. AC Fronsac. Tel: 0557 843418. Owner: Michel Rullier. 14 ha. 85% Merlot,
10% Cabernet Franc, 5% Cabernet Sauvignon. Production: 60,000 bottles

This ancient property, which traces its history back to 1610, was bought by Michel Rullier in 1955, and today it is run by his daughter Brigitte Rullier-Loussert, as is Château de La Huste (*q.v.*). The grapes are picked by hand, and sorted twice before being fermented in concrete tanks. The wine is aged for eighteen months in fifty per cent new oak, then eggwhite-fined and filtered.

I recall a rich and balanced, if somewhat tannic, 1983. The 1998 is quite rich and fleshy, but has a slight green edge. The 2002 has fruit-pastille aromas, but the palate is considerably less confected. It's medium-bodied, supple, and reasonably concentrated. The 2003 and 2004 are better, juicy, plump wines with weight and concentration, and considerable spiciness on the finish. From cask, the 2006 had pleasant fruit but little concentration or flair.

Château de La Dauphine

Fronsac. AC Fronsac. Tel: 0557 740661. Website: www.chateau-dauphine.com. Owner: Jean Halley.
10 ha. 85% Merlot, 15% Cabernet Franc. Production: 60,000 bottles

In late 2000 Bordelais circles were taken aback when Christian Moueix, perceived as the guardian of Right Bank solidarity, sold all four of his Fronsac estates in one go: La Dauphine, Canon de Brem, La Croix Canon, and Canon-Moueix. True, it had already become difficult to sell Fronsac, and no doubt the Moueix portfolio was overstocked, but, all the same, this seemed a savage remedy. It turned out that Moueix had intended to sell only one of the properties, but the purchaser, Jean Halley, was so keen on the job lot that he made an offer Moueix found it impossible to refuse.

The new owner had made a fortune working with the Carrefour supermarket group, and he knew his wines. With great fanfare he set about stamping his imprint on his new estates, especially La Dauphine. This was the most impressive of the four, with its handsome château dating from 1750. In 2001 Halley built a circular *cuvier* that operated by gravity, hired Bernard Lamaud as technical director, and Denis Dubourdieu as his consultant oenologist. Halley's son Guillaume also takes a close interest in managing the estates.

The vines are fairly low down, on sandy clay soils in a single walled block. The vineyards are ploughed and the harvest is manual. After sorting, the grapes are crushed just above the fermentation tanks. Modern vertical presses are used to press the *marc* as gently as possible. After blending, the wine is aged in forty per cent new barriques for twelve months.

The only vintages from the Moueix regime I have tasted are the 1985 and 1986, both in their youth. The 1985 was charming, soft, and forward, yet with piquant fruit and modest concentration. The 1986 was more tannic and dour. The first Halley vintage, the 2001, is very good: there are rich, ripe cherry aromas, ample supple fruit on the palate, yet sufficient tannic grip to give it good structure. The 2002 has some confected aromas, and it's a rather drab wine overall. The 2003 is better despite some jamminess on the nose; it's rich, the texture is silky, and there's plenty of fruit, although it lacks some lift and length. The 2004, with its black-cherry fruit, is reasonably concentrated, discreetly oaky, and has a lively finish. The 2005 is full-bodied and suave but has a curious softness. The 2006 from casks seems similar.

Château Fontenil

Saillans. AC Fronsac. Tel: 0557 512305. Owner: Michel and Dany Rolland. 9 ha. 90% Merlot,
10% Cabernet Franc. Production: 45,000 bottles

The Rollands bought this property in 1986. Its vines, on clay-limestone soils, are over forty years old. The juice is fermented in small wooden vats and some steel tanks, and aged in sixty per cent new oak. Fontenil attracted some notoriety when, in 2000, Rolland unrolled plastic sheeting between the rows of a 1.6-hectare parcel, so that if it rained, the water would not be absorbed and thus would not swell and dilute the grapes. Instead it would drain harmlessly into ditches at the edge of the vineyard. The authorities were not amused, and ruled that the wine made from this parcel would have to be sold as non-vintage *vin de table*. Irritated at what he perceived as bureaucratic meddling, Rolland made the wine anyway. It was fermented in wooden vats with *pigeage*, and aged for sixteen months in new oak. He released the wine as Défi de Fontenil, and charged more for it than for his regular bottling. The plastic sheeting continues to be rolled out, though it seems a fairly pointless exercise given the mostly dry vintages that have followed the completely dry 2000. Could it just possibly be a marketing ploy? Current vintages are released under lot numbers. Thus the 2005 is Lot 2005. I did taste the initial Défi from cask, and found it opulent, but jammy and fatiguing.

The regular Fontenil is a fine wine, benefiting from the effortless expertise and blending skills of the Rollands. The 1998 was impeccable: sweet and oaky but not jammy on the nose, and supple and juicy on the palate yet with a sturdy finish. The 2002 has spice on the nose, a suave texture, and ample fruit backed by firm but ripe tannins. The 2003 oozes cherry and blackberry aromas, while the palate is lush, even broad, yet with sufficient grip to give it interest and length. The 2005 has admirable generosity on the nose, but is a tad overripe for my taste, giving the wine a flat texture. However, I prefer it to the overbearing Défi in 2005. The regular Fontenil is an excellent wine, one of the best from Fronsac and sensibly priced. Défi is an acquired taste.

Château du Gaby

Fronsac. AC Canon-Fronsac. Tel: 0557 512497. Website: www.chateau-du-gaby.com.
Owner: David Curl. 11 ha. 75% Merlot, 15% Cabernet Franc, 10% Cabernet Sauvignon.
Production: 55,000 bottles. Second wine: La Roche Gaby

This fine château is located on a slope overlooking the Dordogne River. The vineyards surrounding the house were planted in the eighteenth century and the property remained in the hands of the same family for 250 years. In 1999 a British financier of Syrian origin called Antoine Khayat bought Château La Roche Gaby, changed its name, and initiated a series of investments, improving the vineyards and building a new *chai*. In 2006 he sold the property to the present owner.

The director, Damien Landouar, points out that the soils around the château are cold, so, although there is no hydric stress, ripening is late; curiously, he uses anti-botrytis sprays to prolong the ripening process even further. Grapes from the lower, and sandier, parts of the property are used for the second wine. The soils are ploughed and only organic fertilizers are added. Yields rarely exceed forty hl/ha. The grapes are sorted twice, then fermented with selected yeasts in cement tanks. Pressing takes place in vertical presses, and the wine is aged for fifteen to eighteen months in forty per cent new barriques, with blending toward the end of the *élevage*.

Wines I have tasted from the early 1980s were soft and easy-going, lacking in character. The 2001 shows a change in direction: rich, plummy, oaky aromas, and a dense, concentrated structure, adding up to a balanced and serious wine. The 2002 is similar but in a lower key, with only moderate acidity and less flair. The 2003 is tannic and rather heavy-handed, yet reasonably balanced and not too extracted.

Château Grand Renouil

St-Michel-de-Fronsac. AC Canon-Fronsac. Tel: 0607 973689. **Owner:** *Michel Ponty. 5.5 ha.*
4.85 ha red: 100% Merlot. 0.65 ha white: 50% Sauvignon Blanc, 50% Sémillon.
Production: *25,000 bottles.* **Second wine:** *Petit Renouil*

Michel Ponty's vineyards are divided between those on the plateau and those on sandier soils lower down, the latter reserved for the second wine. He also owns Château du Pavillon (*q.v.*). Ponty finds that the Cabernets do not ripen consistently enough to warrant their presence in the vineyard. About a third of the vines are seventy years old, so green-harvesting is not systematic, though he has no hesitation about employing it, as he likes to keep yields below forty hl/ha. The vines are picked by hand, with sorting in the vineyard. After a conventional vinification, the wine is aged for twelve months in twenty per cent new oak.

In 1990 Ponty planted a small area with white grapes, which he barrel-ferments; but only twenty-five per cent is aged in oak. The 2003 was broad and lacking in zest and personality, but that probably reflects the vintage.

By 2006, the 1990 red had a rich nose, with some coffee aromas, but the wine was rather rustic. The 1998 showed more complexity, with smoky cherry aromas and modest weight of fruit, yet its quite concentrated and long. The 1999 is a touch green, with a tough finish. In contrast, the 2000, while reserved on the nose, is plump and concentrated, with vigour and ample fruit. New oak is quite noticeable on the 2001, as well as black-cherry fruit; it's suave, concentrated, fresh, and balanced. The 2002 is leaner, more open, and shows a lighter touch, without the richness and length of preceding vintages. The robust 2003 is a success for the vintage, and there are no cooked flavours.

Château Hauchat La Rose

St-Aignan. AC Fronsac. Tel: 0557 247303. **Website:** *www.vignobles-saby.com.*
Owner: *Jean-Bernard Saby. 7 ha. 95% Merlot, 5% Cabernet Franc.*
Production: *30,000 bottles.* **Second wine:** *Ch Hauchat*

The Saby family of Château Rozier (*q.v.*) in St-Emilion also own this property on the St-Aignan plateau. The vines have an average age of forty years, and are picked by hand. The wine is aged in fifty per cent new oak. I have tasted the 2002 and 2003, which, while not that concentrated, are stylish and fruity, if somewhat slack on the finish.

Château Haut-Ballet

St-Michel-de-Fronsac. AC Canon-Fronsac. Tel: 0557 249410. **Owner:** *Olivier Decelle. 2.6 ha.*
95% Merlot, 5% Cabernet Franc. **Production:** *20,000 bottles*

Olivier Decelle has been buying up small, and usually underperforming, properties in all parts of Bordeaux over recent years, and an account of his activities is given under Château Jean Faure (*q.v.*) (St-Emilion). Michel Rolland acts as his consultant oenologist. These vineyards are high up, at eighty metres (262 feet), on clay-limestone soil. The grapes are picked in *cagettes*, then carefully sorted and given a cold soak. After malolactic fermentation in barriques, the wine is aged for up to fourteen months in two-thirds new oak. The oak does show on the nose, in both 2002 and 2003. Yet the oakiness doesn't seem excessive. Both these vintages delivered fruity, forward, reasonably concentrated wines that also had a slight earthiness, which may be a terroir character rather than a winemaking excess. The 2005 is rich but bland.

Château Haut-Lariveau

*St-Michel-de-Fronsac. AC Fronsac. Tel: 0557 511437. **Owner:** Grégoire Hubau. 4.4 ha.*
*100% Merlot. **Production:** 36,000 bottles*

Grégoire Hubau also owns Moulin Pey-Labrie (*q.v.*) in Canon-Fronsac. Here too Merlot is the sole variety planted. The wine is aged in one-third new barriques. The 2001 has discreetly oaky aromas, and offers silky charm rather than weight or concentration. The 2002 is easy-going, quite fleshy, but quite light in structure.

Château de La Huste

*Saillans. AC Fronsac. Tel: 0557 843418. **Owner:** Michel Rullier. 5 ha. 90% Merlot,*
*10% Cabernet Franc. **Production:** 20,000 bottles*

Under the same ownership as Dalem (*q.v.*), this property enjoys views over the river Isle. The vinification is almost identical, except that Huste is aged in a slightly lower proportion of new oak. The only vintage I have tasted is the rather flat and unexciting 2003, which I hope is atypical.

Château Jeandeman

*St-Aignan. AC Fronsac. Tel: 0557 743052. **Website:** www.roy-trocard-vins.com.*
***Owner:** Vignobles Roy-Trocard. 25 ha. 90% Merlot, 5% Cabernet Franc, 5% Cabernet Sauvignon. **Production:** 160,000*
*bottles. **Second wine:** Tonnelles du Roy*

Jean Trocard runs this large estate (as well as other properties in the Libournais), which was acquired by his forebears in 1919. It lies in a single block high up at eighty-three metres (272 feet), and the soils have a lot of limestone. A special *cuvée*, La Chêneraie, from a five-hectare parcel, is picked by hand and aged in one-third new oak. Some 20,000 bottles are produced. I have tasted only the Chêneraie wine, in 2002 and 2003, and neither was inspiring. They had some aromatic charm, but were easy-going and lacking in persistence. Perfectly drinkable, yet unremarkable.

Château Lamarche-Canon

*Fronsac. AC Canon-Fronsac. Tel: 0557 512813. **Owner:** Eric Julien. 4 ha. 80% Merlot,*
*10% Cabernet Franc, 10% Cabernet Sauvignon. **Production:** 28,000 bottles*

This small property is managed by Vignobles Germain, who own and run properties in the Côtes de Blaye. The vines here are old and picked by hand. From 1992 the best lots have been reserved for an old-vine bottling called Candelaire, which is aged in forty per cent new barriques. The 2000, 2002, and 2003 all share jammy aromas that I find confected, but at the same time the flavours show some greenness and a lack of charm and finesse.

Château Magondeau

*Saillans. AC Fronsac. Tel: 0557 843202. **Owner:** André Goujon. 18 ha. 85% Merlot,*
*7.5% Cabernet Franc, 7.5% Cabernet Sauvignon. **Production:** 120,000 bottles*

The vines here are mostly picked by machine. As well as a standard unoaked bottling, there is a *cuvée* called Magondeau-Beau-Site, aged in one-third new barriques for twelve months. In 2000 Olivier Goujon, who makes the wine, created a *garagiste cuvée* called Passion de Magondeau, a selection of the best parcels which is aged entirely in new oak for at least fifteen months. The only wine I have tasted from here is the 2003 Magondeau-Beau-Site, which had a perky red-fruits nose, but the palate was fluid and lacking in zest.

Château Manieu

La Rivière. AC Fronsac. Tel: 0557 249279. Owners: Marlis and Anja Léon. 4 ha. 95% Merlot,
5% Cabernet Sauvignon. Production: 25,000 bottles. Second wine: Ch Roumagnac

This property was acquired by the Léon family in 1987. The vineyards are south-facing and terraced, and picked by hand. The wine is aged in one-third new barriques for eighteen months. The 2002 had smoky, oaky aromas of cherries and redcurrants; it's fairly lean and modest, with freshness rather than concentration. The 2003 has the defects of the vintage: a soupy texture and a lack of vigour.

Château Mayne-Vieil

Saillans. AC Fronsac. Tel: 0557 743006. Owner: Sèze family. 32 ha. 100% Merlot.
Production: 200,000 bottles

This large property, with many old vines, has been owned by the Sèze family since 1918. The gently sloping vineyards are machine-harvested. They produce two wines: an unoaked regular bottling and Cuvée Aliénor, the latter being aged in twenty-five per cent new oak. The 2001 Mayne-Vieil has ripe, plummy aromas; the palate is supple and rounded, with sweet, ripe fruit and fair acidity. The 2002 Aliénor displays black-fruits aromas, plumpness and concentration, and no lack of rich, ripe fruit. The 2003 has a similar opulence, but harsh tannins give a dry finish. The 2004 is supple and easy-going, yet lacks some personality; the 2005 has more energy and concentration if little complexity. The regular 2005 is supple yet vigorous.

Château Mazeris–Bellevue

St-Michel-de-Fronsac. AC Canon-Fronsac. Tel: 0557 249819. Owner: Jacques Bussier. 9 ha.
45% Merlot, 25% Cabernet Franc, 25% Cabernet Sauvignon, 5% Malbec. Production: 60,000 bottles

This property has been in the Bussier family for four generations, and the vines are planted on steep slopes. The wine is aged in tanks as well as in older barrels. I have tasted six vintages since 1998, and find the wines simple and unexciting. Perhaps the high proportion of Cabernet vines presents an obstacle to user-friendly wines? The 2003 is richer and, strangely, better balanced than most other vintages, and the 2004 has some welcome freshness.

Château Moulin Haut Laroque

Saillans. AC Fronsac. Tel: 0557 843207. Website: www.moulinhautlaroque.com.
Owner: Jean-Noël Hervé. 15 ha. 65% Merlot, 20% Cabernet Franc, 10% Cabernet Sauvignon. Production: 80,000
bottles. Second wine: Ch Hervé-Laroque

The impish, good-humoured Jean-Noël Hervé is the latest generation of a family that has been farming here for two centuries. He has been making the wines since 1977, with advice from Christian Veyry. The vineyards are high, at up to ninety metres (295 feet), and some of the Cabernet Franc vines are seventy years old. Yields are low and the harvest is manual, with double sorting before the grapes are deposited without pumping in squat steel tanks. Hervé uses selected yeasts and some micro-oxygenation. The *marc* is pressed in pneumatic presses, and the wine is aged for eighteen months in one-third new oak.

I do not recall tasting a mediocre wine from this estate. The relatively high proportion of Cabernet gives them some austerity when young. The oldest vintage I have encountered is the 1983, where the ripe, supple fruit did fight the pronounced tannins. The 1989, tasted in 2006, was still solid and firm, a touch severe yet rich and weighty. The 1998 is more overtly lush and fleshy, a concentrated wine with slightly dry tannins. I find the 1999 more stylish, with its gentle oakiness, rich fruit, spiciness, and long, graceful finish.

The 2001 is superb, with rich, black-fruits aromas and a good deal of power and concentration, though the essential fruitiness of the wine comes through. There is unusual ripeness on the nose and palate of the 2002, and again a lively finish. The 2003 is burly, and lacks some charm and finesse, but it has ample fruit and length. The freshness and elegance of the delicious 2004 mask the ripe tannins and evident structure of a wine that should age well.

Château Moulin Pey-Labrie

*Fronsac. AC Fronsac. Tel: 0557 511437. Website: www.moulinpeylabrie.com. **Owner**: Grégoire Hubau. 6.5 ha.*
*70% Merlot, 20% Cabernet Sauvignon, 10% Cabernet Franc. **Production**: 35,000 bottles*

Christian Veyry acts as the consultant here. The wine is aged for eighteen months in fifty per cent new barriques. The style is rich and oaky, with considerable density and tannic structure. The 1995 was a touch earthy, but rich and chocolatey; the 1998 has more overt fruitiness. The 2001 is splendid, with sweet, intense oaky aromas, a velvety texture, sumptuous fruit, and admirable concentration and balance. The 2002 is attractively oaky, dense, and full-bodied. Although initially rich and svelte, the 2005 has hefty tannins. From cask, the 2006 showed no greenness and considerable freshness and length.

Château du Pavillon

*Fronsac. AC Canon-Fronsac. Tel: 0607 973689. **Owner**: Michel Ponty. 4 ha. 100% Merlot. **Production**: 20,000 bottles*

Michel Ponty of Grand Renouil (*q.v.*) also owns this small property, with its vineyards well situated on south-facing slopes. As at Grand Renouil, Merlot is the only variety planted. The grapes are picked by hand, sorted, then fermented in cement tanks; the wine is aged for twelve months in fifteen per cent new barriques. The 2001, 2002, and 2003 share firm black-cherry aromas. There is a certain swagger on the palate: the 2001 and 2003 are both rich, mouth-filling wines, yet both are accessible and show no harsh tannins. The 2002 is a touch lighter and more floral, with balance and charm.

Château Renard Mondésir

*La Rivière. AC Fronsac. Tel: 0557 249637. **Owner**: Xavier Chassagnoux. 7 ha. 95% Merlot,*
*5% Cabernet Franc. **Production**: 40,000 bottles. **Second wine**: Ch Renard*

This property was bought by the Chassagnoux family in 1978. The soils here are clay-limestone with some sand. The wine is aged in forty per cent new oak. The 1998 had ripe, elegant, oaky aromas, and an appealing plumpness backed by light tannins. The 2001 is slightly jammy, and its rich fruit is cut by grippy tannins that deprive the wine of charm. The 2003 is initially supple, but the tannins are harsh and give a dry finish.

Château Richelieu

*Fronsac. AC Fronsac. Tel: 0557 511394. Website: www.chateau-richelieu.com. **Owner**: Arjen Pen.*
*12 ha. 74% Merlot, 32% Cabernet Sauvignon, 3% Malbec. **Production**: 80,000 bottles.*
Second wine: Trois Musketeers

Richelieu belonged to the celebrated cardinal in the seventeenth century. It changed hands most recently in 2002, and a new team has been reviving the property. The soils are sandy clay. No herbicides or fertilizers are used. The wine is fermented with natural yeasts and aged for twelve months in one-third new barriques. Richelieu hired Stéphane Derenoncourt to maximize its potential, and in 2003 he created a special *cuvée* called La Favorite. This comes from a three-hectare parcel on the highest slope. The wine is aged for fifteen months in fifty per cent new barriques. Trois Musketeers is in effect the second wine, aged in one-year barrels for ten months. I have not tasted the wines.

Château de La Rivière

La Rivière. AC Fronsac. Tel: 0557 555656. Website: www.chateau-de-la-riviere.com.
***Owner**: James Grégoire. 59 ha. 82% Merlot, 15% Cabernet Sauvignon, 2% Cabernet Franc, 1% Malbec. **Production**:*
*300,000 bottles. **Second wine**: Les Sources du Château de La Rivière*

La Rivière is the largest and the best-known property in Fronsac. The château lords it over south-facing vineyards that descend toward the river. Charlemagne apparently built a fortress on this site. The present château was built in the 1570s, then heavily restored by Viollet-le-Duc in the nineteenth century. After frequent changes of ownership over the centuries, in 1962 La Rivière was bought by Jacques Borie. He renovated the vineyards, put in drainage and repaired the terraces. In 1994 it was sold to Jean Leprince. After he was killed in a plane crash in 2002 the estate was put on the market.

The next buyer was James Grégoire, the inventor of the Oxoline system for rotating barrels during the *élevage*. His family company produced viticultural machinery, and he recalls visiting La Rivière in 1978 and being overwhelmed by its dramatic grandeur. There's an entire hamlet housing the vineyard workers within the estate, and a charming spring-fed ladies' bathing pool from 1736 is hidden in the grounds. This is just one of many springs on the property, an advantage in very dry years, as the vineyards never suffer from hydric stress.

Unsurprisingly, this major manufacturer of harvesting machines continues to pick most of the vineyards mechanically. The grapes are sorted twice, then tipped into the fermentation vats by gravity. The *cuvaison* lasts from three to six weeks, with some recourse to micro-oxygenation. There is no shortage of space here, as there are over three hectares of cellars installed within former limestone quarries beneath the château. The regular wine is aged for twelve to fifteen months in up to forty per cent new oak, including 400-litre barrels.

Michel Rolland used to be the consultant here, but in 2003 was replaced by the Languedoc-based oenologist Claude Gros. It was Rolland who created the special *cuvée*, from a two-hectare parcel, called Aria. This was made from old Merlot vines, cropped at around thirty hl/ha, given a week-long cold soak, then vinified in wooden vats before being aged in new oak for eighteen months. A maximum of 5,000 bottles was produced, and the price tag was high. It's a *garagiste* wine, and Grégoire doesn't seem to like it very much, so its production may be discontinued.

A double magnum of 1986 was still attractive after twenty years. The nose was leafy, yet floral . The palate was not that concentrated but there was some fruit intensity, and the finish was delicate, sweet, and long. The 1989 is slightly dilute, but was still enjoyable in 2001, though it lacked length. The 1998 is good in a discreet style, its succulence supported by a backbone of light tannin and acidity. The 1999 has ripe cherry aromas; on the palate it is supple and attractive, but it's a wine with little grip. The 2001 is fruit-forward and harmonious, with ample fleshy cherry fruit, and some spiciness on the finish. The 2001 Aria has pronounced new oak aromas; the palate is almost brutal in its concentration and lacks elegance. The 2003 is svelte and quite concentrated, yet lacks some persistence, although there is fruit rather than tannin on the finish. The 2005 shows density and grip without any rusticity. From cask, the 2006 seemed rather green.

James Grégoire is still deliberating, I sense, over the direction in which he intends to take La Rivière. Such a large and varied vineyard, perfectly exposed, ought to be able to deliver something more exceptional. The wines thus far are good, sometimes very good, without showing any strong sense of personality.

Château La Rose Garnier

Fronsac. AC Fronsac. Tel: 0608 338111. Owner: Jean-Yves Millaire. 1.5 ha. 90% Merlot,
10% Cabernet Sauvignon. **Production:** *6,000 bottles*

Jean-Yves Millaire is also the owner of the Canon-Fronsac estate of Canon-St-Michel (*q.v.*). Unlike that wine, La Rose Garnier is aged in older barrels. The 2001 was excellent: rich, even flamboyant, with good underlying acidity, and a strong tannic presence on the finish. The 2002 is lean and astringent, and the 2003, despite some slightly cooked aromas, is far better, plump and concentrated but not heavy-handed. The wines are not expensive and offer very good value.

Château La Rousselle

La Rivière. AC Fronsac. Tel: 0557 249673. Owners: Jacques and Viviane Davau. 4.6 ha.
60% Merlot, 25% Cabernet Franc, 15% Cabernet Sauvignon. **Production:** *15,000 bottles*

The Davaus bought this property in 1971. Its vineyards, which they completely replanted, are located both on the clay-limestone plateau and on south-facing slopes. Jacques Davau and his consultant Stéphane Derenoncourt take pains to produce a wine that's robust and concentrated. The vines are usually deleafed on both sides, and green-harvested twice. In 2001 the yield was a miserly thirty hl/ha. The must is fermented with micro-oxygenation *sous marc*. Malolactic fermentation takes place in barriques, and the wine is aged in up to sixty per cent new barriques with just a single racking.

The results are much as one would expect: deeply coloured wines, with oaky, black-fruits aromas and rich, concentrated fruit. The 1998 is fleshy and well balanced. The 2000 is rather soft and lacks some acidity. I prefer the 2001, which has more power and body without any lack of viscosity. The 2002 has aromatic charm despite the oakiness and ample fruit and supple tannins mark the palate.

Château Tour du Moulin

*Saillans. AC Fronsac. Tel: 0557 743426. **Owners:** Josette and Vincent Dupuch. 7 ha. 80% Merlot,*
*10% Cabernet Sauvignon, 10% Cabernet Franc. **Production:** 24,000 bottles*

Vincent Dupuch bought the property in 1987 and replanted much of the vineyard. He makes two wines. The regular bottling is aged in twenty-five per cent new oak for eighteen months. The Cuvée Particulière is cropped at lower yields, vinified at higher temperatures, given a longer *cuvaison*, and aged in a higher proportion of new oak. The only regular Tour du Moulin I have tasted is the 2002, a medium-bodied, moderately concentrated wine of some austerity. The Cuvée Particulière is impressive. The 1998 had finesse despite very marked oakiness on the nose; and despite the extraction, there was enough density of fruit and acidity to carry the wine through to a positive finish. The 2001 too is full-bodied, even weighty, and the power is moderated by its balance and persistence.

Château Les Troix Croix

*Fronsac. AC Fronsac. Tel: 0557 843209. **Owner:** Patrick Léon. 14 ha. 90% Merlot,*
*10% Cabernet Franc. **Production:** 85,000 bottles. **Second wine:** Ch Lamolière*

If the name of the owner rings a bell, that's because for many years he was the chief winemaker for Mouton-Rothschild. Today this ancient property is run by his son Bertrand. Since the Léons bought the property in 1995, the wine has been aged for fifteen months in fifty per cent new oak. The 1998 is oaky on the nose, while the palate is rich and firm with a spicy, rather tannic finish. The oak is well judged on the medium-bodied, well-balanced 2002, which has aromatic charm and elegance. The 2003 is typical of the vintage: a touch flat in texture and rather earthy. The 2004 is concentrated if tarry. From cask, the 2006 seems too extracted.

Château La Vieille Cure

*Saillans. AC Fronsac. Tel: 0557 843205. **Owners:** Colin Ferenbach and associates. 18 ha.*
*75% Merlot, 22% Cabernet Franc, 3% Cabernet Sauvignon. **Production:** 100,000 bottles.*
Second wine: La Sacristie de la Vieille Cure

La Vieille Cure features on the Belleyme map of the 1780s, so the property goes back a long way. It was bought by the current owners, a group of American investment bankers, in 1986, and it is managed by Jean-Noël Hervé of Moulin Haut Laroque, with advice from Christian Veyry. The vines are old, and the harvest manual. There is some use of micro-oxygenation during fermentation, and the wine is aged in one-third new oak.

The 1990 was still going strong after eight years, with considerable aromatic power. New oak dominated the nose in 1998, and the wine is soft and rather bland. Black cherries and liquorice mark the aromas of the 2000, which blends a supple, rounded texture with firm underlying tannins. There's sweet cherry fruit on the nose of the 2001, which has spice and concentration; all it lacks is some flair. Oak also dominates the rather extracted 2002; it has an engaging rusticity and zest rather than elegance. There's ample spicy, delicious fruit on the nose and palate of the lush, concentrated 2004, which has exceptional vigour on the finish.

Château Villars

*Saillans. AC Fronsac. Tel: 0557 843217. **Owners:** Jean-Claude and Thierry Gaudrie. 30 ha.*
*73% Merlot, 18% Cabernet Franc, 9% Cabernet Sauvignon. **Production:** 150,000 bottles.*
Second wine: Ch Moulin-Haut-Villars

This large property has been in the same family since the early nineteenth century. The wine is aged for ten to fourteen months in about one-third new oak and bottled without filtration. The 1982 was still attractive after ten years, medium-bodied and balanced but not very distinctive. The 1993 is lean but elegant and highly drinkable in 2000. I have tasted the 1998 three times: in 2000 it lacked excitement and persistence; in 2001 both bottles were musty and dour. The 2000 sees a return to form, with plummy, toasty aromas; it's rich, dense, and opulent. The 2002 has less power but more elegance, and certainly doesn't lack fruit and length. The 2003 displays black-cherry aromas, richness, and opulence on the palate without soupiness, and surprising length of flavour. The 2004 is a touch jammy but plump and approachable.

26. Côtes de Blaye and Côtes de Bourg

Northwest of Libourne lie these two appellations. Bourg, the more southerly, is much smaller than the sprawling Blaye. They are of ancient origin, since the ports of both Blaye and Bourg occupy strategic positions on the Gironde estuary. The Romans, who built forts along the shore, almost certainly planted vines on the slopes behind both towns. In medieval times wine producers here prospered, since regions such as the Médoc were still undeveloped and there was easy access to northern Europe. Bourg growers would have had a clear view across the estuary to what were then the fields and woodlands of Margaux.

Until a few decades ago, the primary role these wines played was to act as blending components in négociants' generic Bordeaux. This hardly gave any motivation to improve quality. But by the 1980s there were a few properties in each appellation that took a more independent line, usually selling their wines through their own commercial networks, and these estates set the standards to which others gradually aspired.

As in Fronsac, which lies between these regions and Libourne, the enemy is tannin. Without full ripeness, and without the correct choice of grape variety in each location, the tannins can be somewhat coarse. Nonetheless quality has been steadily improving here, but whether there is a market substantial enough to support these vast swathes of vineyards, especially in Blaye, is questionable.

COTES DE BLAYE

Like so many regions within Bordeaux, Blaye has expanded considerably in recent years. In 1994 there were about 4,000 hectares under vine. Today there are 5,200 hectares of red vines, and 400 of white. Historically, the region was better known for its white wines than its reds, but that has clearly changed. The dominant red variety is Merlot, with seventy per cent of the surface, followed by Cabernet Sauvignon with twenty per cent, and Malbec and Cabernet Franc with ten per cent between them. In the past much of the white wine was dispatched to the nearby Charente for distillation into Cognac. However, certain sectors, such as the communes of Blaye, Cars, and Plassac, were always renowned for their red wines. There are some 800 growers, of whom half supply five cooperatives.

The most important communes are Blaye (101 hectares), Plassac (271), Berson (823), Cars (820), St-Martin-Lacaussade (176), St-Paul (500), Mazion (175), St-Genès-de-Blaye (165), St-Seurin-de-Cursac (70), Fours (120), Campugnan (134), Cartelègue (269), Marsas (198), Cubnezais (180), Cézac (321), St-Vivien-de-Blaye (230), St-Mariens (323), St-Christoly-de-Blaye (371), St-Savin (263), St-Girons-d'Aiguivives (215), Anglade (386), Reignac (739), Marcillac (653), St-Aubin-de-Blaye (274), St-Caprais-de-Blaye (156), St-Ciers (521), and St-Palais (390). (The figures refer to the area under vine at each commune, but they are clearly over-estimates and should not be taken as reliable. But they indicate the relative importance of each commune.)

The soils are essentially clay and limestone, but in the northern sectors there is more gravel and less clay. Because of the enormous size of Blaye, which is fifty kilometres (thirty-one miles) from top to bottom, it has a less coherent identity than Bourg. The vineyards can be divided into three sectors: those to the west around Blaye itself, those in the north around St-Ciers, and those farther south and east around St-Savin. Vines around St-Ciers ripen later than in the other areas, and the more gravelly soil is generally regarded as less fine than elsewhere in Blaye. Around St-Savin there are plateaux on more sandy soil planted with vines, and much woodland.

The appellations within the region can be confusing. The most important, Premières Côtes de Blaye, was authorized in 1938. The red is a blend from any of the following varieties: Merlot, Cabernet Sauvignon, Cabernet Franc, and Malbec. Quite a few leading estates have a high opinion of Malbec, which is not widely shared elsewhere in Bordeaux. Petit Verdot is not permitted, except where the plantings already existed within existing vineyards. The white Premières Côtes is mostly Sauvignon Blanc, but there is also some Muscadelle and

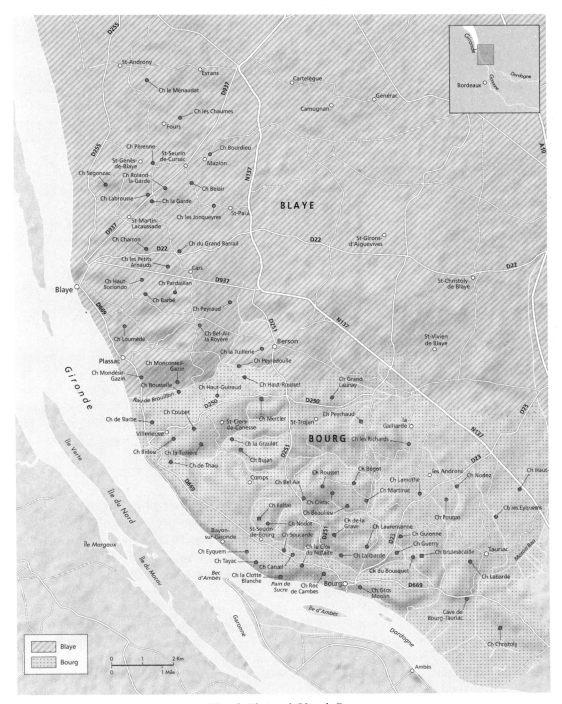

Côtes de Blaye and Côtes de Bourg

Colombard. Although Colombard is not regarded as a noble variety, in Blaye it seems to give highly aromatic wines with an immediate charm, though they rarely age well. However, that scarcely matters since the wines are invariably drunk young.

In 2000 a new appellation was created: Blaye. For this AC a slightly higher minimal ripeness level was required (the scarcely exacting eleven degrees of alcohol), the minimum density is 6,000 vines per hectare (rather than the 4,500 minimum for Premières Côtes), and a maximum yield of fifty-one hectolitres per hectare (in 2005 the authorized maximum yield for Premières Côtes de Blaye was sixty-seven hl/ha). It also requires a double *agrément*, so the wines must pass two tasting panels at different stages of their *élevage*. At the time of writing some twenty estates produce AC Blaye, often as a special *cuvée* in addition to their Premières Côtes. The name has always seemed unsatisfactory, since it would be reasonable for the consumer to assume that Premières Côtes is superior as an appellation to mere Blaye. Marc Pasquet of Mondésir-Gazin views AC Blaye as a kind of laboratory for producers keen to make wines of the highest quality, and he adds that the creation of this new AC put a stop to the proliferation of special *cuvées* that often confused consumers. It is unclear what will happen to the appellation if and when the new AC Côtes de Bordeaux: Blaye comes into being.

Thirteen properties are entitled to use the words *cru bourgeois* on the label. The Médocains objected fiercely to this practice and took the Blayais to court, but lost on the grounds that the Blayais could establish a prior claim to the term. Not all the estates legally entitled to use the term employ it on their labels. It should not be assumed that a *cru bourgeois* is intrinsically superior to a wine without that benediction.

Château Alfa La Bernarde

Marsas. Tel: 0556 560430. Owner: Mähler-Besse. 7 ha. 60% Merlot, 20% Cabernet Sauvignon, 20% Cabernet Franc. Production: 50,000 bottles

This property was bought by the négociant house of Mähler-Besse in 1989. Its best Merlot parcels are harvested manually and used for a special *cuvée* called Blavia. This is aged for twelve months in twenty per cent new barriques. The regular wine in 2000 had some aromatic charm, and was reasonably concentrated, though it had little personality. The 2001 Blavia is more evidently oaky on the nose, and heftier on the palate; it shows more fruit than finesse, but is a satisfying mouthful of wine.

Château Bel Air La Royère

Cars. Tel: 0557 429134. Owners: Xavier and Corinne Loriaud. 23 ha. 22 ha red: 74% Merlot, 20% Malbec, 6% Cabernet Sauvignon. 1 ha white: 100% Sauvignon Blanc. Production: 100,000 bottles. Second wine: Les Ricards

This congenial and communicative couple come from the Charente, and until 2003 Xavier Loriaud managed La Tour-Carnet in the Haut-Médoc. They always wanted to own a Bordeaux vineyard, but the more prestigious regions were unaffordable. In 1992 they found this property, which was then producing bulk wine, and their first vintage was 1995 (a mere 3,000 bottles). The Loriauds have hired Christian Veyry as their consultant oenologist.

In 1992 there were only nine hectares under vine, of which one-third was planted with Malbec. Despite the modest reputation of this variety, they could scarcely afford to pull out a third of their vineyard. They also planted a little Cabernet Sauvignon, which had not been represented in the vineyard. In 2004 they leased ten more hectares. Some of the vines are near the house on the plateau of Les Ricards; other parcels are more scattered. Loriaud controls yields by pruning short; he also green-harvests but mainly to improve aeration and avoid rot.

Some of the rented vineyards are machine-harvested but this goes into a wine produced under a different label. All grapes destined for Bel Air, an AC Blaye, or for the second wine are hand-picked. The major sources for Bel Air are a parcel on the top of a north-facing slope and the old Malbec at Cars. After fermentation in steel and cement tanks, the wine goes through its malolactic fermentation in barriques. It is then aged for eighteen months in eighty per cent new oak. There is very occasional use of *cliquage*, but it is not systematic. The second wine is aged in twenty per cent new oak.

Some Sauvignon Blanc has been planted, and from 2004 there has been a white wine fermented in new barriques and aged for six months.

The oldest vintage I have drunk is the 2001, which seemed rather overripe and fatiguing. The 2002 was concentrated and a serious wine from a difficult vintage. The 2003 is fleshy and full-bodied, with dense, oaky, chocolatey aromas, and a good deal of spice and vigour on the palate – an excellent wine for this baking vintage. The 2004 is similar but more graceful, with a silky texture and good length. The 2005, tasted in June 2006, showed enormous promise, being very rich and sumptuous but also displaying fine acidity. Bel Air La Royère is unquestionably one of the top wines of Blaye, with a spiciness that may well derive from the old Malbec in the blend. Les Ricards is also of very good quality, as well as being considerably less expensive.

In 1997 the Loriauds bought a parcel of Merlot in Cars, which is used to produce an inexpensive wine called Clos Lagassa.

Château Bellevue-Gazin

Plassac. Tel: 0557 420200. Website: www.chateau-bellevue-gazin.com. Owners: Alain and Anne-Sophie Lancereau-Burthey. 15 ha. 70% Merlot, 25% Malbec, 3% Petit Verdot, 2% Cabernet Sauvignon. Production: 40,000 bottles. Second wine: Les Baronnets

The genial Lancereau-Burtheys are newcomers. He is a civil engineer, and they spent much of their early life in Libya, where they made wine from vines planted by Italians. After a spell in Paris, they acquired this property in 2003, and also bought Château Lers Lumède (*q.v.*). Most of the vines here are in a single lofty parcel of gravelly clay soils. Their average age is forty years, with some Malbec that is now fifty years old.

Only the best parcels are picked by hand. After a cold soak, the must is fermented in cement and steel tanks, with pumpovers and *pigeage*. The *marc* is pressed in a vertical press, and the wine goes through its malolactic fermentation in barriques. It is aged for twelve months in up to fifty per cent new oak, with some lees-stirring. Blending takes place late in the *élevage*, and consultant Olivier Dauga assists with this.

The second wine is unoaked. There is also a production of *clairet* from bled tanks. The 2004 was delightful, with pretty aromas of strawberries and raspberries and surprising vinosity and weight. As for the Bellevue-Gazin, the 2003 had a dense nose of plums and liquorice, but a rather burly presence with a touch too much oak; a very robust style with little finesse. The 2004 is more stylish and better balanced, with attractive cherry fruit and a lively attack.

Château Bertinerie

Cubnezais. Tel: 0557 687074. Website: www.chateaubertinerie.com. Owners: Eric and Frantz Bantegnies. 58 ha. 41 ha red: 60% Merlot, 35% Cabernet Sauvignon, 5% Cabernet Franc. 17 ha white: 95% Sauvignon Blanc, 5% Muscadelle. Production: 300,000 bottles. Second wine: Ch Manon La Lagune

This was one of the estates that put Blaye on the map, especially for white wines. Daniel Bantegnies renovated the property from the early 1960s onwards, his blindness not proving the slightest impediment to his energy and dedication to quality. Today the estate is run by his two sons, who built a splendid new underground *chai* in 2003.

Bertinerie is a dispersed estate with vineyards in four blocks, all at about 100 metres (328 feet) in altitude. The soil is essentially clay-limestone, but there are sectors with more clay and sand. A peculiarity here is that many of the Sauvignon vines are lyre-trained, with a canopy divided into two lines of foliage in each row. This has been a research project conducted jointly with INRA since 1987. Frantz Bantegnies says lyre-training gives very good quality, and the grapes ripen a week earlier than those trained more conventionally. The disadvantage is that the split canopy increases considerably the costs of farming. As for the red varieties, the Merlot is planted on clay-limestone, whereas the Cabernet Sauvignon is generally on silty or gravelly clay.

The grapes are picked manually, with sorting in the vineyard. The white grapes receive some skin contact, then descend by gravity into the presses without crushing, whereas the reds are crushed above the tanks.

The white Bertinerie is aged in tanks on the fine lees for about six months. The best fruit is reserved for

Haut-Bertinerie, which comprises about 50,000 bottles in all styles. The white Haut-Bertinerie comes from the oldest Sauvignon vines, cropped at no more than forty hl/ha. It is fermented in eighty per cent new barriques without temperature control, and aged *sur lie* with stirring for eight months.

The red Bertinerie is vinified in enamel and squat steel tanks without recourse to micro-oxygenation. About eighty per cent of the wine is aged in fifty per cent new barriques for twelve months, then aged for six months in tanks. The other twenty per cent stays in tanks. The Haut-Bertinerie is handled similarly, except that the wine is aged in new oak for twelve months, then in tanks for a further eight months. There is a special bottling from a south-facing slope called Landreau, also aged in new oak but for eighteen months.

There are also two *clairets*. The Bertinerie is aged for three months in tanks on the fine lees. The Haut-Bertinerie is fermented in new oak and aged for eight months with lees-stirring.

The white is excellent, and explains the region's former reputation for white wines. The Bertinerie is crisp, fresh, and refreshing. The Haut-Bertinerie predictably has more weight and complexity. The 2003 and the waxy 2006 are rather heavy and ungainly, but the 2004 and 2005 are delicious, with a fine attack, ample fruit, and a long, lemony finish.

The red Bertinerie is piquant and fresh, but can also have some complexity, as in 2004, when there were smoky aromas and good concentration. The Haut-Bertinerie is considerably richer, with plummy aromas often marked by liquorice. The tannins can be rather aggressive, but the texture is usually supple. Of recent vintages my favourites are 2001 and 2004.

Château Les Bertrands

Reignac. Tel: 0557 324136. Website: www.chateau-les-bertrands.com. **Owner:** *Laurent Dubois. 86 ha.*
76 ha red: 60% Merlot, 35% Cabernet Sauvignon, 5% Cabernet Franc. 10 ha white: 85% Sauvignon Blanc,
15% Muscadelle. **Production:** *400,000 bottles*

This very large estate is run on thoroughly commercial lines, providing a range of wines to suit various tastes and wallets. The soil here is well-drained sand and gravel, giving wines that are supple and aromatic. The entire vineyard is picked by machine.

There are two white wines. The Tradition is unoaked, while the Prestige, a pure Sauvignon Blanc, receives skin contact and is fermented and aged for six months in new barriques.

The basic red wine is the unoaked Vieilles Vignes, from vines at least thirty years old. The Prestige is aged for twelve months in one-third new barrels, with some American oak, and the Nectar, which is ninety-five per cent Merlot, is aged for sixteen months in mostly new oak.

Although the wines overall have a reasonable reputation, they are far from being among the stars of the region. Even the top *cuvées* lack concentration and personality.

Château Cantinot

Cars. Tel: 0557 643170. Website: www.chateaucantinot.com. **Owners:** *Yann and Florence Bouscasse. 12 ha.*
55% Merlot, 35% Cabernet Sauvignon, 10% Cabernet Franc. **Production:** *80,000 bottles*

Natives of La Rochelle, the Bouscasses came to the region in 2002 and hired Olivier Dauga to advise them. They found the Cantinot vineyards in need of attention and have been renovating them. The soil is sandy and gravelly, with clay on the slopes. They use no chemical herbicides, and the harvest is manual. After sorting and a cold soak, the juice is fermented in wooden and steel vats with pumpovers and *pigeage*. The wine is aged for twelve months in sixty per cent new oak, with some American oak barrels.

The 2002 had a stylish nose with some menthol notes; on the palate it was fairly rich and moderately concentrated, but not very characterful. The 2003 surprisingly lacks substance and a firm mid-palate, but it is reasonably fresh and juicy for the vintage. It is early days for the Bouscasses, who are keen to make wines of quality. In 2005 they produced a lovely *clairet*, with floral and pear aromas, and a concentrated, creamy palate. The Bouscasses also rent the eight-hectare Château Haut-Boutet.

Château Charron

St-Martin-Lacaussade. Tel: 0557 426666. Website: www.vgas.com. Owner: G.F.A. Ch Charron
(leased by Bernard Germain). 26 ha. 22 ha red: 80% Merlot, 20% Cabernet Sauvignon. 4 ha white: 70% Sémillon,
30% Sauvignon Blanc. Production: 80,000 bottles

This property, though not the eighteenth-century château itself, has been leased by the Germain group since 1980. The vineyards are south-facing, on clay-limestone slopes. The white vines are picked by hand, the reds by machine. As is often the case at the Germain properties, one parcel is singled out for special treatment. Here it is called Les Gruppes, and is picked manually and aged in 400-litre barrels.

The top white is called Acacia and comes from a one-hectare parcel. This is fermented and aged in one-third new oak for six months with lees-stirring. It does not go through malolactic fermentation.

Les Gruppes often has plummy, savoury aromas, sometimes with a touch of black coffee. The 2000 was a plump, super-ripe wine with little complexity but a winning richness. The 2002 is slighter, but is fresh and highly drinkable, with gentle coffee tones as well as cherry fruit. The 2005 from cask shows great promise. The 2005 Acacia had toasty lemony aromas, and its richness was backed by good limy acidity, giving an elegant finish. On this showing, the white has more balance and personality than the red.

Confiance

Fours. Tel: 0557 421825. Owners: Bernard Magrez and Gérard Depardieu. 2.2 ha. 95% Merlot, 5% Malbec.
Production: 6,000 bottles

This *micro-cuvée,* first made in 2002, is produced from vines with a very reduced yield: in 2005, a mere twenty-four hl/ha. Vinification is identical to that of La Croix de Pérenne (*see* Pérenne below). The 2003 had an intense nose of red fruit, new oak, and menthol; the palate was dense and powerful, with a sweet red-fruits character. But the tannins are massive and the alcohol discernibly high, so it's more Barossa than Blaye in style.

La Croix de Pérenne

See *Château Pérenne*

Château Dubraud

St-Christoly-de-Blaye. Tel: 0557 424530. Website: www.chateau-dubraud.com. Owner: Alain Vidal. 25 ha.
23 ha red: 65% Merlot, 30% Cabernet Sauvignon, 5% Cabernet Franc. 2 ha white: 75% Sauvignon Blanc,
12.5% Muscadelle, 12.5% Sémillon. Production: 160,000 bottles

The viticulture here is close to organic, and no chemical fertilizers are used. The wine is vinified in steel tanks with micro-oxygenation, and the top *cuvée,* the Grand Vin, is aged in new oak. The only vintage I have tasted is the regular 2003. Its black-cherry and mint aromas were somewhat muted, but on the palate it is plump and full-bodied, with some weight and tannin, a solid, juicy wine with a hint of liquorice on the long finish.

Château Gigault

Mazion. Tel: 0557 543939. Website: www.the-wine-merchant.com. Owner: Christophe Reboul-Salze.
14 ha. 90% Merlot, 5% Cabernet Sauvignon, 5% Cabernet Franc. Production: 65,000 bottles

The story of how this Bordeaux négociant became the owner of two properties in Blaye is given below under Grands Maréchaux. Grands Maréchaux was the first purchase, but there was no house, and Mme. Reboul-Salze longed for a rural retreat, so in 1998 they bought Gigault and restored it.

He notes the high prices for which the wine was selling in Britain in the 1930s as evidence that the terroir here is exceptional. The vines are in a single block on sandy clay soil over a limestone subsoil. No herbicides or insecticides are used, and the soil is ploughed. Although until 2004 the harvest was manual, Reboul-Salze has had a conversion experience to the mechanical *égreneur* system, and is persuaded that less vegetal matter ends up in the tanks than with hand-picking and hand-sorting. Fermentation takes place mostly in cement tanks with micro-oxygenation. Stéphane Derenoncourt advises on vinification and adapts it to the quality and character of each parcel.

The top bottling here, Cuvée Viva, has now overtaken the regular Gigault in terms of production. Yields are no more than forty hl/ha, and the must is vinified with pumpovers and *pigeage*. Malolactic fermentation takes place in barriques. At first Reboul-Salze aged the wine in 100 per cent new oak, but the very ripe vintages of recent years persuaded him to cut back to about one-third.

The 2003 Gigault has light cherry aromas, and a sharp attack; it's rather hollow and lacks flesh and length. The 2004 is similar, rather dilute and simple but well balanced. Clearly the best fruit is reserved for Cuvée Viva. The 2001 has a lush, oaky nose and a hint of overripeness; the palate is less jammy than the aromas, and there is considerable richness if not a great deal of complexity. The 2003 is similar but with a more pronounced overripeness, though its ample tannin and acidity suggest it will become more harmonious in time.

Château du Grand Barrail

Plassac. Tel: 0557 423304. Owner: Denis Lafon. 35 ha. 33 ha red: 65% Merlot, 25% Cabernet Sauvignon, 10% Malbec. 2 ha white: 50% Sémillon, 50% Sauvignon Blanc. Production: 250,000 bottles

The vines here are picked mechanically, and the red is aged for twelve months in both barrels and tanks. A special Cuvée Renaissance, first produced in 1998, is made from older vines that are hand-picked, and aged in new oak. The 2003 Renaissance had discreet black-cherry aromas, a supple palate with modest concentration, but was refreshed by some acidity and lift on the mid-palate.

Château Grands Maréchaux

St-Grions-d'Aiguevives. Tel: 0557 543939. Website: www.the-wine-merchant.com. Owners: Christophe Reboul-Salze, Etienne Barre, Guillaume Touton. 20 ha. 70% Merlot, 15% Cabernet Sauvignon, 15% Cabernet Franc. Production: 100,000 bottles. Second wine: Les Maréchaux

A successful négociant in Bordeaux, Christophe Reboul-Salze had long had an itch, like so many merchants before him, to produce his own wine. In 1997 he and two partners found this property, but lacked the means to buy it. So he put his commercial skills to use, by selling futures on the basis of a five-year commitment to buy five cases per year. Eighty friends signed on, and he was in business. From the outset Stéphane Derenoncourt acted as consultant oenologist.

As at his other Blaye property, Gigault, the grapes were picked by hand until 2005, when Reboul-Salze changed his mind. After fermentation, malolactic fermentation takes place in barriques, and the wine is aged in twenty-five per cent new oak.

The 1998 was good if straightforward, with spice as well as fruit on the nose; the wine was medium-bodied and fresh. The 2003 is on a larger scale, with a very deep colour, intense ripeness and concentration, and mighty tannins and considerable alcohol.

Domaine des Graves d'Ardonneau

St-Mariens. Tel: 0557 686698. Owner: Christian Rey. 34 ha. 28 ha red: 85% Merlot, 10% Cabernet Sauvignon, 5% Cabernet Franc. 6 ha white: 80% Sauvignon Blanc, 20% Colombard. Production: 100,000 bottles

This inland property dates back to 1763 but was always run as a mixed farm. In 1973 Simon Rey began bottling his wine for the first time. In 1982 his jovial son Christian took over, and since 2006 Christian has been aided by his son Laurent. The soil is gravel and limestone, and ironstone in some sectors warms up fast in sunny weather and accelerates ripening. The vineyards are picked by machine and the grapes vinified in steel tanks.

There are three different red wines. The Tradition is mostly unoaked, although twenty per cent is aged in older barrels. The Cuvée Prestige is aged in thirty per cent new oak, and the Grand Vin, which is always sourced from the same parcel and cropped at thirty-five hl/ha, is aged for eighteen months in new oak.

The basic white wine is almost all Colombard. The rather heavy Prestige is fermented in new oak and is almost entirely Sauvignon; it is aged for seven months on the fine lees. There is also a production of some rosé and *moelleux* under the AC Bordeaux.

The only Tradition I have tasted is the 2002 which, despite some herbaceous aromas, was a supple, lively, and fresh wine. The oak-ageing gives the Prestige more toasty aromas of black cherry and coffee. The 2002 has a more pronounced red-fruits character, and though it lacks some flesh and complexity is quite stylish. The 2003 is quite lively and its ample fruit is supported by a tannic undertow. The 2004 is slightly herbaceous, and although lively on the palate, lacks some concentration and substance.

The 2003 Grand Vin is rich, hefty, and full-bodied, with powerful tannins, but this was not the vintage to aim for extraction, and the wine lacks finesse. The 2004 is much better, a rich, rounded wine with lively cherry fruit and good acidity.

The white Prestige is delicious, with citric aromas and some toastiness, while the palate has ample richness, acidity, and persistence, especially in 2005.

These wines may not be of supreme quality, but they are inexpensive. Even the Grand Vin was only 12 Euros in 2006. They are well-made wines of panache and freshness that will give great pleasure in the short and medium term.

Château Grillet-Beauséjour

Berson. Tel: 0557 543939. Website: www.grillet-beausejour.com. Owner: Franck Jullion. 23 ha.
21.7 ha red: 80% Merlot, 15% Cabernet Sauvignon, 5% Cabernet Franc. 1.3 ha white: 100% Sauvignon Blanc.
Production: 130,000 bottles. Second wine: Ch Le Joncieux

This property has been in the hands of the same family since the 1770s. Its vineyards occupy south-facing slopes on a high plateau. As well as the regular unoaked wine, there is an oak-aged bottling with the AC Blaye. The excellent 2003 Blaye has a complex, savoury nose, with spicy aromas of black cherry and mint; the palate is rich and soft-textured yet not lacking grip and concentration.

Château Haut-Bertinerie

See *Château Bertinerie*

Château Haut-Grélot

St-Ciers. Tel: 0557 326598. Website: www.hautgrelot.verticalwine.com. Owner: Joël Bonneau. 50 ha.
30 ha red: 80% Merlot, 15% Cabernet Sauvignon, 5% Malbec. 20 ha white: 80% Sauvignon Blanc, 10% Muscadelle,
10% Sémillon. Production: 300,000 bottles

Here in the northern sector of Blaye the soil is gravel and sand, and these vineyards are machine-harvested. The regular red wine is aged in older barrels and casks, but the Cuvée Méthez, from pure Merlot, is aged in fifty per cent new oak. A substantial proportion of the production is of white wine. The top white is pure Sauvignon, aged six months in new barriques. The only red I have tasted is the 1999, which was concentrated, quite earthy, and had good length. The 2005 unoaked white has light citric aromas, and ample fresh, crisp fruit, and the palate shows some amplitude and length.

Château Les Jonqueyres

St-Paul. Tel: 0557 423488. Website: www.chateaulesjonqueyres.com. Owner: Pascal Montaut. 15 ha. 90% Merlot,
5% Cabernet Sauvignon, 5% Malbec. Production: 55,000 bottles. Second wine: If de Jonqueyres

If there is one individual who deserves credit for the general improvement in quality in Blaye over recent decades, there is wide agreement that Pascal Montaut is the man. He took over his grandfather's property in 1977 and stopped selling fruit to the cooperative. At that time he had only five hectares and they were not in good shape. He gradually took over other family holdings to expand the property. He pulled out the existing

Ugni Blanc so as to focus on red wines. He was one of the first in Blaye to reduce yields and to buy new oak barrels for part of the crop.

The average age of the vines is fifty years, and they are planted to a fairly high density of 6,800 vines per hectare. Yields tend to be between thirty-five and forty hl/ha. The soil is ploughed and the viticulture essentially organic. The grapes are picked by hand and fermented with indigenous yeasts in steel tanks. Malolactic fermentation takes place in barriques, and the wine is aged in thirty-five per cent new oak. Some years ago half the barrels were new, but Montaut admits that economic conditions in Bordeaux are behind his decision to cut back.

The 1998 is slightly herbaceous on the nose and palate, rather surprisingly, but the wine is fairly rich and shows no sign of tiring. The 2002 is sleek, with bright acidity and considerable elegance. The 2003 is not very aromatic, but has the ripeness and concentration of the year without being heavy-handed; there is fine cherry fruit, ample spice, and a vigorous finish.

Montaut also owns the Clos Alphonse Dubreuil (*q.v.*) in Côtes de Bourg.

Château Lacaussade–St-Martin

St-Martin-Lacaussade. Tel: 0557 426666. Website: www.vgas.com. Owner: Jacques Chardat (leased by Bernard Germain). 22 ha. 18 ha red: 90% Merlot, 10% Cabernet Sauvignon. 4 ha white: 90% Sémillon, 10% Sauvignon Blanc. Production: 150,000 bottles. Second wine: Ch Labrousse

This is one of a number of estates owned or leased by Vignobles Germain in the region. The white grapes are harvested by machine, the red by hand. The top *cuvée* is called Trois Moulins for both red and white. The 2001 white Trois Moulins had bright, firm, oaky aromas, rich fruit on the palate backed by bright acidity, discernible but modest oak, and quite good length. The 2000 red Trois Moulins had smoky, oaky aromas, but was rather hollow on the palate, fresh but only moderately concentrated.

Château Lers–Loumède

Blaye. Tel: 0557 420200. Website: www.chateau-bellevue-gazin.com. Owners: Alain and Anne-Sophie Lancereau-Burthey. 5 ha. 70% Merlot, 25% Malbec, 5% Cabernet Sauvignon. Production: 35,000 bottles

A second property under the same ownership as Bellevue-Gazin (*q.v.*), this was bought in 2002. The vineyards are closer to the river. For the time being the vines are not being taxed: yields are fairly high and the wine is unoaked. Nonetheless the 2004 was plump, quite concentrated, straightforward and enjoyable, especially in view of its low price.

Château Maine–Gazin

Plassac. Tel: 0557 426666. Website: www.vgas.com. Owner: Sylvie Germain. 7.5 ha. 95% Merlot, 5% Cabernet Sauvignon. Production: 45,000 bottles

This property, not far from the estuary, has been owned by the Germain family since 1980. The average age of the vines is forty years, and they are picked by hand. As is the custom at the Germain estates, one parcel, here a single hectare of pure Merlot from seventy-five-year-old vines, is handled separately as a kind of prestige *cuvée*. This Cuvée Livenne is aged in new oak barrels of 400 litres, whereas the regular red is aged partly in new oak but mostly in tanks.

The only wine I have tasted from Maine-Gazin is the Livenne. The 2000 had intriguing leather and liquorice aromas, but was less impressive on the palate, since it lacked depth and character though the black-cherry fruit was attractive. There is sumptuous cherry fruit on the nose of the 2001; it's a delicate wine, fully ready, not especially concentrated but attractive. The oaky, red-fruits aromas of the 2003 were appealing, but the wine's texture was rather soupy and broad, and the tannins tough. The 2005 is far more harmonious, with smoky cherry aromas, and ample weight and spice.

Château Monconseil-Gazin

Plassac. Tel: 0557 421663. Owner: Jean-Michel Baudet. 24 ha. 23 ha red: 60% Merlot, 30% Cabernet Sauvignon, 10% Malbec. 1 ha white: 80% Sauvignon Blanc, 20% Sémillon. Production: 120,000 bottles. Second wine: Ch Le Roc

The château here dates from the sixteenth century though it was much altered in the eighteenth. It has been owned by the Baudet family since 1894. However, in 1927 the property was divided into three sectors to settle an inheritance problem. One became Monconseil, another Haut-Monconseil, and the third is Monconseil-Gazin. Jean-Michel and Françoise Baudet took over in 1989.

The south-facing vineyards, planted on clay-limestone soil over a stony subsoil, are cultivated according to *lutte raisonnée*, and green-harvesting is employed to restrain yields. The harvesting is mostly mechanical, but the white grapes and the Malbec are picked by hand. Baudet prefers to ferment with indigenous yeasts, but does use cultivated yeasts in years such as 2005 when sugar levels were very high. The regular wine, a Premières Côtes, is aged for twelve months in twenty-five per cent new oak.

The top *cuvée*, from a four-hectare block, is released as AC Blaye. The wine is given longer maceration and aged for eighteen months in fifty per cent new barriques. The white wine is unoaked, and although it has been a pure Sauvignon, from 2006 some Sémillon will come on stream and be blended in.

The 2004 white is aromatic, but herbaceous and over-forceful. The regular red lacks some flesh, weight, and length, but it is inexpensive. The Blaye bottling is clearly superior, although the 2002 shows some astringency. In contrast the 2003 has plenty of weight and fruit, with attractive smoky tobacco aromas, good acidity, and quite good length.

Château Mondésir-Gazin

Plassac. Tel: 0557 422980. Website: www.mondesirgazin.com. Owner: Marc Pasquet. 14 ha. 65% Merlot, 20% Cabernet Sauvignon, 15% Malbec. Production: 70,000 bottles. Second wine: Ch Mondésir

When I first met Marc Pasquet in 2000 I thought him rather arrogant. A subsequent visit led me to realize that what I took for arrogance was self-confidence and articulacy, allied to a passionate commitment to quality. In the late 1980s he had been working with Henri Dubosq at Haut-Marbuzet in St-Estèphe. He wanted his own property, but couldn't afford the more prestigious appellations, so he looked in Blaye and found this property in 1990. Before then its wines had been sold in bulk. Most of the vines, many of which are old, are in a single parcel near the river on a south-facing slope.

Pasquet admires Malbec, at least in Blaye. He admits that the selections available twenty years ago were far too productive, but today the clones are of higher quality, so he has been replanting the variety. Density is high for Blaye at 7,400 vines per hectare, and he trains the vines high to increase the surface of foliage. He uses no pesticides, no anti-botrytis sprays, and ploughs the soil. Yields average forty hl/ha for the *grand vin*, and the harvest is manual.

Vinification begins with a week-long cold soak. He ferments with natural yeasts in squat steel tanks at quite high temperatures; the *cuvaison* is usually four to five weeks. Pasquet used to practise micro-oxygenation during maceration, but found that after a few months it made little difference. So he no longer bothers with the technique. The wine is aged in one-third new oak for twenty-two months, as he believes a long *élevage* allows the oak to integrate better with the wine. The second wine is unoaked.

Pasquet also makes a Côtes de Bourg called Haut-Mondésir. This comes from a parcel of 1.8 hectares planted with ninety per cent Merlot and ten per cent Malbec. The production method is much the same as for Mondésir-Gazin. It's an excellent wine, with flavours of blackberries and plums, and has a certain force allied to a graceful presence on the palate and a lively finish. The 1998, 2002, and 2003 were all very good.

It's harmoniousness and elegance that characterize Mondésir-Gazin. Yes, there is ample fruit, and a discreet background of oak, but also spice, concentration, and length. The 1998, 2002, and 2003 are all excellent, and only the 1995 proved disappointing.

Château Pérenne

*St-Genès-de-Blaye. Tel: 0557 421825. Website: www.bernard-magrez.com. **Owner:** Bernard Magrez. 70 ha.*
68.5 ha white: 75% Merlot, 20% Cabernet Sauvignon, 3% Cabernet Franc, 2% Malbec. 1.5 ha white:
*40% Sauvignon Blanc, 40% Sémillon, 20% Sauvignon Gris. **Production:** 350,000 bottles. **Second wine:** Ch St-Genès*

This former ecclesiastical property was sold after the Revolution to an Irish family, and the grand château was built in the nineteenth century by the then-owner, Louis Arnaud. In 1997 it was bought by Bernard Magrez, who restored the château in lavish style. He changed the name to Prieuré Malesan, paying tribute to the highly successful Malesan brand he had created. After he sold the brand in 2003, he restored the original name, which was first used by him for the 2004 vintage. Before 1870 the estate had been known as Château St-Genès, and successive owners had used both that name and Pérenne. Today the former name is that of the second wine.

The vineyards are mostly in a single block around the château on clay-limestone soils. Magrez and his technical director Eric Bardon keep the Cabernet yield down to forty hl/ha to ensure that these varieties ripen fully. The grapes are picked by machine and sorted by an *égreneur*. After a brief cold soak, the must is fermented in steel tanks, with pumpovers and *délestage*. The wine is aged in thirty per cent new oak, some of it American, for twelve to fifteen months.

There is a special *cuvée* of 8,000 bottles called La Croix de Pérenne produced from 2.8 hectares of thirty-five-year-old vines, of which ninety per cent are Merlot and ten per cent Cabernet Sauvignon. In 2005 the yield was a paltry twenty-five hl/ha. The grapes are picked and even destemmed by hand, then fermented in wooden vats with *pigeage* and aged for eighteen months in new barriques.

Even more limited is the production of a pure Sauvignon Blanc from 0.2 hectares of young vines. It is fermented in sixty per cent new oak, and aged with lees-stirring for ten months. Other varieties have been planted, and from 2007 production will be increased to 6,000 bottles. The 2005 white was very good, though oak rather dominated the fresh citric aromas; it is rich and full-bodied, perhaps a touch heavy. The 2006, while still plump and full, had more vigour, and a long, nutty finish.

The Pérenne vintages I have tasted – 2002, 2004, and 2005 – have all been excellent, with ample ripeness, firm tannic extraction, and considerable vigour. The 2005 is particularly fine. I am less convinced by the Croix special *cuvée*. In 2002 it was known as La Croix du Prieuré. Despite the difficulties of the vintage, ruthless yield reduction and concentration resulted in a wine with porty aromas, overripe flavours, and a hot finish that derived from the ludicrous fifteen degrees of alcohol. The 2004 is much better, and even though the alcohol is still high at fourteen degrees, the wine has a beguiling opulence, sumptuous new oak, and fair length of flavour. The 2005, tasted from cask, was similar but had even more weight and power, dense, oaky aromas of chocolate and cloves, more weight than the 2004, and a hot finish. The regular Pérenne is a better-balanced and more enjoyable wine than the blockbuster La Croix, which is clearly directed at palates that equate power with quality.

Château Peyredoulle

*Berson. Tel: 0557 426666. Website: www.vgas.com. **Owner:** Josette Germain. 22 ha. 80% Merlot,*
*20% Cabernet Sauvignon. **Production:** 150,000 bottles*

This attractive property is located just outside Berson on chalky soils over a hard limestone base. There is a regular bottling produced from young vines, but, following the general Vignobles Germain policy, the oldest vines go into a special *cuvée*, here called Maine Criquau. This comes from a two-hectare plot that is picked by hand, unlike the rest of the estate, and this wine is aged in 400-litre barrels for twelve months.

I have tasted only the Maine Criquau bottling. The 2000 had muted plummy aromas and was a touch jammy despite a dash of acidity on the finish. The 2002 is light and lacks substance, and the aromas are a touch herbaceous. There's more gaminess on the nose of the 2003, which is quite rich and chewy; but the acidity is low and the finish blunt. The 2005 has similar aromas, but is more lush and spicy, and shows better potential.

Château Puynard

Berson. Tel: 0557 643321. Owner: Nicolas Grégoire. 16 ha. 65% Merlot, 35% Cabernet Sauvignon.
Production: 100,000 bottles

James Grégoire is the owner of the majestic Château de La Rivière in Fronsac, and his son Nicolas acquired this promising property in 2002. The château itself dates back to the thirteenth century, but was mostly rebuilt in the eighteenth century. From the terrace there is a fine view onto the vineyards, which are in a single block, and the Berson cemetery. The former owner had neglected the vines, and all the wine was sold in bulk. So when Grégoire and his family arrived, he found, in his own words, "no barrels, no stock, and no clients". So he sold most of the 2002 in bulk, and considers the 2003 the first vintage of the new regime.

The soils are varied, with sandy sectors on the plateau and clay-limestone on the slope. The grapes are picked by machine. The basic wine is unoaked. Grégoire also produces an oaked wine called Le Chêne de Château Puynard. The wine is aged for fourteen months in one-third new 400-litre barrels, with minimal racking. Prices are very reasonable. There is also a very pretty *clairet*.

The 2003 Puynard has fresh cherry aromas, some overripe, confected flavours, and moderate length. The 2003 Le Chêne is also rather jammy and fatiguing, and the 2004 is much fresher, with crisper tannins and more evident staying power. Clearly Grégoire is still finding his way and getting his vines and winery into shape, but this is a property with considerable potential.

Château Roland-la-Garde

St-Seurin-de-Cursac. Tel: 0557 423229. Website: www.chateau-roland-la-garde.com. Owner: Bruno Martin.
29 ha. 75% Merlot, 20% Cabernet Sauvignon, 5% Malbec. Production: 160,000 bottles

Bruno Martin took over this substantial property from his father in 1990. There are twenty-five hectares in a single block on clay-limestone soils. Yields are rigorously controlled and average thirty-eight hl/ha. Since 1998 all plantings have been at a density of 7,000 vines per hectare, which is high for Blaye. Martin also shares Marc Pasquet's (of Mondésir-Gazin) enthsiasm for Malbec, believing it can give excellent results if properly managed. He is also committed to *lutte raisonnée* viticulture. In addition, he ploughs, plants green cover in alternate rows, and favours high trellising. Harvesting is both by hand and by machine.

Fermentation takes place in cement tanks with natural yeasts, but Martin, an inveterate experimenter, has also tried fermenting in barriques. The Tradition, his basic red, is aged in older barrels and tanks. The Grand Vin grapes are given a six-day cold soak, and fermented with pumpovers, *délestage*, and *pigeage*. Thanks to vertical presses, the quality of the press wine is very high. The Grand Vin is aged in fifty per cent new oak for eighteen months. Martin blends late, and bottles the wines unfined and unfiltered. Rather confusingly there is also a wine called Cuvée Prestige, which is aged for twelve months in one-third new oak.

The 2003 Tradition had aromas of ripe cherries, but the palate shows jammy fruit with high alcohol – not for me. The 1999 Prestige is still going strong, with lively aromas of cherries, raspberries, and mint; it's quite a rich wine with firm tannins, good acidity, and a refreshing cut. The 2001 Prestige is aromatically similar, but is an odd blend of high ripeness and edgy acidity that's close to astringency. There are no such doubts about the exemplary 2005 Prestige, a generous wine with power and concentration and persistence of flavour.

The Grand Vin lives up to its name, with tremendous depth of colour, intensely oaky as well as fruity aromas, and considerable weight and tannin. The 2000 is still youthful, with an imposing mass of fruit. The 2001 may be a touch too extracted, but has sufficient opulence and power to carry it. The 2003 is both overripe and sumptuous, and the alcohol of 14.9 degrees is overwhelming. But the 2005 is magnificent.

Château La Rose Bellevue

St-Palais. Tel: 0557 326654. Website: www.chateau-larosebellevue.com. Owner: Jérôme Eymas. 45 ha.
38 ha red: 75% Merlot, 20% Cabernet Sauvignon, 5% Cabernet Franc. 7 ha white: 85% Sauvignon Blanc and
Sauvignon Gris, 15% Muscadelle. Production: 300,000 bottles

La Rose Bellevue is in the far north of Blaye, where the landscape is more gently undulating than around Blaye itself. Eymas's grandfather practised polyculture, and his father began acquiring more vines. Jérôme and his wife Valérie have both worked in Australia, so they have an international perspective rare in the Côtes de Bordeaux and a keen understanding of the importance of marketing as well as production.

The vineyards are on the plateau surrounding the house and winery, with sandy, gravelly soils over limestone. The grapes are machine-harvested. After sorting, the red grapes are cold-soaked before vinification with selected yeasts. The red Tradition is unoaked; the Prestige is aged for twelve months in one-third new oak.

The white receives twenty-four hours of skin contact. The Tradition, like the red, is unoaked. The Prestige is barrel-fermented and aged in new oak for six months, with rolling of the barrels on Oxoline racks.

The Tradition wines, including the rosé, are well made and reasonably concentrated, but they are modest and inexpensive. The 2004 red Prestige has jammy, black-cherry aromas; it's plump and spicy, with a slight savoury tone. The 2005 white Prestige has slightly exotic aromas, a creamy texture, well-integrated oak, and moderate length. These are not great wines, but they are well crafted and balanced and give pleasure in the short to medium term.

Château Ste-Luce-Bellevue

Blaye. Tel: 0557 423229. Owner: Bruno Martin. 10 ha. 90% Merlot, 10% Cabernet Sauvignon.
Production: 25,000 bottles

This property is under the same ownership as Château Roland-la-Garde (q.v.), and was bought by Bruno Martin in 2002. The soil has more clay and the wines tend to be more spicy and powerful than Roland-la-Garde. The wine is aged in fifty per cent new barriques. Martin is thinking about planting some white vines here.

The 2002 and 2003 have dense, oaky cherry and blackberry aromas. The 2002 is plump, full-bodied, and muscular, but the wine also has vigour and a long, chewy finish. The 2003 is similar but more tannic, yet there seems to be sufficient fruit to support it and keep the wine in balance.

Château Segonzac

St-Genès-de-Blaye. Tel: 0557 421816. Website: www.chateau-segonzac.com. Owners: Thomas and
Charlotte Herter-Marmet. 33 ha. 54% Merlot, 30% Cabernet Sauvignon, 10% Malbec, 3% Cabernet Franc,
3% Petit Verdot. Production: 220,000 bottles

Segonzac is a property on a baronial scale, with a pompous and rather stumpy château in a lofty position just outside Blaye. It was established in 1887 by Jean Dupuy, later appointed minister of agriculture. The vines were planted in a single block on slopes overlooking the Gironde. In 1990 the estate was bought by Jacques Marmet from Switzerland, who entrusted the running of the property to a management company. Then in 2000 his daughter Charlotte and her husband Thomas Herter took over. One of his first actions was to equip the fermentation tanks with temperature control.

Herter produces a number of bottlings, as he wants to produce varied styles that are drinkable on release. The red wines are the mostly unoaked Tradition, Vieilles Vignes, and, from 2000, Cuvée Héritage. He has also created a wine called LibertIR with only six degrees of alcohol, as a result of technical manipulations performed after fermentation; I am glad to say I have not tasted it. Only the grapes for the top *cuvées* are picked by hand. The grapes are given a cold soak under dry ice (though not for the Tradition), before being fermented with some micro-oxygenation. The Vieilles Vignes is aged for twelve months in one-third new oak, including some American barrels. Héritage is a parcel selection, eighty per cent Merlot, cropped at around forty hl/ha, and aged in new oak for eighteen months.

I recall a sweet, blackcurranty Segonzac from 1983, and there was a Cuvée Barrique, of no great distinction, in 1991. Thomas Herter showed me a range of vintages for which he had been responsible. They are good, sound wines, far from exceptional. Héritage shows the greatest concentration, but in vintages such as 2001 and, especially, 2005, the Vieilles Vignes comes very close in quality. The gutsy 2003 Héritage is particularly opulent and impressive.

There are some other Blaye wines that have impressed me, but my tastings have been too limited to allow a detailed assessment of the properties. I have enjoyed a concentrated and discreetly oaky 2004 white from **Château La Bretonnière**. From **Château Les Graves** I have drunk a complex, aromatic 2003 red, burly on the palate and not for long ageing but packed with upfront fruit. The 2005 whites from **Les Billauds** and from **Haut-Canteloup** were fresh, crisp, and charming, but clearly best drunk young. The same is true of the more tropical white from **Château de la Salle**.

The 2003 red from **Château Les Hives Grillet** is a touch soupy, but there is also a Cuvée Gaby said to be of higher quality. The 2003 Cuvée Prestige from **Château Bois-Vert** had aromas of plums and mint, while the palate was rich and spicy from the oak. The 2003 Cuvée Ulysse from **Château Ferthis** is plummy but tannic. The 2003 AC Blaye from **Château Canteloup** in Fours has muted aromas of plums and liquorice, and a palate with considerable lushness, weight, and flesh, yet also an appealing airiness. Bruno Lafon, the brother of Dominique Lafon of Domaine des Comtes Lafon in Meursault, owns **Château Lafon-Lamartine** in Cars; the only wine I have tasted is the 1999, which was quite rich, reasonably concentrated, but finished with rather dry tannins. The **Château des Tourte**s in St-Caprais has a growing reputation, but I have not tasted its wines.

COTES DE BOURG

The Côtes de Bourg is smaller and more compact than the dispersed Côtes de Blaye, and it has generally been agreed that the quality of its wines has progressed more rapidly than that of Blaye. I think that was true until quite recently. Now quite a large number of Blaye properties have made formidable efforts, and it is not so easy for Bourg to claim any superiority. Stylistically, the Bourg wines seem more robust and structured than the majority of those from Blaye. Despite the perception that Bourg wines are a cut above those from Blaye, there has been no move to emulate the Blayais by creating a superior appellation comparable to AC Blaye. Now any such move would be seen as an irrelevance with the probable creation of the new Côtes de Bordeaux: Bourg appellation. However, in 2007 the Bourg growers voted to opt out of this new appellation in any case.

It was granted its AC status in 1936, and for its white wines in 1945, although only some twenty-five hectares are planted with white grapes. Fifteen communes with 3,900 hectares qualify for the appellation: Bayon-sur-Gironde (190 hectares), Bourg (649), Comps (55), Gauriac (416), Lansac (394), Mombrier (220), Prignac-et-Marcamps (227), Pugnac (326), St-Ciers-de-Canesse (400), St-Seurin-de-Bourg (150), St-Trojan (181), Samonac (264), Tauriac (410), Teuillac (328), and Villeneueve (221). Of the 550 growers, 300 are independent and the remainder supply grapes to four cooperatives. About 180 growers bottle and commercialize their wines. Overall, the red *encépagement* is sixty-seven per cent Merlot, twenty-one per cent Cabernet Sauvignon, six per cent Cabernet Franc, and six per cent Malbec. As in Blaye, Cabernet Franc is less important than Cabernet Sauvignon, but the latter can be difficult to ripen except on warmer soils with a significant gravel content. The white *encépagement* is forty-six per cent Sauvignon Blanc, twenty-three per cent Colombard, twenty-three per cent Sémillon, and eight per cent Muscadelle.

Clay-limestone is the dominant soil type, with some sectors where there is a high gravel and/or sand content, as well as scattered ironstone. Since many of the vineyards are close to the Gironde, frost and hail are rare. Although compared to the Médoc, Bourg is a late-ripening region, the local climate is moderated by the estuary. For some reason wind patterns also keep Bourg significantly drier than some neighbouring areas. Bourg is hillier than Blaye, with a series of ridges hitting the skyline as one moves eastwards; there is no counterpart to the flatter areas of Blaye in the north and east of that region.

François Mitjaville of Roc de Cambes has thought hard about the region he bought into some years ago:

> It's often said that the first slopes overlooking the estuary are the finest terroir here. But even though Roc de Cambes is in this area, it isn't necessarily true. It is certainly one of the best spots. But the lines of slopes farther inland can also produce excellent wines, though they ripen later. The coastal slopes are well ventilated – there are always breezes here – so despite the humidity from the estuary, there is no more mildew or oïdium than there is inland. Bourg has an advantage compared to some other Côtes regions as there has always been quite high density of plantation, and pruning has traditionally been guyot double.

Driving me to a balustraded lookout point near Château Tayac, he pointed across the estuary to Margaux and remarked:

> This is the spot where the Dordogne joins the Gironde and the estuary begins. And it's here that the great Cabernet terroir of the Médoc, with its gravelly soils, comes face to face with the other great terroir of Bordeaux, the clay-limestone of the Côtes.

It's a region of family-owned properties on a moderate scale; the average size of a Bourg estate is twelve hectares. The overall improvement in quality has come about as a realization that moderate yields are essential, and the more conscientious properties now apply techniques such as leaf removal and green-harvesting. The planting of green cover has also helped to reduce vigour and thus yields. In the past, when the wines from here fetched low prices, growers felt compelled to crop at maximum levels just to accumulate sufficient volume in their cellars. Unfortunately, another period of low prices has coincided with a decade when many growers have made costly investments in their vines and *chais*.

The influx of younger growers, unable to afford land in more prestigious appellations, has also contributed to the improvement in quality. It was François Mitjaville of Tertre-Rôteboeuf (St-Emilion, *q.v.*) who first demonstrated that the reds from the Côte de Bourg could rise to great heights, inspiring ambitious young growers to try to follow in his footsteps. Mitjaville recalls that when he began producing his wine, which carried a high price tag, the négociants weren't interested, as what they were looking for from Bourg was inexpensive wine with no concentration or ageability.

Over-extraction has been a problem here, even at quality-conscious estates. The terroir here naturally gives tannic wines, and winemakers must take care not to overdo the extraction. Harsh tannins can also be the consequence of early harvesting, a habit ingrained when the chief customers for the wines were cooperatives and merchants largely indifferent to quality. Today the quality-conscious estates at least make an effort to harvest, whether by hand or by machine, when the fruit is ripe.

The region benefits from a dynamic syndicat, with a well-run Maison du Vin offering a wide range of wines for sale and tasting. The syndicat has also produced a detailed study of the region's soils, which has been of great use to the growers, and has promoted the replanting of Malbec. As in the other Côtes appellations, it is probable that the AC Côtes de Bourg will eventually be replaced with Bourg: Appellation Côtes de Bordeaux Contrôlée.

Château Brulesécaille

*Tauriac. Tel: 0557 684031. Website: www.brulesecaille.com. **Owners:** Martine and Jacques Rodet. 25 ha.*
24.25 ha red: 75% Merlot, 20% Cabernet Sauvignon, 3% Cabernet Franc, 2% Malbec. 0.75 ha white:
*100% Sauvignon Blanc. **Production:** 150,000 bottles. **Second wine:** Ch La Gravière*

Jacques Rodet has been making the wine here since 1974. It is a property that has descended since 1924 through his wife's family. The vines are well located on a clay-limestone hillock around the house. The average age of the vines is thirty-five years, boosted by the presence of some eighty-year-old Merlot. Rodet plants green cover, primarily to counter erosion on the slope. The Merlot is picked by hand, the Cabernets by machine.

After a brief cold soak, the grapes are fermented with cultivated yeasts in steel tanks, with some pumpovers and micro-oxygenation. Rodet saves a high proportion of Cabernet for the main wine, which has only fifty per cent Merlot – low for Côtes de Bourg. The wine is aged for twelve months in twenty-five per cent new barriques, then eggwhite-fined. Rodet seeks to make wines for medium-term ageing, and believes they are generally at their best after five years.

There is a small production, some 6,000 bottles, of Sauvignon Blanc, which is whole-bunch pressed, barrel-fermented, and aged on the fine lees for six months in fifty per cent new oak. The 2005 was full-bodied, with fourteen degrees of alcohol, but the oak was well absorbed and there was some delicate acidity on the finish.

As for the red, the plump 2003 was burly and lacked lift. The 2004 is somewhat slack, with light cherry aromas, but the palate is curiously reticent; it's a sound wine but doesn't shine. The 2005, from cask, was more opulent, a robust wine with good extract rather than verve.

Cave Vinicole de Bourg-Tauriac

Tauriac. Tel: 0557 940707. 450 ha. Production: 3,300,000 bottles

Probably the best of the Bourg cooperatives, Bourg-Tauriac was founded in 1936 and today has 160 members who farm 450 hectares. It rewards growers financially for the quality of their fruit, and uses computers to manage individual parcels of vines. Evidence is a *cuvée* produced from ten hectares of the best parcels, a blend of eighty per cent Merlot and twenty per cent Cabernet. The grapes are picked by hand and fermented with pumpovers and *délestage*, and an extended warm maceration. The wine is aged in new barriques with lees-stirring. Total production is around 35,000 bottles. The 2003 Evidence was aromatically a touch stewed despite some plum and liquorice tones; the palate was fluid and fruity but the wine lacked complexity. Perhaps this was not the ideal vintage to assess the wine.

Clos Alphonse Dubreuil

Villeneuve. Tel: 0557 423488. Website: www.chateaulesjonqueyres.com. Owner: Pascal Montaut.
0.5 ha. 60% Merlot, 40% Cabernet Sauvignon. Production: 3,000 bottles

This *micro-cuvée* is produced by the owner of the leading Blaye estate Les Jonqueyres (*q.v.*). After a length *cuvaison*, the wine is aged for fifteen to eighteen months in new barriques. After almost ten years the 1997 had developed sweet, leafy aromas, and was still evidently ripe and concentrated on the palate, though marked by firm tannins. The 2004 had mentholly aromas and lacked some flesh; the acidity was pronounced too, suggesting a slight lack of ripeness.

Château Le Clos du Notaire

Bourg. Tel: 0557 684436. Website: www.clos-du-notaire.com. Owner: Roland Charbonnier. 20 ha. 76% Merlot,
17% Cabernet Sauvignon, 7% Cabernet Franc. Production: 150,000 bottles

As the evocative name suggests, this property did once belong to a notary, from whom the present owner is descended. Roland Charbonnier took over running the estate in 1974. The vineyards are on south-facing gravelly limestone soils, with some iron traces. There are two red wines. The Tradition is aged in older barrels and tanks. Notaris comes from a five-hectare parcel, and is aged for eighteen months in new barriques. The 2003 Tradition is simple and easy-going; the 2003 Notaris has cherry and vanilla aromas, and is juicy and supple on the palate, with density rather than depth.

Château Falfas

Bayon. Tel: 0557 648041. Owner: John Cochran. 22 ha. 55% Merlot, 30% Cabernet Sauvignon, 10% Cabernet Franc, 5% Malbec. Production: 120,000 bottles. Second wine: Les Demoiselles de Falfas

The American John Cochran was a Europe-based lawyer whose wife Véronique happened to be the daughter of one of France's leading biodynamic viticulture consultants. Her father helped them to find a property where they could make wine as well as drink it. They bought Falfas in 1988. The château itself is one of the loveliest in the region, dating from 1612. A year after they bought the property, the Cochrans began converting its vineyards to biodynamism. Over half the vines are on clay-limestone soils alongside the château, and seven hectares are closer to the river near Tayac, on heavier clay soils.

The strict rules of biodynamic cultivation are not enough to ensure a wine of good quality. The Cochrans have introduced other modifications to improve their wine. New plantings are made at a density of 7,000 vines per hectare, and debudding rather than green-harvesting is favoured as a means of controlling yields to around forty hl/ha. Harvesting is manual.

After a short cold soak, the grapes are fermented in cement tanks with indigenous yeasts. The pomace is pressed in a vertical press, and the wine is aged for up to fourteen months in one-third new barrels, including a few from American oak. In 1990 the Cochrans introduced Cuvée Chevalier, from the oldest Cabernet vines and a mere twenty-five per cent of Merlot. Yields are derisory, at around twenty hl/ha. The wine is aged for eighteen months in new oak.

My experience of Falfas wines is limited, but both the 2002 Falfas and the 2000 Chevalier are excellent. The 2002 is bright and spicy, not the fleshiest of wines but that is made up for by its liveliness and length. The dominance of Cabernet in the Chevalier does mean the wine is both tannic and high in acidity, even in a very ripe year such as 2000. The wine is well made but perhaps too muscular.

Château Fougas

Lansac. Tel: 0557 684215. Website: www.vignoblesbechet.com. Owner: Jean-Yves Béchet. 13 ha. 50% Merlot, 25% Cabernet Sauvignon, 25% Cabernet Franc. Production: 75,000 bottles

Although Jean-Yves Béchet, who comes from a family of négociants, bought this property, with its charming chartreuse, in 1976, it was not until 1993 that he and his wife Michèle began to focus on producing the best possible quality. The vineyards are in a single block of sandy alluvial soils over very varied subsoils. The viticulture is organic, and it is Michèle Béchet who looks after the farming, while her husband attends to the cellar. Her aim is to encourage the roots to descend as deeply as possible into the subsoil. The harvest is mostly manual.

Until 1993 there was a Cuvée Tradition and an oak-aged Cuvée Prestige. When they created Cuvée Maldoror, the Tradition was dropped and the Prestige, somewhat confusingly, became the basic wine. The Prestige is aged for twelve months in barriques, of which few are new.

Maldoror, named by Michèle after Lautréamont's celebrated prose poems *Les Chants de Maldoror*, has a much higher proportion of Merlot in the blend than the Prestige, and it is made from older vines. The Béchets insist they are not looking for overripeness and their goal is to have the wine express the terroir as faithfully as possible. By 2005 the production of Maldoror was greater than that of Prestige. The fruit is carefully sorted, then cold-soaked for almost two weeks so as to maximize the wine's intrinsic fruitiness. Vinification takes place in squat steel tanks with automatic *pigeage*. The *marc* is pressed in vertical presses. The wine is aged for eighteen months in eighty per cent new barriques, which are rolled to keep the lees in suspension. *Cliquage* is preferred to racking.

Of the vintages of the Prestige I have tasted, my preference, rather to my own surprise, is the 2003, which has light cherry aromas, ample fruit and spice on the palate, and restrained tannins and, best of all, a lively finish. The 1998 is slightly herbaceous on the nose, and seems too extracted. I find the extraction too noticeable in the 2002, although the wine certainly doesn't lack fruit. (The 1992 Prestige was still clinging to life in 2007, but only just.)

Cuvée Maldoror has the edge above all when it comes to elegance. The 1993, the debut vintage, tasted recently, had slightly gamey aromas that were far from unpleasant. The palate was medium-bodied and supple, with rather earthy tannins; despite some spiciness on the finish, the wine seems at or just past its peak. The 1998 is magnificent, powerfully oaky and cedary yet allowing the fruit to shine through on the nose and palate. With the similar 2001, everything again seems in harmony: rich fruit, acidity, concentration, a light tannic backbone to give it lift and length. Elegance also marks the 2003, as well as a svelte texture, delicious fruit, light spiciness, and a fair if not exceptional finish. The 2004 seems promising, with ripe aromas of raspberries and cloves; it's medium-bodied, juicy and bright, yet less opulent and vigorous than the first-rate 2005.

Château de la Grave

*Bourg. Tel: 0557 684149. Website: www.chateaudelagrave.com. **Owner:** Philippe Bassereau. 45 ha.*
43.5 ha red: 78% Merlot, 20% Cabernet Sauvignon, 2% Malbec. 1.5 ha white: 70% Sémillon, 30% Colombard.
Production: 320,000 bottles

This important property has been in the hands of the Bassereau family for four generations. They are firm believers in *lutte raisonnée*, and the harvest is manual.

The basic wine is called Caractère and it is aged for twelve months in one- and two-year-old barrels. About 16,000 bottles are made each year of the top Cuvée Nectar, an old-vine selection cropped at under forty hl/ha. It is aged in about fifty per cent new oak for fourteen months. The wine is eggwhite-fined but unfiltered. There is another wine, Château de la Grave Bel Air, which is produced from rented vineyards in St-Seurin-de-Bourg; the vinification is essentially the same as for Caractère. In addition, there is a white wine aged in new American oak.

The only wine I have tasted is the excellent 2003 Nectar. The nose was certainly oaky, with lively touches of cedar and tar; the palate was suave and concentrated, with ample ripe fruit and good length.

Château Guerry

*Tauriac. Tel: 0557 682078. Website: www.bernard-magrez.com. **Owner:** Bernard Magrez. 22 ha. 50% Merlot,*
*20% Malbec, 15% Cabernet Sauvignon, 15% Cabernet Franc. **Production:** 170,000 bottles.*
Second wine: La Chapelle du Ch Guerry

This property, with its charming house of 1790, was acquired from the de Rivoyre family in 2004 by the omnipresent Bernard Magrez. The vines, which are picked manually, are on a single well-exposed slope with clay-limestone and clay-gravel soils. In 2005 the yield was a low thirty-three hl/ha. The wine is aged in one-third new barriques. The only vintage I have tasted is the decidedly rustic 2002.

Château Guionne

*Lansac. Tel: 0557 684217. Website: www.chateauguionne.com. **Owner:** Alain Fabre. 21 ha. 60% Merlot,*
*33% Cabernet Sauvignon, 2% Cabernet Franc, 5% Malbec. **Production:** 120,000 bottles. **Second wine:** Ch Beauguerit*

Alain Fabre was a grower and winemaker in the Corbières, but with each year that went by he felt the region was becoming increasingly inhospitable to fine-wine production. Drought was taking a severe toll on his vineyards, and in any case he did not consider his terroir exceptional. So he looked elsewhere, and found this fine property and house in Lansac, and moved here with his wife Isabelle in 2000.

About half the vines are in a south-facing single parcel on clay-limestone soils close to the house. There are two other major blocks, one of which furnishes the second wine. The vines were not in good condition in 2000, so he has had to renovate them. Fabre is particularly keen on his old-vine Malbec. The vines are picked by machine, and then sorted and passed through an *égreneur*. After a cold soak, the grapes are fermented with selected yeasts, *pigeage*, and some micro-oxygenation for the top *cuvées*.

The Traditionnel is unoaked. Coeur Boisé, a *cuvée* composed of half Cabernet Sauvignon and half Malbec, is aged for twelve months in one- and two-year-old barriques. The top wine, Cuvée Renaissance, is fifty per cent Malbec, and aged in new oak for eighteen months, though Fabre will use less new wood in future. There is also a nouveau-style wine called G with a dash of residual sugar, intended to appeal to younger drinkers. Older drinkers will not care for it.

The 2002 Traditionnel has aromas of cherry and liquorice; it's not especially concentrated, but as an upfront, fruity wine, it delivers the goods. The 2001 Boisé has plenty of fruit yet seemed somewhat lame and incomplete. The 2001 Renaissance, however, has intense aromas of cherries, raspberry coulis, and mint; the wine is suave, full-bodied, and concentrated, and refreshed by good length. The 2002 Renaissance doesn't have the same weight so the oak is more obtrusive, but the fruit is sumptuous. The 2003 Renaissance has baked and chocolatey aromas, and a rich and plump palate, though the tannins are quite dry. The stylishly oaky 2004

Renaissance, with its explosive fruit, sleek texture, and huge concentration promised, when tasted from cask, to be the best yet.

Château Haut-Mondésir

See *Château Mondésir-Gazin (Blaye)*

Château L'Hospital

*St-Trojan. Tel: 0557 643360. Owner: Bruno Duhamel. 6 ha. 5.5 ha red: 80% Merlot, 10% Malbec, 5% Cabernet Sauvignon, 5% Cabernet Franc. 0.5 ha white: 50% Sémillon, 50% Colombard. **Production:** 50,000 bottles*

Bruno Duhamel, a former business manager, and his wife Christine, an archaeologist, exchanged high-pressure work in the city for high-pressure work in the Bourg countryside. They bought this property in 1997. The soil is varied, but all parcels are rich in clay. It's a late-ripening terroir, and the Cabernet Sauvignon does not always ripen fully. The viticulture here is *lutte raisonnée*, and the harvest manual.

For some reason Duhamel produces numerous different *cuvées* from his small vineyards, and I found the experience of visiting the property exasperating, as wine followed wine in a seemingly random order, while Bruno Duhamel philosophized at length. The oaked red wines are aged in barrels of 300 and 500 litres and bottled without filtration.

The basic red is the unoaked Cuvée Merlot-Malbec. In the 2002 and 2003 there were pleasant sour-cherry aromas, and the 2002 had some spice and persistence; the 2003, however, was juicy but confected with high alcohol. His oaked bottling, labelled under the château name, is from eighty per cent Merlot oak-aged for twenty-four months. The 2002 was very good, with smoky oaky aromas tinged with liquorice; the palate was plump and juicy but there was a slightly fierce acidic edge, and the wine overall lacked focus.

A wine called Château de Laplace has even more Merlot, at ninety per cent of the blend, and the yields are very low, at thirty hl/ha. It is cheaper than the oaked Château L'Hospital, even though it is aged in new oak for nine months, as Duhamel sees the *élevage* as a way of seasoning the barrels. The 2002 had aromas of cherries and red fruits as well as substantial oakiness; the wine is plump, concentrated, and spicy, but high alcohol mars the finish.

L'Estocade comes from a parcel on gravelly clay, half Merlot, half Cabernet Franc. This is barrel-fermented with *pigeage*. I have not tasted it.

The white wine is made from Sémillon and Colombard in equal proportions, cropped at thirty hl/ha from old vines, and aged twelve months in new American oak. Rather to my surprise, I enjoyed this wine, with its spicy, apricot aromas, its lush, creamy texture, and its delicate acidity.

Duhamel claims to be enjoying much success at smart restaurants, so he must be doing something right, but I found his range too disparate and inconsistent.

Château Labadie

*Mombrier. Tel: 0557 643665. Owner: Joël Dupuy. 42 ha. 60% Merlot, 20% Cabernet Sauvignon, 20% Cabernet Franc. **Production:** 200,000 bottles. **Second wine:** Ch Laroche Joubert*

This large property has very varied soils, essentially clay-limestone, but there are sectors with heavier clay, and with gravel. The grapes are picked by machine, and when I visited in 2000 there was no temperature control during fermentation. The wine is aged in twenty-five per cent new oak, of which some is American; the second wine is unoaked. The 1995 was too marked by the Cabernets, with some brutal tannins and slightly unripe green-pepper flavours. The 2003 is far riper, with plenty of black-cherry fruit, but it's somewhat hollow and tails off on the finish. A third wine, Château Haut Richards, supplies supermarkets.

Château Martinat

Lansac. Tel: 0557 683498. Owner: Stéphane Donze. 10 ha. 70% Merlot, 20% Cabernet Sauvignon, 10% Malbec. Production: 90,000 bottles

Donze had an earlier career in maritime transport, and his wife Lucie was a golf-course designer. They bought this estate in 1994, having decided to buy vines in the Côtes de Bourg as her family was based at Château Grand Chemin. Christian Veyry acts as their oenological consultant. With the exception of a parcel of old Malbec, the vines are in a single block on clay soils with gravel. New vines are being planted at a density of 6,500 vines per hectare and the trellising has been heightened. Average yields are forty hl/ha, and the grapes are picked by hand.

Donze likes a long *cuvaison* but is wary of excessive extraction, so he goes easy with his pumpovers, and there is no micro-oxygenation. Martinat is aged in one-third new Nadalié barrels for fourteen months, with lees-stirring and minimal racking. He blends very late, and says his stylistic goal is elegance, early drinkability, and ageability – a hard combination to pull off.

Since 1999 Donze has made a special *cuvée* called Epicuréa, which contains twenty per cent Malbec. It is made from late-picked but not overripe grapes. He and Veyry go to the trouble to choose individual vines rather than rows of vines, so the selection and harvesting are labour-intensive. The wine is aged for eighteen months in new oak, with lees-stirring. About 15,000 bottles are made.

The 2003 Martinat has stylish, plummy, toasty aromas, but a strange edginess on the palate as though not entirely ripe; however there is sufficient acidity to give a persistent finish. The 2005 is a complete success, being sumptuous, spicy, and delicious, yet still quite lively on the finish. Any slight greenness in the 2003 Martinat is completely absent from the splendid Epicuréa, with its sweet, intense, oaky aromas, its suave texture, its fine weight of fruit, and peppery aftertaste. In 2005, when tasted just before bottling, I preferred the Martinat, with its freshness and exuberance, to the more grippy, extracted Epicuréa.

Donze leases Grand Chemin, but most of its production is sold in bulk. The 10,000 bottles he commercializes are in a lighter style than Martinat, with freshness and balance more pronounced than richness or extraction.

Château de Monteberiot

Mombrier. Tel: 0557 642096. Owners: Gilles Marsaudon and Marie-Hélène Léonard. 10 ha. 75% Merlot, 20% Cabernet Sauvignon, 3% Cabernet Franc, 2% Malbec. Production: 70,000 bottles

The new owners bought this property in 2002, so their first vintage was in 2003. The soil is a mix of clay-limestone and sandy slopes. They introduced some Malbec, heightened the trellising, and began ploughing the soil. Harvesting is manual and mechanical.

There are three wines. The Cuvée Classique is mostly aged in tanks, though one-third of the crop is briefly aged in barriques. Jour de Cocagne has forty per cent of both Cabernets, and is unoaked. The top wine is the coyly named La Part des Fées, from hand-picked old vines, almost all Merlot, and aged in new barriques for fifteen months. The 2003 Fées was anything but fairy-like. The nose was firm and oaky, oozing black fruits, while the palate was supple and juicy, with some weight and density and an overall heaviness and lack of excitement.

Château Nodoz

Tauriac. Tel: 0557 684103. Owner: Jean-Louis Magdeleine. 42 ha. 60% Merlot, 35% Cabernet Sauvignon, 5% Cabernet Franc. Production: 250,000 bottles. Second wine: Ch Galau

Wines from this large property with its single parcel of vineyards have been gaining recognition in recent years.

M. Magdeleine favours *lutte raisonnée* and picks his grapes by hand and by machine. There are three red wines, and the top Cuvée Spéciale is aged entirely in new barriques. The only wine I have tasted is the 2003 Futs de Chêne, which was splendidly harmonious. Despite oaky black-cherry aromas and a slight herbaceous tone, the nose has elegance, while the palate has a suave, lush texture, ample concentration, and spice and vigour on the finish.

Château Peychaud

Teuillac. Tel: 0557 426666. Website: www.vgas.com. **Owner:** *G.F.A. Ch Peychaud (leased by Bernard Germain).*
29 ha. 90% Merlot, 5% Cabernet Sauvignon, 5% Petit Verdot. **Production:** *200,000 bottles*

As at almost all the properties run by Vignobles Germain, one parcel is set aside for special treatment. Here it is Maisonneuve Vieilles Vignes, a four-hectare block that is hand-picked, unlike the rest of the estate, and aged for twelve to fourteen months in 400-litre barrels. The regular Peychaud is unoaked. The only wine I have tasted is the Maisonneuve. The 2000 was too woody for my taste. The 2003 had a reduced nose in 2006, but the fruit was sweet and rounded, though the wine dried on the finish. The 2005, tasted from cask, is super-ripe, plummy and powerful, and clearly has good potential.

Château Roc de Cambes

Bourg. Tel: 0557 744211. **Owner:** *François Mitjaville. 10 ha. 70% Merlot, 25% Cabernet Sauvignon,*
5% Malbec. **Production:** *45,000 bottles*

The eloquent François Mitjaville is best known as the owner/winemaker who elevated Tertre-Rôteboeuf (*q.v.*) to the top ranks of St-Emilion wines. In the 1980s he was keen to expand his holdings in St-Emilion, but was unable to find suitable vineyards near his own. He saw himself as a specialist in grape-farming on clay-limestone soils, so he had been thinking incessantly about the possibilities. When a friend mentioned that Roc de Cambes was for sale, he went to inspect the vineyards and immediately realized he could make something of them. His friends were sceptical, but he went ahead, even though the purchase required an enormous bank loan. It can't be easy to run two properties far apart from each other, but he insists that he never stops training his seventeen employees so that he can have complete confidence in them.

He makes two wines: Roc de Cambes and Domaines de Cambes. The latter comes from about four hectares of vines that must be declared as AC Bordeaux. The vineyards lie in two blocks on slopes just north of Bourg, mostly on cliff-like shelves overlooking the river. There are some very old vines here, as the vineyards, protected by the flowing Gironde, escaped the 1956 frost. Mitjaville finds the soil here slightly more generous and fertile than that at Tertre-Rôteboeuf.

The viticulture and winemaking are identical to those at Tertre-Rôteboeuf. The wine is vinified in cement tanks and aged in fifty per cent new barriques. He uses natural yeasts because he believes the action of cultivated yeasts is still not properly understood and thus even more complicated. Mitjaville, who combines humility with blazing self-confidence, says he still finds the process of vinification essentially mysterious. He admits that he makes wines that require human intervention, arguing that the only purely natural element in a wine is the fruit itself. However, the nature and quality of that fruit are also determined by human decisions, and part of the stature of Roc de Cambes derives from the fact that Mitjaville tends to pick late and only at optimal ripeness.

Roc de Cambes is marked by its purity of aromas, its silky texture, and its finesse and length. The 1990 was still impeccable by 2006, with elegant, truffley aromas and a sweet spiciness on the palate, which remains balanced and long. The 1993 was good for the vintage, and ready to drink by 2000. The 1995 has sweet, lush, red-fruits aromas; the wine is very rich and concentrated, suave yet spicy, shows a hint of tobacco as it matures, and has a delicious finish. The nose of the 1998 shows a fine balance of red fruits and oak, and it became smokier with aeration. It's a fresh, graceful wine, far from massive but pure and stylish. There are some candied aromas in 2003, but it's fragrant, with charming raspberry and cherry fruit; the palate is opulent and silky, and has good acidity and length. The 2004 is exquisite, again with intense aromatic purity; it's only medium-bodied, but it is stylish, fresh, and spicy, with a lightly peppery finish. A glimpse of the 2005 from cask suggested it would be a sumptuous wine with lovely clean acidity.

François Mitjaville is a man of passion. He is full of notions relating to the history of wine production and wine regions, and philosophizes readily about the processes of winemaking. He decided that the ideal spot at which to expound on the terroir of Bourg was the dead centre of the main road leading north from the town. It wasn't a deliberate choice, it was just that he was in full flow and simply stopped in the road to focus more completely on what he was saying. Fortunately it was a dozy weekend lunchtime, so there was little traffic. His driving is somewhat erratic, alternating between a snail's pace and bursts of speed. "Don't worry," he assured me as I gripped the armrest, "I know every inch of this road." Not quite well enough, as he was pulled over by a *gendarme* as we roared into Bourg. He waved me off to where my own car was parked nearby, and I last saw the brilliant and generous François Mitjaville deep in negotiations with the unsmiling policeman.

Château de Rousselet

*St-Trojan. Tel: 0557 643218. Website: www.chateauderousselet.com. **Owners:** Francis and Emmanuel Sou.*
17 ha. 16.5 ha red: 60% Merlot, 15% Cabernet Sauvignon, 15% Cabernet Franc, 10% Malbec. 0.5 ha white:
*100% Sauvignon Blanc. **Production:** 50,000 bottles*

This property, well known in France, is on gravelly clay soils, and the vineyards include some old Malbec. No herbicides are used. The white grapes are picked by hand, the reds by machine. There are two reds, unoaked and oaked. The latter spends twelve months in one-third new barriques. I have not tasted the wines for some years; they seemed fairly light with rather hard tannins, but may have improved in recent years. There is a simple unoaked white, and a superior bottling that is pure Sauvignon, aged five months in barriques with lees-stirring.

Château Sauman

*Villeneuve. Tel: 0557 421664. Website: www.chateausauman.com. **Owner:** Dominique Braud. 25 ha. 75% Merlot,*
*15% Cabernet Sauvignon, 10% Malbec. **Production:** 180,000 bottles*

Braud is the fifth generation of his family to run this property, which has vineyards on southwest-facing clay-limestone slopes. Most of the vines are picked by machine. The Cuvée Tradition is unoaked. Cuvée Emotion is a rarity in Bordeaux: a pure Malbec. Cuvée Particulière, first made in 1989, comes from two hectares of older vines and has fifty per cent Merlot; it is aged for sixteen months in one-third new oak. The only wine I have tasted is the lightly aromatic 2003 Cuvée Particulière, which is fluid, pleasant, but unremarkable.

Château Tayac

*St-Seurin-de-Bourg. Tel: 0557 684060. Website: www.chateau-tayac.fr. **Owner:** Pierre Saturny. 30 ha.*
29 ha red: 50% Merlot, 45% Cabernet Sauvignon, 5% Cabernet Franc. 1 ha white: Sauvignon Blanc, Sauvignon Gris,
*and Muscadelle. **Production:** 170,000 bottles*

This splendid if rather pompous château was built in the 1830s on a site overlooking the estuary. The family recount the legend that the Black Prince stopped here in 1356 and built four towers, of which two remain. The medieval castle was razed after the Hundred Years War. During the eighteenth century Tayac was owned by *parlementaires* and dispatched its wines to the French court. In 1950 the estate was bought by the present owner. He is semi-retired these days, but his charming wife Annick still welcomes visitors, and their sons Loïc and Philippe run the estate on a daily basis. Pierre Saturny found that the vines needed considerable renovation when he bought the property, and the first vintage with which he was satisfied was 1962.

The vines are planted between the château and the estuary on a shallow clay shelf above a limestone cliff. This parcel is planted with a special selection of Merlot with red stalks. Mme. Saturny says that this sub-type, which they continue to propagate by massal selection, gives stronger, sweeter wines than the regular Merlot. Other blocks of vines lie behind the château and on the far side of the main north–south road. The harvest has always been manual, but from 2006 part of the vines will be picked by machine.

The red wines are fermented in cement tanks, with some micro-oxygenation, and the blends are assembled late. There are various bottlings. Rubis du Prince Noir is the basic wine, Merlot-dominated, unoaked, and made from youngish vines. Cuvée Reservée is half Merlot, half Cabernet Sauvignon; it is aged in older barrels. Cuvée Prestige is made from vines between twenty-five and sixty years old. It is distinctive in containing seventy-five per cent Cabernet Sauvignon, and is aged in one-third new barriques.

A new wine was introduced in 2001: Les Terrasses. In contrast to the Prestige, this is ninety per cent Merlot, aged for twenty-four months in seventy per cent new Taransaud barrels. It is not made every year: none was made in 2002, nor in 2005, as the quantities available were too small. The maximum production is 20,000 bottles.

The 2003 Rubis is a perfectly pleasant wine, medium-bodied, modestly concentrated, and supple. The 2001 Reservée has aromatic charm; it's concentrated and spicy, but quite tannic on the finish. The 2002 is agreeable but lacks grip or personality.

The Cuvée Prestige is austere, no doubt thanks to the high proportion of Cabernet Sauvignon. In many vintages there is a certain stalkiness on the nose, marring the cherry and blackcurrant fruit. There is usually plenty of fruit on the palate and no lack of concentration, but dry tannins can spoil the finish. Nor does it seem to diminish with bottle-age: the 1998, otherwise a fine and robust wine, finishes dry. Of vintages from 1998 to 2003, the finest is the 2001.

Les Terrasses seems more successful. The 2001 is excellent, with its richly oaky nose, its power and concentration, and its long, chewy finish. It's far from elegant, but it's well structured and should age well. The 2003 is equally good, with no trace of over-extraction or jamminess despite the abundance of very ripe Merlot.

There is a small production of white wine, aged in lightly toasted Hungarian oak. I have not tasted it. The Saturny family also own a ten-hectare property called La Joncarde, which they bought in 1989; the wine is Merlot-dominated and mostly sold in Japan.

I have had limited encounters with some other wines in recent vintages.

Château Genibon-Blanchereau This twenty-hectare estate produces a special *cuvée* called Amethyste, aged in oak for twelve months. The 2003 had slightly herbaceous aromas, and lacked some flesh and weight on the palate.

Château Haut-Guiraud The Cuvée Péché du Roy is eighty per cent Merlot, aged for fourteen months in new oak. The 2003 was impressive, opaque in colour, muted but fruity on the nose, and the palate was very lush and full-bodied; although very oaky, there seemed to be enough vigour to prevent the wine from being heavy-handed or over-dense.

Château Lamothe The Grande Réserve here is partially oaked. The 2003 has light cherry aromas, and it's a medium-bodied, rounded wine, with excellent fruit and balance.

Château Mercier There are two red wines here, and the Cuvée Prestige is aged for twelve months in one-third new oak. The only wine I have tasted here is the 2004 white, almost entirely Sauvignon Blanc. Its aromas are apricotty and delicate, and there's plenty of lively acidity and zest on the palate.

Château Reynaud This five-hectare property made a charming 2003, and also produces an oaked *cuvée* called La Volière.

27. Between the Rivers

With so much attention focused on the most prestigious regions, and rightly so, one easily forgets that almost half the wine produced in Bordeaux is generic. When you include the large if amorphous appellations such as Entre-Deux-Mers and Premières Côtes de Bordeaux the proportion is even larger. It is here that the expansion of the Bordelais vineyards over the last two decades has been at its most aggressive – and most reckless. With the foolish but curiously French assumption that if one produces wine, then the public is somehow obliged to buy it, the area under vine was almost doubled, with little thought given to whether a market existed for these reservoirs of mostly unremarkable wine.

The *poulets* have come home to roost with a vengeance. While the prices for top Bordeaux have been soaring, the market and prices for generic Bordeaux have been dwindling. Over-production, inadequate wine-making, appalling marketing, and ever more confident competition from other wine regions, within Europe as well as the much derided *nouveau monde*, have all made their contribution. The plummeting market has also infected regions of genuine merit, such as Fronsac.

Nonetheless there are some very good wines being produced in what I am obliged, rather dismissively, to call "the rest of Bordeaux". There are some shining stars in a galaxy of mediocrity. It is very difficult for these wines to gain recognition, since they must enter the marketplace without the prop of a prestigious appellation. Properties make their mark by stratagems such as a ruthless reduction in yields, resulting in super-concentrated wines that attract the attention of wine critics, or by ingenious and focused marketing. Few properties are likely to prosper, or perhaps survive, if the low prices for generic Bordeaux continue for much longer. One of the few ways to achieve higher prices is to deliver full-bodied, oaky wines that please the critics, and perhaps the consumers too. If the terroir is intrinsically reluctant to produce this style of wine, then the wine must be manipulated until it delivers the correct formula. I note this without disdain, for it must be exceedingly difficult for even the best properties in these regions to thrive.

Rather than discuss each appellation individually, I have grouped them all together. This is because there is so much overlapping between appellations. I have before me two white wines from Château Rauzan-Despagne. One is AC Entre-Deux-Mers, the other is AC Bordeaux Blanc. I have no idea why. No doubt the explanation is tediously bureaucratic. In any event it makes no sense to discuss this property, which does indeed lie within Entre-Deux-Mers, under more than one appellation. Moreover the rules within each appellation are often very confusing: the nuances that determine whether a wine is entitled to be Premières Côtes or plain Bordeaux are too exhausting even to contemplate.

So some notes will follow about each appellation covered by this chapter, and then there follows a selection of properties from all of them.

BORDEAUX AND BORDEAUX SUPERIEUR

In terms of zones of production, there is absolutely no difference between these two appellations. If your land entitles you under INAO rules to produce Bordeaux, you are equally entitled to produce Supérieur. The principal difference is that the former must have a minimum of 9.5 degrees of alcohol, whereas Bordeaux Supérieur must have a staggering ten degrees. Perhaps more significant is that the tastings for the *agrément* for "Bord Sup", as it is cosily known, are later than those for AC Bordeaux, allowing the wines to be commercialized later and after proper ageing. Should a wine fail to make the grade as Bord Sup, it can always be declassified to Bordeaux; clearly the reverse is not possible. A majority of Bord Sup is estate-bottled, which is not the case with AC Bordeaux, most of which finds its way into merchants' blends of generic Bordeaux destined for supermarkets everywhere.

Everything that is not entitled to a superior appellation is automatically Bordeaux. Thus on the riverside fringes of the Médoc, along the alluvial *palus* soils, the vineyards cease to be in Margaux or the Haut-Médoc or wherever, and revert to plain Bordeaux. White wine produced within the vast Entre-Deux-Mers is entitled to that appellation, but not

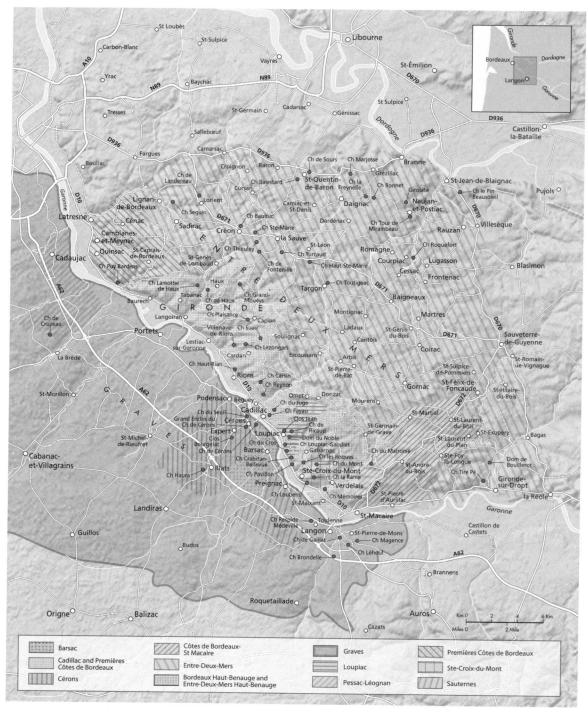

Between the Rivers

the red wine from the same region, which is mere Bordeaux. Large swathes of land north of Libourne or Fronsac are plain Bordeaux. Growers within appellations whose names are utterly unknown outside the immediate neighbourhood – Graves de Vayres, for example – often prefer to use the lowlier Bordeaux appellation since the buyer will at least have some idea about where it comes from. In 2003, according to James Lawther, about 44,000 hectares ended up being declared as AC Bordeaux, and 11,800 as Bord Sup. That's a lot of wine.

There is also sweet Bordeaux Supérieur, produced from seventy-six hectares planted with a range of white varieties. The maximum yield is forty hectolitres per hectare, the minimum alcohol 11.5 degrees, and the grapes can be picked by hand or machine. There are said to be almost fifty producers, but I don't recall ever tasting the wine.

COTES DE BORDEAUX ST-MACAIRE

This small appellation of ten communes, just inland from the sweet wine appellation of Ste-Croix-du-Mont, produces both dry and sweet white wine, but from a mere sixty-four hectares in 2005. The maximum yield for the sweet wine is forty-four hl/ha, and the grapes may be picked either by hand or by machine. There are some fifty producers, and production, rather surprisingly, has been rising slightly in recent years.

ENTRE-DEUX-MERS

This vast region extends, as its name implies, between two sheets of water: the Dordogne, which separates it from St-Emilion, and the Garonne. In fact it never quite makes it as far as the Garonne, as the Premières Côtes blocks its way. This is an area of mixed farming, and vineyards occupy only a fairly small part of the region. In 2006 some 1,529 hectares were declared as Entre-Deux-Mers, which since 1937 has been an appellation for dry white wine only. There are 194 producers; fourteen are cooperatives, which are responsible for about one-third of production.

The major grape varieties are Sauvignon Blanc and Sémillon, with some Muscadelle and minor plantings of Ugni Blanc or Colombard. However, the regulations require the presence of at least seventy per cent of the three major varieties in any blend. Some growers like Sauvignon for its charm and raciness and aromatic zest; others prefer the more long-lived Sémillon (meaning the plant itself, which can live for a century or more, which is not the case with Sauvignon) for its weight, its richness, and its aptitude for long ageing when not overcropped. Most of the grapes are picked by machine, and the majority of vineyards are laid out to make this feasible. Quality-conscious growers believe that higher density and lower yields are the only way to achieve good quality. However, Stéphane Defraine, the president of the Syndicat, notes that maximum yields have been reduced to fifty-six hl/ha but doubts it has made much difference. He argues that the quality is much the same, but the grower must charge a higher price for his wine, which in turn reduces profitability.

The region is essentially an undulating limestone plateau, with numerous soil variations. To the west and southwest there is more sand and gravel; to the east and northeast there is more silt and sand. One geological specialty is *boulbène*, a stony clay-limestone soil with silt, originally deposited, it's said, by erosion and wind. The plateau is in places quite high (for Bordeaux) and at Launay, the *butte* reaches a height of 147 metres (480 feet). With soils that are rich but cool, ripening can be problematic, which is why white wines are often – but not always – more successful than reds.

There is talk, mainly on the part of the Syndicat, of creating an appellation for red Entre-Deux-Mers. It would be differentiated from the existing AC Bordeaux in having more stringent criteria of production, and the resulting higher quality, it is hoped, would add lustre to the region. Certainly in the public mind, Entre-Deux-Mers is associated with white wine, and in the 1970s about ninety per cent of wine was white. A good deal of *moelleux* was produced too, mostly by chaptalizing, so the quality must have been fairly dismal; production seems to have ground to a halt some time in the 1970s in favour of dry wines.

Marc Lurton of Château Reynier argues that Entre-Deux-Mers growers, whether producing white or red wines, need to accept the limitations of the terroir. He believes the region is capable of producing very good wines, but he thinks it an error to opt for extremes of extraction or oak-ageing. Not everyone agrees, and wines such as Reignac and Girolate seem to suggest that some parts of the region are indeed capable of making excellent wine.

GRAVES DE VAYRES

This quite large region, an AC since 1937, lies just south of a loop in the meandering Dordogne in the northwest corner of Entre-Deux-Mers. You traverse it if you take the fast road from Bordeaux to Libourne. It consists of 700 hectares, of which fifteen per cent is planted with white vines. There are some forty producers. I suppose the region justifies its existence because of its soil, which, as the name suggests, is gravel and sandy gravel. There are also deposits of loess and silty loam. Much of the wine is sold under the more recognizable appellation of Bordeaux.

STE-FOY BORDEAUX

This immense region has been an AC since 1937. It is shared by nineteen communes, and is in effect the eastward extension of the Entre-Deux-Mers, as all its vineyards lie south of the Dordogne and the river town of Ste-Foy. At its eastern boundary it lies alongside the vines of Bergerac. The soils are very varied, with *boulbène* and sandy gravel.

Five hundred growers cultivate 7,000 hectares of vines, but only 400 are declared as Ste-Foy. The Syndicat would like to see more of the wines under the appellation, but, as in other obscure appellations, many producers find it easier to sell their wines as AC Bordeaux. And not all those who use the Ste-Foy appellation make good wines.

Until the 1970s almost all the wines were white, and many were sweet. The first red vines went into the ground in 1965. Some sweet wine is still produced, but it is increasingly marginal: in 2005 ten growers declared the production from a total of twelve hectares as sweet.

It seems likely that when the new Côtes de Bordeaux appellation comes into being, Ste-Foy will become one of its constituent parts.

PREMIÈRES COTES DE BORDEAUX

AC Premières Côtes lines the right bank of the Garonne, from Carbon-Blanc in the suburbs of Bordeaux to near Langon in the south, and stretches for some distance inland. The land rises steeply from the shoreline, where the vines are merely AC Bordeaux, onto the plateaux and into the hills that dominate the Côtes. The communes are: Baurech, Beguey, Bouliac, Cadillac, Cambes, Camblanes et Meynac, Capian, Cardan, Carignan, Cénac, Gabarnac, Haux, Langoiran, Latresne, Lestiac, Le Tourne, Monprimblanc, Omet, Paillet, Quinsac, Rions, St-Caprais-de-Bordeaux, St-Germain-de-Grave, St-Maixant, Ste-Eulalie, Semens, Tabanac, Verdelais, Villenave-de-Rions, and Yvrac. The following are not part of the Premières Côtes, but could legally release wines under the AC: Ladoux, La Sauve, Loupiac, Pian sur Garonne, and Ste-Croix-du-Mont.

About 300 properties declare red wine from 3,400 hectares. The grape varieties overall are fifty-five per cent Merlot, twenty-five per cent Cabernet Sauvignon, fifteen per cent Cabernet Franc, and five per cent Malbec.

Sweet white wine is produced from 300 hectares by ninety-five estates. The grapes planted are seventy per cent Sémillon, twenty-five per cent Sauvignon Blanc, and five per cent Muscadelle. The wine is invariably in a *moelleux* style with around thirty grams of residual sugar. The maximum yield is a generous forty-four hl/ha, and some of the crop would be picked by machine.

Like Entre-Deux-Mers, the Premières Côtes is a very attractive region, and this has drawn outside investors, with new owners from Britain, Germany, Finland, and other countries now installed in their pretty châteaux and attempting to make a financial success of their vineyards. The region suffers from a lack of identity, although some excellent wines are produced. At least with its own appellation for red wine, there is some incentive, which is lacking in the Entre-Deux-Mers, to produce serious and well-structured wines at sensible prices.

Château L'Abbaye de Ste-Ferme

Ste-Ferme (Entre-Deux-Mers). Tel: 0556 613144. Owner: Baron Arnaud de Raignac. 50 ha. 40% Merlot, 40% Cabernet Sauvignon, 20% Cabernet Franc. Production: 300,000 bottles. Second wine: Ch de Nardon

Arnaud de Raignac is a progressive winemaker, keen to make wines of individuality as well as quality. His vineyards here are machine-harvested. The 2003 had rich, smoky cherry aromas, and considerable plumpness and concentration on the palate, yet the finish is lively. The 2005 has a crunchy red-fruits character and impeccable ripeness.

Château de Barre Gentillot

Arveyres (Graves de Vayres). Tel: 0557 248026. Owner: Yvette Cazenave-Mahé. 45 ha. 81% Merlot, 16% Cabernet Franc, 2% Malbec. Production: 300,000 bottles

The basic wine here is pure Merlot, aged in tanks for two years. The same base wine, aged in new barriques for eight months, appears as Cuvée Jean Julien. The basic 2000 was rounded and juicy, but lacked weight and finesse. The property also produces Bordeaux Supérieur under the Château de Barre label.

Château Bauduc

Créon (Entre-Deux-Mers and Premières Côtes). Tel: 0556 232222. Website: www.bauduc.com. Owner: Gavin Quinney. 30 ha. 17 ha red: 70% Merlot, 25% Cabernet Sauvignon, 5% Cabernet Franc. 13 ha white: 60% Sauvignon Blanc, 40% Sémillon. Production: 180,000 bottles. Second wine: B de Bauduc

Gavin Quinney enjoyed a high-flying career in London before deciding he wanted to make wine as well as drink it. In 1999 he bought this handsome property just outside Créon, and moved here with his family. They have become familiar to British newspaper readers, as whenever an editor wants to run a story on the joys/miseries of being British residents in France, a photograph of the Quinneys duly accompanies the article.

The vineyards lie within the Premières Côtes as well as Entre-Deux-Mers. The soils are varied, but the Entre-Deux-Mers land is essentially gravelly clay, whereas in the Premières Côtes the soil is clay-limestone. No sooner had Quinney arrived at Bauduc than he replanted ten hectares of Premières Côtes vines to a density of up to 6,600 vines per hectare to improve quality. He makes a wide range of wines under numerous appellations. The Bordeaux Sec is mostly Sauvignon Blanc and vinified in tanks after skin contact. In contrast a barrel-fermented wine called Les Trois Hectares is sourced from a three-hectare parcel of mostly Sémillon planted from 1947 onwards.

The Bordeaux Supérieur is essentially Merlot, made from manually harvested fruit and partly aged in barrels. The more serious red is the barrique-aged Clos des Quinze, from a parcel in the Premières Côtes. (The style of the wine is likely to change slightly in the future, as Quinney plans to remove the Cabernet Sauvignon, which he feels does not work well here.)

The Bordeaux Sec is very aromatic, the 2004 being spicy and lightly grassy, the 2005 more floral and rich. Both show considerable ripeness and concentration, but these are wines intended to be drunk young to appreciate their exuberant fruitiness. The 2003 Trois Hectares showed more apricot aromas, more plumpness on the palate, and an almost excessive ripeness. The 2003 Bordeaux Supérieur has lush black-cherry aromas; it's a supple, rounded wine, with the slightly flat finish often found in this vintage. The 2003 Clos des Quinze has dustier aromas from the oak, and more substance and tannic support.

Quinney admits Bauduc is not immune from the commercial difficulties that affect the region as a whole, but astute marketing, personal charm, sensible pricing, and consistent quality have persuaded some top British restaurants to adopt Bauduc as their house wine.

Château Beaulieu

Salignac (Bordeaux Supérieur). Tel: 0557 977508. Owner: Comte Guillaume de Tastes. 15 ha. 60% Merlot,
30% Cabernet Franc, 10% Cabernet Sauvignon. Production: 80,000 bottles

Salignac lies north of Libourne, and its best-known estate is Beaulieu, made with advice from Stéphane Derenoncourt and soil analyst Claude Bourguignon. The wine is fermented in cement and steel tanks with extended maceration, then aged in at least sixty per cent new barriques.

The new oak was very noticeable on the nose of the 2002, which was sweet and intense; the wine was no heavy-weight but had an attractive graceful quality, and quite good acidity. The 2004 has a delicate red-fruits nose, but the wine lacks some grip and concentration; nonetheless it's medium-bodied and nicely balanced. It is eclipsed by the excellent 2005, which has considerably more concentration, weight, and spice. Attractively priced, Beaulieu offers excellent value.

Château Bel Air Perponcher

Naujan-et-Postiac (Entre-Deux-Mers). Tel: 0557 845508. Website: www.despagne.fr. Owner: Jean-Louis Despagne.
61 ha. 26 ha red: 80% Merlot, 20% Cabernet Sauvignon. 35 ha white: 40% Sauvignon Blanc, 35% Sémillon,
25% Muscadelle. Production: 400,000 bottles

This is one of a number of properties owned by the dynamic Despagne family. Bel Air Perponcher, with its loftily situated château, was bought in 1990. The basic white is fresh, lemony, and fairly simple. More weight is evident in the Grande Cuvée, which shows more weight and length. There was a pretty 2005 rosé with ripe strawberry aromas. The 2004 Bordeaux Supérieur had a very charming red-fruits nose, and although distinctly light, was very attractive and quaffable. More serious is the Grande Cuvée, which in 2003 had more smoky aromas, no baked or jammy flavours, and considerable weight behind the supple texture.

Château Bois Pertuis

St-Christophe-de-Double (Bordeaux). Tel: 0556 263838. Website: www.bernard-magrez.com. Owner: Bernard Magrez.
70 ha. 70% Merlot, 20% Cabernet Sauvignon, 10% Cabernet Franc. Production: 320,000 bottles

St-Christophe-de-Double is a remote village in the far northeastern corner of Bordeaux. Magrez bought the property in 1994 and Michel Rolland acts as his consultant oenologist. The vineyards, on sandy clay soils, are 100 metres (330 feet) high and well suited to Merlot. Much of the vineyard has been replanted, and the trellising heightened. Yields are low: in 2005 they were thirty-six hl/ha. The grapes are machine-harvested and vinified in steel tanks, then aged in ten per cent new barriques for eight months.

Magrez enjoys producing *garagiste cuvées* from many of his properties, and this one is no exception. Here the wine is called Excellence de Bois Pertuis, and it comes from a two-hectare parcel of thirty-year-old Merlot. In 2005 the yield was twenty-six hl/ha. I have not tasted it. The 2003 Bois Pertuis had very plummy aromas; on the palate it was soft, overripe, and forward. However, 2003 was not the best year to assess typicity.

Château Bolaire

Macau (Bordeaux Supérieur). Tel: 0557 881979. Owner: Vincent Mulliez. 5 ha. 39% Petit Verdot, 34% Merlot,
27% Cabernet Sauvignon. Production: 25,000 bottles

The owner of Châteaux Belle-Vue and Gironville (*qq.v.*) acquired this property on the Macau *palus* more recently, and the first vintage was 2003. Like many *palus* vineyards, it has a high proportion of Petit Verdot, here from eighty-year-old vines. Yields on this fertile soil are kept down to around forty hl/ha, and although most of the wine is aged in French and Hungarian oak, of which one-third is new, about one-fifth remains in tanks. The 2004 is packed with fruit, and although not especially complex, has an imposing personality. The 2005 is more complex and spicy. The price is reasonable.

Château Bonnet

*Grézillac (Entre-Deux-Mers). Tel: 0557 255858. Website: www.andrelurton.com. **Owner:** André Lurton.*
250 ha. 130 ha red: 50% Merlot, 50% Cabernet Sauvignon. 120 ha white: 45% Sémillon, 45% Sauvignon Blanc,
*10% Muscadelle. **Production:** 2,000,000 bottles*

This large and sprawling eighteenth-century château is located just a few miles south of St-Emilion. André Lurton is admired as the man who, almost single-handedly, created the Pessac-Léognan appellation and made a success of it. But his roots lie here in Grézillac; Bonnet was bought by his grandfather Léonce Récapet in 1897, and inherited by André Lurton in 1956. It has been his home ever since. In 1956 there were only thirty hectares of vines, but Lurton has bought and integrated neighbouring properties and expanded it to its present size.

If in Pessac-Léognan Lurton is keen to show how superb the white wines can be, here at Bonnet his goal has always been to produce substantial volumes of well-made, reliable, and inexpensive wine. The white grapes are harvested by hand, the reds by machine. The white Réserve spends five months in new oak, and the red Réserve is aged for twelve months in twenty-five per cent new oak. Since 2000 there has been a top *cuvée* called Divinus, which comes from four hectares planted with eighty per cent Merlot and twenty per cent Cabernet Sauvignon. The grapes are picked by hand, and the wine is aged for eighteen months in new barriques. From 2006 a white Divinus, pure Sauvignon Blanc and unoaked, has been produced from the best parcels.

André Lurton, never averse to a headline, attracted attention when he became one of the first major Bordeaux producers to defy the often unthinking conservatism of the French wine drinker by sealing the white Bonnet, the estate's most important wine, with a screwcap closure. I have drunk white Bonnet frequently over two decades. It is not a great wine, and does not aspire to be. It offers aromatic fragrance, with freshness on the palate, and citrus and melon flavours; in some vintages there are varying degrees of grassiness, but the wine is never excessively herbaceous and there is always a good balance of fruit and acidity. The 2006 Divinus is brilliant, with tremendous spice and verve on both nose and palate.

The prettily scented rosé – in 2005 strawberries were to the fore – is a touch bland. The regular red had crushed red-fruits aromas in the 2004, and although light-bodied, was clean, fruity, and invigorating. The red Réserve had ample fruit in 2003, and was discreetly oaky; it's a supple, fleshy wine, unlikely to make old bones. The richly fruity 2005 Réserve has more spice and intensity, but it too is fashioned in a fairly forward style. I prefer the Réserve to the 2003 Divinus, which lacks concentration and is rather slack. The 2005 Divinus, tasted from cask, had sweet, lush blackberry aromas, and considerable richness and concentration, with good acidity behind the black-fruits flavours. It is as close as André Lurton has ever got to making a *garagiste* wine.

Domaine de Bouillerot

*Gironde-sur-Dropt (Entre-Deux-Mers). Tel: 0556 714604. Website: www.bouillerot.com. **Owner:** Thierry Bos.*
14.5 ha. 13 ha red: 55% Merlot, 25% Cabernet Franc, 10% Malbec, 6% Cabernet Sauvignon, 2% Petit Verdot,
*2% Carmenère. 1.5 ha white: 100% Sémillon. **Production:** 85,000 bottles*

The estate produces red Bordeaux and Bordeaux Supérieur, but a sweet 2003 St-Macaire called Palais d'Or. In 2003 this magnificent sweet wine was made from botrytized Sémillon grapes cropped at ten hl/ha; it was aged for eighteen months in new barriques, and has 160 grams of residual sugar. The nose is rich, heady, and peachy, while the palate is truly sumptuous and velvety, with flavours of peach and lemon, and remarkable spice and vigour on the finish. The 2005 is crisp, silky, and elegant; as delicious in its fresher style as the 2003.

Domaine du Bouscat

*St-Romain-la-Virvée (Bordeaux Supérieur). Tel: 0557 582082. **Owner:** François Dubernard. 12 ha. 60% Merlot, 20% Malbec, 18% Cabernet Franc, 2% Cabernet Sauvignon. **Production:** 80,000 bottles*

This village lies just south of St-André-de-Cubzac, and the vines are planted on south-facing slopes. Yields are kept low here, and the grapes are given a four-day cold soak, and micro-oxygenated during fermentation. La Gargone is a *cuvée* aged in seventy-five per cent new oak barrels of various sizes, and bottled without fining or filtration. About 550 cases are produced.

There is also, since 2003, a special *cuvée* from 0.5 hectares called Les Portes de l'Am… (don't ask me why); the grape blend here is fifty per cent Merlot and twenty-five per cent each Malbec and Cabernet Franc. After severe sorting, the must is fermented in 600-litre barrels. Then the wine is aged in 320-litre barrels with *cliquage*. Only 160 cases are produced.

The 2003 La Gargone has a dense, chocolatey nose, and the rich, voluptuous fruit is backed by very firm tannins; like many 2003s, this could use more acidity and zest. I prefer the sweeter, more elegant 2004, supple in texture, with attractive red-fruits flavours and a long, perky finish. The 2005, tasted from cask, is lush and oaky on the nose, and the palate is concentrated and spicy. It's a bit flashy, but the tannins are ripe and the wine is long.

The 2003 Les Portes has splendid floral aromas with black-cherry fruit, and although the palate is voluptuous and highly concentrated, the oak and intensity are a bit overwhelming. The 2004 is too extracted, so the plump, super-concentrated attack gives way to assertive, even coarse tannins and an overall impression of dourness. The 2005, from cask, has super-rich chocolatey aromas, similar to those of the 2003; but there is much more vigour and length, making this the best of the range by a long way.

I don't know anything about the terroir at St-Romain-la-Virvée, but the location is not that promising. Undoubtedly impressive as some of the wines are, they do seem overworked and highly manipulated. They may impress, but they also strive to impress.

Château de Camarsac

*Camarsac (Entre-Deux-Mers). Tel: 0556 301102. **Owner:** Bérénice Lurton. 60 ha. 60% Merlot, 40% Cabernet Sauvignon. **Production:** 400,000 bottles*

This splendid Renaissance pile rose from the ruins of a fourteenth-century fortress on this site. For six centuries it was the home of the Gères family, who gradually added on residential wings to make the buildings habitable. In 1973 it was bought by Lucien Lurton, who, when he divided his estates among his numerous children, handed Camarsac to his daughter Bérénice, who also runs Climens (*q.v.*) in Barsac.

The vineyards here are machine-harvested, and two *cuvées* are produced. Cuvée Bérénice Lurton is the lighter of the two, a stylish wine, not especially concentrated, but, in 2004 and 2005, attractive and balanced, especially when drunk slightly chilled on a warm night. The Sélection, with its charming multi-coloured label, is aged for six months in barriques. The 2003 had a smoky, fruit-cake nose; on the palate it was supple and reasonably concentrated, with a long, oaky finish. Some oak is present on the nose of the 2004, but the wine lacks some flesh and complexity.

Château Carignan

*Carignan (Premières Côtes). Tel: 0556 212130. **Website:** www.chateau-carignan.com. **Owner:** Philippe Pieraerts. 67 ha. 70% Merlot, 20% Cabernet Sauvignon, 10% Cabernet Franc. **Production:** 400,000 bottles.*
Second wine: L'Orangerie de Carignan

Carignan laps at the outskirts of Bordeaux, but the estate has preserved its rural atmosphere. Lording it over the vineyards is the château itself. It dates from the mid-fifteenth century, but there were extensive baronial-style additions in the nineteenth century. Philippe Pieraerts bought the property in 1981, and since 1998 has devoted himself full-time to running the business. In 1981 there were only sixteen hectares under vine, but he was able to expand the property, and has integrated into Carignan the neighbouring Château Léon.

The soil is clay-limestone and gravelly clay. About thirty per cent of the vines are planted to a density of 7,000 per hectare, which is still unusually high here. Viticulture follows the principles of *lutte raisonnée*. The grapes are picked by hand and by machine. There is no crushing, and the fruit is fermented in steel and cement tanks; although these tanks are equipped with micro-oxygenation, the technique is not used systematically. The wine is aged for up to twelve months in fifteen per cent new French oak and ten per cent American oak. The *cuvées* are blended late, and if the wine is not up to standard, Pieraerts won't sell it under the Carignan label, as happened in 1984, 1987, and 1991.

In 1998 Pieraerts and his consultant oenologist, Louis Mitjaville, created a luxury *cuvée* called Prima. This comes from a specific twelve-hectare parcel with a good deal of forty-year-old Merlot. It is aged for eighteen months in new Radoux barrels. A variation on the theme is a wine called Quatuor, exactly the same as Prima, except that it is aged in new oak from four sources, two French, the others Missouri and Russia. Each barrel is bottled separately and the wines are presented in a four-pack. Quatuor was made in 2000 but then the concept was abandoned, for the sound reason that it was too complicated to explain and sell.

I found the 1999 Carignan rather austere, with good fruit but firm tannins that led to a rather dry finish. The 2002 is more stylish and fresher, but it's not complex and is already close to its peak. The 2003 has rich cherry aromas; the texture is silky and the wine reasonably concentrated, with surprising zest on the finish.

The 2001 Prima is delicious, with sweet, oaky, blackcurranty aromas; it's not super-concentrated but it is very spicy and lively. The solid 2002 doesn't seem to have sufficient fruit to absorb the oak, which was very marked when I tasted the wine in 2004 and again in 2006. The 2003 is predictably super-ripe, just the right side of jammy on the nose; the palate is rather chunky and dense, giving the wine weight and substance but little finesse. I prefer the 2004, where the sweet new oak shines out on the nose, while the palate has much more finesse than the 2003. This is a well-structured wine that should age well. The 2005 is a mighty wine, but its power is balanced by its vigour and length. From 2006 Prima will be pure Merlot.

Château Carsin

Rions (Premières Côtes). Tel: 0556 769306. Website: www.carsin.com. Owner: Juha Berglund. 27 ha.
12 ha red: 80% Merlot, 20% Cabernet Sauvignon, Carmenère, and Petit Verdot. 15 ha white: 56% Sémillon,
44% Sauvignon Blanc and Sauvignon Gris. Production: 130,000 bottles. Second wine: Dom de l'Escalade

Mr Berglund is the only Finn in the village. He bought the property in 1990 when, by his own admission, he knew little about wine. He also rented an additional thirty hectares, but in 2003, when the leases expired, he decided not to renew them because of the increasingly difficult economic and commercial situation. Peter Vinding-Diers, the former Graves winemaker, designed the winery, which is encased in a wooden shed, rather like, I am told, a typical Finnish dwelling. Mr Berglund makes the most of his nationality, and during harvest Carsin is a popular destination for wine-loving Finns. Mandy Jones from Australia made the wines until 2003, and since her departure a neighbour has been taking care of the property, which doesn't seem an ideal solution.

Most of the vines are on a *croupe* high above the riverside town of Rions, but there are fifty-two parcels in all, which must make the property hard to manage. One hectare is cultivated biodynamically. With so many blocks, there is little uniformity of soil, but the dominant type is gravelly clay. Green-harvesting keeps yields down to forty hl/ha. The grapes are mostly picked by hand. Fermentation takes place with selected yeasts under a protective blanket of nitrogen.

The white grapes are given skin contact, then chilled to 5°C (41°F), and held at that temperature for a month before fermentation is allowed to begin in steel tanks; a very small proportion of the wine is barrel-fermented. Recent vintages such as 2002 and 2004 have been pleasantly herbaceous, with grapefruit aromas, while the palate has been bright and lively. I also recall some creamy, gently oaky white wines from the early 1990s. With a high Sémillon content, these are wines that can age. There is also a Prestige bottling, which is barrel-fermented and aged for eight months in oak. The only example I have tasted, the 2001, was dour and lacked freshness.

There are three *cuvées* of red Carsin. The regular bottling, aged in older barrels, is fruit-forward and uncomplicated. Cuvée Noire has a higher Merlot content and is aged in one-third new oak. The top wine is the Cuvée Privée, made from parcels with a high clay content. In some years there is a minute production of sweet Cadillac.

The 2002 Carsin is lean and rather green, but I recall a 1990 that, while light, was well balanced and enjoyable. The 2002 Cuvée Noire certainly has more ripeness and flesh than the regular bottling, but there's little complexity here. The 2003 Cuvée Privée is full-bodied and concentrated, with lush black-cherry fruit, and no excessive extraction.

It's hard not to get the impression that Carsin produces too many wines, with the basic wines lacking some stuffing, since the top grapes are reserved for the more prestigious bottlings.

Château Castenet-Greffier

Auriolles (Ste-Foy Bordeaux). Tel: 0556 614067. Owner: François Greffier. 22 ha. 19 ha red: 60% Merlot, 30% Cabernet Sauvignon, 10% Cabernet Franc. 3 ha white: 80% Sauvignon Blanc, 15% Sémillon, 5% Muscadelle.

Production: 150,000 bottles

I have only a fleeting acquaintance with this property, but was very impressed by the 2005 white, which had sufficient aromatic weight to suggest it was dominated by Sémillon rather than Sauvignon, while the palate was juicy, creamy, and full-bodied.

Cave Coopérative: Union des Producteurs de Rauzan

Rauzan (Entre-Deux-Mers). Tel: 0557 841211. Website: www.caves-de-rauzan.fr. 2,100 ha.

Production: 13,000,000 bottles

There are many cooperatives in Entre-Deux-Mers, but this is one of the largest. Founded in 1932, it has 250 members. It worked hard to raise the quality of its white wines from the 1980s onwards. Today an entire team checks the members' vineyards, and a complex system of bonuses and penalties gives incentives to the growers. It is the cooperative, not the individual grower, that decides the harvest date. Grapes are accepted only until 10am to ensure that the fruit does not cook while waiting in hot weather to be processed. It has invested in two very costly Winescan machines that can complete a full analysis of the grapes within seconds of their arrival.

The white grapes are given some skin contact and pressed in pneumatic presses. Fleur is roughly equal parts of Sémillon and Sauvignon Blanc, whereas Comte de Rudel has more Sémillon. There is also an oaked white called Château Haut-Mazières, which is aged for six months in barriques.

The co-op first made red wines in the 1960s, and today they form the largest part of the production. It also produces a large quantity of rosé, usually from Cabernet Franc. Micro-oxygenation has been used systematically for the reds since the late 1990s. Oak-aged reds are put into American as well as French oak. The top wine, first made in 2002, is a parcel selection called Prestige des Vignerons.

In the late 1980s the Rauzan white wines seemed among the best of the appellation, but today they seem less remarkable. The 2005 Fleur is well made and clean, but bland. The Haut-Mazières is too oaky, and the palate not that well balanced. I have sampled a range of reds from 2002 and 2003 and they were unexciting. True, they are very inexpensive, but only 2003 Comte du Rudel had some weight of fruit. The cooperative is very well equipped, so I was hoping for more interesting wines at the top level.

Château Champ des Treilles

*Margueron (Ste-Foy Bordeaux). Tel: 0556 591588. Website: www.champdestreilles.com **Owners:** Jean-Michel and
Corinne Comme. 10 ha. 7 ha red: 60% Merlot, 40% Cabernet Sauvignon, Cabernet Franc, and Petit Verdot.
3 ha white: 50% Semillon, 50% Sauvignon Blanc. **Production:** 40,000 bottles*

Jean-Michel Comme is the winemaker at Pontet-Canet in Pauillac, and it's hard to imagine a property within
Bordeaux farther away from Pauillac than Champ des Treilles, close to the Duras and Bergerac borders. So his
wife Corinne is in charge here. Jean-Michel inherited the property in 1998, and he immediately converted the
estate to biodynamism. This, Corinne Comme explains, is less out of ideological conviction than because a
history of disease in his family had made them very wary of using chemical treatments. She is happy with the
decision, and finds that the vines are healthy and resist all the familiar maladies.

The soil here is clay-limestone over flint. In 1998 there were only five hectares, so they have doubled the
surface, and in some parcels doubled the density by planting between existing rows. She is a fan of Petit Verdot
here, which ripens earlier than Cabernet Sauvignon and usually gives better results. The harvest is manual, in
cagettes. Those vines planted at a density of 10,000 per hectare are used for the *grand vin*. Yields can be very low;
in 2002 the yield for the *grand vin* was a mere eighteen hl/ha.

The wines are fermented with natural yeasts in enamel tanks and also in strange egg-shaped cement tanks that
keep the lees in suspension. Corinne Comme remarks, "My favourite moment is the first pumpover, as it's the first
human intervention in the winemaking process." The wine is aged in one-third new oak, with regular racking.

Given the small size of the property, she makes a lot of wines, as much, it seems, for the pleasure of it than as
the result of any commercial policy. There are two white wines. Le Petit Champs is pure Sémillon, while the *grand
vin* is mostly Sauvignon and aged in one-third new oak. They are both very good. The 2004 Petit Champ had
muted, waxy, peachy aromas, and although slightly neutral was concentrated and long. The 2003 *grand vin* is more
honeyed and oaky on the nose; it's plump but not too oaky, with stone-fruits flavours and good persistence.

As for the reds, Le Petit Champs is made from low-yielding vines but aged in tanks only. The 2003 has plum-
compote aromas; the palate is blunt and lacking in elegance. The 2002 *grand vin* is also rather disappointing and
lacklustre, with herbaceous aromas and some greenness on the palate too. The 2003 also lacks finesse, but it has
dense, plummy aromas, and is hefty on the palate, with ample concentration and fruit but rather low acidity.

She also makes a wine called Le Sens, a *micro-cuvée* of 600 bottles, a blend in equal parts of Merlot and Petit
Verdot, aged in new oak. The 2002 was magnificent: opaque in colour, scented with fine-grained oak which
gave the nose great elegance, and immensely rich and concentrated on the palate, yet with fine tannins and a
wealth of black fruits. A fluke, or the triumph of Petit Verdot on this terroir?

Finally, there is a *moelleux*, not made every year, from Sémillon, with around 100 grams of residual sugar.
This is aged in older barrels. The 2002 has pure apricot aromas, while on the palate it is creamy, lightly sweet,
lacking in weight but marked by fine acidity.

At Champ des Treilles the hand of the winemaker is very evident, but these are wines of individuality and
personality, even if occasionally hit or miss, and well worth looking out for, as prices are very reasonable.

Château des Chapelains

St-André-et-Appelles (Ste-Foy Bordeaux). Tel: 0557 412174. Website: www.chateaudeschapelains.com.
Owner: Pierre Charlot. 35 ha. 23 ha red: 50% Merlot, 41% Cabernet Sauvignon, 9% Cabernet Franc.
12 ha white: 53% Sauvignon Blanc, 32% Sémillon, 12% Sauvignon Gris, 3% Muscadelle.
Production: 250,000 bottles. Second wine: Ch de la Pélissière

Until 1991 all the grapes from Chapelains went to the local cooperative. When Pierre succeeded his father in 1991, he left the cooperative, and today he is president of the Syndicat of Ste-Foy. His vineyards were planted to a very low density, but new plantings have been at 4,600 vines per hectare. The soils are clay and clay-limestone, and the viticulture based on *lutte raisonnée*. The majority of the grapes are picked by machine. Charlot ferments in steel tanks and was an early enthusiast for micro-oxygenation, which he has been using since 1995.

The basic unoaked red is called Prélude. Momus is aged in older barrels. Les Temps Modernes has more Merlot than Momus and is aged in younger barrels though still without any new oak. There is a delicious *clairet*, rich and vinous, for which Charlot deservedly has an established reputation.

The whites go through a period of skin contact before fermentation. The basic white is unoaked. In the mid-1990s Charlot began barrel-fermenting a white from mostly Sémillon and named it Cuvée Découverte. This is aged for twelve months in twenty-five per cent new 300-litre barrels. The basic whites lack some acidity and vigour. Cuvée Découverte is considerably more interesting, with more spice, creaminess, and concentration.

As for the reds, I found the 2001 Momus unremarkable, though it had decent fruit. Les Temps Modernes, with its lively cherry aromas, is more enticing. The 1998, though not complex, has remained fresh and enjoyable; the 2001 is more delicate and stylish, with gentle oakiness; the 2002 is moderately concentrated, quite tannic, but finishes positively. The 2003 has some austerity and greenness, and a slightly bitter finish.

The wines are inexpensive, and the top *cuvées* are excellent value for money.

Château Chapelle Maracan

Mouliets-et-Villemartin (Entre-Deux-Mers). Tel: 0557 560506. Website: www.malet-roquefort.com.
Owner: Alexandre de Malet Roquefort. 15 ha. 10 ha red: 70% Merlot, 15% Cabernet Sauvignon, 15% Cabernet Franc. 5 ha white: 50% Sauvignon Blanc, 25% Sémillon, 25% Muscadelle. **Production: 90,000 bottles**

The personable Alexandre de Malet Roquefort of La Gaffelière (*q.v.*) fell in love with this property in 2000. Just southeast of Castillon, it consists of two sun-drenched slopes with clay-limestone and gravel soils. He makes a special Bordeaux Supérieur *cuvée* called La Chapelle d'Aliénor, named after his wife. This is cropped at a very low twenty-five hl/ha and only 10,000 bottles are produced. The 2003 was rather stewed on the nose, but the palate was weighty and spicy, with ample fruit. The 2004, while unquestionably ripe and lush, has more tannic backbone and vigour and length – an excellent wine.

Clos Nardian

St-Aubin-de-Branne (Entre-Deux-Mers). Tel: 0557 846422. Website: www.teyssier.fr. Owner: Jonathan Maltus.
1 ha. 40% Sauvignon Blanc, 40% Sémillon, 20% Muscadelle. **Production: 3,600 bottles**

Jonathan Maltus owns Château Teyssier in St-Emilion, near the Dordogne River, and on the opposite shore in St-Aubin he found a parcel of forty-year-old Sauvignon and Sémillon and seventy-year-old Muscadelle that took his fancy. He has rented this vineyard, and prunes it hard to four bunches per vine to keep the yield to around twenty-five hl/ha. It is whole-bunch pressed, fermented and aged for about eight months in heavy-toast new oak, with the lees kept in suspension. There is usually a dash of residual sugar to add to the wine's viscosity.

Maltus admits that Clos Nardian is shamelessly manipulated, but it is unquestionably delicious, a big, juicy, peachy, baggy wine that nonetheless has quite good acidity and length. The 2004 was plump and opulent, the 2005 has greater freshness. Clos Nardian is very expensive, but it is a monument to hedonism.

Clos Ste-Anne

Capian (Premières Côtes). Tel: 0556 230001. Owners: Sylvie and Marie Courselle. 7.5 ha. 5 ha red: 90% Merlot,
10% Cabernet Franc. 2.5 ha white: 60% Sémillon, 40% Sauvignon Blanc. Production: 50,000 bottles

The owners are the daughters of Francis Courselle of Château Thieuley (*q.v.*). Here the soil is different, with a great deal of gravel, as well as some limestone and clay. The red wine is aged for fourteen to sixteen months in seventy per cent new barriques. A little dry white wine is made, as well as a Cadillac. The 2001 red showed signs of over-oaking on the nose, but on the palate was a rich, full-bodied, and spicy wine, with some austerity from the oak.

Château Clos de la Tour

See *Château Pey La Tour*

Château Le Conseiller

Lugon (Bordeaux Supérieur). Tel: 0557 259119. Owner: Jean-Philippe Janoueix. 20 ha. 100% Merlot.
Production: 60,000 bottles

Jean-Philippe Janoeuix already owned Château Croix-Mouton (*q.v*) when in 2002 he bought the neighbouring property. The vines were not in good shape and are being renovated. The vinification of this wine is similar to that of Croix-Mouton, but with more *pigeage* and extraction. The 2003 was very burly, certainly impressive but, with fifteen degrees of alcohol, a bit brutal. The 2004 has more overt fruitiness and better length.

Château de la Cour d'Argent

St-Sulpice (Bordeaux Supérieur). Tel: 0557 845473. Owner: Denis Barraud. 20 ha. 90% Merlot, 5% Cabernet Franc,
5% Cabernet Sauvignon. Production: 120,000 bottles

Barraud, the proprietor of Château Les Gravières in St-Emilion, has owned this property since 1971. Half the vines lie just across the boundary with St-Emilion on sandy gravelly soils; the rest are near Genissac on clay-limestone. Since the late 1990s yields have been sharply reduced and the wines have been aged in one-year-old barriques for fourteen months. The 2003 has sound cherry aromas and a rather soupy texture and in general lacks zip. The 2004 is excellent: a rich, plump wine with good acidity supporting it. The 2005 is just as good, potentially better, in a fruit-forward style backed by very good acidity and ripe tannins.

Château Croix-Mouton

Lugon (Bordeaux Supérieur). Tel: 0557 259119. Owner: Jean-Philippe Janoueix. 40 ha. 85% Merlot,
15% Cabernet Franc. Production: 300,000 bottles. Second wine: Réserve du Croix-Mouton

This property just northwest of Fronsac used to be known as Château Mouton, until a certain well-known property in Pauillac took exception. Hence the change of name in 2004. When Janoueix bought the property in 1997 it was abandoned, so it took a lot of work and investment to renovate it. The vines are planted on deep alluvial soils, not usually considered ideal for quality wine production. But Janoueix is specifically trying to produce a fruity, accessible wine ready to drink on release. The wine is aged in fifty per cent new oak for nine months, though twenty per cent of the juice stays in tanks.

In 2000 the innovative Jean-Philippe Janoueix planted 1.4 hectares of Merlot on the property at densities of 10,000, 15,000, and 20,000 vines per hectare. The first crop was in 2005, with a yield of thirty-four hl/ha, and he named the wine 20 Mille. It is aged in new oak with lees-stirring. Only 4,000 bottles are produced.

The 2004 Croix-Mouton has lively aromas with ample fruit; on the palate it is not that concentrated, but it's fresh and quite forceful, though somewhat hollow. The 2005 20 Mille, tasted from cask, has super-ripe black-cherry aromas; it's very tannic and concentrated, quite extracted but with sufficient spice and freshness to give the wine length and complexity.

Vignobles Despagne

Naujan-et-Postiac (Entre-Deux-Mers). Tel: 0557 845508. Website: www.despagne.fr. 310 ha.
Production: 1,800,000 bottles

The Despagnes are a well-established wine-producing family based in Entre-Deux-Mers. In 1970 Jean-Louis Despagne, having inherited the company at the age of twenty-eight, made it his mission to improve the often miserable quality of the region's wines, especially the white wines. The success of Robert Mondavi apparently inspired him to follow this path. It took him a while to find his way. At first he began ripping out alternate rows to facilitate mechanization, but in the 1980s he returned to higher density. The Despagnes' viticultural practice is modelled on the Cousinié method. Today they control 310 hectares dispersed among a number of properties: Girolate, Tour de Mirambeau, Rauzan-Despagne, Mont-Perat, and Bel Air Perponcher (qq.v.).

Château Le Doyenné

St-Caprais (Premières Côtes). Tel: 0556 787575. Website: www.chateauledoyenne.fr. Owner: Dominique Watrin.
9 ha. 70% Merlot, 20% Cabernet Franc, 10% Cabernet Sauvignon. Production: 30,000 bottles.
Second wine: Les Hauts du Doyenné

Dominique Watrin bought this ancient property in 1994, and that was also her first vintage, vinified with advice from Michel Rolland. The vines are on a gravelly plateau with clay and limestone slopes, facing south and southwest. The vines are managed mechanically, but harvested by hand. After fermentation in steel tanks, the wine ages in forty per cent new oak for fifteen to eighteen months.

The 2002 managed to be fairly light and rather dry and short. The 2003 had more fruit but the tannins were rather brutal. The 2004 was better balanced, if slightly hollow on the mid-palate, but some all-too-evident extraction led to a rather hard finish. The 2005 from cask shows promise: the oak is pronounced at this stage, but there is lively acidity as well as firm tannins, and this is easily the best balanced of the vintages I have tasted. The wine is moderately priced.

Château Dubois-Challon

Baigneaux (Entre-Deux-Mers). Tel: 0557 247094. Owner: Pascal Delbeck. 11 ha. 4 ha red: 60% Merlot,
30% Cabernet Franc, 10% Cabernet Sauvignon. 7 ha white: 50% Sauvignon Blanc, 45% Sémillon, 5% Muscadelle.
Production: 50,000 bottles

After the death of Heylette Dubois-Challon, her winemaker Pascal Delbeck inherited not only Bélair in St-Emilion, but her other properties. He had in any case been making the wines here for thirty years. I have not tasted the red wine, but he is especially proud of the white, Fleur Amandine. This is barrel-fermented and aged in oak for eight months. Both the 2002 and 2003 had very flowery aromas, with notes of tropical fruit in the latter; on the palate the wine is quite exotic, even honeyed, with a creamy texture and some weight.

Egrégore

St-Christophe-de-Double (Bordeaux). Tel: 0556 263838. Website: www.bernard-magrez.com.
Owner: Bernard Magrez. 2 ha. 100% Merlot. Production: 5,000 bottles

This is another "*cuvée d'exception*" (as he calls them) from Bernard Magrez, and presumably comes from a vineyard close to Bois Pertuis (q.v.). The soil here is clay with patches of sand or gravel, and the vines are thirty years old. Yields are very low, between seventeen and twenty-eight hl/ha, and the grapes are picked and destemmed by hand. They are fermented with *pigeage* in 4,000-litre wooden vats. The wine goes through its malolactic fermentation in barriques, and is aged for eighteen months in eighty per cent new oak.

The only vintage I have tasted is the first one: 2002. It had sweet, intense oaky aromas, as one would expect, and was rich and opulent, although there was a good deal of tannin on the finish. Not a bad wine, but hard to distinguish from the many other similar wines in M. Magrez's portfolio of *micro-cuvées*.

Château de Fontenille

La Sauve Majeure (Entre-Deux-Mers). Tel: 0556 230326. Website: www.chateau-fontenille.com.
Owner: Stéphane Defraine. 42 ha. 34 ha red: 90% Merlot, 5% Cabernet Franc, 5% Cabernet Sauvignon. 8 ha white:
30% Sauvignon Blanc, 30% Sémillon, 25% Muscadelle, 15% Sauvignon Gris. Production: 300,000 bottles

Stéphane Defraine began his career in wine as a consultant for estates owned by absentee proprietors. Then in 1989 he bought and expanded this property, gradually increasing the density of plantation. The soil is silty clay with some gravel. A particularity of the microclimate is constant wind. This greatly reduces the threat from disease, which is why Defraine has retained a good deal of Muscadelle, as the variety is normally very susceptible to rot. The vineyards are picked mechanically.

The white grapes are given some skin contact, fermented at cool temperatures, and aged three months *sur lie*. From some old Sémillon vines in the Premières Côtes he makes a barrel-fermented white that is aged for six months in oak. The 2005 Entre-Deux-Mers was very aromatic with nuances of Muscat and grapefruit; it's a lively wine that's refreshing rather than profound. I tasted the 2005 barrel-fermented white from barrel; it was fat and rich but not heavy.

Defraine makes a fine *clairet* from mostly Cabernet Franc, and it now accounts for twenty per cent of his production. The red Bordeaux has some charm; it's supple and easy-going, a fruit-forward style intended to be drunk fairly young. He also owns a seven-hectare property nearby called Château La Forêt, which is all dispatched to the thirsty Belgians.

Girolate

Naujan-et-Postiac (Entre-Deux-Mers). Tel: 0557 845508. Website: www.girolate.com. Owner: Jean-Louis Despagne.
10 ha. 100% Merlot. Production: 24,000 bottles

Jean-Louis Despagne and his son Thibault had the risky idea of handling a small parcel of their extensive vineyards as though it was the finest of *crus*. In 1999 they planted ten hectares of Merlot to a density of 10,000 vines per hectare. The vines, planted on dense clay over limestone, were trained very low to absorb the heat from the soil. By retaining only four bunches per vine, the Despagnes keep yields down to twenty hl/ha and thus obtain full ripeness about ten days earlier than in neighbouring vineyards. At such levels overripeness is a risk, but one that they, and their consultant Michel Rolland, were prepared to tolerate.

The grapes are picked by hand and fermented with indigenous yeasts in 150 new barriques. The barrels are rotated on Oxoline racks in order to extract the tannins as gently as possible. The pomace is pressed in a vertical press, and this press wine is blended into the free-run. There is some *cliquage* during the ageing, and the wine is then bottled without filtration after twelve months or so.

It is hard to imagine a more labour-intensive way to make wine, and this is reflected in its high price. Other estates flirt with barrel-fermentation, but only for a portion of the crop or for a *micro-cuvée*. Here the entire crop is handled this way. The Despagnes are not put off. Indeed, they are planning to plant a nearby slope called Cruscant with Cabernet Sauvignon. It will be fascinating to see the results, given the difficulties this variety can have in ripening in the northern Entre-Deux-Mers.

I would normally be sceptical about such over-perfectionist exercises in winemaking, but the vintages of Girolate I have tasted have been excellent, if sharing a very similar profile. There is a dense plumminess on the nose, and a discernible oakiness; yet although the wine is powerful and concentrated, the tannins are supple and there is no sense of over-extraction. Indeed the 2004 also has a beguiling delicacy and fruitiness, and the wine's structure is partly concealed by its evident charm. The 2005 is more voluptuous, teetering on the edge of over-ripeness. Whether Girolate, still made from young vines, is expressing a sense of place or merely the result of some brilliantly judged winemaking it is difficult to say; we will need a few more vintages in bottle before that judgment can be made.

Château Goudichaud

St-Germain-du-Puch (Graves de Vayres). Tel: 0557 245734. Owner: Yves Glotin. 48 ha.
40 ha red: 60% Cabernet Sauvignon, 40% Merlot. 8 ha white: 85% Sauvignon Blanc, 15% Muscadelle.
Production: 400,000 bottles

This estate is graced with a handsome eighteenth-century château and park, and was once a summer residence of the archbishops of Bordeaux. Although the buildings are in St-Germain in Entre-Deux-Mers, the vineyards are in the Graves de Vayres.

The 2002 red was medium-bodied, with light tannins and acidity, and a touch of astringency. Better is the white, at least in 2004, when it was aromatic and citric, with reasonable concentration and very attractive fruit. These are wines to drink young.

Château Grée Larroque

St-Ciers-d'Abzac (Bordeaux Supérieur). Tel: 0557 494542. Owner: Arnaud Benoit de Nyvenheim.
2 ha. 75% Merlot, 20% Cabernet Franc, 5% Cabernet Sauvignon. Production: 9,000 bottles

This small property is located some fifteen kilometres (nine miles) north of Libourne. De Nyvenheim bought it in 1981, but only since 2000 has quality has been to the fore. Stéphane Derenoncourt is the consultant oenologist, and the grapes, planted to a density of 6,000 per hectare, are farmed organically. The vines are old, with an average age of forty-five years. The soils are silty, but with varying combinations of clay, gravel, and limestone. After being picked into *cagettes*, the grapes are fermented in whole bunches with micro-oxygenation. Malolactic fermentation takes place in barriques, and the wine is aged for twelve months in sixty per cent new oak with lees-stirring.

The 2003 has ripe aromas, with hints of milk chocolate; it's a rich, plump, juicy wine with ample grip but no harsh tannins. The 2004 is more low-keyed, with similar chocolatey aromas, but it's less vivid on the palate. The 2005, tasted from cask, was sensational, the nose combining elegant oakiness and fresh charm, while the fruit is mouth-watering and the tannins bold but ripe. This is an excellent property.

Château Hostens-Picant

Les Lèves (Ste-Foy Bordeaux). Tel: 0557 463811. Website: www.chateauhostens-picant.fr. Owner: Yves Picant.
42 ha. 32 ha red: 70% Merlot, 20% Cabernet Franc, 10% Cabernet Sauvignon. 10 ha white: 50% Sémillon,
45% Sauvignon Blanc, 5% Muscadelle. Production: 180,000 bottles. Second wine: Ch de Grangeneuve

This property was bought by Yves Picant in 1986, but the first vintage was 1989. Previously the fruit had been sold to a cooperative. The soils are varied, being mostly limestone but with some gravel and flint as well. In recent years Stéphane Derenoncourt has acted as a consultant, and the estate, despite its remote location, aims high. The harvest is manual.

The fruit for the white Cuvée des Demoiselles goes through skin contact, and after pressing is fermented in new 350-litre barriques, with lees-stirring for around ten months. The varieties are kept separate until late in the *élevage*. The 2004 has rich, oaky pear and apricot aromas; it's supple and lush but lacks a little bite. The 2005 and 2006, tasted from cask, seemed similar.

The regular red is fermented in steel tanks, with bleeding if necessary to improve concentration. It is then aged in one-third new oak for between fourteen and eighteen months. The 2004 has elegant, cedary aromas, and though not especially concentrated, it's graceful and fresh. The 2005, tasted from cask, had very ripe fruit but lively acidity too. The top red is Cuvée Lucullus, mostly Merlot picked at very low yields and vinified in wooden vats with micro-oxygenation, then aged in new oak for eighteen months and bottled unfiltered. The 2002 seemed both too oaky and too ripe, and dry tannins marred the finish, but the 2004 is silky and plump, made in a luxurious style that lacks some cut. The suave 2005 resembles the 2004 but is spicier and shows more length.

Château Lagarosse

Tabanac (Premières Côtes). Tel: 0556 670005. **Owner:** *Stephen Adams. 25 ha. 80% Merlot, 10% Cabernet Franc, 10% Cabernet Sauvignon.* **Production:** *150,000 bottles*

Like Fonplégade (*q.v.*) in St-Emilion, this property is owned by an American investor and its management is entrusted to a company called Wine & Vineyards, with Michel Rolland acting as consultant. Its vineyards, on a single slope, face south and southwest, with clay-limestone on the higher sectors, and more clay and gravel lower down. The grapes are machine-harvested.

The red wine is aged in one-third new oak. There is also a special *cuvée* called Les Comtes, which comes from a 3.5-hectare parcel high on the slope. The 2001 Lagarosse had a pronounced Merlot character, and was very ripe yet well balanced, with good acidity. The 2002 Les Comtes was dominated by oak on the nose, though there was plenty of lush fruit; the texture was silky and the fruit attractive, but it was a touch extracted and overall seemed less well balanced than the regular wine.

Château Lamothe de Haux

Langoiran (Ste-Foy Bordeaux). Tel: 0557 345300. **Website:** *www.chateau-lamothe.com.* **Owners:** *Fabrice and Anne Néel. 80 ha. 59 ha red: 60% Merlot, 30% Cabernet Sauvignon, 10% Cabernet Franc. 21 ha white: 40% Sémillon, 40% Sauvignon Blanc, 20% Muscadelle.* **Production:** *600,000 bottles.* **Second wine:** *Clos Lamothe*

This elegant château stands on a terrace above former quarries where some of the wines are now aged. In 1956 the property was bought by the present family, returning from North Africa, and in 1972 Fabrice and Anne Néel took over. In 1997 they were joined by their daughter Maria and son-in-law Damien Chombart. The vineyards are dispersed, but are mostly on limestone and gravel soils, with very little clay. The grapes are machine-harvested.

The basic red Lamothe is unoaked, but there is also a *cuvée* aged for at least twelve months in thirty per cent new barriques. In 2000 a new wine was introduced, Cuvée Valentine, a parcel selection from fifty per cent Merlot, and aged for fourteen months in eighty per cent new oak.

The basic white is mostly unoaked. Cuvée Valentine is unusual in that most of the grapes are Sauvignon Gris; this is barrel-fermented and aged for a few months in lightly toasted new oak with lees-stirring. The regular white is fresh and reasonably crisp, but lacks excitement. However, I prefer it to the rather dour, grapefruity Valentine.

From 2002 and 2003, the oaked red and the Cuvée Valentine both have elegant cedary aromas, but I find a lack of ripeness on the palate, with rather edgy acidity in both wines and a lack of length.

Château de Launay

Soussac (Entre-Deux-Mers). Tel: 0556 613144. **Owner:** *Baron Arnaud de Raignac. 60 ha. 40 ha red: 80% Merlot, 10% Cabernet Sauvignon, 10% Cabernet Franc. 20 ha white: 40% Sauvignon Blanc, 40% Muscadelle, 20% Sémillon.* **Production:** *100,000 bottles*

Arnaud de Raignac also owns Château de l'Abbaye de Ste-Ferme (*q.v.*). He bought Launay in 1999 from François Greffier, who favoured high yields and aged his wines in tanks only. From his first vintage, 2002, Raignac decided to turn things around, and began by replanting some vines to a higher density of 6,000 vines per hectare. He is assisted and supported by wine consultant Stefano Chioccioli.

Two-thirds of the vineyards are in a single parcel on clay-limestone soil though the limestone here is, says Raignac, rather powdery. Debudding and green-harvesting are used to reduce yields; he aims for a weight per vine of 500 grams, which seems scarcely economical. The grapes are picked as late as possible in *cagettes*; the fruit is sorted twice, then chilled to preserve aromas. Fermentation takes place in very small and squat steel tanks and a few wooden vats, with micro-oxygenation and *pigeage*. Then the red wine is aged in ninety per cent new barriques for fourteen to sixteen months.

There are two white wines. The Launay bottling is ninety per cent Sauvignon Blanc, and Vignes d'Elisa is a pure Muscadelle, fermented and aged in new oak for ten months. The yield for the latter is a derisory fifteen hl/ha, and only 15,000 bottles are made.

I tasted M. Greffier's white wines in 1989 and was unimpressed. The Raignac wines are very different. I tasted three vintages of the white Château de Launay, from 2003 to 2005. I admit to being dismayed. The wines were wildly overoaked, though the 2005 was less planky, and the fruit components suggested stewed peach. On the palate the wines are rich, buttery, oaky, heavy, and lack finesse, although the 2005 had better acidity. These are wines that might impress on the tasting bench, but I would find it hard to get through a bottle over dinner. I also tasted Vignes d'Elisa from 2002 to 2005. Here too the oak aromas were overwhelming, although the 2002 was more discreet and floral. Sadly, these wines too were heavy, oily, and leaden, lacking acidity, and, in the case of the 2005, showing a lot of overripeness and alcohol on the finish.

As for the red, the formidable 2003 had dense black-fruits aromas, with nuances of tobacco and woodsmoke; it's very rich and plump, with a soupy texture and massive tannins. The 2004 had aromas of blackcurrant and blackberry, but again the palate was dominated by bruising tannins. I preferred the 2005, which had more spice and freshness when tasted in June 2006.

I am at a loss to understand the vogue for such over-extracted wines, although I appreciate Arnaud de Raignac's sincerity in seeking to produce wines with more substance and character than those made in earlier decades. However, he claims to be making wines that are accessible young but ageworthy, but I question whether the young reds will give much pleasure until the tannins calm down – if they ever do.

Château Lesparre

Beychau et Caillou and Vayres (Entre-Deux-Mers, Graves de Vayres). Tel: 0557 245123.
Website: www.chateaulesparre.com. Owner: Michel Gonet. 180 ha. 165 ha red: 65% Merlot, 20% Cabernet Franc,
15% Cabernet Sauvignon. 15 ha white: 55% Sémillon, 35% Sauvignon Blanc, 10% Muscadelle.
Production: 2,000,000 bottles

This vast estate was bought in 1986 by Champagne producer Michel Gonet, who also owns properties in Pessac-Léognan. Most of the vineyards, which are on sandy gravelly soil and *boulbène*, are within the Entre-Deux-Mers, but some sixty hectares fall within Graves de Vayres. The majority of the production is of Bordeaux Supérieur. The grapes are picked by machine, and the vinification uses the high-tech *Flash Détente* method (*see* Chapter Three). The oaked red is aged for ten months in fifty per cent new oak, with micro-oxygenation; the Bordeaux Supérieur is unoaked.

The regular white Entre-Deux-Mers, which is unoaked, is pleasant enough, if a touch confected and lacking in some vigour. The 2004 oaked white, aged for six months in fifty per cent new barriques, has rather heavy-handed oaky aromas, with cooked lemon fruit; it's very ripe and plump but less oaky than the nose. The reds are simple, reasonably fresh, and uncomplicated.

Château Lezongars

Villenave-de-Rions (Premières Côtes). Tel: 0556 721806. Website: www.chateau-lezongars.com. Owner: Russell Iles.
48 ha. 44 ha red: 70% Merlot, 15% Cabernet Franc, 15% Cabernet Sauvignon. 4 ha white: 75% Sauvignon Blanc,
25% Sémillon. Production: 200,000 bottles

The Iles family bought this property in 1998 and found it needed a great deal of renovation. But soon they were up and running, and the wines have enjoyed considerable success, aided by the Iles' vigorous marketing of their range. The vines are planted on a south-facing limestone escarpment, and they are picked by hand and by machine.

The range is quite complicated. As well as the Lezongars wines, there is a range under the Château de Roques label, which is not exactly a second label, but a specifically vinified selection of lighter, easy-drinking wines.

The 2004 white Lezongars, from sixty per cent Sémillon, is broad and rich but lacks some zest, but the unoaked 2005 Château de Roques has a better attack if less weight and richness.

Until now the vinification for the red wine has been traditional. From 2006 Russell Iles and winemaker Marielle Cazeau may begin to use micro-oxygenation, at least for Château de Roques. The Lezongars red is aged for nine months in thirty per cent new oak, including some American barrels. A barrel selection called L'Enclos is given slightly longer barrel-ageing. In 2000 the Bordeaux négociant Bill Blatch proposed a Special Cuvée, which is sourced from five densely planted hectares on gravelly slopes; this is almost entirely Merlot, vinified with *pigeage,* and aged in at least seventy per cent new barriques for fifteen to eighteen months.

These are good wines at all levels. The red Lezongars in 2001 was well made, with ample fruit, freshness, and balance. The 2002 is lighter but very enjoyable for medium-term drinking. I prefer L'Enclos to the Special Cuvée, which is rather overworked and extracted. The 2001 Enclos is spicy and complex, well balanced, and long. The 2003 is not quite at this level, since the tannins are a bit too marked.

Château Marjosse

Tizac de Curton (Entre-Deux-Mers). Tel: 0557 555780. Owner: Pierre Lurton. 37 ha. 32 ha red: 65% Merlot, 25% Cabernet Sauvignon, 5% Cabernet Franc, 5% Malbec. 5 ha white: 55% Sauvignon Blanc, 40% Sémillon, 5% Muscadelle. Production: 250,000 bottles

This has been the property of Pierre Lurton since 1990. Lurton has a day job directing Cheval Blanc and Yquem, as well as keeping an eye on properties in South Africa and Argentina. So perhaps not a great deal of time is left over to manage the home farm. The white wine is pleasantly citric and crisp, but lacks some complexity and zest, although the 2006 has more weight and texture than the rather nondescript 2005. The reds are perfumed and bright, but there is little depth or personality here. But these are all well-made wines with freshness and some finesse.

Château Mongiron

Nérigean (Entre-Deux-Mers). Tel: 0557 245461. Owner: Guillaume Quéyron. 10 ha. 8.5 ha red: 95% Merlot, 5% Malbec, Cabernet Franc, and Cabernet Sauvignon. 1.5 ha white: 34% Sauvignon Blanc, 33% Sémillon, 33% Muscadelle. Production: 50,000 bottles

Nérigean, a few miles south of Libourne, is a village built over a network of limestone quarries. Guillaume Quéyron is a skilled viticultural consultant: he advises the estates owned by Clément Fayat, and is a collaborator with Jean-Luc Thunevin.

Quéyron took over from his father in 1999, and immediately made changes to the viticulture by replanting to a higher density. His goal, given that the wines have to be sold at moderate prices, is to balance his vines so as to combine reasonable volumes and good quality. He is no fan of green-harvesting, nor of leaf removal, since many of the leaves drop off anyway in early September. He tends to pick long after his neighbours have finished. There are minimal treatments.

Fermentation takes place in steel tanks, with some *pigeage,* micro-oxygenation, and minimal pumping. The regular wine, Villa Mongiron, is unoaked. The top *cuvée,* La Fleur Mongiron, is from hand-picked grapes and aged in at least eighty per cent new barriques. These are very good wines, with ripe, smoky cherry aromas and nuances of coffee and marzipan; the fruit is evidently very ripe but not jammy, and there is considerable spice and persistence.

Château Mont-Perat

Capian (Premières Côtes). Tel: 0557 845508. Owner: Jean-Louis Despagne. 98 ha. 70 ha red: 70% Merlot,
20% Cabernet Sauvignon, 10% Cabernet Franc. 28 ha white: 80% Sauvignon Blanc, 20% Sémillon.
Production: 700,000 bottles

The other Despagne estates are in Entre-Deux-Mers. Mont-Perat, being in the Premières Côtes, delivers wines with rather more weight. The white is spicy, robustly grassy, and quite full-bodied. The red can be slightly overripe and lacking in vigour and length, although the 2001 had an excellent attack, a tighter structure, and a livelier finish than subsequent vintages.

Château Moutte Blanc

Macau (Bordeaux Supérieur). Tel: 0557 884039. Owner: Patrice de Bortoli. 3 ha: 50% Merlot, 30% Petit Verdot,
20% Cabernet Sauvignon. Production: 18,000 bottles

These vines are planted on fertile *palus* soils. The regular wine contains twenty-five per cent Petit Verdot, but the interest of this property is that it is one of the few to produce a pure Petit Verdot, called Moisin. The 2002, although slightly austere, was concentrated and spicy, with a brooding black-fruits character. It has a strong personality which makes it well worth seeking out.

Château Pénin

Génissac (Entre-Deux-Mers). Tel: 0557 244698. Owner: Patrick Carteyron. Website: www.chateaupenin.com.
40 ha. 37.5 ha red: 95% Merlot, 3% Cabernet Franc, 2% Cabernet Sauvignon. 2.5 ha white: 65% Sauvignon Blanc,
20% Sauvignon Gris, 15% Sémillon. Production: 270,000 bottles

Patrick Carteyron was an oenologist working in Bourg and Blaye when in 1982 he took over a property that had been in his family since the 1850s. He expanded the estate from its then fifteen hectares. The peculiarity of the Pénin vines is that they are planted on deep gravel beds deposited by the Dordogne River, so the soil is very stony and well drained. There are also some sandier sectors, and a higher 2.5-hectare parcel with large stones of glacial rather than alluvial origin; this is the source of his all-Merlot *cuvée* Les Cailloux, first made in 1999. Although Carteyron picks by machine, he works hard in the vineyard to ensure even maturation.

Half of the white must is barrel-fermented in new oak and aged for six months with lees-stirring; the other half ages on its fine lees in tanks, and the two components are then blended. The 2005 was highly aromatic and citric, and had ample fruit and acidity. Carteyron makes both a rosé and a *clairet*, the former being eighty per cent Cabernet Sauvignon, the latter eighty per cent Merlot and showing more vinosity. The rosé and *clairet* together represent about forty per cent of his production.

The red grapes are fermented in steel tanks with micro-oxygenation *sous marc*. The Cuvée Tradition is unoaked. The Grande Sélection is mostly Merlot, aged twelve months in one-third new oak, including about ten per cent American oak. Les Cailloux sees much more new oak, all French.

The Tradition is not of much interest, but the Grande Sélection is a good wine, its aromas drenched in black fruits and olives. The 2003 was very forward but had reasonable freshness, as Carteyron eliminated any raisined berries. The 2004 is more classic, being supple, quite tannic, and reasonable concentrated. The 2003 Cailloux was a bit baked, but the 2004 was impressive, with its plum, blackberry, and liquorice aromas; perhaps it is a touch too dense, but the wine seems in balance and should harmonize with more bottle-age.

Château Peuy-Saincrit

*St-André-de-Cubzac (Bordeaux Supérieur). Tel: 0557 432677. Website: www.vgas.com. **Owner:** Bernard Germain.*
*13 ha. 90% Merlot, 10% Cabernet Sauvignon. **Production:** 90,000 bottles*

Bernard Germain and his extended family own or lease a large number of properties in Bordeaux and in Anjou. Peuy-Saincrit, although by no means the most important, has been the ancestral home since 1843. The average age of the vines is forty years and they are planted to a density of 5,500 vines per hectare on clay-limestone soils. The regular wine is machine-picked and unoaked, but, as is common practice at the Germain estates, a parcel has been isolated for special treatment. Here it is Montalon, 2.5 hectares that are picked by hand; the wine is aged in one-third new oak, using 400-litre barrels, for ten months.

Montalon is a sound, modern-style Bordeaux, with ample lush fruit and a dash of vanilla on the nose, and reasonable richness and spice on the palate. Of recent vintages, the 2002, 2003, and 2005 seem the best.

Château Pey La Tour

*Salleboeuf (Entre-Deux-Mers). Tel: 0556 355300. Website: www.cvbg.com. **Owner:** Dourthe-Kressmann.*
*142 ha. 58% Merlot, 31% Cabernet Sauvignon, 11% Cabernet Franc. **Production:** 1,000,000 bottles*

Until 2005 this immense property was known as Château Clos de la Tour. It was bought by Vignobles Dourthe, a company subsumed within the large négociant house of CVBG, in 1990. The soil is sandy clay over a limestone base. Density was increased to 5,500 vines per hectare, and the trellising heightened. The vines are machine-harvested, and sorted and destemmed with an *égreneur*. Michel Rolland is the consultant oenologist.

The estate produces only Bordeaux Supérieur. The regular bottling is intended for early drinking and is aged in tanks. The Réserve is given a cold soak, then aged for twelve to fifteen months in barriques. The property's reputation for good value is well deserved. Both styles of wine are admirably well made, with a good deal of upfront fruit and, in certain vintages, considerable charm. The Réserve was a touch bland in 2001, but the 2002 and 2004 have sufficient fruit and concentration to carry the oak without being dominated by it.

Château de Pic

*Langoiran (Premières Côtes). Tel: 0556 670751. **Owner:** François Masson Regnault. 33 ha. 31 ha red: 60% Merlot, 35% Cabernet Sauvignon, 5% Cabernet Franc. 2 ha white: 75% Sémillon, 20% Sauvignon Blanc, 5% Muscadelle.*
***Production:** 240,000 bottles*

The soil here is rich in well-drained gravel over a clay-limestone subsoil. The family of the present owner bought the property, which is of medieval origin, in 1975, but had to renovate the buildings and the vineyards. The white grapes are picked by hand, the reds by machine. The red wine is mostly unoaked, although about one-fifth is aged in fifty per cent new barriques. Château de Pic is a bright, fresh wine, modestly concentrated, but with some grip on the finish. It is inexpensive. But avoid the 2003.

Château Pierrail

*Margueron (Ste-Foy Bordeaux). Tel: 0557 412175. Website: www.chateau-pierrail.com. **Owner:** Demonchaux family.*
*58 ha. 48 ha red. 85% Merlot, 10% Cabernet Franc, 5% Cabernet Sauvignon. 10 ha white: 70% Sauvignon Blanc, 30% Sauvignon Gris. **Production:** 300,000 bottles*

Margueron is located about ten kilometres south of Ste-Foy, but the Demonchaux choose not to use the local appellation. The château is a fine seventeenth-century building that once belonged to the barons of Brianson. The estate is best known for white wines. The regular white is a blend of Sauvignon Blanc and Gris; the Cuvée Prestige is fermented and aged for nine months in new barriques, with lees-stirring.

The regular 2003 white was an attractive wine, with tropical fruit aromas and flavours, but not much length. The 2000 white Prestige is heavily oaked and a touch oily, but it has some persistence. The 2001 red, aged twelve months in oak, is sleek and ripe, with a pleasing austerity on the finish to give it some grip.

Château Plaisance

Capian (Premières Côtes). Tel: 0556 721506. Website: www.chateauplaisance.com. Owners: Patrick and Sabine Bayle.
25 ha. 23.5 ha red: 75% Merlot, 20% Cabernet Sauvignon, 5% Cabernet Franc. 1.5 ha white: 100% Sémillon.
Production: 150,000 bottles

This fine eighteenth-century chartreuse is perched high on a south-facing slope, and was purchased by the Bayles in 1985. The vines, in a single parcel, are picked by machine and by hand. There are two white wines, both barrel-fermented. The more luxurious is the Cuvée Alix, which is aged in new oak for twelve months, with lees-stirring. The red wines are all bottled without fining or filtration after being aged in one-third new oak. The two more basic wines are the Tradition and the Cuvée Spéciale, the latter being the more structured. Both Cuvée Sortilège and Cuvée Alix, from older vines, are aged in new oak with *cliquage*, but the latter has more Cabernet Sauvignon.

This has been one of the most ambitious properties in the region for many years, and I recall fine red wines from the late 1980s. The 2001 Alix had bright oaky aromas, and was fresh and rewarding. The 2002 was a touch too oaky, given the fruit, and the tannins were quite extracted. The 2005 white Alix has a lively nose of lemons and passion fruit; it's a wine with plumpness and weight, perhaps a touch too much so, but there is light acidity on the finish. The 2005 white Alix is more melony and less individual. There is an appealing crispness to the red Alix in 2005, which is balanced and judiciously extracted.

Château Rauzan-Despagne

Naujan-et-Postiac (Entre-Deux-Mers). Tel: 0557 845508. Owner: Jean-Louis Despagne. 64 ha.
13 ha red: 75% Merlot, 25% Cabernet Sauvignon. 51 ha white: 40% Sémillon, 35% Sauvignon Blanc, 25% Muscadelle.
Production: 420,000 bottles

This former hunting lodge was bought by the Despagnes in 1990. There are two whites. The Entre-Deux-Mers is citric, reasonably fresh, but somewhat bland. The Bordeaux Blanc Grande Réserve is much more interesting, with attractive and delicate yellow-plum aromas, considerable concentration and spice, and a fetching blend of citrus, apricot, and yellow-plum flavours. There is a charming, strawberry-scented rosé from Cabernet Sauvignon. The 2004 Bordeaux Supérieur was quite herbaceous on the nose, but not worryingly so, while the palate was a touch thin, with hints of glacé cherries. More impressive is the 2003 Grande Réserve, from old vines, with its ultra-ripe but not jammy aromas, its lush yet fresh texture, and its tangy finish.

Château de Reignac

St-Loubès (Entre-Deux-Mers). Tel: 0556 204105. Website: www.reignac.com. Owner: Yves Vatelot.
80 ha. 76 ha red: 75% Merlot, 25% Cabernet Sauvignon. 4 ha white: 60% Sauvignon Blanc, 30% Sémillon,
*5% Muscadelle, 5% Sauvignon Gris. **Production: 350,000 bottles***

Entrepreneur Yves Vatelot arrived here in 1990. Until that time the vineyards had been machine-harvested and most of the wine sold in bulk. (Some must have been bottled, as I recall a very simple 1986 from here.) He put a stop to that. Michel Rolland, who is still his consultant oenologist, came to inspect the vineyards and reported that the terroir was special here, because there are two pronounced soil types. The first is clay-limestone, typical of the Right Bank and well adapted to Merlot; and the other clay-gravel, reminiscent of the Left Bank. Thus, proclaims Vatelot, he can make good wines not only in good Right-Bank vintages, but in good Left-Bank ones too.

In the early 1990s he renovated the vineyards, raising the trellising, increasing density to 6,000 vines per hectare, and setting up controls that allow him to monitor hydric stress within each parcel. At the same time Vatelot's wife Stéphanie was fixing up the spacious château into a modern, slightly zany family home. Yves transformed an older tower into a tasting room, with a pulley device for raising and lowering bottles from an upper storey, where they can be decanted or jacketed if the tasting is to be blind.

The younger vines go into the basic wine, whereas the best fruit is used for the wine simply called Reignac, which he first made in 1996. The average age of the vines for Reignac is about forty years, and the yield a mere thirty hl/ha. The fruit is picked in *cagettes*, thoroughly sorted, then crushed above the steel and wooden vats. Since 1999 the grapes have been cold-soaked for seven days at 6°C (43°F). Vatelot vinifies the wine with pumpovers, *pigeage*, and micro-oxygenation. But one-third of the grapes are fermented in new barrels. Both components of Reignac are aged in new oak for eighteen months with lees-stirring. Reignac is no *garagiste* exercise, despite the labour-intensive vinification. Over 200,000 bottles are produced.

In 2002 Vatelot added another wine to the range: Balthus. This comes from a purchased property two kilometres (just over a mile) away that has three hectares of forty-year-old Merlot on clay-limestone soil, cropped at fifteen hl/ha. After a prolonged cold soak, the whole crop is barrel-fermented at a fairly low temperature. Instead of punching down the cap, the barrels are rolled twice daily for some thirty days. Then the wine is aged for nineteen months in new oak with stirring and rolling on Oxoline racks. I asked Vatelot why he chose the name Balthus. His reply was succinct and jokey. "Balthus. Pétrus. C'est pas compliqué."

He also makes a small quantity of white wine from a very stony lower sector of the vineyards. These vines were planted in 1991, and the first vintage was 1996. Here, too, the yield is low: twenty-seven hl/ha in 2005. After some skin contact, the must is fermented in new oak and aged for eight months with lees-stirring.

In June 2006 the Vatelots kindly invited me to lunch. As I joined the other guests – a Bordeaux négociant and the Bordeaux buyer for one of the largest French supermarket chains – Yves announced that with each course we would be served blind either two or three wines. Each flight would be the same vintage, and we could assume that one of the wines was from Reignac. This is just the kind of occasion that wine writers dread, but all the guests were in the same boat.

The first flight was 2002. The other guests preferred Wine Two; I had a fairly strong preference for Wine One. Wine Two was Reignac; Wine One was Cheval Blanc. The second flight was 1999. Once again, the other guests went for Reignac, while I disgraced myself by preferring Mouton-Rothschild. Finally we had three 2003s. The other guests gave first place to Balthus, while I thought Château Margaux was better; but we agreed that Haut-Brion was the weakest of the trio. Yves Vatelot was hugely amused by our deliberations. If I had failed to flatter my host by choosing his wines, at least I could compliment myself on having a good nose for First Growths.

Whatever my preference, it is clear that Reignac is a very fine wine. We also tasted the first Vatelot vintage, a wine then labelled Reignac Prestige since Reignac did not exist. The nose showed some evolution, with leafy, gamey aromas and a touch of liquorice. The palate was concentrated and a bit rough around the edges, but it still had good fruit and length. As for the 1999 Reignac, the nose showed black fruits and woodsmoke, while the palate was very concentrated, spicy, and savoury, but perhaps lacking some complexity. The 2002 had an elegant, toasty nose; for a young wine it was very supple and sumptuous but a touch heavy and very evidently Merlot. The 2004 seemed better balanced; the nose was closed but the palate was lively and balanced, with upfront juiciness and a good tannic structure.

The 2003 Balthus also had a very savoury nose, and was on the edge of overripeness; but the tannins were well integrated. I preferred it to the 2004, which was just too dense, chocolatey, and over-extracted. The 2005, dour from cask, has since developed superbly into a complex wine with a lifted finish. Yet on the whole, I prefer Reignac to Balthus.

The white shows spicy, oaky aromas, and fruit nuances of dried apricot and peaches, and lanolin. Although a big, creamy wine, there is sufficient spice and acidity to keep it vigorous and ensure good length. The 1998, 2004, and 2005 were all delicious in 2006. The 2006 has more tropical fruit nuances, but is equally appealing.

Château Reynier

Grézillac (Entre-Deux-Mers). Tel: 0557 845202. Owner: Marc Lurton. 35 ha. 28 ha red: 50% Merlot,
50% Cabernet Sauvignon. 7 ha white: 50% Sauvignon Blanc, 45% Sémillon, 5% Muscadelle.
Production: 250,000 bottles

Like Château Bonnet just up the road, Reynier was bought a century ago by the Récapet family, and inherited in 1956 by Dominique Lurton. He separated Reynier from his brother André's Bonnet. In 1996 Dominique's son Marc took over, after having spent many years in the United States. He also owns Château de Bouchet, which produces lighter wines for early drinking.

The vineyards are planted on clay-limestone over a limestone base. Although the older Merlot vines are planted at a low density, Lurton has left them like that, as they never yield more than forty-five hl/ha anyway. The basic wine is aged in tanks, while Cuvée Heritage is aged in new barriques for sixteen months in a quarry a short distance from the buildings.

The white is given some skin contact, and aged on the fine lees for up to six months; there is no malolactic fermentation. The white is spicy and fresh yet doesn't lack weight and substance; there's little depth here but it's well made and balanced. The 2002 Cuvée Heritage also lacks complexity but it's supple, pleasantly fruity, and quite elegant. The Reynier wines don't reach great heights but they are consistently well made.

Château Reynon

Béguey (Premières Côtes). Tel: 0556 170818. Website: www.denisdubourdieu.com. Owners: Denis and
Florence Dubourdieu. 38 ha. 19 ha red: 80% Merlot, 20% Cabernet Sauvignon. 18 ha white: 85% Sauvignon Blanc,
15% Sémillon. Production: 240,000 bottles. Second wine: Le Clos de Reynon

The Reynon vineyards, on a slope close to the Garonne and the nineteenth-century château were acquired by Florence Dubourdieu's father in 1958. She and her husband, Professor Denis Dubourdieu, took over in 1976, and made the château their home. There is clay-limestone on the slopes and deep gravel over a clay subsoil on the plateau above. The vines are planted to a density of 6,000 per hectare and the soil is ploughed; no herbicides are used. The harvest is both mechanical and manual.

Although Reynon makes a pleasant Merlot-dominated red, aged in one-third new barriques, the estate is better known for its white wine, especially the Cuvée Vieilles Vignes. This has been a consistent wine for over twenty years, with its grapefruity aromas, its fine fruit balanced by lively acidity, and good length. But it lacks the complexity of the Dubourdieus' other white wine, Clos Floridène (*q.v.*) from the Graves.

Château Rouquette

Pellegrue (Bordeaux Supérieur). Tel: 0556 613559. Website: www.ch-rouquette.com. Owner: Michael Banton.
32 ha. 55% Cabernet Sauvignon, 38% Merlot, 7% Cabernet Franc. Production: 220,000 bottles.
Second wine: Ch Bel Air de l'Orme

There was a château here in the fourteenth century, though the present buildings date from the seventeenth and eighteenth centuries. In 1997 Rouquette was bought by Briton Michael Banton and his French wife Alia. The vineyards are on southeast-facing slopes. They have been gradually fine-tuning the winemaking. Oak-ageing was begun only in 2000, and since 2001 they have employed some micro-oxygenation *sous marc*. After a short cold soak and fermentation in stainless-steel tanks, the wine is aged in fifty per cent new oak, of which a quarter used to be American oak; since 2004, however, only French oak has been bought. The Bantons have also introduced a *cuvée* called Merigot, which has a much higher proportion of Merlot.

The 2000 had some aromatic charm, but was tannic and coarse on the palate, with some greenness. The 2001 Merigot was disappointing too, lacking vigour and fruit. The 2003 is raw, tannic, and lacks finesse.

Château Ste-Marie

*Targon (Entre-Deux-Mers). Tel: 0556 236430. Website: www.chateau.sainte.marie.com. **Owners:** Gilles and
Stéphane Dupuch. 80 ha. 50 ha red: 72% Merlot, 23% Cabernet Sauvignon, 5% Petit Verdot.*
*30 ha white: 70% Sauvignon Blanc and Sauvignon Gris, 20% Sémillon, 10% Muscadelle. **Production:** 500,000 bottles.*
Second wine: Ch Gravelle

This large estate used to belong to the nearby abbey of La Sauve, and has been in the same family for four
generations. In 1982 there were only eight hectares under vine, so the expansion has been both considerable
and recent. That means there are also vineyards within the Premières Côtes at Capian, where the soil is
gravelly clay, whereas at Targon the soil is clay-limestone with heavier clay below. Although most of the vineyards are planted at a relatively high density of 5,000-6,000 vines per hectare, Stéphane Dupuch has planted
three hectares of white vines at 10,000 vines per hectare. About one-fifth of the grapes are picked by hand.

After skin contact and pressing, the white Cuvée Tradition is aged on the fine lees, half in tanks, half in
barrels, though with very little new oak. In 1992 Dupuch introduced a top *cuvée* called Madlys, fermented and
aged in twenty per cent new oak.

The red grapes are fermented with a discreet use of *pigeage*. Dupuch has tried micro-oxygenation, but is not
convinced that it makes a great deal of difference. Two of the wines – Tradition and Vieilles Vignes – are unoaked.
The other wine is Alios, which comes from Premières Côtes fruit and is aged for twelve months in barriques.

The 2000 Madlys was fading by 2006, but the 2004 had a rich, flowery, white-peach nose with no overt
oakiness; it is rich and spicy, but has quite assertive acidity. In 2005 the Madlys is more textured and oaky than
the Vieilles Vignes, but the latter has lively flowery aromas, and rich stone-fruits flavours and exemplary balance.
The 2006 Madlys is lush and peachy, sumptuous yet balanced and stylish, and clearly more complex than the
regular white. In their different ways, these are among the best white wines of Entre-Deux-Mers.

As for the reds, the 2004 Vieilles Vignes has smoky aromas, with a slight figginess; on the palate it is a touch
rustic, with a hint of underripeness. The 2004 Alios, despite its slight herbaceousness on the nose, is clearly riper
than Vieilles Vignes, with more plump fruit, spice, and length. The 2002 Alios is underpowered in terms of its
fruit, since the tannins are substantial.

Château de Seguin

Lignan de Bordeaux (Entre-Deux-Mers). Tel: 0557 971978. Website: www.chateau-seguin.fr.
***Owners:** Michael and Gert Carl. 126 ha. 121 ha red: 50% Cabernet Sauvignon, 45% Merlot, 5% Cabernet Franc.*
*5 ha white: 50% Sauvignon Blanc, 40% Sémillon, 10% Muscadelle. **Production:** 570,000 bottles*

When the Carl family from Denmark, owners of a wine-importing company, bought this property in
1985, there were only twenty hectares under vine. They promptly replanted, and the expansion has been
considerable. Seguin was a former dairy farm of ancient origin, and a tower supposedly from the Carolingian
era survives. The vineyards are planted on slopes above Lignan on clay-limestone soils, and the newer plantings
are at 6,000 vines per hectare. The Carls favour *lutte raisonnée* and the grapes are picked mechanically.

There are two white wines, the basic Sauvignon de Seguin and the Prestige, which is aged for five months
in new oak with lees-stirring. The latter can be a touch oily from the oak, and even in 2005 the wine was rather
heavy and effortful.

The reds are vinified in steel tanks with, since 2005, some micro-oxygenation. The regular wine is made
from fifty per cent Cabernet Sauvignon, and aged six months in older barrels. The Cuvée Prestige is an
old-vine selection, also dominated by Cabernet, and aged for twelve months in new barriques. Cuvée Carl
is usually pure Merlot, also aged for twelve months in new oak.

I compared the three *cuvées* from 2003, and preferred the Prestige, which, though super-ripe, has firm
tannins to support it; the 2004 was similar. The basic red is ripe but soft, with some flab derived from low
acidity. The Cuvée Carl has aromas of sweet ripe cherries and vanilla, but the palate is both soupy and tannic.

Château de Sours

St-Quentin-de-Baron (Entre-Deux-Mers). Tel: 0557 241926. Website: www.chateaudesours.com.
Owners: Martin Krajewski and partners. 50 ha. 40 ha red: 85% Merlot, 10% Cabernet Franc, 5% Cabernet Sauvignon.
10 ha white: 60% Sémillon, 40% Sauvignon Blanc. Production: 360,000 bottles. Second wine: Dom de Sours

This property, about twelve kilometres (7.5 miles) south of Libourne, was developed by British wine merchant Esmé Johnstone; he sold his shares in 2005 though he remains a consultant. Château de Sours is well known for its delightful Merlot-dominated rosé. The white is made from hand-harvested grapes that are given skin contact for twenty-four hours, then fermented in tanks and aged six months in barrels. The red is eighty per cent Merlot, fermented with micro-oxygenation, and then aged in one-third new barriques for sixteen months. There is also a high-priced *cuvée* called La Source, both red and white.

The 2003 white is a great success, with floral, peachy aromas, and a palate that's rich yet spicy, though only modest in length. The white La Source is similar, though the aromas are more opulent and the texture more lush. The 2002 has uncomplicated fresh raspberry aromas; the wine is medium-bodied, not especially concentrated but lively and balanced. The 2001 La Source is oakier, with a touch of varnish on the nose, and the wine has some elegance but not a great deal of depth or length. In general, the wines are a well-made commercial range, but the special *cuvées* seem overpriced.

Château Suau

Capian (Premières Côtes). Tel: 0556 721906. Website: www.chateausuau.com. Owner: Monique Bonnet. 65 ha.
58 ha red: 50% Merlot, 30% Cabernet Sauvignon, 20% Cabernet Franc. 7 ha white: 40% Sauvignon Blanc,
40% Sémillon, 20% Muscadelle. Production: 450,000 bottles. Second wine: Ch Maubert

Local legend has it that the château here was a hunting lodge of the Duc d'Epernon. A family of *pieds noirs* had owned Suau from 1962 to 1981, when it was bought by Philippe Raoux, owner of the enormous Château d'Arsac. He sold the estate to Monique Bonnet's father in 1986, and they found the vines in poor shape. She tells me that early in the twentieth century the vineyards were planted solely with white vines. In 1986 the vineyards, which are in a single block, were planted to a density of only 3,000 vines per hectare, which by 1990 she was expanding to 5,000, and from 2000 she was planting at 7,000 vines per hectare. The soil is gravelly clay, and the grapes are picked by hand and by machine.

After sorting, the red grapes are cold-soaked and fermented with occasional micro-oxygenation. The Cuvée Tradition is unoaked, while the Cuvée Prestige is aged twelve months in one-third new barriques. The white grapes are given skin contact. Again the Tradition is aged in tanks, the Prestige in new barriques for eight months with lees-stirring. In 2002 Monique Bonnet introduced a Premières Côtes white, and a screwcapped range called Duo aimed at younger drinkers. There is also a Cadillac.

I find the white Premières Côtes silky but insipid. However, the Tradition is grassily aromatic, but on the palate the Sémillon gives body and the Sauvignon a certain raciness and good length. I prefer it to the rather heavy and overoaked Prestige.

The only red Tradition I have tasted is the 2003, which has a baked and earthy nose, and plump fruit on the palate at war with hefty tannins. The Prestige ages very well. The 1996 has meaty aromas, rich fruit, ample freshness and acidity, and a stylish finish. The aromas of the 1999 are smoky and gamey, and there is fine concentrated plummy fruit on the palate with light acidity that keeps it lively. The 2000 is more intense and weightier, with flavours of black fruits and plenty of spiciness on the finish. The 2002, while in the same mould, lacks a little finesse, but it's still a good, solid wine.

The Cadillac is made in a *moelleux* style and lacks some richness and weight, a pleasant but unremarkable wine. Suau is an underrated property, and the red Prestige in particular is excellent and dependable.

Château Thieuley

La Sauve (Entre-Deux-Mers). Tel: 0556 230001. Website: www.thieuley.com. Owner: Francis Courselle. 83 ha.
42 ha red: 70% Merlot, 15% Cabernet Sauvignon, 15% Cabernet Franc. 41 ha white: 50% Sémillon,
40% Sauvignon Blanc, 10% Sauvignon Gris. Production: 520,000 bottles

When I first visited Thieuley in 1990, Francis Courselle was already being hailed as a master of white wine vinification in the Entre-Deux-Mers. His father André had bought the property in 1950, and Francis, an oenologist, took over in 1972. At that time there were a mere six hectares under vine. He planted more vines on three *croupes* with gravelly soil over clay and silt. Recent plantings are at a density of 6,000 vines per hectare, and the trellising is high so as to increase the area of foliage. Almost all the grapes are picked by machine, and in 2003 they were picked at night to avoid cooked flavours.

Courselle is now assisted by his daughters Marie and Sylvie, the former being the winemaker. The basic white wine, a Bordeaux Blanc, is fifty per cent Sémillon, with the fruit given skin contact but no oak-ageing. The best-known wine is the Cuvée Francis Courselle, which comes from vines at least fifty years old. The must is barrel-fermented in a *chai* chilled to 10°C (50°F) to slow down the process, and then aged for eight months in new but lightly toasted oak.

There was no red wine here until 1972. The red vines are planted on soils with the highest clay content, and Marie Courselle says the wines tend to be tannic when young and need some bottle-age. The grapes are fermented in steel and cement tanks with micro-oxygenation, and aged for twelve months in *foudres*, though a third of the wine is aged in new barriques. There is no racking, and the lees are stirred by rolling barrels on Oxoline racks.

There are two special *cuvées*. The Réserve Francis Courselle is mostly made from the best parcels of Merlot. It used to be aged in new oak, but from 2002 the proportion of new wood has been reduced to sixty per cent. Finally, there is Heritage de Thieuley, eighty per cent Merlot and first made in 2000 from the ripest hand-picked grapes. This is aged for fifteen months in new oak.

Over the two decades I have been tasting them, the white wines have been very good. The unoaked bottling is all it should be: aromatic and citric, sometimes slightly herbaceous without being tart, and with engaging vibrancy and length. The Cuvée Francis Courselle is less racy, and the oak is quite pronounced, but there is a lusher texture and ample richness and power. The 2005 and the svelte 2006 are particularly good. I am not entirely convinced by the 2001 white Heritage, with its yeasty, oaky nose; it's medium-bodied, quite oaky, but with modest acidity and a less than dazzling finish.

The 2003 red Thieuley has a light cherry-pie nose, a soft, rounded texture, and adds up to a fairly bland if certainly drinkable glass of wine. The 2001 Réserve has more complexity. The aromas are of red fruits and cranberries, but it's a concentrated and full-bodied wine with considerable weight and enlivening tannins. I prefer it to the 2001 Heritage, which is a tad overripe on the nose, and too extracted on the palate. The Réserve has better balance. The 2005 Réserve is suave and oaky but lacks a certain cut.

Château Tour de Mirambeau

Naujan-et-Postiac (Entre-Deux-Mers). Tel: 0557 845508. Website: www.despagne.fr. Owner: Jean-Louis Despagne. 88 ha. 29 ha red: 80% Merlot, 20% Cabernet Sauvignon. 59 ha white: 34% Sauvignon Blanc, 33% Sémillon, 33% Muscadelle. Production: 650,000 bottles

This is yet another of the prodigious Despagne family's estates. There are two red wines: the medium-bodied, undemanding Réserve, and the Cuvée Passion. The latter comes from a ten-hectare plot of Merlot, planted to a density of 10,000 vines per hectare. It has more oak and density, without being extracted or weighty. Of recent vintages the 2001 was particularly succulent. The whites are straightforward, usually with citrus aromas, and various degrees of weight and richness. In 2005 the regular Entre-Deux-Mers seemed just as good as the Réserve, combining crispness with ripeness and a sleek texture. The property also produces a sweet Sémillon Noble; the 2003 had mandarin flavours and considerable intensity and lushness.

Château de Tressac

La Rivière (Bordeaux). Tel: 0663 157751. Owner: Henri Despeaux. 5 ha. 87% Merlot, 7% Cabernet Sauvignon, 6% Malbec. Production: 24,000 bottles

Henri Despeaux used to be a winemaker for Bernard Magrez, but this is his own property, bordering the Fronsac appellation. The first vintage was 2002. The vines, which have an average age of fifty-five years, are planted on clay soils that have proved advantageous in the hot years of the early twenty-first century. Green-harvesting keeps yields down to thirty-five hl/ha. After a ten-day cold soak, the fruit is fermented without crushing, then aged in forty per cent new barriques with lees-stirring. The oldest vines are dispatched to a special *cuvée* called Carpe Diem, cropped at even lower yields and vinified in 400-litre barrels, of which sixty per cent are new.

The 2003 has a confected bonbons nose, a slack texture, and little persistence. The Carpe Diem had more aromatic purity, and though lush on the palate it was also close to jammy and thus rather fatiguing. The 2004 too is confected, with glacé-cherry flavours; but the acidity is better than in 2003. The 2004 Carpe is close to overripeness but has admirable concentration and a fine texture; if there is something assembled about the wine as a whole, it at least has formidable fruit. The 2005s are a cut above, being full-bodied, super-ripe, and spicy; although there is too much alcohol on the Tressac, the fruit is impressive and the two *cuvées* seem close both in style and quality.

There are plenty of other properties in Entre-Deux-Mers producing good if not characterful white wines. There is no reason to give each of them an individual entry, but it is worth recording that there are good dry whites to be found at **Châteaux Chantelouve, Haut-Garriga, Haut-Pougnan, Lestrille, Mylord, Nardique La Gravière**, and **Vignol**.

28. Sauternes and How it is Made

 A surprising amount of sweet wine is produced in Bordeaux as a whole, and forty years ago the volume was vastly greater. In the postwar years sweetness was considered desirable as much for its nutritional value as for its flavour. From regions such as the Graves, Entre-Deux-Mers, and the Premières Côtes, tanker-loads of sweet wine roared forth. Many of these wines would have been poor: sickly with chaptalization and high in sulphur dioxide, they would have been a short cut to a headache. They also bastardized the great tradition of sweet wine production from Bordeaux.

That tradition had its base in Sauternes but was not exclusive to that region. I recall fabulous sweet wines from what is today the Premières Côtes – but from great vintages such as 1929, so they were probably the exception rather than the rule. Xavier Planty, the director of Château Guiraud, believes the whole territorial concept of the Sauternais is artificial, and that there are other terroirs in the Graves, Toulenne for example, equally capable of producing great sweet wines.

By the 1960s the damage done to Sauternes by the degradation of its authentic style was so severe that it would take decades to overcome. A handful of properties – notably but not solely Yquem – maintained standards, but the great majority, even many First Growths, simply abandoned the criteria indispensable to the production of great sweet wine. Planty recalls that in the early 1980s only Yquem was going through its vineyards more than twice in search of botrytized fruit; and many estates picked everything at once, reversing traditional practice. That practice required low yields, the patience to wait for substantial botrytis infection of the grapes, hand-harvesting, and barrel-ageing if not barrel-fermentation. It was only in 1983 that a revival of authentic Sauternes began, which fortunately has lasted to this day.

One reason why standards can easily slip is that Sauternes is so expensive to produce. Moreover, this is a region almost entirely devoted to sweet wines. In Germany, for example, the production of botrytis wines such as Beerenauslese and Trockenbeerenauslese is the icing on the cake of a great vintage. In lesser years, or in vintages when botrytis is absent, the same grapes can be used to make other styles of wine. This is not the case in Sauternes. (Some estates such as Rieussec, Suduiraut, and Rayne-Vigneau do pick some grapes early to produce a dry white wine, but it is commercially insignificant.)

In years when heavy rain damaged the grapes beyond any hope of recovery, very little or even no wine at all can be made. Vintages such as 1992 and 1993 were washouts. Suduiraut released not a single drop as *grand vin* in 1991, 1992, and 1993. Similarly in 2000, while the Médoc and St-Emilion were basking in yet another superb vintage, heavy rain fell in Sauternes a short time after most properties had begun harvesting, and the crop was severely reduced. No vintage of the century here.

It is hard to say when sweet wine production became a regional specialty here. Other regions renowned for their sweet wines – the Rheingau and Tokaj, for example – have their myths about the "discovery" of the beneficial aspects of noble rot, and perhaps Tokaj got there first in the seventeenth century. The precise moment at which farmers learned to differentiate between noble rot and the myriad other kinds of rot, all of which spell ruin, is difficult to pin down. A nobly rotten grape looks fairly revolting, as does a raisin for that matter, but it would not have required a genius to ascertain that it tasted good and did no damage to health. Certainly by the late eighteenth century this had been understood, as the renown of Château d'Yquem confirms. It is recorded in the Yquem cellar book that the harvest in 1810 continued until November 11. If the aim had been simply to pick sugar-laden overripe grapes, there would have been no need to wait so long. The conclusion is inescapable that the owners were deliberately waiting for botrytis infection. A more detailed account of the history of Sauternes, the region, and its winemaking style is given in my earlier book on the subject.[1]

---

1 Brook, *Sauternes and Other Sweet Wines of Bordeaux*, Faber, London, 1995

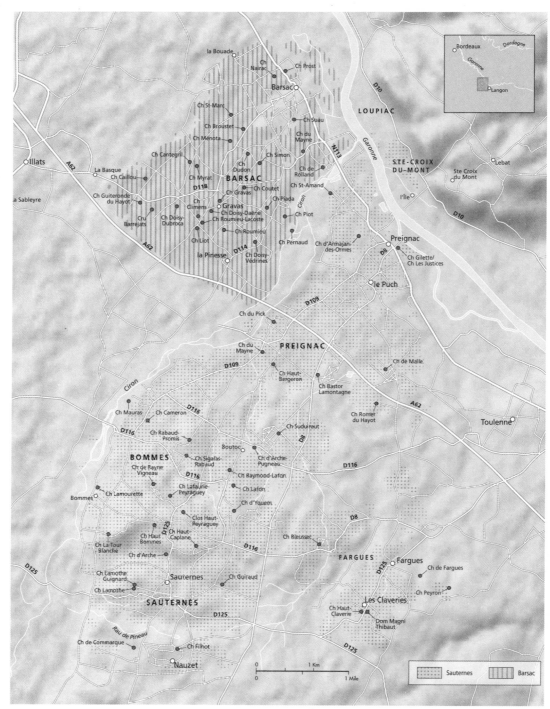

Sauternes and Barsac

The region clearly prospered in the nineteenth century, thanks to strong international demand. Wines such as the 1847 Yquem were legendary and were sold to the Russian court for fabulous prices. Of course the Sauternais suffered as badly as the rest of Bordeaux from diseases such as mildew and, especially, phylloxera. (According to Pierre Dubourdieu of Doisy-Daëne, a lot of red wine was produced in Barsac in the 1860s and the wine was often considered superior to Pomerol.) Nor did it fare well during the decades of crisis such as the 1930s and 1950s. The run of mediocre vintages in the 1960s did not help. Even Yquem nodded, bottling its 1963, whereas today that wine would have been quietly poured away or sold off in bulk. Estates took to producing dry wines as well as sweet ones. When I first visited Guiraud some twenty years ago, I was offered its dry white and its red wine as well as the Sauternes.

THE SAUTERNAIS

The region is simply the southeastern extension of the Graves district, about forty kilometres (twenty-five miles) south of the city of Bordeaux. It is bordered by two rivers: the large Garonne and the stream-like Ciron. Because the Ciron is colder than the Garonne, their confluence encourages the development of early-morning mists, and that is precisely the microclimatic condition most likely to lead to the development of botrytis. The mist usually burns off by lunchtime, and in ideal circumstances afternoon sunshine will dry the bunches and inhibit the development of undesirable forms of rot; warm weather will also assist the concentration of juice and flavour within each grape.

The confluence of two rivers is not the sole factor that produces botrytization in this region, as there are areas distant from the rivers that also succumb to botrytis. In Sauternes itself, some kilometres from the Ciron, differences in the temperature of the subsoil help to provoke a heavy dew that also contributes to the onset of botrytis. Noble rot is, after all, a fungal condition encountered just about everywhere that humid conditions occur, which is why many vineyards in regions where no sweet wine is made are often treated with anti-botrytis sprays. Botrytis is the enemy of red wine, destroying its pigmentation and altering its flavour. It is only in the Sauternais and other sweet wine regions that the vineyards are manipulated to encourage its development.

There are five communes within the region, with about 2,300 hectares of vines. Two of them, Barsac and Preignac, flank the main N113 road that descends from Bordeaux to Langon. The other three – Sauternes, Bommes, and Fargues – lie farther to the west. Barsac enjoys the luxury of being able to choose between two appellations: either its own name or that of Sauternes.

Sauternes About 400 hectares of vines are planted here on soils of gravel, clay, and sand. Because the clay content is high, good drainage is essential. The terrain is gently hilly, with some château-topped outcrops at Yquem and Rayne-Vigneau, and thus there are varied exposures as well as soil types. It is sometimes remarked that Yquem routinely produces four different styles of Sauternes from its vineyards, and these are then carefully blended to produce the style recognizable as Yquem. Those who claim to dislike Sauternes because the wine is "heavy" can make the strongest case by pointing at wines from the Sauternes commune, which can indeed be more full-bodied than those from other villages.

Bommes Its 380 hectares lie fairly close to the Ciron. Gravel soils are important here, but there is also a good deal of clay and, in lower sectors, sand.

Fargues The smallest commune, Fargues is planted with 190 hectares, mostly on clay and limestone slopes; lower-lying land, with higher sand and gravel content, is less propitious. The subsoil is gravelly and here too there is clay.

Preignac With 565 hectares under vine, this is an important commune. A few vineyards lie on the Garonne side of the N113, but the majority stretch westwards to the boundaries with Bommes and Sauternes. Being a large area, the soils are very varied, with alluvial deposits to the north and east, and more clay and gravel in the southern sectors.

Barsac Other than Sauternes itself, Barsac is the most distinctive of the communes. Its 850 hectares of vines are planted on reddish sand and clay over a subsoil of limestone bedrock not commonly found elsewhere in the

Sauternais. The soil itself has a high iron content, which may also contribute to the character of the wine. Equally important are the water-retentive qualities of the limestone, which help to combat hydric stress. Toward the N113 the soils are more alluvial and generally not as prized as those lying farther away from the Garonne, between the railway line and the autoroute. The best sector is the so-called plateau – at twenty metres (sixty-six feet) above sea level the term is a slight exaggeration – known as Haut-Barsac.

Barsac certainly has its own character, being lighter in colour and texture than the other communes; it also has a more citric character and thus more overt freshness. Barsac used to be a wine with higher alcohol and thus slightly less residual sugar than the other communes, but I doubt that is the case any longer. The apparent "lightness" of Barsac is deceptive. Wines from the top estates can live happily for seventy or more years from great vintages, with far less evolved colour, aroma, and flavour than comparable wines from Sauternes or Bommes.

Not too much importance should be placed on communal origin. Many other factors – grape varieties, harvesting dates, winemaking styles, and oak-ageing – come into play in determining the style of any château's wine. In a blind tasting it would be very difficult to identify the communal origin of each wine.

GRAPE VARIETIES

Only three varieties are grown: Sauvignon Blanc, Sémillon, and Muscadelle. Of these Sémillon is easily the most important. Because the bunches are large and the crops generous, dry Sémillon can be bland and dilute. For botrytis wine, its salient feature is having thin skin that allows the botrytis spores to penetrate it with relative ease. It is also a variety that ages well, as admirers of dry Hunter Valley Semillon will recognize, and this too is an important factor. Sémillon is also a long-lived vine and centenarian blocks are by no means rare in Bordeaux; Sauvignon, in contrast, usually tires after about thirty years in the ground (although consultant Denis Dubourdieu says that, if properly cared for, Sauvignon vines can age very well too).

Sauvignon Blanc, growing a tighter bunch than Sémillon, is less susceptible to botrytis and is also more prone to the malady of eutypiose. On the other hand, its aromatic freshness and high acidity are valued as they stand in contrast to the fatter, less acidic Sémillon. Some growers deliberately pick Sauvignon, or some of their Sauvignon, without noble rot precisely to retain its aromatic typicity and prevent their Sauternes from becoming heavy or blowsy. On the other hand, many fine estates contain no Sauvignon at all – Climens is one example – but the most typical *encépagement* in the vineyard is eighty per cent Sémillon and twenty per cent Sauvignon, as at Yquem.

The third variety, Muscadelle, has been falling from favour for many years. It ripens early and is susceptible to the ruinous black rot as well as noble rot. Some producers, such as Alexandre de Lur-Saluces, note that a Muscadelle wine can be very attractive when young but does not age well. Didier Laulan of Broustet says it needs to be picked just as botrytis is becoming established; wait any longer and its typical aromas will diminish. Its few remaining partisans value its aromatic quality, but even they will rarely have more than ten per cent of Muscadelle in their vineyards.

It is interesting that in the mid-nineteenth century Sauvignon was the most prized variety and it dominated the vineyards of Yquem and other properties such as La Tour Blanche. It appears that it was Sémillon's greater resistance to *oïdium* that began to swing the balance. Then after phylloxera, when the vineyards needed to be replanted, the more generous yields of Sémillon struck most growers as a distinct advantage.

The varieties are usually pruned differently. Sauvignon is pruned by the *guyot simple* system, with a single fruit-bearing cane. Sémillon and Muscadelle are usually pruned *à cot*, which is a kind of spur-pruning: the previous year's wood growth is removed, leaving two or three stumps, each with two or three eyes, from which the new shoots will spring and eventually be trained along wires.

Poor clones are often blamed for poor-quality wines, and it is no different in the Sauternais, where over-productive clones were planted in the 1960s. Moreover, many clones are selected to deter disease, whereas in the Sauternais the goal is the opposite. For some years, Château Guiraud, in collaboration with other properties, has been developing massal selections from vines planted before the 1956 frost. This large project includes estates in Pessac-Léognan, so it is not restricted to the Sauternes region. In 2005 Xavier Planty began microvinifying these different selections, so that their merits can be assessed.

GROWING THE GRAPES

Without low yields, a fine botrytis wine cannot be produced. The yields for Cabernet Sauvignon, even in the greatest vineyards of the Médoc and Graves, are often around sixty hectolitres per hectare; those for Merlot on the Right Bank somewhat lower. The yields for the lesser sweet wines such as Loupiac and Cadillac, which are not always botrytized, are forty hl/ha, which the best growers of those regions consider too generous. For Sauternes the maximum yield is twenty-five hl/ha, and top estates rarely achieve it. In general, good Sauternes tends to be made from vines yielding between twelve and eighteen hl/ha but there are vintages in which factors such as the need to eliminate mouldy bunches can reduce yields to single figures.

Low yields are attained by severe pruning. One consequence of overcropping is that having too many bunches retards maturation, and it is important that the grapes are fully ripe by the time botrytis attacks. The balance of a typical Sauternes is 13.5 to fourteen degrees of alcohol, plus eighty to 100 grams of residual sugar. To attain this balance, the grapes must be picked with a potential alcohol of eighteen degrees. Botrytis increases the sugar content of a grape, so with ample noble rot in the vineyard attaining such levels should pose no problem – so long as viticultural practices have maximized the possibility of botrytis infection on ripe fruit.

Nature sometimes offers a helping hand. Spring frost is an ever-present risk, especially in low-lying sectors such as Barsac. Hail is by no means uncommon. Frost damage was extreme in 1991, and again in 1994, when I toured the vineyards the day after a severe frost, and could see that some properties, such as Myrat, would clearly have no crop at all. The problem with hail is that it bruises or gashes the grape skins, and this makes the bunch highly susceptible to all manner of diseases and moulds.

Not only is the grower required to limit yields severely but the evolution of the bunches has to be constantly monitored. Before the harvest begins it is common for vineyard workers to go through the vines removing any bunches that show signs of mould, black rot, insect damage, and uneven ripening. Inevitably this process, known as a *trie de nettoyage*, adds to production costs, as does the ensuing reduction in yield.

Ploughing the soil, a return to traditional practice, was slow to be adopted in the Sauternais, as elsewhere in Bordeaux. Yquem had always ploughed, and Coutet did so from 1989 onwards. By the early 2000s many estates had abandoned, or minimized, the use of herbicides and were working the soil. Mireille Daret of Cru Barréjats believes that, among its other benefits, ploughing helps to retain acidity in the fruit, an advantage in vintages such as 2003.

BOTRYTIS

I have already made many references to *Botrytis cinerea* and it is now time to explain precisely what it is. It is a parasitic fungus of the *Ascomycetes* family and its spores are omnipresent in vineyards. It is by no means confined to the Sauternais. In certain climatic conditions it will attack red as well as white grapes, and I have encountered red botrytis wines from Pinot Noir (in Germany) and from Zweigelt and other varieties (in Austria). Botrytis is the same thing as noble rot, and the French term is *pourriture noble*.

The action of the botrytis spores is complex and even now not properly understood. It appears that the spores' filaments penetrate the skin of the grape, which is gradually invaded by the fungus. By making the skins more permeable, the rate of infection is increased. The skin shrivels and discolours, turning purple-brown; at the same time the fungus consumes the flesh and the berry desiccates as the water content shrinks. As a consequence the sugar content of the grape increases, as does the level of glycerol and dextrin. Thus the resulting juice is both higher in sugar and more viscous in texture.

A fully botrytized berry will have succumbed to weight loss as the inner content of the grape is consumed. What remains, however, whether in the form of sugar or acidity, will have been concentrated. Sugar content (which would be about thirteen degrees of potential alcohol for a dry white wine) will have risen to between sixteen and twenty-six degrees. For most estates, the ideal is between eighteen and twenty-one degrees. Too low, and the wine will lack sweetness and texture; too high, and the must may have difficulty in fermenting and may leave a level of residual sugar that unbalances the wine (as was sometimes the case in 1990 or 2003).

Acidity levels will also be higher, which is important for the balance of the wine. A merely sweet wine would be cloying without acidity to refresh the palate. Denis Dubourdieu summarizes the process as follows:

> *The work done by this fungus on the grape should be considered as hyper-maceration*
> *which "digests" the solid part. At first, the mould carries out selective extraction,*
> *intensifying the fruit content, deteriorating the tannin and erasing rather acidic and bitter*
> *aspects. The second phase is that of concentration.*[2]

Recent research in Switzerland by Roger Pezet and others has refined our understanding of how botrytis functions. I am no specialist in plant biology, and Xavier Planty has kindly acted as an intermediary in explaining this research. It seems to show that flowering is the most crucial period for the generation of botrytis. After the flowers drop off, there remain two slight openings in the green grape to which the stems were attached. These are large enough to allow botrytis spores to enter. They then remain dormant until the grapes begin to mature. Thus at flowering about thirty per cent of grapes are colonized by botrytis spores. Their action is inhibited by the metabolism of the grape, which has its own anti-botrytis mechanisms. Once the grape is fully mature, however, the spores awaken, and start consuming the sugars within the grape. It does this from the inside, whereas before this research it was thought (as I have stated above) that the spores penetrated the skins only from the outside. The "best" botrytis is when the grape is fully mature and the spores can concentrate everything. To retain acidity, a grower should aim for botrytis infection as soon as possible after the grapes mature, rather than three weeks later. Pick at sixteen degrees and you will have less acidity than at twenty-one degrees. Being a parasite, the spores attack the sugar first and can consume fifty per cent of what's in the grape; they then attack the acidity.

Xavier Planty is convinced that the use of treatments against mildew and oïdium inhibit and retard the awakening of the dormant spores. Although the action of botrytis varies from one location to another, Planty believes it is also related to how copiously the vines have been treated. He is also convinced that adding compost and other vegetal organic matter into the soil is positive in terms of encouraging botrytis. He cannot be certain but he suspects that it is the avoidance of treatments at Guiraud that allows him to harvest relatively early. Thus in 2005 he was picking from October 13 onwards, before other estates had even started. And in 2000 he had picked almost half of the crop before the rain began to fall, whereas La Tour Blanche, just one kilometre (about half a mile) away, hadn't even started to pick when the rains began.

What does seem clear is that there is still much to be learned about the action of botrytis. Fabrice Dubourdieu, the clever and articulate son of Denis and Florence, insists, and I dare say he is reflecting rather

2 Denis Dubourdieu, quoted in article in *Flavours from France*, Autumn 2004

than challenging his father's views, that botrytis is not a component or ingredient in a wine but an agent. "Once it has done its work," he says airily, "there is no need to speak of it further." He also maintains that part of the task of botrytis is to extract aromas from the grapes, but at the same time he insists that botrytis aromas as such don't exist. Perhaps he is right, in the sense that there are no aromatic compounds directly linked to botrytis spores, but I occasionally detect an aromatic profile in a wine that I (and others) associate with botrytized fruit, though I find it hard to put that profile into words. Xavier Planty, who has spent a quarter of a century working with botrytized fruit, tells me he associates certain aromas such as spice and saffron with noble rot, and also finds aromas of iodine a tell-tale sign of a botrytis infection that is too advanced and lacks purity.

In ideal circumstances botrytis infection is rapid and even, and there are vintages when this is the case. But they are the exception rather than the rule. Botrytis infection is usually sporadic. It is also highly sensitive to humidity. Without humidity the spores will not be activated, so in very dry years – 1985 is one example – the berries remain healthy until very late in the season. In that year Yquem was still harvesting some plots as late as December, in its perfectionist quest for only botrytized grapes. Growers must reflect on whether to pick ripe, shrivelled grapes with high sugars but no botrytis, or whether to hang on in the hope that eventually conditions will grow more humid and botrytis will perform its task. The risk of waiting, of course, is that the heavens will deliver not just humidity, but torrential autumn rains that will in effect wipe out the crop.

THE HARVEST

Because botrytis infection is irregular, the harvesting process is very complex. Only in exceptional vintages does botrytis swoop so fast that all the bunches can be picked within a week or two. The norm is that certain rows will be botrytized in advance of others, or that one variety will succumb before the others. There are also various stages of infection. In ideal circumstances one would wait for the final stage when the berry is desiccated and known as "*rôti*". Thus the vineyards of Sauternes have to be picked by *tries successives*, which means repeated forays by the harvesters. This is, of course, a prolonged and labour-intensive process. On average a Sauternes harvest requires three or four *tries*. In years such as 1985, when the progress of botrytis is very slow, there can be as many as ten. In practice many estates will, at a certain point, draw the line and declare the harvest over by picking everything that is left, even if those bunches are not ideal.

There is an economic factor that needs to be taken into account. To house and feed a troupe of harvesters for one or two months is very expensive, and there will also be pressure from the harvesters themselves, especially once the weather becomes colder, to bring matters to a conclusion. It is for this reason that the viticultural goal during the growing season is to have the most even possible maturation, so that the harvesting can be as rapid as possible.

The element of risk is one that Sauternes growers live with each year. In 1982 many top estates realized their bunches were not fully botrytized and waited for noble rot to spread further. Then it began to rain, and much of the crop was lost. Meanwhile, at Suduiraut, which at that time was in the habit of harvesting too early rather than too late, almost the entire crop was safely in the vats. The wine may not have been exceptional, but it was decent enough. Its neighbours had been more conscientious but ended up gnashing their teeth.

The harvesters have to be very well trained, and prior experience counts for a lot. As Denis Dubourdieu once told me: "If you're taking a boat out in bad weather, you'd better have a well-equipped vessel and a good crew." I know from personal experience that it can be very difficult to distinguish a properly botrytized bunch from one that is affected by other forms of mould. It is common for part of a bunch to be properly botrytized, while another part, less visible, may be harbouring black rot. The myth of the

Sauternes harvest is that the botrytized berries are picked individually. This may very occasionally be the case — at very small properties or for certain *tries* within certain blocks — but most harvesters will be cutting whole bunches. It is probable that they, or their supervisors, will inspect each bunch and remove any portions that are not cleanly botrytized. But if bad weather threatens, the harvesting teams may be under pressure to pick fast and without sufficient discrimination.

There will also be different views on how to deal with the early stages of botrytis infection. Berries will discolour, turning a kind of purple-green, but they will be full of juice and the chemical transformations provoked by botrytis will be, at best, incomplete. This stage of infection is called "*pourri plein*": the spores will have consumed sugar without increasing concentration of acids and flavours. Thus a *pourri plein* grape may actually be less sweet than one free from botrytis, so clearly it is inadvisable to pick such grapes. There are other types of rot such as *pourriture aigre*, which can be provoked by hail, the pecking of birds, or the activity of wasps. This kind of rot turns the juice into vinegar, and experienced pickers can identify it by smell alone.

It is possible for properties to perform what it is in effect a final *trie* at the *cuvier* by installing a sorting table where workers can eliminate rotten bunches or vegetal matter. This too has an economic cost. When I observed the harvest in 1994, I visited a prestigious estate as the grapes were coming in, and there was no sorting at all. It had been a difficult harvest in uncertain weather, and there was no incentive to employ dozens of workers to sort through the bunches. With grapes high in sugar, harvesters and winery workers also have to put up with some very active insect life, such as clans of wasps, so there is an understandable wish to see the bunches pressed as fast as possible.

Tries successives not only function as an exercise in quality control. They also give each property a wide range of wines from which the final blend can be composed. If there are, for example, five *tries* and two grape varieties, there could well be more than ten lots, each handled separately. Moreover, many estates will differentiate between each day of each *trie*, vinifying each separately. Once fermentation is complete, the winemaker will be able to identify the salient character of each lot and begin to compose the eventual blend. Blending is not only a way to achieve the most perfect aroma and flavour for a particular wine; it also allows a correction of the balance of the wine, for example, blending a lot with rather high alcohol with another lot that is on the low side.

Choices made during harvesting also have stylistic consequences. When I expressed my overall disappointment with the 2006s to Denis Dubourdieu (although his own wine had been a rare exception in a blind tasting of the vintage), he said that many properties were forgetting the need to have freshness and zest in the wine, giving priority to sweetness and breadth of texture. At both Yquem and Doisy-Daëne, harvesting had begun on September 9, although the *ban de vendange* had been announced for September 18. By picking early, and by ensuring the grapes were sufficiently ripe by that time, he had been able to retain that essential liveliness in the wine. Sugar and lushness are necessary but not sufficient in a fine Sauternes.

MAKING SAUTERNES

There is no mystery to the vinification of Sauternes. Denis Dubourdieu points out that the action of botrytis is itself a form of vinification. "The vinification process is one of controlled digestion of sugar, and in the case of sweet wine this has begun on the vine." Thus by far the most important part of the whole sweet wine production process has already taken place by the time the grapes come into the winery.

Nonetheless, there are choices to be made, and they are often linked to economic factors. The bunches may be pressed — as at Yquem, Nairac, Coutet, and many other properties — in vertical presses, which, it is widely agreed, give the most gentle extraction and the finest quality. But it can be a slow and labour-intensive process, and one that some growers would just as soon avoid. There can be as many as three pressings of the same batch in a vertical press, but the third is often discarded as it can show signs of oxidation. Modern pneumatic, or bladder, presses also give good results and are often found at the larger estates.

The best wines are usually fermented in *barriques*. During the 1960s and 1970s many top properties abandoned this practice on grounds of cost and convenience, and fermentation took place in steel tanks or in underground concrete tanks; nor was the wine subsequently aged in barrels. Tank fermentation has advantages: temperature can be easily controlled, and so can volatile acidity. However, when a wine is barrel-fermented, the small volume of the barrel tends to inhibit high temperatures; they rarely exceed 20°C (68°F). Some winemakers will rely on indigenous yeasts to complete the fermentation; others may use selected or cultivated yeasts. The arguments for and against each option are no different to those for dry wines, except that selected yeasts are less likely to impart specific and uniform aromas or flavours, since the sweetness of the wine will tend to mask them.

In a good vintage, when the grapes have eighteen degrees or more of potential alcohol, the result should be a properly balanced wine. But less perfectionist estates may have a potential alcohol of fifteen or sixteen degrees, which will only give a wine in a *moelleux* style. For such properties the solution has always been chaptalization, adding enough sugar to the must to give an additional two degrees, which is then converted into alcohol by the yeasts. The problem is that chaptalization increases the alcoholic degree but not the residual sugar. The result can be an unbalanced wine with excessive alcohol. Some also claim that not all the added sugar is converted into alcohol but remains in the wine as mere sweetness, which is detectable on the palate.

Chaptalization is no more than a tool that any French winemaker is entitled to use. There may be vintages that are improved by the discreet addition of a little sugar during fermentation. But it has to be said that systematic chaptalization amounts to an admission of viticultural failure. A conscientious *chef de culture* and *maître de chai* will do everything possible, from pruning to harvesting to elimination of inadequate lots, to ensure the grapes are sufficiently rich in sugar to make a good wine. Although chaptalization used to be routine at many properties, I think it is safe to say that in recent years top estates would resort to it only in exceptional circumstances.

With a must rich in sugar, there will come a point at which fermentation will grind to a halt, as the alcohol inhibits any further activity on the part of the yeasts. If a winemaker fears that the wine may end up with too much alcohol (and in 1990 there were wines with an excessive sixteen degrees), it is possible to stop the fermentation once the balance is considered ideal. This can be done by chilling the wine or by adding sulphur dioxide, or a combination of the two. Some winemakers have told me that they often have difficulty coaxing the yeasts to keep working after the wine has reached 13.5 or fourteen degrees, so they suspect any wines with over fifteen degrees must have been chaptalized.

After fermentation comes the *élevage*. A good Sauternes will have been aged in barrels. Denis Dubourdieu remarks:

> The process of élevage *is one of protecting and refining. But you don't need to protect Sauternes grapes; a grape that's been attacked by botrytis has seen everything. The art of making white wine is that of constructing aromas, and with reds you construct colour and tannin. To use barriques for dry wines is an art; to use them for sweet wines is easy.*

Nonetheless, choices need to be made: the length of the *élevage*, the level of toasting, the proportion of new wood, and the timing of the blending process. There are no formulae. Mireille Daret at the perfectionist Cru Barréjats favours a very long *élevage* on the grounds that she can minimize filtration before bottling and avoid sterile filtration.

Winemakers need to be vigilant. Just as there is a risk during fermentation of high volatile acidity, so there is a possibility during the *élevage* that the wine will end up with too much sulphur dioxide. It is impossible to eliminate its use in sweet wine production, since it keeps bacterial infection at bay and prevents the reactivation of any dormant yeast cells. But an excess of SO_2 can be unpleasant to the wine drinker, and none too good for our health either. Fortunately in recent decades winemakers have found ways to reduce total sulphur levels, often in response to regulations imposed by importing countries such as Japan.

In the 1980s two Bordeaux professors invented a process called cryo-extraction. It is essentially a chamber that can be installed in the corner of a winery; the interior can be chilled to as low as -5°C (23°F). Some chambers are portable and can be moved according to demand from estate to estate. The theory is that chilling the grapes is an effective way to avoid dilution in vintages that are marred by rain. Rainwater can ascend through the roots into the vines and the berries. Chilling allows the water content, and the water content alone, to turn into ice. After about twenty-four hours the fruit is removed from the chamber and pressed. The moisture content, now frozen, is compacted and can be removed, while the sugar-rich juice, unaffected by the freezing process, emerges in the usual way and can be fermented. Juice from botrytized grapes has a lower freezing point than water, which allows the frozen water to be separated. The result is a more concentrated must.

Cryo-extraction proved very controversial. Alexandre de Lur-Saluces was shaken by articles claiming that his purchase of a cold chamber would lead to a change of style at Yquem, which would henceforth resemble German icewine. This was nonsense, but it did some short-term damage. Those using cryo-extraction pointed out that although the chamber did increase the must weight (potential alcohol) of the fruit by eliminating mere water content, there was also a consequent loss of volume. (Some estates got round this problem by picking *pourri plein* bunches at fourteen to fifteen degrees and then using cryo-extraction to concentrate to twenty degrees. That indeed smacks of excessive manipulation.) If there were not a high proportion of botrytized juice in the chilled fruit, the amount of juice after pressing would be negligible. Cryo-extraction did not absolve properties from obtaining good-quality botrytized bunches in the first place. The best that cryo-extraction can do is restore the original potential of rain-tampered fruit; it cannot improve on it. If there is any black rot on the grapes, its unpleasant aromas and flavours will be highlighted by chilling; thus the technique can only be used when the fruit is essentially healthy.

Today cold chambers are hardly ever used, and properties such as Rayne-Vigneau, which do sometimes employ them, insist that the resulting wine is destined for the second wine. They see it as no more than a way to recover a part of the crop that might otherwise be lost to dilution. Charles Chevallier at Rieussec told me in 2000 that the estate had last used its cold chamber in 1995, and then only for the second wine: "If the weather is bad and cryo seems like the solution, then the chances are that the botrytis won't be of good quality." One proprietor told me he found his cold chamber very useful for chilling beer when he was giving parties.

THE CLASSIFICATION

That Sauternes was included in the 1855 classification is a reminder of how highly regarded these wines had become by the mid-nineteenth century. Elsewhere in the Graves, only Haut-Brion was considered worthy of classification. An unusual feature of the Sauternes section was that one property, Yquem, was given a class of its own: *premier grand cru*, a cut above mere *premier cru*.

The 1855 classification is no longer entirely valid. For example, Château Rabeaud has now been divided into two properties, and Château Doisy into three, and Château Pexoto (a Second Growth) has been absorbed by Château Rabaud-Promis. But the original *classement* (*see* Appendix) remains essentially intact.

Back in the 1970s the wisdom and accuracy of the classification seemed questionable. First Growths such as La Tour Blanche were making awful wine. From 1983 onwards, when the fortunes of Sauternes revived, it became clear that the reason for that had nothing to do with the potential of the vineyards, but had everything to do with short cuts taken in the vineyard and winery. Recent vintages demonstrate that all the classified estates have the potential to make excellent wine, and most of them do. The brokers of 150 years ago knew whereof they spoke.

THE IMAGE OF SAUTERNES

When I wander into the Maison de Barsac or any other institution with a good stock of Sauternes on sale, I leave feeling depressed. These wines have an extraordinary history. I refer not to the history of the region or the style but the individual story each wine has to tell: of perfectionism and financial sacrifice, of pathetically low yields, of the vagaries of the autumnal climate, of the capricious behaviour of *Botrytis cinerea*, of the surgical skills of the harvesters, of the two-month watch on the weather so as to know when to pick and when to desist. And all this results in a wine that costs no more than a good *cru bourgeois* or a lesser classified growth. True, a series of excellent vintages – 1997, 2001, and 2005 – has boosted the market, but Sauternes remains a lamentably underappreciated.

To some extent this is the fault of the Sauternais themselves, who do not work well together, who have little conception of the notion of marketing (the Austrians, whose sweet wine industry was destroyed by scandal in 1985, have shown themselves capable of phoenix-like revival), and who see themselves as victims of indifferent négociants. Yet few châteaux welcome visitors or show any interest in communicating with consumers.

It also has to do with patterns of consumption. When does one drink Sauternes? As an apéritif, say some. But only a wine from a lighter year, an 1987 or perhaps a 2002, is suitable, since a Sauternes from a great vintage is simply too rich to whet the appetite. With foie gras, say others, but how often do we eat foie gras? And when we do there are other contenders to fill the wine glass: Bonnezeaux, Tokaji, Jurançon, and countless others. Ditto Roquefort. It is undeniable that in recent years the average level of residual sugar has been increasing, and wines with 120 or 130 grams are by no means unusual. Such sweetness in a wine makes it even more difficult to match with food, and confirms Sauternes' role as a wine to be consumed with a fruit dessert or on its own after a meal. In the past a Sauternes with eighty grams of sugar might have been a good pairing with foie gras; that is less likely to be the case with a wine with 120 grams. François Amirault of Château de Fargues has given me the following figures for residual sugar in his wines: 125 grams in 2002, 132 in 2003, and 129 in 2004. This is not by choice, as he strives to keep sugars at a moderate level to balance a typical alcoholic degree of 13.8 to 14.1 degrees. Pierre Meslier of Raymond-Lafon believes higher residual sugar levels are the consequence of less chaptalization. Amirault adds that wines with very high sugars tend to attract the highest scores from wine critics, especially, I expect, from those with no historical grasp of the authentic style of Sauternes.

It is also unfortunate, but usually unavoidable, that the great vintages for Sauternes are often poor vintages for claret. Thus 1997, 1999, and 2001 were all excellent for Sauternes, less so for Médoc. This means négociants cannot sell Sauternes on the coat-tails of the sought-after red wines. In 1999, Sauternes producers were obliged to reduce their *prix de sortie*, despite the excellence of the wine, simply because red wine estates had been forced by an unexceptional vintage to bring prices down, and the négociants would not tolerate a different approach from the Sauternais. Unlike red wines, there is, Yquem apart, little speculation in Sauternes; this diminishes the importance of the futures market. One Second-Growth proprietor told me in June 2005 that he had not sold a single case of his 2004, admittedly a difficult vintage, *en primeur*.

Yet the fact remains that Sauternes is one of the great wines of the world, a complex confection of fruit, acidity, and alcohol that gives pleasure at all stages of its very long life. It is a wine that wins lip service from its numerous admirers, but how often is it consumed? Alexandre de Lur-Saluces used to worry, with good reason, that Yquem had become a kind of national monument, but was hardly ever drunk. Sauternes is a luxury product that with a few exceptions – Yquem, Fargues, Climens – is sold at or below cost. Châteaux proprietors tend to be the local aristocracy – as at de Malle, Myrat, Sigalas-Rabaud, or Filhot – or rich corporations – Suduiraut, Lafaurie-Peyraguey, Bastor-Lamontagne, Yquem – or those who have had the good fortune to inherit a property but are not solely dependent on its revenues for their income. As Henri Dubosq of Haut-Marbuzet in St-Estèphe once remarked to me: "Sauternes is the preserve of the very rich. They have to make a choice: they can either have a chorus girl as a mistress or they can have a property in Sauternes."

Sauternes also suffers from the overall denigration of sweet wine as a wine style, and from the proliferation of poorly made examples. Michel Garat, who directs Bastor-Lamontagne, once remarked to me that quality-conscious estates rightly sold off their lesser wines in bulk in order to maintain the standards of their *grand vin*. Unfortunately those lesser lots, which in poor vintages such as 1993 can be truly horrible, usually end up in negociants' blends which in turn furnish supermarket shelves at risibly low prices. It is hardly surprising that the consumer, purchasing one of these rock-bottom Sauternes and tasting it, decides that in future he or she will give Sauternes a miss. One of the more alarming Bordeaux statistics is that forty-seven per cent of the production of Sauternes is sold in bulk.

Similarly, some less-well-known estates simply cannot afford to take the pains necessary to ensure the production of a memorable Sauternes. There are still many properties where the yield is the maximum, where only lip service is paid to the notion of *tries successives*, where chaptalization is routine, where new oak barrels are unknown. Perhaps in 2001 it was possible to make acceptable wine by such methods, but that would be very much the exception. No doubt there is a market for these pallid but inexpensive sweet wines, but they do the image of Sauternes no favours.

Bérénice Lurton, the owner of Climens, decided some years ago to go for broke: to continue to make the wine with the most exacting care, but also to raise its price to a level that reflected the costs of production. I had some personal regrets about this policy, since it meant I could no longer afford to buy this wonderful wine, but I have no doubt that she made the right decision. The words "Sauternes" and "bargain" cannot belong in the same sentence.

In the château profiles that follow in the next chapter, please note that production figures express an average. There are certain vintages, such as 2000, when only a small crop can be harvested and production is far lower than the average.

29. Sauternes Part I

Château d'Arche

*Sauternes. Tel: 0556 766655. Website: www.chateaudarche-sauternes.com. **Owners:** private investors. Deuxième cru.*
*27 ha. 90% Sémillon, 10% Sauvignon Blanc. **Production:** 80,000 bottles. **Second wine:** Prieuré d'Arche*

This finely located estate, one of the highest in Sauternes, was bought by the president of the Bordeaux *parlement*, the Comte d'Arche, in 1727. The property was sold during the Revolution and subsequently broken up. The history of the property in the nineteenth and early twentieth centuries is extremely complex, and readers thirsty for more detailed knowledge should refer to Number 93 of *The Vine* by Clive Coates MW. By 1925 it belonged to a politician called Armand Bastit-St-Martin, who began reconstituting the property's historic vineyards. In 1981, shortly before his death in 1983, Bastit-St-Martin leased the property to Pierre Perromat, a former chairman of INAO. The property remained in the hands of the Bastit-Martin family until 1996, when they sold it to an Irish family. In 2002 part of the château was converted into a small luxury hotel. By 2003 Perromat had turned over management of the property to his son-in-law, Jérôme Cosson. Two years later the estate was in the hands of private investors from Europe and the United States.

When I first visited Arche in the mid-1980s I found Pierre Perromat's enthusiasm infectious. He demanded as many as ten *tries* in certain vintages; often the harvest took six weeks to complete. Later visits were less felicitous, either because I found myself in the hands of an indifferent cellarmaster, or because Perromat failed to keep his appointment with me. The current management team is, fortunately, more helpful.

The soil is quite gravelly, and the subsoil gravelly clay, as is common in Sauternes. Cosson tells me the vineyards were rather neglected until 1996, when new drainage was installed and some parcels replanted. Cosson is no fan of cryo-extraction, which had been used in the early 1990s, but sometimes chills bunches under dry ice, easing the pressure on his team to process the grapes the moment they arrive. Vertical presses are used. There was a period when one-third of the wine remained in tanks, but today the entire crop is barrel-fermented with selected yeasts and aged in one-third new oak for twelve to eighteen months. There is also a special *cuvée* of 3,000 bottles called d'Arche-Lafaurie, which is aged for twenty-four months in 100 per cent new oak.

The oldest Arche I have encountered is from 1936, a poor vintage. At fifty years old its aromas showed some oxidation and it was evidently beginning to dry out on the palate; yet some sweetness and richness lingered on, and the length was impressive. The 1982 had fruity, lanolin aromas, but was rather hot and sulphury, and the fifteen degrees of alcohol were all too evident. I bought the 1983 and have drunk it over a decade, always with pleasure. It had rich apricot aromas, a creamy texture, flavours of apricot and pineapple, moderate acidity, and a clean, precise finish. I tasted the 1986 only once, and in its youth, and found the rich fruit was followed by a bitter, sulphury tone.

The 1988 is disappointing, with no botrytis aromas, and although fairly soft and rich on the palate, it was hard-edged and awkward. The 1989 was very different, a wine of considerable power, with a lush fruitiness; yet it lacked some intensity and had a rather dour, oaky finish. The 1990 was also rich and powerful on the nose, and the palate was juicy and peachy yet spicy too, with a lively aftertaste. The 1995 was quite stylish, with pleasant apricot aromas and flavours, but it lacked concentration and complexity. Rather odd aromas of lemon, tinned pineapple, and furniture wax marked the 1996, but the palate was more engaging, with a creamy texture, reasonable concentration, and decent length. I prefer the peachy 1998, despite a certain slackness on the palate.

There is a full-throttled character to the 1999, a wine with weight rather than finesse. Even finer is the 2001, which is very rich, creamy, and full-bodied yet intrinsically fresh for all its apricotty opulence. I'm not convinced that the d'Arche-Lafaurie of the same year, although richer, is superior. The 2002 is very sweet, with intense apricot aromas, a silky texture, but little complexity or depth. The 2003 is rich but hollow; it lacks length. The 2004 is excellent, with a good deal of oak and power on the nose, but with a good attack and some welcome raciness, and quince and apricot flavours.

Château d'Armajan d'Ormes

Preignac. Tel: 0556 635821. Owner: Jacques Perromat. 15 ha. 70% Sémillon, 25% Sauvignon Blanc, 5% Muscadelle.
Production: 25,000 bottles. Second wine: Ch des Ormes

The Armajan family owned this fine property until the Revolution. In the early twentieth century the property became neglected and dwindled in size. It was acquired by cousins of the present owners and renamed. In 1953 Michel Perromat took over the property. After the frost of 1956 the entire vineyard was replanted. Today the property is owned by Perromat's son Jacques, who also owns Beauregard-Ducasse (*q.v.*) in the Graves.

Michel Perromat (the brother of Jean and Pierre, both big players in this corner of Bordeaux) believed in routine chaptalization, as he liked a wine with around fifteen degrees of alcohol. Under Jacques Perromat this remains a wine with quite high alcohol. The must was usually fermented in tanks, though in exceptional vintages the best lots were barrel-fermented and released as a Crème de Tête, a wine I have never encountered. The regular wine is aged half in barrels, of which a third are new, and half in tanks.

My knowledge of this wine is limited. The 1986 was lean and elegant rather than concentrated, but the fruit and style were attractive. The 1990 was fat but lacked finesse. The 1995 had peachy but elegant aromas; it was soft and rich, moderately concentrated, yet had curiously high acidity. There were aromas of stewed apricots on the 1996, but the palate is much fresher and livelier, though marred by a slightly hot finish. The 2002, 2003, and 2004 show sweet apricot fruit; they are balanced but not very exciting.

Cru Barréjats

Barsac. Tel: 0680 603195. Website: www.cru-barrejats.com. Owner: Mireille Daret. 5 ha. 85% Sémillon,
10% Sauvignon Blanc, 5% Muscadelle. Production: 8,000 bottles. Second wine: Accabailles de Barréjats

Dr. Mireille Daret comes from a family deeply embedded in the region. She inherited a small parcel of vines between Climens and Caillou, although the crop was sold in bulk. In 1990 she went into partnership with another local doctor, Philippe Andurand; they bought more vines to form this small but ambitious property. Now there are additional parcels near Myrat and Coutet, all on the Haut-Barsac plateau.

Mireille Daret is a woman with strong ideas. Severe pruning keeps yields to around twelve hectolitres per hectare, but she is not keen on removing leaves; however, she manually removes any superfluous shoots since they needlessly consume sugar. The rows are ploughed and no herbicides are used. Harvesting is meticulous and the grapes are pressed in a vertical press, settled under dry ice, and then decanted into new barrels. There is no chaptalization, no acidification. There are some vintages such as 2004 when she reduces the proportion of new wood to fifty per cent, but she would rather use all new oak. She also believes in long ageing, usually three years, which allows her to minimize filtration. She adapts vinification to the quality of each vintage. Thus in 2000, a low-acidity year, she shortened the *élevage*. In 2003, she added *verjus* berries to the press, as she needed more acidity from those green berries in the final wine.

Barréjats is expensive, but it is truly hand-crafted. Whenever I taste it in a blind tasting, I score it as highly as many a First Growth. The first vintage, the 1990, lacked some complexity, but was still an elegant wine with fresh, lemony acidity and good length. The 1991, soon after bottling, was elegant but very oaky, but there was great intensity on the palate. The 1992, tasted in 2006, was holding up well, especially given the mediocrity of the vintage: the nose was waxy and oaky, the palate rich and plump with reasonable concentration and fair acidity. The 1995 has tangy citric aromas; it's light and fresh with an attractive piquant finish. The 1998 is disappointing.

The 2001 is magnificent, powerful and sumptuous on the nose, while the palate is very rich and forceful, packed with peachy fruit yet also showing tangy acidity; the long finish is orangey with a peppery tone. The 2002 is opulent, but needs time for the oaky aromas to integrate; there are flavours of Seville orange and apricot, a creamy texture, a firm, acidic backbone, and fine length. Orangey tones emerge again on the nose of the 2003 and 2004, as well as some tropical fruit; in 2004, high acidity gives a bracing sherbetty tone.

Château Bastor-Lamontagne

*Preignac. Tel: 0556 632766. Website: www.bastor-lamontagne.com. **Owner:** Crédit Foncier. 56 ha. 80% Sémillon, 20% Sauvignon Blanc. **Production:** 150,000 bottles. **Second wine:** Remparts de Bastor*

During the Middle Ages this property belonged first to the English Crown, and then after 1453 to the French Crown. It was bought by a Bordeaux *parlementaire*, Vincent de la Montagne, and then passed through various hands. In 1936 it was bought by the Crédit Foncier bank, which also owns Beauregard (*q.v.*) in Pomerol and other Bordeaux estates. Since 1987 it has been managed by Michel Garat. The château is alongside the road that runs from Preignac to Suduiraut. Most of the vineyards surround the buildings on sandy, stony soil. This is not a sector with a high clay content, so Bastor is never one of Preignac's most powerful wines.

It has always been Garat's policy to produce a well-made Sauternes with typicity but at a reasonable price. It succeeds very well. Yields are relatively high, and the vineyard managers are happy with clusters that will give a must weight of twenty degrees of alcohol, even if not all the berries are fully botrytized. Nevertheless improvements in quality are being made all the time. Fermentation takes place with natural yeasts; the old horizontal press has been replaced with a gentler, pneumatic model. The proportion of must that is barrel-fermented has been gradually increasing and now stands at around seventy-five per cent. The wine is aged in ten to twenty per cent new barriques and bottled after about fifteen months. Although Bastor is equipped with a cold chamber, it is never used for the *grand vin*. It says much for the commitment to quality here that no *grand vin* was produced in 1991, 1992, or 1993.

In 2000 Garat began producing a special *cuvée* called Cru Bordenave, replacing a defunct Crème de Tête bottling. Bordenave comes from a 2.5-hectare parcel on gravel and clay soils near Preignac. Once leased by the estate, it has now been bought. The must is fermented in new oak, and aged for twenty months. In 2004 he also introduced a lighter style of Sauternes called Caprice; the grapes are mostly botrytized but they are picked fairly early and aged only in tanks, the idea being to produce a refreshing apéritif style.

I often drank the 1981, and the wine was always sound, if not very botrytized. At last tasting, the plump Sémillon fruit was to the fore on the nose, while the palate was soft, moderately rich, stylish and fruity, but lacking in depth. The 1982 was quite lemony and vigorous in the late 1980s but I have not tasted it since. The 1983 had elegant, citric aromas, and there was good fruit on the silky palate; although the wine lacked intensity overall, it was clean and stylish. The 1984 was forgettable. I never much cared for the 1986, which had some weight of fruit but lacked verve and distinction.

There were dried-apricot aromas on the 1988; it had a sprightly character and dried-fruits flavours; not complex but very attractive. The 1989 is still impressive: fat, peachy, and lush on the nose, broad and unctuous yet far from heavy. The 1989 Crème de Tête, of which only 500 bottles were made, was very rich, unctuous and honeyed, with dried-apricot flavours, and impeccable concentration and balance. The 1990, also last tasted in 2003, had delightful aromas of peach and mango; it remains rich but has become slightly slack; the 1989 has lasted better.

Although the vintages of the early 1990s were released under the Remparts label, there is no point pretending they were particularly good wines. Bastor was back on form with the splendid 1997, with its peach-compote aromas, its concentration and juiciness, and its upfront fruitiness. The 1998 seems leaner, but none the worse for that, since it gained in liveliness, freshness, and finesse. The 1999 has rich apricot aromas, and is reasonably rich and concentrated, but there's not much complexity here. The 2000 is rather muted; the fruit is fairly rich but it's not an arresting wine. This was the first year when Cru Bordenave was made: it is richer and more peachy, but it didn't really stand out as exceptional, not surprisingly when one recalls the sodden harvest.

The 2001 is an outstanding Bastor. The aromas, initially citric, are now more infused with stone fruits; the palate is supple, even svelte, rich without being too unctuous, and there is a welcome spiciness on the long aftertaste. The Cru Bordenave does not strike me as significantly better, though it too is very good. There is less concentration in the 2002 Bastor, but there are zesty pineapple and citrus aromas, a fine texture, some tropical fruit flavours, and fair acidity and length.

In 2003 Garat fermented some of the Sauvignon in tanks to preserve freshness, and he also reduced the oak-ageing as the pH was high and he feared premature oxidation. The wine is decent: supple, quite concentrated, with fair acidity, and reasonably stylish; but not a patch on the 2001. The 2004 is fairly simple and lacks some unctuousness. The 2005 is melony and refined.

Overall, Bastor-Lamontagne can hold its own with many a Second Growth. It is a commercial style of Sauternes, but not a cynical one. It is well made and in top vintages rises to some heights. And it is invariably good value.

Château Broustet

Barsac. Tel: 0556 271687. Owner: Didier Laulan. Deuxième cru. 16.5 ha. 80% Sémillon, 16% Sauvignon Blanc, 4% Muscadelle. Production: 45,000 bottles. Second wine: Les Charmes de Ch Broustet

Broustet has had something of a struggle to maintain its identity. In the mid-nineteenth century it formed part of Nairac, and though it later won its independence it found itself under the same ownership as Château de Myrat. From the late nineteenth century it was owned by the Fournier family, who also owned Château Canon in St-Emilion. Family squabbles led to both properties being put on the market in the early 1990s. Broustet was bought by Didier Laulan, the owner of Château de St-Marc.

One peculiarity at Broustet was the high proportion of Muscadelle in the vineyards, but that proportion has diminished over the years. The vineyards are in a single parcel around the unremarkable estate buildings. The soils vary: toward the railway line there is gravel and sand; elsewhere it is a more classic Barsac soil of clay over limestone. The average yields are fairly high at around twenty-two hl/ha.

Eric Fournier often chaptalized, and Laulan has done the same in years such as 2002 and 2004. There is no acidification, and in a low-acidity year such as 2003, Laulan prepares a tank of wine made from green berries and then sees whether it improves the wine to blend a little in. The juice is fermented in steel tanks, and is aged for twelve months in one-third new barriques and then for a further twelve months in tanks. Eric Fournier liked a lot of alcohol in his wine – up to fifteen degrees – but Laulan likes to keep it under fourteen.

The oldest Broustet I have tasted is from 1980; it was rather lame, easy-going, waxy, and sulphury. The 1981 was hard and aggressive by 1986 but I have not tasted it since. I disliked the flabby, waxy 1982, a wine with no finesse and little length. The 1986 also had a lot of sulphur, and aromas of peaches and wet wool; it was an abrasive wine with some richness but no charm. The 1988 had burly aromas of apricots, oranges, and lanolin; it was a gawky, earthbound wine, creamy in texture but lacking in zest.

If the high alcohol showed on the 1988, it showed even more in 1989, when it was 14.8 degrees. It was rich wine, but there was something leaden about it, with the balance favouring alcohol and power rather than luscious fruit. The 1990 was much the same, a discreet and rather dull wine that finished with a whack of alcohol (15.5 degrees).

Laulan made a decent Broustet in 1994; it had some opulence and quite good acidity, though it was far from elegant. The 1995 was better: quite rich and plump, overtly fruity, with reasonable concentration and acidity. The 1996 was the best Broustet for many years, quite powerful, sumptuous and spicy but with ample acidity and a long, honeyed finish. The 1997 was surprisingly lean, though vigorous, but inexpressive in its youth. There is real complexity on the 2001: peaches and cream and a touch of tar on the nose; the palate is creamy and lush, with a welcome tang of sherbet on the aftertaste. The 2002 is very citric, with marked acidity and less flesh than the 2001; but it's an attractive wine. The 2003 has shed its youthful puppy fat. It has oaky, mandarin aromas, a supple texture, forward fruit, but little complexity. Laulan was unhappy with his 2004, which he decided not to release. The 2005 was very promising in 2006, with delicious fruit, but it's early days.

It must be clear by now that I did not care for the wines during the Fournier years. I found them clumsy and overbearing. Laulan shows a lighter touch, and recent vintages have been good, yet it still seems that the wine could, potentially, be even better if it had more concentration and subtlety.

Château Caillou

Barsac. Tel: 0556 271638. Website: www.chateaucaillou.com. **Owner:** *Marie-Josée Pierre. Deuxième cru. 13 ha.*

90% Sémillon, 10% Sauvignon Blanc. **Production:** *25,000 bottles.* **Second wine:** *Les Erables de Caillou*

Caillou makes me laugh: not the wine, but the Toytown château, which could be a first draft for a Disneyworld version of a French château, with its slender turrets and its grandiose clock on the façade. It was bought in 1909 by Joseph Ballan, from whom the present owner is descended. Apparently the vineyard has not altered since 1855, though other accounts suggest it was much expanded by the Ballans. In the 1980s Caillou was run by the personable Jean-Bernard Bravo. He co-owned the property with his sister Marie-Josée, and the two clearly did not get on. Eventually there was a parting of the ways, and Jean-Bernard left the estate in 1997 and has been written out of the château's website. I last saw him in 2005 on keyboard in a jazz band at a party in Margaux.

The vines are planted on a plateau of clay-limestone over a subsoil rich in boulders. The average age of the vines is twenty-five years. The grapes are pressed in a pneumatic press and fermented partially in steel tanks and partially in new oak; the wine is aged in sixty per cent new barriques for twelve to eighteen months.

There are numerous *cuvées* at Caillou, and as they keep changing names, followers of the wine are kept in a state of confusion. Until twenty-five years ago the most botrytized grapes were vinified separately and produced as a Crème de Tête, the wine for which Caillou was best known. In 1982 the name was changed to Private Cuvée, and the wine was aged for up to three years in oak. In 2002 the name was changed again to Cuvée Prestige. In this version the wine was made from vines over fifty years old, and aged for eighteen months in new oak.

In 1990 the Bravos introduced Cuvée Reine, which is also fermented and aged for eighteen months in new oak. It is not made every year, and since 1990 has been produced only in 1996, 1997, 1999, 2001, and 2003. Only 600 bottles are released, and at a very high price (115 Euros in 2005).

The oldest Caillou I have tasted is the 1943 Crème de Tête, which in the 1980s had a healthy colour and an attractive marmalade nose; it was intense and extremely sweet but lacked depth and length. The 1947 Crème de Tête was also bright in colour but caramelly on the nose; however, the attack was fresh and the wine intense, with flavours of barley sugar and oranges. The wine overall struck me as good rather than great. The 1975 Crème de Tête in 1986 was quite volatile, bland, and alcoholic. Another bottle in 1994 was fresher, with some aromatic charm, and a fresh, spicy palate and long, citric finish.

The 1973 Caillou was showing signs of oxidation and caramel flavours by 1986; perhaps a poor bottle. I have come across the 1976 Sélection de Grains Nobles, though precisely what *cuvée* this label represented I have no idea. Presumably it is a cut above the regular bottling. Nonetheless it lacked fruit and richness and showed a lot of alcohol and oiliness.

There were aromas of lanolin on the rather drab 1979, a soft, hollow wine with modest length. No Caillou was bottled in 1980. The 1983 was lean and citric, and lacked weight and complexity. The 1986 had some charm but tasted dilute and thin. I preferred the superficial but pretty 1987, with its delicate apricot aromas and its light, silky texture. The 1988 was quite good, with some spice and aromas of ripe lemon; the texture was creamy and there was no lack of upfront fruit, and though it was light, it was well balanced.

I have never been impressed by the 1989; despite some power and lushness, it is quite aggressive with a rather coarse, almost meaty character; acidity carries the wine through to a reasonably long finish. The 1990 is far more stylish, with plump apricot flavours, a dried-fruits character, and good length. The 1990 Private Cuvée was richer, oilier, fatter, but also somewhat heavy and lumpish. The 1991 Caillou is pleasant but unmemorable. There was an oaky Cuvée Speciale (perhaps an inaccurately transcribed version of the Private Cuvée in my notebook) in 1991 (1,000 bottles) that was more interesting, with a creamier texture and more elegance. The 1992 Caillou was good for the vintage, with apricot aromas and a lean, spicy, vigorous character. No Caillou was made in 1993, and 1994 was a tiny crop as a consequence of severe frost damage.

The 1995 had fresh, lemony aromas, but was plump and rather dilute, and lacked personality. There were dried-apricot aromas on the 1996, but the wine, though silky, lacked concentration and grip, and its candied finish was a touch cloying. The 1999 is a good if atypical Caillou, with its plump, peachy aromas and its lushness on the palate. Liveliness characterizes the 2001, which had attractive lemon and mandarin aromas, and reasonable concentration, spiciness, and length. The racier 2002 vintage suits the Caillou style well. There are waxy apricot aromas, lemon and apricot flavours, good acidity, and a gently candied finish.

The 2003 has orange and peach aromas, a rather sticky texture, and an overall heaviness. I tasted the 2003 Prestige from cask: it had a more intense peachiness, but a similar flavour profile, and despite more evident acidity than the regular Caillou, it still lacked freshness. I also tasted 2003 Cuvée Reine from cask, and found it similar to the Prestige, though creamier and more honeyed and with flavours of caramelized oranges. The 2004 Caillou is one-dimensional, but has appealing apricot and quince flavours. The 2005, tasted blind from cask, seemed promising.

I don't quite know what to make of Caillou. It is rarely great, and seems at its best when not trying too hard. The regular wine in a good year often seems as enjoyable as the more effortful prestige *cuvées*. Caillou just seems too inconsistent to recommend on a regular basis. There are other properties in this category that offer wines with more personality and dependability.

Château Cantegril

Barsac. Tel: 0556 629651. Website: www.denisdubourdieu.com. Owner: Denis Dubourdieu. 18 ha. 80% Sémillon, 20% Sauvignon Blanc. Production: 50,000 bottles

Cantegril has a long and noble history, having belonged at one time to the Duc d'Epernon, then to the *seigneurs* of Cantegril, one of whom married into the Myrat family and built Château de Myrat. The castle that stood at Cantegril was destroyed in the eighteenth century and replaced by a tall, handsome house in the mid-nineteenth century. In 1854 Cantegril was separated from Myrat and bought by M. Ségur-Montagne, but then changed hands many times. When Pierre Dubourdieu, the father of Denis, ran the property, he picked the grapes fairly early to be sure of a reliable crop (at Doisy-Daëne he was prepared to take more risks) and there was no barrique-ageing until 1988. Today the wine is aged in twenty-five per cent new oak.

Cantegril made a very good wine in 1981, with excellent fruit balanced by good acidity. The 1982 had rather herbaceous aromas, was straightforwardly sweet but also well balanced and clean. The 1983 was citric in its aromas but simple and shallow on the palate. The 2002 has charming apricot and honey aromas; it's a sleek, medium-bodied wine with more charm than depth, but then Cantegril has no pretensions to profundity. The light but elegant 2004 has muted aromas and a certain fluidity on the palate, but lacks body.

Château de Carles

Barsac. Tel: 0556 629651. Website: www.denisdubourdieu.com. Owner: Denis Dubourdieu. 3.5 ha. 80% Sémillon, 20% Sauvignon Blanc. Production: 12,000 bottles

These vineyards are located on a (relatively) high part of the Haut-Barsac plateau between Climens and Gravas. It's an ancient property, and in 1855 belonged to the manager of Château de Myrat, and he apparently blended its wine into Myrat. In 1906 the estate was bought by Fernand Barbe, and it was acquired by Denis Dubourdieu in 2004. The wine is barrique-fermented and aged in twenty-five per cent new oak. The 2004 has appealing aromas of apricot and orange peel; the wine is rich and silky, with a delicate but lively finish.

Château Climens

*Barsac. Tel: 0556 271533. Website: www.chateau-climens.fr. **Owner:** Bérénice Lurton. Premier cru.*

*30 ha. 100% Sémillon. **Production:** 30,000 bottles. **Second wine:** Cyprès de Climens*

The early history of this great property is murky. The historian Henri Enjalbert writes of a mid-fifteenth-century English owner with the unlikely name of Climens. According to the present owner, however, the name Climens is first documented in 1547, when Jacques Roborel bought a grassland property called Climens. Vines were apparently planted from about 1640 onwards. It remained in the Roborel family until 1802, when it was sold to wine merchant Jean Binaud. It was sold again in 1850 and 1871. Then in 1885 Henri Gounouilhou, the owner of Doisy-Dubroca, bought Climens, and it remained in his family until in 1971 it was bought by Lucien Lurton. For a while it was run by his son Louis, and then by his daughter Brigitte. Apparently her relations with her father were far from ideal and she clashed with the Climens guardian, a hereditary post then occupied by a battleaxe called Mme. Janin. About twenty years ago Brigitte Lurton arranged for me to taste some vintages of Climens at the property (she herself being based at Château Bouscaut), but Mme. Janin denied all knowledge of the appointment and chased me away. Fortunately the old lady is no longer manning the gates.

In 1992 Lucien Lurton handed out his numerous estates to his numerous children, and the young Bérénice Lurton took over at Climens. Despite her inexperience, she learned fast and rapidly confirmed its status as the best property in the Sauternais after the untouchable Yquem. She worked for many years with the *maître de chai*, the late Christian Broustaud, who had arrived in 1969 and was to retire in 2003. His successor, Frédéric Nivelle, had come to Climens in 1998, so knew the property well when he took over.

There are thirty hectares of vines around the château, most of them between the house and the motorway on the well-drained Haut-Barsac plateau. The soil is red sand and gravel soil over limestone. The average yield over a decade is thirteen hl/ha and, after selection and blending, the average yield for the *grand vin* is seven hl/ha. Only the first two pressings are used for Climens, and each day's crop forms a separate lot, so there can be as many as twenty-five lots. All the wine is fermented with indigenous yeasts in barriques, of which up to forty-five per cent are new. There is no temperature control, but the simple expedient of opening the windows adequately chills the *chai* at night, should that be necessary. The wine is bottled about two years after the harvest.

Because the wine is blended late, a cask tasting at Climens is a prolonged and challenging experience, but one that is always fascinating. Richness is not the sole criterion for inclusion in the *grand vin*; instead Bérénice Lurton looks for "*éclat et élan*". "Climens never shows well when it is very young. It can seem gawky. It always has fine acidity, but the fruit is never explosive. It needs time." It is true that Climens can be deceptive. It's a Barsac, so it's not as powerful or heavy as a Sauternes. But it ages superbly, and even in mediocre years Climens almost always produces a worthwhile wine.

The oldest vintage I have tasted is from 1918. It was a medium brown, and had a caramelized orange nose; on the palate it was rather light and faded fast, though a second bottle was sweeter and richer. The 1924 was as dark as oloroso sherry; there were fruit-cake aromas, but the palate was a revelation: elegant, spicy, and harmonious, with lovely acidity and remarkable length. In 1993 the 1927 was still going strong, copper-gold in colour, with barley-sugar aromas, raisins and citrus on the palate, but it was just beginning to crack up. The 1928 and 1929 are said to be extraordinary, but I have never tasted them. The 1937 Crème de Tête was copper-gold, and had rich aromas of caramel, banana, stewed peach, and grilled nuts. Although quite rich, it was losing body and fruit and beginning to dry out.

I have not tasted the acclaimed wines from 1947 and 1949, but I did taste the 1959 in 1987. The nose was fat and marmaladey, while the palate was still powerful and intense, with rich fruit; it wasn't the most elegant Climens but it still had good length. I have had better bottles of the 1962, a wonderful wine with toasty botrytis aromas with a twist of lemon, while the palate was sumptuous, creamy, lightly peachy, perfectly bright and fresh, and remarkably long. The 1964 was lighter, and a touch soapy on the nose; by 1984 it was very soft and heading toward flabbiness. The 1966 has always had attractive lemon and barley-sugar aromas, but it disappoints on the palate, which in most bottles I have drunk has been rather bitter and astringent. The 1970, often sampled, is dull despite its acidity; there is no complexity. The 1971, tasted in 1990, is much better, with developed botrytis aromas, a good deal of ripeness and richness, with ample apricot fruit and good length.

The 1972 vintage was poor, but Climens made a decent wine, with stylish aromas though not much botrytis; the creamy palate is a touch flabby. The 1973 has some richness, spiciness, and persistence, a good result for a modest year. I drank the 1974, a vintage many estates chose not to bottle, in 1990 and noted "alive but not going anywhere". But it was still alive in 2001, sweet and supple, but lacking some personality. In 1975 Climens made a great wine. By 2003 it had developed gorgeous aromas of peach and *crème brûlée*; the palate was rich, creamy, and concentrated, and had extraordinary length.

I have always adored the 1976. Many wines from this super-rich vintage are overblown, but not Climens, which is certainly fat and rich but also has enlivening acidity and wonderful elegance. This wine never flags and always surprises with its beauty. Not for the only time, Climens made a fine wine in an abominable year: the 1977, at thirty years old, had honeyed, peachy aromas, moderate weight, and considerable freshness, if little complexity. The 1978, tasted twice in 2000, has developed surprisingly well, given the modesty of the vintage. It has dried-apricot aromas with a slight toastiness; it's soft and full-bodied, with moderate acidity but very much alive. The 1979 took many years to develop its personality. Today it has waxy, honeyed aromas, moderate sweetness and concentration, and some weight and length. The 1980 is even better, with stone fruits on the nose; it's delicious and spicy and intense, with a long, citric finish. I have not tasted the 1981 since 1994, when it had fine fruit with an unusual smoky character.

The 1982 has botrytis on the nose, but the palate is underpowered and by 1999 the fruit was beginning to dry out. There is a good deal of oakiness on the 1983, but there's fine acidity and finesse, and excellent length. There is botrytis and citrus on the nose of the racy 1985; it's lightly candied and tangy, with a creamy texture and excellent length. There are stone-fruits aromas as well as citrus on the more complex 1986, a delicious wine, discreet and elegant and long. Elegance and concentration are the hallmarks of the superb 1988, with its apricot and lemon fruit, its sleek texture, its remarkable length. The finely balanced 1989 is similar but has a touch more fat, weight, and voluptuousness. The 1990 is a worthy successor, with perhaps more aromatic vibrancy, and slightly less power than the 1989; that doesn't make it inferior, however, as the balance, again, is impeccable. This magic touch extends to the superb 1991, when an early harvest became an excellent harvest (Broustaud obtained special permission from INAO to pick early). Last tasted in 2005, it shows no signs of flagging, and is still concentrated, peachy, and spicy.

This great run of vintages was halted by the 1994, which lacks succulence, is distinctly citric and spicy, and has a slightly bitter finish. The 1995 has slightly oily, oaky aromas; on the palate it is rather soft and easy-going, without the usual Climens raciness and finesse. By 2007, the 1996 had developed honeyed aromas, apricot flavours, a velvety texture, and a long, lively finish. The excellent 1997 has discreet aromas of white peaches; it's concentrated and powerful, but also elegant and complex. It still needs quite a few years to show its full potential. Bérénice Lurton believes this is the best Climens since 1990.

The 1998 is more marked by tropical fruit than usual; the palate has a burnished quality and it's slightly less concentrated than usual. But it still has the estate's typical spiciness and elegance. The nose of the 1999 is very rich, with aromas of apricot jelly and peach; it's rich, slightly phenolic, rather closed now but with a long, clean finish. The 2000 is a success for the vintage, with assertive lemony aromas, great freshness and concentration, but its discreet style suggests there is more complexity to come. The 2001 is predictably magnificent, with rich apricot aromas and flavours, a remarkable balance of extract and purity, and intense concentration. The 2002 is one of the best wines of the vintage. It suits the Climens style, which again exudes apricot fruit, purity and elegance, and very good length. The 2003 has gained in stature: predictably rich and unctuous, it also has a seductive quality and a vigour that mark it out from most wines of the vintage. The long, stylish, discreet 2004 is also a great success. The harvest in 2005 was immensely complex, but Climens produced a beautiful wine, though with very high residual sugar (148 grams per litre). It is typical of Lurton's perfectionism that by April 2007 the final blend of the 2005 had yet to be fixed. Initial impressions of the 2006 suggest a wine far above the average for the region.

Clos Dady

*Preignac. Tel: 0556 622001. Website: www.clos-dady.com. **Owners:** Christophe and Catherine Gachet.*
*6.5 ha. 90% Sémillon, 10% Sauvignon Blanc. **Production:** 20,000 bottles. **Second wine:** Ch de Bastard*

The vines belonged to the mother of Catherine Gachet, but until 1999 the wine was unremarkable. That was the year when the couple – he a dentist, she a press attaché – took over the estate. He looks after the vines, she takes care of the vinification, initially with advice from Pierre Dubourdieu. The vineyards are dispersed: there are three hectares near Château de Malle, and other parcels near Raymond-Lafon. Christophe Gachet sees this not as a complication but as a blending opportunity.

They take a rigorous approach to viticulture, aided by the vines' average age of forty-five years. Yields are very low, rarely exceeding twelve hl/ha, and the harvest usually requires between five and seven *tries*. They practise *lutte raisonnée*, but do use some herbicides beneath the rows. The grapes are pressed in a vertical press, settled overnight, and then fermented with both indigenous and selected yeasts. There is no chaptalization. They buy their barrels from Yquem, and although they are two years old, they have seen only one previous wine, and to have your barrels rinsed by Yquem can be no bad thing. However, in top years such as 2001 they also buy some new barrels. The lees are stirred, and the wine aged for at least eighteen months. There is also a prestige *cuvée* called Dolce Vita, offered at a daringly high price. Aware of the indifference of the négoce to Sauternes, the Gachets' commercial strategy is to sell their wines into top restaurants.

The wines are first-rate. The 2001 is magnificent, with powerful aromas of dried apricot, pineapple, and honey; it is very rich, creamy, and spicy, tight and stylish, with flavours reflecting the aromas, and the finish is very long. The 2002 is not far behind in quality, although the aromas are more candied and there is less sweetness; it is also less tropical, less flamboyant, but nonetheless is a very attractive wine that by no means lacks complexity. The 2003 is fresh and lively and tastes of Seville oranges. The 2004 shows aromas of apricot, mango and oak; there are stone-fruits flavours on the palate, a good deal of spice and oak, and orangey tones on the finish. When I tasted it blind alongside other 2004s, it was among the best.

Château Clos Haut-Peyraguey

*Bommes. Tel: 0556 766153. Website: www.closhautpeyraguey.com. **Owner:** Martine Langlais-Pauly. Premier cru.*
*12 ha. 90% Sémillon, 10% Sauvignon Blanc. **Production:** 25,000 bottles. **Second wine:** Ch Haut-Bommes*

This fine property once formed the upper part of Lafaurie-Peyraguey, and became separated from the mother ship in 1879. It was acquired by the Pauly family in 1914. At that time they already owned Haut-Bommes, a five-hectare property that is in effect the second wine. Jacques Pauly took over running the two estates in 1969; he retired in the early 2000s, and was succeeded by his dynamic daughter Martine.

Most of the vines are located at a height of fifty to eighty metres (164 to 262 feet) between Lafaurie-Peyraguey and Rayne-Vigneau, while another parcel adjoins Yquem. The soil is mostly sandy gravel on a clay subsoil. Neighbours tell me that these vineyards consist of one of the best terroirs in the region. The average age of the vines is thirty-five years, and their average yield eighteen hl/ha. There are usually between four and seven *tries*.

Jacques Pauly was modest and quietly spoken, never one to push the merits of his own wine. He was prepared to delay harvesting until botrytis was thoroughly installed, and he was clearly a skilled winemaker, extracting the maximum elegance from his vines. In the 1980s he fermented the wine with natural yeasts in cement tanks, but during the 1990s he vinified a growing proportion of the crop in new barriques. Chaptalization was very rare. He aged the wine for about twenty months in fifty per cent new barriques. His aim was to make wines with finesse rather than conspicuous richness.

The 1983 was shy on the nose, and had lean, appley fruit; it was elegant and attractive though light for the vintage. The 1984 was good for the year, with surprising bite and spice. The 1986 was juicy, upfront, and forward, spicy and balanced but not very complex. The 1987 was sweet and appley though simple. The 1998 has delicate apricot aromas; its elegance derives from high acidity, but it's one-dimensional and essentially an apéritif wine. The 1989 was similar, with waxy aromas with a touch of citrus and an admirable zestiness on the palate. It's balanced and has finesse, but pales beside the best wines of the vintage. The 1990 is marginally better, but has insufficient weight for a great year.

There was a slight vegetal tone on the nose of the 1991; the wine was intense but lean, with high acidity and an appealing stylishness. The 1993 was lively and citric, with no off-flavours from a mould-tainted year.

By 1996 something seems to have changed at Clos Haut-Peyraguey. It's a wine I have tasted often, usually blind, always with positive notes. There is more lushness and botrytis on the nose; the texture has more silk, the acidity is less aggressive than in earlier vintages, there is very stylish apricot fruit and excellent balance. The 1997 is similar, but I have not tasted it since 2000. The aromas were rather different in 1998, more melon and mandarins than apricot, and there was ample sweetness, spice, and vigour, with a lemony finish. The 1999 has aromas of dried apricot and citrus, great refinement on the palate, very pure apricot fruit, a light smokiness, and excellent concentration and length.

By 2001 the property had really hit its stride. This is a wonderful wine with enormous aromatic finesse; it's very sweet and creamy, citric and intense, but there's good acidity to balance the sweetness. The 2002 is admirable too. Oak seems more evident on the nose, but there are also apricot and lemon aromas; the palate is tight and silky, very fresh and delicate, with the merest hint of boiled sweets on the finish. The honeyed 2003 is broader than usual, but the wine supports the greater weight of this vintage without becoming blowsy. The 2004 is more problematic, with pear-drop aromas, some pineapple as well as citric fruit, the usual silkiness, but a lack of complexity on the finish. The 2005 has citrus and pear flavours and a long elegant finish.

Tasting and drinking this wine over two decades have been like watching a flower slowly unfurl. The elegance has always been there, but not until the 1990s did the *cru* start delivering its full potential. It has triumphantly carved out its niche as one of the most refined of Sauternes, a wine one can never accuse of heaviness or coarseness.

Château Closiot

*Barsac. Tel: 0556 270592. **Owner**: Françoise Sirot-Soizeau. 5 ha. 90% Sémillon, 7% Sauvignon Blanc, 3% Muscadelle. **Production**: 12,000 bottles*

Alban Duprat bought this property, which once formed part of the Coutet domaines, in 1934, and it passed to his son; he in turn ceded control to his daughter Françoise in 1988. Until then the wine had been sold in bulk, so she had to make substantial investments to produce and sell her own wines. She has been greatly aided by her husband Bernard Sirot, a well-known Belgian wine writer and, indeed, wine enthusiast. She also owns Château Camperos.

The vineyards are well located, neighbouring the Doisy properties and Coutet. The Sirots practise *lutte raisonnée* and much is done to encourage natural predators. The average age of the vines is forty years, and the average yield eighteen hl/ha. Both indigenous and selected yeasts are used during fermentation, which takes place in twenty per cent new medium-toast barriques, with a total *élevage* of twenty-two months.

In 1994 they created a special *cuvée* called Passion de Closiot. This uses heavily botrytized berries cropped at six hl/ha, and the wine is aged for three years in new oak. It is made only in top vintages.

The first vintage of Closiot I have tasted is the 1990, which was rather grubby – perhaps a bad bottle. The 1996 was cleaner but still modest, with lean citric aromas, pleasant but unremarkable apricot and apple fruit, some elegance, and a slightly dry finish. The 2000 is a pleasant surprise, with smoky, peachy aromas, and a broad, silky texture; all it lacks is some freshness. The 2001 is quite rich but the texture is rather thick, giving a cloying finish. I much preferred the more discreet 2002, with its citrus and apricot aromas and flavours, its liveliness and spice, its poise and length. Despite low acidity and a candied character, it is hard to resist the lush, pineappley 2003.

The 1996 Passion has a spicy nose dominated by new oak; it's sleek and silky, with pronounced oak and dried-apricot flavours, and good concentration and length. The 1999 is even better, but it's a very unctuous style with peach, orange, and passion-fruit flavours balanced by lively acidity.

Château La Clotte-Cazalis

Barsac. Tel: 0556 675427. Website: www.laclotte.com. Owner: Bernadette Lacoste. 5 ha. 95% Sémillon,
5% Sauvignon Blanc. Production: 15,000 bottles

Mme. Lacoste is married to a local doctor, whose family have owned this property since 1779. But for decades the vines were leased to other growers. Inspired by their daughter Marie-Pierre, who used to work at Guiraud, Bernadette Lacoste decided to revive La Clotte. She gave up her career as a medical assistant and took courses in oenology. Her first vintage was 2001. The wine was very well received, and she was up and running.

The vines are over fifty years old, with 1.5 hectares near Château Rolland, and the remainder on the other side of RN113, though she says the soils are very similar. She is preserving the old vines by complanting massal selections to replace individual vines that have died off. The soil is ploughed. The harvesting is meticulous, with seven to eight *tries*. Fermentation takes place in both steel tanks and barriques with indigenous yeasts; there is no chaptalization, and even in 2003 no acidification. At first she aged only half the wine in oak, but since 2004 all the wine has been barrique-aged for eighteen months.

These are delicious wines. The 2001 has aromas of candied lemons and pineapple; it's rich but airy, sleek in texture with flavours of tropical fruit, and a lively finish. It's not a profound wine but it has excellent balance. Pure pleasure. The lush 2002 is close in quality, distinctly sweet but balanced by quite good acidity, though there is an unwelcome boiled-sweets tone on the finish. The 2003 is very sweet and creamy, but it's far from heavy; there are dried-apricot flavours and a long, candied finish.

Château Coutet

Barsac. Tel: 0556 271546. Website: www.chateaucoutet.com. Owners: Philippe and Dominique Baly. Premier cru.
38 ha. 75% Sémillon, 23% Sauvignon Blanc, 2% Muscadelle. Production: 80,000 bottles.
Second wine: Chartreuse de Coutet

Although the château itself includes a thirteenth-century tower and fourteenth-century chapel, the first documentation is from the seventeenth century. A *parlementaire* called Charles de Guérin bought the estate in 1643, and in 1685 it passed to his nephew Jean de Pichard. In 1788 Coutet was bought by Gabriel Barthélémy Romain de Filhot, who also owned Filhot. He had only another five years to enjoy his properties, as he was guillotined during the Revolution. Both Coutet and Filhot remained in the Filhot family, and when Marie-Geneviève de Filhot married into the Lur-Saluces family in 1807, she brought both estates, plus Piada, with her as her dowry. The Lur-Saluces family retained Coutet until 1922. It was sold on a few years later to Henri-Louis Guy, a manufacturer of vertical presses. After he died his daughter, Mme. Rolland, took over, and she remained in charge until 1977. It then came into the hands of the present owners, the Baly family of Strasbourg. Today Philippe Baly is the ever-courteous public face of Coutet, welcoming visitors to the property with a broad smile.

The vineyards, which are unaltered in location and extent since 1855, surround the château. After the frost of 1956 most had to be replanted. The soil is thin but complex, with silt, fine gravel, and weathered sand. The grapes are picked into *cagettes*, and carefully sorted in the vineyard. Coutet still uses its vertical presses, and sometimes the third pressing is discarded. The must is fermented in barriques. In the 1980s about one-third of the barrels were new; but by the late 1990s the proportion had risen to fifty per cent, and today only new oak is used. Blending takes place progressively at each racking. Although Coutet is equipped with a cold chamber, no cryo-extracted wine ever goes into Coutet itself. Indeed, only about half the crop goes into the *grand vin*.

In 1922 a special *cuvée* was created to honour Mme. Rolland, and it became known as Cuvée Madame. The tradition was revived after World War II. It's a selection of old vines from one particular parcel, often picked grape by grape to ensure only fully botrytized fruit is chosen. Philippe Baly notes: "The effort required to produce Cuvée Madame is completely uneconomical, as it ties up forty workers for a whole day just to produce a few barriques of wine. But it's a way for the team to show what can be done here if there were no constraints of any kind. And since we produce so little, it has no detrimental effect on the quality of the regular Coutet." It is not made every year. It was made in 1941, 1943, 1949, 1950, 1959, 1971, 1975, 1981, 1986, 1988, 1989, 1995, and 2001. Curiously none was made in 1990. Quantities vary: there were 1,600 bottles in 1988, 1,000 in 1989. It is sometimes said that Cuvée Madame is never sold, but certainly a few years ago it was possible to buy some vintages directly from the château, though at terrifying prices.

There is also a dry white wine from Coutet, but it has nothing to do with the Barsac vineyards, being sourced from vines at Pujols a few miles away in the Graves.

In 2000 I was able to taste some venerable vintages at a London auction house. The 1906 was still in excellent shape, despite a dark brown colour. It had aromas of tar and Bovril, while the palate was still sweet, very concentrated, and lush; the flavour reminded me of the Dutch coffee sweet called Hopjes. The 1908 had a similar colour and aroma, while the palate was lean and vigorous with surprising freshness and length and, again, a coffee tone. The 1913 smelt of smoke and caramelized oranges; acidity was quite high, but the wine remained fairly sweet and long. The 1914 had clean, vigorous marmalade aromas, while the palate was still rich and assertive, with a slight tarriness but no sign of fatigue. The 1916 was a light copper in colour, had honeyed and smoky aromas, and it too was still fresh and youthful with concentration and delicious orangey fruit.

In 1993 I tasted some more recent vintages. The teak-coloured 1919 had an evolved raisiny, *crème brûlée* nose that was losing freshness; the palate was caramelly yet vigorous. The 1924 smelt of toffee, raisins, and barley sugar, yet the palate showed little sign of age, being sumptuous and very concentrated, with flavours of honey and raisins and a long *rôti* finish. The 1926 was similar but slightly less evolved, and it showed fresh acidity and excellent length. The 1929 was a bright teak-brown; the nose was sumptuous, with honey and raisin aromas; although the flavour was toffeeish and also suggested *beurre noire*, the palate was still racy, a perfect blend of maturity and freshness.

A London bottling of the 1949 had intense honeyed aromas, and was very sweet with moderate acidity. The 1950 and 1959 are also admired vintages from Coutet, but I have not tasted them. In 2005 the 1961 was bright gold, had a lovely peach and honey nose, and tasted of fresh, ripe apricots; the only blemish was a slight phenolic tone. In 1981, the 1971 had attractive pungent, waxy aromas, a lush and silky texture, delicate appley fruit, and a long finish. The 1973, when young, was a pretty wine, with flowery aromas; it is probably past its best. The 1975 is delicate and spicy, with lively acidity and a slight boiled-sweet character on the finish. It used to show better than the rather sulphury 1976, but the latter wine had shed its surliness by 2005, and had aromas of peach and dried apricot, and a typically *rôti* 1976 palate, yet showed no sign of tiring.

The 1979 in 1985 was harmonious but unexciting; it had reasonable length and a dry finish. I have not tasted it since. The 1980 was good if rather lean, sulphury in its youth but with good potential. The 1981 had great charm, plenty of botrytis, and a supple, gentle, honeyed palate, with good length. The 1982 was a bit lame, with moderate sweetness, a creamy texture, and some dried-apricot character, but it lacked vigour. The 1983 was decidedly citric, with modest botrytis and a rather hard, sulphury finish. There were light, delicate botrytis aromas on the 1985, but overall this was bland and lacked flair. The 1986 was better, quite oaky on the nose, but rich and viscous, with pear and lemon flavours and some complexity.

With the 1988 there is a sea change, and Coutet rose to meet the quality of the vintage. When I tasted it in 1992, I noted "Coutet back on form." It evolved well, and by 1996 the nose was delectable, with ripe apricots and botrytis; the palate was racy and intense, with some tropical fruit, and a very long, citric finish. The 1989 maintains that high standard, but has more weight and opulence and a more pronounced *rôti* character. The 1989 Cuvée Madame is similar but more honeyed and orangey, with a touch more weight. But the regular Coutet is almost as fine. The 1990 has great charm. By 2004 the initial apricotty fruit had become slightly raisiny, but the wine had not lost its intensity, and the creamy texture was as sensuous as ever. The 1992 was feeble and rather short. The 1994 was oaky and spicy when young, but by 2005 it had become rather slack, but still had enjoyable mandarin fruit. Curiously there was less overt botrytis in the 1995, a fresh and creamy wine that lacks some complexity. Far better is the 1996, with its botrytis and apricot aromas and flavours; it's not hugely sweet but has great purity. In 2006 the 1997 seemed a touch heavy; there was abundant honey and botrytis, but it didn't have the zest of Coutet at its best. It has taken many years for the 1998 to shed its adolescent awkwardness; by 2007 its aromas blended peachy fruit with elegant oak; a splendid attack ushers in an assertive, spicy wine, with very good length.

However, the 2001 is brilliant and complete; it's rich, oaky, and tight, with citrus and apricot flavours, and great concentration and elegance. The 2002 is surprisingly voluptuous and oaky, but with a fine backbone of acidity, and a very long if slightly candied finish. The straightforward 2004 is balanced but lacks flair, but the velvety, concentrated 2005 shows great promise.

Although Coutet went through a dull patch in the 1970s and 1980s, it is now demonstrating that it is capable again of producing wines of extraordinary quality. It is often compared to Climens, and usually to Coutet's disadvantage. But the wines are different: Climens has more weight, more majesty; Coutet is racier, and dances into the future with a lighter step.

Château Doisy-Daëne

*Barsac. Tel: 0556 629651. Website: www.denisdubourdieu.com. **Owner:** Denis Dubourdieu. Deuxième cru.*
15 ha sweet white, 17ha dry white. 80% Sémillon, 20% Sauvignon Blanc.
***Production:** 45,000 bottles sweet white, 30,000 bottles dry white*

It seems likely that the Doisy estate was first planted in the early eighteenth century. Then in the 1830s the property was divided in three. One part was bought by someone called Daëne, who was apparently English. He died in 1863, and it passed through various hands until it was bought in 1924 by Georges Dubourdieu, grandfather of the present owner. Pierre took over running the property in 1945, although he had been involved in the winemaking since 1942. Inevitably his oenologist son Denis took an interest in the estate, which he did throughout the 1990s, and in 2000 Pierre formally retired. Now Denis's opinionated son Fabrice, also an oenologist, is becoming involved in the family properties (which include Cantegril in Barsac, Reynon in Béguey and Clos Floridène in the Graves (*qq.v.*)).

I always enjoyed meeting Pierre Dubourdieu, as his mission in life, other than making splendid wines, was to goad journalists. He always claimed to be far more interested in making dry wines than sweet wines. "One glass of Yquem is plenty for me," he once muttered, adding: "To me the taste of honey in a wine is an abomination. I don't make Sauternes, I make Doisy-Daëne." He was an enthusiast for cryo-extraction, even in fine vintages, arguing that it was the best way to avoid chaptalization (although in fine vintages one wonders why chaptalization would be necessary in the first place). He admitted that botrytis gave the wine aroma, concentration, and unctuousness, but at the expense of freshness and youthfulness, which he greatly prized.

Pierre Dubourdieu never made voluptuous wines. He liked to pick at must weights of seventeen or eighteen degrees to retain the freshness and acidity he sought. The must was fermented in barriques (at least since the late 1980s) with indigenous yeasts. The proportion of new oak was about one-third. He aged the wine for about eighteen months in chilled cellars, so as to slow down its natural evolution.

What was stimulating about Pierre Dubourdieu was his technical inventiveness. In 1978, according to Clive Coates, he covered part of the vineyard with plastic sheeting in October and harvested in December, to produce a Vin de Noël from shrivelled grapes. Coates found it fat, oily, and somewhat oxidized and spirity, yet complex. Whether the wine was ever commercialized I don't know. Dubourdieu also developed extraordinary techniques. In the days when the Barsac was fermented in tanks, he would add lees from the previously fermented dry wines; this, he argued, helped preserve freshness. Then he devised a system for pumping wines from tanks through a filter and then into barriques and out again, keeping the wine in constant slow circulation; this would avoid the need for racking. To what extent he put such ideas into practice I cannot say, nor can I comment on their efficacy. But it was fun watching him fill scraps of paper with designs I could hardly begin to understand.

During the excellent 1990 vintage he, and Denis, wondered what it would be like to take matters to an extreme. So they left some Sauvignon Blanc on the vine until well into November, and picked it at about forty degrees of potential alcohol. That would not be unusual in Germany for a TBA, but the result would be a wine with six to eight degrees of alcohol and a huge amount of residual sugar. Dubourdieu wanted a wine with the usual alcohol level of Sauternes, and this he achieved, although he would not reveal how he managed to get the yeasts to work that hard. The 1990 had 15.5 degrees and about 350 grams per litre of residual sugar. Dubourdieu justifiably called the wine L'Extravagant de Doisy-Daëne and charged a small fortune for the 2,400 half-bottles he released. He repeated the exercise in 1996, charging even more for the wine, and again in 1997, though in that year the wine was pure Sémillon. L'Extravagant has also been made in 2001, 2002, and 2003.

Pierre Dubourdieu once poured me a glass of the 1943, which had been aged in casks for four years. Botrytis and orange were evident on the nose, which remained fresh; the wine was very concentrated, and despite a hint of oxidation the fruit was delicious. He also poured me the 1970 – "almost too good to give a journalist", he murmured – which smelt ripe and peachy and had wonderful vigour; although concentrated it was still very youthful and had a long, clean finish. The 1971 was more exotic, with aromas of mango and banana; it was a wine of charm as well as vigour. The 1976 was far more *rôti*, with aromas of peach and marmalade; it was rich, spicy, and tangy, and far from tiring in 1993. The 1980 was fairly light and rather acidic – not memorable. The 1981 was also rather lean and graceless, and not especially sweet. The 1982 was far better, with fresh pineapple aromas, more sweetness and fat on the palate, and moderate intensity and length.

The 1983 is not hugely concentrated, but it has always been delectable, with apricot aromas, a creamy palate, and fine acidity. The 1984 had pretty pear aromas, but was one-dimensional and light. The 1986 had melony aromas and seemed to have little botrytis; it was a soft, spicy, plump wine without great concentration. The 1988, however, was delicious, a racy wine of great delicacy and charm. The 1989 has been consistently good over many years. The nose is quite floral, but there are also aromas of peach and honey; it has fine fruit and acidity, some firmness of structure, and an appealing spiciness on the finish. The 1990 is similar, perhaps a touch sweeter and plumper, and with more *confit* fruit. The 1991 wasn't complex, but it was supple and stylish. The 1995 also lacked complexity, but there were fresh aromas of lemon and apple, and the wine, if a touch light, was well balanced and fresh. There is more richness on the 1996, and more evident botrytis; the texture is creamy yet a citric finish keeps it lively.

The 1997 was the best Doisy-Daëne for many years, with elegant apricot and botrytis aromas, exquisite silkiness, and no excessive sweetness; it is made with a light touch yet doesn't lack complexity. I tasted the 1997 L'Extravagant from cask in June 1999. As intended, it was an extraordinary wine, with rich, powerful, peachy aromas; the palate was highly concentrated – no surprise there – but the texture was so syrupy as to be scarcely drinkable despite the delectable lemon and apricot fruit; the length was amazing. A great wine but something of a showpiece.

The 1998 has a good attack, but doesn't quite deliver on the palate, which is not that exciting or expressive. Despite a slight lack of concentration, the 1999 is very attractive, with honeyed passion-fruit aromas, a plumpness on the palate, and ample richness. The 2000 has muted peachy aromas; it's plump, rather low in acidity, and forward, with a hint of boiled sweets on the finish. The 2001 has unusual opulence and body for Doisy-Daëne; it's lush, spicy, and stylish, with oodles of ripe apricot fruit. The 2002, initially disappointing, is now a wine of vigour and precision. The 2003 is very sweet, a touch alcoholic and confected, but it has good length and isn't heavy. The elegant 2004 is supple and spicy, with well-integrated oak and lively citrus and apricot flavours. Silky, citric, and lively, the 2005 has fine potential.

Overall, Doisy-Daëne is a very good and reliable wine, yet only occasionally does it reach great heights. It somehow lacks a little conviction. It doesn't go all out, except with the virtuoso L'Extravagant.

According to Pierre Dubourdieu, Doisy-Daëne Sec was the first dry white wine made in the Sauternes region. It is made by removing golden Sauvignon berries that are unlikely to attract botrytis and thus qualify for the sweet wine. This method both supplies fruit for the dry wine and reduces the crop for the sweet. The wine is aged in twenty-five per cent new barriques for about twelve months. The 1990 was deliciously creamy and spicy when young, and more recently the 2002 had muted aromas of pears and ripe grapefruit, while on the palate there was ample richness, body, and spice, as well as splendid fruit and length.

Château Doisy-Dubroca

*Barsac. Tel: 0556 726974. **Owner:** Louis Lurton. Deuxième cru. 3.8 ha. 100% Sémillon. **Production:** 6,000 bottles.*
Second wine: La Demoiselle de Doisy-Dubroca

For the history of the Doisy estates, see Doisy-Daëne (*q.v.*). This, the smallest of the trio, was bought by the Dubroca family in 1880; later, marriage brought the family into relation with the Gounouilhous, and when the latter acquired Climens, Doisy-Dubroca came with it. In 1971 the twinned properties were acquired by Lucien Lurton, who handed Doisy-Dubroca over to his son Louis in 1992. Its wines were for many years vinified by the Climens team. Since 1997, however, the two properties have been completely separated. The vines lie in a single rectangular parcel between Doisy-Daëne and Doisy-Védrines. Yet the soils are quite varied with red sand and gravel over a limestone base; the drainage is excellent. Since 2000, the grapes have been farmed organically. The wine is fermented and aged in twenty-five per cent new barriques for eighteen to twenty-four months.

Louis Lurton is one of the more eccentric members of this prodigious family. In 2005 he told me how he has been conducting experiments at Doisy-Dubroca to force out vegetal elements (a technique I didn't manage to understand) and has also been working on how to slow down the fermentation without increasing the risk of volatile acidity. In 2001, for example, the fermentation took a year to complete, which irritated INAO, as it meant the wine was not ready for the *agrément* tastings. Lurton was not fazed; he claims the wine gained in richness and *confit* flavours. Lurton also holds back vintages before releasing wines; thus in 2005 the current vintage on sale was 1997.

The 1979 was an attractive wine in 1994, with slightly smoky, lemony aromas, a creamy texture, some nuttiness and good concentration. There was a not altogether pleasant gumminess on the nose of the 1980, which was quite rich and intense, with appley flavours but a rather bitter finish. The 1981, tasted repeatedly, has always been very good, with elegant appley aromas, considerable intensity, good acidity, and a *crème brûlée* finish. There were light honey and apricot aromas on the easy-going 1983, which was soft, sweet, and creamy. But it was still going strong in 1999. The 1985 had marzipan aromas with little evident botrytis; the palate was somewhat oily and lacking in fruit. The 1986 was far better, with delicate citrus and oak aromas; with its sweet, lemony fruit and its elegance, it was quintessential Barsac. There is considerable complexity on the 1988, with very ripe apricot fruit, a creamy texture, and delicious upfront fruit with great freshness. The 1989 was similar and was very accessible from the outset. The 1990 is plumper, with apricot and lemon fruit and considerable elegance but not much grip.

The 1997 is rather strange. The nose is delicate and honeyed, but with a herbal character atypical of Barsac; it's on the palate too, which is moderately rich and not that sweet. The 2001 lacks richness; it's a pretty and svelte wine but hardly worthy of the vintage. Although there were many lacklustre wines from this estate in the past, it does seem that Doisy-Dubroca is losing its way.

Château Doisy-Védrines

*Barsac. Tel: 0556 685981. **Owner:** Olivier Castéja. Deuxième cru. 30 ha. 80% Sémillon, 15% Sauvignon Blanc, 5% Muscadelle. **Production:** 80,000 bottles. **Second wine:** Petit Védrines*

This property is named after a family who sold the estate in 1851 to a family called Boireau. Olivier Castéja is a direct descendant of the Boireaus. This branch of the Castéjas runs the négociant house of Roger Joanne. Olivier's father Pierre Castéja and his wife moved into the charming sixteenth-century manor house here in 1947 and ran the property thereafter, producing many fine vintages, although Pierre always admitted that he was by inclination a Médocain. After his death in 2004, Olivier took over, though his elderly mother still lives in the house. The property was expanded when in 2001 they bought six hectares from Château Bouyot, with vines between Myrat and Ménota, and another parcel near Coutet; at present the production from these vineyards goes into the second wine. The historic Védrines vineyards are on the plateau, on clay-limestone with iron traces, and the Ciron flows some 600 metres (660 yards) away. Pierre told me that any lots with a must weight lower than seventeen degrees were sold off in bulk. Yields are about twenty hl/ha on average, and there has been occasional use of cryo-extraction, most recently in 2004.

Fermentation begins in tanks, and the wine is then transferred to barriques, where it is aged for eighteen months. The proportion of new oak has fluctuated considerably. In 1989 it was all new oak, but by the 2000s it had been reduced to one-third. Olivier Castéja finds that Védrines typically has quite high acidity, so he likes a good deal of residual sugar in the wine (around 130 grams per litre) to balance that acidity. No *grand vin* was made in 1991, and in 1993 only twenty per cent of the crop was usable.

In style Doisy-Védrines tends to be a bit richer and fatter than most other Barsacs, including the other Doisys. Yet it remains a typical Barsac in its acidity, vigour, and longevity. It sometimes seems to be underrated, perhaps because it is run by négociants. But in my experience it is a very satisfying wine that also offers good value. The 1989 was a particular success, yet in 1994 the London wine merchant John Armit discounted the wine by one-third, noting: "Cost price. Lovely wine, but can't sell it."

The oldest vintage I have tasted was the sumptuous 1970, which had a strong orangey character on the nose and the palate; it was still fresh and lively after twenty-five years, though the finish was rather hot. I remember Pierre Castéja remarking as we tasted this wine that if his winery had been as well equipped in 1970 as it was now, this would have been a truly great wine. The 1975 was very good too, but it evolved quite fast. After twenty years it had marked smoky, barley-sugar, and dried-apricot aromas; on the palate it was not especially sweet, but smoky and elegant, with dried-fruits flavours. The 1978, from a difficult year, was clumsy and probably past its best. The same goes for the austere 1981.

The 1982 was rather bland, fairly rich but lacking in character, a vapid wine overall. There was a huge improvement in 1983, with its pronounced dried-fruits aromas, its spiciness, elegance, and length. The 1985 had a light botrytis character and reasonable concentration but not a great deal of stylishness or length. There was far more power and opulence in 1986; the palate was lush but persistent with considerable complexity and length. The 1988 had ample apricot fruit, a marked botrytis character, fair concentration, and a long, juicy finish.

The 1989 was gorgeous from the outset and stayed that way. There were aromas of honey, of peaches and cream, and the oak was quite marked; it was also balanced by fine acidity. The 1990 was similar but had a stronger raisiny character, overt oakiness and botrytis, and perhaps lacked the elegance of the 1989. I found little to like in the 1992, 1993, and 1994; I have not tasted them in many years but doubt they have improved with age. There was complexity on the nose of the 1995, with rich peachy, botrytis aromas, while the palate was sweet and oaky, with excellent acidity and length. The 1997 is delicious: very sweet but with racy acidity, perhaps not complex but very stylish.

The 2001 has immense charm and appeal, with pineapple as well as citrus fruit, a slight candied tone, and zesty acidity. The citric 2002 is not quite at the same level; it's juicy and quite lush but a touch slack compared to the 2001. The 2003 is very sweet and sleek, with apricot and mandarin fruit, and surprising freshness. The 2004 is more stylish and pure, with candied fruit reminiscent of the 2001, and a dash of lime on the finish.

Château de Fargues

Fargues. Tel: 0557 980420. Website: www.chateau-de-fargues.com. **Owner:** *Comte Alexandre de Lur-Saluces.*
15 ha. 80% Sémillon, 20% Sauvignon Blanc. **Production:** *12,000 bottles*

The estate is dominated by the ruinous fourteenth-century castle that stands imposingly on a slope. It has been a Lur-Saluces property since the late sixteenth century. After a son of the family married Françoise-Josephine de Sauvage d'Yquem in the late eighteenth century, the Lur-Saluces headquarters became Yquem, and thereafter it seems that the castle was allowed to decay. After the LVMH group bought Yquem, Fargues remained in the family. Curiously there was no wine production here until the twentieth century, and even then it was red wine. It was not until 1935 that white grapes were planted by Bertrand de Lur-Saluces, and the first vintage was 1942. Since 1993 François Amirault, who used to work at Nairac, has been the winemaker, and even when Yquem was under the same ownership, Fargues was always run more or less autonomously.

Fargues has a different microclimate to Sauternes itself, and the grapes ripen a week later than at Yquem. There is a higher risk of frost and rain (and hail in 2004 wrecked sixty per cent of the crop). Yields are extremely low: 7.5 hl/ha is typical. The low yields may be attributable to the unremarkable soil at Fargues, which is essentially sandy loam. In the 1980s, when Pierre Meslier was making the Fargues as well as Yquem, he told me that it was more difficult to make Fargues than Yquem because of its terroir and microclimate. Amirault finds that precocious vintages suit Fargues best. He also notes that the vineyards can be swept by strong winds, which help dry the grapes after rain or mist. Fargues is equipped with cryo-extraction but Amirault is no fan of the technique; he tried it in 1993 and rejected the results.

The barrels used to come from Yquem after they had been used for about one year, and the wine used to be aged for forty-two months, as at Yquem, although in lighter vintages Amirault has abbreviated the *élevage*. In the past, when one tasted Yquem and Fargues from the same vintage side by side, Fargues often showed better. Meslier used to agree but pointed out that after about five years the difference became more marked, and Yquem, like a trained racehorse, would start to pull ahead. To be fair, neither Meslier nor Amirault like these direct comparisons with Yquem.

No Fargues was bottled in 1964, 1972, 1974, or 1992. The oldest vintage I have tasted is the 1980, which had gentle, lemony botrytis aromas; the wine was soft and creamy with lovely depth of flavour and elegance and a long, spicy finish. The 1983 is delicious, with a rich dried-apricot nose, and concentrated apricot fruit on the palate too. In the modest 1984 vintage, the wine had some aromatic elegance and vanilla tones; it was oaky, with good bite and acidity, but there was some dilution. No such reservations about the 1986, which had an unctuous botrytis nose; very oaky and spicy, it has rich apricot fruit, fine acidity, and very good length. The 1987 had elegant peachy aromas, but lacked the usual concentration and structure.

Oak, honey, and apricots dominate the nose of the splendid 1988, which has 120 grams of residual sugar (compared to ninety in 1987). The palate shows great complexity, with flavours of apricot, mandarins, and barley sugar, but the richness is countered by excellent acidity and length. The 1990 is impeccable, with delicate honeyed aromas; it's assertive but also has enormous freshness and elegance. Despite the difficulties of the 1994 vintage, the wine came out well, elegant rather than rich, and markedly oaky. There are quince as well as peach aromas on the 1996, a rich and unctuous wine with a firm, oaky backbone. The 1997 is creamy and spicy, but lacks a little aromatic freshness, with hints of stewed peach and caramel; however, it still manages to be long and elegant. The 1998 is more voluptuous: the nose is honeyed, the palate rich and peachy and quite powerful. The 1999 has a stronger dried-fruits character; it's an intense wine with fine acidity and no excesses.

The 2001 has 132 grams of residual sugar, but exhibits a bold, powerful style that conceals the sweetness; it's immensely stylish and long. The 2002 has some exotic aromas but more typical stone-fruits flavours, and ample vigour and concentration. The 2003, tasted from cask, lacked some backbone to support the plump, rounded peachy fruit, and the oak was very marked, giving the wine a somewhat dry finish. In 2006 from cask, the 2004 had freshness and citric dash, but the fruit was subdued and inexpressive. The 2005 is sensational: rich, oaky, spicy, and very long.

I don't recall a disappointing vintage of Fargues, which is testimony to the brilliant winemaking skills of Meslier and now Amirault, and to their determination to bottle only wine that is truly worthy of the estate's reputation. Prices are high, and only the first-rate will do.

Château Farluret

Preignac. Tel: 0556 632476. Owner: *Robert Lamothe. 10 ha. 90% Sémillon, 5% Sauvignon Blanc, 5% Muscadelle.*
Production: 30,000 bottles

This property is under the same ownership as the estimable Château Haut-Bergeron (*q.v.*). It produced a delicious 1997, with peachy aromas, a luxurious plumpness saved from flabbiness by good acidity and length.

Château Filhot

Sauternes. Tel: 0556 766109. Website: www.filhot.com. **Owner:** *Gabriel de Vaucelles. Deuxième cru. 62 ha.*
60% Sémillon, 36% Sauvignon Blanc, 4% Muscadelle. **Production:** *100,000 bottles.* **Second wine:** *Ch Pineau du Rey*

This immense château was mostly built in the 1840s, although some sections are older. The estate was established by Romain de Filhot in 1709, when he began planting vineyards. The wine was admired by Thomas Jefferson and sold for high prices. One of Filhot's descendants bought Coutet but the two estates were confiscated during the Revolution, and Filhot was guillotined. However, his daughter, who had married a Lur-Saluces, was able to secure their return. It was her son Romain-Bertrand who expanded the vineyards and the château. In the later part of the nineteenth century the wine was sold as Château Sauternes and the archives preserve wooden case stamps that confirm this. In 1901 the name of Filhot was restored.

After phylloxera the property declined. By 1933 only twenty hectares remained under vine, compared to 120 in the mid-nineteenth century. The sister of Bertrand de Lur-Saluces, Thérèse, had married into the Durieu de Lacarelle family, and she persuaded her brother to sell Filhot to her. One of her daughters married Comte Pierre de Vaucelles, a diplomat, and in 1974 the estate passed to their son Henri. He came from an industrial rather than agricultural background, and was probably dismayed by the enormity of the task he had taken on. He once explained that the upkeep of the mansion included the maintenance of two hectares of roofs alone. On the property there are vestiges of tobacco and cattle sheds, mementoes of other enterprises that had been tried out but failed. Vaucelles admitted: "Filhot is far too large for its place in the local economy."

Henri de Vaucelles could, and did, talk for hours about such matters as the local economy, about the economic, religious, and social forces that dictated the styles of sweet wine and their commercial distribution over the centuries. Once he got started it was difficult to stop him, and I recall standing in the courtyard as he began one of his disquisitions; it started to rain but he kept talking. Some ten minutes later we returned to the château, both completely soaked. Unkind fellow proprietors recall dinner parties at which he held forth for two hours on the Swedish market for agricultural products. Trapped within this kindly estate manager was a historian trying to get out. After the rather sudden death of his wife, Henri de Vaucelles handed over the running of Filhot to their five children.

Unfortunately, he seemed to have a passion for just about everything except the wine he produced. The vineyards, between Guiraud and Lamothe, are somewhat unusual, and their proximity to the forests of the Landes means that they can be quite cool and prone to frost, which is why, he explained, Filhot has always had an unusually high proportion of Sauvignon Blanc. This is sometimes said to explain its light style, but Guiraud nearby also has a good deal of Sauvignon, yet no one would call it light. The soil is a sandy gravel over porous limestone, with the vines on gentle southwest-facing slopes. The vineyards had clearly been capable of making great wine, otherwise the wines would, in the past, not have fetched the high prices they did.

Henri de Vaucelles, however, picked at fairly high yields, as there were vintages when he made 180,000 bottles, whereas today the production is significantly lower. He also fermented the must in fibreglass with frequent chaptalization, and for most of his career there was no barrel-ageing. Once his son Gabriel began running the estate in the 1990s, changes were made. Stainless-steel tanks with temperature control replaced the old fibreglass tanks; fermentation took place with indigenous as well as selected yeasts. And although the wine remained in tanks for about twelve months, it was then aged in barriques, one-third new, for a further twelve months.

The oldest Filhot I have tasted is the 1896, which had a light, sweet, orangey nose; although pleasant, it was clearly fading and drying out. The 1929 vintage was more memorable. In 2000 it was deep amber-gold, raisiny on the nose with a touch of barley sugar, while the palate was burnished and caramelly, but the finish was lively, spicy, and very long. The 1934 has not held up quite as well. The nose is honeyed but rather subdued; it's medium-bodied and not hugely sweet, but the flavours of dried apricots and marmalade are very attractive, and the finish is long. The 1935 is more weary, honeyed on the nose but far from bright; it's soft, lightly sweet, and quite tarry. The 1945 was splendid in 1994, with complex aromas of ripe lemons and stewed apricots; the palate was intense and lean, quite raisiny, lean but very refined, and extremely long.

By 1970 Filhot was no longer at this level of quality. The 1970 showed no botrytis, was sulphury, while the palate was rather dull and bitter. The 1971 was better, citric but mild, with some stylishness but little vigour or length. For some reason, Filhot produced a very attractive 1976, which I bought and drank over many years. It took a while to shed its sulphur, but then revealed a lush, peachy wine, with flavours of marmalade too, a touch of pepper from alcohol, and, as it aged, a tendency to become more tarry and caramelized. The 1978 was pallid, soapy, and lacked fruit. The 1979 was better, with some waxy Sémillon aromas, and some charm though only moderate sweetness. The 1980 was rather washed out and lacked concentration. The 1981 too was bland and lacklustre. The 1982 was soft and lightly sweet but essentially feeble.

Filhot upped its game somewhat in 1983, and the wine had good fruit, a creamy texture, and some structure. The 1985 was similar, but the alcohol showed through and there was no complexity. In this vintage Henri de Vaucelles experimented with an icewine style, picking frozen grapes on November 20, and giving the wine just a bit of barrique-ageing. It tasted rather like a lacklustre Jurançon, having some sweetness and sprightly acidity, but it lacked complexity and length.

The 1986 was too sulphury to give much pleasure; it had simple apricot fruit, little concentration, and a rather hard finish. In its youth it had some raciness, but it didn't last. The 1988 was attractive but undernourished. Far better was the 1989, which is still drinking well. It has citrus and apricot aromas, more weight than usual, considerable freshness, and decent length. The 1990 was not bad either, with melon and pineapple aromas, some richness, and a creamy texture, but not much concentration or length. Vaucelles produced a superb Crème de Tête in 1990, which revealed some of the real potential of Filhot: it had very ripe apricot and orange fruit, far more opulence, creaminess, and sweetness than usual, and in 2007 was still fresh and long.

The 1995 was a return to mediocrity, with an odd tinned-peach flavour and a drab finish. The 1996 lacked concentration, but it was a pretty wine, with good apricot and lemon-drop fruit, and moderate length. The 1997 was disappointing, but more plump and rounded than most Filhots, and it had attractive acidity. With the 1998 there are real signs of improvement, with attractive and even pungent aromas of lemon and apricot, a light but supple texture, good acidity, and an elegant finish. The 1999 is similar, with peachy aromas and fine acidity; although only medium-bodied, it is balanced and elegant. The 2000 is leaner and more citric. The 2001 is good but should be better; it's lush but there isn't much concentration. The 2002 is a lightweight, though with pleasant apricot and mandarin fruit and reasonable length. Rich yet lively stone-fruits aromas and flavours make the 2003 a supple and accessible wine from this luxurious vintage.

Château Gilette

Preignac. Tel: 0556 762844. Owner: Christian Médeville. 4.5 ha. 96% Sémillon, 4% Sauvignon Blanc.
Production: 8,000 bottles

This is the most eccentric wine of Sauternes. As a vineyard it is not that remarkable. It lies on warm and thus precocious soils near the school and cemetery in Preignac, on sandy gravel soil with a subsoil of rock and clay.

The distinctive style of Gilette – a wine aged for many years in concrete tanks – evolved because Christian Médeville's father went into the army in the 1930s and instructed his wife not to touch the wines, which were then stored in concrete tanks. On his return from war he was struck by their freshness and the absence of oxidation. Thus expediency involved into a style and philosophy.

Gilette is made only in outstanding vintages and has never been chaptalized. Yields are usually around nine hl/ha. If the must isn't good enough for Gilette, it is used for the family's other property of Les Justices (*q.v.*) or sold off. Médeville likes a long, slow fermentation in steel tanks, usually with natural yeasts, and aims for an alcohol level of around fifteen degrees. The wine is then racked, filtered, and left alone. In the past Médeville made different categories, such as Demi-Doux (last made in 1958) and Doux (last made in 1962). These were usually disappointing. The legendary Gilettes are Crème de Tête, which for some years has been the only style made.

The wine remains in tanks of 2,000 to 4,000 litres because there is no risk of oxidation. The 1955 and 1959 were not bottled until 1982, so slow was their evolution. In 1993 the current vintage was 1971. Not all the wine is put on the market at once, and Médeville maintains substantial stocks of older vintages.

I didn't care for the 1958 Demi-Doux; it had elegant mango aromas, but the alcohol was harsh and the finish bitter. A 1956 Demi-Sec, tasted in 1985, was light and short and thoroughly unappealing. The disappointing 1950 Doux had sixteen degrees of alcohol, a light body, and a rapid finish. The 1955 Doux was much more attractive, with soft, honeyed aromas, a supple texture, ample fresh fruit, and fine length.

Now to the real Gilette: the Crème de Tête. The 1950 was surprisingly syrupy, and had very rich marmalade aromas; yet there was sufficient acidity to counter the extreme richness and the wine finished long. The 1953 was softer, again with marmalade flavours, but marred by high alcohol (sixteen degrees). Despite a slightly alcoholic finish, the deep golden 1955 was a gorgeous wine, with rich honey and banana aromas, a sumptuous palate with elegance as well as power. The 1959 was more coppery in colour, with aromas of caramelized orange and honey, a creamy voluptuous texture, and excellent length – not a subtle wine but a magnificent one. The 1967 was more raisiny, but very intense and powerful, and it retained a vigorous youthful acidity. The 1970 was similar in flavour but had less weight and persistence.

Despite rich peachy aromas, the 1971 had a good deal of elegance too with a spicy aftertaste and good length. The 1975 had a peachy botrytis nose, great intensity and elegance thanks to its fine acidity, with a hint of raisins on the finish. I prefer the weightier, more *rôti* 1976, with its astonishing depth of flavour. The 1979 is peachy on the nose, more orangey on the palate, lush and concentrated, and the finish is fresh and clean. The 1981 perhaps lacks complexity; the aromas and flavours are orangey, and there's caramel on the finish. The 1982 is rich but only medium-bodied, but it's creamy and fresh and bright, with moderate length. The 1983 is far more botrytized with smoky apricot aromas, and a palate that is racy and pure, with delicious apricot fruit and fine length.

There are some great wines from Gilette, yet I am not sure I see the point of the exercise. We do want wines to evolve, so that they yield up every nuance of whatever complexity they enfold. Gilette does that, but very, very slowly. Surely the same splendour of aroma and fruit could emerge after moderate barrel-ageing. After all, the quality of Gilette derives from its vineyards and how the grapes are harvested, rather than from the ageing process. Today the wines are bottled a few years earlier than used to be the case.

Château Gravas

Barsac. Tel: 0556 271520. Website: www.chateau-gravas.fr. Owner: Michel Bernard. 11 ha. 90% Sémillon, 10% Sauvignon Blanc. Production: 30,000 bottles

The château is a pretty ivy-covered house, and its vineyard enjoys an excellent location on gravelly soil between Climens and Coutet. It was acquired by the Bernard family in 1850. In the mid-1980s, Pierre Bernard cheerfully admitted he chaptalized routinely. The wine was briefly aged in barrels but mostly stored in underground tanks, since, he claimed, his clients didn't want any taste of wood. His personal preference was for a wine higher in alcohol and less rich than Sauternes. I can't say I cared much for his wines in the 1980s and early 1990s, though there was the occasional Special Cuvée, as in 1983, that was considerably richer and more complex. Even by the early 2000s, the wine was still being aged in a combination of tanks and barriques. The 2003 has tropical fruit flavours and a candied finish, as does the unexciting 2004.

Bernard also produces two other wines from different parcels on the property: Château Simon-Carretey and the unoaked Château Hallet. Gravas itself is made from ninety-five per cent Sémillon.

Château Grillon

*Barsac. Tel: 0556 271645. **Owner:** Odile Roumazeilles-Cameleyre. 11 ha. 85% Sémillon, 10% Muscadelle,*
*5% Sauvignon Blanc. **Production:** 30,000 bottles*

A shipowner bought Grillon in 1926 and it is still in his family. I know little about it, but the 2004 was very good from cask and the top *cuvée* in 2003, called Haut-Grillon, is peachy and plump.

Château Guiraud

*Sauternes. Tel: 0556 766101. **Website:** www.chateau-guiraud.fr. **Owner:** consortium of investors. Premier cru.*
*83 ha. 65% Sémillon, 35% Sauvignon Blanc. **Production:** 170,000 bottles. **Second wine:** Dauphin du Château*

In the centre of this enormous property stands the sober château with its panelled salons. In the eighteenth century the estate, then known as Château Bayle, had numerous owners, and in 1766 it was acquired by Pierre Guiraud, a Bordeaux négociant. It remained in his family until 1846, when the Lur-Saluces bought Guiraud at auction, only to be gazumped the following day. Guiraud went through various owners, until in 1932 Paul Rival became the owner. Under Rival's ownership the wine ceased at some point to be barrel-aged.

In 1981 Guiraud was bought by Frank Narby, an Egyptian-Canadian businessman, who entrusted its management to his son Hamilton. Hamilton Narby was determined to make wines that would be a match for those from Yquem. He appointed Xavier Planty as *régisseur*, and today Planty both runs the estate and has become a partner. Hamilton Narby had a falling out with his father and left the property. His brother Jeremy took his place, but as he lived in Switzerland, he had little influence. Planty remained in charge, but answerable to the shareholders. A few years ago he discreetly enquired whether the Narbys would be agreeable to an offer. The answer was yes, and in 2006 Guiraud was bought by Olivier Bernard of Domaine de Chevalier, Stephan von Neipperg of Canon-La-Gaffelière, Planty himself, and by their major financial backers, the FPP group. Planty remains as manager, but with enhanced authority.

As well as eighty-three hectares in the Sauternes appellation, Guiraud owns thirteen hectares used for Bordeaux Blanc. For many years Guiraud was dogged by the errors of Paul Rival. He had planted red grapes, which had to be grubbed up. The density was lower than ideal, and had to be increased. Drainage had to be repaired. Planty also halted the use of herbicides. The soil is sandy and gravelly, with a little clay; the subsoil is varied, with both limestone and clay. When Frank Narby bought Guiraud, over half the vines were Sauvignon Blanc, and this proportion has been reduced, though it remains atypically high nonetheless. Planty admits that in difficult years Sauvignon can be fragile, but in fine years he relishes its rich, smoky flavours and its elegance.

The *grand vin* is never chaptalized, and only batches with a must weight of at least twenty degrees are used. In 1988 only one-third of the wine was barrel-fermented; today it is all fermented and aged for twenty-four months in barriques, of which over half are new. The wine is blended progressively at each racking. In 2003 Planty set up for me thirty-seven barrel samples of the 2002, each being a different lot. My task was to eliminate those not worthy of going into the final blend. It was a fiendishly difficult task, especially for an initiate. However, about seventy-five per cent of my selections matched Planty's, so I didn't completely disgrace myself.

I once tasted the 1921, but there was some maderization as well as *crème brûlée* aromas, and the palate was drying out, leaving raw acidity and alcohol – past its best. The 1929 and 1959 are said to be good. The 1962 was impressive but strange, showing piercing pear aromas, intense sweetness and concentration, and a long, lemony finish. The 1964 was shy on the nose, but luscious and enjoyable. I have often drunk the 1975, but bottles have varied. At best, it had elegant, smoky botrytis aromas, a creamy texture, fine acidity, and considerable spiciness. The 1976 was always deep gold in colour, with a rather baked honey and peach nose; the wine was burly and caramelly and rather coarse. I had mixed experiences of the 1979; at best it was full, supple, and flavoury, but also a bit flabby. The 1981 has always been rather hot and sulphury, with the fruit clobbered into the background. The 1982 too was sulphury and baked, hard at the edges and lacking in generosity.

In 1983 Guiraud produced an excellent wine of remarkable elegance and freshness, not enormously sweet but concentrated and complex with smoky *rôti* flavours. The 1985 had oily aromas, and though rich and supple, lacked some intensity and structure. There was considerable power on the 1986, but it was unusually blowsy and lacked finesse. The 1988 had more floral aromas, more elegance; this is a delicious wine, finely balanced, vivid and fresh, a classic example of the vintage. The 1989 is extremely rich, with botrytized aromas of apricot and pineapple; it's lush, velvety, and full-bodied, yet has good length. The 1990 is a great Guiraud with all the stops out: very rich on the nose, with honey, peaches, and caramelized oranges, almost raisiny but not tarry; the palate is plump, burnished, and concentrated, with a vigour undiminished fifteen years later.

The 1992 is sweet and sappy and reasonably concentrated, but a lightweight by Guiraud standards. I tasted the 1995 only once, and found it tarry and coarse, with a bitter finish; I suspect a poor bottle. The 1996 was similar in its youth, with tarry aromas, a flabby texture, and some oxidation; yet the same wine in 2003 was a marvel of opulence, a touch tarry, it's true, but also with complex peach, mango, and barley-sugar flavours. The 1999 is muted on the nose, but very sweet, intense, and creamy, with a light candied tone to the citrus and pineapple fruit. The 2000 is good for the vintage. The creamy 2001 is splendid, with *rôti* barley-sugar and peach aromas, bright acidity and fine concentration, and a zesty, complex finish. The 2002 has a raciness unusual for Guiraud, and a good attack and some spiciness, leading to a long, lemony finish. The 2003 has heady peachy aromas; broad and opulent, it is reasonably concentrated but rather forward. The 2004 has considerable complexity, with flavours of apricot, quince, oak, and a dash of white pepper. The full-bodied 2005 shows immense promise.

Guiraud is a fine Sauternes, but perhaps not as consistent as it should be. There are vintages when the wine is on the edge of oxidation and tarriness, when the balance is questionable. But when Guiraud gets it right, it's among the most complex and dazzling of Sauternes.

Château Haut-Bergeron

*Preignac. Tel: 0556 632476. **Owner:** Robert Lamothe. 16 ha. 95% Sémillon, 5% Sauvignon Blanc.*
*Production: 50,000 bottles. **Second wine:** Ch Grand Piquey*

This property has been in the Lamothe family since the mid-nineteenth century. Robert is taking a back seat these days in favour of his sons Patrick and Hervé. The vineyards are in no fewer than sixty parcels, including some near Climens, and others near the house and near Lafaurie-Peyraguey. The average age of the vines is fifty-five years, and there are parcels remaining from 1896 and 1903.

The Lamothes wait for as long as possible before harvesting. The first pressing is always in a pneumatic press, but in top years the second pressing takes place in a vertical press to obtain a more concentrated must. Haut-Bergeron is fermented in steel tanks with indigenous yeasts, and aged for eighteen months in up to fifty per cent new oak, including some Hungarian barrels. There is some rotation of the wine between tanks and barrels.

These are very rich wines, deep in colour and *confit* in flavour. Lamothe believes their deep golden colour comes both from the soil and from the concentration of the fruit. In 2001, 2002, and 2003 the wines had 130 grams of residual sugar. In 1996 Lamothe made Cuvée 100 from the very oldest vines; this was barrel-fermented and aged for three years in oak. The 2001 had 200 grams of residual sugar; in 2002 the wine stopped fermenting once it reached eight degrees, so they were unable to use it.

The 1986 was a truly voluptuous wine, with plump, orangey aromas, and a sweet, silky palate refreshed by good acidity; however, the finish was slightly too alcoholic. The 1990 had better balance, with powerful peach and stewed-apricot aromas with a hint of caramel, and a concentrated, creamy palate, flamboyant and long. The 1991 is leaner, and rather flat on the mid-palate, but a good wine nonetheless. So is the 1992, though it lacked length. Haut-Bergeron is back on full unctuous form with the 1995, with its heady, rich, honeyed nose, its splendid fruit and discreet tarriness. The 1996 was similar, but with orangey rather than stone-fruits flavours. The 2000 is less marked by botrytis, with its aromas of honeydew melon and apricot; it's fresh and lively but lacks some weight. The 2003 is far from elegant, with boiled sweets on the nose, while there is lemon and passion fruit on the palate, which is nonetheless rather one-dimensional. The 2005 is sleek and stylish. Haut-Bergeron is not the most subtle of Sauternes but it is hard to resist its super-rich hedonistic fruit.

Château Les Justices

Preignac. Tel: 0556 762844. Owner: Christian Médeville. 9 ha. 90% Sémillon, 10% Sauvignon Blanc.
Production: 20,000 bottles. Second wine: Ch de l'Ecole

Christian Médeville is better known for the remarkable Château Gilette (*q.v.*). Half of the Justices vineyards are on the river side of the N113, the remainder near Bastor-Lamontagne. Until 1985 the wine was aged in tanks, but since then the wine, though fermented in tanks, has been aged in barriques.

In 1976 and 1983 the wines were ripe, fresh, and rounded, but marred by high alcohol and a fairly short finish. Despite the lack of botrytis in 1985, the wine was attractive, with waxy Sémillon aromas and flavours, a creamy texture, and quite good length. The 1986 had a curious almondy nose and lacked some concentration and structure. The 1988 was leaner and more aggressive but also more stylish and better balanced. The 1989 was richer and more sumptuous but had less persistence. The excellent 1990 was more *confit*, with ample botrytis and lovely acidity, a well-balanced wine that by 2005 was near its peak. The 1991 was soft and peachy yet fairly light. The 1992 was lean and short. The 1995 had honeyed aromas, was full on the palate, with apricot and mandarin flavours, but the acidity was edgy. The 1996 had aromas and flavours of apricot and lemon zest, but had a bit too much alcohol. The 1998 was rich but atypically syrupy with a rather cloying finish. There is excellent fruit on the 2001, reasonable concentration without heaviness, and a welcome purity and elegance. The 2002 is more modest but has charm and a clean citric presence and length.

Château Lafaurie-Peyraguey

Bommes. Tel: 0557 195777. Owner: Suez company. Premier cru. 40 ha. 90% Sémillon, 8% Sauvignon Blanc,
2% Muscadelle. Production: 70,000 bottles. Second wine: La Chapelle de Lafaurie

The crenellated walls that surround the château are a reminder that this was originally built as a castle, and its surviving tower dates from the thirteenth century. The ivy-covered house itself is essentially seventeenth century. In the following century it became the property of Nicolas-Pierre de Pichard, a senior *parlementaire* who owned Château Lafite. He named the estate after himself. Pichard fled France during the Revolution and his property was confiscated and sold to two gentlemen named Lafaurie and Mauros. It was Peyraguey who established the reputation of its wine, but he died soon after having the satisfaction of seeing it rated as the third-best Sauternes in 1855.

Thereafter Lafaurie passed through various hands, until in 1879 the property was divided. The higher sector was sold to a M. Grillon, who renamed it Clos Haut-Peyraguey. In 1917 the main sector, Lafaurie-Peyraguey, was bought by the Bordeaux merchant Desiré Cordier. A small part of Château d'Arche, which had at one time also belonged to M. Lafaurie, was later incorporated into Lafaurie-Peyraguey. Cordier managed the property well, especially from the 1980s onwards, when the *régisseur* was Michel Laporte, who has now been succeeded by his son Yannick. The dynasty was unbroken even after the sale of the estate in 1996 to the Suez company, which undertook a major renovation of the buildings in the early 2000s.

The vineyards are dispersed. Twelve hectares are within a walled *clos* around the château; five are on a clay *croupe* near Clos Haut-Peyraguey, five near Arche on gravel soil, and five more behind Rabaud-Promis, plus parcels near Guiraud and in Preignac, and elsewhere. Because all these parcels ripen at different times, the Laportes have always had a large number of lots to work with. The average age of the vines is about forty years. In conjunction with the Gironde chamber of agriculture, Lafaurie has planted a new clone of Sauvignon Rosé which has apparently powerful aromas and gives high must weights; but it delivers only two barrels of wine. The Laportes aim at harvest for must weights of twenty to twenty-one degrees from yields that generally are between sixteen and eighteen hl/ha. Yannick Laporte instituted harvesting in small baskets so that bunches can be swiftly inspected before being tipped onto the sorting table.

From 1967 to 1977 the grapes were pressed in rough horizontal presses and mostly aged in metal vats, with just a few months of barrel-ageing. By 1978 Laporte acknowledged the results were unsatisfactory, and reverted to a more traditional *élevage*; he also installed vertical presses. Michel Laporte realized fermentation in vats risked a loss of aroma. Today fermentation takes place in medium-toast barrels with indigenous yeasts; one-third of the barrels are new and the wine is aged for eighteen months.

The 1912 was still alive seventy years later, though dark in colour; there were marmalade aromas, considerable sweetness and richness, and a touch of dryness. A Belgian-bottled 1926 was copper-gold, lightly caramelly on the nose, and lightly sweet on the palate, with high acidity and a piercing citric aftertaste – yet better than it sounds. Lafaurie seems to have excelled in 1934, 1937, 1945, and 1947, but I have not tasted them. Indeed Lafaurie eluded me until the apricotty 1980, which was rather volatile and had a burnt-almond finish. The 1981 was better, with a sweet, oaky nose and a light but well-balanced palate. The 1982 was quite sharp and aggressive, with citrus flavours and some elegance on the finish.

In 1983, Lafaurie, like so many other Sauternes properties, at last made an outstanding wine. Bright gold, it had fine marmalade and oak aromas, a creamy texture, flavours of orange and peach, and enough acidity and power to carry it through to a stylish finish. The 1984 had some richness and intensity on the palate; a good effort for the vintage. When young the 1985 was very oaky, very sweet, creamy but closed; it seemed very well balanced and packed with fruit, so should have evolved well. The 1986 was impeccable: oaky, scented with honey and quince, elegant, spicy, and deliciously tangy on the finish. The aromas of the 1987 are oaky, elegant, and nutty, while the palate is sweet and creamy and has fine apricot fruit.

The 1988 has weight and power, and superb concentration and acidity, with the oak perfectly integrated. The succession of excellent vintages continues with the brilliant 1989, which is slightly toasty but packed with delicious peachy fruit, remarkable weight and fullness, and fine length. If anything, the 1990 is even better because of its brilliant attack, its weight and power, its dense structure, its terrific acidity and length. Even in 1991, Lafaurie triumphed, delivering a rich, unctuous wine, a touch low in acidity but an excellent wine that was still rich and youthful in 2004. Laporte took his foot off the pedal in 1992, making sure the wine didn't try to deliver more than the raw material contained; the result was a delicious and spicy, apricotty wine. There was ample botrytis on the oaky 1994, but it lacked the elegance of Lafaurie at its best. The 1995 was rich and peachy, a touch plump and heavy, but nonetheless a strong and convincing wine.

By 2007, peaches, honey, and caramel were marking the nose of the 1996, and there's ample vigour and stylishness to sustain the delicious fruit, and the finish is lively. The 1997 has wonderful raciness as well as concentrated citric fruit, well-integrated oak, and excellent length. The silky 1998 is equally delicious, rich in stone-fruits aromas and flavours. It's finely balanced, as is the 1999, which is ripe, spicy, and elegant. The 2000 is sound, but the acidity is a bit low and the wine lacks some flair. The 2001 is zesty, very sweet, creamy, oaky, and delicious, with a long future ahead of it. The 2002 is more floral and delicate, but has freshness and vigour, flavours of ripe citrus, and good length. With 138 grams per litre of residual sugar, the 2003 is plump and opulent and rich, but it does have reasonable acidity that prevents it from being cloying. The 2004 is moderately sweet, silky, rather reserved at present, and lacks a little flair. The supple 2005 is lush but long.

There's something effortless about Lafaurie-Peyraguey. I always have the impression that Michel Laporte, and now his son Yannick, are steeped in the culture of Sauternes winemaking, which holds no perils for them. Whatever the difficulties of the year, they rise to the challenge, making one of the very best wines of the vintage. For consistency, Lafaurie is hard to beat.

30. Sauternes II

Château Lamothe

Sauternes. Tel: 0556 766789. Website: www.guy.despujols.free.fr. Owner: Guy Despujols. Deuxième cru.
7.5 ha. 85% Sémillon, 10% Sauvignon Blanc, 5% Muscadelle. Production: 20,000 bottles.
Second wine: Les Tourelles de Lamothe

The house is on the site of an eighth-century Merovingian fortress, of which a few traces remain. It is a property that has passed through numerous owners, including the Bastit-St-Martin family of Château d'Arche. In 1961 Armand Bastit-St-Martin sold most of the property to Jean Despujols, but retained part of the vineyard, which produced wine labelled Château Lamothe-Bergey. In 1981 this was sold to the Guignard brothers and renamed as Château Lamothe-Guignard (see below). Under Jean Despujols, Lamothe made very ordinary wine, but quality began to improve after his son Guy took over in 1989.

The vineyards are quite high, on gravelly and sandy soils with a clay subsoil; the vines are planted on a steep southwest-facing slope, and their average age is forty years. Yields tend to average twenty hectolitres per hectare. After pressing in a pneumatic press, the must is fermented with indigenous yeasts. In the 1980s the wine was aged in tanks, and gradually a proportion of barrels was introduced. In this century the *élevage* is more conventional, with the wine aged twelve to fifteen months in twenty-five per cent new barriques. In some vintages Guy Despujols produced a Sélection Exceptionelle at a fairly high price.

In 1990 I tasted the 1924, which was a full, golden colour. The nose was dumb, but the palate was sweet and juicy, with considerable freshness despite some caramel and bitter-orange flavours on the finish. The 1986 is peachy but rather cloying. The bland, loosely structured 1989 is seriously disappointing for the vintage. The 1990 was a more vivid wine, with aromas of banana, apricots, and oranges, very sweet and intense but somehow all on the surface and one-dimensional. The 1992 was a fair effort, with gummy, marzipan aromas, reasonable fruit, but little depth or complexity. The 1995 was pleasant, a rounded and forward wine with little grip, but the fruit and acidity were attractive. The 1996 developed into a medium-bodied wine with a rich, waxy nose, good apricot fruit, invigorating acidity, and just a touch of bitterness on the finish.

The 1997 has attractive apricot aromas, and is fairly rich and supple, but there is little evidence of botrytis, so the overall effect is one of simplicity. The 1998 had sulphury aromas, while the palate was merely pleasant and silky; there's not much to the wine, but it beats the 1999, which is hot and alcoholic, but perhaps I had a defective bottle. The 2001 is distinctly sweet, with ripe lemon flavours but little complexity. The 2002 is similar but with less zest and little character. However, the honeyed 2003 is surprizingly good.

Given its location, there seems no reason why Lamothe shouldn't produce very good wine. As it is, the wine is middle of the road, by no means poor but lacking in concentration, flair, and distinction.

Château Lamothe-Guignard

Sauternes. Tel: 0556 766028. Owners: Philippe and Jacques Guignard. Deuxième cru. 19 ha. 90% Sémillon,
5% Sauvignon Gris, 5% Muscadelle. Production: 36,000 bottles. Second wine: L'Ouest de Lamothe-Guignard

As has been mentioned in the previous entry, this was once a single property that was divided in the late nineteenth century. In the twentieth century this portion was known as Lamothe-Bergey, and it was sold by Henri Bastit-St-Martin to the Guignard brothers in 1981. The Guignards are well implanted in the Graves. One branch owns Château Rolland in Barsac, another Roquetaillade-La-Grange in the Graves (*qq.v*).

Jacques Guignard looks after the vines, Philippe takes care of winemaking and sales. In 1981 they found the buildings run-down, as the wine had previously been made at Château d'Arche. The vineyards are in two sectors. One is on a gravelly plateau facing toward Sauternes, the other on clay-limestone slopes overlooking the Ciron valley. There is also a leased parcel near Rieussec. The average yield has been eighteen hl/ha, though some of the crop is sold off in bulk.

In the 1980s the must was fermented in tanks, but there have been vintages when at least part of the crop was barrel-fermented. The wine is aged in twenty per cent new oak for twelve to fifteen months, although in vintages such as 1992 and 1993 no new oak was used. The wines are fairly priced and offer good value, though they rarely scale the greatest heights. In style, they are often less luscious than most Sauternes and have some of the finesse one associates with Bommes.

The 1983 was light on the nose; the wine lacks some concentration and vigour. There was little botrytis evident on the attractive 1985, but it had good acidity and reasonable length. There were light, waxy, Sémillon aromas on the 1986, which is a relatively simple, accessible wine, though with some force and acidity. (Curiously, when I tasted the wine blind in 1988 I noted "almost Germanic nose". Michael Broadbent's tasting note from 1990 remarked "very Germanic nose". There was no collaboration, so we must have been onto something. However, it was not a character I noted in subsequent tastings.)

The 1987 was soft and easy-going, but had an attractive botrytis character and liveliness. There is much more weight on the 1988, which ten years on had retained its powerful Sémillon nose, and a lush and almost syrupy texture. The 1989 was the best Lamothe-Guignard of the decade, with honeyed, apricot-flan aromas, a velvety texture, fat, peachy flavours, and a slightly baked character. The 1990 is even better: sweeter, creamier, more unctuous and honeyed, with real depth and excellent length.

For a mediocre vintage, the 1992 turned out reasonably well, but it was relatively dilute and lacked structure. The 1995 had rich, peachy aromas, a creamy texture, and some weight, but at the expense of concentration and vigour. There are more candied-pineapple aromas on the 1996, a pretty wine that lacks some grip and energy. Lush apricot and mandarin aromas dominate the 1997, which in 2005 was still lean and lively, though it had a slightly bitter lemon-pith finish.

Lamothe-Guignard is back on form with the sumptuous 2001, with its smoky, marmalade nose, its lovely texture and concentration, and flavours of stewed peach and oranges. I detect pear drops on the nose and palate of the 2002, a pretty but not very concentrated wine. There's apricot jam on the palate of the silky 2003, but it's not a lugubrious wine and has fair acidity on the finish. The nose of the 2004 is attractive – apricot and mandarins – but the attack is a bit weak and the perky acidity doesn't seem fully integrated into the fruit.

Château Lamourette

Bommes. Tel: 0556 766358. Owner: Anne-Marie Léglise. 10 ha. 90% Sémillon, 5% Sauvignon Blanc,
5% Muscadelle. Production: 15,000 bottles

These vineyards are on sandy soil with a rocky subsoil, and the owner finds that her wines sometimes resemble Barsac more than Bommes. The wines are aged in tanks for eighteen months. The 1989 and 1990 were distinctly herbaceous in aroma, and the palate lacked structure. The 1989 was mediocre for the vintage, the 1990 sweeter, more intense, and better balanced. Later vintages were little better. The 1995 had fresh lime and apricot aromas, but was simple and lively rather than rich or weighty. The 1996 was dull, light, and lacked length. Sadly, more recent vintages such as 2002 and 2003, continue the lacklustre record.

Château Latrezotte

See *Sauternes de ma Fille*

Château Laville

Preignac. Tel: 0556 632814. Owner: Claude Barbe. 14 ha. 80% Sémillon, 15% Sauvignon Blanc, 5% Muscadelle.
Production: 12,000 bottles. Second wine: Ch Delmond

I know little about this property, but the 2001 is impressive, with its lush apricot aromas; it's fresh, juicy, and delicious on the palate, with attractive spice and acidity. The 2004, tasted young from cask, was almost as good, and had ample weight and concentration and a long, spicy finish.

Château Liot

Barsac. Tel: 0556 271531. Website: www.chateauliot.com. Owner: Jean Gérard David. 21 ha. 85% Sémillon,
8% Muscadelle, 7% Sauvignon Blanc. Production: 50,000 bottles. Second wine: Ch du Levant

How does one pronounce Liot? M. David himself pronounces it with the "t" both silent and spoken, so you can't go wrong. This property has descended through the female line to the present genial owner and his Spanish wife. Much of the vineyard is near the house, and there are other parcels near Climens, all on the Haut-Barsac plateau on reddish soil. Liot has always been a commercial Barsac, uncomplicated and enjoyable, and inexpensive. The wine is aged in fifteen per cent new oak for sixteen months, and the second wine is unoaked.

Back in 1994 he served me the 1961, which was a bright copper-bronze, and inexpressive on the nose. But it was still rich, concentrated, and unctuous, though caramel and candied-orange flavours suggested it was quite evolved. The 1983, like most Liots, is light in colour, with little botrytis evident; it's pleasantly sweet, but there is little verve or complexity. The 1986 was equally simple but fresh. The 1988 was sweet, clean, tangy, and fresh, and had considerable charm. The 1989 and 1990 both had more depth, more evident botrytis, more elegance, and better length.

The 1994 was creamy and attractive but not remarkable; the 1996 is lusher, as is the excellent 1997. The 2001 is a perfectly good wine but with little character. I find the 2003 rather slack, but it's opulent without being heavy and has reasonable length.

Château de Malle

Preignac. Tel: 0556 623686. Website: www.chateau-de-malle.fr. Owner: Comtesse Nancy de Bournazel.
Deuxième cru. 27 ha Sauternes, 3 ha Graves. Sauternes. 75% Sémillon, 23% Sauvignon Blanc, 2% Muscadelle.
Graves: 70% Sauvignon Blanc, 30% Sémillon. Production: 80,000 bottles Sauternes, 15,000 bottles Graves.
Second wine: Ch de Ste-Hélène

Many of the visitors to this exquisite seventeenth-century château come here to admire the architecture, furnishings, and Italianate gardens rather than because of any great interest in wine. However, the Bournazel family have a wide variety of wines with which to tempt visitors, as they also produce dry white and red wines from the Graves. The *parlementaire* Jacques de Malle built the château, and his descendants remained at Malle until 1702, when Jeanne de Malle married Alexandre-Eutrope de Lur-Saluces, the owner of Château de Fargues. The young couple remained at Château de Malle. By the end of the century the Lur-Saluces were installed at Yquem, thanks to another glittering marriage, while the lesser branch of the family remained at Malle. This state of affairs persisted well into the twentieth century, until a bachelor Lur-Saluces bequeathed the property to his nephew, Comte Pierre de Bournazel.

When he inherited in 1956 at the age of twenty-seven, Pierre de Bournazel found the property – both the château and its surrounding vineyards – in poor condition, as his elderly uncle Pierre had rather neglected it. Much of the château was infested with termites. To make matters worse the frost of 1956 wiped out most of the vines, which had to be replanted (with the aid of Pierre Dubourdieu of Doisy-Daëne). As he had no knowledge of winemaking, he went to Bordeaux to study oenology. His family remained based in Paris, but in 1980 they all moved permanently to Malle. But Pierre de Bournazel was an ill man, and in 1985 he died. Fortunately his widow Nancy, a tall, commanding woman of great warmth and humour, was happy to take up the challenge of running the property, which she has done with great success for many years. Today she is assisted by her sons.

In recent years Nancy de Bournazel and her team have been placing much more emphasis on sound viticulture than in the past; the estate is not organic but treatments are kept to the minimum. The microclimate at Malle is fairly precocious, an advantage in years such as 2004 when the harvest is threatened by rain. Since 1986 half the must has been fermented in new barrels, the other half in one-year barrels. Natural yeast fermentation is preferred but not systematic. The must is never chaptalized. The wine is aged in one-third new oak for between twelve and eighteen months. The *régisseur*, Vincent Labergère, works closely with coopers to achieve the right level of toast, which is fairly low as he doesn't want an evidently oaky wine. No wine was bottled in 1992 or 1993.

Malle had a reputation for producing a fairly light wine. I suspect that had much to do with yields and vinification, as in recent vintages Malle has not lacked richness, although it has never been a heavy or massive wine. The oldest wine I have tasted, the 1938, had fierce acidity and a burnt finish; in 1982 it was already way past whatever its best had been. But the 1943, fifty years on, was still lush and plump, with aromas and flavours of oranges; though not especially full-bodied, it wasn't tiring. The 1962 was light, sharp, and rather tart. The 1981 was a pretty wine, distinctly citric, but creamy and elegant, relatively light but finely balanced. The 1986 was soft and rich but lacked complexity or persistence. The 1987 was modest yet gawky.

With the 1988 there is a marked improvement. There is plenty of botrytis on the nose, which is honeyed and peachy; it has evolved quite rapidly but is a soft, plump, hedonistic Sauternes. The 1989 shines because of its freshness and balance, its concentration and persistence. The 1990 is as good, if not better, with more power, more weight, and very good length. There is some botrytis on the nose of the 1991, which is very sweet and intense, with a fine texture and good length. Like the similar 1994, it was probably best enjoyed relatively young. The 1995 has spicy, oaky, apricot aromas, fine apricot fruit, moderate acidity, and discernible alcohol on the finish. The 1996 has more tropical fruit aromas, richness and power, and fair concentration and finesse. Floral and honeyed aromas mark the 1997, which is rich and supple but also has a long, citric finish.

After this string of excellent wines, the 1998 is a slight disappointment; it's easy-going with a pretty touch of oak, but it lacks punch and complexity. I prefer the 1999, with its opulent, peachy aromas, its spice and liveliness. The 2001 is rather one-dimensional now, but it's supple and silky and has ample fruit and freshness, and will surely develop well. There are aromas of honey and apricot on the 2002, which is a rich, bold wine with delicious fruit and a fine backbone of acidity. The 2003 is, of course, more voluptuous; it has delicious apricot and peach fruit but the wine lacks some zest at present. The youthful 2004 is somewhat neutral, but the 2005 is oaky yet succulent.

Although Malle is best known for its Sauternes, it also produces some good dry wines. M de Malle is produced from fifty per cent Sémillon and fifty per cent Sauvignon Blanc, with the grapes vinified together after skin contact. The must is fermented in fifty per cent new oak, and aged for nine months on the fine lees. It's quite a lean wine, sometimes a touch tart, with aromas and flavours of gooseberry and grapefruit. There is also an unoaked white called Chevalier de Malle, which is pure Sauvignon Blanc.

Château Massereau

Barsac. Tel: 0556 274662. Owners: Jean-François and Philippe Chaigneau. 1.2 ha. 85% Sémillon, 15% Muscadelle. Production: 2,000 bottles

Les garagistes sont arrivés! Massereau was originally a fifteenth-century hunting lodge that belonged to a family called Pinson for centuries. When sold in 1986, it had lost most of its vineyards, which had been bought by Doisy-Védrines and often sold on. Massereau was bought in 2000 by Jean-François Chaigneau, an oenologist, and his more commercially minded brother.

They could not earn a living from just over a hectare, so they also produce red Graves, some Bordeaux Supérieur, and a *clairet* from an additional nine hectares. The Sauternes, labelled M de Massereau, comes from vines close to the Ciron. Chaigneau has heightened the trellising and prunes severely; the soil is ploughed and no herbicides are used. Only botrytized grapes are picked, so there can be as many as a dozen *tries*. The fruit is pressed in a vertical press, and there is no chaptalization, acidification, or cryo-extraction. The must is fermented and aged in new oak for about twenty months, and bottled without filtration (which seems risky for a sweet wine).

These are impressive and serious wines, but so they should be with a price tag of around 100 Euros. The 2001 had a curiously buttery, oaky nose; on the palate it was highly concentrated, its lushness balanced by fine acidity. The 2002 lacks some fat, but it has delightful pineapple and apricot fruit and a good deal of freshness and complexity. The 2003 is rich but not heavy, with ripe stone-fruit aromas and flavours. Although quality is high, these wines are hardly good value considering what else is available.

Château du Mont

Fargues. Tel: 0556 620765. Owner: Hervé Chouvac. 1 ha. 100% Sémillon. Production: 3,000 bottles

Chouvac owns a property of the same name in Ste-Croix-du-Mont. Interestingly, he sells the wine from here, known since 2001 as Cuvée Jeanne, for the same price as the Ste-Croix, as he doesn't want his clients to assume that the Sauternes is necessarily of finer quality. There are usually three *tries* and yields tend to be close to the maximum. The must is fermented and aged in new barriques.

The 1996 has burnished aromas of mandarins, apricots, and dried fruits; it is silky and has charm and delicacy, a pretty wine that is still youthful. The 2004 has a slight herbaceous character on the nose; it's medium-bodied and has zest but I don't detect a lot of botrytis and the fruit is rather candied. Given the low price at which the wine is sold, it offers excellent value.

Château Monteils

Preignac. Tel: 0556 761212. Website: www.monteils-vin-sauternes.com. Owner: Hervé le Diascorn.
12 ha. 75% Sémillon, 20% Sauvignon Blanc, 5% Muscadelle. Production: 35,000 bottles

This wine has a growing reputation. It is aged for eighteen months in tanks and barriques. The only vintage I have tasted, other than a green cask sample of the 2004, is the fresh, silky 2001.

Domaine de Monteils

Preignac. Tel: 0556 622405. Website: www.domaine-de-monteils.com. Owners: Marie-Christine and
Jean-Paul Fourcaud. 11 ha. 85% Sémillon, 8% Sauvignon Blanc, 7% Muscadelle. Production: 30,000 bottles.
Second wine: Ch Haut-Monteils

This property was developed in the 1960s by Jean-Claude Cousin but much of the wine was sold in bulk. In 2000 his son-in-law Jean-Paul Fourcaud took over running the estate. The vines are on gravel soil and planted to an unusually high density of 7,000–8,800 vines per hectare. The regular bottling is fermented and aged mostly in tanks for twenty-four months; the Sélection is fermented and aged in barriques. The 1996 Sélection was rich and oaky, with good concentration and a spicy finish. The 2004, tasted from cask, is lighter and less concentrated but attractive nonetheless. The 2003 and 2005 are lush but show good acidity.

Château de Myrat

Barsac. Tel: 0556 270906. Owners: Jacques and Xavier de Pontac. Deuxième cru. 22 ha. 88% Sémillon,
8% Sauvignon Blanc, 4% Muscadelle. Production: 40,000 bottles

In the mid-nineteenth century this property, with its delectable eighteenth-century château, was conjoined with Broustet. In 1936 Myrat alone was acquired by the de Pontac family, related, somehow, to the celebrated Pontacs formerly of Haut-Brion. Unfortunately Maximilian de Pontac became so disillusioned with producing this costly wine for an indifferent market that he stopped bottling the wine and in 1976 took the extraordinary step of up rooting the entire vineyard despite its classified status. It had been ranked at the head of the Second Growths, and was said, according to Xavier de Pontac, to have the best soil in Barsac after Climens: limestone-clay on fissured limestone. On the death of Maximilian in 1988, his sons decided to replant the estate and renovate the cellars, and the old *cuvier* has been attractively converted into a tasting and reception hall. The Pontacs were plagued by the most dreadful luck. In the great vintage of 1990, the vines were still too young to be entitled to produce Sauternes, so the wine was released as AC Bordeaux. In 1991 frost did considerable damage and only 6,000 bottles could be made. In 1992 most of the wine was sold in bulk, again leaving just 6,000 bottles. Some 1993 was bottled, but it was not a good vintage. In April 1994 most of the vineyard was hit by frost on the day I visited Myrat, with a downcast Xavier de Pontac bravely trying to shrug off the disaster. Finally, in 1995 Myrat was in full production for the first time.

The Sémillon is fermented and aged in thirty per cent new barriques, but the Sauvignon component, which is small, is aged in tanks and then the two are blended.

I have not tasted old vintages of Myrat, but those who have done so were impressed by their quality and staying power. The 1990 was interesting to taste, just to see how very young vines cope in a great vintage. It was a charming wine, light and spicy and well made, but it lacked richness and length. The 1991 had little concentration or fruit. The 1995 had tarry aromas from strong botrytization, and on the palate the wine was very rich and full, but a touch blowsy. Myrat seems to find its true expression with the 1996, with its oaky, spicy, peachy aromas, its creamy texture and attractive apricot fruit, and a finesse and concentration absent from previous vintages. The 1997 has barley sugar and although the texture is quite soft there is also bracing acidity and a lively finish.

The 2001 has been consistently excellent, with aromas of orange and peach and a light smokiness; it's plump and full-bodied, with lovely ripe apricot fruit and a very long, almost peppery finish. Far leaner is the 2002, but the texture is silky, it's elegant and has good acidity, and reasonable length. The 2003 rapidly developed peachy, honeyed aromas; it's very rich and broad, almost syrupy, but it does have decent length.

Château Nairac

Barsac. Tel: 0556 271616. Website: www.chateau-nairac.com. Owner: Nicolas Heeter-Tari. Deuxième cru.
16 ha. 90% Sémillon, 6% Sauvignon Blanc, 4% Muscadelle. Production: 15,000 bottles

As you enter Barsac from the north, the broad, low château on the right is Nairac. It was built by a pupil of Victor Louis in the 1770s. It takes its name from Elysée Nairac, who bought the estate in 1777. He belonged to a rich merchant and shipowning family from Bordeaux. The Nairacs fled the country during the Revolution, but after Elysée's death in 1791, the estate was inherited by his daughters. They lived here until the death of the remaining daughter in 1837. It was acquired by the Capdeville family, who already owned Broustet; so the two estates were combined, only to be divided again in 1861 on the death of Bernard Capdeville. The Nairac portion was inherited by his daughter, who was married to Pierre Brunet, the owner of Piada. Perhaps because they already had enough white vines, they chose to plant Nairac with red varieties. In the early twentieth century the childless Brunets died and left the property to a cousin; by this time about one-third of the production was of Sauternes. Under the ownership of a négociant called Jean-Charles Perpezat, the red vines were gradually eliminated. The vines were replanted again after the frost of 1956. Nairac was sold by the Perpezats in 1966, but the new owner neglected the property and sold its wine in bulk.

Nairac was sold in 1972 to Nicole Tari and her American husband Tom Heeter. Her family owned Giscours, where Heeter had been gaining experience of the wine business. After their marriage they had began and began looking out for their own property. Nairac was bought cheaply, but needed complete renovation. The house had been empty for half a century, and it would be a further two years before it was fit for habitation. Tom Heeter was essentially self-taught, though he benefited from advice he sought from Emile Peynaud and Pierre Meslier of Yquem. He would prove to be a perfectionist winemaker, practising the most severe selective harvesting. (It is widely accepted that Nairac's vineyards are not all outstanding, and thus selection is even more important here than at better endowed properties.) He also experimented tirelessly with methods of reducing combined sulphur in the wines, and was fascinated by the permutations offered by oak barrels of various sources and types. He began by using entirely new oak, but by 1980 reduced the proportion to around fifty per cent. His perfectionism meant that he was able to produce good wine in years when most other châteaux gave up trying.

Unfortunately the marriage was not to last. Tom Heeter's last vintage was 1986, and Nicole Tari bought him out in 1987. She hired François Amirault as winemaker, but relations soured after a few years, and in 1993 he left for Château de Fargues. By this time the Heeters' son Nicolas was ready to try his hand, and showed the same perfectionist streak as his father. I have been a frequent visitor at Nairac, enjoying Tom Heeter's rather chaotic hospitality, lavish lunches with Nicolas in the kitchen, and a few nights in the distinctly spartan guest quarters. So I have a soft spot for Nairac, which may influence my judgment.

Nine hectares of vineyards lie behind the château, three more along the RN13 on gravelly soil, and two more next to Climens on more classic Barsac soil. Density is high at around 8,000 vines per hectare, and yields exceedingly low. From 1992 to 2003 the average has been 8.5 hl/ha. Nicolas, like his father, likes to pick the Sauvignon Blanc overripe rather than botrytized, to preserve its freshness and floral aromas, and the variety usually accounts for around fifteen per cent of the final blend. The must is barrel-fermented in up to sixty-five per cent new oak, and the *élevage* can be as long as thirty months. Any barrels with which Nicolas Heeter-Tari is unhappy are sold off. For a Barsac, Nairac can be very lush and powerful, and easily mistaken for a Sauternes.

The only pre-Heeter vintage I have tasted is the 1955, which Nicolas Heeter-Tari brought up from the cellar as a reward for helping him press the grapes in 1994. It was remarkably good, with *confit* aromas of caramelized oranges and honey. It wasn't that sweet, but the texture was rich, and the wine was balanced and quite long, with evolved flavours of caramel and marmalade. The 1972, in 1986, was rather woody, but rich, velvety, and concentrated; it is probably past is best. According to Clive Coates, the 1973 was aged in Yugoslav oak. It was fairly light yet concentrated, with attractive spiciness and acidity, and was still lively and elegant ten years on. Heeter lavished eleven *tries* on the miserable 1974 vintage, but the wine was still dilute and rather short. The 1975, last drunk from magnum in 1986, was always delicious, a racy, elegant wine with impeccable balance and length. The 1976 had much more weight and botrytis, almost to excess; it was sumptuous for many years, but a magnum drunk in 1999 seemed to be drying out.

The 1979 was excellent for the year, with ample honeyed botrytis, a lush texture, ample in body and oaky on the finish. The 1980 displays honeyed aromas, and a palate marked more by charm and elegance than power and weight. The 1981 was rather hard and austere when young and I doubt it has mellowed greatly. The 1982 is a slight disappointment, reasonably concentrated but one-dimensional and lacking in persistence. The 1983 is far more complex, with pronounced oakiness, elegance and raciness, fine concentration, and good length. The 1985 was very sulphury when young, and I have not tasted it since. The 1986 always seemed overoaked, with oily aromas and a lack of finesse and balance. In 1987, a difficult year, Nairac made a pleasant but unremarkable wine.

I tasted the 1988 when fairly young, and then it was an oaky, spicy wine that seemed well structured. The 1989 was far better, a very sweet but discreet style with a good deal of oak but fine acidity and length. The 1990 has the conspicuous oakiness that so often marks Nairac, but it's also luxurious and lush, with ample flair, complexity, and acidity. The 1991 was almost as good, and much in the same style, though with less body. Only 2,900 bottles were produced in 1992; fierce selection delivered an eccentric wine that was lightly honeyed on the nose, juicy on the palate but with bitter orange flavours and high acidity. The 1994, despite my helping hand, turned out very well, with heady botrytis aromas of apricots and orange zest, and a creamy texture, a touch heavy but certainly concentrated.

The 1995 is a triumph, a flamboyant and truly sumptuous wine, very *confit*, resembling liquefied peaches and cream. The 1996 was similar, but perhaps with a dash more spice and acidity to enliven the very rich peach and mandarin fruit. The 1997 is equally admirable, its richness balanced by its fine attack and its purity of flavour. The 1998, drunk in 2005, was odd, with aromas of stewed peach and iodine, and a slight oxidative tone; the palate too lacked some freshness, which suggests the botrytization was not that healthy. No problems with the plump 1999, which has smoky, peachy aromas and fine concentration. But here too there is a slight oxidative tone and a touch of heaviness that may be allied to the long *élevage*. No Nairac was released in 2000. The sumptuous 2001 has the same weight and richness as the 1999 without that oxidative tone; thus it combines power with finesse. The 2002 is surprisingly rich, with aromas of lemons and olive oil; it has weight and considerable power, as well as spiciness, complexity, and length. I was unimpressed by the 2003, admittedly from cask, in late 2005. The 2004 is quite tropical in its fruit profile, but has a silky texture and considerable intensity and sweetness; if it seems one-dimensional, it is also very pretty, with a long, pineappley finish.

Nairac treads a fine line between Barsac intensity and a richness that occasionally veers toward heaviness, perhaps a consequence of Nicolas Heeter-Tari's obsessive search for only the finest botrytized fruit. Yields are uneconomically low, and one wonders how long Nairac can continue to restrict its production to just the finest barrels.

Château Piada

*Barsac. Tel: 0556 271613. **Owner:** Frédéric Lalande. 10 ha. 100% Sémillon. **Production:** 30,000 bottles.*

__Second wine:__ Clos du Roy

Piada adjoins Coutet, and until 1809 formed part of it. It then passed through various families, and was re-established by the Lalandes in 1940. In 1999 Jean Lalande was succeeded by his son Frédéric. They also own Château Hauret-Lalande, which produces white Graves and, occasionally, Cérons. The Barsac vineyards are close to the house on soils of red sand and sandy gravel over limestone. There are four to five *tries* and yields vary considerably according to the vintage. Piada is almost never chaptalized, and is fermented in ten per cent new barriques and aged for twelve months.

The 1986 had citric aromas, and delicacy rather than concentration, an attractive wine for relatively early drinking. The 1988 was more elegant and racy, a vigorous wine with plenty of underlying richness. The 1989 was more plump and peachy; it opened up fast but had plenty of backbone. The 1990 was sweeter, a touch leaner, with good concentration and a lively, peppery finish. The 1991 was creamy but vigorous and surprisingly tight, with some structure, a modest wine but a success for the vintage. The 1995 lacked botrytis character but had pretty, peachy fruit with reasonable freshness on the finish. The 1996, tasted recently, had a rather oily nose, and although dense and peachy, it had a lot of alcohol and faded on the finish. Alcohol also mars the 1999, which is rather heavy and has a dried-fruits character; it's a bit drab. The medium-bodied 2000 lacks sweetness and has low acidity, and Lalande admits he had been uncertain whether to bottle the wine. The 2001 has rich, peachy aromas, but it's rather hefty, with plump apricot fruit, and it lacks freshness and length. I almost prefer the 2002, with its mandarin and apricot aromas, a silky texture, delicacy rather than power, and attractive acidity. The 2003 is opulent and peachy but lacks acidity. The 2004 has a curious sweet-and-sour tone and flavours of Seville oranges; atypical perhaps, and rather assertive, but it's a wine with character. The 2005 seems candied but easygoing.

Piada is inconsistent, and I'm not sure that Lalande is prepared to go the extra mile to deliver the highest quality. Not able to charge the same prices as the classed growths, he may well be reluctant to make further sacrifices.

Château Rabaud-Promis

*Bommes. Tel: 0556 766738. **Owner:** Philippe Dejean. Premier cru. 33 ha. 80% Sémillon, 18% Sauvignon Blanc, 2% Muscadelle. **Production:** 60,000 bottles. **Second wine:** Ch Bequet*

Rabaud has a long and complex history. In 1660 Marie Peyronne de Rabaud married Arnaud de Cazeau, and their descendants retained possession of the estate until 1819, when it was sold to Gabriel Deyme. In 1864 Henri de Sigalas bought and expanded the estate to over forty hectares. During the 1880s Sigalas acquired Château Pexoto, a Second Growth, and its vines were absorbed into Rabaud. Nonetheless Rabaud retained its First-Growth status. Until 1903 Rabaud remained a single estate, but in that year Henri de Sigalas's son Pierre sold part of the estate to Adrien Promis from Loupiac. But in 1930 the divided property was reunited when Fernand Ginestet came to an agreement with the various owners to farm the vineyards and market the wine. The then-owners were the daughters of Adrien Promis and a Sigalas daughter, who married the Marquis Lambert des Granges. In 1949 Rabaud was divided again, René Lambert des Granges decided to buy what had been the Sigalas share, and Raymond-Louis Lanneluc bought what was now known as Rabaud-Promis. It was poorly looked after, but was saved by Philippe Dejean, who had married Lanneluc's granddaughter. Dejean hadn't really intended to be a winemaker, but he was able to follow the example of his brother Patrick, who owned the Domaine du Noble across the river in Loupiac. Philippe Dejean began managing Rabaud-Promis in 1974, and in 1981 he and his wife became the majority shareholders.

Gradually Dejean was able to make the investments the property badly needed. In 1988 the horizontal presses were replaced by pneumatic presses, and he installed stainless-steel vats. Until the later 1980s the wine had been fermented in underground vats with limited barrel-ageing. From 1988 onwards about one-third of the barrels were renewed each year. Dejean also introduced a second wine to allow better selection for Rabaud.

The vineyards surround the property on a *croupe*, and their average age is thirty-five years. Average yields are eighteen hl/ha. The soil is unusually gravelly for this part of Bommes, but there is a good deal of clay too.

I used to visit Rabaud-Promis on a regular basis, but I have not set foot on the property for at least a decade. Philippe Dejean seems a bit of a loner, and rarely submits his wine when blind tastings are organized for me in Sauternes. So I am less up to date on the property and its wines than I would like.

The oldest vintage I have tasted is the 1918, which was full gold with no browning. It had light barley-sugar aromas; the palate was soft and velvety, but it was losing some fruit and sweetness but not interest. The 1937 in 1990 was still bright, but aromatically reserved, with hints of orange; the palate was soft, loose, and rather dour, and there were flavours of apple compote and modest length. There were light marmalade aromas on the 1948, which remained very sweet and full, though it was just beginning to dry out.

The 1975 showed signs of oxidation, with caramelly, barley-sugar aromas, considerable viscosity and body, reasonable sweetness, and a slightly burnt, marmalade finish. The 1983 has always been very good, with lush, honeyed, peachy aromas; it lacks a little complexity and concentration, but it's an attractive, charming wine with some piquancy on the finish. There's little botrytis on the 1985, but it's rich and waxy, reasonably concentrated, and has modest acidity. The 1986 has an appealing raciness on the nose, but it's supple and fairly simple. The 1988 had a classic Sauternes nose, with peaches and honey; it's more lush and creamy than most previous wines from here, but there is no tarriness or oxidation; it's a delicious wine with all the elegance of the vintage.

On the nose the 1989 is lush and quite oaky; the palate is quite *rôti*, with orange and barley-sugar flavours, good acidity, and a dash of spice on the finish. I have consistently good notes on this wine over many years. The 1990, when young, was very attractive, perhaps a touch light and lacking a little concentration, but the texture was creamy and there were appealing flavours of apricot and honey. The 1992 was lean and racy, lacking in fat and depth, but a well-balanced wine for early consumption. The 1995 had oaky aromas but little evident botrytis; the palate was lush and waxy, but the fruit was rather one-dimensional.

The 1996 is light and elegant on the nose; this too is in a lean style with assertive acidity, and rather less plump fruit than one would have expected; it has a long, citric finish. There is a strange lack of concentration and grip on the 1997, which is pleasant enough but bland for a great year. However, the 2001 is back on form, with a complex nose of peaches and oranges and smoky botrytis; the palate is sweet, silky, and properly concentrated, with orangey flavours and good acidity and length. The 2002 has ample weight but not much vigour. The 2003 has plump apricot aromas, and it's lush and broad, though not especially sweet; the alcohol seems high and the balance imperfect.

Château Raymond-Lafon

Sauternes. Tel: 0556 632102. Website: www.chateau-raymond-lafon.fr. Owner: Pierre Meslier. 16 ha. 80% Sémillon, 20% Sauvignon Blanc. Production: 20,000 bottles. Second wine: Harmonie de Raymond-Lafon

This property was created in 1850, but its early history is unclear. Raymond Lafon was the mayor of Sauternes, a relative owned Château Lafon across the road. Raymond-Lafon was highly rated in an unofficial classification made in 1867. The owners, including the present ones, have always made much of the fact that some of the vineyards touch those of Yquem. After the death of Raymond Lafon, the estate came into the hands of his son-in-law Louis Pontallier. The Pontalliers sold it in the 1950s, and the property became run-down. When Pierre Meslier bought the property in 1972, there were fewer than four hectares of vines.

Meslier had managed classed growths in Margaux before being hired by Yquem as general manager in 1963. Thereafter there were mutterings about conflict of interest as Meslier promoted his own wines as well as Yquem's. Eventually matters came to a head and there was a spectacular falling out between Meslier and the Comte de Lur-Saluces. Thereafter Meslier devoted all his energies to his own estate, and in 1990 he ceded some control to his daughter and two sons, one of whom, Charles-Henri, is now the winemaker.

From the outset, Meslier was determined to apply the same demanding standards to Raymond-Lafon that he had maintained at Yquem. Severe pruning kept yields low. Only botrytized fruit was sought after numerous *tris*, giving an average must weight of between nineteen and twenty-one degrees. There was no chaptalization, and the grapes were pressed in a vertical press. The wine was aged for three years in barriques, of which eighty to 100 per cent were new. What was admirable at Raymond-Lafon was the determination to try to make good wine, in however small a quantity, in each year, though even Meslier was defeated by 1974, when no wine was bottled.

A visit to Raymond-Lafon was something of a ceremony. The Mesliers were devoted to their vicious dogs (as well as the black swan and peacocks that roamed the garden of the villa-like château), so the prudent visitor would wait for them to be shackled before venturing to the cellars. The wine was always presented, usually by Pierre's late wife or his daughter, on a small table in a room within the house. Very precise records were kept of climatic and harvest conditions for all vintages, and the Mesliers were only too happy to pass these detailed reports on to interested guests and customers. Prices rose in the 1980s, and by the end of that decade Raymond-Lafon was probably the most expensive Sauternes after Yquem and Fargues. Various marketing wheezes – such as bottling numbered imperials and selling them in silk-lined boxes – were clearly aimed at the American market. Despite this reliance on glitz, it was impossible to deny that the wine was very good indeed.

The oldest vintage I have tasted was the 1933, but by 1984 it had oxidized and dried out. The 1971 was raisiny and rather austere, so the fruit was beginning to tire; it also lacked length. The first Meslier vintage I tasted was the 1975, which by 1988 was orangey and slightly oxidized; orangey flavours, a velvety texture, and rather fierce acidity added up to an impressive if not harmonious wine. The only bottle of the 1978 I have tasted, in 1986, was also oxidizing. Perhaps this tendency to oxidize was a consequence of the very prolonged barrel-ageing practised by Meslier.

However, the 1979, frequently tasted, was excellent, with ample botrytis on the nose; the palate was creamy yet elegant, with delicious peachy fruit and excellent length. The 1980, also tasted over many years, was voluptuous and silky, elegant yet with excellent acidity and, by 2006, no hint of decline. The 1981 was plump and very concentrated but I have not tasted it since 1986. The 1982 is also very rich, with high glycerol levels; the nose, initially scented with peach and citrus, took on slightly caramelly tones by 1996; there is tremendous weight and concentration on the palate. The excellence of the 1982 Raymond-Lafon is probably attributable to the fact that only a third of the grapes, those picked before the heavy rains, were used. The 1983 was initially very good, but there is considerable bottle variation: some went through secondary fermentation in bottle, others were oxidized.

The 1984 had sweet, honeyed aromas, and was very sweet, with marked acidity; but it was essentially lightweight and is probably past its best. The 1985, tasted after bottling, was very fat but too sulphury to enjoy. The 1986 was lush and creamy, but lacked power and weight, and the fruit was rather subdued. The 1987 was true to the vintage, being lively and concentrated yet lacking in some persistence, signalling that this was not a wine for long ageing. There were citric aromas on the 1988, which was rich and intense, with impeccable balance and fine acidity; I last tasted it in 1993 and my hunch is that it should still be excellent. The 1989 was fatter, even richer, and unctuous, with just a hint of oak on the long finish. The 1991 may have lacked some depth, but it had delicious lemony fruit, a creamy texture, and fine acidity. I was impressed by the 1992 from cask, but have not tasted it since.

There was a good deal of oak as well as botrytis on the nose of the 1996, which was plump and rich, but high alcohol diminished its finesse. The 2001 had ripe apricot aromas, while the palate was powerful and concentrated, with flavours of apricot and mint, and the length was stunning. The 2002 was rather heavy-handed for the vintage, with stewed-apricot aromas, a lot of obvious oak, and an ungainly character unusual for Raymond-Lafon. The 2003 has 168 grams per litre of residual sugar, and it was rich in peach and pineapple flavours, yet its intensity and length successfully balance the sweetness. The 2004 from cask has oaky, apricot aromas, a silky texture, considerable intensity of mandarin and pineapple fruit, and a perky and peppery aftertaste.

Raymond-Lafon rarely disappoints. It always has concentration and a lush botrytis character, and the new oak is well integrated; sometimes it lacks finesse, but that's a quibble. Pierre Meslier aimed for the highest quality from the outset, and, apart from an occasional tendency to oxidation that now seems overcome, that is what he and Charles-Henri deliver.

Château Rayne-Vigneau

Bommes. Tel: 0556 766163. Owner: Crédit Agricole Grands Crus. 0. Premier cru. 80 ha. 80% Sémillon,
20% Sauvignon Blanc. Production: 200,000 bottles. Second wine: Clos l'Abeilley

This château sits high on a hilltop while its vineyards pay homage all around. As at Yquem, the vines have a great variety of expositions, giving the winemakers numerous possibilities for blending. It is named after a late-seventeenth-century owner, Etienne de Vigneau, and was known simply as Château Vigneau until 1892, when the prefix was added. From 1834 it belonged to Baron de Reyne, whose wife was a member of the illustrious de Pontac family. The property passed to her brother, who built the rather pompous château in the 1870s, and from him to his son Albert. After Albert's death in the 1920s, his son-in-law, the Vicomte de Roton, inherited the estate. He had some geological training, and it was he who discovered that the vineyards were studded with precious and semi-precious stones, all deposited here by glaciers from the Pyrenees many million years ago.

The Roton family still live here, but in 1961 the vineyards were sold to a wine merchant called Georges Raoux. Ten years later he sold them to the négociant house of Mestrezat. The vines were in poor shape, so much time and money had to be spent in replanting and renovation. Jean Merlaut, also a Bordeaux merchant, was a major investor in Mestrezat and he supervised the substantial investments in a modern winery, set well apart from the château itself. In 2004 Rayne-Vigneau, like other properties once under the Mestrezat umbrella, was bought by a consortium of investors backed by the Crédit Agricole bank. There has been continuity, however, thanks to the presence since 1982 of Patrick Eymery as *régisseur*. More recently, Denis Dubourdieu has been acting as a consultant to the property.

The vineyards rise to an elevation of seventy-three metres (240 feet), and the soil is unusually stony, with gravelly sand over a clay subsoil. The best sector is around the winery and château, where there is more clay in the soil. The incline means that natural drainage is very good. Since 2000 newly planted vines are at a density of 6,600 per hectare. Insiders sometimes remark that the terroir here is potentially almost as great as that of Yquem, but the relatively young age of the vines inhibits the expression of that potential. Young vines and those planted at the base of the hill are never used for the *grand vin* but are used for the dry white wine. According to Eymery, only about fifty hectares out of the eighty planted are on first-rate soils.

The winery is very well equipped. In 1988 the old horizontal presses were replaced by pneumatic presses. It was only since 2001 that the whole crop has been barrel-fermented. Indeed, Rayne-Vigneau has always been run on commercial lines, which is not to imply that the wine is somehow second-rate. Yields may be slightly higher than at other First Growths (around eighteen hl/ha), but the principle of *tries successives* is strictly adhered to. However, selected yeasts are used, and, at least some years ago, chaptalization was practised when Eymery thought it advisable. The estate is also equipped with a cold chamber, although cryo-extracted lots are never used for the *grand vin*. The wine is aged in fifty per cent new barriques for eighteen months. Eymery wants a wine of elegance and drinkability rather than excessive sweetness, and looks for must weights of nineteen to twenty degrees. Nonetheless in recent vintages the wine has often had residual sugar levels of around 130 grams per litre.

Old vintages such as 1893, 1904, 1923, and 1928 are said to be remarkable, but the oldest Rayne-Vigneau I have come across is the 1939 Crème de Tête, which tasted half its age: the colour was yellow-gold, the nose perfectly healthy with aromas of peach, orange, and barleysugar; and the palate was very sweet and intense and long.

The 1981 was loosely structured and disappointing, with little intensity or length. The 1983 was more stylish, but it lacked richness and was almost tart; nor was botrytis much in evidence. By 1986 there were signs of improvement, and although the wine was not that rich or layered – Rayne-Vigneau rarely is – it was elegant and long. After a simple and skeletal 1987, Rayne-Vigneau produced a splendid wine in 1988, surely its best in decades. There was ample botrytis on the nose, while the palate exploded with apricot and peach fruit and racy acidity. The 1989 is oaky and stylish, quite dense but with exemplary balance and very good length. It is slightly better than the more solid 1990, which is sumptuous and concentrated but lacks the freshness and zest of the preceding vintages. Nonetheless, it's a very fine Sauternes.

The 1992 lacks body and richness and structure, and the 1994 seemed quite dilute, with a thin finish. Peachy botrytis aromas grace the 1995, but the wine could use more vigour and concentration. It's surpassed by the powerful 1996, a plump, rounded wine, honeyed, silky, and concentrated, with a long, oaky finish. The 1997 was excellent just before bottling, distinctly sweet but elegant. The 1998 is more citric, a sleek, medium-bodied Sauternes that lacks some concentration. The 1999 is more stylish, with smoky botrytis aromas, bright apricot fruit, a tight structure, and fine length. The 2000, though scented with honey and peach, is light and somewhat dilute, though reasonably fresh.

Rayne-Vigneau produced a magnificent 2001, packed with ripe stone-fruits flavours, a touch *rôti*, yet with ample zest and spice, and a refreshing pineappley finish. The 2002 is very good too, less exuberant than the 2001, but brisk and long. The 2003 seems rather sugary with lush tropical fruit flavours but fine length. The 2004 is disappointingly simple, but perfectly agreeable. Shortly before bottling the 2005 was sleek but lacked complexity.

Château Rieussec

Fargues. Tel: 0557 981414. Website: www.lafite.com. **Owner:** *Domaines Barons de Rothschild. Premier cru. 90 ha.*
95% Sémillon, 3% Sauvignon Blanc, 2% Muscadelle. **Production:** *110,000 bottles.* **Second wine:** *Carmes de Rieussec*

Before the Revolution Rieussec belonged to a Carmelite monastery; it was then confiscated and sold. There were numerous owners through the nineteenth and twentieth centuries. Eventually, a supermarket proprietor called Albert Vuillier bought Rieussec in 1971. He replanted much of the vineyard and introduced new oak for the first time in many years. He sold the property in 1984 to a consortium dominated by the Rothschilds of Lafite, but Albert Frère of Belgium also owns a substantial stake. Before being whisked away to Lafite to run all the Rothschild interests in Bordeaux, Charles Chevallier managed the property. Today it is run by Frédéric Magniez.

Rieussec stands on another of those hills captured by many of the best First Growths. It's said to be the second-highest spot after Yquem. As well as the vineyards around the château, there are leased vines near Château de Fargues. The grapes ripen about five days earlier than at Yquem, which can be an advantage. The soil is varied, as so often in Sauternes, with much gravel and a subsoil of clay and limestone. From the mid-1990s the Rieussec team reduced the use of herbicides and began ploughing the rows. Sauvignon Blanc and Muscadelle are picked at must weights of around seventeen degrees of potential alcohol, as Rieussec does not want excessive concentration or noble rot for these varieties. It used to be said that at Rieussec there was little selection in the vineyard, and that the blending of the *grand vin* was a matter of selecting the very best barrels. I doubt this is still the case.

Since 1997 the whole crop has been barrel-fermented, with some forty-five separate lots. Rieussec has a cold chamber, which they use just for the second wine. The estate has always favoured long barrel-ageing, usually around twenty-four months. The barrels come from the cooperage at Lafite.

There have been stylistic changes at Rieussec. Before the 1970s it was thought of as one of the lighter Sauternes; under Vuillier it became one of the richest and indeed heaviest wines; while under the Rothschilds it has found an ideal balance.

The oldest vintage I have tasted is the 1926: it looked a fresh medium gold, but it was drying out and austere. The 1959 was a splendid wine, with rich barley-sugar and honey aromas, and intense flavours of apricot and barley sugar; it also had some finesse and a long finish. The 1961 lacked allure: it was soft and rounded, but there was little evident botrytis character, and high alcohol marred the finish. The 1962 was sweet and silky, with lively acidity; it was reasonably concentrated but elegant. I had mixed experiences of the 1970, one bottle showing caramel and butterscotch aromas and a baked character on the palate, another being dumb on the nose and lacking flair on the palate. The 1971 is far better, with *rôti* aromas of dried apricot and honey, reasonable concentration, ample vigour, and a long, tangy finish. When young the deep gold 1975 was very much in the Vuillier style, with a palate that was fat and luscious and close to blowsy; however, a bottle drunk in 2007 had delicate orange aromas and was far livlier than expected. The 1976 evolved very fast; it was rich and honeyed but surrendered all its charm at first sip.

The 1978 too was rather hot and overblown, with flavours of stewed oranges; but it was still eminently if surprisingly drinkable in 2000. There was ample botrytis on the 1979, but it lacked sweetness and was rather soupy; high alcohol marred the finish. The 1980 is quite *rôti*, with toffee-apple and caramel aromas, and a rich, honeyed, creamy palate. By 2000 it was very dark, yet the wine, though burnished and evolved, was still reasonably fresh. The 1981 was more lemony and racy, but lacked fat and complexity. The golden 1982 has raisin and banana aromas, and a slight heaviness on the palate; in the 1990s some bottles were spicy and exuberant, but most seemed lacking in grip and finesse. The 1983 was the apotheosis of the Vuillier style: rich in peachy botrytis, a touch raisiny, chunky and unctuous. By 2000 it was still going strong: the colour was a rich gold, a certain tarriness had set in, but the fruit was delicious.

There was less fat and opulence on the 1984, and the wine had elegance and a clean finish. The 1985 was a disappointment, a dumb wine with a clumsy, soapy, alcoholic character. Rieussec returned to greatness with the 1986, which is oaky and opulent with heaps of botrytis on the nose, a wine of fine concentration and power, plump yet not heavy, and brilliantly long. In contrast, the 1987 was a lightweight, but forward and enjoyable young. The 1988, 1989, and 1990 are all great wines. The 1988 may be less rich and concentrated than the other two vintages, but it has fine acidity and a graceful structure. The 1989 is super-rich but not clumsy, and in 2001 it still tasted youthful and vigorous. The 1990 is more *rôti*, with flavours of marmalade and *crème brûlée* not evident on the preceding vintages. But it's unctuous, complex, and hedonistic, and in 2005 still had amazing length.

The 1992 was modest but pleasant. The 1995 was creamy and full-bodied, a forward wine that nonetheless had a good acidic bite on the finish. The 1996 was very good, a ripe, oaky wine with a creamy, sappy texture and peachy fruit; but high alcohol disrupted the finish. The 1998 is impeccable, very sweet but finely balanced, with a long, elegant finish. Oak and botrytis dominate the nose of the 1999, and the palate is rich, harmonious, and concentrated, with excellent length to counter a slight heaviness. The 2000 is maturing fast and is candied; but it does have zest and concentration. The 2001 is brilliant, with so much zest and acidity that one is scarcely aware of the 150 grams per litre of residual sugar. There are aromas and flavours of mandarins and pineapple, but it's the length and tangy and sherbetty finish that give this wine its distinction. It may be the best Rieussec of recent decades.

The 2002 is lush but lacks purity and finesse, and is a touch flabby. The 2003 is voluptuous, spicy, and lively. The 2004 has more exotic fruit, oranges and pineapple, but it also has vigour, complexity, and length.

The uniformly high quality of the top vintages here shows that selection is rigorous. Despite the size of the property, the number of bottles of *grand vin* rarely exceeds 75,000. Rieussec is expensive but undoubtedly one of the very finest wines of the region.

Château de Rolland

Barsac. Tel: 0556 271502. Website: www.chateauderolland.com. Owner: François Guignard. 18 ha. 80% Sémillon, 15% Sauvignon Blanc, 5% Muscadelle. Production: 40,000 bottles. Second wine: Ch Arnaudas

Like Château de Fargues, these vineyards used to be planted with red grapes, but in 1942 white grapes were planted for the first time. The property was bought by Jean and Pierre Guignard in 1971. The soil is well-drained gravel and clay over a limestone subsoil; and the vines lie on the edge of the Barsac plateau close to the River Ciron.

The wine is fermented in tanks with indigenous yeasts, sometimes chaptalized, and aged for twelve months in ten per cent new barriques. The 1982 was quite full on the nose, but lacked concentration and finesse, and had a sticky, blowsy finish. The 1984 had Muscatty aromas, but was mean, sulphury, and hard. I detected no botrytis on the 1986, a soft, rounded wine, pleasant but characterless. The 1990 was better, though there was a good deal of sulphur on the nose as recently as 2003; it's a lightweight for the vintage but is holding up quite well. The 1991 and 1993 were both lean and lacking richness. The 1997 had plenty of spice on the nose, and was fruity and fresh, even if it had little personality. The orangey 2001 doesn't lack botrytis, but it does lack concentration; nonetheless, it's an attractive Sauternes to drink fairly young. The 2003 is floral and supple with a tangy finish.

Château Romer

Fargues. Tel: 0556 632404. Website: www.chateau-romer.com. Owner: Anne Farges. Deuxième cru.

6.5 ha. 90% Sémillon, 5% Sauvignon Blanc, 5% Muscadelle. Production: 5,000 bottles

Romer was bought by the owner's great-grandfather in 1911, but in 1976 the vineyards were leased by Romer du Hayot. It was only in 2002 that Anne Farges regained control; only two hectares are in production at present. The soil is gravel and gravelly clay. The wine is aged for twelve to eighteen months in sixty per cent new barriques. The 2002 is waxy and rather dull. The 2003 is very rich, juicy, peachy, and concentrated.

Château Romer du Hayot

Fargues. Tel: 0556 271537. Owner: Markus du Hayot. Deuxième cru. 11 ha. 75% Sémillon, 25% Sauvignon Blanc.

Production: 30,000 bottles. Second wine: Ch Andoyse du Hayot

Records referring to this estate begin in the late eighteenth century. In 1833 it was bought by Comte August de la Myre-Mory, who married into the Lur-Saluces family. It was divided among their five children in 1881. In 1937 Mme. du Hayot secured a controlling interest in most of the property, although a portion remained in the hands of the Farges family and is now Château Romer. It was her son André who developed the property. When the autoroute was built, the château and the *chais* were demolished, so he built new air-conditioned cellars at Château Guiteronde, another family property, in Barsac.

The vineyards are planted on clay-limestone and gravel soils not far from Château de Malle. Since 1998 any dead Sauvignon Blanc vines have been replaced with Sauvignon Gris, so the proportion of that variety will gradually increase. The wine used to be aged in tanks only but in the 1990s it was aged in one-third new barriques for twelve months. After André du Hayot died in 2001, his son Markus took over, and he changed the *élevage*. Today the wine is aged for three to four years in oak, but only in older barrels. He argues that long wood-ageing stabilizes the wine and allows him to minimize treatments, such as tartrate stabilization and fining.

No wine was bottled in 1974, 1977, or 1984. The 1981 was sweet but thin, with a rather bitter finish. The 1982 was better, with more vigour but a rather hot finish. There was some botrytis on the apricot-scented nose of the 1986, a soft, rounded wine with some charm and fair acidity and length. The 1990, last tasted in 2001, had a lovely peachy botrytis nose, while the palate was svelte and long, with apricot and quince fruit. The 1995 had a rather strange lanolin and face-cream nose, while the palate was plump and peachy and close to flabby. The 1996 was better, with oak and pears on the nose, a lush texture, good citric fruit, and some finesse and vigour. There were broad peachy aromas on the 1999, a broad and supple palate, good apricot fruit, but a lack of vigour and a slightly caramelly finish. There is a pronounced orangey character on the nose and palate of the 2001 and the wine is rich and sumptuous and has plenty of power. The 2002 is rather dilute and lacks character. Marmalade and barley sugar dominate the nose and palate in 2003, which is too evolved and cloying for my taste. However, the 2004 shows more complexity, with orangey fruit, ample botrytis, and considerable power and depth. I am not convinced that Markus du Hayot's devotion to prolonged barrel-ageing is doing the wine any favours: recent vintages seem stewed and rather heavy.

Château Roumieu

Barsac. Tel: 0556 272101. Owner: Catherine Craveia-Goyaud. 17 ha. 80% Sémillon, 19% Sauvignon Blanc,

1% Muscadelle. Production: 40,000 bottles

There are a number of properties with this name in Barsac, as the original estate with this name was divided in three in 1900. This one adjoins Climens and Doisy-Védrines. The wines are aged in large casks and in barriques, of which twenty per cent are new. The 1986 was sulphury, waxy, and hot. No faults mar the 1990, with its attractive Sémillon nose, its sweet grapiness, its good acidity and general succulence. The 1997 is delicious, with mandarin tones on the nose, a bright, fresh fruitiness, gentle oak, and reasonable concentration and freshness. The 1998 had similar weight but was more burnished and smoky – an attractive wine.

Château Roumieu-Lacoste

*Barsac. Tel: 0556 271629. **Owner:** Hervé Dubourdieu. 11 ha. 95% Sémillon, 3% Sauvignon Blanc, 2% Muscadelle.*
***Production:** 35,000 bottles. **Second wine:** Ch Ducasse*

Dubourdieu, the cousin of Denis, bought out his brothers in order to gain control of this estate, which is just across from Climens on clay-limestone soil. There are many old vines and the average age is forty-five years. The must is vinified in tanks, sometimes with selected yeasts but with minimal chaptalization. Then the wine is aged for twelve months, with a rotation between barrel-aged portions and those aged in tanks. Hervé Dubourdieu is serious about his craft, and released no wine from 1991, 1992, or 1993. The only vintage I have tasted is the 1990, which was rather soupy and coarse. He also produces a special *cuvée* called Sélection André Dubourdieu.

Château St-Amand

*Preignac. Tel: 0556 632728. **Owner:** Anne-Marie Facchetti-Ricard. 20 ha. 85% Sémillon, 14% Sauvignon Blanc, 1% Muscadelle. **Production:** 45,000 bottles. **Second wine:** Ch Solon*

St-Amand is one of the oldest estates in the region. Until his death in 1995, it was a pleasure to visit the very gracious Louis Ricard in his beautifully furnished château and to taste the wine in its natural setting. Today his daughter looks after the property. A good proportion of the crop is commercialized by the Sichel négociant house, which uses the Château de la Chartreuse label -- but the wine is essentially the same.

The vineyards are in four parcels, with the largest block on pebbly soil around the house, and two more at a distance of two kilometres (1.2 miles) on soil richer in clay. Many of the vines are very old and replaced by costly complantation. Although St-Amand is harvested in the traditional way, with about four *tries*, the Ricards like a mixture of nobly rotten and overripe grapes so as to avoid any jammy flavours in the wine. The must is rarely chaptalized – it was Ricard's view that if the wine was no good in the first place, chaptalization wouldn't help – and fermented in tanks. Most of the ageing under Louis Ricard was in tanks, with just three months in barriques to round out the wine; today about half the wine is aged in barrels for eighteen months.

The 1981 was very citric and vivid, though not that concentrated or complex. The 1982 was sweeter and plumper, but there was little depth or finesse. There was more botrytis on the 1983, a sweet, sappy, spicy wine that was quite bracing and long. The 1986 was super-ripe yet not cloying, thanks to refreshing acidity that balanced the plump fruit and gave the wine excellent length. The finely balanced 1988 had a strong citric tone on nose and palate, but also some succulence and elegance. The 1989 was more peachy, more opulent, perhaps at the expense of crispness and vigour, but it was nonetheless a delicious wine. The 1990 was similar, not especially concentrated but with delicious peachy fruit and fine length of flavour. There is a slight tarriness on the 1994 which in other respects was attractive and persistent.

The 1995 is disappointing, showing a heaviness and caramelized orange aromas that are unusual in St-Amand. The wine lacks the finesse of the 1996, which was very much in the house style, with delicacy, citric freshness, and good acidity. The 2001 is less flamboyant and imposing than the best wines from great vintages, but it is very charming, and has great purity of fruit and a tangy finish to offset the considerable sweetness.

One should not make excessive claims for St-Amand. Its wine is not at the same level as that from most classed growths, but its freshness and finesse are a welcome hallmark. Although the wine does keep, it often seems at its best at between five and eight years.

Sauternes de ma Fille

*Barsac. Tel: 0556 263838. **Website:** www.bernard-magrez.com. **Owner:** Bernard Magrez. 8 ha. 98% Sémillon, 2% Sauvignon Blanc and Muscadelle. **Production:** 16,000 bottles*

The former Château Latrezotte, bought by Bernard Magrez in 2004 and given its tender new name. The 2004 was a silky wine with attractive fruit but no great depth; the finish had a trace of boiled sweets. The 2005, tasted young from cask, had pretty apricot and mandarin aromas, but was also a touch confected and light.

Château Sigalas-Rabaud

Bommes. Tel: 0556 213143. Owner: Comte Gérard de Lambert des Granges. Premier cru. 14 ha. 80% Sémillon,
19% Sauvignon Blanc, 1% Muscadelle. Production: 30,000 bottles. Second wine: Le Lieutenant de Sigalas

For the history of this property, *see* Château Rabaud-Promis. A daughter married into the aristocratic Lambert des Granges family. For many years Comte Emmanuel de Lambert des Granges lived in the modest seventeenth-century house and ran the property. The feisty, chain-smoking M. de Lambert des Granges always reminded me of a Norman peasant more than a scion of the French aristocracy, and no one could accuse him of giving himself airs. In the 1980s there was some argy-bargy between M. de Lambert and his winemaker, Jean-Louis Vimeney, the latter not seeing the point of barrique-ageing. During that period some of the wine was barrique-aged, but may have rotated with tank-aged lots – it was all very unclear. In 1990 Vimeney left. M. de Lambert told me that although he favoured some new oak his priority was to retain freshness and aroma. At this he was usually very successful. During the 1990s the family were apparently suffering from some financial difficulties and Emmanuel de Lambert's health was poor. In late 1994 the Cordier négociant house took a minority share in the property. As it also owned Lafaurie-Peyraguey, it was Michel Laporte of that ilk who supervised the winemaking here at Sigalas. In 1996 Emmanuel de Lambert and his family left the region, and his less scruffy brother Gérard took over running the property.

The vineyards are planted on a *croupe* with south- and southeast-facing slopes. Laporte admired the terroir here, pointing to the uniform gravelly soil, with Sauvignon Blanc planted in the sectors with more clay. Xavier de Pontac once told me that in an ideal world he would live at Myrat and farm the vineyards at Sigalas. The average age of the vines is forty-five years. It's a precocious soil, and Emmanuel de Lambert used to defend stoutly his practice of picking early because of it. He would also remove leaves to ameliorate access to sunlight and ensure good aeration.

Michel Laporte (now in retirement but replaced by his son Yannick) imposed much the same vinification and *élevage* here as at Lafaurie, but he tightened up harvesting practices and renovated the vineyards. Each day's picking is now kept as a separate lot; thus in 2001 there were nineteen of them. A pneumatic press was purchased to supplement the existing vertical presses, which still function. Laporte also threw out the old barrels, and for the past ten years Sigalas has been barrel-fermented and then aged for eighteen months in one-third new oak. Under the Laportes the wine has become richer and sweeter. Thus in 2001 there were 138 grams per litre of residual sugar, and in the lighter 2002 vintage 128 grams.

The second wine used to be known as Cadet de Sigalas, but when the Rothschild family took exception, its name was changed.

The oldest Sigalas I have tasted is the 1961, which still had a full orange-gold colour in 2005. It had rich marmalade and barley-sugar aromas and flavours; the palate was lush and juicy without being heavy, and though not a subtle wine it had impressive length. The 1967 had similar aromas and flavour but not quite the grip of the 1961; but the fruit was delicious and the length considerable. The next vintage I tasted was the 1983, but the notes of Clive Coates and Michael Broadbent suggest that Sigalas was among the few properties producing really fine wines in the difficult years of the 1960s and 1970s.

When young, the 1983 had pungent and sulphury aromas that took years to burn off; powerful apricot fruit emerged in their place. The wine was soft and lush but neither hugely concentrated nor markedly sweet. The 1986 was charming but light, a tangy wine with a lot of acidity though not aggressive; it was hard to detect any botrytis. The 1987 was racy and citric but had insufficient richness. Sulphur blocked the aromas of the young 1988, which I last tasted in 1992; the wine was delicious and very much in the racy style that Emmanuel de Lambert favoured. The 1989 was light for the vintage, but elegant and not lacking in botrytis.

There seemed to be a good deal of new oak on the nose of the delightful 1990, though it was less evident on the palate, which was plump but spicy, with fine acidity and vigour. The 1991 was extremely successful, with honeyed aromas, lush and concentrated fruit on the palate, and the hallmark freshness of Sigalas. Only 8,000 bottles of the 1992 were produced; it had some intensity and spice, but was fairly simple. The 1995 was quite citric and in a blind tasting I mistook it for Barsac. It was lively and quite complex, and suggested that Laporte was not diverting (yet) much from the style Emmanuel de Lambert had established. But there was a change in 1996, with its splendid aromas of apricot and candied pineapple; it was sleek, tasted of citrus and pineapple, and had some complexity and stylishness. The 1997, tasted just before bottling, was entirely dominated by oak; but it was tight and concentrated and seemed to have tremendous potential.

The 1998 is sweeter than Lafaurie, with charming aromas of apricot and mandarins, great intensity and brightness on the palate, and a dazzlingly fresh if slightly candied finish. I prefer it to the 1999, which is in a slightly more oxidative style, with aromas of stewed peach and a weighty palate. The 2000 has surprising opulence for the vintage, with delicate lemon and apricot aromas, but lush fruit and a silky texture on the palate. The 2001 is enormously rich, rather tropical in its fruit profile, sumptuous on the palate but again with that bright acidity and impressive length of Sigalas at its very best − and this, for me, is the best Sigalas I have come across. The 2002 is elegant and silky, with peachy fruit and good acidity, but it is less dramatic than the complex 2001. The 2003 has surprising charm, a supple texture without any soupiness, unusual refinement for the vintage, and decent length. There are spicy aromas on the lively 2004, which tastes of passion fruit, but seems to lack a little grip and weight. If a cask tasting in April 2006 is to be relied on, the 2005 will be sensational.

Château Suau

*Barsac. Tel: 0556 625146. **Owner**: Corinne Dubourdieu. Deuxième cru. 8 ha. 80% Sémillon, 10% Sauvignon Blanc, 10% Muscadelle. **Production**: 25,000 bottles*

Until the 1840s Suau was part of the Lur-Saluces domaines, but it was sold in 1845. In 1895 it was acquired by Emile Garros, in whose family the château itself still remains. The vineyard was bought by Roger Biarnès in 1961. He was also the owner of Château Navarro at Illats in the Graves, so Suau was made there. It is not clear why he bought Suau, since even his own daughter admits he was never much interested in the wine business. In 1992 he retired and ceded Suau to his daughter Corinne, who is married to Philippe Dubourdieu of Château d'Archambeau (*q.v.*) in the Graves. She moved swiftly to make much-needed changes, since Suau was the weakest of the classed growths. She began pruning more severely to reduce yields, and restored the practice of *tries successives*, which her father had all but abandoned. She also introduced barrel-fermentation for the first time.

The vineyards lie in a single block between the RN113 and the railway line, behind the Barsac stadium, perhaps not the finest soils in the commune. Biarnès always said he didn't like syrupy wines, and no one could accuse him of making them. He would vinify the wine in tanks with indigenous yeasts, and aged the wine in tanks and barrels, of which few were new. Suau was bottled according to demand. He also produced a wine from another property, Domaine du Coy, with vines near Guiraud, which he didn't take seriously either. Since 2002 Coy has been managed by his other daughter.

Bernard Ginestet wrote that "In the nineteenth century England revelled in the wines [of Suau]" but the oldest vintage for which I can find a tasting note is the 1975, and the oldest I have tasted is the 1986, which was sulphury and lacked acidity. The 1989 wasn't too bad, but it was loose in structure and lacked concentration and finesse. The 1990 was better, with some discernible botrytis, ample fruit in a *confit* style, some smokiness, but again little concentration or complexity. The next vintage I tasted from bottle was the 1999, which had broad, peachy aromas; it was moderately rich but slack. The 2002 was silky and had quite good acidity, but lacks structure and persistence. Corinne Dubourdieu's first vintage, 2003, is dumb on the nose, but has a great deal of sweet plump fruit, mostly apricot and lemon. The 2004 also shows promise. Lazarus has not quite risen, but is limbering up.

Château Suduiraut

*Preignac. Tel: 0556 636190. Website: www.suduiraut.com. **Owner:** AXA Millésimes. Premier cru. 92 ha. 90% Sémillon,*
*10% Sauvignon Blanc. **Production:** 170,000 bottles. **Second wine:** Castelnau de Suduiraut*

This magnificent property is one of the finest in all Bordeaux. Its noble château of 1670 is approached along majestic avenues, and its gardens were designed by Le Nôtre. The Suduiraut family owned the property before the Revolution. In the early nineteenth century a daughter of the family married a M. du Roy, which explains the presence of the words "Ancien Cru du Roy" which used to appear on the labels – it had nothing to do with any king. At about the same time the neighbouring property of Castelnau was bought and incorporated, which explains the name of the second wine. There were numerous proprietors in the nineteenth and early twentieth centuries, and then in 1940 a rich industrialist from northern France, Léopold Fonquernie, bought Suduiraut and took a serious interest in improving quality. His daughters later took over. Then in June 1992 AXA Millésimes, a branch of the vast insurance company that was then run by Jean-Michel Cazes, bought a controlling share. AXA transformed the château into a kind of private hotel and conference centre.

Standards had slipped here in the 1970s, when there was no selection and the wine was aged mostly in cement tanks. In 1978 the genial Pierre Pascaud was appointed as director, and he restored barrel-ageing for at least part of the crop. But chaptalization was still common, as certain parcels were being picked at a mere thirteen degrees of potential alcohol. This was no way to make a *premier cru* Sauternes. Nonetheless quality did improve in the 1980s, and continued to do so once AXA took over. Pascaud was actually delighted to be reporting to a professional group under Cazes rather than to five sisters, each with a differing view. From 1992 the whole crop was barrel-fermented, and aged for eighteen to twenty-four months in one-third new barriques. AXA also created a second wine. In 1995 Pascaud retired and was succeeded by his diffident son Alain, who died young from hepatitis in 2004. He was replaced by Pierre Montegut, who had worked for various estates in Vouvray and for the Cave de Buzet. The *maître de chai* is the young Caroline Gendry.

The vineyards surround the château, though there are a few parcels elsewhere. The density is 7,000 vines per hectare and the plants are pruned to five bunches per vine. According to Pierre Pascaud, the soil warms faster than in other parts of Sauternes, which is why Suduiraut often picked earlier than its neighbours. Whether this was really the case, or whether this was an excuse for playing safe, it is hard to say. He also claimed that the sandy soil meant that the wine was never massive, but I have encountered some very powerful wines from here in certain vintages. Under AXA the soil is being ploughed, and no herbicides are used.

The winery is equipped with cryo-extraction but Montegut sees the technique as very much a last resort, and says that wines made this way are almost always eliminated when the various lots are tasted blind.

Under the Fonquernies, Pascaud had occasionally produced a Crème de Tête. He did so in 1982, when his policy of early harvesting paid off, as other châteaux were affected by the rain that fell in October. It had 130 grams per litre of residual sugar rather than the usual eighty, and only 4,800 bottles were produced. Another Crème de Tête was made in 1989, aged for thirty-eight months in new barriques. A third was made in 1990 but Pascaud decided to blend it in with the regular wine. After the AXA purchase, Jean-Michel Cazes discontinued the special *cuvée*. One was attempted in 2001, but it was agreed that selecting the best lots for a special bottling did indeed detract from the quality of the regular Suduiraut.

In 2003 they inaugurated a dry wine called "S" de Suduiraut, made from a parcel of mostly young vines that was not delivering exceptional juice for Sauternes. It was aged in twenty-five per cent new oak, and at first was sold only to AXA employees, but from 2004 it was made commercially available. About 15,000 bottles are produced. It's quite a mineral wine, with a pleasing austerity.

I have not tasted any venerable vintages of Suduiraut, but 1893, 1928, 1959, and 1967 are all said to be magnificent. The 1970, tasted in 1994, had a muted, rather dusty nose, with some elegant apricot fruit; it was sweet and attractive but it was essentially simple. The 1975 always had an intense *rôti* nose, with aromas of caramel and marmalade; the wine is raisiny, a bit tarry, and intense, with excellent length. There are lush *confit* apricot aromas on the 1976, marmalade flavours but surprising freshness for the vintage, but other tasters have come across bottles with varying stages of maderization. The 1978 was soft and juicy, but faded fast, and must be past its best by now.

There was some charm on the nose of the 1979 in 1995, with smoky, dried-apricot fruit; the palate was silky, not especially sweet, but harmonious and quite concentrated. The famous 1982 was always good but not exceptional. Recently, it showed aromas of toffee apple, caramel, and dried apricot, while the palate was plump and spicy, with fair acidity. The nose on the 1983 is quite light, with aromas of apricot and citrus but lacking in intensity; the palate is one-dimensional, but has some intensity and elegance. The 1985 lacks botrytis; it's a burly wine with no finesse. Much the same is true of the 1986, which when young was sulphury and lacked concentration.

There was a significant improvement with the 1988. It was also rich, ripe, and creamy, with good acidity and substantial alcoholic backbone. As it aged it developed some tarriness, and by 2006 it had aromas of marmalade and barley sugar; the richness was still there, and the flavours were complex: *crème brûlée*, oranges, tropical fruit, and raisins. The 1989 has evolved beautifully into a very rich, honeyed wine, with excellent peachy fruit and a slight raisiny tone. It is going in the same direction as the 1988, with *crème brûlée* and barley sugar coming to the fore. The 1989 Crème de Tête is magnificent, with a very powerful honeyed botrytis character, intense sweetness, amazing concentration, no trace of heaviness, and heavenly length. The 1990 was first-rate too, with the rich peachy fruit leaping from the glass; it doesn't quite match the splendour of the 1989 because it is a touch more heavy and the alcohol, weighing in at close to fifteen degrees, does show. Pierre Pascaud considered this was the finest Suduiraut since 1959.

No *grand vin* was made in 1991, 1992, or 1993. The 1994 is soft and quite opulent and silky, but lacks some concentration – sound but not brilliant. The 1995 is marred by a leaden structure and high alcohol, which is a shame, as the wine is rich, full-bodied, and oaky. I have mixed experiences of the 1996: one bottle had bizarre herbal and iodine aromas, but the most recently tasted example had stone-fruits and kirsch aromas, a sleek texture, and fine concentration and acidity. The golden 1997, which took forty-two days to harvest, is great. It is very sweet, with rich stone-fruits aromas, a sumptuous texture, and remarkable intensity. The 1999, despite the honeyed, peachy nose, is airier, with a fine attack, lively mandarin and dried apricot flavours, an opulent texture, and impeccable length. I find the 2001 very similar; both wines are still young, beautifully balanced, with abundant ripeness, richness, or raciness. The 2002 is marked by elegance and purity, with lovely pineapple and apricot fruit on the nose and palate. It doesn't have quite the layered complexity of the 2001, but, given the difference in style, it is an extremely good wine.

I care less for the 2003, which has waxy, apricot aromas, and although rich and rounded, is a touch hollow and finishes quite hot. The 2004, tasted soon after bottling, has passion fruit as well as apricot on the nose and a similar airiness to the 2001, but it seems less complex. (Because of rain, the yield in 2004 was a miserly four hl/ha.) Tasted blind from cask in April 2006, the 2005 was highly impressive, but these are early days. The must weight was twenty-two degrees of potential alcohol, and there were 160 grams per litre of residual sugar.

Château La Tour Blanche

*Bommes. Tel: 0557 980273. Website: www.tour-blanche.com. **Owner:** Ministry of Agriculture. Premier cru.*
*36 ha. 80% Sémillon, 15% Sauvignon Blanc, 5% Muscadelle. **Production:** 65,000 bottles.*
Second wine: Les Charmilles de la Tour Blanche

If La Tour Blanche has an institutional appearance, that's because for almost a century it has been a winemaking college. The estate's early history is obscure, but it seems to have taken its name from a M. du Tourblanche, who died here in 1784. By the 1840s the owner was a M. Focke, who established the wine's reputation: when it was classified in 1855 it headed the list of First Growths. In 1875 Tour Blanche was sold to Daniel Iffla, who sported the nickname of "Osiris". He was an umbrella manufacturer with a keen interest in oenology, and many experiments in vinification were conducted here. He died in 1907, bequeathing the property to the state on condition that it should be converted into an agricultural college. Despite their glorious reputation, the vineyards were leased to the merchant house of Cordier from 1924 to 1955 on a sharecropping basis.

The vineyards are in a single parcel close to the Ciron. The higher sectors, which rise to sixty-seven metres (220 feet), have gravel soils, and as the slope descends there is more sand and clay. Differences in soil and elevation mean that there is considerable variation in ripening dates between different sectors. Yields are low, around ten to twelve hl/ha; thus in 1999 the yield was seven hl/ha, in 2004 eleven hl/ha.

La Tour Blanche made some drab wines in the 1970s, and it was the arrival in 1983 of a new director, Jean-Pierre Jausserand, that turned things around. He air-conditioned the *chais*, which allowed him to barrel-ferment the wine for the first time. He also instituted more severe pruning to control yields, and made the selection process more rigorous. In 1987 he purchased pneumatic presses. He also acquired a cold chamber for cryo-extraction, but apparently it was never used for the *grand vin*. Any lots with a must weight lower than nineteen degrees of potential alcohol were rejected for La Tour Blanche. There is no chaptalization, except for the second wine. By the late 1980s Jausserand was ageing the wine entirely in new oak. There have been years when no Tour Blanche was bottled: 1963, 1964, 1968, 1992, 1993, and 2000.

There is no doubt that Jausserand revived the fortunes of the property, and revealed the potential of its vineyards. La Tour Blanche is not the weightiest of Sauternes; it has the lighter touch of the best Bommes, but nonetheless displays richness and force. Jausserand retired in 2001 and was replaced by Corinne Reulet.

The estate also produces some dry white wines: Osiris is made from botrytized grapes and aged in barriques; almost the entire production ends up in Belgium. There is also a regular dry wine called Isis that is barrel-fermented and aged in new oak. Production is limited to 6,000 bottles of each wine.

The oldest Tour Blanche I have encountered is the 1923, which I have tasted twice. In 1990 it was a coppery gold, and had a rich barley-sugar and caramelized-orange nose and, despite a caramel tone on the palate, the wine was still vigorous and elegant, though only moderately sweet. The 1931 in 1988 was light brown and had delicate toffee-apple aromas; it was lean and light on the palate but still vigorous and long. The 1934 was copper-gold in 1993, and the nose was splendid: citric and elegant, with evident botrytis. It was a touch raisiny, but still fresh and long. The 1935 was much lighter in colour, with a fresh and lightly honeyed nose, but on the palate it was clearly in decline. The 1939 was fairly discreet on the nose, with caramel and honey tones; the flavour was rather baked and the wine lacked concentration, but it still had delicacy and charm. It is worth noting that other than 1934 and 1937, none of these wines came from good vintages.

I leap over the decades to the 1975. It was pleasantly honeyed on the nose, but the palate was poor: light, watery, and short. The medium-sweet 1976 was a bit better, with faint apricot aromas, a wine of little depth but attractive. I didn't care for the 1977 or 1978, which were hot, sulphury, and short. The 1981 had no detectable botrytis, and was soft and rather flabby. Sulphur seriously marred the 1983 and 1985, which, though sweet, had no finesse and little length. There were some signs of improvement in 1986. The nose was quite oaky, but there was lush fruit on the palate and fair acidity, though it lagged far behind the best 1986s. The 1987 was well made for a lighter year. The aromas were honeyed but elegant, and the palate creamy but spicy, with plenty of plump fruit. The 1988 was quite oaky on the nose, and the palate was intense and elegant, with a touch of pineapple fruit and excellent acidity. But I have not tasted it recently. There was no lack of richness and sweetness in 1989, and there was power as well as lushness behind the forthright apricot fruit. Oak rather dominated the 1990, but it was rich, textured, and balanced.

The 1991 had some candied flavours, and though it lacked weight it was lively and had some richness and good acidity. Unlike many 1995s, that from Tour Blanche has ample botrytis on the nose and palate, plus a good deal of oak; although it lacks some bite and finesse, the fruit itself is delicious. The 1996 is very different, far more *rôti* in style, with marmalade and barley-sugar aromas and flavours, a good deal of alcohol, spiciness rather than freshness, and good length. The 1997 is also quite *rôti*, with some passion fruit and raisined aromas, and although there is good fruit on the palate, it does lack some concentration. In 2006 the stylish 1998 had plenty of charm, with mandarins and apricots on the nose, and a good deal of oak; it had more purity and freshness than other good vintages of the 1990s. The 1999 is similar, perhaps more tightly structured and more silky in texture, but a wine with excellent potential.

Flamboyance marked the 2001, with its Cointreau nose fighting the new oak, its sumptuous palate, its high concentration and fine underlying acidity, its pineappley intensity, and its long finish. The 2002 is more citric, a touch leaner, but it's racy and concentrated, though far more modest than the 2001. There's peach syrup on the nose of the 2003; it's creamy and lush, but there is some acidity and mintiness behind the rich fruit and the wine doesn't lack length. The 2004 is sleek and fresh, with some rather odd banana flavours as well as apricot; it's stylish but lacks some weight and structure. The creamy 2005 is piquant, stylish, and long.

Château Les Tuileries

Fargues. Tel: 0556 623814. Website: www.chateaubrondelle.com. Owners: Jean-Noël Belloc and Philippe Rochet.
3 ha. 90% Sémillon, 5% Sauvignon Blanc, 5% Muscadelle. Production: 10,000 bottles

This small property is under the same ownership as Château Brondelle (*q.v.*) in the Graves. The soil is sandy gravel. Part of the wine is aged in barriques for twelve to sixteen months. The 2000 was a pleasant surprise, with waxy, peachy aromas, a lushness on the palate, and good apricot fruit. The 2001 is better, with a similar flavour profile but more concentration and length.

Château d'Yquem

Sauternes. Tel: 0557 980707. Website: www.yquem.fr. Owner: LVMH group. Premier grand cru.
103 ha. 80% Sémillon, 20% Sauvignon Blanc. Production: 140,000 bottles

Yquem has been in a class of its own since the late eighteenth century. In over 200 years it has scarcely faltered, and never come close to relinquishing its reputation as France's finest sweet white wine. The walls around the hilltop property recall the time in the fifteenth century when Yquem was a fortified farm. A chapel was added a century later, and the main block of what are now reception rooms dates from the seventeenth century. By then Yquem already belonged to the Sauvage d'Eyquem family, whose descendants ran the property until 1999. The family acquired the property in 1593. There was a shift in 1785 when the heiress to Yquem, Françoise Josephine, married Comte Louis Amédée de Lur-Saluces, the godson of King Louis XV. Thereafter it was her Lur-Saluces descendants who ran the property, and they also owned Château de Fargues.

If Yquem is prized today, it was just as revered over 200 years ago, when Thomas Jefferson ordered the wine for George Washington in 1787, and a shipment was dispatched to Napoleon Bonaparte in 1802. Its status as a supreme luxury product was confirmed in 1859, when Grande Duke Constantine of Russia, the brother of the Tsar, tasted the 1847 vintage (still in cask!) and offered a colossal price for the wine. (David Peppercorn has established that until 1861 the wine was not blended but the various *tries* were sold separately as different qualities or styles of Yquem.) Astute marriage ties brought Filhot and Coutet into the Yquem fold. In the mid-nineteenth century Romain Bertrand de Lur-Saluces installed the extremely important drainage system in the vineyards. His grandson Marquis Bertrand ran the property for decades, and was succeeded in 1968 by his nephew Alexandre, who directed Yquem until the sale of the estate in 1999. Bertrand's otherwise magisterial management was marred by the release of some unworthy vintages in the 1960s, a mistake not repeated by Alexandre.

Comte Alexandre ran Yquem extremely well, and there was considerable stability during his reign. Guy Latrille was the affable *maître de chai* for forty-five years, and was replaced in 1998 by the highly competent Sandrine Garbay. Pierre Meslier was the *régisseur* from 1962 until 1989, when he retired under controversial circumstances and was replaced by the more reserved Francis Mayeur.

As happens at so many wine properties, shareholders were tempted to cash in their shares rather than settle for some trifling dividend or a few cases of wine each vintage. At Yquem there were fifty-three shareholders, most of them family members. When Alexandre's elder brother, Marquis Eugène de Lur-Saluces, who owned forty-eight per cent of the shares, expressed his wish to realize his assets, many other shareholders followed in his wake, and the writing was on the wall. The savvy LVMH luxury-goods group had its eye on Yquem, and launched its bid for a controlling interest in 1996. Tremendous battles ensued within the family. Alexandre wielded considerable power when it came to running Yquem. This was undoubtedly necessary, as you can't run an important property by committee; but it also caused resentment at his perceived autocratic style. Writs flew, especially when Comte Alexandre was refused the right to buy out some of the rebellious shareholders.[1]

By April 1999 it was all over, and LVMH had acquired sixty-three per cent of the shares. Pierre Lurton – already a known quantity to the head of LVMH, Bernard Arnault, as he had been running Cheval Blanc for many years – was appointed director. He retained the existing team, but also hired Denis Dubourdieu as a consultant. Surprisingly, Comte Alexandre stayed on at Yquem as a kind of roving ambassador for the wine, especially at international tastings, but in 2004 he left the property for good.

Pierre Lurton did not need to worry about quality at Yquem. But he was aware that the wine had become a monument, revered but rarely drunk: the château had substantial stocks of older vintages in the cellars. Lurton decided to kick-start interest in the wines, releasing the excellent but underrated 1999 at a knock-down price, just to show that Yquem could (once in a while) be affordable. However, when it came to releasing the 2001 vintage, which had been widely hyped and justly so, Lurton released it at 200 Euros per bottle. Buyers gasped, but they took out their cheque books. The wine sold fast and Lurton gloried in his commercial coup. Under the Lur-Saluces, Yquem had never been offered *en primeur*; it wasn't even possible to taste the wine until it had been bottled. Now Yquem was back on the market alongside the other First Growths.

Pierre Meslier used to say that the soil at Yquem is so varied that it would be possible to make four distinct wines from the estate. The topsoil is stony with some sand and clay, but the subsoil differs from that of most other parts of Sauternes, being composed of clay mixed with stones and limestone. Pruning is very severe, only the estate's own compost is used, and there is no use of herbicides or chemical treatments. The average age of the vines is about thirty years. In the 2000s the trellising was heightened. No estate takes more pains with the harvesting than Yquem, and it is not unusual for its 140 pickers to spend two months in the vineyards, with, of course, gaps between *tries*. The aim is to have a must weight of around twenty degrees of potential alcohol.

Cryo-extraction was occasionally practised in the past, but under Pierre Lurton the cold chamber has been removed altogether. Pressing takes place initially in pneumatic presses, and then in a vertical press; each day's harvest forms a separate lot, with each pressing also kept apart. The quality of each pressing is assessed, and the lots are either blended or, in some cases, rejected altogether. Thus in 2003 some final pressings were too rich and too high in volatile acidity, so they were eliminated. There is no chaptalization. On the advice of Denis Dubourdieu, fermentation is arrested with sulphur dioxide, whereas in the past chilling was also used, but this, he claims, can diminish aromas. (Meslier used to insist that the fermentation stopped of its own accord and it wasn't necessary to add SO_2, but this seems unlikely.) He also persuaded Sandrine Garbay to stir the lees for about four weeks, though this is done prudently with very rich lots to avoid giving the wine a fat and heavy texture.

Only new barrels are used at Yquem, and blending is progressive. Under Lur-Saluces the wine was aged for forty-two months, but now the ageing period is being shortened slightly to around thirty-six months, or possibly just thirty in lighter years such as 2004. Lurton says that it is now possible to measure oxidation very precisely, so every manipulation of the wine can be analysed to monitor and avoid any negative evolution. Lot selection is ruthless. In 1979 and 1991, sixty per cent of the crop was thrown out; in 1977, seventy per cent. Even in a great year such as 1990, selection can be draconian. The crop was close to the maximum for the first time since 1893; but sixty barrels went through secondary fermentation and were eliminated. In some vintages no Yquem was released: 1910, 1915, 1930, 1951, 1952, 1964, 1972, 1974, and 1992.

Is Yquem still supreme? Well, yes. No other property can match it, on a consistent basis, for richness, elegance, subtlety, and longevity. There may be the odd vintage when a Rieussec or Suduiraut might be considered the equal

1 For a mesmerizing account of the battle for Yquem, *see* Echikson, *Noble Rot: A Bordeaux Wine Revolution*, Norton, New York, 2004

or even superior to Yquem, but it will be the exception rather than the rule. However, the gap between Yquem and the rest of the pack has narrowed. Yquem has not lowered its standards in the slightest, but properties such as Rieussec, Climens, Coutet, and Lafaurie-Peyraguey have significantly raised their game since the 1980s.

My experience of older vintages of Yquem is not as extensive as I would wish, but that is true of most of us. Michael Broadbent has tasted more than most, and his notes and assessment are printed in his *Vintage Wine*. The fabulous vintages of the past include 1784, 1811, 1847, 1861, 1864, 1865, 1869, 1906, 1921, 1924, 1928, 1929, 1937, 1943, 1945, 1947, and 1949. The oldest vintage I have tasted is the legendary 1847. The colour in 2002 was medium gold with no browning. The aromas were still very rich, with caramel and toffee apple dominant. The wine has remained very rich and sweet, intense and spicy, wonderfully concentrated with mocha tones on the extraordinarily long finish. The 1892, ninety years on, was also merely golden, and had a light, soft, honeyed nose; but on the palate it was drying out. Tasted in 1990, the 1923 had a muted barley sugar nose; it was still very sweet, but the acidity was piercingly high, and the fruit was fading away. The 1928 is a great wine. The nose is complex: there's toffee, vanilla, caramel, and apricot fruit; the palate is still fresh, youthful, and vigorous, intense, quite appley, with a tangy finish and very good length.

The 1950 is now a light copper-gold in colour. There are aromas of oranges, barley-sugar, and gingerbread; it's a concentrated wine with Seville-orange flavours, some raisiny nuances, and quite good length. There are lush botrytis aromas on the 1957, which is surprisingly powerful and concentrated, even thick, yet with plenty of acidity to balance the richness. The 1962 is a lovely wine, with honeyed, peachy aromas that steer clear of raisins; it's plump, concentrated, and very rich, with impeccable balance and length. The 1967 is a celebrated Yquem, which I have been fortunate enough to drink frequently over recent years. It is a great wine, but the nose is quite caramelly and raisiny, and thus it lacks some freshness. But the palate has enormous concentration and luminosity; it is supple but spicy, complex and tangy, and the length is extraordinary. The one time I tasted the 1971, there was some oxidation, and although the wine was very lush, concentrated, and long, it lacked purity. The 1973 is a relative lightweight, with fragrance but a sharp, acidic palate.

The 1975 is a classic Yquem, with lush, toasty, stone-fruits aromas and a hint of marmalade; it's a huge wine, plump and majestic, with fine acidity and length. The 1976 is more *rôti*, with barley sugar aromas, but the nose is still dominated by peaches and cream, while the palate is opulent and creamy, powerful but still tight and vigorous. The 1979 has discreet oaky, botrytis aromas, a lean structure but considerable elegance and a long, toasty finish. The 1980 is similar but lacks a little weight and depth. The 1981 has always seemed a touch overoaked, with some oily, resiny, smoky aromas as a consequence. But it's full, spicy, and concentrated, with fine acidity and length. The 1982 has always been aromatically reserved; it's spicy, reasonably concentrated, and has good acidity, but the structure is loose for Yquem.

The 1983 has been superb from the outset. The nose is botrytis-packed, with aromas of dried apricot, honey, and a hint of caramel. It's very rich, smoky, and concentrated, with some *rôti* character, but has tremendous persistence. In contrast the 1986 has been consistently disappointing. It's a good, powerful wine with ample botrytis, but it has never shown much finesse; it's ungainly for Yquem and lacks vigour. No such qualms about the great 1988, which is notable for its exquisite balance, its finesse and its remarkable length. The 1989 is classic, with a powerful peachy, botrytis nose, and great concentration and acidity; but I'm not sure it is better than the supremely elegant 1988. The superb 1990, still very marked by new oak, has powerful dried-apricot aromas; it's lean, creamy, intense, with firm acidity, and its balance is close to perfect.

From its youth the 1994 was honeyed. It's racy for Yquem, sweet and intense, spicy and long; but has yet to show its personality. The 1995 is more sumptuous but it's also reserved on the nose; it's creamy and oaky, highly concentrated, and very long. The 1996 shows more complexity, with *rôti* stone-fruits and barley sugar aromas; it's supple and velvety, yet perhaps lacks a little zest on the finish; nonetheless the length is impressive. All elements are in balance in 1997, which in its purity and persistence comes close to perfection. Oak rather dominates the 1998, which is still rather closed and inexpressive; it's tight in structure but gains in weight and elegance with aeration, with apricot and barley sugar flavours emerging on the finish. But it doesn't seem at the same level as 1997 and 1999. The latter is brilliantly voluptuous, a sensuous wine with great fragrance, concentration, and length. The 2001 is as good, arguably better, because of its tremendous attack and its intense purity; it has power yet the finish is delicate and wonderfully elegant. Nor can one taste the 150 grams of residual sugar. The oaky, silky 2003 has a fine attack, great concentration, and an exceptionally long and pure finish. Very early tastings suggest that Yquem made superb wine in 2004 and 2005, and was at the top of its game in 2006, producing a wine with an intensity and freshness that most other top Sauternes seem to lack.

Yquem also produces a curious dry white wine called Ygrec. It is made only in years when the harvest is problematic. In such years there will be vines that have insufficient botrytis or that never achieve the ripeness Yquem demands. These lots are kept apart, and blended with wine from grapes picked at conventional must weights for a dry wine. The result is a wine with at least fourteen degrees and with a pronounced botrytis aroma. I was once given a glass as an apéritif, took one sniff, and confidently pronounced: Sauternes. It is alarming to then taste the wine, which is dry yet infused with noble rot. Its power allows it to be balanced with about seven grams of residual sugar without that being easily discernible.

The origin of Ygrec, according to Alexandre de Lur-Saluces, was the practice of removing excess bunches to allow the remaining ones to ripen fully and thus profit more from botrytis. In style the wine used to be very oaky, since it spent thirty-six months in new oak, though without *bâtonnage*. It was made in 1959, 1960, 1962, 1964, 1965, 1966, 1968, 1969, 1972, 1973, 1977–80, 1985, 1986 (a mere 3,000 bottles), 1988, 1994, 1996, 2000, 2002, and 2004.

Pierre Lurton and Denis Dubourdieu are no fans of the Ygrec of the past, and are planning some modifications. They intend to increase the proportion of Sauvignon Blanc from fifty to sixty per cent to give the wine more freshness and aroma. They were temped to pick the grapes earlier for the same reasons, but found that in clay soils Sémillon can have bitter flavours if picked too soon. The proportion of new oak has been dramatically reduced to one-third and the *élevage* shortened to twelve months, but with *bâtonnage*.

As already mentioned, Ygrec until recently tasted like a dry Sauternes with a great deal of oak. In 1988 I enjoyed the 1960, 1969, 1977, 1978, 1979, and 1980. More recently I have drunk the 1988, which was too alcoholic, and the 2002, which had less botrytis influence, more grapefruity aromas, and tasted like a heavyweight Graves. The Ygrec of the future will be fresher than those of the past, but it is less likely to be as ageworthy and individual.

31. The Other Sweet Wines of Bordeaux

Occasional glorious sweet wines from the distant past are a reminder that there were other regions of Bordeaux that were capable of producing wines that could sometimes match in quality and style those from Sauternes. Those regions have not changed, and should still be capable of producing excellent sweet wines, even if they rarely do so.

I suspect that in the past those wines were the result of a different approach to sweet wine production. Most of the white vineyards would have been picked at normal must weights to make a dry wine, while a portion of the vineyard, perhaps more susceptible to noble rot than other parcels, would have been left in the hope that botrytis infection would allow a sweet wine to be made. This is still the case in Cérons, where growers have the right to produce dry and sweet wines from the same parcel, the dry wines being AC Graves. The problem with this approach is that growers are disinclined to continue sweet wine production, since the yields for the dry wine are considerably more generous, and in any case the market for the fairly obscure Cérons appellation is very limited.

Yields are higher in all the lesser sweet wine appellations – Cérons, Loupiac, Ste-Croix-du-Mont, Cadillac, the Premières Côtes de Bordeaux, and St-Macaire – than in Sauternes itself. Thus the wines tend to be less concentrated, less liquorous, although there are exceptions, since a handful of dedicated growers are keen to make wines that can indeed go *mano a mano* with Sauternes. This relative lack of concentration, combined with a lack of renown, means that prices for these lesser appellations tend to be considerably lower than those for Sauternes. (I noted on my last visit to Ste-Croix-du-Mont that prices of the wines have scarcely risen at all over the past twelve years.) Low prices mean that growers have little incentive to ratchet up the quality a further notch or two. On the other hand, those lower prices can be attractive to sweet wine enthusiasts seeking a less costly alternative to Sauternes.

Another factor affecting quality is the need for some producers to make the wine year in, year out. They cannot afford to skip a poor vintage, as their regular clients may be tempted to look elsewhere and never return.

With the exception of Cérons, these appellations lie on the east side of the Garonne. From the riverside, the lanes climb quite steeply to the plateaux on which the vineyards are mostly located. The soils are essentially clay-limestone. Clearly there is no collision of river waters to provide the mists hospitable to botrytis, but autumns along the Garonne are not usually short of foggy days, so there is plentiful botrytis in the right conditions, though it may be less uniform and less intense than in Sauternes and Barsac.

The varietal mix is much the same as in Sauternes and Barsac, although there is overall a higher proportion of Muscadelle. Harvesting is also done by *tries successives*, though less rigorously than in Sauternes. Three, occasionally four, *tries* would be the maximum. The harvesting would be less selective too; it is simply too expensive and labour-intensive to pick single berries; if the bunch looks botrytized, or thoroughly overripe or *pourri plein*, it is likely to go whole into the basket. Vinification is similar to that for Sauternes, though, again for economic reasons, there would be less barrel-fermentation and a lower proportion of new oak barrels. Of course, there are exceptions.

Almost all estates welcome visitors and offer opportunities to taste the wines. Cadillac has invested in an impressive Maison du Vin, just south of the town along the main road, which is a good source of further information as well as of wines to taste and buy.

Only the appellations that require exclusively sweet wines are considered here. There are other appellations that permit the production of sweet wines – Graves, Premières Côtes de Bordeaux, St-Macaire, Ste-Foy – but those wines are included in the discussions of individual properties in the relevant chapters.

CERONS

Cérons lies just north of Barsac has enjoyed its own AC since 1936. Under the name of Sirione, Cérons was marked on Gallo-Roman maps, and Jean Perromat, the owner of Château de Cérons and the village's mayor for some decades, maintains that in the past Cérons was better known than Sauternes. But certainly Cérons had a thriving port from which wines could be transported. In the early twentieth century Cérons was part of the Sauternes region, but was then expelled in 1921 to allow for the absorption of the commune of Fargues into Sauternes. Perromat ascribes this to politicking on the part of the Lur-Saluces family, who owned the Château de Fargues (though it was scarcely an important wine property at that time). In 1920 Cérons had already formed its own Syndicat, and was rewarded for its determination by being granted its AC some ten days before Sauternes.

The appellation applies to three villages: Cérons, Podensac, and Illats. All three also produce dry wines under the AC Graves. For economic reasons the production of Cérons has been shrinking, despite valiant efforts by Jean Perromat to maintain the tradition. Nonetheless if there are almost 1,000 hectares of vineyards within the appellation, of which about 550 are white, it is sadly true that only about fifty are used for Cérons. In 2002 sixty-two hectares yielded 1,622 hectolitres of wine; by 2005, forty-one hectares yielded 1,460 hectolitres. (In 1970 21,000 hectolitres were produced.) There are only about twenty producers. Maximum yields are forty hectolitres per hectare, although for years Perromat tried unsuccessfully to persuade the growers to reduce them to twenty-five, so as to put Cérons on the same level as its neighbour Barsac. The soil resembles that of Barsac, being pebbly gravel and sand over a limestone subsoil.

There seems little reason to doubt that Cérons can make wines that rival those of Barsac. The soils are similar and so are the microclimates that spawn botrytis. In the nineteenth century the writer Julien placed the best Cérons on the same level as Second Growths from Sauternes. But to attain that level of quality growers must take the same risks as their neighbours, and very few are prepared to do so. Jean Perromat notes that Cérons often has fine weather in early November, but there cannot be more then two or three properties that would risk waiting that long before harvesting. To justify producing a sweet wine, growers in the appellation would need to charge twice the price as for their dry wines, but Perromat recalls in the 1960s his white Graves obtained higher prices than his sweet wines. But by 1990 the price of Cérons per *tonneau* was roughly double that for white Graves. Even so, fewer and fewer growers are prepared to produce the former.

Château de Cérons

Cérons. Tel: 0556 270113. Website: www.chateaudecerons.com. Owner: Jean Perromat. 12 ha. 70% Sémillon, 25% Sauvignon Blanc, 5% Muscadelle. Production: 40,000 bottles. Second wine: Pavillon du Ch de Cérons

Even in old age Jean Perromat is a tall, imposing figure, exuding the authority he wielded for decades as mayor of Cérons and tireless promoter of its sweet wines. The Perromats are an influential family in the region, and his brother Pierre was for many years president of INAO; other branches are scattered about these southern regions of Bordeaux. The château is a lovely seventeenth-century manor opposite the village's Romanesque church, although the vineyards are farther away from the river. Perromat bought this property in 1958.

Perromat is prepared to wait for as long as it takes to obtain botrytized fruit. Thus in 1998 there were eight *tries*, which is rare outside Sauternes. Yields are around twenty-five hl/ha. It used to be his practice to barrel-age the wine for many years. Thus the 1973 spent five years in oak, and some of the 1979 was still in barrels in 1986. However, a proportion of the wine was aged in tanks. Thus in 1988 half the wine had been barrel-fermented, and in 1990 he made a blend of the two styles (the oaked portion having been fermented in new wood), though he also set aside four barrels of exceptional richness that he intended to bottle separately as a kind of family reserve. (With eight children, he needs a good deal of wine just to supply his family.) I remember arguing with Perromat after I compared different lots of 1990, suggesting that in fine vintages all the wine should be barrel-fermented. By the 2000s half the wine was being aged in tanks and blended with the remainder that had been aged in largely new barriques. Perromat still favours an *élevage* of about twenty-four months.

The wines of the 1970s and 1980s were hit and miss. The aromas were usually of stone fruits, though in some vintages they were more citric. Botrytis aromas alternated with dried-fruits aromas. Sometimes there was a hard, almost dour quality on the palate, and the alcohol could be worryingly high. The best of the vintages I tasted were 1973, 1986, and 1989. The 1990, however, was delicious, being very rich, enticingly oaky, spicy, and complex. Other good, if not exceptional, vintages of the 1990s include the 1995, 1996, 1997, 1998, and 2001.

Jean Perromat is now in his mid eighties and handing over to his son Xavier.

Château de Chantegrive

Podensac. Tel: 0556 171738. Website: www.chantegrive.com. Owners: Henri and Françoise Lévêque.
5 ha. 100% Sémillon. Production: 6,000 bottles

Chantegrive is best known for its fine white Graves, but since 1990 it has made a little Cérons in favourable years. There used to be two *cuvées*, one aged in tanks, the other barrel-fermented and oak-aged. Since 1995 all the wine has been barrel-fermented. The 1990 was very good, with pear aromas and a sweet, plump palate with considerable finesse, if not that much persistence. The 2001 has aromas of candied lemons, and a great deal of freshness and elegance.

Clos Bourgelat

See Chapter Fifteen (Southern Graves)

Château des Deux Moulins

Illats. Tel: 0556 270243. Owners: Bernard and Jean-Jacques Pastol. 8 ha. 90% Sémillon, 8% Sauvignon Blanc,
2% Muscadelle. Production: 6,000 bottles

Only the oldest vines here are used for Cérons, and only in suitable years. Yields don't exceed thirty hl/ha, and the wines are unoaked. Vintage such as 1975 and 1989 suffered from excessive sulphur, but they had attractive fruit, sometimes with a boiled-sweets edge, and good acidity. The 1990 was still too sulphury to enjoy in 1994. The 2001 had rich apricot aromas, reasonable weight and density, and fair acidity, but the 15.5 degrees of alcohol unsettled the finish.

Château de L'Emigré

Cérons. Tel: 0556 270164. Owner: Gérard Despujols. 8 ha. 80% Sémillon, 20% Sauvignon Blanc.
Production: 9,000 bottles. Second wine: Ch de Valdoir

This property began producing sweet wine only in 1997. Most of it is sold to supermarkets under the second label, leaving just some 1,800 bottles for private customers. The 1997 had a rich, creamy palate with ample fruit but little complexity or length. The 2004 is simple and bland.

Grand Enclos du Château de Cérons

See Chapter Fifteen (Southern Graves)

Château Haura

Illats. Tel: 0556 629651. Website: www.denisdubourdieu.com. Owner: Bernard Leppert (leased to Denis Dubourdieu).
2 ha. 80% Sémillon, 20% Sauvignon Blanc. Production: 7,000 bottles

When I visited Haura in 1994 the owner was the garrulous ninety-year-old Mme. Leppert, and the winemaker was her granddaughter, who subsequently married and left the region. So in 2002 the property was leased to Denis Dubourdieu. The Lepperts cropped at fairly high yields and aged the wines only in tanks. However, in exceptional years they produced a Cuvée Madame, which, according to Mme. Leppert, was picked berry by berry. Under Denis Dubourdieu the wines are barrel-fermented and aged in twenty-five per cent new oak for up to eighteen months.

The Leppert wines were patchy, though I recall a spicy and assertive 1976. But even the 1982 Cuvée Madame, though honeyed and floral on the nose, and quite intense on the palate, was poorly balanced, with excessive alcohol. Under Dubourdieu there has been, not surprisingly, a distinct improvement. The 2002 had waxy aromas, and was silky but forward. The 2003 was richer, more unctuous, yet with considerable vigour and reasonable length. The 2004 is better, with lightly honeyed aromas, a creamy texture, fair concentration, and lushness; not a wine of great depth, but well crafted and quite long.

Le Hauret du Piada

Illats. Tel: 0556 271613. Owner: Frédéric Lalande. 0.5 ha. 80% Sémillon, 12% Sauvignon Blanc, 8% Muscadelle.
Production: 1,200 bottles

This property is owned by the proprietors of Château Piada (*q.v.*) in Barsac. It forms part of a ten-hectare property, but only a tiny sector is used for Cérons. Until 2003 it used to be known as Domaine du Hauret-Lalande. Frédéric says he produces the sweet wine here only when the grapes have the same richness as those at Barsac. The vinification is the same as for Piada, but the *élevage* can be as long as eighteen months. The 1998 had light citric aromas, and was a simple, pretty wine of little depth. The 2002 had more intensity, with lemon and apricot flavours, and ample acidity and persistence, and a long, lemony finish. The 2003 is richer, more peachy and a touch syrupy on the palate; its an opulent wine that lacks some acidity and length. Unlike many Cérons, this is competently made and of good quality.

Château Huradin

Cérons. Tel: 0556 270097. Owner: Daniel Lafosse. 3 ha. 80% Sémillon, 10% Sauvignon Blanc, 10% Muscadelle.
Production: 3,500 bottles

This property was run for many years by Yves Ricaud, but he has handed the reins to his son-in-law, who is the brother of Dominique Lafosse of Clos Bourgelat. Only Sémillon is used for the Cérons, and the wine is unoaked. Even in vintages such as 1989 and 1990 this was a dim wine with no trace of complexity, but recent vintages such as 1996 and 2003 have shown more weight, concentration, and balance, as well as enjoyable apple and apricot fruit.

Château du Seuil

Cérons. Tel: 0556 271156. Website: www.chateauduseuil.com. Owner: Robert Watts. 5 ha. 60% Sémillon,
40% Sauvignon Blanc. Production: 5,000 bottles

The 1999 Cérons from this fine Graves property has apricot aromas, and is sleek, lean, and charming, with purity rather than complexity, and an attractive candied-fruit finish. The 2005 is in a similar style, with a raciness and intensity reminiscent of a Mosel wine.

CADILLAC

The Cadillac communes overlap with those that produce Premières Côtes de Bordeaux. There are thirty-seven of the latter, and twenty-two are entitled to produce sweet wine. These are: Baurech, Béguey, Cadillac, Capian, Cardan, Donzac, Gabarnac, Haux, Langoiran, Laroque, Lesiac, Le Tourne, Monprimblanc, Omet, Paillet, Rions, St-Germain-de-Grave, St-Maixant, Semens, Tabanac, Verdelais, and Villenave de Rions.

All Premières Côtes villages can produce a *moelleux* style, which is usually pallid stuff, but only these twenty-two may produce a wine with the minimum of fifty-one grams per litre of residual sugar required by the rules of the appellation. It was created in 1973, when 15,482 hectolitres were declared as Cadillac. By 2005, the production had dropped to 6,000 hectolitres, equivalent to about 800,000 bottles. There are just under 200 hectares declared as Cadillac (although 1,200 hectares fall within the appellation), with seventy-seven growers producing the wine.

The major grape variety is Sémillon (about seventy per cent), the other two being Sauvignon Blanc (twenty per cent) and Muscadelle. The maximum yield is thirty-seven hl/ha (though forty is sometimes permitted), and the wine must be made from nobly rotten fruit (take that with a pinch of salt) and picked by *tries successives*. (In contrast, Premières Côtes may be picked by machine.) The wine can be sold only in bottle, although there is pressure, fiercely resisted by top producers, to permit bulk sales. They point out that growers unhappy with the requirement can declassify the wine to Premières Côtes, which may indeed be sold in bulk.[1] The minimum must weight for Cadillac is thirteen degrees of potential alcohol, but the Syndicat is petitioning the INAO to raise it to fifteen degrees. Ironically, there is opposition from some Sauternes growers, who clearly fear any raising of standards across the board from their neighbours and potential rivals.

Unlike the other sweet wine appellations, Cadillac has created a special category called Grains Nobles. For this style the maximum yield is twenty-eight hl/ha; the must weight has to be at least sixteen degrees of potential alcohol and no chaptalization is permitted. Clearly, most of the top wines fall into this category, even though not all estates use the term on their labels. At the other extreme is the Premières Côtes appellation, which is either used as a dustbin for sweet wines that don't make the grade as Cadillac, or as *moelleux*-style wines produced for a market that values cheapness over quality. With its high yields (fifty hl/ha) and pathetic harvesting requirements – although some Premières Côtes is picked by hand – it is hard to see how the global reputation of Bordeaux is enhanced by its existence. Indeed, the president of one of the other sweet wine Syndicats argues that the appellation should be abolished. I am inclined to agree.

There were some remarkable sweet wines here made in the past but only in exceptional vintages. One grower told me that the region enjoyed great renown in the early twentieth century. Pickers would complete the harvest in Sauternes, then cross the river to continue working in the villages around Cadillac, where the grapes ripened later than in Sauternes. So there was a tradition of late harvesting by *tries successives*. Quality slumped after World War II, when growers opted for volume over quality to respond to the demand for simple sweet wines. The major buyers were négociants, whose payments were directly related to alcoholic degree. This encouraged maximum chaptalization. That unhappy trend went into decline when the Cadillac Syndicat banned bulk sales.

Château de Birot
Béguey. Tel: 0556 626816. Owner: Eric Fournier. 3.5 ha. 82% Sémillon, 18% Sauvignon Blanc.
Production: 4,000 bottles

The Fourniers were the owners of Châteaux Canon in St-Emilion and Broustet in Barsac, but family squabbles forced their sale. Eric Fournier, who ran both properties in the past, has retreated to this property just north of Cadillac. Yields are very low, and the wine is fermented and aged in barriques. The 2002 had a slightly waxy, apricot nose, some lushness and roundness on the palate, ample fruit, and some spice and acidity on the finish. It is very reasonably priced.

Château Carsin
Rions. Tel: 0556 769306. Website: www.carsin.com. Owner: Juha Berglund. 2 ha. 90% Sémillon, 10% Muscadelle.
Production: 9,000 bottles

This large estate produces a range of dry wines, white and red (*see* Chapter Twenty-Seven), and a tiny amount of Cadillac. Average yields are a low fourteen hl/ha, and there are up to six *tries*. The wine is aged in barriques. The 1996 was fresh and lively rather than super-sweet, but it was enjoyable, with a long, citric finish. The 2001 is weightier, with a delicate boiled-sweets and apricot nose, a creamy texture, fair concentration and acidity, and a fresh finish.

Château Cayla
Rions. Tel: 0556 621540. Owner: Patrick Doche. 6 ha. 100% Sémillon. Production: 10,000 bottles

Patrick Doche made fine Cadillac from a parcel of vines with an average age of fifty years. No Cadillac was made in 1991, 1992, 1993, or 2000. The wine was aged for twelve months in new oak. The 1997 Grains Nobles, which had 160 grams per litre of residual sugar, was magnificent, its sweetness beautifully balanced by racy acidity and elegant oak. However, the property was sold in 2005 and its future is still uncertain.

Château La Croix d'Armagnac

Monprimblanc. Tel: 0556 626456. **Owner:** *Didier Arnaud. 11 ha. 100% Sémillon.* **Production:** *50,000 bottles.*
Second wine: Dom de la Martingue

Of the thirty hectares under vine, only one-third are used for Cadillac. Yields are fairly high and the wines are fermented in tanks, then aged in twenty per cent new barrels. Quality is modest, with sulphur dioxide dominating the wines when young, but the 2003 was a success here, with a waxy, peachy nose, and its richness and juiciness balanced by clean, fresh acidity. The wines are very inexpensive.

Château Fayau

Cadillac. Tel: 0556 980808. **Website:** *www.medeville.com.* **Owner:** *Médeville family. 25 ha. 90% Sémillon,*
10% Sauvignon Blanc, 10% Muscadelle. **Production:** *100,000 bottles*

A visit to Fayau is always a pleasure, as one is greeted by any of three exuberant brothers, the Bordelais equivalent of the Cheerybles brothers, and a posse of tail-wagging dogs. This gives a Dickensian air to the property, and its tasting room doesn't seem to have altered much since the nineteenth century either. Their ancestor, cooper Jérôme Médeville, bought Fayau in 1826, and since then the family have acquired a total of twelve properties in eleven appellations. Fayau itself consists of forty-one hectares, making the family the largest proprietor in Cadillac, but the town authorities are threatening to appropriate some of them as building land.

Yields are fairly high and there is chaptalization in weaker vintages. Fermentation and ageing take place in tanks, and the Médevilles like quite a lot of alcohol in the wine. Although the wines will age, they are fashioned to be drinkable young. In 1996 they introduced a barrique-aged *cuvée*, Grains Nobles, made only in exceptional years. This is sourced from the oldest vines, all Sémillon, fermented in new oak, and aged for up to twenty-four months.

Fayau made some superb wines in the past: the 1937 has aromas and flavours of caramelized oranges and is still going strong; the 1929 is frailer, but has attractive barley-sugar flavours. Wines from the 1960s, such as 1961 and 1967, were alcoholic and rather dry. I disliked the wines from the 1970s and 1980s, which were mostly sulphury, alcoholic, and lacking in sweetness and texture; they also tended to be flabby and short. Quality has improved in recent years, but the wine is still rather bland and sulphury, though the 2004 has some sweetness, spice, and a lively finish.

The Grains Nobles *cuvée* got off to a bad start in 1996; the wine was heavy and gummy when young, and oxidizing and flat when tasted in 2006. The 2002 and 2003 are far better, though reserved on the nose. They have mandarin flavours, ample sweetness and fair acidity, and greater freshness than the regular bottling.

The Médevilles produce a huge range of wines from their various properties, so they cannot focus too closely on their Cadillac, but I can't help feeling that the wines, though improved, could still be far better.

1 One complication is that because Cadillac is sweeter than Premières Côtes, the permitted sulphur dioxide levels are higher for the former. This makes it difficult to declassify much Cadillac, should the grower wish to do so, since its SO_2 content may be higher than the legal limit for Premières Côtes.

Château Manos

Haux. Tel: 0557 345300. Website: www.chateau-lamothe.com. Owner: Pierre Niotout. 8.5 ha. 98% Sémillon,
1% Sauvignon Blanc, 1% Muscadelle. Production: 12,000 bottles

These vineyards, opposite the Haux town hall, have been leased by the Néel family of Château Lamothe (*q.v.*) since 1991, although they have been content with the quality only since 1995. The soil is gravel mixed with clay. Some of the vines are between fifty-five and eighty years old. The young white vines and the red vines are incorporated into the production of Lamothe, so the Cadillac is made only in small quantities. The wine is aged in older barrels for twelve months. The oldest vines, when fully botrytized, are used for the Réserve; yields do not exceed ten hl/ha and the must is fermented and aged in new oak. But the last vintage was 1997; even though 2001 was a great vintage they didn't have sufficient fruit to justify a separate Réserve bottling.

The 1995 and 1997 Réserves are lovely wines. The 1995 is more classic and citric, though the oak is quite marked. The 1997 is weightier, with peach-syrup flavours, but it's finely tuned and well balanced by good acidity, which gives a citric finish. The regular 2004 is simpler, with attractive apricot fruit but little complexity.

Château Mémoires

St-Maixant. Tel: 0556 620643. Owner: Jean-François Ménard. 9 ha. 85% Sémillon, 10% Sauvignon Blanc,
5% Muscadelle. Production: 20,000 bottles

This property used to be known as Roumaud or Cru Rondillon, and was created in its present form in 1985. The holdings are quite complex. Ménard owns thirty hectares in all; the Cadillac vines are in St-Maixant and Verdelais on clay and gravelly clay soils. He also owns six hectares in Loupiac, and has been making wines under that appellation since 1988. Here the varietal mix is slightly different: eighty-five per cent Sémillon and fifteen per cent Muscadelle. Other vineyards produce white and red dry wines.

For the sweet wines there are various quality levels. The basic wine is Classique. Here the yields are around thirty-five hl/ha and the wine is fermented in steel tanks and aged for six months in oak. Grains d'Or is cropped at thirty hl/ha; it is fermented in new oak and aged for forty months. Residual sugar levels are very high, at around 180 grams per litre. Finally there is L'Or Cadillac from 100-year-old vines cropped at twenty-seven hl/ha; the vinification is the same as for Grains d'Or.

The three tiers are made for both appellations. In Ménard's view, his Loupiac is fuller and racier than his Cadillac, which he finds more elegant and honeyed. Since both wines have very high residual sugar levels, I find it hard to distinguish between the two appellations.

I have enjoyed some older vintages, both Cadillac and Loupiac, from Mémoires. The 1990 Grains d'Or in particular was very stylish. The 2003 Classiques were delicious: big, plump wines of considerable weight and power, with barley-sugar and *crème brûlée* flavours and a good finish. The special *cuvées* in 2001 are brilliant, with flavours of peach, orange, and passion fruit. I find little difference between Grains d'Or and L'Or; indeed, I prefer the Cadillac Grains d'Or to the L'Or Cadillac, as the latter is a touch heavy. The wines are fairly priced for the quality, and the Classique is a bargain. The 2005s are equally splendid.

Château Reynon

Béguey. Tel: 0556 170818. Website: www.denisdubourdieu.com. Owners: Denis and Florence Dubourdieu.
18 ha. 60% Sauvignon Blanc, 40% Sémillon. Production: 15,000 bottles

Reynon produces a good quantity of dry white wines, but some bunches are left on the vine to ripen further and are then picked a few grapes or bunches at a time as noble rot attacks the fruit. Yields are around fifteen hl/ha, and the average must weight about twenty degrees of potential alcohol. The wine is fermented and aged in barriques. This Cadillac is made only in appropriate vintages, such as 1996, 1998, 1999, and 2001 – which was the latest vintage. The high proportion of Sauvignon gives Reynon a lot of raciness and freshness, and these are delicious zesty wines with fine lemon, apple, and apricot fruit.

Domaine du Roc

Rions. Tel: 0556 626169. Owner: Gérard Operie. 2.5 ha. 80% Sémillon, 15% Sauvignon Blanc, 5% Muscadelle.
Production: 6,500 bottles

Although this Cadillac is vinified entirely in tanks, the one vintage I have tasted, the 1997, was a delightful wine, with fresh, lemony aromas, evident botrytis and richness on the palate, and a long, balanced finish.

I have in recent years tasted good wines from the following properties, but have insufficient experience of them to discuss them in further detail: **Château du Biac** (Langoiran), **Château Frappe-Peyrot** (Gabarnac), **Château Peneau** (Haux), **Château Peybrun**, **Château Renon** (Tabanac), and **Château La Tour Gaugas**.

LOUPIAC

Like the other sweet wine appellations on the right bank, Loupiac is in gentle decline. In 2002 there were 402 hectares yielding 13,167 hectolitres; by 2005 there were 330 hectares yielding 11,346 hectolitres. There are at present some fifty-eight producers. The maximum yield permitted is forty hl/ha. There is more clay in the soil than in the other appellations, which can be an advantage in very dry years. Many of the vineyards face due south, so, according to some producers, the grapes often acquire a *rôti* character. Most growers agree that the wines tend to be less fat and racier than those from Ste-Croix-du-Mont. The soil is essentially clay-limestone, with outcrops of gravel and clay on the higher spots. Sémillon is the dominant variety, and accounts for eighty per cent of plantings.

There have been vines here since at least the thirteenth century, and Roman remains (which gave rise to the legend that Ausonius built a villa here) suggest that it was likely that vineyards were also present during the Gallo-Roman era. In medieval times Loupiac was under the control of the marquis of Cadillac. By the 1870s the area under vine was scarcely different from the present area, suggesting the region recovered quite well after phylloxera and the economic crisis of the 1930s. The Syndicat was founded in 1900 and the AC created in 1937.

While there are a handful of growers who try, climatic conditions permitting, to make the finest wine possible, there are still many producers who – using the excuse that Loupiac should be a delicate wine without too much richness or sweetness – produce rather thin wines closer to *moelleux* in style. Patrick Dejean, former head of the Syndicat, observes that almost all producers are now capable of making correct wine, but the problems remain lightness and dilution. Some producers foolishly argue that in fine vintages they shouldn't make a wine of exceptional richness or quality, as it would show up the contrast with lesser years. Dejean and others have pressed for lower official yields, but it has yet to happen. There is no equivalent here of the Grains Nobles *cuvées* found in Cadillac, and that, I am told, is because the great majority of customers are not looking for a super-rich style here.

Although one would not want to encourage those growers who can't be bothered to make wines of concentration and complexity when conditions permit, it does seem to be the case that Loupiac in general produces wines a touch lighter and less dense than those from its neighbour Ste-Croix.

Clos Jean

Tel: 0556 629983. Website: www.vignoblesbord.com. Owner: Lionel Bord. 11 ha. 80% Sémillon, 20% Sauvignon Blanc.
Production: 75,000 bottles. Second wine: Ch Jean-Fonthenille

This very attractive estate, with lemon trees standing guard in the gravelly courtyard, was once a staging post of the Knights of Malta, and their crosses are omnipresent here. Lionel Bord also owns Château Rondillon (*q.v.*), which is run by his son Josselin. The vines are mostly planted on clay-limestone slopes, but about one-third grow on the gravelly plateau.

Yields have always been high here. The grapes are pressed first in a pneumatic press, and then in a vertical press. Vinification takes place in tanks with selected yeasts and occasional chaptalization. Although a proportion of used barrels has been used from time to time, as in 1990, the regular wine is unoaked. However, there is a special *cuvée*, at first called Cuvée Vin Nu (as the bottle carried no label) and now named, rather ambitiously, Cuvée Sublime. This is made only in top years and from grapes with an average potential alcohol of twenty-two degrees. The must is fermented in tanks, and then aged fifteen months in older barrels. It was produced in 1990, 1995, 2001, and 2003.

In the 1980s and early 1990s the wines were disappointing: light, sulphury, hard, and lacking purity and concentration. The wines of the 2000s are cleaner and fresher but they are still undistinguished. The Cuvée Sublime is certainly richer and silkier, but it too lacks concentration and persistence. The Bords seem content to be run-of-the-mill, which is a pity, as a more conscientious approach in the vineyard (there are only two *tries*) and winery could surely deliver more exciting wines.

Château du Cros

Tel: 0556 629931. Website: www.chateauducros.com. Owner: Michel Boyer. 34 ha. 70% Sémillon,
20% Sauvignon Blanc, 10% Muscadelle. Production: 110,000 bottles. Second wine: Ségur du Cros

You can see the ruins of the fourteenth-century château, built by the Ségur family, perched uneasily on the plateau overlooking the Garonne just south of the village of Loupiac. Michel Boyer's grandfather, François Thévenot, bought the property from the Comte de la Chassaigne. At that time the plateau was planted with wheat, but during the 1920s Thévenot planted vines, and his grandson, after he took over in the 1960s, planted the slopes. Today Michel Boyer is handing over to his daughter Catherine d'Halluin. It's a large property of thirty-four hectares, and produces dry white and red wines too. There are some very old vines here, both Sémillon and Muscadelle, and yields rarely exceed thirty-five hl/ha.

The wine is fermented in tanks with indigenous yeasts. Boyer began oaking the wines in 1985, and now almost all the wine is aged for twelve months in thirty-five to fifty per cent new barriques. However, a small portion usually remains in tanks to give the final blend more freshness.

In 2004 the Boyers introduced a new wine called La Tradition. This is a Loupiac from a 1.58-hectare parcel planted with Sémillon vines that date from 1907. This is aged for twelve months in sixty per cent new oak, and only 2,400 bottles are produced. They also buy in grapes to produce a lighter style they call Fleur du Cros, which is mostly sold to supermarkets. The Château du Cros wine is limited to around 40,000 bottles.

Cros has always been exemplary medium-bodied Loupiac, not aiming for the highest concentration, but by no means dilute or clumsy. Even in less than stellar vintages such as 1973, 1981, and 1994, Boyer managed to make wines with good apricot fruit and ample vigour; they never seem to lack length and elegance. In good years such as 1985, and 1990, 1996, and 1997, the Loupiac is excellent, sometimes, as in 1996, with floral and citric aromas, and in other years, such as 1997, with more botrytized apricot aromas. The palate has freshness and spice as well as abundant fruit. In 1995 it was a touch too *rôti* to be considered elegant, and in 1997 there are some unusual tropical fruit flavours. The 2003 lacks a little vigour. As for La Tradition, the 2004 was very oaky on the nose, while the palate was plump and voluptuous, an imposing wine with flavours of peach and pineapple.

On a previous visit to Cros, the hospitable Boyers had invited me to lunch, and surprised me by serving sardines with Loupiac, a match that was surprisingly good. On our way to lunch at the house on my latest visit, I reminded Michel Boyer of his gastronomic coup; delighted, he raced ahead to dig out his finest tinned sardines, which we polished off with his 1990 Loupiac.

Château Grand Peyruchet

Tel: 0556 626271. **Owner:** *Bernard Queyrens. 9 ha. 80% Sémillon, 20% Sauvignon Blanc.* **Production:** *22,000 bottles*

The Grand Peyruchet vineyards are planted on sandy clay soils, and there are parcels where the clay is mixed with either gravel or limestone. The average age of the vines is forty years, and the density is 7,000 vines per hectare. The average yield is thirty-two hl/ha. The wine is fermented in tanks with indigenous yeasts, and just under half the crop is aged in one-third new oak; then the two wines are blended. In 1990 Queyrens made a special *cuvée* called Marie-Charlotte, since renamed Cuvée Prestige. This wine is entirely barrel-fermented and aged for twenty months in new oak.

The regular wine is good but far from exceptional. The best vintages I have encountered are the creamy, tangerine-flavoured 1985 and the piquant, pineappley 2003. As for the Prestige, the 1990 is marmalady and has a peppery finish, but too much alcohol gives the wine some coarseness. But in 2006 it was still quite impressive. The 1997 has complex aromas of quince and *crème brûlée*, but the palate is odd, with a sweet-and-sour tone, and a lack of weight and complexity. The 2001 is better, more toasty and honeyed on the nose, but it has a sharpness that is bizarre, and although intense it is far from opulent and almost austere.

Château Loupiac-Gaudiet

Tel: 0556 629988. **Website:** *www.chateau-loupiacgaudiet.com.* **Owner:** *Marc Ducau. 24 ha. 95% Sémillon, 5% Sauvignon Blanc.* **Production:** *100,000 bottles.* **Second wine:** *Ch Pontac*

This pretty little château lies close to the main riverside road, and Marc Ducau used to receive his guests in the charming little central hall, with its chequered tiles and painted scenes of rural life high on the walls. Ducau has retired, but his nephew Daniel Sanfourche still pours the wines in the same spot. Marc Ducau's grandfather bought Château Pontac first, and then in 1920 added Loupiac-Gaudiet. The vineyards surround the château, with the best sectors on well-exposed slopes behind the house. Lower down there is clay soil, and higher up more gravel and limestone. Yields here can be quite high, and extreme concentration has never been the stylistic goal.

Marc Ducau was always opposed to barrel-ageing, and preferred to keep his wines for two years in tanks on the fine lees. He maintained that wood-ageing masks the fruit and dries it out. I suspect he had a loyal customer base that liked his style of Loupiac, so he saw no reason to change it. And indeed the wine was very good, albeit in a modest, discreet style. In lighter years it was decidedly an apéritif wine, while in fine vintages such as 1989 it had ample lush fruit. The 1995, tasted in 2006, was delicate but well balanced and stylish. The 2001 was similar, while the lighter 2002 had more citric flavours. The 2004 was concentrated and pure, with attractive mandarin and apricot flavours.

In 1998 Sanfourche produced for the first time an oaked *cuvée*, called Château de Loupiac, sourced from old vines at the top of the slope; the wine is aged for twelve months in fifty per cent new barriques. It was also made in 1999, 2001, and 2003. The maximum production is 7,000 fifty-centilitre bottles. The 2003 is sweeter than the regular wine, with more body and weight, and the oak does not obscure the wine's essential purity.

Château Mémoires

See *Cadillac*

Domaine du Noble

Tel: 0556 629936. **Owner:** *Patrick Dejean. 17 ha. 80% Sémillon, 20% Sauvignon Blanc.* **Production:** *50,000 bottles*

Up on the plateau stands this charming ivy-covered mansion, where one of Patrick Dejean's brothers lives. Most of the vineyards surround the house on gentle south- and southwest-facing slopes on gravelly clay soil. There are many old vines here, including a parcel of Sémillon from 1899. Dejean follows the principles of *lutte raisonnée*, and prunes to reduce vigour so as to attain must weights of around twenty-one degrees of potential alcohol. He tends to pick the Sauvignon relatively early to preserve its aromatic freshness; it is also vinified separately. The average yield is thirty hl/ha, and never exceeds thirty-five. There is no chaptalization.

Rather confusingly, Domaine du Noble produces both an unoaked and an oaked wine under the same label. Dejean insists the latter is of little significance, since it is made only at the request of a handful of private clients in France and never consists of more than fifteen per cent of the crop. The Noble wines are intended to be aged, and sometimes lack aromatic finesse in their youth. They have good extract and acidity and considerable concentration and opulence. The 1986 had a lot of charm, the 1989 (oaked bottling) was succulent and robust. The 1990 lacked some fat and depth, for some reason, and the 1996, while fresh, lacked complexity. The 2001 is first-rate, with honey and apricot on the nose, considerable richness and opulence on the palate, and delicious citrus and apricot fruit. The 2003 is plump and peachy, a touch solid, with only modest acidity, and I prefer the more stylish 2004.

Château de Ricaud

Tel: 0556 626616. Owner: Alain Thiénot. 20 ha. 85% Sémillon, 15% Sauvignon Blanc. Production: 35,000 bottles
Alain Thiénot is also the owner of a Champagne house and of Château Rahoul (*q.v.*) in the Graves. Ricaud is, architecturally, a neo-Gothic horror-film set surrounded by woodlands. During the late nineteenth and for much of the twentieth century it was owned by the Wells family, and was bought by Thiénot in 1980. Maurice Wells was a judge based in Paris, but wrote to the cellarmaster twice a day so as to monitor developments at Ricaud. He died in 1959. Marc Ducau of Loupiac-Gaudiet once told me that this used to be the finest property of Loupiac, but it went through a bad patch in the 1970s.

When Thiénot bought Ricaud, there were only forty hectares under vine. This has since been doubled, though only a quarter of the vines are declared as Loupiac. Ricaud also produces white, red, and rosé wines. The vines are cultivated by *lutte raisonnée* and the average yields are a low twenty-two hl/ha. The must is fermented in tanks, and aged for twelve months in one-third new barriques.

Vintages of the 1980s were not very exciting, though I enjoyed the tangerine-scented 1986. More recently, the 1999, 2001, and 2004 are all good, especially the 2001, with its bracing boiled-sweets and pineapple finish. In general these are medium-bodied wines, fluid rather than super-concentrated, with a gamut of fruit flavours ranging from Seville oranges to apricot to pineapple. Ricaud is not the most thrilling wine, but it is well balanced and dependable.

Château Rondillon

Tel: 0556 629983. Website: www.vignoblesbord.com. Owner: Josselin Bord. 12 ha. 80% Sémillon,
15% Sauvignon Blanc, 5% Muscadelle. Production: 45,000 bottles. Second wine: Ch Loustalot
Josselin Bord is the son of Lionel Bord of Clos Jean (*q.v.*). This property is planted on slopes with a rather heavy clay soil. Bord believes the wines are more *confit* than those of Clos Jean. The vinification is identical. The 2003 has charming apricot aromas and fruit, and the wine has some weight and spice, with a dried-fruits finish.

Château Les Roques

Tel: 0556 620104. Owner: Alain Fertal. 4 ha. 83% Sémillon, 15% Sauvignon Blanc, 2% Muscadelle.
Production: 18,000 bottles
Alain Fertal also owns Château du Pavillon (*q.v.*) just across the border in Ste-Croix-du-Mont. Since the vineyards touch, there is little difference between them, although the Loupiac sector is a bit steeper and has slightly less soil. The average age of the vines is fifty years. The wine is fermented with indigenous yeasts in tanks, and aged for eighteen months. The special *cuvée* called Frantz, from the oldest vines, is barrel-fermented and aged in sixty per cent new oak. Fertal usually blends about five per cent of this oaked wine into the regular wine. The regular Loupiac is very good and consistent. There are usually aromas of apricot or mandarins and the

palate is suave and concentrated, yet without heaviness; it tends to have a lively finish. Since 1995, my favourite vintages have been 1996, 1998, 1999, 2001, and the rather more easy-going 2002. Cuvée Frantz has more richness, spice, and complexity, but there is no overt oakiness; despite its greater body and weight, there is more elegance and length than on the regular wine. This is one of the top wines of the appellation, and all recent vintages have beenexcellent.

Other good wines from Loupiac include **Château Dauphiné-Rondillon** and **Château Vieux Moulin Cazeaux**.

STE-CROIX-DU-MONT

Unlike the other villages that give their names to these sweet wine appellations, Ste-Croix-du-Mont is located on top of the cliff that plunges down to the fertile shores of the Garonne. The tall spire of the neo-Romanesque church is visible for miles around. Inside the cliffs is a so-called grotto, which one can visit for a glimpse of the stacked, compressed fossilized oysters of which the cliff is composed.

The appellation has a potential surface of about 500 hectares of vineyards, though considerably fewer are declared as Ste-Croix-du-Mont. (Red and dry white wines from these sites must be declared and sold as Bordeaux.) In 2002, 400 hectares yielded 13,190 hectolitres; in 2005, 324 hectares yielded 12,147 hectolitres. Thus the decline in production of Cérons and Loupiac is mirrored here in Ste-Croix. There are about 100 properties, but only twenty or so are full-time wine producers. The maximum yield is forty hl/ha. The soil is varied. The plateau is composed of clay over limestone, and, as has already been mentioned, there are many fossils in the soil. However, there are also sectors, mostly in the centre and to the east, with much gravel and little or no limestone; these are warm soils that are almost always harvested well before the vines on clay-limestone. On the other hand, wines from limestone soils tend to age better. Jean-Marie Tinon, who makes wines from both types of terroir, finds that clay-limestone soils give wines with more minerality, while gravel gives wines with more fruitiness. But in some years, he concedes, these distinctions can be blurred.

If Loupiac is characterized by elegance rather than power, Ste-Croix tends to have more weight, though of course much depends on the individual style and approach of each property. I once asked Yves Armand of La Rame if the region could ever make wines that rival Sauternes. He was doubtful, since the soil is richer here and thus more generous; in Sauternes, the soil tends to restrain the vigour of the vines. But with conscientious pruning and harvesting, he believes it is certainly possible to make wines of excellent quality.

There is less enthusiasm in Ste-Croix-du-Mont for a reduction in maximum yields. Arnaud de Sèze of Château Loubens observes that the present yields allow producers to offer wines at an attractive price, and a severe reduction in yields would eliminate this tier of wines, putting Ste-Croix in direct competition with Sauternes, a competition it is likely to lose. Nor is he persuaded that those growers who customarily crop at forty hl/ha would necessarily make better wine at twenty-five or thirty hl/ha.

Château Bel-Air
*Tel: 0556 620119. **Owner:** Jean-Guy Méric. 25 ha. 85% Sémillon, 10% Sauvignon Blanc, 5% Muscadelle.*
Production: 100,000 bottles

This property dates back to 1648, and it includes vines within AC Bordeaux, Premières Côtes, and Cadillac. The sweet wine tends to be made solely from Sémillon. There are two unoaked *cuvées*, of which the Vieilles Vignes is the richer. The Cuvée Prestige (formerly known as Grand Cru) is fermented in tanks, then aged in mostly older barriques for twelve to eighteen months; it is made only in very good years. The Vieilles Vignes is direct and reasonably pure, though the 2003 was lusher than usual; the 2004 is slight but charming. The Prestige has more intensity than the Vieilles Vignes, and better length, but it's not a wine of great complexity. In terms of quality there is little to choose between the 1997, 2001, and 2003.

Château La Caussade

Tel: 0556 620150. Owner: Yves Armand. 10 ha. 80% Sémillon, 20% Sauvignon Blanc. Production: 10,000 bottles

This is under the same ownership as La Rame (*q.v.*), but the vines are young and located on the plateau. Here Armand fashions a wine in a lighter style that he hopes will appeal to younger drinkers. The regular wine is unoaked, and there is also a barrel-aged *cuvée* rather pretentiously called Sublime. The 2002 La Caussade was sweet, lean, and melony, pleasant but not complex. The 2003 Sublime is also lean but considerably sweeter, with a fine, citric finish.

Château Crabitan-Bellevue

Tel: 0556 620153. Owner: Bernard Solane. 22 ha. 95% Sémillon, 5% Muscadelle. Production: 80,000 bottles.
Second wine: Ch Grand Dousprat

This estate has been in the Solane family since 1870, though it has expanded in recent years to a total of forty-eight hectares. There are numerous parcels, so the vines are on varied soils and expositions. There are some centenarian vines, and the average age is forty years. The regular wine is fermented in steel tanks with natural yeasts and is unoaked. In good vintages Bernard Solane and his son Nicolas produce a Cuvée Spéciale, a selection of the best lots aged in twenty-five per cent barriques for twelve months (although in 2003 the ageing was prolonged to twenty-four months). Unfortunately the wines are one-dimensional and dilute, and in some vintages excessively sulphury and herbaceous. Happily, there are exceptions. The Cuvée Spéciale in 1990 was delicious, concentrated, and powerful. The regular 2003 is attractive too, with flavours of pineapple and mango, but it lacks length.

Château Grand Peyrot

Tel: 0556 620165. Owner: Jean-Marie Tinon. 5 ha. 90% Sémillon, 10% Sauvignon Blanc. Production: 20,000 bottles

Jean-Marie Tinon and his daughter Virginie run two properties: Grand Peyrot and La Grave (*q.v.*). At Grand Peyrot the soils are clay-limestone. With an average age of fifty years, the vines are older than at La Grave. Virginie Tinon believes that Grand Peyrot gives silkier wines than La Grave. There have been vintages, such as 1986, when Tinon used some barriques as well as tanks to age the wine, but this is very much the exception. The 1982 and 1983 were both very good, if not outstanding, and vintages such as 1990 and 2001 have considerable opulence and charm. The 2002 is rather feeble.

Château La Grave

Tel: 0556 620165. Owner: Jean-Marie Tinon. 10 ha. 85% Sémillon, 15% Sauvignon Blanc. Production: 40,000 bottles

This is the sister property of Château Grand Peyrot (*q.v.*). The vineyards here are planted mostly on gravelly soils. There are two *cuvées* of La Grave, one unoaked, the other, first made in 1986, aged in barriques. The oaked wine is now known as Sentiers d'Automne.

La Grave is a well-made wine, but except in great years such as 1990, it can be simple, melony, and lacking in character and richness. The barrique-aged wine is more serious, as one would expect; there is considerably more power and concentration. The 1990 and 1998 were particularly good.

Château Loubens

Tel: 0556 620125. Owner: Arnaud de Sèze. 16 ha. 95% Sémillon, 5% Sauvignon Blanc. Production: 40,000 bottles.
Second wine: Ch des Tours

You can spot this clifftop château from the other side of the river, and conversely there is an excellent view from the terrace of Loubens over to Sauternes, where Rayne-Vigneau and Yquem are clearly visible. Loubens rests on a bed of fossilized oyster shells. In the nineteenth century the cliff was tunnelled into to create seven galleries that used to be the property's *chai*. Since Loubens is not aged in barrels, these galleries now stand empty, and envious neighbours wish that they had such a resource on their doorstep.

The de Sèze family bought Loubens in 1927, and the present occupant has been making the wines for decades, without, it seems, the slightest deviation in style or philosophy. The vines are all on clay-limestone slopes with varying depths of clay. Some of the vines were on slopes so steep that they had to be worked with the aid of winches. De Sèze toys with the idea of bringing them back into production, but believes they would be too dangerous for his workers to cultivate.

The wine is usually pure Sémillon, and the average yield is twenty-five hl/ha. His harvesters are aiming to pick at a potential alcohol of eighteen or nineteen degrees. The grapes are sorted and pressed in either a vertical or a pneumatic press, or both. In some years there is light chaptalization. He prefers to use indigenous yeasts, but there is no fixed rule. In 1989, for example, he used cultivated yeasts to avoid a stuck fermentation, so rich was the must. His father used to age Loubens in barrels, but then could not afford to renew them. So to barrel-age the wines would mean starting from scratch, which he is not inclined to do. However he ages the wine for at least three years in tanks, and then gives it a further year's repose after bottling. No wine was bottled in 1991, 1992, and 1993.

Although de Sèze always claims to aim for finesse rather than power or weight, these are surely the richest and most imposing wines of Ste-Croix-du-Mont. They are stylistically very consistent, with a lush, even ponderous, texture, and strong orangey botrytis aromas and flavours. As well as oranges, I often detect barley sugar and tinned pineapple on the nose, and *crème brûlée* flavours. Loubens is an acquired taste. These are not subtle wines and I don't often find the finesse that de Sèze is aiming for. But it is hard not to enjoy wines that are so voluptuous. Quality is very consistent, but the vintages I have admired most include 1981, 1983, 1988, 1989, 1990, 1995, 1996 (livelier and spicier than usual), and 1997.

Château Lousteau-Vieil

Tel: 0556 633927. **Owner:** *Martine Sessacq. 17 ha. 85% Sémillon, 10% Sauvignon Blanc, 5% Muscadelle.*
Production: *50,000 bottles.* **Second wine:** *Ch Cap des Vignots*

This is a fairly large property producing a commercial style of sweet wine, cropped generously. The wine is fermented in tanks and then aged in twenty per cent new oak for about eighteen months. Often the wines have a tropical fruit character, but they are usually loose in structure and somewhat dilute and bland. But Lousteau-Vieil did make more serious wines in 1975, 1976, 1983, and 1988. A more recent tasting of the 2002 proved unrewarding.

Château des Mailles

Tel: 0556 620120. **Owner:** *Daniel Larrieu. 21 ha. 90% Sémillon, 5% Sauvignon Blanc, 5% Muscadelle.*
Production: *100,000 bottles*

The Mailles vineyards are dispersed but most of them are on south-facing clay-limestone slopes. There are some 100-year-old vines, and the average age is forty-five years. Yields are fairly high, and it shows. The basic wine is fermented in cement tanks with natural yeasts, with a rotation between lots kept in tanks and those aged for about nine months in barriques. In 1988 Mailles produced its first barrel-fermented wine, then called Réserve Personnelle; since 1995 it has been known as Cuvée Laurence. This is aged for fifteen months in ten per cent new oak. It is not produced every year. Although the 1990 Réserve Personnelle stood out, most of the wines, whatever the *cuvée*, are dilute, solid, and rather dull.

Château du Mont

Tel: 0556 620765. **Owner:** *Hervé Chouvac. 14 ha. 90% Sémillon, 5% Sauvignon Blanc, 5% Muscadelle.*
Production: *80,000 bottles.* **Second wine:** *L'If du Ch du Mont*

The vineyards here are in three blocks, which happen to represent the major soil types of the appellation. The property is best known for its Cuvée Pierre, which until 1999 was known as Grande Réserve. This is barrel-fermented and aged in new oak for fifteen months. It is made only in top vintages. Cuvée Pierre is a delicious wine, with rich aromas of peaches, honey, and tropical fruit. The palate is rich and opulent, and often has pineapple flavours on the finish. These are among the most sensuous and opulent wines of the region. The 1990, 1997, and 2003 were all outstanding, and the slightly subdued 2004 is not far behind.

Château du Pavillon

Tel: 0556 620104. **Owner:** *Alain Fertal. 8 ha. 85% Sémillon, 12% Sauvignon Blanc, 3% Muscadelle.*
Production: *25,000 bottles*

Alain Fertal owns two adjacent properties, Pavillon and Château Les Roques (*q.v.*) in Loupiac. The estates used to belong to a merchant from Libourne called Maurice Delavelle, and after his death in a car accident his widow tried to run them, but finally put them on the market in 1994. They were bought by Fertal, who is, or was, a physicist. The two properties are vinified in the same way, except that at Pavillon there is no oaked *cuvée*. The average age of the vines is fifty years, and the harvesting rigorous. Thus in 1997 there were six *tries*, but Fertal threw out half the crop, leaving him with a yield of nineteen hl/ha. The average yields are twenty-five hl/ha, though in 2005 nature was more generous and he ended up with thirty-seven hl/ha.

This is quite a rich wine with aromas of oranges and mango; it's not over-sweet but has freshness, concentration, and balance. The 1996 was somewhat neutral and the 2002 was a bit too discreet, but vintages such as 1995, 1998, 1999, and 2001 were very successful here.

Château La Rame

Tel: 0556 620150. **Owner:** *Yves Armand. 20 ha. 80% Sémillon, 20% Sauvignon Blanc.* **Production:** *60,000 bottles*

Together with Loubens, this is probably the best-known estate in Ste-Croix-du-Mont. Yves Armand has been running the property since 1985, and is now assisted by his son-in-law Olivier Allo. The average age of the vines is fifty years and yields rarely exceed thirty hl/ha. For many years he has been collaborating with the local chamber of agriculture, trying out different types of canopy. He finds a lyre canopy works very well, but the high cost of maintenance reduces its attraction as an option. Indeed, he has been a tireless experimenter, working with cryo-extraction since 1987, although it has been used rarely in recent vintages.

At first the wines were aged in a blend of old barrels and tanks. Today, almost half the crop goes into the barrel-fermented Réserve, which is easily his best wine. He also produces a wine called Sublime as an exclusivity for the British supermarket Waitrose; it is essentially the same wine as the Réserve. Given that Armand once told me he had no confidence in his own ability as a taster, he manages to produce an excellent and consistent range of wines.

I have tasted a number of vintages from the 1970s and early 1980s, and with the exception of the delicate, elegant 1975, they were unremarkable. It's with the 1989 Réserve that La Rame begins to make an impression. The ripeness, the texture, the freshness, and the length mark out this wine, and the 1990 was even better, having more opulence and power without being overworked. It is hard to think of other producers in these sweet wine appellations that were making wines of this quality at that time. In a blind tasting, I suspect it would be quite easy to mistake them for Sauternes. Other than the rather sugary 1997, there were other splendid Réserves in 1995, 1996, and 2001. Together with the very different Loubens, this is probably the most expensive Ste-Croix-du-Mont, but it still offers good value.

Bordeaux Vintages

The greatest earlier years for Bordeaux were 1825, 1844, 1846, 1847, 1848, 1859, 1865, 1869, 1870, 1874, 1875, 1878, 1893, 1896, 1899, 1900, 1904, 1906, 1909 (Sauternes), 1920, 1921, 1926, 1928, 1929, 1934, 1937 (Sauternes), 1943 (Sauternes), 1945, 1947, 1948, 1949, 1950 (Pomerol), 1953, 1955, and 1959.

1961: A mild spring led to early flowering, but at the end of May a hard frost hit the vineyards. This did great damage to the Merlot, so that many wines were almost pure Cabernet. July was warm with some late rain, but August and September were hot and dry. Picking began on September 2 in fine weather. Quality was outstanding, with healthy, ripe grapes with thick skins. But quantities were very small. Many wines are still alive and well, and show enormous vibrancy and concentration. The few disappointments tend to be in St-Emilion. Nor does Sauternes, although very concentrated, match the red wines, although the wines were certainly good.

1962: The summer was hot and the crop bountiful. After some helpful September rain, the grapes were picked in October in healthy condition, giving fruity wines, some of which are still drinking well. A good year for Sauternes, which delivered a large crop of excellent quality.

1963: A vintage more or less ruined by rain that led to rot and sharp acidity.

1964: The summer was hot and dry. Then heavy rain fell in October, diluting the juice. Some good wines were made, especially from precocious vineyards where picking began before the downpours, but quality varies from property to property. Overall, the Graves fared much better than the Médoc, while the best wines came from the Right Bank, where much of the harvest was completed by the time the rain began. Most of the Sauternes crop was drenched on the vine.

1965: A dreadful year, with a wet summer followed by a wet September. Rot was widespread.

1966: After a mixed and fairly cool summer, September came in warm and dry, and a good crop was harvested in fine conditions from early October. In style the wines are quite tannic and austere, but have great elegance. There were some good wines from Pomerol, but many lacked weight and may be past their best by now. It was a fine year for white Graves. Light, lean Sauternes that are probably past their best.

1967: A large crop which struggled to ripen in a cool summer. Some good, if fast-evolving, wines were made on the Right Bank, but Médocs were not that structured and did not keep that well. Some excellent white Graves and a memorable year in Sauternes, but only for estates such as Yquem that picked late.

1968: Sopping wet. All wines should have been drunk by now.

1969: Growers were pleased by the warm, dry summer that brought the crop to ripeness, but heavy rain in September wrecked the vintage. Wines should have been drunk up by now. An Indian summer benefited Sauternes, but the wines were marred by excessive acidity and are patchy.

1970: Weather conditions were rather confused, with a warm, dry July, a cool and wet August, and a cold September which gave way to an Indian summer. The crop was both large and of excellent but not uniform quality, and many wines are still drinking well. Excellent white Graves too, though most are probably past their best. The vintage was successful throughout Bordeaux, but St-Emilion and Pomerol produced many of the top wines. A very good year in Sauternes, even though there was little botrytis to add complexity to the luscious fruit.

1971: A small crop, since Merlot was badly affected by *coulure* during flowering, severely reducing the crop. Overall, the Graves and the Right Bank fared better than the Médoc, with rich white wines and some good reds. The wines in general were not that structured and most will be past their best. The exception was in Sauternes, where there was more botrytis than in 1970 and the resulting wines were fresh and elegant. The best should still be holding up well.

1972: The summer was cool and August very wet, so the grapes never ripened properly despite a dry, warm September. Vegetal wines, long past their modest best. Poor in Sauternes too, though there were some pleasant surprises from Barsac, now probably past their best.

1973: A warm summer, interrupted by some wet weather in July, aroused hopes of a fine vintage, but in late September there was steady rain. Grapes were diluted by overcropping. When young, reds and whites had a lightweight, pallid charm, but have long been in decline. Light, pretty wines from Sauternes that should now be drunk up.

1974: Fine weather in the spring and early summer was encouraging, but from August onwards there was a good deal of rain, and September was cool. The wines, mostly from overcropped vines, were lean and hard, though better in the Graves than the Médoc. Thin wines from Sauternes, distinctly lacking in lusciousness.

1975: Good weather during flowering was followed by a hot summer, interrupted occasionally by powerful storms. The harvest began on September 22 and continued under fine conditions until mid-October. From the outset the wines were very tannic because of the thick-skinned grapes. The year was acclaimed as great, but it became apparent that many wines had more tannin than fruit. There is great variation from estate to estate. Many of the best wines came from precocious soils, such as Haut-Brion, Cheval Blanc, and Pétrus. Many growers were tempted to pick too early in order to ensure a decent crop after the preceding difficult vintages. There were some excellent whites from the Graves.

In Sauternes an Indian summer permitted the gradual spread of botrytis. The wines are fruity and stylish and still drinking well.

1976: An exceedingly hot summer, with weeks of very high temperatures and little rain until mid-September, right at the beginning of harvest. The rain diluted the musts. The result was a large crop of wines that matured rapidly; many had a baked character, others were thin from dilution. The whites were rich and powerful, but aged quickly thanks to low acidity. In Sauternes heavy rain in mid-September threatened to spoil the crop and some growers rushed to pick. Those who waited well into October had very luscious fruit, though without the fine acidity that characterized the 1975s. Some wines show premature oxidation, while others are in their prime.

1977: A wet, cold summer saw off this vintage, despite warm and dry weather in September. Mediocre wines, other than some acceptable whites, and all surely past their best. Poor in Sauternes.

1978: The spring was extremely wet, but conditions improved over the summer, and September was warm and dry, allowing the harvest to take place relatively late but in excellent conditions. Some grapes were less than optimally ripe, so there are some wines that are somewhat lean and even herbaceous, especially from the Right Bank. But overall this is a very good if not spectacular year throughout the region, both for red and white wines. Top white Graves had surprising staying power. Fine autumn weather saved the vintage in Sauternes. Although the wines are rich, they mostly lack botrytis.

1979: A late but satisfactory flowering made it clear the crop would be large – too large. The summer was cool, especially in August, but it was mostly dry. September saved the day, with warm conditions that kept the grapes healthy. The excellent Médoc 1979s tended to be overlooked after all the excitement of the previous year, but the best of them have held up as well as the more celebrated 1978s. Very good wines with supple fruit were made in the Graves and on the Right Bank, too. The cool summer hindered ripening in Sauternes, and botrytis came late, but some very good wines were made. Now ready to drink, although the best will still keep.

1980: Cold weather during flowering caused *coulure* and uneven setting. The weather finally warmed up in August, but this was a very slow vintage to mature, and the crop, especially of Merlot, was small. Good weather continued into October, but the harvest began only in mid-October, hampered by wet weather. Some surprisingly good wines were made, as well as many thin, dilute wines. Wines from the Right Bank were somewhat less consistent than those from the Médoc and Graves. There were some excellent white wines, but these should now have been drunk up. In Sauternes, September was worryingly cool, but then fine weather returned in October and continued well into November. Those who delayed picking made some fine, medium-bodied wines with considerable finesse.

1981: This had all the makings of a fine vintage, until unwelcome rain began falling in late September, interrupting the harvest. This caused some dilution, but the red wines, if a touch lean, were well balanced and medium-bodied, and the best of them are still drinking well. Both the Médoc and Graves fared well, and white Graves were fruity but a touch soft. Many Right Bank wines were picked before the rain did much damage, so there were some successes here, especially in Pomerol. A late vintage in Sauternes, and one hampered by erratic autumn rains. Those who waited were rewarded with moderate botrytis and made good wines with fine acidity.

1982: The growing season led to grapes of perfect ripeness and enormous richness. Acidities were fairly low for the Médoc, resulting in wines of unusual opulence from all parts of Bordeaux. Some critics dismissed the wines as "Californian" in style. While they were lush, most of them had sufficient grip and backbone to stay the course. Although the lesser wines are at, or just past, their peak, the top growths are still going strong, with no sign of fatigue. The crop was large, so the wines were available in good quantities. There were some disappointing wines, often from properties that were not equipped to handle high temperatures during fermentation. White grapes were picked from September 10. Like the reds, they tended to be low in acidity and rather broad, but they were richly fruity. The Sauternais experienced the same hot September as the rest of Bordeaux, but torrential rain in October dashed hopes of a great year. Ironically, some less conscientious estates that routinely picked early and did so this year too made very good wines, although with little botrytis.

1983: The spring was wet, but cleared up in time for a satisfactory flowering in June. August was hot and humid, but there was little rot. After some rain in early September, fine weather returned. Cabernet Sauvignon ripened well and was picked in ideal conditions. In the Médoc the wines from Margaux were outstanding, in some cases superior to 1982. In contrast, St-Estèphe produced less interesting wines, perhaps because of high yields. The crop was very large, though not quite as enormous as 1982. In general, the wines were initially quite tannic, but don't have the body of the best wines of the previous vintage. Nonetheless there were many excellent wines, some of which are still highly drinkable. As often happens in Bordeaux, a very good vintage was overshadowed by an even finer preceding vintage. The wines from the Right Bank were more variable than those from the Médoc. Hail diminished the crop in the Graves.

White wines were also very good, with more zest and extract than the 1982s. The best of them are still drinking well. A great year for Sauternes, where perfect weather conditions lasted from late September into late November. Botrytis infection took its time and let rip only in late October. Those estates that waited made the best wines, and for once the benign weather meant there was no pressure to complete the harvest in a rush. This vintage was a wake-up call for underperforming estates; they soon realized the best properties had made excellent wines that revived what had formerly been a fairly moribund market for nobly sweet wines.

1984: Wet weather in spring led to problems at flowering, notably *coulure* among the Merlot vines. The summer was lacklustre, and there was rain in early September; but the weather improved from late September and the harvest took place in good conditions. Nonetheless the wines were rather mean and charmless. Even the well-balanced wines lack fruit and richness. The Right Bank fared worst, and it's unlikely that many remain drinkable today. Most should have been drunk by now. White Graves, however, had good fruit and freshness, but little staying power and were best enjoyed young. Fine weather in October allowed some good Sauternes to be made, but these too were light and best enjoyed young.

1985: The spring was rather wet, and flowering took place in June in rather damp conditions. July was hot and dry; indeed this was the driest summer since 1961, and hotter overall even than 1982. Heat returned in late September, which helped ripen a very large crop, twelve per cent higher than the abundant 1982. Nonetheless the wines were delicious, less ultra-ripe than 1982 and arguably better balanced. From the outset the reds, from both Médoc and Graves, had fragrance, charm, finesse, and excellent balance, so that many of the wines are still delicious today. But many of the top wines of the year come from the Right Bank and from Fronsac, where the Merlot ripened perfectly. However, growers everywhere who allowed yields to run out of control made relatively dilute wines. There were good white wines from the Graves, despite some localized hail damage. However, acidities were quite low, so they were best enjoyed young, when their perfume and overt fruitiness were to the fore. In Sauternes the autumn was fine, too fine. Botrytis stubbornly held back. A very few estates hung on until late November, but most properties had to be content with attractive, generous, sweet wines with little or no noble rot character.

1986: A dry, hot summer came to an end in mid-September, with rain and some storms. It was essential to wait, as the Cabernet was slow to ripen, and the Merlot especially suffered from some dilution. Fine weather in October made it possible for the grapes to ripen fully, though it was important to eliminate early-picked lots, if any, that were either dilute or green. Although the crop was larger than even 1982 or 1985, the berries were very small, leading to very high tannin levels. The outcome was a fine and classic vintage, with tannins that required at least a decade to soften. Although this was a fine vintage in St-Emilion and Fronsac too, few wines can match the 1985s for elegance and lushness.

The rains also affected the white wines, and growers picked fast to bring in the crop before rot set in. Some excellent wines were made in the Graves, but it was not an easy vintage and careful grape selection was required. Many wines suffered from dilution. In Sauternes the summer was equally hot and dry, but the September rains proved beneficial. By October there was ample botrytis and there was no pressure on estates to pick fast. By early November, however, wet weather returned and acidity dropped, so the best lots of wine were produced in October. They were very rich, but acidity was average, and the wines may not have the longevity of the very best vintages.

1987: Flowering was protracted, and there was some *coulure* in the Merlot, decreasing the crop. This year had all the makings of a fine vintage. July was warm but damp, but there was extreme heat through August and September. However, rain fell in early

October and hardly stopped. Much of the Merlot and Cabernet Franc were picked before the rain, but little of the Cabernet was ripe by then. Conditions were better in the Graves and Pomerol, where ripening was about one week ahead of the Médoc. The wines were not bad, but they were decidedly light, with low acidity and little structure. They were attractive to drink within five or ten years of the vintage, but most are now well past their best. Most of the white grapes were picked after September 21, a good week before the rain began. The grapes were healthy and ripe, and the wines were remarkably good, but without the structure for long ageing. Botrytis arrived late in Sauternes after a rainy October, but the crop was tiny and not all estates released a wine. Although relatively light and low in acidity, the wines were better than 1984, but essentially apéritif wines to drink young.

1988: Winter was mild and wet, and spring was warm, though wetter than normal. Some vineyards had to cope with mildew. There was plenty of rain in early July, but August was warm and dry, and anxieties about mildew and rot receded. There was some rain in September, but it did the grapes no harm. The harvest began during the last days of September, and those who waited until mid-October had Cabernet Sauvignon of excellent quality. Thick skins kept the grapes healthy, allowing growers to wait without too much fear, despite occasional showers. Those who picked too early had to chaptalize heavily. The wines proved fairly austere; sugar levels were not that high, but there was a good deal of tannin and acidity. This was true of Merlot as well as Cabernet. The crop was very large, in some places in the Médoc higher even than 1986. It turned out to be a vintage that demanded patience from the consumer, who was eventually rewarded with many classic wines, as well as some that lacked concentration and weight. On the Right Bank, the thick-skinned but ripe Cabernet Franc as well as Merlot also delivered wines of structure and staying power, but perhaps lacking in complexity. Although generalizations are risky, the best St-Emilions were superior to the Pomerols, some of which lacked flesh. Quality was also very good in the Graves, thanks to a slow ripening season.

The whites were picked from mid-September, and Sauvignon Blanc was of high quality. The wines should have been drunk by now. In Sauternes this was a year when it was essential to wait, as botrytis held off until late October. There was little wind and warmth to desiccate the berries, so the wines had exceptional purity without stridently overripe or raisiny characters. Moreover the wines had fine acidity, which added to their elegance. Their exceptional balance means that they are developing slowly and will be delicious for many years to come.

1989: The winter was very mild, and a hot, dry May led to an exceptionally early flowering in June. The summer was very hot and dry, apart from a few unsettled patches in July. Merlot was ready for picking at the very end of August or in early September, and most vines had been harvested by September 17. Some showers during September did no harm at all. Quality was good, with unusually high sugar levels, though acidity was low and some properties overcropped. Once the Merlot was safely in tank, the Cabernet harvest began, and was completed by October 6. Those who picked early had less satisfactory Cabernet, with rather raw tannins, than those who waited for full phenolic maturity. Petit Verdot was also of fine quality, with high sugars. Tannin levels were as high as in 1986, but were less discernible because of the extreme ripeness of the fruit.

The wines are quite burly, but undeniably rich and powerful, and the best of them are superb. In some cases they were superior to the 1982s, not because of climatic conditions but because most wineries were far better equipped to deal with a hot and precocious harvest. Those that still lacked temperature control probably experienced difficulties during the fermentation. Alcohol levels are high (for Bordeaux) and acidities are relatively low, but that has not prevented many of the wines from ageing majestically. Both the Médoc and the Graves did exceptionally well, and the Right Bank benefited greatly from the precocity of the Merlot grapes.

The white harvest in the Graves was very early, with most estates picking by the end of August. Wines from the top estates have the body and concentration to develop further. In Sauternes the harvest began in mid-September, but botrytis did not attack the grapes fully until October. Sugar levels were higher than in 1988, and some wines are a touch heavy, although overall this is a first-rate vintage. In the communes of Sauternes and Bommes there was significant hail damage that reduced the crop. Barsac was especially successful. There is no rush to drink these wines.

1990: After a warm winter, the spring was cool. However, hot weather in May accelerated flowering, which was some ten days earlier than in 1989. The summer was hot and dry, with only half the usual rainfall, making this the driest year since 1961; fortunately the grapes had small berries and conserved good levels of acidity. Because of the size of the crop, many conscientious estates practised green-harvesting in July to reduce the yields. Some rain in August and a cooling trend in September helped avoid the vines shutting down from the heat. Overall this was a hotter and drier year than 1989. Harvesting took place in exemplary conditions, with Merlot being picked from September 10; but Cabernet Sauvignon took its time coming to full ripeness, as maturation had been slowed by the heat. Sugar levels were close to the highs of 1989. Mouton completed its harvest on October 3.

The crop was very large, once again, so there were wines that showed some dilution. But overall, this turned out to be a magnificent year. In analytical terms, there is little to choose between 1989 and 1990; July was hotter in 1989 than 1990, and in August it was the other way round. The harvest was later in 1990, and this may have resulted in some cases in finer tannins. St-Julien did exceptionally well, as did Pessac-Léognan. Quality was also exceptional on the Right Bank, where the clay soils sustained the vines through the dry summer, although some wines exhibit uncharacteristically high alcohol levels. At first it seemed a better Right Bank vintage than 1989, but a lack of acidity has led to some of the lesser wines fading by the early 2000s.

White wines were picked from September 3 in the Graves. The harvest needed to be rapid to conserve acidity. The wines were very rich and aromatic, and Sémillon coped better than Sauvignon Blanc with the hot weather. Nonetheless this was a patchy year for whites, as it was all too easy to pick the grapes too late.

In Sauternes this was an atypical year. Very hot weather ripened the grapes fast, and then rain in late August provoked botrytis, which spread quickly. Warm winds increased fruit concentration further. Most estates were already harvesting by September 11, and it was completed a month later. Some of the first lots were so high in sugar that they had to be blended with less rich batches in order to complete fermentation. Although there are many superb wines, other wineries suffered from an inability to control the vinification, and there are some unbalanced wines with excessive alcohol and insufficient residual sugar.

1991: One night determined the fate of this vintage, as on April 20 there was a severe frost that eliminated up to seventy per cent of the crop. St-Emilion, Pomerol, and Fronsac were particularly badly hit. There was some compensation in the phenomenon of secondary buds, which emerged some three weeks after the frost. Since the summer was fine, with little rain except in July, some of these secondary buds caught up with the surviving first crop in terms of maturation. Many estates, however, chose instead to eliminate the secondary crop altogether to avoid any greenness in the wine. The weather broke in late August, when there was torrential rain, and there was more rain in September. Uneven ripening and some rot made this a tricky harvest. Many estates had to move fast to bring in the grapes before rot became too widespread. Merlot often coped better than the Cabernets with the unusual weather patterns. This was a year when the Graves, especially the northern sectors near the city, had a slight edge on the Médoc, as it suffered less severely from frost damage. Curiously, despite all the problems, some good wines were made, especially in Pauillac and St-Estèphe, with rich fruit, adequate sugars, and ripe tannins. It was certainly a better year overall than 1987, though inferior to all the vintages in between, but they were not wines for extended cellaring. So little wine was made in St-Emilion, where, for example, Figeac's production was seven per cent of its usual crop, that the vintage can be more or less written off.

Whites, what there was of them, were picked from September 19. Yields rarely surpassed twenty hectolitres per hectare. The Sauvignon was considered marginally superior to the Sémillon. The frost affected the Sauternais too. The wines were not only small in quantity but patchy in quality as botrytis infected some insufficiently ripe fruit as well as mature grapes, and by October there was a good deal of grey rot too. But the best wines were superior to the 1987s and are still drinking well.

1992: A hot May led to an early flowering, but storms in June then prolonged it. Yet there was little *coulure* or *millerandage*. Much of the summer was both warm and humid, provoking rot in many places. This was the wettest summer in fifty years. Green-harvesting was essential to reduce potentially enormous yields. Rain fell in late August and again on September 20, the day before harvest was set to begin, and intermittent rain and cool conditions continued for three weeks. Rot made selection essential, and muddy conditions hampered estates used to harvesting by machine. Sugar levels were modest in both Merlot and the Cabernets. The quality of the wines was lacklustre, with much dilution; the northern Médoc fared best. This proved a wretched vintage on the Right Bank, where there was widespread rot, although in Pomerol, where picking was under way before the heaviest rains fell, some adequate wines were made.

It was an early harvest for whites, beginning on September 8 before the principal rainfall, resulting in good-quality Sauvignon and more mixed results for rot-prone Sémillon. They were wines to enjoy young for their bright, fresh fruit. This was a messy year in Sauternes. Botrytis did set in by mid-September after August rains, but there was grey rot too and pickers needed to be vigilant. Long spells of rain, beginning in late September, complicated the harvest, and the first pickings generally proved the best. However, botrytis infection and full maturation were far from uniform, so the wines lack perfect balance. Many are mediocre, and some properties decided not to release the wine.

1993: Spring was quite wet, but conditions improved by the time of flowering, which passed without problems. Damp weather returned, and with it some mildew. The summer, especially August, was hot and mostly dry. The crop was set to be large, and the vintage seemed highly promising by the beginning of September. It was not to last, and after one week rain began to fall and continued intermittently for the whole month, inevitably bloating the bunches and diluting the juice. Nonetheless there was less rain than in 1992. Temperatures were low, which kept rot at bay. Harvesting of red grapes began on September 18 and was completed by October 15. Merlot, more susceptible to rot than the other varieties, was picked rapidly. Not all the Cabernet ripened fully. Although quality was generally higher than in 1991 or 1992, much depended on yields and on selection by individual estates. The Graves was less badly affected than the Médoc, and produced a crop of medium-bodied wines of charm if little structure. The whites, picked from September 10, were of good quality but not for long keeping.

In St Emilion the vintage was considered better than 1991 or 1992, which was not saying much; the wines were reasonably ripe and healthy but yields were low. Pomerol recorded a moderately successful vintage. Overall, the Right Bank produced better and more structured wines than the Left, and many are still enjoyable.

As elsewhere in Bordeaux, the Sauternais enjoyed a fine August and was all set for a fine vintage. By late September heavy rain began to fall and bunches succumbed to grey rot; Barsac fared worst. Some lots had been brought in before the rain, but the grapes, although ripe, lacked concentration and noble rot. Many wines were tainted by grey rot, which the extensive use of cryo-extraction did nothing to alleviate. A handful of good wines were made, but in general this is a vintage to avoid.

1994: After a cool, wet, frosty April, there was an early flowering in good conditions followed by a hot summer with intermittent rain that kept maturation on track. As in 1993, conditions looked highly promising by early September, and then from September 7 the rain began and continued for most of the month. Fortunately temperatures were fairly cool and there was little rot, but the wet weather did cause some dilution. Growers did not delay the harvest, as the grapes, especially Merlot, were as ripe as they were going to get, and there was nothing to be gained by waiting. The red wines turned out to be dark, quite rich, and tannic; but they mostly lacked finesse and flair. Factors such as the varietal make-up of the wine, and the degree of selection, had an effect on quality. There were some good wines from St-Julien and Pauillac and the top growths of St-Estèphe, but Margaux was more uneven. The abundance of ripe Merlot meant that some good wines could be made on the Right Bank. As in 1993 St-Emilion and Pomerol were more consistent overall than the Médoc. Some rushed to acclaim 1994 as very fine, but it has become apparent that it is another vintage that failed to meet its early promise.

Graves whites were mostly picked before the rain and were often of excellent quality. But not every estate was successful, so there were considerable variations. They should now be drunk up.

In the Sauternais a severe frost in mid-April inflicted widespread damage on many Barsac estates. There was early botrytis but also abundant rain in the second half of September, which diluted the musts. Fine weather returned in early October, but by then there was much grey rot. Harvesters had to leave much of the fruit on the vines, reducing the crop. The harvest was completed by mid-October. Although less disastrous than 1992 and 1993, this was another unsatisfactory year, delivering wines patchy in quality, for medium-term consumption.

1995: After a wet winter, there was a little frost in the Graves, but a generally warm spring led to an early and successful flowering. The summer was hot and very dry. Statistics established that there was less rainfall than in torrid 1976, but the winter rains meant that the water table was higher, so the grapes were less stressed. There was some rain in mid-September, which proved useful, and by September 20 dry weather returned. There was little rot. Merlot was picked from September 16 to 23, and Cabernets were picked from the last week in September. Cabernet Sauvignon was robust and tannic, with rich fruit and a firm structure; Cabernet Franc was also very successful. Winemakers reported great satisfaction with the vintage, which delivered very ripe fruit in good conditions; yields were high. Some critics declared themselves unimpressed by 1995, but with time it has become clear that this is easily the best vintage since 1990, and the best wines are evolving slowly but impressively. They will be long-lived. St-Estèphe fared particularly well, thanks to its water-retentive soils, but there was some heat stress in St-Julien. As in 1994, wines from the Right Bank, including Fronsac, were more consistent than those from the Left, with Pomerol more successful than St-Emilion. However there were some dilute wines.

The white Graves harvest began on August 30, and most grapes were picked before the light rainfall in September, but some Sémillon was affected by rot. Quality was high, as ripening was homogeneous, and the wines showed good structure but are now ready to drink. Red Graves have evolved well, and show a good deal of elegance and richness.

Despite rain in mid-September, this was an early harvest in Sauternes, essentially completed by mid-October. Botrytis was patchy, there was some incidence of grey rot at certain properties, and some lots had to be rejected or consigned to the second wine. Nonetheless there are many good, rich, honeyed wines, and overall the vintage has been underrated.

1996: A cold spring was followed by rapid flowering in very warm weather. July began cool and damp, but then the weather improved. During the latter half of August there was some rain in the Graves, but the Médoc was only slightly affected. September was mostly dry but not especially warm; thus the grapes retained their acidity as they continued slowly to reach full maturity. There was some rain in late September. Merlot was picked from September 23, but most estates waited until early October to begin harvesting Cabernet Sauvignon. The crop was large. Sugar levels were high, and so were levels of malic acidity.

Whites were picked before the rain in September, and quality was excellent, with high levels of ripeness balanced by refreshing acidity. There had been fears that the August rains would damage and inflate the bunches, but sunshine and a drying wind brought the grapes to full ripeness, especially where leaves had been removed to improve ventilation. Red Graves were very good, but not quite as superb, perhaps, as those from the Médoc, especially the northern communes. Quality is less even than in 1995, and some wines show a slight herbaceousness, which is not necessarily unattractive. The Right Bank was more severely affected than the Left by the August and September rainfall, and there was some rot and dilution, as rain compounded the consequences of high yields. Results were patchy. Some good wines were made in Bourg and Blaye.

This was a curious year in Sauternes. The rain in August was welcome, but only to a point, as it also caused some dilution. September was cold, which slowed the progress of botrytis, which set in only after rain at the end of the month. Wind helped dry the grapes and concentrate the sugars, and lots picked in October had high must weights. The wines are richer than the 1995s, especially from Sauternes itself. This has emerged as a very good vintage, although overshadowed by the 1997s.

1997: The winter was unusually warm, and the growing season began three weeks earlier than usual. But May was cool and flowering was uneven and prolonged, though Cabernet Sauvignon fared better than Merlot. The summer was unsettled, with cool weather in July, heavy rain in August, and then a very hot spell. The crop was enormous, so green-harvesting was essential. More storms followed at the very end of August. September was fine and cool, and the harvest in the Médoc began with Merlot on September 12. Northern parts of the Médoc with late-ripening Cabernet fared well, though some vineyards had to be picked earlier than they should have been because of spreading rot. This was not a poor vintage, but it was far weaker than others from 1995 to 2002. The cool weather in September made it difficult for some grapes to ripen fully, and problems at flowering led to uneven ripening. The wet weather in August had led to some rot, which complicated the harvest and required careful selection. Although many Right Bank properties produced better wines than in 1996 after careful grape selection, acidity was generally low, so these were not wines for long cellaring. The harvest was prolonged, so stylistically wines varied from simple and dilute to jammy. The finest were supple and velvety.

The hot weather in August ripened the white grapes rapidly, and many Graves estates were harvesting in August. There was some rot, especially among Sauvignon Blanc, so grapes needed to be carefully sorted. Quality was quite good, but these whites were for early drinking. The reds from the Graves were, overall, inferior in quality to those from the Médoc.

In Sauternes, after a hot, humid August, botrytis arrived early – too early as the grapes were not yet ripe, and pickers had to eliminate these bunches. Botrytis returned in late September, and harvesting resumed and continued into early November. As well as noble rot there was *passerillage*. Although quite a tricky and prolonged harvest, the results were mostly excellent, making this the finest vintage since 1990.

1998: After a mild winter, a sunny May led to even flowering, which was completed by mid-June. Dull weather in July was followed by a hot, dry August. This led to some stress, but rainy weather in the first half of September brought that to an end. Much of the rain fell at night, and sunny days helped keep the vines dry. Skins were quite thick and berries were small, so little dilution or rot was prompted by the rain. Merlot was picked during the last week of September, and quality was first-rate. Cabernet Franc too was of good quality. Cabernet Sauvignon had more of a struggle to ripen, as October was cool and damp, and growers were tempted to pick early before any rot set in.

In style these were tannic wines that were distinctly austere and difficult to taste when young. According to Château Palmer, the rain diluted the sugar and acidity, but not the tannins. Some comparisons were made with 1988. The Médoc wines were very variable, some rich and firm and built to last, others rather tough and charmless.

White grapes were picked from mid-September in fine weather. This was a healthy crop that delivered rich wines, although some have low acidity. The red Graves were classic in their structure, and many have proved outstanding. Growers sought to use as much Merlot as they could in the blend, as it was picked before the rain and was very healthy; some were lucky with their late-ripening Cabernet, others had to pick fast, as quality was deteriorating.

St-Emilion and Pomerol enjoyed their best vintage since 1990. Merlot was mostly picked during the last week in September in excellent conditions, giving grapes with high sugars and fairly thick skins. Acidity and pH levels were comparable to 1990. The wines have been consistently enjoyable since release.

In Sauternes picking began in late September, when there was already ample botrytis and good concentration, and continued through October in mostly good conditions. By late October conditions deteriorated with some black rot setting in, but by then most of the harvest had been completed. The acidity was slightly lower than in 1997, and the wines are similar in style and quality to the 1996s and now show very well indeed.

1999: Spring began cool, but warmed up fast, leading to an early and speedy flowering in early June. The set was excellent, promising a very large harvest, so green-harvesting, especially of Merlot, would prove essential at many properties during the summer. Even the most conscientious of properties ended up with high yields. The summer was warm but interrupted by storms in early August, which led to some botrytis and mildew. Good weather returned in late August, and it remained fine until September 12, when there were further storms in the Médoc, followed by very heavy rain a week later. The Médoc and Graves began the harvest on September 17, and it lasted about two weeks. There was some rot, especially among the Merlot, so selection was important. Despite the rain, many Médoc growers did their best to pick Cabernet as late as possible to ensure the grapes were ripe. The last pickings were not necessarily the best. Those who reduced their yields were more likely to end up with ripe fruit in the vats than those who did not.

White Graves were mostly picked in early September before the rain, and were of good quality with high sugar levels and good acidity too. Many red Graves were fairly thin, as yields were extremely high. In the Médoc it was important not to over-extract during vinification. The best reds tend to be easy-going wines with good colour and fruit and supple tannins; high ripeness levels gave the wines considerable sweetness and charm. Many of them are already drinking well, though the best will keep. The best are similar in style to 1985, though are unlikely to age as well. Opinions varied on whether 1999 was better than 1998. It varies considerably from estate to estate, and it also comes down to stylistic preference. Margaux seems to have made particularly good wines this year.

In St-Emilion there was dramatic hail damage to 500 hectares on September 5; this affected Angélus, Canon, Beau-Séjour-Bécot, Grand-Mayne, and Clos Fourtet. Hail-stricken properties were allowed to pick early so as to salvage the remaining fruit. Many Pomerol vineyards were picked before the September downpours, so the wines were very good though less concentrated than in 1998. Late-ripening Cabernet Franc, however, was affected by the humid weather, and there was a good deal of rot. The crop was larger than in 1998, and there were some dilute wines.

In Sauternes, Sauvignon Blanc matured fast and much was being picked in early September. Rain in late September provoked botrytis in the Sémillon, and good conditions in October allowed the harvest to be completed quite quickly, although considerable grape selection was required. There was excellent fruit concentration throughout the region, and the wines had good acidity and were of high quality. Producers compared them to the wines from 1990 or 1997.

2000: Spring was very warm if wet, and flowering took place from late May to mid-June. However, there was a good deal of mildew, which had to be combated with frequent treatments. There was a fair amount of rain in July, but hot, dry weather returned in August and continued with very few interruptions until harvest, which began on September 18, though many estates waited a further week or so. Indeed, the first half of September was very hot, and some vines suffered from hydric stress. Curiously, blocked maturation resulted in overall sugar levels in the Médoc that were lower than in 1999, but the wines had much better balance and structure.

In the Graves some wines show signs of over-maturity, as some growers waited a bit too long to pick their Merlot. Nonetheless this is an excellent year here as in the Médoc. The white wines are very ripe, but some have low acidity and are rather broad in style.

Despite initial worries about the effects of the cool start to the summer and the abundant mildew, it seems clear that this was a glorious vintage, with very ripe tannins. Some wines show rather low acidity, but this is more than compensated for by the vibrant fruit and mature tannins. Recent tastings of classified growths have confirmed that this is an outstanding vintage.

With no rain in Pomerol and St-Emilion from July 19 until harvest, the only problem was blocked maturation in some vineyards. Rain on September 19 did no damage and may even have helped the Cabernets to ripen fully. A few properties picked too early and ended up with some unripe tannins, but they were in the minority. Some estates waited until mid-October to ensure their Cabernets were fully ripe. Despite some initial worries about drought stress, it soon became clear that the wines overall were rich, very ripe, and generous. In Fronsac the wines were unusually compact and powerful.

Picking was under way by late September in Sauternes, but by mid-October heavy rain had terminated the harvest, and row after row of sodden fruit had to be left on the vine. Vineyards on sandy soils did have some botrytis and early lots were satisfactory; later-ripening vines on clay soils mostly had to be abandoned. Only a minuscule crop of good, if not especially complex, wine could be produced, although top estates such as Yquem and Climens were content with the quality of the wine in bottle.

2001: Flowering took place a week later than in 2000 and proceeded well, though there were some problems with the fruit-set of the Merlot. July was rather wet, but August was dry, though less hot than in 2000. Even ripening was aided by dry, warm days in September, and occasional storms did little damage. Merlot came in with high sugar levels from September 20 onwards, followed by Cabernet Sauvignon from early October. However, vines that were carrying too much fruit did struggle to ripen properly. Perfect weather in October meant that there was no rush to complete the harvest. Acidities tended to be higher than in 2000, but tannins were not always as ripe. Some wines approach 2000 in quality, but this is by no means uniform. However, 2001 has certainly suffered in reputation from being in the shadow of the great year that preceded it. Estates with a good deal of Merlot in the blend made particularly succulent wines.

Whites in the Graves were picked from September 7 onwards in fine conditions. The wines were firm but full of fruit. The reds are good too, but not as fine as in the Médoc. The growing season was cooler, so the wines, if less rich than 2000, had considerable elegance. Merlot did particularly well, favouring properties with a high proportion of that variety.

Véraison on the Right Bank was uneven, but the cool, dry, sunny conditions in September and early October allowed the fruit to ripen fully. Despite a couple of downpours, there was no rot during harvest, and sugar levels were very high. Acidity levels were higher than 2000, and with bottle-age many 2001s from the Right Bank are showing more freshness and flair than their 2000 counterparts. In Fronsac the wines had similar ripeness and tannin levels to 2000, but showed more finesse.

In Sauternes the harvest began in mid-September; later that month some rainfall helped spread botrytis throughout the region, and strong winds helped concentrate the bunches. The harvest continued steadily through October, when the great majority of the vines were picked. Musts were close to ideal: strongly marked by botrytis, but with higher sugar levels than usual as well as excellent acidity that meant that the very high residual sugar was not too evident on the palate. This was certainly the finest vintage since the trio at the end of the 1980s.

2002: The year did not begin well. Although spring was fairly dry, there was heavy rain during flowering, provoking much *coulure* and *millerandage*, affecting all varieties, but Merlot in particular. The summer was unusually cool, and August was quite wet too, which provoked some rot. It was essential to pay close attention to the vineyards during the summer, removing small, hard berries, leaves, and excessive bunches. In mid-September the weather improved dramatically. A storm in the Médoc on September 20 did little damage and the grapes continued to ripen. Steady breezes kept rot at bay. The fine weather continued well into October. Some estates delayed the harvest until early October, and benefited by doing so. The crop was small and acidities as well as sugars were high. Selection was important, but overall the quality of the Cabernets and of Petit Verdot was high.

In the Graves too this was to prove a Cabernet year, as the Merlot was more problematic. The grapes had good levels of ripeness and maintained good acidity levels, thanks to cool nights. Many growers were convinced this was the best vintage since 1995 and 1996. White wines were also very good, despite some outbreaks of rot in the Sauvignon Blanc. It now seems apparent that this is a classic, and still somewhat underrated, vintage. The Médoc wines are pure and intense, with flavours of ripe Cabernet. Comparisons have been made with another fine Cabernet year, 1996.

The crop was exceptionally small on the Right Bank, and quality less consistent than on the Left Bank. At Cheval Blanc, for instance, this was the smallest crop since 1991, and even so most of the wine was declassified. Drizzle in early September led to some rot, but it was easily managed. Although Merlot yields were very low, the later-ripening Cabernet Franc did well. The wines are rather lean, but have gained some weight since bottling, and although inconsistent, there are some engaging surprises, especially in Pomerol and Lalande de Pomerol.

In Sauternes harvest conditions were similar to those in 2001, but the crop was smaller because of *coulure* and hydric stress. The wines have good acidity and a refreshing purity, though lots picked in late October contributed fatter, richer flavours. The vintage lacks the weight and structure of 2001, but has an elegance and forward charm that suggest these are highly attractive wines for medium-term drinking.

2003: This was a year of extremes. Flowering was early, but the young vines took a pounding from exceedingly hot temperatures that were six degrees above average. For over fifty successive days, the temperature was over 30°C (86°F) and in August it frequently topped 40°C (104°F). Hailstorms in June and July did considerable damage to the Graves (especially around La Brède) and parts of the Médoc such as Listrac. *Véraison* took place in July, about three weeks earlier than usual. Although the heat wave was almost unprecedented, the year was not that dry (1995, for example, had been drier). As well as sporadic storms during the summer months, a fair amount of rain fell in late August and early September, which benefited the grapes enormously. Berries shrivelled, and in some cases raisined, so there was little juice and yields were low, though only slightly lower than they had been in 2002. Vineyard managers who deleafed too enthusiastically exposed the bunches to sunburn. Those who picked too early ended up with insufficient phenolic ripeness. But with Merlot approaching a potential alcohol of fifteen degrees by early September, it was essential to pick. It was the Cabernet that benefited from the late summer rains and lower temperatures, and this variety was picked from September 18 onwards. By the end of September Petit Verdot was being picked with fifteen degrees of potential alcohol.

White vines were picked from August 13 onwards, as growers feared plummeting acidity. But many top Graves estates waited, and some rain in early September helped with overall maturation. The whites turned out to be atypical, with tropical fruit flavours, broad textures, little acidity, and a short finish. Some of them were quite voluptuous, but didn't taste much like classic Graves. Some estates began picking the red grapes from August 18, for much the same reasons, but in such cases the tannins were invariably unripe. Vines on sandier soils coped poorly with the heat, as maturation was blocked. As in the Médoc, the berries were small, giving wines of great concentration; yet the wines don't have the structure of the best Médoc wines.

This remains a difficult year to assess. That it was a unique vintage does not make it, as many commentators suggest, a great vintage. The growing season was fairly short, and there was often a lack of phenolic ripeness. Tannins were immense but not always fully ripe. Although acidity was low, the wines did mysteriously gain in acidity during fermentation. Many whites were acidified, but most top estates did their best to avoid this. (The technical explanation is that it was the malic acidity that was very low; thus, after malolactic fermentation, the total acidity had hardly dropped at all.) St-Estèphe, with its water-retentive clay soils, fared best. Individual vineyards such as Giscours, with a relatively high clay content, also did reasonably well. More noble terroirs often exposed the vines to hydric stress, which blocked maturation. It was not a year for heavy extraction, and most winemakers throughout the region opted for shorter *cuvaisons* and a lower proportion of new oak.

Despite some welcome storms in August, the extreme heat punished the vines in St-Emilion and especially Pomerol. Sandy and gravelly soils fared far worse than those with a high clay content. The vines shut down, and in some cases lost their leaves, exposing bunches to sunburn. Routine leaf-pulling earlier in the summer also invited disaster for the same reason. As a consequence, tannin development was slow, but plummeting acidity persuaded some growers to delay harvesting, except in cases where the grapes were clearly raisining. In Pomerol the Moueix team recorded both over-maturity and unripe tannins, so extraction had to be undertaken with great care.

It is clear that there are a number of splendid wines in 2003. But, equally, there are many that seem harsh, extracted, ungainly, and lacking in finesse. There's more to a great wine than concentration and high alcohol. Many wines, including top growths from Margaux and St-Estèphe, are evolving fast. Some of the top properties in Pomerol ended up with a vintage they would as soon forget about, while lesser terroirs in the satellites and in Fronsac, Bourg, and Blaye, with their late-ripening clay soils, coped far better with the torrid conditions. Will 2003 turn out to resemble the mighty 1959 or the baked 1976? With so many unusual and atypical factors at play, it is even more difficult than usual to make predictions. The more I taste the wines, the more scepticism I feel about the vintage and the high claims made for many of its wines.

By late August the grapes in Sauternes were fully ripe, and subsequent rain allowed botrytis to develop, with heat and wind contributing excellent fruit concentration. Indeed maturation was almost too rapid, with sugars climbing as liquid content within the berries plummeted. By the end of September the harvest was over, with some lots registering extremely high sugar levels. However, there were some cooked and raisined grapes that needed to be eliminated. As in 1990, some lots were too high in sugar to ferment without the addition of less sweet batches. Although the vintage was acclaimed as a great one, comparable to 1893 or 1929, and the wines had magnificent richness, there were flies in the ointment in the form of high pH and low acidity. Many wines were heavy and lacked the finesse of, say, the 2001s. It will be fascinating to see how these wines develop and whether those, such as myself, who are sceptical about their staying power will be proved wrong.

2004: After a rather wet spring, temperatures rose in May and the flowering was prolonged. June was hot, July was average, and August remained cool, with a fair amount of rainfall. Many estates had to treat against oïdium. Nonetheless, statistically this was another very dry year. The vintage was saved by the September weather, with its hot days and cool nights. Merlot was ripe by the end of the month, but the Cabernet Sauvignon ripened only in mid-October. Fortunately the weather held, and October was unusually warm. There was some rain in October, but Cabernet skins were thick and resisted the moisture. After very low crops in 2002 and 2003, the vines compensated and yields were potentially very high indeed, so green-harvesting was crucial. Even so, this was a record-breaking crop. Dilution was avoided at the top estates, which also recorded high sugar levels for both Merlot and the Cabernets. Indeed, some estates (Durfort-Vivens, La Lagune) recorded higher sugar levels than in 2003. Many growers compared the year to 1996.

In the Graves the August rains swelled many bunches, but the warmer, drier conditions in September allowed some of that excess moisture to dissipate. Merlot was rich and ripe in the Graves, Cabernet Sauvignon was also very ripe and fleshy, and many growers were ecstatic about the quality of the vintage, both for red and white wines.

Because of the lack of commercial interest in 2004, the quality of the vintage has been underrated. Growers in Margaux in particular were thrilled with the quality of their fruit, and initial tastings suggest this will be a very fine vintage, with an unusual character in that all the varieties ripened well and were picked in healthy condition.

On the Right Bank too yields were very high, and most conscientious estates made serious efforts to reduce the crop. The humid weather in August provoked some mildew, but it did little serious damage. The wines, fortunately, show little sign of dilution, at least at the top level. Sugar levels for Merlot were high, and thick skins gave robust tannins that in most cases were balanced by good acidity thanks to cool September nights. Cabernet Franc was also of high quality. There was no pressure to rush the harvest, and the result was a large number of excellent wines of good structure, especially from Pomerol.

Humid August weather in Sauternes provoked an unwelcome outbreak of grey rot within the bunches that proved tricky to deal with. A warm windy September helped to dry the grapes, but both ripening and botrytis infection were uneven, making the harvest difficult and prolonged. A long spell of rain in mid-October, followed by more rain at the end of the month, complicated the harvest further. Meticulous selection was essential, and those who spared no effort or expense to carry this out made some very good wines.

2005: Climatic conditions were close to perfect in 2005. Flowering took place in fine conditions in early June. The summer was hot and sunny, and occasional downpours in August (except in St-Estèphe, which received no rain) were welcome because of the very dry conditions (drier than 2003). The daytime heat was moderated by cool nights, which preserved acidity and minimized any risk of rot. Fine weather continued into September, so the harvest took place in ideal conditions. All varieties ripened well, and the sole fly in the ointment seemed to be some stuck fermentations because of very high sugars.

Conditions were similar on the Right Bank, and a couple of downpours in St-Emilion in early September did no damage and alleviated potential hydric stress. By mid-September the Pomerol harvest was well under way, and that in St-Emilion followed a week later. Throughout the Libournais high sugar levels led to some stuck fermentations, and the malolactic was slow to terminate. The balance of the wines – high sugars, super-ripe tannins, and fairly low pH – suggests the wines will prove very long-lived.

Dry hot weather delayed the onset of botrytis in Sauternes. The harvest began in late September and continued in perfect conditions until the end of October. The botrytis was very pure and chilly nights maintained good acidity. The wines show every sign of being excellent.

2006: The winter was wet and cold, but conditions improved in May, and flowering was uneventful. June and July were exceedingly hot, but then a cool, damp August upset the trend. The drizzly weather from August 16 to 30 caused the grapes to swell and there was some rot. Very hot weather returned in early September, which helped ripen the fruit, but humid nights meant the risk of rot remained. Rainy weather returned in mid-September, but early-ripening areas such as Pessac-Léognan and Pomerol were able to harvest in fairly good conditions. Although some of the Pomerol harvest took place under falling rain, growers moved fast and completed the harvest before the rain could swell the grapes and dilute them. However, Graves estates with a good deal of Sémillon found that the harvest was a race against rot. Rain continued and many growers decided they had to pick the Merlot fast, even though there was some dilution. Cabernet Sauvignon fared better, and those who waited until early October were able to pick in good conditions. For growers this was a frustrating vintage, since by early September sugar levels and anthocyanins were comparable to 2005 levels, but the rain and rot diminished this potential, though very good wines were made by those who invested in meticulous grape-sorting.

In general, Pomerol fared better than St-Emilion, and St-Emilion fared better than the Côtes, with their colder soils. Some estates bled their tanks to improve concentration, thereby sacrificing about one-fifth of the crop; others will have hauled their concentrators out of early retirement. Evidently, this was not a year for great extraction, as the wines lack some richness. Clearly there will be considerable variation in quality from estate to estate. Throughout Bordeaux this was once again a small crop, and at top estates the proportion of *grand vin* was low (thus forty-four per cent at Mouton).

Sauternes had an early harvest, with Rieussec beginning on September 6. Early forays into the vineyard were mostly devoted to removing any unwelcome rot, although some healthy botrytis could also be found and picked on sloping sites. The mid-September downpours complicated the harvest, but there was ample good botrytis as well as undesirable spoilage. So fruit quality was far from uniform. The harvest had ended by the first week of October. Sauternes had an earlier harvest than Barsac.

Initial tastings in spring 2007 suggest that Pomerol has produced wines almost as fine as those from 2005. St-Emilion is patchier, but here too there are good wines from the plateau and from clay-rich soils; down on the plains rot spread rapidly and quality was harder to achieve. There are some good wines from Fronsac. On the Left Bank, the whites from Pessac-Léognan and the Graves are outstanding, but early tastings of Sauternes were unsatisfactory, with many wines flabby and lacking in freshness. Red Pessac-Léognan is lean and inconsistent, as is the Médoc, although there are good wines throughout, thanks to the later-ripening Cabernet.

Bâtonnage	A Burgundian technique of stirring the lees of white wine during ageing in order to give it more richness; increasingly practised with red wines.
Cagette	A small plastic perforated bin used for harvesting.
Chai	Barrel cellar or store.
Cliquage	Technique of micro-oxygenation by which doses of oxygen are added to a wine.
Coulure	A problem of uneven or abortive flowering that has the consequence of reducing the size of the crop.
Courtier	Broker, acting as intermediary between owner and merchant, or merchant and customer.
Cuvier	Vinification centre.
Délestage	A vinification technique that consists of emptying and refilling a tank in order to mix the skins and juice effectively; also known as "rack and return".
Effeuillage	Leaf removal or thinning.
Elevage	Literally "rearing" – the process of ageing the wine after vinification.
En primeur	System by which wines are sold up to a year before bottling (known in the United States as "futures").
Encépagement	Grape varieties present in a vineyard or wine.
Grand vin	That proportion of the wine that is bottled under the name of the château, excluding the second wine and any sales to wholesalers.
Jalle	Small stream flowing into the Gironde; often forms a boundary between ACs.
Lutte raisonnée	System of viticulture whereby chemical treatments are applied only as a last resort.
Maître de chai	Cellarmaster.
Marc	The residue of skins and pips during and after fermentation.
Millerandage	A problem during flowering in which some berries fail to develop and thus ripen.
Palus	The rich alluvial riverbank, with soil too rich for quality wine.
Parlementaire	Rich and powerful lawyers and politicians prominent in pre-revolutionary times.
Passerillage	Desiccation of grapes for sweet white wines by over ripeness rather than by botrytis.
Pigeage	Burgundian technique of punching down the cap during fermentation; increasingly practised in Bordeaux.
Place de Bordeaux	Collective name for the Bordeaux wine business.
Prix de sortie	Price at which an estate offers its wine to the wine trade.
Régisseur	Estate manager.
Remontage	Pumping over to aerate the must during fermentation.
Sous marc	Micro-oxygenation of the newly fermented macerating wine, with injections of oxygen beneath the floating cap.
Table/tapis de trie	Sorting table.
Terroir	Catch-all term to denote soil, drainage, microclimate, elevation, and any other factor in the vineyard that contributes to typicity.
Tranche	Batch of new wine released for sale by an estate; sought-after wines are often released in as many as four *tranches*, with escalating prices.
Tries successives	The process of picking the same parcel at least twice in order to select only the ripest bunches.
Vendange verte	Bunch-thinning or green-harvesting.
Vin de garage	Expensive, limited-production wine made in pseudo-artisanal circumstances.

Brook, Stephen, *Bordeaux: People, Power, Politics*. London: Mitchell Beazley, 2001.

Brook, Stephen, *Sauternes and Other Sweet Wines of Bordeaux*. London: Faber, 1995.

Clarke, Oz, *Oz Clarke's Bordeaux*. London: Webster's International, 2006.

Coates, Clive, *The Wines of Bordeaux*. Berkeley, Calif.: University of California Press, 2004.

Cocks, Charles, and Féret, Edouard, *Bordeaux et Ses Vins*. 16th edition. Bordeaux: Editions Féret, 2004.

Courrian, Philippe, and Creignou, Michel, *Vigneron du Médoc*. Paris: Payot, 1996.

Danflau, Alfred, *Les grands crus bordelais*. Bordeaux: Gaudin, 1867.

De Coster, Benoît, *Bordeaux alternatif*. Oostkamp: Stichting Kunstboek, 2001.

Duijker, Hubrecht, and Broadbent, Michael, *The Bordeaux Atlas and Encyclopaedia of Châteaux*. London: Ebury Press, 1997.

Echikson, William, *Noble Rot: A Bordeaux Wine Revolution*. New York: Norton, 2004.

Enjalbert, Henri, and Enjalbert, Bernard, *History of Wine and the Vine*. Paris: Bardi, 1987.

Faith, Nicholas, *Château Margaux*. London: Christie's, 1980.

Faith, Nicholas, *The Winemasters of Bordeaux*. 2nd edition. London: Carlton Books, 2005.

Fanet, Jacques, *Great Wine Terroirs*. Translated by Florence Brutton. London: University of California Press, 2004.

Ferrand, Franck, *Bordeaux Châteaux: A History of the Grands Crus Classés*. Paris: Flammarion, 2004.

Gryn, Jo, *Bordeaux, Le vin et moi*. Bordeaux: Editions Féret, 2006.

Hervier, Denis, *Le Médoc et ses crus bourgeois*. Bordeaux: Editions Féret, 2003.

Jefford, Andrew, *The New France*. London: Mitchell Beazley, 2005.

Johnson, Hugh, *The Story of Wine*. London: Mitchell Beazley, 1989.

Kladstrup, Don, and Kladstrup, Petie, *Wine and War*. New York: Broadway, 2001.

Lawton, H, and Miailhe, J, *Conversations et souvenirs autour du vin de Bordeaux*. Bordeaux: Editions Confluences, 1999.

Markham, Dewey, Jr., *1855: A History of the Bordeaux Classification*. New York: Wiley, 1998.

Parker, Robert M., Jr., *Bordeaux*. 4th edition. London: Dorling Kindersley, 2003.

Penning-Rowsell, Edmund, *The Wines of Bordeaux*. 6th edition. London: Penguin, 1989.

Peppercorn, David, *Bordeaux*. 2nd edition. London: Faber, 1991.

Pijassou, René, *Château Palmer*. Paris: Stock, 1997.

Pijassou, René, and Ters, Didier, *Gruaud-Larose*. Translated by Sebastian Cresswell-Turner. Paris: Stock, 1997.

Ray, Cyril, *Lafite*. London: Peter Davies, 1968.

Thiney, Marie-José, *Petit guide d'oenologie*. Bordeaux: Mollat, 1992.

Van Leeuwen, Cornelis, *Carte des sols du vignoble de St-Emilion*. St-Emilion: Syndicat Viticole, 1980.

Wilson, James E., *Terroir*. London: Mitchell Beazley, 1998.

2006 ST-EMILION CLASSIFICATION

Premiers Grands Crus Classés

(A) Ausone
Cheval Blanc
(B) Angélus
Beausejour Duffau-Lagarosse
Beau-Séjour Bécot
Bélair
Canon
Clos Fourtet
Figeac
La Gaffelière
Magdelaine
Pavie
Pavie-Macquin (promoted 2006)
Troplong-Mondot (promoted 2006)
Trottevieille

Grands Crus Classés

L'Arrosée
Balestard-la-Tonnelle
Bellefont-Belcier (promoted 2006)
Bergat
Berliquet
Cadet-Piola
Canon la Gaffelière
Cap de Mourlin
Chauvin
Clos des Jacobins
Clos de l'Oratoire
Clos St Martin
La Clotte
La Couspaude
Corbin
Corbin-Michotte
Couvent des Jacobins
Dassault
Destieux (promoted 2006)
La Dominique
Fleur-Cardinale (promoted 2006)
Fonplégade
Fonroque
Franc-Mayne
Grand Corbin (promoted 2006)
Grand-Corbin-Despagne (promoted 2006)
Grand-Mayne
Grand-Pontet
Grandes Murailles
Haut-Corbin
Haut-Sarpe
Laniote

Larcis-Ducasse
Larmande
Laroque
Laroze
Matras
Monbousquet (promoted 2006)
Moulin-du-Cadet
Pavie-Decesse
Petite Faurie de Soutard
Le Prieuré
Ripeau
St Georges Côte Pavie
La Serre
Soutard
La Tour Figeac

SAUTERNES CLASSIFICATION

Premier Grand Cru

Ch d'Yquem	Sauternes

Premiers Crus

Ch Climens	Barsac
Ch Clos Haut-Peyraguey	Bommes
Ch Coutet	Barsac
Ch Guiraud	Sauternes
Ch Lafaurie-Peyraguey	Bommes
Ch La Tour-Blanche	Bommes
Ch Rabaud-Promis	Bommes
Ch Rayne-Vigneau	Bommes
Ch Rieussec	Fargues
Ch Sigalas-Rabaud	Bommes
Ch Suduiraut	Preignac

Deuxièmes Crus

Ch d'Arche	Sauternes
Ch Broustet	Barsac
Ch Caillou	Barsac
Ch Doisy-Daëne	Barsac
Ch Doisy-Dubroca	Barsac
Ch Doisy-Védrines	Barsac
Ch Filhot	Sauternes
Ch Lamothe	Sauternes
Ch Lamothe-Guignard	Sauternes
Ch de Malle	Preignac
Ch de Myrat	Barsac
Ch Nairac	Barsac
Ch Romer	Fargues
Ch Romer-du-Hayot	Fargues
Ch Suau	Barsac

PICTURE ACKNOWLEDGMENTS

COVER
Front cover: Corbis / Charles O'Rear
Back cover: Conseil des Grands Crus Classés en 1855
Spine: Alamy / Cephas Picture Library

Alamy / Cephas Picture Library 1; André Lurton 2; Charmaine Grieger / Anthony Rose 4; Conseil des Grands Crus Classés en 1855 8–9; Charmaine Grieger / Anthony Rose 10–11; Scope / M Guillard 12–13; Alamy / Cephas Picture Library 249; Château Haut Selve 250, 251 top; Scope / J L Barde 251 bottom; Conseil des Grands Crus Classés en 1855 252–253; Scope / M Guillard 254–255; Alamy / Ros Drinkwater 256–257; Alamy / Cephas Picture Library 258; Alamy / Per Karlsson – BKWine.com 259; Château La Lagune 260–261; Scope / M Guillard 261; Alamy / Cephas Picture Library 262 top; Claes Lofgren 262 bottom; Château Smith Haut Lafitte 263; Alamy / Cephas Picture Library 264; Château Pavie 481 top; Alamy / Per Karlsson – BKWine.com 481 bottom; Alamy / Chad Ehlers 482; Alamy / Cephas Picture Library 483; Claes Lofgren 484–485; Alamy / Cephas Picture Library 486, 487; Scope / J L Barde 488–489; Alamy / Peter Horree 489; Claes Lofgren 490–491; Alamy / Cephas Picture Library 492; Alamy / Mark Zylber 493; Mähler-Besse 494–495; Cephas Picture Library / Nigel Blythe 496 top, / Mick Rock 496 bottom.